PRINCIPLES OF
MARKETING

Dr Frances Brassington

Senior Lecturer
Buckinghamshire College of Higher Education

Dr Stephen Pettitt

Dean of Luton Business School
University of Luton

PITMAN PUBLISHING

London · Hong Kong · Johannesburg · Melbourne · Singapore · Washington DC

To Quincy for all the walks he missed.

PITMAN PUBLISHING
128 Long Acre, London WC2E 9AN
Tel: +44 (0)171 447 2000
Fax: +44 (0)171 240 5771

A Division of Pearson Professional Limited

First published in Great Britain in 1997

ISBN 0 273 60513 5

British Library Cataloguing in Publication Data
A CIP catalogue record for this book can be obtained from the British Library

10 9 8 7 6 5 4 3 2

Typeset by Pantek Arts, Maidstone, Kent.
Printed and bound in Great Britain

The Publishers' policy is to use paper manufactured from sustainable forests.

About the Authors

■ ■ ■

Stephen Pettitt is the Dean of Luton Business School at the University of Luton. Previously he was the Director of Corporate Affairs at the University of Teesside and, before that, Associate Dean (External Affairs) in the Business School, Teesside. He also worked at the University of Limerick in Ireland for four years as a Lecturer in Marketing and was the Managing Director of The Marketing Centre for Small Business, a campus company specialising in research and consultancy for the small business sector.

He worked initially in various sales and marketing management posts for Olivetti, Plessey and SKF before taking up a career in higher education. He holds a Bachelor's degree in Geography and an MBA and PhD from Cranfield. In addition to having wide experience in marketing education at all levels, he has undertaken numerous in-company training, research and consultancy assignments. He has lectured in marketing and entrepreneurship in France, Poland, Bulgaria, Slovakia, Switzerland, the USA and Kenya. He has published over 30 papers and articles and major studies in tourism innovation strategies, large buyer–small firm seller relationships and small firm development.

Frances Brassington is a Senior Lecturer in Marketing at Buckinghamshire College of Higher Education. She graduated from the University of Bradford Management Centre with a BSc (Hons) in Business Studies and a PhD. Her first teaching position was at the University of Teesside where she was also MBA dissertation director and marketing section leader. She has taught marketing at all levels and on a wide range of undergraduate marketing modules and programmes. Her research interests include retail marketing, marketing communications, and the evolution of marketing practice in central Europe. She has also designed and delivered marketing programmes for managers and academics in Poland and Bulgaria.

Brief Contents

■ ■ ■

Contents ix

Part I
MARKETING AND ITS ENVIRONMENT

1 Marketing Dynamics 3
2 The European Marketing Environment 37

Part II
CUSTOMERS AND MARKETS

3 Consumer Behaviour 87
4 Organisational Buying Behaviour 126
5 Segmenting Markets 168
6 Marketing Information and Research 199

Part III
PRODUCT

7 Anatomy of a Product 253
8 Product Management 293
9 New Product Development 331

Part IV
PRICE

10 Pricing: Context and Concepts 369
11 Pricing Strategies 407

Part V
PLACE

12 Marketing Channels 449

13 Retailers and Wholesalers 488
14 Physical Distribution and Logistics Management 531

Part VI
PROMOTION

15 Communication and the Promotional Mix 569
16 Advertising 603
17 Sales Promotion 652
18 Personal Selling and Sales Management 697
19 Direct Marketing 739
20 Public Relations, Sponsorship and Exhibitions 779

Part VII
MARKETING MANAGEMENT

21 Strategic Marketing 827
22 Marketing Planning, Management and Control 875

Part VIII
MARKETING APPLICATIONS

23 Services Marketing 917
24 Marketing and the Smaller Business 952
25 International Marketing 990
26 Current Perspectives in Marketing 1028

Glossary 1055

Contents

■ ■ ■

Preface   xv
Acknowledgements   xviii

Part I
MARKETING AND ITS ENVIRONMENT

1   Marketing Dynamics

Introduction   3
Marketing defined   4
Marketing in action Fisherman's Friends   6
Marketing in action Slovenia's struggle   15
The marketing concept in the organisation   17
Marketing management responsibilities   22
Marketing in action Virgin Direct   28
Marketing scope   29
Chapter summary   32
Questions for review   33
Questions for discussion   33
Case study 1.1 Liptonice   34
Case study 1.2 Plasser and Theurer make tracks   35
References   36

2   The European Marketing Environment

Introduction   37
The nature of the European marketing environment   38
The sociocultural environment   41
Marketing in action Bread   50
Marketing in action Environmentally friendly tyres   54
The technological environment   55
The economic and competitive environment   60
Marketing in action Austria plc joins the EU   64
The political and regulatory environment   70
Marketing in action Airline deregulation   74
Chapter summary   78
Questions for review   81
Questions for discussion   81
Case study 2.1 Sanpro   82
Case study 2.2 Kabo   83
References   84

Part II
CUSTOMERS AND MARKETS

3   Consumer Behaviour

Introduction   87
The decision-making process   88
Buying situations   96
Environmental influences   98
Marketing in action The 1990s woman   99
Psychological influences: the individual   100
Marketing in action Savoury snacks   101
Sociocultural influences: the group   109
Marketing in action Reaching the youth market   113
Marketing in action Pester power   118
Chapter summary   120
Questions for review   121
Questions for discussion   121
Case study 3.1 Madame Tussaud's Rock Circus   122
Case study 3.2 Premium lagers   123
References   124

4   Organisational Buying Behaviour

Introduction   126
Defining organisational marketing   127
Organisational customers   129
Characteristics of organisational markets   132
Marketing in action Buying machine tools   135
Marketing in action Automotive component suppliers   139
Buying decision-making process   142
Marketing in action Pendolino – on time, on track   145
Roles in the buying process   148
The buying centre   152
Buying criteria   154
Relationship marketing   157
Marketing in action Buyer–supplier co-operation   159
Chapter summary   161
Questions for review   162
Questions for discussion   162
Case study 4.1 Taurus   163
Case study 4.2 Philips cultivates suppliers   164
References   166

5 Segmenting Markets

Introduction 168
The concept of segmentations 169
Segmenting organisational markets 169
Segmenting consumer markets 172
Marketing in action Go for bust 173
Marketing in action Cola fatigue 175
Marketing in action Are you a yak or a ewe? 179
Implementation of segmentation 184
Marketing in action Blue Circle's standardised boiler 188
Benefits of segmentation 189
Dangers of segmentation 190
Criteria for successful segmentation 191
Chapter summary 192
Questions for review 194
Questions for discussion 194
Case study 5.1 Kings Hotel (A) 195
Case study 5.2 A night at the opera 196
References 198

6 Marketing Information and Research

Introduction 199
Marketing research overview 201
Marketing in action Research for your convenience 202
Secondary research 209
Primary research 214
Marketing in action Big brother is watching you 219
Marketing in action Trouble brewing 224
The marketing research process 230
Marketing in action Business travel 235
Ethics in marketing research 239
Marketing information systems 240
Chapter summary 244
Questions for review 246
Questions for discussion 246
Case study 6.1 Kings Hotel (B) 247
Case study 6.2 Gathering information on an up and coming market 248
References 250

Part III
PRODUCT

7 Anatomy of a Product

Introduction 253
Meaning of a product 254
Product classification 256
Marketing in action Raw material pricing 261
Understanding the product range 263
Branding 265
Marketing in action Moving brands into new markets 271

Marketing in action Own-label manufacture 274
Packaging 278
Marketing in action Ecolabelling 281
Product design, quality and guarantees 282
Chapter summary 287
Questions for review 288
Questions for discussion 288
Case study 7.1 Cott Corporation, Cola and copycatting 289
Case study 7.2 German diesel railcar 290
References 292

8 Product Management

Introduction 293
The product life-cycle 294
Marketing in action Male fragrance 295
Market evolution 303
Marketing in action The evolving PLC of the PC 307
Managing the product mix 308
Marketing in action Repositioning for good health 312
Customer-specified products 318
Marketing in action Making records 318
Product management and organisation 320
European product strategy 321
Chapter summary 324
Questions for review 325
Questions for discussion 325
Case study 8.1 Pubs in peril 326
Case study 8.2 Fokker takes flight 327
References 329

9 New Product Development

Introduction 331
The meaning of a new product 332
Marketing in action Rubbing salt into the market 334
Marketing in action Neutraceuticals 336
The importance of new product development 337
The new product development process 339
Marketing in action Recycled paper 342
New product failure 354
Trends in npd process management 356
Marketing in action Business forums 359
Chapter summary 361
Questions for review 362
Questions for discussion 362
Case study 9.1 Digital compact cassette *vs* MiniDisc 363
Case study 9.2 Soap wars 364
References 366

Part IV
PRICE

10 Pricing: Context and Concepts
Introduction 369
The role and perception of price 370
Marketing in action Putting you in the picture 372
Pricing contexts 375
Marketing in action Budget tyres 377
External influences on the pricing decision 380
Marketing in action Sweet smell of success 387
Internal influences on the pricing decision 391
Marketing in action Pricing a pinta 395
The European influence on pricing 396
Chapter summary 399
Questions for review 400
Questions for discussion 400
Case study 10.1 The net book agreement 401
Case study 10.2 Eurostar 403
References 405

11 Pricing Strategies
Introduction 407
Pricing objectives 409
Pricing policies and strategies 414
Marketing in action Premium sausages 414
Marketing in action Apple turnover 418
Setting the price range 423
Marketing in action Channel Tunnel and freight costs 429
Pricing tactics and adjustments 432
Issues in pricing 434
Marketing in action Deutsche Telekom 435
Chapter summary 440
Questions for review 442
Questions for discussion 442
Case study 11.1 Summer of CD price discontent 443
Case study 11.2 Lucerne Hotel and Conference Centre 444
References 446

Part V
PLACE

12 Marketing Channels
Introduction 449
Definition of marketing channels 450
Marketing in action Telmat 457
Marketing in action Going Dutch 460
Channel strategy 461
Marketing in action Borsalino 466
Emerging forms of channel structure 470
Marketing in action Daewoo 470
Behavioural aspects of channels 474
Chapter summary 481
Questions for review 483
Questions for discussion 483
Case study 12.1 Monaghan Mushrooms 484
Case study 12.2 French hypermarkets and their smaller suppliers 485
References 487

13 Retailers and Wholesalers
Introduction 488
The nature of retailing and wholesaling 490
The structure of the European retail sector 493
Marketing in action Menswear 495
Types of retailers 499
Marketing in action Hypermarkets in Portugal 504
Non-store retailing 509
Retailer strategy 511
Marketing in action Tie Rack 511
Marketing in action Retailing in Poland 522
Wholesalers and distributors 523
Chapter summary 525
Questions for review 526
Questions for discussion 526
Case study 13.1 Sainsbury's 527
Case study 13.2 Amstrad sells direct 528
References 530

14 Physical Distribution and Logistics Management
Introduction 531
The nature of physical distribution and logistics 532
Marketing in action Apple Hollyhill 537
Marketing in action Benetton 539
Customer service concept 540
Logistics functions 543
Marketing in action EDI – a central part of the logistics system 552
Marketing in action Efficient consumer response 558
Marketing strategy and physical distribution 560
Chapter summary 561
Questions for review 563
Questions for discussion 563
Case study 14.1 Putting some fizz into supply chain management 564
Case study 14.2 Fording the channel 565
References 566

Part VI
PROMOTION

15 Communication and the Promotional Mix
Introduction 569
Communications theory 571
Communications planning model 575
Marketing in action A model market 578
Marketing in action Hooper's Hooch 584
Marketing in action Olive oil 589
Marketing in action Crocodile: will consumers snap it up? 590
Communications planning model: review 596
Chapter summary 596
Questions for review 598
Questions for discussion 598
Case study 15.1 Riverdance 599
Case study 15.2 Le Shuttle 600
References 602

16 Advertising
Introduction 603
The role of advertising in the promotional mix 604
Marketing in action Foden trucks 606
Formulating the advertising message 609
Marketing in action Pan-European advertising – east and west 611
Advertising media 624
Using advertising agencies 633
Developing an advertising campaign 636
Marketing in action Christian Cable TV 638
Chapter summary 645
Questions for review 647
Questions for discussion 647
Case study 16.1 Nike 648
Case study 16.2 Anti-drugs advertising 649
References 651

17 Sales Promotion
Introduction 652
The role and definition of sales promotion 653
Marketing in action Trade promotions 655
Consumer sales promotion methods (1): Money based 663
Consumer sales promotion methods (2): Product based 667
Marketing in action Sampling kids 669
Consumer sales promotion methods (3): Gift, prize or merchandise based 672
Consumer sales promotion methods (4): Store based 679
Methods of promotion to the retail trade 680
Sales promotion to organisational markets 684
Marketing in action JCB 685
Managing sales promotion 685
Chapter summary 690
Questions for review 692
Questions for discussion 692
Case study 17.1 Student banking 693
Case study 17.2 Supermarket loyalty cards 694
References 696

18 Personal Selling and Sales Management
Introduction 697
The definition and role of personal selling 698
Tasks of the sales representative 701
Forms of personal selling 704
Marketing in action Is the sales rep an endangered species? 707
The personal selling process 708
Marketing in action The sales force and IT 719
Sales management 721
Marketing in action 'The Man From the Pru' 725
Chapter summary 731
Questions for review 733
Questions for discussion 733
Case study 18.1 Buying a car 734
Case study 18.2 Irish Fire Products 736
References 738

19 Direct Marketing
Introduction 739
The definition of direct marketing 740
The rise of direct marketing 741
Techniques of direct marketing 744
Marketing in action Automated call handling 757
Marketing in action The next generation of mail order catalogues 760
The role of direct marketing in the promotional mix 763
Marketing in action Castle Cement sweeps telemarketing awards 764
Managing a direct marketing campaign 766
Database creation and management 769
Chapter summary 772
Questions for review 774
Questions for discussion 774
Case study 19.1 Hyatt International Hotels 775
Case study 19.2 Into the Internet 776
References 778

20 Public Relations, Sponsorship and Exhibitions

Introduction   779
Definition of public relations   780
The role of public relations   784
Marketing in action Mad cows and Englishmen   786
Techniques in public relations   787
Marketing in action Corporate magazines   791
Evaluation   793
Corporate identity   795
Sponsorship   799
Marketing in action Music sponsorship   806
Evaluating sponsorship   810
Exhibitions and trade shows   810
Chapter summary   817
Questions for review   819
Questions for discussion   819
Case study 20.1 Shell, Greenpeace and Brent Spar   820
Case study 20.2 Antique exhibitions   821
References   823

Part VII
MARKETING MANAGEMENT

21 Strategic Marketing

Introduction   827
Marketing in action Grolsch   828
Definitions and perspectives   829
Marketing in action Tele Danmark makes international calls   835
Strategic marketing analysis   836
Marketing in action Williams Holdings decides to refocus its product portfolio   837
Marketing in action Aérospatiale and Dassault take off   841
Growth strategies for marketing   845
Marketing and competitive strategy   849
Competitive positions and postures   859
Chapter summary   867
Questions for review   869
Questions for discussion   869
Case study 21.1 Chuft Toys and Gifts   870
Case study 21.2 Boots' strategic headaches   871
References   873

22 Marketing Planning, Management and Control

Introduction   875
Strategic marketing plans and planning   876
Marketing in action Behind the Hollywood glitter   880
The marketing planning process   880
Marketing in action The car park environment   884

Marketing in action TI rethinks its portfolio   889
Market potential and sales forecasting   892
Marketing in action Bouygues backs its forecasts   895
Organising marketing activities   901
Marketing in action Restructuring marketing departments   904
Controlling marketing activities   905
Chapter summary   909
Questions for review   910
Questions for discussion   910
Case study 22.1 DHL – a global brand   911
Case study 22.2 Filofax   912
References   914

Part VIII
MARKETING APPLICATIONS

23 Services Marketing

Introduction   917
Perspectives on service markets   918
Marketing in action Multiplex cinemas   921
Services marketing management   926
Marketing in action Novotel design   931
Non-profit marketing   940
Marketing in action Fundraising and image creation   943
Marketing in action The National Missing Persons Helpline   945
Chapter summary   946
Questions for review   947
Questions for discussion   947
Case study 23.1 The Education Catering Service   948
Case study 23 2 Day visitor attractions   949
References   951

24 Marketing and the Smaller Business

Introduction   952
The nature of small businesses   953
Marketing in action A reason to celebrate   955
The stages in small business development   957
Marketing in action Small businesses move into international markets   968
Franchising   969
Marketing in action La Compagnie des Petits   971
Marketing in action Domino's Pizza franchises   983
Chapter summary   984
Questions for review   985
Questions for discussion   985
Case study 24.1 Styles Precision Components Ltd   986
Case study 24.2 Developing a new franchise proposal: budget-priced hostels   987
References   989

25 International Marketing

Introduction 990
The meaning of international marketing 992
Marketing in action Novo Nordisk 996
Understanding international markets 999
Marketing in action Eastern Europe strikes back
1003
Market entry methods 1004
Marketing in action Barco – projecting the future
1010
International marketing strategy 1013
Marketing in action British Airways and
American Airlines take off 1014
Chapter summary 1020
Questions for review 1022
Questions for discussion 1022

Case study 25.1 Martin Joinery 1023
Case study 25.2 Vinprom-C 1025
References 1027

26 Current Perspectives in Marketing

Introduction 1028
Boss Group Ltd 1030
Wilkinson Sword 1033
Vauxhall UK 1036
DMB&B 1039
Continental Microwave Ltd 1042
Graduate trainees in marketing 1047
Conclusion 1049

Glossary 1055
Index 1067
Index of company names 1082

Preface

■ ■ ■

The world within which marketing takes place is a dynamic and potentially very exciting one. By its very nature, marketing reflects social and political change, as well as technological and economic trends. All of these factors, as well as their own experiences, influence customers' attitudes to organisations and the marketing packages on offer. Marketers have to understand this, if they are going to create offerings that will satisfy, or even delight, their customers. There is something of an element of 'magic' to all this, particularly in consumer markets, as the marketer finds the right blend of ingredients to whet the customer's appetite, to stimulate desire and to generate a sale. Marketing helps consumers to develop emotional bonds with the products they purchase, and to gain psychological as well as functional satisfaction from their use.

Organisational markets also have their own magic. Industrial purchasing might well have a greater element of businesslike functionality and cost effectiveness about it, but nevertheless, marketers still have to present the best case to customers, to show them clearly why they should buy from one supplier rather than another. Greater emphasis on long term buyer–supplier relationships means that the marketer not only has to satisfy the organisational buyer's product needs now, but also has to build trust and reassurance so that co-operation can flourish in the future. In essence, this is not too far removed from what the marketer is trying to achieve in a consumer market.

Marketing is not, therefore, a dry, internally focused management function with rigid procedures and sets of rules. It is live, outward looking and interactive. It responds to what is happening both inside and outside the organisation, yet also tries to drive what is happening in order to capitalise on opportunities. This makes marketing fun, but it also makes it dangerous. Marketing's creativity and flexibility has to be harnessed within a disciplined and controlled management structure in order to ensure, as far as is possible, that the 'right' things are being done at the 'right' time for the 'right' reasons. Sometimes that means breaking new ground and taking risks.

Marketing is also in the front line of an organisation's attitude to social reponsibility and corporate citizenship. Society now expects organisations to ensure that their products are safe and to communicate any risks or problems clearly to the consumer. Organisations are also expected to refrain from selling products in inappropriate ways to vulnerable groups. Marketers have to be able to help the organisation to translate these expectations into practice. Marketers thus have to be creative and flexible, yet disciplined and ethical in everything they do.

In academic terms, the marketing field has reached a sophisticated level of development and is still evolving to incorporate the effects of the changing world. The basic tools of marketing are well established and understood, and theories of consumer and organisational behaviour are becoming increasingly complex. One challenge is to show how all these elements interact with each other in different types of situation, hence the emergence of discrete bodies of literature on international marketing, services marketing and small business marketing, for example. Another challenge is to explore the impact of emerging issues on both markets and marketers, hence the interest in relationship marketing, 'green' marketing, interactive marketing (via the Internet, for instance) and marketing ethics.

The job of a good introductory text book, therefore, is to bring together theory and practice, showing how the two feed from each other. It should cover a wide range of applications, industries and markets, exploring the ways in which marketers are responding to new situations and solving marketing problems creatively.

This has to be presented within a strong, logical framework that allows the student to develop knowledge and understanding in a structured way. It is also essential, of course, to stimulate the student's interest and curiosity about marketing. Marketing lecturers are privileged in many ways, because their students have already had experience of marketing as consumers. They might be cynical about it, but they have experienced it, and part of the stimulation for the student can be the process of understanding and analysing their own behaviour and responses to marketing activities.

In the light of these considerations, therefore, this particular textbook aims to be:

● *Comprehensive* in covering a wide range of marketing topics and elements, including the marketing environment, customers and markets, the 4Ps and specialised applications of marketing. There is particularly comprehensive coverage of the promotional mix to reflect the emerging role of direct marketing and the sometimes neglected aspects of public relations. Physical distribution and logistics are also given considerably more attention than normal. In a European context, distribution and customer service provision across national boundaries are often critical factors in gaining a competitive edge against national competitors. The wider aspects of international marketing are also well covered. The dedication of a chapter to small business management and franchising reflects the widening application of marketing and the creation of new marketing forms.

● *European* in design and focus. Marketers in most large organisations no longer regard other EU nations as export markets, but as part of one large, single market. This text aims to give students this wider European perspective. While there is a bias towards the UK, cases and examples are drawn from across the EU, to help demonstrate the underlying principles of marketing in practice, and from eastern Europe, to show the problems arising from operating in markets in transition.

● *Applied*: marketing cannot be approached as a purely theoretical course of study. It is essential to show how it works in practice, within the context of market conditions and customer behaviour that can be difficult to predict. To that end, not only does each chapter have a full range of examples and 'Marketing in Action' vignettes, but the final chapter also includes a number of in-depth interviews with senior marketing managers who outline their views on the difficulties of putting marketing into practice and some of the future problems facing their organisations.

● *Wide ranging in its coverage of markets and organisations*: marketing is not just about fast moving consumer goods operations which employ dedicated marketing specialists. Marketing happens, formally or informally, consciously or unconsciously, on purpose or by accident, in all organisations. It is important, therefore, to present a wide range of industries and sizes of organisations. Examples have thus been drawn from service industries, non-profit organisations and especially from organisational markets, in which increased product and market complexity presents special challenges to the marketer. Small businesses are also well represented, not only in their own dedicated chapter, but throughout the text.

● *A good read*: the text has been written with the needs of the first-time marketing student in mind. The combination of theory, examples and commentary is designed to engage readers' attention and interest, and to lead them painlessly through to a substantial understanding of marketing principles and applications.

Who should use this book

● *Undergraduates*: this is the prime audience for this text, and the book is intended mainly for use on all-purpose introductory marketing modules. The depth and coverage of some topics, however, such as direct marketing, small business and marketing communications generally, makes certain chapters useful references for more advanced, specialist modules.

● *Postgraduates*: the book is also a good background text to remind MBA or DMS level students of basic marketing principles in preparation for more advanced analysis of managerial concepts and case studies. Again, the depth in some of the areas covered provides useful specialist reading.

Distinctive features of this book

● A clearly written and structured text, including learning objectives for each chapter and a summary of each chapter.

● A wide selection of vignettes and examples in each chapter to illustrate the concepts presented. These are drawn from a range of industries, organisations and countries.

● End-of-chapter questions give students the opportunity to revise the material presented and to check their understanding of it. Discussion questions, encouraging students to debate issues or to research further into marketing practice can also be used as the basis for seminar work for students working individually or in small groups.

- Coverage of the complete range of marketing elements, including direct marketing, as well as a selection of specialist applications, such as small business, services marketing, and international marketing.

- It has been compiled from a European perspective and has a wide European orientation in the examples, vignettes and cases.

- Senior mangement perspectives, compiled from lengthy interviews conducted by the authors, have been included in the last chapter to draw the diverse elements of the book together. These perspectives underline the message that marketing elements have to be integrated into purposeful strategies that have to be implemented in a real and often difficult world.

- A glossary of key terms is also included, based on the key words highlighted in each chapter.

A wide range of supplements are available to support lecturers using *Principles of Marketing*. Many of these are free to those choosing to adopt the book as their main text.

A comprehensive and easy-to-use manual, designed to help lecturers make full use of the book. Includes:

  suggested lecture outlines incorporating the OHPs supplied with the text
  outline answers to the end-of-chapter questions for discussion
  detailed answers to the case studies within the text, and some supplementary questions and answers
  a discussion question and outline answer to each of the Marketing in Action vignettes
  suggested assignments
  10 additional case studies.

Price: Free to adopters of the main text.
ISBN 0 273 623 249

100 black and white OHP masters selected from the book.

Price: Free to adopters of the main text
ISBN 0 273 623 222

Contains a comprehensive range of interesting and exciting case material, structured to follow the contents of *Principles of Marketing*. Each of the 26 chapters contains 3–4 cases from the *Financial Times* newspaper relating to a specific topic. The chapters are supported by a brief commentary to explain the theory in that section.

Price: Available separately at £15.99 or, for very large adoptions, available shrink-wrapped with the text for a special price. For more details telephone our marketing department on 0171 447 2000.
ISBN 0 273 620 584   192pp   246 × 189mm

Electronic multiple choice question bank
Contains over 400 multiple choice questions, arranged in accordance with the structure of the book. Students answer each question and get immediate feedback in terms of which answer is correct. At the end of the test they are given their total score for that session. The software is from Question Mark, the world leader in software for computerising tests, quizzes and surveys.

Price : Free to adopters of the main text.
ISBN 0 273 630 92X

The video contains 6 cases - 4 short (5 minutes approximately) and 2 long (20 minutes approximately). The cases cover a number of different industries and issues, and is appropriate for use in seminars.

Each case is preceded by a brief summary of the theoretical areas covered in the case and the chapters of the book to which they relate. A number of questions for discussion are included on the web site – see below for more details.

Price: Free to adopters of the main text
ISBN 0 273 623 230

An exciting and involving web site which opens up new possibilities for innovative teaching:

  feedback/comments section
  OHPs that lecturers can download
  links to pages of related interest
  regular updates on the cases studies within the book
  guidance on the video cases.

Test pages of this site are located on www.pitmanpub.co.uk.

Adopters of the main book can access the entire site using a password. To obtain your password telephone our marketing department on 0171 447 2000.

Acknowledgements

■ ■ ■

In any project that has taken four years from its inception there are bound to be many people who have helped, directly or indirectly, in its development.

Particular thanks are due to the panel of reviewers, especially to Sheila Wright and Mohammed Rafiq, for all their help and patience in reading drafts that seemed always to be incomplete. Ray Brown and Pete Nuttall both gave alarmingly detailed but invaluable feedback, and thus thanks go to them and to other anonymous UK and European reviewers for their constructive and thorough comments.

A number of people from the University of Luton deserve thanks: Neville Hunt for his sterling efforts in both sourcing the illustrations and participating in some of the senior management interviews; Alison Deacon of the library staff for her help on Chapter 6; Brian Mathews for his advice on pricing and on services marketing; Pat Badmin, Gerry Kirkwood and Jean Lafferty for their help in supplying material for some of the cases, and David Wright and Marie Petit-Rafer for ideas and materials.

Colleagues from Buckinghamshire College of Higher Education have offered insights and feedback on various aspects of the book, especially on international marketing, as well as supplying coffee, comradeship and consolation. Affectionate thanks, therefore, go to Sheena Harland, Kaye 'Fozzie' Foskett, George Byars, John Cox and many others. On the technical side, Ruth and Shirley have worked miracles in resurrecting crashed disks and unjamming printers. Heartfelt thanks to them.

The University of Teesside also played a role in this project. Thanks to Julie Glover, Helen Bussell and Alan 'Smiffy' Smith for their friendship, their valuable feedback on chapter drafts and the provision of case studies. Thanks too are due to Eleanor Stone for sourcing materials at the start of this project.

Barra O'Cinneide, of the University of Limerick, deserves sincere thanks for the provision of case study material. Other case study contributors, including Ivan Marchevski, Nicola Yankov and Martin Thompstone must also be thanked. We are grateful to Phil Cooper and Gordon Styles for their courage in allowing us access to their small businesses for case study material. We would like to offer general thanks to those individuals and organisations who directly and indirectly helped to create the case studies and marketing in action profiles.

We are immensely grateful to the people who so willingly gave up time for the senior management perspectives in Chapter 26:

Ian Aizlewood, Managing Director, Continental Microwave Ltd
Dr Robert Bischof, Chairman, The Boss Group
Ian Coomber, Executive Director, Sales and Marketing, Vauxhall UK
Mike Dickson, Board Account Director, DMB&B
Bill Scholes, Market Research Manager, Wilkinson Sword

and also to their graduate management trainees:

Kate Hopkins, Account Executive, DMB&B
John Hopwood, Brand Analyst, Vauxhall UK.

During the course of this project, we have come to appreciate the excellent journalistic teams who produce *Marketing*, *Marketing Week*, *The Grocer*, the *Financial Times*, *The European*, *The Times*, *The Sunday Times*, and many other publications that keep us all up to date with key developments in marketing across Europe. We are also indebted to our friends in Bulgaria and Poland, not only Nicola and Ivan, but also Nick Tsarev, Onik Karapchian and Leslaw Piecuch for helping us to understand the problems of emerging eastern European economies and markets.

The Pitman Publishing team has endured much over the last few years, and we would like to thank all those who have helped to bring this project to fruition. In particular, we thank Jennifer Mair, Keith Stanley and Simon Lake who began it all, and Catriona King, Stuart Hay, Pradeep Jethi, Julianne Mulholland, Annette McFadyen and Simon Lake (again!) who saw it through its final stages.

Last, but certainly not least, we offer our deepest apologies to our friends and family for all the neglect they have had to suffer. Perhaps now they will stop opening their phone conversations with, 'Hi, how's the book going?'

Part I

...

MARKETING AND ITS ENVIRONMENT

Marketing Dynamics `1`

The European Marketing Environment `2`

Ask anybody what marketing is and it is likely that you will get responses such as 'advertising' or 'making people buy things they don't want'. The first chapters of this book should provide you with fuller, more accurate and more useful definitions than these.

Chapter 1 defines and explores marketing as a philosophy of doing business which puts the customer first, and therefore casts the marketing department in the role of 'communicator' between the organisation and the outside world. Marketers have to tackle a surprisingly wide range of tasks on a daily basis to fulfil that function (hence the thickness of this book), and these too are defined.

Communication is, however, a two-way process. The marketing function does not exist only to deliver the organisation's goods and messages, but also to carry information from a dynamic and changing European environment back into the organisation. Chapter 2, therefore, looks at some of the external influences which affect marketing decisions and thus the way in which organisations choose to do business.

After you have read this section, marketing should mean a lot more to you than 'advertising', and you will appreciate that 'making people buy things they don't want' is the one thing that successful marketers do not do.

■   ■   ■

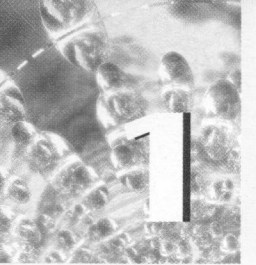

1 Marketing Dynamics

LEARNING OBJECTIVES

This chapter will help you to:

1 define what marketing is;

2 trace the development of marketing as a way of doing business;

3 appreciate the importance and contribution of marketing as both a business function and an interface between the organisation and its customers;

4 understand the scope of tasks undertaken in marketing, and the range of different organisational situations in which marketing is applied; and

5 summarise the structure of this book.

INTRODUCTION

You will have some sort of idea of what marketing is, since you are, after all, exposed to marketing in some form every day of your life. Every time you use a product, buy a product, go window shopping, see an advertising hoarding, watch an advertisement, listen to friends telling you about a wonderful new product they've tried, or even when you go to the library to look at a company's annual report for an assignment, you are reaping the benefits (or being a victim) of marketing activities. When marketing's outputs are so familiar, it is easy to take it for granted and to judge and define it too narrowly by what you see of it close to home. It is a mistake, however, to dismiss marketing as 'just advertising' or 'just selling' or 'making people buy things they don't really want'.

What this book wants to show you is that marketing does, in fact, cover a very wide range of absolutely essential business activities that bring you the products you *do* want, when you want them, where you want them, but at prices you can afford, and with all the information you need to make informed and satisfying consumer choices. And that's only what marketing does for you! Widen your thinking to include what marketing can similarly do for organisations purchasing goods and services from other organisations, and you can begin to see why it is a mistake to be too cynical about professionally practised marketing. None of this is easy. The outputs of marketing, such as the packaging, the advertisements, the glossy brochures, the enticing retail outlets and the incredible bargain value prices, look slick and polished, but a great deal of management planning, analysis and decision making has gone on behind the scenes in order to bring all this to you. By the time you have finished this book, you should appreciate the whole range of marketing activities, and the difficulties of managing them.

Elida Fabergé owns and markets a wide range of toiletry products and fragrances, including Impulse body spray, Organics shampoo, Lynx, Vaseline, Pears and Mentadent. Each brand needs to be properly thought through in terms of what it offers the customer, what the brand name and image communicate to the customer, how it is priced, and how and where it is advertised. Before any of this can happen, however, the organisation has to create, develop and test the product itself, and ensure that it will be accepted by the retail trade. The risks and rewards can be high. Organics is the UK's number two hair-care brand, while Lynx and Impulse are the top-selling body sprays for men and women, respect-ively. Achieving such leadership positions takes a lot of careful planning and management, and usually a lot of investment. Elida Fabergé launched Addiction, a fragrance brand in 1995 which, in addition to its development costs, cost £2 million in television advertising alone. It did, however, earn £4 million in sales in its first three months, but not all products perform so well. Elida Fabergé still faces difficult decisions about Mentadent, Pears and Timotei, all of which are lagging behind in their respective markets (Barnard, 1996).

Before launching further into the detailed descriptions, explanations and analyses of the operational tasks that make up the marketing function, however, it is important to lay a few foundations about what marketing really is, and to give you a more detailed overview of why it is so essential and precisely what it involves in practice.

This chapter will, therefore, start by defining what marketing is, by looking at a couple of widely accepted definitions and discussing their implications for organisations. To see how those definitions have emerged, we provide a brief history of marketing and how it has evolved, both as a business function and as a business orientation or philosophy. Building on that, the chapter can then look at the relationship between marketing, the outside world and the rest of the organisation. This will help to establish the role that marketing departments take on, internally and externally, and to define the tools that they use to fulfil those responsibilities. It is important to remember that marketing has a crucial role in helping to set the organisation's overall strategic objectives, and thus we shall discuss the contribution of marketing to defining strategic direction and how the needs of the customer and the needs of the organisation are reconciled.

Finally, to put all of this into context, there will be a practical section discussing the scope of marketing and looking at the variety of marketing applications that exist. To counter the tendency to think of marketing as being relevant only to consumer markets for fast-moving physical products, there is a timely reminder of other types of market, such as services and non-profit organisations. This section will also outline the influences that are fundamentally changing the way in which academics and managers think about marketing.

MARKETING DEFINED

This section is going to explore what **marketing** is and its evolution. First, we shall look at currently accepted definitions of marketing, then at the history behind those definitions. Linked with that history are the various business orientations outlined on pp. 13–17. These show how marketing is as much a philosophy of doing business as a business function in its own right. It is important to get this concept well established before moving on to the next section where we discuss philosophy and function in the context of the organisation.

What marketing means

Here are two popular and widely accepted definitions of marketing. The first is the definition preferred by the UK's Chartered Institute of Marketing (CIM), while the second is the one offered by the American Marketing Association (AMA):

> Marketing is the management process which identifies, anticipates, and supplies customer requirements efficiently and profitably.   (CIM)

> Marketing is the process of planning and executing the conception, pricing, promotion and distribution of ideas, goods and services to create exchange and satisfy individual and organisational objectives.   (AMA, 1985)

Both definitions make a good attempt at capturing concisely what is actually a wide and complex subject. Although they have a lot in common, each says something important that the other does not emphasise.

Both agree on the following points.

Marketing is a management process

Marketing has just as much legitimacy as any other business function, and involves just as much management skill. It needs planning and analysis, resource allocation, control and investment in terms of money, appropriately skilled people and physical resources. It also, of course, needs implementation, monitoring and evaluation. As with any other management activity, it can be carried out efficiently and successfully – or it can be done poorly, resulting in failure.

Marketing is about giving someone what they want

All marketing activities should be geared towards this. It implies a focus towards the customer or end consumer of the product or service. If 'customer requirements' are not satisfactorily fulfilled, or if customers do not obtain what they want and need, then marketing has failed both the customer and the organisation.

The CIM definition adds a couple of extra insights.

Marketing identifies and anticipates customer requirements

This phrase has a subtle edge to it that does not come through strongly in the AMA definition. It is saying that the marketer creates some sort of offering only after researching the market and pin-pointing exactly what the customer will want. The AMA definition is ambiguous by beginning with the 'planning' process which may or may not be done with reference to the customer.

Example

The launch of digital television services, planned in the UK for 1997, shows some of the difficulties facing marketers trying to predict demand for a new product concept. Hewitt (1995) quoted the Heritage Secretary as claiming that it would be 'the most significant technological and commercial step for television and radio since the development of the cathode-ray tube'. Twenty digital channels can be fitted into the same bandwidth as a conventional channel, but with better picture and sound quality. With this proliferation of channels available, the question is whether the increased capacity will be taken up. This is not so much a matter of supply as one of demand. Even if channels operate on a European scale, where are the new subscribers and the new advertising revenues going to come from to make the services viable? Will current satellite, cable and terrestrial channel subscribers really want to upgrade and pay a minimum of £300 to obtain a digital signal decoder? The potential problem is simple: low numbers of viewers means low advertising revenues, which in turn means poorer programming (more repeats!) and thus even fewer viewers. Identifying wants, or assessing whether people will want something in the future, is therefore an essential first step in any marketing decision, but is not always an easy thing to do.

Marketing fulfils customer requirements efficiently and profitably

This pragmatic phrase warns the marketer against getting too carried away with the altruism of satisfying the customer! In the real world, an organisation cannot please all of the people all of the time, and sometimes even marketers have to make compromises. Efficiency implies working within the resource capabilities of the organisation, and in this case, specifically working within the agreed budgets and performance targets set for the marketing function.

Profitability is a little more questionable. Marketing is now an accepted philosophy within many non-profit-making organisations, such as the UK's National Health Service Trust Hospitals, which would certainly accept the need to manage themselves efficiently and cost effectively, but certainly not profitably. That important context aside, most commercial companies exist to make profits, and thus profitability is a legitimate concern. Even so, some organisations would accept the need, occasionally, to make a loss on a particular product or sector of a market in order to achieve wider strategic objectives. As long as those losses are planned and controlled, and in the longer run provide some other benefit to the organisation, then they are bearable. In general terms, however, if an organisation is consistently failing to make profits, then it will not survive, and thus marketing has a responsibility to sustain and increase profits.

The AMA definition goes further.

Marketing offers and exchanges ideas, goods and services

This statement is close to the CIM's 'profitably', but a little more subtle. The idea of marketing as an **exchange process** is an important one, and was first proposed by Alderson (1957). The basic idea is that I've got something you want, you've got something I want, so let's do a deal. For the most part, the exchange is a simple one.

MARKETING IN ACTION

Fisherman's Friends

Fisherman's Friends, a long established brand, has successfully varied its marketing activities to establish itself in a number of foreign markets. By 1995, 95 per cent of its total sales were generated from overseas markets. The product is sold to the UK and Danish consumer as a lozenge for sore throats, almost as a medicinal product, and sales peak in the winter, reflecting the incidence of colds. In Germany, Norway, Sweden and Switzerland, it is a confectionery product. Interestingly, sales are higher in the markets where it is sold as a sweet than in those where it is sold as a 'medicine'. Once the single European market (SEM) came into existence, the product was launched in France as a confectionery product. Before the SEM, it would have had to have been sold through pharmacies, rather than supermarkets, as a medicinal product because of its menthol content. This case shows the importance of understanding what customers want and expect from products, and making sure that the total marketing offering conforms with it, adapting for local conditions.

Source: Wheatley (1995).

The organisation offers a product or service, and the customer offers a sum of money in return for it. Pepsi offers you a can of cola and you offer payment; you sign a contract to offer your services as an employee, and the organisation pays you a salary; the hospital offers to provide health care and the individual, through taxes or insurance premiums, offers to fund it. A range of further examples is shown diagramatically in Fig 1.1.

What all these examples have in common is the assumption that both parties value what the other has to offer. If they didn't, then they would not be obliged to enter into the bargain. It is up to the marketer to make sure that customers value what the organisation is offering so highly that they are prepared to give the organisation what it wants in return. Whether the marketer is offering a product, a service, or an idea (such as the environmental causes 'sold' by Greenpeace), the essence of the exchange is mutual value. From mutual value can come satisfaction and possible repeat purchases.

FIGURE 1.1

Exchange transactions

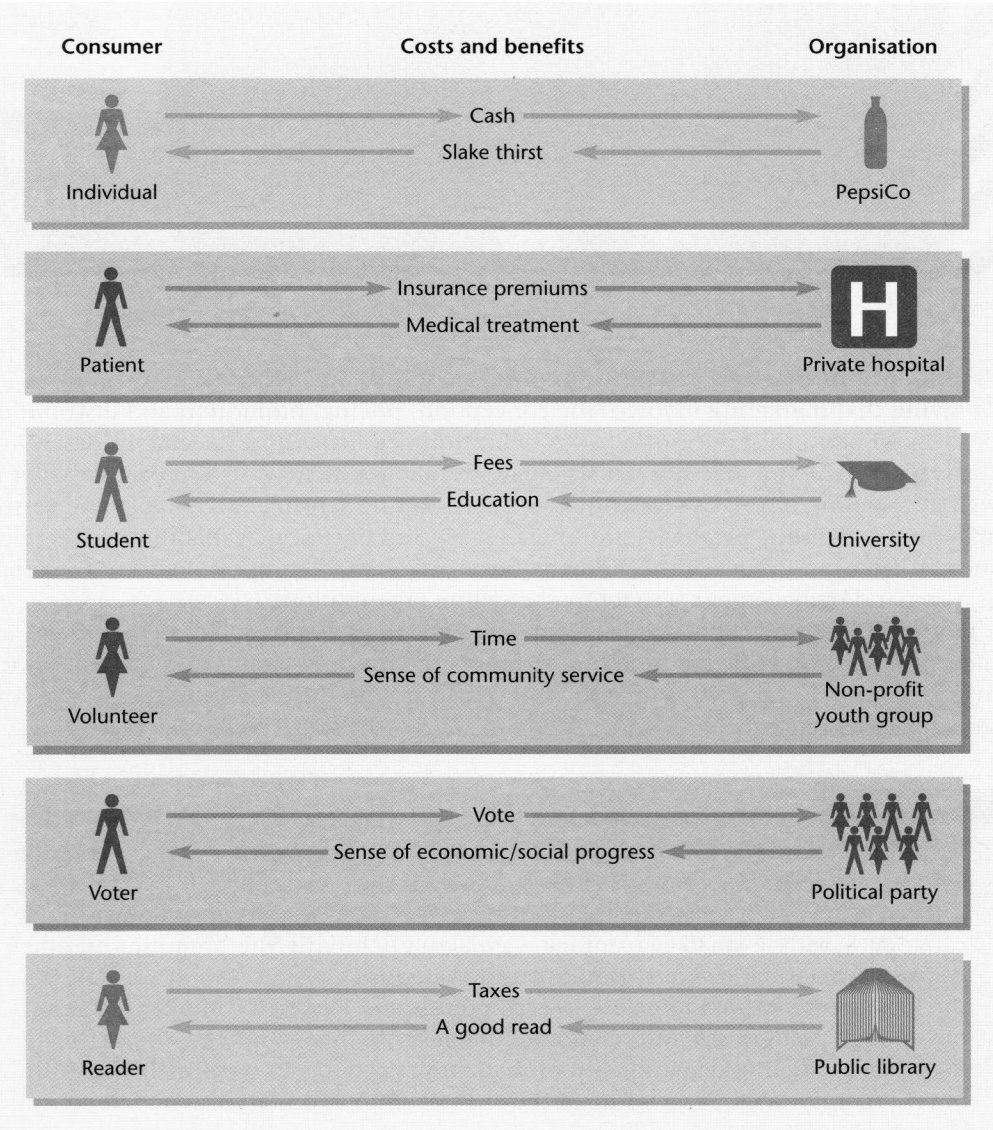

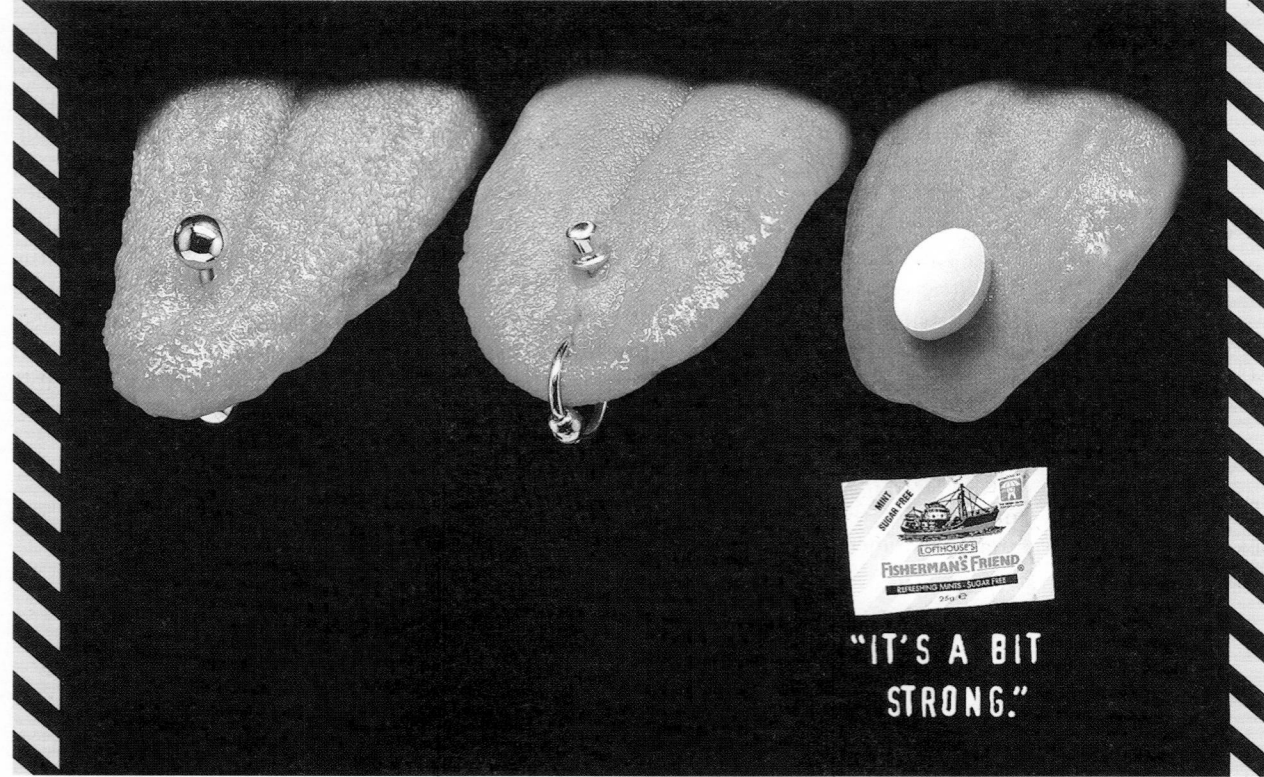

Source: Kelly Weedon Shute Ltd.

Medicine or sweetie? In any event, brace yourself!

Pricing, promotion and distribution of ideas, goods and services

In saying that marketing involves the conception, pricing, promotion and distribution of ideas, goods and services, the AMA definition is a little more specific in describing the ways in which marketers can stimulate exchanges. It suggests a proactive seller as well as a willing buyer. By designing products, setting sensible, acceptable and justifiable prices, creating awareness and preferences, and ensuring availability and service, the marketer can influence the volume of exchanges. Marketing can be seen, therefore, as a demand management activity by the selling organisation.

Both the CIM and the AMA definitions of marketing, despite their popular usage, are increasingly being criticised as failing to reflect the role and reality of marketing in the mid to late 1990s. The two main criticisms centre around the concept of the passive consumer in a discrete exchange, and a failure to address the social context of marketing.

Example

Pulling marketing activities together is not always so easy. Interactive shopping kiosks were withdrawn from Heathrow less than two years after their installation. Although up to 60 000 people per month were browsing through the interactive catalogues, only a small percentage were actually buying the premium-branded goods offered, such as Royal Doulton and Waterford Crystal. Also, it was felt that the kiosks were located too close to cash points, and looked too similar. There was not enough point of sale information to differentiate them. This case shows the difficulty of predicting demand, and of marketing products in ways with which the buyer is comfortable. The closure of the kiosks within two years also underlines the importance of generating sufficient demand quickly enough to sustain business.

Relationship marketing

The traditional definitions of marketing tend to reflect a view that the transaction between buyer and seller is primarily seller orientated, that each exchange is totally discrete, and thus lacking any of the personal and emotional overtones that emerge in a long-term relationship made up of a series of exchanges between the same buyer and seller. Turnbull and Valla (1986) particularly highlight the importance of enduring **buyer–supplier relationships** as a major influence on decision making in international organisational markets.

In some circumstances, however, the traditional non-relationship view is perfectly appropriate. A traveller on an unknown road passing through a foreign country may stop at a wayside café, never visited before, and never to be visited again. The decision to purchase is thus going to be influenced by the ease of parking, the decor and the ambience rather than by any feeling of trust or commitment to the patron. The decision, in short, is based on the immediate and specific marketing offering. Well-lit signs, a menu in your own language, and visibly high hygiene standards will all influence the decision to stop. Such a scenario does not, however, describe the reality in many consumer and organisational markets. As consumers, we often stay loyal to a small number of familiar brands, retailers and suppliers over a number of years. In organisational markets, relationships can be even longer lived. Volvo, for example, has supplier relationships which have lasted for over 50 years.

Easton and Araujo (1994) emphasise that in organisational markets buyer–seller exchanges can no longer be viewed as one-off, discrete, economic transactions, totally uninfluenced by either the social context in which they take place or consideration of past and future transactions between the same two parties.

Example

TR Fastenings, a UK company supplying industrial threaded fastenings, adhesives and turned parts, has developed and nurtured close relationships with its customers. These relationships are based on high levels of communication and understanding of others' needs. This has led to cost reductions in design, production, materials control, purchasing and accounts. The business relies on selling a wide variety of high volume, low unit-cost items, and considers it vital that its customers view the company as a whole, rather than in terms of its individual departments.

The rapid rise of **relationship marketing** (*see* Chapter 19, and p. 157), where organisations develop long-term stable relationships and alliances with other organisations means that:

> **Exchange processes are embedded in the dense fabric of social relations and economic exchange is rarely able to rid itself of non-economic exchange baggage such as social exchange, kinship and friendship networks, altruism and gift giving and a host of other psychological and sociological elements not liable to be reduced to the standardised metric of money.**
>
> (Easton and Araujo, 1994, p. 75)

Although this statement was made strictly in the context of organisational markets, it also has a lot of truth in consumer markets. As Chapter 19 on direct marketing shows, direct relationships between individual consumers in mass markets and the organisations that supply them are starting to develop, and this can only increase the importance of the notion of social processes in the definition of marketing. The UK supermarket chain Tesco, for example, through its Clubcard scheme can track the purchases of individual shoppers, creating a database that allows them to communicate directly with consumers in a way that was not possible a few years ago. Thus 30-something males who are not buying their fair share of wine should watch out for the promotional mailshot that will soon be on its way!

Social marketing

'Social marketing' is a fascinating and thought-provoking phrase that is used by a number of writers (Kotler and Zaltman, 1971; Robin and Reidenbach, 1987, for instance). Social marketing is concerned with ensuring that organisations handle marketing responsibly, and in a way that contributes to the well-being of society. It acknowledges that marketing both draws from and contributes to the society within which it operates, in other words it is not about purely unemotional economic transactions. In order to work, it has to interact with people, it has to reflect what they want and what concerns them, and in turn, marketing's images and values become absorbed into popular culture through a synergistic process. At the worst end of the spectrum, for example, it could be argued that marketing, particularly through advertising, encourages people to aspire to things they cannot really afford, and that it encourages materialism and dissatisfaction with what one has. If that is true, then it is certainly a negative social process. At the best end of the spectrum, it could be argued

Telling us for our own good. Marketing can be used to discourage anti-social behaviour.

Source: DMB&B.

that by developing and opening up mass markets, marketing has brought goods and services that would otherwise only be affordable for few, within the reach of many, and thus marketing is a positive social process. Marketing can also make a positive contribution to the furtherance of altruistic and social causes. The increasing use of marketing techniques by organisations such as Amnesty International, Greenpeace and the International Red Cross, for instance, has had a positive impact in bringing 'issues' to a much wider public and precipitating action.

So definitions of marketing should be moving away from a narrow, organisation-focused perspective, and exchange alone is too narrow a concept for today's approaches and applications of marketing. Further dimensions relating to social contexts and longer-term strategic relationship building are necessary to provide a full understanding of the power of marketing and the influences that shape it.

A definition that includes the important elements of both the AMA and CIM definitions, but perhaps more overtly captures what marketing in 1990s Europe is all about is offered by Gronroos (1990):

> **Marketing is to establish, maintain and enhance long term customer relationships at a profit, so that the objectives of the parties involved are met. This is done by mutual exchange and fulfilment of promises.**

This definition still reflects a managerial orientation towards marketing, but emphasizes the mutually active role that both partners in the exchange play. It does not list the activities that marketers undertake, but instead is more concerned with the partnership idea, the concept that marketing is about doing something *with* someone, not doing something *to* them. Of course, not all transactions between buyers and sellers can be considered to be part of a relationship, especially where the purchase does not involve much risk or commitment from the purchaser and thus there is little to gain from entering a relationship (Berry, 1983). This was clearly shown in the wayside café example cited earlier. Overall, however, marketing is increasingly about relationships. In many organisational markets, the seller or buyer might even adapt their technology, products or production processes to meet the needs of the other party better, and both parties will gain from the stronger relationship formed (Hallén *et al.*, 1987; Pettitt, 1992).

The idea of fulfilling promises is also an important one, as marketing is all about making promises to potential buyers. If the buyer decides, after the event, that the seller did not live up to those promises, the chances are that they will never buy again from that seller. If, on the other hand, the buyer decides that the seller has fulfilled their promises, then the seeds of trust are sown, and the buyer may be prepared to begin a long-term relationship with the seller.

Between them, therefore, the three definitions offered say just about everything there is to say about the substance and basic philosophy of marketing. Few now would argue with any of that, but marketing has not always been so readily accepted in that form, as the next two subsections show.

The development of marketing

The basic idea of marketing as an exchange process has its roots in very ancient history, when people began to produce crops or goods surplus to their own requirements and then to barter them for other things they wanted. Elements of marketing, particularly selling and advertising, have been around as long as trade itself, but it took the industrial revolution, the development of mass production techniques and the separation of buyers and sellers to sow the seeds of what we recognise as marketing today.

In the early days, the late nineteenth and early twentieth centuries, goods were sufficiently scarce and competition sufficiently underdeveloped that producers did not really need marketing. They could easily sell whatever they produced ('the production era' in which a 'production orientation' was adopted). As markets and technology developed, competition became more serious and companies began to produce more than they could easily sell. This led to 'the sales era', therefore, lasting into the 1950s and 1960s, in which organisations developed increasingly large and increasingly pushy sales forces, and more aggressive advertising approaches (the 'selling orientation').

It was not really until the 1960s and 1970s that marketing generally moved away from a heavy emphasis on post-production selling and advertising to become a more comprehensive and integrated field, earning its place as a major influence on corporate strategy ('**marketing orientation**'). This meant that organisations began to move away from a 'sell what we can make' type of thinking, in which 'marketing' was at best a peripheral activity, towards a 'find out what the customer wants and then we'll make it' type of market-driven philosophy. Customers took their rightful place at the centre of the organisation's universe. This finally culminated, in the 1980s, in the wide acceptance of marketing as a strategic concept, and yet there is still room for further development of the **marketing concept**, as new applications and contexts emerge.

Historically, marketing has not developed uniformly across all markets or products. Retailers, along with many consumer goods organisations, have been at the forefront of implementing the marketing concept. Laura Ashley, for instance, developed a strong, unique, international product and retail store image, but within the basic formula is prepared to adapt its merchandising and pricing strategies to suit the demands of different geographic markets. The financial services industry, however, has only very recently truly embraced a marketing orientation, some 10 years or more behind most consumer goods. Knights *et al.* (1994), reviewing the development of a marketing orientation within the UK financial services industry, imply that the transition from a selling to a marketing orientation was 'recent and rapid'. They cite research by Clarke *et al.* (1988) showing that the retail banks were exceptionally early, compared with the rest of the sector, in becoming completely marketing driven. The rest have since followed.

Marketing moves East

This potted history has, so far, presented a sweeping generalisation of what has happened in the evolution of mass produced physical goods within Western European economies. It is interesting to contrast this Western European experience with that of Central and Eastern Europe. For many years, the former Communist command economies had no need of a market orientation, since organisations were told by central government offices what and how much to produce, how much to sell it for and where, and often to whom. In the late 1980s, when all that disappeared, new democratic governments let market forces take over on the Western model, with a consequent revolution in management thinking. Western European academics and practitioners going into former Communist countries to provide management training found generally that although marketing theory and concepts were well known, particularly in the academic sector, they were understood very much in an abstract rather than in an applied sense. There was a widespread feeling that production was the key, as there were many eager potential consumers, but too few goods for them to buy. In Sofia, the capital of Bulgaria, for instance, the growth in the number of high priced restaurants created demand for fresh trout and salmon. Demand far outstripped supply, and so the producers' focus was on raising capital for expansion and improving production capability rather than on marketing. Any firm could sell whatever it could produce, so why waste money on marketing?

The answer to that question began to hit some Eastern European companies very hard, as Western European organisations began to move in on these relatively unexploited markets with their well-developed products and marketing techniques. This serious competition rapidly drove the 'home' companies into a 'selling' perspective, and more recently, towards a more marketing-orientated approach, thus following much the same pattern of development as in Western Europe, but within a much shorter time and benefiting from the experience of the West. Remember, though, that the stage of development reached and the rate of change within various Eastern and Central European economies differ considerably. Shipley and Fonfara (1993), for example, found that many Polish companies have indeed adopted a marketing orientation and have developed appropriate strategic marketing management structures. Nevertheless, they warn that there is still some way to go, and that more training programmes are needed to raise awareness and knowledge of marketing even further. Marinov *et al.* (1993), however, found that in Bulgaria, most organisations are still production orientated, but that there is a move towards a sales orientation. The main barriers, they feel, towards the adoption of a marketing orientation are lack of understanding of what marketing is and lack of resources to do anything about it. Again, Bulgaria is looking towards the West for help and support in overcoming its marketing education problems.

Even in the West, however, the marketing era is not yet over, nor has it stopped developing. The move towards relationship marketing, the increasing importance of international or global marketing and further developments in thinking about 'green' issues, social responsibility and marketing ethics, are all examples of factors that will subtly influence the definition and direction of marketing orientation in the future.

Despite all this, the marketing orientation is not necessarily the only way in which organisations do business, even now. The shift is certainly towards the marketing philosophy, but as the next subsection shows, there are alternative approaches which are still practised.

Business orientations

We discuss below the more precise definitions of the alternative approaches to doing business that were outlined above. We then discribe the characteristic management thinking behind them, and then show how they are used today. Table 1.1 further summarises this information.

TABLE 1.1
Marketing history and business orientations – a summary

Orientation	Focus	Characteristics and aims	Eavesdropping	Main era (generalised)		
				USA	Western Europe	Eastern Europe
Production	Manufacturing	• Increase production • Cost reduction and control • Make profit through volume	'Any colour you want – as long as it's black'	Up to 1940s	Up to 1950s	Late 1980s
Product	Goods	• Quality is all that matters • Improve quality levels • Make profit through volume	'Just look at the quality of the paintwork'	Up to 1940s	Up to 1960s	Largely omitted
Selling	Selling what's produced – seller's needs	• Aggressive sales and promotion • Profit through quick turnover of high volume	'You're not keen on the black? What if I throw in a free sun-roof?'	1940–1950s	1950–1960s	Early 1990s
Marketing	Defining what customers want – buyer's needs	• Integrated marketing • Defining needs in advance of production • Profit through customer satisfaction and loyalty	'Let's find out if they want it in black, and if they would pay a bit more for it'	1960s onwards	1970s onwards	mid-1990s onwards

Production orientation

The emphasis with a **production orientation** is on making products that are affordable and available, and thus the prime task of management is to ensure that the organisation is as efficient as possible in production and distribution techniques. The main assumption is that the market is completely price sensitive, which means that customers are only interested in price as the differentiating factor between competing products and will buy the cheapest. Customers are thus knowledgeable about relative prices, and if the organisation wants to bring prices down, then it must tightly control costs. This is the philosophy of the production era, and was predominant in Central and Eastern Europe in the early stages of the new market economies. Apart from that, it may be a legitimate approach, in the short term, where demand outstrips supply, and companies can put all their effort into improving production and increasing supply and worry about the niceties of marketing later.

A variation on that situation happens when a product is really too expensive for the market, and therefore the means have to be found to bring costs, and thus prices, down. This decision, however, is as likely to be marketing as production driven, and may involve technologically complex, totally new products that neither the producer nor the customer is sure of. Thus CD players, videos, camcorders and home computers were all launched on to unsuspecting markets with limited supply and high prices, but the manufacturers envisaged that with extensive marketing and the benefits gained from progressing along the production and technology learning curve, high volume markets could be opened up for lower priced, more reliable products.

Example

A modern form of production orientation can occur when an organisation becomes too focused on pursuing a low cost strategy in order to achieve economies of scale, and loses sight of the real customer need. Tetra Pak, the Swedish carton manufacturer, makes 68 billion cartons per year for customers such as Del Monte and Gerber worldwide. The problem was that the cartons were difficult to open, and tended to spill their contents all over the floor. Tetra Pak did not invest in innovation to solve this problem, because it was trying to control costs tightly to maintain its position as a low cost operator. The result was that their main rival, Norway's Elo Pak, developed a carton with a proper spout and a plastic cap which better met the customers' needs (Slingsby, 1994). This underlines the necessity for talking to customers and being prepared to respond to their problems and needs.

Product orientation

The **product orientation** assumes that consumers are primarily interested in the product itself, and buy on the basis of quality. Since consumers want the highest level of quality for their money, the organisation must work to increase and improve its quality levels. At first glance, this may seem like a reasonable proposition, but the problem is the assumption that consumers *want this product*. Consumers do not want products, they want solutions to problems, and if the organisation's product does not solve a problem, they will not buy it, however high the quality level is. An organisaton may well produce the best ever record player, but the majority of consumers would rather buy a cheap CD player. In short, customer needs rather than the product should be the focus.

British farmers have often been accused of adopting a product orientation and neglecting marketing, partly as a result of the protection offered by the EU's Common Agricultural Policy (CAP). There are, however, exceptions. G's Fresh Salads in Cambridgeshire achieved a £1 million increase in overseas sales in one year after employing an export sales manager to find out what European customers wanted, in terms of packaging, quality, delivery and pricing. One of their contracts was to supply the Belgian supermarket chain Delhaize le Lion with lettuces and celery, and this was the UK's first direct delivery of fresh produce to an overseas retail chain (Hargreaves, 1994).

Sales orientation

The basis for the **sales orientation** way of thinking is that consumers are inherently reluctant to purchase, and need every encouragement to purchase sufficient quantities to satisfy the organisation's needs. This leads to a heavy emphasis on personal selling and other sales stimulating devices because products 'are sold, not bought', and thus the organisation puts its effort into building strong sales departments, with the focus very much on the needs of the seller, rather than on those of the buyer. Home improvements organisations, selling for example double glazing and cavity wall insulation, have tended to operate like this, as has the timeshare industry.

Timewell (1994) suggests that banks too have followed this kind of philosophy, developing products that are pushed to customers who do not really want them, and do not use them. The banks have discovered that they do not intuitively know what customers want, and thus they will have to adopt a more customer-centred approach to product development. This should mean less of a 'hard sell' in the future, since the products will at least be in tune with customer needs.

Marketing orientation

The organisation that develops and performs its production and marketing activities with the needs of the buyer driving it all, and with the satisfaction of that buyer as the main aim, is marketing orientated. The motivation is to 'find wants and fill them'

MARKETING IN ACTION

Slovenia's struggle

Like many eastern European countries, Slovenia faced a difficult transition to a free market economy, including high, rising unemployment, falling industrial production and economic recession. A particular problem was the loss of its export markets in the former Yugoslavia because of the war. In 1993, exports to the former Yugoslavia halved and thus Slovenia has tried even harder to export into western European markets and to develop free trade links with Poland, Slovakia, the Czech Republic and Hungary.

This has made it all the more important for Slovenian companies to develop a marketing orientation and to streamline their operations. Kovinotehna, for example, is an international trading company, dealing in metal sheets, farming tools and machinery, plumbing and heating products, audio goods, and household equipment among many other areas. The company is primarily a wholesaler, and has concentrated on enlarging and modernising its logistic

and distribution systems in order to deliver its products to customers more quickly, efficiently and cost effectively. It owns its own network of retail stores, including some large superstores, dealing with both consumers and organisational customers, as well as supplying other outlets. It has also managed to penetrate export markets in the Ukraine and Russia, for example. The company recognises the importance of repeat business, and works to develop ongoing relationships with its customers. Kovinotehna is now the fifth largest trading concern in Slovenia.

The company recognised that it would be difficult to achieve all this without outside help, and has sought help from Western business partners. These have supplied the necessary investment and technological help to improve Kovinotehna's competitiveness and the quality of its offering to its customers.

Source: More (1994).

rather than 'create products and sell them'. The assumption is that customers are not necessarily price driven, but are looking for the total offering that best fits their needs, and therefore the organisation has to define those needs and develop appropriate offerings. This is not just about the core product itself, but also about pricing, access to information, availability and peripheral benefits and services that add value to the product. Not all customers, however, necessarily want exactly the same things. They can be grouped according to common needs and wants, and the organisation can produce a specifically targeted marketing package that best suits the needs of one group, thus increasing the chances of satisfying that group and retaining its loyalty.

A marketing orientation is far more, however, than simply matching products and services to customers. It has to emerge from an organisational philosophy, an approach to doing business that naturally places customers and their needs at the heart of what the organisation does. Not all organisations do this to the same extent, although many are trying to move towards it. Hooley *et al.* (1990),

Source: Virgin Financial Services

as a result of an in-depth study of senior marketing executives, suggested that there are different degrees of marketing orientation, as shown in Fig 1.2.

The *marketing philosophers*, the biggest cluster of the four in Fig 1.2, see marketing not only as a function, but as a guiding philosophy of doing business for the whole organisation. In their eyes, marketing is the responsibility of every employee. They also tend to take a more proactive, strategic and planned approach to marketing, and thus have a greater input into corporate strategy.

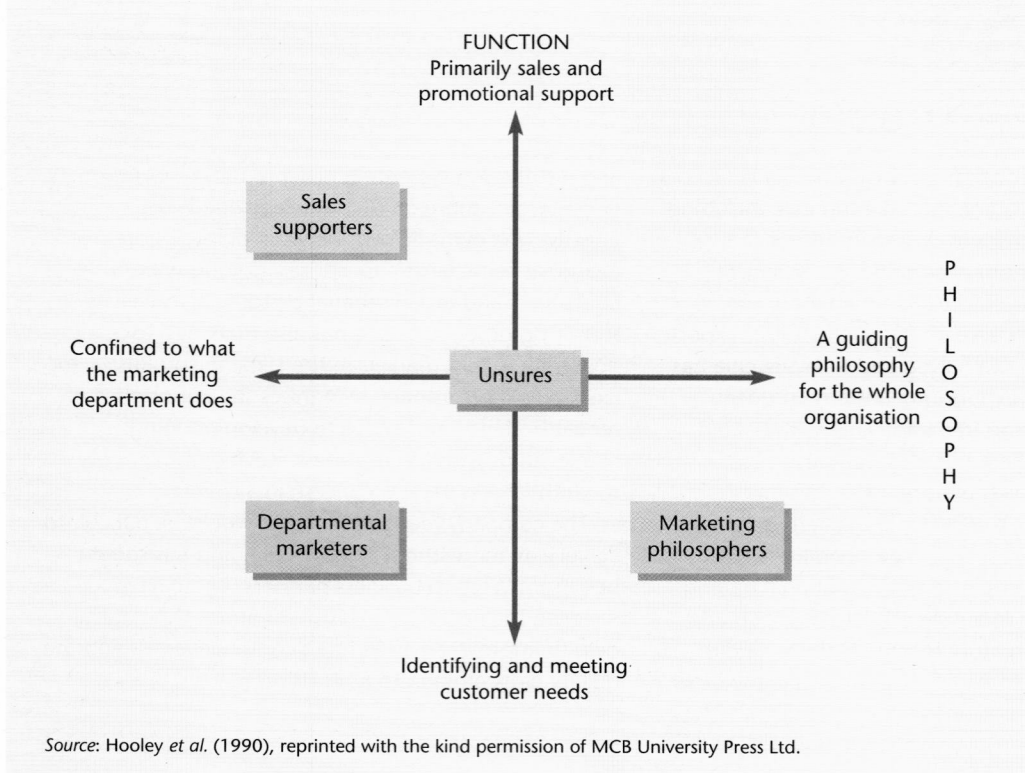

FIGURE 1.2

Marketing approaches

Source: Hooley *et al.* (1990), reprinted with the kind permission of MCB University Press Ltd.

Sales supporters are the smallest cluster, and they see marketing as restricted to the marketing department, with a focus on sales and promotional support.

Departmental marketers see marketing as restricted to the marketing department but, unlike the sales supporters, they also accept the importance of identifying and meeting customer needs.

The '*unsures*' cannot decide exactly what marketing is for. Their attitude reflects elements of sales support and customer orientation, but they do not see marketing as confined to the marketing department nor do they see it as an organisational philosophy. Hooley *et al.* suggest that this implies a laissez-faire attitude to marketing rather than any kind of conscious orientation.

Organisations may evolve from sales support to departmental marketing to the guiding philosophy stage, and organisations that reach the philosophy stage may perform better than those which do not.

The Chief Executive Officer (CEO) of Nestlé fits closely into the marketing philosopher category. His view is that 'Marketing must be a part of general corporate strategy; there is no such thing as isolated marketing' and that 'Marketing is a job for the boss and top management because continuity is important' (Maucher, 1994). He believes strongly in the interaction between marketing function, strategy and philosophy, and longer-term corporate health. He thus feels that the whole organisation can be badly affected when marketing becomes too functional, or 'goes wrong'.

Having thus established the importance of the marketing concept, it is important to look more closely at what its adoption and implementation mean to the organisation.

THE MARKETING CONCEPT IN THE ORGANISATION

What does the philosophy of marketing as a way of doing business mean to a real organisation? In this section we explore the practicalities of implementing the marketing concept, showing just how fundamentally marketing can influence the structure and management of the whole organisation. First, we look at the complexity of the organisational environment, and then think about how marketing can help to manage and make sense of the relationship between the organisation and the outside world. Second, we examine the relationship between marketing and the internal world of the organisation, looking, for example, at the potential conflicts between marketing and other business functions. To bring the external and the internal environments together, this section is summarised by looking at marketing as an interface, i.e. as a linking mechanism between the organisation and various external elements.

The organisational environment

Figure 1.3 summarises the complexity of the external world in which an organisation has to operate. There are many people, groups, elements and forces that have the power to influence, directly or indirectly, the way in which the organisation conducts its business. The organisational environment includes both the immediate operating environment, and the broader issues and trends that affect business in the longer term.

Current and potential customers
Customers are obviously vital to the continued health of the organisation. It is essential, therefore, that it is able to locate customers, find out what they want and then communicate its promises to them. Those promises have to be delivered (i.e. the right product at the right time at the right price in the right place) and followed up to ensure that customers are satisfied.

FIGURE 1.3

The
organisation's
environment

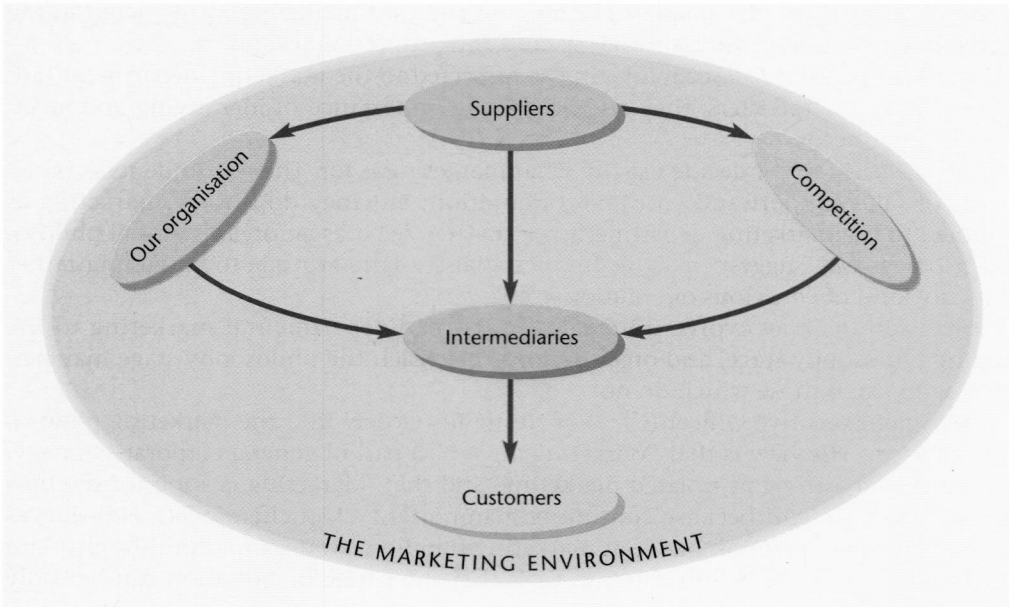

Competitors

Competitors, however, make the organisation's liaison with customer groups a little more difficult, since by definition, they are largely pursuing the same set of customers. Customers will make comparisons between different offerings, and will listen to competitors' messages. The organisation, therefore, has not only to monitor what the competition are actually doing now, but also to try to anticipate what they will do in the future in order to develop counter-measures in advance. European giants Nestlé and Unilever, for example, complete fiercely with each other in several consumer fmcg markets.

Intermediaries

Intermediaries often provide invaluable services in getting goods from manufacturers to the end buyer. Without the co-operation of a network of wholesalers and/or retailers, many manufacturers would have immense problems in getting their goods to the end customer at the right time in the right place. The organisation must, therefore, think carefully about how best to distribute goods, and build appropriate relationships with intermediaries. Again, this is an area in which competition can interfere, and organisations cannot always obtain access to the channels of distribution that they want, or trade on the terms that they want.

Suppliers

Another crucial link in the chain is the supplier. Losing a key supplier of components or raw materials can mean that production flow is interrupted, or that a lower quality or more expensive substitution has to be made. This means that there is a danger that the organisation will fail in its promises to the customer, for example, by not providing the right product at the right time at the right price. Choice of suppliers, negotiation of terms and relationship building all, therefore, become important tasks.

The wider **marketing environment**, which will be discussed in further detail in Chapter 2, covers all the other influences that might provide opportunities or threats to the organisation. These include technological development, legal and regulatory constraints, the economic environment, and sociocultural changes. It is essential for the organisation to keep track of all these things, and to incorporate them into decision making as early as possible if it is to keep ahead of the competition.

This overview of the organisation's world has implied that there are many relationships that matter and that need to be managed if the organisation is to conduct its business successfully. The main responsibility for creating and managing these relationships lies with the marketing function.

Marketing and other business functions

As well as fostering and maintaining relationships with external groups and forces, the marketing function has to interact with other functions within the organisation. Not all organisations have formal marketing departments, and even if they do, they can be set up in different ways, but wherever the responsibility for the planning and implementation of marketing lies, close interaction with other areas of the organisation is essential. Not all business functions, however, operate with the same kind of focus, and sometimes there can be potential conflict where perspectives and concerns do not match up. This subsection looks at just a few other functions typically found in all but the smallest organisations and some of the points of conflict between them and the marketers.

Finance

The finance function, for example, sets budgets, perhaps early in the financial year, and expects other functions to stick to them. They want hard evidence to justify expenditure, and they usually want pricing to cover costs and to contribute towards profit. Marketing, on the other hand, tends to want the flexibility to act intuitively, according to fast-changing needs. Marketing also takes a longer, strategic view of pricing, and may be prepared to make a short-term financial loss in order to develop the market or to further wider strategic objectives.

In terms of accounting and credit, i.e. where finance comes into contact with customers, the finance function would want pricing and procedures to be as standardised as possible, for administrative ease. An accountant would want to impose tough credit terms and short credit periods, preferably only dealing with customers with proven credit records. Marketing, however, would again want some flexibility to allow credit terms to be used as part of a negotiation procedure, and to use pricing discounts as a marketing tool.

Purchasing

The purchasing function can also become somewhat bureaucratic, with too high a priority given to price. A focus on economical purchase quantities, standardisation and the price of materials, along with the desire to purchase as infrequently as possible, can all reduce the flexibility and responsiveness of the organisation. Marketing prefers to think of the quality of the components and raw materials rather than the price, and to go for non-standard parts, to increase their ability to differentiate their product from that of the competition. To be fair to purchasing, this is a somewhat traditional view. The rise of relationship marketing (p. 157) and the increasing acceptance of just in time (JIT) systems (Chapter 14) mean that marketing and purchasing are now working more closely than ever in building long-term, flexible, co-operative relationships with suppliers.

Production

Production has perhaps the greatest potential to clash with marketing. It may be in production's interests to operate long, large production runs with as few variations on the basic product as possible, and with changes to the product as infrequently as possible, at least where mass production is concerned. This also means that production would prefer to deal with standard, rather than customised, orders. If new products are necessary, then the longer the lead time they are given to get production up to speed and running consistently, the better. Marketing has a greater sense of urgency and a greater demand for flexibility. Marketing may look for short production runs of many varied models in order to serve a range of needs in the market. Similarly, changes to the product may be frequent in order to keep the market interested. Marketing, particularly when serving industrial customers, may also be concerned with customisation as a means of better meeting the buyer's needs.

Research and development and engineering

Like production, research and development (R&D) and engineering prefer long lead times. If they are to develop a new product from scratch, then the longer they have to do it, the better. The problem is, however, that marketing will want the new product available as soon as possible, for fear of the competition launching their version first. Being first into a market can allow the organisation to establish market share and customer loyalty, and to set prices freely, before the effects of competition make customers harder to gain and lead to downward pressure on prices. There is also the danger that R&D and engineering may become focused on the product for the product's sake, and lose sight of what the eventual customer is looking for. Marketing, in contrast, will be concentrating on the benefits and selling points of the product rather than purely on its functionality.

Marketing as a business philosophy

The previous subsection took a pretty negative view, highlighting the potential for conflict and clashes of culture between marketing and other internal functions. It need not necessarily be like that, and this subsection will seek to redress the balance a little, by showing how marketing can work with other functions. Many successful organisations such as Sony, Nestlé and Unilever ensure that all functions within their organisation are focused on their customers. These organisations have embraced a marketing philosophy that permeates the whole enterprise and places the customer firmly at the centre of their universe.

What must be remembered is that organisations do not exist for their own sake. They exist primarily to serve the needs of the purchasers and users of their goods and services. If they cannot successfully sell their goods and services, if they cannot create and hold customers (or clients, or passengers, or patients or whoever), then they undermine their reason for existing. All functions within an organisation, whether they have direct contact with customers or not, contribute in some way towards that fundamental purpose. Finance, for example, helps the organisation to be more cost effective; personnel helps to recruit appropriate staff and make sure they are properly trained and remunerated so that they are more productive or serve the customer better; R&D provides better products; and production obviously churns out the product to the required quality and quantity specifications to meet market needs.

All of these functions and tasks are interdependent, i.e. none of them can exist without the others, and none of them has any purpose without customers and markets to serve. Marketing can help to supply all of those functions with the information they need to fulfil their specific tasks better, within a market-orientated framework. Those interdependencies, and the role of marketing in bringing functions together and emphasising the customer focus, are summarised in a simplified example in Fig 1.4.

Although the lists of items in the boxes in Fig 1.4 are far from comprehensive, they do show clearly how marketing can act as a kind of buffer or filter, both collecting information from the outside world then distributing it within the organisation, and presenting the combined efforts of the various internal functions to the external world. The customers box in the figure contains just a few of the issues that concern customers.

Customer concerns

Current product needs. To satisfy current needs, production has to know how much is required, when and to what quality specification. Production, perhaps with the help of the purchasing function, has to have access to the right raw materials or components at the right price. Keeping current products within an acceptable price band for the customer involves production, purchasing, finance and perhaps even R&D. A sales function might take orders from customers and make sure that the right quantity of goods is dispatched quickly to the right place. Marketing brings in those customers, monitoring their satisfaction levels, and brings any problems to the attention of the relevant functions as soon as possible so that they can be rectified with the minimum of disruption.

FIGURE 1.4

Marketing as an interface

Future needs. Marketing, perhaps with the help of R&D, needs to monitor what is happening now and to try to predict what needs to happen in the future. This can be

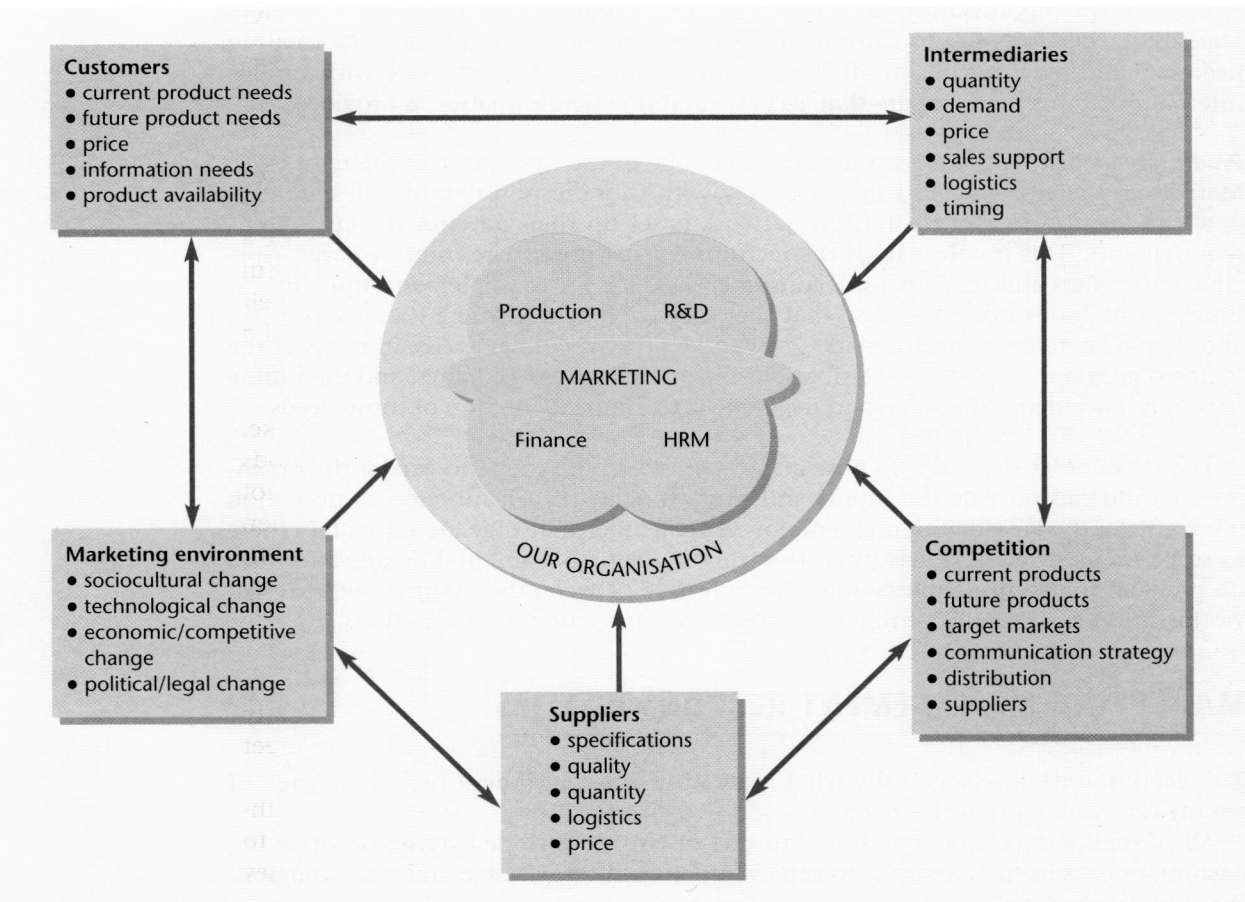

through talking to customers and finding out how their needs are evolving, or working out how new technology can be commercially exploited, or through monitoring competitors' activities and thinking about how they can be imitated, adapted or improved upon. Inevitably, there is a planning lead time, so marketing needs to bring in ideas early, then work with other functions to turn them into reality at the right time. Finance may have to sanction investment in a new product; R&D might have to refine the product or its technology; production may have to invest in new plant, machinery or manufacturing techniques; purchasing may have to start looking for new suppliers, and personnel may have to recruit new staff to help with the development, manufacture or sales of the new product.

When R&D and marketing do share common goals and objectives, it can be a very powerful combination. Marketing can feed ideas from the market that can stimulate innovation, while R&D can work closely with marketing to find and refine commercial applications for its apparently pointless discoveries.

Desired pricing levels. It is rare to find an organisation that can price its products exactly as it wishes without reference to external pressures. Marketing needs to establish what price level the market will bear, and then liaise with production, purchasing and finance to make sure that the organisation can produce the product at that price and still make an adequate profit. If the organisation wants a higher price, then marketing has to make sure that the customer understands and values the benefits they are getting from the product to justify the premium price.

Information needs. If customers do not know about a product or do not understand what benefits it offers them, then they are not going to buy it, and all the internal efforts of the organisation in producing the product will have been wasted. Marketing, therefore, has to liaise with customers to find out what their information needs are and how they fit into the competitive context, and then work with various internal functions to make sure that accurate and timely information is provided.

Product availability. Customers want products to be in the right place at the right time. Marketing, therefore, needs to work closely with those responsible for sales and dispatch to ensure that a distribution network is set up that matches the customer's requirements. This involves both the recruitment of appropriate intermediaries (specific wholesalers and retailers for a consumer product, for example), and the efficient transport of goods from A to B so that they arrive when and where they are wanted, and in good condition. Again, marketing can identify the initial needs, in terms of the required geographic spread of distribution, the preferred intermediaries, and the timing of supply, and then can also help in negotiating the implementation of those needs.

These examples show briefly how marketing can be the eyes and ears of the organisation, and can provide the inputs and support to help each function to do its job more efficiently. Provided that all employees remember that they are ultimately there to serve the customers' needs, then the truly marketing-orientated organisation has no problem in accepting marketing as an interface between the internal and external worlds, and involving marketing in the day-to-day operation of its functions.

MARKETING MANAGEMENT RESPONSIBILITIES

This section outlines specifically what marketing does, and identifies where each of the areas is dealt with in this book.

All of marketing's tasks boil down to one of two things: identifying or satisfying customer needs in such a way as to achieve the organisation's objectives for profitability, survival or growth.

Identifying customer needs

Implicit in this is the idea of identifying the customer. The development of mass markets, more aggressive international competition and the increasing sophistication of the customer have taught marketers that it is unrealistic to expect to be able to satisfy all of the people all of the time. Customers have become more demanding, largely, it must be said, as a result of marketers' efforts, and want products that not only fulfil a basic functional purpose, but also provide positive benefits, sometimes of a psychological nature.

The basic functional purpose of a product, in fact, is often irrelevant as a choice criterion between competing brands – all fridges keep food cold, all brands of cola slake thirst, all cars move people from A to B, regardless of which organisation supplies them. The crucial questions for the customer are how does it fulfil its function, and what extra does it do for me in the process? Thus the choice of a BMW over a Lada may be made because the purchaser feels that the BMW is a better designed and engineered car, gets you from A to B in more comfort and with a lot more style, gives you the power and performance to zip aggressively from A to B if you want, and the BMW name is well respected and its status will reflect on the driver, enhancing self-esteem and standing in other peoples' eyes. The Lada may be preferred by someone who does not want to invest a lot of money in a car, who is happy to potter from A to B steadily without the blaze of glory, who values economy in terms of insurance, running and servicing costs, and who does not feel the need for a car that is an overt status symbol. These profiles of contrasting car buyers point to a mixture of product and psychological benefits, over and above the basic function of the cars, that are influential in the purchasing decision.

This has two enormous implications for the marketer. The first is that if buyers and their motives are so varied, it is important to identify the criteria and variables that distinguish one group of buyers from another. Once that is done, the marketer can then make sure that a product offering is created that matches the needs of one group as closely as possible. If the marketer's organisation does not do this, then someone else's will, and any 'generic' type of product that tries to please most of the people most of the time will sooner or later be pushed out by something better tailored to a narrower group. The second implication is that by grouping customers according to characteristics and benefits sought, the marketer has a better chance of spotting lucrative gaps in the market than if the market is treated as a homogeneous mass.

Identifying customer needs is not, however, just a question of working out what they want now. The marketer has to try to predict what they will want tomorrow, and identify the influences that are changing customer needs. The environmental factors that affect customer needs and wants, as well as the means by which organisations can fulfil them, are discussed further in Chapter 2. The nature of customers, and the motivations and attitudes that affect their buying behaviour are covered in Chapters 3 (consumers) and 4 (organisational buyers), while the idea of grouping customers according to common characteristics and/or desired product features and benefits is discussed in Chapter 5. The techniques of market research, as a prime means of discovering what customers are thinking and what they want now and in the future, is the subject of Chapter 6.

Satisfying customer needs

Understanding the nature of customers and their needs and wants is only the first step, however. The organisation needs to act on that information, in order to develop and implement marketing activities that actually deliver something of value to the customer. The means by which such ideas are turned into reality is the **marketing mix**. Figure 1.5 summarises the areas of responsibility within each element of the mix.

FIGURE 1.5

The marketing mix

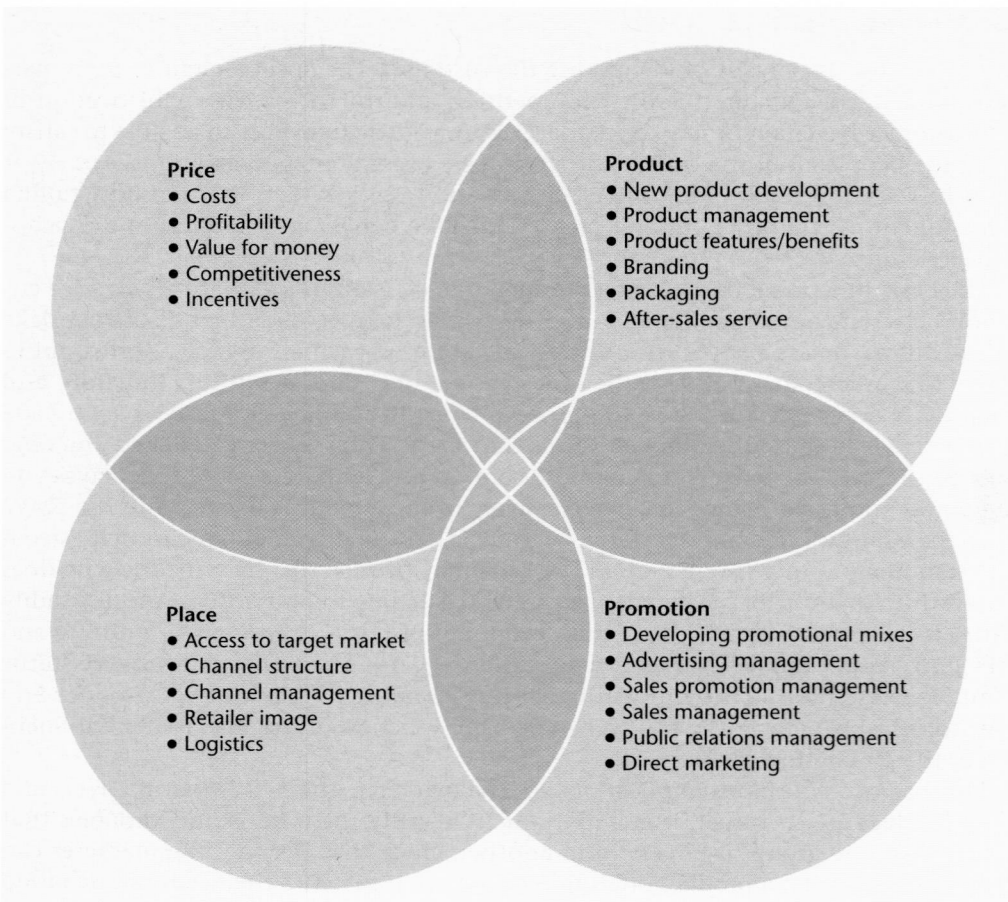

Price
- Costs
- Profitability
- Value for money
- Competitiveness
- Incentives

Product
- New product development
- Product management
- Product features/benefits
- Branding
- Packaging
- After-sales service

Place
- Access to target market
- Channel structure
- Channel management
- Retailer image
- Logistics

Promotion
- Developing promotional mixes
- Advertising management
- Sales promotion management
- Sales management
- Public relations management
- Direct marketing

First defined by Borden (1964), the marketing mix is the combination of four major tools of marketing, otherwise known as '**the 4Ps**' (product, price, promotion and place). This creates an offering for the customer. The use of the words *mix* and *combination* are important here, because successful marketing relies as much on interaction and synergy between marketing mix elements as it does on good decisions within those elements themselves. Häagen Dazs ice cream, for example, is a perfectly good, quality product, but its phenomenal success only came after an innovative and daring advertising campaign that emphasised certain adult-orientated product benefits. A good product with bad communication will not work, and similarly a bad product with the glossiest advertising will not work either. This is because the elements of the marketing mix all depend on each other, and if they are not consistent with each other in what they are saying about the product, then the customer, who is not stupid, will reject it all.

We now look more closely at each element of the marketing mix.

Product

This area, discussed in Part III (Chapters 7, 8 and 9) covers everything to do with the creation, development and management of products. It is about not only what to make, but when to make it, how to make it, and how to ensure that it has a long and profitable life. Furthermore, a product is not just a physical thing. In marketing terms, it includes peripheral, but important elements, such as after-sales service, guarantees, installation and fitting – anything that helps to distinguish the product from its competition and make the customer more likely to buy it.

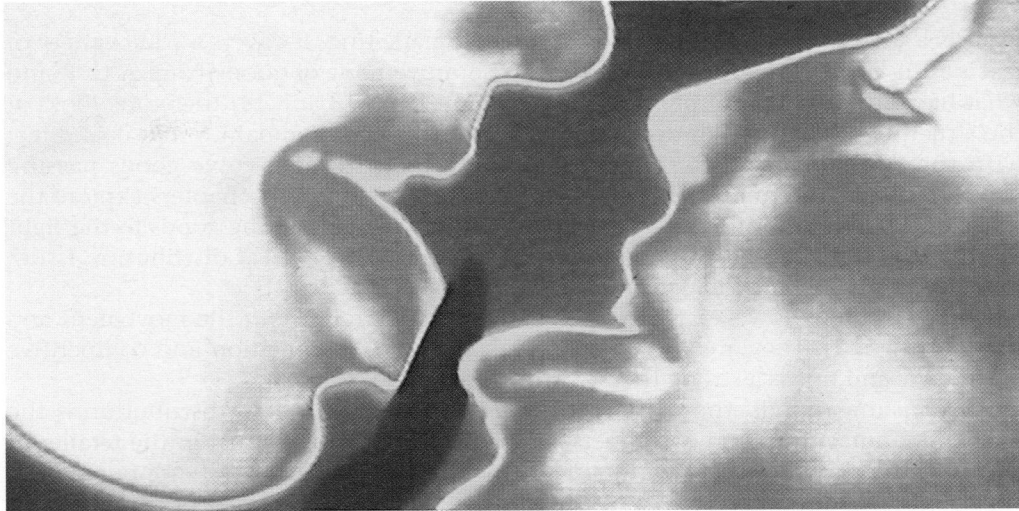

The implied consumer benefit is more than just the taste of Häagen Dazs ice cream.

Source: Bartle Bogle Hegarty.

Particularly with fast-moving consumer goods (**fmcg**), part of a product's attractiveness is, of course, its brand imagery and its packaging. Both of these are likely to emphasise the psychological benefits offered by the product. With organisational purchases, however, the emphasis is more likely to be on fitness for functional purpose, quality and peripheral services (technical support, delivery, customisation etc.). As well as featuring in the product chapters, echoes of these concerns will come through strongly in the chapters on buyer behaviour and segmentation (Chapters 3–5).

Although much of the emphasis is on physical products, it must also be remembered that service markets are an increasingly important growth area of many European economies. The product chapters do cover some aspects of services, but the main discussion of the service product is in Chapter 23, which deals with services marketing.

Price

Price is not perhaps as clear-cut as it might seem at first glance, since price is not necessarily a straightforward calculation of costs and profit margins. As Part IV (Chapters 10 and 11) will show, price has to reflect issues of buyer behaviour, because people judge 'value' in terms of their perceptions of what they are getting for their money, what else they could have had for that money and how much that money meant to them in the first place.

Pricing also has a strategic dimension, in that it gives messages to all sorts of people in the market. Customers, for example, may use price as an indicator of quality and desirability for a particular product, and thus price can reinforce or destroy the work of other elements of the marketing mix. Competitors, on the other hand, may see price as a challenge, because if an organisation prices its products very low it may be signalling its intention to start a price war to the death, whereas very high (premium) prices may signal that there are high profits to be made or that there is room for a competitor to undercut and take market share away.

Overall, price is a very flexible element of the marketing mix, being very easy to tinker with. It is also, however, a dangerous element to play around with, because of its very direct link with revenues and profits, unless management think very carefully and clearly about how they are using it. The focus of the pricing chapters, therefore, is on the factors that influence price setting, the short-term tactical uses of pricing in various kinds of market and the strategic implications of a variety of pricing policies.

Place

Place is a very dynamic and fast-moving area of marketing. It covers a wide variety of fascinating topics largely concerned with the movement of goods from A to B and what happens at the point of sale. Part V (Chapters 12, 13 and 14) therefore, looks at the structure of channels of distribution, from mail order companies that deal direct with the end consumer, to long and complex chains that involve goods passing between several intermediaries before they get to a retailer. The chapters explore the range of different intermediaries, and the roles they play in getting goods to the right place at the right time for the end buyer, as well as the physical distribution issues involved in making it all happen.

Do not assume, however, that these channels are merely about the movement and transfer of goods. They are also about power, control, manipulation and competitive advantage, and this is a strong theme throughout these chapters.

For consumer goods, the most visible player in the channel of distribution is the retailer. Manufacturers and consumers alike have to put a lot of trust in the retailer to do justice to the product, to maintain stocks, and to provide a satisfying purchasing experience. Retailers face many of the same marketing decisions as other types of organisation, and use the same marketing mix tools, but with a slightly different perspective. They also face unique marketing problems, for example, store location, layout and the creation of store image and atmosphere. Retailing has, therefore, been given its own chapter which explores its particular concerns.

Promotion

The longest section of this book, Part VI (Chapters 15–20), is basically about communication, which is often seen as the most glamorous and sexy end of marketing. This does not mean, however, that marketing communication is purely an 'artistic' endeavour, or that it can be used to wallpaper over cracks in the rest of the marketing mix. Communication, because it is so pervasive and high profile, can certainly make or break a marketing mix, and thus it needs wise and constant analysis, planning and management.

Chapters 16–20 look at the whole range of marketing communication techniques, not just advertising, but also sales promotions, personal selling, public relations and direct marketing. The activities undertaken within each area, the objectives each can best achieve, their relative strengths and weaknesses, and the kinds of management and planning processes that have to support them are discussed. To put all that into perspective, however, Chapter 15 first looks at the promotional mix as a whole, thinking about the factors that will influence the relative emphasis put on each individual communications area.

That, then, is the traditional 4Ps approach to marketing that has served very well for many years. More recently, however, it has become apparent that the 4Ps as they stand are not always sufficient. In the services sector in particular, they cannot fully describe the marketing activities that are going on, and so an extended marketing mix, the **7Ps** was proposed by Booms and Bitner (1981), adding people, processes and physical evidence to the traditional 4Ps.

People

Services often depend on people to perform them, creating and delivering the product as the customer waits. A customer's satisfaction with hairdressing and dentistry services, for example, has as much to do with the quality and nature of the interaction between the customer and the service provider as with the end result. If the customer feels comfortable with a particular service provider, trusts them and has a rapport with them, that is a relationship that a competitor would find hard to break into. Even where the service is not quite so personal, sullen assistance in a shop or a fast-food outlet, for example, does not encourage the customer to come back for more. Thus people add value and a dimension to the marketing package way beyond the basic product offering.

Processes

Manufacturing processes, once they are set up, are consistent and predictable and can be left to the production management team, and since they go on out of sight of the customer, any mistakes can be weeded out before distribution. Services, however, are 'manufactured' and consumed live, on the spot, and because they do involve people and the performance of their skills, consistency can be rather more difficult than with normal manufacturing. The marketer, therefore, has to think carefully about how the service is delivered, and what quality controls can be built in so that the customer can be confident that they know what to expect each time they consume the service product. This applies, for example, to banks and other retailers of financial services, fast-food outlets, hairdressers and other personal service providers, and even to professionals such as solicitors and management consultants.

Process can also involve queueing mechanisms, preventing waiting customers from getting so impatient that they leave without purchase; processing customer details and payment, as well as ensuring the high professional quality of whatever service they are buying.

Physical evidence

This final area is of particular relevance to retailers (of any type of product), or those who maintain premises from which a service is sold or delivered. It singles out some of the factors already mentioned when talking about retailers within the place element of the traditional 4Ps approach, such as atmosphere, ambience, image and design of premises. In other service situations, physical evidence would relate to the aircraft in which you fly, the hotel in which you stay, the stadium in which you watch the big match, or the lecture theatre in which you learn.

Other than in the services arena, however, the 4Ps are still widely accepted as defining the marketing mix. This book will, therefore, be structured around them. As you read the subsections on the four elements of the marketing mix, look to see where aspects of people, process and physical evidence are being incorporated or implied within that traditional structure. Relationship marketing, in any type of market for any type of product, is increasingly throwing the emphasis on adding value to products through service. Inevitably, the extra 3Ps are going to impinge on that, and be reflected in discussing applications of the original 4Ps.

The particular combination of the 4Ps used by any one organisation needs to give it **competitive edge**, or **differential advantage**. This means that the marketer is creating something unique, that the potential customer will recognise and value, that distinguishes one organisation's products from another's. In highly competitive, crowded markets, this is absolutely essential for drawing customers towards your product. The edge or advantage may be created mainly through one element of the mix, or through a combination of them. A product may have a combination of high quality and good value (price and product) that a competitor cannot match; an organisation may have established a 24-hour telephone ordering and home delivery service (place) that cannot easily be imitated; an effective and unique communications campaign combined with an excellent product living up to all its promises (promotion and product) can make an organisation's offering stand out above the crowd.

Strategic vision

It is clear that individual marketing activities must be looked at within the context of a coherent and consistent marketing mix, but achieving that mix has to be an out-

Virgin Direct

Many organisations claim to be marketing orientated, with their focus on the needs of the buyer. Virgin Direct, for example, decided that personal equity plans (PEPs) were not being properly designed and marketed to the small UK investor. PEPs are sold by financial services companies who then use the money to buy and sell shares on behalf of their PEPs holders. The income from a PEP is tax free. Virgin felt that the financial services companies selling PEPs were charging small investors too much in management fees and that people felt that the purchasing process was complex and daunting. Virgin, therefore, in partnership with Norwich Union, designed a PEP to suit people whose experience of investment went no further than a bank or building society savings account, cut the management fees to a minimum, cut out intermediaries by selling direct over the phone, and then advertised it in comprehensible English rather than in financial jargon. As Virgin said in an advertisement (*Sunday Times* Money Section, 1 October 1995, p. 3):

> It has none of the things which make most financial products such a drag, such as salesmen, commission and jargon-ridden brochures.

This clearly appealed to the small investor, since by early 1996, within two years of its launch, Virgin Direct had some 65 000 PEP holders and managed PEPs worth around £325 mn. Building on this success, in May 1996, Virgin launched Virgin Life Insurance and the Virgin Survival Plan. The advertising took a similar theme to that used for PEPs (*The Times*, 31 May 1996, p. 5):

> People ask us: 'Why are you getting into life insurance? It's a dreary discredited business'. And we say: 'Yup, that's why'.

For the first few weeks, insurance products were widely advertised, but only offered to existing PEPs customers. Presumably this was because the established customer base might be more likely to buy the new product, particularly because they had been made to feel special by being given priority, and thus would allow volume sales to build more quickly. It could also be a way of testing the market on a limited basis to check what the response would be and to allow the company to fine-tune its product and service offering before a full national launch.

come of a wider framework of strategic marketing planning, implementation and control. Part VII looks at these wider issues, in Chapters 21 and 22.

Strategy is concerned with looking into the future and developing and implementing the plans that will drive the organisation in the desired direction. Implicit in that is the need for strategy to inform (and be informed by) marketing. Strategic marketing thinking also needs a certain amount of unblinkered creativity, and can only be really successful if the marketer thinks not in terms of product, but rather in terms of benefits or solutions delivered to the customer. The organisation that answers the question, 'What business are you in?' with the reply, 'We are in the business of making gloss paint' is in danger of becoming too inwardly focused on the product itself and improving its manufacture (the production orientation). A more correct reply would have been, 'We are in the business of helping people to create beautiful rooms' (the identification of customer needs). The cosmetics executive who said that in the factory they made cosmetics but in the chemist's shop they sold hope, and the power tool manufacturer who said that they did not make drills, they made quarter-inch holes, were both underlining a more creative, outward looking, problem-solving way of marketing thinking. Products are bought by customers to solve problems, and if the product does not solve the problem, or if something else solves it better, then the customer will turn away.

The organisation that cannot see this and defines itself in product rather than market terms could be said to be suffering from *marketing myopia*, a term coined by Levitt (1960). Such an organisation may well be missing out on significant marketing opportunities, and thus may leave itself open to new or more innovative competitors who more closely match customer needs. A classic example of this is slide rule manufacturers. Their definition of the business they were in was 'making slide rules'. Perhaps if they had defined their business as 'taking the pain out of calculation' they would still exist today and be manufacturing electronic calculators. Green (1995) discusses how the pharmaceutical companies are thinking about what business they are in. The realisation that patients are buying 'good health' rather than 'drugs' is broadening the horizons of companies such as Sandoz in Switzerland, SmithKline Beecham in the UK and Merck in the USA, all of which have diversified into areas of health care other than research and development of drugs. SmithKline Beecham in particular wants to spread its efforts across what it sees as the four core elements of health care: prevention, diagnosis, treatment and cure.

Therefore the distinction between the product and the problem it solves matters, because marketing strategy is about managing the organisation's activities within the real world in which it has to survive. In that turbulent and dynamically changing world, a marketing mix that works today may not work tomorrow. If your organisation is too product focused to remember to monitor how customer needs and wants are changing, then it will get left behind by competitors who do have their fingers on the customer's pulse. If your organisation forgets why it is making a particular product and why the consumer buys it, how can it develop marketing strategies that strike a chord with the customers and defend against the competition?

Think about a drill manufacturer that is product focused and invests vast amounts of time and money in developing a better version of the traditional electric drill. How do you think it would feel if a competitor then launched a hand-held, cordless, laser gun that could instantly zap quarter-inch holes (controllably) through any material with no physical effort on the part of the operator, and with no mess because it vaporises the residue? The laser company was thinking ahead, looking at the consumer's problem, looking at the weaknesses in the currently available solutions, and developing a marketing package that would deliver a better solution.

What we are saying here is that it is not enough to formulate a cosy marketing mix that suits the product and is entirely consistent with itself. That marketing mix is only working properly if it has been thought through with due respect to the external environment within which it is to be implemented. As well as justifying the existence of that marketing mix in the light of current internal and external influences, the strategic marketer has to go further by justifying how that mix helps to achieve wider corporate objectives; explaining how it is helping to propel the organisation in its longer-term desired direction, and finally, how it contributes to achieving competitive edge.

Ultimately, competitive edge is the name of the game. If marketers can create and sustain competitive edge, by thinking creatively and strategically about the internal and external marketing environments, then they are well on the way to implementing the marketing concept and fulfilling all the promise of the definitions of marketing with which this chapter began.

MARKETING SCOPE

Marketing plays a part in a wide range of organisations and applications. Some of these are discussed specifically in Part VIII and elsewhere in this book, while others are implicit throughout the text.

Consumer goods

The **consumer goods** field, because it involves potentially large and lucrative markets of so many individuals, has embraced marketing wholeheartedly, and indeed has been at the root of the development and testing of many marketing theories and concepts. Consumer goods and markets will be a major focus of this text, but certainly not to the exclusion of anything else. Since we are all consumers, it is easy to relate our own experience to the theories and concepts presented here, but it is equally important to try to understand the wider applications.

Industrial goods

Industrial, or **organisational goods** ultimately end up serving consumers in some way, directly or indirectly. The cleaned wool that the woolcomber sells to the spinner to make into yarn to sell to the weaver to make into cloth eventually ends up in the shops as clothing; the rubber that Dunlop, Goodyear or Firestone buy to make into tyres to sell to car manufacturers ends up being bought by consumers; the girders sold by British Steel to a civil engineering contractor for a new bridge end up serving the needs of individuals. If these organisations are going to continue to feed the voracious appetite of consumer markets successfully (the right product in the right place at the right time at the right price – remember?), then they also have to manage their relationships with other organisations, in a marketing-orientated way. The buying of goods, raw materials and components by organisations is a crucial influence on what can be promised and offered, especially in terms of price, place and product, to the next buyer down the line. If these inter-organisational relationships fail, then ultimately the consumer, who props up the whole chain, loses out, which is not in the interests of any organisation, however far removed from the end consumer. As Chapter 4 in particular will show, the concerns and emphases in industrial markets are rather different from those of consumer markets, and thus need to be addressed specifically.

Service goods

Service goods, to be discussed in Chapter 23, include personal services (hairdressing, other beauty treatments or medical services, for example) and professional skills (accountancy, management consultancy or legal advice, for example), and are found in all sorts of markets, whether consumer or organisational. As already mentioned p. 26, services have differentiated themselves somewhat from the traditional approach to marketing because of their particular characteristics. These require an extended marketing mix, and cause different kinds of management headaches from physical products. Many marketing managers concerned with physical products are finding that service elements are becoming increasingly important to augment their products and to differentiate them further from the competition. This means that some of the concepts and concerns of services marketing are spreading far wider than their own relatively narrow field, and this is reflected throughout this book. In between the two extremes of a largely service product (a haircut, for instance) and a largely physical product (a machine tool, for instance), are products that have significant elements of both. A fast food outlet, for example, is selling physical products, burger, fries and a coke, and that is primarily what the customer is there for. Service elements, such as speed and friendliness of service, atmosphere and ambience, are nevertheless inextricably linked with those physical products to create an overall package of satisfaction (or otherwise) in the customer's mind. This mixture of physical and service products is common throughout the retail trade, and thus services marketing not only features in its own chapter, but also permeates those chapters dealing with distribution (Chapters 12 to 14).

Non-profit marketing

Non-profit marketing is an area that has increasingly asserted itself in the economic and political climate of the 1980s and 1990s. Hospitals, schools, universities, the arts and charities are all having to compete within their own sectors to obtain, protect and justify their funding and even their existence. The environment within which such organisations exist is increasingly subject to market forces, and altruism is no longer enough. This means that non-profit organisations need to think not only about efficiency and cost effectiveness, but also about their market orientation – defining what their 'customers' need and want and how they can provide it better than their rivals. A small UK example: if a couple seeking family planning advice go to their own doctor rather than to a clinic run by the Family Planning Association (FPA), then the doctor gets paid by the National Health Service for that specific provision and the FPA does not. The FPA, therefore, has a marketing job on its hands to persuade patients to turn to it for that specialist service, as its funding ultimately depends on its number of patients. Chapter 23 looks in more detail at the particular marketing problems that this sort of situation creates.

Small business marketing

Small business marketing also creates its own perspectives. Many of the marketing theories and concepts laid out in this book have been developed with the larger organisation, relatively rich in management resources, in mind. Similarly, the implementation of these concepts is often discussed under the assumption that the organisation *does* have the expertise, flexibility and resources available to do whatever the market dictates to a high and idealistic marketing standard. Many small businesses, however, simply cannot live up to this. They often have only one or two managers who have to carry out a variety of managerial functions; such businesses often come into existence as a result of the owner/manager's manufacturing skills, and therefore have a production rather than marketing orientation; the manager/s have enough to do managing the day-to-day operation of the business without getting bogged down in strategic planning; they have very limited financial resources for investment in researching new markets and developing new products ahead of the rest. These are a few of the many constraints and barriers to the full implementation of the whole range of marketing possibilities. Chapter 24, therefore, takes a closer look at these constraints and considers more pragmatically how marketing theories and practice can be adapted to serve the needs of the small business that wants a long and prosperous future as it develops and grows.

International marketing

International marketing is a well-established field, and with the opening up of Europe as well as the technological improvements that mean it is now easier and cheaper to transfer goods around the world, it is an increasingly important area of marketing theory and practice. Again, it warrants its own chapter (Chapter 25), not only because of its importance, but also because it creates its own problems. Issues of market entry strategies, whether to adapt marketing mixes for different markets and how, and the logistics of serving geographically dispersed markets all provide an interesting perspective on marketing decision making.

Marketing perspectives

Chapter 26 seeks to integrate the concepts introduced elsewhere in the book by presenting discussions with marketing practitioners in a variety of industries. These insights underline the need for clear strategic marketing thinking and an integrated approach to developing the market mix. We also spoke to graduate trainees about why and how they began their careers in marketing. The chapter ends with a few thoughts on the future or marketing and its emergent issues.

CHAPTER SUMMARY

Marketing is about exchange processes, i.e. identifying what potential customers need and want now, or what they are likely to want in the future, and then offering them something that will fulfil those needs and wants. You thus offer them something that they value and in return, they offer you something that you value, usually money. Most (but not all) organisations are in business to make profits, and so it is important that customers' needs and wants are fulfilled cost effectively, efficiently and profitably. This implies that the marketing function has to be properly planned, managed and controlled.

Marketing in some shape or form has been around for a very long time, but it was during the course of the twentieth century that it made its most rapid developments and consolidated itself as an important business function and as a philosophy of doing business. By the late 1990s, all types of organisations in the USA and Western Europe had adopted a marketing orientation and were looking for ways to become even more customer focused, for example through relationship marketing. Emerging markets, such as those of Eastern and Central Europe, are still tending to think in terms of production or selling, but are rapidly aspiring to the Western model of marketing orientation.

The marketing orientation has been a necessary response to an increasingly dynamic and difficult world. Externally, the organisation has to take into account the needs, demands and influences of several different groups such as customers, competitors, suppliers and intermediaries, who all exist within a dynamic business environment. Internally, the organisation has to co-ordinate the efforts of different functions, acting as an interface between them and the customer. When the whole organisation accepts that the customer is absolutely paramount and that all functions within the organisation contribute towards customer satisfaction, then a marketing philosophy has been adopted.

Marketing's main tasks, therefore, are centred around identifying and satisfying customers' needs and wants, in order to offer something to the market that has a *competitive edge* or *differential advantage*, making it more attractive than the competing product(s). These tasks are achieved through the use of the *marketing mix*, a combination of elements that actually create the offering. For most physical goods, the marketing mix consists of four elements, product, price, place and promotion. For service-based products, the mix can be extended to seven elements with the addition of people, processes and physical evidence.

The marketer has to ensure that the marketing mix meets the customer's needs and wants, and that all its elements are consistent with each other, otherwise customers will turn away and competitors will exploit the weakness. Additionally, the marketer has to ensure that the marketing mix fits in with the strategic vision of the organisation, that it is contributing to the achievement of longer-term objectives, or that it is helping to drive the organisation in the desired future direction.

These marketing principles are generally applicable to any kind of organisation operating in any kind of market. But whatever the application, the basic philosophy remains: if marketers can deliver the right product in the right place at the right time at the right price, then they are making a crucial contribution towards creating satisfied customers and successful, efficient and profitable organisations.

QUESTIONS FOR REVIEW

1.1 What essential concepts should a definition of marketing include?

1.2 What is meant by the description of marketing as 'an exchange process'?

1.3 Why are Central and Eastern European countries only just starting to develop a marketing orientation?

1.4 Distinguish between the four main business orientations.

1.5 What are the main groups within the organisational environment that can influence how the organisation operates?

1.6 What factors contribute towards the wider marketing environment?

1.7 How do business functions other than marketing contribute towards satisfying customer needs and wants?

1.8 What is the marketing philosophy?

1.9 What are:

(a) the 4Ps of the marketing mix; and
(b) the 7Ps of the services marketing mix?

1.10 What is competitive edge and why is it so important?

QUESTIONS FOR DISCUSSION

1.1 Which is the most important element of the marketing mix and why?

1.2 Choose a product that you have purchased recently and show how the elements of the marketing mix came together to create the overall offering.

1.3 Choose three different products within the same market and explain how each one is trying to gain a competitive edge over the others.

1.4 Why is the question, 'What business are we in?' so important? How might:

(a) a fast-food retailer;
(b) a national airline;
(c) a car manufacturer; and
(d) a hairdresser

answer that question if they were properly marketing orientated?

1.5 How might the application of the marketing concept differ between a small organisation and a very large multinational?

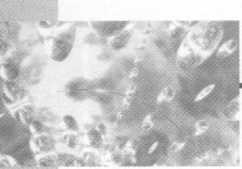

Liptonice

Liptonice, a cold, carbonated, canned lemon tea, is estimated to have cost £2 mn to develop, and was launched into the UK market in March 1994, as a joint venture between PepsiCo, Brooke Bond (a Unilever subsidiary) and Britvic. It was thought that the product would appeal to the UK consumer, who has a strong tradition of tea drinking. Additionally, it was felt that consumers were bored with the usual soft drinks, such as lemonade and coke, and would therefore be receptive to something different. Experience in other European markets was encouraging. A rival product, Nestea, originally developed by Coca Cola and Nestlé, had been launched the previous year in Spain and seemed to be successful. In 1992, however, Brooke Bond had test marketed an iced tea product called CoolBrew in the UK's midlands, but this had failed. Although Liptonice was similar in concept, the company felt that because it was sparkling and because the product was better designed, it would have more success.

The commitment of marketing resources was different too. CoolBrew was launched with little marketing support, whereas Liptonice got a £6 million package, including television advertising and a national sampling programme so that consumers could try the product for themselves and overcome any doubts about it. Problems became apparent soon after the launch of Liptonice, however. Consumers were suspicious of it, and did not really like the taste, hence it failed to achieve anything like its target of £20 mn sales in its first year. A lighthearted taste survey of adult-orientated soft drinks in *The Times*, for example, gave Liptonice a score of 1 out of 10 with the comment, 'The injunction "serve ice cold" is to be taken seriously because it is not at all pleasant otherwise'.

In a rescue attempt, the producers reformulated the product to improve the taste and relaunched it in May 1995. Between them, the original launch and the relaunch are estimated to have cost around £10 mn in marketing. Despite this heavy advertising impact, the product still failed to take off as hoped. By April 1996, the product was in difficulty. PepsiCo and Britvic pulled out of the partnership, leaving Unilever subsidiary Van den Bergh Foods with sole responsibility for the product. The loss of Britvic was particularly crucial, as Britvic had distributed the product to supermarkets and convenience stores. The marketing trade press suggested that Van den Bergh would not be able to achieve the same level of distribution as Britvic had done, and was also reporting rumours, unconfirmed by any of the partners in the product, that Liptonice had been dropped by some supermarkets.

Although the British like tea and drink it throughout the day, they prefer it to be hot and milky. Cold tea as a fizzy drink is thus a strange concept to them. In contrast, in the USA and Europe, tea is drunk black and only at specific times of the day and in the USA in particular, iced tea is a familiar concept, with Americans spending around $850 mn on iced tea in 1995. Independent research suggested that in Europe, iced teas showed a healthy 45 per cent growth in 1994, yet in the UK specifically, there was hardly any growth at all in this sector. All of this meant that it was slightly easier to launch canned (but not carbonated) tea in Europe, initially as a sports drink sold through sports clubs.

Sources: Marketing (1995); Meller (1994); Rees (1996); Young (1995a); Young (1995b).

Questions

1 What market is Liptonice in and what are its competitors?

2 Why was this product less successful than hoped in the UK market?

3 On the basis of the evidence presented in this case, do you think that Liptonice could survive in the UK market?

4 Analyse how soft drink producers use the elements of the marketing mix to create differential advantage.

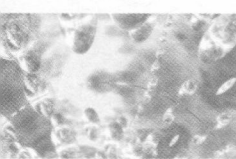

CASE STUDY 1.2

Plasser & Theurer make tracks

Plasser & Theurer are world leaders in track-laying, cleaning and maintenance machines for railways. Although the company is based in Austria, 95 per cent of its sales are generated from foreign markets and it is one of Austria's most profitable companies. Successful marketing has played a major role in establishing the company's position in international markets. The heart of the business is the proposition that productivity and cost efficiency can be improved by applying technology to what was previously a job for manual workers using shovels. Despite a selling price of Sch 20 mn (£1.25 mn), the increased productivity enables the machines, it is claimed, to pay for themselves within a year with a 90 per cent saving on manual costs. The company has invested heavily in R&D to keep ahead of the competition and to keep up with the fast-changing technology of rail construction.

Maintaining the rail infrastructure is vital for national railway systems. In the UK, Railtrack's Infrastructure Maintenance Procurement Unit, for example, spends £1 bn every year on the maintenance of track, signalling, electrification and property. In addition, a further £500 mn is spent per year on major projects, including, for example, the renewal of existing track. Contracts are increasingly being awarded on the basis of a contractor's overall past performance, for example on the successful maintenance of so many miles of track from A to B to appropriate safety, availability and other standards for an agreed sum of money. The specification of the machinery that the contractor uses must, therefore, meet high standards of quality, reliability and operating performance.

Plasser & Theurer does not compete on price, but prefers to plough back its profits into R&D, product development and customer service. Most of its 1700 employees outside Austria are in customer service, including technical support, training and replacement parts. This, along with the product's high quality specification and technical superiority, is consistent with the demands of the market niche occupied.

The company sells its products in 90 countries, and has factories or licensing agreements in 14 of them. Most sales, however, are generated by a highly qualified and trained direct sales force often operating from national sales offices such as the one in Maidenhead, UK. This is essential given the technical complexity of the sale, the need to work closely with a range of buyers and technical staff within the national rail organisations, and not least because of the high price per unit which enables the selling costs to be recovered. As most customer organisations are state owned, close contact at a high level within the organisation and even diplomacy are needed to understand their needs and to ensure a close match with the products available. Although other means of promotion are also used, such as extensive print and brochure material and careful advertising in the trade press such as *Modern Railways* and *Schweizer Eisenbahn Revue*, the amount spent on advertising and promotion is minimal compared with sales force costs.

Sources: Frey (1995); Tulip (1995).

Questions

1 To what extent and why do you think this company is marketing orientated?

2 How does the marketing mix for a company in this kind of organisational market differ from what you might find in a mass market, fast moving consumer goods (fmcg) situation?

3 What lessons can other companies in organisational markets learn from the marketing success of Plasser & Theurer?

REFERENCES FOR CHAPTER 1

Alderson, W. (1957), *Marketing Behaviour and Executive Action: A Functionalist Approach to Marketing*, Homewood, Irwin.

AMA (1985), 'AMA Board Approves New Marketing Definition', *Marketing News*, 1 March 1985, p. 1.

Barnard, S. (1996), 'Driving Force', *The Grocer*, 16 March 1996, pp. 16–17.

Berry, L. L. (1983), 'Relationship Marketing', in *Emerging Perspectives of Services Marketing*, L. L. Berry *et al.* (eds.), American Marketing Association.

Booms, B. H. and Bitner, M. J. (1981), 'Marketing Strategies and Organisation Structures for Service Firms', in *Marketing of Services*, J. Donnelly and W. R. George (eds.), American Marketing Association.

Borden, N. (1964), 'The Concept of the Marketing Mix', *Journal of Advertising Research*, June 1964, pp. 2–7.

Clarke, P. D. *et al.* (1988), 'The Genesis of Strategic Marketing Control in British Retail Banking', *International Journal of Bank Marketing*, 6(2), pp. 5–19.

Easton, G. and Araujo, L. (1994), 'Market Exchange, Social Structures and Time', *European Journal of Marketing*, 28(3), pp. 72–84.

Frey, E. (1995), 'High Tech Solves Low Tech Problem', *Financial Times*, 11 October 1995, p. XVI.

Green, D. (1995), 'Healthcare Vies With Research', *Financial Times*, 25 April 1995, p. 34.

Gronroos, C. (1990), 'Marketing Redefined', *Management Decision*, 28(8), pp. 5–9.

Hallén, L. *et al.* (1987), 'Relationship Strength and Stability in International and Domestic Industrial Marketing', *Industrial Marketing and Purchasing*, 2(3), 22–37.

Hargreaves, D. (1994), 'Granting an End to Food Trade Gap: Farmers and Markets are Drawing Closer', *Financial Times*, 11 August 1994, p. 7.

Hewitt, M. (1995), 'Digital TV Explosion Burning on Long Fuse', *Marketing*, 17 August 1995, p. 10.

Hooley, G. J. *et al.* (1990), 'The Marketing Concept: Putting Theory into Practice', *European Journal of Marketing*, 24(9), p. 7–23.

Knights, D. *et al.* (1994), 'The Consumer Rules? An Examination of the Rhetoric and "Reality" of Marketing in Financial Services', *European Journal of Marketing*, 28(3), pp. 42–54.

Kotler, P. and Zaltman, C. (1971), 'Social Marketing: An Approach to Planned Social Change', *Journal of Marketing*, 35(July), pp. 3–12.

Levitt, T. (1960), 'Marketing Myopia', *Harvard Business Review*, July/Aug 1960, pp. 45–56.

Marinov, M. *et al.* (1993), 'Marketing Approaches in Bulgaria', *European Journal of Marketing*, 27(11/12), pp. 35–46.

Marketing (1995) 'Iced Tea to Shake Up UK Market', *Marketing*, 27 April 1995, p. 2.

Maucher, H. (1994), 'The Marketing Secrets of a Global Giant', *Director*, 48(4), pp. 54–6.

Meller, P. (1994), 'Liptonice Entry Backed by £6m', *Marketing*, 24 February 1994, p. 2.

More, M. (1994), 'New State, New Economy', *European Purchasing and Materials Management*, 1994(3), pp. 375–80.

Pettitt, S. J. (1992), *Small Firms and Their Major Customers: An Interaction and Relationship Approach*, unpublished PhD Thesis, Cranfield University.

Rees, J. (1996), 'PepsiCo Needs New Strategy for Iced Tea', *The Grocer*, 26 April 1996, p. 23.

Robin, D. P. and Reidenbach, R. E. (1987), 'Social Responsibility, Ethics and Marketing Strategy: Closing the Gap Between Concepts and Application', *Journal of Marketing*, 51 (Jan), pp. 44–58.

Shipley, D. and Fonfara, K. (1993), 'Organisation for Marketing Among Polish Companies', *European Journal of Marketing*, 27(11/12), pp. 60–79.

Slingsby, H. (1994), 'Leader of the Pak', *Marketing Week*, 8 July 1994, pp. 36–7.

Timewell, S. (1994), 'Listen to the Customer', *Banker*, 144 (Feb.), pp. 29–30.

Tulip, S. (1995), 'Railtrack Procurement', *Purchasing and Supply Management*, April 1995, pp. 38–40.

Turnbull, P. W. and Valla, J. P. (1986), *Strategies for International Industrial Marketing*, Croom Helm.

Wheatley, M. (1995), 'The Branding of Europe', *Management Today*, April 1995, pp. 66–8.

Young, R. (1995a), 'From Light and Fruity to Sweet and Medicinal', *The Times*, 22 April 1995, p. 8.

Young, R. (1995b), 'Cheers! Here's to a Great Summer', *The Times*, 27 July 1995, p. 36.

2 The European Marketing Environment

LEARNING OBJECTIVES

This chapter will help you to:

1 understand the importance of the external environment to marketing decision making;

2 assess the role and importance of scanning the environment as a means of early identification of opportunities and threats;

3 appreciate the evolving and diverse nature of the European marketing environment;

4 define the broad categories of factors that affect the marketing environment; and

5 understand the influences at work within each of those categories and their implications for marketing.

INTRODUCTION

Marketing, by its very nature, is an outward-looking discipline. As the interface between the organisation and the outside world, it has to balance internal capabilities and resources with the opportunities offered externally. Chapter 1 has already shown, however, that the outside world can be a complex and difficult place to understand. Although the definition and understanding of the customer's needs and wants are at the heart of the marketing philosophy, there are many factors influencing how those customer needs evolve, and affecting or constraining the organisation's ability to meet those needs in a competitive environment. Thus in order to reach an adequate understanding of the customer's future needs and to develop marketing mixes that will satisfy the customer, the marketer has to be able to analyse the external environment and clarify which influences and their implications are most important.

This chapter will dissect the external environment and look closely at the variety of factors and influences that help to shape the direction of marketing thinking. First, the chapter clarifies the nature of the external environment, underlining why it needs to be understood, and what opportunities that understanding offers to the marketer.

In Denmark, a shortage of ecologically produced milk and vegetables was reported in supermarkets in 1995 because farmers had failed to predict the growth in demand for them. It is not, however, only the Danish consumer who is influencing marketing activity. The government is urging its own departments to use 'green' criteria in their purchasing decisions, as well as imposing 'green' taxes on industry to encourage it to reduce its carbon dioxide emissions (Barnes, 1995). Such trends, both in consumer attitudes and in government policy, will clearly influence what is produced, how, and with what cost implications.

Although the environment consists of a wide variety of factors and influences, it is possible to group them under four broad headings: sociocultural, technological, economic and competitive, and political and legal influences. Each will be examined in turn, discussing the various issues they cover and their implications for marketing decision making.

THE NATURE OF THE EUROPEAN MARKETING ENVIRONMENT

This section will first define the broad groupings of environmental influences, and then go on to look at the technique of environmental scanning as a means of identifying the threats and opportunities that will affect marketing planning and implementation within the organisation.

Elements of the marketing environment

Figure 2.1 shows the elements of the external environment in relation to the organisation and its immediate surroundings.

As the figure shows, the elements can be divided into four main groupings, known by the handy acronym **STEP**:

Sociocultural environment
The sociocultural environment is of particular concern to marketers as it has a direct effect on their understanding of customers and what drives them. Not only does it address the demographic structure of markets, but it also looks at the way in which attitudes and opinions are being formed and how they are evolving. A general increase in health consciousness, for instance, has stimulated the launch of a wide variety of products with low levels of fat and sugar, fewer artificial ingredients and no additives.

Technological environment
Technological innovation and technological improvement have had a profound effect in all areas of marketing. Computer technology, for instance, has revolutionised product design, quality control, materials and inventory management, the production of advertising and other promotional materials, and the management and analysis of customer information. The rise in direct marketing as a communication technique, discussed in Chapter 19, owes a lot to the availability of cheap and powerful computerised database management. Technology also affects the development of new processes and materials, as well as the invention of completely new products or applications, such as the multimedia home computer, including a CD-ROM drive, or the development of the low calorie sweeteners that have revolutionised the dieting market.

FIGURE 2.1

Elements of the
external
environment

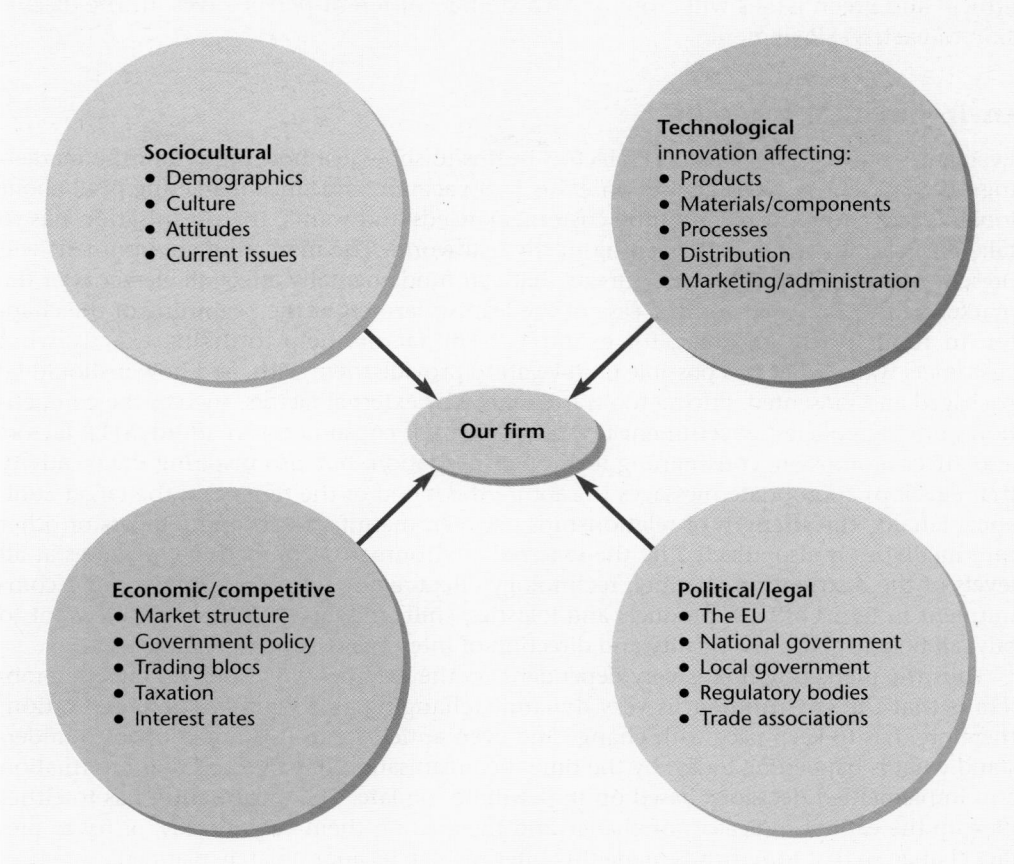

Economic and competitive environment

The economic and competitive environment covers both macro and micro economic conditions which affect the structure of competition in a market, the cost and availability of money for marketing investment in stock and new products, for example, and the economic conditions affecting a customer's propensity to buy. The economic recession of the late 1980s, for instance, caused a significant increase in unemployment at all social levels, and thus affected consumers' willingness and ability to buy many kinds of products.

Political and legal environment

The political and legal environment covers the external forces controlled by governments, both national and European, local authorities, or other trade or activity-orientated regulatory bodies. Some of the rules and regulations developed and implemented by bodies under this heading have the force of law, while others are voluntary, such as advertising codes of practice, for instance. A voluntary agreement covering tobacco advertising in the UK, for example, means (among other things) that the industry has undertaken to reduce its expenditure on poster advertising by 40 per cent. Although the code is voluntary, the government has made it clear that if the industry fails to comply satisfactorily with the agreement, legislation may well be considered.

Each of the STEP areas will be looked at in more detail at pp. 41 *et seq.* There is, of course, much interdependence between them. Rules and regulations concerning 'green' aspects of products, for example, are a result of sociocultural influences pressurising the legislators and regulators. Certain issues, therefore, such as international, ethical and green issues will crop up with slightly different perspectives, in the discussion of each STEP element.

Environmental scanning

Even a brief discussion of the STEP factors begins to show just how important the marketing environment is. No organisation exists in a vacuum, and since marketing is all about looking outwards and meeting the customer's needs and wants, the organisation has to take into account what is happening in the real world. The marketing environment will present many opportunities and threats that can fundamentally affect all elements of the marketing mix, as we saw in the case of the Danish farmers at the beginning of the chapter. In terms of the product, for example, STEP factors help to define exactly what customers want, what it is possible (and legal) to provide them with, and how it should be packaged and presented. Pricing too is influenced by external factors, such as the competition's pricing policies, government taxation and what consumers can afford. STEP factors also affect promotion, constraining it through regulation, but also inspiring the creativity that develops appropriate messages to capture the mood of the times and the target audience. Finally, the strength of relationships between manufacturers and retailers or other intermediaries is also affected by the external environment. Competitive pressures at all levels of the distribution channel; technology encouraging joint development and commitment in terms of both products and logistics; shifts in where and how people want to buy: all help to shape the quality and direction of interorganisational relationships.

Thus the marketing mix is very dependent on the external environment, but the problem is that the environment is very dynamic, changing all the time. The organisation, therefore, has to keep pace with change and even anticipate it. It is not enough to understand what is happening today: by the time the organisation has acted on that information and implemented decisions based on it, it will be too late. The organisation has to either pick up the earliest indicators of change and then act on them very quickly, or try to predict change so that tomorrow's marketing offerings can be appropriately planned.

In order to achieve this successfully, the organisation needs to undertake **environmental scanning,** which is the collection and evaluation of information from the wider marketing environment that might affect the organisation and its strategic marketing activities. Such information may come from a variety of sources, such as experience, personal contacts, published market research studies, government statistics, trade sources or even through specially commissioned market research. Responsibility for collecting and collating the information might lie with individual managers or there could be a committee made up of managers from a range of functions (marketing, R&D, production etc.) which acts as the environmental eyes and ears of the organisation. It is important, however, to limit the amount of incoming information to a manageable quantity, since there is an infinite amount of potentially relevant material out there and a single organisation cannot handle all of it.

The approach to scanning can vary from being extremely organised and purposeful to being random and informal. As Aguilar (1967) pointed out, formal scanning can be very expensive and time consuming as it has to cast its net very wide to catch all the possible influences that might affect the organisation. The key is knowing what is important and should be acted upon, and what can wait.

There is a great deal of skill and perceptiveness involved in assessing the significance of any piece of information and whether it should be acted upon. Volvo, for example, failed to pick up the early signs indicating the emergence of markets for 'people carriers' and four-wheel-drive vehicles, and thus missed out on the growth stages of both markets. Organisations that supply components to the motor industry also have to be alert to changing tastes and trends, in order to plan production. According to Daniels (1994), writing in the *Financial Times*, motor industry analysts predicted that airbags would not be accepted by European motorists. What actually happened was that motorists quickly warmed to the idea and began to demand airbags as standard. The motor manufacturers were caught somewhat unprepared, and consequently put a lot of pressure on suppliers to fulfil demand immediately. The motor industry now faces similar decisions on the likely acceptance and demand for air conditioning, navigation systems and other electronic wizardry. This is all an issue of monitoring both emerging technology and the way in which consumers' tastes and attitudes towards their cars are changing.

Environmental scanning is, therefore, an important task, but often a difficult one, particularly in terms of interpretation and implementation of the information gained. The following looks in more detail at each of the STEP factors, and give a further indication of the range and complexity of the influences and information that can affect the marketing activities of the organisation.

THE SOCIOCULTURAL ENVIRONMENT

It is absolutely essential for organisations serving consumer markets, directly or indirectly, to understand the **sociocultural environment**, since these factors fundamentally influence the customer's needs and wants. Many of the factors discussed here will be looked at again in Chapters 3 and 5, and so this is a brief overview of the demographic and sociocultural influences on marketing thinking and activities.

The demographic environment

Demographics is the study of the measurable aspects of population structures and profiles, including factors such as age, size, gender, race, occupation and location. As the birth rate fluctuates and as life expectancy increases, the breakdown of the population changes, creating challenges and opportunities for marketers, particularly if that information is taken in conjunction with data on family structure and income. Table 2.1, for example, shows birth rates across the EU between 1989 and 1994.

If we look specifically at Portugal or Spain, we can appreciate that European organisations supplying baby-orientated products might feel under threat from a falling birth rate in those countries, and might perhaps look towards Finland or Sweden as more promising markets. This is, however, a very simplistic view. These data may be supported by evidence that people are having smaller families, and additionally

TABLE 2.1
EU birth rates, 1989–1994 per '000 inhabitants

	1989	1990	1991	1992	1993	1994
Austria	11.6	11.7	12.0	12.1	11.8	11.8
Belgium	12.3	12.3	12.6	12.8	11.5	11.4
Denmark	11.5	11.5	12.4	12.5	13.1	13.1
Finland	12.8	12.8	13.2	13.1	13.2	13.3
France	13.5	13.5	13.4	13.3	12.9	12.7
Germany	11.2	11.4	11.3	10.0	9.7	n/a
Greece	9.9	9.9	10.0	10.1	10.1	10.0
Ireland	14.7	14.7	15.1	15.0	14.5	14.3
Italy	9.7	9.7	9.8	9.9	9.6	9.5
Luxembourg	12.4	12.4	13.0	12.9	12.9	13.1
The Netherlands	12.7	12.7	13.3	13.2	13.0	13.1
Portugal	12.0	12.0	11.8	11.8	11.4	11.4
Spain	10.4	10.4	10.2	9.9	9.6	9.4
Sweden	13.7	13.7	14.5	14.4	14.2	14.4
United Kingdom	13.6	13.6	13.9	13.7	13.6	13.6

Sources: Adapted from *Euromonitor* (1995a, p. 125) and *Euromonitor* (1995b, p. 24).

having their children later in life when they are better established economically. All of this would mean that the parents have much more money to spend per child, and additionally, doting grandparents, aunts and uncles might similarly be inclined to spend more. The marketer might, therefore, come to the conclusion that there is still a lucrative upmarket niche to be served. On the other hand, the falling birth rate may be supported by evidence that young, poorer, one-parent families are accounting for an increasing proportion of births, which would mean that if the marketer is not prepared to move downmarket into price-orientated, basic, functional products, then diversification might be an attractive option. It is all a matter of data *interpretation*, made on the basis of the fullest possible picture of both quantitative and qualitative information. At least marketers serving older segments have a few years' grace to plan for the peaks and troughs in population that are heading their way.

At the other end of the scale is what is known as the 'grey market', consisting of the over-55 age group. As Table 2.2 shows, the over-55s represent around one-quarter of the population of most EU countries. Their numbers are increasing, and because of better health care and financial planning, a significant proportion are able to indulge in high levels of leisure-orientated consumption, especially as they are likely to have paid off any mortgage or similar long-term debt, and are not likely to have dependent children. According to Johnson (1990), it has been estimated that in the UK, 30 per cent of men in the 55–64 age group have left the labour market. This trend towards earlier retirement is another positive influence on the leisure-orientated grey market.

Looking at an even older age group, we see that the growth in the numbers of the over-80s has serious social implications. In the UK, for example, this group represented only 2.3 per cent of the population in 1971, but by the year 2000 that is likely to have risen to 4.6 per cent. This group depends extensively on health and social service provision, and yet is the poorest of the retired groups. At the other end of the age spectrum, it is now common for an individual's educational career to begin at the age of three and carry on until 23. Again, this has implications not only for the state, but also for educational institutions (public and private) and providers of educational goods and services.

TABLE 2.2
EU population by age groups (55+) (% of total population)

	55–59	60–69	70–79	80–89	90+	Total
Austria	5.0	10.4	6.4	3.4	0.4	25.6
Belgium	5.5	10.9	6.5	3.3	0.4	26.6
Denmark	5.1	10.1	7.1	3.3	0.5	26.1
Finland	5.0	9.6	6.1	2.6	0.3	23.6
France	5.0	9.8	5.9	3.4	0.5	24.6
Germany (former West)	6.4	10.0	6.4	3.5	0.4	26.7
Germany (former East)	5.7	9.4	5.6	3.1	0.2	24.0
Greece	6.5	11.0	6.3	3.0	0.5	27.3
Ireland	4.1	7.4	5.5	2.1	0.2	19.3
Italy	5.9	11.0	6.7	3.2	0.4	27.2
Luxembourg	5.4	10.0	5.9	2.9	0.3	24.5
The Netherlands	4.8	8.6	5.9	2.6	0.4	22.3
Portugal	5.6	10.3	6.5	2.5	0.2	25.1
Spain	5.4	12.0	6.2	2.7	0.3	26.6
Sweden	4.8	10.1	8.3	3.9	0.5	27.6
United Kingdom	5.0	9.8	7.2	3.3	0.5	25.8

Note: Year 1993, except Austria, Finland and Sweden (1991), and East Germany (1990).
Source: Adapted from *Euromonitor* 1995b, p.143.

We have already made reference to household structure and income as necessary variables for shedding light on the basic population information. Clearly, the size of a household combined with its income is going to be a fundamental determinant of its needs and wants, and its ability to fulfil them. Table 2.3 gives some basic data on trends in average household size across Europe, while Table 2.4 categorises households by the number of occupants.

From Table 2.3, it can be seen that Ireland has a significantly larger average household size than elsewhere in the EU. Unsurprisingly, Table 2.4 also shows that Ireland has the largest proportion of households consisting of five or more occupants. All of this will have a number of implications for marketers selling into Ireland, including the need for larger pack sizes, and more focus on family-orientated products. Across the rest of Europe, differences in average household sizes are less marked, ranging from 2.26 people per household in Denmark to 2.87 people per household in Greece. However, as Table 2.3 shows, some countries are experiencing a pattern of decline in the average household size, for example Austria, Italy and Portugal. Again, marketers

TABLE 2.3

EU average household size, 1989–1994 (persons per unit)

	1989	1990	1991	1992	1993	1994
Austria	2.64	2.63	2.59	2.48	2.45	2.42
Belgium	2.71	2.70	2.70	2.70	2.70	2.70
Denmark	2.31	2.31	2.31	2.31	2.27	2.26
Finland	2.50	2.51	2.43	2.42	2.41	2.40
France	2.63	2.63	2.60	2.60	2.58	2.57
Germany	2.31	2.29	2.29	2.32	2.34	2.34
Greece	2.81	2.85	2.86	2.86	2.86	2.87
Ireland	4.03	4.03	4.05	4.05	4.04	4.04
Italy	3.17	3.17	2.85	2.80	2.66	2.56
Luxembourg	2.79	2.82	2.85	2.85	2.85	2.86
The Netherlands	2.46	2.45	2.44	2.45	2.45	2.44
Portugal	2.94	2.92	2.91	2.84	2.81	2.78
Spain	2.69	2.65	2.61	2.59	2.56	2.53
Sweden	2.27	2.23	2.28	2.28	2.28	2.28
United Kingdom	2.71	2.71	2.72	2.72	2.70	2.70

Sources: Euromonitor Consumer Europe 1995, p. 29.

TABLE 2.4

EU households by number of occupants (% of total households: latest year)

	Year	1 person	2 people	3 people	4 people	5+ people	N.S.
Austria	1993	28.4	30.9	19.1	21.6		
Belgium	1981	23.2	29.7	20.0	15.7	11.4	
Denmark	1993	34.8	33.0	14.7	12.7	4.8	
Finland	1989	31.1	29.1	16.7	15.3	7.9	
France	1992	17.9	32.4	18.3	19.5	12.0	
Germany (former West)	1991	33.6	30.8	17.1	13.4	5.0	
Germay (former East)	1991	30.3	32.2	19.4	14.1	4.0	
Greece	1989	18.5	26.0	19.5	22.5	13.5	
Ireland	1986	18.2	20.3	14.8	16.1	30.6	
Italy	1990	20.7	24.5	23.5	23.5	7.8	
Luxembourg	1988	21.8	29.0	21.0	16.5	11.7	
The Netherlands	1990	29.3	28.9	15.6	18.5	6.0	1.7
Portugal	1988	15.0	23.0	27.0	20.0	15.0	
Spain	1986	12.0	24.0	27.0	18.5	18.5	
Sweden	1990	40.6	31.1	12.3	11.8	4.2	
United Kingdom	1987	25.0	32.0	17.1	13.1	6.0	6.8

Note: N.S. means not specified.
Source: Euromonitor (1995b, p.390).

need to be mindful of these changes and to adapt their offerings accordingly. Sweden in particular has a very large proportion of single-person households (Table 2.4), which will affect a whole range of marketing offerings, for example solo holidays, smaller apartments, pack sizes and advertising approaches and family stereotypes.

What is also important is the level of disposable income available (i.e. what is left after taxes have been paid), and the choices the household makes about saving and/or spending it. Table 2.5 shows how the spending of disposable income varies across Europe.

TABLE 2.5
EU consumer expenditure by object, 1993 (% of total expenditure)

	Food	Alcoholic drinks	Non-alcoholic drinks	Tobacco	Clothing	Footwear	Housing	Fuel	Household goods/ services	Health	Transport	Comm-unications	Leisure	Others
Austria	15.6	2.1	0.8	1.9	7.6	1.7	14.8	4.0	8.3	6.0	15.8	2.4	8.2	10.8
Belgium	16.2	3.1	1.2	1.4	6.7	1.0	12.5	4.0	11.3	12.6	12.0	1.0	4.8	12.3
Denmark	14.3	2.6	0.7	2.6	4.5	0.8	22.5	5.3	6.1	2.2	12.7	2.2	10.4	13.0
Finland	15.1	4.4	0.5	2.2	3.8	0.8	17.0	4.2	5.9	4.9	13.7	–	9.1	18.4
France	14.7	2.0	0.6	1.3	4.9	1.1	17.2	3.9	7.5	10.3	14.2	1.7	7.5	13.0
Germany (former West)	11.6	2.7	0.8	1.7	6.7	1.1	18.5	4.0	9.2	5.2	14.7	2.3	10.4	10.9
Germany (former East)	18.0	3.7	0.7	2.6	3.4	1.1	8.7	7.1	11.7	5.9	20.1	–	7.8	9.2
Greece	29.2	3.1	1.2	3.9	7.4	0.8	10.4	2.6	8.0	4.1	14.2	1.5	5.9	7.8
Ireland	18.8	10.6	2.0	4.2	5.6	1.5	7.9	4.4	7.2	4.2	11.3	1.6	12.5	8.2
Italy	16.8	1.0	0.4	1.4	7.8	2.0	11.4	4.4	9.6	7.0	11.2	1.3	9.0	16.7
Luxembourg	10.9	1.3	0.7	5.7	5.4	0.5	13.8	6.2	11.3	7.7	20.1	–	4.5	11.9
The Netherlands	11.2	1.5	0.6	1.4	5.7	1.1	15.1	2.9	6.9	13.2	11.7	1.5	10.1	17.1
Portugal	29.4	1.3	0.2	1.8	8.4	0.8	7.8	–	5.4	2.6	9.6	2.7	5.3	24.7
Spain	17.7	1.4	0.5	1.4	6.5	2.4	10.3	2.7	6.9	4.6	15.4	1.0	7.0	22.2
Sweden	13.4	2.9	0.6	1.7	5.2	1.0	24.7	4.9	6.6	2.0	13.5	2.0	9.5	11.9
United Kingdom	11.4	6.3	0.8	2.6	4.5	1.0	12.6	3.6	6.1	1.5	7.9	1.9	10.2	29.7

Source: Euromonitor (1995b, pp. 276–7).

Clearly, housing is a fundamental cost, but the proportion of income it takes varies widely across Europe, with the Irish and Portuguese spending the lowest percentage on housing. Looking at the food column, however, it is in the less affluent economies, such as those of Greece and Portugal, that people are spending relatively more on food, as a percentage of their total expenditure. In some of the other categories, the Dutch spend a higher proportion than anyone else on health care; the Luxembourgeois spend more on tobacco (over three times more than the Belgians or French); the Irish seem to enjoy their drink (alcoholic and otherwise) and leisure! Of course, patterns of expenditure will be dictated to some extent by national income levels and relative prices.

Such spending patterns are not fixed: they will vary not only because of changes in the demographic and economic structure of the household, but also because of sociocultural influences, discussed in the next subsection. A further factor which cuts across both demographic and sociocultural issues is employment patterns, specifically the number of working women in a community and the rate of unemployment. This influences not only household income, but also shopping and consumption patterns.

As the data presented here have shown, it is dangerous to generalise about demographic trends across Europe. There are wide variations, particularly between the richer northern and western European states and the poorer southern and eastern states. In 1992, average per capita production in western Europe was $21 000. In Greece, however, it was $7800 and in Russia just $600. This is bound to affect the sociocultural and the socioeconomic environments influencing the marketer. Thus the marketer needs to understand both the differences and the similarities between nations within Europe, as a means of assessing emerging trends and opportunities.

Sociocultural influences

Demographic information only paints a very broad picture of what is happening. If the marketer wants a really three-dimensional feel, then some analysis of sociocultural factors is essential. These factors involve much more qualitative assessment, and can be much harder to measure and interpret than the hard facts of demographics, and may be subject to unpredictable change, but the effort is worth while for a truly marketing-orientated organisation.

One thing that does evolve over time is people's lifestyle expectations. Products that at one time were considered upmarket luxuries, such as televisions and fridges, are now considered to be necessities. Table 2.6, for example, shows the penetration of various types of electrical household goods across Europe.

The home computer, for example, shows much higher penetration in Denmark, the Netherlands and the UK, than in Greece, Portugal or Spain. The marketer now has to decide whether or not this represents a major opportunity in the latter countries. Similarly, in the microwave oven sector, penetration is highest in the more affluent northern countries, such as Sweden and Finland, compared with a very low percentage in Greece and Portugal. Other information is necessary in order to work out why these differences occur. There may be deep-seated cultural factors at work, perhaps associated with attitudes to cooking, food or leisure in the home. However, looking at more established, mature products, such as washing machines and televisions, it is noticeable that there is much more convergence across Europe.

Turning a luxury into a necessity obviously broadens the potential market, and broadens the marketer's scope for creating a variety of products and offerings to suit a wide spectrum of income levels and usage needs. Televisions, for example, come in a wide variety of shapes, sizes and prices, from the pocket-sized portable, to the cheap small set that will do for the children's bedroom, to the very large, technically advanced state of the art status symbol with teletext and stereo sound. This variety has the bonus of encouraging households to own more than one set, further fuelling

TABLE 2.6
EU levels of ownership of electrical household goods, 1990/1991 (% of total households)

	CD player	Home computer	Colour/ mono TV	Video recorder	Phone	Microwave oven	Washing machine	Vacuum cleaner	Dish washer	Deep freezer
Austria	24.0	11.0	96.0	37.0	85.0	31.0	86.0	92.0	35.0	61.0
Belgium	26.0	15.0	97.0	42.0	79.0	21.0	88.0	92.0	26.0	86.0
Denmark	48.0	27.0	98.0	63.0	87.0	31.0	74.0	96.0	36.0	92.0
Finland	19.0	16.0	94.0	46.0	79.0	53.0	76.0	93.0	31.0	52.0
France	23.0	14.0	95.0	35.0	94.0	19.0	88.0	89.0	32.0	43.0
Germany (former West)	24.0	16.0	97.0	42.0	89.0	36.0	88.0	96.0	34.0	73.0
Germany (former East)	–	–	43.0	–	–	–	94.0	65.0	–	40.0
Greece	5.0	6.0	94.0	37.0	75.0	2.0	74.0	52.0	11.0	27.0
Ireland	14.0	12.0	98.0	38.0	53.0	20.0	81.0	87.0	15.0	58.0
Italy	9.0	12.0	98.0	25.0	89.0	6.0	96.0	56.0	18.0	89.0
Luxembourg	30.0	12.0	98.0	39.0	75.0	16.0	93.0	88.0	50.0	91.0
The Netherlands	48.0	25.0	95.0	50.0	96.0	22.0	89.0	98.0	11.0	54.0
Portugal	9.0	7.0	92.0	22.0	52.0	4.0	66.0	62.0	14.0	91.0
Spain	11.0	8.0	98.0	40.0	66.0	9.0	87.0	29.0	11.0	55.0
Sweden	17.0	12.0	97.0	48.0	97.0	37.0	72.0	97.0	31.0	70.0
United Kingdom	20.0	19.0	98.0	69.0	88.0	48.0	88.0	98.0	11.0	84.0

Source: Euromonitor (1995b, pp.392–3).

the volume of the market, particularly as improvements in technology and production processes along with economies of scale further reduce the prices. As Table 2.6 shows, the video recorder is still a little way behind the television in this respect, and the home computer is still at the beginning of the process.

Broadening tastes and demands are another sociocultural influence, partly fuelled by the marketers themselves, and partly emanating from consumers. Marketers, by constant innovation and through their marketing communications, encourage consumers to become bored with the same old standard familiar products and thus to demand more convenience, variety and variation.

Example

The market for hot chocolate drinks dominated for many years by cocoa (made with milk and ceremony) has now evolved into instant drinks (made with hot water) consisting of a plethora of flavoured chocolate powders (banana, mint, toffee, orange, mocha, coconut etc.), in regular or diet forms, in sachets, packets or jars. From the consumer's point of view, much of this proliferation is welcome, as it gives more choice, and more of a feeling that you are buying something tailored to your individual taste, as well as adding interesting variety to life.

As well as demanding variation within product categories, such as with the hot chocolate example above, consumers are also demanding a wider variety of more exotic tastes, particularly in foods. This has emerged partly through the influence of ethnic minorities, partly through cheaper, more widespread international travel which reduces hostility to and suspicion of 'foreign food', and partly through the efforts of marketers who have provided the products that have introduced the average supermarket customer to less well-known cuisines. This has all created growing markets in both premium-priced chilled or frozen ready meals (the UK market for these products is around £300 mn per year), and 'cook-in' sauces which make a wide variety of difficult sounding dishes such as Chicken Tikka and Lamb Rogan Josh easily accessible.

Consumers want variation and variety not only to stave off boredom, but also as a means of asserting their individuality. Although mass markets are necessary to generate the economies of scale that make products affordable, no consumer wants to think they are identical to their neighbours. They want to feel that their purchasing choices, in everything from their car to the contents of their biscuit tin, create a unique profile that gives them the desired status in others' eyes. Marketers like a certain amount of variety and variation (but not too much or the economies of scale are compromised) because it helps to keep customers loyal (you could use a different variety of one manufacturer's cook-in sauces, if you wanted, every night of the week and still not get bored), and allows scope for the premium-priced niches to emerge.

Fashions and fads are also linked with consumer boredom and a desire for new stimulation. The clothing market in particular has an interest in making consumers sufficiently discontented with the perfectly serviceable clothes already in the wardrobe that they go out to buy new ones every season. For some consumers, it is important for their social integration and their status to be seen to have the latest products and the latest fashions, whether it be in clothing, music or alcoholic drinks. In the 1980s, for instance, Guinness managed to shed its UK image as a drink for old men in an old-fashioned pub, and to turn itself into a seriously trendy drink for the young intelligentsia, through its advertising campaign starring Rutger Hauer. Nevertheless, linking a product with fashion may create marketing problems. Fashions, by definition, are short lived, and as soon as they become widespread, the fashion leaders are moving on to something new and different. Marketers, therefore, have to reap rewards while they can, or find a means of shifting the product away from its fashionable associations.

More deeply ingrained in society than the fripperies of fashion are underlying attitudes. These change much more slowly than fashion trends and are much more difficult for the marketer to influence. It is more likely, in fact, that the marketer will assess existing or emerging attitudes and then adapt or develop to fit them. As can be seen in Fig 2.2, there are a number of areas in which changes in societal attitudes have influenced marketing approaches. Each is discussed below.

Environmental issues

Environmental issues have been of major concern in recent years, and this area has caused consumers to think more critically about the origins, content and manufacturing processes of the products they buy. Consumers, for example, want products made with the minimum of pollution and want the reassurance, where applicable, that they come from renewable resources. Many paper products now carry notices stating that they are made from wood from managed forests that are replanted after harvesting. In the same spirit, consumers are also demanding that unnecessary packaging is eliminated and that packaging should be recyclable.

Example

The Body Shop has built its entire marketing approach on these concerns. The organisation emphasizes that the ingredients of its products are as natural as possible, and that its packaging is minimal and can be brought back to the shop for refilling to cut down on waste.

FIGURE 2.2

The impact of societal attitudes on marketing strategy

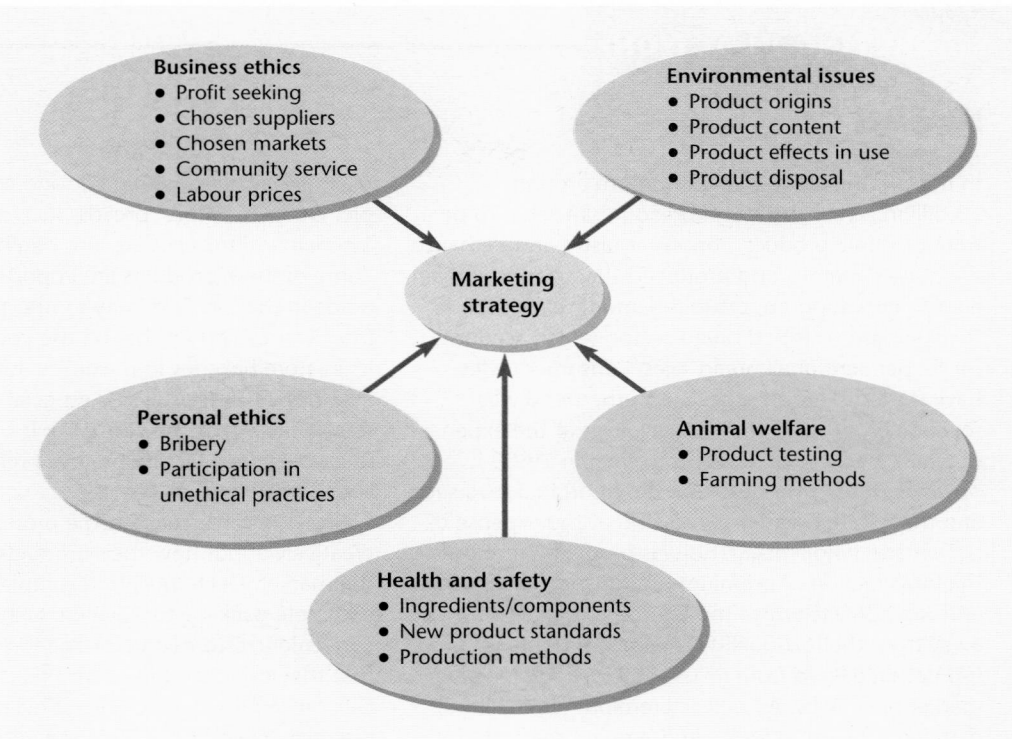

Animal welfare

The issue of animal welfare is linked with environmental concerns, and shows itself in a number of ways. Product testing on animals has become increasingly unacceptable to a large number of vocal consumers, and thus there has been a proliferation of cosmetics and toiletries, for example, which proclaim that they have not been tested on animals. With some products this may only mean that they are made from ingredients that have been separately animal tested and proved safe in the past, but that the current formulation has not itself been tested. Again, The Body Shop has been at the forefront of positioning itself overtly on this issue, reassuring concerned customers about its own products and publicising the worst excesses of animal testing.

Another area of animal welfare which has captured the public imagination is that of intensive farm production methods. Public outcry against battery egg production, for example, opened new marketing opportunities for free range eggs, since consumers wanted the alternative and were prepared to pay for it. Similarly, outdoor reared pork and organic beef are starting to appear in supermarkets. Early in 1995, British seaports and airports saw widely publicised, and sometimes violent, demonstrations against the export of live animals, particularly veal calves. The objection was not only that the travelling conditions and times might be less than ideal, but also that the calves were destined to be kept in veal crates on the Continent, a practice which is no longer allowed in the UK. The force of opinion has affected the attitudes of ferry companies, airlines and road hauliers, some of whom are no longer willing to accept this kind of business. It is now up to the EU to decide whether it wants to further restrict the times and distances that live animals are allowed to be transported, and whether they want to review the veal production industry generally.

While many consumers accept the necessity of farming for meat, there was a much wider backlash against killing and farming for the fur trade. Throughout the 1980s, public revulsion against furs built up and fur products ceased to be regarded as the status symbols they had previously been. Many furriers were driven out of business

Bread

In the UK, the bread market is worth around £3 billion a year. Although bread might seem to be a boring, staple product, consumer tastes and demands are quite dynamic, and producers have had to remain alert to emerging opportunities and threats. Even in the standard wrapped bread sector, which accounts for 52 per cent of all bread sales, consumer tastes have shifted. Through the 1980s, the trend was towards brown and wholemeal loaves at the expense of white, because of health concerns. In 1995, however, it became clear that the trend had reversed, and that white bread was growing at the expense of brown and wholemeal. This was partly the result of the introduction of premium brands such as Kingsmill and Hovis White which moved the product's image away from the low-quality, cheap commodity reputation earned from its use as a weapon in supermarket price wars. As well as premium white bread, demand is growing for malted brown bread and for 'diet' breads.

There are many niches in the market too, arising from the consumer's desire for variety and novelty. 'Ethnic' breads have become popular, and German (pumpernickel; volkornbrot), French (baguettes; petit pain; croissants), Italian (ciabatta; focaccia) and Indian (naan; pitta) breads, among others, are now very easy to find on the supermarket shelves, and there are many variants even within these categories. Ciabatta, for example can be plain, or with olives, or with sun-dried tomatoes, or with pesto. Naans too can be plain or flavoured with garlic and coriander, for example. Other countries' breads, such as those of Spain, Sweden and the USA are also beginning to appear. Some of these products are imported, while others are made in the UK. Sainsbury's imports part-baked bread from France and finishes off the cooking process in its in-store bakeries to maximise authenticity and freshness. This freshness is especially important, as trends show that the consumer is moving away from mass-produced factory breads, preferring products baked fresh on the premises.

This trend has made some producers think more creatively about how their products are delivered to the market. Delifrance, for example, has developed a complete package for retailers such as delicatessens, convenience stores and garage forecourt shops, so that they can bake their own bread on the premises. Delifrance provides a compact oven, promotional material, a wicker display stand and frozen part-baked bread products. The retailer gets 'an authentic French product', the smell of fresh baking in-store to attract customers and whet their appetites, and complete control over supply, in that they can bake more as it is needed and the supply is always fresh. Other companies, such as Country Choice, supply similar systems, and the UK market for these 'bake off' products is estimated to be worth £100mn and growing.

Source: The Grocer (1996).

and many upper class retailers closed their fur departments. There are small signs, however, that in *haute couture* fur is beginning to make a tentative comeback, presumably as public concern has shifted to other issues.

Health concerns

Health consciousness has played a major role in the thinking behind consumer markets. The tobacco market has been particularly hard hit by increased awareness of the risks of smoking, and pressure from health lobbyists and the public has led to increased regulation of that industry. Food products too have been reappraised in the light of health concerns, with more natural ingredients, fewer artificial additives, less salt and less sugar content demanded. Linked with this, the market for low calorie products has also expanded, serving a market that wants to enjoy tasty food in quantity, but lose weight or at least feel that they are eating healthily.

Health concerns also led to a boom in products and services linked with fitness. Health clubs, aerobics classes, exercise videos, sports wear of all kinds, and trainers are just some of the things that profited from the fitness boom.

Personal ethics

Apart from concern about the environment, animal welfare and health, all of which might be seen as ethical issues, there has been a subtle shift in people's attitudes to what is acceptable in other areas of their lives. In Western societies, a manageable level of personal debt is now considered normal. Hire purchase agreements, various types of loans and credit cards provide a means of achieving a desirable lifestyle now and paying for it later. Previous generations might have been more inclined to take the view that if you want something, you save up for it and buy it outright when you can afford it. Consumers today are also more inclined towards self-indulgence and gratification, without too much guilt, through their consumption. This, it must be said, is openly encouraged by marketers who encourage us to believe that we as individuals are special enough to deserve only the best for ourselves.

The early 1990s has seen some conflict between the self-indulgent, self-centred type of conspicuous consumption and external, altruistic concerns about the environment. Although this has curbed some of the worst excesses of the late 1980s, the majority of consumers still seem to be stopping short of radically redefining their attitude to consumption, other than through economic necessity. A study by Dittmar and Pepper (1994) showed that adolescents, regardless of their own social background, generally formed better impressions of people who own rather than lack expensive possessions. In other words, materialism still seems to play a big part in influencing perceptions and attitudes towards others.

Business ethics

Encouraged by various pressure groups and an inquisitive media, consumers now want to see greater levels of corporate responsibility, and more transparency in terms of the openness of companies. Bad publicity about employee relations, environmental records, marketing practices or customer care and welfare now has the potential to move consumers to vote with their pockets and shun an organisation and its products. McDonald's, for example, felt sufficiently concerned about stories circulating about its beef and about its record in the South American rain forests to invest in a considerable marketing communications campaign to re-establish its reputation. The Body Shop again features business ethics strongly in its marketing, emphasising, for example, its 'trade not aid' policy with third world countries and native tribes.

Consumerism and Consumer Forces

Many of the influences discussed above might never have taken hold and become significant had it not been for the efforts of organised groups. They themselves often use marketing techniques as well as generating publicity through the media, quickly raising awareness of issues and providing a focal point for public opinion to form around and gather momentum. Figure 2.3, for example, may remind you of some of the campaigns that have been fought in the interests of raising your awareness of ethical and green issues surrounding the clothing industry.

The UK's Consumers' Association has long campaigned for legislation to protect consumers' rights, such as the right to safe products and the right to full and accurate information about the products we buy. As well as lobbying government and organisations about specific issues, the Consumers' Association also provides independent information to consumers, testing and comparing the features, performance, and value for money of competing products in various categories. This information is published in *Which?* magazine, the June 1995 issue of which carried reports on SLR cameras, telephone charges and car roof and bike racks, for example. In a similar vein,

FIGURE 2.3

Issues affecting green and ethical clothing

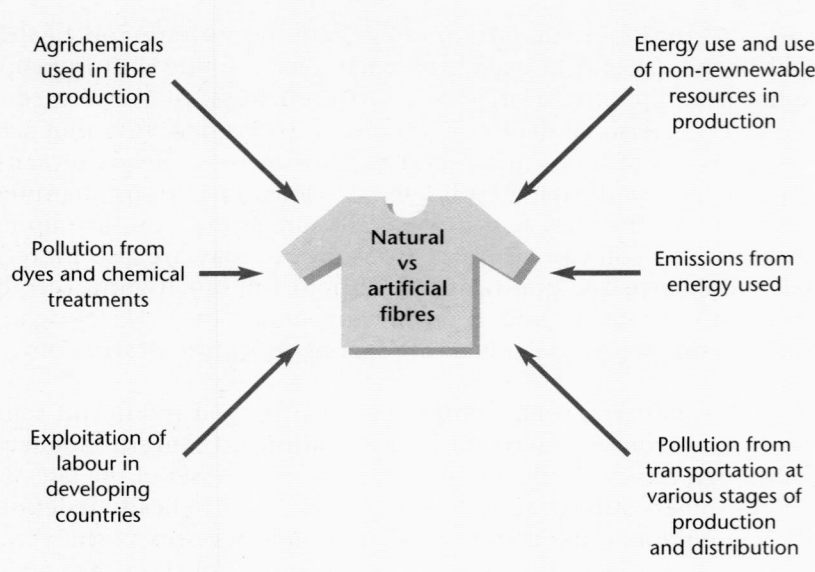

specialist magazines, in fields such as computing and hi-fi, also undertake comparative testing of products of interest to their readership.

High-profile, and sometimes militant pressure has been brought to bear on organisations by green groups such as Friends of the Earth and Greenpeace. Although their interest is a wider, altruistic concern with ecology rather than consumer rights, they recognise that corporate practices that are harmful to the environment, wildlife and ecology can be partly discouraged by 'bottom up' pressure. This means raising awareness, changing attitudes and changing purchasing habits among organisations' core customers.

Example

Tuna fishing is an activity that has been affected by campaigning leading to the exercise of 'consumer power'. The UK public had been happily buying canned tuna for many years without thinking of anything other than the price, the flavour and the quality of the can's contents. Green pressure groups, with the help of the media, then publicised the fact that the nets that were used to catch tuna also caught dolphins, which could not escape and so died pointlessly. A change in the net design would allow the dolphins to be freed without harm. Public outcry was such that the major tuna producers, such as John West, were encouraged to examine their own sources, and to pressurise their suppliers to change their fishing methods. UK consumers now look for 'dolphin friendly' labels on their cans of tuna. The activities of such pressure groups have not only served to change business practices on specific issues, such as tuna fishing, but also accelerated a general cultural change which has awakened the social conscience of organisations (only partly due to the fear of poor publicity and the loss of customers) and has raised the standards of corporate citizenship that consumers expect from business.

Consumers have also been encouraged to think about their personal health as well as that of the planet. Sometimes sponsored by government (for example through the

Continental Tyres have found that an active approach to environmental issues is taking them into exciting new areas.

Source: Continental.

UK government's Department of Health), and sometimes through independent groups such as Action on Smoking and Health (ASH) or the British Heart Foundation with a specific interest, the public are urged to change their lifestyles and diets. Once it is generally and known accepted that too much of this, that or the other is unhealthy, food manufacturers are anxious to jump on the bandwagon and provide products to suit the emerging demand.

Example

Awareness that full fat milk is high in cholesterol has been responsible for a significant shift towards semi-skimmed and skimmed milk which retains most of the vitamin and mineral content but cuts down the fat. Sometimes, a health issue does not even need the support of an organised group to capture the public imagination. A flurry of media coverage about research findings which indicated that eating sugar can actually help weight loss had many of us reaching hopefully for the biscuit tin, purely on medical grounds, of course.

The media have already been mentioned several times as an important channel of communication used by pressure groups to ensure that public awareness is triggered. The media are not, however, passive pawns in all this, simply repeating what they are

Environmentally friendly tyres

The car is not really considered to be one of the more environmentally friendly products available, but many component manufacturers are trying to improve the situation. Tyres, for example, are directly and indirectly responsible for a number of environmental problems. They tend to have a short life span, and are difficult to dispose of or to recycle. They can also affect fuel consumption, accounting for up to 16 per cent of a car's average petrol usage, according to industry estimates. Companies such as Pirelli and Continental are, therefore, working hard to develop more fuel efficient tyres in parallel with looking at ways of improving their durability. Beyond that, they are also thinking about how they can best use tyres that have come to the end of their life. The manufacturers want to develop tyres that can be retreaded more easily and cheaply, and that can be disposed of in a more environmentally friendly way. If a truck tyre can be retreaded several times, its life span can be increased from 150 000 miles to 375 000 miles. There are also possibilities for turning old tyres into rubber powder that can be incorporated into new ones.

All this development activity is spurred not only by an altruistic desire to become 'greener', but also by pressure from motor manufacturers. The motor manufacturers in turn are reflecting consumer concerns and increasing governmental demands for greener motoring.

Source: Simonian (1995).

told. They can magnify a story and give it much more credibility and urgency by the amount and quality of coverage given. Debating issues on current affairs programmes or the publication of editorials and opinion columns in the newspapers stimulate interest and provide the necessary perspectives for the audience to judge how they feel about it all. Some sections of the media behave like pressure groups in their own right. Television consumer programmes, such as the BBC's *Watchdog*, investigate and publicise (usually) bad practice or poor service, highlighting product safety issues, unethical selling methods and fraudulent trading. With audiences in millions, these programmes represent quite a power.

Example

Print media are also adept at whipping up interest in an issue. A series of press articles in August 1995 highlighted the fact that a number of UK universities were admitting students who did not meet the minimum standard for university entrance on to one-year foundation courses. The implication was that this was a way of recruiting degree students by the back door, bypassing normal requirements, and consequently, it was devaluing degree standards. This made dramatic reading, at a time when many students were finalising their university choices. The outcry generated prompted the Secretary of State for Education to demand a formal response from the Higher Education Quality Council (HEQC). A survey of universities revealed that the proportion of students entering higher education by this route was 'tiny', and most of them were mature students who would otherwise be lost to higher education, in other words the intended target group. This story highlights the problems that can arise when the media focus on the sensational aspects of a scenario without presenting the full context.

Pressure groups and consumer bodies are not just there to criticise organisations, of course. They also encourage and endorse good practice, and such an endorsement can be very valuable to the organisation that earns it. A consumer who is inexperienced in buying a particular type of product, or for whom that purchase represents a substantial investment, may well look for independent expert advice, and thus the manufacturer whose product is cited as the *Which?* magazine best buy in that category has a head start over the competition. Organisations may also commission product tests from independent bodies such as the Consumers' Association, or the Good Housekeeping Institute as a means of verifying their product claims and adding the bonus of 'independent expert opinion' to their marketing.

THE TECHNOLOGICAL ENVIRONMENT

In an increasingly dynamic world, where the creation, launch and maintenance of a new product is more expensive and difficult than ever, no organisation can afford to ignore the **technological environment** and its trends. Even if your organisation does not have the inclination or resources to adopt or adapt new technology, understanding it is important because competitors will exploit it sooner or later, with implications for your product and its marketing. Technological advance can be generated from two main sources, as far as the marketer is concerned. The first source is external to the organisation and perhaps even external to the market. Thus technology developed for other purposes, academic, medical or military, for example, may have spin-off commercial benefits. In this case, the skill for the commercial organisation is spotting the potential application early enough, negotiating the rights to use or develop the technology further, and successfully developing a marketable product from it before the competition. The second source of technological advance is market driven, by organisations searching for specific solutions to specific marketing problems. The R&D work may be undertaken in house, or may be commissioned out to specialist agencies or university departments. The range of projects involved may vary from very small to very large, and from the refinement of an existing product to the exploration of completely unknown territory.

The costs and the risks involved can be very high, since there is no guarantee that an R&D project will be successful in delivering a solution that can be commercially implemented. Nevertheless, organisations feel the need to invest in R&D, recognising that they will get left behind if they do not, and optimistic that they will come up with something with an unbeatable differential advantage that will make it all worthwhile.

Example

Ericsson, the Swedish telecommunications equipment supplier, has become the dominant force in the international cellular market through a well thought out approach to technological innovation, with R&D investment in its radio division amounting to about 20 per cent of sales. Ericsson maintains links with many Swedish universities to help new product design and the maintenance of a competitive advantage in a crowded market. Technological innovation is not just the province of new products, however. Ericsson managed to reduce the time taken to assemble a cellular handset from three hours in 1989 to 15 minutes in 1994 (Adonis, 1994).

To get the best out of the commercial exploitation of technology, R&D and marketers have to work closely together. R&D can provide the technical know-how, problem-solving skills and creativity, while the marketer can help guide and refine

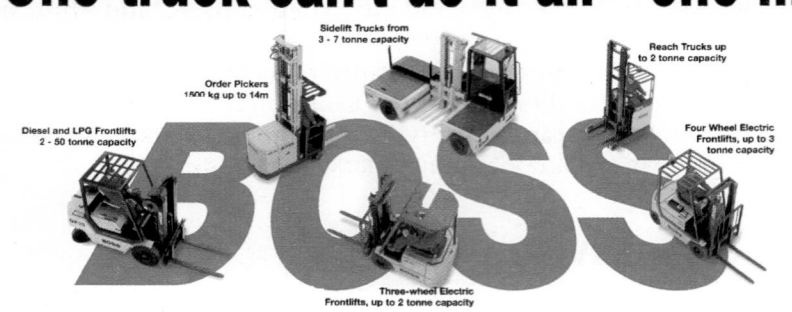

Boss understands the need to invest in product and production technology in order to remain competitive in world markets.

that process through research or knowledge of what the market needs and wants, or through finding ways of creating a market position for a completely innovative product. A lot of this comes back to the question, 'What business are we in?' Any organisations holding the attitude that they exist to solve customers' problems and that they have to strive constantly to find better solutions through higher quality, lower cost or more user-friendly product packages will be active participants in, and observers of, the technological environment. A striking example of this is the Italian firm Olivetti, which began by making manual typewriters, then moved into computers as they saw the likely take-over of the word processor as a means of producing business documentation.

Example

International collaboration in technical development is, however, becoming more common. The European Airbus A300 and A310 projects represent technical and commercial successes that could not have been possible at national level, given the strength of American competition from giants such as Boeing and McDonnell Douglas. By collaboration and pooling their expertise and resources, European companies such as Messerschmitt Belkow-Blohm (Germany), Aérospatiale (France), Casa (Spain), Fokker (Netherlands), Sonana (Belgium) and British Aerospace are able to remain players in world markets. International collaboration does not, however, always work as well as the Airbus project. The European fighter aircraft project, instigated and funded by a consortium of European governments, has suffered serious setbacks in trying to please all partners on political rather than on purely economic or technical grounds. Government interference, bureaucracy and duplication of effort have led to severe cost overruns and delays. Much of this is beyond the control of the various companies involved in the project who are faced with ongoing commitment to developing a product with increasingly questionable commercial viability.

The technological environment is a fast changing one, with far reaching effects on organisations and their products. Technological advances can affect the materials, components and products, the processes by which products are made, administration and distribution systems, product marketing and the interface between the organisation and the customer. Each of these areas will now be looked at briefly, to give just a flavour of the immense impact technology has had on marketing practice.

Materials, components and products

Consumers tend to take products, and the materials and components that go into products, for granted as long as they work and live up to the marketers' promises. Technology does, however, improve and increase the benefits that consumers derive from products, and raise expectations about what a product should be. Some technological applications are invisible to the consumer, affecting raw materials and components hidden within an existing product, while others create completely new products.

Low calorie sweeteners

Artificial low calorie sweeteners, for example, are now found in a wide range of foodstuffs. An extremely successful application has been in fizzy drinks, such as colas and lemonades, creating a new segment among diet-conscious adults. Many claim to be able to taste the difference between the regular and diet (or light) versions of the same product, and thus the next stage of the R&D process might be to eliminate this minor discrepancy.

Unleaded petrol

Pressure from those concerned about the environmental and health effects of motor exhaust fumes has led to the development and widespread acceptance of unleaded petrol. The R&D task here was extensive, not only looking at the formulation and quality of the petrol itself, but also requiring adaptation of existing and proposed car engines to be able to take the new fuel with the minimum effect on performance.

Synthetics in clothing

Synthetic fabrics, fibre mixes and dyes have long been research concerns of the clothing industry. Consumers want easy-care clothes that can stand the rigours of machine washing with the minimum of drying and ironing afterwards. They also want their clothes to be hard wearing and to keep their colours bright, despite repeated washing. In this respect, the textile companies can work closely with the detergent manufacturers. More recently, consumer interest has turned back to natural fabrics, such as linen, cotton and silk, and the technological task has been to find ways of treating these fibres to make them easier to care for without compromising their natural characteristics.

Microchips

Microchips are everywhere! Not only are they the heart and soul of our home computers, but they also program our washing machines, CD players and video recorders, among many things. The incorporation of microchips into products has increased their reliability, their efficiency in operation and the range of sophisticated functions that they can perform, all very cost effectively. This in turn has raised consumers' expectations of what products can do, and revised their attitudes towards cost, quality and value for money.

High-tech products

In terms of brand new, innovative high-tech products, the last 15 years or so have opened up a number of new markets, based on invention and the development of commercial processes to allow its exploitation. This is not always an easy or fast process. CD players, videos, camcorders, computers and software have only begun to become common household possessions as technology improves through the manufacturers' learning experiences, as a wider range of products tailored towards definable market segments emerge and as costs come down through economies of scale.

Packaging

Technology is not just about the physical product itself. It can also affect its packaging. Lightweight plastics and glass, recycled and recyclable materials and cans that incorporate a device to give canned beer the character and quality of draught are examples of packaging innovations that have helped to make products more appealing, enhance their image or keep their cost down. Additionally, developments in areas such as lamination and printing techniques have increased the attractiveness and quality of packaging, again helping to enhance the product image.

Production processes

The fulfilment of marketing promises can be helped or hindered by what happens in the production process. More efficient production can, for instance, increase the volume of product available, thus potentially meeting a bigger demand, or it can reduce the cost of the product, thus giving more scope to the pricing decision. Production can also contribute to better and more consistent product quality, again increasing customer satisfaction. Here are some examples where technology has influenced production processes and indirectly, affected marketing activities.

Computer aided design systems

Computer aided design (CAD) systems have revolutionised product formulation and testing. In terms of design, technology allows ideas to be visualised, tested and accepted/rejected much more quickly than if paper plans and calculations had to be updated. Anything, from the design of a circuit board, through the arrangement of components inside the product, to the external styling and colourways can be fully explored cheaply and quickly. This means that a certain creative impetus can be generated, because the effects of a 'what if?' can be seen almost instantly, and even the wildest ideas can be given space. Sophisticated software can also simulate how the proposed product design might behave in reality under differing conditions, highlighting the probable weak areas and 'bugs'. The outcome for the customer is that products get to the market more quickly, and in a more refined state, and may be cheaper and more reliable.

Computer aided manufacturing systems

Computer aided manufacturing (CAM) systems help to streamline the production process. Computer controlled robotics and other mechanised systems can undertake tasks faster than human operatives, with more consistency and fewer errors. Robots and computers do not get tired or distracted from their tasks! In the long term, this can cut costs, because the labour input is less and there is less wastage through rejects. Again, the customer gets a more reliable, consistent and potentially cheaper product.

Quality assurance and control

Quality assurance (QA) and quality control (QC) are an important part of manufacturing. Technology has improved not only the methods used for testing samples taken from the production line, but also the capacity to detect faults early during the production process. It has also brought the responsibility for QA closer to the shop-floor operative who can monitor process levels and outputs as they happen and take corrective action or call for help as soon as it is needed. The implications for the customer are again related to costs and reliability. The fewer rejects that occur and the fewer rejects that slip through to the customer, the better for the manufacturer's reputation and relationship with the customer. This is particularly important in organisational markets where just in time (JIT) systems operate (*see* Chapter 4 for more on this). This means that a business buying in supplies from another business wants just the right amount to arrive just at the right time to be fed into the production process. There is no scope for error: if a bad batch is delivered, or if there are too many rejects in it, the consequences can be serious as the buyer has no buffer stocks to fall back on. Thus quality has to be right and the buyer has to be able to rely on that quality.

Materials handling

Materials handling and waste minimisation are both concerns of efficient, cost-effective production management, and are again linked with JIT systems. Stocks of materials need to be closely monitored so that further purchases can be triggered when the level gets low; in a large operation, the location of materials needs to be planned so that they can be accessed quickly and spend the minimum amount of time being transported around the site; the packaging and bundling of materials needs to be planned to balance out the sometimes conflicting concerns of adequately protecting and identifying the goods, and making sure that they can be unwrapped and put into the production line quickly. Computerised planning models and advances in packaging technology can both help to increase efficiency in these areas. Waste minimisation is clearly desirable if the manufacturer is going to get the most out of the raw materials. Minimisation through quality control was mentioned earlier, but it can also be achieved through good planning of material usage. A clothing factory, for instance, will use computerised layout planning to work out the best arrangement of the garment components on the cloth before cutting, so that the minimum amount of fabric is discarded.

Benefits to service industries

Even what is essentially a service industry can benefit from technology to improve its ability to serve the customer's needs. The telecommunications industry, for example, has used satellite technology, computerised exchanges and fibre optic cable, for instance, to extend customers' ability to dial direct to virtually any part of the world, relatively cheaply. On the 'hardware' side of the business, telecommunications now encompasses cordless and mobile phones, answering machines, faxes and modems. Technology has also allowed the industry to extend its range of services, such as linking the domestic telephone to burglar alarms, so that the emergency services are automatically alerted to a problem, and the introduction of the chargecard that allows calls made by cardholders from other telephone numbers to be billed to the cardholder's domestic or business number account.

Administration and distribution

There is little point in using technology to streamline the production of goods if the support systems are inefficient or if distribution causes a bottleneck between factory and customer. Distribution has benefited from technology, as has materials handling, through systems for locating and tracking goods in and out. Integrated ordering and dispatch functions mean theoretically that as soon as an order is entered into the computer, goods availability can be checked and the warehouse can get on with the job of fulfilling it, while the computer handles all the paperwork, printing off packing slips and invoices, for example, and updating customer records. All of this speeds up the sending of orders to customers and reduces labour involvement, costs and risks of errors.

Telecommunications linking into computer systems can extend the administration efficiencies even further. Large retail chains, for example, can be linked with their major suppliers, so that as the retailer's stocks reduce, an order can be sent from computer to computer. Similarly, large organisations with sites and depots spread over a wide geographic area can use such technology to link sites, managing and tracking the flow of goods.

Marketing and customers

Much of the technology discussed above has implied benefits for the customer, in producing the right product at the right time in the right place at the right price. Technology also plays a part in the dialogue between buyer and seller, and thus affects the interface between them.

Market research
Market research has benefited from increased and cheaper computer power, which means that large, complex sets of data can be input and analysed quickly and easily.

Databases
Databases are created not only for market research purposes, but also for selling. Relationship marketing, establishing and maintaining a one-to-one dialogue between buyer and seller, is now possible in mass consumer markets. Organisations such as Heinz now see this as an exciting development in consumer marketing, and it is only possible because of database technology that permits the storage, retrieval and maintenance of detailed profiles of many thousands, or even hundreds of thousands, of customers. The technology also allows the creation of tailored, personalised marketing offers to be made to subsets of those customers as appropriate.

Advertising media
The advertising media have improved and proliferated through technology. As well as making use of satellite and cable television channels, advertisers can use teletext pages, video tapes and CDs. Improvements in printing technology have led to better reproduction and thus better quality print advertisements, for example sharply focused, full colour advertising is now commonplace in newspapers. Technology has also made its contribution to the creative side of advertising, for example with computer animation or computer manipulation of images to create special effects.

On-line ordering
As briefly mentioned earlier, on-line ordering is a direct link between buyer and seller, allowing the faster reception and processing of orders. This technology has yet to take widespread hold in consumer markets, although systems such as the French Minitel prove that it is feasible. The nearest to on-line ordering that most consumers experience is through telephone shopping, sometimes in direct response to television or print advertising. This is another spin-off from the telecommunications industry, which can now supply sellers with the capacity to handle many hundreds of calls simultaneously.

Sales force support
Another area that can also be enhanced through computer technology is sales force support. Supplying a sales representative with a laptop computer can give access to current information about products, their availability and prices; it can store customer profiles and relevant information; the representative can update records and write reports while the information is still fresh in the mind, and it can store appropriate graphics to enhance a sales presentation. All of this is easily portable and accessible whether the representative is working in Scotland or Greece.

THE ECONOMIC AND COMPETITIVE ENVIRONMENT

The effects of the **economic and competitive environment** are felt by organisations and consumers alike, and it has a profound effect on their behaviour. In the next few pages we look first at the macroeconomic environment, which provides the overall backdrop against which marketing activities take place. We cover, as well as issues of national interest, such as the effects of government economic policy on commerce, the influence of international trading blocs and trade agreements. All of these things may provide opportunities or threats for an individual organisation. We then turn to the microeconomic environment. This is rather closer to home for the organisation, looking at the extent to which different market structures constrain or widen the organisation's freedom of action in its marketing activities and its ability to influence the nature of the market.

The macroeconomic environment

Figure 2.4 shows a simplified version of the basic economic concept of the circular flow of goods and income that makes a market economy go round. Marketing, as an exchange process, and indeed as a force that actively encourages more exchanges, is an essential fuel to keep that flow going.

The world is not, however, such a simple, balanced, closed, self-sustaining loop as that depicted in Fig 2.4. Its operation is severely affected by the macroeconomic influences generated by government economic policy and by membership of international trading blocs and trade agreements. Figure 2.5 summarises these factors.

FIGURE 2.4

The circular flow of goods and income

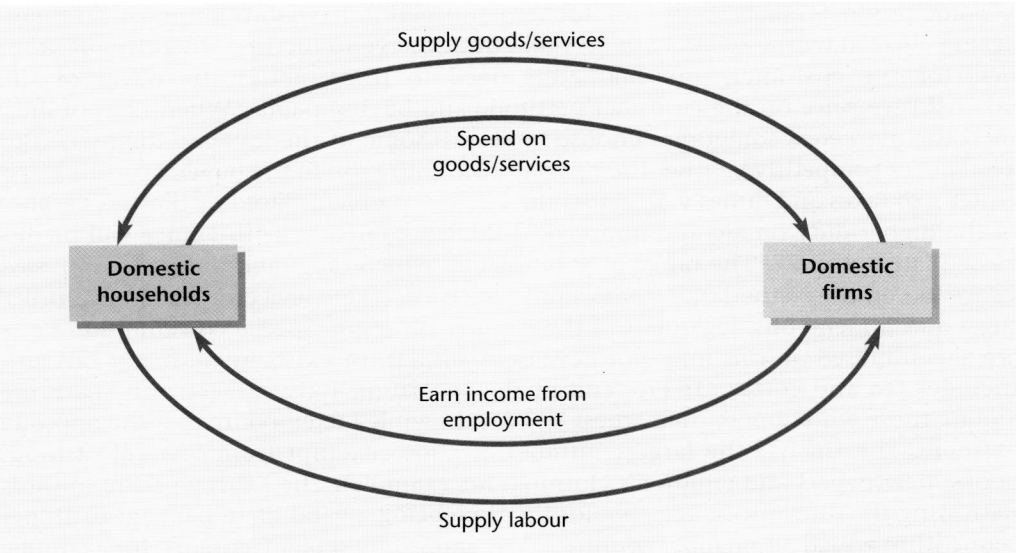

FIGURE 2.5

Marcroeconomic influences on the circular flow

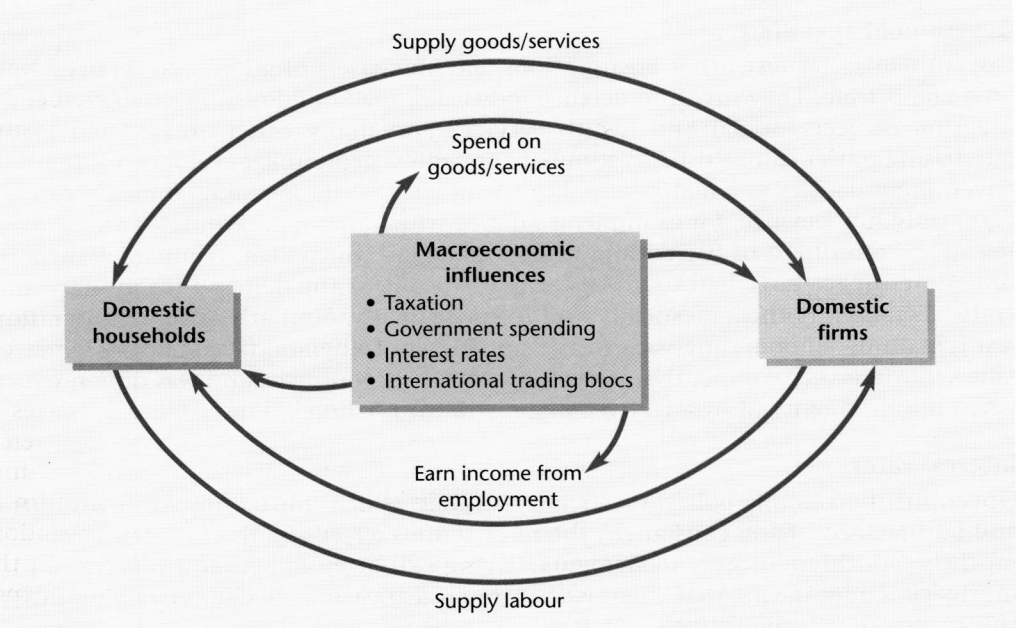

Governments can develop and implement policies in relation to several macroeconomic influences, which in turn affect markets, organisations, and customers. Just a few of these are discussed below.

Taxation

Taxes may be direct or indirect. Direct taxation, such as income tax and national insurance contributions, reduces the amount of money, or disposable income, that a household has available to spend on the goods and services organisations provide. Indirect taxation, such as purchase tax or value added tax (VAT), is collected for the government by the seller, who is obliged to add a percentage to the basic price of the product. Thus a multimedia PC sold in the UK may be advertised with two prices: a basic price of £1300, then £1525 including VAT.

Some products, such as alcohol, tobacco and petrol, have duty imposed on them, again collected by the seller. Both VAT and duties serve to increase the prices of products for the customer, and marketers need to think about the effect of the tax-inclusive price on the customer's attitude and buying habits. When rates of duty increase, marketers sometimes choose to absorb some of the increase themselves to keep prices competitive, rather than pass on the entire rise to the buyer.

Rates of taxes and duties vary across the EU. The problems faced by brewers because of the higher duty on alcohol imposed in the UK compared with France will be discussed later, at p. 77. The range of goods across which taxes and duties are imposed varies too. In the Netherlands, for example, excise taxes are levied on alcoholic drinks, sugar and mineral oils, regardless of the country of origin. Special consumption taxes are also imposed on cars and motorcycles. A similar list exists in Germany, but also includes tea and coffee. At one end of the spectrum, Italy, Greece and Spain are among those who impose the highest VAT levels, while Luxembourg is at the opposite extreme. The UK has the largest number of goods exempt from VAT (most food, books, newspapers and children's clothing, for example). The EU is working towards narrowing the differences, agreeing for the time being a band of 15 per cent to 19 per cent within which all member countries' VAT rates should fall. Germany, for example, adjusted its VAT rate upwards from 14 per cent to 15 per cent, although there is still a 7 per cent rate on items such as food, books and newspapers. A single European VAT system is still some way off, however.

Government spending

Governments, like any other organisations, are purchasers of goods and services, but on a grand scale. They invest in defence industries, road building and other civil engineering projects, social and health services and many other areas. Such large purchasing power can be used to stimulate or depress economic development, but if a government decides as a matter of policy to cut back on its spending, industry can be very badly hit. Defence, for example, is an area which many governments are reviewing in the aftermath of the ending of the 'cold war'. In the UK, companies such as British Aerospace have had to downsize dramatically as the demand for military aircraft has fallen, both domestically and internationally. Similarly, Swan Hunter, the last remaining shipbuilding yard in the north-east of England faced closure when it failed to win a very competitive battle for Royal Navy contracts, and was only rescued when it was bought out by a Dutch company in the offshore oil industry.

Interest rates

Government economic policy affects interest rates, which impact on both consumers and business. For many consumers, the most serious effect of a rise in interest rates is on their monthly mortgage repayments. Paying £20 or more per month extra to the mortgage lender means that there is that much less cash available for buying other things, and across the country, retail sales can be significantly reduced. Interest rate rises can also affect the attractiveness of credit to the consumer, either when buying large expensive items through instalments, or in using credit cards. A consumer thinking about buying a brand new car, for example, may need a loan, and will look at the repayment levels, determined by interest rates, when deciding how expensive a model can be afforded. To try to reduce this potential barrier to purchasing, many car dealers have entered into arrangements with credit companies to offer 0 per cent financing deals to car buyers.

Regional economic development policy

At both European and national levels, governments face the problems of unequal economic performance and opportunity in different regions within their sphere of influence. Governments therefore try to overcome the problems of congestion and rising costs in some areas and underused facilities and infrastructure in others through influencing business decision making with programmes of direct and indirect incentives. In Ireland, for example, the west coast is particularly remote from main European markets, and thus the government offers various tax and capital grant incentives to encourage relocation into the area, indigenous enterprise and business expansion. Similarly, in the Netherlands, a number of assisted areas have been defined to ensure balanced economic growth, including the north-eastern areas of Gronigen, Friesland and Drente, the northern part of Overijssel, and the south-eastern province of Limburg. In these areas, investment premiums are awarded along with cash grants and low interest loans to encourage R&D investment.

The reunification of Germany posed particular problems for the government in trying to privatise eastern German industry and create an integrated free market economy across the whole country. The Treuhandanstalt was set up to manage the privatisation of some 8000 previously state-owned industries, and additionally, a range of incentives, including grants, subsidies, low-cost loans, accelerated depreciation, low tax, labour retraining support and export credit insurance were introduced to encourage both domestic and foreign investment.

At EU level, there is a commitment to reducing the disparities between the various regions, and developing the less favoured areas. Structural funds awarded from the European Regional Development Fund (ERDF) and the European Social Fund (ESF) particularly help the poorer regions of the EU, such as Greece, Spain, Portugal, Ireland and parts of Italy. The appropriateness and benefits of some of the projects awarded funds have been questioned by some critics, however. As Perry (1994) noted, the Court of Auditors in 1993 reported on projects such as the building of a winter ski resort in Crete, the establishment of a school for waiters on the Costa del Sol in Spain, a fur centre and exhibition hall in Greece, and a Spanish wind farm that switched off when the wind blew too hard! Nevertheless, most projects do achieve their stated objectives, and provide a valuable boost to local economies, for example, investment in encouraging high technology enterprise in Ireland.

Governments also negotiate membership of international trading blocs, and the scope, terms and conditions of international trade agreements. Membership of the EU, for example, and particularly the advent of the single European market (**SEM**),

Example

The Swedish dairy comany, Arla, spent two very hard years preparing for Sweden's entry into the EU in 1995 by developing strong relationships with companies within the EU, even though exporting to them was difficult. This meant that on day one of Sweden's EU membership, Arla was very well placed to capitalise on unrestricted trade in key EU markets that it had already defined and begun to penetrate.

Austria plc joins the EU

Austria joined the EU on 1 January 1995. In anticipation of this event, Gütter (1994) looked ahead to estimate what the effects of membership would be on various sectors of Austrian industry. Even before 1995, Austria had considerable trade with the EU, buying 67 per cent of its imports and selling 62 per cent of its exports to EU countries. The amount of trade with the EU is predicted to rise even further following membership. Some industries, however, will find it an easier environment than others, and three examples are presented here.

The construction and building materials sectors, for example, are expected to benefit from EU membership. Although it means more competition for Austrian public sector contracts, it does open up many new opportunities for Austrian firms to compete in other EU countries. Also, EU-funded construction projects will emerge within Austria. Gütter mentions, for example, that the Munich–Verona railway line extension will create £3.4 bn in construction work just on the Austrian section. Suppliers of construction materials will benefit from the removal of trade barriers, and from EU protection from cheap imports from Central and Eastern Europe.

The Austrian brewing industry will also benefit in some ways. Raw material prices will fall, as prices for barley come into line with EU agricultural regulations, and there will be greater export opportunities as again trade barriers are removed. A potential problem, however, is the risk of cross-border shopping. In 1994, taxes on beer in Germany were almost half those levied in Austria, and Austrians living near the border would find it easy and cheap to buy their favourite Austrian beers in Germany.

Within the food processing industry, however, there are mixed fortunes. The agricultural sector in particular is expected to face problems, as farm prices fall by 20 per cent to reach EU levels. Also, the imposition of quotas on milk and sugar production is going to create overcapacity in those areas of agriculture in particular. Secondary food processors, such as jam and fruit juice manufacturers, however, should gain from greater export opportunities as trade barriers fall.

Source: Gütter (1994).

---

has had a profound effect on the wider commercial dealings of organisations operating within the EU, as well as on the economic and competitive environment. Organisations which exist in countries outside the EU have found it increasingly difficult to sell into the EU, since there are now many more EU-based potential suppliers for purchasers to turn to, and also the logistics of purchasing within the EU are easier.

The EU is not, however, the only major European international trading bloc. The European Free Trade Association (EFTA) was formed originally in 1959 by Austria, Denmark, Norway, Sweden, Switzerland and the UK, and was later expanded to include Finland, Iceland and Liechtenstein. Its philosophy was simply to make trade between the member states easier. Since several EFTA members subsequently became members of the EU, and as the prospect of the SEM raised the perceived barriers to entry to EU markets for non-EU organisations, the remaining EFTA countries (except Switzerland) became involved in the idea of the European Economic Area (EEA), formalised by treaty in 1993. Although not full members of the EU, EEA countries now share some of the benefits of the SEM, and certainly face fewer barriers to trade within the EU than they would otherwise have encountered. Participation in the EEA acted as a stepping stone for Austria and Sweden who subsequently became full EU members. Similar co-operation and association agreements are in progress with the former communist states of central and eastern Europe, with the immediate aim of helping to stimulate their economies, and the longer-term aim of eventual EU membership.

Beyond the confines of formalised trading blocs, business is often affected by the existence of trade agreements. Some of these are protectionist, in that they are trying to cushion domestic producers from the effects of an influx of imports, while others are trying to liberalise trade between nations. For many years, for example, the UK's textile industry has benefited from the multi fibre arrangement (MFA), which protected jobs and businesses by basically restricting the imports of low priced clothing from various Far Eastern countries. Similarly, Japan agreed to implement voluntary export restraint (VER) with regard to its car industry's sales to Western Europe and the US. This helped to protect domestic car producers and jobs by imposing quotas on Japanese imports. One way of overcoming the restrictions of this VER was international direct investment, i.e. setting up factories within the EU (taking full advantage, by the way, of various EU investment incentives) to produce cars with sufficient local content to be labelled 'European'. Thus those people owning either a Nissan (built in Washington, Tyne & Wear), a Honda (built in Swindon) or a Toyota (built in Derby), for example, are technically driving a British car. The Nissan range, for example, had in 1995, 83 per cent European content, with the gearbox being the only major component still sourced from Japan. From their British manufacturing bases, the companies can legitimately export, without quota constraints, to the rest of the EU under the terms of the SEM. In 1993, Nissan was the UK's leading car exporter, exporting over 74 per cent of its UK output. The *Financial Times* estimates (Griffiths, 1994) that at least one million Japanese cars will be produced per year in Europe by the turn of the century.

The protectionist stance of agreements like the MFA is, however, being overshadowed by wider moves towards trade liberalisation, through the General Agreement on Tariffs and Trade (GATT), for example. The broad aim of GATT is to get rid of export subsidies and import tariffs (effectively taxes on imports that push their prices up to make them less competitive compared with the domestically produced equivalent product) to make international trade a great deal fairer. This means that negotiated VERs, which do not depend on tariffs to control imports, are becoming an increasingly important tool.

Many of the marketing issues associated with dealing within and with trading blocs, including the SEM, will be considered further in Chapter 26.

The microeconomic environment

The general discussion in Chapter 1 of what marketing is, and the main tools of marketing, did not pay particular attention to the structure of markets. It is nevertheless important to think about market structures, because these will influence what sort of competition the organisation is up against, what scope the organisation has to manipulate the 4Ps and how broad an impact the organisation's marketing activities could have on the market as a whole.

Market structures can be defined in four broad categories, based on the number and size of competitors in the market:

Monopoly

Technically, a monopoly exists where one supplier has sole control over a market, and there is no competition. The lack of competition may be because the monopolist is state owned and/or has a statutory right to be the sole supplier to the market. Traditionally in the UK, this applied to public utilities, such as gas, water, electricity, telephone and postal services, and some key industries such as the railways, steel and coal. Government policy during the 1980s, however, was to privatise and open up some of these industries to competition, with the idea that if they were exposed to market forces and were answerable to shareholders, they would operate more efficiently and cost effectively. By early 1995, the railways and the last part of the electricity generating industry were still in the process of being sold off, while privatisation of the postal service was still uncertain, being a subject of heated political and public debate. Other countries have implemented similar privatisation programmes. The Netherlands, for instance, has privatised post, telephone and telegraph services (PTT) and Postbank.

Example

Even 10 years after deregulation, in 1993/94 British Telecommunications still held around 87 per cent share of retail call revenues, with its main rival Mercury holding around 11.6 per cent. The UK gas market is only just opening up to competition for supply, and thus it is too early to see any long-term effects on market shares. Industrial users of large amounts of gas can now choose whether to be supplied by British Gas or by Kinetica, for example. Even the Post Office, not yet privatised, is seeing parts of its business eroded by competition. Stamps, for instance, can now be purchased at a wide range of retail outlets, not just at post offices, and courier companies, like Securicor, DHL and Federal Express, are competing for guaranteed express delivery services on letters and parcels. Where barriers to entry are too high, an organisation wanting to get into a market can try to do it through take-over. Trafalgar House, a massive industrial conglomerate with interests ranging from engineering to construction to shipping, launched a (hostile) take-over bid in early 1995 for Northern Electric, the privatised company responsible for the sale and distribution of electricity in the North-east of England. That particular bid failed, but that has not deterred other American and European companies making take-over bids for privatised utilities.

In practice, although the privatised companies have restructured themselves internally, and revised their business philosophies to suit their new status, they still face limited competition as yet. This is mainly because of the barriers to entry faced by potential competitors, such as the massive capital investment required, or the monopolist's domination of essential resources or infrastructures.

Mercury Communications has emerged as a significant competitor in the UK since the deregulation of telecommunications.

Source: Mercury Communications/Howell Henry Chaldecott Lury.

The implication of all this is that a true monopoly is hard to find in a modern market economy, although there are several near-monopolies operating. In the UK, a monopoly is deemed to exist where an organisation or a group of collaborating organisations control 25 per cent of a market. Where this occurs, or where a proposed or threatened take-over raises the possibility of it happening, the Monopolies and Mergers Commission (MMC) may undertake an enquiry to establish whether the situation is operating in the public interest and whether there is any unfair competition involved.

In theory, monopolists should not need to be particularly bothered about marketing. After all, they have a captive market with no alternative source of supply, so they should be able to price as highly as they want, and not be too concerned about customer service, corporate image, quality, reliability and all the other things that this book covers. In reality, however, monopolies exist with the consent and acquiescence of the government and public opinion, and thus the monopolist is likely to be subject to some kind of control or supervision to make sure that it operates within the public interest, and thus a strong positive image, good customer service, fair pricing and all the other aspects of marketing soon become essential. Near-monopolies, as we have seen, do face competition, at least in sectors of their businesses, and thus have to be more marketing orientated in their thinking.

This discussion so far has been rather parochial in that it has concentrated on national or regional monopolies. In global markets, however, it is even more difficult, if not impossible, to establish and sustain a monopoly.

Example

British Steel, for example, may be the only major *producer* of steel based in the UK, but it faces severe competition in global *sales* terms from other European and international steel companies. This global view is important, since British Steel generated 49 per cent of its 1992 sales from other European and worldwide markets, and similarly non-domestic sales accounted for over 30 per cent of the 1992 sales of steel companies Usinor Sacilor (France) and Ilva (Italy), while the Belgian firm Cockerill Sambre generated a massive 70 per cent of its sales from the rest of Europe (Lynch 1994, p. 188). In the light of this, along with the pressures of the SEM and GATT against the kind of trade protectionism that would protect and preserve monopoly power within a national market, the true monopoly is an endangered species.

As a final thought, the concept of monopoly depends on how 'market' is defined. While it is true that currently SNCF, for example, holds a monopoly on passenger rail travel in France, it does not have a monopoly on moving people from Paris to Lyon. To travellers, rail is only one option, and they might also consider travelling to their destinations by air, by coach or by car. In that sense, the traveller's perception of rail, in terms of its cost, reliability and convenience, is developed in a very competitive context. British Rail advertising over the last few years has indeed sought to acknowledge this, by comparing the benefits of long distance rail travel with the disadvantages of road and air journeys. The opening of the Channel Tunnel in particular has brought the comparison of different modes of travel to the forefront, as leisure and business travellers decide whether to take the plane, the train or the ferry to and from the UK. It is possible, however, for such competitors to work together. British Midland, the airline, was in the early stages of negotiating an agreement with Eurostar (the operator of the cross channel trains) in 1995 to make tickets transferable between the two services, and a number of airlines were discussing the possibility of arrangements that would mean Eurostar carrying airline passengers if aircraft were grounded through bad weather, for example, and airlines would similarly carry rail passengers if there were problems in the tunnel.

Oligopoly

Well-developed market economies are far more likely to see the emergence of oligopolies than monopolies. In an oligopoly, a small number of firms account for a very large share of the market, and a number of the privatised ex-monopolies discussed above are moving into this category. The oligopoly creates a certain amount of interdependence between the key players, each of which is large enough for its actions to have a big impact on the market and on the behaviour of its competitors. This certainly occurs in large scale, world-wide industrial markets, such as chemicals, oil and pharmaceuticals, because the amount of capital investment required, the levels of production needed to achieve economies of scale and the geographic dispersion of large customers demanding large quantities make this the most efficient way for these markets to be structured.

Example

Oligopolies also occur in consumer markets, however. Petrol retailing in the UK, has largely been concentrated in the hands of a few companies, such as Shell, BP and Esso for example. This has periodically given rise to accusations of collusion, specifically in terms of 'price fixing', which would not be allowed either in UK or EU law. In reality, the organisations within the oligopoly watch each other keenly for signals, and when one makes a price move, the others tend to follow very quickly, because this is a price-sensitive market. It may appear to be orchestrated, but the important thing to emphasise is that each organisation makes its decision independently, on the basis of its analysis of what it sees happening in the market. The petrol oligopoly in the UK became somewhat wider after the entry of the supermarket chains into this market. By late 1993, the supermarkets had taken 16 per cent of the market (Knott, 1993), while by late 1994 it was estimated to be 20 per cent and still growing (Corzine and Buckley, 1994), although by 1996 it seemed to have settled at 22 per cent (Murphy, 1996).

Other consumer oligopolies are less visible to the casual observer. In the supermarket, the shopper may see a wide variety of brands of clothes washing detergents, and thus imagine that there is healthy, widespread competition in that sector. Most brands are, however, owned and managed by either Procter & Gamble (P&G) (Ariel, Daz, Bold etc.) or Lever Brothers (Persil, Radion, Surf etc.), and the proliferation of brands is more to do with fragmented demand, and the creation of discrete segments (*see* Chapter 3), than the fragmentation of supply. Again, the supermarkets are the biggest threat to this oligopoly, with their own brands, such as retailer Sainsbury's own brand Novon.

In marketing terms, it is nevertheless still very difficult for a new brand from a new competitor to enter an oligopolistic market, other than in a small niche. This is because the oligopolists have spent many years and vast amounts of marketing money establishing their brands and shares. In the 1995 Marketing/Nielsen Biggest Brands Survey (Marketing, 1995b), it was reported that P&G had spent £65.2mn advertising its top six brands, while Lever had spent £42.7mn on four brands in the previous year. Add to that the reputed £200mn that Lever Brothers spent on the initial development and launch of Persil Power in 1994, and you can begin to see how such levels of marketing expenditure can act as an effective barrier to entry, and how they can meet any threat from a smaller competitor head-on if they wish.

The supermarket's own brand threat is more serious because of the retailer's inherent control over a major channel of distribution which neither of the oligopolists can afford to lose. All of this really leaves only very small gaps in the market for the smaller competitor, such as that filled by products such as Ark and Ecover, two detergent brands that positioned themselves as more environmentally friendly than anything else available, appealing to the 'dark green' consumer.

Oligopolists spend their time, therefore, watching each other, and developing their marketing strategies and tactics on the basis of what the other main players are doing or are likely to do. If, for example, Lever Brothers launch a new brand, or implement a major new marketing communications strategy, P&G would preferably wish to anticipate it, thus either pre-empting Lever or at least having a calculated response ready when needed. From P&G's point of view, this is essential, even if they are only to maintain the delicate status quo of their relative market shares.

Example

Not all oligopolistic markets are made up of organisations from the private sector. In the European airline industry, for example, there is a combination of state-owned and private operators. While British Airways is a privately owned company, Aer Lingus (Ireland), TAP (Portugal), Air France, Iberia (Spain), Sabena (Belgium) and Alitalia (Italy) are primarily state owned. It is claimed that such companies enjoy a higher level of state aid, and that there is a risk of unfair competition. This may arise from direct subsidy, or through government intervention to slow down the pace of unfavourable change. Despite deregulation designed to create more competition on previously monopolistic routes and to encourage price competition, it can still cost more to travel business class return from London to Hamburg than to New York.

Monopolistic competition

Good marketing practice and the emphasis on differential advantage have created a market structure that might seem a little paradoxical at first sight: monopolistic competition. The idea is that although there are many competitors in the market (with the emphasis on smaller competitors without enough individual influence to create either an oligopoly or a monopoly, as discussed above), each has a product sufficiently differentiated from the rest to create its own monopoly, because to the customer it is unique, or at least any potential substitutes are considered to be inferior. The concept forms the basis of much of the rest of this book.

Perfect competition

Perfect competition is at the opposite end of the spectrum from monopoly, and is about as likely to be found in practice. It involves many small producers, all supplying identical products that can be directly substituted for each other. No producer has the power to influence or determine price, and the market consists of many small buyers, who similarly cannot influence the market individually. There are no barriers to market entry or exit, and all buyers and sellers have complete information about what is happening in the market. All of this is clearly unrealistic. The influence of marketing concepts on even the smallest organisations, along with the development of powerful buyers and sellers in all kinds of markets, consumer and organisational, mean that these conditions cannot hold, and some kind of monopolistic competition or oligopoly soon emerges.

Example

Farm produce, such as vegetables, is often cited as an example of near-perfect competition. While it is true that the market does consist of many small suppliers, i.e. individual farms, the nature of the buyer is more complex, ranging from a family buying a few kilos of carrots from a farm shop, to the fruit and vegetable wholesalers and supermarket chains that buy such quantity that they can influence price and other supply variables. Even the product itself can be differentiated, for example organic and non-organic, or class I and class II quality. The farmer can also differentiate the offering through grading and packaging the produce to suit the retail customer. Even carrots, therefore, can be seen to be moving towards monopolistic competition.

This section has made implicit reference to concepts of supply, demand and pricing. In Chapter 11, which deals with price setting and modification, we go into more detail on the economics on pricing, supply and demand curves and price elasticity.

THE POLITICAL AND REGULATORY ENVIRONMENT

Quite apart from their effect on the economic and competitive environment, governments have a great influence on the character of the general business environment through their policies and the resultant legislation. Organisations have to exist in and operate according to the laws of the societies within which they do business, and thus in addition to the more general laws of contract and commerce, products have to conform to safety laws; manufacturing processes are subject to pollution controls; copyright and patents protect innovation; and retailers' opening hours are restricted in Germany, for example, by the Ladenschlussgesetz, and in the UK by the Sunday trading laws. We look below at the role and influence of national governments and the European Parliament in making such rules that have a direct effect on the marketing mix.

Regulation is not only defined through legislation from national governments or the European Parliament, however. Organisations are also subject to rules passed by regulatory bodies, some of which have statutory powers delegated to them from government, while others are voluntary groupings, such as trade associations, with codes of practice to which the organisation chooses to adhere. We examine the nature and influence of such bodies at p. 75. Inevitably, governments and other regulatory bodies are influenced in their policy making by other sources, such as lobbyists and pressure groups, and at p. 77 we take a wider view of the influences that drive the legislators and rule makers towards their policies.

Overall, therefore, there are three main forces within the **political and regulatory environment**, as shown in Fig 2.6. The degree of relative influence that each force exerts, and the nature of the tensions between them, will vary from country to country and from industry to industry. In general, however, the problem with self-regulation is that it creates tension between what is socially desirable and what those in the industry may consider to restrict commerce unduly. Similarly, there is a risk that the interests of the general public, as represented by pressure groups (the fourth influence shown in Fig 2.6), may also conflict with the needs and desires of commercial organisations, and that too creates tension that the law makers and regulators have to try to resolve.

National and local government

The obvious responsibility of national governments is to determine and maintain the legislative framework within which organisations do business. This will cover areas such as contract law, consumer protection, financial legislation, competition and trading practices, for example. There are still some variations across Europe, however. In Germany, for example, there are no overall government price controls, yet in the Netherlands, the Price Control Act (Prijzenwet) gives government substantial power to control prices for one year at times of high inflation. Nevertheless, increasingly within Europe, national governments are working within EU guidelines with the longer-term aim of achieving as much consistency as possible between member states.

FIGURE 2.6

The European regulatory framework

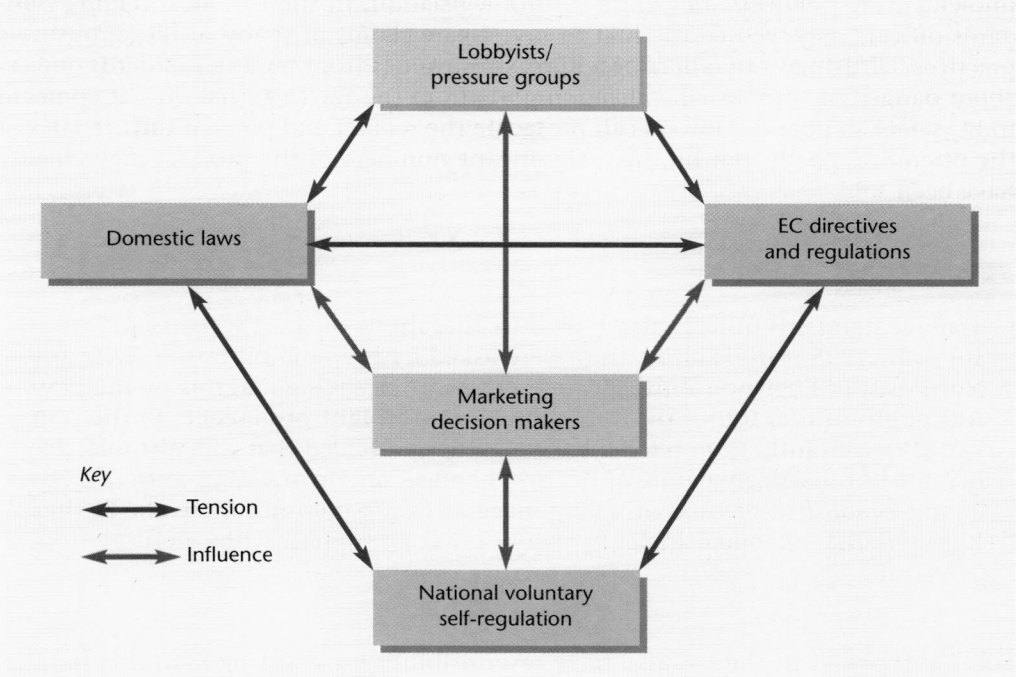

Within the UK, although Parliament passes legislation and puts it on the statute books, the responsibility for implementing and enforcing it is often delegated to specialist bodies, such as the Office of Fair Trading (OFT), the Monopolies and Mergers Commission (MMC), or the Independent Television Commission (ITC), for example. The role of such bodies is discussed further in at p. 75 below.

As well as the legislation they pass that affects the day-to-day business practices of organisations, governments can also have profound effects on the competitive environment. The widespread privatisation of publicly owned utilities and other state- controlled national industries in the 1980s and 1990s, as has already been discussed, presented opportunities for new competitors to enter these markets, as well as profoundly changing the culture and business orientation of the newly privatised companies themselves. In Germany, deregulation and liberalisation of the country's energy sector is a high priority. This is understandable in view of the price of coal. On the world market, the price of coal in 1994 was around 80 DM per tonne, whereas German electricity companies were paying around 280 DM. The difference between the two prices was covered by the Kohlepfennig, a levy on consumers charged by the electricity companies. In short, the German consumer was subsidising the German coal industry. The problem faced by the government, however, is that abolition of the levy would have severe implications in the mining regions, yet failure to act has severe effects on German industry generally and on the consumer (Dempsey, 1994).

Politically driven deregulation has even made its mark on the public sector, particularly in the UK, where hospitals and police forces, for example, now find themselves operating in completely new ways as business units. Hospital pathology laboratories, for example, which traditionally were integrated internal departments, are now being asked to compete against external organisations for their own hospital's business, as well as tendering for contracts from other hospitals and the private sector. These are themes that will be pursued further in Chapter 23.

Local government also carries some responsibility for implementing and enforcing laws made at a national level. In Germany, local government has responsibility for implementing pollution and noise control legislation. In the UK, local trading standards officers may well be the first to investigate claims of shady or illegal business practices. Christmas often heralds a flurry of warnings from trading standards officers about dangerous toys, usually cheap imports from the Far East, that do not conform to EU safety standards. Officers can prosecute the retailer and prevent further sales of the offending goods, but by then, significant numbers of the product may already have been sold.

Example

Trading standards officers also look into allegations of short weights and measures. In 1995, for example, they were asked by the angling fraternity in the North-east of England to investigate the practice of selling maggots by the pint. Although officers found that the number and weight of maggots to the pint varied significantly from retailer to retailer, they decided that this was tolerable because of the wriggly nature of the merchandise, and in any case, since this was a long-established method of selling maggots they would not intervene further. It is up to the individual angler to choose a maggot supplier with care!

Local authorities in the UK also have responsibility for granting planning permission. For businesses, this means that if they want to build a factory or supermarket, or change the usage of a commercial building, then the local authority has to vet the plans and grant permission before anything can be done. Sometimes this poses no problem at all, and local authorities go out of their way to encourage new industrial and commercial investment in their regions, as it provides jobs and encourages local economic regeneration. Establishing the Nissan car plant in Washington, Tyne & Wear, for example, not only provided new jobs in the factory itself, but also encouraged companies supplying goods and services to Nissan to locate and flourish close to the factory.

In other cases, however, planning permission can sometimes be a major barrier. Local authorities are under pressure from small retailers who are worried about the major shift towards out of town superstore shopping. The argument is that town centres and small local businesses are dying because people would rather go to the out of town retail park or shopping mall. This means that local authorities are increasingly reluctant to grant planning permission for further out of town developments, seriously affecting the growth plans of many large retailers. In early 1995, Sainsbury's bought out three Cargo Club warehouse stores, with a view to converting two of the sites to Sainsbury's superstores. Under pressure from the Department of the Environment, it was soon made clear to Sainsbury's that this was regarded as a 'change of use' and thus planning permission would have to be obtained. In the prevailing climate, this is far from a mere administrative detail.

Example

Environmental pressure groups can also raise the profile of a planning issue. Environmentalists and birdlife protectionists won a court injunction to prevent DB, the German state railway, from electrifying the main line from Hamburg to Denmark by forcing a planning enquiry near the border at Flensberg. This set back DB's plans for that line by at least a year.

Although the EU is making considerable progress towards eliminating national regulations that are contrary to fair and free trade, the scale of the task is great. National environmental laws in Germany and Denmark, for example, have been criticised as favouring local rather than international suppliers. The extent to which regulations impact upon business, therefore, varies between countries and industries. There is a slow move towards standardisation, which generally means that the advanced industrialised northern European nations are tending to deregulate, whereas the southern nations are tending to tighten up controls. Moves towards deregulation have been accompanied by increased self-regulation within industries.

The European Union

It is unfortunate that the pronouncements from Brussels that make the headlines tend to be the offbeat or trivial ones such as the proposal to regulate the curve on a cucumber, the redesignation of the carrot as a fruit to allow the Portuguese to carry on their trade in carrot jam, and questions as to whether Cheddar cheese and Swiss rolls can continue to bear those names if they are not made in those places. Despite these delightful eccentricities, the EU works hard towards ensuring free trade and fair competition across member states' boundaries. The development and interpretation of European competition policy has long been an area of debate and controversy. The policy has three main objectives: to create an open and unified European market, to have the 'right' amount of competition in that market and to encourage fair competition unhampered by market abuse and restrictive practices.

The SEM, which officially came into being on 1 January 1993, was the culmination of many years of work in breaking down trade barriers and harmonising legislation across the member states. One area that directly affects marketing, is the abolition of frontier controls, so that goods can be transferred from state to state, or carried in transit through states, without lots of paperwork and customs checks. Additionally, road haulage has been freed from restrictions and quotas so that a haulier with a licence to operate in one EU member state can operate in any other. In terms of products themselves, a set of European standards have been implemented through a series of directives, ensuring common criteria for safety, public health, and environmental protection. Any product adhering to these directives and to the laws of its own country of origin will be acceptable in any member state. Look for the stylised CE symbol on products as the sign that they do conform to European standards.

In other areas of marketing, harmonisation of regulations and codes of practice across member states has not been so easy, particularly in the marketing communications field. At the time of writing, the EC Green Paper on Commercial Communication, which is expected to tackle many of the anomalies in marketing communications practice in different member states, has not yet been published.

Sales promotion, for example, is regulated in very different ways and with very different attitudes across Europe. The UK is very liberal, in that most sales promotion techniques are permitted, and largely regulated through voluntary codes of practice. In Germany, by contrast, many techniques are banned by law or heavily restricted in the way in which they can operate, for instance free gifts are (generally) banned, while there is a restriction on the value of discounts, vouchers or cash refunds. In the Netherlands, free gifts are permitted, but must not exceed 4 per cent of the value of the item to which they are linked. Even these brief examples give an inkling of the nightmares faced by the European marketer trying to trade across borders, and the pressure on the EU to begin to iron out the inconsistencies.

Advertising too is an area of intense debate within the EU. Issues such as the advertising of tobacco and alcohol, advertising aimed at children, comparative advertising and the regulation and control of advertising media are all under consideration. Again, the aim is to find a way of harmonising codes of practice and legislation that

Airline deregulation

The European airline market has long been sheltered from the rigours of a truly free market economy because of the efforts made by various governments to protect their national carriers. This has been done through financial subsidies and tight control over the allocation of 'slots' (i.e., rights of access) at major airports. Air France, Alitalia and Iberia, for example, have all been kept from bankruptcy by state subsidies. In April 1997, however, the market will be fully deregulated, and in theory, any airline will be free to fly to any European destination, and the protection of subsidies and monopolies will end.

The prospect of deregulation has brought a number of new operators into the market and has opened up opportunities for existing airlines. Virgin, for example, acquired a Belgian airline which already had access to 'slots' as a foundation for Virgin Express, planned to be a no-frills, low-fare carrier at the bargain end of the market. Other cut price UK operators, such as EasyJet, Denim and Debonair, also have their eyes on the European market. They face competition from operators from other European countries too, such as Ryanair (Ireland), Air Liberté (France), Spanair (Spain) and Euro Belgium. These so-called peanut airlines (because that is the extent of their in-flight catering) cut costs by paying lower wages to staff and trimming the service offered to a minimum. On the two to three hour flights typical in Europe, small airlines feel that customers will be happy to forego the drinks trolley and the meal in return for rock bottom fares. Southwest, a US peanut airline upon which some of the European companies model themselves, trims its costs by paying its aircrew only while the plane is in the air. This at least guarantees a quick turnaround between flights. Sometimes too, bookings can only be made direct, so that the airline can avoid having to pay commission to agents.

Existing airlines are preparing for deregulation in various ways. Some have entered into strategic alliances to pool their resources, existing routes and expertise, while others, such as Lufthansa, are already discounting their fares. British Airways has bought stakes in other European airlines and is even alleged to be thinking about franchising some routes and licensing its livery to a Scandinavian airline.

Sources: Rees (1996); Kahn (1996).

differ widely from member state to member state. Direct marketing is a relatively new area which has great potential for the marketing of goods across Europe, and yet here too, a variety of national codes are in operation. In the UK, for example, 'cold calling' telephone selling (i.e., an organisation phoning a consumer for sales purposes without the consumer's prior permission) is permitted, but in Germany it is almost totally banned. Data protection laws (i.e., what information organisations are permitted to hold on databases and what they are allowed to do with it) and regulations on list broking (i.e., the sale of lists of names and addresses to other organisations) also vary widely across the EU. Unfortunately, relevant EU directives – the Data Protection Directive, the Distance Selling Directive and the Integrated Digital Services Network Directive – that would resolve some of the inconsistencies, are not expected to reach the statute books until around 1998.

Example

Another area of marketing where the effects of EU intervention are well publicised is in agribusiness. The Common Agricultural Policy (CAP), designed to regulate the supply of produce, has changed the way in which many farmers run their businesses, with subsidies to help certain sectors and quotas to limit others. Milk quotas mean that dairy farmers can only produce so much liquid milk, and thus some have moved into making and selling cheeses, ice creams and yoghurts to use up their excess. Free trade and free movement of goods has also proved contentious at times in the agribusiness sector. Wine producers are worried about the threats caused by free trade in their local markets, while French farmers have campaigned long and hard, and at times violently, against the import of British lamb.

Regulatory bodies

Within the UK, there are many regulatory bodies with greater or lesser powers of regulation over marketing practice. Quasi-governmental bodies such as the Office of Fair Trading (OFT) and the Monopolies and Mergers Commission (MMC) have had statutory duties and powers delegated to them directly by government to ensure the maintenance of free and fair commerce.

Slightly more remote from central government, quasi-autonomous non-governmental organisations (QUANGOs), have a specific remit, and can act much more quickly than a government department. QUANGOs such as Oftel, Ofgas and Ofwat, for instance, exist to regulate the privatised telephone, gas and water industries respectively in the UK. They advise on pricing policies and competition, and also act as ombudsmen if a consumer has reached deadlock in a dispute with the utility supplier. British Telecommunications, for example, under pressure from Oftel had to reduce its tariffs and peg its price rises to the retail price index minus 7.5 per cent because it was felt that it was making too much profit.

Voluntary codes of practice emerge from associations and trade bodies, with which their members agree to comply. The Advertising Standards Authority (ASA), for example oversees the British Code of Advertising Practice which covers a variety of advertising media including print, cinema, video, posters, leaflets and teletext. The ASA also supervises the British Code of Sales Promotion Practice, which lays down guidelines for good practice in sales promotions. The philosophy of the ASA is best summed up in its famous slogan, which states that advertising and promotion should be 'legal, decent, honest and truthful'. The ASA is not a statutory body, and can only *request* an advertiser to amend or withdraw an advertisement that is in breach of the code If the advertiser refuses, the ASA can then *request* the media to refuse to repeat the offending advertisement. Since 1988, however, the Director General of the Office of Fair Trading has had the power under the Control of Misleading Advertisements Regulations to apply for a legal injunction to prevent the re-publication of an advertisement where the ASA's intervention has failed.

Example

An example of an adjudication by the ASA involved a poster campaign developed by Saatchi & Saatchi for the holiday firm Club 18–30 in 1994. Copylines such as 'Beaver Espana', 'Discover Your Erogenous Zones', and 'It's Not Just Sex, Sex, Sex', drew 220 complaints, quite a significant number, which were upheld. The ASA told Club 18–30 to withdraw the advertisements straight away, because they were unacceptable, since they had caused widespread offence, and some of them were irresponsible. See, for example, p. 76 for one of the posters.

One of the problems that the ASA faces, however, is that it has no authority to vet advertisements before publication, and thus by the time the ASA has enough complaints to act on, the offending campaign has had time to be widely seen and to attract a lot of publicity, because of its sensational nature. Then, when the ASA make a

Girls. Can we interest you in a package holiday?

ruling, further publicity is generated, for instance through opinion articles in newspapers discussing advertising standards which include a picture of an offending advertisement so that the readers know what sort of thing they're talking about. Indirectly, therefore, in some cases, ASA involvement rather defeats its own objectives.

The Independent Television Commission (ITC) looks after terrestrial television advertising, while the Radio Authority (RA) supervises radio advertising. These two organisations are statutory bodies and carry much weight since they have the power to issue and control broadcasting licences, and compliance with the advertising codes of practice is effectively part of the licence. Tobacco advertising on British television is not illegal, it is merely prohibited under the code of practice. Pharmaceuticals, alcohol and diet products are also subject to tight restrictions under the code. All of this means that although the basic philosophy of the ITC and RA is the same as that of the ASA, their concerns are a little wider, covering the timing of advertisements, making sure that the advertisements are suitably differentiated from the programmes, protecting children from unsuitable advertising, prohibiting political advertising and regulating programme sponsorship, among other things. In the summer of 1994, the ITC upheld complaints about television advertising for still Tango, a fruit drink. The advertising claimed that the product was not genuine and that consumers should call a given freephone number if they had seen it on sale. Anyone who called the number was told that they had 'been Tangoed' and was offered a voucher for a free can of the drink. The ITC agreed with complainants that television advertising should not be used for such practical jokes, and asked that the advertisement should be withdrawn.

Broadcast advertising can vetted before transmission by the Broadcast Advertising Clearance Centre (BACC). In May 1995, for example, advertisements for Virgin Vodka and for Bell's Scotch Whisky were cleared for transmission, ending a 40-year voluntary ban on advertising spirits on television. It was also reported, however, that an advertisement for Bacardi rum was rejected as being too sexy.

The Institute of Sales Promotion (ISP), the Institute of Practitioners in Advertising (IPA), the Institute of Public Relations (IPR) and the Direct Marketing Association (DMA) are effectively trade associations. All these areas are, of course, subject to prevailing commercial legislation generally, but, in addition, these particular bodies provide detailed voluntary codes of practice setting industry standards for fair dealing with customers. They are not statutory bodies, and only have jurisdiction over their members, with the ultimate sanction of suspending or expelling organisations that breach the code of practice. All of the bodies mentioned here represent organisations with interests in various areas of marketing communications, but trade associations can exist in any industry with similar objectives of regulating the professional practice of their members. There are, for example, the Fencing Contractors Association, the Glass and Glazing Federation, the Association of British Insurers, the British Association of Landscape Industries, and the National House Builders Confederation, to name but a few! As well as regulating business practice, such bodies can also provide other services for members, such as legal indemnities and representation, training and professional development services, and acting as the voice of the industry to government and the media, for example.

Self-regulatory organisations do, of course, exist across Europe, and there are also attempts to introduce internationally accepted codes of practice. In the advertising field, for instance, many national bodies base their codes on the International Code of Advertising Practice issued by ICC in Paris. These guidelines help to harmonise advertising and sales promotion across a range of subscribing countries. The purpose of the code is to ensure that advertising is legal, honest, truthful and socially responsible, and does not hinder fair competition. It also suggests positions on comparative advertising, advertising to children and the avoidance of various types of discrimination. The extent to which the code is adopted varies from country to country. In Germany, for instance, the Deutscher Werberat follows its main provisions, while in Sweden, some legislation goes well beyond the provisions of the international code.

Influences on the political and regulatory environment

The political and regulatory environment is clearly influenced by sociocultural factors, and particularly the pressure of public opinion, the media and pressure groups. Greenpeace and Friends of the Earth, for example, have educated consumers to become more aware of the content, origins and after-effects of the products they buy and use, and this led to the phasing out of Chloro-fluorocarbons (CFCs) as an aerosol propellant and as a refrigerant. The green movement has also spurred the drafting of regulations on the acceptable emissions from car exhausts, which has had a major impact on the product development plans of the motor manufacturers for the next few years. Similarly, the consumer movement, through organisations such as the Consumers' Association, has also played an important role in promoting the rights of the consumer and thus in driving the regulators and legislators towards laws and codes of practice regarding product safety, selling techniques and marketing communications, for instance.

Not all pressure on legislators and regulators originates from pressure groups or consumer-based organisations, of course. Trade associations or groupings lobby the legislators to try to influence regulation in their members' favour. The freedom created by the SEM to import as much alcohol purchased within other EU member countries as you like for your own consumption has created severe problems for the UK brewers. Since duty on alcohol is much lower in France than in the UK, it pays to take a van across the English Channel, stock up on brands of beer and lager that ironically may even have been brewed in the UK, and bring it all back home. The main problem is that some travellers are making a business of it, illegally reselling the goods in the UK at prices that undercut the brewers and their legitimate outlets, yet still making a healthy profit on the trip. The brewers want UK duty reduced so that it is in line with French rates and makes the 'grey' market unprofitable, but as yet, the Chancellor of the Exchequer has not been persuaded.

An area in which the legislators have been pulled in two opposing directions for many years is that of tobacco advertising. On the one hand ASH has lobbied to get tobacco advertising banned completely and to get the taxes on tobacco raised, as a price disincentive to smokers, while on the other hand, the Tobacco Advisory

Council, representing the manufacturers, has waged a counter campaign that has slowed down the pace of restriction and diluted its content. In this case, whatever the legislators do will be unpopular with someone! The current position on this difficult ethical area is that the government do not think that it is right to completely ban the advertising of a product that is itself legal, but they have developed and implemented a five-year voluntary agreement with the industry, which will be tightly monitored, and which details the acceptable range and scope of tobacco marketing activities. In parallel with that, the government will be increasing the budget available for health education campaigns outlining the dangers of smoking.

CHAPTER SUMMARY

This chapter has explored the importance of the external marketing environment as an influence on the way in which organisations do business and make their decisions. The main framework for the chapter is the categorisation of the marketing environment into STEP factors: sociocultural, technological, economic/competitive and political/legal.

Using environmental scanning, a technique for monitoring and evaluating information under each of the STEP headings, organisations can understand their environment more thoroughly, pick up early signs of emerging trends, and thus plan their future activities appropriately. Such information may come from secondary sources, such as trade publications or published research data, or an organisation can commission research to increase their knowledge of the environment. Care must be taken, however, to ensure that all appropriate sources are constantly monitored (but avoiding information overload), and that internal mechanisms exist for disseminating information and acting on it.

The sociocultural environment

The first of the STEP factors is the sociocultural environment. This deals with 'hard' information, such as demographic trends, and with less tangible issues, such as changing tastes, attitudes and cultures. Demographic trends look at how populations are divided in terms of age, sex, income, family size and household structure. Knowledge of these gives the marketer a basic feel for how broad market segments are likely to change in the future, for instance the increase in the number of over-55s, or the increase in one-parent families. To gain the fullest picture, however, the marketer needs to combine demographic information with 'softer' data on how attitudes are changing. A marketer may need to know, for example, how a particular age group's feelings about the environment are developing, so that decisions can be made about product formulation, packaging, recycling and general marketing communication themes. Other similar issues of interest include animal welfare, personal health and both personal and corporate ethics. Some of these concerns can be amplified through the activities of consumer groups, such as the Consumers' Association, and pressure groups such as Greenpeace and Friends of the Earth. The publicity that can be generated through the mass media means that organisations need to be clear about what will and will not be perceived as legitimate, ethical and acceptable business practice, and plan accordingly. Relationships between commercial organisations and pressure groups need not, of course, always be confrontational. The two sides can work together to improve or modify processes, or develop codes of practice that benefit all parties.

Technology

The second STEP factor is technology. An organisation's technological advances may arise from the exploitation of breakthroughs from other organisations, or may be the result of long-term investment in R&D in-house to solve a specific problem. Either way, technology can present the opportunity to create a clear differential advantage that cannot be easily copied by the competition. There are four main areas of an organisation that might be influenced by technology:

Materials, components and products

Advances in these areas can lead to improved products (in terms of quality and performance), or to new products. Examples include artificial sweeteners, opening up the diet market, and the incorporation of microchip control systems into many electrical goods, improving their performance and range of functions.

Production processes

Aided by CAD/CAM systems and improvements in quality control systems, production processes can be made less costly, less wasteful and more reliable and consistent. Materials handling too can be streamlined through technology, again to cut costs and wastage.

Administration and distribution

Technology can improve customer service, by shortening lead times between ordering and delivery, by allowing the seller to tell the buyer instantly whether stock is available or not and by reducing the capacity for human error (lost orders, wrong invoices, mis-dispatched goods etc.). Direct telecommunications links between major buyers with computerised stock control systems and suppliers can also streamline ordering and the flow of goods.

Marketing and customers

As well as improving products themselves and their distribution, technology helps the marketer to understand the customer better. It has extended the power of market research; allowed the rise of database marketing; and increased the range of advertising creativity and media. It also helps to support the sales force, with instant access to information, and has opened the real possibility of on-line ordering for consumers as well as trade customers.

Economic/competitive environment

The economic and competitive environment constitutes the third STEP factor, and can be further divided into the macro- and microeconomic environments. The macro-economic environment analyses the effects of the broader economic picture, looking at issues such as taxation, government spending and interest rates. It also takes account of the threats, opportunities and barriers arising from membership of international trading blocs such as the EU and EFTA, and the trading agreements reached within these blocs.

The microeconomic environment is a little closer to the individual organisation, and is concerned with the structure of the market(s) in which it operates. *Monopolies*, where a market is dominated by a single supplier, are an endangered species. Many of the old state-owned monopolies in areas such as telecommunications and other utilities across Europe have been opened up to competition. In any case, as markets become increasingly global, an organisation that has a monopoly in its home market is not likely to be a monopolist on the world stage. *Oligopolies* occur where most market share is controlled by a small number of firms. Large-scale, world-wide industrial markets tend to be structured like this, but even in branded consumer goods markets, such as petrol retailing and laundry products, oligopolies can be seen.

Monopolistic competition, in contrast, occurs where there are many competitors in the market, but each has a product that is sufficiently differentiated from the rest to create a kind of monopoly, because there is no direct substitute. Finally, *perfect competition* means that there are many small suppliers without any differentiation between their products, but this is an unrealistic situation, as marketers are finding ways of differentiating even the most apparently homogeneous products such as vegetables!

Political/legal environmemt

The final STEP factor is the political and legal environment. Laws, regulations and codes of practice emanate from national governments, the EU, local government, statutory bodies and trade associations to affect the way in which organisations do business.

National governments, as well as passing the legislation that regulates business dealings generally, have also been responsible for privatisation programmes. These have opened up what had hitherto been state-owned monopolies, such as utilities, thus changing the structure of competition in these industries, and changing the way in which customer needs are met. Within the EU, current concerns centre around the establishment of the SEM, and moves towards harmonising laws, regulations and codes of practice across member states to ease cross-border trade. Marketing communications is one particular area where current regulations vary widely between different countries, but it is hoped that the EC Green Paper on Commercial Communication, as at the time of writing, not published, will solve some of the problems.

In the UK, various regulatory bodies exist to oversee activity in particular industries, and thus the government has delegated powers to QUANGOs, such as Ofwat, Ofgas and Oftel, to regulate privatised industries. In the area of non-broadcast advertising, the ASA has no statutory powers, but administers both the British Code of Advertising Practice and the British Code of Sales Promotion Practice. The ASA can only request an offending organisation to withdraw its advertising, although in extreme cases, it can refer a matter to the Director General of the OFT. For television and the radio, the ITC and RA do have statutory powers, however, and oversee broadcast advertising. More generally, trade associations in many industries provide codes of practice for their members, as well as representing their members' interests to government and the media, but again, these associations do not have statutory powers and cannot regulate companies which do not belong to them. Trade associations are not the only bodies trying to influence the political and regulatory environment in terms of lobbying government. Consumer groups and other pressure groups, such as those representing the ecological movement, health issues and animal rights, for example, are active in trying to persuade government to deregulate or legislate, or to influence the scope and content of new legislation.

Key words and phrases

Demographics	SEM
Economic and competitive environment	Sociocultural environment
Environmental scanning	STEP
Political and regulatory environment	Technological environment

QUESTIONS FOR REVIEW

2.1 What does the acronym STEP stand for?

2.2 What is environmental scanning, why is it important, and what are the potential problems of implementing it?

2.3 What kind of information does the study of demographics cover?

2.4 Why might consumer demands for variation and variety in the products they buy cause problems for marketers?

2.5 To what extent have consumer concerns about environmental issues affected organisations' approaches to marketing?

2.6 Why are consumer groups and other pressure groups a major influence in an organisation's marketing environment?

2.7 Summarise the main implications of the SEM for organisations doing business within the EU.

2.8 In what ways can technology contribute to the marketing environment?

2.9 Differentiate between the macro and microeconomic environments.

2.10 What are the four main types of market structure?

QUESTIONS FOR DISCUSSION

2.1 What sources of published demographic data are available in your own university or college library?

2.2 Find and discuss examples of products that are particularly vulnerable to changing consumer tastes.

2.3 To what extent, and why, do you think marketers should be seen to lead the way in addressing 'ethical' issues rather than waiting until consumer concern reaches a level where the organisation is prompted to react?

2.4 What are the differences between the ASA and the ITC? Find and discuss recent examples of adjudications by these two bodies (or equivalent regulatory bodies in your own country). Do you agree with their judgement?

2.5 Using Figure 2.1 as a framework, choose a product and list under each of the STEP factors the relevant influences that have helped to make that product what it is.

Sanpro

Sanpro, otherwise known as female sanitary protection (tampons, towels, and panty liners) is a massive market, but one that is very difficult for marketers to deal with because of the sensitivities involved. Many women, particularly in older age groups, are embarrassed about the nature of the product, and particularly resent having to watch television advertisements for tampons, for instance, in the company of other members of the family. Because of this, until 1986 sanpro products could not be advertised on television in the UK at all, but gradually, the regulatory bodies began to relax the rules. After a large number of complaints about a particular advertisement for Vespré Silhouette, however, the rules were tightened up again and advertisements cannot be shown during 'family viewing times'. One of the unsolved problems arising from this is that the advertisements are now so inoffensive that they do not offer any useful information to women, and clichéd imagery of active young women in tight shorts leading incredibly active and enjoyable lives is felt by many to be patronising. Press advertising in women's magazines can, however, be more explicit and product centred.

The sanpro marketers do not only face communication and attitude problems. The balance of the market between tampons (for internal use) and towels (for external use) has changed, partly because of technological development, and partly because of consumer health worries. Advances in the field of superabsorbents has meant that towels can be much thinner and more discreet, yet still provide reliability and reassurance. This has made them much more acceptable to many women. The growth of the towel sector has been stimulated by the Always brand range, owned by Procter & Gamble, which had about £10 million spent on advertising in 1994 emphasizing comfort and thinness. Added to that, publicity over the risks of toxic shock syndrome (TSS) that can arise from tampon use has put users off these products. This means that in 1995 towels had 51 per cent of the market by value, with tampons lagging behind with only 38 per cent. Panty liners, which have become increasing popular for day-to-day use, held the remaining 11 per cent and their share is growing.

The competitive structure of this market is changing too. Although it is still dominated by one or two large operators such as Tambrands, which claims 58 per cent of the tampon sector with Tampax, and Procter & Gamble, which claims 40 per cent of the towel sector with Always, the threat from supermarket own brands has increased. Originally, the own label products were sold purely on price, and did not provide the quality and the reliability that women need from these products. With manufacturers such as Johnson & Johnson now involved in own brand production, the quality has improved to the point where a significant number of consumers are starting to prefer own brands, which in 1995 accounted for 17 per cent of the market. One result of this is to put pressure on the manufacturer brands to maintain a high level of marketing support. In 1996, Smith & Nephew was estimated to be spending £5m on advertising and promotion for its Lil-lets brand, while Tambrands was spending £10m. This is not just being spent on advertising. Tampax is spending on sales promotions, such as a free tampon container to fit discreetly in a handbag, and discounts for multiple purchases. Similarly, Lil-lets was also giving away tampon containers and also entering into joint promotions with skin care brands.

Sources: Bray (1996); *Marketing* (1995a).

Questions

1 Outline the ways in which the STEP factors affect this market.

2 Why do supermarket own label products pose a threat in this market?

3 Why do you think sales promotions are particularly effective for these products?

4 In terms of the marketing environment, how does this product differ from:
   (a) toilet paper; and
   (b) condoms?

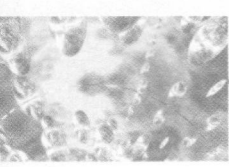

CASE STUDY 2.2

Kabo

The Bulgarian company Kabo processes and sells canned fish and vegetables. Although nationalised in 1947, the company prospered because its home market was sheltered and its export business was handled by the state foreign trade organisation. To Kabo, marketing was of little concern, and its main priority was production. By the 1980s, the company had 32 products and the overall volume of production was 20 000 tonnes. Only 5 per cent of sales were generated in the home market, while 70 per cent came from what was then the USSR, and around 20 per cent came from other markets, especially the UK, Italy and the Middle East.

The prices between the markets varied considerably, with prices in the EU several times higher than those charged in the USSR. That was not a problem for Kabo, as any losses were made up by state subsidies. The first signs of trouble, however, began to show in the 1980s. Mr Lasarov, the executive director, felt that the main problem at that time was too many home competitors who had a distinct advantage by being up to 40 Kilometres nearer the main regions supplying vegetables for canning. This meant higher transport costs for Kabo. These, coupled with reduced state subsidies and restrictions on more innovative marketing and product development activity, led the company to decide to reduce volume and wait for better times.

By 1989 the situation had deteriorated further because of the uncertainty of raw material supply and poor competitiveness. Production had fallen to less than 14 000 tonnes a year and the number of products was down to 12. By the early 1990s, state subsidies had virtually disappeared in the food, tobacco and wine industries. Companies had to become self-sufficient. The free market was now a reality. Many of the problems Kabo faced were common to other central European organisations as they sought to manage the transition to a free enterprise market-based system.

Interest rates soared from around 7 per cent to nearer 45 per cent, making investment problematic. Fuel and energy costs nearly doubled and workers began to look for higher wages. As all this began to affect prices, Kabo's food products became too expensive for the home market, and the former USSR had problems paying even the old price levels. Bartering deals, such as petrol in return for canned vegetables, were proposed at least guaranteeing some form of payment. In other cases, however, no payments were made at all. The state foreign trade organisations disappeared and Kabo had no experience in international marketing and no experience or knowledge or contacts with international distributors and intermediaries.

Faced with all these problems, the decision was made to seek new international markets. Dedicated staff in the newly formed sales department were assigned the task of finding new sales opportunities. The USA, China and France were targeted, importers appointed and test sales carried out. However, none of these markets lived up to sales expectations, as the head of the project Mr Ivanov reluctantly concluded.

> 'These markets are huge enough for us to sell our entire production, but they are too far away which leads to high transportation costs. It would also appear that we cannot offer a product which meets their requirements as far as quality and packaging are concerned. Up until now we have been producing for markets with lower requirements towards quality, yet a failure to invest in the 1980s means that we cannot raise standards easily given our production facilities.'

By 1991, only 6 000 tons were being produced. This fell even further to 1000 tons in 1992, 60 per cent of which was destined for the home market. Debts mounted and suppliers fearing non-payment restricted supplies. The market in the former USSR was lost completely. To Mr Lasarov, the only way out was to make the internal debts a state debt and then to seek privatisation. Then the company would be free to develop.

Adapted from a case prepared by Ivan Marchevski.

Questions

1 In what ways did Kabo's marketing environment change in the transition to a free market economy?

2 Why did Kabo's initial venture into the US, French and Chinese markets fail?

3 If Kabo was thinking of moving into the UK (or other western European) market with its canned fish, what are the key aspects of the marketing environment that it should investigate before entry?

4 From your general knowledge of the market, what do you think might be the biggest barriers to such an entry?

REFERENCES FOR CHAPTER 2

Adonis, A. (1994), 'A Force to be Reckoned With', *Financial Times*, 5 September 1994, VI.

Aguilar, F. J. (1967), *Scanning the Business Environment*, MacMillan.

Barnes, H. (1995), 'Heated Debate Over Danes' Green Tax Plan', *Financial Times*, 21 February 1995.

Bray, L. (1996), 'Privates on Parade', *The Grocer*, 11 May 1996, 35–39.

Corzine, R. and Buckley N. (1994), 'Stores Pump Up the Volume: The Battle for Petrol Sales', *Financial Times*, 12 October 1994.

Daniels, J. (1994), 'Early Sign of a Change in Attitudes', *Financial Times*, 4 October 1994, XI.

Dempsey, J. (1994) 'Big is No Longer Beautiful – Fuel and Power Monopolies Under Scrutiny', *Financial Times*, 21 November 1994, VIII.

Dittmar, H. and Pepper, L. (1994), 'To Have is to Be: Materialism and Person Perception in Working Class and Middle Class British Adolescents', *Journal of Economic Psychology*, 15(2), pp. 233–251.

Euromonitor (1995a), 'Euromonitor Consumer Europe', *Euromonitor*.

Euromonitor (1995b), 'Euromonitor European Marketing Data and Statistics', *Euromonitor*.

Griffiths, J. (1994), 'Transplants Step Up Exports – At Least 1m Japanese Cars Will Be Built in Europe By 2000', *Financial Times*, 4th October 1994, V.

The Grocer (1996), 'Focus on Bread and Morning Goods', *The Grocer*, 6 April 1996, pp. 41–56.

Gütter, S. (1994), 'Austrian Industrial Sectors and the European Union', *European Business Journal*, 6(4), 8–15.

Johnson, P. (1990), 'Our Ageing Population: The Implications for Business and Government', *Long Range Planning*, 23(2), pp. 55–62.

Kahn, F. (1996), 'Crammed in on a Peanut Flight', *Financial Times*, 27 January 1996, X.

Knott, D. (1993), 'Fuel Tests Spark Retail Feud', *Oil and Gas Journal*, 29 November 1993, 33.

Lynch, R. (1994), *European Business Strategies: The European and Global Strategies of Europe's Top Companies*, Kogan Page.

Marketing (1995a), 'Britain's Biggest Brands', *Marketing*, 16 March 1995, pp. 21–24.

Marketing (1995b), 'Britain's Biggest Brands', *Marketing*, 23 March 1995.

Murphy, C. (1996), 'Why Sites are Key to Fuel Fight', *Marketing*, 7 March 1996, 16.

Perry, K. (1994), *Business and the European Community*, Butterworth-Heinemann.

Rees, J. (1996), 'Wings of Desire', *Marketing Week*, 17th May 1996, pp. 36–37.

Simonian, H. (1995), 'Quest for Green Tyre', *Financial Times*, 6 March 1995, III.

Part II

CUSTOMERS AND MARKETS

Consumer Behaviour **3**

Organisational Buying Behaviour **4**

Segmenting Markets **5**

Marketing Information and Research **6**

Part I emphasized that the customer is the hub of the marketer's universe, so it is only fitting that Part II should give further consideration to this VIP. The dilemma is, however, that each customer is an individual with unique needs and wants, and no organisation can hope to please all of the people all of the time.

Chapter 3 focuses further on the individual as a customer, examining the influences on buying choices and habits, both psychological and social, while looking at the kinds of decision-making processes which people might or might not go through in making a purchase. This is particularly important given the range of cultures to be found across Europe. Chapter 4 explores similar themes, but this time for the organisational customers, highlighting the differences between the personal and the corporate shopper.

Additionally, with improvements in distribution and the relaxation of economic barriers, European market potential for many products is unthinkably huge. Organisations, therefore have to find ways of breaking markets down into manageably sized segments for each of which essential needs and wants can be defined. This allows a marketing mix to be designed which can at least please a substantial number of people for most of the time. Chapter 5 looks at ways in which this segmentation process can be designed and implemented. The final chapter in this part, Chapter 6 presents an overview of the role of research in defining, monitoring and assessing buyers, markets and marketing activities.

These four chapters are an important foundation for what follows because context and meaning can only be given to the organisation's decisions on the marketing mix if there are adequate information flows and clear understanding of customer's needs and wants.

■   ■   ■

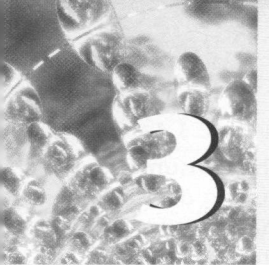

3 Consumer Behaviour

LEARNING OBJECTIVES

This chapter will help you to:

1 understand the decision-making processes that consumers go through as they make a purchase;

2 appreciate how those processes differ between different buying situations;

3 understand the influences which affect decision making, whether environmental, psychological or sociocultural; and

4 appreciate the implications of those processes and influences for marketing strategies.

INTRODUCTION

In contrast to Chapter 2, which looked at the broad backdrop against which marketers have to do business, this chapter focuses closely on the consumer, who is at the centre of many a marketer's universe. While the consumer is part of the marketing environment, and is shaped to some extent by the influences already discussed in Chapter 2, it is also very important to understand the more personal and specific influences affecting consumers and the nature of the decision-making processes they go through.

Figure 3.1 offers a deceptively simple model of buyer behaviour which summarises the content of this chapter. The decision-making process itself is presented as a logical flow of activities, working through from problem recognition to purchase to post-purchase evaluation. The next section of this chapter deals with this in depth. It is important, however, to recognise that it is difficult to generalise about buying situations, as the nature of the decision-making process is bound to differ according to the kind of product or service that is being considered. Later, therefore, (pp. 96 *et seq.*) we discuss how the nature of the product and the situation facing the buyer could change the flow of the decision-making process. Compare, for example, what went into your decision to attend university or college with how you decide whether to visit a Pizza Hut or a nightclub.

The decision-making process is also affected by a number of other more complex influences, as can be seen in Fig 3.1. Some of these influences relate to the wider marketing environment in which the decision is being made (*see* pp. 98–100). Others, however, relate to the individual purchaser and therefore pp. 100–109 will consider those influences emanating from within the individual such as personality, attitudes and learning. Finally pp. 109–119 will look at how the individual decisions are affected by their social context, especially family and cultural groupings.

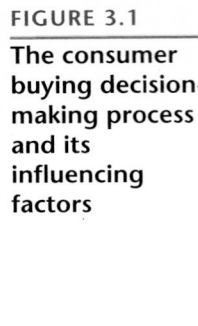

FIGURE 3.1

The consumer buying decision-making process and its influencing factors

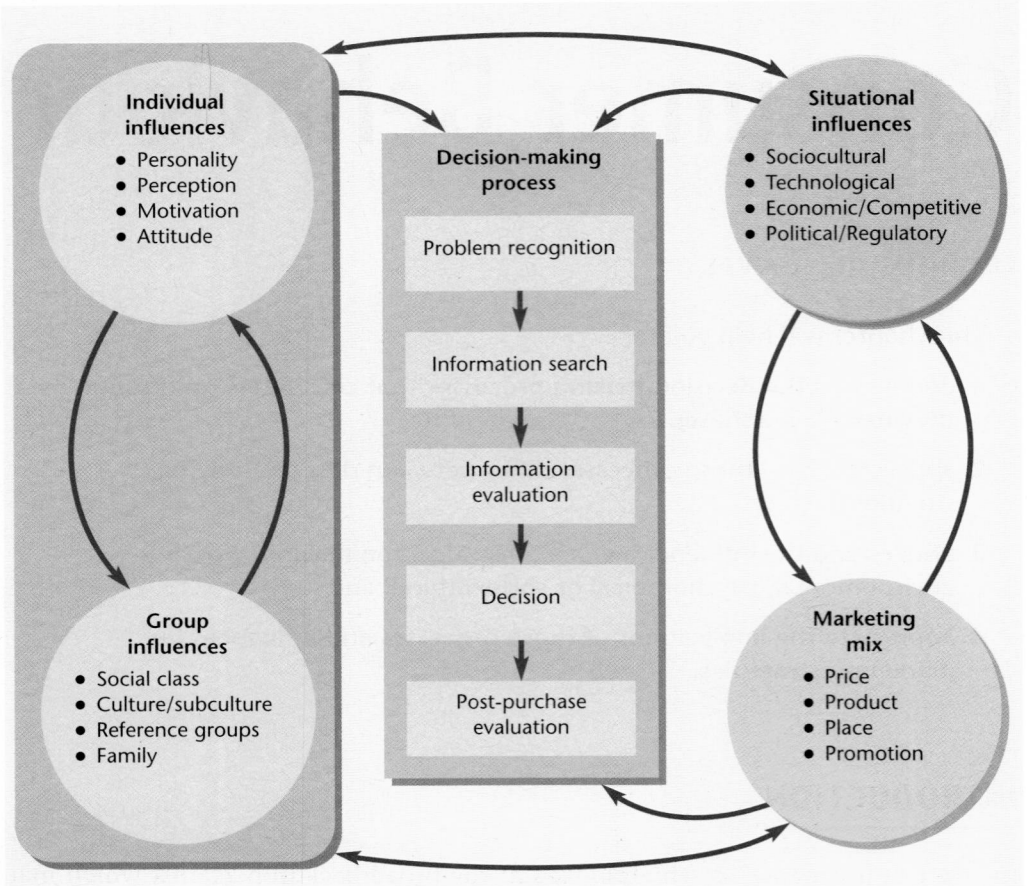

THE DECISION-MAKING PROCESS

Even thinking about your own experiences as a consumer is enough to help you to appreciate the variety of goods people purchase, the individuality of each purchasing episode and the complexity of the influences affecting the final decision. Nevertheless, there have been many attempts to create models of **consumer decision making** of greater or lesser complexity and detail which try to capture the richness of the experience, such as those proposed by Howard and Sheth (1969) and Engel, Kollat and Blackwell (1978). The Engel, Blackwell and Miniard (1990) model presented here, although more concise and simpler in its outline, provides a framework that still allows us to consider, through discussion, many of the more complex elements. It traces the progress of a purchasing event stage by stage from the buyer's point of view, including the definition of likely information needs and a discussion of the level of rationality and analytical behaviour leading to the eventual decision.

We now look at each stage in turn.

Problem recognition

In trying to rationalise the decision-making process, this is a good place to begin. After all, if you are not aware that you have 'a problem', how can you decide to purchase something to solve it? More functional purchases, such as replenishing stocks of washing powder or petrol, may be initiated by a casual glance at current stock levels.

Other purchases may be triggered by a definable event. If, for example, the exhaust falls off your car, you will soon become aware of the nature of the problem and the kind of purchase that will provide the remedy.

Those are a very practical and straightforward examples, but not all situations are quite so self-explanatory. Where psychological needs are involved, the **problem recognition** may be a slow dawning or may lead to a sudden impulse, when the consumer, realising that the current position or feeling is not the desired one, decides to do something to change it through a purchase (Bruner and Pomazal, 1988). Imagine, for instance, that you are wandering round the supermarket after a tough day at work. You're tired, listless and a bit depressed. You've filled your trolley with the potatoes, bread and milk you intended to buy, but you also slip a bar of chocolate (or worse!) in there on the basis that it will cheer you up as you drive home. The 'problem' here is less definable, based on a vague psychological feeling, and it follows that the solution is also less definable – it could be chocolate, cream buns, wine or clothing; whatever takes the purchaser's fancy.

What the examples given so far do have in common, however, is that the impetus to go into a purchasing decision-making routine comes from the consumer. The consumer identifies or recognises the problem, independently from the marketer, and looks for a solution. As will be seen in the following sections, marketers can then use the marketing mix elements to influence the choice of solution. It is also possible, however, for marketers to trigger the process by using the marketing mix to bring a problem to the consumer's attention. If one was to be cynical, one could accuse them of deliberately creating problems in order to stimulate purchase.

Example

The manufacturers of Radion laundry products ran an advertising campaign in the UK featuring a housewife who suddenly realised that even though the shirt she was ironing had just been washed, there was still a sweaty smell clinging to its armpits. Radion, of course has the power to eliminate this in the wash. Housewives across the country supposedly became wracked with fear and guilt, asking themselves 'Do I have this problem? Should I switch to Radion?' A problem had been created in the consumer's mind, and a decision-making process initiated, largely through the marketer's efforts.

There is, of course, a significant difference between being aware of a need or problem and being able to do something about it. Many needs are latent and remain unfulfilled, either because the consumer decides not to do anything about it now, or because they are unable to do anything. Many Polish people may acknowledge that they 'need' a three-week holiday in Spain rather than yet another visit to the Baltic coast, yet even an overland package tour may be unaffordable for them. Problem recognition, if it is to lead anywhere, therefore requires both the willingness and the ability to fulfil the emerging need.

Whether the problem recognition is stimulated internally (i.e., originates within the consumer) or externally (i.e., triggered by marketing or other pressures), there are still several stages left in the decision-making process.

Information Search

Defining the problem is one thing, but defining and implementing the solution is something else. The questions to be answered include those of what kind of purchase will solve the problem, where and how it can be obtained, what information is needed to arrive at a decision and where that information is available. In some cases,

consumers will actively search out relevant information with a view to using it in making a decision, but they can also acquire information passively, storing it away until it is needed. Thus Bloch *et al.* (1986) distinguish between ongoing search (browsing and storing for future reference) and purposeful search with a particular objective in mind. Daily, consumers are exposed to a wide range of media all designed to influence awareness and recall of particular products and services. Thus they 'know' that Radion eliminates sweaty smells before they get anywhere near a conscious choice of laundry product in the supermarket. When they do get to the point of purchasing, the manufacturers hope that they will recall that knowledge and use it in making the brand choice.

The car exhaust example continues to be reasonably straightforward. You need a new exhaust and a supplier must be found. Since consumers usually fall back upon their previous experiences and knowledge before undertaking time-consuming research, you may immediately think of a company that you have used before and have been satisfied with, one whose advertising you have seen, or perhaps you ask a close friend to recommend one. Not all external sources of information are controlled by the marketer – do not forget the power of word of mouth as a marketing tool. Friends, family and colleagues, for example, may all give advice, whether based on experience, knowledge or opinion, to the would-be decision maker in this phase. In choosing a university to study at, for example, many overseas students seek advice from friends who have already studied at the various universities to narrow down the number of options to be considered. Although the type of product and the importance of the purchase may differ, the basic principle is the same. People are more likely to trust information given through word of mouth, because the source is generally assumed to be unbiased and trustworthy, and the information itself often derives from first hand experience.

In other situations, the consumer might seek out information from specialist publications, retailers or even from marketing literature. For example, when buying a car, potential buyers will probably visit competing dealerships to talk to sales staff, look closely at the merchandise and collect brochures. Additionally, they might consult what they consider to be unbiased expert sources of advice such as *What Car?* magazine, and begin to take more notice of car advertisements in all media.

In replacing the car exhaust, of course, you might simply turn to the *Yellow Pages* telephone directory and look under 'Exhaust System Dealers'. The impulse buying of chocolate in the supermarket requires even less information searching than that. It is likely to be restricted to seeing what is available within that particular store at that particular time. Think about why this is the case before you get to the later section of this chapter on buying situations (p. 96), where variations in the extent, rationality and formality of the information search in different situations will be discussed.

Information overload may, however, cause problems for the potential purchaser. There is evidence to suggest that consumers cannot cope with too much information at product level (Keller and Staelin, 1987). Thus the greater the relevance of the information to the consumer, such as the key benefits and applications of the product, the easier it is for consumers to assimilate and process that information as part of their decision making. In other words, better and more extensive information may actually lead to poorer buying decisions! Similarly, at brand level Jacoby *et al.* (1974) found on the one hand that more on-pack information tends to make it more difficult for the consumer to select the most appropriate brand, but on the other hand, that more information positively affected the consumer's level of certainty and satisfaction regarding the selection. There is clearly a fine balance to be achieved between keeping imagery and messages clean, simple and easily understood, and giving consumers enough information to allow them to appreciate the full depth of character of the product and the range of its potential benefits so that they can develop appropriate expectations and post-purchase evaluative criteria.

Whatever form the information search takes, the data gathered are useless until they are evaluated. However, it is likely that many consumers proceed to evaluation with a minimum of information which furthermore may be too partial, biased or poorly structured for the decision that needs to be made. This is bound to influence the quality of the eventual decision.

Information Evaluation

On what criteria do you evaluate the information gathered? A typical *Yellow Pages* may provide up to 10 pages of exhaust system dealerships, featuring over 100 potential outlets within reasonable travelling distance. If you have had no previous experience of any of them, then you have to find a means of differentiating between them. You are unlikely to investigate all of them, since that would take too long, and so you may draw up a shortlist on the basis of those with the biggest feature entries in *Yellow Pages*, or those who also advertise prominently in the local press or on television. Such advertising may emphasise the advantages of using a particular outlet, pointing out to the consumer what the appropriate evaluative criteria are (speed, friendliness or price, for example). Location may be also be an important factor; some outlets are closer to home or work than others. You might telephone three or four of them, dismiss any whose telephone manner is either too surly or too patronising, then compare the rest on the basis of price or their ability to do the job immediately.

Meanwhile, back in the supermarket, the information evaluation is likely to be less time consuming and less systematic. Faced with a set of brands of chocolate that are known and liked, the evaluation is cursory: 'What do I feel like eating?' The nearest to systematic thinking might be (in desperation) the evaluation of which one really represents the most chocolate for the price. Of course, if a new brand has appeared on the chocolate shelf, then that might break the habitual, unconscious grabbing at the familiar wrapper, and make a consumer stop and look closely to evaluate what the new product has to offer in comparison with the old ones.

What has been happening to varying degrees in the above examples is that the consumer has started to narrow down from a wide list of potential options to an **evoked set** (Howard and Sheth, 1969), a final shortlist for serious appraisal. Being a part of the consumer's evoked set, and staying there, is clearly important to the marketer, although it is not always easy. Sutton (1987), for instance, found that it was easier for a new product or brand to enter the evoked set than it was for an existing one that had been considered previously, but rejected.

With the car exhaust, constructing the evoked set means narrowing down to the list of outlets that will be telephoned, whereas with the chocolate purchase the unconscious visual scan across the shelf may lead to a more deliberate choice between a Snickers, a Mars Bar and a Twix. To make a choice from within the evoked set, the consumer needs either a formal or an informal means of selecting from the small number of choices available. This, therefore, implies some definition of evaluative or choice criteria.

Again, marketers will be trying to influence this stage. This can be done, for example, through their communications campaigns (more of this in Chapter 15 and subsequent chapters) which may implant images of products in the consumer's mind so that they seem familiar (and therefore less threatening) at the point of sale. They may also stress particular product attributes, both to increase the importance of that attribute in the consumer's mind, i.e., to make sure that the attribute is number one on the list of evaluative criteria, and to ensure that the consumer believes that a particular brand is unsurpassed in terms of that attribute. Radion and residual armpit smells must be inextricably linked in the consumer's mind, and eradication of armpit smells must be important to the consumer. Point of sale material can also reinforce these things, for example through displays, leaflets, the wording on packaging (Chapter 7), and on-pack promotions.

Generally, therefore, what is happening here is that without necessarily being conscious of it, the potential buyer is constructing a list of performance criteria, then assessing each supplier or available brand against it. This assessment can be based on objective criteria, related to the attributes of the product and its use (price, specification, service etc.), or subjective criteria such as status, fit with self-image or trust of the supplier. This, however, can be a demanding exercise in terms of time and mental effort, and thus the consumer often adopts mental 'rules of thumb' that cut corners and lead to a faster decision. The consumer is especially prepared to compromise on the quality and thoroughness of assessment when the problem-solving situation is less risky and complicated. Table 3.1, based on the work of Duncan (1990), highlights some of the market beliefs widely held by consumers. These beliefs may not relate directly to the specific purchasing situation in hand, but they do act as general decision rules to cut out many of the tedious preliminaries of assessing alternative products. They may focus on brand, store choice, pricing, promotion or packaging, and will serve to limit the size of the evoked set and to eliminate some of the options.

All of this sets the scene for the next stage in the process: the decision.

Decision

The decision may be a natural outcome of the evaluation stage, if one supplier is noticeably more impressive on all the important criteria than the rest. If the choice is not as clear cut as this, the consumer may have to prioritise the criteria further, perhaps deciding that price or convenience is the one overriding factor. In the case of the

TABLE 3.1
Consumer market beliefs

Products and brands
- The best brands are the ones that sell best
- National brands (manufacturer or retail) are always better than local ones unless you know better
- Generic brands are well-known brand names sold under a different label
- Keep clear of products new to the market until 'bugs' have been ironed out

---

Store
- You can tell a store by its window display
- Larger stores offer better prices than smaller ones
- Speciality stores are great for learning about product options, but it is best to buy from a discount store
- A store that offers good value on some of its items probably offers it on all its items
- Small stores give better, more personal service than large ones

---

Price
- Higher prices within a store often mean higher quality
- Sale items can involve seconds and poorer quality merchandise
- Sales are designed to move poor sellers
- Prices will fall soon after the product is launched

Promotion
- When purchasing heavily advertised products you pay for the label and advertising, not higher quality
- The harder the sell, the poorer the product quality
- Free gifts linked to products mean the product may not be up to much

---

Packaging
- Big containers are always cheaper per unit than smaller sizes
- Environmentally friendly packaging adds cost to the product
- Quality packaging means a quality product.

Source: Adapted from Duncan (1990).

car exhaust example, the decision making is a conscious act, whereas with the impulse purchase of chocolate, the decision may be made almost unconsciously.

In any case, at this stage the consumer must finalise the proposed deal, and this may take place in a retail store, over the telephone, by mail or in the consumer's own home. In the supermarket, finalising the deal may be as simple as putting the bar of chocolate into the trolley with the rest of the shopping and then paying for it at the checkout. With more complex purchases, however, the consumer may have the discretion to negotiate the fine details of cash or credit, any trade in, order quantity and delivery dates, for example. This negotiation (*see* Chapter 18 for more on negotiation) may involve further trading of concessions between variables, so that, for instance, you can have your new car within a week as long as you are prepared to accept a red one. If the outcome of the negotiation is not satisfactory, then the consumer may well regretfully decide not to go ahead with the purchase after all, or to rethink the decision in favour of another supplier – you cannot be certain of your customer until they have either handed over their money or signed the contract!

Suppliers can, of course, make it easy or difficult for potential customers to make their purchases. Lack of sales assistants on the shop floor, long queues or bureaucratic purchasing procedures may all tax the patience of consumers, giving them time either to decide to shop elsewhere or not to bother buying at all. Even if they do persist and make the purchase (eventually), their impression of the supplier's service and efficiency is going to be damaged, and may influence their repeat purchasing behaviour negatively. A traveller who has to queue for 20 minutes to buy a rail ticket from a cashier may well decide to travel by car next time, whereas the traveller who can purchase a ticket quickly through an automated ticketing machine, such as those found in railway stations and more recently in airports around Europe, will have no negative impressions of service provision.

Even assuming that all these barriers are overcome, the story does not end here. The consumer's involvement with the product does not finish when cash changes hands, nor should the marketer's involvement with the consumer.

Post-purchase evaluation

Whatever the purchase, there is likely to be some level of **post-purchase evaluation** to assess whether the product or its supplier lived up to the expectations raised in the earlier stages of the process. Particularly if the decision process has been difficult, or if the consumer has invested a lot of time, effort and money in it, then there is a risk of doubt as to whether the right decision has actually been made. This is what Festinger (1957) labelled **cognitive dissonance**, meaning that consumers are 'psychologically uncomfortable', trying to balance the choice made against the doubts still held about it. Such dissonance may be aggravated where consumers are exposed to marketing communication that sings the praises of the features and benefits of the rejected alternatives. Generally speaking, the more alternatives that have been rejected, and the more comparatively attractive those alternatives appear to be, the greater the dissonance. Conversely, the more similar to the chosen product the rejected alternatives are, the less the dissonance. It is also likely that dissonance will occur with more significant purchases, such as extended problem-solving items like cars and houses, because the buyer is far more likely to review and assess the decision consciously afterwards.

Clearly, such psychological discomfort is not pleasant, and the consumer will work towards reducing it, perhaps by trying to filter out the messages that undermine the choice made (for example advertising for a product that was a rejected alternative) and paying extra attention to supportive messages (for example advertising for the chosen alternative). This all underlines the need for post-purchase reassurance, whether through advertising, after-sales follow-up calls, and even the tone of an instruction manual ('Congratulations on choosing the Acme Home Nuclear Reactor Kit, we know it will give you many years' faithful service ...'). Consumers like to be reminded and reassured that they have made a wise choice, that they have made the best choice for them. From the marketer's point of view, as well as offering post-purchase reassurance, they can minimise the risk of dissonance by making sure that potential buyers have a realistic picture of the product, its capabilities and its characteristics. Exaggerated advertising simply raises expectations that cannot possibly be fulfilled in reality, and disappointment and dissonance are almost certain. Another way of making sure that the potential buyer's expectations are rooted in reality is to let them sample the product before purchase, where possible. With fmcg (fast moving consumer goods) products, this is relatively simple to do, and allows consumers to pass judgement on product benefits based on experience, rather than simply on what an advertiser tells them (*see* Chapter 17 for more on sampling). With a higher priced, less frequently purchased product such as a car, it is more difficult to offer samples, but at least a long test drive can go some way to creating realistic expectations, and emphasizing potentially negative points before the customer commits to a purchase.

Thus the post-purchase evaluation stage is important for a number of reasons. Primarily, it will affect whether the consumer ever buys this product again. If expectations have not been met, then the product may not even make the shortlist next time. If, on the other hand, expectations have been met or even exceeded, then a strong possibility of lasting loyalty has been created. The next shortlist may be a shortlist of one! As a result of this, it is important to remember that consumers are not passive, inanimate elements in the marketing process. They do not fade away into insignificance if their relationship with a particular product or supplier ends. According to Smith (1993), dissatisfied customers will tell up to 11 other people about their bad experience, which is two to three times more people than a satisfied customer will talk to. Thus it is important for the marketer to consider how the risks of a poor outcome at the post-purchase phase can best be reduced.

As has been mentioned already, the information evaluation which sets up product performance criteria in the consumer's mind can be influenced by the marketer. Marketing is about making promises, and the post-purchase evaluation is, to some extent, a measure of how true those promises were. If, therefore, the needs and wants of the consumer have been carefully researched and the marketing mix tailored, balanced and implemented accordingly, then the post-purchase stage should be a happy one for all parties.

Monitoring of post-purchase feelings is an important task of marketing, not only to identify areas in which the product (or its associated marketing mix) falls short of expectations, but also to identify any unexpectedly pleasant surprises the purchaser may have had. The product may, for instance, have strengths which are being undersold. This is a natural part of the cycle of product and service development, improvement and evolution.

To recap on the stages in the decision-making process, look at Fig 3.2. This summarises the general process, and then shows its specific application in the context of (a) the impulse purchase of chocolate, and (b) buying and fitting a car exhaust.

There are some points to note about the process as presented here. First, the consumer may choose to end the process at any stage. Perhaps the information search reveals that there is no obvious acceptable solution to the problem, or the information evaluation demonstrates that the cost of solving the problem is too high. It is, of course, the marketer's job to sustain the consumer's interest throughout this process and to

FIGURE 3.2

The decision-making processes for chocolate and car exhausts

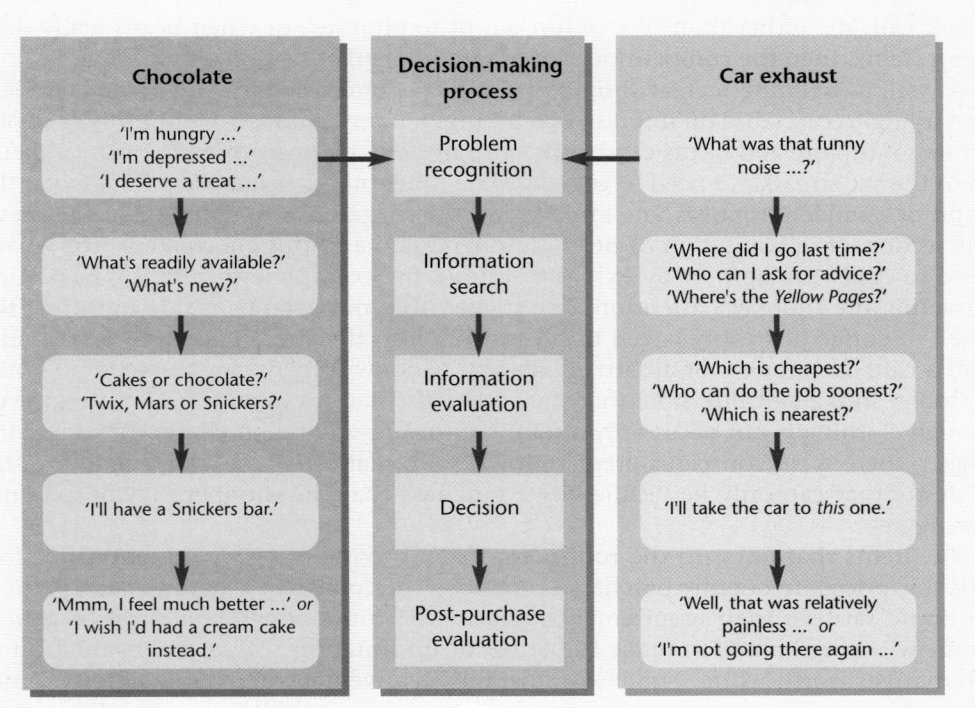

prevent them from opting out of it. Second, the process does not necessarily have to run from stage 1 to stage 5 in an unbroken flow. The consumer may backtrack at any point to an earlier stage and reiterate the process. Even on the verge of decision, it may be felt necessary to go back and get more information, just to make sure. Finally, the time taken over the process may vary enormously, depending on the nature of the purchase and the nature of the purchaser. Many months of agonising may go into making an expensive, important purchase, while only a few seconds may be invested in choosing a bar of chocolate. The next section looks more closely at this issue.

BUYING SITUATIONS

In the discussion of the decision-making process, it has been made clear that both the flow and the formality of the process, and the emphasis that is put on each stage will vary from situation to situation. Some of these variations are to do with the particular environment relevant to the transaction (*see* p. 98), while others emanate from the consumer (p. 100) or from the consumer's immediate social surroundings (p. 109). This current section, however, will look more closely at the effect of the type of *purchasing situation* on the extent and formality of the decision-making process.

Routine problem solving

As the heading of this section implies, a **routine problem solving** purchasing situation is one which the consumer is likely to experience on a regular basis. Most grocery shopping falls into this category, where particular brands are purchased habitually without recourse to any lengthy decision-making process. As with the chocolate buying example above, there is virtually no information search and evaluation, and the buying decision is made simultaneously with (if not in advance of) the problem-recognition stage. This, therefore, explains why many fmcg manufacturers spend so much time and effort trying to generate such loyalty and why it is so difficult for new products to break into an established market. When the consumer thinks 'We've run out of Colgate' rather than 'We've run out of toothpaste', or when beans really does mean Heinz, then the competition have an uphill marketing task on their hands.

As well as building regular shopping habits, i.e. brand loyalty, the manufacturer is also trying to capitalise on impulse purchasing of many products within this category. While toothpaste and beans can be the objective of a planned shopping trip ('When I go to the supermarket, I need to get ...'), some other products may be purchased as the result of a sudden impulse. The impulse may be triggered, as mentioned in the previous section, by a realisation of need ('I'm depressed and this chocolate is just what I need to cheer me up'), or by external stimuli, for example eye-catching packaging attracting the shopper's attention. The trigger need not even be inside the store: the smell of coffee or freshly baked bread wafting into the street may draw a customer into a café on impulse, or an attractive shop window display may attract a potential customer into a clothing store that they otherwise had no intention of visiting (even though clothing is not necessarily a routine problem-solving purchase). Whatever the trigger, there is no conscious preplanning or information search, but a sudden surge of desire that can only be fulfilled by a purchase that the shopper may or may not later regret.

The items that fall into the routine problem-solving category do tend to be low risk, low priced, frequently purchased products. The consumer is happy that a particular brand satisfies their requirements, and there is not enough benefit to be gained from switching brands to make the effort of information search and evaluation of alternatives worth while. These so-called low involvement purchases simply do not carry enough risk, whether measured in terms of financial loss, personal disappointment or damage to social status, for the consumer to get excited about the importance of 'making the right decision'.

Ehrenberg and Goodhart (1980) proposed a simple three-stage model that covers many routine problem-solving purchases. Stage 1 is **awareness** of the brand or product, stage 2 is **trial**, and if the outcome of the trial is satisfactory, stage 3 is **repeat purchase**. Over time, therefore, the repeat purchase becomes habitual, with little or no re-evaluation of the decision. This explains why many manufacturers invest in heavy promotion to generate awareness and trial of new products, as these are necessary foundations for longer-term repeat purchasing behaviour. Later research further supported the relationship between awareness, trial and repeat purchasing, even where consumers indulged in multi-brand and multi-store shopping.

Limited problem solving

Limited problem solving is a little more interesting for the consumer. This is a buying situation which occurs less frequently, and probably involves more deliberate decision making than routine problems do. The goods will be moderately expensive (in the eyes of the individual consumer), and perhaps will be expected to last a long time. Thus the risks inherent in a 'wrong' decision are that much higher. There will, therefore, be some element of information search and evaluation, but this is still unlikely to absorb too much time and effort.

An example of this could be a consumer's purchase of a new piece of hi-fi equipment. If it is some years since they last bought one, they might feel that they need to update their knowledge of who makes what, who sells what, and the price brackets in this market. The information search is likely to include talking to any friends with recent hi-fi buying experience, and a trip round locally accessible electrical goods retailers. To this particular consumer, this is an important decision, but not a crucial one. If they make a 'wrong' choice (as defined in the post-purchase evaluation stage), they will be disappointed, but will feel that they have spent too much money to allow them to simply discard the offending product. Having said that, provided that the hi-fi fulfils its primary function of producing music on demand, they can learn to live with it, and the damage is limited.

Limited problem solving may also be likely to occur with the choice of service products. In purchasing a holiday or choosing a dentist (word of mouth recommendation?) the consumer has one chance to make the right choice. Once you are on the plane or in the dentist's chair, it is too late, and the wrong choice could turn out to be expensive and painful. The necessity to get it right first time is thus likely to lead to a conscious and detailed information search, perhaps even going as far as extended problem solving, to which we now turn.

Extended problem solving

Extended problem solving represents a much more serious investment of money, time and effort from the consumer, and consequently, a much higher risk. Purchases of major capital items such as houses or cars fall into this category. These purchases occur extremely infrequently for most people, and given that they often require the taking out of some kind of a loan, involve a serious long-term commitment. This means that the purchaser is motivated to gather as much information as possible, and to think quite consciously and systematically about what the decision-making criteria should be. That is not to say that the final decision will necessarily be made on purely functional, conscious or rational grounds. If, for example two different makes of car have similar technical specifications, price, delivery and after-sales service terms, then final differentiation may be in terms of 'Which one will most impress the neighbours?'

The significance of buying situations

So what? Why categorise purchases in this way? After all, one consumer's limited problem-solving situation may be another's extended problem. It matters because it may add another dimension to help marketers develop more efficient and appropriate marketing strategies. If a significant group of potential buyers can be defined who clearly regard the purchase of a hi-fi as a limited problem-solving situation, then that has implications for the manufacturers in terms of both how and what to communicate, and where and how to distribute. If consumers are thought to regard a product as a limited problem-solving purchase, then perhaps the marketer will prefer to distribute it through specialist outlets, where the potential buyer can get expert advice, and can spend time making detailed product comparisons. Communication may contain a lot of factual information about technical specifications and product features (i.e. what the product can do), as well as selling product benefits (i.e. what all that means to you). In contrast, the same product as a routine problem-solving exercise may be distributed as widely as possible, to ensure availability, regardless of retailer specialism or expertise, and the communication might centre on product image and benefits, ignoring the detailed information.

ENVIRONMENTAL INFLUENCES

This section is about the wider context in which the decision making is taking place. All of these environmental influences have been covered in some depth already in Chapter 2, so their treatment here will be brief. The important thing is to recognise that decision making is not completely divorced from the environment in which it is happening, whether the consumer is conscious of it or not.

Sociocultural influences

There are many pressures in this category, and pp. 109 *et seq*. looks at them more closely. Individuals are influenced both by current trends in society as a whole and by a need to conform with the norms of the various social groups to which they belong, as well as to enhance their status within those groups.

In wider society, for example, there has been a move in recent years towards demanding more environmentally friendly products, and many consumers who are not necessarily 'deep green' have allowed this to influence their decision making, looking more favourably on CFC-free, recycled, or non-animal-tested products. Examples of social group pressures can be seen in children's markets. Many parents feel unfairly pressured into buying particular goods or brands because the children's friends all have them. There is a fear of the child being marginalised or bullied because of not possessing the 'right' things, whether those are trainers, mountain bikes or computer games.

Technological influences

Technology affects many aspects of consumer decision making. Database technology, for example, as discussed in Chapter 19, allows organisations to create (almost) personal relationships with customers. At its extreme, this means that consumers receive better tailored personalised offerings, and thus that their expectations are raised in terms of the quality of the product, communication and service.

In its wider sense, technology applied to product development and innovation has created whole categories of fast evolving, increasingly cheap consumer 'toys' such as videos, hi-fi formats, camcorders and computer games. Many of these products used to be extended problem-solving goods, but they have moved rapidly towards the limited

The 90s Woman

As women's roles, concerns and expectations have changed, marketers have adapted their approaches, particularly to advertising, in order to keep up. In the 1980s, for example, the emphasis was on the career woman, cool, sophisticated, elegant and in control. She was successful and ruthless, but never lonely since she had somehow found time to develop a relationship with Mr Perfect. She might well 'have it all', but the problem was that the real women looking at these images did not. Of course, a certain amount of fantasy and unreality is acceptable and even expected in advertising, but as the 1990s began, it became clear that current images had become too clichéd and too far removed from what women actually felt and wanted.

In 1993, the advertising agency Ogilvy and Mather (O&M) undertook an extensive survey, using focus groups, of women's attitudes and responses to advertising. The results showed that women resented the typical advertising stereotypes. The harassed housewife of the household products advertisements was particularly unpopular. The advertisements were felt to be 'typical', 'boring' and 'patronising'. Showing a man in the kitchen was no better. Most women cannot relate to this image because it simply does not happen in their households! Women wanted to be portrayed as multidimensional 'caring, sexy, ambitious, daring and independent', yet without losing the reality of their lives as wives, mothers and housekeepers. Finding the right balance between fantasy and reality is not easy, especially when advertisers are so aware of 'political correctness'. Beth Barry of O&M summed up the advertiser's problem,

'If you put beautiful women in exotic locations, female viewers think "That's not me", but if you give them a fat woman on Brighton beach, they will totally reject that too. The answer is to give women a piece of their dreams, but root it in the truth.'

This is a difficult thing to achieve, and many advertisers have failed. A later survey showed that things had not in fact moved much further on. By the mid-1990s, Colgate Palmolive, having realised that they were not getting the message across for their toiletries brands, undertook research to find out about 90s woman. They found that 85 per cent of women are irritated by the glamorous stereotypes of women that appear in advertisements. They also found that power dressing is no longer important and that the thing women most like doing is chatting with their friends. Younger women in particular are more independent and happier to remain single, and find a natural, relaxed look much more acceptable. This led to a much more realistic approach to advertising for the Soft & Gentle deodorant brand from Colgate Palmolive. In contrast, Gillette maintained an element of fantasy with its Natrel Plus advertising, but playing on the brand's 'green' image rather than glamour for glamour's sake.

The beauty editor of *Marie Claire* was quoted in *Marketing* as thinking that advertisers would not abandon images of glamour altogether, but would use them differently:

'Most of the make-up ads are still really glamorous and based around "I can be whatever person I want to be by applying this make-up". The real emerging trend is the strength of the female portrayed: they still show gorgeous girls but they are presented as stronger and it's about doing it for yourself.'

This does, to a great extent, reflect the essence of what O&M found in 1993.

Sources: Bainbridge (1996); Brinkworth (1993).

problem-solving area, as discussed above (p. 97). Such shifts occur for two main sets of reasons, which are interdependent. First, as the manufacturer learns more through experience about the product, its technology, its manufacture and its marketing, they are able to reduce their costs, make better quality products, and expand the product range to offer a number of different models to suit different kinds of customer. Additionally, over time, competition is likely to increase, again acting as an impetus towards better and cheaper products. Second, as a result of all that, the amount of risk inherent in the purchase reduces for the consumer, who does not, therefore, need to spend quite so much time searching for and evaluating alternative options.

Economic and competitive influences

The early 1990s saw recession and economic hardship across Europe, and inevitably, this affected consumers' attitudes, as well as their ability and willingness to spend. With uncertainty about employment prospects, many consumers postponed purchasing decisions, adjusted their decision-making criteria, or cut out certain types of spending altogether. Price, value for money and a conscious assessment of the need to buy become prevalent influences in such circumstances.

Retailers, in turn, had to respond to the slowdown in trade caused by the economic environment. Money-off sales became prevalent in the High Street throughout the year, not just in the traditional post-Christmas period. While this did stimulate sales in the short term, it had one unfortunate effect for the retailers. Consumers began to see the lower sale price as 'normal', and resented paying full prices, preferring to wait for the next sale which they were confident would come along soon.

In terms of competition, very few purchases, mainly low-involvement decisions, are made without any consideration of the competition. The definition of what constitutes competition, however, is in the mind of the consumer. The supplier of car exhaust systems can be fairly sure that the competition consists of other exhaust dealers and garages. The supplier of chocolate, however, may be in competition not only with other chocolate suppliers but also with cream buns, biscuits and potato crisps. The consumer's consideration of the competition, however it is defined, may be extensive, formal and time consuming, or it may be a cursory glance across the supermarket shelf, just to check. Competitors are vying for the consumer's attention through their packaging, their promotional mix and their mailshots, as well as trying to influence or interrupt the decision-making process. This proliferation of products and communication can either confuse the consumer, leading to brand switching and even less rational decision making, or provide the consumer with the information and comparators to allow more discerning decision making.

Political and regulatory influences

Political and regulatory influences too, emanating either from the EU or from national bodies, can affect the consumer. Legislation on minimum levels of product safety and performance, for example, means that the consumer does not need to spend time getting technical information, worrying about analysing it and comparing competing products on those criteria. Legislation and regulation, whether they relate to product descriptions, consumer rights or advertising, also reduce the inherent risks of making a decision. This takes some of the pressure off the customer, leading to better informed decisions, easier decisions and less risk of post-purchase dissonance.

This discussion of the STEP factors is not exhaustive, but simply acts as a reminder that an individual makes decisions within a wider context, created either by society's own dynamics or by the efforts of the market. Having set that context, it is now appropriate to look more closely at the particular influences, internal and external, that affect the individual's buying behaviour and decision making.

PSYCHOLOGICAL INFLUENCES: THE INDIVIDUAL

Although marketers try to define groups of potential customers with common attributes or interests, as a useful unit for the formulation of marketing strategies, it should not be forgotten that such groups or market segments are still made up of individuals who are different from each other. This section, therefore, looks at aspects which will affect an individual's perceptions and handling of the decision-making process, such as personality, perception, learning, motivation and the impact of attitudes.

Savoury snacks

Savoury snacks, such as potato crisps, have always been popular, and the sector is growing faster than ever. It is now worth around £1.4 bn per year. Crisps alone are worth £872 mn, 53 per cent of the market. The reason for this growth seems to be changing lifestyles. Many people no longer have time to sit down for meals regularly and tend to 'graze' on the move. Crisps and other bagged snacks are ideal for this.

Another reason for growth is that those who were children 20 to 30 years ago when the savoury snacks market really began to develop have carried on their snack habits into adulthood and have even passed them on to their own children. As they get older, however, people's tastes and preferences change, opening up new opportunities in the snack market. According to KP Foods, young children are interested in textures and flavours, teenagers want brand credibility, whereas adults want premium good quality brands. Companies such as Golden Wonder, therefore, have developed different products to meet those different needs. Wotsits appeal to the under-10 year olds, then as teenagers they can graduate on to Nik Naks, and finally, as mature adults they can have Wheat Crunchies. All of these are corn-based products, an area that seems to be growing in popularity at the expense of potato-based products. Nevertheless, there are premium brands of potato crisp, such as McCoy's (KP) and Kettle Chips (Kettle Foods), to try to appeal to the more adult purchaser.

In keeping with society's increasing obsession with health, snack manufacturers are trying to develop lower fat, lower salt and lower calorie variants. The low calorie version has not yet become well established, mainly because the manufacturers have had problems getting them to taste good and maintaining the quality consumers expect of the mainstream brands.

Source: Murphy and Bray (1996).

Personality

Personality, consisting of all the features, traits, behaviours and experiences that make each of us distinctive and unique, is a very extensive and deep area of study. Our personalities lie at the heart of all our behaviour as consumers, and thus marketers try to define particular personality traits or characteristics prevalent among a target group of consumers which can then be reflected in the product itself and the marketing effort around it. This is beginning to trespass on the ground which will be covered later in discussion of psychographic or lifestyle segmentation (p. 177), which is hardly surprising, as personality helps to establish lifestyle as much as lifestyle affects personality.

In the mid to late 1980s, advertising in particular was full of images reflecting the personality traits associated with successful lifestyle stereotypes such as the 'yuppie'. Independent, level-headed, ruthless, ambitious, self-centred, materialistic traits were seen as positive characteristics, and thus marketers were anxious to have them associated with users of their products. The 1990s have seen a softening of this approach, featuring images orientated more towards caring, concern, family and sharing as the route to self-fulfilment.

With high-involvement products, where there is a strong emotional and psychological link between the product and the consumer, it is relatively easy to see how personality might affect choice and decision making. In choosing clothing, for instance, an extrovert self-confident achiever with an extravagant streak might select something deliberately *avant garde*, stylishly daring, vibrantly coloured and expensive, as a personality statement. A quiet, insecure character, with under-developed social skills, might prefer to wear something more sober, more conservative, with less attention-seeking potential.

With high involvement products such as the Vauxhall Tigra, psychological factors have a strong influence on consumer choice.

Source: Vauxhall Motors.

Overall, however, the link between personality and purchasing, and thus the ability to predict purchasing patterns from personality traits, is at best tenuous. Kassarjian (1971) probably best summed up the situation in a review of previous studies: some showed a strong relationship between personality and purchasing, the majority showed at best a weak relationship, and a few no relationship at all. Chisnall (1985) takes the more cautious line that personality may influence the decision to buy a certain product type, but not the final brand choice.

Perception

Perception represents the way in which individuals analyse, interpret, and make sense of incoming information, and is affected by personality, experience and mood. No two people will interpret the same stimulus (whether it is a product's packaging, taste, smell, texture or its promotional messages) in exactly the same way. Even the same individual might perceive the stimulus differently at different times. For example, seeing an advertisement for food when you are hungry is more likely to produce a positive response than seeing the same advertisement just after a heavy meal. Immediate needs are affecting the interpretation of the message. Alternatively, relaxing at home on a Sunday afternoon, an individual is more likely to spend time reading a detailed and lengthy print advertisement than they would if they were flicking through the same magazine during a short coffee break in the working day. Naturally, marketers hope that their messages reach target audiences when they are relaxed, at leisure and at ease with the world, because then the individual is more likely to place a positive interpretation on the message and is less likely to be distracted by other pressures and needs.

Other pressures and needs do create problems for marketers to overcome. All consumers are bombarded with marketing messages every day, and if they tried to pay equal attention and interpret them all objectively, then they would rapidly go mad. There are, therefore, a number of defence mechanisms to protect the consumer from over-stimulation and to make the interpretation process less stressful.

Selective attention

Consumers do not pay attention to everything that is going on at once. Attention filters allow the unconscious selection of what incoming information to concentrate on. In daily life we filter out the irrelevant background noise: the hum of the computer, the birds in the garden, the cars in the street, the footsteps in the corridor. As consumers we filter out the irrelevant marketing messages. In reading the newspaper, for instance, a split second glance spots an advertisement, decides that it is irrelevant, and allows the eye to read around it.

This means that marketers have to overcome these filters, either by creating messages that we will decide are relevant, or by building attention grabbing devices into the message. A print advertisement, for example, might use its position on the page, intense colour or startling images to draw the eye, and more importantly the brain, to it.

Selective perception

The problems do not stop once the marketer has got the consumer's attention, since people are infinitely creative in interpreting information in ways that suit them. It is less threatening to interpret things so that they fit nicely and consistently with whatever you already think and feel than to cope with the discomfort of clashes and inconsistency.

One way of creating this consistency or harmony is to allow perception to be coloured by previous experience and existing attitudes. A particularly bad experience with an organisation's offering creates a prejudice which may never be overcome. Whatever positive messages that organisation transmits, the consumer will always be thinking 'Yes, but...'. Similarly, a negative attitude towards a subject will make the consumer interpret messages differently. For example, someone who is deeply opposed to nuclear power will try to read between the lines of the industry's advertising and PR, looking for cover-ups and counter-arguments. This can distort the intended message and even reinforce the negative feelings. Conversely, a good experience makes it a lot easier to form positive perceptions. The good experience from the past creates a solid foundation from which to look for the best in the new experience.

Selective retention

Not all stimuli that make it through the attention filters and the machinery of perception and understanding are remembered. Many stimuli are only transitory, hence one of the reasons for the repetition of advertising: if you did not notice it or remember it the first time round, you might pick it up on subsequent occasions. Jogging the memory, by repeating messages, or by producing familiar stimuli that the consumer can recognise (such as brand names, packaging design, logos or colour schemes) is, therefore, an important marketing task to reduce the reliance on the consumer's memory.

People have the capacity to remember what they want to remember, and to filter out anything else. The reasons for retaining a particular message may be because it touched them emotionally, or it was of immediate relevance, or it was especially entertaining, or it reinforced previously held views. The reasons are many, but the consumer is under no obligation to remember anything.

Learning

Perception and memory are closely linked with **learning**. Marketers want consumers to learn from promotional material, so that they know which product to buy and why, and to learn from experience of the product, so that they will buy it again and pass on the message to others.

Learning has been defined by Hilgard and Marquis (1961) as:

> **the more or less permanent change in behaviour which occurs as a result of practice.**

This implies, from a marketing perspective, that the objective must not only be for the consumer to learn something, but also be for them to remember what has been learned and to act upon it. Therefore advertising materials, for instance, are carefully designed to maximise the learning opportunity. A 30-second television advertisement selling car insurance over the phone repeats the freephone number four times and has it written across the bottom of the screen so that the viewer cannot help but remember it. Demonstrating a product benefit in an advertisement also helps the consumer to learn what they are supposed to notice about the product when they use it. The images from Procter & Gamble's advertisement showing the enormous heap of crockery washed by one bottle of Fairy Liquid next to the pathetic heap achieved with a competing product stay in the mind more easily than a simple verbal message would. More generally, showing a product in a particular usage context, or associating it with certain types of people or situations gives the consumer guidelines about what attitudes to develop towards the product.

Humour, and other methods of provoking an emotional response to an advertisement, can also help a message to stick because the recipient immediately becomes more involved in the process. Similarly, associating a product with something familiar that itself evokes certain emotions can allow those feelings to be transferred to the product. Thus the advertisements for Andrex which feature puppies have helped the British public to learn to think of toilet paper as warm, soft, cuddly and harmless rather than as embarrassing.

Motivation

One definition of marketing puts the emphasis on the satisfaction of customers' needs and wants, but what triggers those needs and wants, and what drives consumers towards their fulfilment? Motives for action, the driving forces, are complex and changeable and can be difficult to research, since individuals themselves often cannot define why they act the way they do. An additional problem is that at different times, different **motivations** might take priority and have more influence over the individual's behaviour. Imagine, for example, a traveller driving from Calais to Marseilles. In the early part of the journey, the main priority is to make good time, find somewhere for lunch and provisionally aim to arrive in Lyon in good time to find a reasonable hotel. Long traffic delays on the southbound motorway throw out these plans. It is getting late and the traveller realises that he will not reach Lyon as planned. After seeing a few 'no vacancies' signs, concern starts to mount about the likelihood of finding a room, rather than sleeping in the car. The many hotels passed earlier in the journey were not considered, but now any hotel is likely to be well received. The priority is no longer distance covered but finding the warmth and relaxation of any hotel room. Our traveller's motives, in terms of both content and intensity, have changed during the events of one long distance car journey. Marketers need to be aware of such influences on patronage motives if they are to market their hotels, restaurants or indeed any business effectively. Think, for example, of the impact on the tired traveller of a well lit, familiar sign that can be clearly seen from the motorway.

Maslow's (1954) *hierarchy of needs* has long been used as a framework for classifying basic motivations. Five groups of needs, as shown in Fig 3.3, are stacked one on top of another, and form a progression. Having achieved satisfaction on the lowest level, the individual can progress to strive to achieve the goals of the next level up. This model does have a certain logic behind it, and the idea, for instance, that true self-actualisation can only grow from solid foundations of security and social acceptance seems reasonable. However, the model was developed in the context of US capitalist culture, where achievement and self-actualisation are often ends in themselves. It is questionable how far these motives can be extended to other cultural contexts.

Examples of consumer behaviour and marketing activity can be found to fit all five levels.

FIGURE 3.3

**Maslow's
hierarchy of
needs**

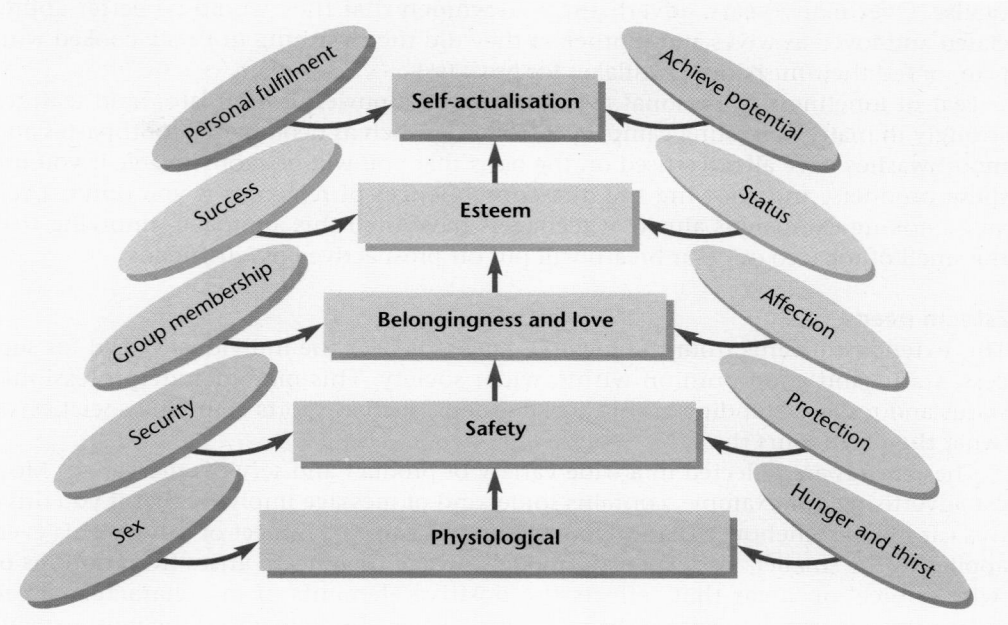

Physiological needs

Basic feelings such as hunger and thirst can be potent driving forces. After a strenuous game of squash, the immediate craving for liquid overrides normal considerations of brand preference. If the sports centre shop only has one type of soft drink in stock, then it will do. Similarly, seasoned shoppers are well aware of the dangers of visiting a supermarket when hungry; so much more seems to go into the trolley.

Marketers can capitalise on such feelings. The soft drink manufacturer can ensure that the sports centre stocks that brand, and that the product image reflects refreshment and thirst-quenching properties. The food manufacturer can advertise at a time of day when the audience is likely to be feeling hungry so that they are more likely to pay attention to the message and remember it.

Safety needs

Once the individual has taken care of the basic necessities of life, food, drink and warmth, the need for self-protection and long-term survival emerges. In modern Western societies this may be interpreted as the desire for a secure home, protected against intrusion and other dangers (floods and fire, for example). It might also cover the desire for health care, insurance services, and consumer protection legislation.

The car market in particular has focused on safety needs as a marketing platform. Driving is an inherently dangerous activity, so the manufacturers try to reassure us that their cars are as safe as possible. Various manufacturers have featured side impact bars, airbags, and/or anti-lock braking systems in their advertising, showing how these things either protect you or help to prevent accidents.

Safety needs in terms of health protection feature strongly in the marketing strategies of products such as bleaches and toilet cleaners. The kind of approach used often appeals to the mother who takes responsibility for safeguarding the health and well-being of the whole family. The threat from bacteria can be eliminated by choosing the right cleanser.

Belongingness and love needs

This is about emotional security, wanting to feel accepted and valued by those closest to you. Marketers again play on this need through the portrayal of the family in particular. Over many years, advertising told women that they would be better appreciated and loved as wives and mothers if they did their washing in Persil, cooked with Oxo, or fed their husbands cornflakes for breakfast.

Fear of loneliness or personal rejection can be a powerful motivator, and features strongly in many marketing campaigns. Toiletries such as deodorants, toothpastes and mouthwashes have all advertised on the basis that you will be more lovable if you use these products, and showing the dire consequences of rejection if you don't. Even anti-smoking campaigns aimed at teenagers have tried this approach, implying that the smell of tobacco on your breath will put off prospective boy/girlfriends.

Esteem needs

This extends outwards from the previous stage to cover the individual's need for success, status and good opinion within wider society. This may include professional status and respect, standing within social groups, such as sports clubs and societies, or 'what the neighbours think'.

These needs are reflected in a wide variety of product and services marketing. Most car advertising, for example, contains some kind of message implying that if you drive this car it will somehow enhance your status and gain the respect of others. This even applies to the smaller, less expensive models, where the esteem arises from notions of 'wise choice' or 'a car that reflects the positive elements of my character'. More overtly, esteem can derive from the individual's sheer ability to afford the most expensive and exclusive items. Perfumes and other luxury products play heavily on the implication that you are a discerning and élite buyer, a cut above the rest, and that using these product makes a statement about who you are and the status you hold. Brand names such as Rolls Royce, Gucci and Rolex have acquired such a cachet that simply saying 'She owns a genuine Rolex' speaks volumes about social status.

Self-actualisation needs

This is the ultimate goal, the achievement of complete satisfaction through successfully fulfiling one's potential. That may mean anything, depending on who you are and what you want out of life. Some will only achieve self-actualisation through becoming the head of a multinational organisation, while others will find it through the successful raising of a happy and healthy family. This is a difficult stage for the marketer to handle, because it is so individual, and thus the hope is that by fulfilling the other needs discussed above, the marketer can help to propel the individual

This Bentley car makes a statement about the owner's status, satisfying esteem needs.

Source: Rolls-Royce Motors.

towards self-actualisation. Only the individual can tell, however, when this stage has been reached.

Interestingly, the traveller from Calais to Marseilles introduced earlier seemed to regress back down from higher order to lower order needs! The initial idea of choosing a nice comfortable hotel that would suitably fulfil his service requirements and match his self-image had to be abandoned. Circumstances brought to the fore the very basic physiological need for sleep and the need for safety, both in terms of stopping driving before tiredness made it dangerous and having a secure roof over his head.

Generally, however, in Western economies, the fulfilment of the very basic needs can be taken for granted. Real physiological hunger, thirst and lack of safety generally do not exist for most people. Manufacturers of food products, for instance, cannot therefore assume that just because their product alleviates hunger it will be purchased and accepted. Any one of hundreds of food brands can do that, and thus the consumer is looking to see how a particular product can fulfil a higher order need, such as love or esteem. Consequently, foods are often marketed on the basis that your family will enjoy it and love you more for providing it (Oxo, for example) or because your dinner party guests will be impressed (Viennetta or After Eights, for example). The emphasis, therefore, is largely on the higher-order needs (belongingness and love, esteem and self-actualisation).

In contrast, emerging market economies are still in the process of moving away from emphasis on the lower-order needs (physiological and safety). When the former Communist states began their difficult transition to market economies, the shortages of basic products meant that people were very concerned simply with survival, acquiring enough bread, tea, milk, meat and other staple items to keep themselves going. Whether a particular product helps you to feel better about yourself is rather irrelevant in those circumstances. Now that the transitions are a few years further on, and because of the impact of the marketing efforts of Western organisations entering these markets, higher order needs are increasingly being considered.

Attitudes

As implied at p. 103 above, an **attitude** is a stance that an individual takes on a subject which predisposes them to react in a certain way to that subject. More formally, an attitude has been defined by Hilgard *et al.* (1975) as:

> **... an orientation towards or away from some object, concept or situation and a readiness to respond in a predetermined manner to these related objects, concepts or situations.**

Thus in marketing terms, consumers can develop attitudes to any kind of product or service, or indeed to any aspect of the marketing mix, and these attitudes will affect behaviour. All of this implies that attitudes play an important part in influencing consumer judgement, whether through their perception, evaluation, information processing or decision making. Attitudes play a key role in shaping learning and while they are fluid, evolving over time, they are nevertheless often difficult to change.

Williams (1981), in summarising the literature, describes attitudes as having three different components.

Cognitive

Cognitive attitudes relate to beliefs or disbeliefs, thus 'I believe that margarine is healthier than butter.' This is a component that the marketer can work on through fairly straightforward advertising. Repeating the message that your product is healthy, or that it represents the best value for money, may well establish an initial belief in those qualities.

Affective

Affective attitudes relate to feelings of a positive or negative nature, involving some emotional content, thus 'I *like* this product' or 'This product makes me *feel* ...' Again, advertising can help the marketer to signal to the consumer why they should like it, or how they should feel when they use it. For some consumers, of course, affective attitudes can overcome cognitive ones. For example I may believe that margarine is healthier than butter, but I buy butter because I like the taste better. Similarly, I believe that snacking on chocolate is 'bad', but it cheers me up so I do it anyway.

Conative

Conative attitudes relate to the link with behaviour, thus attitude *x* is considered likely to lead to behaviour *y*. This is the hardest one for marketers to predict or control, because so many things can prevent behaviour from taking place, even if the cognitive and affective attitudes are positive: 'I believe that BMWs are excellent quality, reliable cars, and I feel that owning one would enhance my status and provide me with many hours of pleasurable driving, but I simply cannot afford it,' or it may even be that 'Audi made me a better offer'.

It is this last link between attitude and behaviour that is of most interest to marketers. Fishbein (1975) developed a model, a further evolution of his earlier 1967 work, based on the proposition that in order to predict a specific behaviour, such as a brand purchase, it is important to measure the individual's attitude towards performing that behaviour, rather than just the attitude towards the product in question. This fits with the BMW example above where the most important thing is not the attitude to the car itself, but the attitude towards *purchasing* the car. As long as the attitude to purchasing is negative, the marketer still has work to do. While it is usually accepted that other factors, both personal and situational, also influence behaviour, many writers, such as Lutz (1981) and Foxall (1984), still argue that attitude is a key link in the causal chain between perceptions of product attributes at one end and purchasing intentions and behaviour at the other end. Others, such as Joyce (1967), see a two-way impact between attitudes and purchasing behaviour so that experience of the product will also influence, through learning, future behaviour.

Attitudes can thus involve feelings (positive or negative), knowledge (complete or partial) and beliefs. A particular female consumer might believe that she is overweight. She knows that cream cakes are fattening, but she likes them. All these things come together to form her attitude towards cream cakes (wicked, but seductive) and her behaviour when confronted by one (five minutes wrestling with her conscience before giving in completely and buying two, knowing that she will regret it later). An advertising campaign for cream cakes, centred around the slogan 'naughty but nice', capitalised brilliantly on what is a common attitude, almost legitimising the guilt and establishing an empathy with the hopeless addict. The really admirable thing about that campaign was that the advertiser did not even attempt to overturn the attitude.

It is possible, but very difficult, to change attitudes, particularly when they are well established and deeply ingrained. Companies like Lada and Aeroflot have been trying for years with varying degrees of success. The nuclear industry too has been trying to overcome hostile and suspicious attitudes with an integrated campaign of advertising, PR and site visits. Many people have indeed been responsive to this openness, and have been prepared to revise attitudes to a greater or lesser extent. There will, however, always be a hard core who will remain entrenched and interpret any 'positive' messages in a negative way.

There is a difference between attitudes that relate to an organisation's philosophy, business ethics or market and those that centre around experience of an organisation's specific product or service. An organisation that has a bad reputation for its employment practices, its environmental record or its dealings with suspect foreign regimes will have created negative attitudes that will be extremely difficult to overturn. Similarly, companies operating in certain markets, such as nuclear power, tobacco and alcohol will never redeem themselves in the eyes of significant groups of the public. People care too much about such things to be easily persuaded to change their outlook. In contrast, negative feelings about a specific product or brand are more amenable to change through skilful marketing. Skoda, for example, launching their new model, the Felicia, tried to overcome the kind of negative attitudes that have led to a plethora of Skoda jokes, through an advertising campaign that admitted to the image problem with gentle good humour, but then tried to establish the positive benefits of the brand: 'We've changed the car. Can you change your mind?'

As the cream cake example quoted earlier shows, defining attitudes can provide valuable insights into target groups of customers, and give a basis for communication with them. Measuring feelings, beliefs and knowledge about an organisation's products and those of its competitors is an essential part of market research (*see* Chapter 6), leading to a more effective and appealing marketing mix. Identifying changes in wider social or cultural attitudes can also provide the marketer with new opportunities, either for products or marketing approaches. In France, for example, a glossy magazine called *Divorce* is available, which focuses on the newly single and the typical problems they face. The advertising within it is for dating agencies and private detectives! Its existence is due not only to the fact that one in three marriages ends in divorce in France, but also to more liberal attitudes towards divorce and the problems it creates. This new openness and acceptability of divorce is also seen in the UK. VW ran a successful advertisement which showed a very happy woman emerging from what the viewer interpreted as a registry office wedding. When she drove away in her VW, however, the slogan painted on the back of the car read 'just divorced'.

In summary, the individual is a complex entity, under pressure to take in, analyse and remember many marketing messages in addition to the other burdens of daily life. Marketers need to understand how individuals think and why they respond in particular ways, if they are going to develop marketing offerings that cut through defence mechanisms and create loyal customers. Individuals' behaviour, however, is not only shaped in accordance with their personalities, abilities, analytical skills etc., as discussed above, but also affected by wider considerations, such as the sociocultural influences which will be discussed next.

SOCIOCULTURAL INFLUENCES: THE GROUP

Individuals are influenced, to a greater or lesser extent, by the social and cultural climate in which they live. Individuals have membership of many social groups, whether these are formally recognised social units such as the family, or informal intangible groupings such as reference groups (*see* p. 114 below). Inevitably, purchasing decisions will be affected by group membership, as these sociocultural influences may help the individual to:

1 differentiate between essential and non-essential purchases;
2 prioritise purchases where resources are limited;
3 define the meaning of the product and its benefits in the context of their own lives; and thus to
4 foresee the post-purchase implications of this decision.

All of these things imply that the individual's decision has as much to do with 'What other people will think' and 'How I will look if I buy this' as with the intrinsic benefits of the product itself. Marketers have, of course, capitalised on this natural wish to express oneself and gain social acceptance through one's consumption habits, both as a basis for psychographic or lifestyle segmentation (which will be discussed later on p. 177) and for many years as a basis of fear appeals in advertising (*see* Chapters 15 onwards).

The following subsections look more closely at some of these sociocultural influences.

Social class

Social class is a form of stratification that attempts to structure and divide a society. Some argue that egalitarianism has become far more pronounced in the modern Europe, making any attempts at social distinction ill-founded, if not meaningless. Nevertheless, these days, social class is established largely according to occupation, and for many years, British marketers have used the grading system outlined in Table 3.2. It has been widely used to group consumers, whether for research or for analysing media readership.

Across the EU different definitions of social class have been used. In the Netherlands, for example, the population is structured into professional and higher managerial, intermediate managerial, clerical and skilled manual, and finally pensioners and the unskilled. In contrast, Germany defines social groups according to monthly household income while France combines the self-employed with senior management and has classes for professional, white collar and blue collar employees. However more fundamental problems can be found in attempting to link consumer behaviour with social class. The usefulness of such systems is limited. They rely on the occupation of the head of the household (more correctly called the main income earner), but fail to put that into the context of the rest of the household. Dual-income households are becoming increasingly common, with the second income having a profound effect on the buying behaviour of both parties, yet most of these systems fail to recognise this. They tell very little about the consumption patterns or attitudes which are of such great use to the marketer. The disposable income of a C2 class household may be just as high as that of an A or B household, and they may have certain upmarket tastes in common. Furthermore, two households in the A or B categories could easily behave very differently. One household might consider status symbols to be important and indulge in conspicuous consumption, whereas the other might have rejected materialistic values and be seeking a cleaner, less cluttered lifestyle. These contrasting outlooks on life make an enormous difference to buying behaviour and choices, hence the necessity for psychographic segmentation (*see* p. 177) to provide marketers with more meaningful frameworks for grouping customers.

TABLE 3.2:
UK socioeconomic groupings

% of population	Group	Social status	Occupation of head of household
3	A	Upper middle	Higher managerial, administrative or professional
14	B	Middle	Intermediate managerial, administrative or professional
27	C1	Lower middle	Supervisory or clerical, junior managerial, administrative or professional
25	C2	Skilled working	Skilled manual workers
19	D	Working	Semi-skilled and unskilled manual workers
12	E	Those at lowest level of subsistance	State pensioners or widows, casual or lowest grade workers

Nevertheless, as Inskip (1995) argues, a deeply rooted sense of class does affect people's perception of the world and their aspirations. In marketing terms, this may mean that middle-class people generally seek out products that will enhance their self-image, self-belief, and sense of success. The working class is more firmly rooted in family values, and although they may still aspire to accumulate possessions, they will not change either those values or themselves fundamentally. Inskip claims that marketers do not understand the working class and its needs properly, and thus have either ignored it completely or failed to address it appropriately as they use patronising and stereotypical marketing activities. Since around 46 per cent of the UK population claim to be working class, this is a serious omission. C2 and D consumers do now have money to spend, even if they choose to spend it in areas such as discount retailers or mail order catalogues that marketers do not find particularly trendy or exciting. Part of the problem is that most marketers are themselves middle class. They thus find it easier to relate to middle-class customers, and carry their own prejudices about the working class into their approaches.

Culture and subculture

Culture can be described as the personality of the society within which an individual lives. It manifests itself through the built environment, art, language, literature, music and the products society consumes, as well as through its prevalent beliefs, value systems and government. As summarised by Chisnall (1985), culture is the total way of life of a society, passed on from generation to generation, deriving from a group of people sharing and transmitting beliefs, values, attitudes and forms of behaviour which are common to that society and considered worthy of retention. Rice (1993, p. 242) similarly defines culture as:

> The values, attitudes, beliefs, ideas, artefacts and other meaningful symbols represented in the pattern of life adopted by people that help them interpret, evaluate and communicate as members of society.

Breaking that definition down further, Fig 3.4 shows diagrammatically the influences that create culture.

FIGURE 3.4

Influences on culture

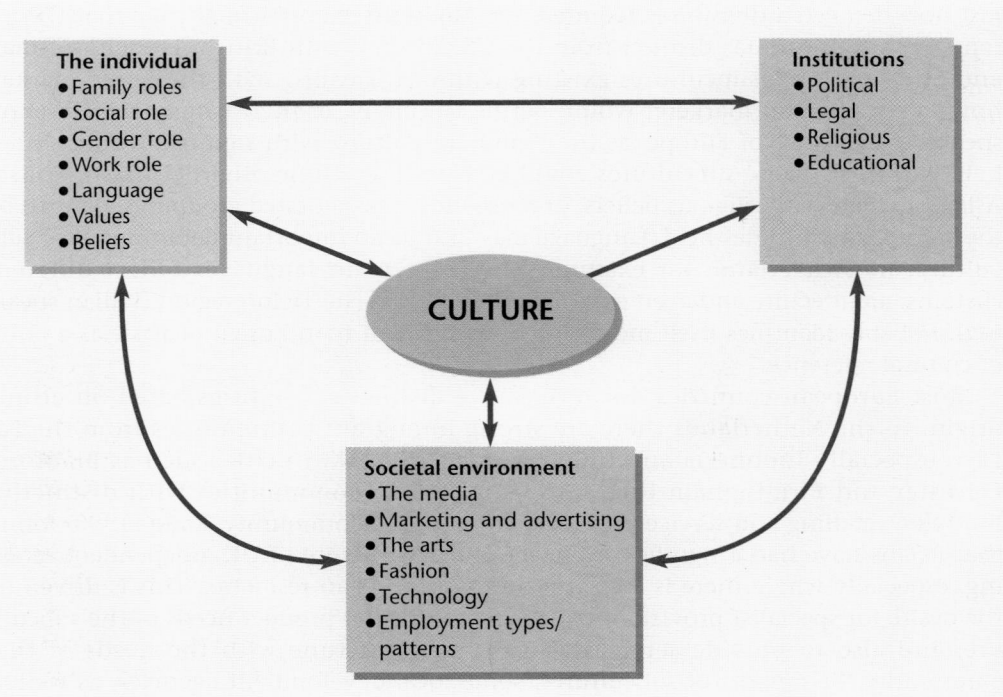

Cultural differences show themselves in very different ways. Although eating, for example, is a very basic natural instinct, what we eat and when is heavily influenced by the culture in which we are brought up. Thus in Spain, it is normal to begin lunch at 4 p.m. and then have dinner after 10 p.m., while in Poland most restaurants would be closing down at those times. Similarly, lunch in Central Europe would almost certainly include sauerkraut, but little fish compared with the wide variety offered on a typical Spanish menu. Even the propensity for eating out may be a cultural factor. Riley (1994), for example, argues that eating out is not a major part of the UK's social culture. Thus the restaurateur has the added marketing task in the UK of overcoming the barrier of the consumer's home orientation and persuading them that eating out is an enjoyable social activity.

Of course culture goes much further in prescribing and describing the values and beliefs of a society. It influences shopping hours, with many Mediterranean supermarkets open for far longer hours in the evening than some of their Northern European counterparts; the beliefs associated with advertising messages and symbols; the lifestyles of the inhabitants, and the products that are more or less acceptable and available in that culture, for example try purchasing an electric kettle in Spain or Italy.

Culture is thus a very important thing for the marketer to understand, first because marketing can only exist within a culture that is prepared to allow it and support it, and second, it has to act within boundaries set by society and culture. Over the past 10 years or so, it has become more and more socially unacceptable in Europe for organisations to use animals for testing cosmetics. Society has informally rewritten one of the rules, and marketers have had to respond. Changing attitudes to tobacco, alcohol and marketing to children are also examples of areas within which cultural change is altering organisations' approaches to business. In the UK, for example, food marketers have been criticised for aiming too much advertising for products such as sweets, soft drinks, sugary cereals, crisps and fast foods at children. These kinds of product are thought to be of dubious nutritional value, if consumed in excess, and are also thought to be contributing to an increase in dental decay among children.

Any culture can be divided into a number of subcultures each with its own specific characteristics, yet existing within the whole. It depends on the onlooker's perspective just how detailed a division is required. An American exporter might say that Europe represents a culture (as distinct from the US culture), with British, French, German and other national subcultures existing within it. Dealing with the home market, however, a German marketer would define Germany, or increasingly the German-speaking territories of Europe, as the dominant culture, with significant subcultures held within it. These subcultures could be based on ethnic origin (Turkish, Polish, Asian or whatever), religious beliefs, or more lifestyle-orientated groupings, defined by the values and attitudes held. Language may also be an important determinant of subculture. In Switzerland, for example, the three main languages reflect different customs, architecture and even external orientations. The Ticino region (Italian speaking) probably identifies itself more closely with Milan than Zurich or Basle as a point of cultural reference.

Most European countries, however, have distinct subcultures based on ethnic origin. In the Netherlands there are strong immigrant communities from the Far East, especially Indonesia and Indo-China. In the UK, in cities such as Bradford, Leicester and Birmingham there are strong Asian communities with distinctive lifestyles, retailing and service provision and sense of community. Rafiq (1990) found that Asians have had a significant impact on the structure of UK independent retailing, especially where there is a high proportion of Asian residents. This is driven by the desire for specialist provision to serve the particular product needs of the subculture, and also to provide services that are more in tune with the needs of that community. In support of subcultures, some local development agencies, as well as universities or colleges, now support specialist units to help new entrepreneurs from minority communities to get started.

In many ways, the tension within ethnic-based subcultures is between cultural assimilation into the main, dominant culture and the preservation of cultural diversity in language, dress, food, family behaviour etc. This tension can be seen even on a European scale, where increased emphasis on travel, rapid communication and pan-European marketing is slowly breaking down barriers at the same time as there is a strong movement towards the preservation of distinct national and regional identities. For example in the west of Ireland, the Gaelic-speaking regions are being heavily supported to prevent relatively small numbers of people from leaving their rural way of life. As far as the immediate future is concerned, even within a united Europe, people are still celebrating and defending their own cultures and subcultures, and marketers need to recognise and empathise with this. One of the reasons (among many) cited for Eurodisney's poor start was that the organisation had underestimated

MARKETING IN ACTION

Reaching the youth market

Marketers are finding it increasingly difficult to reach and communicate with youth markets. It is felt that the young either cannot be contacted through mainstream media or are too cynical and reject the message even if they receive it. This has understandably caused some frustration among marketers, who know that there is a vast lucrative market out there. Some have tried to cut through the barriers to communication with the so-called 'yob' advertising such as the Great Frog and Harley-Davidson campaigns mentioned elsewhere in this chapter. The underlying message is that the advertiser is trying to say, 'Look, we know that you know that advertising is manipulative glossy rubbish, so why don't we laugh at it together? And by the way, why not buy the product since it's been so honest with you?' This is a dangerous approach which not only stretches the boundaries of taste, decency and ethics in advertising, but also risks alienating a substantial proportion of its audience.

Other marketers have found less controversial ways of addressing the youth market. Both Tango and Guinness have used creative, and largely inoffensive television advertising to create a cult following among the young (although Tango had to tone down the exuberance of its early advertisements to make them acceptable). Others were less successful in making an impact through mainstream advertising and sought alternative methods of communication. In August 1995, for example, the brewer Tennent's organised and supported a rock festival in Glasgow, 'T in the Park'. Tennent's had felt that their target market of 18–24 year olds was too cynical about advertising and

that it would be better to communicate with them through a live event. The 1994 'T in the Park' event had increased Tennent's awareness among its target market from 20 per cent to 82 per cent and thus it was decided to make it an annual event. Similarly, in early 1996, Levi jeans decided to withdraw from terrestrial television advertising in the UK for six months. One of its alternative initiatives was to sponsor a rock band, Northern Uproar, on a tour of 21 universities. The objective was to try to build brand credibility by associating it with 'good times' that the target market could relate to.

These are examples of event marketing, and Tennent's and Levi's are not the only brands to use it. Virgin, primarily with its cola brand in mind, sponsored the V96 music festival in the summer of 1996 featuring a range of big-name bands. Virgin anticipated that the event would attract 40 000 visitors each day and hoped that each one of them would leave with a good feeling about the Virgin brand. Alcoholic drinks are being marketed in similar ways. Whisky, for example, faces a very difficult task, because young people tend to view it as 'something boring that Dad drinks'. Ballantine's, therefore, sponsored a gig by a British band in Paris to try to overcome the prejudices of French youth about whisky. Marketers feel that such events are worth while, as long as the branding is strongly presented and as long as the audience goes away happy, feeling that they have had value for money. There will be more on event marketing in Chapter 20.

Sources: Denny (1995); Marsh and Lee (1996).

French resistance, in particular, to an undiluted all-American cultural concept in the heart of Europe. Europeans are happy, and indeed eager, to experience Disney on US soil as part of 'the American experience', but cannot accept it, it would appear, within their own culture.

Subculture need not only be an ethnic phenomenon, however. The existence of a youth subculture, spanning international boundaries, is widely accepted by marketers, and media such as MTV which reach right across Europe allow marketers to communicate efficiently and cost effectively with that subculture. Brands such as Coca-Cola, Pepsi, and Pepe Jeans can create messages that capitalise on the common concerns, interests and attitudes that define this subculture. Pepe Jeans, for example, developed an advertising campaign aimed at the youth market, using MTV, cinema and youth magazines, which featured suicide and alienation from parents, as a reflection of youth angst, anxiety and antipathy. Pepe's chief executive was quoted by Steen (1995) as saying:

> We simply show a world which youth will recognise as being what is around them, one which the older generation may wish wasn't there. It is to be expected that people outside the 12–20 age group may miss the point or be offended.

The core messages strike at something different from, and perhaps deeper than national or ethnic culture, and thus may have pan-European currency without necessarily becoming bland in the process. That is not to say that all 16–25 year olds across Europe should be stereotyped as belonging to a homogeneous 'yoof market'. What it does say is that there are certain attitudes and feelings with which this age group are likely to sympathise, and that these can therefore be used as a foundation for more targeted communication that manages to celebrate both commonalities and differences.

Reference groups

Reference groups are any groups, whether formally or informally constituted, to which an individual either belongs or aspires to belong, for example professional bodies, social or hobby orientated societies, or informal, vaguely defined lifestyle groups ('I want to be a yuppie'). There are three main types of reference group, each of which affects buying behaviour, and these are discussed in turn below.

Membership groups

These are the groups to which the individual already belongs. These groups provide parameters within which individuals make purchasing decisions, whether they are conscious of it or not. In buying clothing, for example, the purchaser might think about the occasion for which it is going to be worn, and consider whether a particular item is 'suitable'. There is great concern here about what other people will think.

Example

Controversially, some advertising agencies are trying to appeal to a certain type of youth subculture through advertising that is deliberately violent, offensive and shocking. As Alderson and Olins (1995) report, opinion within the advertising world is divided as to whether such approaches are 'crass, crude or brilliant'. Advertising for Harley-Davidson motorcycles, under the slogan 'Harley-Davidson. A completely irresponsible thing to do' showed, in one advertisement, a woman forced to work as a prostitute because her husband had bought a motorcycle, and in another, an elderly man was deprived of an electric wheelchair because his son bought a Harley-Davidson instead. Poster slogans also came in for criticism, such as Great Frog jewellery's 'If you don't like it, fuck off' and Club 18–30's 'Summer of 69'. Those who support such advertising approaches maintain that it simply reflects a mood among the target audience and is therefore acceptable. Those who criticise it, however, maintain that it legitimises unacceptable attitudes and behaviour which marketers should not be endorsing.

Buying clothes for work is severely limited by the norms and expectations imposed by colleagues (a membership group) and bosses (an aspirant group?), as well as by the practicalities of the workplace. Similarly, choosing clothes for a party will be influenced by the predicted impact on the social group who will be present: whether they will be impressed; whether the wearer will fit in; whether the wearer will seem to be overdressed or underdressed, or whether anyone else is likely to turn up in the same outfit.

Thus the influence of membership groups on buying behaviour is to set standards to which individuals can conform, thus consolidating their position as group members. Some individuals, of course, with a strong sense of opinion leadership, will seek to extend those standards by exceeding them and challenging the norms with the expectation that others will follow.

Aspirant groups

These are the groups to which the individual would like to belong, and some of these aspirations are more realistic than others. An amateur athlete or musician might aspire to professional status in their dreams, even if they have little talent. An independent professional single female might aspire to become a full-time housewife with a husband and three children; the housewife might aspire to the career and independent lifestyle. A young, junior manager might aspire to the middle management ranks.

People's desire for change, development and growth in their lives is natural, and marketers frequently exploit this in the positioning of their products and the subtle promises they make. Bird's Eye frozen meals will not stop you being a bored housewife, but will give you a little more independence to 'be yourself'; buying Nike, Reebok or Adidas sports gear will not make you into Jurgen Klinsmann or Eric Cantona, but you can feel a little closer to them; Gold Blend coffee, through its ongoing romantic soap opera style advertising also allows you to indulge aspirational fantasies; Martini lets you pretend to be a suave sophisticated jet-setting James Bond type.

The existence of aspirant groups, therefore, attracts consumers towards products that are strongly associated with those groups and will either make it appear that the buyer actually belongs to the group or signal the individual's aspirations to the wider world.

Dissociative groups

These are groups to which the individual does not want to belong or to be seen to belong. A supporter of the England soccer team would not wish to be associated with its notorious hooligan element, for example. Someone who had a violent aversion to 'yuppies' and their values might avoid buying products that are closely associated with them, through fear of being thought to belong to that group. An upmarket shopper might prefer not to be seen in Aldi or Netto just in case anyone thinks they are penny pinching.

Clearly, these dissociations are closely related to the positive influences of both membership and aspirational groups. They are simply the other side of the coin, an attempt to draw closer to the 'desirable' groups, while differentiating oneself from the 'undesirable'.

Family

The family, whether two parent or single parent, nuclear or extended, with or without dependent children, remains a key influence on the buying behaviour of individuals. The needs of the family affect what can be afforded, where the spending priorities lie, and how a purchasing decision is made. All of this evolves as the family matures and moves through the various stages of its life-cycle. Over time, the structure of a family changes, for example as children grow older and eventually leave home, or as events break up families or create new ones. This means that a family's resources and needs also change over time, and that the marketer must understand and respond to these changes.

Traditionally, marketers have looked to the **family life-cycle** as proposed by Wells and Gubar (1966), and shown in Table 3.3. Over the years, however, this has become less and less appropriate, as it reflects a path through life that is becoming less common in the West. It does not, for example, allow for single-parent families, created either voluntarily or through divorce, or for remarriage after divorce which may create new families with children coming together from previous marriages, and/or second families. Other trends too undermine the assumptions of the traditional model of the family life-cycle. According to Lightfoot and Wavell (1995) estimates from the Office of Population Censuses and Surveys (OPCS) in the UK forecast that 20 per cent of women born in the 1960s, 1970s and 1980s may never have children. Those who do currently elect to have children are tending to leave childbearing until later in their lives, so that they can establish their careers first. OPCS has noted that the birth-rate among women in their twenties has dropped, while it has increased rapidly for women in their thirties and forties. At the other end of the spectrum, the number of single, teenage mothers has increased alarmingly in the UK to 3 per cent of girls aged 15–19, the highest figure in the EU. Overall, however, European birth-rates are falling, leading to 'ageing populations' throughout the EU as the proportion of children in the population falls.

All of these trends have major implications for consumers' needs and wants at various stages in their lives, as well as for their disposable incomes, and this will be explored further in Chapter 5. The marketer cannot make trite assumptions based on traditional stereotypes of the nuclear family, and something more complex than the Wells and Gubar model is needed to properly reflect the various routes people's lives can now take. Figure 3.5 offers a revised family life-cycle for the 1990s and beyond.

Regardless of the structure of the family unit, members of a household can participate in each other's purchasing decision making. In some cases, members may be making decisions that affect the whole family, and thus Fig 3.6 shows how a family can act as a decision-making unit where individual members play different roles in reaching the final decision. The roles that any one member takes on will vary from

TABLE 3.3
The family life-cycle Wells and Gubar (1966)

Stage	Title	Characteristics
1	Bachelor	Young, single, not living at home
2	Newly married	Young, no children
3	Full nest I	Youngest child under 6
4	Full nest II	Youngest child 6 or over
5	Full nest III	Older, married with dependent children
6	Empty nest I	Older married, no children living at home
7	Empty nest II	Older married, retired, no children living at home
8	Solitary survivor I	In labour force
9	Solitary survivor II	Retired

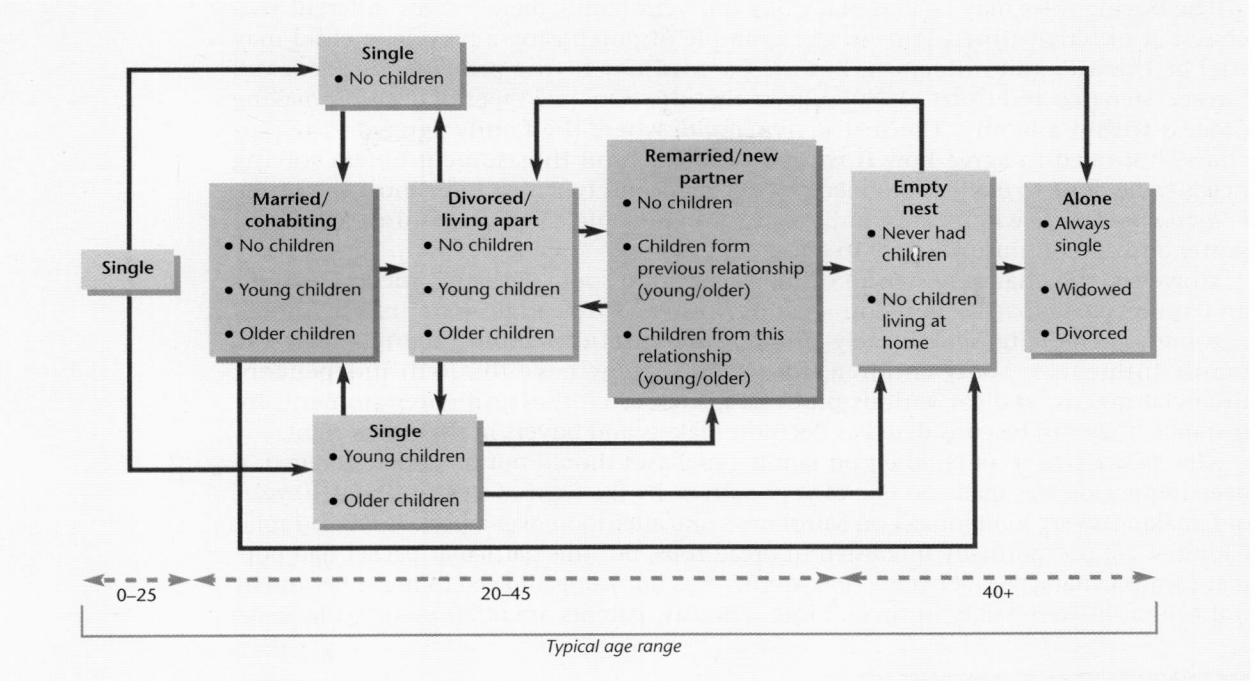

FIGURE 3.5

A family life-cycle model for the 1990s

purchase to purchase, as will the length, complexity and formality of the process. The obvious manifestation of the family decision-making unit is in the ordinary week-to-week grocery shopping. The main shopper is not acting as an individual, pleasing only themselves by their choices, but is reflecting the tastes and requirements of a group of people. In a stereotypical family, Mother may be the ultimate decider and purchaser in the supermarket, but the rest of the family may have acted as initiators ('When you go shopping, will you get me some ...' or 'Do you know that we've run out of ...?' or 'Can we try that new brand of ...?') or influencers ('If you buy THAT, don't expect ME to eat it') either before the shopping trip or at the point of sale.

FIGURE 3.6

The family as a decision-making unit

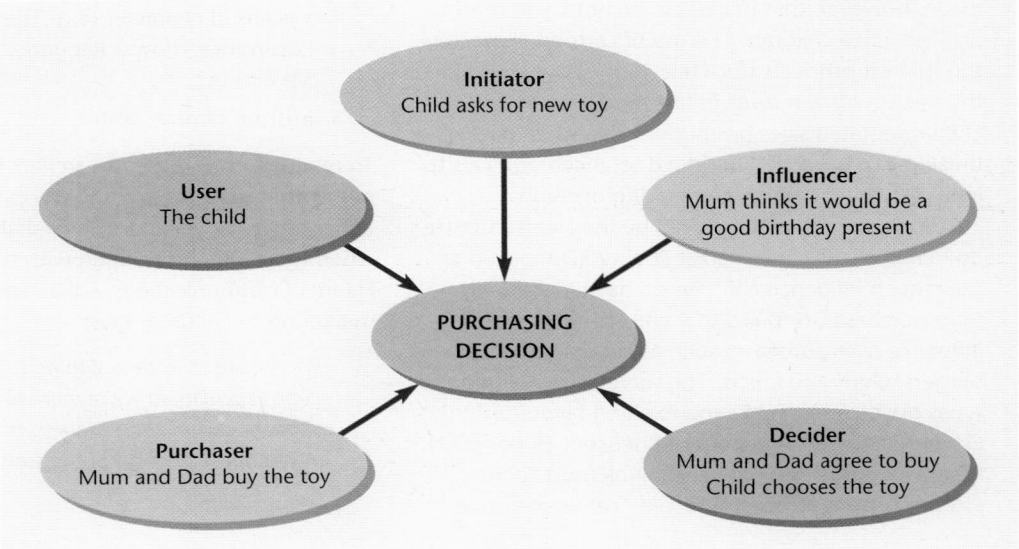

The buying roles may be undertaken by different family members for different purchases at different times. Thus in the example of purchasing a bicycle, a child may well be the user and influencer, but the parents may be the principal deciders and buyers. Menasco and Curry (1989) suggest that there are two types of decision-making process within a family. The first is *consensual*, where the family agree on the purchase, but need to agree how it will be achieved, and thus some problem solving needs to be done to enable it to take place. The second type, felt to be more the norm, is *accommodative*, where the family cannot agree, and thus bargaining, coercion, power and compromise are used to effect a result.

However, the changing nature of many families, some with two income earners and more participative decision making, others with single parents on limited incomes, is challenging relatively simple generalisations about buying habits and family influences. Many children, for example, now have (limited) independent financial means, and for various purchases, such as clothes and entertainment, for instance, they can be considered as decision makers and buyers in their own right.

The 'pester power' of children on family purchases should not be underestimated. A deep impression was made on one of your authors by the sight of a child, about 10 years old, making a very loud impact on Sainsbury's one afternoon over a packet of bread rolls. Children are not normally interested in bread rolls, but this particular packet had popular cartoon characters all over it, and Mother was not being allowed to move her trolley until the rolls were safely in there. More seriously, parents are often prepared to make

MARKETING IN ACTION

Pester power

Those of us who were brought up in the UK during the 1960s remember with affection a television advertisement that had us all chanting, 'Don't Forget the Fruit Gums, Mum'. That is pester power. Since then, the Advertising Code of Practice has been tightened to prevent advertisers from directly encouraging children to ask for things. Fruit Gums cleaned up their act by changing their advertisement to 'Don't Forget the Fruit Gums, chum'. This does not mean, however, that marketers do not try to reach and influence children. The use of cartoon characters, the spin-off products from television shows and films, the free toys given away in fast-food outlets, and the child-orientated sales promotions in and on packets of breakfast cereal are all designed to encourage kids to influence their parents' purchasing decisions.

A survey conducted in 1993 by the Henley Centre on behalf of the supermarket chain ASDA looked at how much influence children do have over family food purchases. It found that children had most influence over purchases such as chocolate, pizza, burgers, chips and crisps. The survey also defined five types of children. 'Fussy and fixed on favourites' (19 per cent); 'strong-willed influencers' (8 per cent); 'gimmick gurus' (26 per cent); 'junk food fiends' (15 per cent), and 'well adjusted "eat what you're

given' (32 per cent). The last category is predicted to be on the decline, while the other four are either stable or increasing in numbers. The Family Market Research Panel suggests that the five biggest influences on pester power at the point of sale are:

1 the child's recall of television advertising;

2 a free promotional gift;

3 attractive packaging;

4 a licensed character (e.g. The Lion King, Pocahontas, Power Rangers, Mickey Mouse or Mr Blobby);

5 in-store samples to try.

To reinforce this, other researchers have found that 74 per cent of mothers find that shopping becomes either much more expensive or slightly more expensive when they take the children with them. As the PR firm Handel Communications, which specialises in marketing to children, says:

'We Brits tend to do anything to avoid causing a scene in public, so we're more likely to give our kids what they want than argue it through with them. A lot of bribing goes on in the supermarket'.

Source: Dwek (1995).

great sacrifices in other areas of the family budget and their own individual spending in order to prioritise children's needs and wants, as suggested at p. 116 above.

Children are an important target group for the marketer, partly because of children's ability to pester their parents and influence family purchasing, and partly because of the marketer's desire to create brand loyalty as early as possible in consumers' lives. Burke (1995) highlighted the fact that marketers are trying to reach children aged between five and 12 through schools, by sponsoring educational packages on the Internet, providing teaching aids and materials, or by the direct distribution of product samples. Kellogg's, for example, gave away 800 000 sample packs of Coco Pops, while McDonald's provide free meal vouchers to be used as prizes. Not surprisingly, many teachers, parents and consumer groups are concerned that the young and vulnerable may be exposed to unreasonable marketing pressures.

The wider family also affects the individual's purchasing in the same way as other reference groups do, with the same anxieties about conformity, approval, acceptance and opinion leadership.

Clearly, groups of all kinds have the potential to act as both facilitators and inhibitors of consumer behaviour. An aspiration to join a particular group might make a purchasing decision easier, if the marketing package clearly reflects that aspiration, while membership of an economically interdependent household might mean that, regretfully, a purchase cannot be justified. For each purchase, the individual has to decide which group's influence is the strongest or most important and act accordingly.

CHAPTER SUMMARY

This chapter has centred on consumer buying behaviour, in terms of both the processes potential buyers pass through in deciding whether to make a purchase and which product to choose, and the factors which influence the decision making itself.

The decision-making process was presented as a number of stages: problem recognition, information search, information evaluation, decision, and finally, post-purchase evaluation. The length of time taken over the process as a whole or over individual stages will vary according to the type of product purchased and the particular consumer concerned. An experienced buyer with past knowledge of the market making a low-risk, low-priced routine purchase will pass through the decision-making process very quickly, almost without realising it has happened. This is a routine problem-solving situation. In contrast, a nervous buyer, lacking knowledge but facing the purchase of a one-off high risk, expensive purchase will prolong the process and consciously seek and analyse information to aid the decision. This is extended problem solving. Decision making is influenced by many factors apart from the type of purchase. Some of these factors are external to the consumer, such as social, economic, legal and technological issues existing within the wider environment

Closer to home, the consumer influences the decision-making process through psychological factors. The type of personality involved; the individual's perceptions of the world and ability to interpret information; the ability to retain and learn from both experience and marketing communication; the driving motivations behind behaviour and finally the individual's attitudes and beliefs all shape their responses to the marketing offering and ultimately their acceptance or rejection of it. In addition to that, the individual's choices and behaviour are affected by sociocultural influences defined by the groups to which the individual either belongs or wishes to belong. Social class as traditionally defined is of limited help to the marketer, but cultural or subcultural groups provide clearly differentiated groups of potential customers. Other membership groups, formed through work, hobbies and leisure pursuits, provide the individual with norms which act as reference points to aid decision making. Similarly, aspirations fuel people's needs and wants, and thus marketers can attract customers through reflecting those dreams and promising products that can help fulfil them or at least visibly associate the individual with the aspirant group for a while. One of the strongest group influences comes from the family, affecting decisions on what is purchased, how that decision is made and how the individual feels about that purchase.

Consumer buying behaviour is a complex area, covering a wide range of concepts, but nevertheless, is an important one for marketers to understand because it lies at the heart of all marketing decisions.

Key words and phrases

Attitude	*Family life-cycle*	*Problem recognition*
Awareness	*Information overload*	*Purchasing situation*
Cognitive dissonance	*Learning*	*Reference groups*
Consumer decision making	*Limited problem solving*	*Repeat purchase*
Culture	*Motivation*	*Routine problem solving*
Evoked set	*Perception*	*Social class*
Extended problem solving	*Personality*	*Trial*
	Post-purchase evaluation	

QUESTIONS FOR REVIEW

3.1 What are the main stages of the consumer buying decision-making process?

3.2 Differentiate between the internal and external stimuli that might trigger the buying process.

3.3 What are the potential sources of information that a consumer might use in the buying process?

3.4 Why is post-purchase evaluation important for:

(a) the consumer; and
(b) the marketer?

3.5 Summarise some of the ways in which marketers can 'help' the consumer at each stage in the decision-making process.

3.6 What are the three different types of buying situation and what kinds of products might be included in each of them?

3.7 How and why might the duration of the decision-making process and the extent of information search differ between the three different types of buying situation?

3.8 How do perception and learning affect consumer decision-making, and how can the marketer influence these processes?

3.9 What is an attitude and why are attitudes so difficult to change?

3.10 Summarise the stages of Maslow's hierarchy of needs and their marketing implications.

QUESTIONS FOR DISCUSSION

3.1 Outline the main sources of information that might be used in purchasing

(a) a new car; and
(b) a packet of biscuits.

3.2 Think of a purchase that you have made recently. What products or brands made up your evoked set of alternatives, and what choice criteria did you use to differentiate between them to lead to your eventual purchase?

3.3 To what extent do you think that social class is a helpful concept in improving the marketer's understanding of consumer behaviour?

3.4 Define the three main types of reference group. Within each type, think of examples that relate to you as a consumer, and analyse how this might affect your own buying behaviour.

3.5 How might the roles undertaken by various members of a two-parent family vary between the buying decisions for:

(a) a house;
(b) something for tonight's dinner; and
(c) a birthday present for a 10-year-old child?

How would your answer change if it was a one-parent family?

Madame Tussaud's Rock Circus

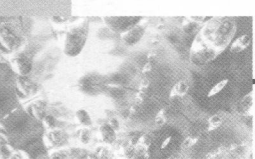

Rock Circus, first opened in 1989, is an exciting extension of the traditional Madame Tussaud's waxworks concept. Sited in London, it provides visitors with a multisensory experience on the theme of 40 years of rock and pop music and is partly a show and partly an exhibition. Its displays include pop memorabilia, more than 50 static and moving figures of rock stars, and 3D handcasts in metal from actual artists which visitors can touch. There is also a 20-minute show with moving performing figures in a huge revolving auditorium. Additionally, a video wall and television monitors show archive footage. To involve visitors further, they have their own stereo headphones activated by infra-red beams as they move through the displays. Typically, it takes visitors about 90 minutes to see and experience it all, and the opening hours extend from late morning well into the evening, seven days a week.

Between 1989 and 1992, Rock Circus attracted a steady 500 000 visitors a year, but management felt that it could achieve more. It was being marketed as 'The Greatest Rock Show in the World', which did not cover the exhibition element, and 'History of Rock' which gave it a traditional, potentially stuffy, museum image. In 1993, therefore, management decided to put more emphasis on its fun, entertainment, and multisensory aspects. Thus in 1993 it was presented as 'Britain's Number One Rock Attraction' and 'Where the Spirit of Rock Speaks to You, Sings to You, Plays for You, Moves and Touches You'. In addition, publicity was generated internationally through the endorsement of artists such as Jon Bon Jovi and Gloria Estefan who gave press conferences at the unveiling of their figures. Joint promotions were undertaken with Virgin Megastores in the West End, and advertisements were displayed on the central London tube network. All this meant that Rock Circus attracted 682, 000 visitors in 1993.

In 1994 there was further refinement of the marketing concept, with Rock Circus now becoming 'The World's Number One Rock Attraction'. Advertising was concentrated on the West End, and there were several events, such as the Annual Music Industry Silver Clef Awards to generate publicity and to reinforce the links between the music industry and Rock Circus. Visitor figures in 1994 rose to 692 000 while it was estimated that 725 000 would visit in 1995.

A survey undertaken in 1993 revealed the following customer profile:

Age group	%
12–15	10
16–24	42
25–34	25
35–44	16
45+	7

Sixty-five per cent of customers were European; 70 per cent visited as individuals, and 30 per cent as organised groups of 10 or more.

Adapted from a case prepared by Jean Lafferty.

Questions

1 Outline how the buyer decision-making process might work for a leisure attraction such as Rock Circus.

2 Why did Rock Circus change its marketing communications messages in 1993 and why was this important to the buyer's decision-making process?

3 What kind of buying situation is this, and what are the implications for the marketer?

4 In terms of individual and sociocultural influences, how would you broadly explain the customer profile presented here?

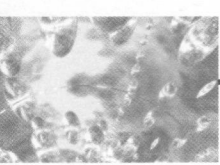

Premium lagers

The shape of the lager and beer markets has changed as drinkers have become increasingly discerning in the brands that they choose. Although people now generally drink less, they are prepared to spend more and the brewers have realised that quality rather than sheer quantity is what a significant segment of the market wants. The competition is fierce, however, as many brewers, both large and small, try to develop brands with European or even global appeal. In the UK alone, the take-home premium lager market is worth over £620 mn and has shown significant growth, although it is beginning to plateau. There are over 400 brands available in the UK although most cannot afford the marketing support to ensure their survival. Matthew Clark Taunton, for example, spent £7 mn marketing its Miller Genuine Draft brand in 1996, while Scottish Courage also spent £7 mn on Kronenbourg 1664 and £16 mn on Holsten Pils. Moctezuma, the Mexican brewer, spent £2.5 mn in the UK in 1995 on its Sol brand, and in 1996, spent £6 mn on a pan-European cinema and poster campaign. Other major brands include Carlsberg, Heineken, Foster's, Becks, Coors and Budweiser.

The market leader in the UK is Stella Artois, a Belgian premium lager owned by the Belgian company Interbrew, but brewed and marketed under licence in the UK by Whitbread. Stella holds about 30 per cent of the UK market, and prides itself on being 'reassuringly expensive'. Other brands are targeting Stella's position, however. A spokesman for Scottish Courage was quoted as saying:

> 'Everything we do on 1664 is designed to give it the most premium of credentials so it sits well alongside Stella Artois'.

A further insight into buyer behaviour in the market from Scottish Courage is that

> 'Consumers are trying to buy into an image. There is an element of taste, but in blind tests consumers find it difficult to tell the difference between brands.'

Many lager drinkers, consciously or not, regard their choice of brand as making some kind of lifestyle statement about themselves. Some will choose a brand because that is what their friends buy, while others will seek out less well-known brands in order to be seen to be different from the crowd. This means that there is room in the market for brands with origins slightly more exotic than Germany, Belgium, or the USA, such as Sol (Mexico), Bajan (Barbados) and Kirin (Japan).

To inject fresh interest into the more mass market established brands, such as Carlsberg and Foster's, 'ice brewed' variants have been introduced. By spring 1996, the ice beer market in the UK was worth £120 mn and was showing 195 per cent year on year growth. Some brewers had held back from this market, unsure whether or not it was a passing fad, allowing Foster's Ice (Scottish Courage) to develop a comfortable 56 per cent share of the sector. In July 1996, however, Anheuser-Busch concluded from its research that the ice beer market did have a long-term future, and thus gave Bud Ice, an extension of the Budweiser brand, a £3 mn launch.

The premium lager market does face threats, however, and not just from internal rivalry between lager brands. Premium ciders are attracting the attention of those who feel that lager is no longer fashionable, and alcoholic lemonades and colas appeal to younger drinkers. The spirits sector has fought back too. Smirnoff Mule, a mixture of vodka, ginger and lime, for example, was launched in April 1996. It is aimed at the male premium lager drinker aged between 20 and 24. Some of the lager companies are experimenting too. Whitbread announced in May 1996 that it was about to test two new products: Kentucky Black (beer containing a shot of bourbon) and Arkansas (beer with a shot of vodka).

Sources: Marketing (1996); Marshall (1996a); Marshall (1996b); Oram (1995); Palmer (1996).

Questions

1 Where does premium lager fit on Maslow's hierarchy of needs and why?

2 Why do you think that the premium lager market is primarily aimed at males aged between 20 and 40?

3 What individual and group influences are likely to affect someone's choice of lager brand?

4 Given the huge range of lagers available, why do you think there is still room for premium ciders and products such as Smirnoff Mule?

REFERENCES FOR CHAPTER 3

Alderson, A. and Olins, R. (1995), 'Yob Commercials Split Ad Agencies', *Sunday Times,* 16 April 1995.

Bainbridge, J. (1996), 'Image Makeover for Stronger 90s Women', *Marketing,* 25 April 1996, p. 7.

Bloch, P. H. *et al.* (1986), 'Consumer Search: An Extended Framework', *Journal of Consumer Research,* 13 (Jun), pp. 119–26.

Brinkworth, L. (1993), 'Housewives Ad Nauseam', *Sunday Times Style and Travel Section*, 28 November 1993, pp. 12–13.

Bruner, G. C. and Pomazal, R. J. (1988), 'Problem Recognition: The Crucial First Stage of the Consumer Decision Process', *Journal of Consumer Marketing,* 5(1), pp. 53–63.

Burke, J. (1995), 'Food Firms Pester Pupils for Sales', *Sunday Times*, 11 June 1995.

Chisnall, P. M. (1985), *Marketing: A Behavioural Analysis*, McGraw-Hill.

Denny, N. (1995), 'Tennent's Taps Into Youth Through Music', *Marketing,* 17 August 1995, p. 12.

Duncan, C. P. (1990), 'Consumer Market Beliefs: A Review of the Literature and an Agenda for Further Research' in G. Marrin *et al.* (eds.), *Advances in Consumer Research*, Association for Consumer Research.

Dwek, R. (1995), 'In Front of the Children', *The Grocer*, 2 December 1995, pp. 45–49.

Ehrenberg, A. S. C. and Goodhart, G. J. (1980), *How Advertising Works*, JWT/MRCA.

Engel, J. F., Blackwell, R. D. and Miniard, P. W. (1990), *Consumer Behaviour*, Dryden.

Engel, J. F., Kollat, D. T. and Blackwell, R. D. (1978), *Consumer Behaviour*, Dryden.

Festinger, L. (1957), *A Theory of Cognitive Dissonance*, Stanford University Press.

Fishbein, M. (1967), 'Attitude and Prediction of Behaviour' in M. Fishbein (ed.), *Readings in Attitude Theory and Measurement*, Wiley.

Fishbein, M. (1975), 'Attitude, Attitude Change and Behaviour: A Theoretical Overview', in P. Levine (ed.) *Attitude Research Bridges the Atlantic*, Chicago: American Marketing Association.

Foxall, G. (1984), 'Consumers' Intentions and Behaviour', *Journal of the Market Research Society*, 26, 231–41.

Hilgard, E. R. *et al.* (1975), *Introduction to Psychology*, (6th edn.) Harcourt Brace Jovanovich.

Hilgard, E. R. and Marquis, D. G. (1961), *Conditioning and Learning*, Appleton Century Crofts.

Howard, J. A. and Sheth, J. N. (1969), *The Theory of Buyer Behaviour*, Wiley.

Inskip, I. (1995), 'Marketers Develop a Class Consciousness', *Marketing Week*, 13 January p. 23.

Jacoby, J. *et al.* (1974), 'Brand Choice as a Function of Information Load', *Journal of Marketing Research*, 11 (Feb), pp. 63–9.

Joyce, T. (1967), 'What do We Know About How Advertising Works?', *Advertising Age*, May/June.

Kassarjian, H. H. (1971), 'Personality and Consumer Behaviour: A Review', *Journal of Marketing Research*, 8 (Nov.), pp. 409–18.

Keller, K. L. and Staelin, R. (1987), 'Effects of Quality and Quantity of Information on Decision Effectiveness', *Journal of Consumer Research*, 14 (Sept.), pp. 200–13.

Lightfoot, L. and Wavell, S. (1995), 'Mum's Not the Word', *Sunday Times*, 16 April 1995.

Lutz, R. J. (1981), 'The Role of Attitude Theory in Marketing', in H. K. Kassarjian and T. S. Robertson (eds.), *Perspectives in Consumer Behaviour*, Scott, Foresman.

Marketing (1996), 'Bud Ice Set for £3m UK Launch', *Marketing*, 30 May, p. 9.

Marsh, H. and Lee, J. (1996), 'Let Good Times Roll to Reach Youth Market', *Marketing*, 16 May, p. 10.

Marshall, S. (1996a), 'New Image for Sol Survivor', *Marketing*, 18 April 1996, p. 10.

Marshall, S. (1996b), 'Whitbread Puts Beer and Spirits Drinks on Trial', *Marketing*, 23 May 1996, p. 1.

Maslow, A. H. (1954), *Motivation and Personality*, Harper and Row.

Menasco, M. B. and Curry, D. J. (1989), 'Utility and Choice: An Empirical Study of Wife/Husband Decision Making', *Journal of Consumer Research*, 16 (June), pp. 87–97.

Murphy, Y. and Bray, L. (1996), 'Savouring the Moment', *The Grocer*, 1 June, pp. 29–33.

Oram, R. (1995), 'Reassuringly Expansive', *Financial Times*, 20 January, p. 17.

Palmer, T. (1996), 'More Cash for Brands', *The Grocer*, 13 April , pp. 31–32.

Rafiq, M. (1990), *Are Asians Taking Over British Retailing?*, Paper 1990:12, Loughborough University Management Research Series.

Rice, C. (1993), *Consumer Behaviour: Behavioural Aspects of Marketing*, Butterworth-Heinemann.

Riley, M. (1994), 'Marketing Eating Out: The Influence of Social Culture and Innovation', *British Food Journal*, 96 (10), pp. 15–18.

Smith, P. R. (1993), *Marketing Communications: An Integrated Approach*, Kogan Page.

Steen, J. (1995), 'Now They're Using Suicide to Sell Jeans', *Sunday Express*, 26 March 1995.

Sutton, R. J. (1987), 'Using Empirical Data to Investigate the Likelihood of Brands Being Admitted or Readmitted into an Established Evoked Set', *Journal of the Academy of Marketing Science*, 15 (Fall), p. 82.

Wells, W. D. and Gubar, R. G. (1966), 'Life Cycle Concepts in Marketing Research', *Journal of Marketing Research*, 3 (Nov.), pp. 355–63.

Williams, K. C. (1981), *Behavioural Aspects of Marketing*, Heinemann Professional Publishing.

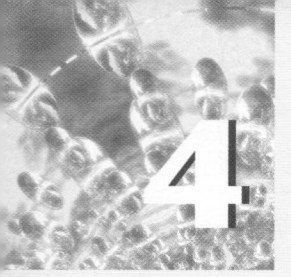

4 Organisational Buying Behaviour

LEARNING OBJECTIVES

This chapter will help you to:

1 understand the nature and structure of organisational buying;

2 appreciate the differences between organisational and consumer buying;

3 analyse the reasons why purchasing varies across different buying situations; and

4 link organisational buying with the development of marketing strategy.

INTRODUCTION

The essence of the marketing philosophy was described at the beginning of this book as the satisfaction of customers' needs and wants through the provision of the right products and services, at the right time, in the right place at the right price. This remains true whether that customer is an individual or an organisation. All organisations, whether making products or delivering services, purchase goods and services from a range of suppliers so that they can run their own operations. Consider, for example, a small local garage. It may purchase not only petrol, but also spare parts, tools, supplies, some capital machinery, confectionery, and accountancy services, for instance. Compare that with a large steel producer or car assembly plant and the thousands of suppliers that are dealt with regularly. There are, therefore, sufficient differences between individuals and organisations in what they purchase and the ways in which they go about their purchasing to make separate consideration worth while.

This chapter, therefore, looks at the special characteristics and problems of organisational markets, beginning with a definition of organisational marketing and a classification of organisational customers. The characteristics of organisational markets are then discussed, and attention is given to the ways in which they differ from consumer markets. The buying decision-making process is analysed, laying the foundations for looking at the roles that individuals and groups play within it. The last two sections examine the criteria, both economic and non-economic, which affect organisational purchasing and the importance of long lasting buyer-seller relationships.

In your wider reading you may come across the terms *business to business marketing* and *industrial marketing*. Generally speaking, these terms are often used interchangeably with 'organisational marketing'. This text, however, uses the term organisational marketing as a constant reminder that not all organisations that make substantial purchases, for example government departments, universities and hospitals, are in business in the profit-making sense of the word, nor are they in industry in the narrow manufacturing sense. Thus, as pp. 129 *et seq.* will show, the term organisational marketing covers a wide range of purchasing relationships between a wide range of organisations without excluding or indeed offending any one of them. First, however, it is important to define more precisely what organisational marketing is.

DEFINING ORGANISATIONAL MARKETING

Organisational marketing is the management process responsible for the facilitation of exchange between producers of goods and services and their organisational customers. This might involve, for example, a clothing manufacturer selling uniforms to the army, a component manufacturer selling microchips to IBM, an advertising agency selling its expertise to Kellogg's, Kellogg's selling its breakfast cereals to a large supermarket chain, or a university selling short management training courses to local firms. Whatever the type of product or organisation, the focus is the same, centred on the exchange, the flow of goods and services that enable other organisations to operate, produce, add value and/or re-sell. Figure 4.1, even though it only offers a simplified view of this flow, gives an idea of the number and complexity of exchanges involved in getting products to the end user or consumer.

The steel producer, for example, takes raw materials (and we will not even begin to consider the mining, refining and transport processes that go into the production of the iron ore and coke that the steel producer buys), and turns them into steel which is then pressed into panels or cast into components to sell on. The car producer can then

FIGURE 4.1

Flows within an organisational market

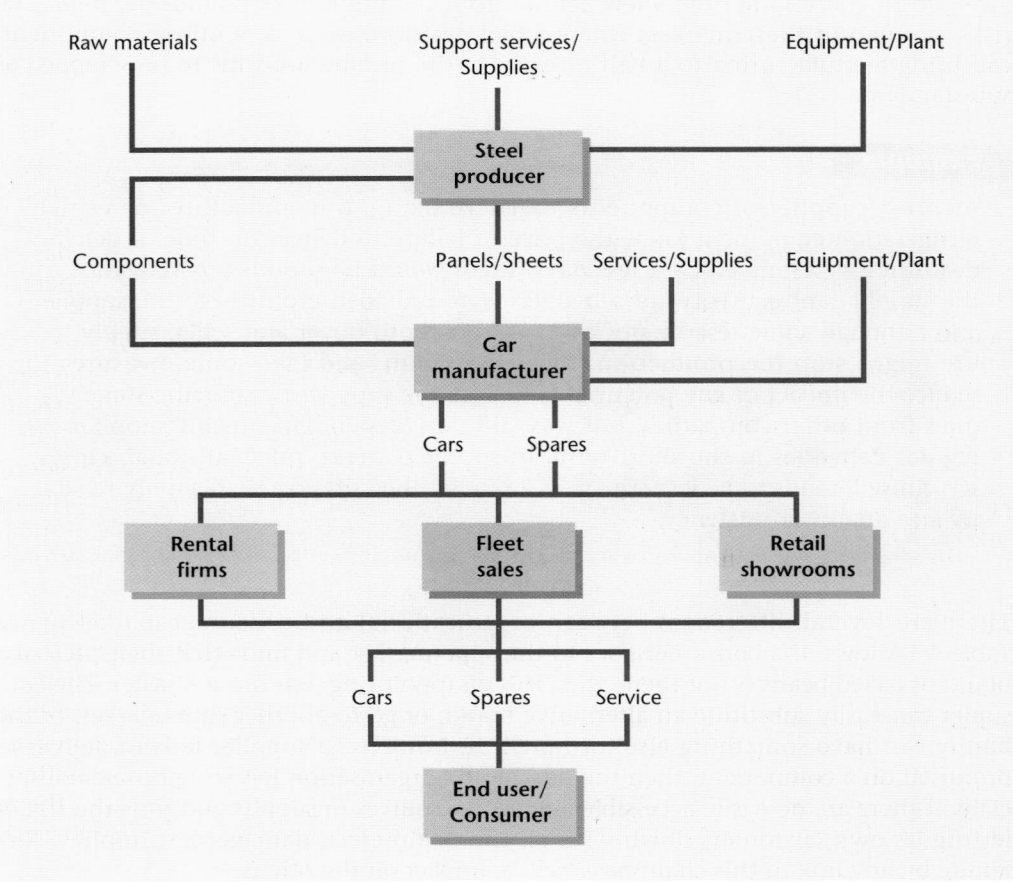

assemble these components, along with others from different sources (glass, plastics, paints, fabrics, tyres, electrics etc.), with the finished car as the output to be sold on.

Both the steel producer and the car manufacturer use more than just the components and raw materials that make the physical product, however. Both of them also buy in various services and supplies which support the main production without directly providing a physical part of it. For example, proper planned maintenance of plant and machinery is essential for safe and consistent production. The steel producer will perhaps use contract engineering service companies to do this work and would consider it as contributing indirectly to the end product. Similarly, the supplies and services used by the quality control function or the managers and administrators that keep a smooth flow of goods and orders in and out of the organisation support the end product indirectly. Thus an organisation may have to purchase not only raw materials and semi-finished goods, but also financial, technical and management consultancy services.

Once the cars or the spares leave the car manufacturer, the retail showroom, i.e. the car dealership, as a *re-seller*, takes the products and sells them to the general public with little change other than perhaps the addition of number plates and fine tuning of the engine. Most of the *value added* comes from intangible elements of customer service.

Even at the re-seller level, there are also other support services to consider. A car dealership selling to the general public, for instance, would put a lot of thought into the design and ambience of the showroom, the training of its sales and service staff and its advertising and other promotional activities. All these services can be bought in and add to the successful sale of the physical product.

All of this goes to show that organisational marketing and purchasing is a complex and risky business. An organisation may buy many thousands of products and services, costing anything from a few pennies to many millions of pounds per item. The risks are high in these markets where a bad decision, even on a minor component, can bring manufacturing to a halt or cause entire production runs to be scrapped as sub-standard.

Example

An Irish supplier of components to Thermoking, a manufacturer of vehicle refrigeration equipment knew the price of failure to deliver on time. If delivery deadlines were missed by a few days, there would be serious repercussions for the supply contract. Forward schedules were provided monthly to the supplier, and although some reserve stock was held by both buyer and seller, supply failure might stop the production line. Thermoking did take some measures to reduce the impact of any potential failure by the supplier by sourcing some supplies from other companies, but was still very dependent on this supplier for regular deliveries in the short term. In such a context, price, although closely scrutinised, tends to be less critical as a purchasing criterion than supply reliability and quality consistency.

There are several differences between organisational and consumer marketing, as Table 4.1 shows. If a consumer goes to the supermarket and finds that their preferred brand of baked beans is not there, then it is disappointing, but not a disaster. The consumer can easily substitute an alternative brand, or go to another supermarket, or the family can have something else for lunch. If, however, a supplier fails to deliver as promised on a component, then the purchasing organisation has a big problem, especially if there are no easily accessible alternative sources of supply, and runs the risk of letting its own customers down with all the commercial damage that implies. Any failure by any link in this chain has a severe impact on the others.

TABLE 4.1

Differences between organisational and consumer marketing

Organisational customers often/usually ...	Consumer customers often/usually ...
• purchase goods and services that meet specific business needs	• purchase goods and services to meet individual or family needs
• need emphasis on economic benefits	• need emphasis on psychological benefits
• use formalised, lengthy purchasing policies and processes	• buy on impulse or with minimal processes
• involve large groups in purchasing decisions	• purchase as individuals or as a family unit
• buy large quantities, and buy infrequently	• buy small quantities and buy frequently
• want a customised product package	• are content with a standardised product package targeted at a specific market segment
• experience major problems if supply fails	• experience minor irritation if supply fails
• find switching to another supplier difficult	• find switching to another supplier easy
• negotiate on price	• accept the stated price
• purchase direct from suppliers	• purchase from intermediaries
• justify an emphasis on personal selling	• justify an emphasis on mass media communication

Thus the links have to be forged carefully, and relationships *managed* over time to minimise the potential problems or to diagnose them early enough for action to be taken. Policy decisions have to made about purchasing, for example whether to source from one supplier only (**single sourcing**) or from several suppliers (**multiple sourcing**), and how the purchasing process should operate (who is authorised to do what and with what safeguards). All these issues will be addressed later in this chapter.

A final reminder of the volume and variety of organisational buyer–seller relationships is provided in Fig 4.2, which shows in detail the wide range of goods and services essential to a clothing manufacturer. All these goods and services represent relationships which have to be established, maintained and sustained.

ORGANISATIONAL CUSTOMERS

So far, only one kind of organisational buying situation has been considered in detail, that of a profit-making organisation involved in transactions with other similarly orientated concerns. There are, however, other kinds of organisation which have different philosophies and approaches to purchasing. Overall, there are three main classes: commercial enterprises, government bodies and institutions, each of which represents a lot of buying power.

Commercial enterprises

Commercial enterprises consist of profit-making organisations which produce and/or re-sell goods and services for a profit. All the members of the flow shown in Fig 4.1 fall into this category, which can be further divided into a number of subgroups, as follows:

Users

Users purchase goods and services to facilitate their own production, although the item purchased does not enter directly into the finished product. Examples of this are things like CAD/CAM systems, office equipment and management consultancy services. Large chemical and steel process manufacturing plants may source a wide range

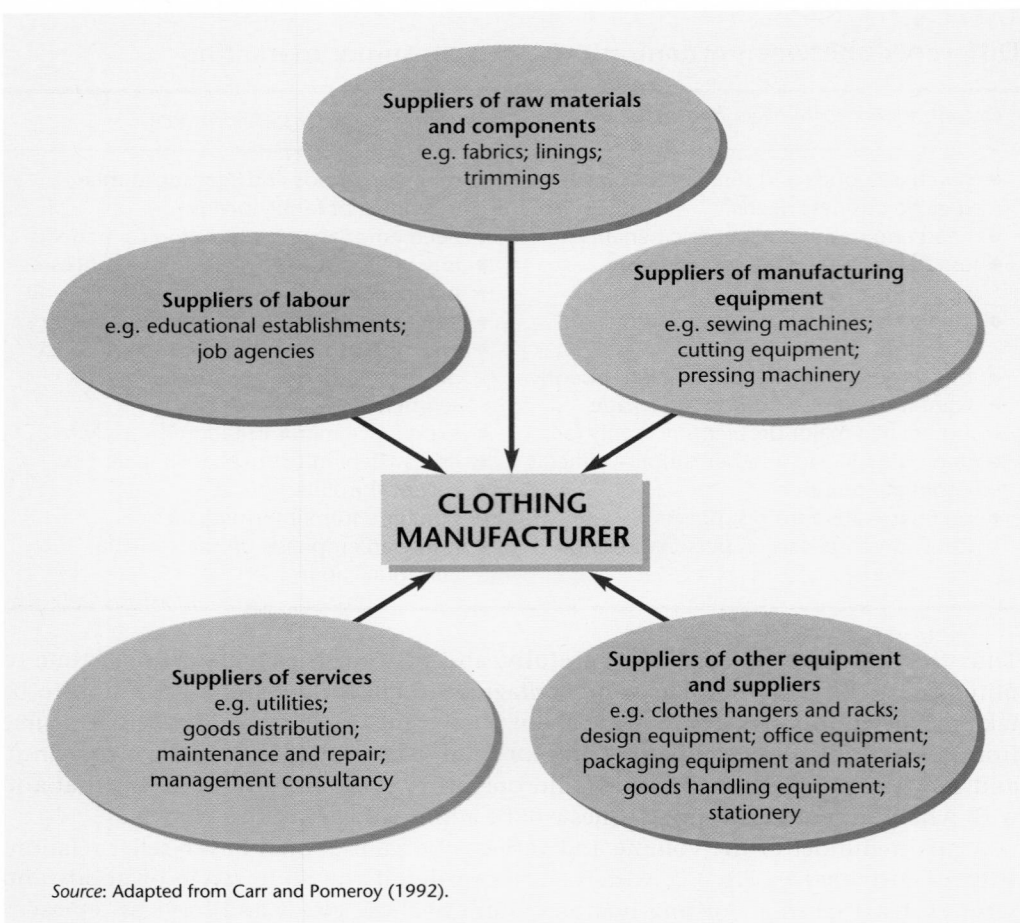

FIGURE 4.2

A clothing
manufacturer
and its suppliers

Source: Adapted from Carr and Pomeroy (1992).

of services from a myriad of local, and often small, suppliers. Plumbers, cleaners, caterers and travel agents thus supply services that are an indirect means to an end rather than a direct influence on production. Although some vetting and inspection may take place before these suppliers are allowed on to the list of approved suppliers, these procedures are far less rigorous than those imposed on companies wishing to supply goods and materials that do directly enter or support the production process.

Original Equipment Manufacturers

Original Equipment Manufacturers (OEMs) incorporate their purchases into their own product, as the car manufacturer does with the electrics, fabrics, plastics, paint, tyres etc. Some of these components will be recognisable even after the OEM has finished with them, for instance a tyre is a recognisable element of a car and is usually strongly branded by the original supplier, whereas others, such as the paint, are incorporated anonymously. Recognisability is important for the tyre manufacturer as a means of developing links with the end consumer and encouraging brand loyalty when it is time to buy new tyres. OEMs' purchasing is very closely linked with forecast demand for their end products, and needs good buyer–seller co-ordination as it has to be tied in with production schedules.

Re-sellers

Re-sellers purchase goods for re-sale, usually making no physical changes to the goods. As mentioned above when discussing the car dealership, the value added stems largely from service elements. A full outline of the role and function of re-sellers can be found in Part V of this book. This group is the closest to the end consumer of the product and should, therefore, be able to feed valuable information back up the chain on what the end market really wants.

Government bodies

Government bodies are very large, important purchasers of goods and services. Within the EU in 1991, for example, public purchasing accounted for 15 per cent of total GDP. In 1992/93, the UK's Ministry of Defence spent some £10.3 mn on defence equipment, spread throughout the international defence industry.

This group of organisational buyers includes both local and national government, as well as EU Commission·purchasing. The range of purchasing is wide, from office supplies to public buildings, from army bootlaces to battleships, from airline tickets to motorways, from refuse collection to management consultancy. Although some purchases may be very large, expensive and high profile, involving international suppliers, as is often seen in defence procurement, others are much more mundane and routine, and involve very little public concern.

Because of the traditional bureaucracy and public accountability surrounding government sector purchasing, there are specialised purchasing procedures which are often more explicit and formal than those found in many commercial organisations. Such a procedure might be:

The development of precise specifications for the good or service

For more innovative and large-scale projects, the development of specifications may be done in conjunction with specialist consultants and the potential suppliers' development personnel.

Tendering for the right to supply

Organisations are requested to bid or tender for the right to supply. Some jobs are only open to tender from organisations already on an approved list while others are open to anyone.

Assessment of tenders

The submitted tenders are assessed, and the winning one is chosen.

Tendering is a very competitive process which demands that the suppliers are well tuned into the procedures and are able to find out early what tenders are on offer. Much of this is down to having the right contacts within the purchasing organisation and maintaining good relationships and communication links with them (within ethical boundaries, of course). These issues of buyer–seller relationships are expanded further at p. 142 and pp. 157 *et seq.* It is often too late to establish contact once formal bidding has begun. The contact and reputation building necessary for next year's bids needs to be done this year.

The EU, as part of the single European market (SEM) initiative issued a Public Services Directive stating that for any of its purchasing needs of 200 000 ECU (five mn ECU for construction bids) or more, the contract must be advertised openly for tender across all community boundaries. The final selection must be made on objective, non-discriminatory criteria within defined European standards.

Example

A good example of the political and economic implications of governments' purchasing decisions was highlighted by the UK Ministry of Defence's decision not to place an order for a naval helicopter carrier with Swan Hunter, a shipyard in Tyne & Wear. The grounds for the government's decision were allegedly based on normal technical and value for money criteria, according to the Defence Procurement Minister. However, as a result of the loss of this order, 2200 jobs were put under threat at the yard, and a further 3500 jobs were at risk in associated industries. There was a large public outcry about the impact of job losses on an area which at the time already had a 29 per cent unemployment level.

Institutions

This group includes (largely) non-profit-making organisations such as universities, churches, and independent schools. These institutions may have an element of government funding, but in purchasing terms, they are autonomous. They are likely to follow some of the same procedures as government bodies, but with a greater degree of flexibility of choice. A university, for example, has to purchase a wide range of products and services in order to teach and undertake research and consultancy. Large capital projects, such as a new lecture theatre, perhaps part financed by government, may be subject to tendering and closed bidding (i.e. a potential supplier makes a bid without knowing what price anyone else has quoted). Many other supplies are purchased with varying degrees of efficiency and formality from a range of different suppliers. A typical university may deal with over 5000 suppliers, although the bulk of purchases may come from just a few of them.

CHARACTERISTICS OF ORGANISATIONAL MARKETS

The differences between consumer and organisational markets do not lie so much in the products themselves as in the context in which those products are exchanged, that is, the use of the marketing mix and the interaction between buyer and seller. The same model of personal computer, for example, can be bought as a one-off by an individual for private use, or in bulk to equip an entire office. The basic product is identical in specification but the way in which it is bought and sold will differ.

Blowspeed Ltd can produce air or water ducting to match a customer's design, however strange the shape.

The following subsections look at some of the characteristics of organisational markets which generate these different approaches.

Nature of demand

Derived demand

All demand in organisational markets is derived from some kind of consumer demand. So, for example, washing machine manufacturers demand electric motors from an engineering factory, and that is an organisational market. The numbers of electric motors demanded, however, depends on predictions of future consumer demand for washing machines. If, as has happened, there is a recession and consumers stop buying the end product, then demand for the component parts of it will also dry up.

Figure 4.3 represents the links in the chain stretching from forestry to reading material. At each stage in the process, there are different influences on the activities and behaviour of the organisations, yet these have implications both up and down the chain. In northern Europe, for

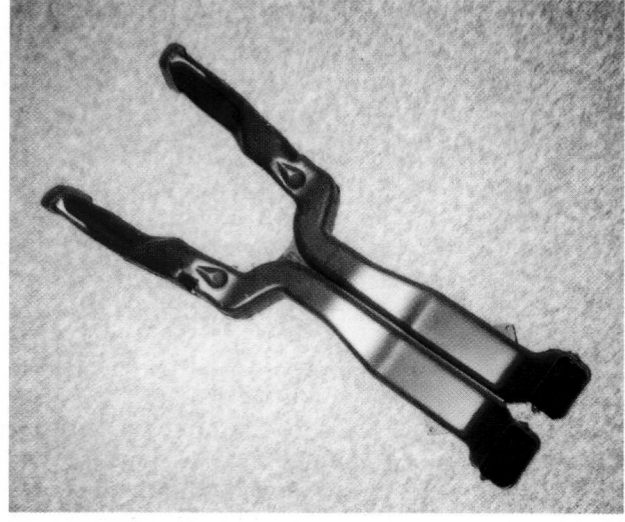

Source: Blowspeed Ltd

FIGURE 4.3

**Influences on an
organisational
purchasing chain**

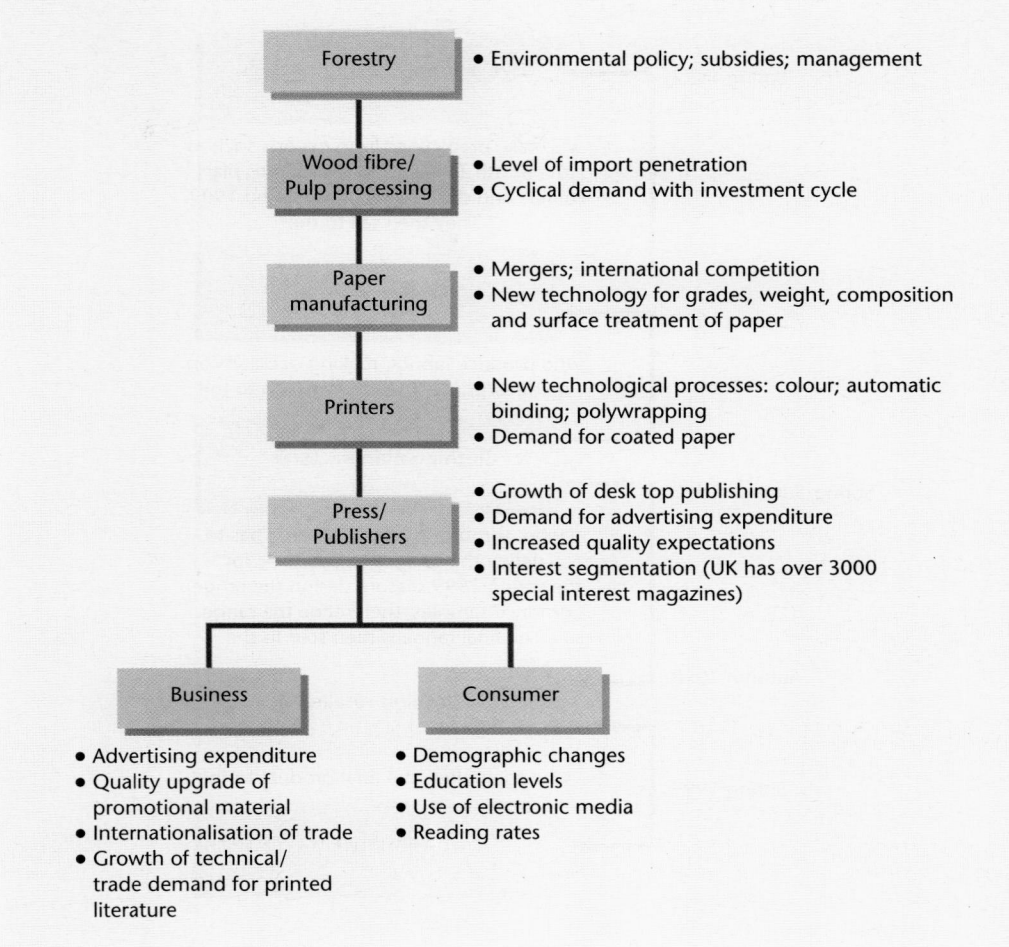

example, between 30 and 40 per cent of the population read newspapers, whereas in southern Europe it is closer to 10 per cent. An increase in that reading rate to bring it closer to the northern level would have a great impact on those supplying paper to the newspaper industry in that region. Similarly, the increase in demand for high quality, full colour special interest publications (for instance CD review magazines) impacts on the type, quality and quantity of paper and printing processes demanded.

Another problem with derived demand is that the further up the supply chain an organisation is, the more remote it is from the end consumer, and the further ahead it has to look in order to predict demand. In the fashion industry, for example, organisations such as ICI and DuPont that produce dyes and fibres have to be two years ahead of the market. This means that in spring 1997 they will be deciding what colours and fabrics will be fashionable in spring 1999! Figure 4.4 shows how those two years are used up in the product development process.

Joint demand
It is also important to note that organisational demand is often closely linked with demand for other organisational products. For example, demand for casings for computers is linked with the availability of disk drives. If there are problems or delays with the supply of disk drives, then the firm assembling the computer might have to stop buying casings temporarily. This emphasizes that there is often a need to plan and co-ordinate production schedules between the buyer and a number of suppliers, not just one.

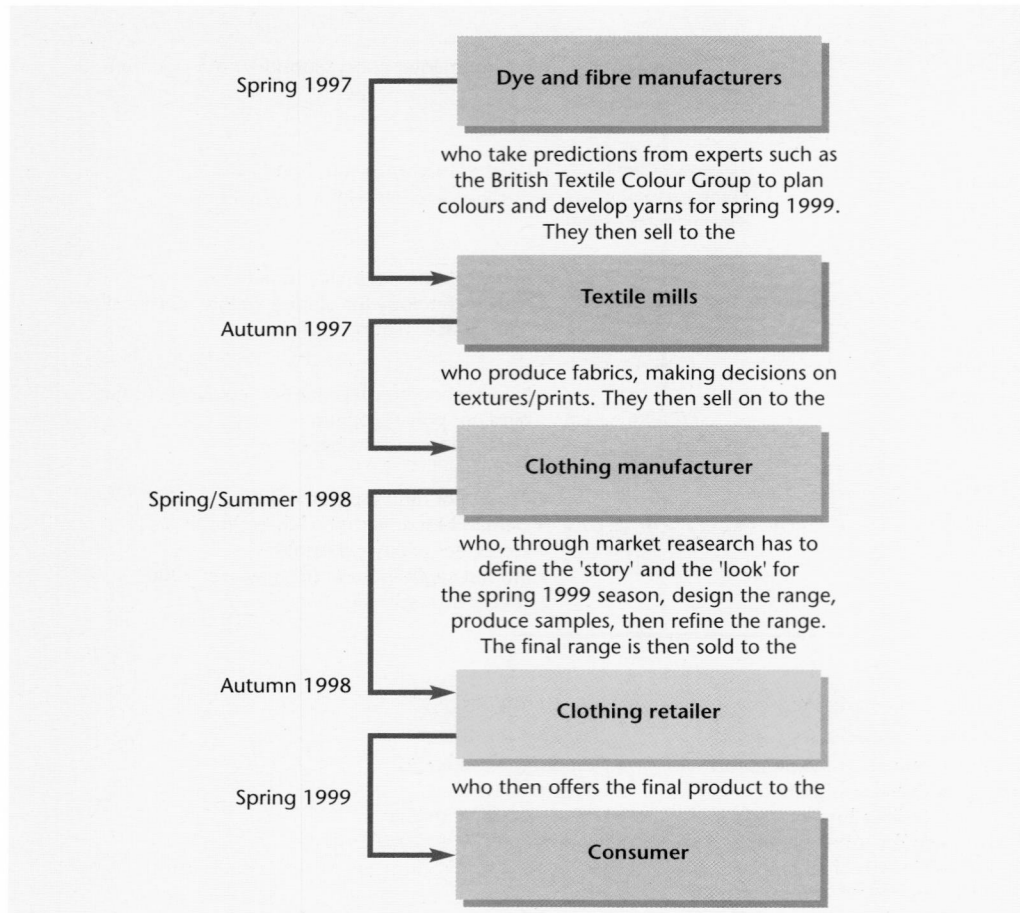

FIGURE 4.4

**Derived demand
in the fashion
industry**

Spring 1997 — **Dye and fibre manufacturers**

who take predictions from experts such as
the British Textile Colour Group to plan
colours and develop yarns for spring 1999.
They then sell to the

Autumn 1997 — **Textile mills**

who produce fabrics, making decisions on
textures/prints. They then sell on to the

Spring/Summer 1998 — **Clothing manufacturer**

who, through market reasearch has to
define the 'story' and the 'look' for
the spring 1999 season, design the range,
produce samples, then refine the range.
The final range is then sold to the

Autumn 1998 — **Clothing retailer**

Spring 1999 — who then offers the final product to the

Consumer

Such tight and crucial links are not common in consumer markets. A close example, however, is that demand for carpets can be linked with the level of buying and selling activity in the housing market, but the two things are not as inextricably tied as in the organisational situation above.

Inelastic demand

Elasticity of demand refers to the extent to which the quantity of a product demanded changes when its price changes. Elastic demand, therefore, means that there is a great deal of price sensitivity in the market. A small increase in price will lead to a relatively large decrease in demand. Conversely, inelastic demand means that an increase in price will make no difference to the quantity demanded.

A car battery, for instance, is just one component of a car. A fall in the price of batteries is not going to have an impact on the quantity of cars demanded, and the car manufacturer will demand neither more nor fewer batteries than before the price change. In this context, and indeed in any manufacturing situation where a large number of components are used, demand is inelastic. Any price changes will be passed on in higher prices charged to the manufacturer's customers or be absorbed into the total costing of the product, or will cause the manufacturer to look for alternative components or cheaper sources of supply (but that takes time and effort and may have implications for production processes, quality and specifications). Whatever happens, demand will not change, and in the short term cannot change, since the manufacturer has obligations and orders to fulfil.

Buying machine tools

MBM Technology, based near Brighton in the UK, operates an Aerospace Equipment Division to provide design and manufacturing services to the aerospace, defence and commercial sectors. In order to produce the high quality and high specification products required by their customers, MBM has to select very carefully the machine tools used to manufacture its specialist assemblies. A detailed assessment of the machine purchase is made before the final selection decision.

At the outset, a detailed assessment is made of the objectives of the purchase. This covers such areas as capacity needed, replacement priority, and the new tool's potential to help MBM serve its own customers better. This could cover reduced lead times, lower manufacturing costs, higher product quality tolerances, or the flexibility to cope with changes in customer needs. After that stage a team is called together, briefed on the project and asked to translate business needs into a technical specification. The team members come from different backgrounds so that they can pool their expertise. The selection criteria cover technical and commercial considerations.

After the specification has been finalised, suppliers are asked to provide quotations. Trade magazines, buyers' directories and guides and exhibitions are used to build a list of reliable sources from which to seek quotes. Some flexibility is offered in the specification to allow for any new ideas or developments that the buying team are unaware of. Typically, an initial list of around 30 suppliers will be drawn up and then a general screening process will reduce that to three. These three will then be invited to detailed negotiations.

At this stage, what is desired is matched with what can be achieved. A distinction is sometimes drawn between 'needs', 'wants' and 'likes'. This enables a guide to be given on those factors in the specification and criteria that are or are not open to negotiation. Firm requirements might involve little discretion, whereas 'likes' can be more flexible. In selecting a supplier, MBM pays particular attention to running costs, spares and maintenance, warranty, health and safety factors, proven track record and long-term stability. MBM also places particular importance on teamwork and the rapport between buyer and seller during the negotiations. The company values the opportunity to develop a relationship based upon trust, commitment and understanding, as even after the supplier selection, after-sales service, installation and maintenance all call for ongoing contact with the supplier.

In the final stages a purpose-built test piece may be used to assess the actual performance of competing machines in technically advanced applications. All these technical factors, along with commercial considerations such as delivery and price are used to guide the final decision. Such a comprehensive buying process is typical of more complex industrial purchases where a range of factors need to be considered in the supplier selection process to find the best match.

Source: Northam (1994).

Structure of demand

One of the characteristics of consumer markets is that for the most part they comprise many potential buyers spread over a wide geographic area, that is, they are diffuse, mass markets. Think of the market for fast food, for example, which McDonald's have shown to have worldwide appeal to many millions of customers. Organisational markets, in contrast, differ in both respects.

Industrial concentration

Organisational markets tend to have a small number of easily identifiable customers, so that it is relatively easy to define who is or is not a potential customer. McDonald's can persuade non-customers to try their product and become customers; in that sense, the boundaries of the market are fuzzy and malleable, whereas a manufacturer of kilns to the brick and roofing tile industry would have problems in trying to extend its customer base beyond very specific types of customer.

This kind of concentration opens up all sorts of marketing possibilities in terms of relationship building and personal contact that just would not be feasible in consumer mass markets. It allows more focused targeting and, in some cases, the dedication of specific members of staff to service that relationship, or the establishment of regional offices and/or distribution facilities.

Considerable knowledge, experience and trust can build up between buyers and suppliers. Where there is a finite number of known customers, most organisations in the trade know what the others are doing, and although negotiations may be private, the outcomes are very public. An example could be an airline's decision to buy an Airbus or a Boeing, and whether to purchase or lease the aircraft.

Geographic concentration

Some industries have a strong geographic bias. Such geographic concentration might develop because of resource availability (both raw materials and labour), available infrastructure or national and EU government incentives. Traditionally, heavy industry and large mass producers, such as shipbuilders, the coal and steel industries and the motor industry, have acted as catalysts for the development of a range of allied suppliers. More recently, airports and seaports have given impetus to organisations concerned with freight storage, movement, insurance and other related services. In Baden-Wüerttemberg in Germany, it is claimed that the regional investment in 36 science parks and high technology research has created the highest number of scientists *per capita* in Europe. Similarly, with 75 patent applications per 100 000 inhabitants, it has produced more innovation than anywhere else in Germany (Genillard, 1993). This new form of geographical concentration provides obvious opportunities for a range of service providers, whether software specialists or marketing consultants!

SKF sells bearings direct to larger OEMs across Europe, especially in the automotive, electrical and mechanical engineering sectors.

Source: SKF.

Concentration can, however, lead to a high degree of mutual dependency. A small, highly specific customer base can leave a supplier very vulnerable if something goes wrong. The closure of a coach works in Shannon, Ireland, resulted in a number of small suppliers also going out of business because they could not find new markets for their skills quickly enough.

Buying Process Complexity

Consumers purchase primarily for themselves and their families. For the most part, these are relatively low-risk, low-involvement decisions which are quickly made, although there may be some economic and psychological influences affecting or constraining them, as Chapter 3 has shown. In contrast, organisational purchasers are always buying on behalf of other people (i.e. the organisation), which implies certain differences from the consumer situation. These differences give rise to much more complexity in the buying process, and the marketer must appreciate them when designing strategies for encouraging trial and reordering. The various dimensions of complexity are as follows.

TABLE 4.2

The advantages and disadvantages of alternative sourcing strategies

(a) Single sourcing

Advantages	Disadvantages
• Improved communications and understanding between buyer and supplier	• Increased costs through lack of competitive pressure
• Increased responsiveness to buyer's needs	• Increased supply vulnerability
• Shared design of quality control systems	• Reduced market intelligence and thus flexibility
• Elimination of supplier switching costs	• Improved supplier appraisal capacity
• Improvement in product cost effectiveness	
• Reduced prices through larger volumes	
• Reduced prices through reduced supplier costs	
• Enhanced ability to implement JIT systems	

Source: Adapted from Treleven (1987).

(b) Multiple sourcing

Advantages	Disadvantages
• Increased competitive pressure	• Perceived lack of commitment
• Improved supply continuity	• Increased costs
• Improved market intelligence	• Less supplier investment
• Improved supplier appraisal effectiveness	• Reduced willingness to adapt
	• Higher operating costs

Source: Adapted from Hahn (1986) and Ramsay and Wilson (1990).

Organisational purchasing policy

Certain systems and procedures for purchasing are likely to be imposed on the organisational buyer. There may be guidelines on favoured suppliers, or rules on single/multiple sourcing, or on the number of quotes required for comparison before a decision can be sanctioned. Often, a purchasing manual is provided for all staff who may be involved in dealing with suppliers. This manual would outline organisational rules and approaches to purchasing, and might list approved suppliers and the procedures to be undertaken for approving a new supplier.

An organisation's decision whether to source from a single supplier or from multiple suppliers is another important aspect of **purchasing policy**. With a single source, the purchaser needs to be assured of the continuity and consistency of supply, as well as value for money. Table 4.2 outlines the advantages and disadvantages of alternative sourcing strategies.

Ramsay and Wilson (1990), in a study of sourcing strategy, challenged the growing belief in Japanese models of long-term single sourcing. They proposed that large, powerful, high-spending organisations might gain more by using competitive pressure to keep a number of suppliers on their toes. This would also reduce the buyer's vulnerability to supply interruption from strikes or breakdowns. Segal (1989) found that the decision whether to adopt single or multiple sourcing was often the result of an overriding organisational attitude to suppliers, arising from whether the buyer wanted close, long-term relationships with suppliers, or an arms-length, competitive type of atmosphere. Segal does concede, however, that other factors, such as product type, market structure and location, might also influence the decision.

Further restraints might also be imposed relating to how much an individual is allowed to spend under particular budget headings on behalf of the organisation before a second or more senior signature is required. Linking individual spending limits with the most appropriate quotation procedure could give rise to a matrix such as that shown in the hypothetical example in Table 4.3.

TABLE 4.3
Purchasing guidelines

Estimated value of order	Method of enquiry	Type of quote	Authorisation
Below £500	Phone/In person	Oral	Junior manager
£500 – £2000	Written/Catalogues	Non-competitive	Middle manager
£2000 – £20 000	Written	Competitive quotes	Senior manager
Above £20 000	Written	Tenders	Board

This matrix provides clear guidelines on who should be involved, for what amount, and the types and methods of quotation required. However, even in this matrix, much would depend on the nature of the organisation. Clearly, for a car manufacturer placing high-volume, repetitive orders, the order value categories would be completely inappropriate.

In addition to the formal requirements associated with purchasing, guidelines are often produced on ethical codes of practice. These do not just cover the obvious concerns of remaining within the law and not abusing authority for personal gain, but also address issues such as confidentiality, business gifts and hospitality, fair competition and the declaration of vested interests.

Professional purchasing

The risk and accountability aspects of organisational purchasing mean that it needs to be done professionally. Much negotiation is required where complex customised technical products are concerned, and even for small components used in manufacturing, defining the terms of supply so that they are consistent and compatible with production requirements (for example performance specification, delivery schedules and quality standards) is a significant job. Most consumer purchasing does not involve so great a degree of flexibility: the product is standard and on the shop shelf, with clearly defined price, usage and function; take it or leave it.

Different types of production and operating systems will help to shape an organisation's purchasing task. An inflexible or technology-driven manufacturing organisation, such as a continuous production plant, allows little scope for varying the types of purchases made, and needs suppliers who will conform to the standards required for maintaining the system (Sheth, 1977). Furthermore, according to Hallén (1980), if there is no guaranteed economic and stable flow of materials at a consistent quality level, the system will be severely impaired. It is thus critical for the suppliers in such a system to be able to meet the demands of the customer's technology.

MARKETING IN ACTION

Automotive components suppliers

The relationships between motor manufacturers and their component suppliers has become increasingly close. Manufacturers are looking for suppliers who can operate cost effectively, but who can also be innovative partners in product development. As the motor manufacturers streamline their own operations, they have become more dependent on outside suppliers. In Japan, for example, 70 per cent of components are out sourced. This means that suppliers have to invest in R&D to keep up with their customers' demands for the latest technology and that they have to be able to deliver reliably and to the right specification.

The international purchasing director of Toyota realises that the eventual cost and quality of a car depend on the components that go into it, and that close communication and co-operation between buyer and supplier is essential. Toyota staff, therefore, are very closely involved in suppliers' product development, production processes and quality systems. With the willing co-operation of the supplier, Toyota will help it to diagnose and overcome its weaknesses, and sets targets for cost, quality and delivery. In essence, Toyota takes as much interest in an out sourced component as it would if it was manufactured in-house, and both parties see this as being in their mutual long-term interests.

The level of interdependence created by this has also led to long-term supply contracts and a move towards single sourcing. The motor manufacturer not only appreciates the investment that the supplier has made on its behalf, but also wants to take advantage of the expertise and creativity that the supplier builds over time. The supplier needs a long-term contract to reassure it that it is worth investing further and to allow it to plan ahead with a measure of certainty. Nevertheless, the motor manufacturer will only risk so much with a single supplier. Toyota, for example, has no problems single sourcing up to 250 000 units of a component a year for one of its models, but as the number rises, one or two other suppliers will be brought in too.

In contrast to the Japanese and European picture, US motor manufacturers are still much more aggressive and adversarial with their suppliers. On average, only 50 per cent of car components are out sourced in the USA and it has been suggested that some of General Motors' problems have been caused in part by its preference for in-house components. US manufacturers have tended to impose targets on their suppliers, for example cost cutting and an insistence that suppliers improve quality by 15 per cent a year, without any negotiation and without any involvement in their achievement.

Source: European Purchasing & Materials Management (1994).

In supplying components for these British built fighter aircraft, suppliers have to be as innovative and as technologically advanced as British Aerospace itself.

Source: British Aerospace.

Mass production systems are often rigid in the short term, although they can be reorganised and modified to accommodate new products, with careful planning. At times of model changes and reorganisation, there may be an opportunity for the supplier to adopt new technical solutions, but often it is the buyer who will determine requirements and dominate the supply situation. This contrasts with unit production, where close discussion and joint development may take place to develop designs and specifications that meet the requirements of the application.

Example

Sometimes, an organisation can rationalise its purchasing activity in order to achieve economies of scale. Pepsi Cola Europe, for example, planned in 1994 to bring some aspects of its purchasing from its various business units under one agreement. Pizza Hut, KFC and Walker's Crisps, therefore, as part of the Pepsi group, were looking to save 5 per cent of their total spend (some £66 mn) by combining their spending power. Items such as cardboard, flour, salt, spices, cooking oil and advertising airtime were all examined for potential scale economies. To achieve these benefits, however, they had to overcome some of the cultural differences across Europe, as well as building integrated supply chains more akin to those found in the US than those that currently exist in Europe (Summers, 1994).

Group decision making

The need for full information, adherence to procedures, and accountability tends to lead towards groups rather than individuals being responsible for purchasing decisions (Johnston and Bonoma, 1981). A full discussion of the role and structure of groups (*buying centres* or *decision-making units*) can be found at pp. 152 *et seq*. While there are group influences in consumer buying, for example the family unit, they are likely to be less formally constituted than in the organisational purchasing situation. It is rare, other than in the smallest organisations, or for the most minor purchases, to find individuals given absolute autonomy in organisational spending. Mattson (1988) found that product-related aspects of the purchase strongly influenced the area of the organisation involved in the purchase, while the size of expenditure influenced the managerial level of those involved.

Purchase significance

The complexity of the process is also dictated by the importance of the purchase and the level of experience the organisation has of that buying situation (Robinson *et al.*, 1967).

For instance, in the case of a **routine rebuy**, the organisation has bought this product before and has already established suppliers. These products may be relatively low- risk, frequently purchased, inexpensive supplies such as office stationery or utilities (water, electricity, gas etc.). The decision-making process here is likely to involve very few people and be more a matter of paperwork than anything else. Increasingly, these types of purchase form part of computer-based automatic reordering systems from approved suppliers. A blanket contract may cover a specific period, and then a schedule of deliveries over that time is agreed. Bearings for the car and electrical motor industries are sold in this way. The schedule may be regarded as definite and binding for one month ahead, for example, but as provisional for the following three months. Precise dates and quantities can then be adjusted and agreed month by month nearer the time. Increasingly, with JIT systems, schedules may even be day or hour specific!

A **modified rebuy** implies that there is some experience of buying this product, but there is also a need to review current practice. Perhaps there have been significant technological developments since the organisation last purchased this item, or a feeling that the current supplier is not the best, or a desire to renegotiate the parameters of the purchase. An example of this is the purchase of a fleet of cars, where new models and price changes make review necessary, as does the fierce competition between suppliers who will therefore be prepared to negotiate hard for the business. The decision making here will be a longer, more formal and involved process, but with the benefit of drawing on past experience.

A technical modified rebuy, therefore, is related to changing design and performance specifications, while a commercial modified rebuy involves issues such as price and delivery. The former type may be decided by technical personnel, whereas the latter is more likely to concern the purchasing department.

New task purchasing is the most complex category. The organisation has no previous experience of this kind of purchase, and therefore needs a great deal of information and wide participation in the process, especially where it involves a high-risk or high-cost product. One example of this might be the sourcing of raw materials for a completely new product. This represents a big opportunity for a supplier, as it could lead to regular future business (i.e., routine or modified re-buys). It is a big decision for the purchaser who will want to take the time and effort to make sure it is the right one. Another situation, which happens less frequently in an organisation's life, is the commissioning of new plant or buildings. This too involves a detailed, many faceted decision-making process with wide involvement from both internal members of staff and external consultants, and high levels of negotiation.

Laws and regulations

As we saw in Chapter 2, regulations affect all areas of business, but in organisational markets, some regulations specifically influence the sourcing of products and services. An obvious example would be the sourcing of goods from nations under various international trade embargoes, such as Iran and Serbia in 1995. More specifically, governments may seek to regulate sourcing within certain industrial sectors, such as utilities.

In Germany in 1994 there was some debate over allowing third parties access to distribution grids to supply electricity and gas. As things stood, the large German utility companies, such as RWE, Bayernwerk and PreussenElektra, had exclusive rights to supply municipalities. This guarantees supply, but restricts choice and price competition. One small town wanted to break its agreement with RWE and seek bids from cheaper alternative suppliers, perhaps even from the Netherlands. The German government, however, is reluctant to deregulate and open its borders unless there is reciprocal access for German utilities into other countries. The case has been referred to the European Commission (Dempsey, 1994).

Buyer–seller relationships

Apart from the tangible characteristics of buyer–seller relationships, as formalised in a negotiated, legally drawn up contract which lays out both parties' responsibilities, obligations and penalty schemes (for late delivery, for instance), there are also less concrete factors, shaping the way in which two organisations do business.

Where there is a small number of identifiable customers, then it is possible for the buyer and the seller to build experience, knowledge and trust in each other to an intimate level that consumer marketers can only dream of. Suppliers can tailor-make their offerings to suit particular buyers, leading to long-term relationships with joint development potential.

One of the problems of such close relationships, however, is dependency. In the short term, the purchaser comes to rely on regular supplies conforming to quality standards, while over a longer period, either party may come to regard the other as essential. For example, a small injection moulding firm found itself selling 80 per cent of its output to a large multinational manufacturer of domestic vacuum cleaners. Since the purchasing organisation also had two alternative suppliers on the sidelines, it was able to exert considerable influence over the small supplier who could not afford to lose the business. These issues are covered more fully at pp. 157 *et seq*.

The result of all the above complex factors working together is to make organisational purchasing a much longer, more formalised process than in consumer markets. Organisational buying decisions have to be justified to managers, accountants and shareholders, and are, therefore, likely to be more rationally made, to be based on more solid information, and to reflect more collective responsibility than a consumer decision. They are also more likely to lead to long-term, mutually valuable, interdependent relationships between specific buyers and sellers.

BUYING DECISION-MAKING PROCESS

It is just as important for marketers to understand the processes that make up the buying decision in organisational markets as it is in consumer markets. The formulation of marketing strategies that will succeed in implementation depends on this understanding. The processes involved are similar to those presented in the model of consumer decision making described in Chapter 3, in that information search, analysis, choice and post-purchase evaluation also exist here, but the interaction of human and organisational elements makes the organisational model more complex.

There are many models of organisational decision-making behaviour, with different levels of detail, for example Sheth (1973), Webster and Wind (1972), and

FIGURE 4.5

**Models of
organisational
buying decision
making**

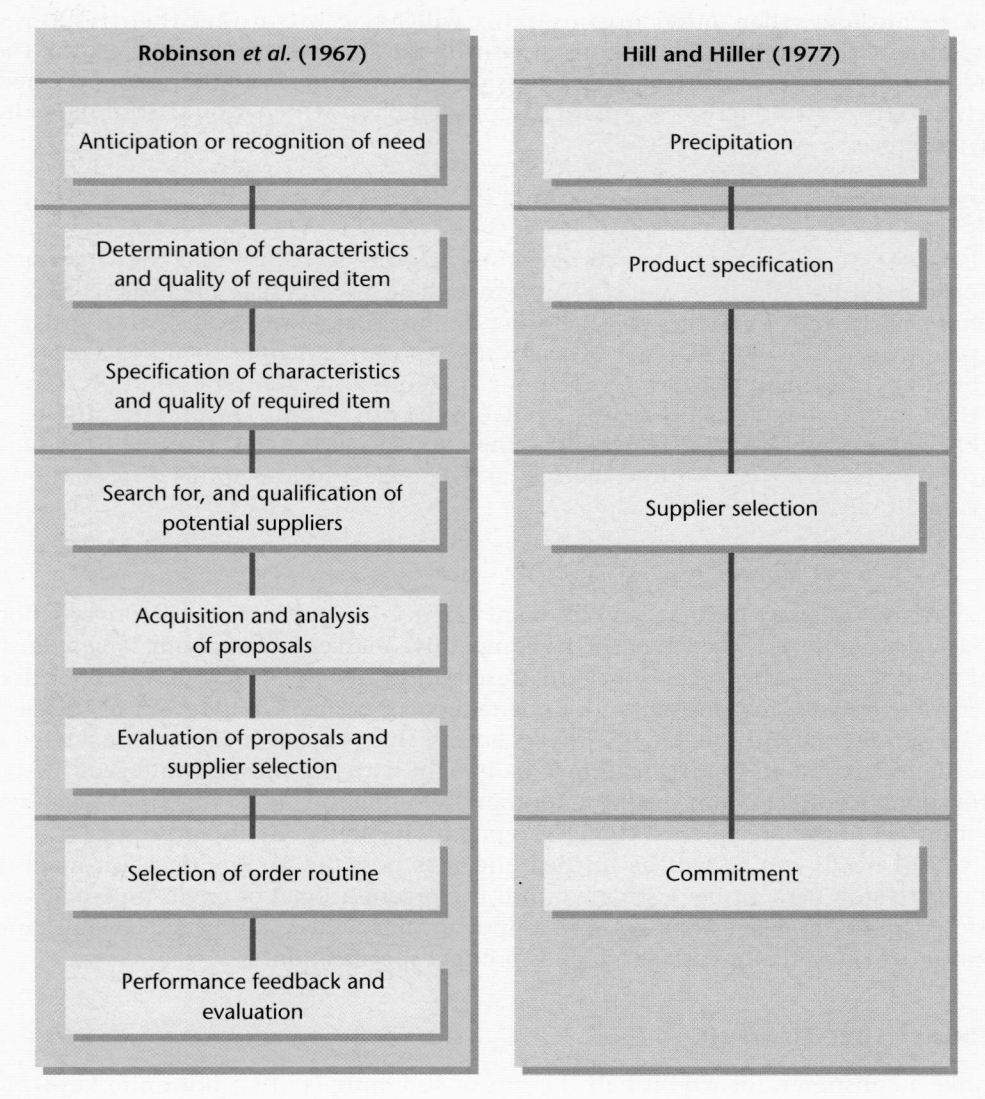

Robinson *et al.* (1967)	Hill and Hiller (1977)
Anticipation or recognition of need	Precipitation
Determination of characteristics and quality of required item	Product specification
Specification of characteristics and quality of required item	
Search for, and qualification of potential suppliers	Supplier selection
Acquisition and analysis of proposals	
Evaluation of proposals and supplier selection	
Selection of order routine	Commitment
Performance feedback and evaluation	

Robinson *et al.* (1967). How the model is formulated depends on the type of organisations and products involved; the level of their experience in purchasing; organisational purchasing policies; the individuals involved; and the formal and informal influences on marketing. Figure 4.5 shows two models of organisational decision making, and on the basis of these, the following subsections discuss the constituent stages.

Precipitation

Clearly, the start of the process has to be the realisation that there is a need, a problem which a purchase can solve. The stimulation could be internal and entirely routine: it is the time of year to renew the photocopier maintenance contract. It could be a planned new buy precipitated, for example, by the implementation of expansion plans or the imminent production of a new product. It could also be something more sudden and dramatic than that, such as the failure of a piece of plant or machinery, or a lack of stock.

External influences can also stimulate a need. If the competition have invested in new technology, then other organisations will have to consider their response. Attending trade exhibitions, talking to visiting sales representatives or reading the trade press might also generate awareness of opportunities, whether based on new technology, cost reduction or quality improvements, which would stimulate the buying process.

Example

Potential suppliers may have to help the customer to realise that they have a need. Security Backup Systems, for instance, have to stimulate potential clients to be aware of the importance of storing essential data away from their normal premises, in case of fire or theft. This means exposing potential clients to a problem that they may not have even thought about, and offering a solution that they may not have realised was available. In offering an automatic off-site backup service for PCs and networks, the company uses telemarketing to raise the awareness of risk, outline the cost and arrange a follow-up meeting to discuss the client's needs in detail.

Changes in the wider business environment can also trigger a need. The privatisation of electricity supply in the UK created a competitive market for supplying large industrial users. Organisations such as Ford, Tesco and Abbey National have appointed energy buyers with responsibility for undertaking a modified rebuy review of the electricity supply market. The energy buyers ensure that what was always considered a routine repurchase in the past can now be bought with the most advantageous long-term supply contracts from the most appropriate supplier. Thus changes in the energy environment have precipitated changes in purchasing decisions and processes.

Not all needs can or will be fulfiled and it is possible for the decision-making process to stop here, or be postponed until the organisational or environmental conditions are better. Nevertheless, some opportunities will be followed through, and these move on to the next stage which is **product specification**.

Product specification

Unlike a consumer, for whom half the fun of shopping is often not quite knowing exactly what is wanted, an organisation must determine in some detail precisely what is required, and the greater the strategic significance of the purchase, the more true this is. Think about buying a component to be incorporated into another end product. The physical characteristics of that component must be specified, in terms of its function, its design, expected quality and performance levels, its relationship and compatibility with other components, but there are also the less tangible, but no less important considerations of quantity required, delivery schedules and service backup, among others.

These specifications will need the combined expertise of engineers, production managers, purchasing specialists and marketers (representing the interests of the end customer), balancing ideals against cost and practicality. A key decision early on will be whether to develop a specification based on known particular needs and then locate a suitable supplier, or to locate the supplier first and then adapt the specifications to suit what they can offer. Even external consultants and suppliers could be involved in particularly complex situations. In the first instance, a general specification will be issued to potential suppliers, but a more detailed one would follow later, perhaps after a shortlist of two or three suppliers has been drawn up.

Where specifications are largely set by the seller rather than the buyer, reports and publications can be used to compare the different features and performance of competing products. The publication *What to Buy for Business*, for example, reviews in detail a wide range of business equipment and services, from franking machines to company health insurance. The October 1993 edition reviewed mobile phones, providing a detailed list of suppliers, technical data on the products themselves and their features, and guidelines on running costs, tariffs, discounts, after-sales service, insurance and safety. All of this helps the organisational buyer to make a more informed choice.

A level of fine detail in specifications is understandable in an engineering context, but is not appropriate in all circumstances. An organisation wanting to develop a corporate brochure, for example, might have a certain amount of in-house expertise within its marketing department, but will issue a general brief to a number of external agencies in order to get a fresh perspective in the light of current practice. The brief may specify the number of pages for the brochure, the scope of the content, the target audience and an indication of the price the organisation is prepared to pay, but the fine detail will be deliberately vague to allow the agency plenty of creative scope. The agency 'interprets' the brief, then makes proposals to the client who can reject or negotiate from there.

It is also worth while at this stage to define the criteria or priorities for choice. It may not necessarily be cost. If a machine has suddenly broken down, then speed of delivery and installation may be of the essence. In the case of new technology, the choice may hinge on compatibility with existing facilities, the future prospects for upgrading it or the service support offered.

MARKETING IN ACTION

Pendolino – on time, on track

As far as the negotiation and delivery of high technology specifications is concerned, the Italians succeeded where the British failed, by managing to develop a high speed train based on tilt technology. Called Pendolino, it was the result of considerable dialogue and trials between Fiat Ferroviaria, the manufacturer, and Italian Railways, the customer. Its main benefit was its ability to run on existing track. Speeds of up to 155 mph were realised on the Rome to Florence line and trials in the Alps, notorious for severe curves, resulted in journey times up to 20 per cent faster. Although track signalling and some installations had to be upgraded to cater for high speeds, the benefit of faster travel often attracted more passengers. The technical requirements were only part of the specification, however. The first class format also required a fine level of attention to detail in the interior design and provision of on-board services.

From humble beginnings in the 1970s, the latest generation of Pendolinos are now sweeping across Europe in an industry traditionally dominated by local suppliers. The approach adopted by Fiat Ferroviaria was often the same: Pendolino was built under licence by local manufacturers with some equipment from Fiat. In Portugal, for example, five of the 10 Pendolinos ordered were to be built in Italy and five in Portugal by Sorefame. In the Czech Republic, Pendolinos were needed for the Berlin–Prague–Vienna service. These were built by a consortium of Fiat, Siemens and Czech railway stock builder, CKD Praha.

When the Finns were interested in purchasing Pendolino, however, a whole new range of customer specifications had to be considered. Finnish track gauge is wider, for instance, the train had to be wider and taller, underfloor air intakes had to be moved to avoid blockages from driving snow and new electrical transmission gear was needed to suit the Finnish railway system. The same building pattern was adopted, however, with Transtech building under licence from Fiat. After Pendolino's introduction in 1996 on the Helsinki–Turku service, a further 23 Pendolinos were planned, at a rate of two to four per year.

Sources: Freeman Allen (1994; 1995a; 1995b; 1996).

A standard Iveco van has been adapted to incorporate broadcasting technology to a customer's specification.

Source: Continental Microwave Ltd.

Supplier selection

The next stage involves the search for a suitable supplier who can best meet all the specified criteria. Sometimes, the inclination to search for potential suppliers can be quite low, and the purchasing department will keep files on who can do what. If existing suppliers can do the job, then they are likely to be favoured. On other occasions, it may be necessary for buyers to be proactive by openly seeking new suppliers and encouraging quotations from those who could meet their requirements. Nevertheless, there is often a bias towards existing suppliers who are known and trusted.

There are some advantages in this approach. Existing suppliers are at least a known quantity, and the purchasing organisation will have experience and a realistic view of their capacity to perform. The existing relationship means that there should be better mutual understanding, good working relationships between members of staff within the two organisations and an appreciation of the constraints under which each of them works. Automatically pushing business towards the existing supplier does, however, have its risks. Is the purchasing organisation becoming too dependent on the one supplier? Will this extra business strain the production capacity of the supplier? Is the purchasing organisation missing out on other suppliers with better technology who are anxious to prove themselves? Some exploration of who and what exists beyond the 'usual' supplier makes sense.

Much depends, of course, on the nature of the purchasing task. A low-risk, frequent purchase might not warrant that kind of search effort, and the existing supplier might be simply asked to tender a price for resupply. One or two other known suppliers might also be asked to quote for the job, just as a checking procedure to make sure that the existing supplier is not taking advantage of the established relationship.

In a high-risk, infrequent purchase (i.e., the new task situation), a more serious, lengthy selection procedure is likely to be implemented. There will be complex discussion, negotiation, revision and reiteration at a high level with a number of potential suppliers before a final decision is made. Additional problems may be caused where different suppliers will be expected to work closely together, such as on the building of a new manufacturing plant, for instance. Their compatibility with each other, their reliability and their ability to complete their part within strict time limits dictated by the overall project schedule, may all affect the decision making.

Commitment

The decision has been made, the contract signed, the order and delivery schedules set. The process does not, however, end here. The situation has to be monitored as it unfolds, in case there are problems with the supplier. Is the supplier fulfiling promises? Is the purchased item living up to expectations? Are deliveries turning up on time? The earlier such problems are diagnosed, the more likely it is that remedial action can be taken with the least disruption to production schedules. Commitment, therefore, comes in two parts, the contractual commitment and the review and evaluation process.

The purchasing manager of a large computer assembly plant in Ireland was clear cut in his requirements. He claimed that 'In my experience, 85 per cent of the business is lost or gained on quality and delivery, not on prices. We want what we order when we want it.' (Pettitt, 1992, p. 208).

With the introduction of new purchasing strategies, such as JIT, the pressure on suppliers increases. Suppliers have to earn customer commitment through consistency, quality and delivery. Failure to live up to these promises can be very costly for production schedules.

Some buyers adopt formal appraisal procedures for their suppliers, covering key elements of performance. The results of this appraisal will be discussed with the supplier concerned in the interests of improving their performance and allowing the existing buyer–seller relationship to be maintained. New suppliers are sometimes eased into critical supply situations so that their performance can be carefully assessed. Small trial orders can grow into larger batches. This approach is especially used where larger firms are dealing with smaller suppliers.

Other buyers are less tolerant, and keep their suppliers under constant threat. A buyer of injection moulded plastic parts, for example, has a policy of withdrawing business from a supplier who fails to meet delivery schedules. Two alternative suppliers are kept in reserve in case this happens. In another company, the buyer of automotive components places the emphasis on quality consistency. If a supplier falls short of quality standards, then again, alternative sources will be activated. Both these examples demonstrate the need for a true marketing orientation among suppliers that is, of fulfiling the customer's needs and wants exactly. These customers are too important to lose, and any complaints have to be handled quickly, efficiently and effectively in order to maintain levels of customer satisfaction.

In a study of the European aircraft industry, Paliwoda and Bonaccorsi (1994) found a trend towards reducing the supplier base to allow closer co-operation and relationships to develop. Airframe manufacturers increasingly expect suppliers to fund development costs from their own resources, and in the avionics and power systems areas, a shift to single (or much reduced) sourcing forms the basis for a preferred supplier system.

In concluding this discussion of the buying process as a whole, we can say that the Hill and Hillier (1977) model has provided a useful framework for discussing the complexities and influences on organisational buying. It is difficult, however, to generalise about such a process, especially where technical and commercial complexity exists. Stages may be compressed or merge into each other, depending on circumstances; the process may end at any stage; there may have to be reiteration: for example if negotiations with a chosen supplier break down at a late stage then the search process may have to begin again.

At each stage, a number of decisions have to be made that may well affect the character of the next stage. These various decision factors are summarised in Table 4.4.

TABLE 4.4
Decision problems in the organisational purchasing decision-making process

Stage	Decision problems
Precipitation	Do we need to make a purchasing decision or not? What benefits (e.g. cost savings) are we looking for?
Product specification	What quantity are we likely to need? How often? What are the 'must have' attributes? What are the 'would like' attributes? What is our required quantity level? What level of service/ support do we want from supplier? What price band are we thinking of?
Supplier selection	Do we want to use existing and/or new suppliers? How do we construct a shortlist of potential suppliers? On what criteria do we select the supplier: price, ability to meet specifications exactly, past experience, solvency, culture? To what extent, and on what features, are we prepared to negotiate?
Commitment	Does the product actually meet our needs? Is the chosen supplier living up to its promises? How do we continue to motivate/ evaluate this supplier? How often do we review their status?

Thus if a decision is taken in the specification stage to adopt a certain type of technology, that may then narrow down the choice of potential suppliers. The process will also vary according to whether the purchase is a new task or a rebuy. Remember too that although organisational buying is assumed to be more rational than consumer buying, it still involves the less than predictable human element, and where groups of people are concerned in the buying process, there is plenty of scope for its smooth flow to be interrupted. The next section looks in more detail at these human elements.

ROLES IN THE BUYING PROCESS

A potential supplier attempting to gain an order from a purchasing firm needs to know just who is involved in the decision-making process. As has already been established, organisational purchasing is unlikely to be the result of one person's deliberation and decision. Thus the aspiring supplier wants to know not only who is involved, but at what point in the process each person is most influential, and how they all interact with each other. Then, the supplier's marketers can deal most effectively with the situation, utilising both the group and individual dynamics to the best of their advantage, for example tailoring specific communication packages to appeal at the right time to the right people, and getting a range of feedback from within the purchasing organisation to allow a comprehensive product offering to be designed.

Clearly, the amount of time and effort the supplier is prepared to devote to this will vary with the importance and complexity of the order. A routine rebuy may consist of a telephone conversation between two individuals to confirm the availability of the product and the fine detail of the transaction in terms of exact price and delivery. A new task situation, however, with the promise of either a large contract or substantial future business, provides much more scope and incentive for the supplier to research and influence the buying decision.

The rest of this section takes a more focused look at some of the functional areas involved in the decision-making process, detailing their interests and concerns. This lays the foundations for the next (p. 152) which then examines how these functional areas operate within a group setting.

Purchasing

The role of the purchasing department is to handle relationships with suppliers by, for instance, sourcing suppliers, soliciting tenders, evaluating offers and negotiating or reviewing performance. Purchasing acts as the interface between other internal functions, such as production and finance, and external suppliers, and thus has to reflect and represent those internal needs. This means that the function cannot act in isolation, except in the case of very well established routines.

The role of purchasing will often vary according to the technology being used and the kind of contact needed with suppliers. In Fig 4.6, where unit or small batch production takes place, such as in building a large gas turbine or specialist vehicles, there may be considerable contact between different departments within the selling and buying organisations. This is because a whole range of specification, quality, design and production issues may have to be discussed before, or even during the transactions. The role of purchasing in such a situation tends to be less central to the whole process, and is more focused towards offering support in such matters as contracts and supplier suitability etc. In mass production, however, given the need for consistency, reliability and possibly frequent and critical exchanges, the role of purchasing may be enhanced to ensure the free flow of goods into the organisation. The other internal departments may channel their efforts and be co-ordinated through the purchasing department.

Purchasing rarely initiates the decision-making process, except for routine rebuys or where they acquire information to suggest that a change of policy or supplier could lead to better efficiency. Thus their key role is in the supplier selection and commitment stages, that is, in locating 'good' suppliers, establishing terms and liaising with them.

The main concerns of purchasing are security and consistency of supply, especially where large-scale production schedules are concerned. Lowest cost is, therefore,

FIGURE 4.6

Models of buyer–seller contact in organisational markets

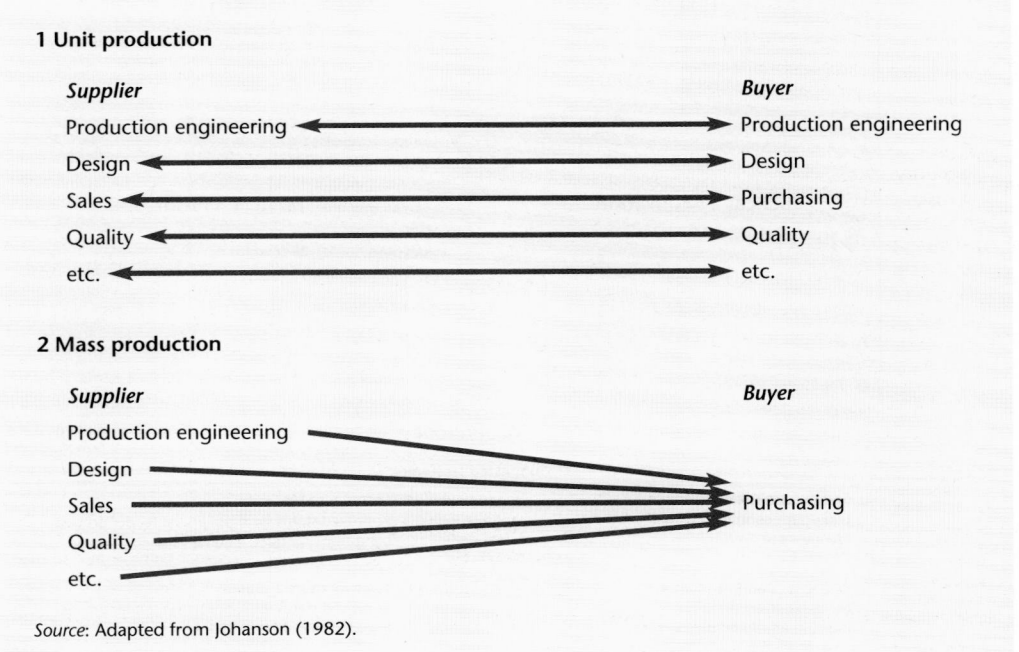

1 Unit production

Supplier		Buyer
Production engineering	← →	Production engineering
Design	← →	Design
Sales	← →	Purchasing
Quality	← →	Quality
etc.	← →	etc.

2 Mass production

Supplier		Buyer
Production engineering		
Design		
Sales	→	Purchasing
Quality		
etc.		

Source: Adapted from Johanson (1982).

unlikely to be their prime criterion. The whole area of purchasing is growing in importance as organisations seek cost savings, raised quality levels and better integration with suppliers to strengthen their overall competitiveness in the supply chain. This means developing a clear understanding of the relative significance of individual purchases and of different types of purchases. Figure 4.7 details the various products and services purchased by a university, classified by the security/risk required and the value of the purchases. Strategic cells SS and SC suggest long-term supply contracts and careful selection of suppliers. The more tactical areas are divided into *acquisition* (TA), where the priority is minimising effort, and *profit* (TP) where the concern is with savings and improving margins through tendering. With business travel in the TP cell, for example, travel agencies would be required to bid on a regular basis, indicating the service level offered and their discount structures. Such a matrix is a valuable guide to an organisation in selecting those product areas that require special attention.

Production/Operations

With prime responsibility for meeting targets for the end product in both quantity and quality terms, the production function also has a great interest in the security and consistency of supply. If a critical component is concerned, then they will be anxious to ensure that the component meets quality and design specifications in order to be entirely compatible with the production flow.

Production staff may, therefore, be mainly involved in the precipitation and specification stages, although if they have an interest as users of the purchased product, they are not going to be entirely absent from the other stages.

In some cases, the production process may have to be adapted to accommodate a particular supplier's technology. This is widespread practice in organisational markets (Johanson and Wootz, 1986; Valla, 1986). While some of these adaptations are driven by logistical concerns alone, issues relating to ease of handling, fit with other organisations' production systems and cost effectiveness may also be considered.

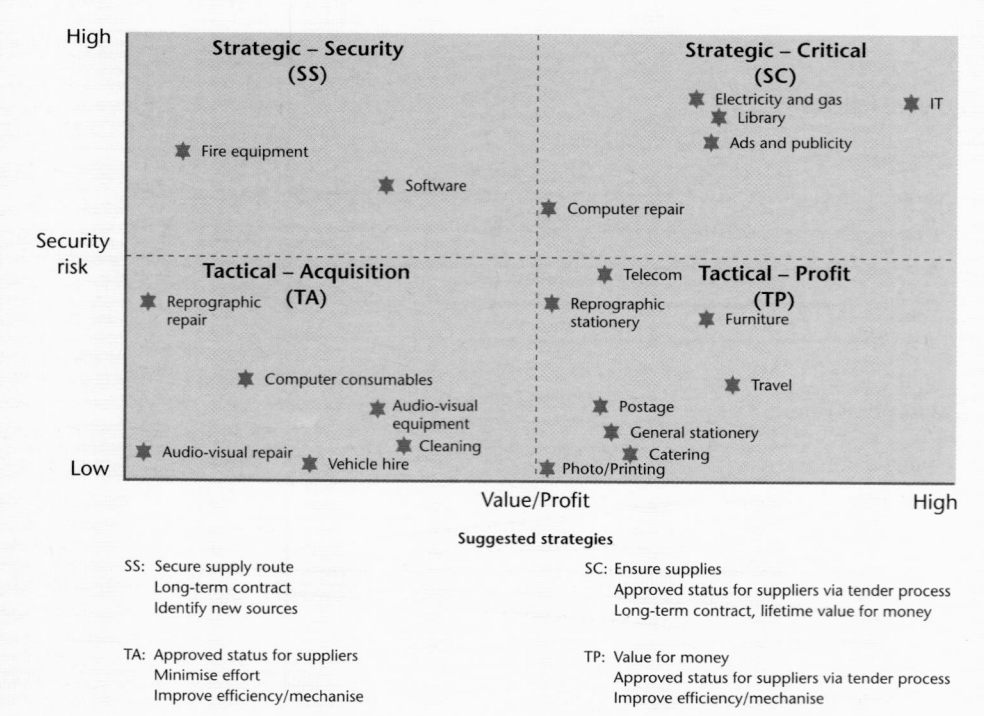

FIGURE 4.7

Commodity positioning matrix

Engineering

Engineering is usually concerned with specification and design, for example when sourcing a component or designing new production facilities, advising production on more efficient methods. Applications engineers may work closely with suppliers to develop solutions to problems, for example pooling their expertise to use CAD systems to design components that both perform to the purchaser's specifications and are feasible, given the supplier's technical capacity and talents. They can also feed specific information back to the supplier to solve a specific end-customer's problem.

R&D

Where R&D has been given a free-ranging brief to look for new, radical solutions to problems, then they are likely, as in the case of engineering, to have close contact with suppliers in the interests of joint development.

Johnson & Johnson, for example were researching new approaches to wound dressings which involved close liaison with textile suppliers to develop fabrics of the right density, texture and quality for medical use and which could withstand sterilisation. At the same time, they also worked with another supplier to develop an adhesive that not only fulfiled its prime functions of being non-allergenic and sufficiently adhesive (but not too much so), but also could be supplied in a form that would allow it to be easily and efficiently incorporated into a production run. This proved to be a somewhat sticky problem.

In addition, development has to be done within given cost parameters. If the proposed solution to an R&D problem looks likely to push the price of the end product up beyond what the market will bear (taking into account the unique selling points offered by the new development), then further development work has to be done to reduce the costs or find alternatives.

In such cases, R&D staff are going to have a strong influence at all stages of the decision-making process, somewhat reducing the role of purchasing to an administrative one.

Finance

For routine production-orientated purchases, is likely that the finance department will devolve budgets to appropriate managers. Finance will simply take on a monitoring role to ensure that there are no irregularities or variances and provide regular internal information.

They take a higher profile role in major capital projects or other large items of expenditure, assessing returns on investments, investigating methods of financing and costing projects, for instance. They may not make the final decision, but they do have an influence in both shaping the feasible options and selecting the most appropriate supplier.

Marketing

The marketing function is primarily concerned with the outputs of the production process, representing the interests of the purchasing organisation's own customers. Marketers' concerns, therefore, are making sure that the implications of whatever is purchased do not compromise the final product offering or its competitive edge. Marketers are likely to approve of options that enhance the offering, perhaps in terms of better quality or improved reliability, thus favouring innovative, reliable suppliers.

Overall, in relation to functional roles in the decision-making process, just who is involved and in what capacity is an amalgam of many factors. The further removed the situation is from routine rebuys, the more people are involved and the more formal and time consuming the process is likely to be. Organisational size, structure and culture will also play a role in defining the process, for instance through the degree of delegation of responsibility and devolved decision making.

THE BUYING CENTRE

The previous section implied that individuals within the purchasing organisation, as well as having functional roles and concerns, can also play different roles within the decision-making process that cross functional boundaries. This section, therefore, looks at these non-functional roles, and how they interact to form a **buying centre** or **decision making unit** (DMU).

Table 4.5 compares buying centres in consumer and organisational markets, indicating the membership, the roles they play and the functional areas which may be involved.

Users

Users are the people who will use the end product, for example an operator who will use production machinery, or a secretary will be use a word processor. These people may trigger the purchasing process through reporting a need, and may also be consulted in setting the specifications for whatever is to be bought.

Influencers

Influencers can affect the outcome of the decision-making process through their influence on others. Influence could stem formally from expertise, for example the advice of an accountant on the return on investment from a piece of capital machinery or that of an engineer on a supplier's technical capability, or it could be an informal, personal influence. Their prime role is in specification, information gathering and assessment.

TABLE 4.5

Comparison of DMUs in consumer and organisational markets

Consumer	Example	Organisation	Example
Initiator	Child pesters parents for a new bike.	**User**	Machine breaks down; the operator reports it, thus initiating the process. May also be asked to help with specs for replacement.
Influencer	Mother thinks about it and says, 'Well, perhaps he has grown out of the old one.'	**Influencer**	User may influence; may also involve R&D staff, accountants, suppliers, sales reps, external consultants.
Decider	Father agrees and they all go to Toys 'Я' Us where the final decision is the child's, but under restraints imposed by parents' credit card limit.	**Decider**	May be a senior manager with either an active or a passive role in the whole process. May also be the buyer and/or influencer
Purchaser	Parents pay the bill.	**Buyer**	Handles the search for, and negotiations with suppliers.
User	The child.	**Gatekeeper**	Secretarial staff preventing influencers reaching the decision maker; R&D staff withholding information.

Deciders

Deciders have the formal or informal authority to make the decision. For routine rebuys, this may be the purchasing officer or someone in a functional role, but organisational structures may dictate that the final decision rests with top management, who are fed information and recommendations from below. The decider's role and level of involvement, therefore, will vary widely, depending on individual circumstances.

Buyers

Buyers have the authority to select and negotiate with suppliers. Buyers with different levels of seniority may exist to handle different types of transaction, for example a routine rebuy could be handled by a relatively junior clerical worker, whereas the high-cost, high-risk new buy might require a senior purchasing manager of many years' experience. Where devolved budgeting exists, the buyer may not belong to a formal purchasing department at all, but be someone who also has a functional role such as R&D or marketing.

Gatekeepers

Gatekeepers have some control over the decision-making process, in that they can control the flow of information by denying access to key members of the buying centre. For example, a secretary or purchasing manager may prevent a sales representative from talking directly to an executive, or intercept brochures and mailshots and throw them in the waste-paper basket before they reach the decision maker. Technical staff can also act as gatekeepers in the way in which they choose to gather, present and interpret information to other members of the buying centre.

Bear in mind that the buying centre is not necessarily a fixed entity from transaction to transaction or even within a single transaction. It can be fluid and dynamic, evolving to meet the changing demands of the unfolding situation; it can be either formally constituted (for a major capital project, for instance) or loosely informal (a chance chat over coffee in the canteen between the purchasing manager and an R&D scientist); it can consist of two or three or many people. In other words, it is what it needs to be to do the job in hand.

When analysing the make-up of the buying centre, we should look not only at the allocation of roles between the different functional areas of the organisation, but also at the seniority of the members. Higher expenditure levels or purchases that have a critical impact on the organisation may involve much more senior management. Of course, input from the lower levels of the hierarchy will help to shape the decision, but the eventual authority may rest at Board level. Thus, for example, a bank's decision to introduce a new account control system may be taken at a very senior level.

Also, an individual's contribution to it may not be limited to one role. In a small business, the owner/manager may be influencer and buyer as well as decider. Similarly, in a larger organisation, where routine rebuys are concerned, the buyer may also be the decider, with very little call for influencers. Whatever the structure, however fluid the buying centre is, it is still important for the aspiring supplier to attempt to identify the pattern within the target organisation in order to create effective communication links.

Having thus established decision-making structures, the next step is to examine the criteria applied during the process.

BUYING CRITERIA

Within the previous sections, the emphasis in terms of decision making has largely been on rational, functionally orientated criteria. These task-related, or economic criteria are certainly important and reinforce the view of the organisation as a rational thinking entity. It is dangerous, however, to fall into the trap of forgetting that behind every job title lurks an individual whose motives and goals are not necessarily geared towards the greater good of the organisation. Such motives and goals may not form a direct, formally recognised part of the decision-making process, but nevertheless, they can certainly cause friction and influence the outcomes of it.

Economic influences

As has been stressed throughout this chapter so far, it is not always a matter of finding the lowest priced supplier. If the purchasing organisation can make the best use of increased reliability, superior performance, better customer service and other technical or logistical supports from its suppliers, then they can offer a better package to their own customers, with the rewards that brings. This route can also result in lower total costs, since it reduces production delays due to substandard components or delivery failures, and also improves the quality consistency of the purchaser's own end product, thus reducing the costs of handling complaints and replacing goods.

The main criteria have already been discussed in the previous sections of this chapter, so here is a summary of them:

Appropriate prices

The appropriate price is necessarily the lowest, but one representing good value for money taking into account the whole service package on offer.

Example

A Health Authority in the UK had to award a training contract for nurses' education. Of the three university bids received, the lowest priced was not chosen, despite being significantly lower than the successful bidder's. The Authority preferred to choose a university with which they felt they could develop close co-operation, and which they were certain would maintain the quality of training over the five-year life of the contract.

Product specification

Product specification involves in finding the right product to meet the purchaser's specified needs, neither more nor less. There are, of course, various trade-offs between specification and price. The main point is the closeness of the match and the certainty that it will be maintained throughout the order cycle, or that the supplier will be able to meet increasing and changing demands as technology progresses. This is particularly important in areas such as electronics where product life cycles are getting shorter and shorter.

Quality consistency

It is important to find a supplier with adequate quality controls to minimise defects so that the purchaser can use the product with confidence. This is especially true for JIT systems, where there is little room for failure.

Example

Velden Engineering (UK) manufacture a wide range of component parts and assemblies for various industries and applications, such as medical and aeronautical. In such sensitive areas, they need to ensure that everything supplied is right first time, as failure can be very expensive indeed. Their customers not only expect compliance with standards such as BS5750 and ISO9002 but also to be supplied with finished components or tested assemblies that can go straight into the production process on a JIT basis. This is a crucial factor in supplier selection.

Supply reliability and continuity

The purchaser needs to be sure that adequate supplies of the product will be available as and when needed, especially where JIT systems are involved. This may mean sacrificing the economies of scale achieved through sourcing from one supplier for the risk-spreading advantages to be had from sourcing smaller amounts from a number of suppliers.

Example

An Irish company that purchased printed circuit boards had an established set of suppliers, used depending on the volume required. For larger volumes, the company tended to source internationally, but smaller volumes for prototype work were sourced within Ireland. In all cases, however, once quality and specification had been assessed, and prices agreed, any failure to maintain supplies to schedule was regarded as a contract termination issue after one initial warning (Pettitt, 1992).

Customer service

Buyers require the reassurance that the supplier is prepared to take responsibility for his product by providing fast and flexible backup service in case of problems. This aspect might also include an appraisal of the supplier's longer-term capacity and willingness to get involved in joint development activities. Some customer service is delivered even before the sale is made.

Example

Nedalo (UK) is a joint venture between Nedalo BV from the Netherlands and Eastern Electricity from the UK, selling small-scale combined heat and power equipment. Nedalo (UK) undertakes free feasibility studies and site assessment to establish for the customer the scale of the savings and the most appropriate usage. The company also offers discounted electricity schemes and the free installation and maintenance of its units. This last area, maintenance, is a good example of the importance of post-sales service. All of these additional services matter to buyers of plant and equipment, but the cost savings also matter. The Edwardian International Hotel near Heathrow airport estimated that the successful installation of a Nedalo unit has saved about £40 000 per year (Guttridge, 1995).

Non-Economic influences

Powers (1991) summarises non-economic influences under four main headings: prestige, career security, friendship and social needs, and other personal needs. We look at each of these in turn.

Status within an office environment is demonstrated through the quality of the furniture. The desire for prestige may overcome economic considerations in the purchasing decision.

Source: Ottantotta executive furniture by Schirolli, tel 0171 836 3636, fax 0171 836 0565.

Prestige

Organisations, or more specifically the individuals who make up organisations, hanker after 'status'. They want to be seen to be doing better than their competitors or other divisions within the same organisation. So, for example, they may be prepared to spend a little more, when the office accommodation is refurbished, on better quality furnishings, decor and facilities to impress, instil confidence or even intimidate visitors to the site.

Career Security

Few people involved in the decision-making process are truly objective about it. They may well be chiefly and genuinely concerned with finding the best solution to the problem, but at the back of the mind there is always the question, 'What does this mean for my job?'

First, there is the risk element. A problem may have two alternative solutions, one which is safe, predictable and unspectacular, and one which is high risk, but promises a high return. If the high-risk decision is made and it all goes wrong, what are the consequences? The individual may not want to be associated with such an outcome and thus will push for the safe route.

Second, there is the awareness of how others are judging the individual's behaviour in the decision-making process: 'Am I prepared to go against the main body of opinion on a particular issue that I feel strongly about or will that brand me as a troublemaker and jeopardise my promotion prospects?'

Friendship and social needs

Needs such as friendship can be dangerous and can sometimes stray very close to ethical boundaries. It is necessary, however, to value trust, confidence and respect built on a personal level between individuals in the buying and selling organisations. It does help to reduce the perceived risk of the buyer–seller relationship.

Other personal factors

The three categories discussed above all provide useful insights into the human elements of organisational behaviour, but their emphasis is still on the relationship between the individual, the job and the organisation. Remember too the individual's personal profile, issues such as demographic characteristics, attitudes and beliefs, discussed in Chapter 3 in the context of consumer behaviour. These, coupled with things like self-confidence and communication skills, can all shape the extent to which that individual is allowed to participate in and influence the outcome of the decision-making process. A young, recent business graduate with forthright views, for example, may provoke negative reactions in older managers who have progressed through more traditional routes, and feel that they have accumulated a wealth of experience, even if the graduate's views are valid.

A further dimension of non-economic forces is trust. Trust is the belief that another organisation will act in such a way that the outcomes will be beneficial to both parties, and that it will not act in such a way as to bring about negative effects (Anderson and Narus, 1986). Trust can be built at an organisational level, but can also stem from a series of personal relationships between employees. Lorenz (1988), for example, found from a study of subcontracting in France that personal contacts were a major cause of organisational trust. From that trust can come a whole series of activities that can enhance the relationship, as considered in the following section.

RELATIONSHIP MARKETING

One matter that has been emphasised repeatedly in this chapter is the potential risks inherent in poor purchasing decisions. The quality of the relationship between the buying organisation and an existing supplier could prove to be a major factor in reducing those risks, and is inevitably going to influence decision-making processes. The history of previous transactions between two organisations leads to understanding, expectations and perhaps an active desire to continue to trade, even at the cost of short-term sacrifice.

There has been, therefore, an increased focus in the recent years on the place of buyer–seller relationships in explanations of marketing and decision making in organisational markets. Porter (1990) goes further in suggesting that an organisation with advantageous relationships with supplier networks has a competitive edge, because of the synergy between them in terms of joint problem solving and information exchange.

This final section of the chapter looks at some of the characteristics of buyer–seller relationships that add a further dimension to the understanding of the decision-making processes already covered.

Durability

Durability refers to the longevity of relationships in organisational markets, that might even outlast individuals and managerial generations. Not all exchanges evolve into long-term durable relationships. In low-cost, low-risk purchasing situations there will be minimal concern about long-term relationships. For example paper clips for the office are a standard product and there is plenty of choice in the market, and thus convenience and possibly low-price will be the major concerns.

However, as complexity increases and as it becomes apparent that value can be created by developing a stable, well-tuned relationship, then there may be mutual advantage in continuity. This may emerge for two types of reason. The first relates to the economic dimension, the second to the social dimension.

Economic Dimension

Joint development has already been mentioned a few times in this chapter. If a supplier has invested time, effort and money in improving quality or products, or in developing special operating processes or services to suit a particular customer, then the supplier will want the relationship to be sustained so that returns on that investment can be realised. Similarly, the purchaser will not want to start the process again from scratch with a new supplier. If the relationship has led to a specialist complex package, then either party may become dependent on the other. In other words, the purchaser cannot easily get the same thing from an alternative supplier, and the supplier cannot easily find an alternative customer.

Social Dimension

There is a certain security and comfort in dealing with someone you know. There is an existing level of trust, knowledge and friendship to build on. Strengths and weaknesses are known quantities, thereby reducing the risks of taking on a new supplier or customer.

Example

Fiat realised at the end of the 1980s that it had weaknesses in its operation that suppliers could help to solve. For many years, Fiat had purchased largely on price, a policy that had encouraged short-term thinking and little innovation in quality from suppliers. Fiat now needed to encourage suppliers to become involved in the design process, and then to invest in their own quality improvement to benefit Fiat. They began to offer a long-term relationship based on trust, and in return for the supplier's investment and commitment, offered them an exclusive contract. Thus 92 per cent of the parts in the Punto were single sourced. This was part of a programme of cutting back the number of main suppliers from 500 to 130, providing 90 per cent of Fiat's parts needs.

Some relationships can be very long lasting and resistant to change, despite the temptations of competitors' marketing wiles. It is difficult for an outsider to break into such well-developed and managed relationships. A number of studies have been undertaken into the duration of buyer–seller relationships. Valla (1986) found that 40 per cent of French buyer–seller relationships studied had lasted for over 20 years; Johanson and Wootz (1986) found that 30 per cent of German relationships studied had lasted for more than 16 years, and in the UK, 40 per cent of relationships studied had been in existence for over 11 years (Cunningham 1986). These results certainly give food for thought. Whether involvement in such relationships has offered protection against the worst ravages of economic recession is a study yet to be undertaken.

Approaches to supplier handling

The way in which the purchasing organisation decides to deal with its suppliers can have a fundamental effect on the future of the buyer–seller relationship. According to Spekman (1988), there are two polarised approaches which lead to very different relationships.

Adversarial approach

The purchasing organisation pressurises the supplier to minimise prices, and by insisting on short-term contracts and using multiple sourcing, keeps the supplier alert and

Buyer–supplier co-operation

A good example of the benefits of collaboration is seen in the relationship between the Lawson Mardon Group (LMG), a plastic blow moulder, and Jeyes, a consumer cleaning goods manufacturer. Jeyes needed 200 different types of plastic bottle in a variety of sizes from 250 ml to 5 litre. Seventeen machines were needed to produce the required volume of containers. Jeyes switched from in-house production to buying in from LMG. The risks of thus extending the supply chain were reduced when LMG located their factory next door to Jeyes'

with a conveyor belt running between the two for continuous production and supply. Both parties benefited from this arrangement. LMG had a long-term seven-year supply contract with flexibility to allow for changing raw material prices, giving them a secure foundation for building a wider customer base. Jeyes were able to focus on their core business, freed of the esponsibility of churning out plastic bottles, yet retaining security and flexibility of supply, delivery reliability, and maintaining quality standards.

sweating. The purchaser is unlikely to be interested in helping the supplier unless there is a direct cost saving to be had. This purchaser will rarely need special products and services and certainly will rarely be prepared to pay for such things. This is a legitimate approach in appropriate circumstances, where there are plenty of alternative sources of supply, the product is fairly standard and price really is the driving criterion.

Collaborative approach

In a collaborative approach, close ties are forged between buyer and seller, and there is much interest and value in close co-operation and integration. Such an approach can support valuable work in product design, specification and quality; advanced production processes; flexible scheduling and delivery; and special inventory. There are, however, the risks of becoming too 'cosy', complacent and blinkered, as well as the inherent dangers of mutual dependency.

Collaborative approaches are particularly crucial in JIT environments, as Table 4.6 shows, neatly summarising the reasons why collaboration rather than confrontation should be considered in critical supply situations.

TABLE 4.6
Collaborative vs adversarial approaches to supplier handling

Adversarial	Collaborative
● Multiple suppliers	● Few suppliers
● Regular price quotes	● Long-term relationship; mutual investment
● Adversarial negotiations	● Partnerships
● Sporadic communication	● Frequent, planned communication
● Little co-operation	● Integrated operations
● Quality and time scales to meet lowest threshold	● Quality and time scales 'designed in'
● Emphasis on lowest unit price	● Emphasis on lowest overall cost

Source: Adapted from Spekman (1988).

Supplier relationship portfolio

The focus so far has been on the relationship between one purchaser and one supplier. In reality, a purchaser is likely to maintain a portfolio of suppliers and to develop different levels and intensity of relationship with each, based on need and value.

Some suppliers have the potential to be long-term important partners in joint innovative development, and therefore the purchaser may encourage co-operation in improving both technical capability and quality, while others will be developed as guaranteed, secure, reliable sources of supply. Both of these will deserve a collaborative approach to handling. Others, however, will merit no special consideration, for example where there are plenty of alternative sources readily available, and will be retained at arm's length somewhere nearer the adversarial end of the handling spectrum. It is the job of purchasing to advise on an appropriate portfolio.

Relationship life-cycle

Much emphasis has been put on the potential durability of a buyer–seller relationships, but as with any kind of relationship, it is dynamic, changes its nature over time and is unlikely to last indefinitely. This evolution can be broken down into five stages of the **relationship life-cycle**, as proposed by Dwyer *et al.* (1987).

Awareness
Awareness occurs as each party learns of each other's existence and potential. This could come about as a result of a sales visit, a trade exhibition or any other means of making an initial contact.

Exploration
Exploration is about discovery, and has all the insecurities of adolescent relationships. It is about gaining experience, testing each other out with no real commitment and with high uncertainty over the outcomes. This could mean small trial orders, and perhaps even some pre-order assessment.

Expansion
Expansion has the characteristics of romance and the early days of marriage. Partners are working together, valuing the benefits, building orders and mutual trust. There is a rising level of commitment and the partners may even be making special adaptations to suit each other better. The uncertainty is much reduced, and members of staff from the two organisations may be starting to build sound working and social relationships.

Commitment
In the commitment stage, the novelty has worn off, but the partners are comfortable with each other and have built a predictable, stable nest round themselves. There is high mutual trust and respect, well-developed personal networks, and the seller has become a major supplier of special products and services, perhaps to the point where there is a high level of mutual dependency. Most relationships remain in this stage, but a few move on to the next stage.

Dissolution
This stage is possibly the equivalent to disillusionment and divorce. If stability and satisfaction have been reached in the maturity stage, then the most likely source of danger is complacency. Lack of innovation or service responsiveness on the seller's part, for example, could encourage the purchaser to turn to a younger, more versatile supplier with a good marketing-orientated approach ('I can tell your current supplier doesn't understand you any more. Let me show you my blueprints ...').

Sometimes the dissolution can be carried out with respect and dignity. A small supplier of engineering components, for example, found that its major customer was going to phase out its purchases from that supplier over the next two years. The customer had decided to make the components itself, but acted responsibly by phasing the supplier out over time rather than all at once. Instant termination of the contract would have had a devastating effect on the supplier, who depended on this customer for 60 per cent of his business. At least he now had two years to find alternative customers or to reorganise the business.

Much remains to be explored in the evolution of buyer–seller relationships. Little is really known about the stages, their underlying determinants, and the specific factors that trigger change. However, it is clear that when the relationship between two parties is examined in depth, patterns of evolution do emerge, and the key decision points that shape the relationship become apparent.

CHAPTER SUMMARY

The focus of this chapter has been organisational buying behaviour and buyer–seller relationships. Organisational marketing is about exchanges between organisations, whether they are commercial enterprises, government bodies or institutions.

Organisational markets have a number of distinct characteristics including: the nature of demand (derived, joint and inelastic), the structure of demand (concentrated in size and in geography), the complexity of the buying process and the risks inherent in it. The decision-making process that organisational purchasers go through has elements in common with consumer decision making, but is likely to be formalised, to take longer and to involve more people. Stages in the decision-making process include:

- *Precipitation:* beginning the process through recognising a need.
- *Product specification:* defining what is required and the priorities or criteria on which a supplier will be selected.
- *Supplier selection:* searching out potential suppliers, soliciting bids and assessing them in order to make a final choice.
- *Commitment:* drawing up contracts, and developing and maintaining a long-term, mutually valuable relationship.

Staff with various functional backgrounds, such as purchasing, marketing, accounting, engineering, production and R&D will be involved in the process, and form a buying centre. The membership of the buying centre, the roles played and who takes the lead may vary from transaction to transaction or even from stage to stage within a single process.

The decision-making process is affected not only by rational, measurable economic criteria (price, specification, quality, service etc.), but also by non-economic influences (prestige, security, social needs, personality) emanating from the individuals involved.

The on-going buyer–seller relationship is increasingly being recognised as a major influencer of organisational marketing strategies. Relationships can be durable and resistant to change, leading to mutual co-operation and the full exploitation of synergy between the two organisations. Other less significant relationships can, however, be kept deliberately superficial. The purchasing organisation has to develop a portfolio of different relationships of varying closeness and depth to suit the whole spectrum of its needs.

Relationships do develop over time, and pass through a number of developmental stages, from the initial *awareness* stage, through *exploration* and *expansion* phases, establishing trust, to *commitment*. Some relationships then pass on to *dissolution*, perhaps through complacency, or one party's neglect of the other.

Key words and phrases

Buying centre	*Modified rebuy*	*Product specification*
Decision-making unit (DMU)	*Multiple sourcing*	*Purchasing policy*
	New task purchasing	*Relationship life-cycle*
Derived demand	*Organisational marketing*	*Routine rebuy*
Joint demand		*Single sourcing*

QUESTIONS FOR REVIEW

4.1 What are the different categories of organisational customer, and how do they differ from each other?

4.2 What is derived demand and how might it affect organisational purchasing?

4.3 Why does organisational buying vary across different types of organisation, sometimes even within the same industry?

4.4 What are the main differences between organisational and consumer buying behaviour?

4.5 Outline the main stages in the organisational buying decision-making process.

4.6 What factors influence the complexity and the amount of time spent on the decision-making process?

4.7 What is a buying centre?

4.8 How might people in different functional roles (for example, R&D or marketing) participate in organisational buying?

4.9 Define the main economic and non-economic influences on organisational decision making.

4.10 Why is it that in some buyer–seller relationships strong bonds and co-operation develop?

QUESTIONS FOR DISCUSSION

4.1 From the supplier's point of view, how might the marketing approaches aimed at a customer making a new task purchase differ from those aimed at a routine rebuy customer?

4.2 How are supplier handling strategies changing as organisations seek to improve their competitiveness?

4.3 What are the stages in the buyer–seller relationship life cycle, and how is each characterised? What difference might the stages make to the seller's marketing approaches?

4.4 You are the purchasing manager of a large organisation with an enormous annual spend.

Most of your contracts are awarded by tender. What would your attitude be to the following offers from potential suppliers, and to what extent would they influence your decision making:
(a) A bottle of whisky at Christmas?
(b) An invitation to lunch to discuss your requirements?
(c) An offer of the free use of the supplier's Managing Director's Spanish villa for two weeks?
(d) £1500?

4.5 What do you think are the advantages and disadvantages of long-term, close buyer–seller relationships?

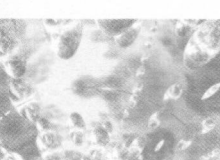

Taurus

The news hit the press on 12 March 1993. It certainly was news for the financial community, although it was not entirely unexpected. The failure of Taurus could be counted on a number of dimensions. First, between seven and 13 years of development work was lost. The cost, sunk without trace, was estimated to be between £100mn and £300mn. Up to 450 people were expected to lose their jobs. The reputation of the Stock Exchange council, the prime movers of the project, suffered a severe jolt, doing little for London as a major centre in the international financial community. The chief executive of the Stock Exchange resigned in a storm of controversy. All this was the result of an organisational buying decision that went sadly wrong.

Taurus, more technically known as the Transfer and Automatic Registration of Uncertified Stock, was meant to revolutionise the transfer of shares through the development and implementation of a fully computerised transfer system. Such a system was meant to reduce dealing costs, save time and eliminate traditional share certificates. The new system was designed to raise the competitiveness of the City of London as a financial centre, and to eliminate paper-based mechanical procedures, replacing them with a computerised system. The brief for the scheme, first conceived in 1981, was to replace share certificates and stock transfer forms with an electronic register so that shareholders would be sent regular statements detailing their recent transactions made through paperless exchanges.

Taurus 1 was meant to provide the comprehensive fully integrated solution to share transfer, fully replacing paper-based systems. However, the initial specification was to be based around simulating the paper system rather than adopting a specification that was based upon actual user requirements. This proved extremely difficult to put into operation, given the range of variables involved. Agreeing a specification was also made more difficult by the composition of the committee designed to progress the project. This included not only the Stock Exchange, but also the banks, the government's Department of Trade and Industry (DTI), pension houses and other parties concerned to protect the rights of small shareholders. Finding consensus was never easy and the project became larger and more complex as its system requirements evolved to cater for the differing interests.

It became increasingly obvious by the mid 1980s that Taurus 1 was in trouble. Operationally, the system failed to meet the demands of the agreed specification. Attention was diverted to other projects and Taurus 1 lapsed until 1987. However, failure to gain acceptance of the idea of a single computerised register to be maintained by the Stock Exchange resulted in major objections and criticisms from the users and providers of the existing paper-based system. Taurus 1 was dead for lack of progress.

Despite its demise, the need for efficiency improvement remained. It needed a champion, however. The launch of Taurus 2 coincided with the arrival of Peter Rawlins in 1989 as the new chief executive of the Stock Exchange. With a brief to modernise the Stock Exchange, he placed considerable importance on Taurus as a means of fully streamlining what were considered to be antiquated support systems. A new committee was formed to represent all the City interests and the idea of a central register was dropped in favour of linking existing commercial databases maintained by brokers, registrars, banks and others into a network. It was hoped that wider participation, including the DTI, would enable the emergence of a consensus on commitment to change.

Again problems emerged with the specification. Delays and complications all added to the cost and fostered a growing feeling that the project was doomed. Critics such as Pro Share (an organisation set up by the Stock Exchange to promote wider share ownership) started arguing for two systems rather than one. One system would cater for the financial institutions and the other for the private investor. However, the final straw came when the consulting company responsible for operating the system conducted practical tests and considered it virtually inoperable. The changes needed would double the development cost again and the project would be delayed until 1996.

To the Stock Exchange council and the banks such further delay was unacceptable. The project was to be abandoned in its present form. According to *The Times*, Mr Rawlins as a fervent supporter of Taurus was 'left with little option but to fall on his sword'.

Even as the press reports gained momentum, the implications were being considered. One banker was quoted as saying, 'We all knew it was an enormous project but were beginning to hope the big building blocks were in place. London clearing systems are completely out of date and archaic'. Others were disappointed at the waste of so much time and money.

Whether there will be a long-term disadvantage to the City remains to be seen. Alternative, allegedly more basic systems are operating in Europe and the USA. These could be licensed for use in London if nothing is salvaged from a major organisational buying decision that went wrong.

Source: The Times (1993).

Questions

1 Outline the problems leading up to the demise of Taurus 1. Could they have been predicted?

2 Given the eventual outcome of Taurus 1, what changes were needed to give Taurus 2 a better chance of successful launch?

3 In a new major project such as Taurus, what consideration should be given to the composition and decision-making style of the buying committee?

4 In what ways do you think that implementation of the purchasing decision-making process in a manufacturing firm investing in new production machinery might differ from that of the Stock Exchange investing in a computer system?

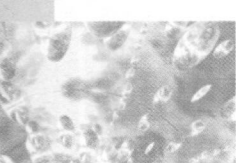

CASE STUDY 4.2

Philips cultivates suppliers

Philips is a global operator in the electronics market with factories all over the world. In order to compete and to ensure customer satisfaction, Philips has to manage its quality and purchasing strategy very carefully. The company recognises that customer satisfaction depends on the quality of what happens on the production line, which in turn depends on the performance of suppliers. If any of the links in the chain break down or fail to meet the required standard, then all the glossy advertising in the world is not going to make up for the customer's disappointment in a product that is unavailable, or does not work properly, or fails to meet their technical expectations.

Total quality, therefore, is an ingrained philosophy throughout Philips' operations, resulting in better products and better processes. 'Philips Quality' has five simple, but important principles:

(a) Strive for excellence.
(b) Customer first.
(c) Demonstrate leadership.
(d) Value people.
(e) Supplier partnership.

Directly or indirectly, many of these principles could not be properly implemented without good relationships with the right suppliers. Philips cultivates supplier relationships based on trust and co-operation, sharing experience and expertise to benefit not only the buyer and the supplier, but also the end customer. Together, Philips and its suppliers develop technology, solve problems, learn from experience and try to avoid errors and misunderstandings.

Clearly, Philips cannot develop and maintain deep relationships with every one of its suppliers. Instead, it assesses its suppliers to discover which ones are the most important in terms of their strategic significance to Philips' business. These receive the most attention and investment in relationship building. Philips has three categories of supplier:

1 *Supplier–partners*: this might be the smallest group, but these are the most important suppliers and Philips builds intense, involved relationships with them. An important focus of the co-operation is innovation, the development of new expertise and new opportunities. These suppliers might well have essential knowledge and/or expertise that Philips could not otherwise access or develop for itself. This makes these suppliers extremely significant strategically as their loss could seriously undermine Philips' current business and future direction.

2 *Preferred suppliers*: these suppliers are less important but there is still good reason for Philips to work closely with them on issues such as quality, logistics

and price to gain mutual benefit. The supplier does adapt itself to suit Philips' requirements, to some extent, but there is not the same mutual dependence as in the first category.

3 *Commercial suppliers*: these are the least important suppliers and although Philips will encourage better performance in terms of quality etc., it is unlikely to get involved in helping the supplier to achieve it.

Philips also emphasizes the importance of supplier revaluation as a basis for improving future performance. A supplier's actual performance is measured against mutually agreed targets in terms of quality, logistics, costs and responsiveness.

Source: European Purchasing and Materials Management (1993/94).

Questions

1 Why should Philips go to all this trouble to develop relationships with suppliers? Why doesn't it just choose suppliers on the basis of the lowest price?

2 What do you think each of the five principles of 'Philips Quality' actually means in practice? How are they consistent with the marketing concept and what impact might they have on the marketing mix?

3 Suggest what criteria Philips might use to decide what category a particular supplier falls into.

4 What is the purpose of supplier evaluation? What do you think Philips might do if they found that a particular supplier had under performed in terms of costs and quality?

REFERENCES TO CHAPTER 4

Anderson, J. C. and Narus, J. A. (1984), 'A Model of the Distributor's Perspective of Distributor–Manufacturer Working Relationships', *Journal of Marketing*, 48 (Fall), pp. 62–74.

Anderson, J. C. and Narus, J. A. (1986), 'Towards a Better Understanding of Distribution Channel Working Relationships' *in* K. Backhaus and D. Wilson (eds.) *Industrial Marketing: A German–American Perspective*, Springer-Verlag.

Carr, H. and Pomeroy, J. (1992), *Fashion Design and Product Development*, Blackwell.

Central Office Of Information (1993), *Britain 1993: An Official Handbook*, HMSO.

Commission of the European Communities (1990), *Public Procurement: Opening Public Service Contracts*, Background Report ISEC/B30/90, 9 November.

Cunningham, M. T. (1986), 'The British Approach to Europe' *in* P. W. Turnbull and J-P. Valla (eds.) *Strategies for International Industrial Marketing*, Croom Helm.

Dempsey, J. (1994), 'Big is No Longer Beautiful', *Financial Times*, 21 November, VIII.

Dwyer, F. R. *et al.* (1987), 'Developing Buyer–Seller Relationships', *Journal of Marketing*, 51(2), pp. 11–27.

European Purchasing and Materials Management (1993/94), 'Philips Quality', *European Purchasing and Materials Management*, 1993/94(2), pp. 51–55.

European Purchasing and Materials Management (1994), 'Many sources, one market', *European Purchasing & Materials Management*, 1994(3), pp. 167–73.

Freeland, J. R. (1991), 'A Survey of JIT Purchasing in the United States', *Production and Inventory Management*, 32(2), pp. 43–50.

Freeman Allen, G. (1994), 'Italy's Pendolino: The Second Generation', *Modern Railways*, April pp. 227–8.

Freeman Allen, G. (1995a), 'Europeview', *Modern Railways*, Nov. p. 707.

Freeman Allen, G. (1995b), 'Europeview', *Modern Railways*, March, p. 165.

Freeman Allen, G. (1996), 'Europeview', *Modern Railways*, June, p. 395.

Genillard, A. (1993), 'Plenty of Scientists But No Monkeys', *Financial Times*, 29 April, p. 39.

Gutteridge, S. (1995), 'Financing Small Scale CHP Schemes', *Purchasing and Supply Management*, Feb. pp. 41–42.

Hallén, L. (1980), 'Stability and Change in Supplier Relationships', in L. Engall and J. Johanson (eds.), *Some Aspects of Control in International Business*, Uppsala.

Hill, R. W. and Hiller, T. J. (1977), *Organisational Buying Behaviour*, MacMillan.

Johanson, J. (1982), 'Production Technology and the User–Supplier Interaction' *in* H. Håkansson (ed.) *International Marketing and Purchasing of Industrial Goods: An Interaction Approach*, John Wiley and Sons.

Johanson, J. and Wootz, B. (1986), 'The German Approach to Europe', in P. W. Turnbull and J-P. Valla (eds.), *Strategies for International Industrial Marketing*, Croom Helm.

Johnson, W. J. and Bonoma, T. V. (1981), 'The Buying Centre: Structure and Interaction Patterns', *Journal of Marketing*, 45 (Summer), pp. 143–56.

Lorenz, E. H. (1988), 'Neither Friends Nor Strangers: Informal Networks of Subcontracting in French Industry', in D. Gambetta (ed.), *Trust: Making and Breaking Cooperative Relations*, Basil Blackwell.

Mattson, M. R. (1988), 'How to Determine the Composition and Influence of A Buying Centre', *Industrial Marketing Management*, 17(3), pp. 205–214.

Northam, S. (1994), 'Look Before You Leap', *European Purchasing and Materials Management*, 1994(3), pp. 251–7.

Paliwoda, S. and Bonaccorsi, A. J. (1994), 'Trends in Procurement Strategies Within the European Aircraft Industry', *Industrial Marketing Management*, 23(3), pp. 235–44.

Pettitt, S. J. (1992), *Small Firms and Their Major Customers: An Interaction and Relationship Approach*, unpublished PhD Thesis, Cranfield University.

Porter, M. E. (1990), *The Competitive Advantage of Nations*, The Free Press.

Powers, T. L. (1991), *Modern Business Marketing: A Strategic Planning Approach to Business and Industrial Markets*, St Paul MN: West.

Ramsay, J. and Wilson, I. (1990), 'Sourcing/Contracting Strategy Selection', *International Journal of Operations and Production Management*, 10(8), pp. 19–28.

Robinson, P. J. *et al.* (1967), *Industrial Buying and Creative Marketing*, Allyn and Bacon.

Segal, M. (1989), 'Implications of Single vs Multiple Buying Sources', *Industrial Marketing Management*, 18(3), pp. 163–178.

Sheth, J. (1973), 'A Model of Industrial Buying Behaviour', *Journal of Marketing*, 37(Oct), 50–6.

Sheth, J. (1977), 'Recent Developments in Organisational Buying Behaviour', in A. G. Woodside *et al.* (eds.), *Consumer and Industrial Buying Behaviour*, Elsevier.

Spekman, R. E. (1988), 'Strategic Supplier Selection: Understanding Long Term Buyer Relationships', *Business Horizons*, 31(4), pp. 75–81.

Summers D. (1994), 'Living Life to the Max', *Financial Times*, 29 September, p. 15.

The Times (1993), 'Taurus Finally Succumbs to Fatal Errors of Conception', *The Times,* 12 March.

Trevelen, M. (1987), 'Single Sourcing: A Management Tool for the Quality Supplier', *Journal of Purchasing and Materials Management*, 23(1), p. 19–24.

Valla, J-P. (1986), 'The French Approach to Europe' *in* P. W. Turnbull and J-P. Valla (eds.), *Strategies for International Industrial Marketing*, Croom Helm.

Webster, F. E. and Wind, Y. (1972), *Organisational Buyer Behaviour*, Prentice Hall.

What To Buy For Business (1993), 'Mobile Phones', *What to Buy for Business*, No. 151, October, Reed Business Publishing.

Wolfe, A. (1992), 'The Eurobuyer: How European Businesses Buy', *European Business Review*, 92(1), pp. 3–10.

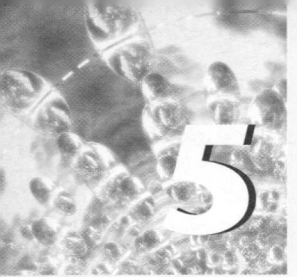

5 Segmenting Markets

LEARNING OBJECTIVES

This chapter will help you to:

1 understand the potential benefits of breaking markets down into smaller, more manageable parts or segments;

2 explain the ways in which market segments are defined in both organisational and consumer markets;

3 understand the effects on the marketing mix of pursuing specific segments; and

4 appreciate the role of segmentation in strategic marketing thinking.

INTRODUCTION

Building on the understanding of buyer behaviour and decision-making processes outlined in Chapters 3 and 4, this chapter concerns a question which should be very close to any true marketer's heart: 'How do we define and profile our customer?' Until an answer is found, no meaningful marketing decisions of any kind can be made. It is not usually enough to define your customer as 'anyone who wants to buy our product' because this implies a product-orientated approach: the product comes first, the customer second. If marketing is everything we have claimed it to be, then the product is only a small part of a total integrated package offered to a customer. Potential customers must, therefore, be defined in terms of what they want, or will accept, in terms of price, what kind of distribution will be most convenient for them and through what communication channels they can best be reached, as well as what they want from the product itself.

Remember too that in a consumer-based society, possession of 'things' can take on a symbolic meaning. A person's possessions and consumption habits make a statement about the kind of person they are, or the kind of person they want you to think they are. The organisation that takes the trouble to understand this and produces a product that not only serves its functional purpose well, but also appears to reflect those less tangible properties of a product in the purchaser's eyes, will gain that purchaser's custom. Thus the sport shoe manufacturers such as Reebok and Nike not only developed shoes for a wide range of specific sports (tennis, soccer, athletics etc.), but also realised that a significant group of customers would never go near a sports facility and just wanted trainers as fashion statements. This meant that they served three distinctly different groups of customers: the professional/serious sports player, the amateur/casual sports player and the fashion victim. The R&D invested in state of the art quality products, combined with the status connected with the first group, and endorsement from leading sports icons helped these companies to build an upmarket image that allowed them to exploit the fashion market to the full with premium-priced products. This in turn led to the expansion of product ranges to include branded sports and leisure clothing.

All this forms the basis of the concept of segmentation, first developed by Smith (1957). Segmentation can be viewed as the art of discerning and defining meaningful differences between groups of customers to form the foundations of a more focused marketing effort. The following section looks at this concept in a little more depth, while the rest of the chapter will examine how the concept can be implemented and its implications for the organisation.

THE CONCEPT OF SEGMENTATION

The introductory section of this chapter has presented the customer-orientated argument for the adoption of the segmentation concept. There is, however, also a practical rationale for adopting it. Mass production, mass communication, increasingly sophisticated technology and increasingly efficient global transportation have all helped in the creation of larger, more temptingly lucrative potential markets. Few organisations, however, have either the resources or the inclination to be a significant force within a loosely defined market. The sensible option, therefore, is to look more closely at the market and find ways of breaking it down into manageable parts, or groups of customers with similar characteristics, and then to concentrate effort on serving the needs of one or two groups really well, rather than trying to be all things to all people.

It may help you to understand this concept better if you think of an orange. It appears to be a single entity, yet when you peel off the skin you find that it is made up of a number of discrete segments, each of which happily exists within the whole. Eating an orange is much easier (and much less wasteful and messy) if you eat it systematically, segment by segment, rather than by attacking the whole fruit at once. Marketers, being creative folk, have adopted this analogy and thus refer to the separate groups of customers that make up a market as **market segments**.

The analogy is misleading, however, in that each segment of an orange is more or less identical in size, shape and taste whereas in a market, segments may be very different from each other in terms of size and character. To determine these things, each segment has its own distinct profile, defined in terms of a number of criteria, referred to as *bases* or *variables*, set by the marketer. The choice of appropriate criteria is very important and thus a significant proportion of this chapter is devoted to thinking about the bases by which segments might be defined in both consumer and organisational markets. Leading on from this, there is also the question of influences which might affect an organisation's choice of segmentation variables. Then, once an organisation has defined its market segments, what is it supposed to do with the information? This too is addressed in this chapter.

Organisational and consumer markets, in general, tend to be segmented differently and will, therefore, be discussed separately, beginning with organisational markets. If you are unsure of the difference between these two types of market, then revise the content of Chapters 3 and 4 before you go any further.

SEGMENTING ORGANISATIONAL MARKETS

The overall concept of segmentation applies equally to both consumer and organisational markets, but the variables by which they are segmented do differ. One major feature of organisational segmentation is that it can focus on both the organisation and the individual buyers within it. Additionally, there is the need to reflect group buying, that is, the involvement of more than one person in the purchasing decision.

All of this can be compared with a family buying situation in a consumer market, but operating on a much larger scale, usually within a more formalised process.

Wind and Cardozo (1974) suggest that segmenting an organisational market can involve two stages:

1 *Identify subgroups* within the whole market which share common general characteristics. These are called **macro segments** and will be discussed further below.

2 *Select target segments* from within the macro segments based on differences in specific buying characteristics. These are called **micro segments**, and are discussed at p. 171.

Macro segmentation bases

Macro segments are based on the characteristics of organisations and the broader purchasing context within which they operate. Defining a macro segment assumes that the organisations within it will exhibit similar patterns and needs which will be reflected in similar buying behaviour and responses to marketing stimuli.

The bases used for macro segmentation tend to be observable or readily obtained from secondary information (i.e., published or existing sources), and can be grouped into two main categories, each of which will now be discussed.

Organisational characteristics

There are three organisational charactistics: size, location and usage rate.

1 *Size*. The size of an organisation will make a difference to the way in which it views its suppliers and goes about its purchasing. A large organisation, for instance, may well have many people involved in decision making; its decision making may be very complex and formalised (because of the risks and level of investment involved), and it may require special treatment in terms of service or technical co-operation. In contrast, a small organisation may operate on a more centralised decision making structure, involving one or two people, and with simpler buying routines. The UK clearing banks, for example, tend to segment their business customers by size. Small businesses need sympathetic local support, and the banks target the new start up segment of the small business market with advice packs and promises of cheap financing along with the support of their own banking adviser.

2 *Location*. Organisations may focus their selling effort according to the geographic concentration of the industries they serve. Such specialisation is, however, slowly breaking down as the old, heavy, geographically based industries, such as ship-building, mining and chemical production, become less predominant. Additionally, there is the emergence of smaller more flexible manufacturers, geographically dispersed in new technology parks, industrial estates and enterprise zones. Nevertheless, there are still examples of geographic segmentation, such as that of computer hardware and software sales, or in the financial sector, which is concentrated in London, Frankfurt, Zurich and the major capitals of the world. Organisations providing certain kinds of services might also look to geographic segments. A haulage company might specialise in certain routes, and thus look for customers at specific points to make collection, delivery and capacity utilisation as efficient as possible.

3 *Usage rate*. The quantity of product purchased may be a legitimate means of categorising potential customers. A purchasing organisation defined as a 'heavy user' will have different needs from a 'light user', perhaps demanding (and deserving) different treatment in terms of special delivery or prices, for example. A supplier may define a threshold point, so that when a customer's usage rate rises above it, their status changes. The customer's account may be handed over to a more senior manager and the supplier may become more flexible in terms of co-operation,

pricing and relationship building. It is generally a better investment to make concessions in order to cultivate a relationship with a single heavy user than to try to attract a number of light users, as implied in Chapter 4.

Product or service application

This second group of segmentation bases acknowledges that the same good can be used in many different ways. This approach looks for customer groupings either within specific industries as defined by standard industrial classification (SIC) codes, each with its own requirements, or by defining a specific application and grouping customers around that.

The SIC code may help to identify sectors with a greater propensity to use particular products for particular applications. Glass, for example has many industrial uses, ranging from packaging to architecture to the motor industry. Each of these application sectors behaves differently in terms of price sensitivity, ease of substitution, quality and performance requirements, for instance. Similarly, cash-and-carry wholesalers serve three broad segments: independent grocers, caterers and pubs. Each segment will purchase different types of goods, in different quantities and for different purposes.

The macro level is a useful starting point for defining some broad boundaries to markets and segments, but it is not sufficient in itself, even if such segmentation does happen too often in practice. Further customer-orientated analysis on the micro level is necessary.

Micro-segmentation bases

Within a macro segment, a number of smaller micro segments may exist. To focus in on these, the organisation needs to have a detailed understanding of individual members of the macro segment, in terms of their management philosophy, decision-making structures, purchasing policies and strategies, as well as their needs and wants. Such information can come from published sources, past experience of the potential buyer, sales force knowledge and experience, word of mouth within the industry, or at first hand from the potential buyer.

Micro segmentation reflects, to some extent, the nested approach to organisational market segmentation suggested by Bonoma and Shapiro (1984). This means starting with broad characteristics, that is, the demographic profile of the customer (understanding the industry; organisational size etc.), and then developing increasingly fine detail by working through their operating variables (product, technology, quality etc.), purchasing approach (DMUs, power, buyer-seller relationships etc.), situational factors (delivery lead times, order size etc.), and finally, personal characteristics (the individuals concerned).

TABLE 5.1

Bases for micro segmentation in organisational markets

- Product
- Applications
- Technology
- Purchasing policies
- DMU structure
- Decision-making process
- Buyer–seller relationships

An overview of common bases for micro segmentation is given in Table 5.1. If some of the terms given within the table seem a little vague, revise Chapter 4 which goes into them all in much more detail.

Gathering, collating and analysing such depth of information is, of course, a time-consuming and sometimes difficult task, and there is always the question of whether it is either feasible or worth while. However, there are benefits in defining such small segments (even segments of one!) if it enables fine tuning of the marketing offering to suit specific needs. Given the volumes of goods and levels of financial investment involved in some organisational markets, the effort is well worth while. An organisation which has a small number of very important customers would almost certainly treat each as a segment of one, particularly in a market such as the supply of organisation-wide computer systems where individual customer needs vary so much. In contrast, in a market such as office stationery, where standard products are sold to perhaps thousands of organisational customers, any segmentation is likely to centre around groups aggregating many tens of customers on the macro level.

Overall, this section has shown that it is useful to be able to segment organisational markets, and that it can be done in a number of ways relating to the nature of both the product sold and the buying organisation. The emphasis here has essentially been a practical one, treating the buying organisation as a rational entity. Chapter 4 (particularly pp. 155 *et seq.*), in looking more deeply at the organisation as the sum of its human parts, demonstrated some of the potential irrationalities which make micro segmentation so fascinating. In consumer markets, rapid progress has also been made towards expanding concepts of segmentation to include what might be termed the less rational influences on purchasing, as the following section shows.

SEGMENTING CONSUMER MARKETS

Segmenting consumer markets does have some similarities with organisational segmentation, as this section indicates. The main difference is that consumer segments are usually very much larger in terms of the number of potential buyers, and it is much more difficult, therefore, to get close to the individual buyer. Consumer segmentation bases also put more emphasis on the buyer's lifestyle and context, because most consumer purchases fulfil higher-order needs (*see,* for example, Maslow's hierarchy of needs, discussed at p. 104) rather than simply functional ones.

Geographic segmentation

Geographic segmentation defines customers according to their location. This can often be a useful starting point. A small business, for example, particularly in the retail or service sector, operating on limited resources, may look initially for custom within its immediate locale. Even multinationals, such as Heinz, often tend to segment geographically by dividing their global organisation into operating units built around specific geographic markets.

In neither case, however, is this the end of the story. For the small business, simply being there on the High Street is not enough. It has to offer something further that a significant group of customers want, whether it is attractively low prices or a high level of customer service. The multinational organisational segments geographically, partly for the sake of creating a manageable organisational structure, and partly in recognition that on a global scale, geographic boundaries herald other, more significant differences in taste, culture, lifestyle and demand. The Single European Market (SEM) may have created a market of some 400 million potential customers, yet the first thing most organisations are likely to do is to segment the SEM into its constituent nations.

> ### Example
>
> Take the marketing of an instant hot chocolate drink, made with boiling water. In the UK, virtually every household owns a kettle, and hot chocolate is viewed either as a bedtime drink or as a substitute through the day for tea or coffee. In France, however, kettles are not common, and hot chocolate is most often made with milk as a nourishing children's breakfast. Thus the benefits of speed, convenience and versatility that would impress the UK market would be less applicable in the French market. France would require a very different marketing strategy at best, or at worst, a completely different product.

Geographic segments are at least easy to define and measure, and information is often freely available from public sources. This kind of segmentation also has an operational advantage, particularly in developing efficient systems for distribution and customer contact, for example. However, in a marketing-orientated organisation, this is not sufficient. Douglas and Craig (1983), for example, emphasise the dangers of being too geographically focused and making assumptions about what customers in a region might have in common. Even within a small geographic area, there is a wide variety of needs and wants, and this method on its own tells you nothing about them. Heinz divides its global operation into geographically based subdivisions because it does recognise the effects of cultural diversity, and believes in 'local marketing' as the best means of fully understanding and serving its various markets. It is also important to note that any organisation segmenting purely on geographic grounds would be vulnerable to competition coming in with a more customer-focused segmentation strategy.

In summary, therefore, there is limited scope for the application of geographic segmentation on its own. It may be useful for service-based products that require the customer to come to you. For example hairdressers attract business from a geographic catchment area centred on their salon, but even so, they still segment further on other criteria (for instance sex, age and trendiness). In manufacturing, geographic segmentation may also be useful for organisations operating with very limited resources. By confining its operations to a small geographic area, the organisation can develop a focus which will allow it to expand gradually as business builds up. In the main, however, it is used as a foundation for other, more customer-focused segmentation methods, such as those described below.

Demographic segmentation

Demographic segmentation tells you a little more about the customer and the customer's household on measurable criteria that are largely descriptive, such as age, sex, race, income, occupation, socioeconomic status and family structure.

Demographics might even extend into classifications of body size and shape! In the UK, for example, the proportion of overweight men has risen to almost 50 per cent of the male population, while 40 per cent of the female population are overweight. The overweight thus represent a significant marketing opportunity. The clothing retailers High and Mighty and Evans primarily target larger men and women respectively. Furniture manufacturers are redesigning their products to cope with bigger and heavier people, while cars, trains and airline seats are also having to be adapted (Palmer and Cohen, 1993).

MARKETING IN ACTION

Go for bust

The British bra and lingerie company, Gossard, has found that a geographic approach to market segmentation can have some validity. The types of product that sell best in various countries are different, partly for the practical reason that women vary in average size across Europe, and partly because of cultural and lifestyle factors. While the British female figure averages around sizes 12–14, German women tend towards sizes 14–16, and the French towards 10–12. Italian women want to be seductive, and thus buy a lot of basques; the Germans are practical and look for support and quality; the French want to be fashionable and impress other women; and the Scandinavians want natural fibres. This is, of course, a grossly generalised survey, but the basic trends are there, and give Gossard a basis for developing appropriate new products and strategies for different markets.

Source: Broadhead (1995).

Source: Gossard.

Gossard designs different products for different European markets as both taste and average sizes differ across regional boundaries.

As with the geographic variable, demographics are relatively easy to define and measure, and the necessary information is often freely available from public sources. The main advantage, however, is that demographics offer a clear profile of the customer on criteria that can be worked into marketing strategies. For example an age profile can provide a foundation for choice of advertising media and creative approach. Magazines, for instance tend to have readerships that are clearly defined in terms of gender, age bands and socioeconomic groups. The under-35 female reader, for example, is more likely to go for magazines such as *Marie Claire*, *Bella* and *Cosmopolitan* than the over-35s who are more likely to read *Prima*, *Good Housekeeping* and *Family Circle*.

One of the problems facing organisations looking to European markets in particular is that socioeconomic definitions vary widely across different countries, as already shown at p. 110. Efforts are, however, being made to develop a uniform scale, applicable across national boundaries, and relevant to the needs of marketers. The outcomes of one such project, reported in Marbeau (1992) and Quatresooz and Vancraeynest

Example

The 1995 British Shoppers Survey in *Marketing*, classified consumers according to age and family status and showed the types of products and brands each group tends to purchase (*Marketing*, 24 August 1995). The groups of shoppers included singles under 35, married under 35 with no kids, married under 35 with kids, single parents, married over 55 with no kids. Single parents, for example, represent 3.2 per cent of all shoppers and tend to shop a little but often, usually at discount retailers like Kwik Save. Their favourite brands include Kellogg's Coco Pops, and while they do buy branded products in some areas, such as coffee and detergents, they gravitate towards supermarket own brands in others. They are least likely to own a car.

(1992) suggest a definition of social grade based on the terminal education age of the main income earner in a household, his or her further education and professional training, and his or her occupation. Additionally, an economic status scale is proposed, based on a household's ownership of 10 carefully chosen consumer durables. This provides a way of comparing different countries without the problems of varying exchange rates, varying purchasing power or income measurement. The extent to which such a system becomes common European currency remains to be seen.

On the negative side, demographics are purely descriptive and, used alone, assume that all people in the same demographic group have similar needs and wants. This is not necessarily true (just think about the variety of people you know within your own age group). Additionally, as with the geographic method, it is still vulnerable to competition coming in with an even more customer-focused segmentation strategy. It is best used, then, for products that have a clear bias towards a particular demographic group. For instance cosmetics are initially segmented into male/female; baby products are primarily aimed at females aged between 20 and 35; school fee endowment policies appeal to households within a higher income bracket at a particular stage of the family life-cycle. In most of these cases, however, again as with the geographic method, the main use of demographic segmentation is as a foundation for other more customer-focused segmentation methods.

Geodemographic segmentation

Increasingly sophisticated data collection techniques and cheaper, more powerful computing facilities have led to the rise of **geodemographics**, a means of either defining the demographic characteristics of a given location or identifying the geographic spread of any given characteristic. A Classification of Residential Neighbourhoods (ACORN), marketed by CACI Information Services, is a well-established and widely used geodemographic system, built in the UK on the basis of national census data combined with market research data. ACORN classifies areas into one of 11 broad groups, each of which has a number of subdivisions. Table 5.2 shows how one of these groups, Group D, 'older terraced housing', is defined and further differentiated to provide detailed profiles. These profiles include a variety of interesting characteristics for the marketer, such as age breakdown, income, employment, car ownership, holiday habits,

MARKETING IN ACTION

Cola fatigue

One area that is showing impressive growth in the 1990s is that of adult-orientated soft drinks. The starting point for this is 'cola fatigue ' in the 20–35 year old age band. This age group is looking for something that is more grown up, more sophisticated, and non-alcoholic, and thus a £600 mn per year market for fruit and herb-based drinks (such as Aqua Libra, Kiri, Amé, and Purdey's), as well as cold teas (Snapple and Liptonice, for instance) has opened up in the UK. Both Coca-Cola and Pepsi Cola, recognising the growth of competing products better tailored towards the adult segment than either Coke or Pepsi, are currently working on developing new products specifically for this age group. Clearly, however, there is more to this sector than simply age segmentation. The products are mainly high priced (compared with other soft drinks), and to some extent, fulfil a desire among certain groups in society to cut back on alcohol consumption and to find a 'healthy' alternative to it. The fruit and herb ones in particular, through ingredients like ginseng, have vague connotations of new age alternative medicinal properties about them that make them attractive to certain life styles. Nevertheless, the primary driving force in the development of this market was originally the complete lack of adult-orientated soft drinks.

newspaper readership, leisure interests, and limited information on consumption habits.

Geodemographic systems are increasingly becoming available as multimedia packages. CACI, for example, market a Windows-based mapping and data analysis package called *InSite*. It includes census and lifestyle data, ACORN, market research and business data, allowing the manager to analyse any geographic area in some depth. CCN's MOSAIC is also available on CD-ROM, giving the manager access to colour maps, spoken commentary on how to use the system, photographs and text. CCN are also working on customised geodemographic packages, tailored to suit a particular client's needs.

Such systems are invaluable to the marketer across all aspects of consumer marketing, for example in planning sampling areas for major market research studies, or assessing locations for new retail outlets, or finding appropriate areas for a direct mail campaign or door-to-door leaflet drop. O'Malley *et al.* (1995) point out that retailers find geodemographics invaluable. This is because setting up a new retail store location is very capital intensive and represents a long-term commitment. Retailers thus need to monitor a trade area in terms of its catchment, shopper profiles, and competitive effects. Geodemographics can help to achieve this.

One of the problems, however, is that the smallest neighbourhood unit ACORN can define consists of about 150 households, and even with 11 major groups subdivided into

TABLE 5.2
ACORN Group D

- Older terraced housing – pre-1914
- Tenement flats
- Low income
- Inadequate ventilation/heating/cooking facilities
- Government grants have led to some modernisation
- Lack of suitable play areas for children
- In larger towns: young families
- In smaller towns: elderly population
- Few modern retail facilities

Source: CACI Information Services.

CCN's MOSAIC geodemographic system is available on CD-ROM, thus enhancing its user-friendliness and flexibility.

TABLE 5.3

Applications of geodemographic and lifestyle data

Application	Percentage of respondents
Targeting direct mail	55.6
Market segmentation	47.0
Customer database building	41.1
Media analysis	34.4
Retail location analysis	29.8
Sales force organisation	13.2
Other applications	12.6

Source: Survey conducted by Peter Sleight, Target Market Consultancy. Reprinted with kind permission.

38 neighbourhood types, it is unlikely that the label put on a neighbourhood is going to be applicable to all 150. Nevertheless, the science of geodemographics is still evolving and trying to break areas down into even smaller units, incorporating more lifestyle data (*see* below) as well. Systems such as Computerised Marketing Technologies (CMTs) *Storescan*, for example, can provide marketers with information about the catchment areas of all supermarkets within a given area, and the projected shopping habits of every consumer within that area.

A survey carried out by Target Market Consultancy and published in *Marketing* magazine (Burnside, 1995) found that 75 per cent of respondents use geodemographic or lifestyle data within their businesses. Table 5.3 lists the most popular applications for the data.

Psychographic segmentation

Psychographics, or **lifestyle segmentation**, is an altogether more difficult area to define, as it involves intangible variables such as the beliefs, attitudes and opinions of the potential customer. It has evolved in answer to some of the shortcomings of the methods described above as a means of getting further under the skin of the customer as a thinking being. The idea is that defining the lifestyle of the consumer allows the marketer to sell the product not on superficial, functional features, but on benefits that can be seen to enhance that lifestyle on a much more emotional level. The term *lifestyle* is used in its widest sense to cover not only demographic characteristics, but also attitudes to life, beliefs and aspirations.

Plummer (1974) was an early exponent of lifestyle segmentation, breaking it down into four main categories: activities, interests, opinions and demographics.

Activities
The activities category includes all the things people do in the course of their lives. It covers, therefore, work, shopping, holidays and social life. Within that, the marketer will be interested in people's hobbies and their preferred forms of entertainment, as well as sports interests, club memberships and their activities within the community (voluntary work, for instance).

Interests
Interests refers to what is important to the consumer, and where their priorities lie. It may include the things very close to them, such as family, home and work, or their interest and involvement in the wider community. It may also include elements of leisure and recreation, and Plummer particularly mentions areas such as fashion, food and media.

Opinions
The category of opinions comes very close to the individual's innermost thoughts, by probing attitudes and feelings about such things as themselves, social and cultural issues and politics. Opinion may also be sought about other influences on society, such as education, economics and business. Closer to home for the marketer, this category will also investigate opinions about products and the individual's view of the future, indicating how their needs and wants are likely to change.

Demographics

Demographic descriptors have already been extensively covered, and this category includes the kinds of demographic elements you would expect, such as age, education, income and occupation, as well as family size, life-cycle stage, and geographic location.

By researching each of these categories thoroughly and carefully, the marketer can build up a very detailed and three-dimensional picture of the consumer. Building such profiles over very large groups of individuals can then allow the marketer to aggregate people with significant similarities in their profiles into named lifestyle segments. As you might expect, because lifestyles are so complex, and the number of contributory variables so large, there is no single universally applicable typology of psychographic segments. Indeed, many different typologies have emerged over the years, emphasising different aspects of lifestyle, striving to provide a set of lifestyle segments which are either generally useful or designed for a specific commercial application.

In the USA, for example, advertising agencies have found the Values And Life Style (VALS-2) typology, based on Mitchell (1983), particularly useful. The typology is based on the individual's *resources*, mainly income and education, and *self-orientation*, i.e. attitude towards one self, one's aspirations, and the things one does to communicate and achieve them. The segments that emerge include, for example, *Achievers*, who fall within the category of 'status orientated'. They have abundant resources, and are career minded with a social life that revolves around work and family. They mind very much what other people think of them, and particularly crave the good opinion of those who they themselves admire. The implication is that Achievers have largely 'made it' in terms of material success, in contrast to *Strivers* (who are likely to be Achievers in the future) and *Strugglers* (who aspire to be Achievers, but may never make it). Both these segments are also status orientated, but are less well endowed with resources, and still have some way to go.

With the advent of the SEM many organisations have been trying to produce lifestyle-based psychographic segment profiles that categorise the whole of Europe. One such study, carried out by Euro Panel, and marketed in the UK by AGB Dialogue, was based on an exhaustive 150-page questionnaire administered across the EU, Switzerland and Scandinavia. The main research areas covered included demographic and economic factors, as well as attitudes, activities and feelings. Analysis of the questionnaire data allowed researchers to identify 16 lifestyle segments based on two main axes, innovation/conservatism and idealism/materialism. The results also identified 20 or so key questions that were crucial to matching a respondent with an appropriate segment. These key questions were then put to a further 20 000 respondents, which then allowed the definition of 16 segments, including for example Euro-Citizen, Euro-Gentry, Euro-Moralist, Euro-Vigilante, Euro-Romantic, and Euro-Business.

Paitra (1993) similarly defines three Euro-segments:

The Moderns

Representing some 30 per cent of Europeans, the Moderns have flexible purchasing power and are open to change, with cosmopolitan tastes and a liking for the exotic and foreign. They have no problem thinking about themselves as European and as nationals of their own country at the same time. They are more likely to be Italian or French than British or German.

The Go-betweens

Representing 40 per cent of Europeans, this group have experienced a change in their attitudes, but not enough to change their buying habits, and thus they are torn between habit and the thrill of the unexpected. They could become Moderns, but are still too tied to their home culture, education and the society within which they live. Marketing approaches that are obviously pan-European are less likely to influence or affect them than approaches that appear to be rooted in their own culture etc. This group are more likely to be British or Spanish than French, Italian or German.

Are you a Yak or a Ewe?

In the UK, Access, the credit card company, came up with six lifestyle segments, built up from profiles of its 10 million credit card holders. Within these segment profiles, it is easy to see the influence of demographic variables, as well as some of the elements defined in Plummer's (1974) activities, interests and opinions categories:

1 *YAKS (Young, Adventurous, Keen and Single).* These are 18 to 24 years old, have no heavy financial burdens yet, since they either live at home with their parents or rent cheaply, and can afford to ski in the winter and seek the sun in the summer. They are status seekers who like eating out, fashion and flash cars.

2 *EWES (Experts With Expensive Style).* Aged between 25 and 34, they have two incomes, a mortgage, but no children. They are high flying, trendy and enjoy a busy and extensive social life. They can still afford two or three holidays a year, despite heavy spending on the home.

3 *BATS (Babies Add The Sparkle).* These couples are similar in age to the EWES, but in addition to the mortgage, they also have the responsibility of children. Their holidays will be more restricted and modest, since most of the spending is home or child orientated.

4 *CLAMS (Carefully Look At Most Spending).* These are 34 to 44 years old with heavy financial burdens, such as mortgages and school fees. Their car is likely to be a second hand estate. Since cash is so tight, they will be high borrowers and will restrict their social life to things like dinner parties with other CLAMS of their acquaintance.

5 *MICE (Money Is Coming Easier).* At 45 to 55, MICE are at the peak of their earning, and because the children are in the process of leaving home and the end of the mortgage is at least in sight, they have more disposable income to enjoy for themselves. They can, therefore, enjoy regular holidays.

6 *OWLS (Older With Less Stress).* These are the over-55s who have paid off most of their long-term debt. Their children are now independent, so the OWLS have more disposable income for themselves, and may even have moved into a smaller house that is cheaper to run and maintain. They have plenty of leisure time and are determined to enjoy it, particularly as they are generally healthy and like travel.

Clearly, such classifications give Access more insight into the particular needs and wants of different groups of customers. By understanding the customer's cash flow pressures, their spending profiles and their usage of the credit card, the organisation can better tailor its customer service and marketing mixes to appeal to each group, thereby forging closer bonds with them.

Source: *Daily Mail* (1991).

The Traditionals

Accounting for the remaining 30 per cent of Europeans, this group holds on tight to local, regional and national traditions. They are very conformist, in that they have a great respect for authority, prefer an ordered existence and resist change, as a bringer of chaos. They are largely unattracted to international or pan-European brands, preferring the very familiar, habitually purchased products that they have always bought. This group is most likely to be German, with some representation in the UK and Italy, and is less likely to be found in France or Spain.

Paitra is convinced, as the above typology shows, that there is no such thing as the generic Euro-consumer. He strongly feels, however, that the Euro-segment which transcends national boundaries does exist, and that international, qualitative studies are going to become increasingly important to marketers in defining and locating such segments.

Despite the extent and depth of research which has gone into defining typologies such as these, they are still of somewhat limited use. When it comes to applying this material in a commercial marketing context, the marketer still needs to understand the underlying national factors that affect the buying decisions for a particular product. These Euro-segments give only a very general flavour of trends and changing attitudes, as part of the sociocultural marketing environment, and are still too simplistic, given the cultural diversity within the EU.

Nevertheless, there are compelling reasons why such methods of segmentation are worth considering and persevering with, despite their difficulties. Primarily, they can open the door to a better tailored, more subtle offering to the customer on all aspects of the marketing mix. This in turn can create a strong emotional bond between customer and product, making it more difficult for competitors to steal customers. Euro-segmentation adds a further dimension, in that it has the potential to create much larger and more profitable segments, assuming that the logistics of distribution allow geographically dispersed members of the segment to be reached cost effectively, of course, and may thus create pan-European marketing opportunities.

The main problem, however, as we have seen, is that psychographic segments are very difficult and expensive to define and measure. Relevant information is much less likely to exist already in the public domain. It is also very easy to get the implementation wrong. For example, the organisation that tries to portray lifestyle elements within advertisements is depending on the audience's ability to interpret the symbols used in the desired way and to reach the desired conclusions from them. There are no guarantees of this, especially if the message is a complex one (more of this in Chapter 15). Additionally, the user of Euro-segments has to be very clear about allowing for national and cultural differences when trying to communicate on lifestyle elements.

In summary, psychographic segmentation works well in conjunction with demographic variables to refine further the offering to the customer, increasing its relevance and defendability against competition. It is also valuable for products that lean towards psychological rather than functional benefits for the customer, for instance perfumes, cars, clothing retailers etc. For such a product to succeed, the marketer needs to create an image that convinces consumers that the product can either enhance their current lifestyle or help them to achieve their aspirations. Solomon (1994) summarises the uses of psychographic segmentation as:

1 to define a target market;
2 to create a new view of the market: breaking away from stereotypes;
3 to position the product: making sure product attributes fit with the deeper needs of the customer;
4 to better communicate product attributes: influencing advertising themes and content;
5 to develop overall strategy: identifying opportunities and trends, for instance;
6 to market social and political issues: to home in on groups with basically sympathetic attitudes and beliefs, or to identify those who need more persuasion.

Behaviour segmentation

All the categories of segmentation talked about so far are centred on the customer, leading to as detailed a profile of the individual as possible. Little mention has been made, however, of the individual's relationship with the product. This needs to be addressed, as it is quite possible that people with similar demographic and/or psychographic profiles may yet interact differently with the same product. Segmenting a market in these terms, therefore, is known as **behaviour segmentation**.

TABLE 5.4

Usage segmentation in the soup market

Use	Brand examples
Dinner party starter	Baxter's soups; Covent Garden soup
Warming snack	Crosse & Blackwell's soups
Meal replacement	Heinz Wholesoups
Recipe ingredient	Campbell's Condensed soups
Easy office lunch	Batchelor's Cuppa soups

End use

What is the product to be used for? The answer to this question has great implications for the whole marketing approach. Think about soup, for instance. This is a very versatile product with a range of potential uses, and a wide variety of brands and product lines have been developed, each of which appeals to a different usage segment. A shopper may well buy two or three different brands of soup, simply because their needs change according to intended use, for example a dinner party or a snack meal. At this point, demographic and psychographic variables may become irrelevant (or at least secondary) if the practicalities of usage are so important to the customer. Table 5.4 defines some of the possible end uses of soup, and examples of products available on the UK market to serve them.

> **Example**
>
> Even the humble potato has become a victim of usage segmentation. The pre-bagged potatoes sold by some supermarkets are now labelled to indicate suitability for various uses, and thus the shopper can see precisely what is best for baking, roasting, chipping or boiling. Although it is still possible to buy a bag of 'general purpose' potatoes, the shopper is left with a vague feeling that these are somehow second best for everything!

Benefits sought

This variable can have more of a psychological slant than end usage and can link in very closely with both demographic and psychographic segments. In the case of a car, for example, the benefits sought may range from the practical ('reliable'; 'economic to run'; 'able to accommodate Mum, Dad, four kids, a granny, a wet dog and the remains of a picnic') to the more psychographically orientated ('environmentally friendly'; 'fast and mean'; 'overt status symbol'). Similarly, the benefits sought from a chilled ready meal might be 'ease of preparation', 'time saving', 'access to dishes I could not make myself', 'a reassuring standby in case I get home late one evening', and for the low-calorie and low-fat versions, 'a tasty and interesting variation on my diet!' It is not difficult to see how defining some of these *benefit segments* can also indicate the kinds of demographic or lifestyle descriptors that apply to people wanting those benefits.

Usage rate

Not everyone who buys a particular product consumes it at the same rate. There will be heavy users, medium users and light users. Figure 5.1 shows the hypothetical categorisation of an organisation's customer base according to usage. In this case, 20 per cent of customers account for 60 per cent of the organisation's sales. This clearly raises questions for marketing strategies, for example should we put all our resources into defending our share of heavy users? Alternatives might be to make light users heavier; to target competitors' heavy users aggressively, or even to develop differentiated products for different usage rates (such as frequent-wash shampoo).

Again, this segmentation variable can best be used in conjunction with others to paint a much more three-dimensional picture of the target customer.

FIGURE 5.1

Consumer product usage categories

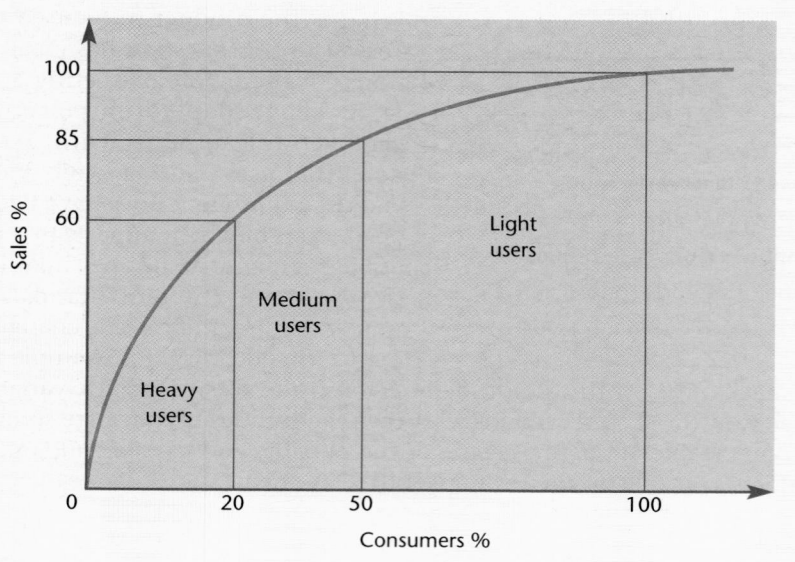

Loyalty

As with usage rate, loyalty could be a useful mechanism, not only for developing detail in the segment profile, but also for developing a better understanding of which segmentation variables are significant. For instance a carefully thought out market research exercise might help an organisation to profile 'loyal to us', 'loyal to them' and '**switchers**', and then discover what other factors seem to differentiate between each of these groups. More specifically, Wind (1982) identified six loyalty segments as:

1 current loyal users who will continue to purchase the brand;

2 current customers who might switch brands or reduce consumption;

3 occasional users who might be persuaded to increase consumption with the right incentives;

4 occasional users who might decrease consumption because of competitors' offerings;

5 non-users who might buy the brand if it was modified;

6 non-users with strong negative attitudes that are unlikely to change.

Alsop (1989), however, in a study of the US market found that the extent of **brand loyalty** was questionable. Brand loyalty was highest for cigarettes, mayonnaise and toothpaste, all with over 60 per cent of respondents claiming to be brand loyal. At the other end of the scale, garbage bags, canned vegetables, athletic shoes (surprisingly), and batteries all showed less that 30 per cent loyalty. Round about the 50 per cent mark came ketchup, beer, laundry detergent and cars. The picture may be different in European markets, but what is certain is that brand loyalty can be a fragile thing, and is under increasing threat. This is partly as a result of the greater number of alternative brands available and incentives or promotions designed by competitors to undermine customer loyalty. The most serious threat in the UK, however, has come from supermarket own brands, many of which look uncannily like the equivalent manufacturer brands, but undercut them on price. Consumers thus believe that the own brands are just as good, if not identical, and are thus prepared to switch to them and to be more price sensitive. There is more on this issue in Chapter 13.

Assuming that loyalty does exist, even a simple combination of usage rate and loyalty begins to make a difference to the organisation's marketing strategy. If, for example, a large group of heavy users who are also brand switchers was identified,

Through strong branding, Uncle Ben's Rice enjoys high brand loyalty in an otherwise 'commodity' market.

Source: Masterfoods.

then there is much to be gained from investing resources in a tightly focused marketing mix designed to turn them into heavy users who are loyal to us.

Attitude

Again, trespassing on the psychographic area, attitude looks at how the potential customer feels about the product (or the organisation). A set of customers who are already enthusiastic about a product, for example, require very different handling from a group who are downright hostile. A hostile group might need an opportunity to sample the product, along with an advertising campaign which addresses and answers the roots of their hostility. Attitude-based segments may be important in marketing charities or causes, or even in health education. Smokers who are hostile to the 'stop smoking' message will need different approaches from those who are amenable to the message and just need reassurance and practical support to put it into practice. Approaches aimed at the 'hostile' smoker have included fear ('Look at these diseased lungs') and altruism ('What about your children?'), but with little noticeable effect.

Buyer readiness stage

Buyer readiness can be a very valuable variable, particularly when one is thinking about the promotional mix. How close to purchasing is the potential customer? For example, at a very early stage, the customer may not even be aware that the product exists, and therefore to get that customer moving closer to purchase, the organisation needs to generate *awareness* of the product. Then there is a need for information to stimulate *interest* in the product. The customer's ability to understand and interpret that information may lead to *desire* for the product, which in turn stimulates *action*: the purchase itself.

Figure 5.2 summarises this progression, and Chapter 15 will consider further its influence on the promotional mix.

Behavioural segmentation, therefore, examines closely the relationship between the potential customer and the product, and there are a number of dimensions upon which this can be done. Its main achievement is to bring the relationship between customer and product into sharper focus, thus providing greater understanding of the customer's specific needs and wants, leading to a better defined marketing mix. Another advantage of this kind of segmentation approach is that it provides opportunities for tailored marketing strategies to target brand switchers or to increase usage rates. All these benefits do justify the use of behavioural segmentation, as long as it does not lead to the organisation becoming product centred to the neglect of the customer's needs. The customer must still come first.

Multivariable segmentation

As has been hinted throughout the previous sections, it is unlikely that any one segmentation variable will be used absolutely on its own. It is more common for marketers to use a **multivariable segmentation** approach, defining a 'portfolio' of relevant segmentation variables, some of which will be prosaic and descriptive while others will tend towards the psychographic, depending on the product and market in question. The market for adult soft drinks, discussed at p. 175 for example, includes age segmentation along with some usage considerations (for example as a substitute for wine as a meal accompaniment), some benefit segmentation (healthy, refreshing, relaxing), and lifestyle elements of health consciousness, sophisticated imagery and a desire for exotic ingredients.

The emergence of geodemographics in recent years, as discussed at p. 175 above, is an indicator of the way in which segmentation is moving, that is, towards multivariable systems incorporating psychographics, demographics and geographics. These things are now possible and affordable, as Chapter 6 will show, because of increasingly sophisticated data collection mechanisms, developments in database creation and maintenance (*see* Chapter 20), and cheaper, more accessible computing facilities. A properly managed database allows the marketer to go even further and to incorporate behavioural variables as the purchaser develops a trading history with a supplier. Thus the marketers are creeping ever closer to the individual consumer. The UK supermarkets that have developed and launched store loyalty cards that are swiped through the checkout so that the customer can accumulate points towards discounts, for example, are collecting incredibly detailed information about each individual shopper's profile. It tells them when we shop, how often, which branches of the store we tend to use, how much we spend per visit, the range of goods we buy, and the choices we make between own brands and manufacturer brands. The supermarkets can use this information to help them define meaningful segments for their own customer base, to further develop and improve their overall marketing mix or to make individually tailored offers to specific customers.

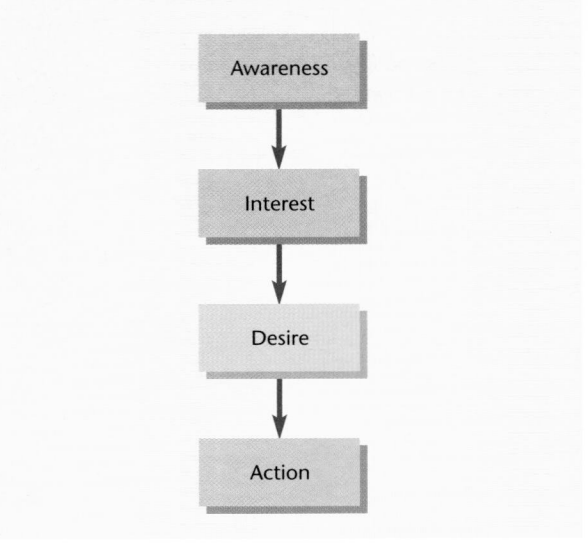

FIGURE 5.2

The AIDA response hierarchy model

IMPLEMENTATION OF SEGMENTATION

This chapter so far has very freely used the phrase 'segmenting the market', but before segmentation can take place, there has to be some definition of the boundaries of that market. Any such definition really has to look at the world through the consumer's eyes, because the consumer makes decisions based on the evaluation of alternatives and substitutes. Thus a margarine manufacturer cannot restrict itself to thinking in terms of 'the margarine market', but has to take a wider view of 'the spreading-fats market' which will include butter and vegetable-oil-based products alongside margarine. This is because, generally speaking, all three of these product groups are contending for the same place on the nation's bread, and the consumer will develop attitudes and feelings towards a selection of brands across all three groups, perhaps through comparing price and product attributes (for example taste, spreadability, cooking versatility and health claims). This opens up a much wider competitive scene, as well as making the margarine manufacturer think more seriously about product positioning and about how and why consumers buy it. Similarly, the adult soft drinks market, introduced earlier, cannot be too restrictive in its market definition. It is still competing to a certain extent with the more traditional soft drinks (both the fizzy ones such as colas and lemonades and the still fruit juices) and alcoholic drinks, as a substitute. The key to its continued growth and success lies in pulling it away further from the wider, mainstream beverages markets (alcoholic and non-alcoholic), through clear differentiation in terms of all elements of the marketing mix, to reduce the 'substitute' effect. The various manufacturers involved can then concentrate more on competition and further segmentation within the adult market.

This whole issue of market definition and its implications for segmentation comes back, yet again, to what should now be the familiar question of 'What business are we in?' It is a timely reminder that consumers basically buy solutions to problems, not products, and thus in defining market segments, the marketer should take into account any type of product that will provide a solution. Hence we are not in 'the margarine market', but in the 'lubricating bread' market, which brings us back full circle to the inclusion of butter and vegetable-oil-based spreads as direct competitors.

It is still not enough to have gone through the interesting exercise of segmenting a market, however it is defined. How is that information going to be used by the organisation to develop marketing strategies? One decision which must be made is that of how many segments within the market the organisation intends to target. We look first at **targeting**:

Targeting

There are three broad approaches available, summarised in Fig 5.3, and discussed in detail below.

FIGURE 5.3

Segmentation targeting strategies

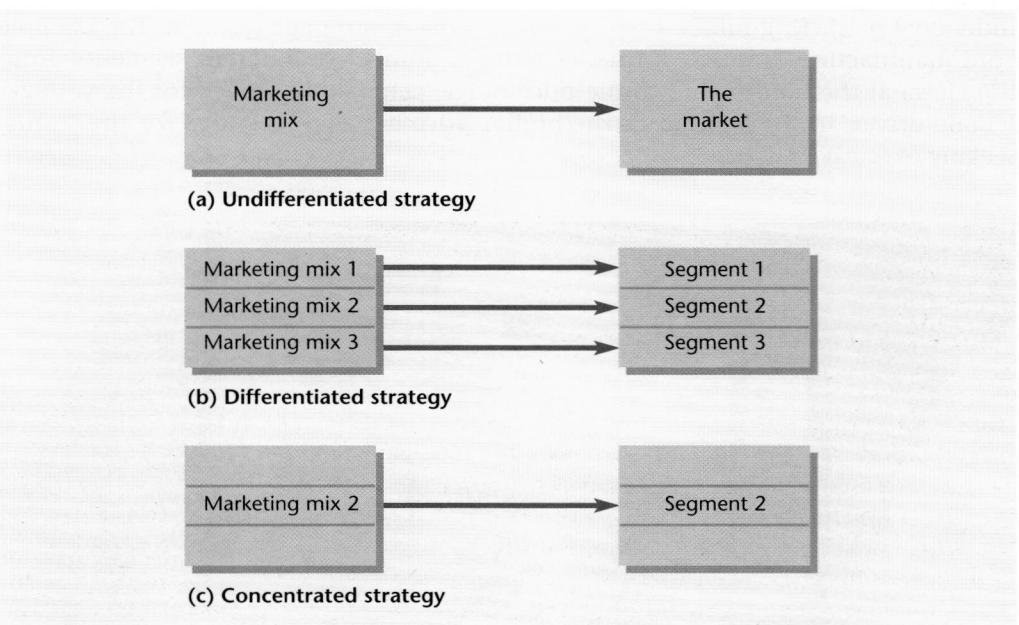

(a) Undifferentiated strategy

(b) Differentiated strategy

(c) Concentrated strategy

Concentrated

The concentrated approach is the most focused approach of the three, and involves specialising in serving one specific segment. This can lead to very detailed knowledge of the target segment's needs and wants, with the added benefit that the organisation is seen as a specialist, giving it an advantage over its more mass market competitors. This, however, carries a risk of complacency, leaving the organisation vulnerable to competitive entry into the segment.

Example

The Body Shop concentrates on manufacturing and retailing cosmetics and toiletries made from natural ingredients, with overt 'green' environmentally friendly overtones. Although they were pioneers in this segment and created a strongly differentiated image for themselves and their products, they are now facing aggressive competition from more mainstream retailers. Chains such as Boot's, for example, have introduced similar ranges into their stores to tempt at least the 'light green' or price-conscious shopper away from The Body Shop.

In terms of management, concentration is attractive because costs are kept down, as there is only one marketing mix to manage, and there is still the potential for economies of scale. Strategically, the concentration of resources into one segment may lead to a stronger, more defendable position than that achievable by competitors who are spreading their effort more thinly. However, being a niche specialist may make it more difficult for an organisation to diversify into other segments, whether through lack of experience and knowledge, or through problems of acceptance arising from being identified with the original niche.

The benefits also need to be weighed against the other potential risks. First, all the organisation's eggs are in one basket, and if that segment fails, then there is no fall-back position. The second risk is that if competitors see a rival establishing and clearly succeeding in a segment like this, then they may try to take some of it.

Differentiated

As Fig 5.3 implies, a differentiated strategy involves the development of a number of individual marketing mixes, each of which serves a different segment. For example Ford manufactures a range of cars, covering a number of different segments, from the Fiesta at the bottom end of the price range, generally intended for the younger female driver, to the Scorpio in the higher price bracket, intended for the status-seeking executive.

Daewoo's interactive screen allows each customer to 'design' their own car, within limits.

Source: Daewoo.

As with the concentrated strategy, this approach does allow the organisation to tailor its offerings to suit the individual segments, thus maintaining satisfaction. It also overcomes one of the problems of concentration by spreading risk across the market, so that if one segment declines, the organisation still has revenue from others.

To be implemented properly, this approach requires a detailed overview of the market and how it is developing, perhaps leading to the early detection of new opportunities or emerging segments. This knowledge is valuable for an organisation with a healthy curiosity about its environment, but is acquired at a cost (in terms of both finance and managerial time). It also leads to increased costs in trying to manage the marketing mixes for a number of products, with possible diseconomies of scale.

Overall, a differentiated strategy dilutes the organisation's efforts through the thin spreading of resources. The organisation must, therefore, be very careful not to overreach itself in the number of segments it attempts to cover. Nevertheless, it can help an organisation to survive in highly competitive markets.

Example

H J Hall Sock Group manufactures branded socks, but found the UK market of the early 1990s very difficult. Quite apart from the fact that the average British male acquires only five new pairs of socks a year, there is fierce competition from cheap imports, market traders and stores' own brands (Marks & Spencer, for example, cornered 20 per cent of the sock market in 1990). H J Hall Sock group has survived by targeting a number of specialised segments that the bulk manufacturers would not consider worthwhile. Thus the firm has supplied soccer teams (including the English, Irish and Scottish national sides), Middle Eastern armies and the top end of the fashion market. In fact the company claims that economic recession has helped them. Since fashion-conscious men can no longer afford new suits, they are buying expensive new socks instead, which they *can* afford (Darwent, 1993).

Undifferentiated

The undifferentiated approach is the least demanding of the three approaches in that it assumes that the market is one great homogeneous unit, with no significant differences between individuals within that market. Thus a single marketing mix is required which serves the needs of the entire market. The emphasis is likely to be, therefore, on developing mass communication, mass distribution and as wide an appeal as possible.

An undifferentiated approach does have some apparent advantages. It involves relatively low costs, as there is only one marketing mix which does not require the depth of research, fine tuning and updating that a concentrated or differentiated strategy would entail. It could also lead to the possible maximisation of economies of scale, because of having a single product in a potentially large market.

It is naive to hope that you can please everyone. What is likely to happen in reality is that some people will like your product offering more than others, and thus a segment (not of your own definition) will emerge by default. Because your product has not been tailored to that segment, it is unlikely to be exactly what that segment wants, and therefore any competitor who does target the segment more closely will attract those customers. This is similar to what is happening in the potato example cited at p. 181 above, where the 'general purpose' product is becoming overshadowed and pushed into a perceived 'second best' position by usage-specific varieties.

If an undifferentiated approach is possible at all, then it might best be suited for products with little psychological appeal. For example petrol is essentially a very ordi-

Blue Circle's standardised boiler

The market for gas-fired domestic central heating boilers is fragmented across Europe, largely on a geographic basis. This is not only because the climate and the nature of housing vary so widely in different places, but also because plumbing standards and techniques are different. Consequently, there are thousands of different types of boiler available but each one is mainly focused on its home country. Those companies that do try to achieve a pan-European approach tend to take an existing product and make significant adaptations to make it suitable for other countries.

Blue Circle, a UK company, has boiler interests in France, Germany and the Netherlands, as well as in the UK, but each national division largely pursues its own home market. The parent company, however, spotted an opportunity to create a truly pan-European boiler for a niche segment and put together a team of 40 engineers and marketers from across Europe to develop the product. Condensing boilers save energy and cut carbon dioxide emissions, but only account for about 5 per cent of the European market. Other companies make them, but on a country by country basis. Blue Circle thought that if they could develop a product that was 90 per cent standardised for any country, it could achieve economies of scale in manufacture as well as saving on the development costs normally associated in the industry with redesigning the product for each

market. They also felt that the product would have a cross-border appeal to a market segment looking for 'greener' approaches to heating and that this segment would have considerable future potential.

The design process, with its target of 90 per cent standardisation, was not easy. The design had to be flexible enough to be easily adapted with the minimum of fuss to suit different national preferences and conventions on, for example, the type of boiler, the type of gas used, design and safety regulations, location within the house (apparently in the UK, gas boilers tend to be in the kitchen; in the Netherlands they are in the attic; in Germany, in the cellar) and electronic controls. Nevertheless, the target was achieved through a kind of modular design, with the added benefit that the interaction between engineers from different countries led to many improvements and simplifications in boiler design generally.

The product was launched in 1995, first in the UK and the Netherlands, then later in Germany and France. Although the product itself was standardised, other elements of the marketing mix were tailored for different countries. Even the product name varied, from Envoy in the UK to Runner in the Netherlands and Ecotherm in Germany.

Source: Marsh (1995).

nary product which many of us purchase regularly but never even see (unless we are not very adept with a self-service pump). It makes the car go, regardless of whether it is a Rolls-Royce or a Lada, and traditionally, the only discriminating factor between brands has been price. Petrol retailers have now begun to create market segments, through the petrol itself (as with unleaded and petrols with extra additives); through the extended product (providing car washes, mini-supermarkets etc.), and also through strong corporate images which create brands and engender loyalty. All of this is moving the petrol retailers away from undifferentiated strategies.

Quite apart from the advantages and disadvantages connected with each of the alternative approaches above, there are a number of factors influencing the choice of targeting strategy.

Marketing theory may well point to a particular strategy as being ideal, but if an organisation's resources cannot support and sustain that strategy, then an alternative must be found. A smaller organisation may, for example, need to adopt a concentrated strategy (perhaps based on a geographic segment in a consumer market, or on a specialist niche in an organisational market) to generate the growth required to allow a wider coverage of the market.

TABLE 5.5

Differentiation in the salt market

- Table salt
- Cooking salt
- Sea salt
- Rock salt
- Alpine rock salt
- Iodised salt
- Low-sodium salt
- Garlic salt
- Celery salt

et cetera!

It is also important to make the choice of strategy in the context of the product itself. As has already been indicated, certain types of product lend themselves more readily to certain approaches, for example a product with many of potential variations which involve a high level of psychological relationship with the customer (such as clothing or cosmetics) is better suited to a differentiated or concentrated approach. Other products with a more functional bias can be treated in a more undifferentiated way.

It must be reiterated, though, that undifferentiated approaches are becoming increasingly rare. Salt used to be held up to marketing students as the prime example of a commodity product sold in an undifferentiated way. Table 5.5 demonstrates how all that has changed.

The product's life-cycle stage (*see* Chapter 8 for a full definition of this concept) might also affect the choice of strategy. For example, an innovative new product, of which neither the industry nor the consumer has past experience, may first be marketed with an undifferentiated strategy in order to gain practical knowledge of the market's behaviour and reactions. It is very difficult to undertake meaningful market research in advance of launching such a new product, because the market may have problems conceptualising the product or putting it into context. It will be in the growth and maturity stages of the life-cycle that differentiated strategies will emerge as competitors enter the market and organisations learn from experience.

That last comment is a reminder that strategic decisions cannot be taken in isolation from the activities of the competition. If competitors are clearly implementing differentiated strategies, then it is dangerous for you to adopt a more dilute undifferentiated approach. It may make more sense to identify the segments within which the competition is strong and then to assess whether it would be possible to attack them head-on in those segments or to find a different niche and make that your own. Thus competition is affecting not only the choice of approach, but the actual choice of segment(s) to target.

BENEFITS OF SEGMENTATION

The previous sections of this chapter should at least have served to show that market segmentation is a complex and dangerous activity in the sense that the process of choosing of variables, their measurement and their implementation leaves plenty of scope for poor management and disappointment. Nevertheless, there are few, if any, markets in which segmentation has no role to play, and it is important to remember the potential benefits to be gained, whether looking at the customer, the marketing mix or the competition.

The customer

The obvious gain to customers is that they can find products that seem to fit more closely with what they want. These needs and wants, remember, are not only related to product function, but also to psychological fulfilment. Customers may feel that a particular supplier is more sympathetic towards them, or is speaking more directly to them, and therefore they will be more responsive and eventually more loyal to that supplier. The organisation that fails to segment deeply enough on significant criteria will lose custom to competitors who do.

The marketing mix

This is a timely reminder that the marketing mix should itself be a product of understanding the customer. Market segmentation helps the organisation to target its marketing mix more closely on the potential customer, and thus to meet the customer's needs and wants more exactly. Segmentation helps to define shopping habits (in terms of place, frequency and volume), price sensitivity, required product benefits and features, as well as laying the foundations for advertising and promotional decisions. The customer is at the core of all decisions relating to the 4Ps, and those decisions will be both easier to make and more consistent with each other if a clear and detailed definition of the target segments exists.

In the same vein, segmentation can also help the organisation to allocate its resources more efficiently. If a segment is well defined, then the organisation will have sufficient understanding to develop very precise marketing objectives and an accompanying strategy to achieve them, with a minimum of wastage. The organisation is doing neither more nor less than it needs to do in order to satisfy the customer's needs and wants.

This level of understanding of segments that exist in the market also forms a very sound foundation for strategic decisions. The organisation can prioritise across segments in line with its resources, objectives and desired position within the market.

The competition

Finally, the use of segmentation will help the organisation to achieve a better understanding of itself and the environment within which it exists. By looking outwards, to the customer, the organisation has to ask itself some very difficult questions about its capacity to serve that customer better than the competition. Also, by analysing the competitors' offerings in the context of the customer, the organisation should begin to appreciate the competition's real strengths and weaknesses, as well as identifying gaps in the market.

DANGERS OF SEGMENTATION

The benefits of segmentation need to be balanced against the dangers inherent in it. Some of these, such as the risks of poor definition and implementation of psychographic segmentation, have already been mentioned.

Other dangers are connected with the essence of segmentation: breaking markets down into ever smaller segments. Where should it stop? Catering for the differing needs of a large number of segments can lead to fragmentation of the market, with additional problems arising from the loss of economies of scale (through shorter production runs or loss of bulk purchasing discounts on raw materials, for instance), as mentioned at p. 186 above. Detail needs to be balanced against viability.

Within the market as a whole, if there are a number of organisations in direct competition for a number of segments, then the potential proliferation of brands may simply serve to confuse the customer. Imagine five competitors each trying to compete in five market segments. That gives the customer 25 brands to sort out. Even if customers can find their way through the maze of brands, the administration and marketing difficulties involved in getting those brands on to the supermarket shelves can be very costly.

As Chapter 4 showed, such problems are less likely to occur in organisational markets. Where an organisation has a very small number of high-spending customers, each one can legitimately be treated as a separate segment with its own marketing mix tailored to it.

CRITERIA FOR SUCCESSFUL SEGMENTATION

Cutting through the detail of how to segment, and regardless of the complexities of segmentation in different types of market, are four absolute requirements for any successful segmentation exercise. Unless these four conditions prevail, the exercise will either look good on paper but be impossible to implement, or fail to deliver any marked strategic advantage.

Distinctiveness

Any segment defined has to be *distinctive*, that is, significantly different from any other segment. The basis of that difference depends on the type of product or the circumstances prevailing in the market at the time. It may be rooted in any of the segmentation variables discussed above, whether geographic, demographic or psychographic. Note too the use of the word *significant*. The choice of segmentation variables has to be relevant to the product in question.

Without a significant difference, segment boundaries become too blurred, and there is a risk that an organisation's offerings will not be sufficiently well tailored to attract the required customers.

Tangibility

It must be remembered that distinctiveness can be taken too far. Too much detail in segmentation, without sound commercial reasoning behind it, leads to fragmentation of effort and inefficiency. A defined segment must, therefore, be of a sufficient *size* to make its pursuit worthwhile. Again, the notion of size here is somewhat vague. For fmcg goods, viable size may entail many thousands of customers purchasing many tens of thousands of units, but in an organisational market, it may entail a handful of customers purchasing a handful of units.

Proving that a segment actually exists is also important. Analysis of a market may indicate that there is a gap which existing products do not appear to fill, whether defined in terms of the product itself or the customer profile. The next stage is to ask why that gap is there. Is it because no organisation has yet got round to filling it, or because the segment in that gap is too small to be commercially viable? Does that segment even exist, or are you segmenting in too much detail and creating opportunities on paper that will not work in practice?

Accessibility

As well as existing, a defined segment has to be *accessible*. The first aspect of this is connected with distribution. An organisation has to be able to find the means of delivering its goods and services to the customer, but this may not be so easy, for example, for a small organisation targeting a geographically spread segment with a low-priced infrequently purchased product. Issues of access may then become an extension of the segment profile, perhaps limiting the segment to those customers within a defined catchment area, or those who are prepared to order direct through particular media. Whatever the solution to problems of access, it does mean that the potential size of the segment has to be reassessed.

The second aspect of access is that of communication. Certain customers may be very difficult to make contact with, and if the promotional message cannot be communicated, then the chances of capturing those customers are much slimmer. Again, the segment profile may have to be extended to cover the media most likely to access those customers, and again, this will lead to a smaller segment.

Defendability

In talking about targeting strategies at pp. 185 *et seq.* above, one of the recurrent themes was that of the competition. Even with a concentrated strategy, targeting only one segment, there is a risk of competitors poaching customers. In defining and choosing segments, therefore, it is important to consider whether the organisation can develop a sufficiently strong differential advantage to defend its presence in that segment against competitive incursions.

> **Example**
>
> Sock Shop in the UK, a niche retailer selling a vast variety of both 'fun' and serious products for feet could not, in the end, defend its position against high street retailers such as Marks & Spencer copying the basic idea and selling similar products more cheaply and more conveniently.

Organisational Markets

Most of the above discussion has centred on consumer markets. With specific reference to organisational markets, Hlavacek and Ames (1986) suggest a similar set of criteria for good segmentation practice. They suggest, for example, that each segment should be characterised by a common set of customer requirements, and that customer requirements and characteristics should be measurable. Segments should have identifiable competition, but be small enough to allow the supplier to reduce the competitive threat, or to build a defendable position against competition. In strategic terms, Hlavacek and Ames also propose that the members of a segment should have some logistical characteristic in common, for example that they are served by the same kind of distribution channel, or the same kind of sales effort. Finally, the critical success factors for each segment should be defined, and the supplier should ensure that it has the skills, assets and capabilities to meet the segment's needs, and to sustain that in the future.

CHAPTER SUMMARY

This chapter has focused on the complexities and methods involved in dividing markets into relevant, manageable and targetable segments in order to allow better tailored offerings to be developed.

In organisational markets, segmentation techniques are divided into macro and micro variables or bases. Macro variables include both organisational characteristics, such as size, location and purchasing patterns, and product or service applications, defining the ways in which the product or service is used by the buyer. Micro segmentation variables lead to the definition, in some cases, of segments of one customer, and focus on the buyer's management philosophy, decision-making structures, purchasing policies and strategies, as well as needs and wants.

In consumer markets, five main categories of segmentation are defined: geographic, demographic, geodemographic, psychographic and behaviour based. Between them, they cover a full range of characteristics, whether descriptive, measurable, tangible or intangible, relating to the buyer, the buyer's lifestyle and the buyer's relationship with the product. In practice, a multivariable approach to segmentation is likely to be implemented, defining a portfolio of relevant characteristics from all categories to suit the market under consideration.

The implications of segmentation are wide reaching. It forms the basis for strategic thinking, in terms of the choice of segment(s) to target in order to achieve internal and competitive objectives. The possibilities range from a niche strategy, specialising in only one segment, to a differentiated strategy, targeting two or more segments with different marketing mixes. The undifferentiated strategy, hoping to cover the whole market with only one marketing mix, is becoming increasingly less appropriate as consumers become more demanding, and although it does appear to ease the managerial burden, it is very vulnerable to focused competition.

Segmentation offers a number of benefits to both the consumer and the organisation. Consumers get an offering that is better tailored to their specific needs, as well as the satisfaction of feeling that the market is offering them a wider range of products to choose from. The organisation is more likely to engender customer loyalty because of the tailored offering, as well as the benefits of more efficient resource allocation, and improved knowledge of the market. The organisation can also use its segmentation as a basis for building a strong competitive edge, by understanding its customers on a deeper psychological level and reflecting that in its marketing mix(es). This forms bonds between organisation/product and customer that are very difficult for competition to break.

There are, however, dangers in segmentation, if it is not done well. Poor definition of segments, inappropriate choice of key variables or poor analysis and implementation of the outcomes of a segmentation exercise can all be disastrous. There is also the danger that if competing marketers become too enthusiastic in trying to 'out-segment' each other, the market will fragment to an unviable extent and consumers will become confused by the variety of choice open to them.

On balance, segmentation is a good and necessary activity in any market, whether it is a mass fmcg market of international proportions, or a select organisational market involving two or three well-known customers. In either case, any segment defined has to be distinctive (i.e., features at least one characteristic pulling it away from the rest that can be used to create a focused marketing mix); tangible (i.e., commercially viable); accessible (i.e., both the product and the promotional mix can reach it) and finally, defendable (i.e., against competition).

Key words and phrases

Behaviour segmentation	Macro segments
Brand loyalty	Market segments
Buyer readiness stages	Micro segments
Demographic segmentation	Multivariable segmentation
Geodemographics	Psychographics
Geographic segmentation	Switchers
Lifestyle segmentation	Targeting

QUESTIONS FOR REVIEW

5.1 What is the difference between macro and micro segmentation in organisational markets?

5.2 What variables might be included in micro segmentation?

5.3 What is geographic segmentation and how is it used in consumer and organisational markets?

5.4 What are the main demographic variables used in consumer markets?

5.5 What is geodemographic segmentation and how can it help the marketer?

5.6 What, according to Plummer, are the four main components of psychographic, or lifestyle, segmentation?

5.7 Why is psychographic segmentation so difficult and so risky to do?

5.8 In what major way does behavioural segmentation differ from the other methods? Outline the variables that can be used in behavioural segmentation.

5.9 What are the three approaches to targeting available to marketers?

5.10 What factors might affect the marketer's choice of targeting strategy?

QUESTIONS FOR DISCUSSION

5.1 How might the market for personal computers, sold to organisational markets, be segmented?

5.2 Find examples of products that depend strongly on demographic segmentation, making sure that you find at least one example for each of the main demographic variables.

5.3 Choose a consumer market and discuss how it might be segmented in terms of benefits sought.

5.4 For each targeting strategy, find examples of organisations that use it. Discuss why you think they have chosen this strategy and how they implement it.

5.5 How can market segmentation influence decisions about the marketing mix?

Kings Hotel (A)

As a rough guide, assume that £1 = 25 Polish złoty (zł) approximately.

The Kings Hotel is situated on the inner ring road, some 10 minutes walk from the historic centre of the Polish city of Kraków. It is opposite the Wavel castle, the ancient Polish Royal Palace which is a major tourist attraction. Unlike a number of other Polish cities, Kraków avoided widespread destruction during the Second World War, and so although some buildings declined somewhat during the Communist era, it has largely retained its historical character.

The Kings Hotel is the second oldest hotel in Kraków, but up until 1989 it had been used as apartments, barracks and a hostel for the Polish army. In 1989, the rooms and exterior were refurbished by army personnel so that the establishment could become an army hotel. The front part of the hotel catered for high-ranking visiting officers, and lesser ranks were accommodated at the rear. The hotel was split into four operating units:

1 A three star hotel (the front part) with 72 beds. The price of a double room was 1200 zł per night, and that price remained the same all year.

2 A two star hotel (the rear part), with a mix of bedrooms sleeping up to four per room, and a total capacity of 78. The price was 600 zł per night for a double room, and again the price was constant all year round.

As a comparison, prices at the nearby Hotel Forum, one of the best in Kraków, were 1455 zł in the low season and 2190 zł in the high season.

3 A disco bar with a street entrance. This is rented out privately, but infrequently.

4 A restaurant at the front of the hotel at ground floor level, primarily serving hotel guests.

Although this is primarily an army hotel, since 1989 independent guests have been allowed in to supplement revenue and it is envisaged that this side of the business will continue to grow. A number of sensible compromises have been made to allow both sides of the business to develop. Army personnel do not use the hotel during the summer months, for example, so that the potential income from the tourist market can be maximised. Army bookings also tend to be made well in advance so that independent bookings can be made around them to enable higher occupancy levels. At present, all profits are returned to the army. Repairs and modernisation are the responsibility of the army, although little is currently being spent on improvement.

The hotel management has avoided tour bookings wherever possible. They did deal with the Polish airline LOT a few years ago for block bookings, but found that more profitable business from independent travellers had reached a sufficient level to reduce the need for such trade. Prices are already comparatively low, and no discounts are offered to private individuals or groups. The army however, receives a 40 per cent discount on all rooms and food. Most of the customers in the summer season are tourists and outside that period they tend to be business travellers, especially visiting university staff and local government officers.

Little promotion is undertaken, but a multi-language brochure has been designed. Good relations are maintained with the Kraków tourist office, which finds accommodation for travellers, and the hotel advertises in any tourist board publications. The hotel also advertises on a poster site at the local airport. The real concern facing the management team is that the army might withdraw from the hotel business in the near future. If privatisation did take place, the manager was not sure whether the hotel could survive the growing competition in the city as other hotels had already been modernised to achieve Western European standards. Kings Hotel would no longer be assured of a steady flow of army personnel as guests.

The following extracts from a report by an independent guest perhaps help to clarify the magnitude of the task facing any new owner.

> 'I arrived at 11p.m. from the airport at a small crowded car park which fronts the dimly lit entrance to the Kings Hotel. The stone floor, poor lighting and decoration gave a hollow feel to the reception area as did the two small utility tables and the bench seating in front of a small television set. Along the far wall was a chest high reception desk. Booking was swift, but there was no one to help me take my luggage upstairs. There was a largish man watching television who might or might not be an hotel employee. He turned out to be "security"'.

> 'I eventually found my room. I was surprised how large it was. It had twin beds, a high ceiling and old fashioned utility furniture. The wallpaper and curtains were plain and uninspiring. There was a TV, a porch area with wardrobe, and a shower and toilet in the bathroom. Water flowed down the toilet bowl

constantly. The small hand basin did, however, provide plentiful hot water through a modern chrome mixer unit. The shower curtain was missing, as were some wall tiles, although they did look modern. There were no drinking facilities or refrigerator in the room. Overall, the room was kept clean and tidy'.

'I found few additional facilities in the hotel. Telephone calls to any EU country had to be made through the operator, although most international lines were always engaged. There was no shop or bar where drinks or food could be obtained. Fortunately, the receptionist kept small supplies of beer, crisps and chocolate to sell from behind the counter. At breakfast, it was necessary to collect a voucher from the receptionist, go out of the hotel to the far end of the building and enter the hotel restaurant. The self-service restaurant offered a small selection of cold meats, cheese, eggs, bread, jam and cool tea or coffee.'

Adapted from a case prepared by Pat Badmin.

Questions

1 How might the needs of the army segment differ from those of the independent traveller?

2 Evaluate Kings Hotel's strengths and weaknesses in terms of what it currently offers
   (a) the army guest;
   (b) the independent tourist;
   (c) the business traveller.

3 How might the hotel's marketing task differ if it targeted tourists travelling in organised groups as opposed to the independent traveller? Is the hotel wise to avoid block bookings from tour operators, as it does currently?

4 If the army business was lost, what market segment do you think Kings Hotel is currently best equipped to target?

CASE STUDY 5.2

A night at the opera

Opera has traditionally been seen as a 'difficult' art form, appealing to a wealthy élite audience. As far as the UK is concerned, it comes from an alien culture, and because it is mostly sung in Italian and German, is hard to follow if you are not familiar with the story.

There has, however, been a great surge of interest in opera in the UK since 1990. Some of this is due to the BBC's use of Puccini's 'Nessun Dorma', sung by Pavarotti, as its theme for its coverage of the 1990 soccer World Cup tournament in Italy. The tournament ended with the highly successful Three Tenors Concert (Pavarotti, Domingo and Carreras), the CD and video of which turned into massive best sellers worldwide. Other singers, such as Lesley Garrett and Kiri Te Kanawa, have been shrewdly marketed to create popular appeal through 'crossover' albums of lighter music. This can then lead fans towards the heavier, more operatic side of the singer's repertoire. Classical music generally has also been helped in the UK by the populist efforts of the radio station Classic FM and publications such as *Classic CD* and the *BBC Music magazine*. Much of opera's mystique has gone. A 1990 survey on behalf of the magazine *Opera Now* suggested that newcomers to opera were mainly the under-35 year olds, and that they were more responsive to radical stagings and contemporary works.

It is possible, therefore, that a new potential audience for live performance of opera has been created, beyond the traditional segment of those aged over 55 in the A and B socioeconomic groups. Currie and Hobart (1994), therefore, developed a profile of the audiences attending performances of *Carmen* at the National Indoor Arena in Birmingham in 1992 to find out just how wide its appeal actually was. The audience's age profile was as follows:

Age	Per cent
16–18	1
19–24	3
25–34	12
35–44	18
45+	66

Sixty-five-per cent of the audience was female, and in socioeconomic terms, 61 per cent of the audience was from groups A and B. Ninety-five per cent attended opera regularly (between one and three times a year), and 90 per cent also attend the theatre. Forty-eight per cent of the audience found out about the production from the quality newspapers. Just under 20 per cent found out through word of mouth, but no other medium of communication (television, radio, posters, leaflets etc.) scored even as high as 10 per cent. Forty-six per cent had travelled less than 21 miles to attend the performance, and 24 per cent had travelled between 21 and 40 miles.

Eighty per cent of the audience felt that price was an important factor. The ticket price for *Carmen* in Birmingham was £30, less than half the price of an equivalent production at Covent Garden in London. This is still fairly expensive, though, compared with theatre, for instance. The problem is, however, that opera is expensive to stage and the producers felt that £30 was a rock bottom price, even for an 8000 seat arena.

Adapted from a case prepared by Currie and Hobart (1994).

Questions

1 What benefits is the opera-goer buying?

2 Given that opera has indeed widened its appeal over the 1990s, why do you think the *Carmen* audience was still so 'traditional'?

3 What marketing advice would you give opera promoters to help them improve the mass appeal of live performances?

4 Do you ever attend live concerts? If not, why not? If you do, how would you define the target market segment for those events?

REFERENCES FOR CHAPTER 5

Abratt, R. (1993), 'Market Segmentation Practices of Industrial Marketers', *Industrial Marketing Management*, 22, pp. 79–84.

Alsop, R. (1989), 'Brand Loyalty is Rarely Blind Loyalty', *Wall Street Journal*, 19 October, p. B1.

Bonoma, T. V. and Shapiro, B. P. (1984), 'How to Segment Industrial Markets', *Harvard Business Review*, May/June, pp. 104–110.

Broadhead, S. (1995), 'European Cup Winners', *Sunday Express*, 7 May, p. 31.

Burnside, A. (1995), 'Homing Devices on Target', *Marketing*, 19 October, pp. 29–32.

CACI Information Services, (1992), *The Acorn User Guide*, CACI Ltd.

Currie, G. and Hobart, C. (1994), 'Can Opera Be Brought to the Masses?, *Marketing Intelligence and Planning*, 12(2), pp. 13–18.

Daily Mail (1991), 4 November.

Darwent, C. (1993), 'A Socking Success', *Management Today*, February, pp. 44–46.

Douglas, S. P. and Craig, C. S. (1983), *International Marketing Research*, Prentice-Hall.

Hlavacek, J. D. and Ames, B. C. (1986), 'Segmenting Industrial and High Tech Markets', *Journal of Business Strategy*, 7(2), pp. 39–50.

Marbeau, Y. (1992), 'Harmonisation of Demographics in Europe 1991: The State of the Art. Part 1: Eurodemographics? Nearly There!' *Marketing and Research Today*, 20(1), pp. 33–40.

Marketing (1995), 'The 1995 British Shopper Survey', *Marketing*, 24 August, pp. 17–19.

Marsh, P. (1995), 'Down in the Boiler Room', *Financial Times*, 21 August, p. 8.

Mitchell, A. (1983), *The Nine American Lifestyles: Who Are We and Where Are We Going?*, MacMillan.

O'Malley, L. *et al.* (1995), 'Retailing Applications of Geodemographics: A Preliminary Investigation', *Marketing Intelligence and Planning*, 13(2), pp. 29–35.

Paitra, J. (1993), 'The Euro-consumer: Myth or Reality?', in C. Halliburton and R. Hunerberg (eds.), *European Marketing: Readings and Cases*, Addison-Wesley.

Palmer, R. and Cohen, J. (1993), 'Bunter's Back as Model Shape for the Future', *Sunday Times*, 25 April.

Plummer, J. T. (1974), 'The Concept and Application of Lifestyle Segmentation' *Journal of Marketing*, 38 (Jan.), pp. 33–7.

Quatresooz, J. and Vancraeynest, D. (1992), 'Harmonisation of Demographics in Europe 1991: The State of the Art. Part 2: Using the ESOMAR Harmonised Demographics: External and Internal Validation of the EUROBAROMETER Test', *Marketing and Research Today*, 20(1), pp. 41–50.

Smith, W. R. (1957), 'Product Differentiation and Market Segmentation as Alternative Marketing Strategies', *Journal of Marketing*, 21 (July).

Solomon, M. R. (1994), *Consumer Behaviour*, (2nd edn.) Allyn and Bacon.

Sunday Times (1989), 17 September.

Windy, J. (1982), *Product Policy and Concepts, Methods and Strategy*, Addison-Wesley.

Wind, Y. J. and Cardozo, R. (1974), 'Industrial Marketing Segmentation', 3 (March), pp. 153–66.

6 Marketing Information and Research

LEARNING OBJECTIVES

This chapter will help you to:

1 recognise the importance of information to an organisation and the role information plays in effective marketing decision making;

2 outline the sources of secondary data, understand the role of secondary data and the issues involved in its collection and analysis;

3 outline the sources of primary data, understand the role of primary data and the issues involved in its collection and analysis;

4 become familiar with the various steps involved in the marketing research process;

5 appreciate some of the ethical concerns surrounding marketing research; and

6 understand the role of a marketing information system and a decision support system, and develop an awareness of the various types of information available.

INTRODUCTION

The nature and role of market research in Europe has seen significant changes in recent years, as organisations increasingly look to do business in a wider range of EU markets. To be effective in penetrating these markets requires specialised and sophisticated approaches to identifying, assessing and satisfying market demands in a competitive environment. In a community with 15 member states, each with subtly different needs and market characteristics, effective information on the markets that are of interest is essential to help the organisation to make a better decision on the most appropriate market entry and competitive strategies. To support all this, the organisation also needs a properly designed and managed information system to enable timely and appropriate information to be available for the marketing decision maker.

Every aspect of marketing considered in this book, including the definition of markets and market segments, the formulation of an integrated strategy based on the 4Ps and planning and control mechanisms, requires the collection and analysis of information. The better the planning, data collection, information management and analysis, the more reliable and useful the outputs become, and thus marketers are able to make decisions that are more likely to satisfy the needs and wants of selected market segments. The organisation that is prepared to contemplate making a significant change to its marketing effort, without first assessing likely market reaction, is running a very high risk of failure.

> ### Example
>
> As an example of research-driven marketing decisions, in 1995 McDonald's screened a television advertisement showing a boy who has arranged for a meeting of his separated parents in a McDonald's restaurant. This scenario emerged from research which showed that the number of families in the UK with single parents had risen from 8 per cent in 1971 to 21 per cent in 1992. McDonald's wanted to run a campaign that reflected a family situation other than the traditional nuclear one. However, in this case it would appear that the boy's efforts were not in vain, since the parents looked as if they might get back together again (*Marketing*, 1995).

In general, gathering information on the actual or potential market-place not only allows the organisation to monitor trends and issues concerning its current customers, but also helps it to identify and profile potential customers and new markets, and to keep track of its competition, their strategies, tactics and future plans. In this context, market research and information handling offer the organisation a foundation upon which it can adjust to the changing environment in which it operates.

> ### Example
>
> A Polish engineering company suddenly found that its traditional markets in the former Soviet Union had collapsed with the break up of the eastern European trading bloc. Market research played a major role in identifying potential segments in Germany, the main customer buying criteria, and the marketing mix strategy that would best provide an opportunity to establish a niche in an already competitive market.

Marketing information and research principles and practice are often similar across a wide range of situations in consumer and organisational market contexts, although they may, of course, become market specific in terms of their focus. Thus assessing the market for machine tools in Germany and Spain, for example, may differ in terms of the sources of data and information used, but the need for the careful selection of key information sources and the design of a user survey of key potential buyers may well follow similar lines.

This chapter first considers the role of marketing research in assisting decision making and identifies a number of broad alternative approaches. The chapter looks in detail at sourcing and collecting secondary (or desk) research, from existing or published sources, and primary (or field) research, derived from scratch, through surveys, observation or experimentation, for a specific purpose. The important aspects of designing samples and data collection instruments are explored in some depth, since however well managed the rest of the research process is, asking the wrong questions in the wrong manner to the wrong people is a recipe for poor quality marketing information. After thus exploring the practicalities of data collection, the chapter then puts it all into the broader managerial context of a marketing research planning framework. The stages in designing and implementing a marketing research project are considered from establishing objectives, writing a brief, through to project execution and the dissemination of the findings. Because marketing research is potentially such a complex process, with so much riding on its findings, and because organisations often delegate it to agencies, it is important that it is carried out professionally and ethically. There is therefore a section on the ethical issues involved in marketing research at p. 239.

The focus then shifts to managerial problems surrounding information handling. After a summary of the main sources of information used by marketing decision makers, there is a discussion of the use of a marketing information system, designed to generate the kind of information needed on a timely basis. For some organisations this may be a well-organised, formal system, whereas for others it may be much more random, *ad hoc* and chaotic. Finally, consideration is given to the impact of decision support systems in helping the marketing manager to make sense of the information, and to use it as a decision-making tool.

Throughout this chapter, the terms *client* and *researchers* have been used. Client means the organisation that has commissioned the marketing research, whether from an external agency or from an in-house department. Researchers mean the individual or the team responsible for actually undertaking the research task, regardless of whether they are internal or external to the client organisation.

MARKETING RESEARCH OVERVIEW

Marketing research is at the heart of marketing decision making, and because of this, careful consideration should be given to how its processes and methods can be used to the best advantage. This section offers an overview of some of the foundations of marketing research and of the various alternative strategies available before the commissioning of a major survey.

Definitions and types of marketing research

Marketing research is a critical input into marketing and management decisions. Marketing research can be defined as:

> '**the process of defining a marketing problem and opportunity, systematically collecting and analysing information, and recommending actions to improve an organisation's marketing activities.**' (Berkowitz *et al.*, 1992 p. 168).

Marketing research links the organisation with the environment in which it is operating and involves specifying the problem, gathering data then analysing and interpreting those data to facilitate the decision-making process. Marketing research is an essential link between the outside world and the marketer through the information used to identify and define marketing opportunities and problems, generate, refine and evaluate marketing actions, monitor marketing performance and improve understanding of marketing as a process. Marketing research thus specifies the information required to address these issues and designs the methods for collecting the necessary data. It implements the research plan, and then analyses and interprets the collected data. After that, the findings and their implications can be communicated.

Marketing research can be split into two broad areas.

Primary research

Sometimes also called *field* research, primary research is undertaken by, or commissioned by, an organisation for a specific purpose. The required information does not already exist in any available format, and so the research has to be undertaken from scratch. If an fmcg manufacturer, for example, wants to find out in detail about what motivated consumers to try their brand specifically, then it is likely that they will have to undertake primary research. The advantage of primary research is that it is exactly tailored to the problem in hand, but it can be expensive and time consuming to undertake. We will look in detail at methods of primary research at pp. 214 *et seq.*

Secondary research

Sometimes also referred to as *desk research*, secondary research consists of data and information that already exist and can be accessed by an organisation. Thus, for example, they would include published government statistics and published market research reports. All of the data included in the tables in Chapter 2, for example, come from secondary sources. The advantage of secondary research is that it can be much cheaper and quicker to access, and may provide information that the organisation would not otherwise have the time, resources or inclination to gather. The organisation does, however, need to be careful that secondary data are current and that they are appropriate and applicable to the problem in hand. We will look in detail at secondary research at pp. 209 *et seq.*

Clearly, if secondary research is available that answers the question or solves the problem, then that is the quickest and most efficient way of gathering the necessary data. In many cases, however, secondary data may not be directly applicable, or may only give half the picture. This means that a market research project will often incorporate both primary and secondary research, each complementing the other.

The role of marketing research

The role of marketing research in consumer markets has become well established across the EU. It is particularly important for manufacturers, because of the way in which retailers and other intermediaries act as a buffer between manufacturers and their end consumers. If the manufacturer is not to become isolated from market trends and changing preferences, it is important that an accurate, reliable flow of information reaches the marketing decision maker. It might be very limiting if only feedback from the trade were used in making new product and marketing-mix decisions.

MARKETING IN ACTION

Research for your convenience

J C Decaux (UK) Ltd is a subsidiary of J C Decaux International, a French-owned company. In 1983, the company introduced the Automatic Public Convenience (APC) to the streets of the UK. The company has always considered market research, highlighting the concerns of the UK public, to be very important. Based on past research, the company has adopted a standard policy of organising a demonstration every time a new APC is installed, which is open to all who are interested to 'relieve' any concerns.

As the company's managing director says,

'If any person has a concern, we will, as a standard measure, explain and show how the unit operates'.

The company's R&D department is dedicated to improving design and addressing the public's changing needs.

Source: J C Decaux UK Ltd.

On the face of it, this is an unlikely subject for research, but UK attitudes to these automatic public conveniences are different from those of their French neighbours.

Source: J C Decaux UK Ltd.

Another factor facing the consumer goods marketer is the size of the customer base. With such a potentially large number of users and potential users, the onus is on the organisation to make sure that it generates a backward flow of communication from those customers. The potential size of consumer markets also opens up the prospect of adapting products and the general marketing offering to suit different target groups. Decisions on product range, packaging, pricing and promotion will all arise from a well-understood profile of the different types of need in the market. Think back to Chapter 5, where the links between market segments and marketing mixes were discussed in more detail. Marketing research is essential for ensuring that segments exist and that they are viable, and for establishing what they want and how to reach them. As markets become increasingly European and global in their scope, marketing research plays an even more crucial role in helping the organisation to Europeanise its marketing effort, and to decide when to standardise and when to vary its approaches as new markets are opened up.

In organisational markets, the role of marketing research is still very similar to that in consumer markets, in that it helps the organisation to understand the marketing environment better and to make better informed decisions about marketing strategies. Where the two types of market may differ is in the actual design and implementation of marketing research, because of some of the underlying factors peculiar to organisational markets, such as the smaller number of customers, and the closer buyer–seller relationships, as introduced in Chapter 4. Despite any differences, the role of marketing research is still to provide an essential insight into opportunities, markets and customers.

A larger organisation, such as KLM, tends to be better equipped for formal marketing research, as it recognises that it can become remote from customers, whereas a smaller organisation has more day-to-day contact with its customers, although that can lead to a narrow view, oblivious to new ideas and opportunities. Regardless of whether the marketing research function is highly formalised and structured or whether it is informal and *ad hoc*, the organisation must be confident that it is sufficiently well informed to be able to make marketing decisions with the support of timely and accurate information.

KLM, the Dutch airline, carries out two different annual research surveys among business travellers. The first survey focuses on the 50 000 Dutch business people who are members of its frequent flyer programme, and looks at issues such as check-in procedures, in-flight service and value for money. The second survey is much wider. It is undertaken in conjunction with two magazines, *Time* and *Newsweek*, which have 175 000 readers between them who are also business travellers. This survey looks at attitudes towards KLM as a business airline compared with other carriers (Rijkens, 1992). Between the two surveys, KLM can begin to build a picture of how well it is meeting the needs of existing customers and how it can improve its service to them, and can also monitor perceptions of its perceived position in the market as a basis for developing strategies for attracting new customers.

Marketing research can take many forms, from being a highly specialised project requiring expert knowledge and considerable expense, to being quite informal and inexpensive. Compare, for example, the decision to develop a new aircraft such as the Boeing 777 with an airline's decision to introduce in-flight telephone facilities. The former would take many years, and would formally involve both regulatory bodies and airlines at all stages of the aircraft's development to make sure that the highest standards of technical efficiency and reliability were achieved. Both Boeing and the airlines would also, however, be interested in detailed consideration of passenger reaction to a two engined plane crossing the Atlantic. The telephone facilities, on the other hand, might be introduced on an experimental basis on some planes, perhaps after a preliminary survey of business travellers, and an assessment made of usage. In both cases, the purpose is the same: to gather and assess information on customer needs, likes and dislikes, attitudes, interests, behaviour and opinions, before, during and after product development. That information can then be used to find the best match between what the market is demanding and what the organisation can provide, given its own resources and capabilities. The amount of time and cost to allow for each project will, of course, vary considerably. An organisation with a proper respect for marketing research and the support it offers to decision makers will allow a project to take as long as it needs, and to cost as much as it needs, to solve the defined problem, without getting lost in irrelevant fine detail.

The need for marketing research sometimes arises because the organisation needs specific details about a target market, which is a well-defined, straightforward descriptive research task. Sometimes, though, the research need arises from a much broader question, such as why a new product is not achieving expected market share. The organisation may have a theory about the nature of the problem, but it is up to marketing research to establish whether any assumptions are correct, and to check out other possibilities. In practice, most marketing researchers spend a fair proportion of their time on informal projects, undertaken in reaction to specific requests for marketing information. Often these projects lack the scientific rigour associated with the more formal definition of market research. However, problems of a more innovative and complex nature have to be solved through major, formal pieces of market research, simply because of the risks involved in going ahead without the fullest possible insights. International market research, is becoming increasingly important as organisations expand into new, unfamiliar markets. A survey among 557 buyers of market research in 12 different countries, showed that half the respondents regularly buy international market research. The Finns came out on top, with 47 of their 50 respondents buying international data, while the Greeks came bottom. The British and French were about average, just ahead of the Dutch and Italians (Gofton, 1994).

Types of research

So far, the discussion of marketing research has been very general, and has not distinguished between different types of research. There are, however, three major types of research, each one suitable as an approach to different kinds of problem.

Exploratory research

Exploratory research is often undertaken in order to collect preliminary data to help clarify or identify a problem, rather than for generating problem solutions. Before preparing a major proposal, some exploratory work may be undertaken to establish the critical areas to be highlighted in the main body of the research.

Example

An American manufacturer of high-pressure fire-fighting hose nozzles wanted to enter the European market with their most recent innovative design. Before they made a serious commitment to detailed market research across Europe to establish customer reaction and the market entry strategy, some exploratory research was undertaken. This made use of secondary data to establish who the competition would be, what the safety and product standards across Europe were, and not least, what the trends and profile of purchasing by the different fire-fighting authorities were. In addition, a small number of key interviews were held with purchasing bodies in Germany, France and the UK to establish the procedures for trial and adoption in those markets. This survey of knowledgeable persons provided a valuable insight into the characteristics of European markets and revealed to the manufacturer that significant differences existed in what they had at first believed to be a relatively homogeneous market. As a result of the exploratory research, the manufacturer decided to survey one country at a time in depth with the focus on product specification and trial procedures, which is what the exploratory research had found to vary markedly across the countries surveyed, and then to launch the product country by country.

In this case, exploratory research was used as a means of identifying the areas that the main survey would consider in more depth. It also ensured that the organisation's original expectations and assessments were tested before detailed surveys were designed.

Exploratory research can be conducted through a number of different techniques. Secondary sources of information may be enough (*see* p. 209), or the organisation may wish to undertake small-scale qualitative research such as surveys of knowledgeable persons, or small group discussions (*see* p. 216). In some circumstances, the organisation may even choose to use observational research (*see* p. 219) for its exploratory data. However, whatever the method chosen, in each case the purpose is to make an initial assessment of the nature of a marketing problem, so that more detailed research work can be planned appropriately.

Descriptive research

Descriptive research aims to provide the marketer with a better understanding of a particular issue or problem. Descriptive research can range from quite specific briefs, for example profiling the consumers of a particular brand, assessing the actual purchase and repurchase behaviour associated with that brand, and the reasons behind the behaviour exhibited. Most research in this category tends to be of a large-scale survey type, designed to provide a means of better understanding of marketing problems through the presentation of both quantitative and qualitative data (*see* pp. 206–207).

Causal or predictive research

This type of research is undertaken to test a cause and effect relationship so that reasonably accurate predictions about the probable outcome of particular actions can be made. The difficulty with this kind of research for the marketing manager is that to be confident that more of x does cause more of y, all the other variables that influence y must be held constant. The real world laboratory is rarely so obliging, with competitors, retailers and other middlemen, and the marketing environment generally, all acting independently, doing things that will change the background conditions. Thus researchers trying to establish, for instance, whether or not a promotional 10 per cent price reduction would increase sales volume by 15 per cent during a specified period are faced with the problem of ensuring that all the other variables that might influence sales volume are held constant during the research. Random sampling may help in this process, so that the 10 per cent offer would only be made in a random selection of stores, with the other stores offering normal terms. Any difference in the performance of the product in the two groups of stores is likely to have been caused by the special promotion, since both the 'normal' and the 'promotional' product have been subjected to identical environmental factors, impacting on all the stores, during the same period.

The origins of research data

There are two main types of data, which are generated by fundamentally different research approaches.

Qualitative Research

Qualitative research involves the collection of data that are open to interpretation, for example people's opinions, where there is no intention of establishing statistical validity. This type of research is especially useful for investigating motivation, attitudes, beliefs and intentions, rather than utilising probability-based samples. With this approach, many of the methods used to generate data are grounded in the behavioural sciences. They are often based on very small-scale samples and as a result, cannot be generalised in numerical terms. Although the results are often subjective, tentative and impressionistic, they can reflect the complexity that underlies consumer decision making, capturing the richness and depth of how and why consumers act in the way they do. According to Chisnall (1986, p. 147)

> **for all its limitations, qualitative research is able to provide unique insights to inspire and guide the development of marketing strategy and tactics.**

Quantitative techniques, despite their statistical rigour, are rarely able to capture the full complexity and the wealth of interrelationships associated with marketing activity.

Example

A university market research company in Ireland was commissioned by the local development agency to examine the factors that caused tourism firms to innovate. This required detailed consideration of the barriers to, and facilitators of, innovation. A qualitative research survey of 30 of the more significant tourism operators in Ireland revealed much useful information about the innovation process and the ways that the local development agency could assist in that process (Pettitt 1989).

A range of methods can be adopted within the qualitative framework. These include:

- survey research/questionnaires
- focus groups
- in-depth interviews
- observational techniques
- experimentation,

All of these are discussed further in at pp. 214 *et seq.*

Quantitative Research

Quantitative research involves the collection of information that is quantifiable and is not open to the same level of interpretation as qualitative research. It includes data such as sales figures, market share, market size, consumer product returns or complaints, and demographic information (*see* p. 173) and can be collected through primary research, such as questionnaire-based surveys and interviews, and through secondary sources, including published data.

Quantitative research usually involves larger-scale surveys or research that enable a factual base to be developed with sufficient strength to allow statistically rigorous analysis. Most of us have been on the receiving end of quantitative research at some time or another, having been collared by the interviewer armed with a clipboard interviewing respondents in the street. The success of quantitative research depends in part on establishing a representative sample that is large enough to allow researchers to be confident that the results can be generalised to apply to the wider population. It is then possible to specify that 'Forty-five per cent of the market think that ... whereas 29 per cent believe ...' The research can be undertaken through telephone interviews, face-to-face interviews, or mail questionnaires (*see* p. 217), and can also utilise secondary data sources (*see* p. 209).

Continuous research

A large number of research projects are developed specifically to better understand and to overcome marketing problems as they are identified. At pp. 230 *et seq.* we trace the development of such projects from inception through to final evaluation. Some research, however, is conducted on a continuous basis. **Continuous research** is available on an ongoing basis for a subscription or agreement to purchase the updated findings. Usually offered by market research agencies, syndicated research provides much useful data on an ongoing basis. In the UK, retail purchases by consumers are tracked by A C Nielsen, while Target Group Index (TGI) produced by MRB, plots the fortunes of some 5000 brands. Similar services are available in all the main European markets. The quality of such research is very high, but the important advantage is shared cost, since Nielsen data, for example, are essential to any large multiple retailer or brand manufacturer, and they will all buy the data. The price for each organisation is still far, far less than the cost of doing or commissioning the research individually. The big disadvantage, of course, is that competitors also have access to exactly the same information.

There are a number of different approaches to generating continuous data.

Consumer panels

Market research companies recruit large numbers of households which are prepared to provide information on their actual buying and consumption patterns on a regular basis. The panel may be constituted to provide as wide a coverage of the population as possible, or it may be defined to home in on a particular segment. The make-up of a consumer panel can be quite specific. The Pre- and Post-Natal Survey (PNS), operated in the UK, runs a regular survey of 700 pregnant women and 600 mothers with babies up to six months old. For manufacturers of baby foods, nappies, toiletries and infant medicines, such inside information can be invaluable. At the other extreme, Taylor Nelson AGB offer Superpanel, claimed to be the largest in Europe with 8500 households and 28 000 individuals providing purchasing information weekly.

Data can be extracted from consumer panels in two main ways: home audits and omnibus surveys.

Home Audits. The consumer is expected to throw nothing away, and that includes cans, wrappers and all other forms of packaging. Refuse is placed in a special container that is checked at regular intervals by an independent auditor, who also checks the food cupboard and fridge/freezer. Sometimes additional questions are asked to supplement the survey. Increasingly, electronic terminals are installed in homes to allow regular tracking of brand usage. Nielsen Homescan have around 9000 homes linked to in-home scanners that record grocery purchases as well as collecting answers to survey questions. Information is simply downloaded to the research company on a regular basis using a modem. This method is increasingly replacing the old style consumer diary, which recorded the same kind of information, but using pen and paper technology!

Television viewership panels are very similar, in that they involve the recruitment of households and the installation of in-home monitoring equipment. This time, the objective is to use the equipment to enable minute-by-minute recording of audience viewing by channel. From these data, organisations such as AGB and RSMB are able to provide detailed ratings for programmes and viewing patterns during commercial breaks, a critical factor in the sale of advertising time.

Consumer panels enable buying profiles to be built up over time, and provide much useful information for brand managers. Panel data are particularly useful for assessing consumer loyalty, brand switching and the frequency and quantities purchased.

Omnibus surveys. An omnibus survey, as the term suggests, enables an organisation to participate in an existing research programme whenever it is felt appropriate. When an organisation wants to take part, it can add a few extra questions to the next round of questionnaires sent to the large number of respondents who are regularly contacted. The big advantage is cost, although normally the number of questions that can be asked on behalf of a specific organisation is very small. The speed with which answers are received is also an important factor. OMNIMAS, offered by Research Services (GB), offers the result of a weekly survey of 2100 British adults within seven days of the commission. NOP use CATI (computer aided telephone interviewing) based services, and according to their director of omnibus research,

> **'provided clients give us their questions by Friday morning, we can contact consumers over the weekend and provide results by Monday afternoon'** (as reported by Fletcher, 1995, p. 25).

An even faster service is Telenight which allows three to six fairly straightforward questions to be asked and a next-day report is provided. This can be useful in advertising and PR situations, where quick managerial decisions may be needed.

CAPIBUS Europe represents a new pan-European omnibus survey which covers 5000 adults per week across the UK, Germany, France, Italy and Spain. As the latest CAPI (computer aided personal interviewing) technology is used, the results can be delivered in a standard format within four weeks. The service is delivered through the co-operation of five market research companies, one representing each country. Standardisation is important for building confidence in the results. If the sample definition across Europe is similar, and if the fieldwork is designed and delivered in a similar manner, then the findings from different markets become far more comparable. This could be especially important during a launch of a new brand or a pan-European advertising campaign.

Retail audits

The retail audit concept is perhaps the easiest to implement as it relies on trained auditors visiting selected retail stores and undertaking regular stock checks. Increasingly, the use of barcode scanning is providing even more up-to-date information on what is sold where and when. Changes in stock, both on the shelf and in the warehouse, indicate an accurate figure for actual sales to consumers by pack size. This information is especially useful for assessing brand shares, response to sales promotions and the amount of stock being held within the retail trade. Along with information on price levels, the brand manager has much useful information with which to make revised marketing mix decisions.

Sources of marketing research

Marketing research can come from a varied range of sources. These include commercial marketing research companies who can be consulted for specific primary research projects. They can vary considerably in size and specialisation, depending on whether they are large multinationals or small operations. Some will offer the full range of services, but others may choose to specialise. Some, for example, concentrate on large-scale field surveys and have a well-developed infrastructure to accommodate such activity, while others focus on research in depth and specialised psychological, motivational and attitudinal research.

However, marketing research can also be undertaken by the organisation's own marketing research department, if it has one, and secondary data can be obtained from a range of commercial and government sponsored bodies. If it is decided to undertake the research internally, the organisation has to be sure that the range of expertise exists to cope with the problem in hand. The problem is that the greater the in-house expertise available, the more expensive and difficult it is to keep it employed throughout the year. According to Litherland (1994), the number of in-house marketing research departments has decreased considerably across Europe in recent years. In addition to the cost considerations, one of the other problems was the tendency of in-house departments to provide data rather than sound strategic and tactical advice based upon well-analysed and considered information. At Whitbread, the UK brewing and leisure group, the market research department has been retained as a support to the operational marketing decision makers, i.e. the brand managers for such products as Stella Artois, Murphys and Beefeater steakhouses. One of the key benefits is considered to be the depth of understanding that the researchers gain of the Whitbread business.

SECONDARY RESEARCH

There is little point commissioning expensive primary research if the data needed have already been obtained by other organisations, either on a commercial basis or as part of their normal information gathering and dissemination activity. Secondary data can be either internal or external to the organisation. The former is considered to be part of the normal MIS (marketing information system), as outlined later in at p. 240. External secondary data offer valuable information to researchers, once sourced. There is a wide variety of sources to consider, such as government departments and agencies, university libraries, higher education research organisations, other libraries, industry associations, trade and professional bodies, commercial information sold to industry or published in magazines or newspapers, to name but a few. Of course, as already mentioned, the major drawback with secondary data is that the information has been collected for purposes other than this particular research project, and may not be in a suitable or usable form.

Secondary data can nevertheless play a variety of roles in the research process. The main role of secondary data is probably in providing background information on industries and markets, in terms of trends, dynamics and structure. Some of this information may be useful in its own right in informing management decision making, although it is more likely to provide pointers for further primary research. It can also provide useful information that may assist sample selection for surveys by indicating the main competitor and customer groups.

Sources of secondary data

It would be impossible to list all potential sources of data as the number of sources is vast, and much will depend upon the type of research project in question. A discussion with a business librarian will soon reveal how extensive such a list can be! However, a number of the more commonly used sources are listed below:

Government published data

Government, through its various departments and agencies, is one of the most important sources of information on general economic, social and trade statistics. Most European nations have a central statistical office to disseminate information and it is important for researchers to tap this source early in a project. In the UK, the Central Statistical Office (CSO) produces a range of statistics, both general and specific. The general category includes *Annual Abstract of Statistics, Regional Trends, Monthly Digest of Statistics* and *Social Trends*. Specific publications include *Census of Production* (manufacturing industry) and *Census of Distribution* (retailers and wholesalers). These may be a little out of date when published, but they do reveal basic information about market potential and trends. The *Guide to Official Statistics* lists the full range of government publications available in the UK.

The *Business Monitor* (UK, DTI) series is a useful source of reference for product-based information, while the *Digest of Tourist Statistics* gives basic information on the UK tourism industry. The *Business Monitor* series is used to estimate market size, but some care needs to be taken in interpreting the data to ensure that the boundaries defined in the published statistics are relevant to the product market being researched.

Government-based reports are, of course, available across the rest of Europe. In France, the Institut National de la Statistique et des Études Economiques (INSEE) produces a range of data including an on-line database detailing French household consumption. In the Netherlands, the Central Bureau voor de Statistiek produces a wide range of demographic and socioeconomic statistics. The Spanish Instituto Naçional de Estadistica publishes data every two months on the major industrial sectors, prices, employment etc. Although information is available from the central statistical office in most EU nations, often it will be in the native language.

European Commission

Over the years, the EU has become a major provider of secondary data on its member states. *Eurostat* (the Statistical Office of the European Community) provides a range of publications on a regular basis that are often also available on CD-ROM. A wide range of areas related to the socioeconomic and political environment are covered and it would pay researchers to familiarise themselves with just what is available. *European Economy* outlines in a quarterly bulletin economic trends in the member states, while *Panorama of EC Industry* details trends in over 100 product groups. *CRONOS* regularly carries statistics concerning the industrial, economic, financial and social environment in all member states. *REGIO* is a demographic database focusing on employment, unemployment and other population characteristics across the community. *COMEXT* is concerned with intra-community and external trade, and so is a useful source for identifying possible export opportunities. Such databases are, however, very expensive to access on-line.

The European Documentation Centres and Euro-info Centres in all member states provide a useful one-stop shop, where a wide range of European official publications as well as other sources can be viewed at leisure.

Trade published data

Most trades or industries, under the umbrella of their trade association, also produce information that either has been especially commissioned or is compiled from members' submissions. Some have their own libraries of articles and journals relevant to the industry, with some co-operation extending across national boundaries. Most trade associations, however, publish very little and tend to restrict circulation to their own members.

Chambers of commerce

The strength and role of chambers of commerce vary widely across Europe, and even within different member states. In France, for example, they play a very active role in industry for promotion and training, as well as network building. The advantage in contacting a chamber of commerce is that the information is local and comprehensive for narrowly defined areas.

Directories and publications

Directories, the majority of which are commercially produced, can be found on most topics that interest researchers, and are often available from good commercial libraries. A few are worthy of special mention:

Kompass. *Kompass* is a comprehensive international source, published country by country, which is widely used for company and product information, especially during the sampling process. If you want to generate a list of companies that manufacture pig feed, then this is the directory for you. The European *Kompass* can be obtained on-line and on a country-by-country basis, for example *Kompass Netherlands* lists 25 000 Dutch companies, and *Kompass France* details 56 000 firms.

Dun and Bradstreet. Dun and Bradstreet's *Key British Enterprises* lists the top 20 000 firms in the UK with financial data, trade names, trading styles, SIC grouping and location. Along similar lines, they also publish *Dun's Europa*. The financial information provided is especially useful for obtaining a quick profile of an organisation of interest. Additional publications include *Who Owns Whom* (Continental Europe) and, on a country basis, such publications as *Nederlands Ondernemingen en hun Financiale Kenmerken* (Dutch companies and their financial characteristics) and in France a publication that covers the 30 000 largest companies with such information as location, SIC and brand names. Dun and Bradstreet also have several databases covering different regions of the world which are available on-line via *DataStar*.

Yellow Pages. Basically a business telephone directory, classified by goods and services, versions of *Yellow Pages* can be found across the EU, and are now appearing in the central European states. Although the coverage can be very comprehensive, detailing a wide range of products and services, the information is sparse and not always up to date, especially given the short life span of many small businesses.

Euromonitor. Euromonitor publishes various European directories and journals of market research, including the *European Directory of Retailers and Wholesalers*, containing key information on 3000 distribution companies across Europe. Euromonitor also produces *Retail Monitor International* on a monthly basis, reporting on international retailing and trends across Europe.

NTC Publications Ltd. *European Marketing Pocket Book* gives interesting information on demographic, economic and promotional issues for marketers across Europe. There are five other pocket books in the series, for example *Retail Pocket Book* and *British Shopper*, focused more on the UK market.

Newman Books. Directory of European Retailers provides useful information on buyers, location, floor space etc. of around 4000 larger European retailing organisations.

Graham and Trotmans. The Major Companies of Europe details over 8000 European companies.

Price Waterhouse. Price Waterhouse produces *Guide to European Companies*.

ELC International. ELC produces *Europe's 15 000 Largest Companies*.

CBB Research Ltd. CBB research produces *Directory of European Industrial and Trade Associations*.

Manor House Press. Manor House publishes *Store Buyer International* which lists around 9000 buyers in European retail stores.

Market research agencies

A number of specialist providers of market information have emerged. They often sell the information on a subscription basis. A number of the more important providers are:

Euromonitor Publications. Euromonitor Publications is a major provider of reports and statistics across Europe including:

- *European Marketing Data and Statistics:* an annual publication that details Europe-wide information on market size, spending patterns, ownership etc.
- *The Book of European Forecasts*: this provides data on lifestyles and consumption pattern trends across Europe.
- *Consumer Europe:* provides statistics on 250 consumer products sold across Europe.
- *European Consumer Lifestyles: 1985–1995:* presents much useful information on European shopping habits, spending patterns, and leisure activities.
- *Young Britain:* considers the attitudes and lifestyles of 16–24 year olds.

Euromonitor regularly produces market reports on a wide range of consumer products including food and drink, cosmetics, travel and financial services. Its biannual publication, *European Directory of Consumer Market Reports and Surveys,* provides an essential guide to recently completed research projects across a number of European markets.

Euromonitor's monthly journals also include *Market Research Europe, Market Research International* and *Market Research GB*. Other important publications from Euromonitor include *International Marketing Data and Statistics, Consumer International, Consumer Eastern Europe, Retail Trade International*, and *World Marketing Data and Statistic*s on CD-ROM.

Mintel Publications. Mintel Market Intelligence produces market research reports on a monthly basis, especially on consumer goods markets. More specialist themes in retailing and market sectors are also produced on a subscription basis. *European Lifestyles* examines seven EU markets from a consumer shopping pattern and lifestyle consumption perspective. Mintel reports are also available on CD-ROM.

Key Note Reports. These are similar to Mintel reports, but cover more non-consumer markets. Key Note produce *Market Sector Overviews*, for example fitted kitchens, and

Industry Trends and Forecasts, for example the UK pharmaceutical industry. Reports are also available on-line.

The Economist Intelligence Unit. The EIU produces market research reports on a monthly basis in *Retail Business*.

Libraire du Commerce International (LCI). LCI presents data on consumer attitudes, brand awareness and product preferences across French-speaking Europe, plus an analysis of food and wine markets in some other EU countries that may be relevant to French manufacturers.

Market Research Burda GmbH. Influences on Buying Decisions and *Typology of Consumer Demands* examine German consumer shopping patterns.

Press published data

Not only do specialist market research organisations produce regular reports, but the quality press and especially the financial press, also produce reports on a wide variety of markets and sectors. The *Economist Intelligence Unit* annually produces a large number of reports, and the *Financial Times* offers a Business Information service to answer specific queries. The *Financial Times* also produces surveys, covering both individual countries and product markets.

Financial institutions data

The major banks and leading finance houses in many European markets produce regular reports on industries and sectors as a guide to investors.

Electronic data sources

An increasing amount of information for researchers can be found on databases. Organisations such as Kompass, Dun and Bradstreet, trade associations, the business press, and not least Eurostat and the government statistical services are providing information in computerised form, either using CD-ROM, or through on-line services. Alternatively, database hosts act as intermediaries offering information access by subscription. For example *DIALOG* holds such files as *Kompass* and the *FT Company Abstracts* and *DataStar* has the largest on-line EU system offering 60 separate databases associated with market research, as well as industry and company reports. *MAID* contains the extensive range of *Euromonitor* market research reports. These databases are normally offered on the basis of a licence fee plus an hourly charge. Two examples indicate the power contained within this emerging form of secondary data searching. *DataStar's Hoppenstedt* in the Netherlands allows access to key statistics on 20 000 Dutch companies, while *BODAC* (the French government's official company and trade register) contains over one million entries for the enthusiastic researcher!

Syndicated data services

Two forms of syndicated data service can be found: those where manufacturers agree to jointly fund continuous research in their product area to the benefit of all parties, and those where a research agency deliberately sells a research programme to interested parties in the sector. The advantage of the syndication approach is that it shares the cost, although it also shares the results. Nowadays, most syndicated services are driven by the research agencies, although the users do have a major say in the design and implementation of the research. There are many services available, ranging from advertising to veterinary products, that involve panels, surveys and audits. We looked at these at p. 207.

Bond (1994) reported how IBM used a syndicated service offered by Opinion Leader research to explore the views of the UK's opinion leaders on the question of what big business can do for the community. The study was shared with other participants, such as Whitbread and Texaco, and involved contacting senior people in politics, industry, education, the civil service etc. The advantage of pursuing the syndicated route was that the participating organisations could exert much more influence on the questionnaire and study than would have been possible with an omnibus study (provided that the contributors could agree, of course).

Some syndicated services are offered across international boundaries. Taylor Nelson AGB operates a syndicate for drugs manufacturers, including Merck Sharp and Dohme and Pfizer, called *CardioMonitor* which follows diagnosis and drug therapy in 10 European markets, as well as in the USA and Japan.

Using secondary data

Secondary data vary widely in terms of relevance and quality. Boyd *et al.* (1977) suggest four criteria for evaluating secondary data sources:

1 pertinency of the data;
2 who collects the data and why;
3 method of collecting data;
4 evidence of careful work.

Although secondary sources of data are widely used, as they tend to be low cost and usually easily obtainable once a source has been identified, the criteria above do suggest some potential problem areas. Often the data fail to get down to the micro level necessary to support management decisions. The focus is often at industry level rather than the sector or segment of particular interest, perhaps within a defined geographical area. Some data may have been collected to promote the well-being of the industry, rather than to provide wholly accurate figures, and sometimes they are not always accurate because of their source, their age, or the way they were collected. However, for most surveys the sorting, sifting and analysis of secondary data are useful for purposes ranging from developing sample frames (*see* p. 221) to providing comprehensive insights into market size, structure and trends.

PRIMARY RESEARCH

Once the decision to use primary research has been made, researchers have to define what data need to be collected, and how. This section looks specifically at 'how'. First, there is an overview of primary research methods. For example the data needed may be drawn from personal interviews, telephone or mail surveys, involving customers, non-customers, suppliers, retailers or any other group of interest. These are not, however, the only methods of data collection, and thus the section also looks at observational and experimental research methods.

Whatever method is chosen as most appropriate to the client's information needs, researchers then have to think about defining a sample of individuals or organisations from the total population of interest (defined as a market segment or an industry, for instance). This topic is covered in some depth at p. 221. Finally, of particular interest to those conducting surveys, pp. 225–30 look specifically at questionnaires.

Research methods

The three most commonly used methods for collecting primary data are interviews and surveys, observation and experiments.

In order to achieve its mission of being the most customer-focused brand in the car market, Daewoo has invested heavily in research into customer service expectations.

Source: Daewoo.

Interviews and surveys

Interviews and surveys involve the collection of data directly from individuals. This may be by direct face-to-face personal interview, either individually or in a group, by telephone or by a mail questionnaire. Each of these techniques, considered in turn below, has its own set of advantages and disadvantages which are summarised in Table 6.1.

Personal interviews. A personal interview is a face-to-face meeting between an interviewer and a respondent. It may take place in the home, the office, the street, a shopping mall, or at any prearranged venue. In one extreme case, a holiday company decided to interview respondents who were at leisure on the beach. One can imagine the varied responses!

TABLE 6.1
Comparative performance of interview and survey techniques

	Personal interviews	Group interviews	Telephone survey	Mail survey
Cost per response	High	Fairly high	Low	Very low
Speed of data collection	Fast	Fast	Very fast	Slow
Quantity of data collectable	Large	Large	Moderate	Moderate
Ability to reach dispersed population	Low	Low	High	High
Likely response rate	High	Very high	Fairly high	Low
Potential for interviewer bias	High	Very high	Fairly high	None
Ability to probe	High	High	Fairly high	None
Ability to use visual aids	High	High	None	Fairly high
Flexibility of questioning	High	Very high	Fairly high	None
Ability to ask complex questions	High	High	Fairly high	Low
Ability to get truth on sensitive questions	Fairly low	Fairly high	Fairly high	High
Respondent anonymity	Possible	Fairly possible	None	None
Likely respondent co-operation	Good	Very good	Good	Poor
Potential for respondent misunderstanding	Low	Low	Fairly low	High

There are three broad types of personal interview:

(a) the in-depth, largely **unstructured interview**, taking almost a conversational form;
(b) the **structured interview**, which allows the interviewer far less flexibility to explore responses further and results in a more programmed, almost superficial interview;
(c) a combination of these, the **semi-structured interview**, which is based around a programmed script, but the inclusion of some open-ended questions gives the interviewer scope to pursue certain issues more flexibly.

The unstructured interview can be used for collecting quantitative data, but is rather more useful for exploring attitudinal and motivational issues. Although a standard set of questions may be used as a guide, there is often considerable scope for the interviewer to explore some topics in more depth if additional unforeseen themes emerge in the interview. Generally, the questions are more of a checklist than a rigid format to follow. Given that an unstructured interview may provide one or two hours of intense exploration, it is important that the interviewer is properly briefed, can judge whether the respondent is starting to go off at a tangent or raising new issues of real relevance, and can adjust to the changing pattern of the interview. Often high-level interviewing skills are needed, along with a sound knowledge of the product-market concept being examined. These interviewing skills must also include the ability to record the interview accurately if a tape recorder or video recorder is not being used. Further problems that can emerge in the data analysis stage will be considered below.

The major advantage of the unstructured interview is the depth that can be explored and the ability to push the respondent on meaning and accuracy. However, the time taken to complete an interview, and the cost of each interview, make large-scale surveys of this nature prohibitively expensive. In organisational markets, they are often used on a small-scale basis to fill gaps left by other approaches such as mail or telephone surveys.

The structured personal interview adopts a standard questionnaire in wording, layout and order that the interviewer must follow strictly. Little use is made of open-ended questions and the questionnaire is carefully designed for ease of recording information and progress through the interview. This may be especially important if the questionnaire is being administered in the street, thus interrupting a respondent's planned shopping trip. The use of a standardised questionnaire means that the responses from a large number of individuals can be handled with considerable ease as there is no need for further interpretation and analysis. Furthermore, the interviewer retains control over the completion of the questionnaire. This approach is used by opinion pollsters and organisations seeking to quantify responses to predetermined questions. As less-skilled interviewers are needed, the whole process can be completed more quickly than the unstructured interview, in terms of both field work and data processing. The limitations stem mainly from the need to design and pilot the questionnaire very carefully to ensure that it meets the specification expected of it. We look more closely at some of these questionnaire issues at p. 225 *et seq.*

Group interviews and focus groups. Group interviews are used to produce qualitative data which are not capable of generalisation to the wider population, but do provide useful insights into underlying attitudes and behaviours relevant to the marketer. A group interview normally involves between six and eight respondents considered to be representative of the target group being examined. The role of the interviewer is to introduce topics, encourage and clarify responses and generally guide proceedings in a manner which is effective without being intrusive.

In this kind of group situation, individuals can express their views either in response to directed questions or, preferably, in response to general discussion on the themes that have been introduced. Often it is the interaction and dialogue between respondents that is more revealing of opinions. So that participants will relax enough to open out like this, it is often helpful to select the group concerned to include people of a similar status. For example a manufacturer of an innovative protective gum shield for sports persons organised different group interviews for sports players (users) and dentists (specifiers). Further subdivision could have been possible by type of sport, or to distinguish the casual player from the professional.

Group interviews are especially useful where budgets are limited or if the research topic is not yet fully understood. If secondary data have clearly indicated in quantitative terms that there is a gap in the market, group interviews may be useful in providing some initial insights into why that gap exists, whether customers are willing to see it filled, and with what. This could then provide the basis for more detailed and structured investigation. There are of course dangers in generalisation, but if between four and six different discussion groups have been held, some patterns may begin to emerge. For the smaller business with limited funds, group interviews may provide a useful alternative to more costly field techniques.

Telephone interviews. Telephone interviews are primarily used in industrial markets in Europe as a means of reaching a large number of respondents relatively quickly and directly. Whereas there is variation across Europe in home telephone ownership, virtually every business is connected, and so a readymade network exists to reach targeted respondent groups. It is far more difficult to ignore a telephone call than a mail survey, although the amount and complexity of information that can be gathered is often limited. In the absence of any visual prompts and with a maximum attention span of probably no more than 10 minutes, the design of the questionnaire needs to be given great care, and piloting is essential to ensure that the information required is obtainable.

The range of applications is wide but the telephone is especially useful for usage and purchase surveys where market size, trends and competitive share are to be assessed. Other applications include assessing advertising and promotional impact, customer satisfaction studies and establishing a response to a very specific phenomenon, such as the launch of a new export assistance scheme. Kwik Fit Exhausts telephone their recent customers to establish the degree of satisfaction with their recent purchase.

The interviewing process itself is highly demanding. Being able to generate interest and to keep the attention of the respondent is critical, yet at the same time the information required must be collected in an effective and unbiased manner. The use of software packages can enable the interviewer to record the findings more effectively and formally and to steer through the questionnaire, using loops and routing through, depending on the nature of the response. With the demand for such surveys, a number of agencies specialise in telephone research techniques.

Mail questionnaires. This popular form of research involves sending a questionnaire through the post to the respondent for self-completion and return to the researchers. Questionnaires can, of course, also be handed out at the point of sale, or included in product packaging, for the buyer to fill in at their own convenience and then post back to the researchers. Hotels and airlines assess their service provision through this special kind of mail survey, and many electrical goods manufacturers use them to investigate purchasing decisions.

While the mail survey has the advantage of wide coverage, the lack of control over response poses a major problem. Researchers cannot control who responds and when, and the level of non-response can create difficulties. Response rates can drop to less than 10 per cent in some surveys, although the more pertinent the research topic to the respondent, and the more 'user friendly' the questionnaire, the higher the response rate. Offering a special incentive can also work (Brennan *et al.*, 1991). In a survey of Irish hotel and guest house owners, the offer of free tickets to a local enter-tainment facility proved an attractive incentive. Other larger-scale consumer surveys promise to enter all respondents into a draw for a substantial prize.

There are other obvious things that can be done to ensure higher response rates. A clear, spacious and user-friendly layout, gentle reminders and follow-up approaches to non-respondents, and a supportive, persuasive covering letter all assist in increasing the responses. However, the non-respondents in themselves may pose a problem. It is important to assess whether the respondents, as a group, may be different from the late and non-respondents. Those who think more strongly about a topic, for example, are more likely to respond than those with a more marginal interest, perhaps repre-senting casual or light users.

Mail surveys are especially prevalent in organisational markets, where target respondents can be more easily identified from contacts or mailing lists. The process of mailing can also be readily implemented and controlled using the organisation's normal administrative and mailing infrastructure already set up for response logging, address label generation, folding, and franking etc. One way of trying to improve response rates for organisational mail surveys is to warn or notify the desired respond-ent in advance that the survey is on its way. Haggett and Mitchell (1994), reviewing the literature on pre-notification, found that overall it increases response rates by around 6 per cent, and on average reduces by one the number of days taken to respond. The telephone shows the best results, increasing responses by 16 per cent, while postcards only manage a 2.5 per cent improvement. There is, however, no evi-dence to suggest that the quality of the response is also improved.

There is no one best method to select from the group discussed above. Much will depend upon the nature of the research brief, especially in the light of the resources available and the quality and quantity of information required for decision making. A direct face-to-face interview, for example, allows for deeper exploration by the inter-viewer, an evaluation of body language, and generally higher response rates, but it has the disadvantages of possible misinterpretation, distortion or bias in the interviewer's report, especially if the interviewer is inexperienced, poorly trained or poorly super-vised. There is also a chance that the interviewee will give what they feel to be more acceptable responses, rather than their genuine belief about a particular question. All of these factors, including the type of questions asked and the structure of the inter-view, have the potential to influence and distort the results of the survey.

The other factor that has become of significant concern is the cost of the research survey. Face-to-face interviews, especially if conducted on an in-depth basis, tend to be the most costly and time consuming, thus making this form of survey less attrac-tive. Other survey techniques, such as group interviews, telephone surveys and mail questionnaires, all provide alternative, cheaper ways of gathering data. Each of them, however, also has its own set of limitations, and ultimately, the decision on choice of technique has to put aside absolute cost considerations and think in terms of finding the most cost-effective way of collecting those vital data.

Churchill (1976) suggested three criteria for assessing alternative survey techniques: information control, sample control and administrative control. *Information control* refers to the amount, type and complexity of data required, and how accurate the responses need to be. As already indicated, if attitudes, opinions or motivations are to be examined, then more personal, face-to-face methods usually need to be used. However, personal interview and telephone surveys may produce data tainted by interviewer bias. Telephone surveys offer little potential for generating lengthy answers to questions, while there is evidence to suggest that the length of a mail ques-tionnaire does not affect the response rate.

Sample control again varies by method. Each method has its own inherent problems of identifying sample members and, not least, generating a response from them.

Non-response is often much lower with personal interviews than with mail questionnaires, for example. Finally, time and cost constraints clearly affect each method, although the differences can be exaggerated. For example mail surveys may be quicker than personal interviews, but if non-response means that second or third mailings have to be sent, it adds to the time taken, and the costs incurred.

What is obvious to researchers is that the decision involves a trade-off between the different methods. There are many factors, and all must be considered in the light of the survey objectives and data needs.

Observational research

This method involves, as its name implies, the observation of particular individuals or groups, whether they are staff, consumers, potential consumers, members of the general public, children, or whoever, by trained observers. The intention is to understand some aspect of their behaviour that will provide an insight into the problem that has been identified by the marketing research plan. For example, trials are often conducted with new products in which consumers are asked to use a particular product and are observed while they do so, thus giving information about design, utility, durability and other aspects, such as ease of use by different age groups, and whether people naturally use it in the intended way. This provides an opportunity to test the product and observe how it is used first hand.

Another form of observational research that deliberately seeks feedback on employee performance is *mystery shopping*. Mystery shopping allows a researcher to go through the same experience as a normal customer, whether in a store, restaurant, plane or showroom. As far as the employees are concerned, they are just dealing with another customer and they are not aware that they are being closely observed. The 'shopper' is trained to ask certain questions and to measure performance on such things as service time, customer handling and question answering. The more objec-

MARKETING IN ACTION

Big brother is watching you

One method of observational research uses security cameras, installed in many stores, to observe consumer traffic patterns as they move about the store. This information can be used to help design the layout of the store, probably with the intention of keeping you in the store longer and exposing you to more products. The advertising agency J Walter Thompson (JWT) have taken this concept a stage further with their *InSitu* research technique. Shoppers are filmed, without their knowledge, as they shop in a store, and then they are interviewed in depth about their shopping decisions. The combination of video and interview is very important, because seeing the video reminds shoppers of what they were thinking at the time of the purchase. JWT claim that the system can highlight those brands which are examined but then rejected at the point of sale. The interview can discover precisely what it was that put the shopper off. Major brand owners such as Kellogg's and Lever

Brothers signed up to use the system as soon as it was launched.

This whole system does, however, raise ethical issues about invasion of privacy. First, the shopper is warned by signs at the store entrance that the premises are under video surveillance for research purposes. Then, if the customer raises any objection when approached by the researcher for the post-video interview, the video-tape of that customer is wiped clean. The researchers do claim that there have been few objections:

'People like the idea of being on TV and generally they are flattered. Once I was filming a couple and they started having a fight about which paint to buy. I made my presence known and the chap said it was fine to film them and carried on with the argument.'

Source: Snowdon (1995a).

tive the measures the more valuable they are to marketing managers to ensure that certain benchmark standards are being achieved. In a survey of 80 of the UK's largest retailers, almost all claimed to use mystery shopping with the aim of identifying training needs, improving company standards and improving staff performance (Cramp, 1994).

The potential problems that can be experienced with interviews are also likely with observation where human observers are used. That is, the training and supervision of the observers is of great importance and since it is more subjective, the likelihood of misinterpretation is higher. On the other hand, mechanical observation tools may be used to overcome bias problems, such as supermarket scanners monitoring the purchases of particular consumers or groups of consumers, and the Neilsen people meters, used to monitor the viewing and listening habits of television watchers and radio listeners.

Other devices can be used to observe or monitor closely the physiological responses of individuals, such as their pupil dilation (using a tachistoscope) when watching advertisements, to indicate degree of interest. A galvanometer, which measures minute changes in perspiration, can also help to gauge a subject's interest in advertisements.

In some ways, observation is a more reliable predictor of behaviour than verbal assertions or intentions. Where interaction is not needed with the respondent, or where the respondent may be unable to recall the minutiae of their own behaviour, direct observation may be a valuable additional tool in the researcher's armoury. It is particularly informative when people are not aware that they are being observed, and are thus acting totally naturally, rather than changing their behaviour or framing responses to suit what they think researchers want to see or hear. Observation can be relevant in both consumer and industrial markets. In the latter, observation at exhibitions and shows can provide useful insights to behaviour. Also, the actual tracking of buyer decisions and experiences as they work through the system (i.e., order processing, packaging, delivery, invoicing, after-sale service etc.) can reveal much about operating procedures for usage, buying and logistics in a way that would be difficult to discover and fully understand through post-purchase questioning.

Experimentation

The third method through which primary data can be collected is by conducting an experiment. This may involve the use of a laboratory (or other artificial environment), or the experiment may be set in its real-world situation, for example test marketing a product (more on that in Chapter 9). In the experimental situation, researchers manipulate the independent variable(s), for example price, promotions or product position on a store shelf, and monitor the impact on the dependent variable, for example sales, to try to determine if any change in the dependent variable occurs. The important aspect of an experiment is to hold most of the independent variables constant (as well as other potentially confounding factors) while manipulating one independent variable and monitoring its impact on the dependent variable. This is usually possible in a laboratory, where control of the environment is within the power of researchers, but far less possible in a real-world situation where a myriad of external complications can occur which can confuse the results.

For example a manufacturer may want to find out whether new packaging will increase sales of an existing product, before going to the expense of changing over to the new packaging. The manufacturer could conduct an experiment in a laboratory, perhaps by setting up a mock supermarket aisle, inviting consumers in and then observing whether their eyes were drawn to the new packaging, whether they picked it up, how long they looked at it, and whether they eventually chose it in preference to the competition. The problem with this, however, is that it is still a very artificial situation, with no guarantees that it can replicate what would have happened in real life. Alternatively, therefore, the manufacturer could set up a field experiment, trialling the new packaging in real stores in one or more geographic regions and/or specific market segments, and then monitoring the results.

The key to successful experimentation is being able to replicate market conditions as closely as possible in an experimental setting. As will be shown in Chapter 9, in discussing test marketing, many things can go wrong that are well beyond the control of the researching organisation. Not least might be the deliberate attempts by competitors to distort the findings through tactical actions of their own. A carefully timed sales promotion, for example, on a directly competing product, may completely distort the experiment's outcomes.

Not all experimental research designs need to be highly structured, formal or set up for statistical validation purposes. For example side-by-side experiments where shop A offers a different range or mix from shop B, which in all other respects is identical to shop A, can still reveal interesting insights into marketing problems, even though the rigour of more formal experimental designs is not present.

Sampling

Particularly in mass consumer markets, time and cost constraints mean that it is impractical to include every single target customer in whatever data-gathering method has been chosen. It is not necessary even to begin to try to do this, because a carefully chosen representative sample of the whole population (usually a target market) will be enough to give the researchers confidence that they are getting a true picture that can be generalised. In most cases, researchers are able to draw conclusions about the whole population (i.e., the group or target market) based on the study of a sample. The skill, therefore, lies in making sure that the selected sample is indeed representative. If it is not, then the results of the research may not give an accurate picture of the relevant population and decisions made are likely to be wrong. While it is true that a sample is never absolutely identical to the population it is supposed to represent, if selected correctly it will tend to have the same characteristics as that population and conclusions drawn about the sample should reflect those of the population. In other words, the reliability of the results from the sample is high, and decisions can be based on those results with confidence.

Figure 6.1, based on Tull and Hawkins (1990), shows the main stages in the **sampling process**, and each one will be considered briefly in turn:

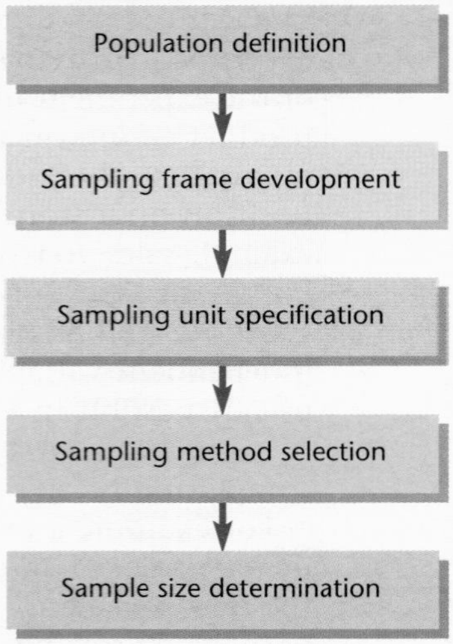

Population definition

The population to be surveyed will derive from the overall research objectives. Often this will be based upon a target market or segment, but even then further definition based on markets, products, or behaviours is unlikely to be necessary to create a tightly defined population. In consumer markets, the population may be defined by any of the variables considered in Chapter 5, provided that researchers can use them operationally. In organisational markets the population is usually defined in terms of organisational characteristics and industries.

Sampling frame

The sampling frame is the means of access to the population to be surveyed. It is basically a list from which individual names can be drawn. Registers of electors or lists of organisations compiled from directories such as *Kompass* and *Dun and Bradstreet* are examples of possible sampling frames. Internal customer records may also provide a sampling frame, although researchers need to be very sure that such records give a complete picture, and that there is no doubt that this is the required population for the study, rather than just a cheap, quick and easy way of generating an extensive list of names.

Sampling unit

The sampling unit is the actual individual from whom researchers want a response. In consumer markets, the sampling unit is usually the name attached to the address in the sampling frame. In organisational markets, however, this stage can be complex because, as we saw in Chapter 4, organisations have a number of individuals concerned with decision making. So if an organisation wanted to survey builders' merchants across Germany, a two-stage process might have to be used. First, the sample unit might be represented by the individual firm selected, and then a secondary stage might focus the individual within that organisation who should be the subject of attention (the sampling element). It is very important to identify the right individual, as the responses of the purchasing manager in this case may be different from those of the managing director.

Sampling method selection

The next step in the process is to select the sample method, which is the means by which individual sample units and elements are selected from the larger sampling frame. The major and early decision is whether to use probability or non-probability sampling methods.

Probability sampling. Random, or *probability sampling*, where each member of the population has an equal or known chance of being selected for the sample, offers specified levels of confidence about the limits of accuracy of the results. So if a retailer wanted to do a survey to establish satisfaction levels with checkout services, they might decide to interview every thirtieth customer coming through the checkouts during research sessions held at different times of the week. At the end of the process, the retailer might be able to conclude that the findings were correct to the 95 per cent

Population definition

↓

Sampling frame development

↓

Sampling unit specification

↓

Sampling method selection

↓

Sample size determination

Source: Adapted from Tull and Hawkins (1990).

FIGURE 6.1

Stages in the sampling process

level of confidence – in other words there was only a one in 20 chance that the sample was biased or unrepresentative.

Stratified sampling is an important method of probability sampling, which involves the division of the sampling frame into defined strata or groups which are mutually exclusive. Random probability samples are then drawn independently from each group. This method is widely used in organisational markets, as they naturally divide into discrete layers or bands, reflecting for example company size, geographic location, market shares or purchase volumes. Researchers could decide, therefore to take a 100 per cent sample (census) of all the larger firms (defined perhaps by turnover or number of employees, for instance) and then use random sampling with the rest. By effectively restructuring the sample frame in a manner best suited to the project, greater confidence can be enjoyed that the sample closely reflects the population in question.

An alternative form of stratified sampling is *area sampling*. Returning to our survey of German builders' merchants, the first stage would be to divide Germany into regions, and then randomly select a small number of those regions as the basis for the sample. Within each chosen region, researchers will then randomly select the organisations for the sample. They may end up studying merchants in the Leipzig, Karlsruhe and Hannover areas, rather than a sample from across Germany that would involve considerable time and expense to follow up.

With a random sampling method, it is important for researchers to ensure that the sampling frame used does enable each member to have an equal chance of being selected. Furthermore, actually obtaining responses from the selected sample can be quite difficult. What if the thirtieth customer through the checkout doesn't want to stop? What if there's nobody at home when the interviewer calls round or phones? What if the sampling frame is out of date and the selected consumer has moved house or died? Any of these circumstances violate the ideal of the random sample.

Non random sampling. *Non random samples* are much easier to identify than random samples because they are not based on the same strict selection requirements, and allow researchers a little more flexibility. The results from these samples are not representative of the population being studied and may lack the statistical rigour generated by random sampling, but they are still often of considerable use to researchers. Two main non-random sampling methods may be used:

1 *Judgemental sampling.* This method is widely used in organisational market research. Sample units are selected deliberately by researchers, because they are felt to represent better sources of the required information. Given the concentrated nature of many industries, if a contracting company for pipework cleaning wanted to enter a new geographical market, for example, it would probably make sense to survey the heavy users if that was the target segment of interest, rather than draw at random from all users, large and small. Of course, no inference could be drawn about the wider population from such a sample method.

2 *Quota sampling.* Quota samples are formed when researchers decide that a certain proportion of the total sample should be made up of respondents conforming to certain characteristics. It may be decided, for example, that for a particular study, the sample should consist of 400 non-working women aged between 25 and 35, 250 full-time working, and 350 part-time working women in the same age group. This breakdown may reflect the actual structure of the market under consideration. Each interviewer is then told how many completed questionnaires to bring back within each quota category. The choice of respondents is not random, since the interviewer is actively looking for people who fulfil the quota definitions, and once the quota is full, will reject any further respondents in that category. The criteria for defining quotas often use geographic or demographic factors, for example age bands, employment, the structure of the family unit, location, car owners etc., whatever is felt to reflect the structure of the market.

The advantage of quota sampling is that it is quicker and cheaper to do than a full random sample would be, as no sample frame has to be devised, and researchers do not have to worry whether the sampling frame is up to date or not. Furthermore, interviewers are not committed to following up specific respondents. Under a quota sample, if a particular respondent does not want to co-operate, then that's fine – the interviewer will look for another one.

Sample size

A final yet very important consideration in the sampling process is sample size. While it may be true that the larger the sample, the greater the confidence that the sample truly represents the population of interest, there is no point in spending more time and money pursuing any bigger sample than you have to. With random sampling based on statistical analysis, researchers can have confidence within prescribed limits that the sample elements are representative of the population being studied. It is not so much the size of the sample selected that matters, as the tolerated risk of sampling error that researchers are prepared to accept and the cost that is incurred in adding to the number of sampling elements.

As one would expect, the higher the levels of confidence required, the greater the size of the sample needed. In Europe, surveys of consumer buying habits are often around 2000 units, which would typically yield a 95 per cent confidence level that the sample reflects the characteristics of the population. In organisational markets, sample sizes of between 300 and 1000 can be used to produce high levels of confidence. With stratified samples, provided that the strata have been carefully defined according to relevant characteristics, even smaller sample sizes may be permissible, especially if they are supported by a full census of some of the more critical groups.

MARKETING IN ACTION

Trouble brewing

The rate of change in the UK beer market is very fast and seems to be speeding up. In the 1980s, for example, it took low and no-alcohol beer two years to become established, whereas in 1995, it took alcopops (Hooper's Hooch etc.) only six months. Brewers thus have to use market research so that they can be alert to new trends and product opportunities. They need to know how consumers' tastes are changing, how they perceive current products on the market and how they would respond to new product concepts. As Whitbread found, consumer' perceptions of brands do not always coincide with what the marketer intended, and the sooner this can be diagnosed and remedied, the better. Researching new products is no easier. Whitbread also realises that historical preferences and purchasing patterns are of limited use in a fast-changing market, and thus faces the task of defining tomorrow's customer.

It is not just the consumer who is of interest. The brewers also need information for analysing the performance of their channels of distribution. Research has shown that the take-home market grew by 8 per cent, (by value) in 1995, and that multiple grocers are the main channel, with the Scottish market growing faster than any other area of the UK. Intermediaries also need information to help them decide which products should be stocked and in what quantities. One of the problems with the rate of change in the beer market is that there are too many brands chasing too little shelf space. In the premium lager sector alone there are 400 brands, far too many for any one retailer to stock. Thus the intermediaries also have to analyse historical sales data, predict consumer trends and estimate the likely effects of brewers' promotional and other marketing activities in order to allocate what space they do have available.

Source: The Grocer, 1996.

Questionnaire design

The questionnaire is a commonly used research instrument for gathering and recording information from interviews, whether face to face, mail or telephone surveys, as described earlier. Researchers soon learn that the best planned surveys soon fall apart if the questionnaire is poorly designed and fails to gather the data originally anticipated. Even the most professional researchers can still make mistakes which only come to light when the responses come back, i.e. when it is too late. To minimise the risk of disappointment, however, there are several dimensions to consider in questionnaire design.

Objectives

The aim of a questionnaire is closely linked with the overall purpose of the research. It is tailormade to meet the information requirements of the study and therefore lies at the heart of the research process. If the questionnaire is to fulfil its role properly as a means of data collection, then there are five detailed areas that need to be analysed carefully. The aims of a questionnaire are:

To link with purpose of the research. The questionnaire should fit closely with the survey method chosen and take account of the likely impact upon the population being sampled, the number of respondents required and not least the research problem being investigated. For example a questionnaire may have a very different style if it is to be directed at trade experts rather than the public. Similarly, there will be other differences depending on whether the focus is on attitudes and preferences rather than buying patterns.

To collect data. The questionnaire must elicit accurate responses that do shed light on the topic being studied. The quality of the response is all-important, and this is heavily influenced by the design of the questionnaire and the specific construction of the questions. There are several types of data that a questionnaire can collect.

1 *Classification data* are concerned with facts and the recording of actual behaviour. Demographic, ownership and usage behaviour all fall into this category. Sometimes the questions are easy to answer, assuming of course that the respondent wishes to provide accurate responses. For example, age and income are often under- or overestimated. However, questions asking whether you have purchased, when you last purchased, and how frequently you purchase, may at first glance seem reasonable but they do rely on accurate memory and truthfulness. The more personal and sensitive the classification data required, the more wary researchers need to be.

2 *Opinion based data* are more difficult to gather. We all lock away our opinions, beliefs, attitudes and feelings and only allow them out when we have confidence that their expression will not do us any harm. Respondents may, therefore, even be conscious of the image they are creating in the eyes of the interviewer. A respondent may have no views or no ideas, for example, on the merits and demerits of Chilean wine, as compared with Portuguese wine, but may not wish to show ignorance! Where views are expressed, it is often difficult to capture the strength and range of beliefs, let alone ascertain how they might influence a brand attitude or image. Attitudes and opinions consist of a number of dimensions, some of which are conflicting. Finding the right research instrument to unravel that complexity is a major challenge.

3 The study of *motivation*, trying to understand why people express the views they do, is an even greater challenge to researchers. The reasons can be extremely diverse, complex, muddled, contradictory and inconsistent, yet researchers often need to fully understand this area if the reasons for brand preference and buying

behaviour are themselves to be better understood. Often, this area is best explored by the use of in-depth and focus group interviews.

To enable the efficient and effective analysis of data. The questionnaire needs to be prepared with data analysis in mind. The presentation of raw data is fine, but rarely assists with a more detailed consideration of causation, and the relationship between the factors being considered. Think about the possible differences between a wide- ranging in-depth interview report and a structured questionnaire when it comes to analysis.

To minimise errors and bias. A questionnaire allows the same format to be used across a large number of respondents, regardless of where and when the survey is administered. The more tightly controlled the questionnaire, the less the scope for interviewer variation, and thus the more comparable become the data. This means that the procedures followed, the language used, and the interviewer role should not vary significantly across the survey.

To encourage accurate and full responses. Linked with the above point on standardisation is the need to ensure that the questions asked are answerable and that respondents will not mind giving a truthful and accurate response. Keeping the wording neutral, by avoiding 'leading' questions that seem to hint at there being a 'right' answer, may help. As already mentioned, this is particularly important with sensitive or personal issues.

Some thought also needs to be given to ensuring that the questionnaire will retain the interest of the respondent, so that full completion takes place. It is easy with self-administered questionnaires for the respondent to give up if the questionnaire becomes tedious, seems to be poorly explained, or is too long or complex. When an interviewer is involved, the motivation can still be lost, despite the best efforts of the interviewer, although it takes more courage for a respondent to terminate a face-to-face interview in mid flow than simply to put a pen down.

Types of questions

There are two main types of question that can be asked in a questionnaire: **open-ended questions** and **closed questions**. The category of open-ended questions has many significant style variations within it, but they all allow considerable scope for the respondent to express views on the selected theme (and in some cases, on other themes!). Closed questions force the respondent to choose one or more responses from a number of possible replies provided in the questionnaire.

Open ended questions. Questions such as 'In the buying of garden furniture, what factors do you find important?' or 'What do you think of the trend towards out-of-town shopping centres?' are open ended because they do not give a range of potential answers for the respondent to choose from. In both cases, interviewers could be faced with as many different answers as there are respondents. Using such questions can, therefore, be rewarding, because of the rich insights given in a relatively unrestrained manner. The difficulties, however, emerge in recording and analysing the responses, given their potential length and wide variations. Nevertheless, it has been argued that using open-ended questions can help to build the goodwill of the respondent through allowing an unrestricted response (Chisnall, 1986).

Closed questions. Closed questions fall into two broad groups, dichotomous and multiple-choice questions. *Dichotomous questions* allow only two choices, such as 'yes or no' or 'good or bad', for example. These questions are easy to ask and easy to answer.

With careful pre-coding, it is also relatively easy to analyse responses and to use them for cross tabulation with another variable, for example to find out whether those who say that they do use a product pay more attention to product-specific advertising than those who say that they do not use it. The problem with dichotomous questions is that it can take very many questions to obtain a relatively small amount of information. This can be critical where the length of the questionnaire needs to be constrained.

Multiple choice questions are a more sophisticated form of closed question, because they can present a list of possible answers for the respondent to choose from. This could be, for example, a list of alternative factors that might influence a purchasing decision (price, quality, availability etc.), or it could reflect alternative levels of strength of feeling, degree of importance or other shades of variation in response to the variable under consideration. Figure 6.2 gives examples of different types of multiple-choice question.

These questions need to be designed carefully, to incorporate and group as wide a range of answers as possible, since restraining the amount of choice available creates a potential source of bias. The alternative responses need to reflect the likely range, without overlap or duplication, since this too may create bias. By offering an 'other, please specify' category, these questions provide some opportunity to collect responses not originally conceived (but which should have been identified in the pilot stage), or responses that do not fit neatly into the imposed structure. However, the advantage of multiple-choice questions is that again they are relatively straightforward to analyse, if pre-coding has been used.

Multiple choices can also be used to overcome some respondent sensitivities. If asked 'How old are you?' or 'What do you earn?' as open questions, many people may refuse to answer because the questions are too specific and personal. Phrasing the question thus, 'To which of these age groups do you belong, 17 or under, 18–24, 25–34, 35–44, 45 or over?', allows the respondent to feel that they have not given quite so much away. It is unlikely in any case that knowing a respondent's exact age would be of any greater use to researchers. The bands need to be defined to reflect the likely scope of responses from the target respondents, and to be easy for them to relate to. Professionals, for example, will be more likely to relate to bands based on annual salary, than manual workers, who are more likely to know what their weekly wage is. The scope of responses will also vary between these two groups. The bottom band in a survey aimed at ABC1 socioeconomic groups may be 'less than £15 000', whereas the equivalent of this figure in weekly wage terms may provide the top band for a C2DE orientated survey.

FIGURE 6.2

Examples of multiple-choice questions

To which of the following age groups do you belong?
- (a) 17 or under
- (b) 18 – 24
- (c) 25 – 34
- (d) 35 – 44
- (e) 45 or over

Which of these daily newspapers do you regularly read?
- (a) *The Times*
- (b) The *Daily Telegraph*
- (c) The *Daily Mail*
- (d) The *Sun*
- (e) Other (please specify)

How do you travel to work?
- (a) Private car
- (b) Taxi
- (c) Bus
- (d) Train
- (e) Other (please specify)

On average, how often do you go to the supermarket?
- (a) More than 4 times a week
- (b) 2 or 3 times a week
- (c) Once a week
- (d) Once a month
- (e) Less than once a month

Rating Scales are a form of multiple-choice question, widely used in attitude measurement, motivational research and in situations where a number of complex, interacting factors are likely to influence a situation. There are a number of scaling methods, including:

1 *Likert summated ratings.* A large number of statements, relevant to the research study, are built up from preliminary research and piloting. These statements are then given to respondents who are asked to respond on a five- or seven-point scale, for example 'strongly agree', 'agree', 'neither agree nor disagree', 'disagree' and 'strongly disagree'. The responses are scored from 5 (strongly agree) down to 1 (strongly disagree). The average score across all respondents can then be used to establish the general strength of attitude towards the variable under consideration. An examination of the pattern of individual responses may also reveal issues of interest to the marketer.

  Likert scales are very popular with researchers because of their relative ease of implementation. The statements must, however, be carefully derived and relevant to the phenomena being studied. The scale itself must accurately reflect the range of respondents' views.

2 *Semantic differential scales.* These scales were developed to measure differences in the meaning of words or concepts. This method involves a bipolar five- or seven-point rating scale, with each extreme defined by carefully selected adjectives representing opposite extremes of feeling. A study of retail store atmosphere might offer a series of scales including 'warm – cold', 'friendly – unfriendly', or 'fashionable – unfashionable', for example. Once the scales have been defined, the product (or whatever) is rated on each of them to reveal a profile of the respondent's opinion. Such scales can also be used for measuring corporate image or advertising image and for comparing different brands. In the latter case, if two products are plotted at the same time on the same scales, significant differences may emerge, and help the marketer to understand better the relative positioning of products in consumers' minds.

Examples of both types of rating scale can be found in Fig 6.3.

The wording of questions. The success or failure of a questionnaire lies as much in the detail as in the grand scheme and design. This includes the detailed wording of questions so that the respondent fully understands what is required, and accurate responses are encouraged. The next few paragraphs raise a number of pertinent issues.

  It is always important to ensure that the *meaning of words and phrases* is fully understood by the respondent. Particular effort should be made to avoid the use of jargon and technical language that may be unfamiliar to the respondent. Additional complications arise from surveys that are intended for pan-European implementation, as commonly used phrases may not translate well into different cultures.

  Ambiguity can lead to misunderstandings, and thus poor or inaccurate responses. A question such as 'Do you buy this product frequently, sometimes, seldom or never?' seems to be very clear and unambiguous, but think about it for a minute. What does 'frequently' mean? To one respondent, it might mean weekly, to another it might mean monthly. Researchers should therefore be as specific as possible.

  A further source of ambiguity or confusion occurs when the respondent is asked to cope with too many concepts at once. Two questions should, therefore, never be *piggy backed*, i.e. asked in one question, such as, 'How important is price to you, and how do you think we could improve on value for money?'

  As already mentioned, *leading questions* may tempt the respondent to favour a particular answer. This is not, of course, the essence of good research. Thus asking, 'Are you, or are you not, in favour of capital punishment?' is more balanced than, 'Are you in favour of capital punishment?', which is edging the respondent towards 'Yes' as an answer. Even the choice of one word in a question may be seen as leading. 'Should

Likert scale

	Strongly agree	Agree	Neither agree nor disagree	Disagree	Strongly disagree
Safeway's prices are generally lower than those of other supermarkets					
Safeway's offers the widest range of groceries					
Safeway's staff are always friendly and helpful					
I never have to queue too long at the checkout					
Supermarket own brands are just as good as manufacturers' brands					
Low prices are important to me in choosing a supermarket					
Supermarkets should provide more personal services					

Semantic differential scale

	1	2	3	4	5	6	7	
Modern								Old-fashioned
Friendly								Unfriendly
Attractive								Unattractive
Spacious								Crowded
High quality goods								Low quality goods
Wide choice of goods								Limited choice of goods
Convenient opening hours								Inconvenient opening hours
Tidy								Untidy
Short queues								Long queues
Low prices								High prices

FIGURE 6.3

Examples of rating scales

the UK stay in the EU, or not?' is a very different question from, 'Should the UK leave the EU, or not', because each question triggers different associations and emotions.

Questions that are *too closed* are a kind of leading question that may also frustrate researchers. 'Is price an important factor in your purchase?' begs the answer 'Yes', but even if it was a balanced question, the responses tell very little. It does not indicate how important price is to the respondent, or what other factors influence the purchase. An open-ended or multiple-choice question might tell much more.

Researchers need to be sympathetic to people's *sensitivity*. Some areas are highly personal so building up slowly may be important, and 'soft' rather than 'hard' words should be used, for example 'financial difficulties' rather than 'debt'. Of course, the more sensitive the information, the more likely the respondent is to refuse to answer, lie, or even terminate the interview.

Coding and rules. It is more important to obtain accurate and pertinent information, than to design a questionnaire that embraces everything but rarely gets completed. Hague (1992) proposes an *ideal length* for three different types of questionnaire:

- telephone interviews: 5 to 30 minutes
- visit interviews: 30 minutes to two hours
- self-completion: four sides of A4, 20–30 questions.

A street interview would need to be very much shorter than 30 minutes to retain interest and prevent irritation.

The *layout* of the questionnaire is especially important for self-administered questionnaires. A cramped page looks unappealing, as well as making it difficult to respond. Where an interviewer is in control of the questionnaire, the layout should assist the recording and coding of responses, and ease of flow through the interview to maintain momentum. Most questionnaires are now designed with *data coding* and ease of analysis in mind. This means that all responses to closed questions and multiple choices need to be categorised before the questionnaire is released, and that the layout must also be user friendly for whoever has to transfer the data from the completed questionnaire into a database.

The *order of the questions* is important for the respondent, as the more confusing the flow and the more jumping around they have to do, the less likely they are to see it through to completion. Similarly, to assist the interviewer, the more routing and skipping that is built into the questionnaire, the easier it is to administer.

Support materials and explanation can be very important. For a mail survey a covering letter can be reassuring and persuasive, while, at an interview, the interviewer needs to gain the respondent's attention and interest in participation. Visual aids, such as packaging or stills from advertising, can also get the respondent more involved, as well as prompting their memories.

Piloting Whatever care has been taken in the design of the questionnaire, problems usually emerge as soon as the questionnaire is tried on innocent respondents. Piloting a questionnaire on a small-scale sample can help to iron out any 'bugs', so that it can be refined before the full survey goes ahead. Initially, a fresh eye from colleagues can eliminate the worst howlers, but for most projects, it is best to set aside time for a full field pilot. This would mean testing the questionnaire on a small sub-sample (who will usually not then participate in the main survey) to check its meaning, layout and structure, and furthermore, to check whether it yields the required data, and whether it can be analysed in the intended manner.

THE MARKETING RESEARCH PROCESS

When an organisation has decided to undertake a research project, it is important to make sure that it is planned and executed systematically and logically, so that the 'right' objectives are defined and achieved as quickly, efficiently and cost effectively as possible. A general model of the marketing research process is presented here, which can be applied to a wide range of real situations with minor adaptations. The broad stages, and the decisions and problems associated with them, from the initiation of the research through to the final review of the outcomes, should be common to most research exercises. The model is shown in Fig 6.4, and although it may suggest a logic and neatness that is rarely found in practice, it does at the very least offer a framework that can be tailored to meet different clients, situations and resources. Each stage in the process will now be discussed in turn.

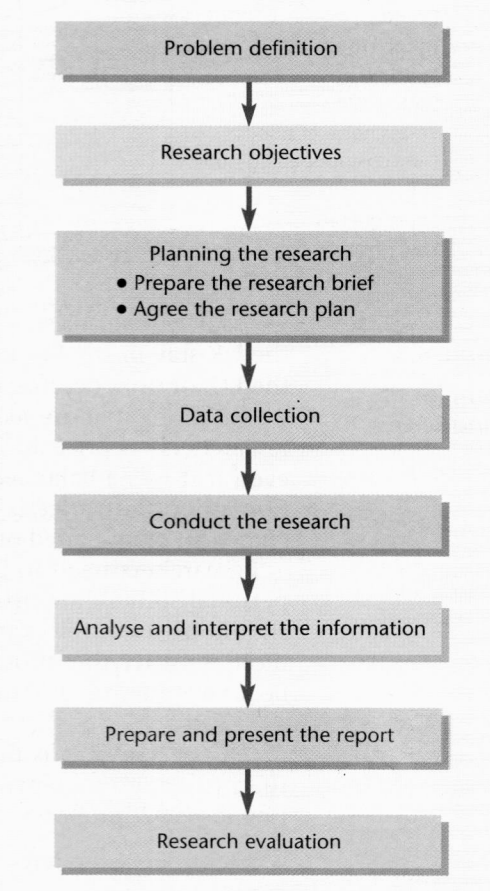

FIGURE 6.4

The marketing research process

Problem definition

Problem definition is the first and one of the most important stages in the research process, because it defines exactly what the project is about, and as such influences how the subsequent stages are conducted, and ultimately influences the success of the project itself. The organisation sponsoring the research, whether it intends to use in-house researchers or an agency, needs to define precisely what the problem is and how that translates into research objectives. This may also lead to the identification of other concerns or problems that need to be included in the project. For example if the fundamental problem has been defined as 'People are not buying our product', the organisation may feel that it should not only explore people's attitudes to the product itself, but also look at how they rate the product on other aspects of the marketing mix in comparison with the competition.

Once the broad nature of the problem has been established, the next stage involves more precise definition of objectives.

Example

Tetley Tea when thinking about launching the revolutionary circular tea bag in the mid-1980s, wanted three questions answered before committing to the enormous expense of the product launch and manufacture. First, they wanted to know whether the round tea bags would attract enough non-Tetley customers to compensate for any cannibalisation of Tetley's existing brands. Second, they wanted to know whether round tea bags would be a short-term novelty, and third, whether the likely gain in share would be enough to justify and cover the launch costs (Phillips *et al.*, 1991).

Research objectives

The tight specification of research objectives is important to ensure that the project is developed along the right lines. Usually, primary objectives need to be distinguished from secondary objectives. The primary objective for an electric components manufacturer seeking to enter the French market, for example, might be to establish the market potential for the products specified and to indicate appropriate market entry strategies. The secondary objectives tend to be more specific and comprehensive. For the components manufacturer they might include:

- defining market trends and competitive structure over the past five years
- profiling the existing main suppliers in terms of strengths and weaknesses (products, prices, distribution, branding, service etc.)
- identifying the main buying criteria when purchasing
- identifying the main buyers of electrical components
- surveying potential trade and end users for willingness to switch supply source.

The list above is not exhaustive, but the main point is that objectives clearly drive the whole research process, and should provide the necessary foundations for whatever management decisions will have to be taken at the end. In all cases, the research objectives need to be clearly and concisely stated in writing to ensure that the research brief can be adequately prepared.

The skill at this stage lies in being sufficiently broad minded and flexible to avoid being misled by assumptions and prejudices that may not be valid, yet being focused enough to allow the project a strong sense of direction and a chance of being achieved within time and cost constraints. To be successful at this stage, the project team needs good communication and a solid understanding of the issues involved.

This is where exploratory research may be useful, in eliminating some of the possibilities or filling some basic gaps in knowledge and understanding. This could involve some preliminary discussions with distributors, experts or customers. The information collected, including any secondary data, can then be used to prepare the research brief for the formal commissioning of work.

Planning the research

The planning stage falls into two main parts: first, the preparation of the research brief, and second, agreeing the research plan. This applies equally whether the research is conducted in-house or not.

Prepare the research brief

The research brief originates from the client. Its quality and precision can vary widely. In some cases, the client has a vague idea of what the problem is, but is not sure what the underlying causes or dynamics are. They thus rely heavily on researchers to specify the problem and then decide on the best research design, effectively asking them to undertake the first two stages of the research process. In many ways, the development of this kind of brief is rather like consultancy and may be part of that kind of overall process.

In other cases, however, the brief may be highly specified for researchers. The organisation has already undertaken the first two stages of the research process, and thus has made a detailed analysis of the current situation, identified the problem that needs to be addressed and then formulated its exact requirements. The brief can then be handed over complete to either a marketing research agency or the in-house department.

The main points of the research brief (adapted from Hague, 1992) will be:

- a definition of the problem, including its history
- a description of the product to be researched
- a description of the market to be researched
- specific research objectives
- time and financial budget
- reporting requirements.

This brief may be the subject of modification and negotiation during the meetings.

Agree the research plan

On the basis of the brief, a research plan needs to be agreed before the project begins. Not only is this important for cost and timing considerations, but it also ensures that the data generated will enable management decisions to be resolved without the need for further analysis. There is nothing worse than completing a major research project only to find that the results are at best of only partial use to managers!

The details of the research plan will vary according to the project. Many of the points that will be covered in the subsequent stages of the research process need to be outlined in the plan. This will help the clients to appreciate the specification they are contracting for, and indeed open any debate about the time and cost constraints early enough to negotiate changes. The research plan ideally should contain:

- background information for the research
- research objectives (based on decisions that need to be made and the criteria to be used)
- research methods (secondary and/or primary)
- type of analysis to be employed
- degree of client involvement
- data ownership
- details of subcontractors (if any)
- level and timing of ongoing reporting

- format of final report
- timing and cost of research.

An organisation with a major research project may well ask a number of research agencies to tender for the business. Each agency will obviously propose different research plans. These need to be evaluated alongside the organisation's more usual buying criteria. The final decision by the clients should be based on confidence that the chosen agency can best meet its information needs through the research plan proposed, but within any constraints imposed.

Data collection

The first requirement in preparing the research plan is to identify clearly what additional data are needed and then to establish how they are to be collected. This may involve collecting both primary and secondary data, or just primary data.

Once the researchers have recognised that information is needed that is not currently available, they must decide from what source they can most effectively get that information. It is well worth checking secondary data sources first to see what has already been done. The pursuit of secondary data should be exhaustive, as secondary data are usually far more cost effective and quicker to collect than primary data. However, because secondary data were collected for another purpose they are not always in a form that is useful or appropriate, and thus they often have to be re-analysed to convert them into a form that can be used for a particular project. Even if secondary data are available, or can be converted, they may still not be sufficient to meet all the researchers' needs, and thus a primary research study may still have to be developed to fill the gaps or further explore the issues. If there are no appropriate secondary data commercially available, then a primary research study will have to be developed from scratch.

Conduct the research

Once the research plan has been developed and the methods of collection and proposed analysis identified, it is necessary to go about conducting the research itself.

Primary data collection is a familiar sight in the majority of high streets and shopping centres. The interviewer relies on interviewees being amenable and giving up some time.

This stage will vary according to the type of research. The demands of a consumer survey involving perhaps thousands of respondents over a wide geographical area are very different from those of a select number of interviews in depth.

Particularly in primary research, it is this part of the process that often presents the biggest problem because the collection of the data should not be left to poorly trained or badly briefed field researchers. Using people who do not recognise the importance of their role may cause them to take less care, allow bias to be introduced into the process, or at the extreme, to cheat in some way so that they can ostensibly fulfil their obligations, but with the minimum effort, and with no regard for truth or accuracy.

During the development of the research plan, those involved, who are usually well qualified and trained, are at pains to ensure the accuracy of data collection, realising that important decisions may be made on the results. They are therefore very careful in what they do and how they go about structuring the research. On the other hand, those who will be responsible for actually collecting the data, field workers, interviewers, and even their supervisors, are more removed from the design and development process, and less aware of the implications of data quality (or lack of it). Furthermore, they may not be adequately prepared in terms of training (poor interviewing skills or data recording techniques), they may not be motivated (often being poorly paid and employed on a part-time basis) or they may not be appropriately or adequately supervised (such as when conducting research over a wide geographic area). Each of these shortfalls has the potential to distort the results of the research itself. It must be said, however, that the research industry is well aware of these problems and has developed quality control standards, especially with regard to interviews and contact with the general public, and that reputable suppliers of marketing research comply with them.

There are a number of areas, in any kind of face-to-face research, where careful attention to detail can pay dividends. The prime purpose of the interviewer is to deliver the questions in an orderly, structured and accurate manner, where appropriate asking secondary questions, and finally accurately recording the responses of the respondent in line with the measurement instruments selected. The greater the need for the interviewer to depart from a carefully prepared script and *modus operandi*, the greater the skill involved and the higher the cost of the interview. This is particularly emphasized in the implementation role of the interviewer who conducts a group discussion or an in-depth interview. The dangers of interview bias are always present where the interviewer records what they think has been said or meant, not what has actually been said in response to a question. This sort of bias can be particularly pronounced where open-ended questions are being used.

Example

An entrepreneur wanted to assess whether a high quality dog kennel service would prove popular in his area. Although he was well aware of existing kennel services, none offered the five-star pampered pooch treatment envisaged. He was advised by a 'business counsellor' to select one of the better neighbourhoods and undertake a door-to-door survey personally to deliver a short questionnaire. Needless to say, the research never got off the ground using that method. Can you think why?

The whole area of data collection can be particularly difficult for a new business that does not have the resources to employ field researchers. It is bad enough that the entrepreneur has to design the research, perhaps as part of a feasibility study, without having to find the time and develop the expertise to carry it out accurately.

New technology is making a big impact in the implementation of field research by assisting in the questioning and recording process. Computer-aided telephone interviewing **(CATI)** and computer-aided personal interviewing **(CAPI)** mean that interviewers using laptop computers and modems can download questions from the central system, and then quickly return completed data by the same route. By entering data as the interview is being conducted, and using the screen to move between questions, the interviewer can achieve marked improvements in efficiency, recording accuracy and control of the process. Most of the fast turnaround in syndicated research services is due to the impact of CAPI and CATI (Fletcher, 1995).

Analyse and interpret the information

While the quality of the research data is essential, it is the analysis of the data, i.e., turning raw data into useful information, that provides the most value to the organisation. It is on the basis of the reports prepared from the data analysis that significant managerial decisions are likely to be made. Few surveys are undertaken nowadays without a detailed consideration of how to code, enter and classify the data generated. The use of sophisticated computer hardware and software packages, provides a powerful means of processing large quantities of data relatively easily. CAPI, CATI, scanners that can read completed questionnaires, complex statistical analysis and data manipulation have improved the speed, accuracy and depth of the analysis itself. However, it is still the human element, the researcher's expertise in identifying a trend or relationship, or some other nugget hidden within the results, that provides the key component for decision makers and transforms the data and techniques used into valuable information.

Researchers need to be conversant with such statistical techniques as correlation analysis, regression analysis, multivariate analysis, factor analysis, cluster analysis and the repertoire of significance tests. These techniques fall into either the descriptive category or relational, ranging from simple cross tabulations through to highly sophisticated multivariate analysis.

Some care needs to be exercised in the interpretation of quantitative data. Outputs of calculations should never overrule sound common sense in assessing the significance and relevance of the data generated. There is sometimes the danger of analysis paralysis, where the use of highly sophisticated techniques almost becomes an end in itself, rather than simply a means of identifying new relationships and providing significant new insights for management. While the old saying, that trends, differences or relationships are only meaningful if they are obvious to even the untrained

Business travel

Competition between airlines for business travellers is intense, because they are profitable and tend to repeat purchase. The emphasis is on luxury and high-quality service, but there is no point investing in providing things that the passenger either does not want or does not appreciate. Before launching its Club World concept, therefore, British Airways (BA) undertook extensive research. It gave customers a long list of service options and then asked them to allocate 100 points between the options to reflect their own priorities. Customers might appreciate having an extremely comfortable seat, a limousine to take them to

the airport, a private departure lounge, speedier priority check-in procedures or frequent flyer incentives. This research will have helped BA to decide what its customers 'must have', what they 'would like' and what is irrelevant to them. Many customers, especially on long-haul flights, value comfort and privacy so that they can sleep. BA has thus even undertaken research into sleep patterns to design a seat that converts into a bed. With the use of screens, the passenger can virtually have a private cabin and a long undisturbed sleep.

Source: Luckhurst (1996).

statistical eye, may be going too far, it does highlight the danger of the misinterpretation of cause and effect and the differences between groups of consumers, arising from over-reliance on finely balanced statistics pursued by researchers.

Not all data are quantitative, of course. Qualitative data arising from in-depth interviews or group discussions pose a different kind of challenge to researchers. Whereas quantitative data have to prove their reliability when compared with the wider population, qualitative data can never be claimed to be representative of what a wider sample of respondents might indicate. The main task of qualitative data, therefore, is to present attitudes, feelings and motivations in some depth, whether or not they are representative of the wider population.

To handle qualitative data analysis, great care must be taken in the recording of information. Video or taped interviews are thus helpful in enabling classification and categorisation of the main points to be checked and explored in depth. Similarly, issue or content analysis enables particular themes to be explored across a range of interviews. For example if researchers wanted to identify the barriers to exporting in small firms, they might define such themes as market entry, market knowledge, finance or using agents as indicative of the main barriers to be assessed. The data analysis might be supported by a range of quotations from the interviews. Because of the richness and complexity of this kind of data, skilled psychologists are often used to explore and explain much of what is said and, indeed, not said.

So although the risks of bias are great in qualitative analysis, both in data selection and analysis, and although the results can, in untrained hands, be rather subjective and conjectural, the advantage arises from the fresh insights and perspectives that more rigorous statistical techniques would simply not generate.

Prepare and present report

The information provided by researchers must be in a form that is useful to the decision makers. Too often, research reports are written in highly technical language or research jargon that, to a layman, is confusing or meaningless. Marketers who want to use these reports to make decisions need them to be easily understandable. A report that is too complex is all but useless. The language and the use of visual aids, such as graphs and charts, become critical elements in the presentation and interpretation of research reports. Various software packages, such as Microsoft's Powerpoint, greatly assist presentation through incorporating graphs, pie charts, histograms and other illustrations, often in full colour. All of this helps the marketing decision maker to understand the main points of the research findings. That is why the formal presentation of the report, whether written or verbal (which allows the client to ask questions and seek clarification of points made), should be given as much thought, care and attention as any previous stage in the research process.

Although a verbal presentation can play an important part in sharing understanding, it is the report itself that has the power to influence thinking significantly. Arguments can be carefully presented with data used appropriately in their support, and the detail surrounding the main findings can be displayed to increase the client's confidence that the research was well executed to plan. There are no standard report formats, as much will depend upon the nature of the research task undertaken. The following headings are simply indicative of the main areas that need to be covered, and they closely follow the issues discussed in this section.

Title page
The title page includes details of the report title, the client, the researchers and the date of completion. Often, the title page is also the front cover so it is important that all information is presented in a clear, professional manner.

Table of contents

The table of contents varies according to the main and sub-heading system used. It is important to convey clearly to the reader the structure of the report and where to find the relevant sections.

Preface

The preface is the beginning of the main body of the report. The preface should state why the research was undertaken and outline the marketing problems requiring solutions, the basis of the research design and the plan selected. Typically, any previous research should be quoted, whether secondary or primary, and the specific research objectives agreed at the briefing stage should be specified, to avoid any ambiguity. Often, the signed research brief is appended to this section as a gentle reminder to the client. The danger for researchers is that on more substantial projects taking place over several months, the marketing environment and events move on, making some of the assumptions originally incorporated into the brief questionable. The final part of the preface is a detailed description of the research plan and, most importantly, the rationale for the plan selected.

Executive summary

Busy executives do not always find the time to read the full report. This is especially true when senior management within the client organisation may need to reflect on some of the findings. The executive summary needs to be carefully prepared to highlight the main points of the research and to draw the reader's attention to the main conclusions and recommendations.

There is no ideal length for an executive summary. In a short report of between 15 and 25 pages it may be possible to detail the main points in a page or two. A major study of 100 or more pages may require five to 10 summary pages, depending on the complexity of the research brief.

Research methods

The findings are only as good as the appropriateness to the problem in hand of the research design and the data collection methods. This section should, therefore, indicate the secondary and primary research methods used, and why. Details and comments on the research execution should be contained within this section, and any deviations from the original plan highlighted and explained. A challenge in this part of the report is to decide how much material should be contained within the main body of the text and how much should be relegated to the appendices. For example, detailed sampling methods, response profiles and even questionnaire design may all be placed in the appendices, to retain the focus and flow in the main body of the report.

Findings

The findings constitute the main body of the report and what the client is really paying for. At this stage the data, information, facts and opinions are all presented in a neutral manner, without comment. The findings should be in sufficient detail to enable the reader to assess the information, to check its accuracy and validity and, not least, to fully understand what has been generated. A full range of display techniques may be used to present the findings and again, heavy use of the appendices may focus the reader on the main issues rather than on areas that are too detailed or minor to be worthy of critical consideration.

Conclusions

The conclusions are the creative part for researchers, as the report moves from the presentation of data and information to interpretation. A combination of problem appreciation, research evaluation and an ability to advise is required at this stage.

Although clients will draw their own conclusions, the research findings should be solid enough and compelling enough to mean that the two sets of conclusions do not differ significantly!

Recommendations

Depending on the nature of the research objectives, it may be necessary for researchers to move beyond the findings and conclusions, and give firm recommendations to the client. It is, of course, critical that the recommendations flow from the research findings and conclusions, and are not reflections of the researchers' partiality or misconceptions. At this stage, the research becomes a part of the managerial decision-making process, as the emphasis is on what, if any, action should be taken.

Appendices

The appendices contain data that may be relevant to a detailed understanding of the research, but need not be read to establish the link between the research plan and the recommendations. Appendices should always relate back to key parts of the text to guide the interested reader. A wealth of information could be contained in the appendices such as questionnaires, tables, literature, summaries or sub-reports, sampling methods and so on.

It should be clear from the above that a well-presented and formulated report is vital if it is to build the confidence of the reader and to have any chance of actually influencing the management decision maker.

Research evaluation

Research projects rarely go completely to plan. Although greater care in conducting pilot studies and exploratory research will make it more likely that the actual outcomes will match those planned, problems may still emerge that will require careful consideration in weighing up the value of the project. Thoughtful analysis of the planning, conduct and outcomes of the project will also teach valuable lessons for the future to both clients and researchers.

This stage can involve a review of all aspects of the research plan described above. Any deviations need to be understood, both in terms of the current results and for designing future research. With regard to the research project undertaken, the most important point is whether the research actually provided a sufficient quality and quantity of information to assist management decision making. Sometimes, the research objectives may have been ambiguous or poorly framed in the context of the marketing problem being addressed. Ultimately, it is the marketing manager who must take responsibility for ensuring that the objectives and research plan were compatible and reflected the requirements, although researchers can help in this task.

Example

Perhaps the ultimate test for the value of the research is what action or decisions were made as a result of it. A small manufacturer of made-to-order fabricated metal cabinets had seen sales and profitability decline over several years. Market research identified changes in customer buying preferences away from the specifications offered by the firm, and profiled a more competitive climate, caused by new entrants. This study led to a fundamental rethink of the quality of the products being offered, and the need to open up new markets.

Far too often, research is undertaken but the findings are only partially accepted, or at worst ignored, as not conforming to preconceived notions and prejudices. Although poorly designed and executed research is best ignored, and researchers have the responsibility for presenting the findings of the research accurately and persuasively, the true value of the project lies in the extent to which it offers added power to the manager for making better decisions. This kind of evaluation helps the client to understand better when research was a 'good buy' or a 'bad buy', and how to improve things next time around.

ETHICS IN MARKETING RESEARCH

The ethical concerns surrounding market research have been the subject of an ongoing debate in the industry for a long time. Because much consumer research involves specific groups of consumers, including children and other groups that might be considered vulnerable, it is essential that the researchers' credibility is maintained and that the highest standards of professional practice are demonstrated. This is vital if researchers are to maintain the confidence of their clients, as well as that of the general public and the government, and so the industry has established a set of professional ethical guidelines. Members are expected to comply with these guidelines, although there is still some debate about their interpretation. The market research guidelines include such matters as protecting the confidentiality of respondents or clients, not distorting or misrepresenting research findings (for example two major newspapers could both claim to be the market leader by using readership figures gathered over different time spans and failing to mention the time period), using tricks to gain information from respondents, conducting an experiment and not telling those being studied, and using research as a guise for selling and sales lead building. Recently, your authors were stopped in the street by a market researcher with an appaling questionnaire that broke every guideline within this chapter, but it soon emerged that the real purpose was to generate sales leads for a time share operator. The European Society for Opinion and Marketing Research (ESOMAR), a leading marketing research association, is actively trying to encourage members to stamp out the practice of 'sugging' (selling under the guise of market research) through an agreed code of practice.

There is a conflict of interest between selling and research. Selling needs clear, persuasive communication outwards from the organisation, while research needs to preserve a neutrality if the respondent is to open up fully. Research can certainly inform the selling process, helping the marketer to make better, more effective decisions, but if the two become confused or merged with each other, then neither functions particularly well. For example, a new small business entrepreneur organised interviews with potential customers for 'market research purposes'. However, although the session began with a face-to-face in-depth interview based around a questionnaire, the respondent started to 'freeze' half-way through, as the 'researcher' started to enthuse about the benefits of the new manufacturing service planned. That respondent would not take kindly to being manipulated into listening to a sales pitch when he thought that he was doing a new business a favour by participating in research. Any goodwill (or potential sales) will almost certainly have been destroyed.

Codes of conduct are therefore especially useful in influencing the behaviour of the more responsible organisations within the industry. Within the UK, the Market Research Society has an extensive code of conduct covering such areas as professional ethics, sampling conditions and practice and the presentation of findings. ESOMAR has developed a similar internationally based code of practice to augment local specifications. Of course, not all providers of market research are committed to compliance, and not all bad practice can be eliminated, but considerable progress is being made across Europe.

MARKETING INFORMATION SYSTEMS

It has been argued throughout this chapter that sound marketing information is an effective prerequisite for sound marketing decisions. The alternative is intuition and informed opinion (which itself may be based on no more than intuition). The increased complexity, international orientation and competitiveness of markets now place a high premium on timely information. Marketers need information about existing and emerging market segments and their likely responses to various marketing strategies. They also need ongoing information about changing market conditions, new behaviour by consumers, new market opportunities, competitors, technological advances, changing government policy at a national or European level, distribution channel developments and requirements, as well as sociological and cultural changes. All of these have the potential to affect the success of an organisation. The sooner the opportunities or threats are spotted, the earlier the management team can decide what to do. The availability and effective use of information is therefore critical for successful marketing decision making.

The previous sections of this chapter have looked at the various sources of external data and information, and how data can be obtained from a variety of secondary and primary methods. There is still the problem, however, once the data have been collected and analysed, of structuring information into a meaningful form to provide timely flows to managers, whether on an *ad hoc* or a continuous basis. The complexity of managing a continuous flow of information into the organisation demands a well thought out information gathering, storage and retrieval system. There is little point in having a highly complex information system that cannot readily deliver what managers want, when they want it, and how they want it. Any system must be responsive to the needs of the users.

A marketing information system **(MIS)** has been defined as:

> **an organised set of procedures and methods by which pertinent, timely and accurate information is continually gathered, sorted, analysed, evaluated, stored and distributed for use by marketing decision makers'** (Zikmund and d'Amico, 1993, p. 108).

Nowadays, most of these systems are data based and use high-powered computers. System requirements need to co-ordinate data collection and decision support, as shown in Fig 6.5. The MIS should be tailored to the specific requirements of the organisation. These will be influenced by the size of the organisation and the resources available as well as the specific needs of decision makers. While these needs are likely to be broadly similar between organisations, they will not be exactly the same and therefore the design of the systems and their sophistication will vary. What is important is that the information is managed in a way that facilitates the decision-making process rather than just being a collection of data gathering dust.

It can be seen from Fig 6.5 that an MIS provides a comprehensive framework for managing information. Information comes in a variety of forms and from a range of sources, any of which can be of critical importance to any organisation, whether large or small, profit or non-profit orientated, government or private, local, national or multinational. In the current fast changing, information-rich, technological environment, organisations tend to be overwhelmed with information. Along with generating huge amounts of data about their day-to-day activities (sales, customer details, incoming and outgoing orders, transactions, service requirements etc.), organisations are usually in various stages of gathering other data about competitors, new product tests, improved service requirements and changing regulations, for example. The problem often becomes not how to get the data but what to do with them, and how they should be managed to turn them into useful information. This is where the MIS comes

FIGURE 6.5

The marketing information system

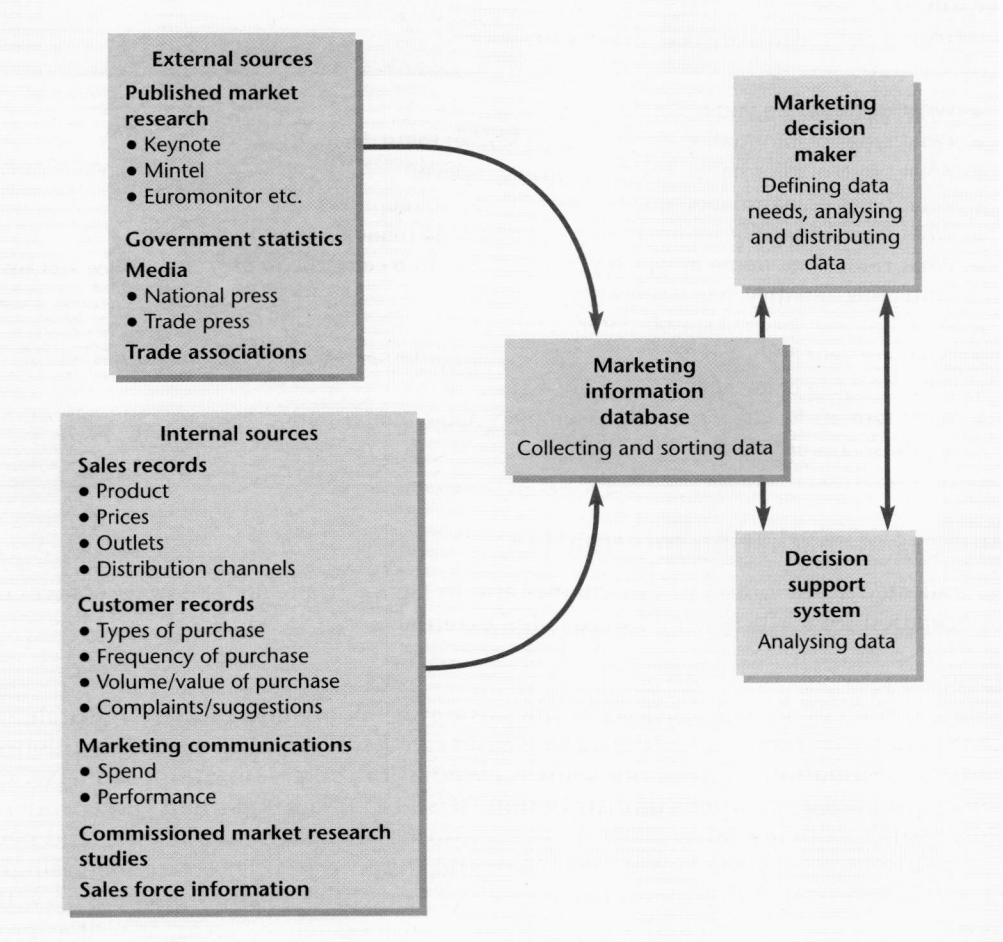

in, to provide a means of managing information, even for small or medium-sized organisations. Unless the organisation has a system that can collect, evaluate, analyse and distribute this information, providing it in a form that is useful, the organisation is not getting the maximum benefit from what it has. Timeliness of information, whether it be for short- or long-term decision making, is also of importance, as the provision of immediate feedback or projected trend details to decision makers can provide a competitive advantage in the market-place.

The other requirement of information is that it should be appropriate to the needs of the those using it. Just as you may have difficulty identifying the information you need to make decisions about a range of options facing you, such as whether to update your computer, buy the new software version of your word-processing package, go on an overseas holiday, or even look for a new job, organisations encounter the same problems, but usually on a much larger scale. They have to manage the information they have, identify what information they need, and present it in the form that the various decision makers require. Not all information the organisation has is necessarily appropriate for all marketing decision makers. It is therefore important to identify the various needs of those decision makers and to ensure they are supplied only the information that meets their needs. This facilitates decision making and helps to avoid information overload. The questions in Table 6.2 help to identify information requirements by getting managers to answer a range of questions relating to their own individual needs. The same process could work for you as an individual.

TABLE 6.2
Defining information requirements

- What decisions do you make on a regular basis?
- What types of information do you need to make these decisions?
- What types of information do you regularly receive?
- What types of information do you need but do not currently get?
- What types of specific information are you likely to request?
- What is the time frame in which you would like to receive the information (daily, weekly, fortnightly, monthly, half-yearly etc.)?
- What are your areas of specific interest?
- What are your likely sources of that information (internal reports, trade magazines, etc.)?
- What are your data analysis requirements?
- What formats for the information (summary, table, graphs, print, computer disk/file, etc.) are most appropriate for you?

Sources of marketing information

As indicated at the outset of this chapter and in Fig 6.5, there are two main sources of information for a MIS system, internal and external:

External sources

External sources are either *ad hoc* studies using secondary and primary research, or continuous data provided by the various syndicated and omnibus studies mentioned earlier. Information comes from sources external to the organisation, such as customers, suppliers, channels of distribution, strategic alliance partners, independent third parties, commercial agencies, industry associations, CSO, Eurostat etc., and new external sources like the World Wide Web and the Internet. These are increasingly being recognised by the business community as a potential means of keeping up with developments in research and a range of other business-related areas, as well as providing a computer link with many millions of computer users, both individual and organisational. The challenge for the marketing manager is to integrate these findings into the organisation to effect change. Much will depend upon the purpose of the research. Some may be specifically designed to support decisions of a tactical nature that need to be addressed as a matter of some urgency, others are part of a longer-term strategic development process indicating trends and opportunities. Externally sourced information may have to be disseminated widely throughout the organisation, so that all functions can think about its implications and contribute to focused senior management strategic decision making.

Internal sources

Information also comes from internal sources within the organisation. These include the internal record keeping system (production, accounting, sales records, purchase details etc.), marketing research, sales representatives' field reports, call details, customer enquiries and complaints, product returns etc. All of this information, again, must be managed appropriately and distributed in a timely fashion if it is going to be used effectively to assist decision making.

The development of Electronic Point of Sale (EPOS) technology has revolutionised the flow of information within retail operations, providing a base for fast and reliable information on emerging trends. Either by using a laser barcode scanner or by keying in a six-figure code, retailers can be right up to date in what is moving, where, and what the immediate impact will be on stock levels. Retail managers can monitor movement on different product lines on a daily basis and adjust stock, orders and even in-store promotions, based on information either from individual stores, or across all the branches. Tesco, with its Clubcard loyalty scheme, can now even track and record the purchasing and shopping habits of millions of individual customers, and tailor its marketing offerings, both locally and nationally, based on solid internally generated information. Direct response marketing, as will be discussed further in Chapter 19, similarly allows a wide range of organisations to build databases of information about individual customers. This too can be used as a resource for developing longer-term strategic plans as well as for fine tuning shorter-term marketing tactics aimed at individuals or sub-segments within the customer base.

The flow of sales force information into a MIS provides access to up-to-date profiles on customers' expectations, account problems and competitive activity. The key is to structure the data entry at sales representative level so that there is as little delay as possible in the flow. Gathered as part of the sales representative's daily reporting routine, information on calls made, orders, new accounts plus other interesting snippets, all enable a closer link between sales and marketing decision making.

Organisations thus get everyday information, often as a matter of course, from a variety of sources that can influence their decision making, but *intelligence* means developing a perspective on the information that provides a competitive edge, perhaps in new product opportunities or the opening up of a new market segment.

Example

Camelot, the company responsible for launching the UK's national lottery in 1994, undertook extensive market research and analysis to underpin its business plan and marketing strategy. They combined the effects of the number of outlets where lottery tickets would be available, advertising and media activity to assess likely consumer awareness and frequency of purchase. That then led to a forecast of sales and thus to an assessment of commercial viability (Kent-Smith and Thomas, 1995).

Sometimes environmental scanning can provide useful insights. By deliberately looking at the various influences on product markets, an organisation may spot early warning signs before the competitors are aware of them. This will help in the forward planning process, and will be especially useful as an input to strategic development decisions.

Example

Shingleton (1994) reports, for example, how Lex Vehicle Leasing used research to underpin a turnaround from a £7 mn loss to a £13 mn profit within 18 months. The research thoroughly investigated the car leasing market, identified and justified a number of business opportunities, and then advised Lex on how it should reposition itself to take advantage of them.

Decision support systems

The availability and use of a range of computer-based decision support systems **(DSS)** are changing the way information is used and presented to decision makers, and the way in which they interpret it. While a MIS organises and presents information, the DSS actually aids decision making by allowing the marketer to manipulate information and explore 'What if ...' type questions. A DSS usually comprises a software package designed for a personal computer, including statistical analysis tools, spreadsheets, databases and other programs that assist in gathering, analysing and interpreting information to facilitate marketing decision making. By having the DSS connected to the MIS, marketers further enhance their ability to use the information available. Effectively, this brings the MIS to the desk top, and even to the personal lap top, with the appropriate connections, servers and modems. This can encourage wide use of information, although there may be some problems about restricting access to more sensitive areas, and ensuring that the complexity can be handled from a systems perspective.

The use of simple spreadsheets and databases, for example, allows an organisation to keep track of customers' ordering details, payments, returns and product complaints on an individual basis. From this information, marketers can project future sales, keep track of complaints, identify who their regular customers are, what quantities they are buying, as well as patterns of purchase etc. One of your authors failed to visit her local supermarket as frequently as the retailer would have liked, despite having a store loyalty card. This resulted in a very polite letter reminding her of the benefits of buying at that store rather than elsewhere, and telling her about a few promotional offers that might be of interest. Thus overall the DSS can be used with statistical analysis to try to identify significant patterns and trends, in both sales and customer behaviour, as well as for predicting the future course of those trends and the impact of marketing decisions upon them.

The MIS or the DSS will never replace decision makers, only help them. Marketing decisions still need the imagination and flair that can interpret 'hard' information and turn it into implementable tactics and strategies that will maintain competitive edge.

CHAPTER SUMMARY

Marketing managers find it impossible to make decisions effectively without a constant flow of information on every aspect of marketing. Everything, from defining target markets, to developing marketing mixes, to making long-term strategic plans has to be supported with appropriate information. The key question, however, is whether the organisation recognises the worth of the information it has, and whether it is prepared to use information intelligently to make decisions, rather than putting more value on its own prejudices about how the market works.

There are three different types of market research, exploratory, descriptive and causal, each one serving different purposes. Depending on the nature of the problem under investigation, any of the three types of market research may use qualitative or quantitative data. Rather than individually pursuing a series of marketing research studies, an organisation can participate in *continuous research*, undertaken by a market research agency on an ongoing basis and usually syndicated.

Secondary research provides a means of sourcing marketing information that already exists in some form, whether internal or external to the organisation. Secondary data can be used to paint an overall background picture to a more specific marketing problem, or to help to focus primary research objectives. Secondary data can be very wide ranging, and can provide much depth, but the organisation needs to be sure of how and why the data were originally collected, and that the data are relevant and up to date before relying on them totally. The data may thus need to be re-analysed or worked over before they can be used with confidence.

Gaps in secondary data can be filled through *primary research*. The main methods of primary research are interviews and surveys, observation, and experiments. Surveys may take place through face-to-face interviews, by telephone or by mail. Group interviews or focus groups allow interviewers to explore issues with several people at once. The group interaction often adds another interesting dimension to the research, with members debating with each other, and generating ideas from each other. Observational research can be used to collect information about how people react to products and how they use them. Experimentation can also be used, although it is orientated more towards causal research allowing, for example, researchers to test whether manipulating one marketing mix variable will have a significant effect on sales. Experiments may take place under artificial laboratory conditions, or they may take place in the field.

Sampling is a crucial area for successful market research. There is no need to survey an entire population in order to find answers to questions. As long as a representative sample is drawn, answers can be generalised to apply to the whole population. There are five important areas connected with sampling: population definition, drawing up the sampling frame, defining the sampling unit, the sampling method and the sample size.

Questionnaires are often used as a means of collecting data from the sample selected, but they need to be carefully designed with a number of issues in mind. They must reflect the purpose of the research, collect the appropriate data, whether those are factual classification data or opinion-based data, accurately and efficiently, and facilitate the analysis of data. Inherent in all that is the need to minimise errors and bias, and to encourage full and accurate responses.

Whether primary or secondary data are envisaged, their collection fits into a general framework for the conduct of a marketing research project that can be applied to almost any kind of market or situation. It consists of eight stages: problem definition, research objectives, planning the research, data collection, research implementation, data analysis, reporting findings and research evaluation.

The organisation needs to co-ordinate its information, collected from a variety of sources, including primary research, into a MIS. A formal MIS brings everything together under one umbrella, and provides timely and comprehensive information to aid managers' decision making. DSS build on the MIS to help decision making. The DSS uses a variety of computer tools and packages to allow a manager to manipulate information, to explore possible outcomes of courses of action, and to experiment in a risk-free environment.

Key words and phrases

CAPI (computer-aided personal interviewing)

CATI (computer-aided telephone interviewing)

Closed questions

Continuous research

DSS (decision support system)

Focus groups

Marketing research

MIS (marketing information system)

Open ended questions

Primary research

Qualitative research

Quantitative research

Rating scales

Sampling Process

Secondary research

Semi-structured interview

Structured interview

Unstructured interview

QUESTIONS FOR REVIEW

6.1 Why is *marketing research* an essential tool for the marketing manager?

6.2 What is the difference between *primary* and *secondary* research?

6.3 What kinds of marketing problems might be addressed through:

(a) *exploratory*;

(b) *descriptive*; and

(c) *causal* research projects?

6.4 Differentiate between *qualitative* and *quantitative* research, highlighting their relative advantages and disadvantages.

6.5 What are the *criteria for evaluating secondary sources*, and why are they important?

6.6 What is *observational research*, and in what circumstances might it be more appropriate than interviews or surveys?

6.7 What are the main stages in the *sampling process*, and what does each involve?

6.8 How does *quota sampling* work, and what are its advantages?

6.9 Define the stages of the *marketing research process* and outline what each one involves.

6.10 Discuss the role and content of a *MIS* and how it might relate to a *DSS*.

QUESTIONS FOR DISCUSSION

6.1 Without looking back at pp. 210–14, how many of the ten different categories of *sources of secondary data* can you list? Check your list against pp. 210–14, and then investigate what your library has to offer under each category.

6.2 Evaluate the appropriateness of each of the different *interview and survey-based primary research methods* for:

(a) investigating the buying criteria used by organisational purchasers;

(b) defining the attitudes of a target market towards a brand of breakfast cereal;

(c) profiling purchasers of small electrical goods; and

(d) measuring levels of post-purchase satisfaction among customers.

Clearly define any assumptions you make about each of the situations.

6.3 Design a questionnaire. It should contain about 20 questions, and you should use as many of the different types of question as possible. Pay particular attention to the concerns discussed at pp. 225–230 of the chapter. The objective is to investigate respondents' attitudes to music CDs and their purchasing habits. Pilot your questionnaire on 12 to 15 people (but preferably not people on the same course as you), analyse the results and then make any adjustments. Within your seminar group, be prepared to discuss the rationale behind your questionnaire, the outcome of the pilot, and any data analysis problems.

6.4 Why is an ethical approach to marketing research important, and what are the main areas of concern?

6.5 Why is a sound *research brief* important, what should it contain, and how does it influence each of the subsequent stages in the process?

CASE STUDY 6.1

Kings Hotel (B)

This follows on from the situation described in Case study 5.1.

The manager decided that some development would be necessary if the hotel was to better meet the needs of the independent customer. He hoped that a questionnaire for independent guests would provide a valuable insight into the type of customers visiting the hotel and what new facilities they would like to see.

The manager asked his two teenaged children, who were students on a tourism management course, to prepare a questionnaire that could be given to guests as they arrived at the hotel. The questionnaire would be given to them as they checked in along with a letter explaining the purpose of the exercise. A box would be provided at reception for completed questionnaires. He briefed the students on the type of information required and suggested that they should have a summary report of the data analysis and information ready in two months' time. This would give him some ideas before the start of the summer season in four months' time.

Adapted from a case prepared by Pat Badmin.

Questions

1 What marketing problem is this research trying to help solve?

2 What information do you think the hotel manager would actually need in order to investigate this problem?

3 To what extent and why do you feel that the research method employed is appropriate for gathering the information needed?

4 Criticise the questionnaire outlined in the case in terms of the choice of questions, their wording and their response mechanism.

QUESTIONNAIRE

1 Are you male or female?

2 How old are you? ☐ years ☐ months

3 How did you travel to the hotel

Car ☐

Airline ☐

Train ☐

Coach/bus ☐

Other ☐

4 How long do you normally stay in a hotel?

1 week ☐

2 weeks ☐

More than 2 weeks ☐

5 Have you been to this hotel before?   yes/no

6 If you had to choose between the following, which do you think are the most important for the hotel to provide?

A larger car park ☐ bath in every room ☐

computerised booking ☐ shop ☐ bar ☐

an automatic telephone system ☐ don't know ☐

Thank you for helping with this questionnaire, which when completed should be put in the box at the reception desk.

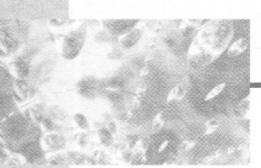

CASE STUDY 6.2

Gathering information on an up and coming market

The condom market can be viewed as a bit of a laugh, as a bit of an embarrassment, as a moral outrage, or as deadly serious, given the risks of sexually transmitted diseases or unwanted pregnancy. To condom manufacturers, however, it is a commercial business just like any other, with consumers, segments, trade customers, competitors and the need to manage marketing activity. This must be based, as with any company, on sound marketing information. Manufacturers have had to track changing attitudes, for example. Largely thanks to government health campaigns over the last 10 years, people in the UK have become less embarrassed about buying condoms and their purchase has become more socially acceptable. This has also led to a change in emphasis in channels of distribution, as this case will later show.

Condom purchases vary between planned and impulse buys. An NOP Health Monitor survey found that travelling abroad either for business or for pleasure often led to planned purchases before the trip. The report found that 81 per cent of people thought a holiday to be the most likely occasion for casual sex, while in the 48–55 age group, 18 per cent thought a business trip more likely. Although men were the larger group of pre-holiday purchasers, nevertheless, 58 per cent of women expecting a sexual experience on holiday travelled with condoms purchased at home. Such planned purchases are actively encouraged by condom manufacturers, as the customer can be assured of a quality product and a familiar brand by buying at home.

Impulse or reminder purchases represent the second group, where availability is essential for continued sales. The policy of Durex is to suggest to retailers that condoms should be easy to find, self-selected, preferably from special displays, and clearly priced to avoid any interaction with sales staff or at the checkout. This reflects the changes taking place in distribution patterns. Condoms are no longer sold exclusively in chemists or barbers' shops, but also in supermarkets as a toiletry alongside razors and shampoos. This exposes the product to both men and women, and encourages customers to treat condoms as a normal part of the regular shopping routine. ASDA believes that women represent the largest purchase group in its stores. A variety of different types of outlet have been targeted to accommodate the change in purchase patterns, such as late-night grocery stores and vending machines in 'strategic places' such as discos, pubs and student

social facilities. Despite these changes, it has been estimated that 30 per cent of consumers still have some reservations about purchasing condoms.

In parallel with changes in distribution patterns, condoms have experienced considerable expansion in the range of products available. In recent years, they have become stronger, more sensitive and more reliable. Variations in strength, colour, texture and flavour have all been offered to the market. Products such as Ultra Strong, Extra Safe, Arouser, Safe Play and Fetherlite are all offered by the clear market leader, London International Group (LIG) as variants within the Durex brand family. Durex has 21 per cent of the world market for condoms, and 40 per cent of the European market. Jiffi represents the other main player in the market with such names as Rainbow (nine colours), Cocktail (four flavours) and Flavours (eight fragrances). Mates, launched in 1987 and now owned by Ansell International, is another key player in the UK market.

Research has also indicated that consumers need to be assured of the product quality. A new European standard, EN600, will be introduced in 1998 as a guide to size and quality. Interestingly, retailers are not giving any priority to developing own brands in this market, because of the emphasis on reliability and quality.

Government health campaign advertising has worked well for the manufacturers in creating generic demand for the product. In 1993, for example, the UK government spent around £10 million on sexual health advertising. In 1984, only 31 per cent of males and 35 per cent of females said that they would use a condom the first time they had sex with someone, but by the early 1990s, the percentages had increased to 69 per cent of men and 78 per cent of women. This change has also made it easier for manufacturers to advertise directly and more explicitly, although they still have to be careful not to offend people too much or else they will not listen to the message. Despite the efforts of government-sponsored advertising in increasing condom use, it was still expected that with the range of brands on the market, more marketing support would be needed from individual manufacturers to retain brand loyalty and to improve market penetration.

LIG, for example, was reported to have spent £34 million in 1995 worldwide on marketing, with most of it going on the Durex range, and including advertisements on MTV. LIG had reviewed its advertising approaches and researched consumer attitudes, and felt that it was not quite getting it right:

People don't want to be told they're going to die if they don't use condoms. We have to tell them there's a new with-it way, put a bit of oomph into the product.

Sources: Kelly (1996); Lane Fox (1995); Snowdon (1995b); Snowdon (1995c).

Questions

1 Briefly outline the types of market research information that might be useful to a condom manufacturer.

2 What are the problems of undertaking primary consumer research for a product like this? How can these problems be overcome?

3 Thirty per cent of buyers still have some reservations about purchasing condoms. Suggest a programme of primary research that might tell the manufacturers why this is.

4 To what extent do you think it would be ethical for condom manufacturers to undertake a survey of 14–16 year olds?

REFERENCES TO CHAPTER 6

Berkowitz, E. N. *et al.* (1992), *Marketing*, (3rd edn.) Irwin.

Bond, C. (1994), 'Leap Off the Omnibus', *Marketing*, 20 October, pp. 28–30.

Boyd, H. W. *et al.* (1977), *Marketing Research*, (4th edn.) Irwin.

Brennan, M. *et al.* (1991), 'The Effects of Monetary Incentives on the Response Rate and Cost Effectiveness of a Mail Survey', *Journal of the Market Research Society*, 33(3), pp. 229–41.

Chisnall, P. M. (1986), *Marketing Research*, (3rd edn.) McGraw-Hill.

Churchill, G. A. (1976), *Marketing Research: Methodological Foundations*, (5th edn.) Dryden Press.

Cramp, B. (1994), 'Industrious Espionage', *Marketing*, 18 August, pp. 17–18.

Darwent, C. (1993), 'All Cisterns Go', *Management Today*, April, pp. 52–4.

Fletcher, K. (1995), 'Jump on the Omnibus', *Marketing*, 15 June , pp. 25–8.

Gofton, K. (1994), 'Moving in on More Markets', *Marketing*, 10 March, pp. 26–9.

The Grocer (1996), 'Brewers Must Think Again to Keep Up', *The Grocer*, 27 April.

Haggett, S. and Mitchell, V. W. (1994), 'Effect of Industrial Prenotification on Response Rate, Speed, Quality, Bias and Cost', *Industrial Marketing Management*, 23(2), pp. 101–10.

Hague, P. (1992), *The Industrial Market Research Handbook*, (3rd edn.) Kogan Page.

Kelly, J. (1996), 'Something for the Weekend', *The Grocer*, 27 January, pp. 43–5.

Kent-Smith, E. and Thomas, S. (1995), 'Luck Had Nothing To Do With It: Launching the UK's Largest Consumer Brand', *Journal of the Market Research Society*, 37(2), pp. 127–41.

Lane Fox, H. (1995), 'Durex Stretches its Brief', *Marketing*, 10 August , p. 14.

Litherland, S. (1994), 'Time to Weigh the Internal Evidence', *Marketing*, 17 November, pp. V–VI.

Luckhurst, J. (1996), 'Upwardly Mobile', *Marketing Week*, 23 February, pp. 47–8.

Marketing (1995), 'Single Parents at McDonald's', *Marketing*, 16 March, p. 3.

Pettitt, S. J. (1989), *Innovation in Tourism*, Unpublished report for Shannon Development Co., Ireland.

Phillips, A. *et al.* (1991), 'Developing a Rounder Tea', *Marketing and Research Today*, 19(1), pp. 3–13.

Rijkens, R. (1992), *European Advertising Strategies: The Profiles and Policies of Multinational Companies Operating in Europe,* Cassell.

Shingleton, J. (1994), 'Black Rhino to Leaping Gazelle: How an Integrated Research Programme Helped Rejuvenate Lex Vehicle Leasing Limited', *Journal of the Market Research Society*, 36(3), pp. 205–16.

Snowdon, R. (1995a), 'Why JWT Is Now Asking the Obvious', *Marketing*, 14 September, p. 16.

Snowdon, R. (1995b), 'Aids Ads Expand in Approach', *Marketing*, 30 November, p. 6.

Snowdon, R. (1995c), 'Durex Feels its Way to Erotica', *Marketing*, 29 June, p. 5.

Tull, D. S. and Hawkins, D. T. (1990), *Marketing Research: Measurement and Method*, MacMillan.

Zikmund, W. G. and d'Amico, M. (1993), *Marketing*, West.

Part III

. . .

PRODUCT

Anatomy of a Product **7**

Product Management **8**

New Product Development **9**

Chapter 7 poses a very simple question, 'What is a product?' and finds that the answer is somewhat less simple. It is related to what the buyer really wants from the product, whether that consists of practical performance, psychological benefits or both, and the ways in which marketers choose to communicate that through the product via branding, packaging, design and quality.

Following an analysis of this complex anatomy of the product, Chapter 8 can then look critically at more detailed product management issues, such as the product life cycle and its influence on marketing decision making, the importance of developing a balanced portfolio of products and brand management. It also opens the debate about the advantages or otherwise of pan-European branding.

One of the lessons to be learned from the product life-cycle theory is that most products have a finite lifespan. As a product matures, therefore, decisions have to be made about what to do next. Chapter 8 examines some possibilities, such as relaunching an improved version of the product, while Chapter 9 takes the route of new product development, that is, allowing the product to die and replacing it with something new. The processes and problems of new product development are fully explored.

■   ■   ■

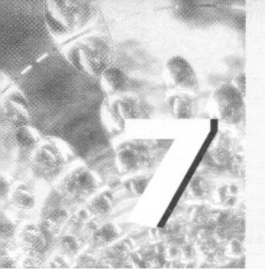

Anatomy of a Product

LEARNING OBJECTIVES

This chapter will help you to:

1 define and classify products and the key terms associated with them;

2 understand the nature, benefits and implementation of branding;

3 appreciate the functional and psychological roles of packaging;

4 understand the broad issues relating to product design and quality and their contribution to marketing.

INTRODUCTION

The product is at the heart of the marketing exchange. If the product does not deliver the benefits the customer wanted or if it does not live up to the expectations created by the other elements of the marketing mix then the whole exercise has been in vain. Remember that customers buy products to solve problems or to enhance their lives and thus the marketer has to ensure that the product can fully satisfy the customer, not just in functional terms, but also in psychological terms. The product is import-ant, therefore, because it is the ultimate test of whether the organisation has understood its customer's needs.

Example

Compare two types of car, the Lambourghini and the Trabant, for example. The Lambourghini is sleek, powerful, expensive, carefully designed and hand built. It delivers status to the customer in terms of the name, the look, the quality and the élitism associated with it. The Trabant, in contrast, at the time of the fall of the Berlin Wall, was regarded as being cheap, smelly, unsophisticated and under-powered. The brand image was so poor that the owners were selling them off for less than £45 and looking for second-hand BMW, Mercedes, and VW models. Several years later, in 1995, the Trabant's reputation had been restored some-what. Particularly in the former East Germany, people were realising that the Trabant is a cheap, reliable, easily maintained car which is well suited to the poorer state of the eastern roads, and makes an ideal second family car. Since Trabants were no longer produced, however, they became difficult to find, giving them a rarity and cult value. When a consignment of 444 brand-new Trabants were returned from a bankrupt Turkish dealer, they were selling on the German market for almost 20 000 DM (about £8800) each.

The above example raises a number of interesting questions about what makes a product, the importance of brand image and customer perceptions of it, and the interaction between the product and other elements of the marketing mix. Clearly, marketers have to understand the nature of these questions, and base strategic decisions about the development and management of product offerings on the answers. To start the process of thinking about these issues, therefore, this chapter examines some fundamental concepts. The definition of product and ways of classifying products lead to some basic definitions of product ranges. Then, the underlying concepts that give the product its character and essential appeal to the buyer will be examined. These include branding, packaging and labelling, design, style and quality, and the role of peripheral areas such as guarantees in enhancing the product offering. The wider issues of product management and new product development will then be discussed in the following two chapters. The first task for this chapter, meanwhile, is to define the meaning of the term *product*.

MEANING OF A PRODUCT

The product is one half of the exchange that interests marketers (price is the other half; *see* Chapters 10 and 11). A formal definition of product may be that

> **a product is a physical good, service, idea, person or place that is capable of offering tangible and intangible attributes that individuals or organisations regard as so necessary, worthwhile or satisfying that they are prepared to exchange money, patronage or some other unit of value in order to acquire it.**

A product is, therefore, a powerful and varied thing. The definition includes tangible products (tins of baked beans, aircraft engines), intangible products (services such as hairdressing or management consultancy), and ideas (public health messages, for instance). It even includes trade in people, for example, the creation and hard selling of pop groups and idols is less about music than about the promotion of a personality to which the target audience can relate. Does a Michael Jackson fan buy his latest album for its intrinsic musical qualities or because of the Michael Jackson name on the sleeve? Politicians too try to sell themselves as people with caring personalities in exchange for your vote at election time. Places are also saleable products. Holiday resorts and capital cities, for example, have long exploited their natural geographic or cultural advantages, building service industries that in some cases become essential to the local economy.

Whatever the product is, whether tangible, intangible or Michael Jackson, it can always be broken down into bundles of benefits which mean different things to different buyers. Figure 7.1 shows the basic anatomy of a product as a series of four concentric rings representing the **core product**, the **tangible product**, the **augmented product**, and finally the **potential product**.

The *core product* represents the heart of the product, the main reason for its existence and purchase. The core benefit of any product may be functional or psychological, and its definition must provide something for the marketer to work on to develop a differential advantage. Any make of car will get the purchaser from A to B, but add on to that the required benefits of spaciousness, or fuel economy, or status enhancement, and a definition of a core product to which a market segment will relate begins to emerge. The core benefit of a holiday could be to lie in the sun doing absolutely nothing, being pampered for two weeks, at one end of the spectrum, or, at the other end, to escape from the world by seeking adventure and danger in unknown terrain. Although it might be argued that an 18–30 Club holiday could satisfy both those core benefit requirements, generally speaking, very different packages will emerge to meet those needs.

FIGURE 7.1

**The anatomy of
a product**

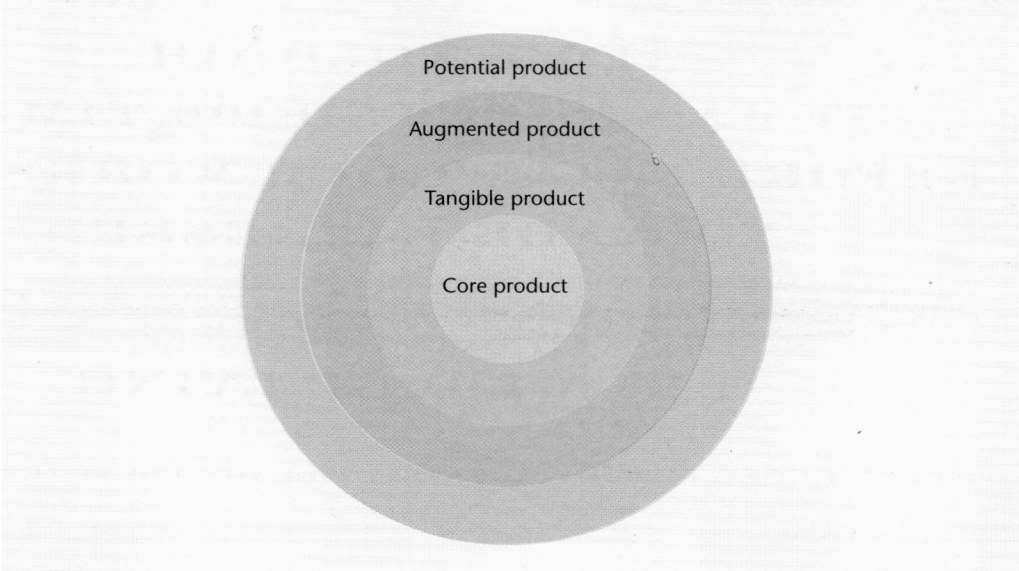

The definition of the core benefit is important because it influences the next layer, the *tangible product*. The tangible product is essentially the means by which the marketer puts flesh on the core product, making it a real product that clearly represents and communicates the offer of the core benefit. The tools used to create the product include design specification, product features, quality level, branding and packaging. A car that embodies the core benefit of 'fast and mean status symbol', for example, is likely to have a larger engine, sexy design, leather upholstery, lots of electric gadgets, built-in CD player, definitely be available in black or red metallic paint (among other choices), and certainly carry a marque such as BMW rather than Lada.

The *augmented product* represents add-on extras which do not themselves form an intrinsic element of the product but may be used by producers or retailers to increase the product's benefits or attractiveness. A computer manufacturer may offer installation, user training and after-sales service, for instance, to enhance the attractiveness of the product package. None of this affects the actual computer system itself, but will affect the satisfaction and benefits the buyer gets from the exchange. Retailers also offer augmented products. An electrical retailer selling national and widely available brands such as Hoover, Zanussi, Indesit or Hotpoint needs to make its own mark on each transaction so that the buyer will want to shop there again in the future. Augmenting the product through extra guarantees, cheap financing, delivery and breakdown insurance is more likely to provide memorable, competitively defendable and relatively inexpensive mechanisms for creating a relationship with the consumer than price competition.

Finally, the *potential product* layer acknowledges the dynamic and strategic nature of the product. The first three layers have described the product as it is now, but the marketer also needs to think about what the product could be and should be in the future. Kotler (1994) defines the potential product in terms of its possible evolution, for example new ways of differentiating itself from the competition. Thus British Airways' recent introduction of first class seats that convert into 'beds' is a means of retaining and attracting travellers in a very competitive and profitable segment. Doyle (1994), however, takes a slightly different view. He considers that the potential product reflects such high levels of added value and differentiation that the product is better protected against competitors and substitutes. Achieving this kind of potential has been one of the foundations of success for such organisations as Marks & Spencer,

IF WE TOLD YOU
IT WAS CHECKED 100 TIMES
BEFORE IT LEFT OUR WORKSHOPS
YOU'D BE IMPRESSED...

BUT WE'D BE LYING.

EVERY CROSS PEN IS CHECKED AT LEAST 150 TIMES. **CROSS**®

SINCE 1846.

10 carat Rolled Gold Ball Pen, available in jewellers, stationers, pen specialists and all leading department stores.

Source: Travis Sennet Sully Ross.

Quality is a key element in Cross Pens' tangible product.

Kellogg's, and Levi's over many years. Thus Kotler is saying that potential simply reflects what might be done with the product in the future, whereas Doyle is saying that it provides a strategic focus in itself.

In summary, all four layers of product contribute to the buyer's satisfaction, but the outer two depend on the definition of core product to determine how they are realised. The core itself may be functionally based, in terms of what the product is supposed to do, or it may be benefit or promise based, in terms of how this product will make you feel. It is, however, in the outer layers, the tangible and augmented product, that most of the overt marketing competition takes place.

PRODUCT CLASSIFICATION

To bring order to a wide and complex area of marketing, it is useful to be able to define groups of products that either have similar characteristics, or generate similar buying behaviour within a market. Such classification schemes allow some generalisations to be made about appropriate marketing strategies for each group.

Product-based classification

A product-based classification groups together products that have similar characteristics, although they may serve very different purposes and markets. There are three main categories: **durable products, non-durable products** and service products.

Durable products
Durable products last for many uses and over a long period of time before having to be replaced. Products such as domestic electrical goods, cars and capital machinery fall into this group.

Non-durable products
Non-durable products can only be used once or a few times before they have to be replaced. Food and other fmcg goods fall into this category, as do office consumables such as stationery and computer printer cartridges.

Service products

Services represent intangible products comprising activities, benefits or satisfactions that are not embodied in physical products. Items such as financial services, holidays, travel and personal services create problems for marketers, because of their intangibility and inherent perishability. Services are so different that they warrant their own chapter within this book (Chapter 23).

The nature and implementation of the marketing mix is likely to be very different for each of these categories of product. A durable is likely to be an infrequently purchased, relatively expensive good. It may require selective distribution through specialist channels, and a communications approach that is primarily centred on information and function rather than psychological benefits. In contrast, a non-durable is likely to be a frequently purchased, relatively low-priced item requiring mass distribution through as wide a variety of outlets as possible and mass communication centred on psychological benefits. Services have to find ways of either bringing the service to the consumer or persuading the consumer to come to the service delivery point. Communication has to develop both functional and psychological benefit themes as well as reassuring the potential customer of the quality and consistency of the service offered.

These outlines are, of course, broad generalisations of limited use, and it is not difficult to think of exceptions within each category (compare cars and washing machines in the durable group, for instance). Although these classifications are ostensibly based on product characteristics, it has proved to be impossible to talk about them without some reference to buyer behaviour, so perhaps it is time to make this dimension more explicit, and instead to think about user-based classifications of products.

The following subsections deal in turn with consumer markets (goods purchased for personal or family consumption – *see* Chapter 3) and organisational markets (goods purchased for business or institutional use – *see* Chapter 4). Although both groups look for satisfaction from their purchases, the kinds of products they buy and the buying influences and behaviour that predominate are very different, thus meriting separate treatment. It is important to note that even the same product can be marketed very differently, depending on whether it is aimed at a consumer or an organisational purchaser, as will be shown, for example, at p. 260 *et seq.*

User-based classifications: consumer goods and services

The contents of this section are very closely linked with the content of pp. 96 *et seq.*, where differences in buyer behaviour were based on whether the purchase was a routine response situation (i.e., a familiar, low-risk and frequently encountered situation), a limited problem-solving situation (some unfamiliarity, medium risk, less frequently encountered) or an extended problem-solving situation (no experience, very infrequent, high-risk purchase). If we begin with these behavioural categories, it is possible to identify parallel groups of goods and services that fit into those situations, giving a very powerful combination of buyer and product characteristics for outlining the basic shape of the marketing mix.

Convenience goods

Convenience goods correspond with the routine response buying situation. They are relatively inexpensive, frequent purchases. The buyer puts little effort into the purchasing decision and convenience often takes priority over brand loyalty. This is especially true of supermarket-based shopping. If the desired brand of breakfast cereal is inexplicably unavailable within the store the shopper is visiting, they will probably buy an alternative brand or do without rather than take the trouble to go to another shop.

The marketing implications of such a product definition are similar to those outlined for the non-durable in p. 256 above. Wide distribution needs to be assured to make it as likely as possible that the product will be under the consumer's nose. Communication needs to be aimed directly at the consumers to get them as involved as possible with the product through the creation of brand image to offset brand-switching indifference. Packaging and brand imagery need to be as attention grabbing and as memorable as possible to facilitate recognition and positive brand choice at the point of sale. The market may well be price sensitive and thus the producer and retailer should be prepared to accept low margins and to seek profit through volume.

The types of goods involved may be staple items, such as groceries, but could also include impulse purchases or emergency purchases. For example a consumer browsing through a bookshop with no particular intention to buy may be caught suddenly by a particular title, jacket design or author's name and make an immediate decision to buy. In an emergency, such as dealing with a burst water pipe in the home, convenience takes on a less lazy definition. The need for a solution to the consumer's problem takes on an urgency that precludes extensive shopping around. In both the impulse and the emergency situations, the key to making a sale is essentially the same: be in the right place at the right time with the right product and be ready to ambush the unsuspecting customer.

Shopping goods

Linked with limited problem-solving behaviour, **shopping goods** represent something more of a risk and an adventure to consumers, who are thus more willing to shop around and plan their purchases, and even to enjoy the shopping process. Comparison through advertisements and visits to retail outlets may be supplemented with information from easily accessible sources, such as consumer organisations' published reports, word of mouth from family and friends and brochures, as well as advice from sales assistants in the retail setting. A moderately rational assessment of the alternative products based on function, features, service promises, and guarantees will lead to a decision.

The effort required by this process is worth it if the purchase is significant or if the consumer will have to live for a long time with the consequences of the decision (*see* the hi-fi example at p. 97). Whether a purchase falls into this category depends on the individual consumer's perceptions of the importance and complexity of the purchase, as well as their previous experience within the market concerned. One consumer's shopping good is another's convenience or speciality good. Within the shopping goods classification, there may be brand and/or store loyalty involved, or no loyalty at all. There may also be a pre-existing short-list of preferred brands within which the detailed comparison and final choice will be made.

The implications of all this for the marketer impact on all aspects of the marketing mix, not just product. The mass distribution strategies of the convenience good may no longer be appropriate. The consumer is more likely to seek out certain specialist retailers and see what they have available than to purchase impulsively from a supermarket shelf, because of the nature of the product and the buying behaviour it invokes. This makes the careful targeting of key retailers essential. A hair-dryer manufacturer needs a presence in Curry's, Comet and Argos because those are the places the consumer will go to seek market information. Hair-dryers are a grey area, in the sense that for a significant number of consumers they are closer to convenience items than shopping goods. In that case, a major manufacturer with a recognisable, reassuring name such as Braun or Philips can display and sell products very successfully through a supermarket type of outlet.

The volume of goods sold will be less than for a convenience item, but the margin on each unit will be much higher. Price sensitivity could go either way with these products. A consumer who is confused by the amount of information to be analysed and is having difficulty comparing competing products on the basis of performance and features, may resort to price as the deciding factor. A more expensive one may be purchased on the basis that it must be a better quality product, or a cheaper one may be bought on the basis that it will do the job and there's no point spending more on fancy frills.

Communication might also take two directions. Establishing a strong corporate name is important so that when the consumer enters the market, the name either springs to mind as an obvious choice or at least seems very familiar, and therefore comforting, when it is encountered. Organisations such as Ariston, Zanussi and Hotpoint have used mass advertising in this way, so that even consumers who are not currently interested in buying kitchen appliances are aware that they exist and have some perception of what the company name stands for. The hope is that these percept-ions will be transferred to the actual products at the appropriate time.

The other direction for communication is that of working closely with the retail trade. If a consumer seeks information at the point of sale to guide product choice then obviously any manufacturer wants their product to be the one with the strongest retailer backing. Providing training or incentives (*see* Chapter 17 on trade sales pro-motion) to retailers or individual sales assistants, as well as help with point of sale displays and provision for joint promotion (*see* Chapter 17) all help to forge stronger links between producer and retailer with a view to developing a competitive edge.

Speciality goods

Speciality goods equate with the consumer's extensive problem-solving situation. The high-risk, expensive, very infrequently purchased products in this category evoke the most rational consumer response a manufacturer could hope to find. It is still not entirely rational, however. The psychological and emotive pull of a brand name like Porsche could still override objective assessment of information, leading to a biased, but happy decision for the consumer. If you allow the inclusion in this category of products like designer perfumes, the ones that cost several hundred pounds for 50 ml. and would be a once (or never) in a lifetime purchase for most consumers, then ration-ality goes right out of the window and the purchase is made entirely on the basis of the dream and the imagery woven around the product.

The products in this category need very specialist retailing which will provide a high level of augmented product services, both before and after the sale. Limiting dis-tribution to a small number of exclusive and well-monitored outlets not only protects the product from abuse (for example inappropriate display or sales advice), but also helps to enhance the product's special image and the status of the buyer.

The (relatively) very low volumes sold of these products are compensated for through their high profit margins. Prices are high not only to reward the producer and retailer for their care for the product and its buyer, but also because the buyer is likely to perceive a high price as a positive benefit (*see* Chapter 11 on the pricing of luxury goods and on psychological pricing), enhancing the status of the purchase.

Communication will be a more extreme version of the shopping goods scenario, with much emphasis on name and image building. This is likely to focus more on the psychological benefits of choosing that manufacturer or that product rather than on the functional benefits as such. At these price levels, function and quality can almost be taken for granted: it is the extra intangible psychological 'something' that differen-tiates between competing products. There is also going to be even closer co-operation between manufacturer and retailer, who will take care that any joint promotional efforts do not compromise the product's quality or status level.

Unsought goods

Within the **unsought good**s category, there are two types of situation. The first is the sudden emergency, such as the burst water pipe or the flat tyre. The organisation's job here is to ensure that the consumer either thinks of their name first or that they are the most accessible provider of the solution to the problem.

The second unsought situation arises with the kinds of products that people would not normally buy without aggressive hard selling techniques, such as timeshare properties and some home improvements.

Example

The timeshare industry in particular has earned a bad reputation over the last 10 years or so for what society generally regards as unethical pressure selling. (The selling techniques themselves are further discussed in Chapter 18 on personal selling). This has led to some individuals committing themselves to what, in the cold light of day, are actually unwanted, very expensive purchases. Some legislation, such as a mandatory 'cooling-off' period after the signing of the contract, does protect the consumer, but the fact remains that the developers are faced with the necessity of selling timeshares quickly, and they will continue to develop ever more subtle ways of pressurising consumers into an unsought purchase.

User-based classifications: organisational goods and services

This type of classification of organisational goods and services is linked closely with the discussion at p. 141, where the spectrum of buying situations from routine rebuy to new task purchasing was discussed. The novelty of the purchase influences the time, effort and human resources put into the purchasing decision. If that is then combined with the role and importance of the purchase within the production environment, it is possible to develop a classification system that is both widely applicable and indicative of particular marketing approaches.

Capital goods

Capital equipment consists of all the buildings and fixed equipment that have to be in place for production to happen. Such items tend to be infrequently purchased, and given that they are expected to support production over a long lifetime, and that they can represent a substantial investment, they are usually regarded as a high-risk decision in the new task category. This category might also include government-funded capital projects such as the building of motorways, bridges, housing and public buildings like hospitals and theatres. Tenders from companies throughout Europe were sought in 1995 for projects such as motorway construction in Bari, Italy; educational buildings in Charleroi, Belgium; and multi-dwelling buildings in Pinto, Spain.

The purchasing organisation, will, therefore use extensive decision making, involving a wide range of personnel from all levels of the organisation, and perhaps independent external consultants as well. The seller will also have to be prepared to spend a lot of time and effort researching the buying organisation and cultivating a relationship with its key personnel during the decision-making process. In some cases, the seller might have to become involved in developing a tailor-made product for the

Example

Siemens wanted to manufacture microchips on Tyneside in the UK, but first of all needed a factory. The £1.1 bn contract for designing and managing the construction project was awarded to the British company McAlpine and the German company Hochtief as a joint venture. This partnership of two powerful names, as well as the fact Hochtief has worked successfully for Siemens in the UK before, is thought to have had a major influence on Siemens' decision.

buyer. Such purchasing is likely to centre on rational criteria, so the seller will have to bid for the contract, communicating the quantifiable benefits of the product, in competition with a number of alternative suppliers.

Accessory goods

Accessory goods are items which give peripheral support to the production process without direct involvement. Included in this group, therefore, will be items such as hand tools, fork-lift trucks, storage bins and any other portable or light equipment. Office equipment is also included here, such as word processors, desks, chairs, and filing cabinets.

Generally speaking, these items are not quite as expensive or as infrequently purchased as the capital goods. The risk factor is lower, too. Buying the 'wrong' desk will not jeopardise the organisation in the same way as buying the 'wrong' production machinery would. An unreliable fork-lift truck can disrupt production, but even so, it is relatively quick and simple to replace. All of this indicates that the length of and the degree of involvement in the purchasing process will be scaled down accordingly into something closer to the modified rebuy situation.

The seller's main task, therefore, would appear to be to ensure that the prospective purchaser has all the relevant up-to-date information to hand. The purchase of office equipment, for example, might be delegated to the office manager without reference to more senior management, within an overall budget. The office equipment supplier then needs to maintain regular contact, making sure that the latest catalogue is in the office manager's hands, so that when a purchasing decision is due, that is the catalogue that is used. Regular visits from a sales representative can help to communicate or negotiate special offers and deals, as well as providing a human point of contact for the office manager.

Raw materials

Raw materials arrive more or less in their natural state, having been processed only sufficiently to ensure their safe and economical transport to the factory. Thus iron ore is delivered to British Steel; fish arrives at the Findus fish-finger factory; beans and tomatoes are delivered to Heinz, and fleeces arrive at the textile mill. The raw materials then go on to further processing within the purchaser's own production line. The challenge for the supplier of raw materials is how to distinguish their product from the competition's, given that there are often few specification differences between them. Often, the differentiating factors in the purchaser's mind relate to non-product features, such as service, handling convenience, trust and terms of payment, for example.

MARKETING IN ACTION

Raw material pricing

Price can be a major factor in the purchasing of raw materials in organisational markets. In early 1995, a dispute arose between US and European aluminium groups about the price of can sheet, the material used to make drinks cans. The largest US firm, Alcoa, introduced a new pricing formula linked to the volatile price of aluminium, traded as a commodity on the London Metal Exchange. This new formula raised can sheet prices by 50 per cent. The can makers calculated that this added 2 cents to the cost of each can, and

threatened to turn to plastic, glass, or tin-plated steel instead. Pechiney Rhenalu, a French producer of can sheet, disagreed with Alcoa's approach, claiming that long-term, stable prices, fixed within narrow bands for three to five years ahead, would be far more attractive to the customers and would better protect the can sheet industry against substitution, i.e., the glass, plastic and steel options.

Source: Gooding (1995).

Semi-finished goods

Unlike raw materials, semi-finished goods have already been subject to a significant level of processing before arriving at the purchaser's factory. They still, however, need further processing before incorporation into the ultimate product. A clothing manufacturer, therefore, will purchase cloth (i.e., the product of spinning, weaving and dyeing processes) which still needs to be cut and sewn to create the ultimate product.

Components and parts

Components and parts are finished goods in their own right, which simply have to be incorporated into the assembly of the final product with no further processing. Car manufacturers, for example, buy in headlamp units, alarm systems and microchips as complete components or parts, and then fit them to the cars on the assembly line.

There is an important distinction to be drawn here between products specified by the supplier and those specified by the buyer. If the components are buyer specified, then the sales representative's major responsibility is to make sure that the right people are talking to each other. This might mean, for instance, co-ordinating the efforts of applications engineering personnel within the selling organisation with the engineering and specifying staff within the buying organisation. Even when the product has been agreed, there is still a need to maintain the relationship. This would be particularly critical if specific capital investments have been made by either party. Buyer-specified products will be discussed further at p. 318 *et seq.*

In contrast, supplier-specified products demand clear appreciation of customer needs, carefully designed and priced products and effective selling and promotion to exploit the opportunities identified by market research. Often, the competitive edge comes from designing unique parts for targeted applications, which can be delivered to a standard and consistent quality level to meet customer requirements.

Supplies and services

Finally, there are several categories of minor consumable items (as distinct from the accessory goods discussed above) and services that facilitate production and the smooth running of the organisation without any direct input.

Operating Supplies. Operating supplies are frequently purchased consumable items that do not end up in the finished product. On the factory floor, these will include things like the lubrication oils for the production machinery. In the office, this group mainly includes stationery items such as pens, paper and envelopes, as well as computer consumables such as printer toner or ink cartridges, and floppy disks.

Maintenance and Repair. Maintenance and repair services ensure that all the capital and accessory goods continue to operate smoothly and efficiently. Maintenance and repair may take place on a planned basis, regularly servicing and checking equipment. They may also be called in on a trouble-shooter basis, when an actual problem develops. Remember, though, that maintenance and repair are not just about looking after equipment, but also about looking after the working environment, from mending the roof to emptying the office waste-paper baskets. This category can also include minor consumable items, such as cleaning materials, which assist in providing this service.

Business Services. Business services may well be a major category of purchases for an organisation, involving a great deal of expenditure and decision-making effort, since they involve the purchase of services like management consultancy, accounting and legal advice and advertising agency expertise. This takes the discussion back to new task purchasing and its associated problems of involvement and risk.

UNDERSTANDING THE PRODUCT RANGE

Very few organisations are single-product companies. Most offer a variety of different products and perhaps a number of variations of each individual product, designed to meet the needs of different market segments. Car companies clearly do this, producing different models of car to suit different price expectations, different power and performance requirements, and different usage conditions from the long-distance sales representative to the family wanting a car largely for short journeys in a busy suburban area. The same happens in organisational markets. Ingersoll-Rand, for example, have developed a whole range of portable compressors for use on construction sites. These range from small units that will run a single tool to high- capacity, high-pressure specialist units. A construction or engineering contractor can then choose the appropriate unit to do the job in hand most cost effectively and most efficiently. Service companies also vary their products to suit different customer groups. A business school will offer undergraduate and postgraduate courses; post- experience courses for practising managers; full-time and part-time courses; tailored training packages for industry; and consultancy.

To understand any product fully, it is essential to appreciate its position in the wider family of the organisation's products. The marketing literature uses a number of terms when talking about the product family which are easy to confuse because of their similarity. Here are some definitions which sort out the confusion and offer some insight into the complexity of the product family. Figure 7.2 shows how all of these terms apply to the products produced within the Consumer Healthcare division of SmithKline Beecham in 1994.

FIGURE 7.2

SmithKline Beecham consumer healthcare product mix, 1994

Product mix

The **product mix** is the total sum of all the products and variants offered by an organisation. A small company serving a specialist need in an organisational market may have a very small, tightly focused product mix.

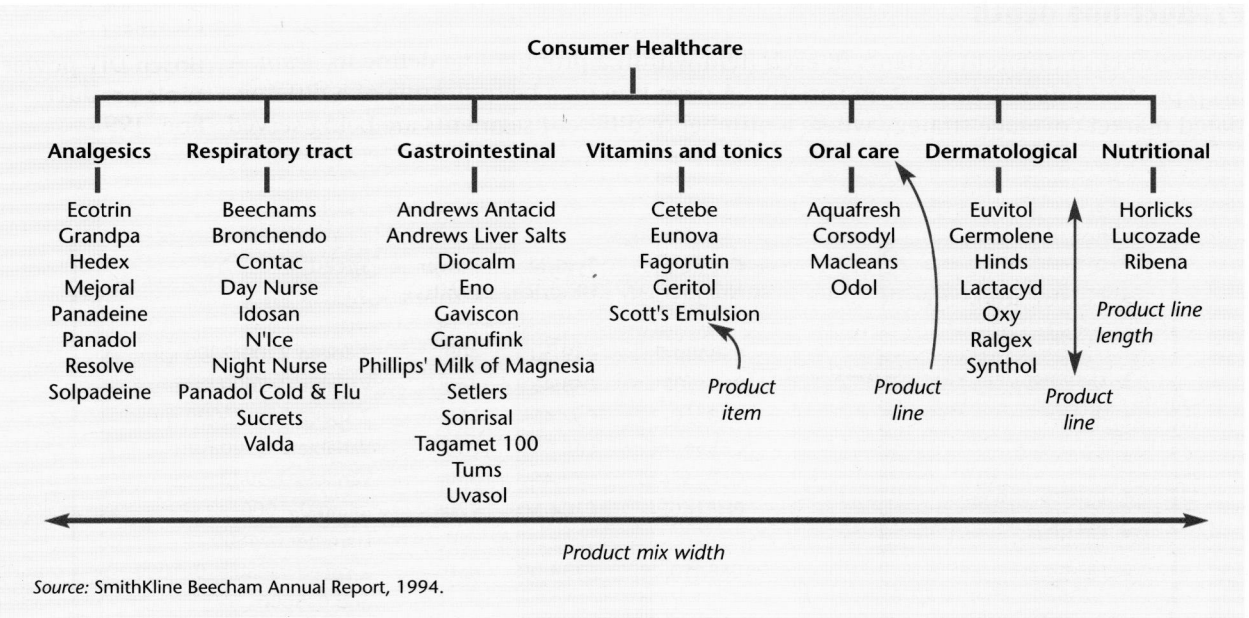

Source: SmithKline Beecham Annual Report, 1994.

Specialist companies also exist in consumer markets, of course. Van Dyck Belgian Chocolates, for example, offer boxed chocolates, chocolate bars, liqueur chocolates, fruit-flavoured chocolate, nut chocolates etc. A large multinational supplier of fmcg goods, such as Nestlé, has a very large and varied product mix, from confectionery to coffee to canned goods.

Product line

To impose some order on to the product mix, it can be divided into a number of **product lines**. A product line is a group of products that are closely related to each other. This relationship may be production orientated, in that the products have similar production requirements or problems. Alternatively, the relationship may be market orientated, in that the products fulfil similar needs, or are sold to the same customer group or have similar product management requirements. A company such as Minolta may define three of its product lines as still cameras, video cameras and photocopiers. These labels make sense because those three groups involve different technologies, and also because they sell to very different customers and markets.

Product item

A product line consists of a number of **product items**. These are the individual products or brands, each with its own features, benefits, price etc. In the fmcg area, therefore, if Heinz had a product line called table sauces, the product items within it might be tomato ketchup, salad cream, mayonnaise, reduced calorie mayonnaise etc.

Product line length

The total number of items within the product line is the **product line length**. Bosch, for example, might have a product line of DIY power tools as shown in Fig 7.3. Their equivalent industrial range of power tools would probably be even longer.

Product line depth

The number of different variants of each item within a product line define its *depth*. A deep product line has many item variants. A deep line may be indicative of a differentiated market coverage strategy where a number of different segments are being served

FIGURE 7.3

Bosch DIY power tools product line, 1995

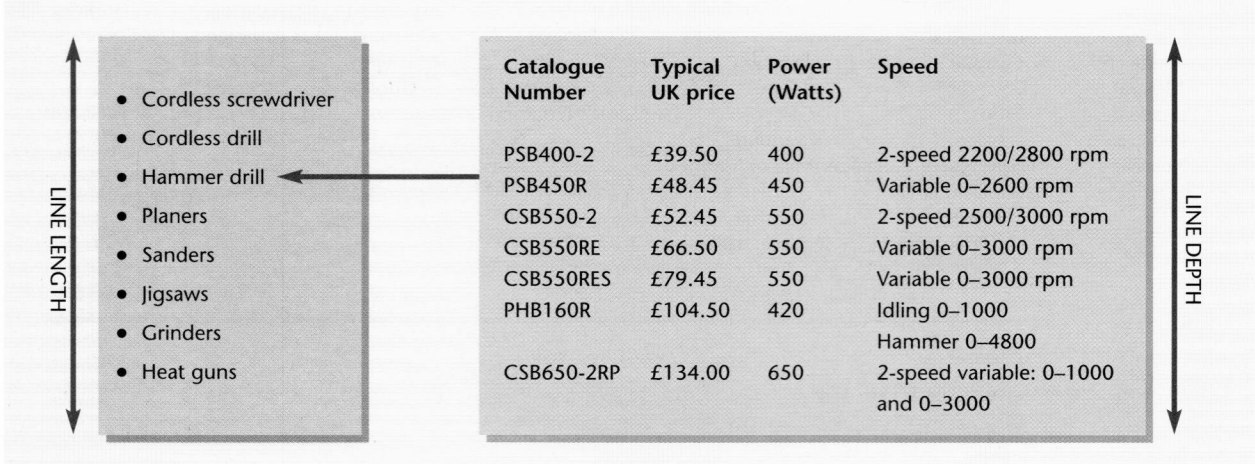

	Catalogue Number	Typical UK price	Power (Watts)	Speed
• Cordless screwdriver				
• Cordless drill				
• Hammer drill ←	PSB400-2	£39.50	400	2-speed 2200/2800 rpm
• Planers	PSB450R	£48.45	450	Variable 0–2600 rpm
• Sanders	CSB550-2	£52.45	550	2-speed 2500/3000 rpm
• Jigsaws	CSB550RE	£66.50	550	Variable 0–3000 rpm
• Grinders	CSB550RES	£79.45	550	Variable 0–3000 rpm
• Heat guns	PHB160R	£104.50	420	Idling 0–1000 Hammer 0–4800
	CSB650-2RP	£134.00	650	2-speed variable: 0–1000 and 0–3000

LINE LENGTH

LINE DEPTH

with tailored products. If we look again at the Bosch example in Fig 7.3, we can break hammer drills down into a number of variants, giving a depth of seven, each of which has different performance and application capabilities, as well as fitting into different price segments.

Similarly, in an fmcg market, Table 7.1 shows the Lynx brand produced by Elida Gibbs. Taking into account the various combinations of product type and fragrance, Lynx has a depth of 25. This depth does not aim to cover different market segments, but does offer sufficient variation and choice to keep the target segment interested and loyal. The line includes all the basic male toiletry products so that the customer does not need to purchase anything from outside the line, and the variety of fragrances allows the customer to experiment and have a change from time to time!

TABLE 7.1
The Lynx brand, 1995

Product type	Fragrance					
	Africa	Mirage	Java	Tempest	Oriental	Nevada
Body spray	○	○	○	○	○	○
Shower gel	○	○	○	○	○	○
Aftershave	○	○	○	○		
Roll-on deodorant	○	○	○	○		
Deodorant stick	○	○	○			
Aftershave gel	○	○				

Source: Elida Gibbs, *Male Toiletries Retailing*, Spring/Summer 1995, p. 1.

Product mix width

The *width* of the product mix is defined by the number of product lines offered. Depending on how broadly or narrowly defined the product lines are, a wide mix might indicate an organisation with a diverse interest in a number of different markets, such as Nestlé. A wide mix in an organisational market might indicate a specialist technology being supplied for very different applications to customers in different industries.

These definitions will be important for the next chapter's discussion of managing the product mix.

BRANDING

Branding is an important element of the tangible product and, particularly in consumer markets, is a means of linking items within a product line or emphasizing the individuality of product items. Branding can also help in the development of a new product by facilitating the extension of a product line or mix, through building on the consumer's perceptions of the values and character represented by the brand name. This points to the most important function of branding: the creation and communication of a three-dimensional character for a product that is not easily copied or damaged by competitors' efforts. The prosaic definition of brand, accepted by most marketers, is that it consists of any name, design, style, words, or symbols, singly or in any combination that distinguish one product from another in the eyes of customer.

Branding is a very important activity in consumer markets. *Marketing's* annual survey of Britain's biggest brands shows how much business a brand can bring to its owner, and the level of advertising support that brands can command. Table 7.2 gives details of the top 10 brands from the 1994 survey, while Table 7.3 shows the top 10 fastest growing brands in the UK in 1994.

An organisation's approach to branding depends on its overall product mix and individual line strategy, as will be shown at pp. 275 *et seq*. First, however, it is necessary to look a little more closely at the meaning of branding, beyond the raw definition already presented.

The meaning of branding

The definition of brand provided above offered a variety of mechanisms through which branding could be developed, the most obvious of which are the name and the logo. As with the product mix jargon discussed in the previous section, you are likely to meet a number of terms in the course of your reading, and it is important to differentiate between them.

TABLE 7.2
The UK's top 10 brands, 1994

Brand	Owner	Sales (£m)	Ad. spend (£m)
Coca-Cola	Coca-Cola	Over 440	12.7
Walker's Crisps	PepsiCo	240–245	3.7
Ariel	Procter & Gamble	225–230	26.9
Persil	Lever Brothers	215–220	24.2
Nescafé	Nestlé	215–220	7.5
Pampers	Procter & Gamble	190–200	17.3
Andrex Toilet Tissue	Scott Paper	165–170	8.4
Pepsi	PepsiCo	160–165	6.4
Whiskas	Pedigree Petfood	150–155	10.2
Bells	United Distillers	150–155	4.7

Source: Adapted from *Marketing* 16 March 1995, p. 22. Copyright A C Nielsen, reprinted with kind permission.

TABLE 7.3
The UK's 10 fastest growing brands, 1994

Brand	Owner	Sales (£m)	Change (%)	Ad. spend (£m)
Huggies	Kimberly–Clark	35–40	988	8.2
Action Man	Hasbro	10–15	142	0.7
Pantene Shampoo	Procter & Gamble	30–35	95	11.0
Andrex Kitchen Towels	Scott Paper	5–10	60	0.3
Pringles	Procter & Gamble	40–45	60	1.7
Dune	Christian Dior	5–10	55	0.9
Paco Rabane	Creative Fragrances	5–10	55	0.9
Lynx	Elida Gibbs	10–15	50	0.6
Fisher-Price Pre-School	Fisher-Price	20–25	49	2.9
Patak's Indian Foods	Patak (Spices)	5–10	43	0.3

Source: Adapted from *Marketing* 16 March 1995, p. 23. Copyright A C Nielsen, reprinted with kind permission.

Brand name

A brand name is any word or illustration that clearly distinguishes one seller's goods from another. It can take the form of words, such as Weetabix and Ferrero Rocher or initials, such as AA. Numbers can be used to create an effective brand name, such as 7-Up. A browse through the telephone directory of any British town is likely to reveal a small company called A1 Taxis. The A1 name is popular with small operators partly because it has connotations of quality, but mainly because the quirks of alphabetical order mean that it comes very early in the telephone book listing and is thus more likely to attract a potential customer's attention. Brand names can also be enhanced by the use of an associated logo, such as the one used by Apple computers, to reinforce the name, or through the particular style in which the name is presented. The classic example of this is the Coca-Cola brand name, where the visual impact of the written name is so strong that the onlooker recognises the design rather than reads the words. Thus Coca-Cola is instantly identifiable whether the name is written in English, Russian, Chinese or Arabic because it always somehow *looks* the same.

The strategic issues surrounding the choice and use of brand name are examined further at p. 274.

Trade name

The trade name is the legal name of an organisation which may or may not relate directly to the branding of its products.

> ### Example
>
> Cadbury's, as an organisation, have deliberately developed a strong image for the Cadbury corporate name to act as an umbrella for all their product brands. Hence their products benefit both from the affection that consumers hold for the corporate name and from the individual character developed for Cadbury's Flake, Cadbury's Dairy Milk, Cadbury's Drinking Chocolate and all their other products. In the car market, Ford similarly use their corporate name in conjunction with individual identities for their models (Ford Escort, Ford Fiesta, Ford Mondeo etc.), whereas both Volvo and Peugeot rely more on the company name and do not try to build character through model names. Thus Volvo have produced the Volvo 440 series, while Peugeot also label their individual models by numbers, such as 106, 309, 405.

Some companies prefer to let the brands speak for themselves and do not give any prominence to the product's parentage. Washing powder brands produced by either Lever Brothers or Procter & Gamble do not prominently display the company name, although it is shown on the back or side of the pack. Few consumers would realise that Persil, Surf and Radion come from the same stable. Similarly, RHM produce brands such as Paxo that have no obvious corporate identity.

There is more on the strategic implications of the degree of corporate branding used at pp. 275 *et seq*.

Trade mark

A trade mark is a brand name, symbol or logo, which is registered and protected for the owner's sole use. To bring the UK into line with EU legislation, the Trades Marks Act, 1994 allows organisations to register smells, sounds, product shapes and packaging, as well as brand names and logos. This means, as discussed by Slingsby (1994), that the Coca-Cola bottle, the Toblerone bar, and Heinz's tomato ketchup bottle are now as protectable as their respective brand names. Also, for the first time, advertising slogans, jingles, and even movements or gestures associated with a brand, can be

The packaging helps to communicate a strong brand identity for the Jif lemon.

Source: Van den Berghs Food Ltd.

registered as trade marks. The Act prevents competitors from legally using any of these things in a way which may confuse or mislead buyers, and also makes the registration process and action over infringement much easier. By 1996 it was also possible to register trade marks for the whole of Europe by filing a single application to the Community Trade Mark Office in Alicante, Spain, rather than having to apply for registration country by country. The workings of this office are covered in detail by De Ulloa (1995).

Trade marks are valuable properties, as organisations invest much time and money in creating them and educating consumers about what they stand for. This means that there is also value in trade which capitalises on the illegal use of brand names. Companies such as Nike and Reebok have put a great deal of effort into trying to stem the flow on to the market of counterfeit, low-cost copies of their brands. These counterfeits, allegedly sourced from the Far East, are poor quality goods which damage the company name and image if purchased as 'originals'. Even organisational markets are not immune to this trend which has been seen in the markets for motor spare parts and aircraft parts, among others.

Example

A European manufacturer of insecticides found that there was widespread counterfeiting and dilution of its products in developing countries. Some unscrupulous distributors were diluting the product with water or alcohol, or simply refilling old packaging with anything! According to Luesby (1995), in 1992 the counterfeit market as a whole accounted for 5 per cent of world trade. The EU claimed that it was costing 100 000 jobs a year in Europe, while the USA calculated that counterfeits from China alone were costing $1 bn a year.

Brand mark

The brand mark is specifically the element of the visual brand identity that does not consist of words, but of design and symbols. This would include things like the McDonald's golden arches, the Apple's computer symbol, or Audi's interlocking circles. These things are also protectable, as discussed under the trade marks above.

The benefits of branding

Branding carries benefits for all parties involved in the exchange process and in theory at least makes it easier to buy or sell products. This section, summarised in Fig 7.4, looks at the benefits of branding from different perspectives, beginning with that of the buyer.

Consumer perspective

Branding is of particular value to the buyer in a complex and crowded market-place. In a supermarket, for example, brand names and visual images make it easier to locate and identify required products. Strong branding can speak volumes about the function and character of the product and help consumers to judge whether it is their sort of product, delivering the functional and psychological benefits sought. This is especially true for a new, untried product. The branding can at least help the evaluation of product suitability, and if there is an element of corporate branding (as discussed with Cadbury's and Ford above) it can also offer reassurance about the product's quality pedigree.

This all aids the shopping process and reduces some of its risks, but it goes further. Giving a product what amounts to a three-dimensional personality makes it easier for consumers to form attitudes and feelings about the product. It gets them sufficiently interested to want to be bothered to do that. This has the double effect of creating brand loyalty (the product as a trusted friend) and of creating something special in the consumer's mind that the competition would find difficult to touch.

A final slant on this issue of relationship between buyer and brand is that the brand's name and image are as individual and as evocative as a person's name and facial features. If you mention the name of a mutual friend to someone, the name triggers the recall of the friend's face and personality as well as the listener's attitude towards that person. The name acts as a shorthand label for a large bundle of complicated descriptors and emotions. The brand's name serves the same purpose. This means that for an established brand, relatively short, sharp communication can achieve a wealth of response from the target audience.

Manufacturer perspective

The manufacturer benefits, of course, from the relationship of the buyer with branding. The ease of identification of the product at the point of sale, the connotations of quality and familiarity, and the creation of a three-dimensional product personality

FIGURE 7.4

The benefits of branding

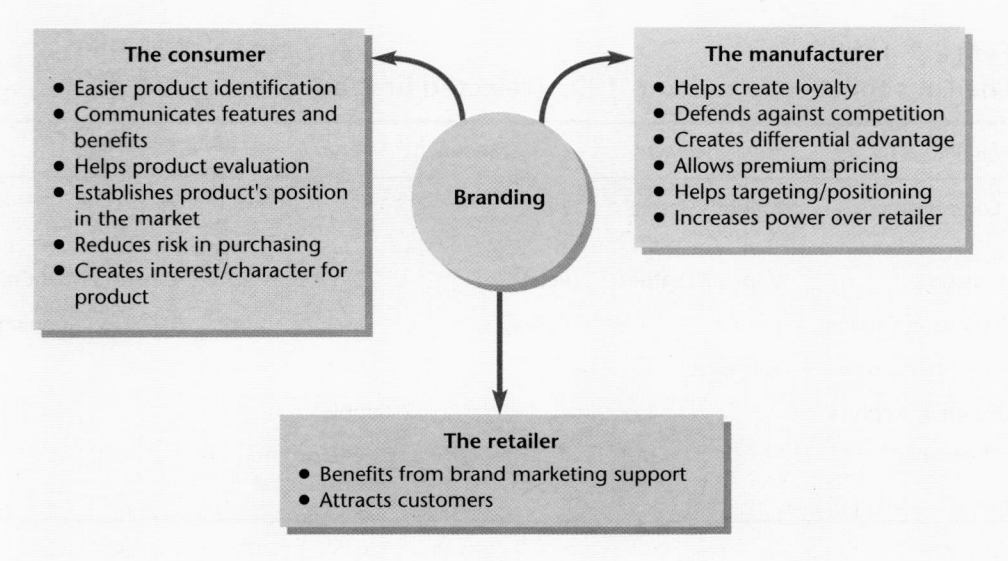

all help the manufacturer. The manufacturer's key interest is in the building of defendable brand loyalty to the point where the trust, liking and preference for the brand overcome any lingering price sensitivity, thus allowing a reasonable measure of premium pricing and the prevention of brand switching.

> ### Example
>
> Late in 1994 we saw the ultimate example of the use of branding as a means of commanding premium prices with the launch of 'designer water'. The fashion designer Donna Karan launched her own brand of water, available for £1.50 per small bottle, exclusively from her fashion outlet in Bond Street, London. A company executive was quoted in a newspaper article as saying, 'Water is international. It's real. It's part of you' (Green, 1994).

Other more subtle advantages of branding for the manufacturer are linked with segmentation and competitive positioning strategies. Different brands can be used by one organisation to target different segments. Because the different brands have clearly defined individual characteristics, the consumer does not necessarily link them, and thus does not become confused about what the organisation stands for. Even where there is a strong corporate element to the branding, as with Ford cars, the individual models within the range are seen clearly as separate products, serving different market needs, with price differences justified in terms of design and technical specification. Consumers view this wide range of brands positively, as a way of offering as tailored a choice as possible within the confines of a mass market.

Strong branding is also important for providing competitive advantage, not just in terms of generating consumer loyalty, but also as a means of competing head-on, competing generally across the whole market in an almost undifferentiated way or finding a niche in which to dominate. Brand imagery can help to define the extent of competition or exaggerate the differentiating features that pull it away from the competition. Table 7.4 examines the toilet soap market, identifying the different levels of competitive activity in different market segments, as represented by available brands.

Retailer perspective

The retailer benefits from branding to a certain extent. Branded products are well supported by advertising and other marketing activities, and so the retailer has some

TABLE 7.4
The UK's toilet soap market, 1993 (selected brands)

Manufacturer	Family segment	Luxury/beauty	Skincare	Cosmetic	Deodorant
Lever Brothers	Knight's Castile	Lux		Dove	Shield Lifebuoy
Cusson's	Imperial Leather	Pearl		Cusson's Mild Cream	
Procter & Gamble	Fairy	Camay		Ulay Conditioning Bar	
Colgate Palmolive	Palmolive				Fresh
Smith & Nephew			Simple		
Own label			The Body Shop Boots Natural		

Source: Based on information from Mintel Market Intelligence (September 1994), 'Soap, Bath and Shower Additives'.

Moving brands into new markets

Many bigger brand owners have turned to the emerging market economies of central and eastern Europe, partly as a way of expanding, and partly as a means of escaping highly competitive and cluttered markets in the West which were beginning to suffer from consumer resistance. Building and maintaining brands in countries such as Russia has not proved to be easy, despite the wealth of opportunity available. In many sectors, competition built up quickly. In confectionery, for example, Mars were in Russia first, followed by Cadbury, Nestlé, Suchard, and many other European and US firms. Companies have also suffered from economic factors, such as the devaluation of the rouble and increasing duties and taxes.

A major problem is the lack of the kind of marketing infrastructure that is fundamental to brand management and that Western companies take for granted. Brands depend on mass distribution, and yet the Russian retail industry is still in a state of transition. Brands also depend on targeted TV advertising, yet there is no accurate means of measuring audience figures. Brand owners cannot even turn to alternative means of communication, as direct mail, telemarketing, and database marketing systems either do not exist or are largely unreliable. Russian manufacturers tried to fight back with a 'Made in Russia' campaign, but the influx of Western companies has pushed the cost of advertising media far beyond the reach of any Russian company. A survey of brand awareness in Russia reveals a string of names familiar to the Western consumer, such as Pepsi Cola, Mars, Whiskas, Mercedes, Sony, Colgate, IBM and Samsung, for example.

Source: Teather (1995).

assurance that they will sell. Branded products do draw customers into the store, but the disadvantage is that if a brand is unavailable in one store, then the shopper is likely to patronise another instead. The retailer may prefer the shopper to be less brand loyal and more store loyal! Supermarkets have always recognised the value and necessity of manufacturer branded goods, but they have also looked for ways of reducing the power that this gives the brand owner. This issue will be looked at in detail in the next subsection.

Lest this discussion should seem too enthusiastic about branding, we now turn to some of the disadvantages. Echoing one of the risks of segmentation (discussed in Chapter 5, p. 190), there is the danger of proliferation if brands are created to serve every possible market niche. Retailers are under pressure to stock increasing numbers of lines within a product area, which means in turn that either less shelf space is devoted to each brand, or retailers refuse to stock some brands. Both options are unpleasant for the manufacturer. The consumer may also begin to see too much choice, and at some point, there is a risk that the differences between brands become imperceptible to the consumer and confusion sets in.

Types of brands

The discussion so far has centred on the brands created and marketed by manufacturers and sold through retail outlets. An area of growing importance, however, is the brand created by a wholesaler or retailer for that organisation's sole use. This development has taken place partly because of conflicts and power struggles between manufacturers and retailers (*see* Chapter 12), and partly because the retailers also need to generate store loyalty (*see* Chapter 13) in a highly competitive retail sector.

This section, therefore, distinguishes between the brands emanating from different types of organisation.

Manufacturer brands

Most manufacturers, particularly in the fmcg sector, are at arm's length from the end buyer and consumer of their product. The retail sector is in between and can make the difference between a product's success and failure through the way the product is displayed or made available to the public. The manufacturer can attempt to impose some control over this through trade promotions, but the manufacturer's best weapon is direct communication with the end buyer. Planting brand names and recognition of brand imagery in the consumer's mind through advertising or sales promotion gives the manufacturer a fighting chance of recognition and selection at the point of sale. Furthermore, the creation of a strong brand which has hard core loyalty can tip the balance of power back in favour of the manufacturer, because any retailer not stocking that brand runs the risk of losing custom to its competitors.

The creation and management of a manufacturer brand generates many responsibilities and costs in terms of promotion, distribution, quality control and product development, but if the process is managed effectively, then it does represent a valuable asset, both financially and strategically.

Retailer and wholesaler brands

The growth of **own label brands** (i.e., those bearing the retailer's name) has become a major factor in retailing. Supermarkets and clothing stores, in particular, have been very active in creating physical products exclusive to the store, reflecting the retailer's name. The responsibility for the development and maintenance of the brand falls on the retailer. The retailer may or may not manufacture the products directly, but either way, the product will not admit its provenance. 'Manufactured in the UK for J Sainsbury PLC' is the nearest you are likely to get.

Why do it? One possible problem a retailer has is that if a consumer is buying a recognised manufacturer's brand, then the source of that purchase is less relevant. A can of Heinz baked beans represents the same values whether it is purchased from a corner shop or from Harrod's. Retailers can differentiate from each other on the basis of price or service, but they are looking for more than that. The existence of a range of exclusive retailer brands that the consumer comes to value creates a physical reason for visiting that retailer and no other. These brands also serve the purpose of giving the consumer 'the retailer in a tin', where the product in the kitchen cupboard is a constant reminder of the retailer and embodies the retailer's values in a more tangible form, reinforcing loyalty and positive attitudes.

Other reasons include the fact that the retailer can earn a better margin on an own brand, and still sell it more cheaply than a manufacturer's brand. This is because they do not face the product development, brand creation and marketing costs that the manufacturers incur. The retailer's own brand is sold on the back of the retailer's normal marketing activity, and not with the massive advertising, promotion and selling costs that each manufacturer's brand has to bear. Even the comparatively small production runs involved with retailer's brands need not increase costs too much, if the own brand is either the manufacturer's brand with a different label, or a slight variation.

The use of own label varies across different retailers. Some retailers, such as Kwik Save, use their own label to create a no-nonsense, no-frills, value for money generic range. Others, such as Marks & Spencer, Sainsbury's and the Albert Heijn chain in the Netherlands have created own brands that are actually perceived as superior in quality to the manufacturer's offerings. The penetration of own labels also differs. Table 7.5 shows the percentage of own-label business across different products.

It is apparent that some supermarkets are using own-brand products increasingly as a central pivot around which to cluster a select but small number of manufacturer brands. Given that own-label products seem to put so much power into the hands of the retailers, why do manufacturers co-operate in their production? For a manufacturer of second-string brands (i.e., not the biggest names in the market), it might be a

TABLE 7.5

UK grocery own-label trends, 1991–1993 (own-label market share %)

	1991	1992	1993
Pre-packed salads	74	79	86
Aluminium foil	73	74	75
Pre-cooked sliced meat	80	79	72
Cream	66	67	70
Honey	57	60	64
Dry pasta	53	57	60
Household cleaning and sponges	55	57	60
Facial tissue	48	47	47
Toilet tissue	40	39	40
Squashes	34	34	36
Mineral water	29	33	36
Indian foods	19	18	22
Lavatory cleaners	17	18	20
Mustard	14	16	19
Coffee	15	17	17
Detergents	8	7	8

Source. Adapted from *The Retail Pocket Book* 1994, p. 54. Published by NTC Publications, Henley-on-Thames. Reprinted with kind permission.

good way of developing closer links with a retailer and earning some sort of protection for the manufacturer's brands. In return for the supply, at attractive prices, of own-brand products, the retailer might undertake to display the manufacturer's brands more favourably, or promise not to delist them, for example. The extra volume provides some predictability for the manufacturer and it also could help to achieve economies of scale of benefit to both parties.

The danger, of course, is that of the manufacturer becoming too dependent on the retailer's own-brand business. The supplier–buyer relationship needs to be carefully monitored and handled (*see* pp. 142 *et seq.*). Some retailers, such as Marks & Spencer, and the Irish retailer Dunne's demand a high level of influence over the operations of their own-label suppliers, to the point of expecting to take a significant proportion of the supplier's output, yet retaining the right to drop a supplier who fails to live up to expectations. The smaller, more vulnerable organisation in particular needs to develop an active policy of diversification to offset the strategic risks of over-dependency.

A final twist in the evolution of the own-brand scene over the past few years has been an increasing consumer cynicism, giving credence to the view that retailers' own brands are only the manufacturers' brands with different labels, but much cheaper. To counter this, some big manufacturers have made it explicit that they do not operate in the own-brand market. Nescafé and Procter & Gamble have advertised on this basis, and Kellogg's packaging actually states, 'We don't make cereals for anyone else'. Their fear is understandable. Why continue to spend more on manufacturer brands when you can get the same goods cheaper with an ASDA label on it?

Branding strategy

This chapter has already hinted at a number of important dimensions to be considered in developing and maintaining a branding strategy. Each one will now be treated separately.

Own-label manufacture

Some major brand manufacturers have begun to recognise the opportunities offered by own-label manufacture. In June 1995, for example, Mars announced that it was to move into own-label manufacture of 'wet cooking sauces' (for example, Dolmio bolognese sauce in a jar) after 60 years of resistance to such supply. One reason is probably aggressive competition in the sector. In 1994, for example, 60 branded products were launched in this sector, and 83 delisted. A further reason is overcapacity at the Dutch manufacturing plant. Own-label manufacture will create an extra market share that will reduce the overcapacity (assuming that the own label does not simply take share away from Mars' existing brands), and will give Mars more total supermarket shelf space than its competitors. Heinz too have developed own-label business, offering beans, spaghetti and tuna to UK supermarkets, but with different recipes, 'inferior' to the normal Heinz brands. By September 1995, Heinz were also looking for European retailers to whom they could sell own-label products.

Source: Richards (1995a); Richards (1995b).

Selecting a brand name

If all the benefits to the buyer mentioned at p. 269 are going to be achieved through branding, then the name becomes a crucial choice. It must be memorable, easy to pronounce and meaningful (whether in real or emotional terms). As manufacturers look increasingly towards wider European and international markets, there is a much greater need to check that a proposed name does not lead to unintended ridicule in a foreign language. Neither the French breakfast cereal *Plopsies* (chocolate- flavoured puffed rice) nor the gloriously evocative Slovakian pasta brand *Kuk & Fuk* are serious contenders for launch into an English-speaking market. From a linguistic point of view, care must be taken to avoid certain combinations of letters that are difficult to pronounce in some languages. The combination 'th' is fine in English, but not in French, while the combination 'cz' poses no problem to a Polish speaker, but challenges most of western Europe. The danger is, of course, that by trying to avoid challenging anyone linguistically, imagination is lost and the Eurobrand becomes the Eurobland. Some brand names such as Adidas, Findus, Mars and Lego have nevertheless managed to avoid the pitfalls.

Language problems apart, the ability of a brand name to communicate something about the product's character or functional benefits could be important. Blackett (1985) suggests that approaches to this can vary, falling within a spectrum ranging from freestanding names, through associative names, to names which are baldly descriptive. This spectrum is shown with examples of actual brand names in Fig 7.5. Names which are totally *freestanding* are completely abstract and bear no relation to the product or its character. Kodak is a classic example of such a name. *Associative* names suggest some characteristic, image or benefit of the product, but often in an indirect way. Pledge (furniture polish), Finesse (shampoo), and Impulse (body spray) are all names that make some kind of statement about the product's positioning though the consumer's understanding of the word(s) used in the name. The extremely prosaic end of the spectrum is represented by *descriptive* names. Names such as Chocolate Orange, Shredded Wheat and Cling Film certainly tell you about what the product is, but they are neither imaginative nor easy to protect. Bitter Lemon, for example, began as a brand name and was so apt that it soon became a generic title for any old bottle of lemon-flavoured mixer. Somewhere between associative and descriptive names come a group with names that are descriptive, but with a distinctive twist. Ex-Lax (laxative), Lucozade (fizzy glucose drink) and Bacofoil (aluminium cooking foil) are names that manage to describe without losing the individuality of the brand.

FIGURE 7.5

**The brand name
spectrum**

In summary, there are four 'rules' for good brand naming. As far as possible, they need to be:

1 *distinctive*, standing out from the competition while being appealing to the target market and appropriate to the character of the product;
2 *supportive* of the product's positioning with respect to its competitors (pp. 308 *et seq.* will discuss positioning in further detail), while remaining consistent with the organisation's overall branding policy;
3 *acceptable*, recognisable, pronounceable and memorisable, in other words user-friendly to the consumer; and finally,
4 *available*, registerable, protectable (i.e., yours and only yours).

With respect to this last point, it is important to ensure that the suggested brand name is not infringing the rights of existing brands. This is particularly difficult with international brands. In 1995, for example, a French court ruled that Eurostar, the cross-channel passenger rail service, should change its name to protect the rights of a firm called Eurostart (the two names are, of course, pronounced the same in French).

As mentioned earlier, the establishment of the Community Trade Mark Office means that a single registration can protect all aspects of a brand's identity across Europe. A trade mark search carried out by an agent, costing anything from £200 (for checking out a proposed name) to £2000 (for a detailed search), can help to reassure an organisation that it is not likely to infringe the rights of others. This all suggests that great care needs to be taken when developing brand identities. In order to minimise the risk of either choosing an inappropriate name or the inadvertent breach of another organisation's registered trade marks, many organisations do use professional consultants who specialise in brand concept development and testing, and trade mark searches.

Product range brand policy

For most fmcg organisations, the decision on whether to brand the product range or not is an easy one. Branding is essential for most products in these markets. Difficulty arises with some homogeneous products because in theory the customer does not perceive sufficient difference between competing products to make branding feasible. As suggested at p. 187 in the discussion on undifferentiated products, however, there are fewer and fewer truly homogeneous products to be found. Petrol brands, for example, have now been created which differentiate on the basis of service factors and the use of sales promotions as an integral part of the offering.

Branding is of even less significance when supplying organisational markets, because of the differences in buyer behaviour. There is, however, increasing interest in branding in some sectors. Computer systems are heavily branded for instance, and at the other end of the purchasing spectrum, organisations supplying consumables are turning to branding as a means of trying to engender customer loyalty. Stationery companies, such as Arjo Wiggins Fine papers with its Conqueror, Connoisseur and Keay Kolour brands, are branding paper and other office goods.

Once the decision to brand has been made, there are still a number of choices, one of which is the degree of independence the brand is to be given in terms of its relationship with both other brands and the originating organisation.

Generic brands represent one extreme, where a single brand image covers a wide range of different products. This is mainly found in supermarkets where a range of very low-priced, basic staple products are packaged with the minimum of frills and often the minimum permissible information on the packaging, such as Tesco's Value Lines. This is still a form of branding, in the sense that it is creating a distinctive character for a set of products.

At the opposite extreme, individual products are given entirely separate individual brand identities. There is thus no obvious relationship between different products produced by the same organisation. This is known as *discreet branding*. It is a useful policy to adopt if the intention is to compete in a number of different segments because it reduces the risk of one product's positioning affecting the consumer's perception of another product. It also means that if one product gets into trouble, perhaps through a product tampering scare, or through production problems causing variable quality, the other products are better insulated against the bad reputation rubbing off on to them too. The big disadvantage of the discreet approach to branding, however, is that each brand has to be set up from scratch, with all the expense and marketing problems associated with it. The new brand cannot benefit from the established reputation of any other brand.

One way of allowing brands to support each other is by using a *monolithic* approach to branding, which uses a family name (usually linked with the corporate name) with a single brand identity for the whole product range.

Example

Heinz is a prime example of the monolithic approach. The Heinz brand is well respected and very strong, but individual Heinz products have little identity of their own. Brand names are descriptive, and always include the word Heinz to link them, such as Heinz Cream of Tomato Soup, Heinz Baked Beans, Heinz Low Calorie Mayonnaise etc. Even the label design of each product shows that it clearly belongs to the Heinz family, further drawing the products together. Such family unity creates a strong overall image, and allows new products easy entry into the existing product lines (although it might take consumers a while to notice a new flavour of soup in among the rest). It is also possible to achieve economies of scale in communication, if desired, and distribution, through treating the family as a unit rather than as a number of independent products. The danger is, however, that if one product fails or gains a bad reputation, the rest may suffer with it.

A compromise between monolithic and discreet branding is an approach that allows individual brand images, but uses a corporate or family name as a prominent umbrella to endorse the product. Some organisations, such as Ford and Kellogg's use a *fixed endorsed* approach. Here, there is a rigid relationship between the company name and the brand, with a high degree of consistency between the presentation of different brands (but not as extreme as the Heinz approach). A *flexible endorsed* approach, such as that practised by Cadbury's, gives the brand more latitude to express its individuality. The company name may be more or less prominent, depending on how much independence the organisation wants the brand to have. These products seem to enjoy the best of both worlds. The family name gives the products and any new products a measure of credibility, yet the individuality of the products allows variety, imagination and creativity without being too stifled by the 'house style'. Marketing costs are, however, going to be higher because of the need to develop and launch individual identities for products and then to communicate both the family image and the individual brand images.

Developing a brand extension policy

A kind of flexible endorsement that does not involve the corporate name is where a brand name is developed to cover a limited number of products within a product line.

Example

Reckitt and Colman established the Dettol brand name in 1933. This name has now been expanded to include a whole range of clearly related products, such as Dettox, Dettol antiseptic soap, foam bath, antiseptic cream, wipes, and mouthwash in a mini-family, again capitalising on the established reputation of the 'parent' product.

This example raises the issue of *brand extension*. Dettol has been very successful in launching variants or new products. Such a policy is cost efficient in that it saves the cost of developing totally new images and promoting and building them up from nothing. Consideration of brand extension also begins to highlight some of the marketing issues involved in branding which will be discussed further in the next chapter on product management.

In summary, any individual organisation is faced with a range of decisions including whether or not to brand, the character of its brands and the degree of independence each brand is given. A smaller organisation with limited resources and a limited number of products may take a monolithic approach, whereas a larger organisation may be better able to create discreet brands if it chooses. Whatever the situation, however, the branding and brand management decisions have to be made in the context of market segments, positioning and the competitive environment. Branding can be a strain on resources if the brand identity is not well established or if it is under threat.

An organisation that uses branding effectively, whether creating a monolithic brand family, a fixed or flexible endorsed set of brands, or taking a discreet branding approach, is in a powerful position with the retail trade in gaining shelf space and co-operation. It can also be in a better position to engender consumer loyalty, whether to

The strength of the Dettol brand has allowed numerous extentions.

Source: Cowan Kemsley Taylor.

an individual product or to a range (which would allow product switching within the variety offered in the range, without the loss of overall sales). All of this helps to make branding a very active and strategically important area in marketing.

PACKAGING

Packaging is an important part of the product which not only serves a functional purpose, but also acts as a means of communicating product information and brand character. The packaging is often the consumer's first point of contact with the actual product and so it is essential to make it attractive and appropriate for both the product's and the customer's needs.

> **Example**
>
> McVitie's have managed to differentiate their Jaffa Cakes brand from supermarket 'look-alike' own brands by producing innovative packaging for mini-Jaffa Cakes. The pack consists of six individually sealed plastic segments, joined by perforations, which can be easily separated. The pack is bright orange, with the texture of orange peel to emphasise the nature of the product. Each segment provides a portion of Jaffa Cakes, and can be packed into a lunch box or just used as a convenient snack. Meanwhile, the other five segments remain sealed and therefore stay fresh until required.

Packaging is any container or wrapping in which the product is offered for sale and can consist of a variety of materials such as glass, paper, metal or plastic, depending on what is to be contained. The choice of materials and the design of the packaging may have to take account of the texture, appearance and viscosity of the product, as well as its perishability. Dangerous products such as medicines or corrosive household cleaners need special attention. Other design issues might include the role of the packaging in keeping the product ready for use, the means of dispensing the product, and the graphic design, presenting the brand imagery and the statutory and desired on-pack information.

Naturally, there is a cost involved in all of this, and thus the organisation needs to be reassured that a particular solution to its packaging needs and problems will either serve a functional purpose or enhance the product's image and competitive standing in the market. Equally, trying to save money by skimping on packaging could be a false economy. If the packaging does not work (literally or metaphorically), then the customer is likely to reject the whole product. Although it can cost £100 000 to create a packaging design for an fmcg product, it seems a very reasonable sum compared with the £3 million or more that will be spent on the advertising to launch that same product. Gilgrist (1994), who interviewed a number of consultants in the packaging design field, found that they expressed similar sentiments: that packaging design is often neglected for new products, with all the time and resources going into advertising; that packaging is a powerful tool in helping to create a solid and distinctive brand image; that packaging is a crucial communicator at the point of sale.

With the rise of the self-service ethos in consumer markets, packaging has indeed grown in importance. It has to communicate product information to help the consumer make a choice, to communicate brand image and positioning, and mostly, to attract attention at the point of sale and invite the consumer to explore the product further. Even in organisational markets, packaging is important. To serve organisational customers' needs, suppliers have to think about how best to bundle quantities of product together for ease of handling for fast moving products, how best to protect products which will be held for a time in storage, or how to make it as easy as possible for a customer to unpack and introduce a component or product into a production line.

Thus packaging is an important part of the overall product offering and has a number of marketing and technical dimensions, some of which are discussed below.

Functions of packaging

Functional

First among the functions of packaging are the practicalities. Packaging must be *functional*: it must protect the product in storage, in shipment and often in use. Packaging may consist of a number of layers, each serving a different purpose. A packet of frozen beefburgers, for example, may have an outer cardboard box. This protects the product in transit and handling, creating units of a standard size that can easily be packaged together for delivery to the retailer. The outer box also allows the retail display to be attractive and tidy, presenting necessary product information, cooking instructions, and selling points to be presented to the consumer. Inside the box, the burgers may be sealed in groups of six inside clear plastic wrapping. This prevents them from suffering 'freezer burn', a natural process of deterioration in unprotected frozen food. The individual burgers are finally separated from each other with a single sheet of film to prevent them from sticking together.

Frozen food is not the only area in which it is necessary to preserve freshness. Jars of coffee and cans of dried milk, such as Marvel, have an inner seal which serves the double purpose of keeping the product fresh until it is opened and reassuring the customer that the product has not been tampered with before purchase.

Other packaging functions centre on convenience for the consumer, both in terms of ease of access and ease of use. The ring-pull tins now used for canned sardines, for example, have made the sweat and (usually) bloodshed associated with the old style key-operated tins a thing of the past (corned beef canners take note!). An example of packaging that also helps the usage of the product is shower gel. The lid of the pack, incorporating a hook, is removed and clipped to the bottom of the pack to allow it to be hung in the shower. A self-sealing mechanism in some packs means that the contents do not drip out unless the pack is purposefully squeezed. In the convenience food sector, ease of use has come with the development of packaging that can be placed straight inside a microwave oven and thus serves as a cooking utensil. These last examples also underline the necessity for packaging materials, design and technology to develop in parallel with markets and emerging market needs. Consumer pressure for fewer preservatives and additives in food products has also encouraged the development of packaging that better preserves pack content. Conversely, advances in packaging technology can themselves lead to the opening up of new opportunities. The development of the 'widget', a device incorporated into beer cans, has opened up the market for canned beer that behaves and tastes like draught.

A less positive driving force behind packaging development in the late 1980s was the sad spate of attempts at corporate blackmail through product tampering scares. Manufacturers and retailers alike became very concerned to hasten the development of packaging that was difficult to interfere with without leaving an obvious trace. Many jars or packages now have at least a visually prominent seal on the outer pack with the verbal warning that the product should not be used if the seal is damaged.

Promotional

In addition to offering functional information about product identity and use, packaging also serves a *promotional* purpose. It needs to grab and hold the consumer's attention and involve them with the product. This means that the packaging is actually adding value to the brand; this can be achieved through the combination of materials, shape, graphics and colour.

With some products, the added psychological value of the packaging is an absolutely essential part of the product. Perfumes, for example, rely heavily on their packaging to endorse the qualities of luxury, expense, exclusivity, mystery and self-indulgence that they try to represent. Champagne, a perfume by Yves St Laurent, comes in a crimson-lined gold box, which opens out like a kind of casket to reveal an elegant bottle representing a champagne cork, complete with gold wire. It is estimated that the packaging for such a product actually costs about three times as much as the content of the bottle itself. Closer to the mass market, Easter eggs are also an example of the packaging outshining the content. Novelty carton shapes, bright graphics, ribbons and bows are central to the purchasing decision, and dull any natural inclination to compare the price with the actual chocolate content.

Finally, packaging can literally be used for promotional purposes. It gives the manufacturer a powerful medium of communication. It can be used, for example, as a means of distributing coupons, for advertising other related products, announcing new products, presenting on-pack offers, or distributing samples and gifts. A special can was developed for Lucozade Sport, for example, that allowed 'instant win' vouchers to be sealed into the packaging, separate from the liquid. There is more on all of this in Chapter 17 on sales promotion.

Packaging in the marketing mix

Packaging plays an important part in the marketing mix. This chapter has already outlined its functional importance, its communication possibilities and its crucial role as a first point of physical contact between the buyer and the product. Effective and thoughtful packaging is recognised as means of increasing sales.

Even the choice of the range of pack sizes to offer the market can reinforce the objectives of the marketing mix. Trial size packs, clearly labelled as such, help with new product launch (*see also* Chapter 17) by encouraging low-risk product trial. Small-sized packs of an established product may reinforce a commitment to a market segment comprising single-person households, or infrequent users. Larger packs target family usage, heavy users generally, or the cost-conscious segment who see the large pack as better value for money. The increase in out-of-town shopping by car means that consumers are far better able than ever before to buy large, bulky items. This trend has developed further into the demand for multiple packs. When the US warehouse club Costco first opened in the UK, it only sold in bulk quantities such as gallon jars of HP Sauce, 10-kilo packs of dishwashing powder and 4 kilo packs of minced beef. These sizes were, however, later found to be somewhat larger than the customer really wanted, even when buying in bulk. Pack sizes may also be closely linked with end use segmentation (*see* p. 181). Ice-cream could be packaged as either an individual treat, a family block, or a party-sized tub. The consumer selects the appropriate size depending on the end use, but the choice must be there or else the consumer will turn to another brand.

Any organisation needs to appreciate the changing demands made on packaging as consumers change. These trends can be anticipated or followed, and treated as another tool of competitive strategy. One particular trend over recent years has been pressure on manufacturers to improve the recyclability of their packaging. The European Commission introduced a Directive stipulating that a minimum of half of all waste packaging must be recovered, and at least a quarter must be recycled (but with a minimum of 15 per cent for each different material). The Commission's next step is to look at technical standards, and to decide what can and cannot legally be used in packaging. Some countries already take a more stringent approach to recycling than others, however. As the *Economist* (28 January 1995) pointed out, Germany's rule that at least 72 per cent of drinks bottles should be refillable may be very environmentally laudable, but it does tend to favour local drinks suppliers, against the spirit of the SEM and unrestricted competition. Similarly, Denmark's ban on drinks cans again protects its domestic bottlers against competition.

In developing a new product or planning a product relaunch, an organisation thus needs to think carefully about all aspects of packaging and its integration into the overall marketing mix of the product. The technical and design considerations, along with the likely trade and consumer reactions, need to be assessed. Consumers in particular can become very attached to packaging. It can be as recognisable and as cherished as a friend's face, and consumers may not, therefore, take kindly to plastic surgery! Sudden packaging changes may lead to a suspicion that other things about the product have changed for the worse, too. All of this goes to show that, as with any aspect of marketing, packaging design and concepts need careful research and testing, using where possible one of the growing number of professional consultancies in the field.

Labelling

Labelling is a particular area within the packaging field which represents the outermost layer of the product. Labels have a strong functional dimension, in that they include warnings and instructions, as well as information required by law or best industry practice. Labels state, at the very least the weight or volume of the product (often including a stylised letter 'e' which means that the variation in weight or volume between packs is within certain tolerances laid down by the EU), a barcode and the name and contact address of the producer. Consumer demand has also led to the inclusion of far more product information, such as ingredients, nutritional information and the environmental friendliness of the product. Information about the extent to which the packaging is made of recycled materials or can be recycled is also much more common now.

The EU has turned its attention to nutritional labelling on food products, and issued a Directive offering manufacturers two alternative standard formats for nutritional information on packaging. As Williams (1993) reports, however, consumers

---

MARKETING IN ACTION

Ecolabelling

The European Commission is attempting to develop common standards for various aspects of product labelling. The Ecolabel, for example, based on Germany's well-established *Blue Angel* labelling scheme, gives a consumer reassurance that the product displaying it conforms to EU environmental standards. According to Harding (1995), after Hoover attached a European Ecolabel to its washing machines, it increased its market share in Germany and at the top end of the UK market. There are, however, some reservations about the scheme. First, there is a fear that consumers will think that all washing machines carrying the Ecolabel are the same in terms of their environmental record, and that this

will blur the distinction between the bottom and top ends of the market. Second, the requirements for qualifying for an Ecolabel are not tough enough since they only relate to the machine in use (i.e., energy, water and detergent consumption) rather than to the wider issues of its manufacture and the company's environmental record. Third, the manufacturers are worried about the cost of the Ecolabel, as those using the label have to pay 0.15 per cent of their European turnover to the Ecolabel Board. Kirchenstein and Jump (1993) offer further discussion of the philosophy and implementation of the Ecolabel scheme.

Source: Harding (1995).

have not found either of these formats particularly helpful, because although the consumer is told, for example, how much fat a product contains, there is nothing to indicate whether that quantity constitutes 'a lot of fat'. Williams suggests that a system that provides more interpretation in a graphical way, in the context of health recommendations, would allow consumers to make more informed choices of foods. Shannon (1994) similarly feels that the regulations are still too complex and confusing for the consumer, and need simplifying to provide a system of labelling that is meaningful and useful.

The prominence and detail of health and safety instructions are also becoming increasingly important, as organisations seek to protect themselves against prosecution or civil liability should the product be misused. These instructions range from general warnings to keep a product out of the reach of children, to prohibitions on inhaling solvent-based products, through to detailed instructions about the use of protective clothing.

Clear labelling in terms of the matters discussed in this section is important and necessary. The information may be incorporated into the outer packaging as a whole, or there may be a distinctive and separate label. Many organisational products, for example, may be plainly wrapped and bear a very functional label, serving to identify only the product and its use.

PRODUCT DESIGN, QUALITY AND GUARANTEES

Design

The preceding discussion of packaging has already mentioned one aspect of design. But there is far more to design than just pretty logos, graphics and attractive packaging. Design is an integral part of the product itself, affecting not only its overall aesthetic qualities, but also its ergonomic properties (i.e., the ease and comfort with which it can be used), and even its components and materials. All of this together can enhance the product's visual appeal, its ability to fulfil its function and its reliability and life span.

Industrial designers have to tread a fine line between innovativeness and customer expectations. Microsoft, for example, have designed an ergonomic computer keyboard which allows the wrists and hands to maintain a much more natural position while typing, reducing the risk of strain and making the typist more relaxed. The new keyboard looks good too, with gentle curves replacing the familiar boxy shape of traditional keyboards. The benefits are unquestionable, yet people are so used to the old design that despite the discomforts, they are slow to make the change. Innovative design can, nevertheless, be the making of a product.

Example

Dyson vacuum cleaners are designed to operate without a dust bag, giving the technical benefits of better suction and no risk of blockages or burst bags. The design innovation goes further, however, affecting the aesthetics of the product too. The upright model, the Dyson Dual Cyclone, is generally the same kind of shape as the traditional uprights of companies such as Hoover, yet there are subtle details of styling, colouring and design (for instance the see-through dust collection chamber), that clearly differentiate it from the competition and give the message that here is something more advanced, more futuristic, more exciting than you are used to. All these design advantages allowed Dyson to price their initial product at double the price of the best selling units, and 25 per cent higher than even the highest priced competitor. Despite the price premium, they achieved a 60 per cent share of the upright cleaner segment, including strong sales to the C and D socioeconomic groups (Miles, 1995).

The motor industry is another area in which design plays an important role, since the 'look' of a car says a lot about its distinctiveness and its character. Since the 1980s, European car manufacturers have regained some of the ground lost to Japanese companies by re-emphasizing design individuality in their new models. Renault, for example, with the Twingo, took the risky decision to move away from trying to design a Eurocar, that would offend nobody, towards designing something quirky and unashamedly French. According to Rawsthorne (1994), prelaunch research showed that 40 per cent of the market actively disliked the Twingo, but Renault went ahead anyway and within a year of its launch it had become France's second best selling car. Essentially, what Renault have done is come back to some basics of market segmentation, the philosophy of appealing completely to a small number of customers rather than trying to be all things to all people. Ford, however, still believes that there can be such a thing as a 'world car', that can suit all tastes internationally. It will be interesting to watch this battle between nationalism and internationalism unfold!

Despite the success stories, it must nevertheless be said that design is often not given the recognition or priority that it deserves. Lorenz (1994) gives two broad reasons for this. First, design does not have a clear place in strategic planning, or indeed in the set of strategic concepts that many managers use. Design and its potential contribution is simply not well enough understood by most managers. Second, because design has traditionally been a lowly function, smothered by marketing or engineering departments, it is not given a proper weighting in decision-making processes. Governments have, however, recognised the importance of design in helping industry to gain a sustainable competitive edge in global markets. Bodies such as the UK's Design Council, the Netherlands Design Institute, and the French Agence pour la Promotion de la Création Industrielle promote and support good design practice. The EU also encourages design with initiatives such as the biannual European Community Design Prize aimed at small and medium-sized businesses. The winners in 1994 were Kompan (Denmark: children's playground equipment), Luceplan (Italy: lighting), and Vitra (Swiss, with a German manufacturing base: office furniture).

Quality

Unlike design, quality is a very well understood concept among managers. Many organisations now recognise the importance of quality and have adopted the philosophy of total quality management (TQM), which means that all employees take responsibility for building quality into whatever they do. TQM affects all aspects of the organisation's work, from materials handling to the production process, from the product itself to the administrative procedures that provide customer service. Marketers, of course, have a vested interest in all these manifestations of quality, because creating and holding on to customers means not only providing the quality of product that they want (and providing it consistently), but also supporting the product with quality administrative, technical and after-sales service.

In judging the quality of the product itself, a number of dimensions may be considered, as shown in Fig 7.6.

Performance

Performance is about what the product can actually *do*. Thus with the Bosch hammer drills mentioned earlier (*see* Fig 7.3), a customer might perceive the more expensive

FIGURE 7.6

Product quality dimensions

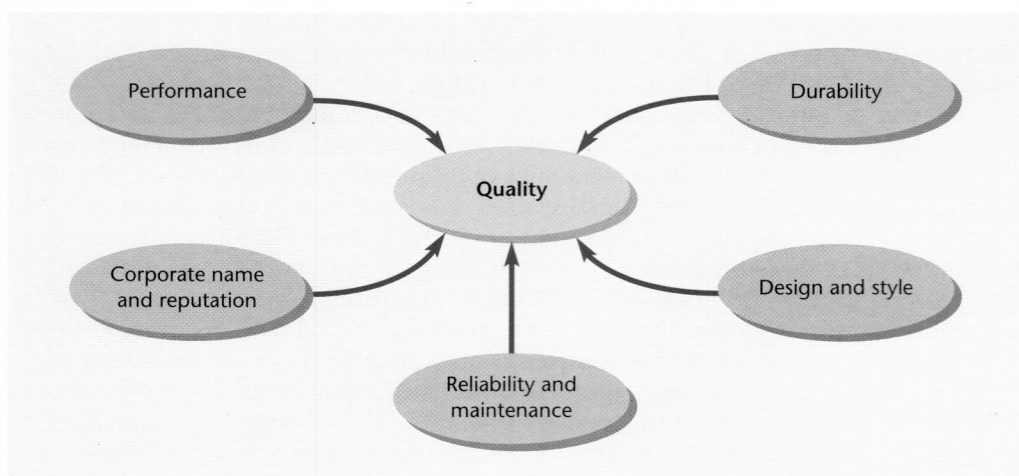

model with a variable speed of 0–4800 rpm as being of 'better quality' than the more basic 2-speed drill. The customer might have more difficulty judging between competing products, however. Black & Decker, for example, produce a range of hammer drills that are very similar to the Bosch ones, with minor variations in specification and price levels. If both the Bosch model and the equivalent Black & Decker model offer the same functions, features, benefits and pricing levels, the customer might have problems differentiating between them in terms of performance and will have to judge on other characteristics.

Durability

Some products are expected to have a longer life span than others, and some customers are prepared to pay more for what they perceive to be a better quality, more *durable* product. Thus the quality level built into the product needs to be suited to its expected life and projected usage. Thus a child's digital watch fitted into a plastic strap featuring a licensed character such as Barbie or Batman, retailing at around £5, is not expected to have the same durability or quality level as a Swiss Tissot retailing at £125. Disposable products in particular, such as razors, biros and cigarette lighters, need to be manufactured to a quality level that is high enough to allow them to perform the required function for the required number of uses or for the required time span, yet low enough to keep the price down to a level where the customer accepts the concept of frequent replacement.

Reliability and maintenance

Many customers are concerned about the probability of a product breaking down or otherwise failing, and about the ease and economy of repairs. As with durability, some customers will pay a price premium for what are perceived to be more *reliable* products or for the peace of mind offered by comprehensive after-sales support. These days most makes of car, for example, are pretty reliable if they are properly maintained, and so car buyers may differentiate on the basis of the cost and ease of servicing, and the cost and availability of spare parts. As mentioned at the beginning of this chapter, among the appealing features of the Trabant are its durability, its reliability, and a mechanical simplicity that allows many repairs to be done by the owner.

Design and style

As mentioned earlier, the visual and ergonomic appeal of a product may influence perceptions of its quality. The sleek, stylish, aerodynamic lines of the Lambourghini contrast sharply with the functional boxiness of the Trabant. Packaging design can also enhance quality perceptions. In the 1995 Design Effectiveness Awards, Coley Porter Bell were commended for their work in redesigning the Cadbury's Milk Tray packaging. Cadbury's had decided that the brand had lost some of its quality image over the years, and so the box was made more rigid and more square, with a framed edge to improve the quality feel. The presentation of the chocolates was improved and the logo made more feminine, to make Milk Tray more appropriate as a gift. The outcome of the relaunch was a sales increase of 20 per cent. (DBA, 1995).

Corporate name and reputation

If, after all that, customers are still uncertain about the relative quality offerings of the alternative products under consideration, they may fall back on their *perceptions of the organisation*. Some may feel that Black & Decker is a well-established, familiar name, and if they have had other Black & Decker products that have served well in the past, then that might swing the quality decision in Black & Decker's favour. Others may decide in favour of Bosch because of its associations with high quality German engineering.

Marketers recognise that quality in the market-place is a matter of perception rather than technical specification. This is particularly true in consumer markets where the potential customer may not have the expertise to judge quality objectively, and will use all sorts of cues, such as price, packaging, or comparison with competitors, to form an opinion about quality level. A survey by Total Research called EquiTrend, reported in *Marketing* magazine (Lane Fox, 1995), measured brand quality perception among consumers of over 170 brands in some 30 product and service categories. Table 7.6 shows the top 10 brands from the 1995 EquiTrend and their overall quality ratings out of a maximum possible score of 10. Incidentally, Bosch power tools came 13th in the list, and Black & Decker power tools came 19th.

Even in organisational markets, the quality agenda is still set by the customer, who will soon let the manufactuer know if their product is unacceptably inconsistent, or

The high quality German engineering heritage enhances a quality reputation.

Source: Robert Bosch.

TABLE 7.6
Brand quality ratings, 1994

Brand	Perceived Quality
Mercedes-Benz	8.57
BMW	8.29
Lego Toys	8.25
Fisher-Price	8.17
Marks & Spencer stores	8.15
Disney World, Florida	8.08
Kellogg's Corn Flakes	7.97
Levi Jeans	7.91
Duracell	7.91
Kodak photographic film	7.86

Source: EquiTrend, Total Research, London. Reprinted with kind permission.

if their response to complaints or queries is too slow or inadequate. If the manufacturer is lucky, the customer will give them warning of their discontent and give them a chance to do something about it, but if the manufactuer is unlucky, the customer will simply stop buying from them. This further underlines the need for some kind of constant dialogue with customers to ensure that the warning signs are picked up early. In general, investment in quality is good for business, creating satisfied and loyal customers.

Guarantees

One way in which an organisation can emphasise its commitment to quality and its confidence in its own products and procedures is through the *guarantees* it offers. Although customers are protected under national and EC laws against misleading product claims and goods which are not fit for their intended purpose, many organisations choose to extend their responsibility beyond the legal minimum. Some will offer extended warranties. Double-glazing companies, for example, routinely offer 10 or 15-year guarantees on their windows, which is fine as long as the company is still in existance in 10 or 15 years' time! Others are less ambitious and simply offer 'no questions asked' refunds or replacements if the customer is unhappy with a product for any reason at all. Retailer Marks & Spencer has operated such a policy for many years, and although it can be abused, it is generally highly valued by customers. In a completely different market, Rover cars offered a similar scheme in which the customer was entitled to a full refund within a month of purchase, regardless of their reasons for returning the car. Such schemes not only reflect the organisation's confidence in its product and its commitment to customer service, but also reduce the risk to the customer in trying the product.

It may also be possible for the organisation to use its guarantees to create a differential advantage over its competitors. The danger is, however, that promises can be copied. The largest UK supermarket chains, for example, trying to shift the emphasis away from price competition to quality of service, are all now offering very similar packages, including refund and replacement schemes on any product that fails to satisfy. Perhaps the real differentiator will be the speed, efficiency and courtesy with which those promises are fulfiled. In strategic terms, the biggest potential problem is that once similar guarantees have become widespread within a particular market or industry, they start to be seen as a normal part of the product package, and their impact may be lost as customers look for other differentiating factors.

CHAPTER SUMMARY

This chapter has provided a broad introduction to the product element of the marketing mix. Product is *defined* as covering a wide variety of goods, services and ideas which can be the subject of a marketing exchange. The product itself is layered, consisting of the core product, the tangible product and, finally, the augmented product. Using the tangible and augmented product, manufacturers, service providers and retailers can create differential advantage.

Products can be *classified* according to either their own characteristics (durable, non-durable or service) or buyer-orientated characteristics. In consumer markets these are linked with the frequency of purchase and the length and depth of the information search. In organisational markets, they are more likely to relate to the final use of the product. An organisation's product mix, made up of individual product items, can be divided into product lines. These are groups of items which have some common link, either operational or marketing based. Product mix width is established by the number of product lines, while product line depth is defined according to the number of individual items within a line.

Branding is an important way of creating differentiated tangible products. It helps the manufacturer to establish loyalty through the three-dimensional character imposed on the product, as well as deflecting consumer attention away from price. The buyer develops a relationship with the product, thus forming strong attitudes and preferences which the competition will find hard to break. The buyer can also identify the product easily at the point of sale, and the manufacturer can use the brand image as an instantly recognisable element in advertising and other communication. Branding is carried out not only by manufacturers, but also by retailers who want to create a more tangible character for themselves, as well as wanting consumers to consciously prefer to shop at their outlets.

Branding issues concerning manufacturers include the choice of *brand name* and the choice of product range *brand policy*. *Packaging* is another important element of the tangible product. It serves the practical purposes of product protection and preservation, and as a source of information about the product and its safe use. It also helps to attract the consumer's attention and to enhance the brand image through its design and materials. The package can also be used for promotional purposes, offering a medium for the distribution of coupons, for instance, or for advertising other products in the range. The organisation's choice of the pack size, or range of sizes to offer, links packaging very closely to aspects of buyer behaviour, perceptions and desired frequency of purchase. *Labelling*, as a specific area of packaging, covers the legally necessary information to be included on the pack as well as the additional information the consumer demands.

Product *design* is an important but often underestimated function, as it can help to create differential advantage, by building in new useful features or benefits, and emphasizing the way in which the product differs. Where potential customers have too little technical knowledge to judge competing products, good design can both appeal on an emotional level and emphasize important features and benefits. In many organisations, however, design is not given the priority, resources or consideration that it deserves, partly because of its traditionally lowly status, and partly because it does not feature strongly in the kinds of strategic planning frameworks that managers commonly use.

Quality is also an important concept, but its contribution, unlike that of design, has been fully recognised, and through TQM programmes it has been integrated into all aspects of organisational performance. In marketing terms, quality is a natural concern, because it is closely linked with satisfying the customer's needs and wants, and creating repeat business. Desired quality standards, in both products and customer service provision, are set by the customers themselves, and thus it is all the more important for the organisation to listen to its customers.

Guarantees reflect the organisation's confidence in its products and its procedures, and reduce the perceived risk to the potential customer in trying a product. These guarantees or manufacturers' warranties are over and above any legal protection to which the customer is entitled. Guarantees can create a differential advantage, provided that the competition cannot copy them, or they might be necessary simply to keep pace with competitors who implemented them first.

Key words and phrases

Augmented product	*Non-durable products*	*Shopping goods*
Branding	*Own label brands*	*Speciality goods*
Convenience goods	*Potential product*	*Tangible product*
Core product	*Product items*	*Unsought goods*
Durable products	*Product lines*	
Manufacturer brands	*Product mix*	

QUESTIONS FOR REVIEW

7.1 What, other than physical goods, might be classed as products?

7.2 What is the *augmented product*, and why might it be important?

7.3 Define *durable* and *non-durable* products, and summarise the likely marketing differences between them.

7.4 What is a *speciality product* and how might its marketing mix and the kind of buying behaviour associated with it differ from those found with other products?

7.5 What are the six different categories within the *user-based product classification system* for organisational products?

7.6 Why do you think the EU felt it necessary to extend the range of things that can be registered as trade marks?

7.7 What benefits does branding offer the consumer?

7.8 Why do retailers develop *own-brand products*?

7.9 What are the advantages and disadvantages of *monolithic* branding compared with *discreet* branding?

7.10 How can design contribute to the success of a new product?

QUESTIONS FOR DISCUSSION

7.1 Choose three different brands of shampoo which you think incorporate different *core products*.

(a) Define the *core product* for each brand.
(b) How does the *tangible product* for each brand reflect the *core product*?

7.2 Adapt Fig 7.1 to suit the specific example of a personal computer:

(a) for family use; and
(b) for the use of a small business.

How do your two diagrams differ from each other, and why?

7.3 Choose a manufacturer of consumer products and list all the brands they sell. How might these brands be grouped into product lines and why? (You might find Fig 7.2 helpful.)

7.4 List as many functions of packaging as you can.

7.5 Develop a weighted set of five or six criteria for 'good' labelling. Collect a number of competing brands of the same product and rate each of them against your criteria. Which brand comes out best? As a result of this exercise, would you adjust your weightings or change the criteria included?

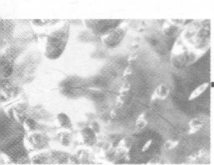

Cott Corporation, cola and copycatting

The Cott Corporation is a Canadian company that specialises in own label manufacture. It deals with over 90 retail chains worldwide, in countries that include Canada, the USA, Japan, France, Spain and the UK. One of its objectives is to challenge Coca-Cola and Pepsi by developing a share of the cola market through own-label products. In some regions of its home market, Canada, for example, it has managed to take a 30 per cent share. Cott has developed a number of slightly different cola concentrates, varying in flavour or sweetness etc. A retailer will choose which one it prefers and then will have exclusive rights to that particular concentrate in its own market. The concentrate is then shipped to a bottling plant which turns it into a drinkable carbonated liquid and bottles or cans it to the retailer's specification.

By concentrating on own label rather than trying to establish a manufacturer brand, Cott gains several advantages. The main one is that its marketing and advertising spend is minimal. This is particularly important in a market in which the two key players, Coca-Cola and Pepsi, commit such vast resources to marketing communication. In the UK alone, Pepsi and Coca-Cola spent £6.2 mn and £8.5 mn respectively on their core brands in 1993. This would make it very difficult and very expensive for a new manufacturer brand to make any impact on its launch. Because Cott's products are own brands, the responsibility for promotion lies with the retailer rather than with Cott. The brand can benefit from the retailer's established corporate image and thus there are not the same problems of having to create a brand image and develop a market position from nothing. There can also be more emphasis on point of sale promotion, and the own brand product can be given adequate shelf space. Similarly, because the product belongs to the retailer, Cott can benefit from the retailer's logistic systems to get the product into the distribution channel.

The retailer benefits too, and not just from having an exclusive product that offers customers a wider choice than just Coca-Cola or Pepsi. Cott's cola concentrates are about one-sixth the price of Coca-Cola or Pepsi, and overall, the retailer can earn around 15 per cent more profit. In Canada, Coca-Cola and Pepsi both lowered their prices and widened retailer margins, but these responses were not sufficient to overcome the attractions of the Cott own brands.

The first Cott brand to hit the UK was Sainsbury's Classic Cola in 1993. Supermarkets had not had notable success with own-label colas up until then. In the take-home market, Coca-Cola had over 60 per cent of the market, Pepsi over 20 per cent and retailer own labels less than 10 per cent. To try to overcome the shoppers' resistance to own-label colas, Sainsbury's decided to go for a relatively discreet approach in that the cola was given a brand identity and character of its own. Although the Sainsbury's name was clearly visible on the packaging, and although everybody knew that it was an own-label product, the Classic Cola brand name, along with a packaging design and colour scheme that was remarkably similar to that of Coca-Cola, persuaded the public that this was a quality product worth trying and not just another second-rate supermarket own label. Sainsbury's also threw itself wholeheartedly into the launch, with substantial advertising in the run-up to it. At the time of the launch, Classic Cola dominated Sainsbury's shelf space and was offered at introductory prices that significantly undercut the competition to generate trial of the product. The launch was extremely successful. Nine weeks after the launch, Classic Cola had captured 25 per cent of the UK's take-home cola sales, and within Sainsbury's stores, accounted for 75 per cent of sales with Coca-Cola dropping from 44 per cent to 9 per cent of Sainsbury's cola sales.

Much of this shift in share was, of course, a result of the launch hype and was bound to settle down. Even so, by August 1994, Sainsbury's still held nearly 16 per cent of the take-home cola market, and Coca-Cola was down to around 40 per cent with Pepsi just over 15 per cent. By the autumn of 1994, Cott had two more colas on the UK market: Woolworths' Genuine American Cola, and Virgin Cola, a joint venture between Cott and Virgin, and initially sold exclusively through Tesco supermarkets.

One issue that the launch of Classic Cola brought to the fore was that of copycat brands, that is, retailer own-label products that look very similar to established manufacturer brands and often even have similar sounding names. Coca-Cola objected to Classic Cola's cans, which, in Coca-Cola's opinion, looked so similar to Coca-Cola's that shoppers might easily confuse the two. Under pressure from Coca-Cola, Sainsbury's did redesign the packaging to differentiate it further from

Coca-Cola, but nevertheless, retained the distinctive red and white colour scheme. Both sides quoted research to support their point of view. Sainsbury's maintained that their product could not possibly be mistaken for Coca-Cola, whereas Coca-Cola said that its surveys showed that consumers were easily confused. Similarly, as part of the wider debate on copycat brands generally, the brand manufacturers' independent survey showed that over 20 per cent of shoppers had actually bought own labels in mistake for manufacturer brands and that 42 per cent had at least picked up own labels from the shelf thinking that they were manufacturer brands. In contrast, the retailers' independent survey showed that 70 per cent of shoppers never get the two types of brand confused.

Sources: Marketing (1994); FT, 24/3/94; FT, 11/5/94; FT, 20/7/94; FT, 15/6/94; FT, 6/5/95.

Questions

1 Why did Cott choose to challenge Coca-Cola's and Pepsi's dominance through own-label products rather than through a mainstream manufacturer brand?

2 Given that both Coca-Cola and Pepsi are good quality, popular brands, why should a retailer such as Sainsbury's want an own-label cola?

3 What contribution do you think the branding and packaging strategy adopted by Sainsbury's made to the success of the product launch? Was Coca-Cola right to object to the packaging's similarity to its own? Why?

4 What are the risks arising from copycatting for:
(a) the retailer; and
(b) the manufacturer whose brand has been copycatted?

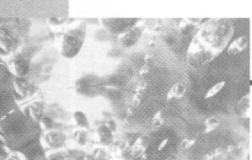

CASE STUDY 7.2

German diesel railcar

The German railway system still has a relatively high density of small branch lines. They do not carry many passengers, but they do provide an important social benefit to the communities they serve. The service operators, however, are coming under increasing pressure to improve their efficiency and cut their costs. One way of doing this is to update and improve the rolling stock on these lines, and a number of railcar builders have risen to the challenge of designing new stock.

The changing political and legislative environment was the main stimulus for this development. The country's regional railways were passed to the 15 Länder (regional government) from the start of 1996 as part of the process of developing a unified German system and in preparation for privatisation in the late 1990s. The Länder became responsible for planning and raising finance for regional lines, although the operation of services still primarily rested with the Deutsche Bundesbahn (DBAG). This was done to make it easier to integrate regional railways with city tramways and local bus services, thus improving the service offered and encouraging greater use of public transport.

Central government gave DM 8.2 bn to be split between the Länder for local rail services. Out of this, the Länder have to pay DBAG to run the train services.

The Länder do get the passengers' ticket revenue, but on branch lines, this is unlikely to cover the cost of providing the service. The Länder are thus subsidising the service, and if the grant from central government runs out, the Länder have to meet any extra outgoings from their own funds. As a result of this, the Länder are naturally seeking cost-effective ways of maintaining the level of service within the constraints of the central government grant. One solution was to invest in new railcars with lower operating costs, since the Länder were now free to make their own purchasing decisions, independently of DBAG.

A new lightweight passenger railcar design was therefore necessary. It had to be capable of carrying around 70 passengers over poorer quality lines. It also had to be able to travel over urban tramways, thus the need for a lightweight design. After the announcement of the changes in railway management in 1994, a number of manufacturers saw an opportunity to develop a new product concept that met the Länder usage criteria as well as the technical operating criteria imposed by DBAG and other train operating companies who would actually be running and maintaining the equipment.

Nine manufacturers had lightweight railcars to offer by 1995 including, for example:

1 *RegioSprinter*: Duewag, part of the Siemens group, was the first entrant into the market with a prototype railcar. The operating specification included a three section aluminium body, a low floor for urban use and a maximum speed of 100 kph. The cost was DM 1.58 mn for a 74-seater compared with DM 3.8 mn for a conventional 136-seater. The first order for 16 units soon came from the Dürener Kreisbahn (DKB), an urban rail and bus company based at Düren, between Aachen and Köln. A further order followed from the Saschen region for railcars to be used on branch lines in the Chemnitz area.

2 *Eurailbus*: this was a joint venture between Neoplan, a bus builder based in Stuttgart, SüdBadenBus, a bus operator from Freiburg and De Dietrich, a French manufacturer of passenger rolling stock. Each partner brought different experiences to the product design process. Offering a similar specification to the RegioSprinter, it had a top speed of 120 kph and like other designs it offered flexibility in seating, standing space etc. The design was still at the prototype stage and no commercial orders had been received by early 1996.

3 *GTW2/6*: this was an adaptation of a design used successfully in Switzerland. It was developed by AEG Schienenfahrzeuge, part of the ABB-Daimler Benz transport group, in partnership with two Swiss companies, Stadler and SLM. The railcar seats 104, again in a three-module aluminium body. The maximum speed is 120 kph. This design has a technical advantage in that it can cope better with poor and curving branch lines.

4 *Regio-Shuttle*: this was considered to be a more traditional design than the rest, less of a cross between a train and a tram. The prototype was planned for launch in 1996 by ABB Henschel. Its maximum speed is 120 kph and the powerful motors in either single, two- or three-car formats were designed for German rural routes. Even before serious prototype testing, the Bavarian Land had committed itself to 11 units at DM 1.9 mn each. Interest was also being expressed by local railways in Baden-Württemberg, south of Stuttgart.

5 *Double decker railbus*: this design emanated from DWA and its Berlin research institute. As a double decker, it is a major departure from conventional designs and can carry between 138 and 177 passengers in various configurations. It was also promoted as leading to greater cost savings than any of the other competitors. The operational prototype was shown at the Hannover Spring Fair in 1994 with a price tag of around DM 1.8 mn. The first commercial order was from Thuringen Land.

Other entrants to the market offered their own design alternative, to suit the customer's needs.

These new products are not just a result of the opportunity emerging from the Länder's new-found purchasing power. Overcapacity in the rolling stock industry has led to much more aggressive competition, and also, DBAG has allowed manufacturers much more design freedom. All of this has created considerable interest from the manufacturers and has resulted in a number of radical design departures and the adaptation of technologies from tram and bus systems.

Sources: Freeman Allen (1995); *Modern Railways* (1995).

Questions

1 What is the core product and what is the tangible product offered:
   (a) to the Länder; and
   (b) to the rail passengers?

2 What are the main influences that have impacted on the design of the various railcars on offer?

3 What quality dimensions are likely to be most important to the Länder?

4 In what ways do you think the design process might differ for a consumer good compared with an organisational product such as the railcar?

REFERENCES TO CHAPTER 7

Blackett, T. (1985), 'Brand Name Research – Getting it Right', *Marketing and Research Today*, May, pp. 89–93.

DBA (1995), *Design Effectiveness Awards*, Design Business Association/Marketing.

De Ulloa, G. (1995), 'The Community Trade Mark Office', *Managing Intellectual Property*, Litigation Yearbook, pp. 17–18.

Doyle, P. (1994), *Marketing Management and Strategy*, Prentice Hall.

Economist (1995), 'Tied up in Knots', 28 January, p. 62.

Freeman Allen, G. (1995), 'New German Lightweight Railcars', *Modern Railways*, June, pp. 355–7.

Gilgrist, A. (1994), 'Pack to the Future', *Marketing Week*, 18 November, pp. 48–50.

Gilmour, F. (1989), 'Brand Blueprint', *Marketing*, 28 September, pp. 34–5.

Gooding, K. (1995), 'Alcoa Shifts Goalposts for Drinks Packaging', *Financial Times*, 24 January, p. 27.

Green, J. (1994), 'Make Sure You Wear Some Water', *Daily Express*, 26 October, p. 21.

Harding, J. (1995), 'Sticking Point for Fresh Green Products', *Financial Times*, 29 March, p. 16.

Kirchenstein, J. J. and Jump, R. (1993), 'The European Ecolabels and Audits Scheme: New Environmental Standards for Competing Abroad', *Total Quality Environmental Management*, 3(1), pp. 53–62.

Kotler, P. (1994), *Marketing Management: Analysis, Planning, Implementation and Control*, (8th edn), Prentice Hall International.

Lane Fox, H. (1995), 'As You Like It', *Marketing*, 22 June, pp. 18–19.

Lorenz, C. (1994), 'Skin-deep Styling is Not Enough', *Financial Times*, 13 June, p. 17.

Luesby, J. (1995), 'Mystery Markers to Unmask Copycats', *Financial Times*, 28 April, p. 13.

Marketing (1994), 'CopyCotting Catches On', *Marketing*, 20 October, p. 17.

Miles, L. (1995), 'Mothers and Fathers of Invention', *Marketing*, 1 June, pp. 26–7.

Modern Railways (1995), 'EuropeView', *Modern Railways*, July, pp. 421–2.

Rawsthorn, A. (1994), 'Talent Needs Intelligence Too', *Financial Times*, 13 June, p. 16.

Richards, A. (1995a), 'Mars: Never Say Never', *Marketing*, 15 June, p. 13.

Richards, A. (1995b), 'Heinz B Brands Turn to Europe', *Marketing*, 28 September, p. 4.

Shannon, B. (1994), 'Nutrition Labelling: Putting the Consumer First', *British Food Journal*, 96(4), pp. 40–4.

Slingsby, H. (1994), 'Distinguishing Marks', *Marketing Week*, 11 November, pp. 40–1.

Sunday Times (1993), 'Adult Disneyland', *Sunday Times*, 28 November.

Teather, D. (1995), 'Out of the Cold', *Marketing*, 2 November, pp. 26–9.

Williams, C. (1993), 'Graphical Nutritional Labelling: The Need for Consumer Research', *British Food Journal*, 95(6), pp. 25–30.

8 Product Management

LEARNING OBJECTIVES

This chapter will help you to:

1 understand the product life-cycle concept, its influence on marketing strategies and its limitations;

2 appreciate the importance of product positioning and how it both affects and is affected by marketing strategies;

3 understand the scope and implications of the various decisions that management can take with regard to product ranges, including deletion;

4 define the role and responsibilities of the product or brand manager; and

5 outline the issues surrounding pan-European branding.

INTRODUCTION

The previous chapter defined what a product is and some of the terms that are used in talking about products within organisations and markets. Even that general overview raised a number of strategic issues relating to how an organisation is supposed to manage such an important resource as its product range. This chapter addresses those issues.

Products need managing throughout their working lives. Someone has to decide what products should be created and when is the best time to launch them. Someone has to help the product to capitalise on its strengths and iron out its weaknesses. Someone has to decide whether an older product, past its prime, should have its life extended through modification or marketing strategy or whether it should be allowed to die peacefully. Such decisions are critical to an organisation's strategy, since after all, the product range is at the heart of the supplier–buyer relationship. Product management, therefore, needs clear lines of authority and effective and efficient organisation. In consumer markets, many product management decisions are made by the marketing manager, but in organisational markets, responsibility is shared across a range of functional areas, including research and development (R&D), engineering and the after-sales service personnel.

This chapter is concerned with the strategic concepts and tools that help those managers, whether marketers or engineers, to make the best decisions about their products. The first concept presented is that of the product life-cycle. This traces the life story of the product, helping managers to understand the pressures and opportunities affecting products as they mature. The important area of new product development is considered in the next chapter, but the difficulties of supporting a product in its early stages are addressed here as being crucial to the future well-being of the product. Within a product range, some products can live very long and profitable lives, such as Smarties, Dettol, Bovril, Mars Bar, and, of course, Coca-Cola.

To create and sustain long-lived brands such as those listed above, the product range needs to be managed in sympathy with changes in the customer and competitive environment through the concept of product positioning and repositioning. This may involve changes in marketing strategies including promotion, packaging, design, or even in the target market profile. In the 1960s, for example, Coca-Cola introduced the can of coke for the first time in addition to the traditional bottle. This changed the way in which the product was purchased and consumed, and thus its image. Every product has to be assessed and managed according to how the consumer perceives it in relation to the competition. This is a natural extension of the targeting decision discussed at p. 185.

The natural processes of product maturity and decline lead to the discussion of product deletion issues. No product has an infinite life span, and deciding the best time either to refresh and relaunch a product or to withdraw it altogether is a difficult one. It requires a critical review of the product's market performance, an analysis of its past (and potential future) contribution to overall profitability, and a sound grasp of what is happening in the market.

Finally, this chapter returns to the practical problems of managing these processes, presenting a brief overview of product management structures as a foretaste of the more detailed review in Chapter 22.

THE PRODUCT LIFE-CYCLE

The **product life-cycle** (PLC) concept reflects the theory that products, like people, live a life. They are born, they grow up, they mature and eventually, they die. During its life, a product goes through many different experiences, achieving varying levels of success in the market. This naturally means that the product's marketing support needs also vary, depending on what is necessary both to secure the present and to work towards the future. Figure 8.1 shows the theoretical progress of a PLC, indicating the pattern of sales and profits earned. The diagram may be applied either to an individual product or brand (for example Kellogg's Cornflakes), or to a product class (breakfast cereals).

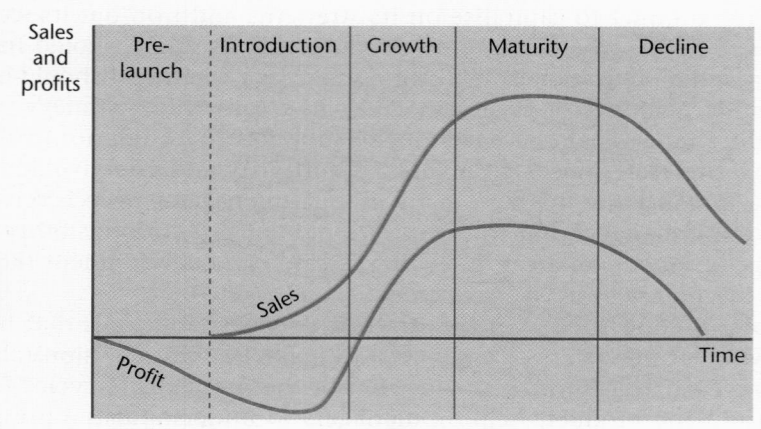

FIGURE 8.1

The product life-cycle

The PLC concept offers no hard and fast rules for product management, but it can act as a useful guide for thinking about what a product has achieved and where it is heading in the future. There are, however, some reservations about the usefulness of this concept (Dhalla and Yuspeh, 1976). As you read the rest of this section, think about what those reservations might be, then compare your thoughts with the critical appraisal of the concept at pp. 300 *et seq*. First, it is important to describe in some detail the stages of the PLC. Figure 8.1 indicates that there are four main stages in the PLC: introduction, growth, maturity and decline, and these are now discussed in turn along with their implications for marketing strategy.

Stage 1: Introduction

At the very start of the product's life as it enters the market, sales will begin build slowly and profit may be small (even negative). A slow build-up of sales reflects the lead time required for marketing efforts to take effect and for people to hear about the product and try it. Low profits are partly an effect of the low initial sales and partly a reflection of the possible need to recoup development and launch costs.

The marketer's main priority at this stage is to generate widespread awareness of the product among the target segment and to stimulate trial. If the product is truly innovative, there may be no competitors yet and so there is the added problem of building primary demand (i.e., demand for the class of product rather than simply demand for a specific brand) as a background to the actual brand choice.

In most cases, the new product is an addition to an existing market and will either be targeted at a different segment or be offering additional features and benefits. There are a number of problems facing the marketer. First, there is a need to gain distribution. With new fmcg goods, the retail trade may be hard to convince unless the product has a real USP (unique selling point), because of the pressure on shelf space and the proliferation of available brands. In parallel with that, there is still the task of generating awareness among consumers and moving them through towards a purchase. The decision on the product's price, whether to price high or low, or whether to offer an introductory trial price, could be an important element in achieving that first purchase.

Given the failure rate of new products and the importance of giving a product the best possible start in life, the introduction stage is likely to make heavy demands on marketing resources. This can be especially draining for a smaller organisation, but nevertheless is necessary if the product is to survive into the next stage: growth.

MARKETING IN ACTION

Male fragrance

It has taken 40 years to build a substantial market for male aftershave in the UK. Brands such as Old Spice and Brut have helped to create a mass market, reassuring men that smelling nice is not just for wimps. This was reinforced by the overtly male brand imagery of products like Hai Karate, Pagan Man and Cossack in the 1970s. Now that aftershave is established as a normal part of the male bathroom cabinet, the marketers are trying to broaden the scope of male grooming products, to include fragrances, body sprays, and cosmetics. Many of these newer products carry designer names, such as Issy Miyake, Armani, Calvin Klein, and Yves St Laurent, emphasising their fashionability and stylishness rather than functional manliness. These markets are no longer to be sniffed at! The more mature aftershave market, for instance, was worth some £212 mn in 1993, while fragrances were worth £145 mn and body sprays £39 mn.

Source: Moir (1994).

It didn't need a designer's name to make Lynx the UK's best selling male toiletry brand.

Source: Elida Fabergé Ltd.

Stage 2: growth

In the growth stage, there is rapid increase in sales. One reason for this might be that word is getting around about the product and the rate of recruitment of new triers accelerates. Another reason is that the effects of repeat purchases are starting to be seen. There is some urgency at this stage to build as much brand preference and loyalty as possible. Competitors will now have had time to assess the product, its potential and its effect on the overall market, and will thus have decided their response. They may be modifying or improving their existing products, or entering a new product of their own into the market. Whatever they do, they will deflect interest and attention away from the product, and there is a risk that this will flatten the growth curve prematurely unless the company takes defensive steps.

Example

Virgin decided to enter the growing Personal Equity Plans (PEPs) market by setting up a completely new company, Virgin Direct Personal Financial Services, in partnership with Norwich Union. The attraction of the market for Richard Branson was clear, as *The Sunday Times* reported:

> 'I **cannot walk past a fat and complacent business sector without wanting to shake it up a bit.**'

The company felt there was an opportunity to offer direct sales to the consumer, with no high pressure selling, no hidden charges, and no jargon, unlike many of the more traditional financial services organisations. Thus the growth stage of the PEPs market could support a new entrant, with sufficient untapped potential to allow the opening up of a new segment of uncertain investors looking for the reassurance of a trustworthy name (Hinde, 1995).

Figure 8.1 shows that profits start to rise rapidly in this stage. This too might be affected by competitive pressure, if other organisations choose to compete on price, forcing margins down. Again, repeat purchases which build brand loyalty are the best defence in these circumstances.

Even though the product might seem to be still very young and only just starting to deliver its potential, towards the close of the growth stage might be a good time to think about product modifications or improvements either to reinforce existing segments or to open up new ones. This is about keeping one step ahead of the competition. If the initial novelty of your product has worn off, buyers might be vulnerable to competitors' new products. This might also threaten the security of your distribution channels, as heavy competition for shelf space squeezes out weaker products perceived as heading nowhere. This all reinforces, yet again, the need for constant attention to brand building and the generation of consumer loyalty, as well as the necessity for the cultivation of good relationships with distributors.

Another good reason for considering modifying the product is that by now you have real experience of producing and marketing the product. The more innovative the product (whether innovative for your organisation or innovative within the market), the more likely it is that experience will have highlighted unforeseen strengths and weaknesses in the product and its marketing. This is the time to learn from that experience and fine tune the whole offering or extend the product range to attract new segments.

> ### Example
>
> Forte decided to develop its Travelodge concept, with budget-priced, but well-appointed hotels sited close to motorways and other major trunk routes to cater for the long-haul traveller. This is in contrast to their more luxurious and traditional hotels sited in cities and tourist centres.

This is not to imply that an organisation should advocate change for the sake of change. Any changes must be the result of detailed analysis of what is happening in the market and projections of what is likely to happen in the event of various developments taking place. It is strategic change, it is planned change, it is purposeful change in the best interests of the organisation, the product and the customer.

At some point, the growth period comes to an end as the product begins to reach its peak and enters into the next stage: maturity.

Stage 3: Maturity

During the maturity stage, the product achieves as much as it is going to. The accelerated growth levels off, as everyone who is likely to be interested in the product should have tried it by now, and a stable set of loyal repeat buyers should have emerged. This is not a cause for complacency, however. There are few new customers available, and even the laggards have purchased by now. This means that there is a high degree of customer understanding of the product and possibly of the market. They know what they want, and if your product starts to look dated or becomes unexciting compared with newer offerings from the competition, then they might well switch brands. Certainly, the smaller or more poorly positioned brands are going to be squeezed out. In these circumstances, the best hope is to consolidate the hard-core loyal buyers, encouraging heavier consumption from them. It may also be possible to convert some brand switchers into loyal customers through the use of sales promotions and advertising.

At this stage, there is likely to be heavy price competition and increased marketing expenditure from all competitors in order to retain brand loyalty. Much of this expenditure will be focused on marketing communication, but some may be channelled into minor product improvements to refresh the brand. Distribution channels may also need careful handling at this stage. Unless the product remains a steady seller, the retailer may be looking to delist it to make room on the shelves for younger products.

The sales curve has reached a plateau, as the market is saturated and largely stable. Any short-term gains will be offset by similar losses, and profits may start to decline because of price competition pressure. It is thus very important to try, at least, to retain existing buyers. Sooner or later, however, the stability of the maturity phase will break, either through competitive pressure (they are better at poaching your customers than you are at poaching theirs) or through new developments in the market that make your product increasingly inappropriate, pushing the product into the decline stage.

Example

It is possible for the marketer to take action to extend the maturity stage, or even to stimulate new growth in the market. Scotch whisky is a mature product (in all senses of the phrase) in its biggest markets, the UK and France. This is partly because of the high level of competition in the market, over 2000 brands, and partly because of the image of whisky as 'something your parents drink'. The potential to inject new life into the market has come from the trend in countries such as Portugal, Spain and Greece, where whisky is commonly drunk with water, ice or cola by the under-30 years age group. If whisky manufacturers can successfully give their brands a more youthful emphasis and a more consistent European image then they may be able to extend the life-cycle still further. United Distillers, for example, are using advertising for their Johnny Walker Red brand in Belgium, the Netherlands, Portugal, Italy and eastern Europe to appeal to younger, more discerning drinkers (Mazur, 1994).

Berenson and Mohr-Jackson (1994) suggest that organisations often turn to new products rather than rejuvenating existing ones to extend their life-cycles. They consider that rejuvenation can be a better option, provided that the organisation thinks about five issues:

1 Why the product is going into decline.
2 Whether the marketing environment is right for a rejuvenation strategy.
3 What the product name communicates to the market.
4 Whether there is still a potential segment worth reaching.
5 Whether there is any possibility of creating value for customers.

These questions can help the organisation to assess the relative advantages of rejuvenation over a full new product launch.

Stage 4: Decline

Once a product goes into decline for market-based reasons, it is almost impossible to stop it. The rate of decline can be controlled, to some extent, but inevitably, sales and profits will fall regardless of marketing effort.

Example

Butlin's holiday camps grew rapidly in the 1950s as the C2, D and E socioeconomic groups in particular had more leisure time and more disposable income for family holidays. However, by the 1970s, trends in the marketing environment were working against the established Butlin's concept. Holiday-makers found cheaper and sunnier alternatives in Spain, rejected the highly regimented and enclosed atmosphere of the holiday camp, and came to expect much higher standards of facilities and entertainment. Although some camps were modernised, repositioned and relaunched to suit changing tastes, others such as the one in Filey had to be closed.

Decline can often be environment related rather than a result of poor management decisions. Technological developments or changes in consumer tastes, for example, can lead to the demise of the best managed product.

Example

The introduction into the mass market of CD players led to the virtual extinction of vinyl records as the record companies exploited the growth of the new medium. There was a deliberate strategic decision to pull resources and marketing expertise away from vinyl, based on analysis of market trends. In this example, vinyl was an innocent victim of the changing technological environment.

Some products are deliberately sacrificed on the altar of consumer demand. Fashion products with a naturally short PLC capitalise on shifting consumer tastes and the rise and fall of popular icons, and are managed with the expectation of a short maturity and a quick decline.

Faced with a product in decline, the marketer has a difficult decision of whether to try slowing down the decline with some marketing expenditure, or to milk the product by withdrawing support and making as much profit out of it as possible as it heads towards a natural death. In the latter case, the withdrawing of marketing support aimed at distributors in particular is quite likely to speed up the delisting process.

The problem with a declining product is that it can absorb a great deal of management time for relatively little reward. Decisive action is called for so that management effort can go into the newer products that need it. There are a number of possible options for dealing with declining products. The option of complete deletion is considered separately at p. 317.

Milking or harvesting

The strategy of milking or harvesting centres around the idea of allowing nature to run its course with little or no marketing support. The product is allowed to fade away naturally while the profits are reaped. After all, if a product has had a long and useful life, and has built up a good solid core of loyal users, it is not going to die overnight and the organisation might as well extract the last little bit of return on the investment it has made in the product over the years. Let the buyers drift away gradually and let the product die when it is no longer economic to produce it or when the retailers drop it.

This strategy has the advantage of maximising the useful life of the product, as well as generating the cash and the time to help establish new products. The slow decline of the product gives the organisation adjustment time to get used to the declining cash flow and to find other means of generating revenue. It is also less of a shock to the consumer (and other interested parties in the market) than the sudden disappearance of what might still be a popular product, with all the resentment that would cause.

Phased withdrawal

The milking strategy has a certain amount of drift attached to it. The product can continue indefinitely, as long as there is a purchaser out there. With a phased withdrawal, however, the ultimate cut-off date for the product is set, along with a number of interim staging posts. The interim stages might involve pulling the product gradually from different channels of distribution, or might focus on withdrawal from geographic areas.

The planned withdrawal does have some certainty about it. The organisation knows in advance what is going to happen to the product and can take that into account when planning its marketing strategies. It also allows time to plan replacement products (with the possibility of phasing them in as the old product is phased out), and does not cut off the income from the declining product prematurely. For the customer, however, there is an element of unpleasant surprise if the product disappears from their favourite retailer or from their area suddenly.

Car manufacturers normally operate on a phased withdrawal basis, so that both dealers and the public are well aware of when new models will be launched. Renault thus phased out the Renault 25 in readiness for the launch of the Safrane in 1993.

Contracting out or selling

A way of keeping loyal users of the product happy is to sell the brand to a niche operator or to subcontract its marketing and/or production. To a smaller, perhaps more flexible firm, the remains of the product's market might represent a manageable challenge which could earn what seems to them to be a satisfactory return. This way, the originating organisation is rid of a product it no longer wants, consumers do not lose a product that they do want, and the subcontractor or buyer gains access to, and experience with, a brand that they could probably never have built for themselves.

Example

A large organisation might buy a brand if it feels that it can do a better marketing job than the original owner. Quaker, for example, bought Snapple, a US fruit drink brand in 1994 for $1.7 bn. The product was already in decline at the time of the purchase, but sales fell by a further 17 per cent in the first half of 1995. Quaker were still optimistic about the potential future of the brand in the UK, claiming to be working on establishing solid distribution networks and gradually building consumer loyalty by rolling out the product region by region (Teather, 1995).

Once the decision is made and the implementation plans drawn up, the process can be allowed to run its course with the minimum of managerial interference.

Facets of the PLC

The PLC is more of a guide to what could happen rather than a prescription of what will happen. At its best, it does provide some useful indications at each stage of some of the marketing problems and issues that could arise. It is, after all, a form of collective wisdom based on the history of many brands.

In reality, however, it is too general and superficial a concept to stand alone as it is. Before applying the concept in practice, it is necessary to dig deeper and think about a number of issues before the PLC becomes a really useful tool.

Length of PLC

How long is a piece of string? It is very difficult to predict how long it will take a product to move through its life. The length of the PLC varies not only from market to market, but also from brand to brand within a market. Some board games, for example, such as Monopoly, Scrabble and more recently Trivial Pursuit are well-established, long-term sellers, whereas other games, particularly those linked with television shows (remember Countdown, Blockbusters, and Neighbours board games?) have much shorter spans.

It is even more difficult to predict when the key transition periods from one stage to the next will happen, yet this is critical information for planning strategy changes. The problem is that the length of the PLC is affected by so many things. It is not only the pace of change in the external environment, but also the organisation's handling of the product throughout its life. The organisation's willingness and ability to communicate effectively and efficiently with both the trade and the consumer, their policy of supporting the product in the critical early period, and their approach to defending and refreshing their products will all affect how the PLC develops.

Self-fulfilling prophecy

Linked with the previous point, there is a real danger that the PLC can become a self-fulfilling prophecy. A marketing manager might, for example, imagine that a product is about to move from growth into maturity. Theory may suggest appropriate marketing strategies for this transition, and if these are implemented, the product will start to behave as though it is mature, whether it was really ready for it or not. This demonstrates a basic marketing dilemma: should the PLC drive marketing strategies, or should the PLC be defined as an outcome of strategies derived through other means?

The shape of the PLC

The shape of the PLC offered in Fig 8.1 is necessarily a generalisation. Products which get into marketing problems at any PLC stage will certainly not follow this pattern. Products which spend relatively longer in one stage than another will also have distorted PLC curves. A product which has a long and stable maturity, for instance, will show a long flat plateau in maturity rather than Fig 8.1's gentle hillock. Different market circumstances could also distort this hypothetical curve. Five different scenarios, the innovative product, the imitative product, the fashion product, the product failure, and the revitalisation, each with its own PLC shape, are shown in Fig 8.2.

Innovative product. The innovative product is breaking totally new ground and cannot really utilise consumers' previous experience as a short cut to acceptance. The marketer will have to overcome ignorance, suspicion and scepticism, thus extending the introduction stage. People feel that they have managed perfectly well without this product in the past, so why do they need it now? This is a question that both microwave oven producers and 3M, the manufacturers of Post-It Notes, have managed to answer to the customer's satisfaction. Having to educate the market from scratch is neither easy nor cheap. Sony, in introducing the Walkman, had to undertake this task, and of course, they not only laid the foundations for their own product, but also broke the ground for 'me too' subsequent imitative entrants.

As said at p. 295, the introductory stage does hinge on creating awareness, encouraging trial of the product and winning over the retail trade. In the case of innovative products, this is an even more crucial, but much longer process.

Imitative product. Imitative products, such as new confectionery brands, or the first non-Sony walkman, do not require as much spadework as the innovative product. They take advantage of the established market and the buyer's existing knowledge and past experience, and thus will move into the growth stage very quickly. The main considerations for the imitative marketer are establishing clear, differentiated positioning of the product against existing brands, encouraging trial and making repeat purchase as easy as possible.

Fashion product. Fashion products have a naturally short PLC. Fads are an extreme form of fashion product, accentuating the rapid sales increase followed by the rapid decline. The timing of entry into the market is critical, and those who succeed in

FIGURE 8.2

**PLC Variations of
a theme**

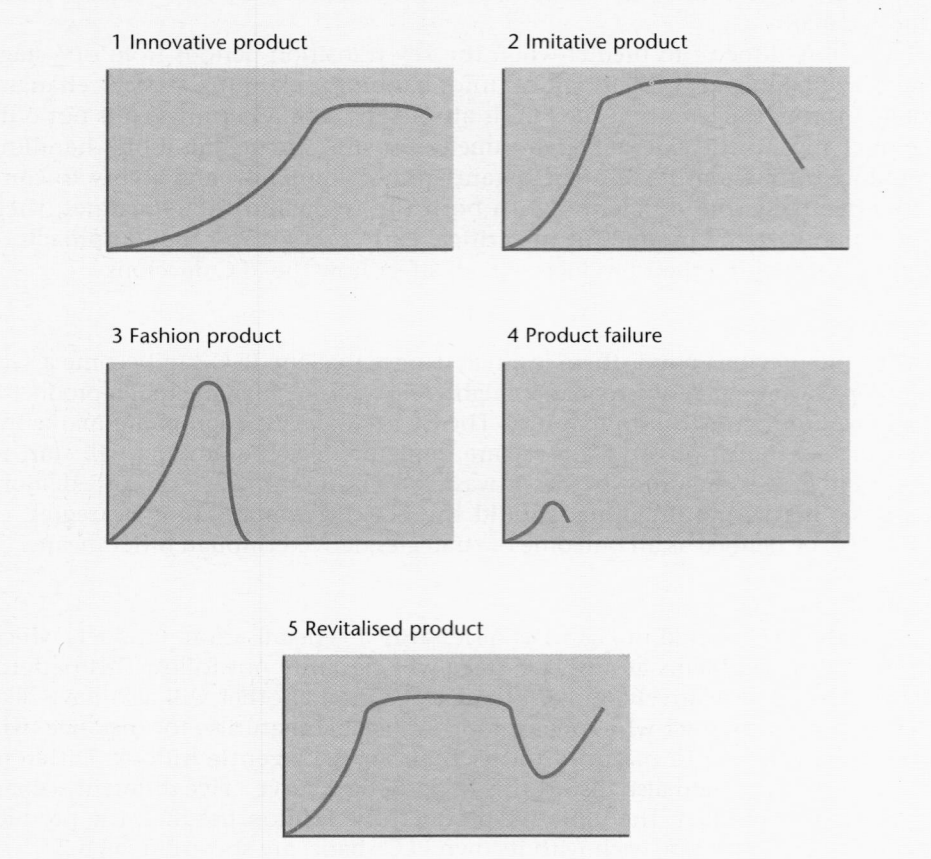

Example

The party dresses designed for the Christmas market appear in the High Street shops in late autumn and disappear again after the January sales. This implies a Matterhorn-shaped PLC curve as shown in Fig 8.2(3), with a very rapid rise to a short maturity and an equally rapid decline. Such an ephemeral existence requires a lot of forward planning, as there is no time to adjust the marketing mix once the product is launched. Note, however, that not all clothing products conform to this model. Women's tights, for example, are a staple product enjoying a long and fairly stable maturity, with minor adjustments to packaging and colour ranges.

---

making a quick return in these markets are those who spot the trend early. There is little opportunity for late entrants. It is interesting to note that some fads retain a hard core of enthusiasts, for example skateboarding.

Product failure. Some products never even achieve a growth stage: they fail. This may be because the product itself is badly thought through, or because it never gained awareness or distribution. New food products from small manufacturers without the resources to create strong brands may fail because they simply cannot gain mass distribution from retailers unwilling to take risks with unknown producers or brands.

Revitalisation product. The revitalisation phase of the PLC shows that marketing effort can indeed influence the course of a life-cycle. By updating a product, either through design or through a fresh marketing approach, new life can be injected to regenerate customer and retailer interest and loyalty. Tango, for example, was a standard, uninteresting fizzy orange drink until some surreal, controversial and imaginative advertising repositioned it as a trendy teenage drink.

Product level, class, form and brand

As said at the beginning of this section, the PLC can operate on a number of different levels. It is important to distinguish between the PLCs of total industries (such as the motor industry), product classes (such as petrol-driven private vehicles), product forms (such as hatchback cars) and individual brands (such as the Fiat Uno). Rink and Swan (1979) argue that there is a need for a clear definition of the distinction between these four categories of PLC so that the manager can fully understand the context within which the brand is evolving.

Industries and product classes tend to have the longest PLCs, because they are an aggregate of the efforts of many organisations and many individual products over time. An industry, such as the motor industry, can be in an overall state of fairly steady maturity for many years even as individual product forms and brands come and go. In the motor industry, for example, the hatchback is probably a mature product form, while the people carrier is still in its growth stage. Although a number of hatchback 'brands' have come and gone, the number of people carrier 'brands' is still growing. At the same time the earliest entrants in the European market are starting to reach maturity.

Focusing down further to the individual brand level, it can be even more difficult to judge the nature of the PLC because there are so many competitive factors to take into consideration. Each factor, for example a competitor's pricing or promotional approach, has an influence on the strategies formulated for the brand and a direct effect on its success or failure. A brand's growth phase, may not be as rapid as hoped or may not achieve as high a level of share as planned if a major competitor can find a way of distracting the market's attention during the critical launch period. To some extent, a predictable range of likely competitor actions and their outcomes can be foreseen, and contingencies can be built into product planning to account for them. Nevertheless, it is still very difficult to forecast sales, to define the best strategies for each stage, the duration of each stage and the overall curve dynamic. The PLC concept provides no guarantees, despite its neatness. There are too many unpredictable factors influencing a product's life, and too much depends on the quality of the care, commitment and imagination with which the product is managed.

Despite these weaknesses, the PLC is a well-used concept. Product marketing strategies should, however, take into account other considerations as well as the PLC, as the next section shows.

MARKET EVOLUTION

The marketing manager needs to understand how markets develop over time, in order to plan and manage products, their life-cycles and their marketing strategies better. Three components are involved in market evolution: the way in which customers adopt new products, the evolution and acceptance of technology and, finally, the impact of competition.

The diffusion of innovation

The product life cycle is clearly driven by changes in consumer behaviour as the new product becomes established. The rate at which the growth stage develops is linked in particular with the speed with which customers can be led through from

FIGURE 8.3

**Diffusion of
innovation:
adopter
categories**

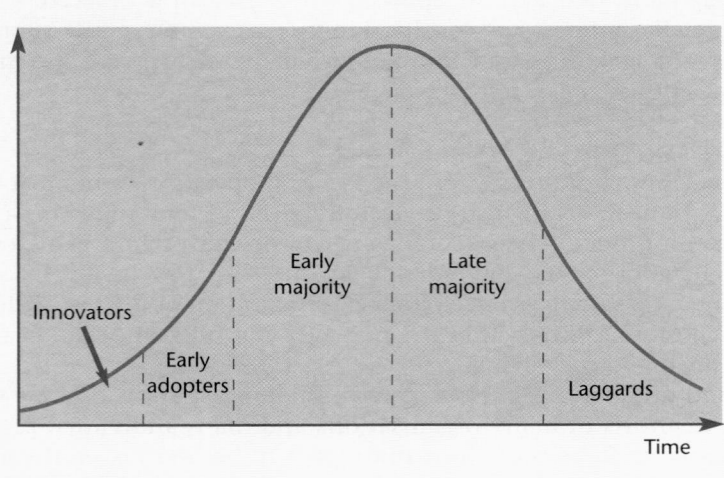

Source: Based on Rogers (1962).

awareness of the product to trial and eventual adoption of the product, in other
words how fast the AIDA model (*see* Fig 5.2 on p. 184) works. The problem is, however, that not all customers move through it with equal speed and eagerness, and
some will adopt innovation more quickly than others. This has led to the concept of
the **diffusion of innovation** (Rogers, 1962), which looks at the rate at which innovation spreads across a market as a whole. Effectively, it allows the grouping or
classification of customers depending on their speed of adoption into one of five
adopter categories, as shown in Fig 8.3.

Innovators

Innovators are important in the early stages of a product's life-cycle to help get the
product off the ground and start the process of gaining acceptance. They form only a
small group, but they buy early and are prepared to take a risk. In consumer markets,
innovators tend to be younger, better educated, more affluent and confident. In
organisational markets, innovators are likely to be profitable, and again, willing to
take risks in return for the potential benefits to be gained from being first.

   Innovators may be category specific. A consumer who is an innovator in the hi-fi
market, for example, may be a laggard when it comes to small kitchen appliances or
photographic equipment. It depends on the individual's interests and inclinations,
and to some extent on what kinds of product they think are important in establishing
their status in other people's eyes. Within a particular product category, the innovator
may continue to show innovative tendencies over time, wanting to be the first with a
series of new products. Thus those who were the first to adopt car phones may also be
the first to adopt in-car computerised navigation systems.

Early adopters

Early adopters enter the market early, but are content to let the innovators take the real
pioneering risks with a new product. They do, however, soon follow the lead of the innovators and are always alert to new developments in markets of interest to them. Once the
early adopters begin to enter the market, the growth stage of a PLC can then develop.

   Both innovators and early adopters tend to be opinion leaders, and thus it is important for the promoter of a new product to target them and win them over. The mass
market, however, looks particularly to the early adopters for a lead as they are more of
a mainstream group than the innovators. The early adopters are thus critical for
making a product generally acceptable, and for spreading word of mouth recommendations about the product's value and benefits.

Early majority

With the *early majority* the mass market starts to build up, as more and more people enter the market. The early majority are more risk averse than the previous groups, and want some reassurance that the product is tried and tested before they will commit themselves to it. This group may be relatively well educated, with above average incomes, but that may depend on the nature of the product concerned. CD-ROM drives for home computers, for example, have entered this stage, but many consumers may be holding back until the price comes down. When a product does reach the early majority, social pressure may begin to build: 'You really must get yourself an ice cream maker – you can't possibly manage without one'. This begins to move the product towards the late majority.

Late majority

The *late majority* customers are perhaps less interested or bothered about the product category, or are content to wait until they see how the market develops. They are a little way behind the early majority, and want even more reassurance about the product's benefits and worth. The late majority may have more choice of alternative products in the market, as competition builds, and will certainly have the benefit of the accumulated knowledge and experience of the previous groups. Once the late majority have been converted, the product is likely to be reaching its mature stage, a steady plateau of repeat purchases, with very few new customers left to enter the market.

Late adopters or laggards

The last remaining converts are the *late adopters*, or *laggards*. They may be very averse to change, and therefore have resisted adopting a new product, or they may have had attitudinal or even economic problems coming to terms with it. Alternatively, they may just have been very slow in hearing about the product or in relating its benefits to their own life-styles. They may be in the lower socioeconomic groups, or they may be older consumers.

Which stage of the diffusion model do you think this product has reached?

The benefits of being among the late adopters are that others have taken all the risks; the ephemeral brands or manufacturers are likely to have disappeared; it may thus be easier to identify the best products on the market, and the price may be falling as competitors fight for share among a shrinking market. By the time the late adopters get into the market, however, the innovators and early adopters are likely to have moved on to something else, and thus the whole cycle begins again!

As this discussion has implied, diffusion of innovation has strong links with the product life-cycle concept, and can be used both as a means of segmenting a market, and for suggesting appropriate marketing strategies. In the early stages, for example, it is important to understand the needs and motivations of the innovators and early adopters, and then to attract attention and generate trial among these groups. Other than knowing that they have innovative tendencies, however, it can be difficult to profile the groups using more concrete demographic or psychographic variables. In that case, it is important for the marketer to think in product terms. Perhaps hi-fi innovators and early adopters may be reached through specialist magazines which review new products, for example.

According to Gatignon and Robertson (1985), building on the work of Rogers (1962), six main factors affect the rate of product adoption:

Source: Sony UK.

1 *Relative advantage*: additional benefits and value added compared with alternatives.
2 *Compatibility*: fit with consumer tastes, needs, attitudes etc.
3 *Complexity*: the less complex the product or the more user friendly it is, the quicker the rate of adoption.
4 *Divisibility*: whether it can be tried on a limited basis to reduce the risk of trial, e.g. computer software demonstration disks.
5 *Communicability*: ease of communicating benefits.
6 *Perceived risk*: what it will cost the buyer in terms of both money and pride if the purchase turns out to be a 'wrong' decision.

The marketer can consider these factors when developing products and their marketing mixes. Market research can help to define compatibility and to determine the most attractive relative advantage. Risk can be reduced through warranties, free samples, trial prices and pack sizes or 'satisfaction or your money back' promotions. Communication can be helped through product demonstrations or samples.

Technological impact

Technology also evolves over time. Sometimes this evolution is gradual, allowing the product to develop incrementally through new models and upgrades, but with no major shocks to the customer. Sometimes, however, technical breakthroughs occur which radically alter the expectations of the market and its competitive structure. Such technological discontinuities tend to create a period of intense change and disturbance to the *status quo* as new products emerge that capitalise on the breakthrough. Whole industries can be wiped out by these changes if adaptation does not take place (Tushman and Anderson, 1986). The demand for black and white televisions, steam locomotives and mechanical cash registers all changed dramatically as a result of technological discontinuity. Fortunately for many organisations, such radical changes are rare and take some time to work through to the market. It took nearly 15 years for British Rail to replace all its steam locomotives (1953–68), a further 25 years in Poland (until 1993), and China still builds steam locomotives for industrial applications.

Technological innovation can thus be used to extend the product life cycle, by helping to refresh and update the product, but it can also shorten a life-cycle by rendering a product obsolete.

Competitor entry timing

In the same way that consumers can be classified according to their willingness and ability to adopt innovation, competitors can be classified according to their timing in entering a market. In any specific product market, competitors can be categorised into five main groups:

Pioneers
Pioneers are the innovative organisations that create new markets or are the first to get to the market. They may invest heavily in R&D and marketing to keep the new ideas flowing and to commercialise them. This group might include organisations such as Sony, 3M and Philips.

Early imitators
Organisations that are *early imitators* see what the pioneers have done, recognise the market's potential, and then copy them. An early imitator's product is likely to be a 'me too' product, with very little to differentiate it from the pioneer. Any differentiation is likely to arise from elements of the marketing mix other than product. The entry of early imitators may coincide with the growth stage of the life-cycle when there is enough demand and enthusiasm to support a number of very similar competing products.

The evolving PLC of the PC

The PLC of the computer market has so far only lasted about 30 years, but it has certainly been dynamic and eventful. The industry's PLC has been a rapid series of introductions, growths and early maturities as products have been rendered obsolete by new or improved technologies; generally, microprocessors double in power and capacity within two years. Such rapid rates of change and product improvement are enough to give a headache to the innovators and early adopters among customers who want to keep ahead of the rest!

One specific sector of the market is the personal computer (PC), first introduced in the late 1970s. Initially, its introduction and growth were slow. PCs were relatively expensive, not particularly user friendly, and limited in what they could do. Larger organisations saw no need for them because they had established mainframes to do their computing, and smaller organisations felt that they would be either no better than established manual systems or not cost effective. The general public, apart from a few technically minded innovators, was not convinced either.

The growth stage took off in the early to mid-1980s with competition between IBM and Apple. Apple pioneered user-friendly graphics and mouse-driven menus, while IBM, in conjunction with

Microsoft, managed to establish MS-DOS as the standard operating system, and introduced Windows. IBM also stimulated the market because its PCs were made from standard components, available to any manufacturer. This meant that anyone could make an IBM-compatible 'clone' – and they did. The proliferation of similar machines meant not only that prices of PCs fell, but also that the software market became more attractive and lucrative. The availability of cheaper machines and a wider range of more sophisticated software, coupled with the fact that computer companies began to market the benefits of PCs rather than trying to sell the technology, opened up both the consumer and organisational markets to rapid expansion.

The growth stage is not yet over. Within the European market, there are still many households without PCs and there is no reason why the PC should not eventually become as much of a standard household item as the television. Technology is still advancing, and so even those households and organisations that do already own PCs are under pressure to upgrade to gain the full benefits of the CD-ROM drive and access to the Internet.

Source: Bird (1996).

Early differentiators

An organisation that takes the basic product and improves it or adds new features is a *early differentiator*. The early differentiator's product does, therefore, offer distinct features and benefits, but builds upon the pioneer's original product concept. The entry of such competitors is likely to happen during the growth stage.

Early nichers

As a market moves towards saturation and maturity, the level of general competition becomes intense, and any new entrant is likely to look for a specific *niche* segment. This segmentation could be based on any of the variables examined in Chapter 5, such as product benefits, price sensitivity, or psychographics.

Late entrants

In an established mature market, it will be difficult for a new entrant to compete unless it has some means of clear differential advantage. This could be in terms of price, distribution or promotional weight. A *late imitator* is unlikely to be able to achieve these things without the strong financial backing provided by its other products in other markets, or by acquiring an established product in the market as with Quaker's acquisition of Snapple mentioned earlier. For a small organisation without such backing, entering a market at this stage could be a high risk, unfeasible strategy.

Clearly, these categorisations are somewhat generalised, but they do add another dimension to the PLC. They help in understanding how a market's PLC might evolve, and what kinds of marketing strategies are appropriate at each stage given the competitive environment. Many of these issues will be further explored in Chapter 21.

Managerial responses

By using the PLC together with analysis of customers, technology and competitors, as outlined above, the marketing manager can begin to paint a detailed picture of the factors that are likely to influence the shape of the PLC, its duration and the strategies that might be appropriate at each stage. Table 8.1 summarises this approach from the point of view of a pioneer organisation, looking at the projected PLC of a radically new consumer product. As the PLC's externally generated characteristics unfold, the organisation's strategies also develop, as a means of either minimising threats or maximising opportunities. However, the manager needs to exercise caution in assuming that the future will unfold neatly according to plan. In a marketing environment that is witnessing reduced new product development cycle times, customer-driven product development and increasing global competition, there is less certainty than ever. Models which appear to be conceptually very simple and predictive then become very dangerous managerial tools.

MANAGING THE PRODUCT MIX

In a dynamic marketing environment, the product mix is not static. The effects of changing technology, evolving competition and changes in customer needs mean that it is most important for an organisation to find ways of keeping its product ranges fresh and interesting. This opens up a number of management problems, requiring planned procedures and strategies in order to:

1 retain and maintain existing products so that they continue to meet their objectives;
2 modify and adapt existing products to take advantage of new technology, emerging opportunities or changing market conditions;
3 delete old products that are close to the end of their working lives and no longer serve their purpose; and finally,
4 introduce a flow of new products to maintain or improve sales and profit levels, and to form a firm foundation for tomorrow's markets. This latter point will be dealt with separately in Chapter 9.

An organisation, therefore, needs a balanced **product portfolio**, capable of sustaining it satisfactorily over its planning horizons. Note that the portfolio ideally must be *balanced*, containing neither too many new nor too many declining products. Too many new products could put an organisation at risk, as product launch is resource intensive with no guarantee of success. At the other extreme, too many declining products could threaten the future of the business, as sales and profits start to fall. Even if replacement or diversification plans are in place, unless they are implemented over a longer period of time, the organisation could find itself coping with too much change and new product risk. In an ideal world, mature, but still strong products can provide the stable cash flow against which a planned programme of new product establishment and declining product deletion can take place.

Positioning products

A crucial decision, which could affect the length of a product's life and its resilience in a market over time, concerns the product's positioning. **Product positioning** means

TABLE 8.1
PLC Stages: Characteristics and strategies

	Introduction	Growth	Maturity	Decline
Market characteristics				
Type of customer entering market	Innovators	Early adopters	Early majority / Late majority	Late adopters
Type of competitor entering market	Pioneer	Early imitators / Early differentiators / Early nichers	Late entrants	
Numer of products on the market	One	Few	Many	Declining
Technological development	Discontinuity – radically new concept	Incremental – fine tuning – differentiation	Incremental – possibility of interruption by discontinuity?	None or minor
Financial characteristics				
Sales	Low	Growing rapidly	Growing slowly	Declining
Costs per customer	High	Average	Low	Low
Cash flow	Negative	Acceptable	High	Acceptable
Profit	Negative	Rising rapidly	High	Declining
Main marketing objectives				
Re consumer	Gain awareness / Generate trial	Widen acceptance / Generate trial/repeat sales	Remind/reinforce / Encourage loyalty	Milk last sales
Re competition	Establish premier position	Defend	Compete	
Re distribution	Gain acceptance	Widen distribution / Increase shelf space	Maintain shelf space	Keep product available
Re product	Establish	Fine tune	Refresh/relaunch/vary / Maintain	Drop/sell
Marketing mix				
Product range	Basic / Brand building	Enhanced	Extension/variety / Brand image reinforcement	Rationalisation
Price	Skimming – capitalise on early entry	Lower Penetration	Low Match/beat compeititon	Steady
Channels of distribution	Limited	Increasing	Maximum	Declining
Consumer promotion focus				
• Advertising	High: Awareness	High: Image building	Modererate: Remind/reinforce	Minimal: Remind
• Sales promotion	High: Trial	High: Repeat purchase	Moderate: Short-term share gain	Low: Reward loyalty
Trade promotion				
• Ads/promotions	High: Awareness/acceptance	Minimal: Reinforce/defend	Moderate: Defend/relaunch	Minimal: Remind
• Personal selling	High: Awareness/acceptance	Lower: Repeat orders	Moderate: Reinforce/relaunch	Minimal: Repeat orders

thinking about a product in the context of the competitive space it occupies in its market, defined in terms of attributes that matter to the target market. The important criterion is how close to the ideal on each of those attributes, compared with competing products, your product is judged to be by the target market. Harrod's, for example, is positioned as a high quality, exclusive departmental store. In order to reinforce this positioning with its target market, Harrod's makes sure that its product ranges, its staff expertise, its displays and overall store ambience are of equally high quality.

It is the target customer's definition of important attributes, and their perception of how your product compares on them that matter. Marketing managers have to stand back from their own feelings and must ensure that the attributes selected are those that are critical to the customer, not those that marketing managers would like to be critical. The range of attributes judged to be important will vary according to the particular market segments under consideration. Chapter 5 offered further insights into the relationship between segmentation and product characteristics.

Further need for managerial objectivity arises when a positioning exercise is carried out. While managers may take steps to create a product and marketing package that they think will fill a previously defined position, they still need to ensure that they closely monitor the target market's opinions to make certain that the required image and message are being conveyed.

The concept of product positioning is clearly focused on a customer-based perspective, but it still has serious implications for product design and development. The decision about positioning is made during the product's development, and will be reflected in a whole range of the product's characteristics, including brand image, packaging and quality, as well as in the pricing and communication elements of the marketing mix.

Defining and selecting an appropriate position for a product involves three stages.

Stage 1

Detailed market research needs to be carried out during the first stage in order to establish what attributes are important to any given market segment, and their order of preference. This background research will centre on a class of products rather than on individual brands within the class. Thus a particular segment, for example, might regard softness, absorbency and a high number of sheets on the roll as the three most important attributes of toilet tissue, in that order of preference.

Stage 2

Having identified the important attributes, in the second stage further research now shortlists the existing products that offer those attributes. Brands such as Kleenex Velvet and Andrex might be seen as fulfilling the needs of the toilet tissue segment mentioned above.

Stage 3

In the third stage, it is necessary to find out:

(a) what the target market considers to be the ideal level for each of the defined attributes; and
(b) how they rate each brand's attributes in relation to the ideal and to each other.

The conclusions from this hypothetical research may be, for instance, that while Andrex has more sheets per roll than Kleenex (thus apparently achieving a better rating for Andrex on an important attribute), in relation to the ideal, Andrex is perceived to have too many (too bulky for the roll holder), whereas Kleenex might be perceived to have too few (runs out too quickly). Both products could thus improve their offering.

Once the positioning process has been completed for all the relevant attributes, it is useful to be able to visualise the complete picture graphically, by creating a *perceptual map* of the market. Figure 8.4 shows such a hypothetical map of the toilet tissue market, using price and softness as two dimensions which might represent important attributes. This shows that Brand A is serving the bottom end of the market in Segment 1, offering a cheap, purely functional product, whereas Brand B is aimed at the discerning customer in Segment 2 who is prepared to pay a little more for a gentler experience. Brand C seems to be closer to Segment 1 than Segment 2, but is overpriced compared with Brand A for a similar quality of product. Brand D is floating between the two segments, with nothing to offer that is particularly appealing to either.

In some cases, of course, two dimensions are insufficient to represent the complexities of target market opinion. Although this creates a far more difficult mapping task,

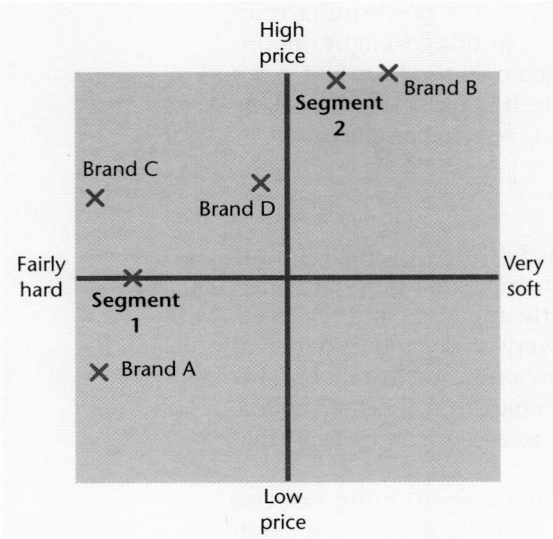

FIGURE 8.4

Perceptual map of the toilet tissue market

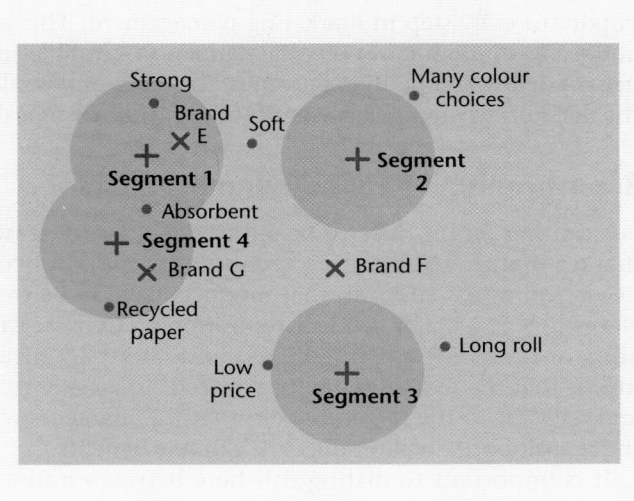

FIGURE 8.5

Multidimensional perceptual map of the toilet tissue market

any number of further dimensions can be included using multidimensional scaling techniques (Green and Carmone, 1970). Figure 8.5 expands the mapping of the toilet tissue example to include additional dimensions. In such a case, the map is an invaluable aid to understanding complex product relationships, almost at a glance, saving many pages of confusing verbal description.

As can be seen from Fig 8.5, Segment 1 wants high performance, and Brand E is well positioned to serve its needs. Segment 2 is fairly concerned about performance characteristics, but also thinks that the aesthetics of the tissue are important, so that it co-ordinates with bathroom decor and fittings. Brand E might be able to better serve this segment by expanding its colour range, without alienating Segment 1. Segment 3 is the value-conscious economy segment that wants the largest number of sheets per roll for the least amount of money. Segment 4 has more of an environmental conscience than the others, and Brand G is well positioned for them. Brand F, however, is poorly positioned to serve any of the existing segments and its managers need to think carefully about which direction to take with it.

Perceptual mapping helps to provide insights into appropriate competitive actions. For instance, a fundamental decision could be whether to try to meet the competition head-on or to differentiate your product away from them. The map can show just how far away from the competition your product is perceived to be, and where its weaknesses lie, leading to an understanding of the marketing tasks involved in improving the product offering. If the intention is to differentiate, the map can indicate whether your product is sufficiently different in terms of attributes that matter, and whether market niches exist that your product could be adapted to fill.

Example

Volvo focused on safety as an important attribute of a family car at a time when its competitors were communicating performance and value for money. Volvo were not perceived as providing outstanding performance or value, so they decided to differentiate and create a niche for themselves in a segment for which safety was a very high priority.

All of this implies that assessing and defining meaningful product positioning is an important early step in marketing management. This process can bring to light opportunities, it can highlight potential dangers of cannibalising one's own products and it can help to define competitive pressures, strengths and weaknesses. It is also a step in making the decision to modify a current product range by repositioning selected products.

Repositioning and modifying products

Positioning might have to be adjusted for many reasons as both the product and its market mature. Developing technology, evolving competition, changing customer needs and wants all mean that products have to be constantly appraised and reviewed. Nevertheless, a major **product repositioning** exercise can be very costly and risky (alienating or confusing existing buyers and failing to attract new ones, for instance). This means that the marketing manager needs to be sure that the changes will be perceptible and relevant to the target market, that the market is willing to accept change, and that the repositioning will produce measurable benefits.

It is important to distinguish here between a fundamental repositioning exercise and minor product refreshment. The latter is a natural part of the PLC, when small changes which suggest progress and improvement are implemented to prevent the product image from becoming stale. Car manufacturers for instance, will change their colour ranges and redesign various accessories each year, but the market does not interpret these as anywhere nearly as radical as a repositioning would be. Fine tuning the product itself can be done without seeking to reposition, and conversely, repositioning can take place through pricing, promotion or distribution without any change to the product. Kellogg's, for example, used advertising to reposition their Cornflakes brand as an adult snack that can be eaten at any time of day rather than as a basic and rather boring children's breakfast. The slogan, 'Have you forgotten how good they taste?' implies a long-established brand heritage, with connotations of familiarity, reassurance and quality.

Repositioning has a number of serious implications. It might involve redefining or enlarging segments, and it may well involve redesigning an entire marketing strategy. Such a fundamental revamp of a product is most likely to take place in the maturity stage of the PLC, when the product is beginning to fade a little.

There are three main areas for repositioning and product improvement.

MARKETING IN ACTION

Repositioning for good health

Lucozade used to be positioned as an invalid's drink, with the slogan 'Lucozade aids recovery'. Its advertising in the 1960s used to show a poorly child being tended by a caring mother who gave him Lucozade. As general health and living conditions have improved, however, this became too much of a niche position. If people only bought Lucozade when there was sickness in the household, the purchase frequency and volume would be very low, especially when compared with other more mainstream fizzy drinks. In the 1980s, therefore, Lucozade was repositioned to capitalise on the growing health boom. Instead of being a semi-medicinal 'illness' drink, with all the negative connotations that implies, it became a specially formulated, glucose-rich, energy drink for active and busy people, and this positioning was endorsed by sports celebrities, e.g. Daley Thompson. It still retained its premium price and quality image, but created much more positive connotations and a rationale for more frequent purchase and consumption. The repositioning was achieved partly through packaging, for instance, in a 'one shot' bottle (no longer just the large size bottle), selling alongside other soft drinks (colas, etc.) and partly through powerful celebrity advertising featuring current sports heroes.

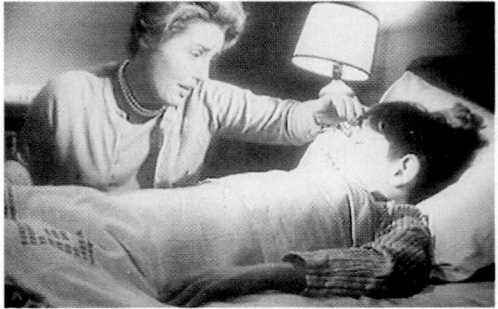

Lucozade was very successfully repositioned as a fitness drink.

Source: Olgivy & Mather/ SmithKline Beecham.

Quality

As discussed at pp. 283 *et seq.*, quality has a number of dimensions. With physical products, quality can be defined in terms of reliability, durability and dependability, which are generally applicable across most products. There are, however, product-specific quality dimensions which the target market could use as indicators of a quality product, such as speed, taste, colour, materials, ingredients and even price and packaging (*see* Chapter 11 and pp. 280 *et seq.*).

Quality for service products tends to arise from the customer's perceptions of the physical support mechanisms and the infrastructure that help to create an appropriate interactive environment. An efficient appointments system, friendly reception and provision of coffee and magazines in a pleasant waiting area, for example, all add to the perceived quality of a service operation in the minds of customers. Naturally, this must be reinforced by consistent, reliable and satisfactory delivery of the service itself.

In changing the quality of a product, the movement can be towards either relatively higher quality or relatively lower quality. Lowering the quality is likely to lose existing customers, but at the same time could open up an expanded market if it brings the product into a more affordable price range. Lowering the quality does not necessarily mean making actual changes to the product; it can be an act of omission. An organisation could make a conscious decision to withhold any further development and modification resources from a product, despite seeing competing products improve. This means that the organisation's product quality is declining relative to the rest, and may indicate that the product is being phased out, and that resources are being saved for investment in future products.

Raising the quality of a physical product could be achieved perhaps through better components or refined manufacturing. For a service product, it could mean major refurbishment for the premises or developing the way in which the experience is packaged. Whatever the product or the means employed, raising the quality offers the prospect of charging higher prices and increasing profit margins. It might, however, lead to increased competition from other organisations greedy for a share of that prosperity. The other point to consider carefully is whether the target market will either recognise or value the newly raised quality.

Skoda, an organisation with a well-established image of being at the bottom or at best edging towards the middle of its product class within the EU, produced massive, real improvements in its product quality as a result of its partnership with VW. Nevertheless, it still faced an uphill task in persuading a sceptical public to reposition its attitudes accordingly.

Design

Thinking in an aesthetic rather than an engineering context, design affects the impact of the product on the senses. This concept can be difficult to handle, as it covers areas such as the appearance, texture, taste, smell, feel or sound of the product, all of which involve the customer in some very subjective assessments. These areas do, however, provide many combinations of variables that could offer the opportunity for change. If the objective is to reposition a product, just changing its visual appearance or its packaging (probably with 'new improved...' splashed across it) could give customers sufficient cues and justification for revising their opinions of it.

Design is clearly an important factor in fashion clothing markets. Brand names become closely associated with certain characteristics or a certain 'look' which helps to position them in the 1990s, Jaeger, for example, was closely associated with traditional, classic looks, but the organisation felt that it needed to be more fashionable and stylish as the brand's growth had slowed compared with its competitors. The solution was to retain a core classic range, so as not to alienate loyal customers, but to supplement it with capsule collections of more fashionable merchandise. This signalled a subtle rather than radical shift in Jaeger's positioning to widen and refresh its appeal.

It must be stressed that any design changes are a waste of time and resources unless they matter to the market, can be communicated to that market and are implemented to achieve defined objectives.

Performance

Like design, performance relies on the customer's initial, rather impressionistic assessment. A more concrete appreciation of performance may only come after product use. The kind of things under consideration here include convenience, safety, ease of handling, efficiency, effectiveness and adaptability to different situations. A car's performance, for instance, can be measured in terms of its acceleration, braking ability or fuel economy, depending on what is important to the buyer. Improving the fuel economy at the expense of acceleration might change the character of the car, making it less appealing to a 'boy racer' type of segment, but positioning it more firmly and more positively in the 'heavy urban usage' segment. Even the fuel itself has been repositioned in terms of its performance-enhancing capabilities, with some brands promising to be more engine-friendly or to improve engine performance.

Quality, design and performance are often inextricably interlinked. Proposed changes under one heading have implications for the others. Improving a car's fuel economy may involve better quality components under the bonnet as well as a more aerodynamic body design.

It does not really matter whether a proposed change is classified as relating to quality, design or performance, or all three. What does matter is that as part of the product management process, all the relevant options are assessed to make sure that the product continues to achieve its maximum potential, either within its existing segment(s) or through repositioning into a new one. Quality, design and performance all provide possibilities for the major or minor changes that will ensure this.

Product range management

The discussion above concentrated on the adjustment and adaptation of existing products and their marketing mixes to reposition the offering in the customer's mind. Taking this concept a step further, the organisation may wish to leave existing products as they are, and use the assessment of positioning to identify opportunities for new products to fill or extend the current range. This approach to new product development may use existing products as a basis, rather than the more radical departures envisaged in the next chapter. These decisions are all part of the ongoing product audit, constantly checking to make sure that product offerings continue to serve the market's needs and wants. A major advantage is that all the positive attitudes and perceptions of the original brand's customers can be transferred to the new product that evolves (Aaker and Keller, 1990).

Two broad options are available: extending the product line and filling the product range.

Extending the product line length and depth

Extending the product line involves looking at the current range and deciding whether to extend it upwards, downwards or in both directions. An upwards extension might involve introducing a higher priced, higher quality, more exclusive product, while a downwards extension might require a basic, no-frills product at a rock bottom, mass market price.

In thinking about such an extension, the marketer needs to be sure that the gaps thus filled are worth filling. Will sufficient customers emerge to take up the new product? Will the trade accept it? Is it a significant profit opportunity? Will it simply cannibalise existing products? This last issue is particularly important; there is no point in extending a product range downwards if the major effect is to pull customers away from an existing mid-range product.

Extending upwards. Extending upwards has a number of attractions, assuming that the organisation has the ability to produce a suitably attractive and consistently high-quality product offering. An upwards extension could create a product with higher margins (*see* Chapter 11) as well as enhancing the organisation's image. It also helps to build a kind of staircase for the customer to climb. As the customer becomes more affluent or as their needs and wants become more sophisticated, they can trade up to the next product in the range and still maintain their loyalty to one organisation. A business school, for example, with established post-experience management programmes at certificate and diploma levels might extend its product range upwards to include an MBA. The intention would be that students should work their way through all three qualifications in the course of their management careers. Similarly, a bank might create a new savings scheme offering higher rates of interest for balances over £10 000 to prevent a customer with such funds from taking their money elsewhere.

> ### Example
>
> Pringle, the Scottish knitwear firm, best known for its sweaters and golf sponsorship, tried to extend upwards into luxury goods, such as high-quality luggage and accessories. At the same time, it was also expanding sideways into non-knitwear clothing and its own retail outlets. This combination of upwards and sideways expansion did not work well. The Pringle brand name was appearing on too

many items that were too far removed from its core image. This diluted the impact and exclusivity of the name, and meant that customers did not perceive the luxury goods as being suitably classy or élite. Luxury brands in particular have thus to be careful about how widely they spread their name. One of the reasons why Pierre Cardin is now a mass market name rather than the élite brand that it was in the 1970s is that the brand was stretched over too many different product categories, losing its focus and its core values (Richards, 1995).

Extending downwards. The downwards extension can be used to attack competitors operating at the volume end of the market. It can build a larger base of sales if a lower priced product broadens the number of potential customers. Then, by introducing people to the bottom of the range product and forming some kind of relationship with them, it may be possible to get them to trade up, thus assisting sales of the mid-range product. This would be the ideal situation, but do remember the risks of cannibalisation if the bottom of the range product acts as a magnet to existing mid-range customers. Careful thought also needs to be given to the logistic implications of extending downwards if it opens up bigger markets. This might mean shifting higher volumes of goods to more outlets, as well as increased commitment to mass communication in order to reach the greater number of potential buyers.

Example

Mercedes launched its 190 car as a means of extending downwards into a lower price bracket segment. This brought people on to the first rung of the Mercedes product range ladder much earlier. The average age of a first-time Mercedes buyer fell by about 10 years! This is important, as the company estimates that about 80 per cent of its customers remain loyal once they have owned a Mercedes.

As mentioned at p. 274, Heinz have managed to extend downwards in the beans market by undertaking own-label manufacture for retailers. This has allowed them to gain a position at the price sensitive, discount end of the market without damaging the overall brand image.

Both kinds of range extension clearly have benefits and risks which need to be assessed before a decision can be made. The biggest danger, perhaps, is that of stretching scarce management and cash resources so thinly that current products suffer from neglect and new extensions to the range never have a real chance of becoming established on a firm foundation.

Filling the product range

The option of **filling the product range** involves a very close examination of the current range, then creating new products to fill in any gaps between existing products. This could be a relatively low-cost option as it would be likely that existing distribution and promotional activity could be applied to the new products. As implied in the previous section, the range extension option is opening new ground, thus requiring a possible review of distribution and promotional activity.

One way of filling out the range could be to increase the number of variants available. The product remains the same, but it has a range of different presentations. Thus a food product might be available in single-serving packs, family-sized packs or catering-sized freezer packs. Tomato ketchup is now available in squeezy bottles as well as in glass ones.

Manufacturers of laundry detergents have long used range filling as a means of keeping consumer interest and persuading them to buy different products for different uses. This means that when the UK supermarket Safeway launched its own brand of laundry products, Cyclon, it had to provide a wide range of variants in order to compete with the established brands in the market. Thus the range included biological, biological with fabric conditioner, non-biological and coloureds-washing products. All of these are available as powder or liquid, standard or concentrated, in boxes and bottles or in refill bags and pouches, and in different sizes. Excluding different pack sizes, this provided the shopper with over 30 different choices!

Filling the range can be a useful strategy for keeping the competition out, by offering the consumer some novelty and a more detailed range of products closer to their needs, and to add incrementally to profits at relatively low risk. The danger, however, is the risk of adding to costs, but with no overall increase in sales. This is the risk of cannibalisation, of fragmenting existing market share across too many similar products. There is the added irony that the consumer might well be indifferent to these variants, being perfectly satisfied with the original range.

Deleting products

The final stages of a product's life are often the hardest for management to contemplate. The decision to eliminate a poor seller that may be generating low or even negative profits is a tough one to make. The economic rationale for being ruthless is clear. A product making poor returns absorbs management time and can quickly drain resources if it is being kept alive by aggressive selling and promotion. Such a product may also have a marginal competitive position, and be unlikely to recover any significant share in the market. As the product's sales volumes inevitably decline, its unit costs start to increase (*see* Chapter 11), and the product becomes a burden.

There is, however, often a reluctance to take action. There are various reasons for this, some of which are purely personal or political. Managers often form emotional attachments to the products they have looked after: 'I introduced this product, I backed it and built my career on it'. If the offending product was launched more recently, then its deletion might be seen as an admission of failure on the part of its managers. They would, therefore, prefer to try just once more to turn the product round, and to retain their reputations intact.

Other reasons for being reluctant to delete a product are based on a desire to offer as wide as range as possible, regardless of the additional costs incurred. While there is still some demand (however small) for a particular product, the organisation feels obliged to continue to provide it, as a service to its customers. Suddenly deleting that product might result in negative feelings with some customers. Car owners in particular become attached to certain models and react badly when a manufacturer decides to withdraw them from the available range.

Managers may also find it difficult to calculate the full product cost. Where costs are shared between several different products, for example, there may be a number of justifiable ways of splitting those costs, depending on what you want to prove. Coming to an agreement that a product is covering its variable costs and making at least a contribution to fixed costs and overheads is useful, but it is only a beginning. Opportunity costs also have to be considered, which means defining what else could be done with the resources (manufacturing, financial, labour and management) that are being invested in this product. If those resources could be employed more profitably on something else within the strategic context of the business, then the product in question may be less secure.

All of this means that there is a need for a regular systematic review to identify the more marginal products, to assess their current contribution, and to decide how they fit with future plans.

If new life can be injected into a product, then all well and good, but if not, then there are three broad options.

Phase Out

Phasing out means allowing a gradual decline of the product with little change during the year, as long as it is making some contribution. There will then be a review at the end of the year to decide whether to continue with the product any longer or not.

Run Out

Running out entails a deliberate effort to sell more in the product's main markets, but without heavy marketing expenditure. Self-financing promotions may be the most that the organisation will allow. In this situation, the organisation expects to lose sales, but will make a greater return on each sale because of the lack of investment in marketing support.

Drop or Sell

In the worst case, the organisation finds that it can no longer sustain a product which is making little or no contribution. Major customers may be notified in advance to allow them adjustment, stocking or re-sourcing time. With fair warning of the product's demise, customers are less likely to be caught by surprise and thus less likely to feel angry that they have not been informed. They may not like the decision, but at least they have time to discuss it and get used to it.

As a general rule, many companies have not introduced regular deletion procedures (Avlonitis, 1985; Greenley and Bayus, 1994). The price of this failure is long, and sometimes unprofitable product ranges, which serve the needs of neither the customer nor the manufacturer.

CUSTOMER-SPECIFIED PRODUCTS

So far, the assumption has been made that the manufacturer or the service provider specifies the product. Particularly in organisational markets, this is not always the case, as a specific customer might have such unique requirements that standard

---

MARKETING IN ACTION

Making records

The recording industry has particular problems with increasingly short product life-cycles and thus products that become obsolete very quickly. In 1988, for example, 668 singles entered the UK charts, whereas in 1993, the number was 1052. Singles enter the charts at a higher point, but stay there for a much shorter length of time than previously. Another problem is that traditionally, singles were used almost as a marketing device to sell albums, which generated the real profits. In the mid-1990s, however, the singles charts were dominated by dance acts which generally do not sell albums. There is concern within the industry that these acts are too ephemeral and that

the record companies are not able to do enough to nurture and develop talent over time because they are under too much pressure to churn out immediate, short-term hits. Parallels are drawn with bands such as Pink Floyd, the Rolling Stones and other big names from the 1960s and 1970s. Recording companies took risks and these artists were given the space and time to develop. As a result, they still sell, and their record companies have rich back catalogues of their material that earn a steady profit. The question is, where are the Rolling Stones of the future going to come from?

Source: Wroe (1995).

product offerings will not suffice. The supplier's skill lies in designing and developing a standard specification that can be used as a basis for fine tuning and compromise in accordance with individual customer needs.

To provide customised products, the supplier needs to develop technical capabilities. This might mean investment in capital goods, machinery and plant to allow customer specifications to be met. A heavy haulage company, for example, will have to be able to load large items on to trailers but may only have the ability to handle items up to 500 tonnes. Any heavier object that a customer may want to have transported is beyond the haulier's technical capability. As well as technical capability, a supplier might have to be able and willing to be responsive in the design, production and delivery of the product or service. In the case of the haulier, extensive negotiation will be necessary on the collection, movement and installation of any load, although what is possible is restricted by the haulier's available technology. If suppliers claim to be prepared to be responsive to special requirements, they must be sure that their own suppliers can be equally responsive if necessary.

In some organisational markets, a supplier might have to adapt facilities or even invest in new facilities, just to serve the needs of one or two customers. Small manufacturing subcontractors often invest in new machinery to service one or two major customers in the hope that further business may then be found, given their expanded capabilities and capacity. In this case, the supplier's investment in its ability to meet customised needs can give it a means of generating customer loyalty. However, if those customers can still easily source the same goods from elsewhere, then such specific investment might be dangerous (Blois, 1980). Nevertheless, preparedness to adapt and invest for a specific customer is widespread in organisational markets. Sometimes it is instigated by the customer, and sometimes by the supplier as a means of winning orders (Cunningham, 1986; Turnbull and Valla, 1986). Often, however, a smaller supplier does not have the luxury of choice, and is expected to adapt itself as a sign of commitment to a larger customer. In return, the supplier perhaps gets slightly longer-term contracts and other forms of co-operation from the customer.

Example

A small manufacturer of engineering components and assemblies had the production facilities to machine parts and maintain quality within very tight specifications set by customers. One customer was a manufacturer of arrester gear for military aircraft and space shuttles, and clearly any component failure would have disastrous consequences. The customer, therefore, took great care in ensuring that the supplier was completely reliable and could meet and maintain very high standards. Before placing any order, the customer would inspect in detail the equipment that the supplier intended to use, and insist on trials and test orders before a final supplier selection was made and a major contract awarded.

(Pettitt, 1992)

This example highlights the amount of time and effort that a buyer might have to put into sourcing a customised product successfully. It also explains why some buyers may be prepared to sacrifice precision of specification and make do with a standardised product instead, where possible. To develop a specification, and then find and assess suppliers who are willing and able to meet them may be too time consuming and expensive to be justified. In some cases, however, it cannot be avoided. A crucial component of a larger system, such as a unique printed circuit board (PCB) for a machine-tool operating system will have to be customised. Interestingly, there are suppliers of PCBs who specialise in the low-volume, prototype, customised end of the market. They provide fast service and technical responsiveness, and then as soon as the PCB moves out of the development stage and into full scale mass production, the contract is handed over to other high-volume, low unit cost manufacturers.

The break-up of the Warsaw Pact meant that Russia had no source of training air-craft because most of their needs had previously been met by Czech and Romanian companies. The Russian Ministry of Defence then entered into negoti-ation with Russian industry to look for a domestically produced product. The problem was, however, that there were no suppliers experienced in trainer design and manufacture. Eventually, the ministry teamed up with two manufacturers of aerobatic competition aircraft, Sukhoi and Yakovlev, to develop a new supply source co-operatively. The key to the success of the resulting trainer, the Sukhoi Su-39 was the companies' willingness to adapt and invest in design, technical and manufacturing capabilities jointly and with the operating requirements of the Russian air force in mind (Braybrook, 1995).

Even if a supplier has the capability to produce to customer specifications, the job still has to be done efficiently and within a cost structure that leads to an acceptable price from both parties' perspectives. The trade-off between price and specification will depend on many factors, such as how critical the product is to the buyer, whether high prices can be passed on to the buyer's ultimate customer and the nature of the market niche occupied by the buyer. In some situations, the product is not completely customer specified, but is a compromise between customer needs and suppliers' tech-nical capabilities. This means that there has to be 'give and take' in the advice and design stage to produce a valued and cost-effective package. This is especially true where physical products are purchased that do not actually enter into the buyer's own product, but help the buyer to enhance their service or production capability offering to their own customers.

Even consumer markets may be able to offer customer-specified products, within limits. Fitted furniture has to be supplied to fit room dimensions, although the cust-omer is likely to choose from a range of pre-fabricated types of unit which will then undergo minor adjustments to make them fit. Clothes can be tailor-made to fit an individual, although again, the range of styles and fabrics within which that can be done may be predetermined and limited. In Pizza Hut, customers have plenty of flexi-bility to design their own pizzas, but within a range of toppings specified by the organisation. This strikes a successful yet delicate balance between cost-effective pro-duction and the personal touch so valued and so difficult to achieve in mass markets.

PRODUCT MANAGEMENT AND ORGANISATION

There is a range of management structures for marketing, depending on the tasks required and the environmental opportunities and threats. A traditional functional organisation which emphasizes sales and distribution lacks the holistic approach to marketing so necessary for successful brand development. Also, in some organisa-tions, the number of products to be managed may be large. This means that some kind of focus is needed to ensure that each product gets appropriate management sup-port and attention, as well as to exploit the synergies between products and between their marketing strategies.

Products are extremely important as revenue earners, and so they need careful management. Product-centred management structures can help to ensure that they do get the care they deserve. A product or brand manager handles part of a range or even an individual brand if it is very critical. **Product managers** operate across all func-tional areas, especially marketing, but also liaise with R&D, production and logistics to ensure the best opportunities and treatment for their product(s). Their job is to manage the product throughout its life cycle, from launch, through any modifications, to its eventual demise. It can often be a total commitment and may include commissioning research, liaising with distribution and even handling sales with major account negotiations. The product manager will also be involved in planning advertising approaches, media selection and packaging.

Product managers clearly cannot undertake all this alone. They play a key role in a project team, taking the product through from idea to commercialisation. These teams are always multifunctional, because of the need to consider project viability from all angles. If the launch is successful, then the day-to-day management of the product will be turned over to the product manager, with less input from the initial team.

In terms of planning, controlling and monitoring product performance, the product manager is likely to have to produce an annual product plan, specifying actions, resources and strategies for the coming trading period. This helps the manager to justify the investment of resources in the product and also allows the early recognition of problems with the product and proposed corrective action.

This kind of product management structure is used in larger fmcg organisations in particular, where there is significant emphasis on new product development and major mass market brands. It may also be applicable in some organisational markets, but as Davis (1984) suggests, the structure and complexity of some organisational markets means that other options may also have to be considered. If, for example, the same product or component is sold to a range of different end users, then it may be better to divide management responsibility by end user (or segment) rather than by product. A car component, for example, may be sold to car manufacturers, servicing and repair workshops or specialist retailers. Each of these customer groups needs different handling, and the component manufacturer may prefer to have specialist marketing managers for each one. A different approach is to divide marketing management responsibility on a geographic basis, particularly where international marketing is the norm. The logic is the same as for the end user focus: each territory has a unique profile, and very different demands and handling needs, requiring a specialist manager. Both of these alternatives, allocating responsibility by end user or geographic area take account of the day-to-day marketing needs' of the organisation's products, but potentially leave an unfilled gap for a 'product champion'. The last thing the organisation wants is for managers to develop the attitude that they only sell the product, and that its wider strategic development is 'somebody else's problem'.

EUROPEAN PRODUCT STRATEGY

Creating a brand that can be established across Europe, a **Eurobrand**, is neither easy nor cheap, and indeed the car industry's dilemma of whether or not to aim for the 'world car' has already been mentioned at p. 283. Many smaller companies feel that they have a sufficiently difficult job on their hands creating and maintaining a presence in their own local national market without worrying about the rest of Europe. Even some of the bigger household name organisations, such as Nestlé, have consolidated their European presence as much through the acquisition of companies in each local market as through establishing pan-European brands.

Lynch (1994) is uncompromisingly blunt in defining the criteria essential for Eurobrand building:

1 *Resources*: Lynch estimates that a marketing communications budget of no less than $60 million is needed for three years to establish the brand, unless, of course, a much longer-term phased introduction is planned.
2 *Quality*: The need for consistent quality in both the product itself and the production, logistical and administrative procedures that support it should not be underestimated.

Operating on a pan-European basis is more difficult than operating within a national market.

3 *Timing*: According to Lynch, it will take at least five years to establish a Eurobrand, and short-term returns on investment should not be expected.

These three criteria alone put Eurobranding out of the reach of most organisations. There are also practical considerations, for example culture and language. These can affect everything from the brand name (remember Plopsies and Kuk & Fuk; not to mention other gems from non-English speaking markets, such as Fanny, Spunk, Bum and Crap?), to the imagery associated with the brand, to the advertising. The marketer has to decide whether to use an identical approach in all corners of the European market, or whether to make adaptations, perhaps to the advertising or the packaging, for particular local or cultural conditions. (More detailed discussion on these issues will be found in Chapter 25 on international marketing.) As Wolfe (1991) points out, only around 40 per cent of European adults understand English, the most widespread language, which means that packaging will have to be multilingual, or as non-verbal as possible, or produced in a number of different language versions.

Example

Scott Worldwide, manufacturers of the Baby Fresh brand of baby wipes found a compromise solution (Cramp, 1995). Because they had expanded into various international markets over a number of years, there was no consistent brand image. Pack sizes, colours and graphics varied greatly from country to country. After much research, the pack size, colour and basic graphic imagery were standardised, and a series of animal icons designed to signify product variants. Within that framework, there were designated areas on the pack where local flexibility was allowed, for colour or message variation.

Halliburton and Hunerberg (1987) found that strategic variables such as positioning and product range transferred more readily across borders than pricing, which needs to reflect local conditions. Advertising and distribution tended to vary between standardised and differentiated approaches. It is, however, difficult to generalise. Nescafé, while giving the impression of being a standardised international brand, actually varies in blend, flavour and product description to suit local taste (Rijkens, 1992). This highlights the difference between the concept and the brand in terms of standardisation. For Nescafé, there is often considerable conformity across Europe on packaging, labelling and basic communications mix strategies whereas specific message design and pricing are subject to more local control. Bolz (1992) also found more of a standardised, pan-European approach in the areas of product specification, brand name, design and packaging than in pricing and promotion. The decision to standardise is also influenced by external factors, such as the homogenisation of demand, the existence of global segments, economies of scale and global competition in the sector. Factors such as retail structure and the legal and technological environments, however, tend to create barriers to standardisation.

All of this assumes that there is a pan-European market for the product, demanding volumes that justify the investment. Despite the potential problems, however, there are many pan-European brands (some of which are also global brands). The car manufacturers successfully sell the same model across Europe, while Procter & Gamble, Johnson & Johnson, Colgate Palmolive, Heinz and Nestlé all maintain pan-European fmcg brands. Although many of those brands have been around for many years, it is still possible to launch a new brand on a pan-European basis. Gillette's Natrel deodourant was launched with heavy marketing support across the EU, using not only identical product and brand imagery in all countries, but also identical packaging and advertising.

Outside the fmcg area, many organisations with well-established products have restructured themselves to make the most of the opportunities offered by the SEM. Whirlpool Europe, for example, which makes domestic appliances such as dishwashers and washing machines, has spent several years restructuring itself on a pan-European basis. According to Baxter (1994), this has meant centralising and streamlining production and administrative support as well as reorganising the sales effort. Rather than maintaining a sales force for each European country, they now have two pan-European sales organisations, each concentrating on different types of distribution channel because, as the company itself says:

'Channels across borders have a lot more in common than different channels within a country.'

All of this not only increases production and administrative efficiency, and provides a sales force better tailored to the market's needs, but also allows the organisation to use its European size to compete effectively against national competitors in each country. In organisational markets, as Chapters 4 and 7 have already indicated, there is a far higher propensity to adapt product offerings to suit individual customers, regardless of geographic boundaries. The nature and significance of these product adaptations will vary according to market structure, technological forces and the importance of the buyer–seller relationship. However, Europroducts have been developed in some organisational markets such as software, computers, trucks, and machine tools, where any adaptations tend to be minor, for example trucks for the UK market need to be right-hand drive!

In summary, the advantages of pan-European branding are:

● defining segments across borders increases the size of the potential market
● achieving economies of scale in production, administration, marketing and sales effort
● gaining competitive advantage over nationally orientated competition.

The potential dangers of pan-European branding are:

● a segment too geographically spread to be served efficiently
● presenting a bland product through trying to be all things to all people and trying to avoid cultural or linguistic problems
● high investment and long lead times stretching resources and patience to breaking point
● making so many concessions to local differences that you end up with a series of loosely related products rather than a single pan-European brand.

Colgate toothpaste, recognisable anywhere in Europe.

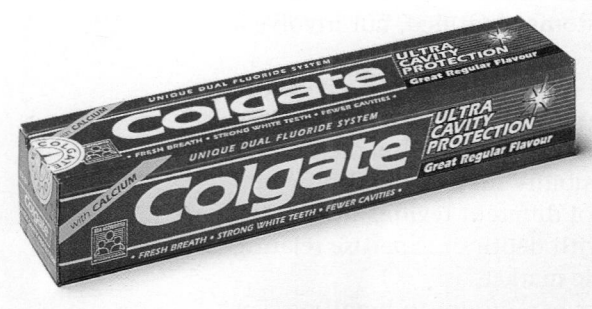

Source: Colgate Palmolive Ltd.

As more Eurobrands evolve, it has been argued, there will be fewer new brands introduced at a national level, and more that are targeted across wider European markets to appeal to Eurosegments, using common brand names, packaging and positioning (Guido, 1991). In support of this view, Doyle (1994) considers that the focus should be on appealing to a particular segment rather than focusing on standardisation or adaptation issues. Thus there may be a wide diversity of products, appealing to segments that are free of geographic boundaries.

CHAPTER SUMMARY

This chapter has tackled some of the more detailed issues connected with managing products from their conception to their eventual decline. The product life-cycle (PLC) concept is the foundation for the idea that products do move through stages in their lives, and that they may, therefore, have different marketing needs over time. The PLC suggests four stages: introduction, growth, maturity and decline. Inevitably, the PLC is a very general concept, perhaps too general to be of real use, and there are many practical problems in using it.

For an organisation, product management is important not only for making sure that existing products live profitable and efficient lives, and that they are deleted at the most appropriate time, but also to enable it to plan for the future and the flow of new products, taking advantage of new technologies and other opportunities. This implies the need for a balanced portfolio of products: some still in development, some in the early stages of their lives, some more mature and some heading for decline.

One way of ensuring that products get the most out of their life-cycles is to think about how they are positioned. This means defining what attributes or benefits are important to the market, then researching how your product, its competitors and a hypothetical ideal product are rated against those criteria, then analysing each brand's position in relation to the others and in relation to the ideal. Perceptual mapping, using two or more dimensions, can help to visualise the state of the market. All of this can stimulate debate as to whether a product needs to be further differentiated from its competitors, or whether it needs to be brought closer to the market segment's ideal.

Rather than repositioning existing products, an organisation may choose to introduce new products, based on existing ones, to fill perceived gaps. Current ranges may be extended upmarket, downmarket or in both directions. The organisation needs to make sure, however, that any such extensions are acceptable to the trade and to customers, do not stretch resources too thinly and will not compromise or cannibalise existing products. A further option is to fill out an existing product range, without moving up- or downmarket, perhaps by increasing the number of variants available, for example in terms of pack sizes or packaging formats.

The decision to delete a product can be a difficult one. Emotional attachment to products, a reluctance to admit defeat or difficulty in proving that a product is making a loss may all delay deletion. When a product is to be deleted, there are several options. Phasing out allows gradual decline; running out means a deliberate selling effort in main markets but without heavy support; drop or sell means deleting the product completely.

Customer-specified products cause their own marketing difficulties for manufacturers, as the product has to be produced efficiently, to specification, and within cost constraints. The manufacturer may have to adapt facilities in order to make what the customer wants. Sometimes products are not totally customer specified, but involve a compromise between manufacturer and buyer.

In fmcg companies in particular, product or brand managers may be given the responsibility of looking after a particular product or group of products. Although a similar product management structure may be found in organisational markets, alternative options may be considered. Management responsibility may be divided by end user, or on a geographic basis, again, because the needs of different regions may differ. In either case, the organisation can develop managers with depth of expertise relating to a specific group of end users, or a particular geographic market.

The creation of the SEM has opened opportunities for pan-European branding. For many smaller organisations, however, this is not a serious issue, and they do not have the resources, or the real desire to move beyond their own national boundaries. Organisations interested in pan-European branding need, abundant resources, to be sure that they can deliver consistent quality in all aspects of the operations and marketing, and that they are prepared to support the brand through a long lead time before the product begins to make a return on its investment.

QUESTIONS FOR REVIEW

8.1 Define the four stages of the *product life-cycle*.

8.2 What might be the main concerns for a marketing manager dealing with a *mature* product?

8.3 To what extent is the *PLC* limited in its applicability as a management tool?

8.4 What are the alternative ways of allocating *product management* responsibility in organisational markets?

8.5 Discuss the relationship between *product adopter categories* and the *stages of the PLC*. What are the implications for the marketer?

8.6 Define *product positioning*, and summarise the reasons why it is important.

8.7 Why might *product repositioning* be necessary, and in what ways can the organisation achieve it?

8.8 Differentiate between *product line extension* and *filling out the product range*. In what circumstances might each be appropriate?

8.9 Find examples of *product line extension*, both upmarket and downmarket. Try to analyse the marketing thinking behind the extensions.

8.10 Outline the alternative *product deletion methods* available, and the advantages and disadvantages of each.

QUESTIONS FOR DISCUSSION

8.1 In what ways might *customer-specified products* complicate the product management task?

8.2 Why is *product management* essential?

8.3 Choose a consumer product area (be very specific – for example choose shampoo rather than hair care products) and list as many brands available within it as you can.
(a) What stage in the *PLC* has each product reached?
(b) What stage has the *product class* or *form* reached?

(c) Does any one organisation own several of the brands, and if so, how are these brands distributed across the different *PLC stages*?

8.4 What circumstances might lead an organisation towards *pan-European branding*?

8.5 Find an example of:
(a) a successful *pan-European brand*; and
(b) an unsuccessful *pan-European brand*.
What do you think has contributed to the success/failure?

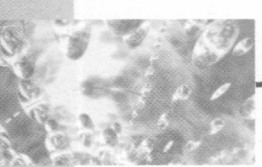

CASE STUDY 8.1

Pubs in peril

The traditional British pub is an endangered species, hovering between maturity and decline, for a number of reasons. It faces more competition than ever from other leisure activities, such as cinemas, theatres, nightclubs, sport, restaurants etc. Furthermore, the wide range of competitively priced take-home beers and lagers means that for many, crashing out on the sofa with a few cans and a really good video is an attractive alternative. The attempts of retailers and brewers to establish a home delivery beer market makes this an even bigger threat. Going down to 'the local' to while away an evening with friends is simply not enough any more. People are not visiting the pub as frequently as they used to because they want more from their social lives and their leisure time.

The pub is also a victim of shifting demographic trends in the UK. Its traditional target market of young males is declining, with the 18–24s forecast to provide only 20 per cent of pub goers by the year 2000. It is further forecast that by the turn of the century, women will make up 40 per cent of pub clientele. Demographic trends also mean that the centre of population is shifting. Many older town centre pubs in particular are now badly located, either because they are no longer in a residential area or because that area is too economically poor to provide an adequate turnover.

For all these reasons, over 500 pubs are closing down every year. The big operators who own chains of pubs, therefore, have had to modify their products (i.e., the pubs) to reposition them, and fill out and extend the product line. Organisations such as Allied Domecq Leisure and Whitbread have developed concept pubs, which build a range of themed activities on to the basic function of a pub to make it more of a 'leisure experience' rather than a 'night out at the pub'. Sports themes are popular, for example Domecq's *Football Football* and Whitbread's *Pitchers* concepts. Domecq also owns *Smiling Sam's*, which it refers to as a 'one stop licensed leisure concept'. The theme is the American deep south and as well as food and drink, it offers video games and bowling. The chains have not entirely abandoned the traditional pub, however, but they have redesigned it to make it more markedly traditional to appeal to particular market segments. In the UK market,

for example, Domecq owns 90 Firkin pubs focused on real ale and a younger, student clientele. Internationally, Domecq runs a chain of 50 John Bull authentic English pubs across Europe, and is now expanding into Asia. Families are also a target segment, catered for by Domecq's Big Steak Pubs with Wacky Warehouse play areas attached.

Greenalls takes a more flexible approach, using 'occasions' segmentation. It recognises that a single pub might have to fulfil a number of different roles, depending on the time of day at which it is used. A city centre pub might be seen primarily as somewhere to get a substantial hot meal at lunchtime, as somewhere to stop off for a quick drink in the early evening on the way home, and as a trendy place to have a good time in the evening. It has entered the concept pub market with Square Venues, which try to create more of a nightclub atmosphere within a pub setting. But even these are targeted at specific occasions: the Thursday to Saturday night town centre pub crawl with a gang of mates.

Adapted from Benady (1996).

Questions

1 At what stage in the PLC are the following, and why?
   (a) Pubs, generally?
   (b) The traditional 'local'?
   (c) The concept pub?

2 If you were to develop a two-dimensional perceptual map of the pub market, how would you label the axes? Where would the following be positioned on your map, and why?
   (a) A sports-themed concept pub?
   (b) A real ale traditional type pub?
   (c) A family-orientated pub?

3 How do you think Domecq's marketing mix will differ for each of its types of pub? To what extent do you think these differences might be driven by PLC theory or by segmentation considerations?

4 Is Greenalls right to try to use 'occasions' segmentation? Can a pub be all things to all people and survive?

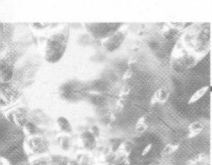

CASE STUDY 8.2

Fokker takes flight

Fokker, the Dutch planemaker first entered the jet airliner business in 1965 with the launch of the F-28. This proved to be a highly successful product, with 242 aircraft delivered before production ceased on this model in 1987, and it established Fokker in the passenger jet as well as the turboprop business. As is often the case with aircraft manufacturers, the F-28 model evolved into four types offering different fuselage lengths (i.e., passenger capacity) and wing spans (i.e., operating performance). Like any product, aircraft have life-cycles, which although longer than many consumer products, still require careful management to maintain market share. In the 1970s, a new product development programme was introduced which sought to improve significantly on the F-28, by using new engines and aircraft technology. This eventually resulted in the launch of the Fokker 100 some 10 years after its initial conception. The first orders came in 1986 from Swissair and USAir even before the prototype had made its maiden flight, but it was not until 1988 that Swissair took delivery of its first aircraft. Thus the F-28 was replaced by the 100, serving the same product niche.

The completion of this programme allowed Fokker to think about filling out the product range, by moving into other areas of the jet market. Product niches are in part determined by the passenger capacity of the aircraft and so Fokker considered stretching the 100 to create a 130-seat plane or shrinking the fuselage to create an 80-seater. Market research in 1991 suggested that the priority was the development of a smaller jet aircraft to cater for the expected increase in demand for short-haul regional travel. The research focused on the traffic expectations of a number of operators, especially in Europe and the Far East where demand for a 70-seater appeared to be strongest. In America, regional jet travel is commonplace, but in Europe, with its well developed road and rail systems, progress in shifting to air travel has been slower. Thus the decision to develop a new Fokker 70 was made, with the expectation of selling 350 aircraft by the year 2000, roughly 50 per cent of world demand. Such optimism was considered to be justified, as American aircraft manufacturers had already pulled out of regional jets in favour of a focus on long haul. The remaining serious competition for Fokker was in Europe, and more recently in Brazil and Indonesia. In total, there are 17 companies involved in the regional jet business but not all offer a 70-seater aircraft serving the niche that interested Fokker.

Rather than incur the considerable time and expense of starting from scratch, it is common practice in the aircraft industry, to 'derive' a new plane from parts and systems designed for existing models. This considerably cuts down development costs and risks. Thus the wing design, the Tay engines from Rolls-Royce, and the electronic guidance systems from the Fokker 100 were to be used, suitably modified for a shorter-fuselage jet. The use of sophisticated navigation and landing systems from the 100 gave the 70, it was claimed, a competitive advantage over other offerings. The 70 was planned to be around 25 per cent cheaper to operate than the 100, an important factor in regional aircraft purchases. The decision to go ahead with production was made in 1992 to allow a year for test flights. The formal launch took place at the Paris Air Show in June 1993 and the first order, 15 planes for Indonesian regional operators, was signed to coincide with the show. Further orders that year came from British Midland and the US Mesa Air group. The first delivery took place in 1995 and the new aircraft was truly born. By the end of 1995 orders stood at 63 aircraft for 15 different customers, including a large order from Alitalia for 15 Fokker 70s.

Despite the initial success of the 70, storm clouds were gathering over the company's future in a highly competitive market. The five aircraft manufacturers in Europe were all experiencing problems arising from failure to rationalise and to combine their efforts to achieve meaningful economies of scale. National pride often overwhelmed economic common sense. The recession that hit regional airlines in the USA in the early 1990s saw orders cancelled, and demand slumped. The knock-on effect on European producers was severe. Saab needed to build 50 (models 340 and 2000) planes per year to be profitable, but often managed only 15. The British Aerospace Jetstream (19–64 seats) was also thought to have lost money.

Fokker was not immune to the problems of overcapacity and weak demand, whatever the long term potential, and tough price competition. DASA (now Daimler-Benz Aerospace), which had partnered Fokker in the late 1980s on the 100, took a controlling stake in Fokker from 1993. Unfortunately, Fokker's losses mounted, and despite many attempts to lower costs and to improve sales, considerable difficulty was experienced in returning Fokker to profitability. To make matters worse planes are sold in dollars, although costs are incurred in local currencies, leading to further losses on exchange rate fluctuations. DASA were losing patience with Fokker, despite the positive start made by the 70. Experts in the industry suggested that a single European regional jet company was needed, building on the approach that was so successful with the Airbus. However Fokker was still selling in direct competition with British Aerospace's Bae146 which was later relaunched as the RJ at allegedly very low prices to regain lost share. In the light of this unfavourable environment and the pressure from DASA, it was absolutely critical for Fokker that the 70 should achieve its expected 50 per cent market penetration.

Sources: Relman (1995); Skapinker (1995); Tieman (1995); van der Krol (1995a); van der Krol (1995b).

Questions

1 How do you think the PLC for an aircraft model differs from that of a car, and why?

2 What factors within the marketing environment have affected Fokker's product range decisions for jets?

3 The rationale for the Fokker 70 was an assumption that demand for regional jets from European airlines would grow. What factors are likely to influence that growth?

4 How relevant do you think the concept of product positioning is in an organisational market such as this one? Against what criteria would an aircraft be positioned?

REFERENCES TO CHAPTER 8

Aaker, D. A. and Keller, K. L. (1990), 'Consumer Evaluation of Brand Extensions', *Journal of Marketing*, 54 (June), pp. 27–41.

Avlonitis, G. J. (1985), 'Product Elimination Decision Making: Does Formality Matter?', *Journal of Marketing*, 49, pp. 41–52.

Baxter, A. (1994), 'Putting Sales in a Spin After Costs Squeeze', *Financial Times*, 29 December, p. 11.

Benady, D. (1996), 'Inn Jeopardy', *Marketing Week*, 15 March, pp. 38–41.

Berenson, C. and Mohr-Jackson, I. (1994), 'Product Rejuvenation: A Less Risky Alternative to Product Innovation', *Business Horizons*, 37(6), pp. 51–7.

Bird, J. (1996), 'Tales of the Unexpected', *Management Today*, May, pp. 54–6.

Blois, K. J. (1980), 'Quasi-integration as a Mechanism for Controlling External Dependencies', *Management Decision*, 18(1), pp. 55–63.

Bolz, J. (1992), *Wettbewerbsorientierte Standardisierung der Internationalen Marktbearbeitung*, Darmstadt.

Braybrook, R. (1995), 'The New Russian Trainers', *Air International*, 49(5), pp. 305–8.

Cramp, B. (1995), 'Refreshing Change', *Marketing*, 19 January, pp. 21–23.

Cunningham, M. T. (1986), 'The British Approach to Europe', in P. W. Turnbull and J.P. Valla (eds.), *Strategies for International Industrial Marketing*, Croom Helm.

Davis, E. J. (1984), 'Managing Marketing', in N. A. Hart (ed.) *The Marketing of Industrial Products*, McGraw-Hill.

Dhalla, N. K. and Yuspeh, S. (1976), 'Forget the Product Life Cycle Concept', *Harvard Business Review*, Jan–Feb, pp. 102–12.

Doyle, P. (1994), *Marketing Management and Strategy*, Prentice-Hall.

Gatignon, H. and Robertson, T. S. (1985), 'A Propositional Inventory for New Diffusion Research', *Journal of Consumer Research*, 11 (March), pp. 849–67.

Guido, G. (1991), 'Implementing a Pan-European Marketing Strategy', *Long Range Planning*, 24(5), pp. 23–33.

Green, P. E. and Carmone, F. J. (1970), *Multidimensional Scaling and Related Techniques in Marketing Analysis*, Allyn and Bacon.

Greenley, G. E. and Bayus, B. L. (1994), 'A Comparative Study of Product Launch and Elimination Decisions in UK and US Companies', *European Journal of Marketing*, 28(2), pp. 5–29.

Halliburton, C. and Hunerberg, R. (1987), 'The Globalisation Dispute in Marketing', *European Management Journal*, 4 (Winter), pp. 243–9.

Halliburton, C. and Hunerberg, R. (1993), 'Pan-European Marketing: Myth or Reality?', in C. Halliburton and R. Hunerberg (eds.), *European Marketing: Readings and Cases*, Addison-Wesley.

Hinde, S. (1995), 'Virgin Moves From Selling Pop to Selling PEPs', *Sunday Times*, 1 January.

Lambkin, M. and Day, G. (1984), 'Evolutionary Processes in Competitive Markets Beyond the Product Life-Cycle', *Journal of Marketing*, 53 (July), pp. 4–20.

Lynch, R. (1994), *European Business Strategies: The European and Global Strategies of Europe's Top Companies*, Kogan Page.

Mazur, L. (1994), 'Whisky Too Galore', *EuroBusiness*, Dec. 1994/Jan. 1995, pp. 46–9.

Moir, J. (1994), 'Kiss and Smell', *Guardian*, 21 December. p. 10.

Pettitt, S. J. (1992), *Small Firms and their Major Customers: An Interaction and Relationship Approach*, unpublished PhD Thesis, Cranfield University.

Relman, P. (1995), 'Fokker 70 ... Fellowship Too', *Air International*, November, pp. 267–73.

Richards, A. (1995), 'The Knitwear Brand that Stretched Too Far', *Marketing*, 6 April, p. 13.

Rijkens, R. (1992), *European Advertising Strategies: The Profiles and Policies of Multinational Companies Operating in Europe*, Cassell.

Rink, D. R. and Swan, J.E. (1979), 'Product Life Cycle Research: A Literature Review', *Journal of Business Research*, 78 (Sept.), pp. 219–42.

Rogers, E. M. (1962), *Diffusion of Innovation*, The Free Press.

Skapinker, M. (1995), 'Consolidation Seen as the Way Forward', *Financial Times*, 12 June, p. 2.

Teather, D. (1995), 'Will Snapple Crumble Here After Its US Dive?', *Marketing*, 17 August, pp. 14–15.

Tieman, R. (1995), 'Regional Plane Makers Are Coming Down to Earth', *The Times*, 6 January.

Turnbull, P. and Valla, J.P. (1986), 'The Strategic Role of Industrial Marketing Management' in P. W. Turnbull and J.P. Valla (eds.), *Strategies for International Industrial Marketing*, Croom Helm.

Tushman, M. L. and Anderson, P. (1986), 'Technological Discontinuities and Organisational Environments', *Administrative Science Quarterly*, Winter, pp. 439–65.

Van Der Krol, R. (1995a), 'Looking Forward to the Benefits', *Financial Times*, 12 June, p. 7.

Van Der Krol, R. (1995b), 'Fokker to Cut 1,760 Jobs', *Financial Times*, 28 February, p. 35.

Wolfe, A. (1991), 'The Single European Market: National or Euro-Brands?', *International Journal of Advertising*, 10, pp. 49–58.

Wroe, M. (1995). 'Slipped Discs', *Marketing Business*, February, pp. 18–22.

9

New Product Development

LEARNING OBJECTIVES

This chapter will help you to:

1 define the various types of product 'newness' and the marketing implications of each;

2 understand the reasons for new product development;

3 analyse the eight stages in the new product development process;

4 appreciate the reasons for new product failure; and

5 outline some current trends in R&D management.

INTRODUCTION

Chapter 8 considered issues of product development, modification and deletion within the context of an existing product portfolio. Sometimes, however, to satisfy strategic objectives it is not enough just to manipulate existing products. Organisations need a flow of new products to keep their portfolios fresh, their customers interested, and their sales growing. This chapter, therefore, is devoted entirely to **new product development** (NPD).

Obviously, the pace of NPD will vary depending on the pressures to change and the scale of change required. Complex, technology-based products, such as new drugs, may be launched and then continue as stable products for a number of years, with any further development effort focusing on minor changes and improvements. In fmcg markets, however, there is more likely to be a rapid rate of NPD. Despite the promising hopes held for some of these new products, it is a stark fact that most, up to 90 per cent, will fail to achieve their potential and will not survive. This is a sobering thought, given the amount of time, resources and money that often goes into developing a new product. A new brand of cheese, Churnton, launched into the UK market in 1994, for example, cost £500 000 to develop, plus a further £2.5 mn for the advertising and promotion for its launch (Maitland, 1994). These sums are not unusual. According to OC&C Strategy Consultants, the marketing cost of a typical food product launch in the UK averages about £3 mn (Mitchell, 1994). In some markets, the stakes are even greater. It costs something like $40 mn (£27 mn) to launch a new fragrance worldwide (Rawsthorn, 1994).

The fact is that nobody can give any guarantees that any new product will succeed, and the more radical the new product idea, the more true this becomes. NPD is not just about *invention*, it is also about *innovation*. Invention is about the creation of ideas and physical products, but innovation is about finding appropriate applications and commercialising those ideas and products. It is something of a cliché, but the British are generally felt to be good at invention, but very poor at innovation, whereas the Japanese are astute when it comes to defining and exploiting the commercial possibilities of an idea or product.

It is, however, possible to assess or minimise the risks of NPD through effective and efficient planning and management of the NPD process. This chapter will later outline a framework, identifying the stages of NPD and the relevant questions that should be asked of any NPD project. First, however, it is necessary to discuss in more detail the definition of 'new products', as it is always important to clarify the context within which NPD is being undertaken. We consider also the rationale for pursuing an active programme of planned new product launches, and point out that in some circumstances, organisations could be failing strategically through their inaction and reluctance to commit themselves to NPD.

The particular emphasis of this chapter is on the introduction of the framework to guide NPD from initiation through to commercialisation. It can be argued that such a procedure can reduce but not eliminate the risks associated with new product launch. An examination of the causes of new product failure reveals that many failures could be avoided with better analysis and research in the development stage. In reality, not all new products are manufacturer initiated and driven. In some organisational markets, the NPD approach may be customer led or a joint effort between buyer and supplier. The final section in this chapter, therefore, examines the underlying approach and rationale for various types of co-operative new product development.

THE MEANING OF A NEW PRODUCT

This section looks at precisely what a new product is, exploring definitions of 'new' from the organisation's point of view, and then discussing the problem from the buyer's perspective.

Types of newness

The term 'new product' appears to be pretty clear cut. There are, however, differing degrees of newness which can make a significant difference to the way in which an organisation handles that product. The risks, opportunities and strategies associated with that product will partly depend upon the type of newness in question. At one extreme, newness could simply involve a new pack size or colour, while at the other extreme, the product could represent a radical, mould-breaking innovation. There are, of course, many options between these two extremes.

A number of these options are of particular interest, and will now be discussed in turn:

New to the company; new to the market
The most exciting option is the product that is new to the company and new to the market; it represents a completely new idea that has never been offered before. Technological breakthroughs often provide the basis for such radical new products. Within the last 20 years or so, the invention and commercialisation of the home video recorder, the CD player and the personal computer (to name but three) have created vast new markets and made a huge impact on the lifestyles of many individuals.

The delicate task with such radical new products is gaining the market's acceptance. In the summer of 1995, for example, Bass launched alcoholic lemonade on to the UK market under the brand name *Hooper's Hooch*, just beating Merrydown Wine's *Two Dogs*. Although alcoholic lemonade had been successfully established in the Australian market, it was a completely new concept for the UK. At the time of the launch, much media coverage and debate was generated about whether such a product would present alcohol too appealingly and attractively to children, thus encouraging them to start drinking. While this publicity may have raised doubts about its acceptability, it did generate awareness and trial of the product among the curious. Manufacturers justified the ethics of alcoholic lemonade by saying that it was targeted at the young premium lager drinker, closer to the adult soft drinks market, and that the flavour was too bitter to appeal to children.

One problem with this category of new product is that potential buyers might be suspicious of a totally new concept – will it be reliable, will it be superseded, will I look a fool in two years' time for having bought it? The second problem is in persuading potential buyers that they actually need this product. After all, if one had lived one's life without a video recorder, why get excited about its invention? Marketers have to address both these problems. The key to them both, perhaps, lies in targeting a segment of innovators and opinion leaders (*see* pp. 303 *et seq.*). If they accept the product, then maybe the suspicion of the rest of the market will be reduced because they can see that other people have bought it. Furthermore, when the rest of the market sees that people they look to (opinion leaders) have embraced the new product, desire for the product becomes a social need for its intangible status benefits rather than a real need for its

With Hooper's Hooch, Bass successfully introduced a new category of alcoholic drink to the UK.

Source: Bass Brewers Ltd.

core function. Generally, the whole marketing mix needs to be handled with care. If the market has no experience of anything quite like this, there is no clear reference point against which to develop a market-orientated marketing mix.

If the risks and marketing problems are so great, then why engage in this kind of innovation? Well, if it works, then there is the respect and reputation gained from being first, not only with the market, but also with shareholders, potential investors and even potential employees (visibly successful organisations attract the brightest candidates). In marketing terms, there is the opportunity to establish a strong, prime position in the market before the real competition starts. Against this, the innovative organisation is bearing the costs and risks of development and market creation, and has to face the prospect of competitors coming in later with cheaper imitative products (*see* pp. 306 *et seq*.), unless they pursue proactive further development to stay ahead.

New to the company; a significant innovation for the market

Where a product represents a significant innovation for the market, the core product concept itself is familiar, but there is a new twist to it that makes it innovative and exciting. Examples of this might be the first combined washer-dryer, the first fax machine to operate with ordinary paper, or the first car fitted with a catalytic converter.

MARKETING IN ACTION

Rubbing salt into the market

Salt can be regarded as a very long life-cycle product that has been used for generations. Salt has not been without its critics from a medical point of view, however. Although it is an essential component of a healthy diet, too much may lead to problems such as raised blood pressure. Consumers are aware that they should cut back on their salt intake, but they also know that much of their salt intake is indirect, through the consumption of processed foods such as bread and hamburgers. Direct intake of salt can be controlled, and health awareness has thus opened up opportunities for 'healthier' versions of salt, such as low-sodium variants.

PanSalt is produced by the Kallo Group from Finland, and was launched into the UK market in the summer of 1996. It was hoped that it would achieve brand leadership within two years because of its advantages when compared with conventional salts. PanSalt's innovation was to reduce the sodium content of the salt by 43 per cent, thus considerably lowering one of the most harmful agents in salt. Other product features include a lower potassium content. The flavour is still salty, but has no unpleasant after-taste. The product was first marketed in Finland in 1986 following a new formulation by a scientist. Subsequent studies all concluded that PanSalt was an effective substitute for traditional salt. It passed rigorous testing in the USA, where it is also classed as a medicine that can be purchased over the counter.

As in Finland, PanSalt is sold in the UK to consumers as a salt for domestic use, as well as being sold to other manufacturers as an ingredient for processed food products. If the success in Finland is repeated, the brand could well achieve its aim of becoming market leader within two years. It does, however, face competition, for example from LoSalt, although Kallo feels that PanSalt is more likely to expand the 'salt alternative' sector than simply to steal share from competitors.

There are two main channels that Kallo had to develop to ensure satisfactory market entry. First it had to be listed by some of the major supermarkets and health food multiples. This would enable the company to build a market presence in the retail sector. This effort would have to be supported by in-store promotion, point of sale promotion, and advertising to the consumer and the trade. Second, the processed food sector had to be developed, for example by encouraging trials with bread and snack manufacturers. This would then allow them to make claims to other organisational customers of reduced sodium content with no loss in product acceptability. New product innovation, therefore, has to be carefully marketed to ensure that trial and market acceptance takes place to justify the investment.

Source: The Grocer (1996b).

The marketing task is perhaps a little easier here, because the basic product concept is a familiar one. The main job is one of communicating the nature of the innovation and the added benefits it confers on the product. The consumer can compare the new product with the old from their own experience, and thus reach an opinion as to the value of the innovation. A family which has had to live with the inconvenience of the space taken up by a washing machine and a tumble dryer in a small house would not need much persuading about the benefits of a combined machine.

New to the company; a minor innovation for the market

A product that represents only a minor innovation for the market is less exciting than the previous option from the market's point of view, as the product offered is not particularly different from what already exists. The challenge and the burden of newness rests much more heavily on the organisation than on the market. An organisation might, for example, enter the existing video recorder market for the first time with a machine that is easier to program than any competitor's product. While this is a worthwhile feature that will attract interest, it is not sufficiently innovative to turn the market upside-down.

In this situation, there should not be too much risk involved in the product concept itself, as that is largely established, tried and tested. The risks and problems arise from trying to gain distribution and break into an established market which may consist of a number of powerful competitors who will use marketing counter-measures to prevent the successful entry of a new product.

New to the company; no innovation for the market

An organisation that offers a product that represents no innovation is offering a completely imitative product, based on a competitor's approach and technology, and the market perceives little difference between them. Many organisations consciously decide to take this 'me too' approach to NPD (see pp. 337 et seq.). For a smaller organisation with limited resources, it makes sense to let the bigger competitor spend the time, effort and money developing the radical new concepts (as with products that are either new to the market or significant innovations), then when the market is established and known, it can launch a slightly cheaper imitation and get a foothold in the lower end of the market. The imitator may be able to achieve a cost advantage, if it has learned from the experience of the innovator. Sony suffered from this with the Walkman. They invented the concept, developed it into a viable commercial proposition, created the market, and launched the first product, yet within a couple of years, they were facing stiff competition from a whole range of cheaper 'me too' imitations offering no signif- icant new features. See also pp. 306 et seq. for further discussion about imitative products.

Customer-orientated perspectives

As implied in the previous section, it is the customers' view of newness and their reaction to that newness that count. This section looks more specifically at the buyers' degree of learning and adjustment to the new product as reflected in their buying behaviour, and their use of the product or service, linking all of this with the supplier's perspective discussed above.

The buyer's approach to dealing with new products has to be put into the context of the level of innovation within a market, which can be categorised in three ways, **continuous innovation**, **dynamically continuous innovation**, and **discontinuous innovation**, as shown in Fig 9.1.

Continuous innovation

In a market characterised by continuous innovation, new product introductions are regular occurrences. No new behaviour is really required of the consumer, who is used to

FIGURE 9.1

The innovation
continuum

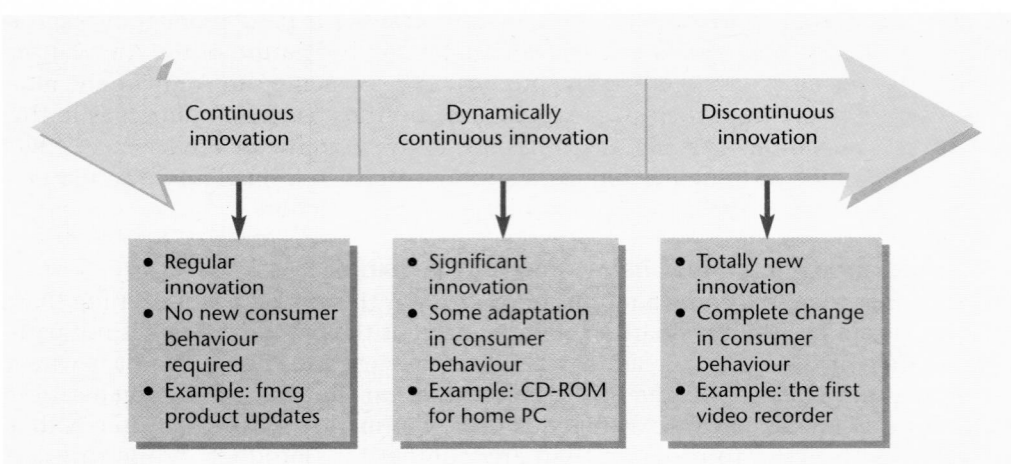

sizing up new products regularly, and includes that activity as a matter of course in the decision-making process. It imposes a small amount of low-risk, limited decision making on what would normally be a routine response situation (*see* pp. 96 and 257 *et seq.*).

Fmcg markets, such as that for laundry detergents, often see new product launches, usually with minor or no innovation incorporated in them. 'Now washes even whiter', 'Washes cleaner at even lower temperatures', 'More concentrated cleaning power than ever', 'With added stain digesters' are the types of phrase that appears on laundry products to signify some level of continuous innovation. Consumers may see them in the supermarket, look at them, then make a decision as to whether to try them or remain loyal to their existing brand. This emphasizes that the key task for the marketer with such new products is to generate awareness and gain distribution.

Dynamically continuous innovation

A market characterised by dynamically continuous innovation tends to involve new products with a degree of significant innovation. Because the innovation represents a big change in a familiar product, it is likely to require some change in buying behaviour. While the buyer has a familiar frame of reference for the product, the new features and benefits have to be understood and integrated into that familiar picture.

MARKETING IN ACTION

Neutraceutials

Continuous innovation can capitalise on changing consumer tastes and concerns. Food manufacturers for example have produced lower-fat, lower-sugar or lower-calorie versions of familiar products over the years. In some cases, they are now moving towards adding more ingredients to their foods. As Oram (1995) reports, there is a growing market for 'neutraceutical' foods with added health-giving ingredients. Thus SmithKline Beecham has introduced Ribena Juice and Fibre, which the company claims can help to reduce cholesterol levels; MD Foods, a Danish company, has introduced Gaio, a yoghurt containing a particular cholesterol-reducing culture, and a French company has launched Carres Memoire, a brand of chocolate that is supposed to improve memory. Raisio is a Finnish company manufacturing Benecol, a margarine product. It claims that the margarine can cut blood cholesterol levels by between 10 per cent and 14 per cent. Such is its appeal, that it sells out as soon as it appears on the supermarket shelves in Finland. This also allows the manufacturer to charge a premium price for it – about six times the price of a normal margarine.

Sources: The Grocer (1996a); Oram (1995).

The introduction of the electric toothbrush, for instance, might have caused problems for some consumers. The function would be well understood, but what are the advantages of an electric one over a manual brush? How do I know it's safe? This is related to limited decision-making situations (*see* p. 97), and thus emphasizes the need for the marketer to provide information and to explain the new benefits to the prospective purchaser. In selling a fax machine which does not require special paper in order to receive incoming messages, marketers do not need to explain the function and benefits of the fax itself, which is very well established, but they do need to show how the plain paper feature differentiates the machine from the competition, and how it saves money and time etc.

Discontinuous innovation

Discontinuous innovation represents the biggest upheaval for the potential customer, and relates most closely to extensive decision making (*see* p. 97). It requires a whole new learning experience for the customer, with new patterns of consumption behaviour. The consumer has to understand the underlying concept of the product and then relate it to their own life, visualising how it will fit in. This process is linked to the issues of suspicion and acceptance raised in the discussion of the marketing problems of products new to both the market and the organisation. Customers need hard information about what the product is and what it does, but they also need guidance on its benefits and what that means to them. There is also a role here for product demonstrations. The microwave oven, for example, was greeted with incredulity when it was launched, because it was difficult to believe that it could do all the things promised without compromising the quality of the food. The advertisements could achieve a certain amount, but 'seeing is believing', and seeing the machine in action and tasting the results were essential for proving that it did live up to its promises.

THE IMPORTANCE OF NEW PRODUCT DEVELOPMENT

Having looked at the outcomes of NPD, in terms of degrees of innovation and their impact on the potential customer, it is now time to think more clearly about why NPD is so important. Organisations do not operate in a static environment, but are constantly facing the consequences of changing technology, changing customer tastes and preferences and changing competitor product ranges. Any organisation that is positively managing its product portfolio will recognise that its existing products are in different stages of their life cycles, and can be modified to maximise their potential, but inevitably, new products will be needed to replace the mature and declining ones.

Although it is an important part of a product strategy, NPD can be a very risky business. The commercial and financial risks can be very high, with many new products failing. As reported in a newspaper article by Mitchell (1994), of 12 000 new grocery and toiletry products launched in the UK during 1995, 90 per cent will be dropped within months of their launch. The failure rates can thus be very high, yet organisations are increasingly driven to NPD as a means of gaining competitive edge. The investment in NPD can be very substantial in some industries. According to Elliott and Beavis (1994), for example, the UK pharmaceutical industry invests 12 per cent of its sales revenue in R&D, compared with the UK average of 1.6 per cent. Furthermore, analysis undertaken by the Department of Trade and Industry of the R&D investment of the UK's listed companies showed that the pharmaceutical companies accounted between them for nearly one-third of all UK R&D spending in 1993 (Caulkin, 1994). The added ingredients for the 'neutraceutical' products mentioned earlier can take up to 15 years to develop, and cost anything from $10 mn to $100 mn.

Saes Getters is an Italian company that makes the component that maintains the vacuum within a television or computer monitor cathode ray tube. The company invests 10 per cent of its turnover in R&D, which has two important benefits. First, R&D allows the company to stay one step ahead of the competition in terms of evolving and improving the core product, which means that many competitors fall by the wayside because their products are rendered obsolete by Saes Getters. Second, R&D allows the company to diversify into different industrial applications, which means that there is a constant flow of new products for new markets, again, ahead of the competition. This diversification also reduces the company's dependency on a single product for one specific market (Hill, 1995).

The organisation, therefore, needs a new product strategy which is linked with the overall strategic plan of business. It is essential to look ahead and assess how much sales or profit will have to be generated from today's or tomorrow's new products in three or five years' time. Our discussion of the product life-cycle (*see* pp. 294 *et seq*.), pointed out that it takes time to get a new product established, and the one that is intended to be the big revenue earner in five years' time might have to be launched now, and therefore should already have spent some time in development.

The approach to NPD can be either reactive or proactive.

Reactive approach

The *reactive* approach is taken by the organisation that is happy to respond to what others do, rather than seeking to outmanoeuvre its competitors. This organisation is happy to let others take risks and face the problems of breaking new ground, then it will enter the market when it is clear that further opportunities exist. The organisation may be late into the market, but may have the production or marketing muscle to capitalise on the situation. This organisation avoids costly launch errors, and can even eventually use that experience to extend the technology.

The reactive organisation is most likely to have its emphasis on application and design engineering. As said earlier, however, the imitative market entrant does have the problems of breaking into an established market in which others may already have built reputation and market share. With the Walkman market, Sony had the established lead and the quality reputation, so the imitators concentrated on getting manufacturing costs down to allow them to produce cheaper, lower quality products to create a new segment at the bottom end of the market.

Proactive approach

The *proactive* organisation deliberately sets out to find new ideas and seeks to commercialise them early before the competition step in. This approach requires a strong commitment to R&D, consumer research and market awareness. It also needs willingness to take risks and the kind of organisational culture that encourages enterprise. Such an organisation may deliberately scan the environment for opportunities and then develop products to fit the perceived gap in the market. If the organisation, however, has insufficient resources to develop an idea from scratch, it may then seek or initiate joint ventures, or licences.

Proactive NPD is far from easy, and there are a number of considerations to be taken into account when thinking about this approach. First, such an investment in NPD is expensive and time consuming, with no guarantees of success. This commitment, therefore, really needs to take place against a backdrop of an existing portfolio comprising steady profit-earning products, in order to keep the organisation and the NPD process ticking over. Furthermore, a new product in the early days after its launch may continue to consume more resources than it generates, so the organisation needs to be sure of its short-term cash flow. Finally, fast moving changes in the marketing environment mean that there is an increasing tendency for life cycles to shorten, with the result that organisations are under pressure to produce successful new products more often, yet with shorter payback periods (*see* Chapter 11).

Example

Canon is an example of an organisation that has successfully taken a proactive approach to NPD. In the 1960s and 1970s, Canon was primarily a camera company, but had the foresight to apply its optics knowledge to office products. In the 1970s it became a serious competitor, threatening Xerox in the copier market, and also began to develop laser printers. By the 1980s, Canon had also developed the Bubble-Jet printer. Every year, Canon adds something like 800 patents to its portfolio.

Either way, perhaps one of the main motivating forces for NPD is a justifiable paranoia: if our organisation does not invest in NPD, the competition certainly will, and that will place us at a longer-term disadvantage. It is important, however, to manage the NPD process appropriately within the organisational context and structure.

Cooper and Kleinschmidt (1987) compared product successes and failures against various factors that might affect the likelihood of success. The most important factor was having a good-quality, well-managed NPD process. This was closely followed by a need for the new product to offer a clear competitive advantage. Other important factors included synergy between the new product and the organisation's technological and marketing strengths; the quality and thoroughness of the early stages of the NPD process; the effectiveness of the technological and marketing inputs into the NPD process, and of course having top management support. This, then, emphasizes the importance of the NPD framework, the subject of the next section.

THE NEW PRODUCT DEVELOPMENT PROCESS

This section develops an eight-stage framework which can guide the NPD process. Shown in Fig 9.2, it is presented as a logical sequence, narrowing down from a broad spread of potential general ideas in the first stage to the commercialisation of a single highly developed concept in the final stage. Clearly, the implementation of the process will vary according to the particular organisation involved and the market context within which it is operating. Some stages may be truncated, others may be extended, according to circumstance. In a complex, high-technology market, the process may be extremely formal and take many years to complete, while in a fast moving fashion market, the process may be reiterated three or four times a year, for each new season. Nevertheless, despite the variations, it is still important to recognise that such a framework or process brings a degree of rigour to NPD that can help to reduce the risks and problems of failure (Booz-Allen, Hamilton Inc., 1982).

Each stage in the NPD process will now be discussed in turn.

Idea generation

Any new product has to start somewhere as the germ of an idea. In view of the investment and commitment that will to be given to this process, it is important in the early stages to let the corporate imagination range as freely as possible, just to make sure that all the options have been thought of. There is a need for an ongoing flow of new ideas. It does not matter how ridiculous some of them might sound; at this stage anything goes, and you never know what potential an idea might have. Ideas can always be abandoned at the next stage if serious appraisal shows them to be inappropriate. Rarely do these ideas emerge out of nowhere, however. Some ideas develop from a combination of recognising emerging market needs and exploring technical feasibility. Thus ideas may be either problem or opportunity driven. Whatever the source of ideas, however, some kind of formal mechanism is usually needed to generate and collect them.

There are a number of main sources of new product ideas:

FIGURE 9.2

The new product development process

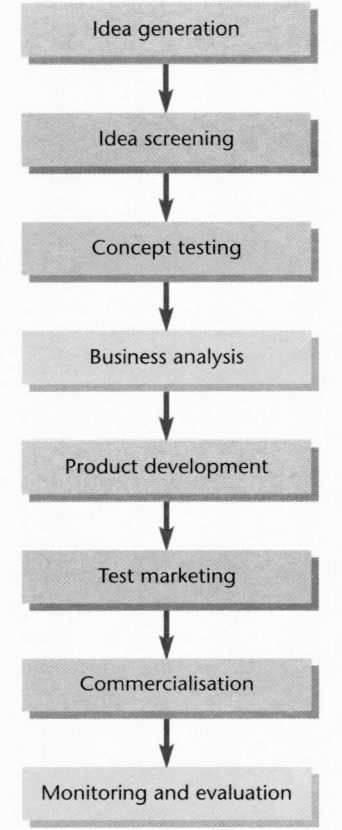

Research and development

R&D is the obvious source of new product ideas. After all, that is what an organisation's R&D staff are paid to do. In some organisations, the R&D department can be given a very tight brief ('Develop something that conforms to these specifications'), in others, they can be given freedom to range widely ('Do what you want, as long as you deliver something we consider commercially viable'). The first approach has the advantage of making sure that R&D activity and expenditure are controlled, since it is problem or project driven and has defined aims and objectives. The second approach, however, allows R&D scientists full creative scope to do what they are good at, and it does throw up products that otherwise would never have been conceived.

R&D work can also vary from being completely self-sufficient, working only within the company environment, to collaborative research with other organisations, external institutes or universities. This latter approach allows the organisation to draw on a much wider pool of expertise on a particular project than they could ever reasonably hope to employ for themselves, but has the drawback of placing the work in a more public arena where the competition might detect it. There is more on this at pp. 356 *et seq.*

Generating and developing ideas through R&D can involve fairly long time-scales, with far from certain reward. Maintaining an R&D department is thus expensive, yet essential for a proactive organisation. Sometimes, external inventors approach an organisation with their own ideas. They might wish to sell the idea to the organisation, or to enter into a collaborative development deal, splitting the profits. The Black & Decker Workmate began life as such an idea.

Competitors

There are two categories of competitor to consider here: actual and potential. Actual competitors are those who operate in your existing market and have products there already. Looking in detail at the products themselves and assessing the marketing strategies around them can lead to an understanding of the concept's strengths and weaknesses, and thus how it can be improved. This analysis can form the basis of a new improved version, albeit a potential 'me too' product, with a more focused marketing strategy.

Potential competitors operate in areas from which others are currently absent. If the organisation's strategic plan suggests a need to redefine the market then potential competitors may become actual competitors. This could, for example, apply to export markets. An organisation thinking of entering a foreign market would need to assess existing coverage of that market and develop its own product and marketing offering accordingly.

In some situations, there may be no intention of entering into direct competition with the potential competitors studied, but every intention of lifting ideas from them. A study of tourism innovation in Ireland (Pettitt, 1989) found that a common source of new products was visits by entrepreneurs to other countries, where they picked up new ideas. Also in Ireland, efforts have been made by the Irish Development Authority and the Irish

Goods Council to build up an ideas bank from looking at import substitution possibilities. This involved identifying product sectors such as foodstuffs and electronics where home producers could be given help to develop products and thus enter the market.

Employees

Employees can be encouraged to suggest new product ideas through suggestion boxes and competitions. Organisations such as Toyota, Kodak and General Motors operate such schemes. Employees may be able to think of improved ways of producing the product or new features to incorporate. It is very easy to underestimate the vested interest of the work-force in the organisation's products and their knowledge. After all, they work with the organisation's products on a daily basis, and their jobs depend on continued progress and development within the market.

Employees who have regular contact with customers and the trade should be given special attention. Service engineers and sales representatives, for example, come into contact with customer problems as a normal part of their working day, and may thus generate potential ideas that can offer product opportunities. It is important, therefore, to make sure that such employees are encouraged to have such discussions with customers and that the reporting mechanisms are in place to capture and collate the information arising.

Customers

The organisation is in business to serve the customer's needs and wants, and so it is crucial to be in touch with customers, not only on the informal basis discussed above, but also through formal research techniques. Monitoring changing consumer attitudes and feelings about products and markets, and their usage patterns provides fertile ground for new ideas. Whether this research is regularly purchased secondary data or opportunity-driven commissioned research, it may reveal important gaps early enough to allow the organisation to gain competitive advantage in its NPD programme.

Recycled paper

Recycled paper was introduced in the late 1980s as part of the general trend towards 'green' products. Although some progress was made in the greeting cards and large format notepaper sectors overall no significant impact was made on virgin fibre products. There was an image of cheapness and unattractiveness about recycled papers that failed to persuade buyers. However one company, Weir Paper Products in Scotland, believes that the market is now ready for growth as a result of paper producers' changes in technology and production techniques.

Technological improvement means that the finished quality of recycled papers is better. Paper buyers were often highly critical of the appearance and performance of recycled products. The loss of presentation had to be compensated for by a clear demonstration of a concern for the environment, which did not appeal to many buyers. But as the difference between virgin fibre and recycled paper narrows, and quality improves, recycled paper can gain more popularity. Weir went one stage further by installing new equipment that allowed high-quality papers to be produced from lower-grade raw material, thus producing an even more acceptable product. Top-quality recycled papers can now be used confidently for any type of printing requirement, including reports, brochures or mailshots, where image and quality matter. Technological improvement is not the only factor that is encouraging a wider use of recycled papers. An increase in the price of the pulp that goes into virgin fibre paper, and a fall in the price of the waste that goes into recycled paper mean that a wide price differential has opened up.

Source: McAtear (1995).

In organisational markets, customers are a particularly important source of product improvement and innovation ideas. Von Hippel (1978), looking at scientific instrument markets, found that 82 per cent of major improvements and 70 per cent of minor improvements in four different instruments arose from customer suggestions. Some organisations go as far as to identify lead users, those customers whose needs are evolving ahead of the market in general. Working with lead users, organisations can develop their innovative ideas and products early, and then adapt them for the wider market (Von Hippel, 1986). Similarly, Bonaccorsi and Lipparini (1994) found that a leading Italian firm derived significant improvements in NPD through close, co-operative partnerships with innovative suppliers.

Licensing

Licensing can be a useful way of getting access to new products without the time and expense of full-scale NPD. Licensing is a contractual relationship in which a manufacturer (licensor) who owns trade mark or patent rights over a product or technology allows another organisation (licensee) to manufacture and market that product in return for royalties or other payments. Licences are often used as a means of entering international markets without direct investment, and are further considered in that context in Chapter 25. A small US manufacturer of orthopaedic aids and specialist hospital equipment, for example, had neither the resources nor the know-how to get into the European market. It thus searched for an English-speaking organisation based in Europe that would act as a licensee for the products.

A licensing agreement may cover the use of patents, manufacturing expertise or technical services, but a major issue is often whether or not the licensor's trade mark will be used. Nevertheless, a co-operative agreement between licensor and licensee can generate benefits in terms of new technology and ideas for both parties. The licensing route is attractive for smaller organisations with limited resources, either as an exporting strategy (as a licensor) or as a means of product range development (as a licensee) (*see* Chapter 24).

Organised creativity

A number of techniques for encouraging staff to develop new ideas exist. Majaro (1991) suggests brainstorming, synectics, attribute listing, forced relationships and morphological analysis.

Brainstorming. Brainstorming involves a group of 6 to 10 people in an intensive session focusing on a specific problem. The purpose is to generate as many ideas as possible, however wild they are. The benefit of the group session is that one person's idea may spark off other ideas from the rest of the group. In discussing brainstorming, Osborn (1963) suggests that there should be no negative comments about any idea during the sessions; that outlandish ideas should be accepted; that the more ideas generated, the better, and that ideas can be combined to create better ones.

Synectics. Synectics is a group technique similar to brainstorming, but less problem specific. This frees the group from any mental strait-jacket and allows it to enter into more exploratory thinking.

Attribute listing. Attribute listing means listing all the attributes of a product and then changing each one in search of a new combination. Osborn (1963) suggests thinking in terms of other uses, adaptation, rearrangement, reversal, magnifying or minimising attributes, combination or substitution.

Forced relationships. Forced relationships as a technique considers products in relation to each other. Manufacturers of telephones, computers and hi-fi equipment, for example, may generate new product ideas by thinking of their products in relation to a car, for example, and considering the technology involved, the design and styling and how the product would fit into the car's cockpit fascia.

Morphological analysis. Morphological analysis means looking at a problem and its components, and then finding connections and solutions. Thus thinking about a golf buggy might lead to consideration of options relating to fuel source, power transmission, body shape and surface contact.

Agencies and consultants

Many agencies and consultancies specialise in providing information to organisations to assist in the generation of new product ideas. In the fashion industry, for example, agencies exist to predict colour and fabric trends so that designers and manufacturers can develop appropriate ranges for future seasons.

General Intelligence

Apart from the specific sources already mentioned, there is also a range of external sources, most of which are not specific to the organisation. These sources provide very general information which can be interpreted by the organisation to reveal possible new ideas. Such sources include trade magazines, exhibitions, distributor comments, government agencies, libraries and general research publications.

Despite the range of sources of new ideas, only a few ideas are likely to amount to anything. A large and regular supply is therefore needed. If an organisation really wants a successful NPD programme, it must ensure a systematic and ongoing effort.

Once the pool of ideas has been collected, it is time to move on to the next stage, idea screening.

Screening ideas

This second stage of NPD is where a preliminary scan of the ideas is conducted, in order to eliminate those that are unlikely to prove appropriate or successful. This means undertaking an assessment of an idea's potential, using information that is already available within the organisation. If the idea does not seem to fit within what is already known, or if nobody seems prepared to make out a case for following it through, there is little point in investing in more serious and costly external research and testing. It is best to drop bad ideas (after a fair hearing) as soon as possible, partly to allow concentration on the better ideas, and partly to prevent a bad idea gaining unjustified management momentum as time goes on.

The objective of this stage then is to assess whether the idea fits with the broad strategic plans and development directions of the organisation. It is also important to establish whether the idea's implementation is technically feasible. Usually, the idea and its preliminary screening analysis are presented to management as a proposal. This will describe the product arising from the idea, outline how it complements existing products, analyse its market segments, define and analyse the competition, and forecast its likely margin and its sales profile over time so that recommendations can be made whether or not to proceed.

Many organisations use a semi-formal weighting procedure to establish the relative importance of various screening criteria. This produces a score for each idea, allowing them to compared with each other. Table 9.1 shows an example, suggesting main criteria that might be applied for screening-assessment purposes. In this case, Idea 1 scores significantly better than the other two.

It can be seen that each specific factor assumes a different weighting, according to its overall importance in a successful launch. In some cases, management have a maximum of 100 points to divide between all the relevant criteria. Having such a limited number of points to distribute means that there is likely to be an overt, critical discussion on why particular criteria have been included and why certain criteria deserve more points than others. This in itself is a useful process, forcing managers to think hard about how their market ticks.

Some care clearly needs to be taken in assessing ideas on such criteria. Ideas at the extreme ends of the spectrum (the excellent or the complete non-starters) pass

TABLE 9.1
Idea-screening criteria

Criterion	Weighting	Idea 1		Idea 2		Idea 3	
		Raw score	Weighted score	Raw score	Weighted score	Raw score	Weighted score
Fit with corporate strategic goals	15	8	1.20	3	0.45	5	0.75
Fit with marketing strategic goals	15	7	1.05	3	0.45	5	0.75
Market growth	5	9	0.45	9	0.45	3	0.15
Size of target market	10	6	0.60	8	0.80	9	0.9
Access to market	10	4	0.40	9	0.90	7	0.7
Differential advantage offered	10	9	0.90	5	0.50	7	0.7
Profitability potential	10	7	0.70	7	0.70	4	0.4
Timing	5	8	0.40	7	0.35	9	0.45
Synergy with existing products	5	7	0.35	3	0.15	6	0.3
Synergy with existing technology	5	7	0.35	3	0.15	2	0.1
Synergy with existing distribution channels	5	3	0.15	8	0.40	8	0.4
Synergy with existing skills and assets	5	6	0.30	4	0.20	5	0.25
Total	100	81	6.85	69	5.50	70	5.85

Note: Raw score = marks out of 10; Weighted score = (raw score × weighting)/100

through this process very easily, but the ones in the middle, on the borderline between 'accept' and 'reject', could be more difficult to assess. The numerical score itself has a spurious certainty about it, and in reality, for a borderline idea, it should be possible to override the score and argue about its strengths and weaknesses on a more qualitative level. Remember that the assessment criteria and their weightings are in themselves management judgements, based on perceptions of previous experience, and thus there is always room for doubt or argument.

Concept testing

Once an idea has been accepted in principle at the internal screening stage, it needs to have some external endorsement. This, then, is the third stage of NPD: **concept testing**, which can be defined as:

> **'A printed or filmed representation of a product or service. It is simply a device to communicate the subject's benefits, strengths and reasons for being'.**
> (Schwartz, 1987)

Concept testing starts to describe, profile and visualise the product in a way that potential customers would understand. What is presented to potential buyers at this stage may still only be sketch concepts, in the form of working statements, drawings or storyboards, or it may go as far as models and mock-up packaging. There are two main types of concept statement: core ideas and positioning statements. Core ideas consist of short, general statements of what the product can do. There is no attempt to sell, as such, and all this type of statement is doing is testing whether the basic idea is acceptable or attractive. Positioning statements may comprise several paragraphs, focusing on main and secondary benefits, as well as outlining aspects of the product's marketing mix. Here, the researcher is trying to get as close as possible to assessing a realistic package that the potential customer might encounter in the market-place.

The overall objective, then, is to assess the relative attractiveness of each idea to the people who the organisation hopes will eventually buy the product. The kinds of questions asked are included in Table 9.2. Such an assessment provides management

TABLE 9.2
Concept testing

Hypothetical concept statement for a self-chilling beer can

'A can of beer that cools itself, whatever the outside temperature. When the sealed can is opened by pulling a tab, the pressure releases a special capsule that can chill a can from a room temperature of 23°C down to 5°C in thirty seconds. The taste of the beer is unaltered and it will feel as if it has come straight from the fridge. The can will still be fully recyclable and requires no special storage. The price of the drink may rise by around 5%.'

A group of consumers may then be asked the following questions to establish such factors as need, perceived value, the impact on trial, how to communicate benefits, and likely usage rates:

- 'What problems do you find with the temperature of beer served from a can?'
- 'Do you understand the benefits of the new can?'
- 'Do you believe in the benefits offered?'
- 'Will these benefits be important to you?'
- 'Would you require any more evidence to support the claims made?'
- 'Do you think that the new price of the beer is fair for the value offered?'
- 'Would you certainly/probably/not sure/probably not/ certainly not buy beer in these cans?'
- 'Would the new can increase your total purchases of beer or would they remain the same?'

with further information about the strengths and weaknesses of each idea and a rating on a scale from 'definitely would buy' to 'definitely would not buy'.

This stage of the process sometimes produces surprises (there would be no point doing it if it did not). Management's favourite ideas can be rejected by the consumer, while apparently weak or borderline ideas emerge with hidden appeal. Whatever the outcomes, management should now have a fuller picture of each idea and may, therefore, reject a few more, and carry a small number through to the next stage, a thorough business analysis.

Business analysis

The fourth stage of NPD requires the product concept to be specified in greater detail so that production, marketing and financial projections can be made. It may involve, for example, forecasting new product sales and the rate of repeat purchase. Some of the issues addressed at this stage may well be the same as those included in the preliminary screening earlier, but here, the organisation is looking for more depth, more rigour and more evidence. Beyond this stage, it can become very expensive to drop an idea because of the capital investment and management time involved in developing and creating prototypes of both the product and its marketing strategy. It is important, therefore, that this stage should be thorough and that management are fully convinced and committed to any idea carried beyond it.

There are three main dimensions to consider: marketing, finance and production.

Marketing strategy

It is particularly important to show evidence of the nature of the *market*, its shape, size, dynamics, competitors and likely competitor reaction, along with any customer feedback gained so far. Further research may be undertaken at this point to clarify or further explore specific areas of concern. All of that activity looks at the external picture. It is also essential to demonstrate the internal strategic benefits to be gained and the demands their will be made on marketing resources by continuing with a particular product idea. Thus the product's relationship with the existing product portfolio, its distribution, sales and promotional needs all have to be addressed in some detail. None of those considerations, however, can make sense without some kind of outline of the marketing programme envisaged for launching and sustaining the product, considering all elements of the marketing mix.

All of these elements have to be fully costed and linked with a range of alternative sales and profit projections that are realistic, and both optimistic and pessimistic.

Production

Satisfactory marketing of the product is not enough. The organisation has to be able to *produce* it as well. Detailed analysis, therefore, is needed on all aspects of manufacturing, such as material and component sourcing and storage, factory space, labour and machinery requirements. Thought also needs to be given to whether introducing this product will affect other production lines and schedules. Again, all this needs to be costed in the context of various possible levels of production. Only then can the sales and profit projections be appreciated. The sales figures projected may look healthy in themselves, but may actually be below the threshold for economies of scale to operate on the production side. This might mean that the product can only just break even at best, unless its production costs can be brought down, or its marketing strategy is revised radically to open up a bigger market at a higher price.

If the costs of production are thought to be too high, or if the disruption to current activities is too great, then it might be decided that it would be better to sub-contract manufacture to another organisation, in which case an extremely careful and detailed analysis of the risks and benefits would have to be undertaken, along with a detailed search for potential suppliers.

Financial analysis

Both of the areas discussed so far, marketing and production, have *cost* implications. These need to be fed into detailed calculations of the costs associated with different volumes, and a breakeven analysis. Decisions also need to be made on the level of fixed costs and overheads that would need to be apportioned to the product. The financial analysis would also have to decide how to treat the R&D and development costs associated with the product, in terms of the amount to be charged to the product and over how many years it should be recovered.

The objective of the financial analysis is to provide information on the return on the investment in development, the likely payback period, and the product's profit sensitivity should its market share develop in various ways, both good and bad. Chapter 11, on pricing, will develop these concepts further and look at how they might impact on the pricing decision.

Competitive response

One of the most difficult things to gauge in all of this is competitive reaction. That is why all of these analyses have to include an element of 'what if?' about them and take account of good, average and poor sales performance. Patent protection or heavy branding may help to protect against the competition launching a 'me too' product too quickly, but if a product launch threatens the competition's existing market shares, then the organisation concerned will have to be prepared for swift and damaging competitive response. That will reflect not only on its sales, but also on its marketing costs if, for example, an advertising or price war results.

Product development

The business analysis has brought through one or two ideas with real potential. Now, it is time to commit significant investment to produce the actual product. Everything that can be done theoretically has been done. Any further analysis requires a *real* product in order to allow demonstration, product trials, performance assessment and usage testing.

Just how problematic this fifth stage of NPD is, depends on how innovative the new product is. The process may be more straightforward if the product utilises known technology. With a new shape of potato crisp, for example, more of the risk will lie in the organisation's ability to create a market presence than in its ability to produce a consistent quality product. With new engineering products (such as components), capital investment items (such as production machinery), or even new food types (such as microwavable frozen chips), extensive development work will be required before production reaches an acceptable level of efficiency, quality and consistency.

> ### Example
>
> Paxman is a supplier of high-powered diesel engines for locomotives, yachts and electrical generators. In 1993 it launched a new engine, the VP185 which performed 15–20 per cent better than the company's previous model which had been used in Intercity 125 locomotives. Before launch, however, the VP185 had to undergo extensive testing. In 1991 it underwent a British Rail type test, where its performance and ratings under different power demands were examined. Once it had passed these tests and gained British Rail Type Approval, it was fitted into a locomotive for further testing in the field for some 8000 hours under realistic operating conditions (Ford, 1994). Similarly, Siemens spent five years and between DM 100 mn and 200 mn developing a new series of gas turbines. These too underwent extensive testing trials, the results of which, in terms of thermal efficiency and electrical output, were used by Siemens as part of its marketing approach (Baxter, 1995).

In the product development stage, this Paxman VP186 diesel engine underwent extensive testing.

Source: GEC Alsthom Diesels.

The staff involved at this stage will depend on the nature of the technology concerned. Design engineers, development engineers, R&D scientists, manufacturing and tooling experts may all play a part with an engineering or capital product. With foodstuffs, extensive laboratory testing, along with initial taste trials, may be required. The organisation will call on any type of expertise, whether available internally or consulted externally, in order to get it right. In any case, a sound appreciation of product specification and legal requirements (touching on safety, health or performance, for example) is necessary.

It is impossible to specify a length of time for this development process. An aircraft takes many years to develop and involves many different areas of expertise from interior design to micro-electronics. A fashion product may take a matter of weeks, by necessity. However long it takes, the objective is to answer questions on whether the product can be made cost effectively, within business plan guidelines, and whether it is capable of performing consistently under realistic conditions.

Towards the end of the development phase, if the product is looking good, plans can be made for market and customer testing. In fmcg markets, this means developing brand identity, packaging, labelling, promotion, pricing and launch strategy etc. Churnton, the new cheese mentioned at the beginning of this chapter, for example, was subjected to trial tasting sessions in Safeway supermarkets, which allowed the company to gauge likely repeat purchase rates (80 per cent), and to refine its promotional pitch ('After one taste, you'll turn to Churnton'). In organisational markets, it is more likely to involve the development of appropriate support manuals and associated training, or installation guides so that a realistic test can go ahead.

Test marketing

Particularly in consumer markets, before the decision is made to proceed with a full launch, the potential product can be offered on a limited basis in a defined geographic area, under conditions that are as realistic as possible. Within the UK, this geographic area is likely to correspond with a regional TV area to allow advertising to run only within the boundaries of the test market. This enables an assessment to be made of the likely outcomes of a full national launch.

Test marketing, the sixth NPD stage, answers a number of critical questions about the product. It gives an indication of whether the target market will actually buy the product and whether they will repeat the purchase or not. It shows the trade response to the product and how it performs in reality against the competition. Conducting market research to monitor the progress and outcomes of the test market can assess trade and consumer response to elements of the marketing mix, identifying which aspects are successful and which might need revision, and it can also offer valuable information on how the market rates the various product attributes and benefits. Again, this can identify where product improvements need to be made before the full launch.

Example

Although test marketing involves a major commitment, it is still cheaper to stop now than to face the embarrassment of a full-scale national failure. McDonald's, for example, test marketed a product called McPloughman's (bread, cheese and pickle) in the UK. They found that customers were not interested in it, and that staff did not like to mention it or try to sell it to customers. The company felt that it had not researched the product sufficiently well, and abandoned the idea.

Test marketing is not an extension of the development stage. Much of the product testing should already have been undertaken and the obvious bugs ironed out. This stage may be seen as a trial run for the major launch, in which all the elements of the planned marketing offering are assessed.

In summary, test marketing offers a number of benefits:

1 it is a real test in a real environment;
2 it offers a last chance for fine tuning;
3 it gives the opportunity to vary some of the mix variables. For example, a test market might take place in two geographically different (but demographically similar) regions, each of which has a different advertising approach, with all other elements of the marketing mix held constant. This might help to decide which advertising approach is the more effective in terms of generating sales or creating the right product image;
4 it allows the assessment of things that are difficult to predict on paper, such as awareness generated, propensity for repeat buying, etc.

All of this allows the adjustment of the overall business plan and the launch strategy. It is especially important as a guide for the fine detail, such as how much to produce initially, where to supply, whether to run more or less advertising etc.

Test marketing seems like a good idea, but there are a number of areas that need careful consideration before a decision is made on whether to test market or go straight into a national launch.

Test area selection

If the results of the test market are going to be scaled up to give a picture of the total market, then the organisation needs to be absolutely sure that the test market is indeed representative of the overall target market. The criteria for selection will vary from product to product, taking into account things like distribution structure, media availability, competitor activity, and the detailed breakdown of the target market profile.

Competitive response

Even within an area selected as being as typical as possible, there are risks that the test marketing may go wrong. Competitors will not sit back passively and let another organisation proceed with test marketing. If they find out that test marketing is to be conducted in a particular region, they may at least try to distort the results. They could do this quite simply by running sales promotions, either aimed at the trade, so that the retailers stock up with competitors' products and will be less willing to take on large quantities of the test-marketed product, or aimed at consumers to divert their attention from the test product.

A potentially more serious problem of test marketing is that it gives the competition a great deal of warning and much detail about what is planned. This might just give them enough lead time to bring forward their own plans and launch their own version of the product with full knowledge of the test marketers' position. This is especially easy if the basis for the new product lies in relatively superficial aspects such as packaging or branding rather than in fundamental product attributes or technicalities.

Timing and duration

Other problems relate to the timing and the duration of the test market. The organisation needs to ensure that any seasonal factors affecting sales are taken into account when planning and evaluating the test market. Also, the duration of the test market needs to be carefully considered. If it goes on for too long, then all that happens is that the organisation stops learning anything useful or new, and this unduly delays the big launch. A prolonged test market means that the competition are being given a longer lead time to think of a response to the national launch. Too short a test market period, however, might mean that important effects are missed. Enough time must be allowed to enable the target market to become aware of the product, try it, then settle down into a regular purchasing pattern. It may also take some time for advertising and other promotional efforts to reach their full potential.

All three of the areas discussed above must be taken into account when planning and evaluating the effects of a test marketing exercise. In particular, the typicality of the test area and the possible effects of untypical behaviour or spoiling tactics from the competition need to temper the way in which the results are scaled up to reflect the national picture.

If the risks of test marketing are too great, especially with the delay and the danger of competitors' alternatives coming on to the market, then there are a number of alternatives.

1 *Simulated test market.* This is a much reduced version of the full test market discussed above and involves the introduction of a brand to a number of selected stores. Free samples might be distributed, and consumers questioned about their buying habits and brand preferences. These consumers are then tracked through their product usage, questioned on their assessment of the product's attributes and repurchasing behaviour.
2 *Controlled distribution minimarkets.* Again, this technique is often store specific. Purchase of the new product is monitored electronically, and if possible, repurchases are also tracked.

Both of these methods lower the costs of test marketing, as well as being quicker to produce results. Most importantly, however, they make a less public impact, allowing the organisation to keep elements of its product launch plans away from the competition's direct scrutiny.

Overall, provided it is carried through with thought, and sufficient time is available to do it properly, test marketing can be a very valuable step in the launch process, especially for products which eventually pass through mass distribution channels.

Its role is less clear cut, however, with services and organisational products.

Test marketing for services

Cowell (1984) points out that test marketing for services is not always possible. Large service providers, such as airlines or banks, who produce mass market services can test a new service package on an individual route or in an individual region. This will help them to answer the question of whether they have developed a product that is really attractive to the people it was designed for, and whether they are selling it effectively. There will then be an opportunity for refining the service itself and its delivery, and perhaps its marketing strategy, before offering the product from all the organisation's service outlets.

Many small service providers, however, are geographically centred anyway, and thus the test market is the entire real market! In this case it may be less a matter of test marketing and more a matter of pacing the development of the business. Thus the market may be tested initially with a compact range of core services, and then the organisation can open out to a greater range of services when viability has been established.

Test marketing for organisational products

According to Moore and Pessemier (1993), there are several reasons why test marketing may not be appropriate for organisational products:

1 *Market structure.* The market may consist of a small number of potential customers in total, or a very small number of customers may account for a large proportion of sales in this market. Either way, a test market would become tantamount to a full launch.
2 *Buyer–seller relationships and customisation.* In many organisational markets, close and durable working relationships develop, which in turn lead to joint product development. This means that the potential buyer is involved in NPD from the start, with an implied commitment to purchase what is effectively a customised product at the end of it. Since the buyer is involved in prototype testing as part of the joint development process, and since issues such as price and availability are also negotiated as part of the development, test marketing as such is a rather redundant concept.
3 *The product's life span and purchase frequency.* Some organisational products, such as capital equipment for example, have very long life spans and are thus purchased very infrequently. This means that although there may be many potential customers in total, at the time that an organisation with a new product is ready to test market it, there may actually be very few potential customers ready to consider the product *now*. Again, this effectively means, therefore, that the test market would consist of all potential customers who are able and willing to buy.

Clearly, much depends on the type of product. Low-cost, low-risk, relatively frequently purchased goods which are applicable across a range of business customers lend themselves to consumer type test marketing. On the other hand, test marketing is less applicable to customer-specified or high-cost, high-risk capital items (which tend to be developed with the co-operation of the customer anyway) with a very limited number of customers in the whole market. Where test marketing is appropriate, Hart (1993) suggests that it can be done geographically, in a particular region or in a small foreign market, or that it can be tested in a particular industry or market segment. Moore and Pessemier (1993) advocate the use of trade shows and exhibitions (of which more in Chapter 20) as a means of exposing new products or prototypes to a range of 'expert' scrutiny to get feedback on what amendments might have to be made before full commercialisation. The problem with this, of course, is that the ideas are exposed to competitors as well as to potential customers.

Commercialisation

By the seventh stage, commercialisation, everything that can be done to ensure the successful launch of the new product has been done. The surviving product is now ready for its full launch.

Any significant changes to the product after the test marketing stage can be very expensive, not just in terms of direct costs, but also in opportunity cost terms if a competitor gets in sooner. This is especially true with products that have a short life cycle, such as high technology consumer products. It is also true that significant changes after the test market effectively take the whole NPD process back a stage or two, if the changes fundamentally change the concept so that further business analysis, product development and test marketing have to take place.

Assuming, however, that no significant changes happen, the product is now ready to launch. Many of the topics covered in this book as a whole apply to the details of the marketing programme for the product launch. Areas such as positioning (pp. 308 *et seq.*), strategies for the introduction stage of the product life-cycle (p. 295), price setting (Chapter 11), and the initial promotional programme (all the chapters in Part VI) are of particular relevance to new product launch.

In terms of how to go about launching the product, there are two main alternatives at this stage:

Immediate national launch

Making the product available in all areas of the country, in all the planned outlets at the same time achieves two things. First, it makes a big impact, providing a single focus for a large PR, advertising and promotional blitz. Second, it allows little scope for the competition to sneak in, either with a launch of its own to eclipse yours, or with a loud promotional voice to distract the market from your new product. If you are investing considerable promotional resources in making a big issue out of the national launch, it will be difficult and expensive for the competition to shout louder than you.

The risk of a national launch, however, is that it leaves the organisation open to teething troubles. A test market can reduce those risks, but it cannot guarantee against them. Working in a carefully managed test market is different from day-to-day operation on a national scale. Production routines that work well on the sort of quantities required for a test region may not scale up as well or as efficiently as planned, for example. Both consumers and the trade have long memories, and early problems with supply or quality will taint an organisation's and a brand's reputations.

Rolling launch

A **rolling launch** is an alternative to the full national launch. It involves building towards full national coverage by starting with one or two recognised distribution areas, then gradually adding new regions to those already served as experience and success accumulate. This means that the organisation can concentrate on getting the logistics of distribution and production right, and can also fine tune marketing strategies in the light of experience.

Whether to use this approach depends a great deal on the resources available. A smaller or less well-established company could have difficulty in financing and managing a full national launch, yet could make an effective impact within a limited region. Success within that limited region would then finance the addition of further areas to the new product's distribution. The decision might also depend on the organisation's experience in NPD and any similarity between the new product and existing ones. If the new product is part of a family of related brands, then it might make

This novel product started its UK life among trend-setters in London.

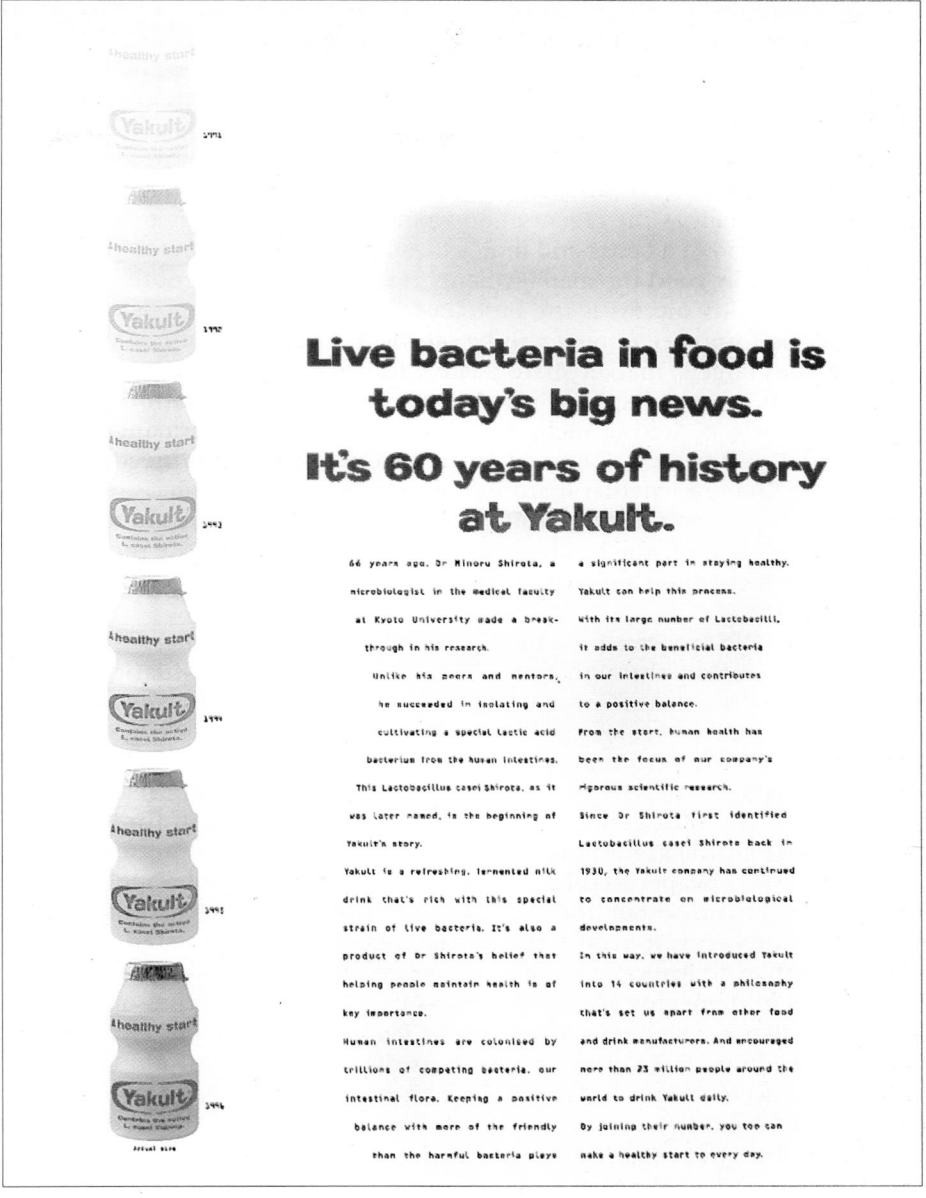

Source: Travis Sennet Sully Ross.

sense to go for the national launch through the same distribution channels and with a similar marketing stratergies as are used for the other brands. Even if the brand is free standing, i.e., unrelated to existing products, if it makes use of the same sales or distribution channels, then again, a national launch might be feasible.

In some cases, rolling out can have an international dimension. In Ireland, with a small domestic market, organisations can start with that home base as almost a test market, but to achieve significant volume sales, they then have to roll out to attack the UK and other European markets as they gain experience.

Monitoring and evaluation

As with any marketing activity, the story does not end just because all the practical tasks within a particular framework have been completed. There always has to be time given over to reflection on how well the process itself has been implemented, and how successful or otherwise the outcomes have been. NPD, as a particularly difficult activity to manage and get right, deserves that kind of review more than most.

Part of this final NPD stage will relate to the *process* and part to the *performance* of the product itself after launch. The process may be reviewed in terms of whether each stage was given due consideration, whether the right kinds of people were involved in it, whether it needed more time or resources, whether it took more time and resources than it need have done or whether the quality of the information, analysis and decision making was as high as the organisation would wish. Taking time to address such issues might at least lead to a better and more efficient NPD exercise on the next occasion.

No matter how good the management and implementation of the NPD process, the real measure of its success is the product to which it gave rise. Before the product is launched, performance criteria will be set for it. These criteria might include volume or value sales targets, market share relative to competition, trade take-up of the product, or promotion objectives linked with awareness generation, product trial or attitude formation. Setting such criteria allows forecast performance to be compared with actual performance. Any mismatch between the two needs to be carefully analysed to find out whether it arose from poor management decision making, lack of information, poor forecasting or unforeseen market conditions. In any event, lessons need to be learned for the future. Some further insights into the problems of evaluating new product failure are given at p. 355.

The entire NPD process presented here follows a logical pattern of stages, from initial idea generation through to commercialisation and evaluation. As each stage progresses, the number of ideas being followed through reduces, and the investment of money and time becomes greater and more serious. At any stage, it is possible for the organisation to terminate the process or to backtrack to an earlier stage. If, for example, business analysis shows that the favoured idea is not feasible for whatever reason, then the idea generation stage may be run again to find something on a slightly different track. Although the longer the process goes on, the more expensive it gets, it is still cheaper to drop a new product just before it is launched than to face the public embarrassment and the massive costs of a market failure. The aim of the whole NPD process is to reduce the considerable risks of failure, but each stage is sufficiently complex to leave plenty of scope for an organisation to get it wrong.

Mistakes in managing the NPD process can lead to two types of wrong outcome, broadly speaking. The first is a decision to launch when the product should not have been allowed out (a *go error*), and this is discussed in the following section. The second is a decision not to launch a new product which eventually turns out to be successful (a *drop error*).

All the time, the organisation is having to balance the risk of rushing the NPD process and making either of those two types of error, against the costs of prolonging it. The organisation also has to decide how much commercial risk it is prepared to take. If it is too risk averse, then there is a greater danger of a drop error, while if it is too daring, there is a greater risk of a go error.

NEW PRODUCT FAILURE

New product failure is a very real and very common phenomenon. The introduction to this chapter stated that something like 90 per cent of new products fail. Failure can also be very expensive. While a larger organisation can carry a certain level of loss from a failure (although that does not mean that they either encourage or enjoy it), a small newly formed organisation may go out of business completely if its one and only project fails.

Failure is sometimes a difficult thing for managers to cope with sometimes, especially if they think that it will reflect badly on either their status or their career prospects. Failure is, therefore, sometimes rationalised or hidden. Failure might be justified, by saying that the failed product was not really not part of the organisation's objectives or that it did not really fit with the organisation's capabilities. Poor top management support or lack of development resources are commonly cited as reasons for failure. Deeper analysis often reveals many other reasons.

Failure defined

Even the term 'failure' needs to be more precisely defined, as it can carry shades of meaning.

Outright failure – lost money

A product may be a failure because it is not covering its variable costs and it is not making any contribution to fixed costs and profit (*see* Chapter 11). Such failures could arise either because the sales volumes are too low (*see* below), or because there was a major miscalculation of unit production or distribution costs.

Outright failure – major negative market response

Another type of outright failure occurs when the market has rejected the product outright. It has not come anywhere near its sales targets, and therefore is likely to be either losing money or not earning as much as the organisation forecast.

Partial failure – failure to make contribution to fixed costs and profit

A partial failure occurs when the product has been accepted by the market, but for some reason is not living up to financial expectation. Again, this may be a result of the miscalculation of costs. This is only a partial failure, because the product's standing in the market seems to be satisfactory, and while that is the case, and while the product is managing to cover its variable costs at least, it might be redeemable with a certain amount of effort.

Partial failure – failure to achieve its set objectives

When a product fails to achieve its set objectives, the issues involved are similar to those discussed above in relation to monitoring and evaluation. Failure is a relative term, and thus a product can superficially seem to be performing well in the market and making a comfortable contribution to fixed costs and profit, yet still be labelled a failure because it is performing below expectations. The question is, of course, whether those expectations were realistic in the first place.

Partial failure – no longer fits organisational strategy

A product cannot be blamed for failing to fit in with organisational strategy. Particularly if the NPD process has been long and difficult, by the time the product is launched, the organisation might have moved on strategically. This may mean that the product no longer fits easily into the desired product portfolio, or that the management view it as out of keeping with the kind of image they now wish to project. At this point, the organisation faces a number of options such as repositioning (*see* pp. 308 *et seq.*) or deletion (*see* pp. 317 *et seq.*).

There are many reasons why products fail, and some of the more frequently quoted include:

1 Too small a target market, which is too specialised for the volumes originally planned, or those needed for breakeven.
2 Insufficient differentiation from existing offerings, leading to another 'me too' imitative product.
3 Poor or inconsistent product quality.

4 No access to the market, because the organisation is unable to get trade distribution, and does not have sufficient resources to sell direct.
5 Poor timing in terms of the industry life cycle. Launching too early (before the market is fully formed and ready) or too late (after the peak has passed) has an impact both on the resources needed for a successful launch and on the investment pay-back period.
6 Poor marketing, through either an insufficient spend or a badly allocated spend. It may be that not enough attention was paid to the main competitive alternatives, leading to a marketing strategy that was unable to cut through competitors' activities.

In an ideal world, every one of these reasons for failure is avoidable. Within the NPD framework presented, all these issues of competitive activity, state of the market, market size, production capability should be addressed, and the organisation should not be caught out by such failures after launch. In the real world, however, time is short, managers are under pressure to make decisions within very tight dealines, information is expensive and incomplete, corners are cut, assumptions are made, risks are taken, and sometimes, a product launch simply does not work out. It also needs to be emphasized that although the process presented in this chapter is a cool, rational approach to the NPD problem, it has to be implemented by people who often have their own agendas. (Refer back to pp. 155 *et seq.* to remind yourself of the issues involved.) Managers become emotionally attached to their own pet projects, and will sometimes take the risk of seeing a product through to launch come what may, rationalising away any warning signs. Some may see the new product as their big career break, or as a means of differentiating themselves from their colleagues in the eyes of senior management. Some may take a gamble on a borderline project for the personal rewards and status that success would bring. Such human interest might well drive a difficult launch to success, but equally, it might drive it to an inevitable failure.

TRENDS IN NPD PROCESS MANAGEMENT

The main message from this chapter should be that NPD is a necessary, costly and risky process. It needs adequate levels of investment and management commitment if it is going to succeed in ensuring that tomorrow's products are ready when needed. It also needs time, however, which perhaps is the scarcest commodity of all. As competitive pressures increase, and as the life-cycles of products become shorter, the temptation is to push a new product out on to the market as quickly as possible. This sense of urgency is further heightened by financial pressure, particularly in periods of recession, where the emphasis is on keeping development costs as low as possible, and putting a new product out to begin to recoup its development costs as soon as possible. In fmcg markets, for example, the NPD time has been reduced from around two years to between three and six months in some cases (Matthews, 1995). Clearly, there is a great risk here of launching an under-developed, under-researched second rate product, which may well fail before the marketers can fine tune the offering after launch.

Research and development

> **Example**
>
> Reducing the NPD time need not mean compromising on the quality of the NPD process. Renault has managed to cut both the costs and the time taken in NPD through restructuring the way in which it manages the process

(Ridding, 1995). In February 1995, Renault opened its Technocentre, a design and development plant which brought together the whole NPD process from conception, through prototyping, to the final development process, on a single dedicated site. Previously, these stages had been sequential and dispersed, but now they are co-ordinated and simultaneous. The outcome is that Renault claims that it will reduce the development time for a new car from 58 to 38 months, and save between 1 and 1.5 bn francs per model, which represents anything from 10 per cent to 25 per cent of the launch costs of a new vehicle.

Not all organisations have the funds to invest in that kind of long-term R&D commitment themselves, however. Faced with difficult economic and competitive conditions, many organisations are tempted to cut back on R&D, to make immediate savings. Taylor (1995), looking at the electronics market, for example, noted that organisations such as Hitachi (3 per cent reduction), Matsushita Electric (5 per cent), Fujitsu (15 per cent) and Sony (1 per cent) all cut their R&D spends in 1994. Computer companies have also cut back severely on R&D, for example IBM (33 per cent reduction over the previous two years), Apple (15 per cent reduction), and ICL (17 per cent). The strongest growth in R&D was among companies in semiconductor and telecommunications markets, such as Motorola (22 per cent increase), Ericsson (23 per cent), and Nokia (32 per cent).

Looking to reduce costs, yet to tap into as wide a range of innovative technology as possible, organisations are increasingly turning to **outsourcing R&D**, i.e., contracting out R&D to other organisations such as commercial or government laboratories, consultants and universities. There is indeed little point in an organisation's trying to re-invent or develop a technology for itself if there is another organisation that can do that work better, and whose expertise can be bought. A survey reported by Houlder (1995a) indicated that by 1996, European businesses would be 24 per cent reliant on external technology. There are, however, a number of potential problems arising from outsourcing. The contracting organisation may not ultimately have total control of what might become a critical technology for its business, and furthermore, may run a higher risk of details of that technology being leaked to competitors than if the R&D was totally in-house. Time lags too might be a problem, since it takes time for an organisation to realise it has a problem that is worth outsourcing; to locate a suitable contractor; to brief them on the background to the organisation and its R&D needs; then to discuss and refine the terms and conditions of the required work. The internal implications of outsourcing also need to be carefully thought through. The organisation may lose its internal R&D impetus altogether, becoming rather too dependent on external bodies for its innovation. Where internal R&D and outsourcing do exist in parallel, the organisation will also have to be careful to avoid attitude problems towards the external ideas (for example, internally sourced ideas might be given priority in terms of implementation, time and resources).

Half-way between outsourcing and the Renault approach is the idea of partnership, or **collaborative R&D** (Houlder, 1995b). This means that two or more organisations pool their resources and their expertise to undertake a specific project that will benefit both/all of them.

Example

In 1992, Siemens Environmental Systems and Yorkshire Water jointly developed a sensor for monitoring toxic waste. The water company needed the sensor, but did not have the technological expertise, while Siemens had the technology but wanted ideas for diversifying its business.

The robot supplier must collaborate with the car manufacturers to develop the right production system.

Source: Vauxhall Motors Ltd.

As with outsourcing, collaboration is a way of sharing costs and tapping into a wider field of expertise, but unlike outsourcing, both the risks and the potential commercial benefits are also shared. Before matters reach this stage, however, a big problem with collaboration can be finding an appropriate partner in the first place. In industries where there is close buyer–supplier co-operation, collaborative R&D partnerships can emerge naturally within the supply chain. Intel, for example, the manufacturer of microprocessors, has entered into a joint development venture with Hewlett-Packard.

With the exception of companies whose circumstances are similar to those described above, most smaller, low profile companies do not find collaborators easily, particularly where the nature of the R&D concerned may cut across industries or scientific disciplines. This all, however, further assumes that organisations know precisely what kind of partner they are looking for and for what purpose or objective.

Business forums

One of the problems of collaborative R&D mentioned elsewhere in this chapter is that of finding a suitable partner. Yorkshire Water and Siemens met at a business forum, an increasingly popular method of exchanging ideas, floating potential ideas and locating expertise. Scottish Enterprise, an economic development organisation, regularly runs forums all over Scotland. They felt that Scottish businesses needed a focus to help them build networks and test ideas before committing themselves to the market. A typical Scottish Enterprise forum is tightly structured. An entrepreneur makes a 20-minute presentation, then two experienced assessors make their comments on it. After that, the wider audience, around 90 people, ask questions and give their views. There would be no more than two such presentations at one meeting. One entrepreneur who went through this process to present a new product idea came out with offers of finance, practical expert advice and comments that helped to improve the business plan. Others use it as a confidence booster, to fine tune their ideas and to get a feel for how others respond to them. They can find out what aspects of the project need more explanation or justification, and what others see as the drawbacks. This might help an entrepreneur to make a much more professional pitch later, when presenting the project to bank managers or other financiers!

Source: Buxton (1996).

Some ideas for collaboration only emerge after organisations have come together and talked to each other about their respective problems and areas of expertise. With this in mind, national governments, the EU, universities and other bodies with an interest in promoting innovation have promoted conferences, forums and clubs (e.g. the European Industrial Research Managers' Association) to allow dialogue between organisations which otherwise might never even think of talking to each other. It was at such a forum organised by the government-backed Centre for the Exploitation of Science and Technology that Yorkshire Water and Siemens came together.

Finally, as a form of summary of this section, Table 9.3 brings together the advantages and disadvantages of using the three types of R&D approach discussed: in-house, outsourcing and collaboration.

Organisation for NPD

As this chapter has made clear throughout, NPD is a serious and necessary business, and accordingly needs the right kind of management support and organisational structures if it is to flourish and produce results. This section looks in further detail at the kinds of teams and individuals who might be involved in NPD.

Product or brand manager

A product or brand manager has responsibility for a single product or brand family, and thus has developed extensive knowledge of a specific market. The brand manager may be able to spot new opportunities in that market, or ways of stretching or filling product lines. The risk, of course, is that the brand manager is too involved in managing the current product, or is too emotionally attached to it to threaten its future with a new product. Quite apart from that, the individual who is a good brand manager may not necessarily be equally good at developing and appraising new product opportunities. Thus although the brand manager has a valuable role to play, the NPD process is likely to involve others.

TABLE 9.3
Advantages and disadvantages of various ways of organising R&D

	Advantages	*Disadvantages*
Outsourcing	Reduced costs Access to wider technology Access to a wide pool of R&D talent Use only when needed Solves specifically defined problems Access to facilities	Information leaks Requires trust Lose in-house R&D impetus Time lags Lack of control/motivation Lack of control over critical technologies Good communication needed
Collaboration	Shared costs Access to wider technology Access to wider facilities Access to a wide pool of R&D talent Shared risks Multi-industry/cross-disciplinary synergy possible Involvement/development of in-house R&D function	Shared benefits Needs trust Danger of domination by one partner Danger of unequal benefits Locating a suitable partner
In-house	Secrecy Total control over process Total control over critical technology Industry/company/product knowledge among researchers Quick response/always available Reap all the rewards	Cost Limited expertise Limited facilities May be too close to the problem Permanent resource to be funded and maintained

Market manager

A market manager has responsibility for a particular market, which may be defined in terms of customer type or product type. An organisation manufacturing and selling motor spares may define its markets as independent garages, franchised car dealerships, multiple chains such as Kwik-Fit and mass retailers such as Halfords. Market managers develop deep knowledge of the customer needs and wants within their own markets, but as with the brand managers, their expertise is best deployed as part of a wider team.

New product manager

A new product manager is employed specifically to seek out new product opportunities, and is likely to be found in a consumer market where the emphasis is on marketing rather than technical innovation. The existence of such a post formalises commitment to new products, and ensures that the NPD process is in the hands of one who understands how it works and will take responsibility for implementing it. Nevertheless, the new product manager may need to draw on the expertise of others within the organisation.

Venture team

The Renault approach discussed above is an example of the venture team. This is a group of selected individuals from various functional areas who are given the freedom to work solely on NPD, unhindered by other responsibilities and relatively independent of the rest of the organisation. In the Renault case, this went as far as providing a separate, purpose-built site for the team to work in. Such an approach clearly signals a long-term, serious investment and commitment to NPD.

New product committee

A new product committee may take responsibility for defining the organisation's new product policies, aims and objectives, and may also make the ultimate decision about which new products to launch. Such a committee is likely to consist of senior managers from a range of functional areas, thus not only co-ordinating NPD strategy and effort through out the organisation, but also visibly endorsing commitment to NPD at top level.

Task force

A task force is a temporary team, brought together from the various functional areas of the organisation, to tackle a specifically defined NPD project. Unlike members of a venture team, however, the task force members may have to cope with their involvement in NPD in addition to their normal duties, although in some cases they may be temporarily seconded to the task-force full time. Once the NPD problem is solved, the task force disbands.

Clearly, the number of individuals concerned and the range of functional areas involved in an NPD exercise will vary according to the size of organisation and the nature of the NPD task in hand. Thus within a single organisation, a variety of flexible NPD approaches may be employed to suit different conditions.

CHAPTER SUMMARY

This chapter has been concerned with new product development (NPD) as a means of enabling organisations to maintain the pace of innovation in their industries and to keep themselves ahead of the competition. There are, however, different degrees of newness. A product might be completely *new to the market*. Such products are totally innovative, and can emerge from technological advances. Alternatively, a product might be a *significant innovation for the market*, where the basic product concept is familiar, but there is a new twist to it. The other two options represent *minor* or *no* innovation to the market. These are products that either offer little change (of minor but not fundamental interest to the market) or are purely imitative.

The buyer's attitude to new products may also be influenced by the rate at which new products are introduced into the market. In fmcg markets, for instance, there is *continuous innovation*, where new product launches are fairly common, and it is difficult (and expensive) to get the consumer deeply excited about any single launch.

New product development is important to organisations for many reasons, including the need to maintain competitive advantage through innovation and better serving the customer's changing needs and wants. There are two types of approach to NPD. The first is to be *reactive*, to wait and see what others do and then follow or imitate, and the second is to be *proactive*, to set the pace and standard, and be the one whom others follow or imitate. Whatever the approach, NPD is not an easy activity, and there are many potential problems that can arise. In order to minimise the risks, therefore, the NPD process needs careful and skilful management. An eight-stage framework, building from the initial idea generation through to actual product development, test marketing and launch, helps to define the necessary NPD activities and shows how they fit together in a logical sequence.

Even with a well-planned, resourced and managed NPD framework, things can go wrong. An organisation may decide to launch a product that should have been rejected (a *go error*) or to dump a product that could have succeeded (a *drop error*). Such errors reflect the delicate balancing act that NPD represents: risk vs. safety, investment vs. uncertain rewards, speed to market vs. taking enough time to make a considered and well-researched decision, proactiveness vs. reactiveness.

Many new products do fail, for a variety of reasons. It should be emphasized, though, that many common reasons for failure, such as too small a target market, insufficient differentiation, poor quality, poor distribution, poor timing or poor marketing, are entirely avoidable if the NPD process is researched and handled correctly. The reality is, however, that many organisations are under pressure and do not feel that they have the time and resources to do things as thoroughly as they should.

It is possible to cut the time spent on the NPD process by more effective and efficient management, although this requires long-term commitment and investment. Other organisations have attempted to reduce the costs of NPD by outsourcing their R&D, that is, by using external bodies to undertake work on their behalf. While this allows the organisation to tap into wider technology and expertise, it may compromise commercial secrecy, increase the time taken for the NPD process and remove much control away from the organisation. Another trend is that of collaborative R&D, where organisations enter into complementary partnerships to achieve specific R&D goals. Both partners benefit from shared risks and from synergy between their respective skills and industrial experience.

Key words and phrases

Collaborative R&D	*New product development (NPD)*
Continuous innovation	*Outsourcing R&D*
Concept testing	*Rolling launch*
Discontinuous innovation	*Test marketing*
Dynamically continuous innovation	

QUESTIONS FOR REVIEW

9.1 What is the difference between *dynamically continuous innovation* and *discontinuous innovation*?

9.2 What is the difference between *reactive* and *proactive* NPD?

9.3 What are the eight stages of the NPD process?

9.4 List as many potential general sources of new product ideas as you can.

9.5 What kind of criteria are likely to be taken into account during the *idea screening* stage?

9.6 What is *concept testing* and why is it a crucial stage in the NPD process?

9.7 How are marketing, production and financial concerns brought together at the *business analysis* stage?

9.8 What might be the main causes of uncertainty at the *business analysis* stage?

9.9 What is the role of the *product development* stage for an fmcg product?

9.10 What is the difference between *outsourced* and *collaborative* R&D?

QUESTIONS FOR DISCUSSION

9.1 Find an example of a new product for each of the *types of newness* categories discussed at pp. 332 *et seq*. What particular marketing problems do you think the organisations launching each of those products might have had?

9.2 What are the potential benefits and pitfalls of using a screening approach based on rating ideas against weighted criteria?

9.3 How might the *product development* stage differ for:

(a) an fmcg product; and
(b) an organisational product?

9.4 To what extent do you think that *test marketing* is a good idea?

9.5 Find examples of two recently launched fmcg products, one of which was given a *full national launch*, and the other of which was *rolled out* gradually. Why do you think the particular approach chosen was appropriate for each product?

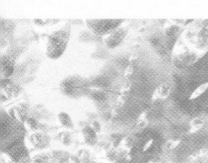

Digital compact cassette
vs MiniDisc

Music formats tend to have long life-cycles as consumers build collections that they do not want to become obsolete simply because a change in format occurs. Vinyl records were only partially replaced by cassette tapes in the 1970s, after having been around for some 50 years. The 1980s saw the introduction of the compact disc player which, after a slow start, with only 30,000 sold worldwide in the first year, rapidly became the main music format. The clear advantages in terms of durability and sound quality of CDs compared with vinyl and tapes were important aspects of that success. Now Sony and Matsushita with Philips are locked in a battle to develop what each believes to be the eventual replacement for the CD in the next century. The early results, however, do not augur well for either camp.

Sony launched the MiniDisc in 1992. The main advantages are that the compact discs are miniaturised and it is possible to record on to the CD, something that cannot be done with conventional CDs. World-wide sales for the system increased from 39 000 in 1992 to 388 000 in 1994, well below a level that would suggest a serious threat to the established CD format. Even if sales rose to one million, the MiniDisc would still have only 1 per cent of the hi-fi sector, well short of the 5 per cent that would give it the status of a mass market product in the eyes of the industry.

Meanwhile, an alternative system was offered by Matsushita and Philips: the Digital Compact Cassette (DCC). The main attraction of this system is that it offers sound of equivalent quality to CDs and could be regarded as a successor to analogue cassettes through the use of digital technology. Matsushita indicated that sales of all DCC systems were 20 000 in 1992, 160 000 in 1993, but fell back to 120 000 in 1994. These figures were also below expectations.

There are a number of reasons for the disappointing performance so far of both formats and their failure to make a serious attack on the traditional CD or cassette tape market.

1 Consumers' built-in resistance to change in music formats, especially as many replaced their collections in the 1980s with the introduction of the CD.
2 Record companies have only slowly committed production to the new format and, in contrast to their response to the introduction of the CD, have not invested in converting their catalogues to either MiniDisc or DCC. Polygram, controlled by Philips has introduced material on the DCC system, while Sony's music subsidiaries have released titles on MiniDisc. However, by 1995 there were still only 1200 albums on DCC.
3 Music retailers seeking fast stock turn were reluctant to dedicate much space to albums from either system.
4 Hi-fi retailers of the 'hardware' often appeared to be unenthusiastic about heavily promoting the new systems. Philips recognised this problem and rationalised the number of retailers involved across Europe. Thus the number of retailers stocking the system was been cut from 900 in the UK alone to 300 across the whole of Europe.

The manufacturers of the alternative systems were unperturbed by the slow start, but they did take some action to try to stimulate sales. Philips cut the price of the DCC by almost 50 per cent. It also decided to switch from advertising to specific point of sale promotions and direct support for retailers in both the 'hardware' and 'software' aspects, supported by a £150 000 spend in the specialist press. Philips also developed in-store demonstration units, accompanied where needed by demonstrators. Sony was considering redefining the MiniDisc as a niche product for CD recording, rather than as a potential mass-market format product, while Philips decided to present the DCC as a more modern alternative. Sales over the next few years will be critical. The prices of both systems also fell, to assist market penetration.

Sources: Marketing (1995); Rawsthorn (1995a); Rawsthorn (1995b).

Questions

1 Outline the reasons why the MiniDisc and the DCC are having greater problems making an impact on the market than the CD did originally.

2 Could these problems have been predicted and avoided?

3 Why do you think Philips cut the number of retailers stocking DCC?

4 Are these products failures?

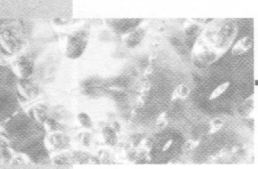

CASE STUDY 9.2

Soap wars

This is a fairly grubby story of a head-to-head clash between two powerful rivals who have effectively carved up the entire multi-million pound European market in clothes washing detergents between them. Competition between Lever and Procter & Gamble (P&G) is fierce, with each trying to outpace the other in terms of development, innovation and market share.

The battle between them reached new heights after Lever's launch of Persil Power, a micro powder enhanced with an 'accelerator', in the UK. Lever spent some £100 mn on new production facilities, and £250 mn across Europe on the product launch. The initial launch advertising spend in the UK in May 1994 was reported to be £25 mn. The launch was also supported by a 10-page mailshot, emphasizing the stain-shifting power of the product, with a 'green' message as the secondary selling point.

Persil Power was launched in the UK after two years of product testing across Europe. The product had already been launched in the Netherlands in April 1994, and towards the end of that month, a P&G executive was quoted as saying that the new product caused damage to fabrics. Despite the fact that Lever took out full-page advertisements to refute the claims and to display undamaged clothing, the story took hold and the unfavourable publicity grew. P&G denied that it had deliberately planted hostile stories in the press, but did admit to commissioning research to test Persil Power. Before the product was even launched, P&G had commissioned tests from six different European research institutes, each of which returned results unfavourable to Lever.

Mid-June 1994 saw the start of a campaign to distribute 11 million free samples of Persil Power over the summer to virtually every household in the UK with a washing machine. This was a direct response to the P&G smear campaign. The counter-campaign by Lever was reputed to be costing £25 mn, and included a Persil Roadshow designed to reach customers directly at shopping centres. Despite all this, by early July, Persil Power's market share had fallen from its peak of 5 per cent of all powders to 3.4 per cent, partly because Lever had reduced its promotional spend, and partly because of the bad publicity. By the end of July, Lever had reduced the level of accelerator in the powder by three-quarters, but P&G was still claiming that damage could occur, and the media were still interested. The *Sun*, for example, on 27 July ran a headline:

'Persil Pays £200 for Ruined Undies – Shorts Eaten'

Meanwhile, P&G really did stop messing about and launched an advertising campaign featuring comparisons between faded, tatty, shredded clothes washed in 'a powder with accelerator' (no prizes for guessing which brand they meant) with vibrant, clean clothes washed in Ariel.

All along, Lever claimed that P&G was deliberately trying to spoil the launch to clear the way for Ariel Future, due to hit the market in September 1994. P&G, however, preferred to take the moral high ground, claiming only to have the industry's reputation and the welfare of the nation's undies at heart. By the end of August, reports appeared suggesting that P&G's criticisms were well founded. The Consumers' Association, for example, after carrying out tests on Persil Power, found that it did cause problems. Since the Consumers' Association is a widely respected independent judge of products, any adverse comment from them was likely to be a serious blow for Lever. By the end of September 1994, the news on Persil Power was gloomy. Its market share had fallen further to 2.5 per cent, while the Persil family of brands had fallen back from 27.4 per cent share before the launch of Persil Power to 24.2 per cent.

By early 1995, the retail trade had also become concerned about the product, to the point where one major supermarket chain decided not to sell it any more. Once this had happened, Lever was really running out of options. The product was repositioned as a niche heavy-duty powder for whites only, but this did not convince the public and in the spring, Lever decided to abandon Persil Power. Meanwhile, work had begun on rebuilding the Persil brand through the launch of New Generation Persil, clearly different from Persil Power, and clearly distanced from it. A significant sum, £20 mn, was put into its launch to make sure that the message got across. Overall, Persil Power cost Lever a great deal of money, not only the initial investment and marketing costs, but also £57 mn in unusable stock that had to be written off. Perhaps more seriously, it cost Lever market share. Even in 1996, a year after the withdrawal of Persil Power and the launch of New Generation Persil, Persil's market share was still slightly lower than in the pre-Persil Power days.

Sources: Hamilton (1994); Hamilton and Lynn (1994); Hamilton and Ryan (1994); Lynn (1995); *Marketing* (1994); Meller (1994); Richards and Meller (1994).

Questions

1 Why do you think Lever launched the new product using the Persil name? What were the risks and benefits of doing this?

2 How, and to what extent, do you think P&G was successful in spoiling Lever's new product launch? What counter-attack measures did Lever have to take?

3 Was Lever right to maintain the Persil Power brand for as long as it did? What are the problems associated with deleting a brand like this?

4 What are the lessons to be learned from this case about new product development?

REFERENCES TO CHAPTER 9

Baxter, R. A. (1995), 'Birthday in Berlin', *Financial Times*, 16 May, p. VII.

Bonaccorsi, A. and Lipparini, A. (1994), 'Strategic Partnerships in New Product Development', *Journal of Product Innovation Management*, 11(2), pp. 134–45.

Booz-Allen, Hamilton INC. (1982), *New Product Management for the 1980s*, Booz-Allen, Hamilton Inc.

Buxton, J. (1996), 'Toe in the Water', *Financial Times*, 26 March, p. 16.

Caulkin, S. (1994), 'Research into R&D Spending Pays Off', *Observer*, 19 June, p. 8.

Cooper, R. G. and Kleinschmidt, E. J. (1987), 'New Products: What Separates Winners From Losers?', *Journal of Product Innovation Management*, 5 (Sept.), pp. 169–84.

Cowell, D. (1984), *The Marketing of Services*, Butterworth-Heinemann.

Elliott, L. and Beavis, S. (1994), 'Feeling Frail After 15 Year Slimdown', *Guardian*, 8 November, p. 14.

Ford, R. (1994), 'VP185 – Paxman's Powerful New Diesel Engine', *Modern Railways*, March, pp. 141–2.

The Grocer (1996a), 'Wonder Spread From Finland', *The Grocer*, 18 May, p. 9.

The Grocer (1996b), 'Finnish Brand Leader Enters the Fray', *The Grocer*, 1 June, p. 25.

Hamilton, K. (1994), 'P&G Blows Holes in Washday Rivals', *Sunday Times*, 31 July.

Hamilton, K. and Lynn, M. (1994), 'Power Plays', *Sunday Times*, 12 June.

Hamilton, K. and Ryan, M. (1994), 'Persil Soap War Hits 11m Homes', *Sunday Times*, 12 June.

Hart, N. A. (1993), *Industrial Marketing Communications*, Kogan Page.

Hill, A. (1995), 'Saes Getters – Fast Track', *Financial Times*, 27 February, p. 11.

Houlder, V. (1995a), 'Revolution in Outsourcing', *Financial Times*, 6 January, p. 7.

Houlder, V. (1995b), 'Partners in Innovation', *Financial Times*, 24 March, p. 16.

Lynn, M. (1995), 'Unilever Puts New Power into Persil', *Sunday Times*, 15 January.

McAtear, F. (1995), 'Recycled Papers Come of Age', *Purchasing and Supply Management*, July/August, pp. 24–5.

Maitland, A. (1994), 'Hard Sell for a New British Cheese', *Financial Times*, 10 March, p. 11.

Majaro, S. (1991), *The Creative Process*, Allen & Unwin.

Marketing (1994), 'Persil Power Takes Toll on Persil', *Marketing*, 29 September.

Marketing (1995), 'DCC 'Mistakes' Lead Philips To Relaunch', *Marketing*, 6 October.

Matthews, V. (1995), 'Innovators Out to Beat the Odds', *Financial Times*, 9 February, p. 19.

Meller, P. (1994), 'Levers Tops P&G in War of Words', *Marketing*, 5 May.

Mitchell, A. (1994), 'A Costly Presence – New Research into the Price of Promoting and Maintaining Brands', *Financial Times*, 1 September, p. 20.

Moore, W. L. and Pessmier, E. A. (1993), *Product Planning and Management: Designing and Delivering Value*, McGraw-Hill.

Oram, R. (1995), 'Food Companies Serve Up Anti-Disease Dishes', *Financial Times*, 3 August, p. 6.

Osborn, A. F. (1963), *Applied Imagination*, (3rd edn), Schreiber.

Pettitt, S. J. (1989), *Innovation in Tourism*, Unpublished report for Shannon Development Co., Ireland.

Rawsthorn, A. (1994), 'A Nose for Innovation', *Financial Times*, 4 August, p. 11.

Rawsthorn, A. (1995a), 'A New Strategy for Sounder Position', *Financial Times*, 16 February, p. 18.

Rawsthorn, A. (1995b), 'Sony Looks to Solve its MiniDisc Dilemma', *Financial Times*, 18 May, p. 6.

Richards, A. and Meller, P. (1994), 'Truth Behind the Soap Wars Hype', *Marketing*, 7 July.

Ridding, J. (1995), 'Renault Unveils Plant to Speed Launches', *Financial Times*, 17 February, p. 24.

Schwartz, D. (1987), *Concept Testing: How to Test New Product Ideas Before You Go to Market*, American Marketing Association.

Taylor, P. (1995), 'Mania for Mergers', *Financial Times*, 22 June, p. 36.

Von Hippel, E. (1978), 'Successful Industrial Products from Customers' Ideas', *Journal of Marketing*, 42 (Jan.), pp. 39–49.

Von Hippel, E. (1986), 'Lead users: A Source of Novel New Product Concepts', *Management Science*, 32 (July), pp. 791–805.

Part IV

. . .

PRICE

Pricing: Context and Concepts **10**

Pricing Strategies **11**

It is natural to assume that the price of a product is very closely related to the cost of producing it. Since the purpose of marketing is to create and hold a customer at a profit, pricing polices have to reflect a reward to the organisation for its efforts. Manufacturing costs, however, are only the beginning of the story. Chapter 10 looks into a number of influences on pricing decisions, such as distribution channels, long-term marketing and corporate objectives, competitor pricing and customer expectations and finds that it is far from being a simple arithmetic 'cost plus' calculation.

Price is an important indicator of the positioning of the product for potential customers who sometimes have too little experience of the product or the market to judge it by other factors. Price is often equated with quality or used as a means of comparing competing products. For some products, such as motor insurance, price can even be the primary criterion for choice with wide implications for the organisation. A price-sensitive market means that the organisation might have to find ways of cutting costs or increasing volume to maintain profits or it might be able to use creative marketing to reposition into less sensitive segments.

Linking with this, Chapter 11 examines the rationale behind a number of pricing strategies open to organisations, from deliberately setting high prices through to aggressive low-price strategies. Pricing can also be used as a short-term tactical tool, as a means of diverting customers' attention away from competitive products, for example, and trying to influence their behaviour. Whatever is done, however, pricing must be consistent with the message generated by the other elements of the marketing mix or else the buyer may become confused or suspicious.

10 Pricing: Context and Concepts

LEARNING OBJECTIVES

This chapter will help you to:

1 define the meaning of price;

2 understand the different roles price can play for buyers and sellers and in different kinds of market;

3 appreciate the nature of the external factors that influence pricing decisions;

4 explore the internal organisational forces that influence pricing decisions;

5 understand the impact of the single European market on pricing.

INTRODUCTION

At first glance, **price** might seem to be the least complicated and perhaps the least interesting element of the marketing mix, not having the tangibility of the product, the glamour of advertising or the atmosphere of retailing. It does, however, play a very important role in the lives of both marketers and customers, and deserves as much strategic consideration as any other marketing tool. Price not only directly generates the revenues that allow organisations to create and retain customers at a profit (in accordance with one of the definitions of marketing in Chapter 1), but also can be used as a communicator, as a bargaining tool and as a competitive weapon. The customer can use price as a means of comparing products, judging relative value for money or judging product quality.

Ultimately, the customer is being asked to accept the product offering and (usually) to hand money over in exchange for it. If the product has been carefully thought out with the customer's needs in mind, if the distribution channels chosen are convenient and appropriate to that customer, if the promotional mix has been sufficiently seductive, then there is a good chance that the customer will be willing to hand over some amount of money for the pleasure of owning that product. But even then, the price that is placed on the product is crucial: set too high a price, and the customer will reject the offering and all the good work done with the rest of the marketing mix is wasted; too low, and the customer is suspicious ('too good to be true'). What constitutes 'a high price' or 'a low price' depends on the buyer, and has to be put into the context of their perceptions of themselves, of the entire marketing package and of the competitors' offerings. Pricing has a spurious certainty about it because it involves numbers, but do not be misled by this; it is as emotive and as open to misinterpretation as any other marketing activity.

It is thus important to the marketer to understand the meaning of price from the customer's point of view, and to price products in accordance with the 'value' the customer places on the benefits offered.

> ### Example
>
> An ordinary Barbie doll sells through the toys section of a mail order catalogue for around £8.50. A Barbie doll dressed as Scarlett O'Hara from the film *Gone With the Wind* sells through an advertisement in a Sunday newspaper colour supplement for £69.95. The higher price is justified because the Scarlett doll is a limited edition collector's item, with her own certificate of authenticity, and her dress has been copied exactly from the film. The advertisement sells Scarlett as an heirloom or as an investment, suggesting that it is possible that her value might increase over time. It is not a toy, and thus the features and benefits offered are very different from those offered by the £8.50 doll and valued much more highly by the adult target market.

This chapter expands on these initial concepts of price. It will look further at what price is, and what it means to marketers and customers in various contexts. It will also examine more closely the role of price in the marketing mix, and how it interacts with other marketing activities. This sets the scene for a focus on some of the internal factors and external pressures which influence pricing thinking within an organisation. The final section of the chapter tackles some of the issues affecting pricing on a Europe-wide basis.

THE ROLE AND PERCEPTION OF PRICE

Price is the *value* that is placed on something. What is someone prepared to give in order to gain something else? Usually, price is measured in money, as a convenient medium of exchange which allows prices to be set quite precisely. This is not necessarily always the case, however. Goods and services may be bartered ('I will help you with the marketing plan for your car repair business if you service my car for me'), or there may be circumstances where monetary exchange is not appropriate, for example at election time when politicians make promises in return for your vote. Any such transactions, even if they do not directly involve money, are exchange processes and thus can use marketing principles (go back to Chapter 1 for the discussion of marketing as an exchange process). Price is any common currency of value to both buyer and seller.

Even money-based pricing comes under many names, depending on the circumstances of its use: solicitors charge fees; landlords charge rent; bankers charge interest; railways charge fares; hotels charge a room rate; consultants charge retainers; agents charge commission; insurance companies charge premiums; and over bridges or through tunnels tolls may be charged. Whatever the label, it is still a price for a good or a service, and the same principles apply.

Price does not necessarily mean the same things to different people, just because it is usually expressed as a number. You have to look beyond the price, at what it represents to both the buyer and the seller if you want to grasp its significance in any transaction. Buyer and seller may well have different perspectives on what price means. We now turn to that of the buyer.

The customer's perspective

From the buyer's perspective, price represents the value they attach to whatever is being exchanged. Up to the point of purchase, the marketer has been making promises to the potential buyer about what this product is and what it can do for that customer. The customer is going to weigh up those promises against the price and decide whether it is worth paying (Zeithaml, 1988).

In assessing price, the customer is looking specifically at the expected benefits of the product, as shown in Fig 10.1.

Functional

Functional benefits relate to the design of the product and its ability to fulfil its desired function. For example a washing machine's price might be judged on whether or not it can handle different washing temperatures, operate economically and dry as well as wash.

Quality

The customer may expect price to reflect the quality level of the product (Erickson and Johansson, 1985). Thus a customer may be prepared to pay more for leather upholstery in a car, or for solid wood furniture rather than veneer, or for hand-made Belgian chocolates rather than mass produced. Quality perceptions may be to do with the materials or components used in the product, as in these examples, or with the labour involved in making it. Quality may also, however, be a less tangible judgement made on the basis of corporate image. BMW, Heinz and Cadbury's are perceived as quality companies, and therefore they are perceived as producing quality products. The consumer can thus accept that those organisations might charge higher prices.

Operational

In organisational markets, price may be judged in relation to the product's ability to influence the production process. For example a new piece of machinery might be assessed on its ability to increase productivity, make the production line more efficient or reduce the labour content of the finished goods. Even in a consumer market, operational issues might be considered. For instance the purchase of a microwave oven increases the operational efficiency of the kitchen, both making it easier to cater for the staggered mealtimes resulting from the modern family's fragmented lifestyle, and giving the chief cook more time to pursue other interests.

FIGURE 10.1

Factors influencing customers' price assessments

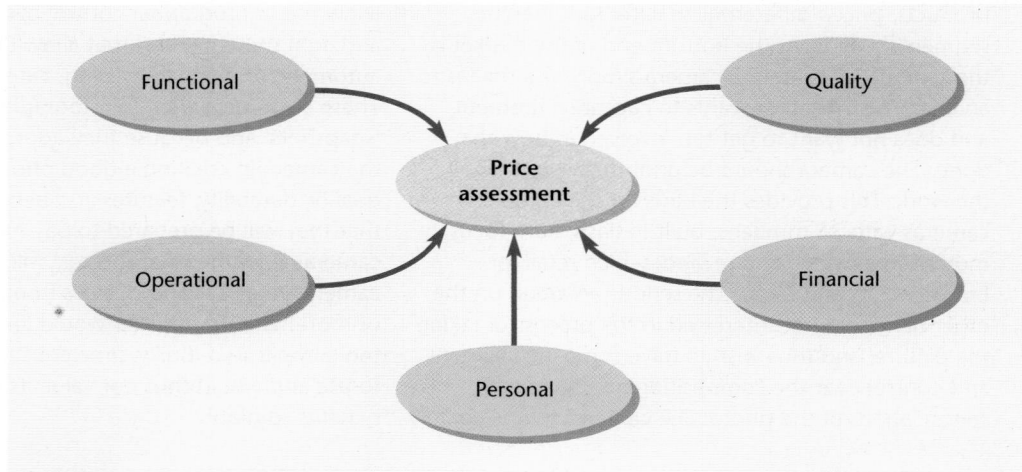

Financial

Particularly in organisational markets, many purchases are seen as investments, and therefore the expected return on that investment is important in judging whether the price is worthwhile or not. New machinery, for example, is expected to pay for itself over time in terms of increased efficiency, output, labour saving etc. Note that this judgement is made not only in terms of production outputs, but also in terms of long-term cost savings, efficiency gains and productivity improvements. Even some consumer products are sold on the basis of their money-saving potential. Orange, for example, ran an aggressive advertising campaign in 1995 showing how their mobile phone system could work out £20 per month cheaper than Cellnet or Vodaphone.

Personal

Personal benefit is a difficult category for the marketer to gauge, as it attempts to measure price against intangible, individual, psychological benefits such as status, comfort, self-image (Chapter 3 will remind you about these benefits) etc. Some high involvement products, such as perfumes, use high pricing deliberately as a means of amplifying the upmarket, sophisticated, exclusive images portrayed in their packaging, distribution and advertising strategies, thus increasing the status enhancement and 'feel good' factor of the purchase. Chapter 11 will examine aspects of psychological factors in price setting further.

Remember too that organisational markets are not immune from the effects of personal factors. Purchasing can be influenced by the individual motivations of people involved (as discussed at pp. 155 *et seq.*), and even by a desire to enhance a corporate self-image.

The problem is, of course, that different buyers put different values on different benefits. This endorses the need for market segmentation (*see* Chapter 5), which can begin to sort out groupings of like-minded customers so that appropriately tailored marketing mixes (including price) can be developed.

So far, it has been assumed that **price perceptions** and judgements of value are constant in the mind of the potential buyer. They are, however, variable according to circumstances. For example, a householder thinking of replacing water pipes would probably be very price sensitive and get quotes from a number of plumbers before

---

MARKETING IN ACTION

Putting you in the picture

Camera manufacturers produce wide ranges of products, priced differently, to cater for different segments' needs. At the bottom end of the market is the customer who sees a camera simply as a means to an end. This customer wants to capture a moment, and does not want to get too involved in how that is done. The camera should be unobtrusive but do all the work. This provides the basis for the compact cameras with 35 mm lens, built-in flash, auto focus, motorised advance and rewind, which retail for between £25 and £140. The serious amateur, on the other hand, may be interested in the process of taking the picture, and thus wish to have some involvement and control over the composition and technical specifications of the photo. SLR cameras that allow

lenses with different focal lengths to be attached, that allow the photographer control over shutter speed and light metering and that allow the choice of automatic or manual focusing, cater for this market. These customers want 'photographs' rather than 'snapshots' and because they appreciate the role of the camera in creating a good photo, they want more quality, durability, features and benefits. This means that they will be prepared to pay more for their cameras than the 'snapshotter' will, and thus SLR cameras retail at various levels from £200 up to £2000 or more. The snapshotter would find such a camera too complicated, bulky, time consuming and irritating to use and would thus not value its features and benefits so highly.

making a decision. A burst pipe in the winter, however, would have that same householder paying almost any price to get a plumber round immediately. In any such distress purchase, the value placed on immediate problem solution justifies paying a **premium price**.

Another factor influencing price perception is scarcity. Where supply is severely limited and demand is high, prices can take on a life of their own and begin to spiral.

Example

Tickets with a face value of £36 for Sir Andrew Lloyd Webber's *Sunset Boulevard* were being advertised by touts at £100, three months before the show was even due to open. In London, theatre-goers clearly placed a higher value on being amongst the first to see a new show than on waiting until after the show had opened to buy a ticket for £36 direct from the box office.

The seller's perspective

Price is a distinctive element of the marketing mix for the *seller*, because it is the only one that generates revenue. All the other elements represent outgoing costs. Price is also important, therefore, because it provides the basis of both recovering those costs and creating profit.

$$\text{Profit} = \text{Total Revenue} - \text{Total Cost},$$

Where total revenue is the quantity sold multiplied by the unit price, and total cost represents the costs of producing, marketing and selling the product. Quantity sold is itself dependent on price as well as on the other marketing mix elements. Table 10.1 shows the percentage of revenue generated by each operational area within a sample of car dealers. It also shows what percentage of the dealers' profits each area contributes. It is noticeable that for a high volume dealership although car sales represent a large proportion of the total revenue, they only contribute one-third of the profit. In comparison, the workshop generates only around 5 per cent of revenue but over 25 per cent of profit. This reflects the fact that for some products, competitive pressures may keep margins tight. To increase profit in such areas, therefore, the organisation may have to find a way of either reducing the costs involved, or justifying higher prices.

Photographs, and not 'snapshots', are what this camera's buyers are paying for.

The seller, however, must always take care to think about price from the perspective of the customer. In pure economic terms, it would be assumed that reducing a price would lead to higher sales because more people could then afford and want the product. As the introduction to this chapter suggested, however, a low price may be interpreted as making a negative statement about the product's quality, and a sudden reduction in price of an established product may be taken to mean that the product's quality has been compromised in some way. Even petrol, the stereotypical homogeneous product has been a victim of this.

Similarly, a high price may not always be a bad thing for a seller. If buyers equate price with quality (and in the absence of information or knowledge of the market, it may be the only indicator they pick up), then a higher price might actually attract customers. Part of the psychological benefit of the purchase for the customer might well be derived from its expense, for example in

Source: Olympus Optical Company (UK) Ltd.

TABLE 10.1
Car dealer turnover and profit broken down by operating area, 1991

	High volume (%)	Medium volume (%)	Japanese (%)	Specialist (%)
Turnover				
Car sales	78.3	80.0	80.4	80.7
Parts	8.2	8.9	6.8	8.7
Workshop	4.7	5.0	3.6	5.4
Bodyshop	1.8	0.8	2.2	1.2
Forecourt	6.1	4.5	6.7	3.5
Other	0.9	0.8	0.3	0.5
Total	100.0	100.0	100.0	100.0
Profit				
Car sales	36.2	37.6	56.0	61.9
Parts	18.4	19.9	12.2	13.8
Workshop	28.4	30.6	20.0	17.7
Bodyshop	10.5	6.6	7.0	2.6
Forecourt	4.9	4.7	3.2	3.1
Other	1.6	0.6	1.6	0.9
Total	100.0	100.0	100.0	100.0

Note: Totals rounded.
Source: MMC, as published in Mullineux (1995).

purchasing gifts where one feels obliged to spend a certain amount on the recipient either to fulfil social expectations or to signal affection. The higher the price, the more exclusive the market segment able to afford the product or service. Many more rail travellers, for example, choose to travel second class than in the higher-priced first class accommodation.

The seller also needs to remember that sometimes the cost to the customer of purchasing a product can be much greater than its price. These broader considerations might have an inhibiting effect on purchase. A consumer buying a CD player for the first time, for example, will not only look at the ticket price of the machine, but also weigh up the costs of replacing favourite records with CDs. A business buying a new computer system has to consider the costs of transferring records, staff training and the initial decrease in productivity as they learn to find their way around the new system, and the costs of installation (and of removing the old equipment). The whole marketing strategy for a product has to recognise the real cost to the customer of accepting the offering, and work to overcome such objections whether through pricing, a better tailored product offering, or through effective communication and persuasion.

Example

In the UK in November 1993, Shell advertised on the basis that supermarket chains were selling petrol that damaged engines. The accusation was that they had removed a detergent additive from the petrol to cut the cost so that they could sell at around 46p per litre as compared with the standard forecourt price of around 49p at that time. Stickers immediately appeared on Sainsbury's supermarket petrol pumps to reassure customers that their product did contain the additive.

Example

The roller towel had been replaced by hot-air dryers and paper towels in many organisations' washrooms on the basis that these were cheaper, easier to service and more hygienic. The cotton towel industry has fought back, however, demonstrating that when consumables, transport, labour, dispenser costs and disposal are taken into account, the roller towel system can be up to 58 per cent cheaper to operate per month (Smith, 1994). Added to that, the industry has improved the design of roller dispenser cabinets and the laundering standards to overcome the poor hygiene image, and has proved that cotton is much more efficient and consistent at drying. In industries such as food processing, catering and pharmaceuticals where hygiene standards are becoming increasingly stringent, and in a world where environmental friendliness is a serious concern, it is not surprising that the combination of cost advantage and performance benefits found in cotton roller towels is irresistible!

Whatever type of market an organisation is in, whatever market segments it seeks to serve, it must always be aware that price can never stand apart from the other elements of the marketing mix. It interacts with those elements and must, therefore, give out signals consistent with those given by the product itself, place and promotion. Price is often quoted as a reason for not purchasing a product, but this reflects a tendency to use price as a scapegoat for other failings in the marketing mix. Price is a highly visible factor, and at the point of purchase it hits the buyer where it hurts – in the pocket. As has been said before in this chapter, if the rest of the marketing mix has worked well up to the point of sale, then the price should not be too great an issue, because the buyer will have been convinced that the benefits supplied are commensurate with the price asked. Price is seen here as a natural, integrated element in harmony with the rest of the offering. It could be argued that a buyer who is wavering and uses price as the ultimate determinant of whether to purchase is either shopping in the wrong market segment or being ill served by sloppy marketing.

PRICING CONTEXTS

This section summarises the impact on pricing of the issues and characteristics prevailing in various kinds of market. It highlights the fact that pricing is not just a cost-driven exercise, but a skill that requires knowledge and understanding of both the customer and the external environment.

Consumer markets

There is much competition for *consumers'* disposable income. This is reflected in both the range of different product markets available for them to spend in, and the variety of products competing in any one market. Consumers also have a great deal of discretion over whether they spend or not. There are very few real necessities and, on many occasions consumers buy because they want to, rather than because they need to.

Also, as a result of the fact that consumers are largely buying to please themselves, their assessment of competing products in most markets is often informal, irrational or even non-existent. As discussed in Chapter 3, psychological factors can play a much greater role than analytical skills. Even where hard product information is provided, the consumer does not necessarily make the effort to digest it properly or retain it. It may simply be used selectively as support for a decision that has already been made. Price too, as has already been pointed out, may be interpreted variously, depending on the individual customer. If you want the product badly enough, then you will justify the expense somehow.

All of this makes it very difficult to identify scope for *price negotiation*, and indeed, in most consumer markets, the unit price of the goods is so low that, there is no need for such a tool. The price is on the product; take it or leave it. There are some exceptions, however. Consumers expect to negotiate the price of a new car with the dealer, and the dealer recognises this and sets the opening price at a level where he can afford to be beaten down 10 or 15 per cent. This has almost taken on the aura of a ritual, and in many cases, it actually adds to the psychological benefits of car buying because the consumers feel that they have been astute enough to drive a hard bargain, and it enhances their self-image.

Nevertheless, price is still an important element of the consumer product's marketing mix. **Price banding** can be a useful addition to a market segmentation exercise, as a segment that is prepared to spend £10 to £20 on a product needs to be served differently from a segment prepared to pay £30 to £40. In making planned purchases of clothes, for example, consumers will sometimes decide to buy a certain item and set the price band within which they are prepared to shop. They then seek out the item within the band that offers the best value in terms of colour, fabric, style etc. If they cannot find anything satisfactory within that band, only then will they consider shifting to another price band.

A consumer for whom price is the primary consideration in comparing competing offerings is said to be **price sensitive**. In dealing with such consumers, marketers have to be particularly careful to get the price right because customers are less likely to be seduced by non-price factors into moving outside their preconceived price band.

Example

The sales and marketing director of a pasta company was hoping that the increases in potato prices in 1995 would increase pasta consumption in UK households. Unfortunately for him, this was unlikely to happen to any significant extent because potatoes are perceived as a staple part of the UK diet and will be purchased regularly regardless of the price. Ninety-five per cent of the UK population eat potatoes at least three times a week, and potatoes are not price sensitive (Gilbert, 1995).

Price sensitivity can, therefore, be a meaningful way of differentiating between groups of customers.

Retail and wholesale markets

Retail and wholesale markets take a far more rational approach to price interpretation than do consumer groups. As intermediaries, they have to look in two directions, at both the manufacturer and the consumer. They have to be realistic about what price they themselves can charge for a product to their customers, and this in turn establishes what kind of price they are looking to pay to the manufacturer, if they are to maintain a reasonable profit margin. This price also needs to reflect the services in respect of selling the product that the intermediary has to perform. Table 10.2 shows car dealers' margins on Vauxhall/Opel models in 1990 across various European countries.

Looking in the opposite direction at the consumer, retailers and wholesalers will also expect pricing structures to reflect demand. For example if a product is going to have mass market appeal and will sell in high volumes, then the intermediaries will need to be able to sell it at a competitive price, especially if it is a new brand entering an established market.

TABLE 10.2

Car dealer margins on Vauxhall/Opel models across Europe, 1990

	Nova (%)	Astra (%)	Cavalier (%)	Carlton (%)
United Kingdom	16.00	17.00	17.00	17.00
Germany	16.00	16.00	16.40	16.80
France	13.00	14.50	15.50	16.50
Spain	10.25	10.25	10.25	12.00
Italy	14.00	16.00	17.00	19.00
Belgium	14.00	14.00	15.50	17.50
The Netherlands	12.70	13.90	14.50	14.90

Source: MMC from General Motors, as published in Mullineux (1995).

Price discipline is also expected, in the sense that manufacturers should not be seen to be selling direct to the public at lower prices than the retailers could set. Price discipline sometimes goes further than this, and retailers become upset if they think that manufacturers are selling to other retailers at lower prices. The major UK supermarket chains, for example, were incensed when they thought that manufacturers were selling branded lines to warehouse clubs such as Costco more cheaply than to themselves. The manufacturers justified any lower prices on the basis of the quantities ordered. Manufacturers also expect price discipline from retailers, however. Kellogg's decision to stop supplying a discount chain because it was selling Kellogg's products at below cost was upheld in the courts.

Intermediaries are also knowledgeable about alternative product offerings, and therefore will use price as a bargaining weapon where they can. Manufacturers in turn may well be willing to make price concessions in order to gain distribution through a powerful retail chain. Another means by which the retailer can keep prices lower is by

MARKETING IN ACTION

Budget tyres

In the tyre market, the budget segment represented something like 25 per cent of the European market in 1995, largely thanks to the increasing number of own brands and the influx of cheaper non-European products. In response to this, the manufacturers of the top brands are expanding their product ranges to cater for the price-sensitive segment, either by manufacturing own brands for tyre retailers, or by creating new budget brands. In 1995, for example, Michelin and Continental agreed to produce and distribute jointly a low-cost brand. Many tyre manufacturers also have own-label supply agreements. Goodyear manufactures the Suburbanite brand for the UK wholesaler Tyreco Trading, Rainbow for the French Arc-en-Ciel retailing group, and also manufactures for the Swiss ESA buying group. This last agreement has the potential to open up a wide own-label market for

Goodyear because ESA is a member of the Tecar buying co-operative with 5500 partners across France, Germany, Switzerland, Austria, Italy and Denmark. It would thus be very lucrative for Goodyear if the ESA deal could be expanded to the other Tecar members. The own-label market thus allows the manufacturers to participate in the budget end of the market without compromising their premium brand images. As the marketing and sales director of Pirelli Reifenwerk in Germany was quoted as saying:

'A top of the line brand will never or only seldom be an option for the price conscious consumer. However, we don't want to overlook this price sensitive market segment, leaving it to bargain suppliers'

Source: Davis (1995).

offering own-brand goods. These compete directly with the manufacturers' brands, but tend to be sold at lower prices. Where a market is under severe price pressure, manufacturers may have to rethink their product policies. Chapters 12, 13 and 14 explore many of these points in more detail, looking closely at the often complex relationships between manufacturers, intermediaries and consumers.

Service markets

Services, as Chapter 23 will show, are different from tangible goods. Because a service is intangible, it is very difficult to assess its quality before purchasing it. Often, **price comparison** is the nearest a potential buyer can get to working out the relative quality of similar competing offerings. A hungry traveller stopping in a strange town may be faced with two restaurants on opposite sides of the road. Both have similar menus, both look to be equally clean, attractive and well patronised. The traveller may then look at their relative prices and decide that the more expensive of the two might give bigger portions, use better ingredients or offer better service.

Another peculiar feature of services is that they are perishable, in that they happen at a particular time and place, and if there is no customer there, the 'product' is lost. A service is not like a packet of cornflakes that can sit on a supermarket shelf until it is sold. If, for example, there are empty seats on a flight from Amsterdam to Berlin, then those unsold tickets represent wasted product and therefore lost revenue because that same flight can never take place again. Pricing, however, can help to ensure that these losses are minimised. Reducing the cost of a ticket as the flight time gets closer may encourage someone to purchase it. The airline may not make as much profit on that ticket as they would like, but as long as they are covering their variable costs and making a contribution to fixed costs and profit, then it is better than no sale at all.

An airline represents service marketing on a very large scale, with many skilled employees able to deliver consistent quality service to many customers simultaneously. Many service businesses, particularly in the field of personal services such as hairdressing or dentistry, are reliant on the skills of one or two individual service providers. In such cases, price may be used as a means of restricting demand, by excluding those who cannot afford the price (or those who do not place sufficient value on that service).

Non-profit markets

Non-profit organisations, discussed further in Chapter 23, differ in that they see themselves as existing and operating for the benefit of the public rather than for the creation of profits. Their objectives, therefore, are to encourage people to use their services or products, or to participate in their activities. Pricing can have a major role in achieving that, if goods and services are sold at cost or subsidised to a point where they are visibly below market rates. Some activities, such as minority interest arts events, could not be produced on a commercial basis unless ticket prices were astronomically high, and therefore public subsidy or sponsorship are essential to keep prices down to an affordable and accessible level.

Public benefit need not always be about increasing and encouraging demand. Environmental awareness means that many pressure groups are concerned about the impact of visitor numbers on popular beauty spots. The provision of access, facilities and amenities, along with the erosion of footpaths, have a devastating effect on the place. This has led to consideration of using entry fees or high car-parking fees as a means of discouraging visitors. Similarly, the city of Oxford has implemented very high car-parking charges to deter shoppers from bringing their cars into a congested city centre and to encourage the use of 'park and ride' public transport. Zermatt has gone one step further and has banned all vehicles unless they have a special permit.

This is to protect the local environment and the ambience of the town, in view of the large number of tourists who visit the area every year.

Unlike the practice in most ordinary consumer markets, where the price is directly exchanged between buyer and seller, in the non-profit sector price sometimes passes through a third party. When this happens it can blunt the consumer's price sensitivity. Where medical services are paid for through an insurance policy, for example, the consumer can begin to think that the visit to the Doctor is 'free' and the connection between the service and its price is lost. Such disconnection can lead to overuse of a 'free' service, causing pricing problems for the service provider. Next year's insurance premiums rise to compensate and consumers grumble about it, becoming even more determined to get their money's worth.

In public services, paid for through taxation, moves have been made to reduce the disconnection between price and service by imposing direct charges which contribute towards the cost of maintaining and improving service provision. Prescription charges made under the UK's National Health Service do not in most cases cover the full cost of the drugs supplied but serve to contribute towards it and to remind the user that the service is not 'free'. In some cases, the charges levied do not even recoup the costs of collecting them, such as the tolls on the Humber Bridge. Raising these charges to a more economic level would potentially cause both political difficulties and public outcry, as happened when the tolls were set on the newly opened Skye bridge. In France, however, the tolls on the Loire bridge between St. Nazaire and St. Brevin have been abolished to encourage economic regeneration in the region. The private consortium that built the bridge still had 16 years left of its rights to collect tolls, but the two local authorities concerned bought up those rights, thus giving them the freedom to drop the toll.

Organisational markets

In organisational markets, the difference between price and real cost is particularly marked. As mentioned above at p. 374, the costs of installation, training, scrap, financing etc. are all used to put the price of major purchases into perspective. Add to this the costs and risks incurred if it turns out that a bad purchasing decision has been made, and you can begin to appreciate why organisational buyers spend so much time and effort analysing potential purchases from all angles. It is rarely the case that the lowest price on paper wins the order. Deeper analysis may reveal that the lowest price actually incurs the highest cost. Mehta (1995), for example, in discussing capital investments, suggests 12 points that affect the total cost, and which should form part of the buying centre's evaluation criteria. These points refer to technological and commercial factors, and are listed in Table 10.3.

An organisation's sensitivity to price may well vary according to the type of item being purchased. More time will be spent considering the price of a component (such as an aircraft engine) that represents a high percentage of the cost of the finished product than on one that represents a fraction of 1 per cent (such as the rivets that hold the engine on the aircraft).

Many organisations try to eliminate unnecessary cost and waste by using **value management**. Value management involves teams who look very closely at processes and products to analyse where the greatest costs are being incurred, and where the greatest value is added. This focuses attention on the critical areas of the production process where cost savings in terms of bought-in components, production methods or systems will yield the greatest benefits. Value management teams are likely to include members from all the different organisational functions, and may also include representatives of suppliers' companies. Once priority areas for cost saving have been identified, the supplier can be instrumental in helping to find solutions, perhaps by looking critically at their own cost profile or by working co-operatively with the buyer to develop new, more efficient components. It has been claimed that value management can achieve savings

TABLE 10.3

Technological and commercial factors affecting the total cost of a capital investment

1	Cost of necessary accessories to achieve full capacity	Transport; installation; commissioning costs; manuals
2	Cost and need for spares	Cost of spares including sourcing; importing; delivery time/cost
3	Actual performance of same equipment in other companies	Assess reliability; running costs; operator problems; maintenance
4	Demonstration and guarantees	Supplier's ability to 'prove' what the equipment can do; promises on spares availability; servicing
5	Eco-friendliness	Dust, noise, smoke, fumes and other pollutant outputs; cost of safe effluent disposal
6	Safety	Safety of operators and others; long- and short-term effects on health
7	Cost of providing special operating conditions	Provision of new facilities, e.g. air-conditioning or pressurised chamber
8	Any supplier's costs associated with installation/trials	Travel and accommodation costs incurred while supplier sets up equipment and runs tests. Is the buyer responsible for this?
9	Training costs	Training operators; costs incurred until they become efficient and achieve output/quality level required
10	Other service costs	Other service needed during installation
11	After-sales service costs	Repairs; maintenance; downtime while awaiting repair
12	Cost of preventative maintenance	Frequency of servicing required; complexity and time needed for scheduled maintenance; cost of downtime and staffing

Source: Adapted from Mehta (1995).

of between 20 per cent and 30 per cent of the cost of bought-in parts (*Purchasing and Supply Management*, 1995).

It is also characteristic of organisational markets that many prices are negotiated, particularly with critical components, custom-made goods, or high-volume bulk purchases. It is common to find that purchases are put out to tender, putting the onus on the seller to design an acceptable offering at a good value price. Both of these areas are considered at Chapter 11 and in Chapter 4.

All of this highlights one of the distinctions between consumer and organisational markets: consumer markets tend towards fixed prices set and controlled by the seller, whereas organisational markets tend to operate more flexibly, with the buyer having a lot more bargaining power.

EXTERNAL INFLUENCES ON THE PRICING DECISION

The previous sections of this chapter have shown that there is more to pricing than meets the eye. It is not a precise science because of the complexities of the marketing environment and the human perceptions of the parties involved in the marketing exchange. There will always be some uncertainty over the effect of a pricing decision, whether on distribution channels, competitors or the customer. Nevertheless, to reduce that uncertainty, it is important to analyse the range of issues affecting pricing decisions. Some of these are internal to the selling organisation, and are thus perhaps more predictable, but others arise from external pressures, and are therefore more difficult to define precisely. There is also some variation in the extent to which the organisation can control or influence these issues. Figure 10.2 summarises the main areas of *external influence*, while this section of the chapter defines them and gives an overview of their impact on the pricing decision, in preparation for the more detailed scrutiny of price setting and strategies in Chapter 11.

Customers and consumers

As p. 371 and p. 375 showed, pricing cannot be considered without taking into account the feelings and sensitivities of the *end buyer*. Different market segments react to price levels and price changes differently depending on the nature of the product, its desirability and the level of product loyalty established.

> **Example**
>
> The discerning coffee drinker who likes the taste of Nescafé and always buys that brand may not notice when the price rises, but even if they do spot the price rise, they might still continue to purchase Nescafé because they value the brand's benefits so highly. A segment that perceives coffee as a commodity and does not mind what it tastes like as long as it is hot and wet, might be more inclined to be price sensitive. They might have been buying the same brand on a regular basis, but if its price rises then they certainly will notice and switch to something cheaper.

The marketer has to be careful to set prices within an area bounded at the bottom end by costs and at the top end by what the market will tolerate. The bigger that area, the more discretion the marketer has in setting price. The organisation can increase its pricing discretion either by reducing costs (thereby lowering the bottom boundary) or by raising the consumers' threshold (by better targeted communication or by improving the product offering).

The consumers' upper threshold is difficult to define as it is linked closely with perceptions of the product and its competitive standing. A product perceived as

FIGURE 10.2

External influences on the pricing decision

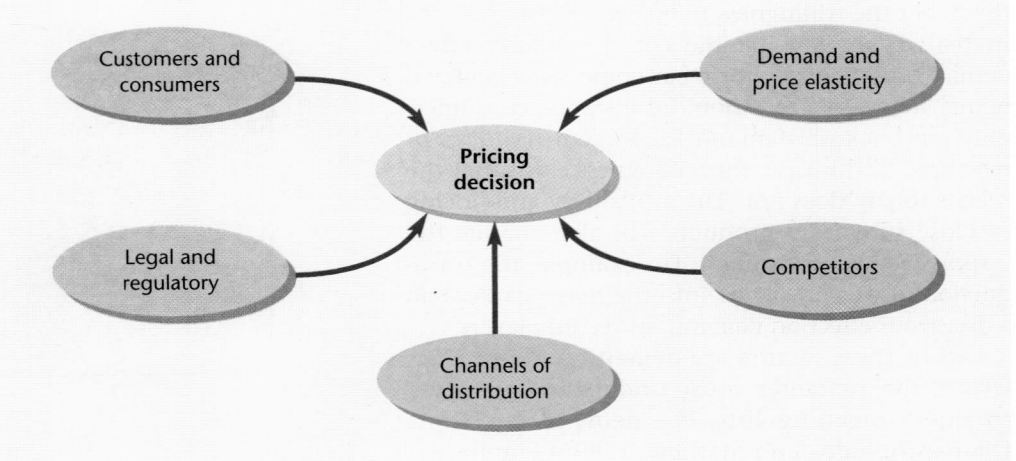

better than the competition will have a higher upper thresh-old than one perceived as poor value. In the latter case, the upper limit on price may be very close to cost. Similarly, a product with strong brand loyalty attached to it can push its upper limit higher because the product's desirability blunts any price sensitivity, enabling a price premium to be achieved.

Demand and price elasticity

Customers' attitudes towards price and their responsiveness to it are reflected to some extent in economic theories of *demand*. Marketers' pricing objectives and the estimation of demand are thus very closely linked (Montgomery, 1988). As pricing objectives change, for example if there is a decision to move upmarket into a premium-priced segment, the nature and size of potential demand will also change. Similarly, it is important for the marketer to able to estimate demand for new product. The definition of demand is flexible here; it may mean demand across an entire product market, or demand within a specific market segment, or be organisation specific.

Chapter 22 will look at some of the techniques used to estab-lish sales and market potential in terms of usage or product sales with different market conditions. Using this information, it is possible to address an issue that has long been concern of economists: the relationship between price and demand.

Source: Nestlé UK Ltd/McCann Erickson.

Brand values justify a premium price.

Demand determinants

For most products, it seems logical that if the price goes up, then demand falls and conversely, if the price falls, then demand rises. This is the basic premise behind the standard demand curve shown in Fig 10.3, which shows the number of units sold (Q1) at a given price (P1). As price increases from P1 to P2, demand is expected to fall from Q1 to Q2. This classic demand curve may relate either to a market or to an individual product. As an example, in 1992 the relative price of a UK holiday for Americans rose because of the weak dollar and so there was a decline in the numbers purchasing those holidays.

The shape of the demand curve, however, will be influenced by a range of factors other than price. Changing consumer tastes and needs, for example, might make a prod-uct more or less desirable regardless of the price. The economic ability to pay is still there, but the willingness to buy is not. Fluctuations in real disposable income could similarly affect demand, particularly for what could be considered luxury items. In a recession, for instance, consumers may cut back on demand for foreign holidays or new cars. In this case, the willingness exists, but the means to pay does not. The availability and pricing of close substitute products will also change the responsiveness of demand. For example, the intro-duction of the CD player into the mass market had a disastrous effect on demand for record players.

All of these factors are demand determinants which the marketer must understand in order to inject meaning into the demand curve. As Diamantopoulos and Mathews (1995) emphasise,

FIGURE 10.3

The classic demand curve

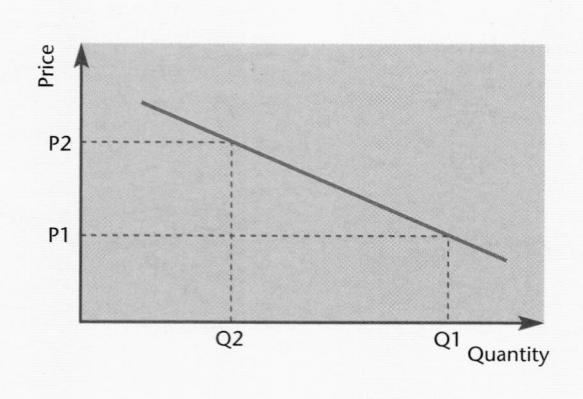

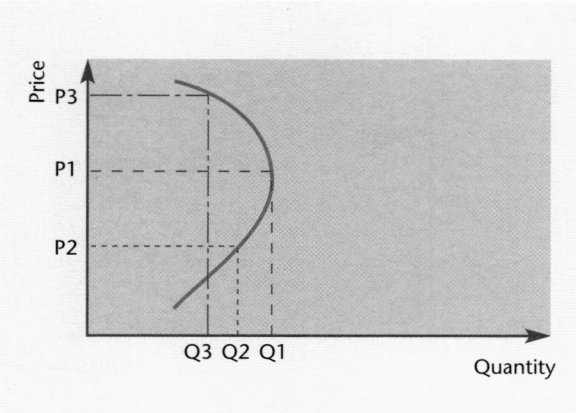

FIGURE 10.4

**The boomerang
demand curve**

however, demand curves are very subjective in nature. They depend very much on managerial judgements of the likely impact of price changes on demand, since most organisations do not have the kind of sophisticated information systems that would allow a more objective calculation. In reality, then, it is a *perceived* demand curve that drives managerial decisions rather than a 'real' one.

Not all products conform to the classic demand curve shown in Fig 10.3. Some products with a deep psychological relationship with the consumer, perhaps with a high status dimension, can show a reverse price–demand curve in which the higher the price the higher the demand. As Fig 10.4 shows, as the price goes down from P1 to P2 and demand falls from Q1 to Q2, the product loses its mystique and demand falls. There is, however, still an upper threshold beyond which the good becomes too expensive for even a status-conscious market. Then as the price rises higher, beyond P3, a more normal relationship holds true in which higher price leads to lower demand. This creates a boomerang-shaped demand curve. Knowing at what point the curve begins to turn back on itself could be useful for a marketer wishing to skim the market. Price too high and you could have turned the corner, becoming too exclusive.

Example

Fine fragrances, especially those with designer names on them, might fall into this category of demand curve. The fragrance houses have been careful to price them sufficiently highly to position them well away from ordinary toiletries. This means that fine fragrances appeal not only to a well-to-do segment who can easily afford this sort of product on a regular basis but also to those who aspire to be part of this élite and are prepared to splash out what seems to them to be a large sum of money occasionally to bring themselves closer to a world of luxury and sophistication. In either case, the high price is part of the appeal and the excitement of the product. The higher the price, the bigger the thrill. If the price became too high, however, the aspiring segment would probably fall away and live out their fantasies with something more affordable. They might find £30 to £80 acceptable, but £70 to £120 might be perceived as too extravagant. Even the élite segment might have its upper threshold. If the price of designer-label fine fragrances becomes too high, then they might as well buy the designer's clothes instead if they want to flaunt their wealth and status!

Another dimension of the demand curve is that marketers can themselves seek to influence its shape. Figure 10.5 shows how the demand curve can be shifted upwards through marketing efforts. If the marketer can offer better value to the customer or change the customer's perceptions of the product, then a higher quantity will be demanded without any reduction in the price. It is valuable for the marketer to be able to find ways of using non-price-based mechanisms of responding to a competitor's price cut or seeking to improve demand, to avoid the kind of mutually damaging price wars that erode margins and profits. This may create a new demand curve, parallel to the old one so that demand can be increased from Q1 to Q2 while retaining the price at P1.

Price elasticity of demand

It is also important for the marketer to have some understanding of the sensitivity of demand to price changes. This is shown by the steepness of the demand curve. A very steep demand curve shows a great deal of price sensitivity, in that a small change in price, all other things remaining equal, leads to a big change in demand. For some essential products, such as electricity, the demand curve is much more shallow; changes in price do not lead to big changes in demand. In this case, demand is said to be *inelastic* because it does not stretch a lot if pulled either way by price. The term *price elasticity of demand* thus refers to the ratio of percentage change in quantity over percentage change in price:

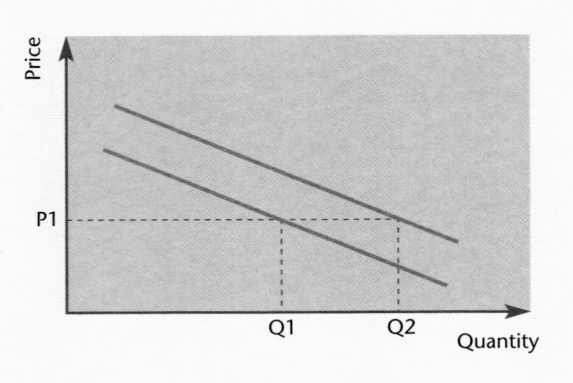

FIGURE 10.5

The parallel demand curve

$$\text{Price elasticity} = \frac{\%\ \text{change in quantity demanded}}{\%\ \text{change in price}}$$

thus the higher the price elasticity of demand, the more sensitive the market. Goods like electricity will have a price elasticity much closer to zero than goods like convenience foods. For most goods, as the quantity demanded usually falls if the price rises, price elasticity is often negative, but by convention, the minus sign is usually ignored. To summarise, there are three possible forms of elasticity:

Elastic demand. Where demand is elastic, a small percentage increase in price (from P1 to P2) produces a large percentage decrease in quantity demanded (from Q1 to Q2), as shown in Fig 10.6. The price elasticity is greater than one (ignoring the minus sign). The effect on total revenue is that a rise in price leads to a reduction in revenue, because the extra income from the price rise does not fully compensate for the fall in demand. Conversely, a fall in price increases demand to the point where total revenue rises, because the income from the new customers more than compensates for the decrease in revenue from existing ones.

Inelastic demand. Where a demand in inelastic, a small percentage increase in price (from P1 to P2) produces a very small percentage change in quantity demanded (from Q1 to Q2) as shown in Fig 10.7. The price elasticity will be between zero and one. In total revenue terms, income increases as the price increases, and falls as the price falls. The change in demand is not sufficient to compensate, as it is with elastic situations.

FIGURE 10.6

The elastic demand curve

Unitary demand. An unlikely, but theoretically possible, situation is that where the percentage change in price leads to an identical percentage change in quantity demanded. The price elasticity is exactly one, and total revenue will remain the same.

It is important for the marketer to understand price elasticity and its causes, whether for an organisation's brand or within the market as a whole, as a basis for marketing mix decisions. There are a number of factors which will influence the price sensitivity (i.e., the price elasticity of demand) of customers. According to economic theory, the emergence of more, or closer, substitutes for a product will increase its price elasticity

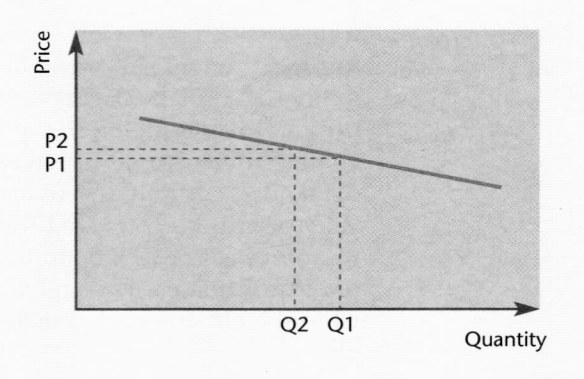

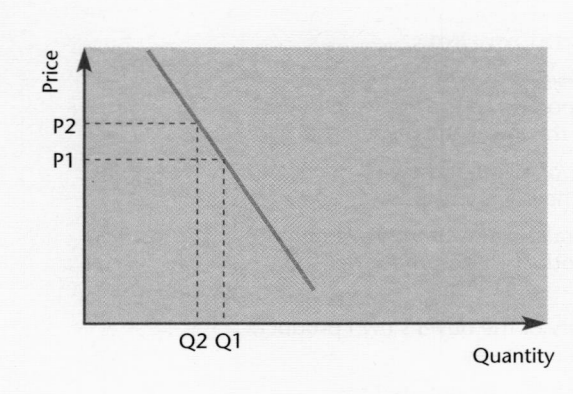

FIGURE 10.7

**The inelastic
demand curve**

as buyers have the option of switching to the substitute as the price of the original product rises. From a marketing perspective, however, it does not seem quite so simple. The emergence of vegetable-based spreadable fats, for example, has offered consumers an alternative to butter and thus something with which to compare the price of butter. Further than that, however, it has completely changed the character of butter's demand curve from that of a necessity (a fairly flat straight line) to that of a luxury (more of a boomerang shape). Those who now choose to buy butter because of its superior taste or because of the status it bestows on the contents of the buyer's fridge will be no more price sensitive now than they ever were, and indeed, may even be less so.

As well as looking at the influence of substitutes on the shape and steepness of demand curves, it is also interesting to consider the relative importance of the purchase to the buyer. A purchase involving a relatively large cash outlay compared with the buyer's income will make that buyer more price sensitive. As discussed in Chapter 3, the more risky and infrequent the purchase, the more rational the buyer becomes, and more important the value for money aspects of the offering become. A rise in the price of cars, for example, might deter a potential buyer from replacing an old car. Table 10.4, based on the work of Nagle (1987) lists nine factors that affect price sensitivity generally, while Table 10.5, based on Porter (1980), looks at sensitivity specifically in the context of organisational markets.

TABLE 10.4
Factors influencing price sensitivity

1	The unique value effect	The better differentiated the product, the lower the price sensitivity
2	The substitute awareness effect	The greater the number of substitutes available, the greater the price sensitivity
3	The difficult comparison effect	The more difficult it is to make a direct comparison between different products, the lower the price sensitivity
4	The total expenditure effect	The smaller the proportion of total spend this product represents, the lower the price sensitivity
5	The end benefit effect	The greater and more valued the end benefit of the product, the lower the price sensitivity
6	The shared cost effect	A buyer bearing only part of the cost of a product will be less price sensitive
7	The sunk investment effect	Buyers who have already bought complementary products or who are 'locked in' to a system will be price sensitive
8	The price–quality effect	The higher the quality and the prestige image of the product, the lower the price sensitivity
9	The inventory effect	Buyers who hold stocks of the product are more likely to be price sensitive than those who purchase for immediate consumption

Source: Based on Nagle (1987).

TABLE 10.5

Factors influencing price sensitivity in organisational markets

1	The total expenditure effect	The smaller the proportion of the total spend this product represents, the lower the price sensitivity
2	The penalty for failure effect	The greater the cost of failure if the wrong choice is made, the lower the price sensitivity
3	The overall saving effect	The greater the overall savings or improvement in performance the product makes, the lower the price sensitivity
4	The contribution to quality effect	The higher the quality of the buyer's own product, the lower their price sensitivity
5	The degree of customisation effect	The more customised or differentiated the product, the lower the price sensitivity
6	The end customer sensitivity	The more price sensitive the buyer's own customer, the more price sensitive the buyer becomes
7	The buyer's ability to absorb costs	The more profitable the buyer and the better able to absorb costs, the lower the price sensitivity
8	The buyer's ignorance effect	The less the buyer knows and the looser their purchasing specifications, the lower their price sensitivity
9	The decision maker's motivation effect	The less motivated the decision maker in terms of cost minimisation, the lower the price sensitivity

Source: Based on Porter (1980).

Elasticity of demand will vary greatly between different types of product. Within the food sector, Bolton (1989) found that whereas coffee brands and convenience foods are very price elastic, certain types of fresh fruit and vegetables are price inelastic. As a final thought on price elasticity, it is interesting to consider how it has been deliberately manipulated in the case of tobacco products. The UK government has pursued a consistent policy over the years of imposing increasingly punitive taxes on tobacco as a social welfare issue. Basically, the aim has been to push tobacco prices up to the point where price elasticity comes into operation and smokers give up the habit because it is too expensive. This point has not yet been reached, as addicts are proving to be remarkably resilient in absorbing the price rises and maintaining their inelasticity.

Channels of distribution

An organisation's approach to pricing has also to take into account the needs and expectations of the other members of the *distribution chain*. Each of them will have a desired level of profit margin and a requirement to cover the costs associated with handling and reselling the product, such as transport, warehousing, insurance and retail display, for example. Even with a service product, such as insurance or a holiday, distributing through agents who claim commission on sales to cover premises, staffing, administration and profit has an impact on the price of the service.

All of this tends to erode the manufacturer's pricing discretion because effectively it adds to the producer's costs and takes the total much nearer to the consumer's upper limit. How much erosion there is will depend on the balance of power between manufacturer and intermediaries.

Competitors

The point has been made several times during the course of this chapter that pricing decisions have to be made in a *competitive* context. The level and intensity of competition and the pricing decisions that other organisations make in the market will influence any producer's own pricing. It is not just about relative positioning ('If the budget version is £10 and the premium quality version is £70 then if we want to signal a mid-range product we have to charge £45'). It also concerns strategic decisions about the extent to which the organisation wishes to use price as an aggressive competitive weapon. Price and non-price competition will be further discussed in Chapter 11.

The influence of competition on price will depend on the nature of the product and the number and size of competitors within the market.

Monopoly

Few monopoly situations, where there is only one supplier serving the whole market, exist. Traditionally, monopolies have been large state-owned enterprises providing public services such as utilities, telecommunications and mail, or operating economically crucial industries such as steel and coal. Legislation protected the monopoly from competition. In theory, monopolists have no competitive framework for pricing

MARKETING IN ACTION

Sweet smell of success

Honey demand appears to have been quite sticky, despite changes in prices. Total world-wide demand has varied little over recent years, but fluctuations in raw material prices can be very high. In 1995, prices rose by 50 per cent because of poor harvests from the main producers.

Germany is the leading nation in per capita consumption of honey for spreading and for use in cooking, demanding 90 000 tonnes every year. Only 20 000 tonnes of that comes from home producers and the rest is imported, mainly from Mexico and Argentina. European honey production is small compared with that of China (150 000 tonnes) and the former Soviet Union (231 000 tonnes). Total UK production is just 4000 tonnes and that of France 30 000 tonnes. European beekeepers who are in serious production operate in a sheltered market behind tariffs on imports from the main non-EU producers. Other factors also restrict the import of supplies from these producers, such as poor quality consistency and lack of continuity of supply.

Honey packers and importers are in the front line in adapting to changes in prices. The 1996 price of Chinese honey was around $1200 per tonne. It had dropped as low as $700 per tonne in the early 1990s. Since China is the market leader, producers from Argentina, Mexico and Australia tend to follow

Chinese prices. The former Soviet Union is not yet fully organised to make a serious entry into world-wide markets, despite its high-quality Siberian honey, and only exports about 2.5 per cent of its output.

A number of factors influence prices. Poor harvests are a major factor. In 1995, for example, the Mexican honey crop dropped by 50 per cent. Hurricanes, drought and disease all take their toll on production. Chinese beekeepers tend to operate as small scale enterprises, each with an average of 50 hives and an annual yield of only 25 kg. There are 7.5 million bee colonies in China, but the potential exists to increase this to 25 million. The Chinese government has imposed a system of export licences to seek to stabilise prices, since the price of honey has a direct effect on the level of interest shown in beekeeping by Chinese farmers. Another factor influencing European prices for honey has been the success of Chinese producers in meeting the product range requirements and quality levels demanded by the US market. The increase in Chinese exports to the USA means that there is less available for export to Europe, thus increasing prices. Supply considerations thus tend to be the main influences on honey prices, as well as the lead taken by the major producing nations.

Source: Guild (1996).

and can, therefore, set whatever prices they like as the customer has no choice but to source from them. In practice, however, governments and independent watchdog bodies have imposed regulations and pressurised monopolists into keeping prices within socially acceptable limits. Even if that was not enough, the growth of international competition and the availability of alternatives also have an impact. The price and availability of fuel, oil, gas or nuclear power for instance, all affect the price and demand for coal.

The last 10 years or so have seen UK government policy moving towards privatising state-owned organisations and creating conditions that will allow free market competition to emerge. This is already evident in the telecommunications market where the emergence of new competition has changed the way in which British Telecommunications develops its service and pricing policies.

Oligopoly

The UK's deregulated telecommunications market described above is an oligopoly, where a small number of powerful providers dominate the market between them. Each player in the market is very conscious of the rest and makes no move without due consideration of the likely competitive response. Pricing is a particularly sensitive issue in such markets, and where oligopolists choose to price very closely with each other, accusations of collusion are bound to arise. Sudden changes in price by one organisation might be construed as a threat by the rest, but prior and public notification of price rises, as will be discussed at Chapter 11 can be used to defuse suspicion.

Example

In the early 1990s, the media accused the biggest UK supermarket chains of keeping their basic prices artificially high to maintain their profits. The entry of discounters and warehouse clubs was thus seen as disturbing the established oligopoly, with the media hopeful (and the supermarkets fearful) that this would trigger a price war. In the short term, price did indeed become a prominent feature of the supermarkets' marketing mixes, with Sainsbury's advertising that 'Good Food Costs Less at Sainsbury's' and Tesco introducing its *Value Lines*, generic products selling at bottom of the range prices, for example. Over time, however, the supermarkets managed to reassert themselves as an oligopoly by managing to focus the customer's attention on quality, consistency and service rather than price, thus differentiating themselves as a group further from the discounters. The price issue did not entirely go away, but was subtly reformulated as a 'value for money' message, largely communicated through selected own-brand items and specific short-term price-orientated promotions rather than price wars across the whole range.

These developments are not surprising, as a price war between oligopolists is something that all parties involved would prefer to avoid. Since oligopolists are likely to be fairly evenly matched, it is difficult for any one of them to be sure that it can win. While the war goes on, the consumer may be happy, but the oligopolists are simply eroding their profit margins to dangerously thin levels, not gaining any competitive ground, and causing themselves much stress about the eventual outcome.

Monopolistic competition

Most markets fall into the category of monopolistic competition where there are many competitors, but each has a product differentiated from the rest. Price is not necessarily a key factor in these markets as product features and benefits serve to differentiate a product and diffuse the competitive effect. The emphasis in these markets is on branding or adding value so that the customer is prepared to accept a different price from its competitors. Miele, the German manufacturer of kitchen and laundry appliances, for example, has developed a reputation for selling very high quality goods at a price premium. It can thus price its products substantially higher than those of its competitors because Miele's customers believe that they are getting good value for money in terms of quality, durability and service.

Perfect competition

As with its direct opposite, the monopoly, perfect competition is hard to find. It implies that there are very many sellers in the market with products that are indistinguishable from each other in the eyes of the buyer. There is, therefore, little flexibility on price because no one seller has either enough power to lead the rest or the ability to differentiate the product sufficiently to justify a different price. If one seller increases the price, either the rest will follow suit or customers will change suppliers, bringing the aberrant supplier back into line. One supplier's reduction in price will attract custom until such time as other suppliers follow suit.

To avoid this kind of powerless stalemate, most markets have evolved into offering differentiated products, even with the most uninteresting commodities (*see* the example at p. 189 on salt, for instance). Nor does the equality of suppliers last for long in most markets. One or two more astute or powerful suppliers usually emerge to lead the market into monopolistic competition.

> ### Example
>
> A visit to the local fruit and vegetable market demonstrates a near perfect market at work. Products are clearly priced, the merchandise is usually visible for comparison and competing suppliers are contained within a defined area. Depending on the season, many prices are set at similar levels. If any differentiation does take place, it could be with a smile, the free provision of a carrying box, or a discount for buying particular goods in quantity (if carrots, for instance, are priced on every stall at 18p per kg., one might differentiate by offering 2 kg. for 30p).

Legal and regulatory

European marketers increasingly need to understand the national and European *legal and regulatory framework* when setting and adjusting prices. Aspects of this were discussed at pp. 70 *et seq*. earlier. Some organisations, such as public utilities, tend to have their pricing policies carefully scrutinised by the government to make sure that they are in the public interest, especially where a near monopoly is operating. Even after privatisation, such organisations are not entirely free to price as they wish. As mentioned in Chapter 2, for example, the privatised water, gas, telephone and electricity companies in the UK are answerable to quasi non-governmental organisations (QUANGOs), watchdog bodies set up by the government. Even the National Lottery has its pricing, distribution of funds and profits overseen by a QUANGO, Oflot.

These are high-profile cases involving large and important organisations whose activities fundamentally affect the whole population and the economy. For the most part, however, Europe subscribes to the idea that a free market should determine prices without governmental interference. Authorities, whether national or EU-based, will nevertheless become involved in pricing issues where they feel that unfair competition or price fixing is taking place. In the UK for example, the Office of Fair Trading (OFT) is the first port of call for complaints about pricing and if the OFT cannot resolve the problem, they may refer the case to the Monopolies and Mergers Commission (MMC). They in turn may refer a case to the EC.

In March 1995, the MMC reported its findings on the case of video consoles and games. The MMC decided that Sega and Nintendo both operate discriminatory pricing, concluding that:

> . . . [it] is a step taken by Nintendo UK and Sega Europe for maintaining and exploiting the complex monopoly situation. We further conclude that this operates against the public interest with the particular adverse effects of raising the price of software to consumers and thus over time the total cost of games, and of impeding the entry of new games systems (Cane, 1995).

The MMC focused particularly on the control that the two companies exercised over the development and pricing of the software for their systems through the licences that they sell to third-party software developers. The problem is that the software developers want to write software for these systems because they know it will sell, and so they accept the terms laid down by Sega and Nintendo. The consumer too is locked into the software because of having bought the console, and so has no real choice but to pay the going rate.

In a slightly more recent case, it was announced in April 1995 that the OFT had referred allegations of price fixing on electrical goods to the MMC. Discount retailers, such as warehouse clubs, had complained that the big name manufacturers of televisions, videos, hi-fis, camcorders and white goods had refused to supply them because they were reselling the goods at prices below the manufacturers' recommended retail prices. If this actually is found to be the case, then the manufacturers do have a case to answer because such attempts to control the retail price and keep it artificially high are no longer allowed. Sony, however, is categorical in its claim that its refusal to supply warehouse clubs is because of the clubs' inadequate display space and staff training, not because of their pricing policies (Buckley and Baxter, 1995a ; 1995b).

Petrol prices are heavily influenced by government taxes and duty, as well as crude oil prices.

Source: DMB&B.

In the UK, resale price maintenance, that is, the power of manufacturers to determine what the retail price of their products should be, was abolished in the early 1960s, although it was retained in a few selected product areas. The Net Book Agreement (NBA), until its abolition in 1995, allowed publishers to control bookshop prices. Once the NBA had collapsed, retailers started looking at another area where resale price maintenance was still practised: vitamins, minerals and dietary supplements. The supermarket chain ASDA cut up to 20 per cent off the prices of brands in those categories, forcing the manufacturers to take ASDA to court to uphold their right to dictate the price. The case went against ASDA which then had to increase prices again, and await the outcome of an OFT review of the situation. In the meantime, all the major supermarkets pointedly and heavily discounted their own-label vitamins, minerals and supplements, as they are perfectly entitled to do.

Example

It was a selective distribution agreement that allowed the perfume houses to refuse to supply the UK discount chemist chain Superdrug in 1993. The perfume houses argued that Superdrug's discount policy would undermine the products' images and turn fine fragrance into another ordinary toiletry (look back to p. 383 where we discussed perfume and pricing). The perfume houses also felt that Superdrug's retail premises and staff training were not consistent with the luxury image of fine fragrances. Superdrug challenged the perfume houses, initially through the OFT, then through the MMC, which in turn referred the case to the EU.

Within the EU, some industries have negotiated selective distribution agreements which effectively allow them to control prices by having the right to decide who should or should not be allowed to sell their products.

Finally, at a more mundane level, manufacturers and retailers may be obliged by law to include duty or tax as part of their pricing. Alcohol and tobacco in particular are targeted by many governments for high rates of duty, partly as a public health measure (keep the prices high to discourage over-consumption), and partly as an excellent revenue earner. In the UK, petrol is also subject to high rates of duty (with a higher rate on leaded petrol than on unleaded or diesel).

As mentioned at p. 62, varying rates of VAT are charged on various categories of products across the EU. When the UK government decided to impose VAT on domestic fuel, the gas and electric companies had no choice but to add it to their customers' bills, thus increasing the overall price of these utilities.

INTERNAL INFLUENCES ON THE PRICING DECISION

Pricing is, of course, also influenced by various *internal factors*. Pricing needs to reflect both corporate and marketing objectives, for example, as well as being consistent with the rest of the marketing mix. It is also important to remember, however, that pricing may also be related to costs, if the organisation is looking to generate an acceptable margin of profit. Figure 10.8 summarises the internal influences on price, and the rest of this section discusses each of them in further detail.

Organisational objectives

The area of *organisational objectives* is an internal influence, linked with corporate strategy. Marketing plans and objectives have to be set not only to best satisfy the customer's needs and wants, but also to reflect the aspirations of the organisation. These two aims should not be incompatible! Organisational objectives such as target

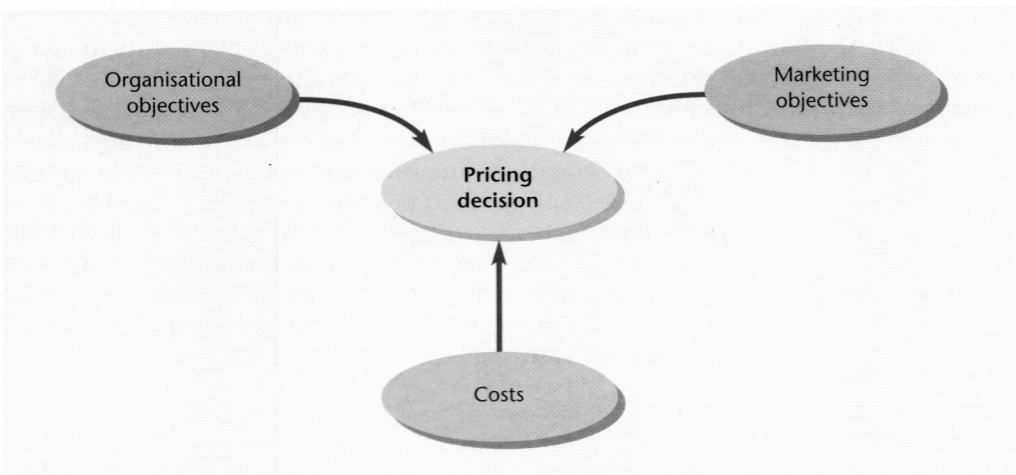

FIGURE 10.8

Internal influences on the pricing decision

volume sales, target value sales, target growth in various market segments and target profit figures can all be made more or less attainable through the deployment of the marketing mix and particularly through price.

Corporate strategy is not simply concerned with quantifiable target setting. It is also concerned with the organisation's relative position in the market compared with the competition. Pricing may be used to help either to signal a desire for leadership (whether in terms of lowest cost or price, or superior quality) or to establish a clearly differentiated niche which can then be emphasized and consolidated through the other elements of the marketing mix. In launching the *Midnight Sun* brand of butter on to the UK market, the Finnish company Valio used high-quality silver packaging as well as pricing the product to match the market leader, Lurpak, to communicate an upmarket image to the customer.

At the other end of the pricing spectrum, discount supermarket chains, such as Netto, Aldi, Lidl and Kwik Save, are trying to achieve objectives relating to price leadership in the market. Obviously, low pricing within their stores is their primary tool, but this can only be achieved through cost reduction (hence the minimalist retail environment and low levels of customer service) and accepting lower profit margins (1 per cent, compared with the industry average of between 5 per cent and 8 per cent). Achieving all of this is also dependent on attracting many more customers through the doors to generate the higher volume of sales needed to make a reasonable profit. The higher volumes also give the discount retailer scope for negotiating more favourable terms with the manufacturers for bulk buying.

Organisational objectives can change over time as the organisation and its markets evolve. A new business, or a new entrant into a market, faces initial problems of survival. There is a need to generate orders to use excess capacity and to establish a foothold in the market. Relatively low pricing (at the sacrifice of profit margins rather than quality) is just one possible way of doing that. Once established, the organisation can begin to think in terms of target profits and building a competitive position, which may involve a revised approach to pricing. Using price as part of an integrated marketing mix, the organisation can aim to achieve market leadership in terms of whatever criteria are important. Once leadership is achieved, objectives have to be redefined to maintain and defend that leadership, thus keeping competition at arm's length.

Corporate objectives can also have both short- and long-term dimensions to them. In the short term, for example, a small business on the verge of collapse might use low price as a survival tactic to keep it afloat, even if its longer-term ambitions include quality leadership at a higher price.

Marketing objectives

As the previous subsection has implied, marketing and organisational objectives are very closely interrelated, and influence each other to a great extent. The distinction, though, is that while organisational objectives relate primarily to the operation, the well-being, and the personality of the organisation as a whole, *marketing objectives* are more closely focused on specific target markets and the position desired within them.

Marketing objectives are achieved through the use of the whole marketing mix, not just the price element, emphasizing again the need for an integrated and harmonious marketing mix. An organisation may have a portfolio of products (*see* pp. 308 *et seq.*) serving different segments, each of which requires a different approach to pricing. Such a differentiated strategy can be seen in telecommunications, with British Telecommunications, developing a range of tariffs for both domestic and business users to suit different needs and priorities.

> **Example**
>
> In 1993, the manufacturers of Castle loudspeakers for hi-fi systems had six models in their range, priced from around £200 (value for money, basic, functional product) to around £1500 (premium product in terms of sound quality and manufacture). As long as the market recognises the functional and quality differences between the models in such a range, the wide spread of prices need not cause confusion or conflict as to what the organisation stands for.

In that sense, it is no different from Renault manufacturing the Renault 5 Campus at one end of the range and the Safrane at the other. The key is to use the other elements of the marketing mix to support the price or to provide a rationale for it. The concept of the product portfolio and the management issues surrounding it are fully covered in Chapter 21.

With each individual volume attractively priced at 60p, these Penguin books are high volume sellers.

Source: Penguin Books.

Another product concept which might influence the pricing of a particular product over a period of time is the product life cycle (*see* pp. 294 *et seq.*). In the introductory stage, a lower price might be necessary as part of a marketing strategy to encourage trial. Advertising this as 'an introductory trial price' would be one way of preventing 'low price = low quality' judgements. As the product becomes established through the growth and early maturity stages, and gains loyal buyers, the organisation may feel confident enough to raise the price. As indicated earlier, this has to be done with due reference to the competitive situation and the desired positioning for both product and organisation. In late maturity and decline, it is possible that price reductions could be used to squeeze the last breath out of the dying product.

Costs

From a marketing perspective, price is primarily related to what the customer will be prepared to pay for a particular product offering. The actual *cost* of providing that offering cannot, however, be completely ignored. Marketing is about creating and holding a customer at a profit, and if an organisation cannot produce the product for less than it can sell it for, then its presence in that market is questionable.

The cost of producing the product, therefore, represents a floor below which the product cannot be sold profitably. However, defining cost may not be so straightforward. In a hotel, for example, the majority of its costs are fixed in the short term (staffing, facilities provision, maintenance etc.) and are incurred regardless of the room occupancy. The variable costs associated with an actual guest (such as laundry and consumables) are relatively low. In setting the price of a room, therefore, the organisation has to reflect both the estimated variable costs and an element of contribution towards fixed costs and profit based on predicted levels of business so that in the long run all costs are met and an acceptable level of profit made.

In the short term, however, it may not be possible to adhere strictly to a cost-recovery formula. The price has to stand in a competitive and unpredictable environment, and may have to be flexible enough to be used as a competitive weapon or as a promotional tool to maintain volume of sales. Thus a hotel may be prepared to let a room at a discount of anything up to 40 per cent of the normal rate at a quiet time of the year when the supply of hotel rooms far exceeds the demand. This is acceptable as long as the price covers the variable costs of letting that room and makes some contribution towards fixed costs and profit. Similarly, at busy times when rooms are hard to find, the hotels can afford to stand by their published rates.

Another important dimension of cost is the concept of joint or shared costs which are divided between a number of products produced by one organisation. Central provision of, for example, R&D facilities, maintenance, quality assurance and administrative costs has to be paid for through revenue generated and therefore has to be reflected in prices. Often the rules for allocating these costs across product lines are arbitrary, and not necessarily closely linked with predicted sales and the market's price sensitivity.

It is therefore clear that costs do play an important role in price setting. They will be further discussed in Chapter 11.

Pricing a pinta

Most consumers in the UK have two main choices when it comes to buying milk. Either they can have it delivered daily to their doorsteps, in traditional one pint bottles, priced at about 41p per pint, or they can buy in cartons or plastic bottles from the supermarket, priced between 24p and 31p per pint, depending on the size of the container. The price of the doorstep pint partly reflects the cost and value of the service provided, and partly reflects the higher operating costs of a relatively inefficient distribution system. Doorstep delivery companies, such as Unigate and Northern Foods, have to run and maintain fleets of milk floats and employ people to make the deliveries, pick up the empty bottles and collect the money from individual households. In contrast, supermarkets are buying in bulk and having deliveries made in bulk to regional depots, which is much more cost effective.

The basic price of milk used to be controlled by the Milk Marketing Board, which had a monopoly over supply. In 1994, however, the milk market was deregulated, opening the market up to free competition. The immediate effect was an increase of between 8 per cent and 11 per cent in milk prices. Most dairy farmers in England and Wales joined a co-operative called Milk Marque which, with control over 65 per cent of supplies, could easily push for higher prices in the interests of its members. Upward pressure on prices has also arisen from EU agricultural policy, with the introduction of milk quotas. Because of this, it is estimated that supply in the UK only meets 85 per cent of demand.

Against this general background, supermarkets have also faced increased prices from their suppliers, because, in 1995, packaging prices increased by about 10 per cent. Although this led to an increase in the price of a four pint bottle of milk to around 99p in early 1996, the supermarket prices were still lower than they had been in the early 1990s. In the early 1990s, a four pint bottle cost about £1.10. This fell to less than 80p in 1993/94 when the discount chains, such as Aldi and Netto, used milk in a price war. The supermarkets watch each others' milk prices carefully, and try to match them. If one breaks ranks, the others soon follow. A result of this is that the supermarkets are barely breaking even on milk. They are buying it in

at around 22p per pint, and selling much of it for as little as 24p per pint, which is not sufficient even to cover the cost of the chilled storage. The supermarkets, however, clearly see milk as a valuable loss leader, bringing customers into the store and reinforcing 'value for money' images.

One other major reason why supermarket milk is still cheaper than in the early 1990s, despite the best efforts of Milk Marque and rising raw material costs, is to do with changing consumer habits and lifestyles. The more milk consumers buy from supermarkets, the greater the supermarkets' economies of scale and price negotiation power. The supermarkets' share of the milk market has risen rapidly:

	Supermarket (% market share)	Doorstep delivery (% market share)
1980	10%	90%
1990	38%	62%
1995	55%	45%
1996	>60%	<40%

Some industry pessimists estimate that eventually the supermarkets will capture 85 per cent of the market. Many consumers find that purchasing milk from the supermarket is actually more convenient than a doorstep delivery. Improvements in milk quality and its processing means that its shelf life has increased, so that consumers can buy enough milk in bulk to last up to ten days. The four and six plastic pint bottles take up less room in the fridge than the equivalent number of glass bottles would, and consumers can buy as much as they want whenever they want rather than being tied to a certain number of pints per day. The customer does not have to worry about being at home either to take the milk in every day, or to pay the delivery person weekly (and check the bill, of course).

If consumers do not want or appreciate the service offered by the doorstep delivery, they will not be prepared to pay a premium for it. Also, as the gap between doorstep and supermarket prices widens, the bigger that premium becomes, and the smaller the number of consumers becomes who will pay it.

Sources: Cowe (1995); Gilchrist and Hornsby (1995); Harding and Oram (1995); Maitland (1996a; 1996b).

THE EUROPEAN INFLUENCE ON PRICING

Much of the general discussion on pricing in this chapter and the next is applicable to any organisation, whether it is trading solely within its own national boundary or on a Europe-wide basis. Nevertheless, it is still interesting to look specifically at the impact of the single European market (SEM), and at how it might influence organisations' attitudes and approaches to pricing decisions.

The impact of the SEM

The creation of the SEM meant the removal of fiscal, physical and technical barriers to trade, and an increase in the number of organisations operating in more than one country. In marketing terms, as discussed in earlier chapters, the SEM has opened up the possibility of pan-European products, or at least of products that are largely standardised across Europe but with adaptations to suit local tastes, preferences or marketing environments. Price may be one element of the marketing mix that is most likely to be adapted for local conditions, as incomes, spending patterns and price sensitivities vary widely across the EU. Price is also a very flexible tool, far easier to adapt than a product!

Quelch and Buzzell (1989) predicted that after the SEM came into being prices would be forced down because of:

1 *decreased costs* through higher-volume sales with more common packaging (and other marketing elements) across the EU and cheaper logistics (since technically there are no import/export regulations and paperwork to fulfil) that also tend towards uniformity;
2 *the opening up of public procurement contracts* to broader competition from across the EU, hence leading to keener prices;
3 *foreign investment,* raising production capacity;
4 *the rigorous enforcement of competition policy*, fewer trade restrictions, less opportunity for building monopolies;
5 *a general increase in competitive activity*, forcing prices down.

The EU itself estimated that prices would fall by around 8 per cent because of the SEM in some sectors such as consumer goods, chemicals and financial services.

Price differentials

Organisations might charge different prices for more or less the same product in different regions of Europe for a number of reasons. Such **price differentials** might, for instance, reflect subtle differences in product positioning; different stages of market development in different countries; fluctuating exchange rates; differing distribution channel structures and trade margins; and local operating costs.

Prices might also be affected by differing tax rates. As mentioned in Chapter 2, VAT and excise rates do vary considerably across the EU, and moves towards harmonisation still have some way to go, with the result that countries such as Denmark and Ireland still implement a VAT rate well above the average of around 15 per cent. Even within a particular country, different rates of VAT might apply to different products. Most higher VAT rates on luxury products, such as France's 22 per cent VAT on cars and electronics, have been abolished, but reduced rates of around 5 per cent or even 0 per cent can still be found within the VAT structures of various nations.

Excise duties, especially on alcohol and tobacco products, are subject to bigger differences, particularly between nothern and southern European countries. The EU members have, however, agreed to abolish duty in all areas except tobacco, alcoholic drink and petrol/oil. Minimum percentage rates of duty have also been agreed for these products, but on beer, for example, the minimum rate is much lower than the EU originally wanted and certainly much lower than the rates actually charged in the UK, Denmark, Ireland and Italy. This means that it is financially worth while for the British, for example, to go on 'booze cruises' to France and load the car up with beers and wines which in France attract minimal or zero excise duty, as long as exchange-rate fluctuations do not wipe out the advantage. The French beer St. Omer, for example, with a minimal amount of duty added to its price, proved very popular in the south-east of England from where shopping trips across the channel are fairly easy to make. Provided that the goods are not resold, i.e., that they are for personal consumption, this is perfectly legal.

Price differentials might also arise according to consumers' willingness and ability to pay. The price of tea and coffee in Swiss cafés is something of a shock to the foreign traveller, but is widely accepted by the Swiss themselves who are willing and able to pay such prices. Implicit in all this is the necessity for the marketer to understand the pricing context of the local market, and to see it through the consumer's eyes. This means understanding the consumer's living standards, life-style, aspirations and purchasing patterns, as well as the alternatives open to that consumer in terms of competitors and substitutes. The organisation might also have a brand-building job to do to establish credibility in the European consumer's eyes. The brand that has been carefully nurtured over the years in its home market to achieve a position where it can command a handsome price premium may mean nothing to the consumer in another European country. The organisation might even have to price low to get into that market against strong local competition, and then begin to build reputation.

Simon and Kucher (1992) argue that it will become increasingly difficult to retain wide price differentials. They predict that over time European differentials will erode, stabilising to a fairly narrow 'price corridor'.

There are still, however, wide differentials between car prices in different parts of Europe. A 1994 EU report found that the number of models where price differentials are higher than 20 per cent amounted to more than half (Eurobusiness, 1995). Italy had the lowest prices, with 51 out of 75 models priced lowest. While prices were increasing in markets such as France and Germany, Austria had the distinction of being the highest priced member state on 33 out of 75 models. The findings included, for example:

(a) *Ford Fiesta*: 47.9 per cent differential between Italy and the Netherlands;
(b) *Rover 214*: around 50 per cent differential between Italy and Sweden, and between Germany and Austria;
(c) *Subaru Legacy Sedan 2 litre*: 53.6 per cent differential between the Netherlands and Austria.

Reducing car price differentials is clearly still a major challenge in Europe, but does not appear to have the manufacturers' support.

Price management

As trade barriers decrease and Eurosegments open up, pricing will become more centralised. An organisation cannot have local management destroying European price levels. Quelch and Buzzell (1989) suggest that there is a need for the marketing manager to understand the price elasticity of different markets and the best price positions. Then, the manager should assess the degree of product movement across borders and relate that to the cost to the customer of crossing a border in order to purchase. In some cases, such as in the border zones between France and Germany, locals develop detailed knowledge of what to buy and in which country, depending on minor currency movements and other price-influencing factors. Such purchasing is now increasingly happening between the UK and France, although the cost of cross channel transport needs to be carefully assessed as part of the price.

In reality, the risks of products 'leaking' from lower-priced countries into higher-priced ones make European pricing a carefully balanced decision. Leakage from Portugal may not be a major problem, but leakage from the Benelux countries into France and Germany may be more of a problem. Simon and Kucher (1992) consider it better not to enter or develop a low-priced country if it undermines prices in a more valuable market. Thus they consider that the larger, higher-priced market should determine price levels. An organisation's European price range will therefore develop, with differences reflecting transport, distribution and other country-specific factors.

Quelch and Buzzell (1992) also propose that as part of building a strong European pricing strategy, marketing managers should undertake product development and branding in European markets. This would help to develop premium-priced segments alongside the lower-priced brands that can protect to some extent against the effects of parallel importing, as discussed below.

Parallel trading

Parallel trading takes place when products sold in one country find their way into another country where they are resold at higher prices. Such trading can even apply to services. In autumn 1995, it was much cheaper for a UK traveller to buy a UK–France Euroshuttle excursion ticket by phone from Calais than in person at Dover.

Parallel trading is increasingly difficult to avoid, especially as retailers source more widely, looking for price bargains across Europe and beyond. Consumers too may be tempted by parallel trading, for example, as they notice the car price differentials already outlined, or if they value the differences in alcohol and tobacco prices. Pressure is building for some national governments to set up legislative barriers to make parallel trading less attractive, despite the fact that this might go against the spirit of the SEM. Such barriers might include the payment of local VAT rates when bringing back into the country, goods that command high prices at home but which are available more cheaply in neighbouring countries. Denmark, for instance, is concerned about cross-border parallel imports from Germany.

Example

There can be a fine line between parallel trading and illegal trade. The brewery group Scottish & Newcastle, for example, hold the UK licence for Beck's beer. They found out, however, that large quantities of German Beck's, originally destined for eastern Europe, were coming on to the UK market. Opportunists were buying beer on the Continent and then selling it to the UK trade at a discount. This is not necessarily illegal, but it does undermine the UK licensee's ability to support the brand, effectively cannibalising it. In this particular case, there was an illegality, not because of the parallel trade, but because of a breach in the labelling requirements. The imports did not state the alcohol content, as required by law (*The Grocer*, 1995).

CHAPTER SUMMARY

This chapter has discussed the basic principles behind an element of the marketing mix that is often neglected or given insufficient strategic consideration. Pricing is a broad area, defined as covering anything of value that is given in exchange for something else. 'Price' is a blanket term to cover a variety of labels and is a key element in the marketing exchange. Price is usually measured in money, but can also involve the bartering of goods and services.

Price serves a number of purposes. It is a measure against which buyers can assess the product's promised features and benefits and then decide whether the functional, operational, financial or personal advantages of purchase are worth while or not. This assessment opens up the difficult area of price perception. Price may well be communicated as a fixed amount of money, but what that sum really represents is a very individual thing which can change as the buyer's needs and circumstances change.

The seller faces the difficult job of setting the price in the context of the buyers' price perceptions and sensitivities. In a price-sensitive market, finding exactly the right price is essential if customers are to be attracted and retained. The seller also needs to remember that price may involve the buyer in more than the handing over of a sum of money. Associated costs of installation, training and disposal of old equipment, for example, are taken into account in assessing the price of an organisational purchase.

The relationship between buyer and price differs according to the type of customer and the type of market. Consumers are likely to be more influenced by non-price factors in making their personal purchasing decisions within preconceived price bands. Nevertheless, there are some price-sensitive segments who will use price as a primary purchasing criterion. Wholesalers and retailers are more pragmatic about price. They know what the consumer is willing to pay and thus seek prices from manufacturers that allow them to sell competitively to the public, yet still cover their costs and an acceptable profit margin. In service markets, price may be used as a means of regulating the demand pattern, either dropping the price to ensure the fullest take-up of the service, or increasing the price to limit the number of customers to a level that the service provider can cope with. Non-profit organisations may also use this latter strategy, for example to protect conservation areas from 'human pollution'. Organisational markets represent the situation where both buyer and seller are likely to take as rational a view of price as possible.

The pricing decision is influenced by a number of factors, some of which are external to the organisation, and some of which are internal. The external influences include customers, channels of distribution, competition and legal and regulatory constraints. Corporate and marketing objectives set the internal agenda in terms of what pricing is expected to achieve, both for the organisation as a whole and for the specific product. The organisation's costs relating to the development, manufacture and marketing of the product will also affect price.

The creation of the SEM opened up new opportunities for pan-European marketing, with lower costs, but also with more price competition. Currently, price differentials can be quite wide in some product sectors across Europe. This might be because of differing local market conditions or because of differing tax rates. Tax harmonisation has not yet been achieved in the EU. Price differentials might also arise from different consumer profiles, knowledge and attitudes to brands and products. Wide differentials in prices across Europe might create a discerning shopper who crosses borders in search of bargains, particularly for high-priced infrequent purchases such as cars. In developing local pricing strategies, therefore, marketing managers should take into account the effects of possible 'leakage' of goods from lower-priced neighbouring countries.

QUESTIONS FOR REVIEW

10.1 What factors affect the customer's interpretation of price?

10.2 In what kind of circumstances might a high price actually be better for a seller than a low one?

10.3 How can a seller distract the customer's attention from a high price?

10.4 Define price discipline and explain what it means to both manufacturers and retailers.

10.5 What are the particular problems of pricing service products?

10.6 List the internal and external influences on pricing decisions.

10.7 Define price elasticity. Why is this an important concept for the marketer?

10.8 In what ways can competition influence pricing decisions?

10.9 To what extent and why do you think that costs should influence pricing?

10.10 What factors influencing European prices are likely to increase or reduce price differentials over the next five years?

QUESTIONS FOR DISCUSSION

10.1 Choose a manufacturer that produces a range of products serving different price segments in a consumer market. How does the manufacturer 'justify' the different prices?

10.2 Find an example of a price sensitive consumer market. Why do you think this market is price sensitive and is there anything that the manufacturers or retailers could do to make it less so?

10.3 Compare consumer and organisational attitudes to price, explaining how and why they differ.

10.4 To what extent do you think the classic demand curve as shown in Fig 10.3 is a useful guide for the marketing manager in practice?

10.5 Choose a consumer product and explain the role that pricing plays in its marketing mix and market positioning.

The net book agreement

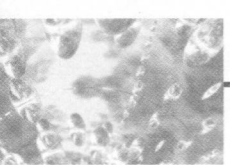

The net book agreement (NBA) came into being in the early twentieth century in the UK to fix the price of books, thus preventing price competition between booksellers and allowing publishers to offer a very wide range of titles. In early 1995, however, it was under pressure. Some major publishers no longer felt that the NBA benefited the industry and had decided to pull out of it. One of the first to go was Hodder Headline. Its chief executive said that the NBA had the effect of keeping hardback prices high and volume low because readers preferred to wait for the cheaper paperback to come out. He estimated that because of the NBA, UK book buyers were paying 70 per cent more for hardback bestsellers than the US customer and 40 per cent more for paperbacks. As a result of this, Hodder had decided to leave the NBA and allow discounting on its titles.

In May 1995, therefore, the supermarket chain ASDA was selling John le Carré's latest novel, published by Hodder Headline, at 50 per cent of the cover price. ASDA was selling the book at £8.49 compared with a cover price of £16.99. Some other retailers followed suit. Dillons, a large chain of booksellers, for example, was selling it for £12.99 and had increased its order for the book to 10 000 copies. Other retailers held back. W. H. Smith, for example, with a market share of 25 per cent, did not wish to enter a price war and actually reduced its order for the book. Overall, however, Hodder increased the print run to 185 000 (from around 100 000). That print run sold out within months, and ASDA, after selling 5000 copies of that novel, broke the NBA on 10 other titles as other publishers took out injunctions to try to stop them.

By the autumn of 1995, things had changed, and the NBA had virtually collapsed, as other large publishers and retailers started to discount. Some bookshops, including W. H. Smith, were discounting by 50 per cent on some titles. Opinions varied as to whether the death of the NBA was 'a good thing' or not. The managing director of W. H. Smith Retail said that there had never been a better time to buy books. W. H. Smith was hoping for a 5 per cent increase in sales and was looking forward to using books flexibly as a means of encouraging sales of other products. Dillons cut prices on 200 titles (but not academic titles) and estimated that a 33 per cent cut in the price of a bestseller could increase its sales fourfold. The marketing director of Dillons said,

'The new trading conditions are good news for book lovers, good news for authors and good news for the industry' (Caine, 1995).

Generally, authors were not going to suffer, because they receive a percentage of the cover price (not the discount price), and the industry was forecasting a big sales rise for bestsellers. Jeffrey Archer, with sales running into millions world-wide, felt that there were 'too many publishers publishing books that no one buys' (Alberge, 1995), and that the end of the NBA would thus make publishers rationalise their lists. He further thought that if publishers made more profit from selling larger volumes of cheaper books, they would plough more back into developing new writing talent.

Although retailer profit margins were under pressure from discounting, they hoped that higher volume sales would compensate. And as volume sales rose, publisher margins would come under pressure too as big retailers, like W. H. Smith and the supermarket chains, used bulk buying power to negotiate better prices. Some larger retailers were demanding up to 70 per cent discount from the publishers. The publishers, however, do not seem to have too much leeway. According to Fairbairn (1995), the price of a book can be broken down as follows:

50%	to the retailer
20%	manufacturing cost
10%	to the author
20%	to the publisher to cover marketing, distribution and profit.

The publishers not only faced downward price pressure from the retail trade, they also faced upward pressure on costs because of a 60 per cent rise in the price of paper between 1993 and 1995. This means that they have had to become more selective in what they publish, with some publishers halving the number of titles offered as they look for larger, more economic print runs. The publishers have gained in one respect, however. Previously, books were sold to retailers on a 'sale or return' basis, reducing the risk to the retailer of being left with unsold stock. Now, where publishers have given discounts, they will only accept returns after a minimum level of sales has been achieved. In extreme cases, such as the supermarkets, where the discounts are much bigger, no returns are accepted at all.

Waterstones, a chain of booksellers, believed that the end of the NBA would generally benefit the bookseller, since 50 per cent of books are bought on impulse, and discounts would encourage that process. Waterstones also felt not only that discounts would be available on bestsellers but that bookshops and publishers would also use them to boost new writers. Nevertheless, Waterstones estimated that only 10 per cent of all books sold would be discounted, and that small bookshops would not be particularly threatened as long as they continued to differentiate on service. They could be right: 10 per cent of people account for 40 per cent of books sales, and they are not necessarily driven by price. The Booksellers' Association was less sure, however, feeling that although the price of bestsellers would inevitably fall, prices of other books would actually rise in compensation. A rise of 20 per cent in the price of paperbacks was expected for 1996.

By early November 1995, about four weeks after the total collapse of the NBA, book sales had risen by nearly 50 per cent, but there were some warning signs. Industry experts felt that the increase in volume sales would not be enough to compensate for lost margins. To maintain profit levels, retailers would have had to sell three or four discounted copies for every full price copy they would otherwise have sold. Few were actually achieving this. By January 1996, it was clear that the discounting was restricted to a few very large multiple retailers. As far as small independent booksellers were concerned, it appeared that there was little change in the number of books they were selling, despite the fact that they could not match the bigger retailers' discounted prices. Some books were on sale in the supermarkets at prices lower than the wholesale price that an independent bookshop would have to pay!

The managing director of Waterstones, interviewed by May (1995), summarised the situation neatly. He said that historically, the NBA was maintained because publishers wanted stability and did not want the smaller bookshop to be put out of business by price cutting by the big multiple stores. In his view, however, there were overwhelming reasons why the NBA had to go. Channels of distribution were changing. Publishers could no longer ignore the mass market appeal of the supermarkets and the opportunity they provided for the impulse buying of books along with the weekly shopping. Furthermore, consumers were looking increasingly for value for money and the book market was suffering from not being able to use price promotion as a marketing tool to give customers what they wanted. Against a background of falling book sales, and media pressure whipping up anti-NBA feeling amongst the book-buying public, Hodder's decision to leave the NBA and ASDA's moves were bound to cause fatal cracks in the fabric of the NBA.

As a final thought on the NBA, Wheatcroft (1995) draws an interesting parallel with the wine market. He points out that since the abolition of price maintenance on a wide range of goods in the 1960s, sales of wines have risen dramatically in the UK, at all price points in the market. Much of the wine bought is cheap and cheerful plonk, but there is still a significant amount of fine wine purchased, and there are many good, specialist, independent wine retailers to be found.

Sources: Alberge (1995); Bennett (1995); Buckingham (1995); Caine (1995); Fairbairn (1995); Hewitt (1996); *Marketing* (1995a; 1995b); May (1995); Narbrough (1995); Rawsthorn (1996); Wainwright (1995); Wheatcroft (1995).

Questions

1 Summarise the reasons for the NBA's collapse.

2 What are the internal and external influences on a book's price from a publisher's perspective?

3 Summarise the advantages and disadvantages to:
   (a) the book-buying public; and
   (b) the booksellers;
   arising from the ending of the NBA.

4 Is the wine analogy appropriate? How do you see the book market in the UK developing over the next few years?

5 Can there be any justification for the artificial maintenance of price levels, such as those represented by the NBA, or should all prices be driven by market forces?

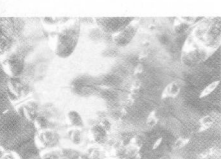

Eurostar

Eurostar is the cross-channel passenger rail service run jointly by French, Belgian and British rail companies. It runs between London and Paris, and between London and Brussels. Eurostar pays Eurotunnel a fee every time one of its trains uses the tunnel. The original estimate for cross-channel rail passenger traffic was 16.5 mn passengers in the first year of operation in 1993, although the delayed opening of the tunnel itself meant that Eurostar did not actually begin operation until November 1994. Eurostar intended to take its customers from the highly profitable business traveller segment as well as from the leisure travel sector. Both involved attracting new business and drawing traffic from the airlines and the ferries. Its longer-term objective was a half-hourly service to Paris and Brussels, with a journey time of less than three hours. Initially, however, Eurostar only ran two trains to each city per day. By 1996, the service had expanded to become virtually an hourly service to Paris during the daytime period. Eurostar was not afraid of emphasizing its unique appeal in its promotional material:

> 'A journey on Eurostar transports you into the 21st century – speeding you through the Channel Tunnel which has been the dream over the centuries and is at last a reality. 1995 is the year to experience the historic link and see for yourself the impact Eurostar and the Tunnel will have on the future of European transport'. (Eurostar, 1995/96)

But in 1995, the first full year of operation, only three million customers were carried. The number of passengers using the service passed the 1 million mark in May 1995. The forecast for 1996 was just five million. Despite a carrying capacity of 200 000 per week, actual passenger numbers often fell well short of expectations. Operating losses to the year ending March 1995 were £102 mn.

At the launch of Eurostar in November 1994, first-class return tickets were priced at around £195 (including meals) and standard-class return fares began at £95 for those able to book 14 days in advance. The last-minute standard-class traveller, however, would have to find £155. Eurostar's expectation was that the extra convenience and preference for rail travel for relatively short distances would soon fill the available seats, so that more services could be added. There was also an assumption that a small premium could be charged for the extra convenience.

By early 1995, it was clear that all was not well. Both the airlines and the ferry companies claimed to have been hardly affected by Eurostar's launch. British Airways in February 1995 claimed a minimal impact, despite offering 13 flights a day to Paris, but Air France had experienced a 7 per cent decline on the London – Paris route. On the Brussels rail route, where Eurostar's capacity at that time was 2400 seats per day, at times the trains were operating almost empty! Given the low level of use, price changes were introduced in February 1995 in an effort to attract tourists from the airlines. Revised prices of £79 return to Paris and £84 to Brussels (both apex – advance purchase – fares), along with big reductions for those aged over 60 and those aged under 25 were introduced. Standard fares remained at £155 and first class at £195, with reductions for booking 14 days in advance. These fares compared with the normal airline fares of £91 (apex) to Paris with advance booking, and a standard fare of around £130. Cheaper airlines offering less service sometimes offered prices as low as £65.

Eurostar's view of its progress at that time was more upbeat than that of the pundits. Although the company recognised that the number of passengers on the Brussels route was disappointing, it claimed that the Paris service was generating 6000 passengers per day, equivalent to around 20 aircraft journeys. The growth in passenger traffic was further thought to have been hindered by some high-profile media coverage of technical problems and delays. Customers cared little that the trains were the most technically sophisticated ever, being able to deal with the requirements of three countries as well as the tunnel. Customers did, however, remember the pre-opening press trip when the train never left Waterloo station in London! In reality, Eurostar's punctuality actually compared well with that of the airlines, even though it was in the first year of its operation.

After a difficult start, by the autumn of 1995 Eurostar had begun to make a greater impact on passenger traffic between London and Paris/Brussels. EPS (European Passenger Services – the British partner) estimated that Eurostar was now carrying around 40 per cent of travellers (air plus rail) between the three cities. Some airlines had reduced the frequency of services on the route, although overall the impact on the airlines was claimed not to be very significant. British Airways (BA), for example, scrapped its Luton to Paris flight and British Midland (BM) also reduced services. BM estimated that airline traffic to the two destinations had fallen by 13 per cent and revenue by

16 per cent because of Eurostar. The real impact might, however, have been hidden by the airlines' traditional non-price response to competition. They tend to reduce flight frequency and/or the size of aircraft rather than reduce price in order to protect margins. Air France, for example, reduced capacity by 38 per cent on the London – Paris route and switched from Airbuses to 737-300s. Meanwhile, Eurostar had by now increased its services to six weekday departures to Brussels and 11 to Paris. Demand for the Paris service still outstripped that for the Brussels service by two to one. At the leisure and off-peak end of the market, prices had fallen further to £69 to Brussels, compared with £76 to Paris.

Still further price cuts were introduced early in 1996 at the lower price end of the market. The 'Getaway Return' was introduced for travel between Monday and Thursday, with at least three nights to be spent away. Day return tickets for a Saturday were introduced at £69 (or £129 for first class). The business traveller market was still a hard one to capture, however. Eurostar's market share of that segment was estimated to be just 20 per cent, well below the original expectation.

With a continued lowering of prices in some segments, by May 1996 travelling by train had become significantly cheaper than travelling by plane. The standard fare could be as low as £65 as long as the booking was made well in advance of travel, and it had the added advantage that the traveller was not obliged to stay away over a Saturday night, as would be required by an airline's cheaper apex fare. The comparable BA fare, 'Eurobudget,' would be over £200. Furthermore, train travellers had no airport departure tax, no long journeys from the city centre, and often less hassle when checking in or collecting baggage than they would have had at an airport.

Nevertheless, the impact on business travellers was still disappointing, and Williams (1996) suggested a number of reasons why. First, flights arrive earlier and depart later than the train, an important consideration for the business executive. The airlines are also renowned for providing additional services to higher-paying customers. Through VIP lounges, telephones, newspapers, refreshments or whatever, the airlines appeared to have the edge. Ticketing systems were also a problem. Whereas airlines could handle open-ended business tickets, Eurostar had to have the outward and return times specified on the ticket. Through-ticketing to other destinations after the Eurostar journey is also a problem, meaning that a separate ticket to the onward destination has to be purchased. Finally, with three rail companies involved in Eurostar, even agreeing a common strategy is never easy, and Eurostar faces the additional problem that all its fares, other than short-term promotional offers, need EU approval as part of EU competition policy.

Further expansion in services during 1996 meant that the battle between the airlines and Eurostar was set to continue. The campaign was to include improving reliability, improved ticketing systems, raised advertising spend and the continued use of a flexible pricing approach.

Sources: Abbott (1995); Batchelor (1996); Elliott (1995); Eurostar (1995/96); Keenan (1995); Prynn and Tieman (1995); Williams (1996).

Questions

1 How might the business traveller's attitude and reaction to price differ from those of the leisure traveller?

2 Why did Eurostar begin its services in 1994 with a premium price? Do you think that this was the right strategy?

3 What are the internal and external influences on Eurostar's ticket pricing?

4 Should Eurostar continue to use price as a major weapon in competition with the airlines?

REFERENCES TO CHAPTER 10

Abbott, J. (1995), 'Eurostar One Year On', *Modern Railways*, November, pp. 687–9.

Alberge, D. (1995), 'Book Trade Turns Over a New Leaf at Last', *The Times*, 27 September, p. 3.

Batchelor, C. (1996), 'Eurostar Fails to Meet Passenger Target', *Financial Times*, 11 January, p. 5.

Bennett, N. (1995), 'Cliffhanger as le Carré Price War is Declared', *The Times*, 1 May, p. 1.

Bolton, R. N. (1989), 'The Robustness of Retail Level Price Elasticity Estimates', *Journal of Retailing*, Summer, pp. 193–219.

Buckingham, L. (1995), 'Book Sales Soar But Profits Fall', *Guardian*, 2 November, p. 1.

Buckley, N. and Baxter, A. (1995a), 'Electrical Goods Groups Face Probe Over Prices', *Financial Times*, 28 April, p. 1

Buckley, N. and Baxter, A. (1995b), 'Electrical Sector Indignant at Pricing Enquiry', *Financial Times*, 28 April, p. 8.

Caine, N. (1995a), 'Exciting New Chapter Opens for Book Buyers', *Sunday Times*, 8 October, p. 5.

Cane, A. (1995a), 'Nintendo and Sega Attacked by MMC for "Inflated Prices"', *Financial Times*, 10 March, p. 22.

Cane, A. (1995b), 'Parent Power Prompts Video Games Probe', *Financial Times*, 10 March, p. 10.

Cower, R. (1995), 'Milk Giant Axes 2,200 Jobs as Stores Price War Bites', *Guardian*, 24 March, p. 28.

Davis, B. (1995), 'An Upheaval in the Retail Market', *Financial Times*, 6 March, p. II.

Diamantopoulos, A. and Mathews, B. (1995), *Making Pricing Decisions: A Study of Managerial Practice*, Chapman & Hall.

Elliott, H. (1995), 'Eurostar Cuts Fares to Fill Weekend Trains', *The Times*, 25 February, p. 10.

Erickson, G. M. and Johansson, J. K. (1985), 'The Role of Price in Multi-attribute Product Evaluations', *Journal of Consumer Research*, 12, pp. 195–9.

Eurobusiness (1995), 'Euro Round Up', *Eurobusiness*, 3(5), p. 15.

Eurostar (1995/96), 'Holidays By Eurostar, 28th May 1995–31st March 1996', travel brochure.

Fairbairn, S. (1995), 'Final Chapter for Book Price Fixing', *Sunday Times*, 1 October, p. 4.

Gilbert, A. (1995), 'Will Potatoes Be Replaced By Pasta on the Dinner Table?', *The Grocer*, 10 June, p. 18.

Gilchrist, S. and Hornsby, M. (1995), 'The Vanishing Milkman Means Loss of 2200 Jobs', *The Times*, 24 March, p. 1.

The Grocer (1995), 'S&N Puts Spotlight on Illegal Parallel Trading', *The Grocer*, 23 September, p. 29.

Guild, A. (1996), 'Honey Market Hits A Sticky Patch', *Financial Times*, 19 March, p. 29.

Harding, J. and Oram, R. (1995), 'Churning of Dairy Sales Sours', *Financial Times*, 15 June, p. 11.

Hewitt, M. (1996), 'Searching For Volume Sales', *Marketing*, 25 January, p. 12.

HiFi Choice (1993), 'The Directory: Loudspeakers', *HiFi Choice*, December, p. 153.

Keenan, S. (1995), 'On the Right Railway Track', *The Times*, 3 November, p. 8.

Kortge, G. D. and Okonkwo, P. A. (1993), 'Perceived Value Approach to Pricing', *Industrial Marketing Management*, 22, pp. 133–40.

Maitland, A. (1996a), 'Price Rise Prompts Fresh Outcry Over Milk Marque', *Financial Times*, 16 January, p. 7.

Maitland, A. (1996b), 'Surge in Supermarket Milk Price Eases Squeeze on Processors', *Financial Times*, 28 February, p. 9.

Marketing (1993), 'Sainsbury Hits Back at Shell Ad', *Marketing*, 18 November, p. 6.

Marketing (1995a), 'A New Chapter in Discounting?', *Marketing*, 15 June, p. 12.

Marketing (1995b), 'Let's Bury, Not Praise, the NBA', *Marketing*, 28 September, p. 5.

May, D. (1995), 'There are Major New Outlets that Publishers Couldn't Ignore', *The Times*, 5 October, p .3.

Mehta, S. (1995), 'Investing in Capital Assets', *Purchasing and Supply Management*, March, pp. 16–19.

Montgomery, S. L. (1988), *Profitable Pricing Strategies*, McGraw-Hill.

Mullineux, N. (1995), *Car Retailing in Europe: Opportunities for the Next Decade, A Financial Times Management Report*, Pearson Professional Ltd.

Nagle, T. T. (1987), *The Strategy and Tactics of Pricing*, Prentice–Hall.

Narbrough, C. (1995), 'Book Rules "Raising Prices" ', *The Times*, 20 March, p. 37.

Porter, M. E. (1980), *Competitive Strategy*, Free Press.

Prynn, J. and Tieman, R. (1995), 'Tunnel Trains Having Little Effect, Say Rivals', *The Times*, 20 February, p. 41.

Purchasing and supply management (1995), 'Value In, Cost Out', *Purchasing and Supply Management*, June, p. 29.

Quelch, J. A. and Buzzell, R. D. (1989), 'Marketing Moves Through EC Crossroads', *Sloan Management Review*, 31(1), pp. 63–74.

Rawsthorn, A. (1996), 'New Leaf Turned Over', *Financial Times*, 13 January, p. 7.

Simon, H. and Kucher, E. (1992), 'The European Pricing Time Bomb and How to Cope With It', *European Management Journal*, 10(2), pp. 136–45.

Smith, R. (1994), 'Hand Drying for the Future', *European Purchasing and Materials Management*, No. 3, pp. 119–25.

The Times (1993), 'Ticket Touts in Sunset Rip-Off', *The Times*, 8 April.

Wainwright, M. (1995), 'Warning on the Dangers of Supping with Supermarkets', *Guardian*, 27 September, p. 3.

Wheatcroft, G. (1995), 'A Cosy Book Cartel is Remaindered', *The Times*, 27 September , p. 16.

Williams, A. (1996), 'Eurostar Fails to Keep Pace with Streamlined Competition', *European*, 2–8 May, p. 25.

Zeithaml, V. A. (1988), 'Consumer Perceptions of Price, Quality and Value', *Journal of Marketing*, 52 (July), pp. 2–22.

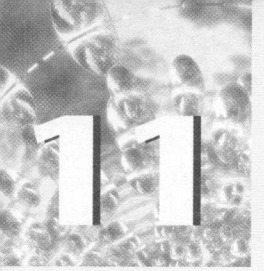

11 Pricing Strategies

LEARNING OBJECTIVES

This chapter will help you to:

1 understand the managerial process that leads to price setting and the influences that affect its outcomes;

2 appreciate the multiple and sometimes conflicting objectives impacting on pricing decisions;

3 define a range of available pricing strategies and their application in different market and competitive situations;

4 understand the available pricing methods and tactics, and their most appropriate use; and

5 appreciate some of the special issues affecting pricing in organisational markets.

INTRODUCTION

Economists' models of pricing tend to be based on costs and simplified models of demand structures without taking into account the reality of the marketing situation. It is rare to find that pricing can be achieved through the simple application of a formula, since the actions of marketers and competitors, as well as the perceptions and behaviour of consumers all have an influence on the pricing decision. Chapter 10 outlined many of these internal and external influences. The reality of pricing is that organisations do not have perfect information, as the economists assume, nor are consumers and competitors passive players in the process. Thus a certain amount of skill is required to assess how both consumers and competitors will respond to a particular pricing decision in the context of a particular marketing mix. The pricing decision is only simple for an organisation that consciously follows the rest of the market rather than tries to lead it.

Many organisations are realising the benefits of giving price proper consideration early on in the product development process. Daimler-Benz, for example, used to think about price almost as an afterthought, basing price on what the engineers decided ought to be included in each new model developed. This situation is now reversed and price is the starting point. The organisation calculates what the market can bear for the kind of product that is to be developed, what the competition are doing in the same area and what kind of profit margin the organisation is seeking from the product. The engineers and the rest of the project team then have to deliver a new vehicle that meets those pricing targets (Parkes, 1993).

Building on the foundations of price influences laid down in Chapter 10, this chapter examines the stages which organisations go through to establish the price range and to set the final prices for their products. Figure 11.1 gives an overview of the process. Setting price objectives, stage 1, ensures that the corporate and marketing objectives of the organisation are taken into consideration in the pricing decision. Stage 2, estimating demand, assesses likely market potential and consumer reaction to different price levels, and was covered in at pp. 381 *et seq*. Within this structure, marketing managers can then begin to define pricing policy in stage 3. This is the guiding philosophical framework within which pricing strategies and decisions are determined. Pricing strategies deal with the long-term issues of positioning within the market and the achievement of corporate and marketing objectives. Establishing cost–volume–profit relationships at stage 4 checks that the estimated sales of the product can generate acceptable levels of income at any given price in order to cover costs and make an adequate profit. Implicit in all of this is the fact that pricing has to take place in a competitive environment, and thus the marketing manager must assess how competitors will react to various possible prices, and the extent to which the proposed price reflects the desired competitive positioning of the organisation and its products.

These first four stages culminate in stage 5, pricing tactics and final adjustments which focus on the practical application of pricing in the marketing mix and in the context of the market segments to be served. Pricing procedures set the method by which prices are calculated in the light of strategies to arrive at the final figure. Tactics, however, allow those prices to be varied on a planned, structured basis or in the shorter term on a one-off or irregular basis, perhaps to take advantage of sudden market opportunities or to overcome unforeseen difficulties.

Although Fig 11.1 presents a neat, logical flow, in reality, the pricing decision is likely to involve many reiterations and merging of stages. Some stages may be omitted, others may be extended to take into account special conditions within a market. There may also be conflict, for example between corporate level pressure to maximise profit and competitive assessment that indicates a market that is already well served at the higher-priced end. Such conflicts need to be resolved to avoid the risks of inconsistent pricing within a poorly defined marketing mix. It is also difficult to generalise about the price-setting process, not only because it operates uniquely in every organisation, but also because it will vary greatly between different types of product and market depending on the dynamics and maturity of the specific situation.

Finally, this chapter reviews some of the special considerations connected with price setting in organisational markets, such as negotiation, tendering and the setting of internally derived transfer prices between different departments or divisions of an organisation.

First, however, we discuss the general stages of the pricing process outlined in Fig 11.1, beginning with pricing objectives.

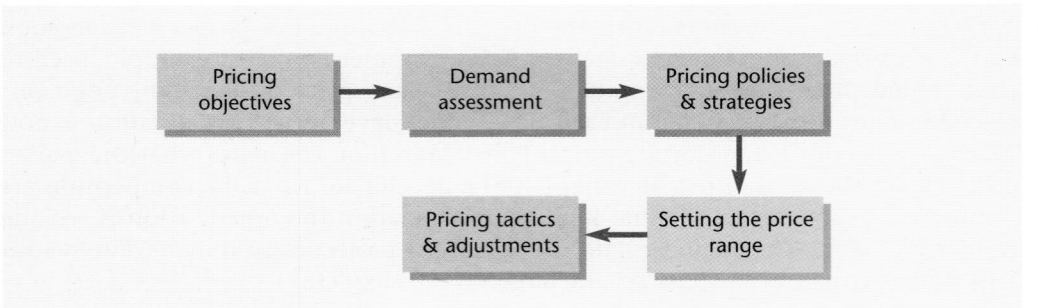

FIGURE 11.1

Determining a price range – overview

PRICING OBJECTIVES

Any planned approach needs to be founded on what has to be achieved, and that applies as much to pricing as to anything else. Its role in the marketing mix as well as its role as the generator of revenue and profit has to be defined. In that sense, price is a delicate balance between serving the customer's needs and wants and serving the need of the organisation to recoup its costs of manufacturing and marketing and to make a profit.

Price objectives, therefore, should be closely linked with organisational and marketing objectives (Baumol, 1965). Some of these may be financially based whereas others may be related to volume of sales. Pricing objectives thus have implications for many functional areas of the business, such as finance, production and distribution, as well as for marketing. Those other functional areas may also influence pricing. If in the short term, for example, finance detects a cash-flow problem, marketers may be pressurised into dropping prices to convert products into cash quickly. In the longer term, the corporate strategists may see the organisation's only means of survival to be the defeat of a major competitor, and price may be a key weapon in that. This also underlines the fact that objectives need not be absolutely fixed; they can vary in the short or long term to meet changing needs and pressures.

Example

The Times, looking to boost its circulation, in 1993 cut its price on weekdays to 20p. Competitors at the quality end of the newspaper market followed suit with their own price cuts, but could not match the 20p offer. In the two years that followed, *The Times* claimed to have increased its daily circulation by 88 per cent as well as having helped to broaden and stimulate the market for all quality newspapers (MacArthur, 1995).

Inevitably, where there are so many objectives relating to so many functional areas, conflicts will arise. In that case, management must work to ensure that compromises and decisions are made, and priorities set in the best interests of the organisation and its customers.

As with objectives in any area of management, pricing objectives must be clearly defined, detailed, time specific and never inconsistent with each other (Diamantopoulos and Mathews, 1995). Clearly, these ideals are easier to achieve in an organisation dealing with a small number of large transactions or a few products. The complexity increases, however, for an organisation dealing in a number of markets, with a large number of customers, or with a number of products.

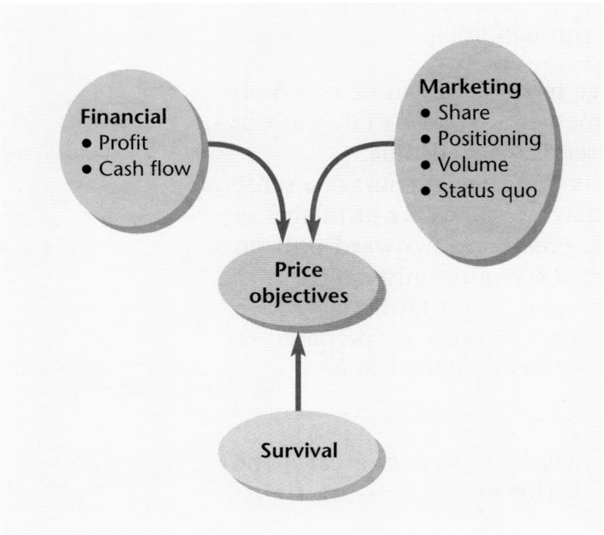

In summary, Fig 11.2 shows the basis of conflicting objectives between different functional areas of the organisation, and each of these will be further discussed below, starting with financial objectives.

FIGURE 11.2

Conflicting price objectives

Financial objectives

Financial objectives can have both short and long-term dimensions. For instance the necessity to generate sufficient cash flow to fund the day-to-day operation of the organisation is a short-term objective whereas the need to generate funds to allow reinvestment in research and development is a longer-term goal. Long-term objectives ultimately provide the means of satisfying shareholder expectations and generating the means of investing in sound foundations for the future.

Most financial objectives centre on either profit or cash flow. We look at profit-based objectives first.

Profit

Return on investment. Pricing is used in the context of return on investment as the means of achieving a specified rate of return on the investment made in the product. One of the interesting questions relating to return on investment (ROI) is the length of time it should take to recoup that investment and begin generating clear profit. If a long-term ROI is acceptable, that gives the marketer the opportunity to build the product strategically, creating and protecting market share through planned market penetration with strong marketing support. It means that the product can be allowed to develop at its own pace with less risk of its existence or position being threatened by management looking for a quick clear profit.

Short-term ROI implies more of a performance orientation. The product is under pressure to generate large amounts of cash to pay for itself and make a clear profit quickly. The danger is that these pressures can lead to inappropriate marketing strategies, for example setting too high a price or attempting to make a niche product into a mass market item to generate volume sales in order to bring in revenue. This lack of patience can, therefore, jeopardise the product's success and thus severely reduce the eventual return on the organisation's investment.

There is a skill involved in setting target ROI, not only because it assumes a degree of knowledge of revenue and cost behaviour that may not be possessed, but also because it has to balance the short-term pressure to bring money in against the possible longer-term strategic desire to build market position slowly but thoroughly. The more volatile and the less predictable the market environment into which the product is being launched, the more problematic becomes the ROI decision.

Profit maximisation. Economics texts often talk of profit maximisation as an organisation's ultimate goal. In reality, an organisation may actually settle for profit satisfaction based on whatever targets have been negotiated through the short- and long-term business plan. Maximisation is an impossible ideal as it implies a perfect knowledge of the cost and demand function beyond the organisation's previous experience. It is particularly impracticable, for example, in a smaller organisation where the owners may not have the time or the inclination, let alone the expertise, to build a maximisation model. Satisfaction based on knowledge of the market and previous experience, however imperfect, may be the main objective to be fulfilled through pricing.

Profit targets can be measured in actual or percentage terms, and can be based on expectations of the way in which the product and its market are likely to develop or expectations of year-on-year growth, namely that past trends will continue.

The problem with profit-based objectives for pricing is that they encourage a sense of control over the environment or predictability that may not be either justifiable or sustainable. Competitive pressures, for instance, may create a downward pull on prices during the course of the accounting period which will compromise target profits. Alternatively, an organisation that sets its profit targets too high may create a pricing structure within the market that attracts new entrants who are prepared to undercut and accept lower profit expectations in order to develop market share.

Cash flow

The pressure to generate cash quickly from a product may be especially great if the product has a short life-cycle, such as goods utilising the merchandising rights associated with a film (e.g., *Jurassic Park*, *The Lion King* or *Pocahontas)*. There may also be pressure if a producer feels that there is only a short lead time available to capitalise on a new product before heavy competition enters the market.

Cash flow considerations are also strong where an organisation has high operating costs and/or fluctuating or seasonal demand. A retailer who stocks lawnmowers, for example, may be prepared to sell the machines at a lower price at the end of the summer in order turn the stock into hard cash, to avoid the costs of keeping the stock over the winter, and to clear the warehouse in preparation for the latest models to be introduced next spring. All of this is worth the reduced margins on the mowers sold cheaply.

This product's heritage helps to justify its premium positioning.

Source: Tate & Lyle plc.

Sales and marketing objectives

Clearly, sales and marketing objectives are important influencers of the pricing decision. Target market share, relative position within the market and target volume sales can all be affected through pricing choices.

Market share and positioning

An organisation's marketing objectives may relate to either maintaining or increasing market share. The implications of this for pricing need to be carefully considered. Maintenance of market share in a highly competitive market may mean that prices cannot be increased for the next trading period, or even that they have to be reduced to face competitors who undercut. Increasing market share may mean aggressively low pricing to attract switchers from competing products. Alternatively, high prices might help to establish a high quality position that appeals to more discerning customers.

> ### Example
>
> In Germany, for instance, consumers are paying between 30 per cent and 50 per cent more for various pork products, including mettwurst, leberwurst, rotwurst, hams and pork steaks, which are retailed under a particular label. These products promise that they are
>
> **'Meat made to Granny's recipes from the sort of pigs that Grandpa kept'**
> (*The Grocer*, 1995).
>
> The price premium emphasizes the quality of the products as well as capitalising on the German propensity towards traditional products that hark back to a bygone age (*see* at p. 179).

The interaction between price and quality, and the need for consistency between them is shown in Fig 11.3. Where price and quality are equal, or where quality level exceeds price, the consumer certainly benefits and thus the seller may have established a useful position. If the price exceeds the quality, however, to the bottom left of the matrix, the offering represents bad value for money and the seller is likely to lose customers unless something is done to remedy the inconsistency.

Obviously, price is not the only factor affecting performance. Astute use of advertising, for example, may help to achieve market share objectives without giving way so much on price. Using price this way as a competitive weapon may be less effective than hoped, since price moves are too easily copied by other organisations.

FIGURE 11.3

Price–quality matrix

		Product quality		
		Low	**Medium**	**High**
Price	**Low**	Economy position	Value position	Excellent value strategy Underpriced?
	Medium	Poor value position Overpriced?	Medium value position	Value position Underpriced?
	High	Poor value strategy Overpriced?	Poor value position Unsupported price premium	Premium positioning

Volume sales

Seeking volume sales may well be related to market share objectives, but arises more from an operational focus on capacity. In different kinds of production activity, pricing may be used as a means of maintaining the operational smooth running of the organisation. With continuous production, involving the mass production of identical products, there is the ability to pile up stocks of the finished product until it is sold. At some point, however, the stockpiles may become unacceptably large, leading to pressure to sell at a discount to clear them. Many car manufacturers faced this problem in the recessionary early 1990s because they kept their production lines running at more or less normal levels, hoping that the market would pick up.

Batch or unit production, involving the production of small numbers (even down to one-off jobs) of different goods at a time, is more concerned with keeping the business afloat than with the running of a particular line. Shipbuilding operates in this way; while one job is being carried out, management are looking to fill the order book for the future, whether with large multimillion pound projects or with small maintenance jobs just to keep the work-force occupied and make a contribution to overheads. Pricing is used very aggressively in such markets to win the contract that will secure the short- or long-term future of the organisation.

In a service industry, because of the inherent perishability of the product, price becomes more important as the deadline for service delivery approaches. In a hotel, for example, if it means the difference between letting a room tonight and not letting it, then price may become negotiable for an eleventh-hour potential guest. Pricing is also used extensively in service situations as a means of evening out fluctuating demand. Again, in the hotel industry, weekend or midweek special deals help to direct demand to the quieter parts of the week, allowing the hotelier to maintain occupancy rates while still recouping the variable costs of so doing.

Status quo

Linked closely with maintaining market share, the objective of preserving the *status quo* implies an organisation that is happy for things to continue as they are and does not want the market's boat to be rocked. Even a market leader may be happy simply to retain share rather than seek even more, and may prefer not to challenge a smaller, lower-priced competitor for fear of damaging its own position in the process.

One of the problems of using pricing as a means of gaining share is indeed the risk of a price war. One organisation reduces its prices and then all the others start a downward spiral of undercutting. The ultimate outcome of this is that margins become increasingly small, the weakest organisations fall by the wayside, relative

Example

Icelandair's average fare to the USA is 35 per cent lower than that of bigger airlines such as SAS, and it carries more Norwegians and Swedes to Florida than any other airline (Carnegy, 1995). The other airlines are happy for Icelandair to do this, however, since the airline is not perceived as a serious threat because of the small scale of its operations, and because a significant proportion of transatlantic travellers would prefer to pay a little more not to visit Reykjavik! On Far East routes, however, the competitive situation is somewhat different, and in January 1995 it was predicted that a price war, cutting ticket prices by up to 25 per cent, would begin as the major airlines struggled to retain share (Ashworth, 1995).

market shares are unlikely to change, and nobody wins other than the consumer. This is a very expensive way of maintaining the *status quo*. Even a smaller supplier may elect to maintain the *status quo* by matching rather than challenging competitors' prices. According to Perks (1993), to win a price war, an organisation should only target weaker competitors, fight from a position of strength and extend the war over a long period to wear down the competition.

An organisation may, of course, choose to match prices in some product areas, but not in others. Even the upmarket UK supermarkets, for example, are seen to compete aggressively on price on a select number of basic product lines, yet quietly make up for this by charging price premiums on others.

Price as a stabiliser can, therefore, be a very powerful force. It also strengthens the arguments for a philosophy of profit satisfaction rather than maximisation, as discussed at p. 410 above, through the trade-off between the perceived gains and losses of failing to follow on price.

Price matching rather than undercutting may well maintain the *status quo*, but it also opens the door for non-price competition, where the focus is on the other elements of the marketing mix. An organisation that can demonstrate that it offers a better product (by whatever criteria which matter to the target market) can neutralise, to some extent, the market's sensitivity to price. This is a difficult thing to do, but it does mean that it is easier to build and retain loyalty, thus defending against competitive erosion of both market share and margins. The more price sensitive the customers, the less loyal they are.

Survival

In difficult economic circumstances, survival can become the only motivating objective for an organisation. Long-term strategic objectives have no currency if you are likely to be out of business tomorrow. Imagine a small company that has found that its market does not have the potential it originally predicted. Price is a very obvious and flexible marketing mix element to change in order to keep goods flowing out and cash flowing in. As discussed at p. 412 above, even a larger firm, such as a shipbuilder, may be prepared to suffer short-term losses to keep the operation intact, even though this cannot be sustained indefinitely without reducing the size of the operation in some way.

Example

The American airline Pan Am, in its last few years before bankruptcy, attempted heavy price discounting and frequent flyer bonus mileage points as a means of staving off collapse. The consumer gained from the lower fares and incentives, but even at those prices, the company did not generate sufficient traffic to pull it out of its financial problems.

PRICING POLICIES AND STRATEGIES

Pricing policies and strategies guide and inform the pricing decision, providing a framework within which decisions can be made with consistency and with the approval of the organisation as a whole. Policies and strategies help to specify the role of pricing and its use in context of the marketing mix (Nagle, 1987). Such frameworks are especially important in larger organisations where pricing decisions may be delegated with some discretion to line managers or sales representatives. They need sufficient rules to maintain a consistent corporate image in front of the market without being unduly restricted.

There are many situations in which a sales representative, for instance, may need policy guidance. Imagine a sales representative visiting a customer who tells him that a competitor is offering a similar product more cheaply. Company policy will help the representative to decide whether or not to get involved in undercutting or whether to sell the product benefits harder.

Other situations where policy and strategy guidelines may be of use include responding to a competitive price threat in a mass market, setting prices for new or relaunched products, modifying price in accordance with prevailing environmental conditions, using price with other marketing mix elements and, finally, using price across the product range to achieve overall revenue and profit targets. Some of these situations are discussed in more detail below. In any situation, guidelines can provide the basis for more detailed pricing strategies designed to achieve price objectives.

MARKETING IN ACTION

Premium sausages

Lazenby's has helped to create a premium-priced, upmarket niche within a sausage market that was dominated by mass-produced products sold on low price. The company has become the market leader in the premium sausage niche market, a move that has proved highly profitable for a relatively small firm in the market. The business started in 1983 with just one Dicker-filler, a hand-operated sausage machine. At that time, UK supermarket sausage prices were between 49p and 69p per pack. Lazenby's positioned itself at around the £1 mark, a price that meant that it took five years before the first supermarket contract was won. Meanwhile, the brand image developed, centred on a traditional image of a smiling butcher, Mr Lazenby, suitably attired in a clean, white butcher's apron.

Demand soon grew for premium sausages. In 1983, the sector was worth around £5 million per year, and by 1996 it was worth £100 mn, 25 per cent of the whole UK sausage market. Lazenby's was well placed to exploit this growth, offering a clear identity for a high quality sausage with flavour variants as diverse as cajun and tandoori. The quality theme extends throughout the raw material and production process. The combination is simple: 100 per cent pork, natural skins and real flavourings. Price tends to be used by consumers as a quality indicator in the sausage market, although in reality, higher-priced products do not always use higher-quality ingredients.

Despite occupying a premium position Lazenby's still had some tough negotiating to do with the larger supermarket chains as it expanded its distribution. Richard Lazenby, the owner claimed,

> *'I know for a fact that one major UK supermarket chain is making margins of 45% on our products and 90 per cent of that is profit – but it's always the supplier who ends up having to carry the can.'*

Pressures on margins and the need to reinvest in new equipment to retain the leadership position in a growth market means that premium prices are an essential part of the overall strategy.

Source: Darwent (1996).

New product pricing strategies

In addition to all the other pressures and risks inherent in new product development, as discussed in Chapter 9, it is important to get the launch price right as it can be difficult to change it later. It can be easy and tempting to set a low price to attract customers to a new launch, but this can establish attitudes and perceptions of the quality and positioning of the brand that would be difficult to overturn. A subsequent price rise might be viewed with some hostility by the customer. The safest route to low price entry with an option of raising it later is to make the price a promotional issue. Clearly signalling the low price as an introductory offer, a short-term trial price, both attracts attention and encourages trial of the new product, and when the price does rise to its 'normal' level, there is no confusion or suspicion in the customer's mind.

> ### Example
>
> When the summer fruit variant of Aqua Libra, the adult-orientated new age non-alcoholic drink was launched in cans, it was priced at 49p. This was clearly shown on the cans as an introductory price which would not therefore compromise any later moves towards the premium pricing normally associated with this brand.

Another aspect of the high or low price setting decision is the likely impact on the competition. A high price might encourage them to enter the market too, as they see potentially high profit margins. The organisation launching the new product may not, however, have too much choice. Internal pressure to recoup development costs quickly, as discussed at p. 410, may force a high price, or alternatively, a price-sensitive market might simply reject a high price and force prices lower.

According to Monroe and Della Bitta (1978), much depends on how innovative the new product is. A new brand in a crowded market can be precise with its price positioning as there are many competitors to compare with, and both the price setter and the consumer can 'read' the price signals clearly. A completely unknown product, such as the very first domestic video recorder, has no such frame of reference. The price setter can work on three things. First, the prices of other domestic electrical goods might give clues as to the sort of prices consumers expect to pay. This is a tenuous link because this new product is so obviously different it may not be comparable, especially in the mind of an opinion-leading consumer. Second, market research may have been carried out to discover how enthusiastic consumers are about the new idea, and hypothetically what they would pay to possess it. Again, this may be misleading because the consumers have no experience of this product and may not themselves be able to foresee in theory how they would respond in practice. Third, the price setter can work on internal factors such as costs, breakeven analysis and return on investment. This serves as a starting point and experience and emerging competition will allow a more realistic price structure to evolve. It is a dangerous route, however. If that cost-based price turns out to be inappropriate, rescuing the product could be almost impossible, particularly if astute competitors are learning from your mistakes and launching realistically priced products themselves.

With all this in mind, the high or low entry price decision boils down to two alternative strategies, **skimming** or **penetration**, first proposed by Dean (1950).

Price skimming

In order to skim, prices are set high to attract the least price-sensitive market segments. Such pricing might appeal, for instance, to opinion leaders who want to be seen to be first with any new product regardless of the price, or to those who seek status and see high price as the mark of an exclusive product.

Skimming has a number of advantages. It allows the organisation to establish a quality brand image that could serve as a stepping stone to future development of lower-priced, more mass market versions. If the product in question is a difficult one to produce, then pricing to keep the market small and exclusive can also give breathing space to gain learning experience on lower volumes while still marketing the product in a real market. The risk here, of course, is that high price raises high expectations, and if that learning experience does not go well, then the market will think that the product quality is too poor or inconsistent to justify the price, a bad reputation will stick and the future of the product becomes questionable. Finally, it is easier to reduce price than to raise it. If an initial high price does not generate the required response, it can be slowly lowered until an appropriate level is found.

Price skimming was short but sweet.

Example

Organisations with new products may not have long to enjoy the fruits of skimming. The Sony Walkman, for example, had a honeymoon period as the only product of its type, and could thus price itself high. As competitors began to infiltrate the market with imitations, the market's price profile began to develop and although Sony remained a premium-priced brand, it would never again have the freedom to skim as it chose.

Source: Sony UK Ltd.

Penetration pricing

In an attempt to gain as big a market share as possible in the shortest possible time, an organisation may price aggressively below existing competition, deliberately paring its margins for the sake of volume. This is *penetration pricing*. It may be a necessary strategy if cost structures are such that a very large volume of sales is required to break even or to achieve economies of scale in production or marketing terms. It is a risky strategy because it could establish a poor-quality brand image and also, if it does not work, it would be very difficult to raise the price.

It is, nevertheless, a legitimate strategy to seek to deny the competition volume share within the market. Penetration pricing of a new product, particularly in a market where product differentiation is difficult, reduces the attractiveness of market entry to competitors unless they can be sure that they can produce and market much more efficiently and on a tighter cost base. Penetration pricing is also useful in elastic demand situations where price is a critical factor for the buyer.

As emphasized above, the choice of launch price should take into account future plans for the pricing and positioning of the product. Some products can enter a market with a skimming price and retain it, particularly luxury goods that are well differentiated from each other and have an element of uniqueness about them. The Swiss company Bueche Girod, for example, advertised a 9 carat gold and diamond ladies' watch for £1675 with a matching necklace for a further £2975 for Christmas 1995. In markets where a new product has a high level of technological innovation and customers have no benchmark against which to compare prices, the introductory price may skim, but this will give way to something more competitive as rival products enter the market, economies of scale are achieved and costs reduce with the learning curve. In contrast, penetration pricing at launch sets an aggressive, value for money stance that the manufacturer would find hard to break away from, regardless of what the competition do. This product will always have to be priced competitively.

Product mix pricing strategies

A product which is part of a product range cannot be priced in isolation from the rest of the range. The range has to be viewed as an entity, and different products serve different purposes which come together to benefit the whole. In seeking to serve the needs of a number of market segments and build a strong competitive defence across the market, one product may be allowed to earn a relatively low return while another is skimming.

Within an individual product line (*see* pp. 263 *et seq.* for the distinction between range and line), such as SLR cameras, each product within the line offers additional features and their pricing needs to be spaced out accordingly. Customers see the set of products within the line and relate the price steps with additional features, benefits or quality. This may also encourage consumers to trade up to a more expensive model in the line as they begin to indulge in a type of marginal analysis: 'For an extra £20 I can have a zoom facility as well. Seems like a better deal ...'. The process may not be so rational. As discussed at p. 373, price may be used as an indicator of quality in the absence of other knowledge or indicators. Thus a buyer may find a model within the product line at (or slightly beyond) the preconceived spending limit and feel that the best possible quality purchase has been made, regardless of whether the product benefits and features are useful or appropriate.

Rather than presenting a predetermind collection of standard products with standard prices, some organisations prefer to offer a basic-priced product to which the consumer can then add extras, each of which adds to the overall price. The beauty of this is that the basic price seems very reasonable and affordable, and thus the consumer can easily get to the stage of wanting the product. Once that stage is reached, the odd few pounds here and there for extra features seems insignificant even though the final total price may be somewhat higher than the consumer would have been comfortable with in the first place. At least the customer is getting a personally tailored purchase.

Example

Holiday packages prominently feature low prices on their brochures to attract attention and make themselves seem eminently affordable. Two weeks in the sun for only £99 per person soon increases to something closer to £300 when airport transfers and taxes are added, along with the supplements for a local departure, insurance, better quality accommodation with a sea view, full board, and an August rather than May holiday. Buying a car is also a minefield of extras. Delivery charges, taxes, registration plates, metallic paint, sunroof, alarm system, central locking are among the items that may not necessarily be quoted in the advertised price.

The problem with any such approach is knowing what to leave out and what to include in the basic price. A basic price that does not include non-optional items such as tax is likely to lead to an unimpressed customer. There is also the danger that a competitor who comes in with an all-inclusive price may be seen as attractive by customers who feel that they have been deceived by overpriced extras that are actually essentials. In the USA, both General Motors and Ford led the car market in offering *one-price selling* or *value pricing* where they offered vehicles with a fixed set of options at a fixed, non-negotiable price. Such moves take away the uncertainty about what the real price will be and what is or is not included in the price, as well as relieving the buyer of the ordeal of having to haggle over price (Moskal, 1994).

This discussion has raised issues of the psychology of pricing which will be further discussed at p. 429.

Managing price changes

Prices are rarely static for long periods. Competitive pressures may force prices down, either temporarily or permanently, or new market opportunities might increase the price premium on a product. The pressure of cost inflation means that the marketing manager has to decide whether to pass these cost increases on to customers through prices charged, and when. However, changing prices can have a serious effect on profit margins and on market stability. If the changes are too significant, whether on transatlantic air fares or the price of vegetables in the local market, it is almost inevitable that competitors will respond in some way. Price changes not only cause ripples through the market, but also have an impact on sales volume. Normally, it is likely that a price cut will increase volume, and it is sometimes a very fine calculation to predict whether the profit margin earned on the extra volume gained more than compensates for the lost margin caused by the price cut. At various times, an organisation might be faced with the prospect of initiating price changes, or of responding to competitors' price changes.

Initiating price cuts

Initiating price cuts can be a very dangerous activity. Any organisation considering such a move needs to think through carefully the likely impact of any changes on both customers and competitors. Table 11.1 shows how much extra volume needs to be sold to make up for the lost margin on any given price cut. It can be seen that if the initial gross profit margin was 30 per cent and a price cut of 10 per cent was introduced, unit sales would need to increase by 50 per cent just to maintain the original profit level. For even the best of organisations, assessing the likely impact of such a price cut on the market is a tough challenge.

Nevertheless, organisations still do cut prices from time to time. They may do so for short-term tactical reasons, such as clearing excess stock, or as part of a more fundamental strategic 'value for money' repositioning. Much depends on whether the organisation sees itself as a price leader or follower in the market. A leader may wish

---

MARKETING IN ACTION

Apple turnover

Apple Computers was forced to reappraise its pricing strategy in a number of world markets because of severe price competition and the launch of Microsoft's Windows 95 software.

Apple had always tried to occupy a premium price position based upon customers' belief that the system was easier to use and, in some applications, offered more advanced capability than other PC products. The launch of Windows 95 narrowed the competitive advantage, however, and forced Apple to cut prices in the tougher markets of the USA and Japan. In the latter market, some Apple products were sold below cost. Price cutting cannot be maintained as a long-term strategy, because Apple has high R&D costs to recoup. This is because Apple products are based on hardware and software technology specific to Apple, rather than being based on industry-wide components.

Other PCs make heavy use of common components such as Intel microprocessors.

Given the tough environment, Apple might have to leave the price-competitive, entry level, mass market for low-priced machines in favour of higher performance machines that can sustain higher margins. At the higher end of the market, potential customers become more sensitive to the product benefits offered and more knowledgeable about the advantages and disadvantages of competing systems. This could eventually mean that Apple might become a niche operator in selected segments such as publishing. Such a move would not be without problems, however, if the loyalty of existing customers were lost and associated software companies decided to withdraw as market volume declined.

Source: Kehoe and Taylor (1996).

TABLE 11.1

The impact of price reductions on sales volume

If you cut your price by: %	If your gross profit margin is (%)						
	5	10	15	20	25	30	40
	you need an increase in unit sales of (%):						
1	25.0	11.1	7.1	5.3	4.2	3.4	2.6
2	66.7	25.0	15.4	11.1	8.7	7.1	5.3
3	150.0	42.9	25.0	17.6	13.6	11.1	8.1
4		66.7	36.4	25.0	19.0	15.4	11.1
5		100.0	50.0	33.3	25.0	20.0	14.3
6		150.0	66.7	42.9	31.6	25.0	17.6
7		233.3	87.5	53.8	38.9	30.4	21.2
8			114.3	66.7	47.1	36.4	25.0
9			150.0	81.8	56.3	42.9	29.0
10			200.0	100.0	66.7	50.0	33.3
11			275.5	122.2	78.6	57.9	37.9
12			400.0	150.0	92.3	66.7	42.9
13				185.7	108.3	76.5	48.1
14				233.3	127.3	87.5	53.8
15				300.0	150.0	100.0	60.0
16				400.0	177.8	114.3	66.7
17				566.7	212.5	130.8	73.9
18					275.1	150.0	81.8
19					316.7	172.7	90.5
20					400.0	200.0	100.0
21					525.0	233.3	110.5
22					733.3	275.0	122.2
23						328.6	135.3
24						400.0	150.0
25						500.0	166.7

to make the first move, leaving competitors with the problem of whether to respond, and how. There are a number of reasons for cutting price, including the following.

Capacity utilisation. Where excess production capacity is found in a market, there is a temptation to lower prices to levels that do not cover full costs, but at least cover the variable cost and make some contribution towards fixed overheads, just to keep the production lines busy. Such price cutting cannot carry on indefinitely, but might serve a useful purpose in the short term until either recovery or shakeout.

Example

In 1994, Club Méditerranée found it necessary to instigate price cuts up to 15 per cent at some of its resorts. Accompanied by an aggressive marketing campaign, this was designed to attract more European customers in order to fill unused capacity (Walker, 1994).

Market dominance. If an organisation enjoys a strong price and cost leadership position and is not likely to fall foul of competition legislation, it may pay to seek an even more dominant position through selective or across the board price cuts. Such action could help to eliminate or at least squeeze some competitors, but an organisation following this strategy also runs the risk of making customers more price sensitive.

Market defence. If a market segment is under attack or if demand is weak compared with other alternatives, it may pay an organisation to defend its position by lowering prices to minimise the impact of the threat. It could be a dangerous strategy in the long term, but by creating short-term difficulties for the attacker, it may help the organisation to retain share.

A sudden unsignalled price cut might be seen by competitors as the first move in a price war. An organisation needs to be sure that it can win and be sure of what it is going to achieve by such an aggressive act. An advance warning of a price increase is less likely to be viewed with hostility. It gives the competition time to reflect on its implications and to make a considered response, which does not necessarily mean a panic descent into further undercutting. It also allows good customers to stock up at the old prices or allows further negotiation time in organisational markets. Many annual subscriptions to magazines are offered to readers at the existing rate, with a clear indication that the subscription rate will rise in the near future. This is an incentive to 'act now'. An early notification of price increases, often associated with the introduction of new and revised products, gives a short-term flurry of excitement to the market as customers aim to beat the deadline.

Example

Discount grocery retailers effectively acted as initiators of price cuts, challenging the established supermarkets' pricing policies and trying to focus the British shopper's attention on price. They assumed that they could sell the high volumes required to make a profit at low price levels, and that their 'no frills' low service retailing formats would give them a cost advantage that would make it very difficult for the established supermarkets to compete by undercutting them. What they had not properly foreseen, however, was the supermarkets' response to the discounters' price cutting. Instead of following on price and effectively becoming discounters themselves, the supermarkets responded with selective price cuts overtly signalling competitiveness, but at the same time invested in customer service, loyalty schemes and quality image building to dull the customer's price sensitivity. Any losses made on the selective price cuts could be absorbed by the margins on more premium-priced merchandise. By 1995 it appeared that the supermarkets were winning the price war, as the discounters accounted for only 7 per cent of food sales, and there were rumours that the supermarkets were even feeling confident enough to consider price rises (Hinde, 1995).

Responding to competitors' price cuts

The above example demonstrates that when a competitor initiates price cuts, whether selective or across the board, a very careful response needs to be planned. Much again will depend upon how and why the change has taken place. Is it overt and threatening, covert and threatening or clearly signalled with some attempt at justification, for example spare capacity?

The response to a competitor's price cut can take three broad forms: ignoring the decrease, responding head-on by matching or undercutting the competitor or deflecting the decrease, as the supermarkets did, by emphasizing added value rather than price.

Ignoring the decrease. This can be a high-risk strategy if the price cut is significant and clearly related to an aggressive campaign to gain market share. Once share is lost it is very difficult to win it back.

Many years ago, Bic created turmoil in the pen industry with low pricing, disposability and heavy promotion through mass distribution. Many traditional suppliers failed to spot the threat emerging across Europe quickly enough and lost substantial market share by not responding. The desirability of matching a price cut may depend upon whether it is perceived to be a short-term or long-term measure. If it is longer term, there may be a case for introducing an economy brand and repositioning the threatened product slightly more upmarket. This is effectively what happened in the pen industry as suppliers introduced higher quality, well differentiated pens, while seeking to match the lower Bic prices through new cheap alternatives based on a similar competitive formula.

Undercutting. Responding by *undercutting the competitor* might easily lead to a flurry of price cuts, stimulating a price war in which the consumer may well be the only winner. Sectors such as petrol, transatlantic air fares, supermarkets and cross-channel travel have all experienced price wars in recent years. Price war threats are especially prevalent in oligopolistic markets, but many organisations seek to avoid them for the kind of reasons discussed on p. 412 (Lambin, 1993).

Deflecting the cut. *Deflecting the price cut* may be an appropriate option if the cut is not very severe and sufficient brand loyalty and differentiation has reduced customers' price sensitivities. Various options can be used to add value to the product at existing prices. This could include larger pack sizes, more features, more services, better packaging or promoting the product quality and benefits more aggressively. In extreme circumstances, of course, the only commercially sensible option may be to concede defeat and move on.

In 1993, the Dutch flower industry faced severe price competition from cheap imports of flowers, mainly from Africa. These imports reduced the price of cut roses by 40 per cent, and the Dutch growers could no longer compete, since the African growers had the cost advantages of low wages, no heating costs and no restrictions on the use of fertilisers or pesticides. Instead of trying to combat the lower prices, therefore, the Dutch growers have increasingly turned to higher quality, more expensive niche markets, in which the Africans could not compete (Griffin, 1994).

The main difficulty with responding to price increases is that decisions often have to be made quickly in order to protect short-term volumes and there might be too little time for detailed 'what if ...?' planning. Thus the surprise of a sudden price cut from a competitor and the speed of response needed can lead to poor decisions in the long run. The nature of the response will, in part, reflect the organisation's strategic plans and the importance of the product under threat. If it is central to future development, then careful but decisive action may be needed. If it is a marginal product, perhaps in the later stages of its life cycle, there may be less sense of urgency.

Initiating price increases

Not all price changes involve cuts. Price increases may also be initiated, whether because of cost pressures or for legitimate strategic reasons. As with initiating price cuts, however, any move to raise prices needs to be considered very carefully, to assess customer and competitor response. The likelihood of customer acceptance of the price increase can be estimated from previous experience and from known sensitivity within price ranges. Much, however, will ultimately depend upon whether competitors choose to ignore the increase or to follow suit. This assessment need not be based entirely on guesswork. Previous experience, actual and anticipated market conditions, demand stability or volatility and not least an estimation of production capacity within the industry might all influence the likely reaction. Sometimes cost pressures, perhaps arising from increases in wage rates or in raw material prices, affect all competitors in the market, making a general price increase more likely.

Cost pressures. Manufacturers can no longer assume that higher raw material prices can be passed on automatically to customers through higher prices. On average, fuel and raw material costs rose by 11.5 per cent in 1994, while manufacturers achieved average price increases of only 3.4 per cent. This indicates that customers further down the supply chain are not necessarily prepared to accept price increases (Cheeseright, 1995). The calculations presented in Table 11.1 operate in reverse when a price increase is contemplated. The price rise is likely to cause a fall in demand, and the question to assess is whether the extra margin earned through the higher price compensates for the profit sacrificed on the lost volume. There could be a loss of volume if competitors choose not to replicate the price increase. If an organisation feels that a price rise is unwise, then it might have to find ways of absorbing cost increases, perhaps through cutting costs or increasing efficiency in other areas.

Curbing demand. Not all price increases are cost driven. In situations where demand is buoyant and shortages are starting to emerge, the supplier can use price to curb demand or to capitalise on the profit opportunity. This can be achieved in several ways other than through a straight price rise. One method is to withdraw concessions or discounts. Thus, for example, the number of cheap seats available on a particular flight often reflects the likely level of overall demand. This emphasizes the flexibility and responsiveness of pricing as a marketing tool, since thanks to on-line booking systems, the airline can adjust its discounts in accordance with sales levels. An indirect way of raising prices is to 'unbundle' the product or service so that elements that were originally included in the price are now charged as extras. What used to be an all-inclusive price for a restaurant meal, for instance, may suddenly no longer include drinks or a service charge. Similarly, installation and training might begin to be charged to the purchaser as an additional cost on a new office word processing network.

Responding to competitors' price increases

When an organisation is faced with a competitor's price rise, it has to decide whether and how to respond. There are three possible responses: respond in kind by matching the competitor's move; maintain price levels, but differentiate the product by emphasizing how much better value it now represents; or refuse to respond at all. Responding in kind is perhaps the safest option from a market stability perspective. Many organisations prefer to follow others in implementing price rises, rather than taking the leadership risks. Smaller firms may use the leader's price as a reference point, follow the price and continue to compete on non-price factors such as location, service and adaptability. Promoting further differentiation may be the best option for defending a niche.

Even if the price increase is replicated, the higher margins can be ploughed back into adding value. This could mean offering more product per sale, or including services that were originally charged for or increasing promotional activity to develop stronger product loyalty. Not responding at all is perhaps the highest risk option, if it is perceived as an aggressive response designed to gain market share. Smaller firms may have more flexibility in their response, as their actions are likely to have only a marginal impact. For example, larger airlines are unlikely to care whether or not Icelandair follows their price increases.

The specific response selected will primarily depend upon how much the other organisations in the market want market stability and to shelter under the price umbrella created by the price leader.

SETTING THE PRICE RANGE

Once the strategic direction of the pricing decision has been specified, a price range needs to be set within which the final detail of price can be established. A pricing method is needed that can generate purposeful and sound prices throughout the year. The method and its rigidity will obviously vary depending on whether the organisation is setting one-off prices for a few products or many prices for a large product range or is in a fast moving retailing environment.

There are three main pricing methods, which take into account some of the key pricing issues already discussed. They are cost based, demand based and competition based. The organisation may adopt one main method of operation or use a flexible combination depending on circumstance. Each method will be discussed in turn, once the general principles of cost–volume–profit relationships have been established.

The cost–volume–profit relationship

The demand patterns discussed at pp. 382 *et seq.*, although established and understood in their own right, also need to be understood in the context of their relationship with costs, volume of production and profit. The marketer needs to understand how the organisation's costs behave under different conditions, internally and externally generated, in order to appreciate fully the implications of marketing decisions on the operation of the organisation. The marketer should understand the different types of costs and their contribution to the pricing decision. The four most important cost concepts are fixed costs, variable costs, marginal cost and total cost. These are now defined.

Definitions of costs

Fixed costs. Fixed costs are those which do not vary with output in the short term. This category thus includes management salaries, insurance, rent, buildings and machine maintenance etc. Once output passes a certain threshold, however, extra production facilities might have to be brought on stream and so fixed costs will then show a step-like increase.

Variable costs. Variable costs are those which vary according to the quantity produced. These costs are incurred through raw materials, components, and direct labour used for assembly or manufacture. Variable costs can be expressed as a total or on a per unit basis.

Marginal costs. The change that occurs to total cost if one more unit is added to the production total is the marginal cost.

Total cost. Total cost is all the cost incurred by an organisation in manufacturing, marketing, administering and delivering the product to the customer. Total cost thus adds the fixed costs and the variable costs together.

To reiterate what was said in Chapter 10, costs may not be the only factor involved in setting prices, but they are an important one. No organisation would wish to operate for very long at a level where its selling price was not completely recovering its costs and making some contribution towards profit.

There are two main approaches to examining the cost–volume–profit relationship: marginal analysis and breakeven analysis.

Marginal analysis

Marginal analysis is concerned with what happens to a business when production or sales change by just one unit. The focus is, therefore, on what is happening to costs and revenues at the very edge or margin of operations. Thus the marginal cost is the additional cost incurred by the production of one more unit, and similarly, the marginal revenue is the extra income derived from selling one extra unit.

FIGURE 11.4

Marginal cost and revenue

Figure 11.4 shows a situation where the marginal cost is high at low quantity production levels. As production levels increase, marginal cost then decreases because of both production and marketing economies. Then, however, a point is reached where the organisation is overstretching its production capacity, and inefficiencies arising from overworked labour and machinery send the marginal cost upwards again.

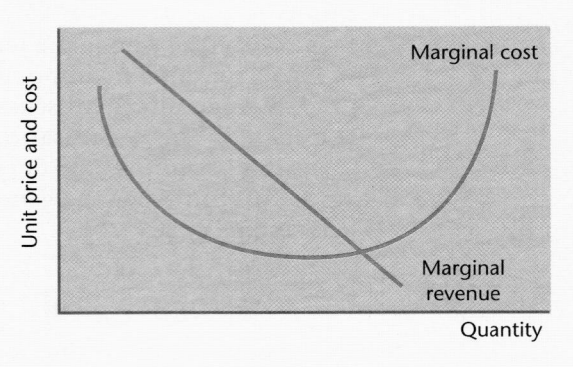

Meanwhile, the marginal revenue curve in the same figure shows how each additional unit sale affects total revenue. The pressure to expand sales, thus broadening the market, leads to lower prices, to make the product more affordable and therefore to lower revenue. Thus marginal revenue usually shows a downward slope. The message is simple: each additional unit sale, at least theoretically, generates less revenue than the previous unit sold because the price is falling.

At the heart of marginal analysis lies the search for the point where marginal revenue is equal to marginal cost. Up to that point, each additional unit sale generates more revenue than it incurs costs, and therefore it is worth producing and selling that unit. Beyond that point, however, the situation is different. Each additional unit begins to incur more cost than it can earn in revenue. Thus it becomes increasingly uneconomic to carry on producing extra units. This is all summarised in Fig 11.5 which shows the relationship between profit and price, total revenue, and total cost.

FIGURE 11.5

Profit maximisation

All of this may seem to be somewhat theoretical and far removed from the realities of pricing in real markets. Emerging strategic opportunities or changing competitive situations may be more urgent motivators of pricing decisions than whether producing one more unit is economic or not. No organisation can operate without due consideration of competitors' actions and price threats which can soon change the best laid revenue analysis.

The model can have some bearing in more stable, less dynamic markets, where there is reasonable and predictable

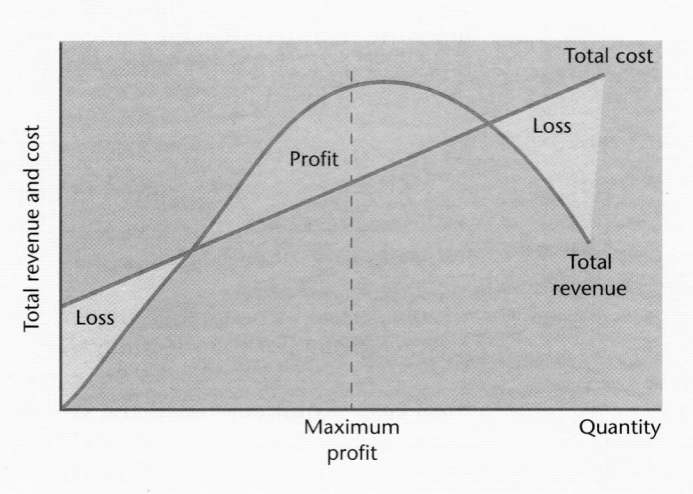

knowledge of cost schedules and demand sensitivity. Marginal analysis can at least certainly demonstrate the folly of chasing sales for the sake of sales. In most new product situations where information is scarce or incomplete, or where a competitive market is very volatile, however, such analysis becomes rather more academic.

Breakeven analysis

Breakeven analysis offers a simpler, more convenient approach to examining the cost–volume–profit relationship. It is a technique that shows the relationship between total revenue and total cost in order to determine the profitability of different levels of output. The breakeven point is the point at which total revenue and total cost are equal (i.e., no profit is made, nor are any losses incurred). Producing beyond this point generates increasing levels of profit.

Knowing how many units at any given price would have to be made and sold in order to break even is important, especially in new product and small business situations where an organisation has limited resources to fall back on if losses are incurred. Combining the breakeven analysis with known market and competitive conditions may make an organisation realise that it cannot compete unless it either reduces costs or develops a marketing strategy to increase volume sales.

Take, for example, a small engineering company wishing to produce a component to be priced at £200. The average variable cost per unit is £100 while the total fixed costs to be recovered are £200 000 per year.

$$\text{The breakeven point} = \frac{\text{total fixed costs}}{\text{unit price} - \text{variable costs}}$$

$$= \frac{£200\ 000}{£200 - £100}$$

$$= 2000 \text{ units per year.}$$

Figure 11.6 shows this information in a breakeven chart.

Breakeven analysis helps to show the impact on contribution to fixed costs and profit of alternative price levels. It is mechanically very simple to calculate, provided that costs are known, and any spreadsheet package can be used to set up a model to test the impact of different prices or cost structures. Breakeven is particularly useful in situations where fixed costs represent a high proportion of total costs. Once the breakeven point is reached, the fixed costs are all covered and any sales beyond that are mostly profit (because the variable cost component is so low). If this is a price-competitive market, therefore, it is useful to know where the breakeven point is so that prices can be set as low as possible, but without crossing the break-even point into loss.

The problem with the approach is that it focuses internally on cost structures and externally on a potentially simplistic relationship between price and sales. It must always be tempered by an appreciation of realistic market and competitive conditions, and put into the context of how the organisation can use other marketing techniques to bolster or develop demand to achieve sales more effectively.

FIGURE 11.6

Breakeven chart

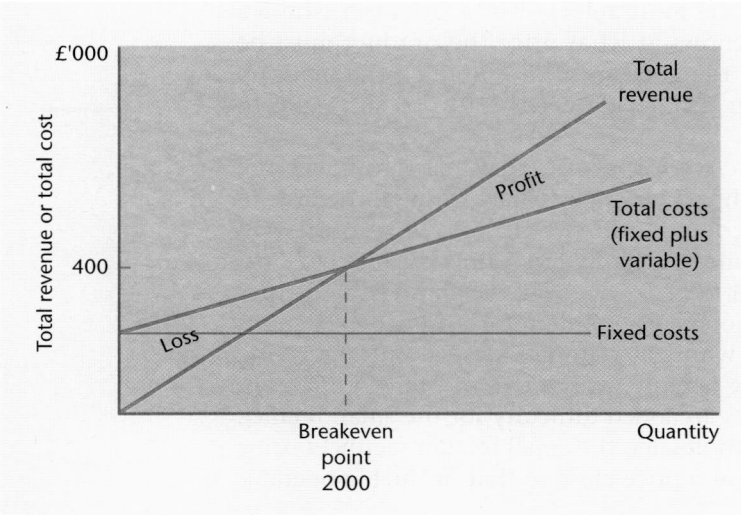

Cost-based methods

The emphasis in *cost based* pricing methods is on the organisation's production and marketing costs. Analysis of these costs leads to an attempt to set a price that generates a sufficient profit. The obvious disadvantage is the lack of focus on the external situation. An organisation implementing such a method would need to be very sure of the market's response. It is, however, a simple method to use, drawing the sort of direct parallels between cost and price that make accountants very happy. There are some variations in cost-based pricing.

Mark-up

Especially in the retail sector, where it can be difficult to estimate demand patterns for each product line, percentage mark-up is used as a means of price setting. This means that the retailer starts with the price paid to the supplier for the goods and then adds a percentage to that to reach the retail price to the customer. In fmcg high volume markets this can be as low as 8 per cent, whereas in low volume fashion clothing markets it can be 200 per cent or more. Mark-ups may be standard across all retailers in a particular sector, although the smaller business may have to accept a lower mark-up to compete with the retail prices of bigger operators who can negotiate better cost prices from suppliers. A retailer such as Costco that deliberately violates the mark-up traditions of its sector can be seen as initiating an all-out price war.

Mark-up can be expressed as a percentage of cost or as a percentage of the retail selling price. If a French wine merchant, for instance, buys a bottle of wine from a vineyard for 20F and adds 15F as the mark-up, thus achieving a retail price of 35F, then the mark-up as a percentage of the cost is:

$$\text{mark-up}/\text{cost price} \times 100.$$

That is:

$$15/20 \times 100 = 75\%.$$

Expressed as a percentage of retail price the mark-up is:

$$(\text{retail price} - \text{cost price})/\text{retail price} \times 100.$$

This gives:

$$15/35 \times 100 = 43\% \text{ (approximately)}.$$

It is thus important to be clear which kind of mark-up is being considered. The latter type, percentage of retail price, may be more relevant in a situation where a market is price sensitive and the retailer knows at what price the product must be sold. Using the retail price and the cost of the good from the supplier, the mark-up achieved can be calculated and the retailer can decide whether this is sufficient to cover selling costs and profit.

Mark-ups must work hard. As well as covering profit, they have to cover the retailer's operating costs. Figure 11.7 shows how mark-ups operate through the distribution chain. Sometimes the mark-ups become bigger the closer one is to the end consumer because of all the services the retailer is expected to supply, such as personal selling and attractive product displays. Each mark-up down the chain may be considered a reward for services rendered. The wholesaler's mark-up for instance, recognises the efficiency brought to the market by the wholesaler, in providing a central meeting point for manufacturers and retailers (there is more on the role of the wholesaler in Chapter 14). The wholesaler's mark-up poses an added difficulty for the small retailer. In paying for the services rendered by the wholesaler, the small retailer sacrifices some of his own mark-up if he still wishes to sell at a price close to that of the big operator who buys direct from the manufacturer.

FIGURE 11.7

Mark-up in the distribution chain

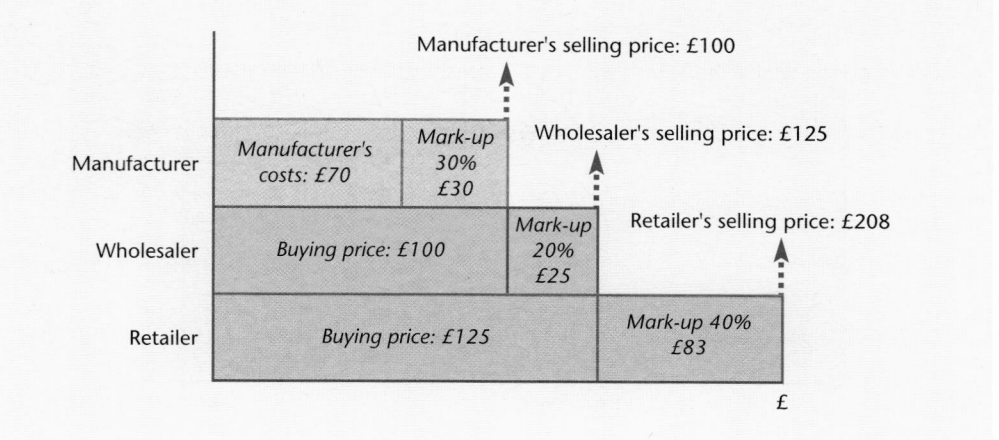

Although this is basically a cost-based pricing method, it does not operate in isolation from external events. Retailers will be wary of implementing a mark-up that leads to a retail price way out of line with the competition, or violates the consumer's expectations. This is particularly evident in the comments on the small retailer in the preceding paragraphs.

Cost-plus pricing

Cost-plus pricing involves adding a fixed percentage to production or construction costs. It is mainly used on large projects or for custom-built items where it is difficult to estimate costs in advance. The percentage will be agreed between buyer and seller in advance, and then just before, or after, the project's completion, buyer and seller agree the admissible costs and calculate the final price. It sounds straightforward enough, but in large complex construction projects, it is not so easy to pin down precise costs. Problems arise where the seller is inflating prices, perhaps through the use of transfer pricing (*see* p. 439), and it can take some time for buyer and seller to negotiate a final settlement.

An industry operating on this kind of pricing method, using a standard percentage, is orientated less towards price competition, and more towards achieving competitiveness through cost efficiency

Experience curve pricing

Over time, and as an organisation produces more units, its experience and learning lead to more efficiency. Cost savings of between 10 per cent and 30 per cent per unit can be achieved each time the organisation doubles its experience, as shown in Fig 11.8. In Fig 11.8 (a), an aggressive pricing strategy is being adopted, as prices are being set in anticipation of future cost savings to be derived from increased experience. In Fig 11.8 (b), however, a more moderate approach is being adopted, in which prices fall with cost savings as they are achieved.

Some organisations use this learning curve, essentially predicting how costs are going to change over time, as part of the price planning process. Such planning means not only that the organisation is under pressure to build the volume in order to gain the experience benefits but also that if it can gain a high market share early on in the product's life, it can achieve a strong competitive position because it gains the cost savings from learning sooner. It can thus withstand price competition.

Although the savings are made mainly in production, there is still a close link with the volume share and price dominating strategies discussed earlier. Fax machines and mobile phones are examples of products that are reducing their relative prices, partly because of the experience-curve effect.

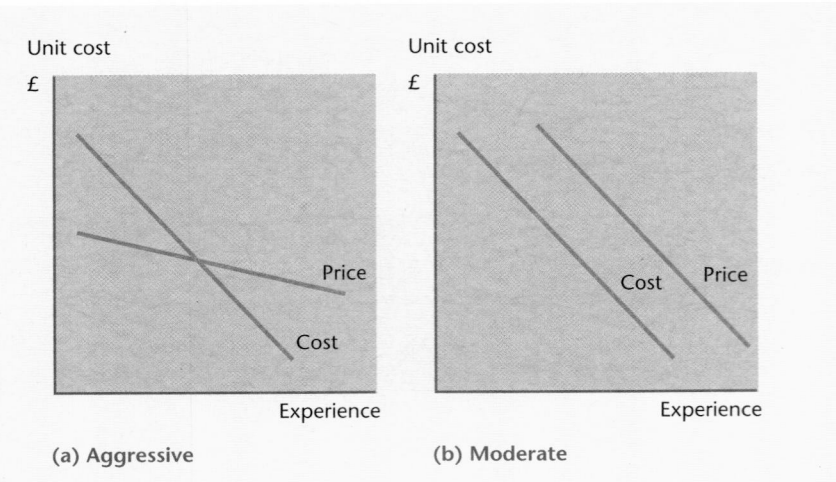

FIGURE 11.8

Experience curve pricing strategies

Unit cost
£

Price

Cost

Experience

(a) Aggressive

Unit cost
£

Cost   Price

Experience

(b) Moderate

The problem with cost-based methods is that they are too internally focused. The price determined has to survive in a market-place where customers and competitors have their own views of what pricing should be. An organisation's price may thus make perfect sense in cost terms and generate a respectable profit contribution, but be perceived as far too high or far too low by customers in comparison with the features and benefits offered. The price may also be way out of line compared with a competitor with a different kind of cost base.

Demand-based pricing

Demand-based pricing looks outwards from the production line and focuses on customers and their responsiveness to different price levels. Even this approach may not be enough on its own, but when it is linked with an appreciation of competition-based pricing, it provides a powerful market-orientated perspective that cost-based methods just do not provide.

At its simplest, demand-based pricing indicates that when demand is strong, the price goes up, and when it is weak, the price goes down. This can be seen in some service industries, for example, where demand fluctuates depending on time. Package holidays taken during school holidays at Christmas, Easter or in the summer when demand is high, are more expensive than those taken at other times of the year when it is more difficult for families to get away. Similarly, holidays taken when weather conditions at the destination are less predictable or less pleasant are cheaper because there is less demand. Even within the course of a single day, travel prices can vary according to demand. Tickets on shuttle flights between Heathrow and UK regional airports vary in price depending on when the peak times for business travellers occur.

The effect of time savings on freight costs is just one of the benefits of the Channel Tunnel.

le Shuttle

Freight
services

Lorem ipsum dolor sit amet

Lorem ipsum dolor sit amet, consectetuer adipiscing elit, sed diam nonummy nibh euismod tincidunt ut laoreet dolore magna aliquam erat volutpat. Ut wisi enim ad minim veniam, quis nostrud exerci tation Lorem ipsum dolor sit amet, consectetuer adipiscing elit, sed diam nonummy nibh euismod tincidunt ut laoreet dolore magna aliquam erat volutpat.

Source: Le Shuttle.

Channel Tunnel and freight costs

The opening of the Channel Tunnel has made organisations reappraise their freight arrangements, in view of the new ways of moving goods between the UK and mainland Europe. There are three ways of getting goods through the tunnel: by road vehicles on Le Shuttle, by Eurofreight rail service and by next-day package service using Eurostar. By far the most important mode is the carrying of trucks and trailers on Le Shuttle in direct competition with the ferries. To TNT Express Worldwide the advantage of the tunnel was not price as such, but the savings in time that have a consequential impact on costs. A trip on Le Shuttle takes 45 minutes, including unloading, compared with 80 minutes by ferry. In 1996, therefore, TNT was sending 150 trailers per week, or 130 tonnes per night, through the tunnel.

Egger, a German manufacturer of fibreboard and chipboard looked at direct rail movement to a depot in Yorkshire. With 40 000 tonnes of a heavy product to move every year, Egger thought that they could replicate their European pattern of mainly rail deliveries. After a detailed analysis, they found that it was more cost effective to use trucks on Le Shuttle than a through-rail link using wagons. Taking a truck and trailer carrying 22 pallets through the tunnel would cost between £100 and £120, compared with £660 for a rail wagon carrying 48 pallets. That means that a pallet moved by Le Shuttle through the tunnel would cost £4.70, whereas one carried by rail wagon would cost £12.83. Although the total cost of movement is the main determinant of the overall cost, in this case Le Shuttle won hands down!

Although Le Shuttle has made an impact in drawing truck traffic away from the ferries, attracting rail freight has proved more difficult. With rail freight, tonnage rose from 109 000 tonnes per month to 209 000 per month in one year, but the complexity of pricing to cover bulk (£3.75 per tonne) and non-bulk (£10 per tonne) rates has made the movement of non-bulk loads less competitive over shorter distances. Often it is only on the longer movements to Spain and Italy that the economies start to favour through-rail for non-bulk loads.

Sources: Batchelor (1996); Cater (1995).

There is an underlying assumption that an organisation operating such a flexible pricing policy has a good understanding of the nature and elasticity of demand in their market, as already outlined at pp. 382 *et seq.*

There are a number of interesting and more subtle forms of demand-based pricing.

Psychological pricing

Psychological pricing is very much a customer-based pricing method, relying as it does on the consumer's emotive responses, subjective assessments and feelings towards specific purchases. Clearly, this is particularly applicable to products with a higher involvement focus, i.e. those that appeal more to psychological than to practical motives for purchase. All the following are examples of psychological pricing.

Prestige pricing. Prestige pricing is used by the consumer as a means of assessing quality, as discussed at p. 373. The high price attracts the status-conscious consumer, the discerning customer for whom price is no object. Luxury goods such as fine jewellery, designer clothing and porcelain all need to be priced at high prestige levels. A lower price would deter that group of customers from buying.

Odd-even pricing. Odd-even pricing is the technique of ending a price with certain numbers, usually odd ones, for example £4.99 or 199 pesetas. It is a widely practised method, which seems to have an effect on the buying public. The research on the subject is far from conclusive, but among others Blattberg and Neslin (1990), for example, found that an increase in sales could be achieved simply by ending the price of the goods with a 9 rather than any other digit. It would appear that consumers view prices ending in 9 as lower prices and think that retailers offering such prices are better value. Further, when consumers were asked to recall the prices later, the prices ending with 9 were recalled as lower than they really were. In some situations, retailers can strive for the opposite effect. If £4.99 is a bargain, then £5.00 emanates quality. This is all far from being proved conclusively, however.

Price lining. Price lining is a technique that is favoured with a product mix strategy in which a number of products are sold at specific price points. Sometimes an organisation will work back from these price points regardless of the cost differences between the products in the line. For example, a clothing retailer might sell ladies' skirts at £25, £40 and £55, capitalising on customers' ideas of price banding (*see* p. 376). At

one extreme, the skirts at each of these prices might all be purchased from the supplier at the same price, but they are marked up to price points on the basis of style, colour and the expected response of the typical customer.

FIGURE 11.9

The stepped demand curve

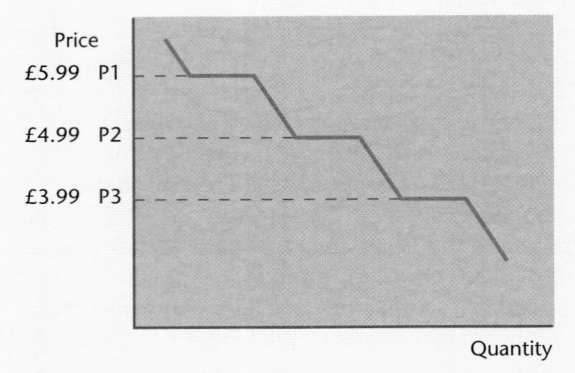

Too many price points may confuse customers and may prevent differentiation. Three or four price points is better than trying to operate eight or nine. Figure 11.9 shows a stepped demand curve where demand is inelastic within particular price bands represented by different price points. Price lining works because it makes it easier for the customer to choose. As the price is held constant within the band, choice can be made on other, perhaps aesthetic, grounds such as fabric, style or colour.

Bundle pricing. Bundle pricing involves assembling a number of products in a single package to save the consumer the trouble of searching out and buying each one separately. It makes it easier to buy, attracting the shopper who is short of time or is risk averse. Personal computers are often sold in this way, with all the hardware, software and peripherals bundled as a package that will enable the user to start some serious computing within minutes. Bundling has a psychological benefit, but it also has an economic rationale, perhaps leading to a lower overall price to the consumer or lower marketing costs for the supplier.

Promotional pricing. Promotional pricing is closely linked with the discussion in Chapter 17 on sales promotion. It can be used to stimulate a market or to reinforce perceptions of value in the short term. Selecting a limited number of lines for a price promotion, as practised in the retail sector, for example, attracts consumers' attention, draws them into the store and makes them feel as though they are benefiting from a bargain. The retailer hopes that the costs of providing a number of such price leaders is recouped by the sales of full-priced items, either to new customers or to existing customers spending the money they saved on the bargains (sales that would not otherwise have been made).

Time specific markdowns. End-of-season sales, one-day sales, sales of the type, 'sale ends Saturday', are common in the retail sector. A greater level of psychological excitement can be created among customers by providing a limited number of cut-price goods on a first-come first-served basis. Those who do not get the bargain of their choice still spend in the store and enjoy the thrill of the chase. More sedately, retailers and manufacturers use price promotions based on rewards for spending over a certain amount, or coupons rewarding repeat purchase as a means of offering the customer that little something extra.

Whether intended to stimulate demand, to encourage product trial, to take the risk out of purchase or to reward consistent and loyal behaviour, all these price promotion techniques show the flexible use of price as a tactical weapon in the marketing mix, supporting and supported by the other mix elements.

Price differentiation. Price differentiation involves the use of different prices for different segments. The same basic product is offered, but the associated services differ. A drink from a vending machine, for example, is more expensive than one from a supermarket because of the convenience, the machinery and its maintenance and the refrigeration. First class travel on an aircraft costs much more than economy class not because it gets travellers to their destination any more quickly, but because of the extra comfort and easier check-in procedure. In both cases, the same core product is being offered, a can of Coke or a journey from A to B, but price variations are justified by both peripheral services and psychological benefits.

Overall, demand-orientated pricing, regardless of how it is implemented, can be very powerful in achieving strong defendable market position. It can also lead to higher profit levels. The problem, however, lies in the difficulty of estimating demand response.

Competition-based pricing

This chapter has frequently warned of the danger of setting prices without knowing what is happening in the market, particularly with respect to one's competitors. According to Lambin (1993) there are two aspects of competition that influence an organisation's pricing. The first is the *structure of the market*. Generally speaking, the greater the number of competitors, i.e. the closer to perfect competition the market comes, the less autonomy the organisation has in price setting. The second competitive factor is the product's *perceived value* in the market. In other words, the more differentiated an organisation's product is from the competition, the more autonomy the organisation has in pricing it, because buyers come to value its unique benefits.

Most markets are becoming increasingly competitive, and a focus on competitive strategy in business planning emphasizes the importance of understanding the role of price as a means of competing. An organisation that decides to become a cost leader in its market and to take a price-orientated approach to maintaining its position needs an especially efficient intelligence system to monitor its competitors. Levy (1994) looks at organisations that offer price guarantees in organisational markets. Any supplier promising to match the lowest price offered by any of its rivals, needs to know as much as possible about those rivals and their cost and pricing structures in order to assess the likely cost of such a promise.

In consumer markets, market research can certainly help to provide intelligence, whether this means shopping audits to monitor the comparative retail prices of goods, or consumer surveys or focus groups to monitor price perceptions and evolving sensitivity relative to the rest of the marketing mix. Data gathering and analysis can be more difficult in organisational markets, because of the flexibility of pricing and the degree of customisation of marketing packages to an individual customer's needs in these markets. There is a heavy reliance on sales representatives' reports, information gained through informal networks within the industry and qualitative assessment of all those data.

Competitive analysis can focus on a number of levels, at one end of the spectrum involving a general overview of the market, and at the other end focusing on individual product lines or items. Whatever the market, whatever the focus of competitive analysis, the same decision has to be made: whether to price at the same level as the competition, or above or below them.

An organisation that has decided to be a price follower must, by definition, look to the market for guidance. The decision to position at the same level as the competition, or above or below them, requires information about what is happening in the market. This is pricing based on 'the going rate' for the product. Conventional pricing behaviour in the market is used as a reference point for comparing what is offered, and the price is varied from that. Each supplier to the market is thus acting as a marker for the others, taking into account relative positioning and relative offering. Effectively, pricing is based on collective wisdom, and certainly for the smaller business it is easier to do what everyone else does rather than pay for market research to prove what the price ought to be, and run the risk of getting it wrong. In a seaside resort, for example, a small bed and breakfast hotel is unlikely to price itself differently from the one next door, unless it can justify doing so by offering significantly better services. Within an accepted price range, however, any one organisation's move may not be seen as either significant or threatening by the rest.

The dangers of excessive price competition, both in terms of the cost to the competitors and the risk to a product's reputation, thus attracting the 'wrong' kind of customer, have already been indicated. But if neither the organisation nor the product has a particulary high reputation, or if the product has few differentiating features, then price competition may be the only avenue open unless there is a commitment to working on the product and the marketing mix as a whole. An extreme form of competitive pricing is practised through tendering, which is discussed at p. 437.

PRICING TACTICS AND ADJUSTMENTS

Pricing tactics and adjustments are concerned with the last steps towards arriving at the final price. There is no such thing as a fixed price; price can be varied to reflect specific customer needs, the market position within the channel of distribution or the economic aspects of the deal.

Price structures

Particularly in organisational markets, *price structures* give guidelines to the sales representative to help in negotiating a final price with the customer. The concern is not only to avoid overcharging or inconsistent charging, but to set up a framework for pricing discretion that is linked with the significance of the customer or the purchase situation.

> ### Example
>
> At one extreme, price structure may involve a take it or leave it, single-price policy such as IKEA operates. They offer no trade discount for organisational purchasers, seeing themselves largely as a consumer-orientated retailer. Compare this with some industrial distributorships, who offer different levels of discount to different customers. Most try to find a middle ground, between consistent pricing and flexibility for certain key customers.

Special adjustments

A variation on price structures, *special adjustments* to list or quoted prices can be made either for short-term promotional purposes or as part of a regular deal to reward a trade customer for services rendered. Figure 11.10 shows the range of discounts and other incentives that can mean that the price paid for an item (for example home appliances) is significantly less that the list price.

As the channel of distribution becomes deeper or wider, there is a need for more structure and careful planning of special adjustments to price structures. There are three main types of special adjustment, none of which is mutually exclusive.

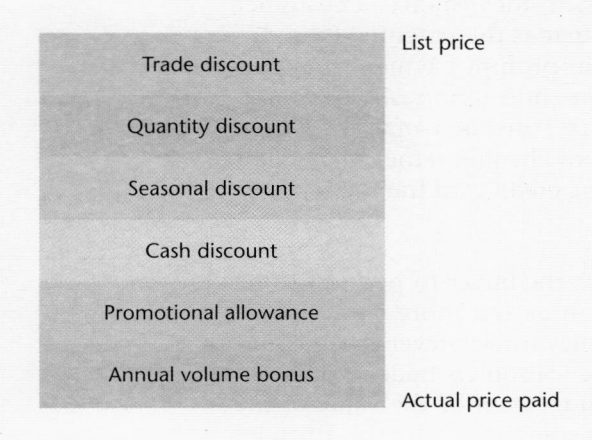

List price

Trade discount

Quantity discount

Seasonal discount

Cash discount

Promotional allowance

Annual volume bonus

Actual price paid

FIGURE 11.10

From list price to actual price

Discounts

Discounts consist of reductions from the normal or list price as a reward for bulk purchases or the range of distribution services offered. The level and frequency of discounts will vary according to individual circumstances. Blois (1994) points out that most organisations offer discounts from list prices and that these discounts form an important part of pricing strategies. There are also different types of discount.

Trade discounts. Trade discounts, sometimes called functional discounts, are based on the services the buyer (a retailer or wholesaler) is expected to perform in the future in reselling the goods. They are normally well understood between buyer and seller, and may be agreed as part of an annual negotiation. The value of the discounts depends on the services to be performed and the location of the buyer in the distribution channel. The closer the buyer is to the end consumer, the higher the service charges and the greater the discount. Different markets have their own traditional discount structures established, but of course any member may seek to violate tradition for competitive reasons.

Quantity discounts. Quantity discounts encourage bulk purchases. Bulk discounts come into force if a single order exceeds a certain volume or value level. Cumulative discounts build up over time. At the end of a trading period, the quantity purchased is totalled and a percentage rebate given back to the buyer. Both types of discount encourage larger purchase quantities, and the cumulative discount also encourages loyalty over time.

There are examples of both types of discount in consumer and organisational markets. The promotional technique of 'buy two and get a third one free' is effectively a bulk discount and is found on many products in many supermarkets. Similarly, a promotion that requires a consumer to collect tokens then send them off for a cash rebate is a form of cumulative discount. In organisational markets, a retailer may be offered a twelfth case of a product free if 11 are initially purchased (quantity discount), or a rebate on the number of cases of a product sold by the end of the trading period (cumulative discount).

Seasonal discounts. Seasonal discounts are usually offered to offset cash-flow difficulties, as discussed earlier at p. 410, or to overcome the problems of utilising capacity in quieter periods. Examples are discounts for buying heating fuel in the summer, retailers being offered discounts for stocking up on seasonal merchandise earlier, or car hire tariff reductions over weekends. Such discounts could be seen as a form of reward to the purchaser for taking on the risks of an early purchase.

Cash Discounts. Cash discounts encourage prompt payment in a form that is easiest and cheapest for the seller to handle. They can operate at all levels of all types of market. A small retailer, buying supplies from a wholesaler, may be offered a better price per case of a product if immediate payment is made than if a 30-day invoice has to be sent. A small retailer, for example, might purchase goods to the value of £1000 and the bill might specify: '£1000, 2/10 net 30'. This means that if the bill is paid within 10 days, the customer can have a 2 per cent discount on the total of £1000; otherwise the £1000 is payable in full within 30 days of the invoice date. In some cases interest may be charged if the bill is not settled after 30 days.

It can sometimes be difficult to make the rules stick. If, for instance, a customer takes the discount but pays after the 10-day deadline, there is the potential for a dispute. From the customer's perspective, the discount for prompt payment may not always be particularly attractive when compared with the short-term cash flow implications of losing the use of that money. Sometimes in consumer markets a cash discount will even be given to consumers who use cash or cheques rather than credit cards, reflecting the extra cost to the retailer of processing credit card transactions.

Allowances

Allowances are similar to discounts, but usually require the buyer to perform some additional service. Trade-in, for example, makes a transaction more complicated because it involves the exchange of a good as well as money for whatever is being purchased. It is a common practice in the car market, where consumers trade in their old cars as part exchange for a new one. The qualitative judgement of the value of the trade-in disguises the discount offered, and it is further complicated by the attitudes of the respective parties. A car that is an unreliable liability to the owner may have potential to a dealer with a particular customer in mind or a good eye for scrap. The owner thinks he is getting a good deal on the old car, while the dealer thinks he can actually recoup the trade-in value and make a bit more besides.

Promotional allowances, often used as trade incentives, mean that a retailer can be rewarded for participating in point of sale promotions, or joint advertising, through cheaper or free goods. The retailer also reaps the added benefit of the synergy gained from being associated with the promotional activities of leading brands.

Geographic adjustments

Geographic adjustments are those made, especially in organisational markets, to reflect the costs of transport and insurance involved in getting the goods from buyer to seller. In consumer markets, they can be seen in the case of mail order goods, which carry an extra charge for postage and packing.

In organisational markets, the terms of delivery and what is or is not included in the price need to be established in advance as part of the negotiated contract. An ex-works price does not include any delivery costs; effectively the buyer collects. A price quoted as FOB (free on board) means that the seller is obliged to deliver the goods to some agreed point, be that an airport, a railhead, a goods depot or whatever, and then the buyer bears the charges from there. A price quoted as CIF (cargo, insurance, freight) generally means that the seller incurs all costs to the buyer's door.

Zoned pricing relates price to the geographic distance between buyer and seller. A DIY warehouse, for example, might add a £5 delivery charge to any destination within five miles, £7.50 for up to 10 miles, £10 for up to 15 miles and so on, reflecting the extra time and petrol involved in delivering to more distant locations. Operating a single zone means that the delivery price is the same regardless of distance, as is the case with the domestic postal service, that charges on the weight of letters rather than the destination. The international mail service does, however, operate on a multiple zone basis, dividing the world up into areas and pricing to reflect different transport costs.

From a marketing perspective, the key decision is the extent to which freight costs can be absorbed, and the extent to which they can be used as a negotiating tool with customers. It is an especially critical question for a smaller organisation as it begins to develop business outside its home market.

ISSUES IN PRICING

There are several issues connected with pricing that should be considered in the setting and managing of prices in organisational markets.

Deutsche Telekom

The controversy surrounding the German government's decision to allow Deutsche Telekom (DT) to reduce prices by up to 39 per cent for corporate accounts is typical of reactions in markets that are regulated to protect them from unfair competition. The reduction followed cuts of 30 per cent in call rates to Scandinavia and the USA in 1995.

Increasing deregulation across Europe in telecommunications has created the opportunity for new private operators to enter the market, usually alongside a dominant operator that either is state owned or has been recently privatised. In Germany, companies such as Veba, RWE and Mannesmann were encouraged to enter the market to create competition, but they later felt that they had been betrayed. The decision to allow DT to cut prices threatened to undermine the competitors' own operations because of pressure on margins. The group of private operators complained to the EC that allowing these discounts to be given was anti-competitive, as it distorted competition. Furthermore, they felt that it might even

force them to leave the market, and would thus create an even stronger long-term dominance for DT. DT had debts of DM 125 bn in 1995, and so, as competitors claimed, could hardly justify such heavy price discounting from a profitability perspective. The chief executive of DT, Ron Sommer, however, hoped that 'the pleasure of using the phone will be increased by using these discounts'. In other words, the increased volume of calls would compensate for the lower margin made on each call.

The German minister of telecommunication granted permission for the new discount structure for heavier phone users, as long as DT agreed to spend DM 10 bn in completing the digitalisation of the country's telecom network. Such digitalisation is necessary for more advanced applications, such as the Internet in the home. The prime beneficiaries would be residential rather than business users who were, in the main, already networked.

Sources: Lindermann (1996); Narbrough (1995).

Negotiating prices

In organisational markets and even in some consumer situations where high-value purchases such as cars are involved, *negotiation* usually takes place. This determines the final price agreed between the parties and the nature of the offer package that will be provided for that price. Negotiation is therefore concerned with the communication processes that take place between the two parties to arrive at a mutually acceptable bargain. Lysons (1993, p. 215) defined negotiation as:

> **'any form of verbal communication in which the participants seek to exploit the relative strengths of their bargaining positions to achieve explicit or implicit objectives within the overall purpose of seeking to resolve the identified areas of disagreement.'**

Many negotiations revolve around price and/or cost trade-offs with the rest of the commercial package offered. Thus a buyer may agree to pay a slightly higher price than he had intended if the seller agrees to deliver more quickly than originally suggested.

Baily (1987) identified four main situations where negotiation may be used:

1 an established supplier wants to increase the price or to change the offer package;
2 the buyer wants an established supplier to reduce the price or to change the offer package;
3 a potential supplier wants to oust the existing supplier;
4 there is no regular supplier and it is a new task purchase.

On a slightly smaller scale, hotel managers regularly have to negotiate deals with organisations for conference and banqueting contracts. Issues such as accommodation, menus, local transport, facilities and the overall price all have to be agreed and offer considerable scope for discussion.

Rolls-Royce was seeking to cut production costs by 30 per cent in order to remain competitive in the aero-engine market. Cuts of that magnitude could only be achieved, however, if suppliers were also prepared to cut their prices to Rolls-Royce, as components account for 80 per cent of the cost of an engine. This would all require extensive negotiation with suppliers, who might be prepared to drop prices in return for guaranteed orders over a long period. At that time Rolls-Royce had just won a 157-engine deal with Singapore Airlines, their largest in 25 years (Lorenz, 1995).

Increasingly, negotiation is part of the continual exchange process that characterises a long-term business relationship. In these situations both parties may seek co-operative negotiation. This is where a win–win deal, with both parties getting something that they want, is the best outcome, as it is in the interests of both parties for the relationship to continue. There is little point in one party obtaining a short- term advantage that might lead to longer-term mistrust and poor supply from the other. If, for example, a buyer who purchases a large proportion of the total output of a small firm drives prices down to a level that is uneconomic for the small supplier, supply problems and even discontinuities might start to occur. Such problems might arise because the small supplier compromises on quality or processes in order to meet the new tighter cost targets.

In other situations, there may be competitive negotiation, where neither party has any real intention of creating a long-term relationship. These deals can easily become win–lose deals where one or other party gains at the expense of the other. For example an organisation purchasing a second-hand piece of capital machinery cannot expect the seller to be concerned with the long-term reliability of that equipment. It is up to the buyer to check out and assess the state of that machinery. Sometimes, competitive negotiations break down completely and neither party gains anything. The seller fails to sell and the buyer fails to buy, and effectively this is a lose–lose arrangement!

There are many potential areas of the offer that might have to be negotiated, and Fig 11.11 highlights typical areas of concern. Of course these will vary from situation to situation. The key skill in effective negotiation is the ability to negotiate elements of the package in terms of a trade-off. Thus the trade-in allowance may be increased if payment is made in total up front, or a discount may be increased if the customer collects the item at their own expense. Not all elements of negotiation will involve price, but virtually all of them will involve cost. A good negotiator will concede on areas that cost a little, but are highly valued by the other party. An organisation selling a photocopier

FIGURE 11.11

Negotiation variables

might agree to send out an engineer within two hours of any repair call, in order to secure a higher price for the machine. The buyer gets the peace of mind of knowing that they will not be left with a broken-down photocopier for too long and will feel that the slightly higher purchase price is thus justified, while the seller will be confident that the machine is so reliable that the agreement will never, or rarely, be put to the test!

Generally, the more the buyer is locked in to the supplier's specification, the more limited the alternative sources and the greater the urgency of demand. This tends to enhance the negotiating position of the supplier. There is more on negotiation, and the relative power balance between the negotiating parties in Chapter 18.

Tendering and bidding

Tendering is another feature of pricing in organisational markets. Tenders are offers made by suppliers concerning the price, terms and conditions of supply. The successful supplier's tender then may form the basis of detailed negotiation to finalise the terms of the deal, but with the clear understanding that they will be awarded the contract. Tendering is widely used in capital goods purchasing where large sums are involved. Many services ranging from training contracts and management consultancy to cleaning and plumbing can be purchased through tenders. Some invitations to tender are restricted to approved or selected suppliers, while others are open to any organisation that wants to bid. A large organisation, for example, may encourage a wide range of smaller businesses to bid for its catering or cleaning services, although fairly strict criteria may be applied to eliminate the weaker bids. Tenders are often advertised in the relevant trade press. *Construction News*, for example, contains details of private and public tenders called for, both in the UK and in the EU. Thus invitations to tender may range from a request to bid in Spanish for multi-dwellings in Pinto (Spain) requiring a 24-month completion, to a request for bids to join a select number of contractors undertaking environmental improvement through road and landscaping work at Waterloo station in London.

The first phase of the tendering process is normally an initial expression of interest. The buyer will let it be known, perhaps through advertisements in relevant trade publications, that they are about to begin a particular purchasing process, and will invite potential suppliers to express an interest in submitting a tender. This is effectively a pre-qualification stage, as the buyer can weed out potential suppliers with a dubious reputation or those who are unlikely to be able to meet the technical or commercial requirements. The remaining potential suppliers who have expressed an interest in the contract can then be invited to prepare and submit a formal tender, a process that in itself can involve much time, effort and expense.

Example

When Railtrack called for expressions of interest in the development and supply of a signalling system for the West Coast main line, 17 expressions of interest from across the world were received. Only nine organisations were selected to prepare formal tenders, including Siemens, ABB and GEC Alsthom. All nine were based in Europe. Railtrack, after the eight-week bidding period, intended to offer contracts to at least three of the bidders. This is because the work required was so wide ranging and complex that no one organisation would be likely to be able to do it all better than anyone else (*Modern Railways*, 1995).

Not all tendering involves a pre-qualification stage or a multi-tiered process. It may be a one-attempt offer where the supplier must estimate likely competitor prices and bids, depending on how badly they want the business. Wimpey won a £6 mn contract to build a new hospital in Wigan. In a five-horse race, only £650 000 separated the lowest from the highest bidder, and Wimpey's happened to be the lowest bid. The highest was around £7 mn.

It is not always the lowest tender that wins, however. A buyer might consider a certain bid too low, and might doubt the bidder's ability to deliver what they promised at an acceptable quality level. Sometimes, therefore, a buyer might feel that a higher price is worth paying to be more certain of the outcome and to cut down the risk of potential problems as the project unfolds.

Contracts for the supply of industrial machinery will invariably involve tendering.

Source: Vauxhall Motors Ltd.

The tendering might end, as in many of the examples quoted above, with further negotiation to finalise the fine detail of the contract. It is also possible, however, usually where smaller jobs are involved, for the buyer to ask for sealed bids. This means that the winning supplier is selected with a minimum of contact, and thus there is no further negotiation of terms. The buyer either takes or leaves the supplier's original offer. In these cases, potential suppliers seek to influence the tendering process well before the formal invitations to tender are issued. By building contacts, influencing specifications and raising its reputation, a supplier may feel that its total offering, not just its price, might receive a more sympathetic hearing from the buyer when it comes to analysing the formal tenders. This, of course, raises issues of what constitutes fair and ethical practice, as discussed in Chapter 4.

Transfer pricing

In larger organisations, there is often a considerable amount of internal trading between different divisions of the company and across national boundaries. A typical car manufacturer may concentrate production of engines, body parts and transmission systems in different divisions and in different locations. Fiat and SKF both have transfer price arrangements for 'selling' parts and finished products respectively to other parts of their own organisations. Transfer prices are thus used to cover the movement of goods or services across organisational boundaries. These prices may be set at commercial rates, based on full overhead recovery and profit criteria, or at a reduced rate agreed within the group. Where transfer prices cover the movement of goods across national or trading bloc boundaries, there is clearly scope to use them creatively as a means of shifting funds around the world with the maximum tax advantages. With different rates of corporation tax in different countries, prices can be manipulated to minimise the organisation's total tax liability.

According to Livesey (1976), there are three different types of transfer prices:

Negotiated prices

With *negotiated prices*, business units or divisions are encouraged to act in a semi-commercial manner in determining transfer prices to other business units. This means negotiation between the two parties, but there are dangers in this approach. If one buying unit decides that it can get a better deal elsewhere, another part of its own organisation may be left with idle capacity, with the result that overall profits suffer. The organisation may avoid this problem by making it compulsory to source internally. This, however, distorts the negotiating position by creating a captive buyer and a captive seller, both of whom know that they will have to reach some kind of agreement.

Market prices

External (*market*) prices are used as a guide to what the buying unit should be prepared to pay. They are commonly used in organisations where business units act as profit centres and therefore cannot afford to give away their outputs too cheaply to other business units. Unfortunately, as this and the last chapter have shown, there may be some debate as to what exactly constitutes a representative price, given the various trade-offs that are possible. List prices or average prices rarely reflect market reality.

> ### Example
>
> Nokia Data, the Finnish computer company that is part of the Nokia group, built its European growth strategy around an approach that gives considerable pricing discretion to local managers in each country. However, the organisation still needed to develop a fair transfer price arrangement that took into account the various local pricing conditions across Europe. It was thus agreed that each local business unit would pay a transfer price set at its local market price less the appropriate local margin of 30 per cent to 40 per cent.

Cost-based systems

The previous methods of transfer pricing have taken the line that the transfer price should reflect what the component concerned is worth either to the buying unit of the organisation or to the end customer. In contrast, the *cost-based systems* approach looks simply at what it cost to produce the component. There are many options within this approach, based on marginal cost, full cost or marginal cost plus a percentage for overhead recovery. The problem with this approach is that it does not reflect market changes or lower cost structures elsewhere. It also does not reflect the opportunity cost of the production capacity used, especially where limits are being reached. In other words, the business unit supplying the component might have external customers clamouring to buy more at much higher commercial prices than the internal cost-based market pays. If the supplying unit cannot expand its capacity or divert sales from the internal to the external market, then it might be losing out severely on a profit opportunity. With a cost-based pricing method, it cannot make up for any of that lost external business through higher internal prices. Despite these weaknesses, this approach is the most popular of all those on offer.

Given all these complications and the lack of any ideal method of transfer pricing, some organisations are happy to allow business units to purchase from the best source, whether internal or external to the organisation. Across Europe, different nations have different policies towards intra-organisational transactions. In the Netherlands, for example, special provisions for determining taxable profit can eliminate distortions caused by transfer pricing so that, for tax purposes, the terms and conditions are comparable to those imposed on transactions between unrelated parties. If there is a doubt, therefore, market prices can be used to ascertain appropriate prices for tax purposes. Similar principles apply in Germany and controls can be stringent. If a German subsidiary company is burdened with costs and expenses that do not reflect the market situation or conditions that could reasonably be imposed on third parties, then the tax authorities can become involved.

CHAPTER SUMMARY

This chapter focuses on the process of setting prices and managing the pricing process. The first step in price setting is the consideration of the organisation's pricing objectives, whether they relate to *financial targets* or *sales targets*. Financial targets can centre on either profit or cash flow. Sales objectives can relate to desired market share and the organisation's position within the market, or to volume sales targets. Pricing, along with the other elements of the marketing mix, can be used to influence both sales and consumers' perceptions of products.

Other influences on pricing objectives involve strategic assessment of the market and the organisation's position within it, and analysis of competitors' likely response to price decisions. Organisations have to weigh up the risks, however, of triggering a price war where price competition leads to a downward spiral of price cutting, risking the health of all parties. For organisations in trouble, the possibility of dropping prices as a temporary survival mechanism might be a means of keeping the business intact.

Any estimates of demand in the market have to be put into the context of what the individual organisation can be expected to achieve. *Marginal analysis* is one method of finding an optimum level of production that covers costs and makes a profit. A simpler, more realistic approach to looking at the relationship between costs, profit and production volume is *breakeven analysis*. This calculates the volume of sales required, at a given price, to cover costs and begin to make a profit. It is then up to the organisation to work out whether it can produce (at least) that volume and whether it has the marketing skills to sell so much.

This information, along with an evaluation of competitors' activities, can guide the organisation towards appropriate pricing strategies, methods and tactics. *Skimming* (high, premium pricing signalling a quality good) and *penetration* (pricing low to gain large market share quickly) are examples of possible strategies for launching new products on to the market. Pricing an individual product also has to take the context of the rest of the *product mix* into account, as well as the pricing moves made by *competitors* within the market.

Methods of arriving at prices can either be cost based (operationally centred), demand based (customer centred), or competition based (copying or differentiating from the rest). In practice, some consideration is given to all three methods as all these elements are central to successful marketing strategy. Pricing tactics allow the organisation to take advantage of short-term or unique opportunities by manipulating price to offer discounts, allowances or geographic adjustments to individual customers or groups of customers.

In most organisational markets and in some consumer purchasing situations, *negotiation* may be necessary to arrive at a final price. Negotiation tends to trade off price against other elements of the total offering, in that the seller is trying to obtain the highest price possible in return for features, benefits or services that are valuable to the buyer, but cost little to the seller. In an ideal situation, therefore, both parties come away from the negotiation feeling reasonably happy that they have achieved a bargain that gives them most of what they want. This is particularly important if the buyer and seller are part of an ongoing business relationship, and will have to trade with each other again in the future.

In organisational markets, potential suppliers are sometimes asked to *tender* or bid for a contract. This means that the supplier offers a price along with details of what the buyer can expect for that price, and the buyer decides which supplier should get the contract. Sometimes invitations to tender are open to any bidder, sometimes they are restricted to a chosen few, selected on the basis past history, areas of expertise or reputation. Contracts are not always awarded to the lowest bidder, as issues of risk reduction, quality of service and reliability may enter the decision. Very large companies with a number of different operating divisions or with multinational subsidiaries might also become involved in *transfer pricing*. Transfer prices may be used as a means of moving money from one country to another, or from one profit centre to another, and thus do not necessarily relate closely to open market prices.

Key words and phrases

Breakeven	*Pricing method*	*Skimming*
Discount	*Pricing policies and strategies*	*Tendering*
Mark-up		*Transfer pricing*
Penetration	*Pricing tactics*	
Price objectives	*Psychological pricing*	

QUESTIONS FOR REVIEW

11.1 Define the various stages involved in *setting prices*.

11.2 List the *financial objectives* that might be achieved through pricing decisions and outline the ways in which pricing might help to achieve them.

11.3 How can pricing help to achieve *marketing* and *sales objectives*?

11.4 In what circumstances might a high price be justified for a *new product launch*?

11.5 What factors might prompt an organisation to initiate either a *price cut* or a *price rise*?

11.6 What are the possible responses for an organisation facing a *competitor's price cut*?

11.7 What contribution can:

(a) marginal analysis; and

(b) breakeven analysis

make to the pricing decision?

11.8 What are the advantages and disadvantages of *cost-based pricing methods*?

11.9 Why are *discounts* an important feature of organisational product pricing for both the seller and the buyer?

11.10 Define *transfer pricing* and summarise the various available methods of calculating a transfer price.

QUESTIONS FOR DISCUSSION

11.1 Define *penetration pricing* and find an example of an organisation that has used it for one of its products.

11.2 How can organisations justify charging *different prices* for different products within their product ranges?

11.3 Define three methods of *psychological pricing*, then find and discuss examples of each one in practice.

11.4 To what extent and why do you think that a marketing manager's pricing decision should be influenced by the competition's pricing?

11.5 Develop a checklist of five important points that you would like a sales representative to bear in mind when trying to achieve a favourable outcome from price negotiation with a potential customer.

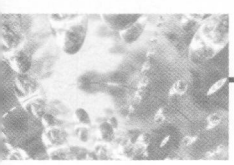

Summer of CD price discontent

The CD as a recorded music format was launched in 1983, and by 1994 enjoyed a 70 per cent share of the UK's £800 million recorded music market. Within this market, however, a few very large organisations dominated. EMI, PolyGram, WEA/Warner and CBS/Sony together accounted for about 62 per cent of CD sales on the supply side, while W. H. Smith, Our Price, Virgin, Woolworth and HMV dominated the High Street. There had been a background rumbling of discontent about CD prices for some time, however. Table A shows a range of estimates of how the price of a CD breaks down. The media picked up on this in the summer of 1993 and fuelled the debate, pointing out that a chart CD cost £12.99, whereas a vinyl record, which cost about the same to produce, cost only £8.50. It was suggested that consumers were well aware of this differential and were annoyed by it.

TABLE A

Estimates of the price breakdown of a CD

	A	B	C
Manufacture	£1.05	£1.00	£0.58
VAT	£2.27	£2.45	£1.93
Artist		£0.69	£1.02
Publisher	£1.76*	£0.64	£0.64
Producer			
Packaging and distribution		£1.13	
Record company	£4.66	£3.38	£5.32
Retailer	£3.25	£4.70	£3.50
Total Price	£12.99	£13.99	£12.99

* Covers artist; publisher and producer.
Sources: A: Ashworth (1993); B: Lynn and Olins (1993); C: Hidalgo (1993).

As well as making the kind of price comparison across formats that is shown in Table A, the media were also quick to point out that a CD selling at £11.99 in the UK can be bought in the USA for £8.54. Perhaps more seriously, the industry also came under pressure from its retailers. W. H. Smith openly said that CDs were overpriced and that this had led to a 10 per cent decline in recorded music sales between 1991 and 1993. They wanted to see an immediate £2.00 price cut by the manufacturers. W. H. Smith were adamant that the root of the pricing problem lay with the suppliers:

> 'We have got to find a way of getting prices down enough to change the perception among 80 per cent of customers that CDs are expensive. We have only 30p profit left after the price cuts we make.' (Murray, 1993)

Woolworth too were critical of the industry,

> 'We guarantee that the price of our CDs is the cheapest on the High Street, but we can't go any lower unless the industry cuts its prices too.' (Murray, 1993)

But the British Phonographic Industry (BPI), which represents the recording companies, stood its ground on pricing levels. BPI argued that prices had actually fallen by 33 per cent in real terms. If prices of CDs had kept in line with inflation since their launch, by 1993, the average price of a CD would have been £19.52 rather than £12.99. They also argued that the recording business is such a high-risk business that many of the gains are wiped out. They alleged that about 80–85 per cent of all new recordings are unsuccessful, so that one successful CD has to carry the losses of nine others.

BPI also maintained that advances and royalties to artists had soared since CDs were introduced, thus increasing costs. A House of Commons National Heritage Select Committee, however, heard evidence from Andy Dodd, of *Simply Red*, that the BPI figures on artists' earnings were overinflated. He also questioned the BPI figure for the cost of manufacturing a CD. BPI quoted £1.05, whereas Mr Dodd said that he knew of a company that could do a production run of 10 000 units for 58p each.

The issue becomes further confused if the question of the cost of actually recording the material is considered. As David Mellor, the former National Heritage Secretary pointed out, record companies produce a wide variety of material, often at a high initial investment. An opera might cost £250 000 to record, yet only sell a few thousand copies.

As far as the comparison of prices in the UK and the USA goes, BPI argued that UK prices for most goods are generally much higher than those in the USA and so CDs are not actually out of line. BPI further pointed out that although the UK is the fourth-largest music market in the world, it is still only one-quarter of the size of the US market in which overheads, such as transport and energy, are lower and catalogues are more limited. UK record shops stock a much wider range of titles, but sell fewer of them, thus increasing costs.

Let us leave the last word on a contentious issue to a columnist writing in *The Times*:

> '*The simple fact is that CDs are sold everywhere in the world at precisely the price which the local market will stand. They are luxury items. If you think they are too expensive, don't buy them.' (Morrison, 1993)*

Sources: Ashworth (1993); Hidalgo (1993); Lynn and Olins (1993); Morrison (1993); Murray (1993); Sherman (1993); *Sunday Times* (1994).

Questions

1 What pricing strategy are the manufacturers adopting on CDs and what conditions allow them to maintain this strategy?

2 What do you think of the BPI's defence of CD prices?

3 Evaluate the options open to the manufacturers in terms of:
(a) short-term pricing tactics; and
(b) longer-term pricing strategies.

4 To what extent do you agree with the sentiment expressed by *The Times* columnist in the last paragraph?

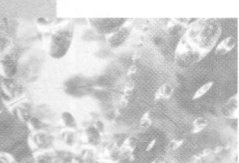

CASE STUDY 11.2

Lucerne Hotel and Conference Centre

The Lucerne Hotel and Conference Centre is situated near Lucerne in Switzerland. Originally, it was a hotel offering both short- and long-stay accommodation to tourists, whether as part of a tour package or as passing trade. The hotel only had 90 beds, thus making it small by international standards, and a fairly limited range of amenities. Nevertheless, it managed to achieve nearly full occupancy between June and September. A high proportion of the hotel's business came from tour operators, offering high occupancy but low prices. The main attraction of the hotel is its setting. Facing south, overlooking Lake Lucerne with the Alps beyond, the restaurant, the compact grounds and many of the bedrooms offer breathtaking views. The management feel that this helps to compensate for the smaller number of amenities on offer. Unlike some other hotels, they cannot offer a swimming pool, choice of restaurants,

or easy access to Lucerne. Travelling times are around 25 minutes to Lucerne and 50 minutes to Zurich.

In 1995, to try to overcome the problems of seasonality, and to generate higher margin business than that brought by the tour operators, the owner, Mr Fischer, decided to convert the hotel to an international conference centre. From his contacts in the trade, he knew that this was a growth market around Europe, and he felt that with its superior location, his hotel could exploit this opportunity. Although a number of hotels attracted conference business, there were no direct competitors in the immediate area. The Lucerne Hotel and Conference Centre was, therefore, launched after a number of modifications and improvements to the premises had been completed. Although the number of bedrooms dropped to 80, the full specification offered was as shown in Table B.

TABLE B

Facilities of the Lucerne Hotel and Conference Centre

Room name	Size (m²)	Boardroom layout (seats)	Theatre layout (seats)	Location (floor)	Daylight	Lake view	Syndicate rooms
Lucerne	240	75	230	Ground	Yes	Yes	Yes
Brigg	170	65	90	1st	Yes	Yes	No
Chur	90	20	40	Ground	Yes	Yes	Yes
Interlaken	62	18	35	Ground	Yes	No	Yes
Zermatt	43	16	30	Ground	Yes	No	Yes

The syndicate rooms tended to be small, holding around 10 to 15 people. The conference centre offered modern furnishings, extensive audio-visual equipment, unlimited coffee and home-made biscuits and pastries and a degree of privacy that is considered essential for a successful conference. The remaining 80 bedrooms were set at a standard somewhere between those found in three and four star hotels and included a desk, individually controlled central heating, colour television, direct dial telephone, private bathroom and an electric blanket.

The promotional material of the centre also claimed to offer healthy eating and an international cuisine to suit all tastes. Special dietary needs could be catered for and the timing and meal plan could be varied according to the needs of the corporate client. The amenities, although limited, included a games room, offering table tennis, a piano, sauna/solarium in a small fitness centre, and arrangements could be made to use the facilities at a local indoor tennis club. Finally excursions could be arranged to local beauty spots and transport from the international airport at Zurich could also be arranged for a client through a local company.

An enquiry was received for an international conference from a major Swiss food manufacturer. The potential client wanted to hold a European sales conference in just three months' time, starting on a Tuesday evening and extending to Friday lunchtime.

Delegates would be arriving from all over Europe for the four-day, three-night conference. The expected number would be 60, but this could rise to nearer 70 if local Swiss HQ staff decided to stop over for some of the nights. Although a large number of rooms would be single occupancy, a number of guests were expected to bring their partners and could extend their stay over the weekend.

The conference requirement specified in the original letter of enquiry was for a large room holding at least 90 and three rooms holding 30. A detailed timetable for the conference suggested full board, i.e., breakfast, a buffet lunch and full evening meal plus accommodation. Mr Fischer contemplated asking the client's events manager to visit the centre to see whether a deal could be finalised.

Questions

1 How should Mr Fischer respond to the client? Should he simply quote them a price for the conference or should he be prepared to negotiate a price for the conference?

2 If he decided to negotiate, what factors would Mr Fischer have to consider in preparing for the meeting?

3 What information would each party ideally like to have about the other before negotiations begin?

REFERENCES TO CHAPTER 11

Ashworth, J. (1993), 'Critics Turn Up the Volume Over Compact Disc Prices', *The Times*, 15 May.

Ashworth, J. (1995), 'Declaration of Air Fare War on Routes to the Far East', *The Times*, 4 January.

Baily, P. J. H. (1987), *Purchasing and Supply Management*, (5th edn.), Chapman & Hall.

Batchelor, C. (1996), 'Price War Forces Freight on to Roads' *Financial Times*, 13 June, p. 25.

Baumol, W. J. (1965), *Economic Theory and Operations Analysis*, Prentice Hall.

Blatterg, R. C. and Neslin, S. A. (1990), *Sales Promotion: Concepts, Methods and Strategies*, Prentice Hall.

Blois, K. (1994), 'Discounts in Business Marketing Management', *Industrial Marketing Management*, 23(2), pp. 93–100.

Carnegy, H. (1995), 'Low Costs and High Ideals Hold Icelandair on Course', *Financial Times*, 12 April.

Cater, B. (1995), 'Tunnel Tempts Time Savers', *The Times*, 12 October, p. 33.

Cheeseright, P. (1995), 'Price Chill Leaves Manufacturers in the Cold', *Financial Times*, 24 February, p. 10.

Darwent, C. (1996), 'Bangers and Cash', *Management Today*, June, pp. 72–4.

Dean, J. (1950), 'Pricing Policies for New Products', *Harvard Business Review*, 28 (Nov.), pp. 45–53.

Diamantopoulos, A. and Mathews, B. (1995), *Making Pricing Decisions: A Study of Managerial Practice*, Chapman & Hall.

Griffin, M. (1994), 'Imports Cut into Dutch Flower Power', *Financial Times*, 5 August, p. 22.

The Grocer (1995), 'Building on an Old Fashioned Image', *The Grocer*, 4 November, p. 41.

Hidalgo, L. (1993), 'Recording Industry is at War Over High British Retail Costs', *The Times*, 16 April.

Hinde, S. (1995), 'Retail Giants Rout Cut-Price Rivals', *Sunday Times*, 25 June, p. 1–18.

Kehoe, L. and Taylor, P. (1996), 'Apple Left With Few Options as Strategy Turns Sour', *Financial Times*, 12 January.

Lambin, J. J. (1993) *Strategic Marketing: A European Approach*, McGraw-Hill.

Levy, D. T. (1994), 'Guaranteed Pricing in Industrial Purchases: Making Use of Markets in Contractual Relations', *Industrial Marketing Management*, 23(4), pp. 307–13.

Lindermann, M. (1996), 'Deutsche Telekom Discounts Approved', *Financial Times*, 12 March, p. 2.

Livesey, F. (1976), *Pricing*, MacMillan.

Lorenz, A. (1995), 'Cut Prices, Rolls Tells Its Suppliers', *Sunday Times*, 19 November, p. 2.2.

Lynn, M. and Olins, R. (1993), 'Music Giants Tremble as George Battles Sony', *Sunday Times*, 17 October.

Lysons, C. K. (1993), Purchasing, *M&E Handbooks*, (3rd edn.), Pitman Publishing.

MacArthur, B. (1995), 'Readers Win the Price War', *The Times*, 14 June, p. 32.

Modern Railways, (1995). 'Railtrack Shortlists West Coast Main Line Signalling Bidders', *Modern Railways*, August, p. 506.

Monroe, K. B. and Della Bitta, A. J. (1978), 'Models for Pricing Decisions', *Journal of Marketing Research*, 15 (Aug.), pp. 413–28.

Morrison, R. (1993), 'Perfect Sound – But Too Much Interference', *The Times*, 15 May.

Moskal, B. (1994), 'Consumer Age Begets Value Pricing', *Industry Week*, 21 February, pp. 36–40.

Murray, I. (1993), 'Monopolies Commission to Investigate CD Prices', *The Times*, 15 May.

Nagle, T. T. (1987), *The Strategies and Tactics of Pricing*, Prentice Hall.

Narbrough, C. (1995), 'Telekom Forecasts Trebled Profits', *The Times*, 9 June, p. 28.

Parkes, C. (1993), 'Heavyweight Feels the Pain of Recession', *Financial Times*, 29 April.

Perks, R. (1993), 'How to Win a Price War', *Investor's Chronicle*, 22 October, pp. 14–15.

Sherman, J. (1993), 'Pop's Millionaires Lead Clamour for Cheaper CDs', *The Times*, 16 April.

Sunday Times (1994). 'Flawless CDs Show Record Damage', *Sunday Times*, 7 August.

Walker, A. (1994), 'Club Med Revises Pricing Strategy', *Hotel and Motel Management*, 4 April, pp. 6 and 45.

Part V

. . .

PLACE

Marketing Channels **12**

Retailers and Wholesalers **13**

Physical Distribution and Logistics Management **14**

Place, or distribution, can become the element of the marketing mix which causes the biggest headache to a manufacturer. The other three mix elements remain under the manufacturer's control, but once the product is out of the factory gate, it is at the mercy of the middlemen within the distribution channel. Chapter 12 defines the main types of distribution channel available to manufacturers and discusses the advantages or otherwise of each. There are, of course, strategies through which the manufacturer can minimise the risks inherent in poor channel management, and Chapter 12, therefore, also focuses on both the importance of cultivating good relationships within distribution channels and where possible, ways of gaining and maintaining control over channel members.

Chapter 13, in contrast, centres on the retailer as the main interface between manufacturer and end consumer. Retailers face particular problems, such as choice of location, merchandising and image development, which are all discussed in this chapter. Many of these problems are, at heart, centred on making decisions on elements of the marketing mix, but the application in retailing gives them a different and interesting angle.

Chapter 14 looks at the logistics function. This involves the way in which orders are processed and how goods are moved most cost effectively from the manufacturer through the distribution channel to the end customer. As markets become geographically bigger, ensuring that the logistics function operates fficiently and smoothly becomes even more important if customers are going to receive what they want, when they want and where they want it.

■ ■ ■

12 Marketing Channels

LEARNING OBJECTIVES

This chapter will help you to:

1 define what a channel of distribution is;

2 understand the role of the channel and its important contribution to efficient and effective marketing effort;

3 differentiate between types of intermediary and their roles;

4 appreciate the factors influencing channel design, structure and strategy; and

5 understand the potential for co-operation and conflict within channels, and the effects of both positive and negative uses of power.

INTRODUCTION

Part of the responsibility of a marketing-orientated organisation is to get the product to the customer in the right place at the right time. This has led to the development of extremely efficient and sophisticated distribution systems. Imagine what life would be like for a consumer without those familiar distribution systems. The onus would be on us as consumers to find out what is being supplied, when and where. Without the back-up of a customer orientation, issues of supply, location, timing, quantity and assortment would all be resolved to suit the supplier's, not the customer's, abilities and preferences. This is fine, as long as demand outstrips supply and consumers are prepared to invest considerable time and even money in sourcing goods. Such a scenario is not impossible. Before the changes in eastern Europe, a consumer's first activity after finishing work was often to join the queues for essential items of food such as bread.

This indicates the importance of a sound distribution infrastructure both in the structure of a modern economy and as a tool in the marketing mix, and provides the main theme of this chapter. This topic is often referred to as 'place' to cover the decisions and strategies that enable the product to flow to the consumer, whether from the market, direct to the home, via a wholesaler or from a retail outlet.

Example

The motor industry in Europe is a good example of the complexity surrounding the design, building and maintenance of distribution channels. Europe has over 470 million people and of 155 million cars. It also has over 30 manufacturers supplying national sales organisations in each of 24 countries, who in turn supply more than 100 000 retail outlets. In Germany alone, there are 17 000 dealers and 9000 sub dealers, while in France there are 4000 main dealers and

19 000 sub-dealers. In the UK, the figures stand at 6700 and 600, respectively. Assuming that around 13 million cars are sold each year in Europe, that means an average of around 130 cars per outlet, although this will vary widely between different countries and car manufacturers. If this is compared with an optimal average of 600 new cars per outlet to justify the necessary investment in premises, equipment and staffing, there is clearly considerable scope for change and rationalisation (Mullineux, 1995). The car manufacturers, therefore, are concerned with a whole range of decisions in order to remain competitive, yet provide good customer service and achieve marketing objectives through their distribution channels.

The chapter begins with a definition of channels of distribution, highlighting the role played by different types of intermediaries, and looks at the relative merits of using intermediaries compared with direct selling. Attention then turns to the strategic decision making necessary to design and implement a channel strategy. While the main emphasis will be on the manufacturer selecting a channel structure and strategy to achieve market coverage and marketing objectives, the power of the intermediary should not be forgotten. In many countries, the power of negotiation rests with the intermediary who may select or deselect manufacturers' products. Such action has a major impact on the manufacturer, but little impact upon the intermediary.

Although channels of distribution are important economic structures, they are also social systems involving individuals and organisations. This chapter, therefore, also considers issues associated with the general conduct of the relationship. Such relationships may be characterised by conflict, co-operation, trust or a climate of mutual hostility and discontent, despite the economic pragmatism that binds both parties together.

Of course in service situations, there is no product movement or storage because production and consumption are normally simultaneous. In that case, the channel of distribution is primarily concerned with providing access to the booking and reservation system and in handling the sales and negotiating process associated with such access (*see* Chapter 23). The emphasis in this chapter, therefore, will be the movements of physical goods.

DEFINITION OF MARKETING CHANNELS

A **marketing channel** can be defined as the structure linking a group of individuals or organisations through which a product or service is made available to the consumer or industrial user. The degree of formality in the relationships between the channel members can vary significantly from the highly organised arrangements in the distribution of fmcg products through supermarkets, through to the more speculative and transient position of roadside sellers of fruit and vegetables.

Example

It is interesting to compare the highly developed food distribution systems in western Europe with those struggling to emerge in Romania. The Netherlands Bacon Association, for example, has introduced a *Royal Crest* quality assurance scheme, covering all parties in the distribution chain from the pig farmer to the consumer, including pig traders, slaughterhouses and the retail trade. This guarantees a level of quality that both multiple retail chains and consumers demand. Thus not only is the product available when and where the consumer demands it, but the standards in quality, taste and consistency also provide extra reassurance (*The Grocer*, 1995a). Meanwhile, in Romania, products do make their way through the food chain, but there is little feedback from customers and an unsophisticated retail structure that involves few regular supportive trading relationships (Morton, 1993)

There are several different types of **intermediary**, each with a slightly different role. These will now be defined, and then we shall look at the ways in which these intermediaries come together to create different kinds of distribution channels between manufacturer and consumer. As a means of summarising all of this, this section will finally consider the rationale for using intermediaries at all.

Types of intermediary

Many marketing channels involve the physical movement of goods and the transfer of legal title to the goods, although the physical movement may be separate from the change of title, especially if external transport carriers are used. As the goods pass from hand to hand, each intermediary adds a *margin* to the price of the goods which may or may not reflect the value added. Various functions are performed by the various types of intermediaries in return for their margins. Some purchase an assortment of products from various suppliers and then add value by storing, breaking bulk, and then adding services (e.g., credit, delivery) during the resale process. In some situations, product transformation may take place, especially in packaging and in the image of the product which may be enhanced by in-store promotion.

However, not all intermediaries between the manufacturer and consumer necessarily take legal title to the goods, or even physical possession of them, as the following descriptions show.

Wholesalers

Wholesalers do not normally deal with the end consumer but with other intermediaries, usually retailers. However in some situations sales are made directly to the end user, especially in organisational markets, with no further resale taking place. An organisation may purchase its catering or cleaning supplies from a local cash and carry business that serves the retail trade. A wholesaler does take legal title to the goods as well as taking physical possession of them.

Retailers

Retailers sell direct to the consumer and may either purchase direct from the manufacturer or deal with a wholesaler, depending on purchasing power and volume. Retailers come in many different formats, sizes and locations as we shall see in Chapter 13.

Distributors and dealers

Distributors and dealers are intermediaries who add value through special services associated with stocking or selling inventory, credit and after-sales service. Although these intermediaries are often used in organisational markets, they can also be found in direct dealing with consumers, for example computer or motor dealers. The term usually signifies a more structured and closer tie between the manufacturers and intermediary in order that the product may be delivered efficiently and with the appropriate level of expertise. Clearly, some retail outlets also are closely associated with dealerships and the distinction between them may be somewhat blurred.

Franchisees

A franchisee holds a contract to supply and market a product or service to the design or blueprint of the franchisor (the owner or originator of the product or service). The franchise agreement covers not only the precise specification of the product or service, but also the selling and marketing aspects of the business. The uniformity of, different branches of McDonald's is an indication of the level of detail covered by a franchise agreement. There are many products and services currently offered through franchise arrangements, especially in the retail and home services sector, considered in Chapter 24.

Agents and brokers

Agents and brokers are intermediaries who have the legal authority to act on behalf of the manufacturer, although they do not take legal title to the goods or indeed handle the product directly in any way. They do, however, make the product more accessible to the customer and in some cases provide appropriate add-on benefits. Their prime function is to bring buyer and seller together. Universities often use agents to recruit students in overseas markets.

The specific role of each channel member will vary depending on a range of market and strategy issues. The next subsection looks at how these intermediaries relate to each other, and discusses further the specific roles that each plays in getting goods to end users.

Channel structure

The route selected to move a product to market through different intermediaries is known as the *channel structure*. The chosen route varies according to whether the organisation is dealing with consumer or organisational goods. Even within these broad sectors, different products might require different distribution channels.

Consumer goods

The four most common channel structures in consumer markets are shown in Fig 12.1. As can be seen, each alternative involves a different number of intermediaries, and each is appropriate to different kinds of markets or selling situations. Each one will now be discussed in turn.

Producer–consumer (direct supply). In the producer–consumer channel, the manufacturer and consumer deal directly with each other. There are many variants on this theme. It could be a factory shop, or a pick-your-own fruit farm. Some manufacturers sell direct to the public through mail order. The increasing cheapness and ease of setting up customer databases (to be discussed in detail in Chapter 19) mean that direct selling by telephone or mail order is becoming a more attractive distribution option.

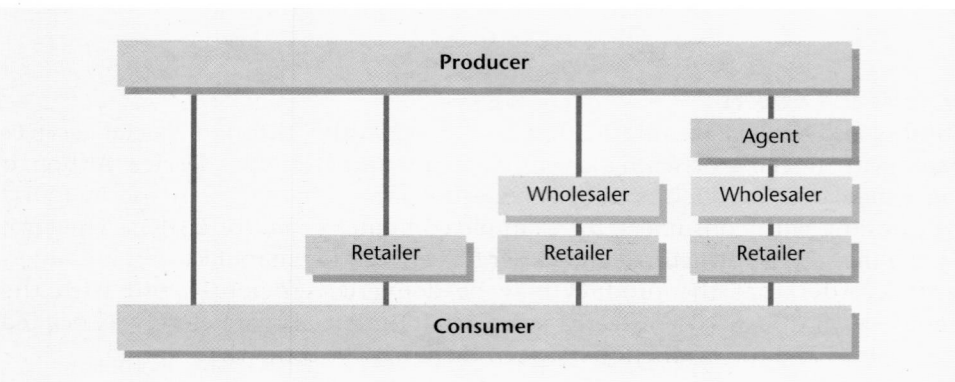

FIGURE 12.1

Channel structures for consumer goods

Alternatively, goods may be sold through a network of sales offices. Door-to-door selling, such as that practiced by double-glazing companies, and party-plan selling, such as Tupperware and Ann Summers parties, are all attempts by producers to eliminate intermediaries. Clearly this route has the advantage of control and simplicity, but this must be weighed against the cost and resource efficiency of directly building a company-owned sales and distribution force.

Producer–retailer–consumer (short channel). The producer–retailer–consumer route is the most popular with the larger retailers, since they can buy in large quantities, obtaining special prices and often with tailormade stock handling and delivery arrangements. This route is typically used by large supermarket chains and is most appropriate for large manufacturers and large retailers who deal in such huge quantities that a direct relationship is efficient.

Figure 12.2 shows a highly simplified form of the goods and information flow between a manufacturer and a retailer. The fast capture and processing of information is critical for the efficient and effective functioning of such systems. Tesco, for example, has automated its business chain to such a degree that orders, invoicing and payments are all triggered by shoppers passing through the checkouts.

In the car trade, a local dealer usually deals directly with the manufacturer, because unlike fmcg products, there is a need for significant support in the supply infrastructure and expertise in the sales and service process. This is an example of the grey area between retailing and distributorships, discussed at p. 451.

Producer–wholesaler–retailer–consumer (long channel). The advantage of adding a wholesaler level can be significant where small manufacturers and/or small retailers are involved. A small manufacturing organisation does not necessarily have the skills or

FIGURE 12.2

The flow of products and information between a large manufacturer and a large retailer

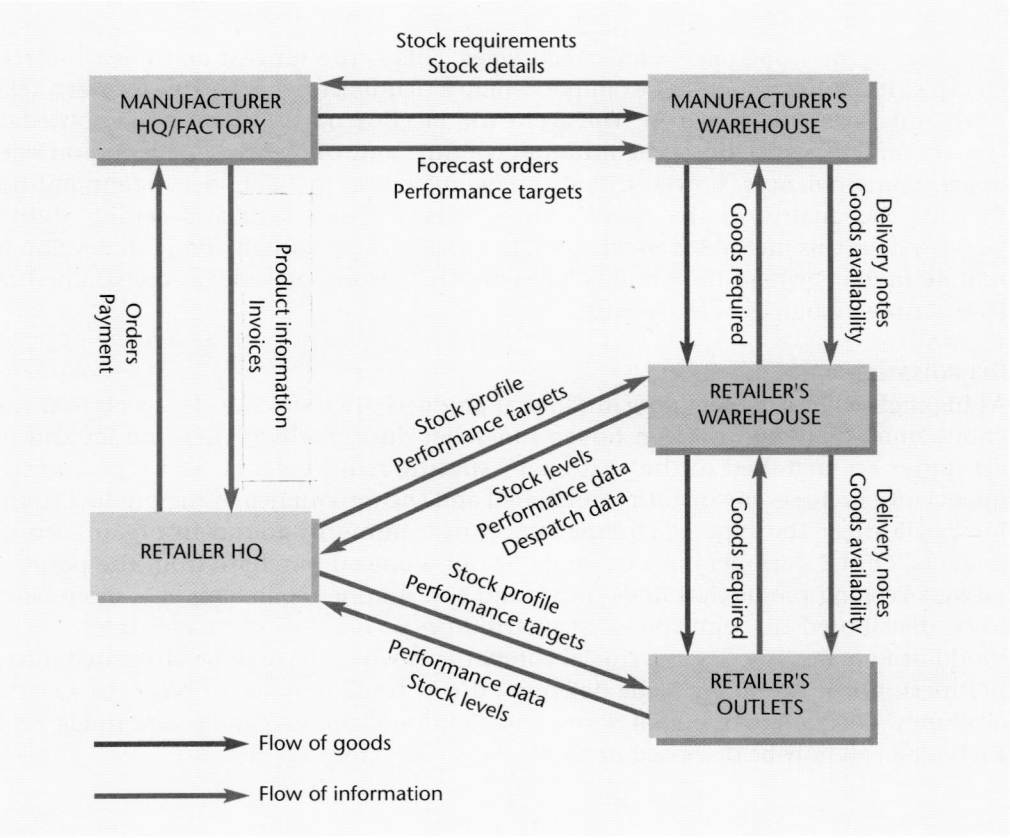

resources to reach a wide range of retail customers, and similarly, the small corner shop does not have the resources to source relatively small quantities direct from many manufactures. The wholesaler can provide a focal point for both sides, by buying in bulk from manufactures, then splitting that bulk into manageable quantities for small retailers; bringing a wider assortment of goods together for the retailer under one roof; providing access to a wider range of retail customers for the small manufacturer; and similarly providing access to a wider range of manufacturers' goods for the small retailer. Effectively, the wholesaler is marketing on behalf of the manufacturer.

Example

Sugro UK, a Nantwich-based wholesale group which is part of a German-based parent company, is an amalgam of 84 wholesalers and cash and carry operators specialising mainly in confectionery, snacks and soft drinks. They service 43 000 outlets including 16 000 CTNs (confectionery, tobacco, news establishments), 6500 convenience stores, 2400 petrol forecourts, and around 5000 pubs. The advantages for small independent retailers sourcing from the group are mainly linked with the group's centralised bulk buying from major manufacturers, the availability of Sugro own brands on some lines, as well as an efficient and comprehensive stocking and delivery service (Gilbert, 1995).

The wholesaler can also act on behalf of relatively large manufacturers trying to sell large volumes of frequently reordered products to a wide retail network. Daily national newspapers, for example, are delivered from the presses to the wholesalers who can then break bulk, and assemble tailormade orders involving many different titles for their own retail customers. This is far more efficient than each newspaper producer trying to deal direct with each small corner shop newsagent.

Producer–agent–wholesaler–retailer–consumer. This is the longest and most indirect channel. It might be used, for example, where a manufacturer is trying to enter a relatively unknown export market. The agent will be chosen because of local knowledge, contacts and expertise in selling into that country, and will earn commission on sales made. The problem is, however, that the manufacturer is totally dependent and has to trust the quality of the agent's knowledge, commitment and selling ability. Nevertheless, this method is widely used by smaller organisations trying to develop in remote markets where their ability to establish a strong presence is constrained by lack of time, resources or knowledge.

Organisational goods

As highlighted in Chapter 4, organisational products often involve close technical and commercial dialogue between buyer and seller during which the product and its attributes are matched to the customer's specific requirements. The type and frequency of purchase, the quantity purchased and the importance of the product to the buyer all affect the type of channel structure commonly found in organisational markets. Office stationery, for example, is not a crucial purchase from the point of view of keeping production lines going, and as a routine repurchase, it is more likely to be distributed through specialist distributors or retailers such as Staples, Office World or Rymans. In contrast, crucial components which have to be integrated into a production line are likely to be delivered direct from supplier to buyer to specific deadlines. The variety of organisational distribution channels can be seen in Fig 12.3. Each type will now be discussed in turn.

FIGURE 12.3

Channels structures for organisational markets

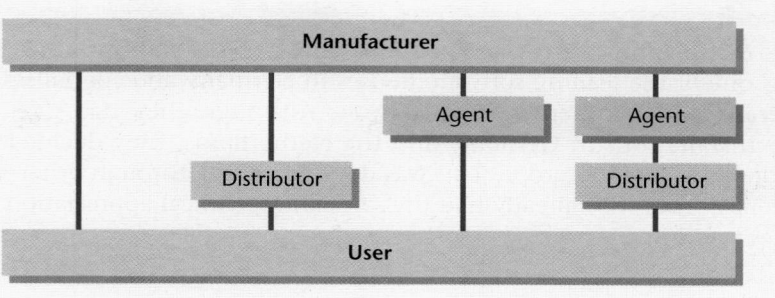

Manufacturer–user. The direct channel is most appropriate where the goods being sold have a high unit cost and perhaps a high technical content. There is likely to be a small number of buyers who are perhaps confined to clearly defined geographical areas. To operate such a channel, the manufacturer must be prepared to build and manage a sales and distribution force that can negotiate sales, provide service and administer customer needs. In some cases, the sales representative will both sell and install the product, as happens with computer software applications.

Manufacturers may also operate their own sales branches or offices. These organisations are owned and operated by the manufacturer, but fulfil many of the functions and roles of a wholesale operation. They allow the manufacturer to retain more control over the way in which the distribution channel works, and can increase the effectiveness and efficiency of the links between manufacturers and their customers, but they also may be a necessity if the manufacturer needs wholesale services that are not available on the open market.

Example

AB Konstruktions-Bakelit, one of Sweden's largest manufacturers of industrial plastic components, deals directly with customers such as Volvo, Saab and Alfa Laval. This is because of the need for considerable dialogue during the design and development stage to ensure a close fit between the customer's specification and components that are made to order. There would be a very high risk of misunderstanding if a third party were introduced.

Sales branches tend to be situated away from the manufacturer's head office in areas where demand is particularly high. They are a conveniently situated focal point for the area's sales force, providing them with products and support services so that they in turn can better meet their customers' needs more quickly. Sales branches may also sell products themselves directly to small retailers or wholesalers.

Sales offices do not carry stock, so, although they might take orders from local customers, they are only acting as agents and will pass the order on to head office. Again, they provide a locally convenient focus in busy areas.

Manufacturer–distributor–user. Less direct channels tend to be adopted as the number of customers grows, the size of customers reduces, and the number of intermediary functions also increases. Building materials, for example, are often sold to builders' merchants, who then sell to the building trade based on lower order quantities, and consequently with a greater range of stock availability but greater proximity to local need. The philosophy is similar to that of the short channel of distribution discussed in the consumer context above.

This less direct type of structure can also apply to software products. Moser GmbH is one of the leading software houses in Germany and specialises in selling to trade and handicraft organisations. Although they had over 10 000 software installations in Germany and the Netherlands, they decided to seek expansion elsewhere in Europe. This was done by selling through other software and system houses who already had the sales and technical appreciation to generate sales for Moser.

Manufacturer–agent–user. Sometimes an agent is introduced to act on behalf of a group of manufacturers in dealing with users in situations where it would not be economically viable to create a direct selling effort, but where there is a need for selling expertise to generate and complete transactions.

Teijo Pesukoneet from Nakkila in Finland specialise in technically advanced cleaning machines for metal components in enclosed cabinets. Although they have their own sales offices in Sweden and Norway, they operate through agents in other main European markets such as the UK and Germany. Agents are trained to handle technical queries and sales enquiries but relay orders to Finland for direct delivery.

Generally speaking, agents do not take title to goods, but may buy and sell, usually on a commission basis, on behalf of manufacturers and retailers. They facilitate an exchange process rather than participating fully in it. They tend to specialise in particular markets or product lines and are used because of their knowledge, or their superior purchasing or selling skills, or because of their well-established contacts within the market. The distinction between an agent and a broker is a fine one. Agents tend to be retained on a long-term basis to act on behalf of a client, and thus build up working rapport. A broker tends to be used on a one-off, temporary, basis to fulfil a specific need or deal.

The main problem with agents is the amount of commission that has to be paid, as this can push selling costs up. This cost has to be looked at in context and with a sense of proportion. That commission is buying sales performance, market knowledge and a degree of flexibility that would take a lot of time and money to build for yourself, even if you wanted to do it. The alternative to using agents, therefore, may not be so effective or cost efficient.

Manufacturer–agent–distributor–user. A model comprising manufacturer–agent–distributor–user links is particularly useful in fast moving export markets. The sales agent co-ordinates sales in a specified market, while the distributors provide inventory and fast restocking facilities close to the point of customer need. The comments on the longest channel of distribution in the consumer context (*see* p. 454) are also applicable here.

The type of structure adopted in a particular sector, whether industrial or consumer will ultimately depend on the product and market characteristics which produce differing cost and servicing profiles. These issues will be further explored in the context of the main justification for using marketing intermediaries, described next.

Telmat

Telmat is a pharmaceutical intermediary that can act as both agent and distributor, offering trading and consultancy networks. Although based in Switzerland, it serves the needs of distribution channels in eastern Europe. In January 1993, for example, the main manufacturer of the drug Digoxin in the Czech Republic encountered problems and could not distribute the required amount. The Ministry of Health asked Telmat to source extra supplies. Using its contacts, Telmat was quickly able to negotiate with Procter & Gamble, who own a French manufacturer of Digoxin, to fulfil the need. Telmat claims that within 30 days it was able to:

- acquire 250 000 extra boxes of Digoxin
- translate the instruction leaflets into both Czech and Slovakian
- obtain the necessary drug registration certificates
- transport the goods to Prague and then within 24 hours to other parts of the republic.

Thus the organisation not only acted as an intermediary linking buyers and sellers (i.e., an agent), but also provided the kind of logistical services expected of a wholesaler or distributor.

Source: European Purchasing and Materials Management (1994).

Rationale for using intermediaries

Every transaction between a buyer and a seller costs money. There are delivery costs, order picking and packing costs, marketing costs, and almost certainly administrative costs associated with processing an order and receiving or making payment. The role of the intermediary is to increase the efficiency and to reduce the costs of individual transactions. This can be clearly seen in Fig 12.4.

If six manufacturers wished to deal with six buyers a total of 36 links would be necessary. All of these transaction links cost time and money to service, and require a certain level of administrative and marketing expertise. If volumes and profit margins are sufficient, then this may be a viable proposition. However, in many situations this would add considerably to the cost of the product. By using an intermediary, the number of links falls to just 12, and each buyer and each seller only needs to maintain and service one link. If this makes sense when considering only six potential buyers, just imagine how much more sensible it is with fmcg goods where there are millions of potential buyers! On economic grounds alone, the rationale for intermediaries in creating transaction efficiency is demonstrated.

However there are other reasons for using intermediaries, because they add value for the manufacturer and customer alike. These value added services fall into three main groups (Webster, 1979), as shown in Fig 12.5.

FIGURE 12.4

The role of intermediaries

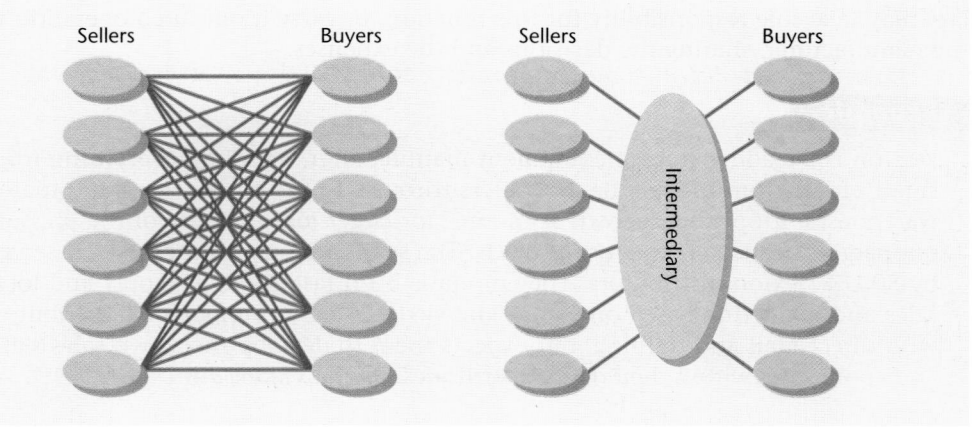

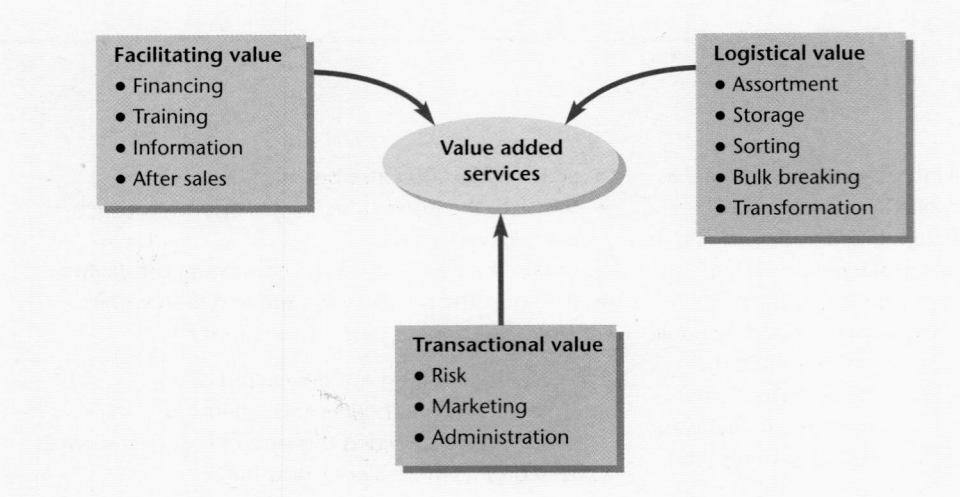

FIGURE 12.5

Value added
services provided
by intermediaries

Transactional value

The role of intermediaries in assisting transaction efficiency has already been highlighted. To perform this role adequately, the intermediary, as an interconnected but separate entity, must decide upon its own strategic position in the market-place, and therefore assemble products that it believes its own desired customers need and then market them effectively. The selection is extremely important, and requires careful purchasing in terms of type, quantity and cost to fit the intermediary's own product strategy.

The *risks* move to the intermediary, who takes *title* to the goods and as legal owner, is responsible for their resale. Of course, it is in the manufacturer's interest to see the product moving through the distribution system in order to achieve sales and profit objectives. However, the risk of being lumbered with obsolete, damaged or slow moving stock rests with the intermediary, not the manufacturer. This is a valuable service to that manufacturer.

With the transfer of title and risk, the need to *market effectively* increases. Intermediaries may recruit and train their own sales forces to resell the products they have assembled. This is another valuable service to the manufacturer as it means that the product may have a greater chance of being brought to the attention of the prospective customer, especially in organisational markets. An intermediary can use the full range of promotional weapons available, including advertising, point of sale promotion and direct mail (*see* Chapters 16, 17 and 19). An industrial distributor may have a sales counter or a telephone sales operation, or it may have an external field sales force to sell the product in question (Anderson and Narus, 1986). The intermediary may take sole responsibility for this function, or carry it out in co-operation with the manufacturer, sharing the decisions and the expenses.

Example

Dexion is a leading storage equipment manufacturer, handling everything from small orders from independent retailers through to fitting out large automated warehouses. It operates its own sales force for larger jobs, because of the pressure on margins in such competitive projects. The small user market, however, is served by 50 UK Dexion distributors. The emphasis is on fast ex-stock supply and local sales and marketing based on sound knowledge. Dexion supports its distributors with direct mail and training, but expects them to develop their own sales skills and approaches within their defined territories (*Business Marketing Digest*, 1991).

Logistical value

A critical role for the intermediary is the assembly of an *assortment of products* from different sources that is compatible with the needs of the intermediary's own customers. This assortment can operate at product or brand level. A drinks wholesaler, for example, may offer a full range of merchandise from beer to cognac, but within each category considerable brand choice may also be offered. The benefit to the customer is the wide choice available from one source, supported perhaps by a competitive and comprehensive pre and post-sales service. However, for other intermediaries the choice of assortment may be more limited. If one manufacturer occupies a dominant position, the choice of competing brands may be severely restricted to just complementary products. In many car dealerships, for example, only one manufacturer's new cars can be sold, although there might be more flexibility over second-hand cars.

Assortment strategy is a critical variable in a retailer's marketing strategy. The key is to build an assortment to reflect the needs of the target market.

Example

Assortment strategy can be clearly seen in the music business. Some stores specialise only in classical or rock and associated sheet music. Others aim to provide a little of everything, but primarily concentrate on the best sellers in CD and tape. A further group aim to provide depth of range by covering many older, slower moving titles.

There are risks in any of these strategies of misjudging changes in customer fads or tastes. This is particularly noticeable in high fashion areas where even the sale rails do not move assortments that have been left behind. The trend, however, in a society where disposable incomes are increasing, is for deeper choice within more specialised assortments, whether the all-Japanese store in North London or cuckoo clock shops in Berne.

A further dimension of logistical value is the *accumulation and storing of products* at locations which are appropriate and convenient to the customer. The small manufacturer can make one large delivery of output to the wholesaler's warehouse, where it can be stored until a retailer wants it, and broken down into smaller lots as necessary. The hassles of transporting small quantities to many different locations, finding storage space and insuring the goods are taken away from the manufacturer.

Example

A walk around a back-street market in Sofia, reveals row upon row of sellers with small tables offering piles of undifferentiated home-grown carrots or turnips and little else, a far cry from the town centre markets in the UK or France. By using intermediaries, farmers or market gardeners do not need to find their own markets. A fruit and vegetable wholesaler can accumulate small quantities of different products from specialist growers, sort them, and then make larger deliveries of assorted goods to the next point in the chain, thus gaining economies in transport costs. This can also open up opportunities for wider variety within the retail chain. A typical French supermarket, for example, might offer 200 different types of cheese and over 80 charcuterie items.

Sorting is a very basic step in the logistical process, and means grouping many different diverse products into more uniform, homogeneous groups. These groups may be based on product class and further subdivided by such factors as size, shape, weight and colour. This process may also add value by *grading*, which means inspecting,

Going Dutch

In 1997, the Dutch are introducing a radically new way of distributing fresh produce into their major markets in order to improve competitiveness. Traditionally, growers supplied foreign importers through an auction system, from which produce was then moved on into international markets. Prices could vary considerably at auction because of fluctuations in supply and demand. From January 1997, supermarkets around Europe will be able to buy Dutch produce direct, on long-term fixed prices rather than through importers. Initially, VTN (a new marketing organisation) will operate in six product areas, including fruit, tomatoes, cucumbers and field vegetables. Although prices will vary on a weekly basis, there is an opportunity for buyers to deal directly with the growers via VTN, and for growers to become more closely involved in the movement of their products.

VTN will operate direct sales teams to handle enquiries and to process orders. It will also designate distribution depots in the Netherlands and in its main European markets in order to offer cost savings and shorter delivery periods. These centres will also add value by packing and grading and gathering produce from the growers. Not all growers, however, agreed to participate in the new system, preferring to retain the old auction system. It thus remains to be seen how the system will work and whether the proposed benefits will be realised.

Source: *The Grocer* (1996).

testing or judging products so that they can be placed into more homogeneous quality grades. These standards may be based on intermediary or industry predetermined standards. Large supermarket chains, for example, are particularly demanding about the standardisation of the fruit and vegetables that they retail. If you look at a carton of apples in a supermarket, you will see that they are all of a standard size, colour and quality. Mother Nature hasn't quite worked out how to ensure such uniformity, so the producers and wholesalers have to put the effort into sorting out and grading the top quality produce for the High Street. The second class produce ends up in less choosy retail outlets, while the most irregular specimens end up in soup, fruit juices and ready meals.

A further important role for the intermediary, as already implied, is **bulk breaking**, the division of large units into the smaller, more manageable quantities required by the next step in the chain. Whereas a builder's merchant may purchase sand by the lorry load, the small builder may purchase by the bagged pallet load, and the individual consumer by the individual bag. The value of bulk breaking is clear to the DIY enthusiast who certainly would not wish to purchase by the pallet load. There is, of course, a price to pay for this convenience, and the consumer would expect to pay a higher price per bag purchased individually than the builder would pay per bag purchased by the pallet load.

A final role is in actually *transporting the product* to the next point in the chain. Lorry loads may be made up of deliveries to several customers in the same area, thus maximising the payload, and with careful siting of warehouse facilities, minimising the distances the products have to travel. Again, this is more efficient that having each manufacturer sending out delivery vans to every customer throughout the country.

Facilitating value

The intermediary also offers a range of other added value services either to the manufacturer or to the customer. Not only do intermediaries share the risks, as outlined above, they also provide a valuable *financing* benefit. The manufacturer only has to manage a small number of accounts (for example with two or three wholesalers rather than with 200 or more individual retailers) and can keep tighter control over credit periods, thus improving cash flow. As part of the service to the consumer, retailers may offer credit or other financial services such as credit card acceptance, easy payment terms and insurance. Manufacturers selling direct would not necessarily be interested in such financial services.

Other activities also add value. Local demonstrations and consumer *training* provided by intermediaries enable the manufacturer to avoid costly labour inputs. Market *information* and *feedback* are precious commodities, as we saw in Chapter 6. The intermediary is much closer to the market-place, and therefore alert to changes in consumer needs and competitive conditions. Passing on this information up the channel of distribution can enable manufacturers to modify their marketing strategies for the benefit of all parties. While there is no replacement for systematic, organised market research, information derived from sales contacts and meetings with intermediaries provides specific, often relevant intelligence. For the small manufacturer, with very limited market research resources, this can be particularly invaluable.

All the above functions need to be performed at some point within the marketing channel. The key decision concerns which member undertakes what role. This decision may be reached by *negotiation*, where the power in the channel is reasonably balanced, or by *imposition,* when either manufacturer or retailer dominates. Whatever the outcome, the compensation system in terms of margins needs to be designed to reflect the added value role performed.

An appreciation of added value dispels the commonly held belief that involving intermediaries simply increases the price of goods to the consumer. It also dispels the view of some small business marketers that they cannot afford to pay a margin to the intermediary, and so must deal direct. Clearly if intermediaries, especially wholesalers, were eliminated, the services provided would still need to be performed and in many cases, this would be done somewhat less efficiently. The result could be a rise in prices or a severe limitation on the availability of less popular products, or perhaps even to put smaller manufacturers out of business. If, for example, wine distributors were eliminated, retailers then would have to create trading relationships with individual wineries world-wide, and might never find out about new minor specialist wines. At the same time, immense problems would be created for wine producers in finding retail outlets, organising delivery and absorbing distribution costs.

Ultimately, the existence of intermediaries gives everyone a fighting chance of concentrating on what they are best at doing, whether that is producing, selling or consuming.

CHANNEL STRATEGY

With the various added value roles implicit in the marketing channel, decisions need to be taken about the allocation and performance of these roles, the basis of remuneration within the system and the effectiveness of alternative configurations in enabling market penetration to be achieved competitively and efficiently. This is **channel strategy**. As indicated earlier, these decisions do not necessarily revolve around the manufacturer, despite the origins of the product.

Channel structures

The basic forms of channel design were outlined in Figs 12.1 and 12.2. These are known as conventional channels, in which the various channel activities are agreed by negotiation and compromise, recognising that both sides need each other. The particular structure adopted should reflect the market and product characteristics, taking into consideration such factors as **market coverage**, value, quantity sold, margin available etc. (Sharma and Dominguez, 1992). The structure can be described by the number of levels utilised, ranging from the simplest (two layers) through to the most complex (five or more layers).

Where a manufacturer needs to reach distinct target markets, a dual or multiple distribution approach may be adopted, which means that each target market may be reached by two or more different routes. For example IBM will sell direct to large users and organisations, but will go through the retail trade to reach the consumer segment. This pattern works well, provided discreteness is maintained and as long as the arrangement reflects the various buyers' differing pre- and post-purchase servicing needs. However, problems can emerge if the same product is sold to the same target market through different channels. A book publisher, for example, may create some friction with the book trade if it actively encourages direct ordering and other subscription services at lower prices than the retail trade can manage. This potential for conflict may well increase as direct marketing and home shopping gain in popularity.

Market coverage

One way of thinking about which types of channel are appropriate is to start at the end and work backwards. The sort of questions to ask relate not only to the identity of the end customer, but also to their expectations, demand patterns, frequency of ordering, degree of comparison shopping, degree of convenience, and the associated services required. All of these elements influence the added value created by place, and the density and type of intermediaries to be used, whether at wholesaler or disributor or retail level. Market coverage, therefore, is about reaching the end customer as cost effectively and as efficiently as possible, while maximising customer satisfaction. To achieve this, three alternative models of distribution intensity can be adopted, as shown in Table 12.1, each of which reflects different product and customer requirements from place. They are discussed below, in turn.

Intensive distribution

Intensive distribution occurs where the product or service is placed in as many outlets as possible, and no interested intermediary is barred from stocking the product. Typical products include bread, newspapers and confectionery, but more generally, most convenience goods (see p. 257) fall into this category. The advantage to the consumer is that convenience and availability may be just around the corner, and they can invest a minimum of time and effort in the purchasing process. Using this kind of market coverage also assumes that availability is more important than the type of

TABLE 12.1
Alternative distribution intensities: General characteristics

	Intensive	Selective	Exclusive
Total number of outlets covered	Maximum	Possibly many	Relatively few
Number of outlets per region	As many as possible	A small number	One or very few
Distribution focus	Maximum availability	Some specialist retailer knowledge	Close retailer/ consumer relationship
Type of consumer product	Convenience	Shopping	Speciality
Number of potential purchasers	High	Medium	Low
Purchase frequency	Often	Occasionally	Seldom
Level of planned purchasing by consumers	Low	Medium	High
Typical price	Low	Medium	High

store selling the product, hence the growth of non-petrol products on sale in garages. However, if a product is on sale in every corner shop, it can be difficult for the manufacturer to ensure that the product is being maintained to the desired standard. This may not be a problem with canned or packaged goods, but with more perishable refrigerated or frozen foods, for example, the manufacturer's quality standards may be seriously compromised by poor handling. Even minor irritations can affect the consumer's attitude and satisfaction. In Poland, for example, many small shops do not have the refrigeration facilities to allow them to sell ice-cold cans of Coke.

Example

In Moscow the situation is far worse. Although food and other products are now widely available for those with money, the majority of Muscovites are locked in to more primitive systems. With very low levels of car ownership, weekly supermarket shopping presents major 'logistical' problems. There are still, therefore, many small local stores, 1600 small mixed grocery shops and 2300 specialists such as butchers, bakers, fruiterers and 8000 'kiosks' providing the main source of CTN goods. The whole market is ripe for change (Whitworth, 1995).

Intensive distribution usually involves a long chain of distribution (manufacturer–wholesaler–retailer–consumer). It is an efficient means of getting the product as widely available as possible, but total distribution costs may be high, especially where small retailers are concerned and unit orders are low.

Selective distribution

As the term suggests, a more selective approach is designed to use a small number of carefully chosen outlets within a defined geographic area. These are often found with shopping products (again, *see* p. 258) where the consumer may be more willing to search for the most appropriate product and then to undertake a detailed comparison of alternatives. Unlike intensively distributed goods, which can virtually be put on a shop shelf to sell themselves, selectively distributed products might need a little more help from the intermediary, perhaps because they have a higher technical content that needs demonstrating, for instance. Manufacturers may also need to invest more in the distribution infrastructure, point of sale materials, and after sales service. It may thus pay to select a smaller number of intermediaries, where support such as training and joint promotions can be offered and controlled.

Example

The major fine fragrance manufacturers have long adopted a selective distribution strategy. Their rationale for this is that they are selling a luxury, upmarket product which needs to have an appropriate level of personal selling support and the right kind of retail ambience to reinforce and enhance the product's expensive image. In the early 1990s, they repeatedly refused to supply discount chemist chains such as Superdrug in the UK, who wanted to sell fine fragrances off the shelf like any other ordinary toiletry, undercutting the upmarket department stores and other existing fragrance retailers. Eventually, Superdrug resorted to obtaining supplies via the 'grey market' (i.e., not directly from the manufacturers) and provoked an extremely aggressive response from the manufacturers.

The selective distribution approach is not unique to consumer goods. An Irish distributor of tractor seats for a UK organisation was required to carry local stocks and to fit the replacement seats to conform with European safety standards. Such regulation and control is only possible if a manageable number of outlets are allowed to handle the product. The Irish distributor, therefore, had major territorial rights across the west and south-west of Ireland. It was meant to handle all replacement sales by building up relationships with farmers, farm equipment repair shops and service agents.

Exclusive distribution

Exclusive distribution is the opposite of intensive distribution, and means that only one outlet covers a relatively large geographical area. This type of distribution may reflect very large infrastructure investments, a scattered low density of demand or infrequently purchased products. In organisational markets, the impact on the customer may not be particularly significant if a sales force and customer service network is in place. However, in consumer markets there may be some inconvenience to the customer who may have to travel some distance to source the product and may effectively have no choice about who to purchase from.

> **Example**
>
> In consumer markets, the obvious example of exclusive distribution is new cars. A particular dealership will have the right to sell brand-new Ford cars, for example, within a defined geographic area. Ford goes even further in that it will not consider any multi-franchise proposal. This means that the dealer cannot sell Ford cars and Fiat cars, for example, from the same premises. Similarly, Ford will not give permission for any of its dealers to operate any motor-related business within 50 kilometres of the Ford franchise. If consumers do not like that dealership for some reason, then they will have to travel some distance to find the next Ford dealer, or else buy a Renault locally instead.

Such an exclusive approach may even fit in with the product's own exclusivity. It would also be appropriate where high degrees of co-operation in inventory management, service standards and selling effort are required between manufacturer and intermediary.

> **Example**
>
> When Mustang, an American-based manufacturer of small four-wheeled construction vehicles, wanted to build a presence in the UK market, it appointed a sole distributor offering a sales force experienced in selling small equipment into the building trade.

Influences on channel strategy

There are several alternative channel design decisions facing the manufacturer who has a choice, but there are also several factors which may constrain these choices. These factors are outlined below, and are shown in Fig 12.6. While it may be desirable to adopt an optimal design in terms of marketing effectiveness and efficiency, rarely do organisations have the luxury of a clean sheet of paper. More often, they inherit the consequences of previous decisions, and the risks of changing design midstream need to be carefully considered before any planned improvement.

Organisational objectives, capabilities and resources

The channel strategy selected needs to fit in with the organisation's objectives, capabilities and resources. If the objective is to generate mass appeal and rapid market penetration, then an intensive distribution approach would be necessary. This would have to be supported, however, with an equally intense investment in other market-

FIGURE 12.6

**Factors
influencing
channel strategy**

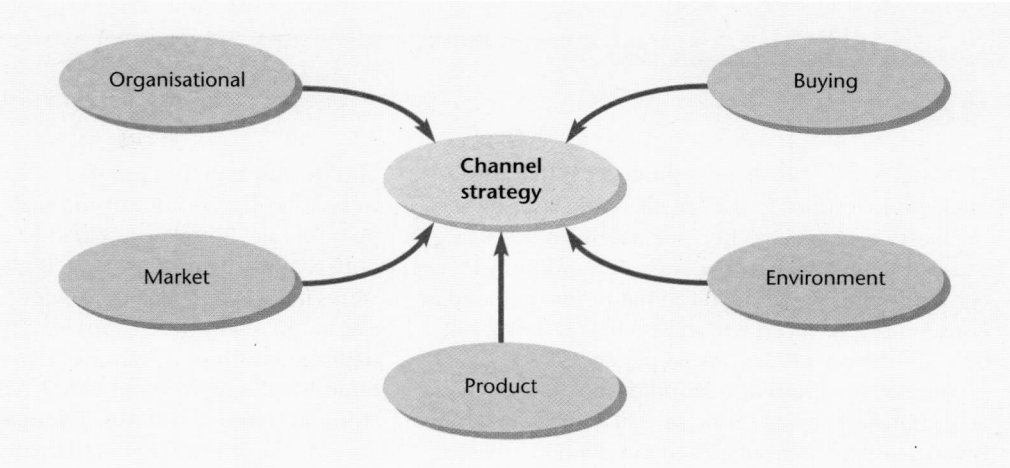

ing activities such as promotion. If the focus was on repositioning up-market into a more exclusive niche, then a selective or even an exclusive distribution approach would be called for.

An organisation that wishes to control marketing activities, and is well endowed with resources, may assume many of the channel functions directly. A small organisation with a small market share may have little choice but to concentrate on manufacture and direct dealing with an intermediary. A lack of resources and a lack of expertise and contacts may leave no option.

Objectives may change over time as environmental circumstances evolve. For example demands for an improved delivery service or increased geographical coverage may require new distributors, more distributors or incorporating better service levels in the service structure of existing distributors.

Example

The recent changes in Bulgaria present a fascinating case of how environmental factors can influence channel strategy radically. Until 1989, cars came from elsewhere in eastern Europe and distribution was completely centralised. Rarely did supply keep up with demand and there was a backlog of 600000 cars on order, in a country where car ownership reaches only just over 1 million. Despite the fact that firm orders had been placed and deposits paid, there was a strong likelihood that the cars would never be delivered. Following the changes in eastern Europe, most manufacturers now have a sales office in Sofia but there is little in the way of formal dealer networks. The nearest Bulgaria comes to that is the informal networks of car mechanics throughout the country. It remains to be seen whether this network will evolve into a franchised dealer network (Mullineux, 1995).

Market size, dispersion and remoteness

No channel strategy decision can ignore the impact of the market. If a manufacturer wishes to penetrate a market some distance from its base it may lack the contacts, market knowledge or distribution infrastructure to deal directly. There may be little choice but to deal with intermediaries. Similarly, a small organisation might lack the resources necessary for building sales contacts and maintaining customer service, especially if resources are limited and there is a need to develop sales volume quickly.

When demand is more highly concentrated, or where there are a few readily identifiable customers, it may be possible to build a direct operation, keep full control and eliminate intermediaries. Efficiency may be obtained in negotiation, delivery and

Borsalino

The trouble with being a hat producer is that the market is in long-term decline. Over the last 50 years, the wearing of hats has become a rarity in social situations and hats are now often only worn on special occasions. Borsalino, the Italian hat producer based in Alessandria, produced two million hats in 1913, but only 200 000 in 1995. Over 65 per cent of its production is exported to far-off destinations such as Seoul, Osaka and New York, as well as around Europe. When Guiseppe Petrone joined Borsalino in 1993 as Managing Director, he decided to try to relaunch the company, building on its premium image. He was quoted as saying, 'Other manufacturers produce hats – we make a Borsalino'. Borsalino is positioned alongside Ferrari, Campari and Gucci as a status product. Prices can go up to L500 000 for a man's hat.

The renewed marketing effort gave rise to a review of the marketing channel strategy. Previously, Borsalino had sold through 300 designated retailers outside Italy and through 400 retailers in Italy. In order to give itself more control and marketing push at the point of sale, Borsalino decided to open its own outlets at key centres. In 1996 it planned to open stores in locations such as Moscow, Tokyo, Berlin and Hamburg, along with 'shops within shops' in department stores in Paris, Seoul and New York. It refurbished its own shops in Milan and opened new stores in Florence and Asti. The opening of these outlets enabled closer contract with customers and an opportunity to launch new lines in the women's and youth markets where the company had a weaker presence. It also enabled a co-ordinated store identity to be developed, from which new accessories and lines such as Ecuadorian straw hats and Montecristi Panamas could be launched, drawing upon the established reputation.

Source: Simkins (1996).

support services. By way of contrast, a large dispersed market, such as that for magazines, may require a well structured, efficient chain of intermediaries.

Buying complexity and behaviour

Understanding customer needs and buying criteria goes to the heart of effective marketing and has a major influence on channel selection (Butaney and Wortzel, 1988). Questions such as who buys, where they buy, and how frequently they buy, all indicate the kind of intermediary best suited to reach target customers. Matching the intermediary with customer needs, buyer expectations and product position is a challenging task. The move to out of town shopping, with its advantages of easy parking, convenience and large assortments under one roof, has meant a refocusing of effort by some manufacturers to ensure they are well represented. Similarly, if a product occupies a specialist position, there is little point in dealing with a wholesaler who is primarily concerned with mass distribution.

Understanding the product classifications presented in Chapter 7 is also likely to influence design. Convenience, routine decisions may require much more widespread distribution than shopping goods where a more systematic evaluation of the selection criteria may suggest the type of intermediary required in terms of service, range, display and demonstration etc.

Product characteristics

Products that are complex to purchase, install or operate, products that are of high unit value and products that are customer specific tend to be distributed directly to the customer or through highly specialised intermediaries. This reflects the need for close dialogue during the pre- and post-sale situation that may be lost if additional parties are involved. By way of contrast, fairly standard, routinely purchased, low unit value products tend to be distributed intensively through intermediaries.

An important distribution channel for UK drinks and luxury products is through duty free shops and may be affected by EC regulations in the future.

Source: Le Shuttle.

Other product factors also may impact. Highly perishable products need short distribution channels to maintain product quality or to assist in rapid turnover. Items which are non-standard or difficult to handle or items that have the potential to create transport problems may be less attractive to intermediaries (Rosenbloom, 1987).

Changing environment

The changing business environment, discussed in Chapter 2, creates new problems and opportunities for channel design. Three issues demonstrate the effect.

Technology. Technology offers the potential for closer integration between the manufacturer and the intermediary. On-line systems may enable direct access to stock availability, electronic ordering and automated dispatch with the minimum of negotiation, if any. Electronic point of sale (EPOS) data can facilitate very rapid responses within the distribution system. Smaller organisations still relying on older technology such as the telephone and manual checking may soon become marginalised.

Working patterns. The growth in the number of women working has had a profound effect on some distribution channels, making some channels more difficult to operate, such as door-to-door selling during the daytime, while home shopping and convenience shopping outside usual trading hours have become much more widely accepted.

European Community regulations. Generally speaking, manufacturers have the right to decide which intermediaries should or should not distribute their products. Both national and European regulatory bodies start to become interested, however, where exclusion of certain intermediaries might be seen as a deliberate attempt to distort competition or to achieve price fixing. Chapter 10 (at p. 390) referred to the MMC's investigation of the refusal of major manufacturers to supply electrical goods to discount retailers. The outcome hinges on whether the refusal to supply is based on a legitimate concern over the quality of the retail premises and staff, or whether it is an illegal attempt to prevent retail prices falling.

Manufacturers also need to be careful over the restrictions they try to impose on intermediaries as part of a contract. They might, for example, insist that an intermediary does not carry competing products. This is usually permissible, depending on the market structure, the definition of what constitutes competition and whether there is any direct alternative available to an intermediary who does not wish to accept such a clause.

Selecting a channel member

The final phase of the channel design strategy is the selection of specific intermediaries. There may be a number of reasons why a selection decision needs to be made, some of which are not part of a new strategic formulation or realignment. Typical examples would be:

● to add more intermediaries to increase market penetration
● to replace existing intermediaries because of poor performance or contract termination
● to add new intermediaries to service a new product range
● to create a network of intermediaries for market entry.

Whatever the reason, the selection decision should be compatible with the overall channel strategy. The selection decision tends to become more critical as the intensity of distribution itself becomes more selective or exclusive. In mass distribution decisions, such as those concerning products like confectionery, any willing outlet will be considered. However, where a selective distribution approach is adopted, great care must be taken over the final selection of intermediary, as a poor decision may lead to strategic failure. For example, the selection of a wholesaler to allow entry into a new European market may be critical to the degree and speed of penetration achieved.

Example

Klemm is part of the Ingersoll-Rand group and specialises in a range of German-built piling and drilling rigs for construction sites. Klemm wanted to develop sales in the UK by more proactive methods, and so appointed a UK distributor, Skelair International, which had experience in this area, although mainly in second-hand machines. Klemm was seeking a close and effective relationship in order to penetrate the UK market, which although relatively small, demands considerable selling effort and sometimes the ability of suppliers to recommend purpose-built models for special applications (Woof, 1995).

In situations where organisations need to select intermediaries on a fairly frequent basis, it would be useful to select on the basis of predetermined criteria. Table 12.2 highlights a range of issues that should be examined as part of an appraisal process.

The relative importance of the various criteria will vary from sector to sector and

TABLE 12.2
Selection criteria for intermediaries

Strategic	Operational
• Expansion plans	• Local market knowledge
• Resource building	• Adequate premises/equipment
• Management quality/competence	• Stockholding policy
• Market coverage	• Customer convenience
• Partnership willingness	• Product knowledge
• Loyalty/co-operation	• Realistic credit/payment terms
	• Sales force capability
	• Efficient customer service

indeed over time. Inevitably, there is still a need for management judgement, and a trading off of pros and cons, as the 'ideal' distributor that is both willing and able to proceed will rarely be found.

Reverse selection

Not all manufacturers have the power or ability to design their channel strategy and to select the ideal members. Effectively, the intermediaries have the choice of whether or not they will sell the products offered. This luxury of choice is not just restricted to supermarkets and large multiple retailers. Travel agents can only stock a limited number of holidays, and are very careful about offering new packages from smaller tour operators. In some industrial distribution channels, the intermediary can decide whether or not to stock ancillary products around the main products it sells on a dealership basis.

Reverse selection also suggests that intermediaries are proactive in looking for new manufacturers to complement their supply sources, or at a minimum that they are considering whether to extend the assortment being offered. In many organisational situations it is the buyer that initiates the contact process with suppliers.

Klemm used the drilling rig expertise of its UK distributors, Skelair International, to develop sales in the UK.

Source: Skelair International.

EMERGING FORMS OF CHANNEL STRUCTURE

The traditional view of channels of distribution suggests a group of independent manufacturers and intermediaries working together within negotiated guidelines and operating functions to exploit a market opportunity. This does reflect the situation in many cases, where mutual benefit forces consensus rather than competitive behaviour between channel members.

However, a growing number of channels are being effectively led and managed by one channel member who can control the policies, strategies, actions and returns of the other members. These are called **vertical marketing systems** (VMS), and represent an advanced form of channel integration. Such integration may improve supply consistency, lower costs and lead to more effective marketing. Before we examine in more detail the various forms of channel integration, we now provide a brief review of the types of competition that may be experienced in channels. This review forms the basis for an appraisal of the benefits of integration.

Competition in channels

Not all competition in channels comes from traditionally expected direct sources, as we see from Fig 12.7. Sometimes, internal channel competition can reduce the efficiency of the whole channel system. Each of the four types of competition identified by Palamountain (1955) is considered in turn below.

Horizontal competition
Horizontal competition as can be seen in Fig 12.7, is competition between intermediaries of the same type. This type of competition, for example between supermarkets, is

---

MARKETING IN ACTION

Daewoo

Daewoo launched its cars in the UK in 1995 with a new approach to distribution. It decided to operate with its own network of sales points rather than operate through franchised dealers. The direct approach was an important part of the overall sales proposition, based on customer care and developing close relationships with customers in a way that was not considered possible through franchised arrangements. By the admission of the Daewoo Marketing Director, the car itself had no extra features: 'It's a very good bread and butter product. They are not earth-shattering cars, but they are very reliable and tremendous value for money.' The policy was that there were to be no hidden extras added to the advertised price, no price haggling, and servicing would be handled directly by Daewoo, with the customer being given complimentary use of a service car.

Despite the decision to sell direct through 12 showrooms, Daewoo also experimented with other new ways of selling cars that did not involve dealerships. A pilot scheme with Sainsbury's was developed to test car retailing from a supermarket, although it would use Daewoo's own sales staff. Literature was to be made available throughout the supermarket, and a touch screen presentation enabled more detailed information to be obtained on Daewoo. Test drives were also readily available at the store. Daewoo also launched 123 support centres in branches of Halford's, a car parts and accessories retailer, again in order to improve contact with customers.

Initial results were encouraging for Daewoo, in that the company achieved a share of the car market of just under 1 per cent in their first year. The real test perhaps would come when customers consider replacing their vehicles. Would they again buy a Daewoo?

Sources: Barrett (1996); Snowdon (1996).

readily visible. Each one develops marketing and product range strategies to gain competitive advantage over the others.

Intertype competition

Intertype competition refers to competition at the same level in the channel but between different types of outlet. Thus, for example, the battle between the department stores, the high street electrical retailers and large out of town warehouse operations to sell hi-fi equipment to the same customer base is a form of intertype competition. The manufacturer who has a choice may need to develop different approaches to handle each retailer type. Of course, there are dangers if a manufacturer is seen to give unwarranted preference to one type over another, given the intense rivalries that can develop. This may start to lead to dysfunctional channel behaviour.

The supermarket chains, for instance, were dismayed by the fact that the big brand manufacturers agreed to supply Costco, the warehouse club open to the general public, when it first set up in the UK. The argument was that the manufacturers were supplying Costco at lower prices than those offered to the supermarkets, and thus Costco could further undercut them. The supermarkets threatened to delist brands if the manufacturer did not even out the price differentials, but in the end did not carry out the threat. Even the strongest supermarket chain cannot risk being without certain key brands.

FIGURE 12.7

Competition in channels

Vertical competition

Vertical competition can soon become a serious threat to the integrity and effectiveness of a channel. Here, the competition is between different levels in the channel,

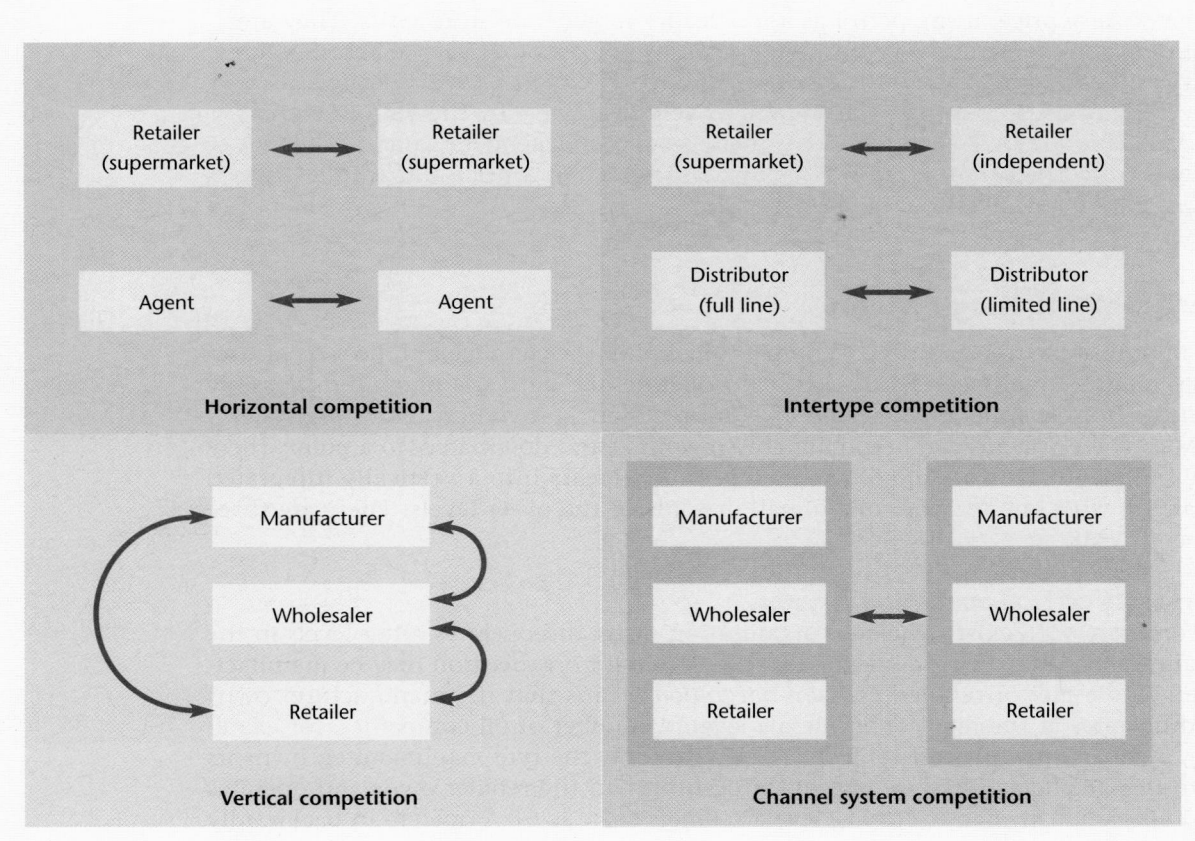

such as wholesaler and retailer, or even retailer and manufacturer. This type of competition can soon lead to internal rivalry, where the focus shifts from co-operative market penetration, focused outwards, to mutual cannibalism, focused inwards.

Channel system competition

The last form of channel competition is where a particular channel is in competition with different, parallel channels. The focus for the operator, therefore, is on ensuring that their system is more efficient and competitive than the others. The emphasis is on total channel efficiency, which may, however, involve some suboptimisation in the interests of a more effective chain.

Vertical marketing systems

To minimise the risks of internal competition within the channel and the risks of conflict, channel members, who wish to co-operate and gain the maximum possible benefits from channel membership, may form closely knit vertical marketing systems (VMS). These systems can become highly organised and dominated, to a point where the independence of some of the members disappears into a vertically integrated channel, with one member owning all or some of the other levels. There are three types of VMS.

Corporate vertical marketing systems

A corporate VMS exists where an organisation owns and operates other levels in the channel. This may be at any level, and the dominant organisation may be manufacturer, wholesaler or retailer. *Forward integration* means that the manufacturer owns and operates at the retail or wholesale level. A number of oil companies, for example, own their own petrol stations, while Firestone, the tyre manufacturer, owns its own tyre retailers. *Backward integration* occurs when the retailer owns and operates at a wholesale or manufacturing level. Retailers such as C&A operate in backwardly integrated markets.

The corporate VMS has the advantage of creating a channel that is tailormade for the owner's product and marketing objectives. Furthermore, that those objectives are shared throughout the channel. The owner also has ultimate control over the activities of the channel and its members. This situation is not always viewed favourably, however. The UK's Office of Fair Trading began to look more closely at the travel industry in late 1995, after complaints from the Consumers' Association and independent operators. The basis of the complaints was that the three top tour operators, Thomson, Airtours and First Choice each had equity links with one of the top three travel agents. Thus the Thomson group owned Thomson holidays (the UK's largest), Britannia charter airline (the UK's biggest) and Lunn Poly travel agency (also the UK's biggest). The tour operator Airtours similarly owned a charter airline, Airtours International, and a travel agency, Going Places (the UK's second-largest). Finally, the UK's third-largest travel agent, Thomas Cook, owned 21 per cent of the tour operator First Choice, and Air 2000, a charter airline. These links raised concerns as to whether consumers, unaware of the vertical integration, would really get unbiased advice or whether one tour operator's products would be sold in preference to another's (Walters, 1995).

Contractual vertical marketing systems

The most prevalent form of VMS is the contractual VMS. Members of the channel retain their independence, but negotiate contractual agreements that specify their rights, duties and obligations, covering issues such as stock levels and pricing policies, for example. This prevents unnecessary internal conflict and suboptimal behaviour. Three types of contractual system are commonly found.

Retail co-operatives. A retail co-operative exsits where groups of retailers agree to work together and to combine and increase their purchasing power by supporting their own wholesaling operation. This sort of agreement helps the small independent retailers who are members of the co-operative with greater range, access to promotion and more competitive pricing.

Wholesaler voluntary chains. A wholesaler voluntary chain is one where a wholesaler promotes a contractual relationship with independent retailers, whereby the latter agree to co-ordinated purchasing, inventory and merchandising programmes. The co-ordination enables some of the benefits of bulk buying and group promotion to be realised by smaller operators. Mace and the Independent Grocers' Alliance are UK examples.

Franchise systems. Franchising is fast becoming a major model of contractual arrangement across Europe. Franchising is an ongoing contractual relationship between a franchisor who owns the product concept and a franchisee who is allowed to operate a business, within an agreed territory, in line with the methods, procedures and overall blueprint provided by the franchisor. Managerial support, training, merchandising and access to finance are effectively exchanged for conformity and a specified fee and/or royalties on sales. Franchising will be considered again in Chapter 24.

Administered vertical marketing systems

Co-ordination and control are achieved in an administered VMS through the power of one of the channel members. It is, in reality, a conventional channel within which a dominant force has emerged. Therefore although each member is autonomous, there is a willingness to agree to interorganisational management by one of its members. Contracts may or may not be used to govern the parameters of behaviour.

Wholesaler, Spar, offers the independent grocery trade the advantages of buying power and group promotion.

Source: Spar.

Example

Marks & Spencer uses an administered VMS to forge very close links with its suppliers, and to dominate decisions about what is supplied, how it is manufactured, quality levels, and pricing. Suppliers accept this dominance because they regard M&S as a prestigious and trustworthy customer, and respect their experience of the market. Similarly, Ahold, the Dutch retailer, offers leadership within its distribution channels in terms of product development, manufacturing and purchasing.

The emergence of these integrated forms of channel system is increasingly questioning the traditional approach to channel management. They also provide a context within which behavioural aspects of channel relationships can be examined.

BEHAVIOURAL ASPECTS OF CHANNELS

Most of this chapter so far has concentrated largely on economic issues involved in channel decisions. However, all channel decisions are ultimately made between people in organisations. There is, therefore, always the potential for disagreement over the many decisions needed to ensure that the system operates effectively. Issues such as expected roles, allocation of effort, reward structures, product and marketing strategies are among those that deserve close attention. A channel is an interorganisational social system comprised of members who are tied together by a belief that by working together (for the time being at least), they can improve the individual benefits gained. The channel also offers the potential for one member to have significant impact on the position of another member, for example, the appointment by a manufacturer of a competing retailer in a town.

It is necessary, therefore, to examine the behavioural processes at work and how they are influenced by, and exert influence on channel decision making.

Co-operation and partnerships

A climate of co-operation is perhaps the most desirable within a channel system. It does not just happen, but needs to be worked on and cultivated with positive co-operation signs and signals. Co-operation can be defined as:

> 'Similar or complementary co-ordinated action taken by a firm in interdependent relationships to achieve mutual outcomes or singular outcomes with expected reciprocation over time' (Anderson and Narus, 1990).

In other words, you scratch my back and I'll scratch yours, and we shall both be better off. Boyd and Walker (1990), for example, suggest a variety of ways in which the functional performance of channel members in terms of quantities purchased, selling and promotional effort, and after sales service levels, can be enhanced by incentives.

Some view conflict and co-operation as being at opposite ends of a continuum, while others view them as distinct concepts. Whatever the view, strong co-operation can lead to a feeling of satisfaction and partnership, one of give and take. Co-operation may lead to strong personal and organisational ties that are difficult for outsiders to break. However, not all co-operation need be voluntary. A weaker channel member may think it best to co-operate and comply with the wishes of a more powerful member, rather than risk retribution.

There are many areas of potential co-operation, and Table 12.3 lists some of them.

It is best to assess co-operation in terms of who does what, an approach that requires a clear view of expected roles and functions. An overall agreed package or programme may guide the way in which channel members work together for their common benefit. This programme should be based on obtaining competitive advantage for the whole system, as well as benefiting particular links. The whole approach embodies the notion of partnership rather than competitive relationships. After all, the system is pointless unless it leads to synergies, that is, unless the members feel that they are gaining more by membership than they could achieve alone or by membership of a different system.

TABLE 12.3
Areas of co-operation

Advertising allowance	Training staff
Payment for retailer displays	Support for new store openings
Contests/competitions	Joint advertising
Merchandisers	Joint selling
Demonstrators	Joint maillings
Samples/bonus goods	Delivery costs
Local market research	Sales promotions
Special packaging/displays	Own label supply
Automatic reordering	Support with store fixtures
Returns allowance	Price promotions

Example

Such a philosophy lies behind the way in which the Francis Nicholls (FN) group operates its wholesale business. The group specialises in providing fresh fruit and vegetables to specialist fruiterers, independent retailers and convenience stores. FN's chief executive was quoted as saying,

> 'Wholesalers have the knowledge and the skill. If they are progressive they can provide a much needed service to these types of outlets ... It all adds up to substantial untapped business' (*The Grocer*, 1995c, p. 42).

FN believes that it helps to bring a wider variety of better quality merchandise to its customers as well as helping with marketing and promotions. It is also branching out into chilled and convenience foods, and will even help a retailer to buy a display cabinet.

Conflict

Conflict is a natural part of any social system. A definition of conflict is:

> 'Tensions between two or more social entities (individuals, groups or larger organisations) which arise from incompatibility of actual or desired responses' (Raven and Kruglanski, 1970).

Conflict may exist where, for example, one channel member feels that another member is not dealing fairly with it, or that the system is not working sufficiently in its favour. The key to dealing with conflict is not to allow it to continue until it reduces channel efficiency or effectiveness, or even results in legal problems. Channel conflict may be issue specific, such as discontent related to changes in margins, or may involve general confrontation on a range of issues. Clark's shoes, for instance, need to be aware of the potential for conflict as they operate a parallel distribution system. They distribute partly through their own shops, and partly through other shoe retailers. They must support both channels equally.

There are two different types of conflict, each capable of generating varying degrees of intensity in dysfunctional behaviour:

1 *Manifest conflict,* which is overt between channel members and may block goal achievement.
2 *Underlying conflict,* which, although not overt, is capable of developing into manifest conflict, but can still shape willingness to co-operate.

There are numerous possible causes of conflict, some arising from poor understanding, others from a fundamental difference of opinion that goes to the heart of the relationship. The kinds of operational problems either caused by conflict or triggering conflict are shown in Table 12.4. These problems may, however, be symptomatic of deeper pressures which can be broadly catergorised into five areas, described below.

Incompatible goals

Different channel members want different things. One, for example, may be seeking growth, while another is looking towards consolidation and stability. Their goals are incompatiable.

Role conflict

Where there is disagreement about who should do what, role conflict may arise. A manufacturer, for example, may feel that a wholesaler is not putting enough promotional effort into reselling a particular product, while the wholesaler may feel that it is the manufacturer's responsibility to promote the product overtly to the retail trade.

TABLE 12.4
Areas of conflict

• Manufacturer/retailer brands	• Delivery arrangements/schedules
• Prices/margins/discounts	• Product exclusivity
• Quality	• Contract flexibility
• Special services	• Display/promotion prominence
• Territory exclusivity	• General compliance
• Market information	• Listing money
• Direct sales	

Decision domain conflict

This is disagreement about who is in the best position to make marketing decisions. Retailers may feel that because they are closer to the end consumer than the manufacturer, they are better positioned to know what kind of point of sale material would perform well, whereas manufacturers, closer to the product, may feel that they should dictate what should be done.

Perceptions of reality

Different channel members may interpret the same phenomena in different ways and may have different perceptions of reality. The Costco example, (p. 471), for instance, shows how the brand manufacturers saw Costco as a beneficial influence in expanding their intensive distribution and better serving the consumer, while the retailers saw it as a threat to their margins and well being. This certainly caused channel conflict.

Expectations

Different channel members may have different expectations about what should happen in the future. Such conflict may include definition of the best outcomes from a situation, how to overcome resource scarcity, how to allocate resources better, or how profit margins should change in the light of a changing business environment.

Example

The danger of conflict in a channel is ever present. Sometimes, disputes can become very public. A headline in the *Observer* newspaper revealed that old milk returned unsold from retailers was being recycled and sold again to supermarkets by a supplier in the south of England. Retail giants such as Tesco, Sainsbury and Safeway, all of whom are proud of their quality image, were involved. The Department of Health and the supermarkets sent their experts to the dairy. Claims were made by an informer that the practice had grown out of the supermarkets using their buying power to obtain milk at very low prices, pressurising suppliers to cut corners. The supermarkets claimed to be unaware of what was happening, and Tesco stated that such practices were strictly against procedures and, if proven, they would take any action to ensure the integrity of supply to re-establish customers' faith in fresh milk. (*Observer*, 1995)

Sometimes policy changes can lead to potential conflicts. Dixons, the electrical retailer, decided to relaunch its own-brand PC called Advent in response to a perceived threat that the German manufacturer and retailer Vobis, Europe's largest, was planning to enter the UK market directly in 1996. Originally, Vobis had supplied an own-brand product to Dixons, but it was felt that Vobis would be planning a direct push in order to improve market share when the agreement expired in 1996 (Lee, 1995).

A similar problem could arise as Mars reconsiders its policy of not supplying own-label products. The decision to allow the Master Foods division in the Netherlands to pursue own-label opportunities for wet sauces alongside brands such as Dolmio reflected spare production capacity and uncertain prospects for the division. Mars had always resisted such a move for fear of compromising its position with retailers. Mars had not wanted to pass sensitive information to retailers, create brand cannibalisation, or lose valuable bargaining power. If Mars was also to make a similar move towards own label in its pet food and confectionery businesses, it could potentially upset the retailers who are not supplied with own labels through Mars and who would then be competing with other retailers' Mars own labels produced to high standards (*Marketing*, 1995).

The response to conflict can even worsen the situation. The exercise of power can be a great source of conflict (Stern and Gorman, 1969), for instance where the strongest member of the channel seeks to impose a solution against the wishes of the others. In contrast, unexercised power could be seen as benevolent restraint and a sign of willingness to co-operate (Frazier, 1983), thus reducing the tensions.

Conflicts can vary in frequency, intensity, duration, content and impact (Magrath and Hardy, 1988). Some conflict can be a powerful reforming pressure, resulting in a stronger, more efficient channel, but too much becomes dysfunctional. This may involve a refusal to co-operate.

Conflict needs to spotted early and dealt with before it becomes too overt. This can be helped by regular meetings, frequent communication, and ensuring that all parties emerge satisfied from negotiations. It is critical that each channel member should fully understand their role and what is expected of them, and that this is agreed in advance. If conflict does become overt, communication, formation of channel committees, a fast arbitration service and top management commitment to resolution are all essential to prevent an irrevocable breakdown of the channel.

In any channel, there are likely to be periods of manifest conflict and periods of calm and co-operation. Similarly, there may be conflict in one area, for example profit margin split, but co-operation in others, for example promotion.

Source: Master Foods Ltd.

Master Foods is now producing own label pasta sauces in addition to its Dolmio brand.

Power–dependency

Power has received considerable attention in the behavioural science literature as a basis for explaining the interaction between two individuals or organisations. It was defined by El-Ansary and Stern (1972) as:

> 'The power of a buyer or seller is his ability to control the decision variables in the marketing or purchasing strategy of another member in the supply chain. For this control to qualify as power, it should be different from the influenced member's original level of control over his marketing or purchasing strategy.'

This means that one channel member might wield considerable power over other members, and might clearly be able to exercise that power to the cost of the others, yet can choose not to use that power. Power can be possessed to influence events without it actually being used (Bacharach and Lawler, 1980). Marks & Spencer possess a great deal of power over their suppliers, but although pursuing rigorous standards and tough bargaining, they value the building of longer-term relationships that do not depend on aggressive or hostile acts.

In a distribution channel, any member might seek to use power-based strategies to influence the others. Power can derive from many sources, real or perceived. A most popular classification comes from French and Raven (1959).

Reward power

Reward power is based on B's perception that A has the ability to provide rewards for B. Such rewards might include volume of business, higher margins or sales and promotional support. As mentioned earlier a small supplier might feel that a large retailer such as Marks & Spencer has reward power. If the supplier complies exactly with the M&S way of doing things, then that will bring them increased or at least repeat M&S business next season.

Coercive power

Coercive power is based on B's perception that A has the ability to mediate punishments for B. The withdrawal of many of the above-mentioned rewards by A could constitute the use of coercive power, for instance the threat of delisting a particular product line. The Costco example given earlier might again be relevant here. The retailers' threats to boycott the brands of certain manufacturers who were also supplying Costco could be interpreted as an attempted exercise of coercive power.

Legitimate power

Legitimate power is based on B's perception that A has the legitimate right to prescribe behaviour for B. This legitimacy could arise from the existence of clauses in formal contracts, or less clearly through the norms or expectations of either party. A contractual VMS, or franchise, often gives one member legitimate power. A franchisee expects the franchisor to specify how the business should be set up and run, since that is part of what the franchisee is investing in.

Referent power

Referent power is based on B's identification with A. In other words, B respects A and might wish to be associated with A to reap reputational and other spin-off effects. A's power might also arise from B's acceptance that both parties are inextricably linked, so that they must succeed or fail together. This kind of power calls for a high degree of empathy and shared communication.

Expert power

Expert power is based on B's perception that A has some special knowledge or expertise, perhaps in market insights, product development or promotion, which gives A influence over B's actions. A small manufacturer or a small retailer might regard an experienced wholesaler as having expert power.

In any channel situation, there may be several different power sources operating, and they may not all be in the hands of the same channel member. When combined, they could provide a basis for an administered VMS, as described earlier. In some situations, one source of power could be cancelled out or counterbalanced by another source wielded by a different channel member.

Example

A classic example of the exercise of power is the relationship between the large supermarket chains and the major brand manufacturers. Over the years, each side has tried to exploit power over the other, to the point where the balance of power between them is now a delicate see-saw, tipping slightly in favour of one, and then the other. The brand manufacturers have, through brand building, made sure that their products are indispensable to the consumer, and thus essential to the retailer, while the retailers have tried to exploit their intensive coverage of the market, making them indispensable to the brand manufacturers. In almost every European country, a small number of distributors account for a very large proportion of business, and this concentration is increasing as retailers join forces, entering into international strategic alliances for purchasing and distribution.

Each party has tried to reduce the power of the other at various times. The manufacturers, for example, have tried to limit their dependence on the big supermarkets by co-operating with the emergent discount chains (Costco springs to mind again), while the retailers have tried to wean consumers off the big brands on to good quality own-brand products (*see* pp. 272 *et seq*.). The uneasy balance, however, remains.

This last scenario raises another concept, *dependency*, that is very closely linked to the development and exercise of power. This is where one party becomes highly dependent for its well-being on the actions of the other party. What is actually happening between the manufacturers and the retailers is that neither in reality can manage without the other, and there is a mutual dependency that limits what each dare do.

Dependency might also be derived from the relative importance of the transactions to the parties involved. If a retailer takes large share of one supplier's output (say 80 per cent), yet that only represents a small proportion of the retailer's overall needs (say 5 per cent), then that supplier is extremely dependent on the retailer who immediately has the basis for coercive power at least. If the supplier does not comply, the retailer can easily drop the supplier with relatively little inconvenience to themselves, but with devastating consequences for the supplier.

Finally, B might become dependent on A because there is no obvious alternative, or because the costs and time involved in switching would be too great. As A occupies such a specialist niche in its own market, A may well possess expert or referent power, and the dependency might tempt A to try to exercise coercive power over B. If A pushes this too far, however, B might rebel and decide that locating or developing an alternative partner would now be worthwhile.

All of these tensions and influencing strategies tend to encourage the emergence of channel leaders who regulate and control events. Sainsbury, Tesco and ASDA all exercise leadership from the retail end, although as discussed earlier, some aspects of this leadership are questionable. Some wholesale systems, such as those matching up small manufacturers and small retailers develop leadership at that level rather than at the retail level. Car manufacturers still provide leadership within the automotive trade, because exclusive dealerships and selective distribution mean that the dealers have much to lose if a manufacturer decides not to deal with them any more.

Atmosphere

The tendency towards power–dependency relationships, conflict–co-operation and the general level of trust in the relationships within a channel are important variables affecting the overall climate that governs ongoing relationships and decision making. The way in which all these elements come together sets the scene for the channel either to flourish for the benefit of all parties, or to be plagued by internal strife and inefficiency.

The atmosphere reflects the history of the relationship between the channel members. It is the accumulation of all the positive and negative feelings that have developed during the exchange and operation of the contracts. The atmosphere is, therefore, an outcome of a relationship, and plays a part in influencing future events. (Håkansson, 1982). A climate of hard bargaining may well lead to defensive behaviour if one party feels hard done by. In another situation, problems may be solved not so much by confrontation as by discussion and compromise.

At the heart of the relationships between channel members is trust, defined as:

'**The firm's belief that another company will perform actions that will result in positive outcomes for the firm, as well as not take unexpected actions that would result in negative outcomes for the firm**' (Anderson and Narus, 1986).

The level of trust existing within a channel can vary from a complete absence to very high degree of completeness. It can also be very long lasting and set the scene for the conduct of the relationship. Trust can lead to co-operation, good communication and an ability to resolve differences speedily and effectively. Trust is therefore, an essential requirement for the implementation of relationship marketing within a channel, which in turn should lead to better synergy between channel members. There is a need to understand more fully the role of trust and expectations in channel behaviour in order to explain why some relationships are remarkably well adjusted and others are almost a constant battle between buyer and seller.

CHAPTER SUMMARY

The channel of distribution is the means through which products are moved from the manufacturer to the end consumer. It might involve direct supply from a manufacturer to a buyer, or it might involve one or more intermediaries. The structure of channels can vary considerably depending on the type of market, the needs of the end customer and the type of product. Consumer goods might be supplied direct, but in mass markets for convenience goods, however, this might not be feasible and longer channels might be used.

Organisational markets are far more likely to involve direct supply from manufacturer to organisational buyer, especially where the purchase is large, technically complex, customised and critical from the buyer's point of view. Some organisational purchases, however, particularly routine repurchases of non-critical items such as office stationery might be distributed in ways that are similar to those used in consumer markets, with various intermediaries involved.

Intermediaries play an important role in increasing efficiency and reducing costs, despite the fact that each intermediary needs to earn a profit margin. Intermediaries can also take some of the risk away from the manufacturer. Intermediaries can bring together a wide assortment of goods from different sources, then store, sort and transport them. Finally, the intermediary can help to ease the cash flow of both their manufacturers, by turning goods into liquid cash more quickly, and their customers, by offering credit terms or accounts. These functions are not all necessarily performed by the same member of the distribution channel and the decision as to who does what may be made by consensus or by the use of power in the channel. Ultimately, the channel should give all parties a chance to specialise in what they are best at, whether manufacturing, buying and selling or consuming!

Manufacturers are not restricted to using only one channel. Dual or multiple channels can help to reach 'pockets' of a target segment or can help to spread distribution for a mass market product as widely as possible. There are three broad levels of intensity of distribution, each implying a different set of channels and different types of intermediary: intensive distribution, selective distribution and exclusive distribution.

Channel design will be influenced by a number of factors, including organisational objectives, capabilities and resources. Market size might also constrain the choice of channel, as might the buying complexity associated with the product and the buying behaviour of the target market. The changing environment can also influence the choice of channel, through evolving technology, changing consumer lifestyles or through changes in regulations.

Selecting specific intermediaries to join a channel can be difficult, especially where selective or exclusive channels are used. This choice can be a critical success factor since, for example, the speed of entry and the degree of penetration into a new market can depend on the right choice of intermediary. Sometimes, however, the intermediary has the power to reject a manufacturer or a specific product. Large supermarket chains, are prime targets for manufacturers with new grocery products to offer, but such retailers are likely to drive hard bargains, if they decide to accept the product at all.

Increasingly, channels of distribution are becoming more than just sets of transactions between unrelated organisations, and vertical marketing systems (VMS) have evolved to create a channel that is more efficient and effective for all parties, ideally working towards the common good in a long-term relationship. The VMS also tries to overcome the threats posed by the various types of channel competition: *horizontal* (between intermediaries of the same type), *intertype* (between different types of the same intermediary), *vertical* (between different members of the same channel) and *channel system competition* (between parallel channels). There are different types of VMS: corporate, contractual, and administered.

Clearly, voluntary co-operation is the best way of achieving an effective and efficient channel. This can lead to strong mutual ties between the members of the channel, creating competitive advantage for all of them. However conflict might arise if one member feels that it is getting a raw deal or being coerced into taking responsibilities that it is reluctant to accept. If not dealt with promptly and sensitively, channel conflict might lead, sooner or later, to the dissolution of that channel.

Behaviour within channels is also influenced by power–dependency relationships. Power might be finely balanced within a channel, sometimes tipping in favour of one party, sometimes another, and both parties will do all they can to reduce the power of the other. Dependency, where one party becomes reliant on another for its well-being, is closely linked with power. Dependency might occur where both parties are large and powerful and cannot exist without the other (e.g., supermarkets and brand manufacturers), or where there is an imbalance in the size of the parties and their importance to each other. Finally, dependency might occur where one party simply has no alternative party to turn to.

The interplay of co-operation–conflict and power–dependency creates the climate within which the channel operates. It also determines the level of trust within the channel which can affect the quality of relationships, the longevity of the channel and its efficiency and effectiveness.

Key words and phrases

Agents and brokers	*Distributors and dealers*	*Marketing channel*
Bulk breaking	*Franchisees*	*Retailers*
Channel strategy	*Intermediary*	*Vertical marketing systems*
Direct supply	*Market coverage*	*Wholesalers*

QUESTIONS FOR REVIEW

12.1 What are the different types of *intermediary* that might be found in a distribution channel?

12.2 What is *the short channel of distribution* in consumer markets and what benefits does it offer the manufacturer?

12.3 Why might *agents* be used in organisational channels of distribution?

12.4 In what ways can intermediaries make a channel of distribution more *cost efficient*?

12.5 What specific functions can intermediaries undertake that are of benefit to the *manufacturer*?

12.6 What are the five factors influencing *channel strategy*?

12.7 In what ways might *product characteristics* influence channel strategy? Give examples.

12.8 Define the different types of *channel conflict*.

12.9 What are the relative advantages and disadvantages of an *administered VMS* compared with the other two types?

12.10 Define the different sources of *power* and explain how each might influence the *atmosphere* within which a channel conducts its business.

QUESTIONS FOR DISCUSSION

12.1 To what extent and why do you think that the creation of a VMS can improve the performance of a channel and its members?

12.2 What kind of market coverage strategy might be appropriate for:

(a) a bar of chocolate;
(b) a toothbrush;
(c) a home computer;
(d) a marketing textbook;

and why?

12.3 Using Table 12.2 as a starting point, develop lists of criteria that a manufacturer might use in defining:

(a) 'good' retailers; and
(b) 'good' wholesalers to recruit for consumer market channels.

12.4 List the potential areas of co-operation and conflict between:

(a) a large brand manufacturer and a large supermarket chain; and
(b) a small manufacturer and a wholesaler.

12.5 Discuss how a power–dependency relationship might work between:

(a) a large brand manufacturer and a large supermarket chain;
(b) a small manufacturer and a large supermarket chain;
(c) a multinational manufacturer of hi-fi equipment and a UK-based high street electrical retailer; and
(d) a small manufacturer of high technology, specialised components and an export agent.

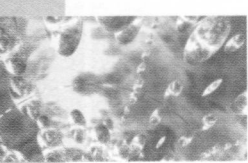

CASE STUDY 12.1

Monaghan Mushrooms

Monaghan Mushrooms Ltd is a wholly owned subsidiary of the Pleroma group, one of the leading mushroom companies in the UK and Ireland. Based in the north-east of Ireland, Monaghan Mushrooms sells most of its output to the UK and a little to continental Europe. Monaghan Mushrooms, despite being an Irish company, does not supply its own domestic market. Its main distribution problem is linking the network of small mushroom producers in Ireland, who operate within a kind of franchised system, with the main grocery buyers in the UK.

Until the 1980s, mushroom producers tended to be large, self-contained organisations which not only grew the mushrooms, but also produced their own high-quality compost as a growing medium, and marketed the mushrooms to the trade. As individual organisations, however, they had problems dealing with large, demanding buyers, and they also had problems maintaining consistency and quality at the premium end of the market. There was room in the market, therefore, for a new system of mushroom growing. The Monaghan Mushroom system enabled a large number of smaller producers to enter the market with minimal capital investment. The system meant that mushrooms were grown in plastic tunnels and growbags as opposed to larger wooden sheds containing locally produced compost, often of variable quality. The key to the Monaghan approach was the production of high-quality compost for the small independent growing units, and the provision of advisory services and centralised marketing. The system enabled the product to have a longer shelf life, an important point considering the distance to the UK market. Also important was the introduction of quality and grading systems that enabled the producers to match their production closely with a buyer's requirements.

The distribution channel linked the producer with the buyer. The product flow moves mushrooms into the grower's cold store from where they are collected by Monaghan Mushroom's own specialised transport fleet. They are then taken to five 'added value' plants where further processing operations take place. These are based in Monaghan (supplied by 132 growers), Donegal (29 growers), Cavan (49 growers), Tyrone in Northern Ireland (38 growers) and Fenton Barnes in Scotland (three larger growers). The centralised operations included grading, packaging and canning.

The range includes baby button, button, closed cup, open cup and flat mushrooms, in white and brown varieties. Packed products include cans and glass jars in a range of sizes for the retail and catering trades, and bulk supplies for other food processors.

A wide range of retail customers are supplied, including the large UK multiple supermarkets such as Sainsbury's, Tesco, Safeway, ASDA and Somerfield, with mushrooms graded and packed to suit requirements. In order to satisfy the demands of these buyers, a rigorous quality control and assurance system is needed to ensure both a quality product to the required freshness, grading and consistency, and high standards of customer service. This includes operating a JIT system to multiple retailers' depots in a temperature-controlled fleet on a daily basis. A split delivery system is used, with 50 per cent company-owned vehicles and 50 per cent contract hauliers.

Despite the competitive advantages of the Monaghan system, the mushroom market is highly competitive. In 1993, for example, the Netherlands was a major European supplier, producing 190 000 tonnes, compared with Ireland's 44 000 tons. Around 50 000 tonnes of Dutch mushrooms were exported, with the UK as the second-largest customer. Irish exports to the UK accounted for around 26 500 tonnes, or around 15 per cent of the market. The overall market for mushrooms in the UK is estimated to be worth £250 million, the majority of which is accounted for by white closed cup mushrooms. A second source of competitive pressure came from the large retailers. Price battles between the multiples often forced mushroom suppliers to seek greater efficiency in order to meet downward pressure on prices. Finally, material costs rose by 25 per cent between 1990 and 1995 and fluctuations in the punt– pound exchange rate created further pressure on producers' margins.

Sources: Adapted from a case prepared by Professor Barra O'Cinneide, University of Limerick; Shapley (1995).

Questions

1 Outline the kind of channel structure appropriate for supplying mushrooms from the producer to:

(a) an individual consumer; and

(b) your university or college catering department.

What kind of market coverage strategies do you think these channels represent?

2 What do you think are the particular problems of producing and distributing a product like mushrooms?

3 What kind of VMS is represented in this case, and what benefits do you think it gives:

   (a) Monaghan Mushrooms; and

   (b) the individual growers?

4 Where do you think the balance of power lies in the relationship between Monaghan Mushrooms and the UK supermarket chains? What could either party do to increase their power?

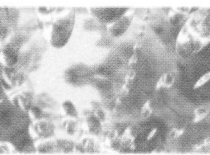

CASE STUDY 12.2

French hypermarkets and their smaller suppliers

Many French small and medium sized enterprises (SMEs) which manufacture consumer goods see the hypermarkets as an appropriate and easy way of reaching a mass market. It is not so easy, however, to get a product accepted by the hypermarkets in the first place, nor is it always easy to survive the pressure of dealing with powerful retailers. The hypermarkets put increasing pressure on suppliers to cut prices and to provide more support services, and many smaller companies, especially those who depend too much on a small number of large retailers, cannot survive.

Duarig, for example, was a manufacturer of sports equipment which was forced out of business completely because of the pressure on its profit margins. Over 80 per cent of its output was sold to the hypermarkets. Cipem, a supplier of artificial flowers, realised that it was too small to resist the pressure from the hypermarkets or to negotiate better terms for itself. The hypermarkets demanded more and more services from Cipem, which eventually got to the point where it could no longer deliver. Others found that the only way to survive when dealing with hypermarkets was to make fundamental, and not necessarily welcome changes in their operations. Lewinger, for example, a manufacturer of knitwear, found that to maintain profit margins, it had to begin to manufacture in low-cost countries such as Poland and Vietnam. Palladium (shoes) tried to maintain control by supplying its goods in limited quantities to the hypermarkets, so that it could get the benefits of mass market distribution without the risk of compromising its exclusive image. The hypermarkets responded by producing copies of Palladium's canvas shoes, which meant that Palladium then had to get involved in litigation about the alleged 'counterfeiting'.

Not all SMEs have bad experiences with hypermarkets, however. Those who work closely with retailers can use the relationship as a means of strategic development.

Routin, for example, began by supplying own-brand fruit concentrates and juices to Carrefour. As the managing director said, it allowed the company to show what it could do and to demonstrate the quality of its goods. It now also supplies other major hypermarket chains, such as Système U, Auchan and Continent, and had a turnover of 215 million francs in 1995. The success of the own-label products gave Routin the experience and the retail contacts to launch a manufacturer brand, Fruiss, a range of fruit syrups. Fruiss was accepted by the hypermarkets for a number of reasons, and not just because it came from a tried and trusted supplier. Fruiss was carefully positioned so that it did not directly compete with any of the own-label products Routin already supplied. It was thus not seen as a threat. In case there were any residual doubts in the retailers' minds, Routin ensured that the hypermarkets could make a healthy profit margin on the brand. As a final inducement, Routin also developed and installed imaginative point of sale display material to reassure the retailers that the product would be noticed by consumers and would be attractive to them.

Acting as an own-label manufacturer, therefore, can be a good way for an SME to develop and grow, and indirectly to become an important force in its product market. Carrefour, for example, has signed up a small company with 70 employees to provide all its own-label gherkins! The hypermarkets seem happy enough to deal with small enterprises and to be an influence on their growth. In 1994, Carrefour claimed to have direct relationships with 25 000 SMEs, although in some product areas, supply is quite concentrated. Carrefour, for example, source seven million pairs of socks from eight suppliers, and five million items of underwear from seven other suppliers.

To be successful, any SME has to appreciate how the hypermarkets work in terms of purchasing, and

TABLE 12.5
Factors in the success of a new product

	Consumers	Retailers	manufacturers
Attractive price	1	1	6
Quality/performance	2	5	1
Ease of use	3	6	3
Known brand name	4	3	5
Technological innovation	5	4	2
Promotional support	6	2	4

Ranked in order of importance where 1 = most important.

what both the hypermarkets and their customers want. To have a fighting chance of survival, the SME has to try to divert negotiation away from price. Concessions on delivery, quantity, promotion or point of sale material, for example, might be easier for the SME to maintain than wafer-thin margins which can then be put under further pressure later. None of this is easy. A survey of manufacturers, consumers and retailers (*see* Table 12.5) found that each group had different ideas about what factors were most important in the success of a new product.

Metronic, a manufacturer of television aerials, satellite dishes and related products, overcame the focus on price by offering the hypermarkets more in the way of service. To make life easier for the retailer, Metronic offered a complete product line management package, as well as taking responsibility for product display in the stores, and giving the retailer regular data on the market and the competition.

Source: Declairieux (1995).

Questions

1 What kind of power do the hypermarkets tend to exert over their small suppliers?

2 What are a small supplier's risks and rewards in dealing with a hypermarket?

3 How can own-label products provide an opportunity for the small manufacturer?

4 Other than going down the own-label route, what can a small supplier do to improve its chances of getting its products listed by the hypermarkets? Are there any potential problems with the strategies you are suggesting?

REFERENCES TO CHAPTER 12

Anderson, J. C. and Narus, J. A. (1986), 'Towards a Better Understanding of Distribution Channel Working Relationships' in K. Backhaus and D. Wilson (eds.), *Industrial Marketing: A German–American Perspective*, Springer-Verlag.

Anderson, J. C. and Narus, J. A. (1990), 'A Model of Distributor Firm and Manufacturer Firm Working Partnerships', *Journal of Marketing*, 54 (Jan.), pp. 42–58.

Bacharach, S. B. and Lawler, E. J. (1980), *Power and Politics in Organisations*, Jossey-Bass Inc.

Barrett, P. (1996), 'Daewoo Tests Store Sales', *Marketing*, 4 April, p. 4.

Boyd, H. W. and Walker, O. C. (1990), *Marketing Management: A Strategic Approach*, Irwin.

Business Marketing Digest (1991), 'Getting the Most Out of the Dealer Relationship', *Business Marketing Digest*, 16(4), pp. 85–8.

Butaney, G. and Wortzel, L. H. (1988), 'Distribution Power Versus Manufacturer Power: The Customer Role', *Journal of Marketing*, 52 (Jan.), pp. 52–63.

Declairieux, B. (1995), 'Comment se faire références', L'Enterprise, No. 119, Septembre 1995, pp. 26–40.

El-Ansary, A. I. and Stern, L. W. (1972), 'Power Measurement in Distribution Channels', *Journal of Marketing Research*, 9 (Feb.), pp. 47–52.

European Purchasing and Materials Management (1994), 'Vaccines Just in Time', *European Purchasing and Materials Management*, 3, p. 182.

Frazier, G. L. (1983), 'On the Measurement of Interfirm Power in Channels of Distribution', *Journal of Marketing Research*, 20 (May), pp. 158–66.

French, J. R. P. and Raven, B. (1959), 'The Bases of Social Power' in D. Cartwright (ed.), *Studies in Social Power*, Ann Arbor, University of Michigan Press.

Gilbert, M. (1995), 'Keeping Them Sweet', *The Grocer*, 28 October, p. 16.

The Grocer (1995a), 'IKB – The Dutch Formula for Integrated Quality Control', *The Grocer*, 25 November, p. 64.

The Grocer (1995b), Boycott Ends as Trial Stops, *The Grocer*, 25 November, p. 13.

The Grocer (1995c) 'Giving Retailers Tools to do the Job', *The Grocer*, 28 October, p. 42.

The Grocer (1996) 'Dutch Direct Sales Vote Revolutionises Trade', *The Grocer*, 8 June, p. 51.

Håkansson, H. (1982), 'An Interaction Approach' in H. Håkansson (ed.) *International Marketing and Purchasing of Industrial Goods: An Interaction Approach*, John Wiley & Sons.

Lee, J. (1995), 'Dixons resists PC Import Tide', *Marketing*, 20 July, p. 7.

Magrath, A. J. and Hardy, K. G. (1988), 'Ten Ways for Manufacturers to Improve Distribution Management', *Business Horizons*, Nov./Dec., p. 68.

Marketing (1995) 'Mars: Never Say Never', *Marketing*, 15 June, p. 13.

Morton, C. (1993), 'Food Distribution in Eastern Europe', *British Food Journal*, 95(7), pp. 16–20.

Mullineux, N. (1995), Car Retailing in Europe: Opportunities for the Next Decade, *A Financial Times Management Report*, Pearson Professional Ltd.

Narus, J. A. and Anderson, J. C. (1986), 'Industrial Distributor Selling: The Roles of Outside and Inside Sales', *Industrial Marketing Management*, 15(1), pp. 55–62.

Nielsen, A.C. (1990), *L'Univers Alimentaire en Belgique*, A. C. Nielsen Belgium.

Observer (1995), 'Revealed: How Old Milk is Recycled and Sold Again', *Observer*, 12 November, p. 1.

Palamountain, J. C. (1955), *The Politics of Distribution*, Harvard University Press.

Raven, B. H. and Kruglanski, A. W. (1970), 'Conflict and Power' in P. Swingle (ed.), *The Structure of Conflict*, Academic Press.

Rosenbloom, B. (1987), *Marketing Channels: A Management View*, Dryden.

Shapley, D. (1995), 'Confidence in Quality Keeps Away the Clouds', *The Grocer*, 25 November, pp. 50–1.

Sharma, A. and Dominguez, L. (1992), 'Channel Evolution: A Framework for Analysis', *Journal of the Academy of Marketing Science*, 20 (Winter), p. 1–16.

Simkins, J. (1996), 'Borsalino Aims to Recapture Past Glories', *Financial Times*, 19 March, p. 24.

Snowdon, R. (1996), 'Driver Focus Puts Daewoo on Right Road', *Marketing*, 11 January, p. 13.

Stern, L. W. and Gorman, R. H. (1969), *Marketing Channels* (2nd ed.), Prentice Hall.

Walters, J. (1995), 'Ticket to Trouble', *Observer*, 12 November, *Business Section*, p. 1.

Webster, F. E. (1979), *Industrial Marketing Strategy*, John Wiley & Sons.

Whitworth, M. (1995), 'Feeding the Hungry Russian Bear is Challenge for the Brave', *The Grocer*, 25 November.

Woof, M. (1995), 'Skelair is dedicated to Klemm', *Construction News*, 30 November, p. 38.

13 Retailers and Wholesalers

LEARNING OBJECTIVES

This chapter will help you to:

1 understand the role and importance of retailers and wholesalers within the distribution channel;

2 classify retailers according to a number of different organisational and operating dimensions;

3 differentiate between types of retailer, appreciating their individual contribution to the retailing scene and their problems;

4 analyse the particular strategic and operational marketing concerns of retailers; and

5 understand the role played by different types of wholesaler.

INTRODUCTION

Shopaholics of the world unite! Retailing is one of the highest profile areas of marketing and, like advertising, has had a tremendous impact on society, culture and lifestyles. To some, shopping is an essential social and leisure activity, while to others, it is a chore. It offers some a chance to dream, and for most of us, an opportunity at some time or other to indulge ourselves. We often take for granted the availability of wide ranges of goods, and know that if we search hard enough, we will find just what we are looking for. Some people, indeed, find that half the fun is in the searching rather than the ultimate purchase.

Although retailing means fun, excitement and the opportunity to splash out vast quantities of cash (thanks to plastic cards!) to us as consumers, it is a very serious business for the managers and organisations that make it happen. It is often the last stage in the channel of distribution before consumption, which means that there is an important role for the retailer in being so close to the final consumer. Not only do retailers have to buy, sort, store and promote goods, they also have to take the risk of being left with poorly selling and loss-making product lines. To avoid this, retailers have to ensure a close match between their capabilities and the merchandise offered, which in turn arises from a clear understanding of their own market appeal, reflected in such areas as store location, merchandise selection, customer service and general ambience and image. Compare the shopping experience provided by, for example, a large hypermarket and a small clothes boutique. One is large, cheap, cheerful, convenient, busy and impersonal while the other is small, relatively expensive, cosy, and places a distinct emphasis on personal service. These differences are the result of careful retailer strategy decisions focused towards developing their individual competitive strengths.

This emphasis on the retailer's strategic thinking in terms of merchandise sourcing reinforces the point made in the previous chapter, that the choice of outlet may not be a completely free decision for the manufacturer. This is because the power balance has progressively swung towards the retailers, given their concentration of purchasing power.

> ### Example
>
> Ahold is a large Dutch retailing conglomerate which operates over 450 Albert Heijn stores in the Netherlands and also has stores in the USA and across the rest of Europe. In order to increase its buying power, it joined forces with Groupe Casino (France) and Argyll Stores (UK) in the European Retail Association (ERA). ERA not only centralised purchasing on behalf of its three members, but also created a focus for co-operation in terms of marketing and logistics (Cooper *et al.*, 1991). As a means of further streamlining the logistics function and reducing its cost, the members of ERA entered agreements with Allkauf (Germany), Edeka (Germany), Hagen (Norway), ICA (Sweden), Jer. Martins (Portugal), Kesko Oy (Finland), La Rinascente (Italy), Mercadona (Spain), Superquinn (Ireland), and Migros (Switzerland) to create Associated Marketing Services (Robinson and Clarke-Hill, 1995). There are many such retail alliances across Europe, offering their members better buying power and cost-effective logistics while the manufacturer gains from relatively easy access to potentially Europe-wide distribution coverage.

Wholesalers are less evident to the general public, yet they play a vital role in servicing both retail outlets and industrial users, as discussed in Chapter 12. The key to successful wholesaling is to have a clear focus on which target customers are to be served, and then to become highly responsive in terms of stock, service and buying and selling efficiency. For many manufacturers, wholesalers and agents are essential intermediaries, as access to the retail or industrial user could become highly expensive and difficult without their services.

However, the role of retailers and wholesalers is not just restricted to the forward movement and promotion of goods. They also send information back up the distribution channel by providing feedback to the manufacturer about market changes, customer preferences and opportunity areas. Sometimes this feedback can be implicit in a retailer's actions, for instance refusing to reorder, or through established sales patterns. More systematic research and information gathering, however, as described in Chapter 6, may provide especially rich explicit insights sooner and in more depth.

This chapter starts with a review of the importance of retailing and wholesaling in the distribution channel. It then examines in some detail the different forms of retail outlet. Non-store retailing is also considered as what we are seeing now in this area may lead to significant new developments and fundamental structural change in the retailing world over the next 10 years or so. Finally within the retail sector, current trends and their impact on the main strategy dimensions are considered, with particular regard to such areas as location, merchandising and competitive positioning. The chapter concludes with a more detailed look at wholesaling. Particular attention is given to the different types of wholesaler and their potential for taking up an effective role within the channel of distribution.

THE NATURE OF RETAILING AND WHOLESALING

Retailing and wholesaling are both about buying and selling for a profit. Of course, that is a gross simplification of the very important roles both play in bridging the gap between producers and consumers. Both receive goods from a wide range of different sources and then (often) redistribute them to convenient locations along with a marketing package that is valued by their customers or the final consumer. Usually, these locations are shops and warehouses but increasingly, other forms of non-store retailing are becoming evident, as will be seen later. The main distinction between the wholesaler and retailer is that the wholesaler is primarily focused on other resellers or organisational users, whereas the retailer is focused primarily on the much larger, but highly differentiated, consumer market.

Retailing and wholesaling can be best defined in terms of the main functions that both perform.

Assembling a range of goods

The main function of a retailer is to *assemble a range of products and services* that complement its own strengths and matches the needs of the target market. Within a particular product area or market, variety is ensured, as retailers seek to differentiate their offerings from those of their competitors, although increasingly this is becoming more difficult.

Example

Think about the variations between record stores in the high street, for instance. Some retailers specialise in a particular style of music, going for depth without breadth, while others go for breadth of coverage without the depth, stocking the best selling popular items from a variety of music styles, but not much more. Others have heavily diversified into videos and computer games. HMV in the UK, however, has chosen to maintain a tight focus on music, claiming that customers should be able to find any current recording they want at least within the larger HMV stores. Its computerised stock control system means that HMV can assess demand and track the availability of the 270 000 releases which are current in the UK at any one time. HMV's chairman was quoted as saying.

'It means that we can have the right stock, in the right place, at the right time, so that our marketing expenditure has every possibility of being maximised.' (Fraser, 1995, p. 36).

Thus by assembling goods, retailers provide both *place utility* and *time utility*. Place utility means that the goods are at a convenient location that reduces the effort that the customer has to make in finding and purchasing a desired range of goods. It may take place either through providing mail order facilities or home delivery or through providing handy retail premises to receive visiting customers. In the case of home shopping, the catalogue or television channel provides the 'showroom' so that customers, from the comfort of their own armchairs, can order by mail or telephone for home delivery. This must be the ultimate in place utility. Time utility similarly means reducing the amount of time the customer has to invest in the purchasing process, and is linked with place utility.

Wholesalers can play a major role in providing the wide assortment of goods required. While some retailers deal directly with manufacturers, others, particularly smaller stores, may prefer the convenience and accessibility of the wholesaler, especially where fast, responsive supply is assured. In the book trade, for example, it is difficult for a retailer to offer anything like the total number of titles available. Instead, the retailer acts as an order conduit, so that either the wholesaler or the publisher can service individual orders that have been consolidated into economic shipment sizes. The wholesaler can maintain a much wider range of products than is possible in all but the largest retail groups, and can provide efficient support activities for rapid stock replenishment.

Providing storage and transportation

The provision of *storage and transportation* has become increasingly important with the widening distance, in terms of both geography and the length of distribution channels, between producer and consumer. Purchasing patterns increasingly include products sourced from wherever the best deal can be offered, whether local or international. As production becomes more concentrated into a relatively small number of larger operations, the need to move products large distances increases. The distance can be even greater in the foodstuffs area, with the demand for exotic and fresh foods from elsewhere in Europe and well beyond. The availability of Chilean grapes in the UK supermarket in winter, for example, is the end point of a long series of distribution decisions including a number of intermediaries.

Retailers and wholesalers, by allowing larger shipments to be made and then breaking bulk, play an important role in establishing economies of scale in channels of physical distribution. Some wholesalers are themselves heavily involved in performing physical distribution roles such as inventory planning, packing, transportation and order processing in line with customer service objectives. This assists the manufacturer as well as the retailer. Often the wholesaler will incur costs in inward bound transportation, maintain a safety stock buffer and absorb associated inventory and material handling expenses, all of which represent savings for the manufacturer.

Giving advice and information

Both retailers and wholesalers are part of the forward *information flow* that advises customers and persuades them to buy. Although in the supermarket environment the role of personal advice is minimal, many retailers, especially those in product lines such as clothing, hobbies, electrical goods and cars are expected to assist the consumer directly in making a purchase decision and to advise on subsequent use. These are the kinds of goods that require limited or extensive decision-making behaviour, as discussed at p. 97 earlier. While retailers might be attentive and responsive to their customers' information and advice needs in the store, there is some evidence that they are less adept at handling telephone enquiries. A survey conducted by the Henley Centre (reported in Summers, 1994) had researchers posing as customers telephoning 800 outlets in various retail sectors for information. Twenty per cent failed to get any answer at all, and another 20 per cent had to wait more than five rings for an answer. Getting through to the right department often proved a lengthy and difficult process, and even then, retail staff did not have the necessary information readily available. The study found little to fault in the retailers' manners, friendliness or willingness to help, but clearly the systems for handling telephone queries are less than efficient. Henley estimates that the number of calls will grow in the UK to around 400 million by the end of the 1990s, and thus retailers need to revise their approach.

Wholesalers are also important sources of advice for some retailers and users. The more specialised a wholesaler, the greater the opportunity for developing an in-depth market understanding, tracking new or declining products, analysing competitive actions, defining promotions needed and advising on best buys. This role may be especially valuable to the smaller retailer who has less direct access to quality information on broader trends in a specific market. Similarly, an industrial distributor may be expected to advise customers on applications and to assist in low-level technical problem solving.

Transferring title

Both wholesalers and retailers (but not agents) take title to goods and services. Within the context of warranty restrictions, the intermediary accepts legal responsibility for the product including its storage, security and resale. This has a direct bearing on the pricing, display and control of the products offered, the processing of cash and/or credit transactions, and the implementation of materials handling into and around the showroom, and if necessary, out to the customer. Some of these functions can be passed on to the customer. In IKEA, for instance, the customer can see display products in a showroom and then pick the required products unassisted from warehouse storage racks before going on to the checkout.

When the wholesaler takes title to goods, there are direct financial and other benefits to the producer, for which the wholesaler is rewarded through a profit margin. These benefits include lower distribution and logistics costs, credit and cash flow benefits, reduced selling and administration costs as a result of dealing with a relatively small number of customers, and a valuable information flow back to the manufacturer.

Providing an appropriate environment

Both wholesalers and retailers receive customers in their premises. The wholesaler in the grocery trade will probably operate like an overgrown supermarket, allowing selected and vetted trade customers to choose and even collect goods during their visit. In other situations, such as a builder's merchant, a mixed operation may exist. Some high-value, low-bulk products will be sold by counter service only, rather than on a self-service basis.

In most retail situations, the consumer enters a carefully planned and controlled environment designed to create a retail environment that helps to establish and reinforce the ambience and image desired. In some, this may be a low-cost minimalist approach that reinforces a no frills, value for money philosophy, with simple picking from racks and pallets or drums. In others, music, decor and display are all subtly developed and designed around themes to create a more up market, higher quality shopping experience. The whole area of retail atmosphere will be readdressed on p. 515.

This builder's merchant provides easy access to materials and supplies.

Source: Gibbs and Dandy Ltd.

The retail environment can also include a range of additional services. Convenient parking is a critical issue where customers are buying in bulk, or want fast take away services (the 'drive-through' fast food operator has found the logical solution to this one!). Additional services in the form of credit, delivery, returns and purchasing assistance can help to differentiate a retailer.

> ### Example
>
> The owner of a small travel agency in Hartlepool personally delivers travel tickets to his main business customers within a wide radius, if necessary on a daily basis. Some music stores have installed computerised lists of albums produced by a wide cross-section of recording companies and artists to assist back-ordering. As mentioned earlier, HMV can call up information on any of the 270 000 recordings currently available in the UK. Additionally, the organisation launched an additional service, HMV Direct, in spring 1996. This is essentially a mail order operation, but HMV are open to the idea of eventually extending the concept to embrace higher tech. distribution methods. This might mean, for example, downloading digitised music from computer to computer either direct or via the Internet. The organisation is prepared to wait, however, until such systems become commercially viable rather than investing directly in their development (Fraser, 1995).

THE STRUCTURE OF THE EUROPEAN RETAIL SECTOR

Retailing across Europe is big business. Table 13.1 shows the value of retail sales across Europe in 1993. In total value terms, Germany, France, Italy and the UK are the leading nations, accounting for 77 per cent of total retail sales between them. On a per capita basis, however, the top five are Austria, Belgium, France, Italy and Luxembourg.

Table 13.2 shows the top 20 west European retailers, ranked by sales. It is interesting to note that no fewer than 16 of them are grocery retailers while the remainder consist of one grocery/variety retailer, two multisector operators and one department store group. In geographic terms, the list is dominated by German and French organisations. When we look at the top 10 retailers in terms of profit in Table 13.3, however, there is much less emphasis on grocery and the list is dominated by the UK.

Retailers can be classified on a number of criteria, not all of which are immediately obvious to the average shopper. A later section of this Chapter (pp. 499 *et seq.*) will concentrate on store types, but this section discusses other classification criteria, which will also help to shed further light on what retailers actually do and why they are important to both manufacturer and consumer.

Form of ownership

Retailing was for many years the realm of the small independent business. Some grew by adding more branches and some grew by acquisition, but it is only since the 1950s that the retail structure of the high street has evolved significantly, favouring the larger organisation. Nevertheless, there are still several predominant forms of ownership to be found:

TABLE 13.1
European retail sales, 1993

	Total ($bn)	Per capita ($)
Austria	41.3	5293
Belgium	55.2	5491
Denmark	25.3	4877
Finland	20.3	4011
France	311.5	5402
Germany	385.5	4748
Greece	25.8	2499
Ireland	12.8	3638
Italy	334.2	5857
Luxembourg	2.8	7170
Netherlands	67.7	4430
Portugal	15.4	1567
Spain	96.5	2531
Sweden	28.4	3258
UK	301.9	5237

Source: Euromonitor, *(1995a)*, p. 311. Reprinted with kind permission.

TABLE 13.2

Top 20 European retailers by sales

	Organisation	Country	Core area	Turnover (£m)	Year
1	Tengelmann	Germany	Grocery	17 812	1991/92
2	Metro/Kaufhof	Switzerland/Germany	Multisector	17 775	1991
3	Rewe Zentral	Germany	Grocery	15 560	1992
4	Carrefour	France	Grocery	12 562	1992
5	Leclerc	France	Grocery	12 204	1992
6	Intermarché	France	Grocery	12 183	1992
7	Edeka Zentrale	Germany	Grocery	10 359	1992
8	J Sainsbury	UK	Grocery	9 686	1992/93
9	Promodès	France	Grocery	9 030	1992
10	Aldi	Germany	Grocery	8 532	1991
11	Tesco	UK	Grocery	7 582	1992/93
12	Pinault-Printemps	France	Multisector	7 532	1992
13	Ahold	Netherlands	Grocery	7 204	1992
14	Karstadt	Germany	Department store	6 724	1992
15	Auchan	France	Grocery	6 681	1992
16	Co-operative societies	UK	Grocery	6 611	1991
17	Casino	France	Grocery	6 605	1992
18	ICA	Sweden	Grocery	5 847	1991
19	Marks & Spencer	UK	Grocery/variety	5 793	1992/93
20	Delhaize Le Lion	Belgium	Grocery	5 768	1992

Source: Adapted from Tordjman (1995) p. 19.

TABLE 13.3

Top 10 European retailers by profit

	Organisation	Country	Core area	Profit (mill. ecu)
1	J Sainsbury	UK	Grocery	880
2	Marks & Spencer	UK	Variety	870
3	Tesco	UK	Grocery	760
4	Great Universal Stores	UK	Multisector	600
5	Boots	UK	Multisector	520
6	Argyll	UK	Grocery	500
7	Spar	Germany	Grocery	370
8	Kingfisher	UK	Multisector	315
9	Delhaize Le Lion	Belgium	Grocery	310
10	Carrefour	France	Grocery	250

Source: Tordjman (1995) p. 34.

Independent

Still the most common form of ownership in terms of number of retail outlets is independent, with over 62 per cent of UK outlets falling into this category. In sales volume terms, however, this group accounts for less than 30 per cent. Marked variances exist between retail categories, with a significant role for the small independent in the drinks sector and in CTN (confectionery, tobacco and news) retailing. Similar patterns exist across Europe, especially in France, Spain and the Benelux countries which have above average densities of small retailers. Typically, the **independent retail outlet** is managed by a sole trader or a family business. For the consumer, the main benefits are the personalised attention and flexibility that can be offered. These operations can be highly individualistic in terms of the variety and quality of merchandise stocked, ranging from very upmarket to bargain basement.

Although it may not be possible for the small independent to compete on price and breadth of range offered, the key is to complement the big multiples rather than to try to compete head-on. Howe (1992) is clear about forces, such as changing population patterns, the drift towards out of town shopping, supply and resource problems and the sheer scale and professionalism of the large multiple chains, that work against the small retailer. To combat this, the small retailer thus needs to look for niches, specialised merchandise, flexible opening hours, special services and to make more effective use of suppliers. This boils down to sound management and marketing thinking.

Example

Many small village grocery shops faced with losing business to the supermarkets, are trying to maintain their place in the community by expanding the range of services offered. Some, for instance, offer fax and photocopying facilities to their customers, and while these services do not make a profit in their own right, they keep people coming into the store and making other grocery purchases while they are there.

In a different retail sector, but working on the same general principles, Germany has a healthy segment of small, independent furniture design stores. These stores provide innovative and individual merchandise, and surveys have shown that 72 per cent of purchasers prefer these outlets to the bigger retailers of mass produced furniture (Myerson, 1993).

Corporate chain

A corporate chain has multiple outlets under common ownership. The operation of the chain will reflect corporate strategy, and many will centralise decisions where economies of scale can be gained. The most obvious activity to be centralised is purchasing, so that volume discounts and greater power over suppliers can be gained. There are, of course, other benefits to be derived from a regional, national or even international presence in terms of image and brand building. Typical examples include Laura Ashley and C&A. Some chains do allow a degree of discretion at a

MARKETING IN ACTION

Menswear

Independent menswear retailers in London face fierce competition from the multiples for both the best labels and the best sites. A trade journal article, in which a number of independents were interviewed, suggested the following advice:

- offer personal service
- find a niche – the independent retailer Manlee stocks a high proportion of larger sizes, for instance
- invest in attractive design and display
- provide entertainment value within the shopping experience

- think carefully about the product mix – Carlyle and Forge, for instance, sell accessories and furniture as well as clothing, catering for their target customer's total lifestyle
- try to find exclusive labels
- think about own label – for Carlyle and Forge, own label represents 75 per cent of its business
- work hard on getting sourcing right and keeping margins under control.

Source: Rice (1995).

local level to reflect different operating environments, in terms of opening hours, merchandise or services provided, but the main strength comes from unity rather than diversity.

Contractual system

The linking of members of distribution channels through formal agreements rather than ownership (i.e., a contractual system) was included in the discussion of vertical marketing systems in Chapter 12. For retail or wholesale sponsored co-operatives or franchises, the main benefit is the ability to draw from collective strength, whether in management, marketing or operational procedures. In some cases, the collective strength, as with franchises, can provide a valuable tool for promoting customer awareness and familiarity, leading in turn to retail loyalty. The trade-off for the franchisee is some loss of discretion, both operationally and strategically, but this may be countered by the benefits of unity. **Franchising** might also pass on the retailing risk to the franchisee. When Benetton's performance was poor in the US market, 300 stores closed, with all the losses borne by the franchisees rather than by Benetton (Davidson, 1993).

If the independent retailer wants to avoid the risks of franchising, yet wants to benefit from collective power, then affiliation to either a buying group or a voluntary chain might be the answer. Buying groups are usually found in food retailing and their purpose is to centralise the purchasing function and to achieve economies of scale on behalf of their members.

> ### Example
>
> Buying groups are particularly strong in Germany, and the two largest, Rewe and Edeka, both appear in the top 20 list of European retailers in Table 13.2. Voluntary chains usually centre around a wholesaler who provides the centralised buying power on behalf of its retail members. The retailers benefit not only from the streamlined purchasing, but also from the corporate image that they are allowed to use, such as that of Spar and VG.

Level of service

The range and quality of services offered varies considerably from retailer to retailer. Some, such as department stores, offer gift wrapping services, and some DIY stores offer home delivery, but in others most of the obligation for picking, assessing and taking the product home rests with the customer.

Three types of service level highlight the main options.

Full service

Stores such as Harrods provide the full range of customer services. This includes close personal attention on the shop floor, a full range of account and delivery services, and a clear objective to treat each customer as a valued individual. Such high levels of service are reflected in the premium pricing policy adopted.

Limited service

The number of customers handled and the competitive prices that need to be charged prevent the implementation of the full range of services, but the services that are offered make purchasing easier. Credit, no quibble returns, telephone orders and home delivery may be offered. This is a question of deciding what the target market 'must have' rather than what they 'would like', or defining what is essential for competitive edge. A retailer, such as Next, which claims to sell quality clothing at competitive prices cannot offer too many extra services because that would increase the retailer's costs. They do, however, have to offer a limited range of services in order to remain competitive with similar retailers

Self service

In self-service stores, the customer performs many of the in-store functions including picking goods, queueing at the checkout, paying by cash or perhaps credit card, and then struggling to the car park with a loaded trolley. Some food stores and discount stores operate in this mode, but the trend is towards offering more service to ease bottleneck points that are particularly frustrating to the customer. This could include the provision of more staff at the delicatessen counter, more checkouts to guarantee short queues, and assistance with packing.

Merchandise lines

Retailers can be distinguished by the merchandise they carry, assessed in terms of the breadth and depth of range.

Breadth of range

The breadth of range represents the variety of different product lines stocked. A department store (*see* pp. 499 *et seq.* for a fuller discussion) will carry a wide variety of product lines, perhaps including electrical goods, household goods, designer clothing, hairdressing and even holidays.

Depth of range

The depth of range defines the amount of choice or assortment within a product line, on whatever dimensions are relevant to that kind of product. A record store stocking CDs, tapes, minidiscs and vinyl records could be said to have depth in its range. Similarly, a clothing store which stocks cashmere jumpers might be said to have a shallow range if the jumpers are available only in one style, or a deep range if they are available in five different styles. Introducing further assortment criteria, such as size range and colour creates a very complex definition of depth. A specialty or niche retailer (*see* pp. 505–507), such as Sock Shop or Tie Rack would be expected to provide depth in its product lines on a number of assortment criteria.

Figure 13.1 shows the difference between these two terms. It is easy to see, in this figure, how tensions can arise between breadth and depth. Since retailers have limited resources and limited space at their disposal, there is a basic choice to be made between breadth and depth. If they go for breadth, they can provide a wide variety of different kinds of goods, but probably would not be able to stock those products in significant depth. Limits may be placed on the number of different brands, or the range of styles, sizes or colours available within a product area. Sacrificing breadth for depth means that the retailer can satisfy demand for a whole variety of different brands, sizes, colours or styles, but only within a very narrowly defined range of goods.

> **Example**
>
> Hennes and Mauritz (H&M), the Swedish fashion chain operates over a dozen own labels covering men's, women's and children's clothing, casual and classic wear, and underwear and outerwear (Krienke, 1993b). Although it is a speciality retailer in the sense that it specialises in fashion, it provides a broad but shallow range, compared with other fashion retailers who specialise in women's wear only or jeans only (narrow and deep). Soldier Blue, an independent 'jeanerie' in London, for example, stocks every size and colour of jeans imaginable.

FIGURE 13.1

Breadth *vs* depth

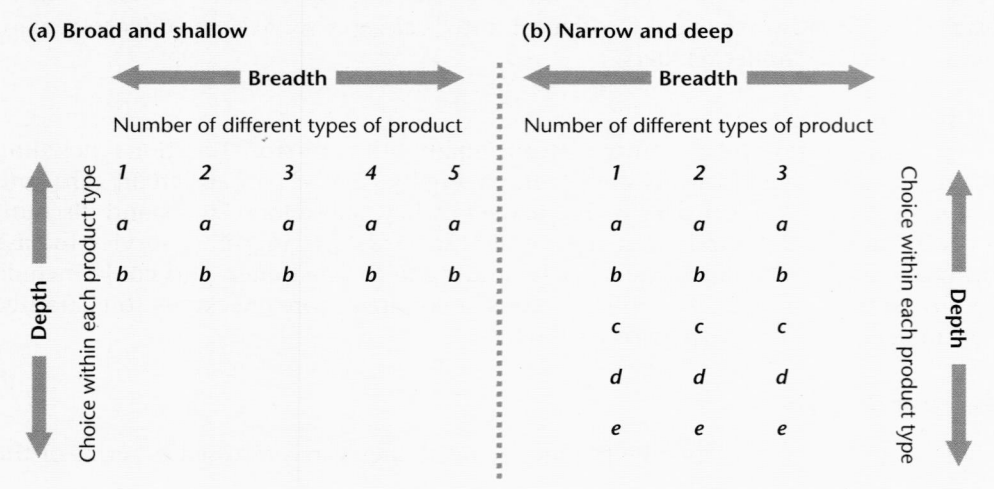

In many cases, customers are happy to accept a polarised choice, patronising department stores when depth of range does not really matter to them, or where the level of customer service they know they will get from the store matters more. Speciality retailers attract custom from those who do want the depth of choice, perhaps because they are engaged in extended problem solving and want access to as many alternatives as possible, or because they want an unusual combination of size, colour and style, for example, that only a specialist stockist would keep. The specialty retailer might also be seen as more knowledgeable and committed to the product area, and this might reduce the risk inherent in the purchase in the customer's mind.

As Fig 13.2 shows, some retailers do try to compromise by offering a mixed approach. Some products, perhaps popular fast-moving lines, will be stocked in depth.

Example

A clothing store might stock a much wider range of colours and sizes for a classic, polo-neck jumper selling at a competitive price, than for an extremely fashionable (and therefore short shelf life) velvet jacket selling at a premium price. Breadth and depth might also vary through the year. At Christmas, for instance, most ladies' clothing retailers expand in terms of both breadth and depth for party wear.

The problems caused by the choice of breadth or depth can also be reduced by careful choice of retailing format. A traditional department store has to restrict itself because of the pressures of space and display requirements.

Example

A catalogue retail showroom (see p. 508), however, such as Argos, is not expected to display its whole range of stock 'live' and is thus able to provide much greater breadth and depth of range than its department store rivals. It is limited only by its logistical systems and ability to update and replenish its in-store warehouses quickly. Nevertheless, Argos offers 95 per cent availability on 3500 products in 250 catalogue showrooms.

FIGURE 13.2

The mixed approach

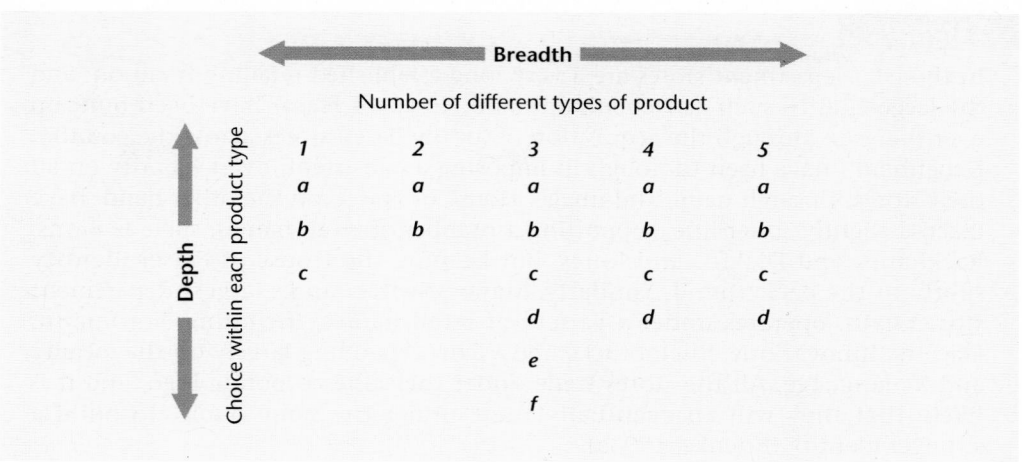

Operating methods

The area of operating methods has seen significant change, with the recent growth of alternatives to the traditional approach. Traditional store retailing, which itself includes a wide number of types of retailer still predominates. These various types are considered in the next section. Non-store retailing, however, where the customer does not physically travel to visit the retailer, has become increasingly popular. This is partly because of changing customer attitudes, partly because of the drive upmarket made by the mail order companies in particular, and partly because of technological advances in logistics. The whole area of non-store shopping will be further discussed at p. 509.

TYPES OF RETAILERS

A walk down any high street or a drive around the outskirts of any large town reveals a wide range of approaches to selling us things. There are retailers of all shapes and sizes, enticing us in with what they hope are clearly differentiated marketing mixes. Taking into account the large number of small independents, there are many thousands of retailers in the UK alone, and yet the 10 top retailers generate 27 per cent of retail sales, while in the grocery sector, the top five supermarkets (Sainsbury's, Tesco etc.) have 64 per cent of the market.

The following discussion groups retailers according to the type of retail operation they run. Each type will be defined, and the role it plays within the retail sector will be discussed. This should help to clarify why it is important for the health of the retail sector to support the diversity of shapes and sizes of retailer, and why the small corner shop is just as valuable in its way as the top 10 retailers.

Department Stores

Department stores usually occupy a prominent prime position within a town centre or a large out of town shopping mall. Most towns have one, and some centres, such as London's Oxford Street, support several.

Examples of department stores are:

- UK: Debenham's, House of Fraser, John Lewis
- France: Printemps, Galeries Lafayette
- Germany: Karstadt
- Netherlands: Vendex
- Switzerland: Manor

In the UK, department stores are a very long-established retailing tradition, and the large chains, such as Debenham's and House of Fraser have been built up over the years through the acquisition of locally based stores across the country. Debenham's have been thorough in imposing a consistent, overt identity on all their stores, through name and image. House of Fraser, on the other hand, have taken a slightly softer line, supporting a number of retail names, such as Binns, Rackhams, and Dickins and Jones, but keeping the House of Fraser identity subtly in the background. Similarly, Manor, Switzerland's largest department store chain, operates under a variety of retail names, including Nordmann, Placette, Innovazione, Rheinbrucke and Vilan, depending largely on the locality and its language. All the stores trade under the same corporate logo, and it is likely that they will all eventually trade under the same name, to build a stronger identity (Krienke, 1993a).

Department stores are large and are organised into discrete departments consisting of related product lines, such as sports, ladies' fashions, toys, electrical goods etc. Manor, for example, stocks clothing for all the family, food, cosmetics, entertainment goods, electrical appliances, toys, kitchenware, home furnishing, decorative objects, gifts and accessories, as well as running restaurants in its stores.

To support the concept of providing everything that the customer could possibly want, department stores extend themselves into services as well as physical products, operating hairdressing and beauty parlours, restaurants, and travel agencies. In some stores, individual departments are treated as business units in their own right. Taking that concept a little further, it is not surprising that **concessions** or 'stores within a store' have become common. With these a manufacturer or another retail name purchases space within a department store, paying either a fixed rental per square metre or a percentage commission on turnover, to set up and operate a distinct trading area of its own. Jaeger, the classic fashion manufacturer and retailer, operates a number of its own stores throughout the UK, but also generates over one-third of its turnover from concessions within department stores such as House of Fraser.

There are sound reasons on both sides for the operation of concessions.

The department store perspective. A concession brings a bit of extra variety and life to a store, and may bring in customers who would not otherwise have patronised that department store. A concession might also trade in a product that the department store owners themselves would not want to take a risk on. Given the uncertainties facing the retail sector, concessions take up what might otherwise be excess floor capacity, and provide a steady income per square metre. Overall, because concessions are clearly distinct from the rest of the store, they are a good way of extending the variety and scope of the store without necessarily compromising its core image.

The manufacturer's perspective. There are two broad reasons why a manufacturer might wish to operate a concession within a department store. The first is a general desire to reduce the influence of the intermediaries and thus have a High Street presence, but without going through the lengthy and expensive rigmarole of setting up a retail operation from scratch. One deal, head office to head office, gives the manufacturer a stake in a number of prime sites across the country, as well as giving them access to the department store's facilities and support systems if required. More specifically, the second reason for taking out a concession is that a manufacturer might wish to have tighter control over the way in which its product is displayed and sold. There is always a risk that if your product is only one of many hundreds that a department store sells, it will not get the handling, display or personal selling attention that you think it deserves.

Another retail name's perspective. Why should a department store allow another established high street retailer to have space on its premises? Often, it is because they are both owned by the same parent company. Debenham's, for example, is owned by the Burton Group, as are Top Shop and Principles. While both Top Shop and Principles have extensive high street presence in their own right, they also run as concessions within some branches of Debenham's. In general terms, there are several possible reasons for this kind of cohabitation:

1 *Encouraging cross-trading*: customers who go into the department store specifically to visit the concession might get drawn into browsing in the wider store (and vice versa).
2 *Lack of suitable sites*: in a particular town, there may not be a suitable property available for opening a new branch. Taking a concession at least establishes a presence in that town until something more appropriate can be found. It also reduces the risk of rushing into a less than desirable property for the sake of it.
3 *Shortage of space*: even if the retailer does have a branch in the town, the shop might not be big enough to display the full range of merchandise. If the original branch cannot be extended, then a concession in the department store in the same town gives some expansion of trading space, although it is a far from optimal solution.
4 *Corporate rationalisation*: high street shops are expensive to operate and maintain. A corporate decision might be made, therefore, to cut back on the number of 'free standing' branches by closing some down and relocating them in local department stores as concessions. Similarly, if the department store is having a rough time, putting concessions into it might increase its turnover and performance as well as mopping up excess capacity.

The department store is not without problems. In the UK, it is under threat from out of town shopping and the general growth of specialist retailers. There are also difficulties with the high cost of city centre location and operation. The department stores' answer to these threats has been a concerted effort to improve their purchasing policies, to update their images and provide a higher quality ambience through refurbishment of existing stores, and to locate new stores in out of town retail parks. According to Tordjman (1995), department stores are a stable format in the UK, weak in Italy, dynamic in Spain, declining in France, but are leaders in non-food retailing in Germany.

Variety stores

Variety stores are smaller than department stores, and they stock a more limited number of ranges in greater depth. C&A, for example, sells only clothing, but provides a great deal of choice within that limited definition, covering ladies' wear, menswear, children's clothing, party wear, sportswear, lingerie etc. Some retailers offer all that in the clothing sector, but add extra ranges too. BhS in the UK, for example, offer housewares and lighting as well as extensive clothing ranges, while Marks & Spencer are respected as much for their groceries as their clothing. Again, according to Tordjman (1995), variety stores have suffered mixed fortunes across Europe. In the UK, largely thanks to Marks & Spencer, it is a powerful sector. In Germany and Italy, however, it is very weak, while in Spain it is marginal and in France declining but stabilising.

Example

Like department stores, the major variety stores such as Monoprix in France and Kaufhalle in Germany operate as national chains, maintaining a consistent image across the country. Some, such as C&A and M&S, also operate internationally. Whatever the geographical coverage of the variety store chain, given the size of the stores, they need volume traffic (i.e., lots of customers) and thus to develop a mass-market appeal, offering quality merchandise at no more than mid-range price points.

Variety stores tend to offer limited additional services, with a tendency towards self-service, and centralised cashier points. In that sense, they are something between a department store and a supermarket.

Supermarkets

Over the last few years, the **supermarket** has been accused of being the major culprit in changing the face of the high street. The first generation of supermarkets, some 30 years ago, were relatively small town centre operations. As they expanded and cut their costs through self-service, bulk buying and heavy merchandising, they began to replace the small traditional independent grocer. More recently, they have expanded on to out of town sites, with easy free parking, and have taken the customers with them, thus (allegedly) threatening the health of the high street.

> ### Example
>
> Generally, supermarkets are large, self-service stores, carrying a comprehensive range of fmcg products, sometimes including in-store bakeries, delicatessens and fishmongers. A typical supermarket is clearly zoned by product group, but always has central checkout facilities. Branches often also stock some convenience items, such as pharmaceuticals, newspapers, hardware etc. The larger branches of retailers such as Auchan, Carrefour or Tesco may carry clothes, small DIY, electrical etc. Others, such as Sainsbury's, have developed parallel chains (Sainsbury's Homebase) to deal specifically with the less frequently purchased hardware, DIY and gardening goods. Similarly, Auchan has diversified into DIY (Leroy Merlin), sport (Decathlon), electrical goods (Boulanger) and into many other areas.

The dominance of supermarkets is hardly surprising, considering that because of their size and operating structures their labour costs are something like 10–20 per cent lower than those of independent grocers, and their buying advantage 15 per cent better. This means that they can offer a significant price advantage. Additionally, they have made efficiency gains and increased their cost effectiveness through their commitment to developing and implementing new technology in the areas of EPOS, shelf allocation models, forecasting and physical distribution management systems.

The challenge of discount operators

British supermarket retailing is at a crossroads. The new wave of discount supermarkets, such as Aldi, Netto and Lidl severely damaged the established operators' value for money image when they first opened in the UK. Aldi and Lidl are both German and Netto is Danish. All three established their operating practices in their home markets before expanding into other parts of Europe. Their main attraction is their low prices, which are achieved in a number of ways (The Economist, 1993):

- limited number of products thus keeping distribution and administration costs low
- concentration on very fast moving lines, thus maximising volume and minimising stock holding costs
- negotiating cheap own label goods
- opportunistic purchasing of one-off consignments of cheap goods
- renting small, cheap sites closer to customers
- minimal service, thus reducing staffing costs
- minimal in-store displays, e.g. selling goods straight out of the cartons in which they were delivered, again reducing costs.

Thus the combination of careful sourcing and the minimisation of operating costs means that the discounter can potentially undercut a 'normal' supermarket's prices by up to 40 per cent on some lines.

The traditional supermarkets are trying to regain some of the 'value for money' ground (through campaigns such as Tesco's Value Lines), but at the same time, they are also trying to clearly differentiate themselves as being upmarket from the discounters. Kaas (1994) suggests that retailers will have to increase their own-label activity as well as developing both price and value-driven offerings to the consumer. The retailers are indeed following that advice among a number of other tactics they are using in their fight against the discounters.

Increased service. Although a supermarket is primarily a self-service operation, there are some service aspects that can be offered to make life easier for the shopper without compromising the supermarket's ethos. Providing more cashiers and more checkouts to reduce the queueing time, helping with packing and carrying goods to the car, personal service at delicatessen, bakery and fish counters may be valued services that encourage store loyalty and reduce the emphasis on price alone. Similarly, providing disabled and mother-and-child parking spaces close to the doors, and specially adapted trolleys, add to the impression of a customer-orientated, caring organisation.

Developing additional products. Another way of extending service or convenience to customers is through extending the range of services provided for sale within the precincts of the supermarket. Dry cleaners, pharmacies, photo processors and cafeterias are among the services offered.

Developing premium tastes. The discounters rely on bulk sales of very fast-moving staple brands and products. The supermarkets, therefore, have seen an opportunity in encouraging customers to try out more 'exotic' and unusual products that are less price sensitive and sell in lower quantities. In fresh foods, for example, this might be done through sourcing fruit and vegetables that are not commonly available in this country, or stocking unusual varieties of common items like apples. More imaginative approaches to chilled or frozen ready meals have also helped to make the consumer more adventurous and more willing to demand extensive choice. The Sainsbury's recipe series of advertisements made the most of some unusual products, whetting the consumer's appetite and, more importantly, showing the product in use.

Emphasizing own brands. As discussed in Chapter 7, retailers have put much time and effort into the development of their own brands, partly as a defence against the power of the brand manufacturers, but also partly as a defence against the discounters. If retailers can convince consumers that their own brands are good quality value for money substitutes for the manufacturer brands, then they stand a chance of achieving two things:

1 removing the emphasis from price on the supermarket shelves, as consumers will seek out the own brand they like rather than hunting for the cheapest bargain, and linked with that;
2 increasing store loyalty, as consumers will want to shop at a particular supermarket because that is the only place they can get the own brand they like.

All of this underlines the fact that discounters compete most successfully where product ranges are virtually identical across all retailers, allowing price to be the differentiating factor, and service provision and service products are of no interest to the shopper. It is in the traditional supermarkets' interests to make sure that the consumer does not adopt that view.

As discussed in Chapter 10, all-out price wars are dangerous unless you know that you can win. The margins on traditional supermarket product ranges are so low (because supermarkets depend on shifting very large volumes of low-margin products to make their profits) that there is little room for price cutting across the board anyway. Furthermore, discounters, through minimal investment in service and display, are already offering prices that the other retailers, with their higher overheads, would have difficulty in matching and sustaining. In comparison with pruning their operations to compete head-on with the discounters, therefore, the defensive tactics outlined above seem far less suicidal, and thus far at least seem to be effective. Hogarth-Scott and Parkinson (1994) researched the effects of a discounter opening a store close to an established supermarket. They found that although 57 per cent of shoppers had tried the discounter once, only 4 per cent of customers had been lost to the discounter, representing 4.7 per cent of turnover. It appears that the British shopper is still more attracted to the high levels of service and the premium offerings provided by the traditional supermarkets.

Hypermarkets

The **hypermarket** is a natural extension of the supermarket. While the average supermarket covers up to 2500 m^2, a superstore is between 2500 and 5000 m^2 and a hypermarket is anything over 5000 m^2 (URPI, 1988). It provides even more choice and depth of range, but usually centres mainly around groceries. Table 13.4 shows the penetration of the different kinds of food retailing format in various European countries (Tordjman, 1995). Examples of hypermarket operators are Intermarché and Carrefour in France, Tengelmann in Germany and ASDA in the UK.

Because of their size, hypermarkets tend to occupy new sites on **out of town** retail parks. They need easy access and a large amount of space for parking not only because of the volume of customers they have to attract, but also because their size means that customers will buy a great deal and will therefore need to be able to bring the car close to the store.

MARKETING IN ACTION

Hypermarkets in Portugal

The retail structure in Portugal is in transition. Traditionally, it has been a country of small retailers, especially in the food sector. There are 3.8 small grocers per 1000 people in Portugal, compared with a European average of 1.4. In just five years, however, from 1989 to 1994, the share of food sales held by small food outlets fell from 64 per cent to 34 per cent and an estimated five shops were going out of business every day. A strong political lobby from the small retailers managed to influence the restriction of Sunday opening hours for larger stores and the control of planning permission. The rationale was an attempt by the smaller stores to get back lost share by seeking the all-day Sunday closure of the larger stores. In a Catholic country, this stance gained much sympathy, supported by those who argued on religious grounds for the maintenance of Sunday as a day of rest.

Despite this minor victory, the small stores appear to be losing the fight for consumer patronage. The supermarket and hypermarket chains such as the Sonae group (consisting of eight Continente stores, 26 Modelo stores and 75 Dia%), Jeronimo Martins, Pao de Acucar and Carrefour have gained market share very quickly. In 1996, there were 44 hypermarkets in Portugal, which is only one hypermarket per 212 000 people, compared with one hypermarket per 32 000 in France. The variety, convenience, low prices and even the attraction of Sunday leisure shopping are powerful forces for change. As with many other European countries, the real answer is for the small stores to become more attractive and competitive, capitalising on personalised service. This means greater specialisation as convenience stores, discount stores, or franchised outlets. These stores, however, more often than not only succeed in taking share from each other rather than seriously affecting the larger stores.

Sources: The Grocer (1996b); Wise (1996).

TABLE 13.4
Penetration of types of food retailing format

	France	UK	Spain	Germany	Italy
Strong	Hypermarket	Superstore	Hypermarket	Hard discount Hypermarket	Supermarket Independents
Medium	Supermarket	Hard discount	Independents Supermarket	Supermarket	
Weak	Hard discount superstore	Hypermarket	Hard discount	Superstore	Hypermarket Hard discount

Source: Tordjman (1995), p. 29.

According to *Euromonitor* (1995b), between 1990 and 1994 the number of hypermarkets in Spain and Italy more than doubled, from 128 to 271 in Spain and from 134 to 299 in Italy. In northern European countries, however, the increase was much less dramatic. In 1994 in France, only 30 new stores opened, although France still has over 2000 hypermarkets. This slowdown in growth has as much to do with the changing regulatory environment as with saturation within the format. In late 1995, the French government proposed even tighter planning restrictions on large retail sites. Previously, it was only sites of over 1000 m² (or 1500 m² in cities) that faced rigorous planning scrutiny. The proposal is to bring that limit down to 300 m² and that a public enquiry will be held for any development of over 6000 m² (*The Grocer*, 1995). It is easy to see the roots of the government's concern by looking at Table 13.5. This shows the top 10 hypermarket and superstore operators in France and the number and average size of their stores.

Out of town speciality stores

An out of town **speciality store** tends to specialise in one broad product group, for example furniture, carpets, DIY or electrical. It tends to operate on an out of town site, which is cheaper than a town centre site and also offers good parking and general accessibility. It concentrates on discounted prices and promotional lines, thus emphasizing price and value for money. A product sold in an out of town speciality store is

TABLE 13.5
The French hypermarket and superstore sector, 1993

	Turnover in France (Fr mill.)	Number of stores	Total selling area (m²)	Average store size (m²)
Leclerc	119.0	525	1 700 000	3 238
Intermarché	117.0	1600	2 150 000	1 344
Carrefour	92.0	111	1 000 000	9 009
Promodès	91.5	990	1 260 000	1 273
Casino	67.5	580	1 200 000	2 069
Auchan	50.0	49	500 000	10 204
Système U	41.0	510	720 000	1 412
Docks de France	37.5	300	780 000	2 600
Cora	26.0	195	620 000	3 179
Compt. Modernes	23.5	325	390 000	1 200

Source: Adapted from *Marketing Vente*, July/August 1994, p. 23.

likely to be cheaper than the same item sold through a town centre speciality or department store.

The store itself can be single storey, with no windows. Some care is taken, however, over the attractiveness of the in-store displays and the layout. Depending on the kind of product area involved, the store may be self-service, or it may need to provide knowledge-able staff to help customers with choice and ordering processes. Recent years have seen efforts to improve the ambience of such stores and even greater care over their design.

> ### Example
>
> IKEA provides an extremely pleasant and user friendly display area, with mock room settings so that customers can see products in context, free pencils and tape measures for making notes and checking dimensions, and a relaxing restaurant area. This is backed up, however, by an extremely functional and efficient warehouse operation in which customers can self select the products they want from pallets and then proceed to a checkout, although service is available to help with bulkier items or larger orders.

Toy 'Я' Us in particular has become known as a *category killer* because it offers so much choice and such low prices that other retailers cannot compete. Its large out of town site mean that it is efficient in terms of its operating costs, and its global bulk buying means that it can source extremely cheaply. Shoppers wanting to buy a particular toy know that Toys 'Я' Us will probably have it in stock, and shoppers who are unsure about what they want have a wonderful browsing opportunity. Additionally, the out of town sites are easily accessible and make transporting bulky items a lot easier. The small independent toy retailer, in contrast, cannot match buying power, cost control, accessibility or choice and is likely to be driven out of business.

Town centre speciality stores

Like out of town speciality stores, town centre speciality stores concentrate on a narrow product group as a means of building a differentiated offering. They are smaller than the out of town speciality stores, averaging about 250 m². Within this

Toys 'Я' Us *used out of town sites to establish itself as a category killer*

Source: Toys 'Я' Us.

sector, however, there are retailers such as florists, lingerie retailers, bakeries and confectioners that operate on much smaller premises.

Other examples of products sold through town centre speciality stores are footwear, toys, books and clothing (although often segmented by sex, age, lifestyle or even size). Most are comparison products, for which the fact of being displayed alongside similar items can be an advantage, as the customer wants to be able to examine and deliberate over a wider choice of alternatives before making a purchase decision. Given their central locations, and the need to build consumer traffic with competitive merchandise, the sector has seen the growth of multiple chains, serving clearly defined target market segments with clearly defined product mixes, such as most of the high street fashion stores. To reinforce the concept of specialisation and differentiation, some, especially the clothing multiples, have developed their own-label brands.

Town centre speciality stores are usually a mixture of browsing and self-service, but with personnel available to help if required. The creation of a retail atmosphere or ambience appropriate to the target market is very important, including for instance the use of window display and store layout. This allows the town centre speciality store to feed off consumer traffic generated by larger stores, since passing shoppers are attracted in on impulse by what they see in the window or through the door. The multiples can use uniform formulae to replicate success over a wide area, but because of their buying power and expertise, they have taken much business away from small independents.

Convenience stores

Despite the decline of the small independent grocer in the UK, there is still a niche that can be filled by **convenience stores**. Operating mainly in the groceries, drink, and CTN sectors, they open long hours, not just 9 a.m. until 6 p.m.

They fill a gap left by the supermarkets, which are fine for the weekly or monthly shopping trip, if the consumer can be bothered to drive out to one. The convenience stores, however, satisfy needs that arise in the meantime. If the consumer has run out of something, forgotten to get something at the supermarket, wants freshness, or finds six unexpected guests on the doorstep who want feeding, the local convenience store is invaluable. If the emergency happens outside normal shopping times, then the advantages of a local, late night shop become obvious. Such benefits, however, do tend to come at a price premium. To try to become more price competitive, some 'open all hours' convenience stores operate as voluntary chains, such as Spar, VG and Mace, in which the retailers retain their independence but benefit from bulk purchasing and centralised marketing activities.

The latest development in the convenience sector has been the expansion of the shops operating at petrol stations. Many petrol retailers, such as Jet and Shell, have developed their non-petrol retailing areas into attractive mini-supermarkets that pull in custom in their own right. In some cases, they are even attracting customers who go in to buy milk or bread and end up purchasing petrol as an afterthought.

Discount clubs

Discount clubs are rather like cash and carries for the general public, where they can buy in bulk at extremely competitive prices. Discount clubs do, however, have membership requirements, related to occupation and income.

The discount clubs achieve their low prices and competitive edge through minimal service and the negotiation of keen bulk deals with the major manufacturers, beyond anything offered to the established supermarkets. Added to this, they pare their margins to the bone, relying on volume turnover, and they purchase speculatively. For instance, they may purchase a one-off consignment of a manufacturer's surplus stock at a very low price, or they may buy stock cheaply from a bankrupt company. While this allows them to offer incredible bargains, they cannot guarantee consistency of supply, thus they may have a heap of televisions one week, but once they have been sold, that is it, there are no more. The following week the same space in the store may be occupied by hi-fis. At least such a policy keeps customers coming back to see what new bargains there are.

The major problem for consumers is that unless they have large families, or a very spacious garage for storage, the minimum purchase quantities for any single item are intimidating. One solution is to form an informal co-operative with a number of like-minded friends, and acting as a mini-wholesaler, break bulk and resell to them. Most consumers however, would probably not be interested in the management and administration involved, and would prefer to pay the slightly higher prices for the convenience of the local supermarket.

Markets

Most towns have markets, as a last link with an ancient form of retailing. There are now different types of market, not only those selling different kinds of products, but street markets, held on certain days only; permanent markets occupying dedicated sites under cover or in the open; and Sunday markets for more specialised products.

Typical market products include fresh food, clothing and housewares. Some goods are downmarket, but others are simply unusual, for example a craftsman or craftswoman selling items they have made themselves.

Example

The value of the market stall as a first step on the retailing ladder is well under-stood. The management of the Gateshead Metro Centre, for example, not only rent out permanent retail space, but also hire out a number of mobile barrows, situated throughout the shopping centre, at relatively low rents. This gives a more lively, market type of character to the public areas, but more importantly, gives an opening for small traders, or individuals with little cash but a lot of entrepreneurial flair, to test a retail concept and to begin to develop a business. Many barrow retailers then build up sufficient confidence and resources to take on a permanent shop unit.

Catalogue showrooms

A fairly recent development, **catalogue showrooms** try to combine the benefits of a high street presence with the best in logistics technology and physical distribution management. The central focus of the showroom is the catalogue, and many copies are displayed around the store as well as being available for the customer to take home for browsing. Some items are on live display, but by no means the whole product range. The consumer selects from the catalogue, then goes to a checkout where an assistant inputs the order into the central computer. If the item is immediately available, the cashier takes payment. The consumer then joins a queue at a collection point, while the purchased product is brought round from the warehouse behind the scenes, usually very quickly.

A prime example of this type of operation is Argos, which offers a very wide range of household, electrical and leisure goods. They offer relatively competitive prices through bulk purchasing, and savings on operating costs, damage and pilfering (because of the limited displays).

NON-STORE RETAILING

A growing amount of selling to individual consumers is now taking place outside the traditional retailing structures. Non-store selling may involve personal selling (to be dealt with in Chapter 18), selling to the consumer at home through television, computer or telephone links, or most impersonally selling through vending machines. Some of these areas clearly have strong roots in direct marketing, which is the subject of Chapter 19, but they will be briefly introduced here.

In-home selling

The longest established means of selling to the consumer at home is through door-to-door selling, where the representative calls at the house either trying to sell from a suitcase (brushes, for example), or trying to do some preliminary selling to pave the way for a more concerted effort later (with higher cost items such as double glazing, burglar alarms, and other home improvements). Cold calling (i.e., turning up unexpectedly and unannounced) is not a particularly efficient use of the representative's time, nor is it likely to evoke a positive response from the customer. Organisations are more likely now to qualify leads in advance, thus sending representives out to people who have already expressed an interest, for example by returning a 'more information please' coupon from an advertisement, or using the cheaper method of telephone selling to arrange an initial interview.

A more acceptable method of in-home selling that has really taken off is the party plan. Here, the organisation recruits ordinary consumers to act as agents and do the selling for them in a relaxed sociable atmosphere. The agent, or a willing friend, will host a party at a house and provide light refreshments. Guests are invited to attend, and during the course of the evening, when everyone is relaxed, the agent will demonstrate the goods and take orders.

Since the pioneering days of the Tupperware party, many other products have used the same sort of technique. Cabouchon sells jewellery across Europe in this kind of way. With a more downmarket product range, Ann Summers is an organisation that sells erotic lingerie and sex aids and toys through parties. The majority of the customers are women who would otherwise never dream of going into 'that kind of shop', let alone buying that kind of merchandise. A party is an ideal way of selling those products to that particular target market, because the atmosphere is relaxed, the customer is among friends, and purchases can be made without embarrassment amidst lots of giggling. One of the best features of party selling is the ability to show and demonstrate the product. This kind of hands-on, interactive approach is a powerful way of involving the potential customer and thus getting them interested and in a mood to buy.

The main problem with party selling, however, is that it can be difficult to recruit agents, and their quality and selling abilities will be variable. Supporting and motivating a pyramid of agents, and paying their commission can make selling costs very high.

Mail order and teleshopping

Both mail order and teleshopping will be explored in more detail in Chapter 19. This section, therefore, gives only a brief introduction in order to acknowledge their place as alternative forms of selling or retailing to consumers. **Mail order** has a long history and traditionally consists of a printed catalogue from which customers select goods which are then delivered to the home either through the postal service or through couriers. This form of selling has, however, developed and diversified over the years.

Offers are now made through magazine or newspaper advertisements, as well as through the traditional catalogue, and database marketing now means that specially tailored offers can be made to individual customers. Orders no longer have to be mailed in by the customer, but can be telephoned, with payment being made immediately by credit card. The strength of mail order varies across Europe, but is generally stronger in northern Europe than in the south. It is very strong in Germany through companies such as Otto Versand, Quelle and Nekermann. Otto Versand also has interests in the strong UK mail order sector, with its 1991 acquisition of Grattan.

Teleshopping represents a much wider range of activities. It includes shopping by telephone in response to television advertisements, whether on cable, satellite or terrestrial channels. Some cable and satellite operators run home shopping channels, such as QVC, where the primary objective is to sell goods to viewers. Teleshopping also covers interactive shopping by computer, using mechanisms such as the French Minitel system or the Internet. The Internet in particular offers interesting opportunities to a variety of sellers, including established retailers. Many, such as Toys 'Я' Us and Blackwell's Bookshop have set up 'virtual' stores on Internet sites, so that a potential customer can browse through the merchandise, select items, pay by credit card and then wait for the goods to be delivered.

Through the development of video catalogues and 'specialogues', and through further exploitation of other direct marketing techniques such as telephone ordering and selling via the Internet, mail order and related forms of non-store retailing could have an interesting future, complementing high street retailing in the eyes of the shopper.

Vending

Vending machines account for a very small percentage of retail sales, less than 1 per cent. They are mainly based in workplaces and public locations, for example offices, factories, staff rooms, bus and rail stations etc. They are best used for small, standard, low-priced, repeat purchase products, such as hot and cold drinks, cans of pop, chocolate and snacks, bank cash dispensers and postage stamps. They have the advantage of allowing customers to purchase at highly convenient locations, at any time of the day or night. Vending machines can also help to deliver the product in prime condition for consumption, for example the refrigerated machines that deliver a can of ice-cold Coke. A human retailer cannot always maintain those conditions.

In the workplace, vending machines can be a valuable complement to normal catering services. If the machine is situated near to the shopfloor or working area, then employees do not have to waste time trekking across to a remote part of the site to get a drink, for instance. Similarly, the vending machine can help to save time and reduce queues in the canteen by dealing with employees' minor purchases, leaving the canteen staff to handle larger purchases.

Although vending machines take up little space, and do not require staff in constant attendance, they do need regular and frequent servicing, whether to replenish stocks or empty the cash box or simply for preventative maintenance to ensure that the service is sustained. Nevertheless, vending machines represent significant business.

Example

In France there are around 170 000 machines for canned drinks, representing a market of F700 million; up to 50 000 machines for cartons and bottles (F400 million), and 15 000 for snacks (F300 million). Evian, producers of mineral water, have some 4500 machines in France distributing bottles of Evian and Badoit, while Perrier operates about 1500 machines (Tanguy, 1994).

RETAILER STRATEGY

This section looks more closely at some of the strategic issues and decisions facing retailers, including location, product mix, competitive positioning, store image and atmosphere, merchandising, the use of technology and, finally, strategic alliances. All these areas could be critical to the marketing success of retailers (Davies, 1992).

Location

Location is a very important area for decision, since if the wrong location is chosen for a store (or worse, a series of wrong locations for a chain of stores), the retailer can lose a great deal of business by failing to reach or attract the right kind of customer to generate a viable level of trade (Anderson, 1993). In addition to lost business, there is also the waste of the money invested in acquiring the site or premises and building and/or shopfitting. A supermarket chain such as Tesco or Sainsbury's can spend up to £20 million per new store, including site acquisition costs.

Choice of location is linked to social and demographic changes. For example, increasing rates of car ownership and the rising number of working women with too little time to shop for their families have helped the rise of the out of town superstore site. But there are other more general factors which also affect the location decision. Some of these are considered in turn.

Catchment

For a given location, the retailer needs to know the size of the population that the store can draw on, and more specifically, what proportion of that population matches the desired market segment profile. Some estimate also needs to be made of the likely average expenditure per customer to see if the store will generate sufficient turnover, given the likely competitive response to the store opening. Further work may also be undertaken to assess the market's response to the retailer's presence and promotional activity (Davies and Rogers, 1984; Wrigley, 1988). Catchment is not only about resident population, but about the location's accessibility and proximity to other attractions, such as railway or bus stations, that will generate passing consumer traffic.

MARKETING IN ACTION

Tie Rack

By the mid-1990s, Tie Rack had managed to turn its fortunes around after a series of poor results caused by a need to restructure and by overextending itself in its US and Canadian operations. Tie Rack was formed in 1982 as a niche retailer selling quality ties and scarves, especially at airports. In the UK, out of 167 shops, 59 are in airport lounges and a further 40 shops are at airports in 14 different countries. Although Tie Rack can be found in the high street, its significant growth has come from its airport locations.

Tie Rack expects its products to be purchased as gifts rather than as last minute emergency purchases. Ties and scarves are small, light and easily slipped into a suitcase or hand luggage. At an airport, customers are captive either because it is too far for them to go to shop elsewhere, or they have limited time available for shopping before their flights. Although many alternatives exist for shopping within an airport, there is usually only one retailer selling goods within each category type. Thus a Tie Rack within an airport effectively has exclusive rights over a captive audience for its merchandise. The real keys to its success, however, have been focusing on a narrow product line and resisting some of the high margin, exclusive product approaches found in some other airport retailers who hope to exploit the captive, price-insensitive customer.

Source: Hall (1995).

Type of goods

Different locations suit different kinds of goods and shopping needs or habits. Think about the difference between convenience and shopping goods, for instance (defined at pp. 257–59). Convenience goods need to be readily available, geographically close to people to buy almost at whim, whereas shopping goods involve a more deliberate purchasing decision, and the consumer is more prepared to travel and invest time and money. Convenience goods, therefore, favour locations with a nearby, dense catchment area or at least a lot of passing, impluse buying traffic, and shopping goods can be a little more remote, providing there is the space to present an extensive range of goods for the customer to compare and choose from.

McGoldrick (1990) classifies the factors affecting location decisions as population, accessibility, competition and costs. Figure 13.3 gives examples of some of the factors that might be considered within each category. This figure also outlines the three major stages in an ideal retail location strategy (Bowlby *et al*, 1984).

Location decision-making process

The location decision-making process consists of three stages.

Search for good locations. At the broadest level, the retailer has to decide which regions, cities or towns to locate in. *Spatial marketing* helps to profile defined geographical areas by socioeconomic categories. It can also establish retail spend potential, thus linking in to minimum threshold requirements, that is, the lowest forecast spend level that makes further investigation worth while.

Assessment of viability. Narrowing down a little, the retailer focuses on the *viability* of a specific site. At this stage, store turnover forecasting using multiple regression techniques may be implemented. This will take into account determinants of sales levels and it is especially important where location is seen as a particularly critical factor. It focuses on the type of customers, public transport, and proximity to competitors,

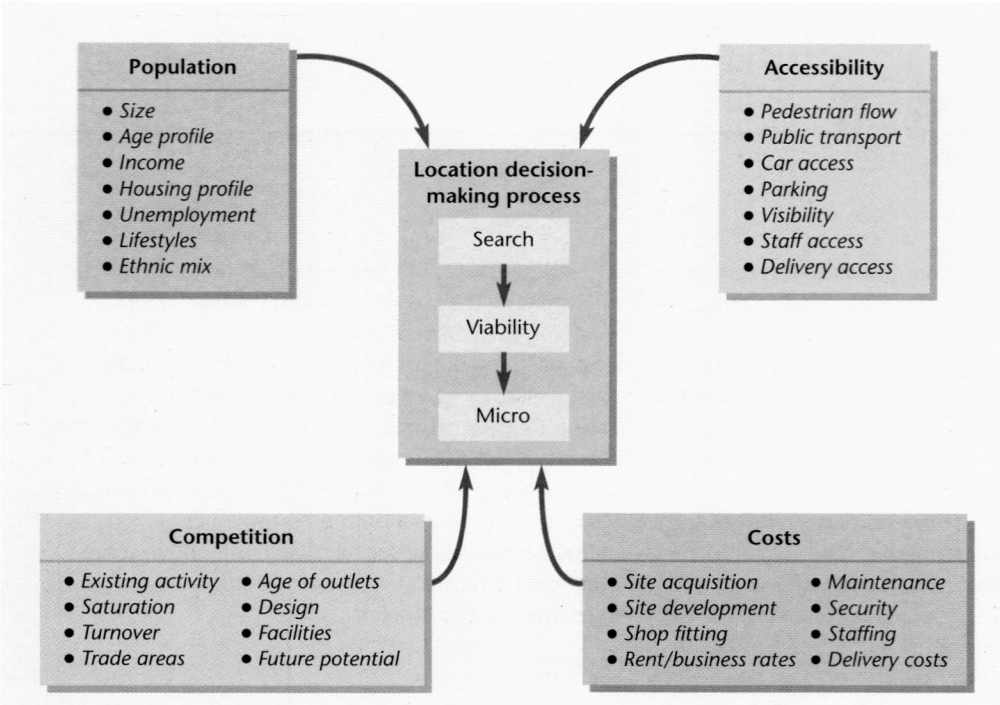

FIGURE 13.3

Factors influencing the location decision-making process

among many other things. Being close to competitors may be a good or a bad thing. Generally, for convenience goods it is not good, but with a shopping product, the closeness may encourage consumers to visit both stores and make comparisons, and the 'better' retailer will win.

Assessment of micro factors. At the most detailed level, the retailer fine tunes by looking at the impact of micro factors, such as pedestrian flows, the profile of local shops, the proximity of other key retailers (such as Marks & Spencer, which always generates plenty of passing consumer traffic), nearness of car parks and the ease of parking and the site's overall appearance. As well as factors that are related to the environment around the site in question, the retailer will consider micro factors relating to the site itself, such as ease of access for loading and unloading, the length and terms of the lease or ownership conditions, and any planning permission needed. The challenge is to establish which micro factors are the most important.

Given the level of investment involved, and the high costs of failure or poor decisions, the larger retail chains use sophisticated, often tailormade, computerised planning models rather than rules of thumb, or hunches. At the very least, the smaller retailer can gain access to material such as the CACI database which profiles shopping centres.

Classification of locations

In general terms, available locations can be classified into three broad areas.

City centre. In the centre of a town or city, the focus is on offices, shopping and public transport termini. There are usually designated retailing zones within such centres. Famous shopping areas in Europe include Oxford Street in London, the Kurfurstendamm in Berlin and Grafton Street in Dublin. City centres attract the largest stores, and often feature shopping malls and pedestrian precincts, covered or open. The presence of a number of big name retailers does generate extra consumer traffic, thus they act as magnets for smaller retailers. Such sites are, however, expensive to occupy and maintain, and are dominated by products such as clothing, footwear, jewellery and financial services.

Suburban. In suburban locations, neighbourhood corner shops or small shopping parades are often found at road intersections or on the edges of large housing estates. They largely serve local needs for convenience goods, and to a lesser extent, shopping goods, through shops of about 200 m^2. Some shopping parades are owned and operated by local authorities who rent the shops to the retailers, others are owned by property companies.

Out of town. First developed in the UK in the 1970s, out of town sites are located at the edges of towns and cities, often next to major roads or at the intersections of major trunk routes. A site either can be dedicated to one massive superstore, such as a supermarket, or can be home to a small range of purpose-built stores (say up to 10). The kinds of products sold on out of town sites are typically groceries, furniture, electrical goods and DIY, retailed through well known supermarkets and discount multiples. The sites are easily accessible, and compared with city centre stores, have lower rents and local authority rates. Most large towns and cities now have them.

The 1980s saw the logical extension of out of town sites into retail parks with much larger numbers of free standing stores of 2500 m^2 or more. Under cover, retail parks have developed along the US model into very large complexes indeed. Out of town shopping malls, such as the Metro Centre at Gateshead and Meadowhall, just off the M1 near Sheffield, have taken the traditional mix and range of stores out of the city centre, and reproduced it on a much bigger scale on a purpose-built site with easy access. The Metro Centre, for example, on two storeys, provides nearly 150 000 m² of retail space, with the additional bonus of 10 000 car parking spaces (which can all be occupied at peak times near Christmas) and a whole range of leisure activities, such as a multiscreen cinema and a bowling alley.

Product range

Breadth and depth of product range stocked was mentioned earlier (*see* p. 497) as a means of classifying retailers. Speciality stores and niche retailers, such as Sock Shop and Tie Rack, concentrate on a few product lines, stocked in considerable depth. Supermarkets and department stores carry a wide product mix. Migros, for example, the Swiss co-operative group, not only retails food, but stocks some 22 000 non-food items. Migros is also into travel, printing, publishing, oil, insurance and many other products and services. It is difficult, however, to keep a broad-ranging product mix and substantial product line depth without investing in large quantities of stock and all the associated costs that go with that.

Product assortment

Most retailers, therefore, will have to compromise, considering product assortment in terms of purpose, status and completeness. *Purpose* means the fit between customer needs and the retailer's revenue requirements. *Status* refers to the relative importance of different products or depths of line. Thus the retailer will define the prime product and then the things that are accessories or add-ons to that. The prime product in a petrol station, for example, is obviously petrol, while food and snacks are desirable, but of secondary importance. That last example links into *completeness*, which is the need to meet customer expectations. Thus motorists expect to be able to buy sweets or cigarettes in a petrol station, and feel that they are receiving inferior service if those kinds of goods are not available.

Product type

The type of products stocked is also important. The retailer may wish to fill only a particular quality niche, or may select a range of products covering different quality levels and price points to fulfil the needs of a wider range of customers. Whether to occupy a niche or to develop a wider specialism is an important decision. If the niche is tightly defined with a very deep assortment, then the retailer will have to hold a large quantity of slow-moving stock, tying up working capital and storage space. Going for a broader, shallower mix might help things to move a little more quickly. Figure 13.4 summarises various influences on product assortment strategy.

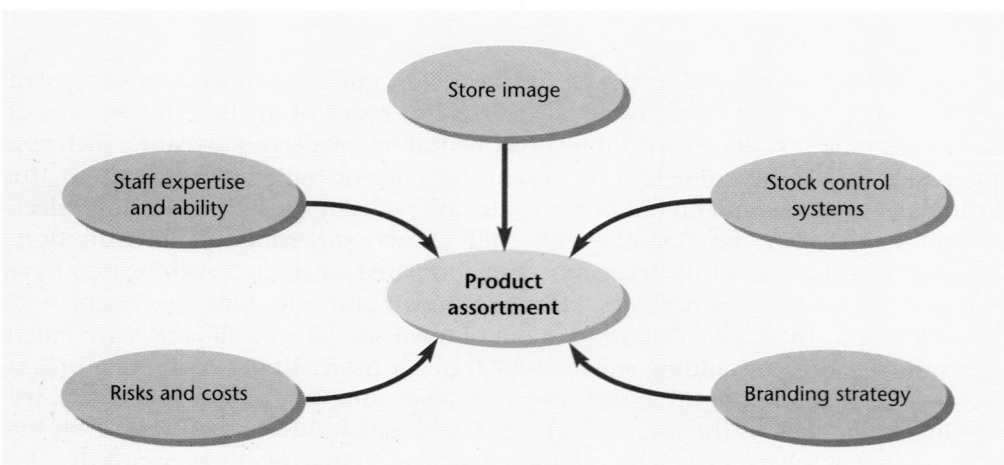

FIGURE 13.4

Factors influencing product assortment strategy

Some retailers do not specialise at all, but take a *scrambled* merchandising approach, by buying in fast-moving items that sell in volume, but are not necessarily related. This achieves a number of things:

1 *It assists impulse purchases.* As with discount clubs (mentioned at p. 507), consumers come in to see what there is and buy while it is still available.
2 *It can generate more sales and profit.* A careful selection of seasonal items for Christmas that are outside the normal product mix in a convenience store can lead to extra sales.
3 *It can improve convenience.* The petrol stations, for example, through developing the range of merchandise and services offered in the forecourt shop have effectively created one-stop shops that can meet most impulse needs of the motorist and those who live close to the garage.
4 *It assists traffic generation.* A wider mix of merchandise attracts a wider mix of customer, certainly for convenience goods.

The retailer does, however, run the risk of losing its distinct image in the mind of the customer. It is also possible to get it wrong, since widening the product mix can project the retailer into unrelated, unknown areas away from its core business, for example a decision to stock CDs in garage forecourt shops, or the newsagent that stocks Christmas trees.

Walters and White (1987) argue that a wide range of issues should be allowed to influence assortment policy. These include careful research, planning, and links with corporate stragey. All of this should be focused towards meeting the needs of the target market and is just as important as merchandise style and service.

Retail competitive positioning

Retailers do not operate in vacuum, and they do have to consider how they shape up against their perceived competitors, and how well they differentiate their offering. This clearly means looking at the market, especially at other retailers, in terms of the criteria that distinguishes one retailer from another in the customer's mind. This analysis reflects the totality of the offer, in terms of merchandising, brand image, products, pricing, atmosphere and image, and service quality (Davies and Brooks, 1989). An independent clothing retailer specialising in designer labels, for example, will position itself as an exclusive, refined, high-priced outlet, with a high level of personal service. In contrast, a high street multiple targeting the teenage market might position itself as a good value for money, lively, vibrant outlet which keeps up with fashion trends. In general, the kind of philosophy applied to product positioning, discussed at pp. 308 *et seq.*, applies equally to retail positioning, although the contributing factors will differ.

Store image and atmosphere

The image and atmosphere of a store is the sum of the physical elements of interior and exterior design, and the layout and displays that create an environment and ambience that consumers find attractive.

Exterior factors that influence perceptions of **store image** include the shop front itself, window displays, the entrance and perhaps even ease of access (traffic congestion in the car park, or closeness to car park). The overall impression these make is especially important to new customers, who may feel either that the store is exciting and welcoming and thus worth a visit, or that it is dirty, dingy and worth walking past. A store may, of course, suffer from influences outside its control, such as the seediness or cleanliness of the surrounding area and nearby retailers, which all impact on a buyer's mood and perception.

Interior factors contributing to **atmosphere** include lighting, wall and floor coverings, and fixtures and fittings, and the effects are very much linked to the senses.

Sight

Sight is stimulated by the use of colour, for example. For a restaurant, red and yellow attract customers and make them feel hungrier and eat faster. Lighting too affects mood and perceptions of products and can help to highlight particular items or ranges or draw customers' attention to the remoter parts of the shop. The general 'look' of a store as customers walk through the door can either lift their spirits and make them want to go in and browse, or underwhelm them to the point where they walk straight out again or only focus functionally on a specific item of interest.

Sound

Total silence is all too rare in retail settings. Most have some sort of music playing, even if the customer does not consciously notice it. Whether it is pop, middle of the road, classical or muzak will depend on the retailer's assessment of the preferences of the target market and the image that is to be projected. Soft music may relax shoppers and make them stay in the store longer, while loud music can reinforce a stimulating, vibrant atmosphere that deliberately sets out to excite the customer.

Scent

Smells are very important. Supermarkets make sure that the cooking smells from the in-store bakery are filtered back into the store so that customers can enjoy the smell of fresh bread, start feeling hungry, and buy more food. Department stores often site the cosmetics counters near the main entrance so that the customer is hit with an exotic blend of upmarket perfume smells. This can be very pleasant, but they need to be careful that the smell isn't so overpowering that it overloads the senses and makes customers feel nauseous! Some smells communicate cleanliness (pine, for example), some communicate luxury (wood or leather, for example), while others are pleasantly stimulating (coffee and bread, for example). All, however, can be used to create and fix a particular impression in the consumer's mind.

Other sensory experiences

As well as the things already mentioned, the consumer does have other, largely tactile, experiences in the retail setting. The feeling of walking on carpet rather than lino, the look and feel of natural wood fittings, and the texture and feel of fabrics around the store, for example, again enhance or detract from the perceived image of the store. Finally, the retailer must bear in mind the comfort of the customer and how it is affected by the temperature of the store. If it is too hot or too cold, the customer will not feel at ease, and will leave the premises more quickly.

It is hard to separate any of those factors from the rest, since the consumer tends to experience them as an integrated whole. The consumer will, however, certainly notice if one factor is out of keeping with the rest. The atmosphere thus created can be

Laura Ashley presents a highly distinctive shop front befitting its upmarket image.

Source: Laura Ashley.

enhanced by the customer's feeling of the 'user friendliness' of the store. The provision of spacious cool changing rooms with adequate lighting and mirrors for trying on clothes, easy access for disabled people, enough room to move between the displays without feeling cramped or lost, displays that make it easy to see the goods properly and to their best advantage, and fast efficient packing and payment handling, all help to make the customer feel more relaxed, and thus willing to spend more time in the store, and thus more likely to spend money in the store.

Other shoppers

A less controllable factor that can have a profound effect on a customer's behaviour is the degree of crowding in a store. Shoppers, walking past an upmarket fashion boutique, might be tempted to go in but, if there is no other customer inside, may feel self-conscious, not wanting to be the focus of the sales assistants' attention. Similarly, an empty restaurant might put potential customers off, either because they feel self-conscious about going in, or because they think that the emptiness is a reflection on the quality of the food. The only kind of store that might possibly benefit from lack of crowds is a supermarket, because of its more impersonal atmosphere. There is something inherently satisfying about having a branch of Sainsbury's virtually to yourself and experiencing hassle-free shopping! At the other extreme, overcrowding is no more attractive. Customers cannot move freely or examine the merchandise properly, and the queues at the checkouts get longer.

It is not only the number of other shoppers that matters. In some situations, the types of other shoppers affect the consumer. Some people would feel very awkward about going into a fashion store, if they felt that they were very different from the shoppers already in there. Similarly, if a shopper was trying to decide whether to buy a particular item of clothing and saw someone old enough to be their grandmother, and four sizes bigger choosing the same item it could make them feel differently about the garment.

As a final thought, remember that store image is not simply a function of the atmosphere factors discussed in this section. It is also affected by additional services offered, merchandise, location, advertising and promotion, brands stocked and pricing. In other words, store atmosphere and store image are simply elements deep inside a detailed marketing mix that must hang together and must be linked in with a strategically defined competitive position, as well as meeting the expectations of target customers.

Merchandising strategies

Store image and atmosphere are also affected by the retailer's approach to *layout* and *display*, which can influence both the customer's behaviour within the store and their perception of the retailer's positioning. They affect how people move around the store, which items attract their attention, and their propensity to interact with the merchandise. Retailers might, however, be restrained in what they can do with layout and display by the kind of factors shown in Fig 13.5.

Store layout

McGoldrick (1990) suggests that most store layouts conform to one of three broad types, or combine elements of them. The alternative layouts are shown in Fig 13.6.

Grid pattern. The grid pattern is the kind of layout adopted by most supermarkets, with systematically arranged aisles. These tend to lead the shopper around the retail space along a largely predictable route that covers most of the store. Supermarkets try to prevent the shopper from taking short cuts by making sure that staple essential items, such as sugar, bread, milk etc. are placed well apart from each other and

FIGURE 13.5

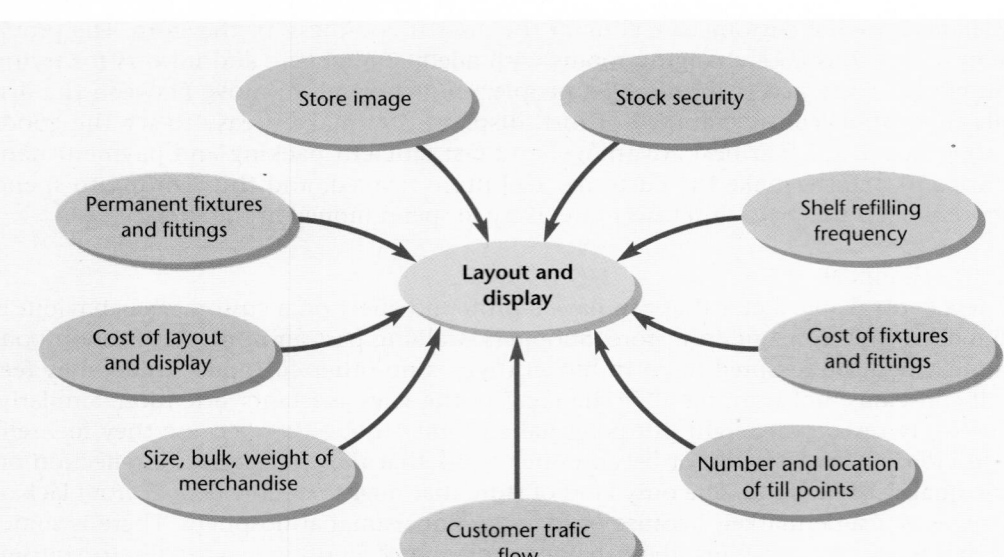

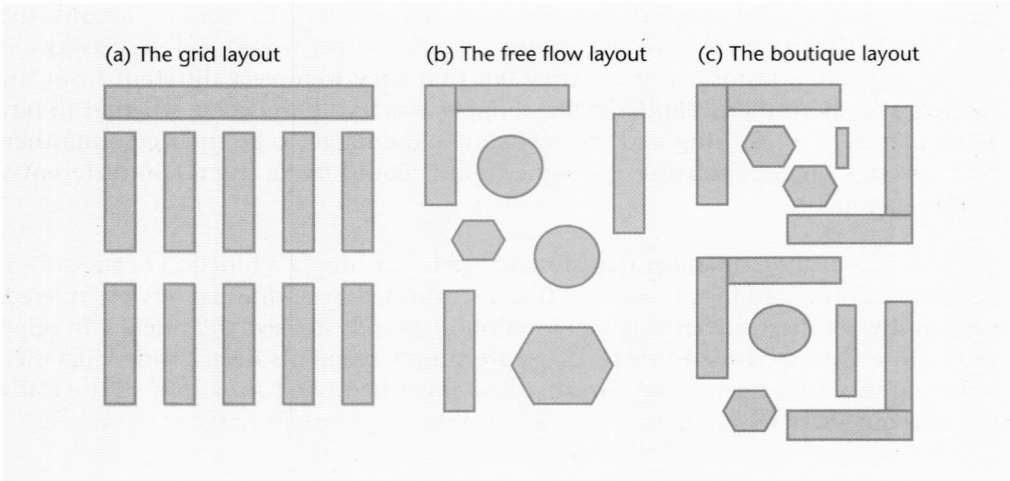

FIGURE 13.6

Alternative approaches to layout

scattered around the store. Thus the shopper who only wants a few basic things still has to pass lots of tempting items that might just lead to a few extra impluse purchases. Routine response staple items are also piled high to reduce the frequency of shelf re-filling, and are placed in narrow aisles to keep shoppers moving, since they do not need to browse around these goods. In contrast, wider aisles are used for the more exotic, less frequently purchased premium goods, such as meals, so that shoppers can move more slowly, have their attention captured, and browse comfortably.

Grid layouts do make sure that the shopper covers as much of the store as possible, and they are easy and cheap to install and maintain. They can, however, be rather boring and regimental, giving the impression of 'functional' shopping. The shopper might also be inclined to associate them with 'pile it high and sell it cheap' discount approaches to retailing, although the quality of the fixtures and fittings and the lighting used by some supermarket chains does give a better quality feel.

Free flow. The free flow pattern is more irregular, involving a variety of different sizes, shapes and heights of fixtures and fittings. Shoppers are free to take any route around the store, and can thus either browse around everything in any order they choose or cut through directly to one display at the back of the store if they prefer. Fashion retailers and others trying to achieve a strong visual 'look' that stimulates customers but encourages them to take their time browsing use this kind of layout. It can, however, be expensive to set up and maintain, and it does not use the available floor space as efficiently as a grid layout.

Boutique. Whereas in a free flow layout the customer perceives the selling area as essentially a single space, in a boutique layout, the perception is one of a number of discrete, separate spaces. This might be particularly useful in a large selling space, such as a department store, where very different departments and concessionaires want to create their own unique and more intimate character.

Many stores combine elements of the three types of layout. A superstore might well use a grid layout for its groceries and other fast-moving lines, but use a free flow approach for clothing, books or videos, for example. Similarly, a variety store such as Boots will vary its approach. Boots uses a supermarket style grid layout for fast-moving staple items such as tights, shampoos, soaps and sticking plasters, but uses a free flow approach for gift-orientated toiletries, toys and household goods. In some larger stores, the gift department, for example, might even be a boutique layout.

Display
Whatever the type of layout adopted, the retailer also has to think about the way in which merchandise is displayed within it. Rosenbloom (1981), as cited by McGoldrick (1990), suggests five alternatives.

Open display. Open displays make the merchandise easily accessible to shoppers and encourage them to pick up and examine goods closely. Fashion stores in particular like to encourage such involvement, so that customers can feel the texture and quality of the fabric, can hold a garment up in front of themselves to check its length or whether it suits them, or can be encouraged to try it on.

Theme display. Themes are commonly used in all kinds of retailers to create a focal point to attract a customer's attention. Events such as Christmas, Easter, and Mother's Day all provide natural themes for the display of gifts and other merchandise. A supermarket might perhaps build an end-of-aisle display around a theme such as Chinese cookery, for example. Such displays are usually temporary, and thus provide something new and different for the regular customer to look at, as well as bringing related merchandise together.

Lifestyle display. Lifestyle displays try to create a more natural setting for the product, giving an idea of how it might be used or by whom, through the subtle use of pictures and other props. IKEA and other furniture retailers, for example, show their goods in room settings, with books in the bookcases, lamps on the tables, and pictures on the walls! Fashion retailers also use lifestyle displays, perhaps using large photographs at the point of sale showing a particular type of person in a particular type of setting wearing a particular outfit. The mail order catalogues have, of course, been doing this sort of thing for years.

Co-ordinated display. A co-ordinated display is similar to lifestyle and themed displays in that it brings together related goods. In a co-ordinated display, goods that are usually sold together or are used together are displayed together. Thus a women's clothing store might display co-ordinating jackets, skirts and trousers together, or include accessories in a clothing display. Even supermarkets might use co-ordination, for example by displaying marzipan, icing sugar, ready-made icing, food colourings and edible cake decorations together near the flour, dried fruit and other home baking goods.

Displaying by product type helps customers find their way round a large out of town store.

Source: Toys 'Я' Us.

Classification dominance display. The aim of a classification dominance display is to suggest specialisation and expertise within a particular product group through the sheer choice of goods displayed. Thus a branch of W. H. Smith, for instance, might have a display of biros and fountain pens covering a wide range of prices, colours, designs and brands. Displays like this are meant to give the customer the impression that THIS is the only place to shop for these kinds of goods.

Technology

Technological advances have allowed retailers to improve the services they offer their customers and to increase their productivity for a better competitive edge.

Barcode scanning not only helps to get customers through the checkout more quickly, but also streamlines stock management. Electronic point of sale (**EPOS**) systems can monitor exactly what products are being sold and how fast, and can trigger reordering or shelf replenishment through direct links often to centrally located warehouses.

Example

Curry's, the electrical retailer, delivers small goods to stores in line with EPOS data. Orders for less frequently purchased larger goods can be sent from the store to a central depot via computer, and then the goods are delivered direct to the customer. Such systems can cost upwards of £50 000, but are essential for giving the customers what they want and expect. Some supermarkets are currently experimenting with self-scanning systems, whereby the customer scans goods as they are put into the trolley. This means that when the customer gets to the checkout, the bill has already been calculated and thus just needs to be paid. This saves on both time and staffing costs.

More strategically, the information gained through EPOS about spending patterns, by brand and by retailer branch, can be used for negotiation with manufacturers or suppliers, or for planning store promotion.

Technology has also fundamentally changed the way in which consumers pay for their purchases. EFTPOS (electronic funds transfer at point of sale) systems have made the use of debit and credit cards very much easier and more acceptable to the retailer and customer alike. Sweeping a card through a reader and letting the till print out the cheque or voucher is much faster and much less prone to error than the old manual systems. For the retailer, it means shorter checkout queues and also faster cash flow, because the day's financial data are downloaded to the bank's computer overnight instead of the retailer having to pay cheques and credit card slips into the bank manually and then waiting for them to go through the three-day clearing system.

Retailer own brands

There is a fine balance of negotiating power between retailers and suppliers. There are some manufacturer brands that the retailers cannot afford to miss out on, and some retail chains that the manufacturer brands cannot afford to be absent from. One tactic that the retailers have used to tip the balance in their favour a little more is the own brand. Over the last few years, certain supermarkets have been proactive in developing good quality, good value for money own brand products across all the major lines they carry. In conjunction with that, they have rationalised the number of brands of any particular product they stock, deleting the minor ones, so that they now have a major manufacturer brand, their own brand, and perhaps one minor brand of a product. The percentage of shelf space and the proportion of sales accounted for by the own brands have been steadily creeping upwards.

In clothing, most retailers are, and always have been, dominated by own brands, for example M&S, BhS, Principles etc. As discussed at p. 472, this has also allowed the emergence of the kind of VMS in which the retailer is the dominant force, dictating quality, service levels, packaging and delivery from its suppliers.

Europeanisation and strategic alliances

Many retailers see international activity as an important part of their businesses, and for some, it represents a significant proportion of their total turnover. As reported by McGoldrick (1995), for example, IKEA generates over 75 per cent of its turnover from international business, Delhaize le Lion, the Belgian food retailer, just over 70 per cent,

TABLE 13.6
Push and pull factors influencing retail internationalisation

Push factors	Pull factors
Economic instability	Economic stability
Low market growth	High market growth
High operating costs	Underdeveloped retail structure
Poor operating environment	Favourable operating environment
Need for economies of scale	Large market
Hostile competition	Innovative retail culture
Mature domestic market	Investment potential
Small domestic market	Niche opportunities
Format saturation	Company owned facilities/operations
Restrictive regulatory environment	Relaxed regulatory environment
Consumer credit restrictions	Positive social environment
Political instability	Political stability

Source: Based on Anderson (1995, p. 85).

Some retailers, such as Marks & Spencer, Laura Ashley, IKEA, Benetton, Aldi and Netto, internationalise by opening their own stores or selling 'branded' franchises to local operators. IKEA, for example, owns virtually all of its 125 stores spread across 26 countries, and deliberately does as little as possible to tailor its ranges to local tastes. It wants to retain the essential 'Swedishness' that permeates all its product design and its retailing approach. As the chain spreads further into the Far East, however, it may have to compromise further (Carnegy, 1995). Other retailers prefer to internationalise through acquisition, with the acquired company retaining its name and local image. Tesco, for example, acquired the French supermarket chain Catteau and has a significant share in the Hungarian chain Global. Similarly, Tengelmann (Germany) bought a stake in Superal (Italy) in order to get into the Italian market. Alternatively, joint ventures mean that two or more retailers join forces to create a new identity. The UK DIY chain, Homebase, is a joint venture between Sainsbury and the Belgian retailer GIB, for example.

whilst for both Tengelmann and Ahold, the figure is between 50 and 60 per cent. The reasons for internationalisation are many and varied. Some are 'push' factors, arising from conditions within the domestic marketing environment that leave the retailer little choice but to internationalise, while others are 'pull' factors, favourable conditions within foreign markets that make them attractive to the retailer. Alexander (1995) neatly summarises the push and pull factors, as shown in Table 13.6.

As mentioned earlier, retailers also form looser international alliances, based on contracts and agreements rather than on degrees of total or co-ownership. These are often geared towards the streamlining of purchasing and logistics rather than direct involvement or interference in each other's retailing operations.

MARKETING IN ACTION

Retailing in Poland

The wholesale and retail sectors in Poland are attracting much interest from EU organisations. Although changes are taking place in the retail structure, Polish retailers still have a long way to go to match the technological and merchandising sophistication achieved by successful EU retailers. Polish stores still tend to be small and many need refurbishment. More than 80 per cent of the retail market is held by small independents and the average size of stores is less than 400 m², sometimes located at the base of blocks of flats or on market stalls. In-store merchandising, themed integration of goods and presentation are only sparsely developed and trading arrangements vary considerably. The wholesaling and distribution system is also very underdeveloped. Surpluses and shortages are common, and quality can be very inconsistent.

This is not, however, deterring incoming investment. A grocery market of £14 billion, a population of 38 million and an above-average central European salary level of £4500 a year, are powerful motivators to enter the market early. Docks de France is thus planning to open 10 Mammouth hypermarkets, regarding the window of opportunity for market entry as narrow. Tesco purchased a 79 per cent share in Savia, a medium-sized retailer and wholesaler in southern Poland; Globi from Belgium is planning 20 outlets, and Norway's Rema already owns 18 stores with 12 more planned. Jeronimo Martins, Portugal's second largest retail group, has bought into the cash and carry business Elektromis of Poznan. With 48 outlets, little serious competition as yet and a low market entry price, they were able to double revenue within a year and broke even on the investment within nine months. Part of the venture means training a new breed of store manager. Young Polish graduates are taken to Portugal for 12 months for extensive training in retail and business management.

Sources: Grain (1996); *The Grocer* (1996c); Provan (1996).

Eurogroup, consisting of GIB (Belgium), Coop Schweiz (Switzerland), Rewe (Germany) and Vendex (Netherlands), was formed as a purchasing alliance. Some alliances, however, go a little further than just purchasing. SEDD, for example, was created early in 1994 as an alliance between Sainsbury (UK), Esselunga (Italy), Docks de France (France) and Delhaize le Lion (Belgium) to pool their 'experience, best practice and buying power' (*Business Europe*, 1994, p. 7). The members of this alliance found that they were individually paying very different prices for the same goods from the same suppliers, and they felt that collectively they could drive much harder bargains. The supplier gains from being able to access markets in four different countries simultaneously.

Buckley (1994) raises a few potential problems with alliances that do not involve ownership. While joint buying power may achieve lower prices, that power cannot be used most effectively unless the retailers can threaten the supplier with delisting in *all* the alliance members' stores. Such unanimity might be difficult to achieve. There might also be cultural differences. Products that might be popular and acceptable in one country might not be wanted in another, thus limiting the buying scope of the alliance. Finally, Buckley points out that membership of an alliance might hinder a retailer's ability to expand into its partners' domestic markets, or eventually to take over a partner. Nevertheless, the number of such alliances is increasing, not just in food and grocery retailing, but in DIY, electrical appliances and toys, among many sectors (Neilsen, 1994).

WHOLESALERS AND DISTRIBUTORS

The emphasis of the chapter now shifts up the distribution channel, away from the retailer to the wholesaler. As consumers, we already know a great deal about the structure of retailing and the variety of retailers who exist to serve our needs. We know much less, however, about the organisations who make sure that the retailers have access to the goods we want to buy. Wholesaling is just as complex a world as that of retailing, with as much variety in the sizes, structures and roles undertaken by its organisations. This section, therefore, will define the range of different types of wholesaler.

Full service wholesalers

As the name implies, full service wholsalers offer the fullest range of wholesaling services, from sourcing and bulk breaking to transportation to marketing and management advice. They are of particular value to the smaller manufacturer or retailer which does not have the necessary expertise to do many of these things for itself. Häagen Dazs, for example, used to deliver ice cream direct to independent retailers, but found that the minimum order quantity, or *drop*, required to make it viable was far too high for many small independents. They switched, therefore, to distribution through specialist frozen food wholesalers so that shopkeepers could buy only one case at a time if they wanted.

Full service wholesale merchants may carry a wide range of product lines, or they might choose to focus on a few lines in depth, or they might be speciality wholesalers, such as the frozen food specialists mentioned above. All of them, however, sell mainly to retailers. Full service wholesalers who sell to manufacturers or non-retailing organisations are called industrial distributors. Again, they might choose to carry a range of products or to specialise.

RS Components is an industrial distributor that buys in electronic components and then sells them on to small manufacturers, prototype designers or repair firms. It defines itself as 'an outsourced purchasing department' because most of its customers are very small organisations that do not want to tie their own money up in stockholding. The other characteristics of the business are the small order size (average £90), the large number of orders handled (average 16 000 per day) and the high level of customer service offered. Service means that orders are dispatched on the same day as they are received, that 58 000 different lines are stocked, that a heavy catalogue is issued three times a year with printed prices guaranteed for the life of the catalogue, and that helplines are provided to advise customers on the appropriate use of components. A more recent innovation is a CD-ROM based catalogue, and on-line ordering for customers via a modem. RS is now internationalising its operations by moving into France, Germany and Italy and further afield into Asia and the Far East (Lynn, 1995).

Limited service wholesalers

In contrast to the full service operators, limited service wholesalers only undertake clearly defined services, as a means of keeping their costs down. They may for, example, choose not to provide transport services, or not to stock large quantities of products.

A typical kind of limited service wholesaler, commonly found across Europe, is the *cash and carry*. These wholesalers serve the needs of the very small retailer, who uses them rather as an individual consumer would use a supermarket. The retailer goes to the cash and carry, browses and selects the required goods, organises payment (either cash or on account), then takes the goods away with whatever transport they have organised for themselves. It is an efficient way for a small retailer to get access to a wide range of branded and other goods at reasonable prices. The cash and carry buys in bulk, and then passes on some of the savings to their customers so that they can also make a return or keep their prices lower. Even so, it is still difficult for the small independent retailer to compete with supermarkets who can sell items to the public at lower prices than the independent can even purchase them at. To try to help with this, many cash and carry operators produce own-brand goods, such as Bestway's 'Best-in' range and Nurdin and Peacock's 'Happy Shopper' label, and generic lines, such as Bestway's 'Save-on' products that allow the small retailer to offer low prices while retaining their margins.

Nurdin and Peacock (N&P) operates a chain of over 50 cash and carry depots, averaging about 7000 m² each, in the UK. The chief executive does feel, however, that N&P needs to further develop its customer service by offering delivery because,

> '... there are many successful customers who either do not have the time or the transport facilities to fetch the goods. They need deliveries and, if we do not provide them, they will go elsewhere' (de Angeli, 1995. p. 14).

Makro is an international chain of self-service cash and carries, which originated in the Netherlands, but now has over 110 stores in 15 countries. Averaging about 9000 m², each store carries around 50 000 food and non-food product lines. Makro supplies not only independent retailers and caterers, but also other types of businesses such as nursing homes or offices, any business, in fact, that is registered for VAT (Fraser, 1994).

CHAPTER SUMMARY

Both retailers and wholesalers bridge the gap between manufacturer and end consumer, but whereas retailers tend to deal directly with end consumers, wholesalers tend to deal with retailers and other organisational buyers. Nevertheless, both can perform broadly similar functions and provide suitable premises for the sale of goods. Suitability can relate to the ambience of the place, services and the facilities provided for customers, as well as the synergy between different manufacturers' products.

Retailers can be classified according to a number of criteria: form of ownership (independents, corporate chains or contractual systems), level of service (full or limited), merchandise lines (breadth and depth) and operating methods (type of store, whether department store, supermarket, variety store or other). Non-store retailing, closely linked with direct marketing, has also become increasingly popular and widespread. It includes in-home selling, parties, mail order operations, teleshopping, and vending machines.

Retailers have particular strategic and operational marketing decisions to make on location, product range, positioning etc. Store image and atmosphere create the character of the store and are important in influencing the customer's perception of it. Both exterior factors (frontage, site, window displays etc) and interior factors (affecting sight, sound, scent and other tactile experiences) make a contribution. The aim is to stimulate the customer, yet make them relaxed enough to want to stay in the store, browsing and buying. Layout and display can also affect the customer's behaviour. Technology too plays a major role in the retailer's ability to service customers and to supply them with what they want when they want it. Retailer own brands can also help to enhance the image of the store as well as giving the retailer extra bargaining power over suppliers. Some larger retailers have also begun to internationalise their operations in various ways. Some have acquired foreign retailers, some have entered into joint ventures and others have entered into looser contractual alliances, usually geared towards pooling purchasing power and offering mutual marketing support.

There are two broad types of wholesaler. Full service wholesalers offer a full range of services, including bulk breaking, transportation, delivery and management advice. Limited service wholesalers keep their costs down by providing only a few, clearly defined services for their customers. They will not usually, for example, undertake deliveries. Cash and carries are the commonest form, serving the needs of small retailers who use the cash and carry just as a consumer uses a supermarket. The wholesaler can buy in bulk and pass on some of the cost savings to the small retailer. Cash and carries also sell own-label goods to give the smaller retailer an opportunity to sell price-competitive goods and to give them a point of differentiation from the large supermarket chains.

Key words and phrases

Atmosphere	Depth of range	Out of town
Breadth of range	Discount clubs	Speciality stores
Catalogue showrooms	EPOS	Store image
Concessions	Franchising	Supermarkets
Convenience stores	Hypermarkets	Teleshopping
Corporate chain	Independent retail outlet	Variety stores
Department stores	Mail order	

QUESTIONS FOR REVIEW

13.1 Summarise the main functions of *wholesalers* and *retailers*.

13.2 Define *place utility* and *time utility*. Why do these concepts matter to customers?

13.3 What factors might be considered in providing an appropriate *selling environment*? How might the importance and the decisions made about these factors differ between retailers and wholesalers?

13.4 What are the predominant forms of *retail ownership*, and what are the major problems facing each of them?

13.5 What are the advantages and disadvantages of allowing *concessions* within a department store?

13.6 What is a *variety store* and what particular advantages does it offer to the shopper?

13.7 What advantages does *out of town retailing* offer to a speciality retailer and its customers?

13.8 Why is choice of *location* so important for a retailer, and what factors are likely to be taken into account when making a location decision?

13.9 What factors influence the *assortment of goods* stocked by a retailer?

13.10 What are the advantages for a retailer or wholesaler of *internationalisation* through strategic alliances? What are the potential drawbacks of such an approach?

QUESTIONS FOR DISCUSSION

13.1 Find examples of:

(a) full service;
(b) limited service; and
(c) self-service stores in the same retail sector.

What contribution does the level of service make to each of those stores' marketing approaches?

13.2 What is a *category killer* and how might its activities affect other retailers? Give examples.

13.3 In what ways and to what extent do you think that *non-store retailing* poses a threat to conventional retailers?

13.4 Choose a retailer and analyse how its store atmosphere is made up.

13.5 Find examples of retailers that use:

(a) grid layout;
(b) free flow layout; and
(c) boutique layout.

Explain how each layout seems to affect shoppers' behaviour within those stores and what contribution it makes to the overall image and atmosphere of the stores.

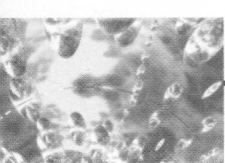

CASE STUDY 13.1

Sainsbury's

Sainsbury's is a long established and well respected grocery retailer in the UK, with a reputation for quality. With sales of £13.5 billion in 1995, a 12.5 per cent share of the UK grocery market, and 20 000 product lines, 10 000 of which are own label, Sainsbury's has to manage all aspects of its retail marketing very carefully.

One very important issue for a retailer such as Sainsbury's is store location. In fact, a former chairman of Sainsbury's said that the four most important things about retailing are location, location, location and location! During the 1980s, the multiple grocery retailers concentrated on large out of town developments, but in the 1990s, not only has the country become some-what saturated with these developments, but local councils have also become far less willing to give planning permission for them. Partly in answer to the critics who hold the multiples responsible for 'the death of the high street', and partly to fill a perceived need in the market, Sainsbury's (and other supermarkets) are also investing in smaller town centre outlets with selections of goods that suit the non-car shopper.

Sainsbury's takes store location very seriously and has a whole department dedicated to finding and assessing potential sites for new stores or for relocated stores. The department has invested about £330 000 in installing store location technology. They use GIS (Geographical Information System) software which contains all the UK Ordnance Survey maps and can plot isochrones on them. An isochrone is a line that joins places of equal 'drive time' from any store or location. Thus an isochrone will join all the places that are 5 minutes drive time from a store at an average speed, and another one will join places that are 10 minutes away, etc. GIS also uses National Census data to give a full demographic and socioeconomic profile of geographic areas, and finally, the government's Family Expenditure Survey gives data on the average weekly expenditure per person on groceries.

From all this, the potential turnover for a new store can be calculated for each of the isochrones (5, 10, 15 and 20 minutes – generally, people will not travel for longer than 20 minutes to do their grocery shopping). The figures can then be adjusted to take into account the effects of competitors who are also operating within the 20-minute catchment area to arrive at an estimate of a new store's turnover. According to Sainsbury's, the system is usually proved correct within 5 per cent either way.

As this perhaps implies, the target segment for any given store is largely and primarily geographic. The move towards fewer, larger out of town stores means that many people just shop at the nearest one for convenience, and thus the profile of the store's customers is largely dependent on the profile of the catchment area, which could be very mixed. Sainsbury's is unlikely to attract the segment that is completely price orientated and cares little for brands, quality or service, but with that exception, Sainsbury's has to cater for the needs of a broad cross-section of customers.

Once the decision has been made to go ahead with a new store, it will be advertised and promoted for a year before it actually opens, and heavy local promotion will continue until the store is established. 'First Brick to First Birthday' is their general guideline.

Marketing communication is an important area for Sainsbury's. In 1995, Sainsbury's spent £40 million just on advertising in a range of media and with a range of objectives. The Sainsbury's name is itself a valuable 'brand' that needs to be supported and maintained in terms of its positioning in the market. One of the problems of Sainsbury's historical reputation for quality is that it is perceived as more expensive than its closest rivals. The dilemma is how to overturn the high price perception without damaging the quality image. National television and newspaper campaigns have been used to try to achieve this, with price-led advertising, featuring products where the prices are very clearly low under the heading, 'Where Good Food Costs Less', and customer service-led advertising under the heading, 'Everyone's Favourite Ingredient', running in parallel.

Despite this emphasis on price, Sainsbury's is not a discounter and would not like to be thought of as such. It does, however, try to price its goods broadly in line with the main competitors (such as Tesco, Safeway and ASDA) and to try to reinforce the 'costs less' aspects of its advertising, it ensures that it always has around six really good price-based promotional offers, or 'stonkers' as Sainsbury's calls them, available to customers at any one time.

There is no room for complacency in this market, however. Tesco has been a major rival to Sainsbury's for many years. Tesco's success in repositioning itself as a good value, good quality retailer has brought it closer to Sainsbury's market position, and by 1995, Tesco had overtaken Sainsbury's to become the number one grocery retailer with 13.9 per cent market share. In 1996, Sainsbury's was thus diagnosing its problems and fine tuning its strategy for regaining the initiative in the market. Sainsbury's intensified its market research, interviewing 1000 customers a week. As a result of this, it was decided to review the number of own label products and to broaden the choice of branded goods; to extend the Economy range (generic products at very low prices) from 60 to 100 lines; to introduce a loyalty card and a credit card; to take on 5000 extra staff and improve training, and to put more focus in their advertising on quality and choice. As their marketing director said:

> 'What you will see is a significant improvement in our strategy. The strategy is essentially sound. What is at issue here is the need to improve the execution of that strategy' (Lee, 1996).

Sources: Notes taken by Neville Hunt at a lecture given by A. Tasker of Sainsbury's (18 January 1995); *The Grocer* (1996a); Lee (1996).

Questions

1 Why is store location so important for a grocery retailer? Assess the way in which Sainsbury's evaluates potential locations.

2 How would you define Sainsbury's market segment? What are the marketing implications of that definition?

3 What factors might encourage a grocery multiple to vary the product mix, promotional offers or pricing from store to store?

4 Why are own-label products so important to Sainsbury's? Can a grocery outlet have too many own-label products?

CASE STUDY 13.2

Amstrad sells direct

In 1994 Alan Sugar, the high-profile entrepreneur who founded Amstrad and still runs it, made a major decision: Amstrad would no longer sell its branded computers and fax machines through electrical retailers. These products would henceforth only be sold direct. This decision was the outcome of several years of difficulty for Amstrad. The company felt that it had not been able to achieve its targets by selling through the large multiple retailers such as Comet and Dixons.

The root of the problem was the tough, competitive market faced by retailers in the consumer electronics industry. Price competition and bargain hunting consumers meant that retailers were often not making much profit on the products themselves, although they were making up for it to some extent through the sale of extended warranties with much bigger margins. Nevertheless, to try to improve margins and share, the retailers put a great deal of pressure on manufacturers to cut their prices, if they wanted to remain as listed suppliers. The chairman of Dixons, Sir Stanley Kalms said in a speech to industrialists,

> 'Suppliers must understand that if they want national distribution through a group like Dixons, which puts emphasis on a high level of customer service, then there is a consequence ... Suppliers cannot ride both horses. There is a choice between working with high service retailers and low cost operations.'

In other words, 'meet our requirements or risk losing the business'. Not only was price squeezed, but demands for advertising support, supply on a 'sale or return' basis, and trial orders, all helped to put even more pressure on the manufacturers. Amstrad, as one of these manufacturers, felt the need to reconsider its distribution strategy fundamentally, deciding to develop its own direct sales operation, Amstrad Business Direct. The proposition, primarily targeting small businesses buying computers, was that by buying direct, significant savings could be made. National advertising featured an invitation to order a free 12-page catalogue, PCs and faxes at factory prices, and a direct ordering facility with a 30-day money back guarantee. The proposition from Alan Sugar featured in the advertisements was,

> 'At Amstrad, we've built our success on making the latest innovations truly user-friendly, truly affordable. Now we're doing the same for buying, by bringing you the massive benefits of dealing direct with the experts. Better advice, better service, better support and all at factory prices.'

The decision to sell direct is not of course without its problems. The marketing costs of informing and persuading consumers now fall on Amstrad, as does the need for pre- and post-sale product support in terms of order handling, product trial, and after sales service. Part of the offering was a 48-hour repair service.

Although Amstrad does have a recognised brand name, the range of competition and rapidly changing technology mean that just keeping up with developments is a challenge. Throughout Europe, a number of direct sales operations in the same industry had been making losses and they were competing not only with each other, but also against the traditional retail sector. Some experts suggested that the real problems with Amstrad stemmed not from retail relationships, but from their loss of a commanding reputation for innovation in the 1980s, which, when coupled with aggressive marketing, proved a powerful combination. The losses experienced in the early 1990s reflected some unsuccessful launches and a market where foreign competition soon catches up, sometimes with a better quality product at a lower manufactured price.

Sources: Randall (1994); Randall and Lloyd (1994).

Questions

1 Why did Amstrad decide to stop selling products through retailers such as Dixons? Is this any great loss to Dixons?

2 What can retailing offer in the PC market that direct supply cannot?

3 Initially, Amstrad targeted its direct supply at small businesses. What would be the problems of extending the direct supply concept to individual consumers?

4 Do you think Amstrad has made the right move? What else could it have done?

REFERENCES TO CHAPTER 13

Alexander, N. (1995), 'Internationalisation: Interpreting the Motives', in P. McGoldrick and G. Davies (eds.), *International Retailing: Trends and Strategies*, Pitman Publishing.

Anderson, C. H. (1993), *Retailing*, West.

Bowlby, S. *et al* . (1984), 'Store Location: Problems and Methods 1', *Retail and Distribution Management*, 12(5), pp. 31–3.

Buckley, N. (1994), 'Baked Beans Across Europe', *Financial Times*, 14 April, p. 19.

Business Europe (1994), 'Stores Form New Euro-retail Alliance', *Business Europe*, 18–24 April, p. 7.

Carnegy, H. (1995), 'Struggle to Save the Soul of IKEA', *Financial Times*, 27 March, p. 12.

Cooper, J. *et al.* (1991), *European Logistics: Markets Management and Strategy*, Blackwell Publishers.

Davidson, H. (1993), 'Bubbling Benetton Beats Recession', *Sunday Times*, 4 April, p. 3–11.

Davies, G. (1992), 'Positioning, Image and the Marketing of Multiple Retailers', *International Review of Retail Distribution and Consumer Research*, 2(1), p. 13.

Davies, G. J. and Brooks, J. M. (1989), *Positioning Strategy in Retailing*, Paul Chapman.

Davies, R. L. and Rogers, D. S. (1984), *Store Location and Store Assessment Research*, John Wiley.

De Angeli, T. (1995),' Deliveries Have Joined C&C on N&P Agenda', *The Grocer*, 16 December, pp. 14–15.

The Economist (1993), 'Europe's Discount Dogfight', *The Economist*, 8 May, pp. 69–70.

Euromonitor (1995a), *European Marketing Data and Statistics 1995*, Euromonitor Publications.

Euromonitor (1995b), *Hypermarkets and Superstores*, Euromonitor Publications.

Fraser, I. (1994), 'Retailer to the World', *Director*, June, pp. 48–51.

Fraser, I. (1995), 'Sight and Sound', *Marketing Business*, October, pp. 36–9.

Grain, A. (1996), 'Costcutter Franchising For Polish Grocers', *The Grocer*, 3 February, p. 6.

The Grocer (1995), 'Grocers Face Stonewalling Planners', *The Grocer*, 16 December, p. 29.

The Grocer (1996a),'Loyalty and Credit Card to Lead Fightback', *The Grocer*, 11 May, p. 4.

The Grocer (1996b), 'Sonae Sets High Target for Trading', *The Grocer*, 11 May, p. 22.

The Grocer (1996c), 'Ten Mammoths Bound For Poland', *The Grocer*, 27 January, p. 5.

Hall, L. (1995), 'Tie Rack's International Departure Puts It Back On Course', *Marketing*, 26 October, pp. 14–15.

Hogarth-Scott, S. and Parkinson, S. P. (1994), 'The New Food Discounters: Are They a Threat to the Major Multiples?', *International Journal of Retail and Distribution Management*, 22(1), pp. 20–8.

Howe, W. S. (1992), *Retailing Management*, MacMillan.

Kaas, P. (1994), 'The Rise of Discount: How to Survive the Profit Squeeze', *British Food Journal*, 96 (2), pp. 18–23.

Krienke, M. (1993a), 'Manor AG: Talented Cast, Excellent Performance', *Stores*, January, pp. 52–4.

Krienke, M. (1993b), 'Hennes and Mauritz', *Stores*, February, pp. 34–7.

Lee, J. (1996), 'Sainsbury's Battles Back', *Marketing*, 16 May, p. 13.

Lynn, M. (1995), 'Where Now, Cash Cow?', *Management Today*, March, pp. 46–50.

McGoldrick, P. (1990), *Retail Marketing*, McGraw-Hill.

McGoldrick, P. (1995), 'Introduction to International Retailing', in P. McGoldrick and G. Davies (eds.) *International Retailing: Trends and Strategies*, Pitman Publishing.

Myerson, J. (1993), 'Germany: Parallel Lines', *Design*, March, pp. 38–40.

Neilsen, A. C. (1994), *Retail Pocket Book 1994*, NTC Publications.

Provan, S. (1996), 'In Gear For Expansion', *Financial Times*, 26 March, p. V.

Randall, J. (1994), 'Sugar Sells Direct', *Sunday Times*, 13 November.

Randall, J. and Lloyd, C. (1994), 'Amstrad to Ditch High Street Sales', *Sunday Times*, 6 November.

Rice, S. (1995), 'The Independents' Lot', *Menswear*, 7 December.

Robinson, T. and Clarke–Hill, C. (1995), 'International Alliances in European Retailing', in P. McGoldrick and G. Davies (eds.) *International Retailing: Trends and Strategies*, Pitman Publishing.

Rosenbloom, B. (1981), *Retail Marketing*, Random House.

Summers, D. (1994), 'Ringing the Tills: Retailers Should Focus on the Phone', *Financial Times*, 8 December, p. 21.

Tanguy, A. (1994), 'Vitrine des Marques', *Marketing Vente*, 84 (Juillet/Août) 1994, pp. 16–17.

Tordjman, A. (1995), 'European Retailing: Convergences, Differences and perspectives', in P. McGoldrick and G. Davies (eds.) *International Retailing: Trends and Strategies*, Pitman Publishing.

URPI (1988), *List of UK Hypermarkets and Superstores*, Unit for Retail Planning Information.

Walters, D. and White, D. (1987), *Retail Marketing Management*, MacMillan.

Wise, P. (1996), 'Corner Shop Feels the Pinch', *Financial Times*, 26 March p. V.

Wrigley, N. (1988), *Store Choice, Store Location and Market Analysis*, Routledge.

14 Physical Distribution and Logistics Management

LEARNING OBJECTIVES

This chapter will help you to:

1 understand the distinction between physical distribution management and logistics;

2 appreciate the importance of customer service as an integral part of logistics and distribution;

3 analyse how customer service elements can be built into the distribution channel;

4 identify the functions involved in logistics and appreciate the decisions contributing to their management; and

5 assess the importance of physical distribution within an integrated marketing mix.

INTRODUCTION

The movement of goods to points where they are actually wanted is an accepted part of our economic system. Only when things break down do we perhaps appreciate a highly sophisticated system that is often taken for granted. The immense problems faced by commuters trying to get to work during a rail strike, a flight delayed because of a mechanical failure, the non-availability of an essential part for repairing the television, or a six-week wait for a much wanted CD, are all examples of the need to ensure that products are available in the right place at the right time for customers who may be already committed to spend. It shows the importance of the movement, storage and availability of products as a key part of a marketing strategy. However good the claims for a product or service, however effective the promotional programme, they will all be in vain if the goods are not available when and where the customer needs and wants them. If an organisation has paid careful attention to customer service needs and cost effectiveness in designing its distribution programme, all members of that channel can benefit not just from the cost efficiency, but also from the improved market effectiveness created.

The act of purchase and consumption of the product is only the final stage of a potentially long chain of distribution that may have involved several carriers and intermediaries stocking, handling and processing orders, as well as making many of the decisions highlighted in Chapter 12.

A survey by the Cranfield Centre for Logistics and Transportation estimated the total UK spend on logistics-related activities as £100 billion, the European market at £570 billion and the world market at £2500 billion. These figures include warehousing, holding stock, transport, administration and packaging. There is plenty of scope, therefore, for cost savings to be made and for service benefits to be created through careful examination of distribution and logistics strategies.

Example

Both SKF, the Swedish bearing manufacturer and Nike, the US manufacturer of trainers and sportswear, chose Belgium as a main European hub, replacing in the latter case 20 national and local warehouses. Customer service was also expected to increase, despite reduced overall stock levels as a wider range of both fast and slower moving items could be held. In both cases, considerable competitive benefits were realised as a result of these moves.

Service products also benefit from careful distribution decisions. Even though production and consumption may occur simultaneously, important 'place' decisions need to be taken. For example the organisers of a rock concert need to think about location, timing and booking facilities (including speed of response and ease of payment), as well as capacity. The more difficult it is to book seats, the more trouble it is to park and the poorer the facilities on offer, the less inclined customers will be to visit. A good example is the state of many soccer grounds in the UK, sited for access by public transport rather than by car. These stadia sometimes offer substandard hygiene and poor protection from the weather and find it difficult to cope with the peaks and troughs in demand caused perhaps when the club suddenly has a good cup or league run. This contrasts with the general standard of stadia found in the USA and elsewhere in Europe. Of course things are changing; ask any Middlesbrough, Newcastle, Spurs or Manchester United supporter!

This chapter examines the processes of physical distribution that enable products to flow from manufacturer to consumer. After an initial review of some of the key concepts, the difficulty of balancing customer service against distribution costs is considered in terms of the total logistics system, which highlights the need for adopting a 'total' approach to distribution management. The various functions and management decisions are then examined in the context of the main choices that lead to different distribution cost and service profiles. These include transportation modes, storage and materials handling. Finally, the role of physical distribution is revisited in the context of the options it generates for a competitive marketing strategy. Distributing service products will be considered in Chapter 23.

THE NATURE OF PHYSICAL DISTRIBUTION AND LOGISTICS

First of all, it is important to distinguish between the two main terms introduced in this chapter. Broadly speaking, **physical distribution** is about the handling and movement of outbound goods from an organisation to its customers. Distribution might be direct, using company owned transport, or indirect using external agencies and the kinds of channel structures considered at pp. 450 *et seq*. **Logistics** has a wider brief, since it is concerned with inbound raw materials and other supplies and their movement through the plant as well as with the outbound goods. It also concerns itself with strategic issues such as warehouse location, the management of materials and stock levels and information systems.

The next two subsections look in a little more detail at each of the two areas.

Physical distribution management

Physical distribution management (PDM) is concerned with the organisation and management of the storage and movement of goods from the end of the production line (finished goods) to the end customer. The range of functions undertaken includes receiving and processing orders, picking and packing (materials handling), managing the infrastructure such as warehouses, managing stock and the selection of transportation methods either direct to the end customer or to a point where bulk will be broken prior to shipment to the individual customer.

Distribution costs as a percentage of revenue vary across Europe from a level of around 8 per cent in the UK and France to around 11 per cent in Sweden (Thomas, 1994). These costs can be broken down further by activity. In the same study it was found that on average across Europe warehousing was 3.03 per cent, transportation 2.79 per cent, inventory 1.73 per cent, customer service 0.83 per cent and administration 0.79 per cent of revenue. Warehousing and transportation are obvious areas of concern within which to seek greater efficiency, given their relative cost and the changes that are taking place in the single European market (SEM). While there is increasing movement of low-value part-finished goods across European boundaries, the movement of high-value goods still tends to be within countries. This means that internal distribution systems are being replicated in different countries, thereby increasing distribution costs. The Nike and SKF examples mentioned earlier, by adopting a pan-European approach, are the exceptions to the rule (Thomas, 1994).

Taking an overview of PDM as it relates to a particular channel of distribution, it is important to note that the structure of the *physical* distribution channel may not coincide exactly with that presented earlier in Chapter 12, unless one or more members decides to undertake those roles directly. Figure 14.1 compares the two structures, showing the increased level of detail needed to describe physical distribution from manufacturer to consumer.

FIGURE 14.1

Channel management and physical distribution management

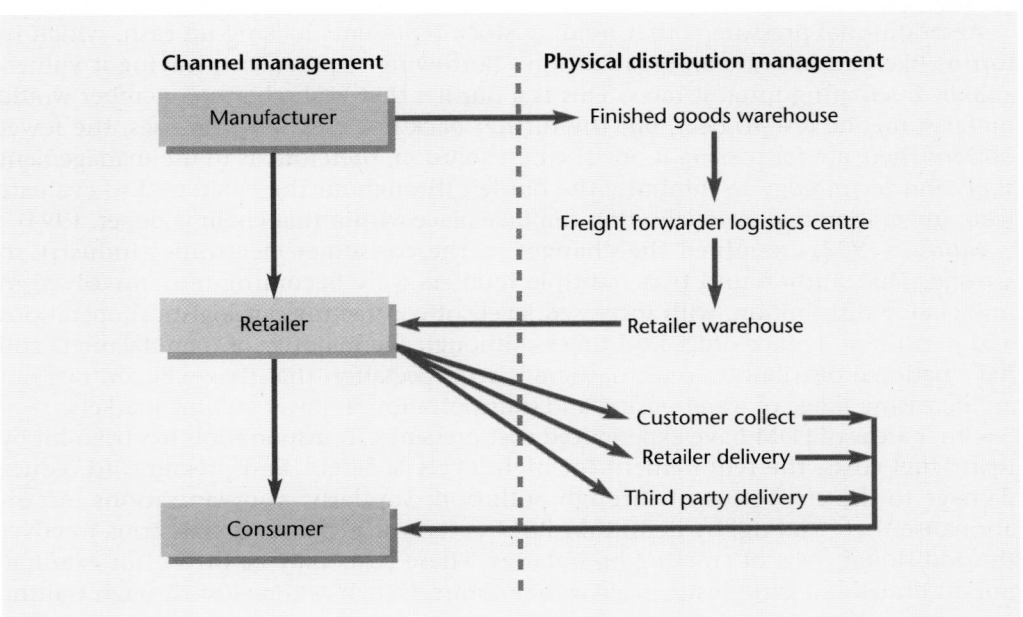

The extra intermediaries in a physical distribution channel do not take title to the goods, or take any direct part in their own right in transformation, adding product value or promotion. Such intermediaries are called **facilitators**, as their main function is to undertake the storage and movement of goods to ensure a free flow, and to help the main members of the distribution channel to achieve their objective of having the right goods in the right place at the right time, as cost effectively as possible. Typically, these intermediaries include transportation companies, those who rent out warehouse space and insurance and administration agents.

Although these facilitators might not add product value through transformation, they do add it through creating availability and service.

Example

Tibbett and Britten is one of the UK's leading facilitators in contract distribution and warehousing. One of its major activities is transporting hanging garments for multiple and independent clothing retailers. Increasingly, Tibbett and Britten regard Europe as their business area, operating 80 sites in nine countries, with 8.5 million ft² of warehousing, and 3600 vehicles. They claim that they add value by dovetailing their operation exactly to customer requirements and then operating extremely efficiently using specialised IT-based tracking of product movement and location (Robson, 1993).

PDM has emerged as an important variable in the marketing mix in recent years. The links with customer service are obvious. A fast, reliable, timely level of service where and when customers want it can be an important way of adding value, enhancing customer satisfaction and strengthening relationships (Mentzer *et al.*, 1989). However, there are other implications arising from increasingly global and competitive markets. Some stem from retailers managing inventory levels more effectively in order to increase stock turnover, as seen at pp. 490 *et seq.* By stocking less and relying on fast, frequent delivery, they have increasingly passed the burden of storage backwards to the manufacturer and wholesaler, so that they are responsible for coping with fluctuations in demand. With the aid of computer technology, many items can be controlled at a level of sophistication not possible a few years ago. Such changes have cost implications that demand careful assessment by the manufacturer or wholesaler.

An additional pressure is that holding stock represents locking up cash, which in turn is likely to increase an organisation's borrowing requirement, leaving it vulnerable to fluctuating interest rates. This is a burden that each channel member would prefer someone else to bear, but the further back up the chain it passes, the fewer options there are for passing it on. The best solution, therefore, is to use management skills and technology to minimise the burden throughout the chain and to evaluate what integration and rationalisation can take place within that chain (Cooper, 1994).

Moffat (1992) examined the changes in the consumer electronics industry in Europe. This study found that multiple retailers were becoming more involved in influencing distribution, with increased levels of contracting out logistical operations and pressure to reduce order lead times. Although the majority of manufacturers still have national distribution centres, there is an expectation that they will contract out an increasing range of warehousing and transportation in lower volume markets.

Other areas of PDM have experienced cost pressures. Transportation has been hit by rising fuel costs, the requirement for high levels of safety, and pressures to reduce damage to the environment through pollution. Similarly, as organisations internationalise their trading, by definition PDM costs will increase in real terms to cover the additional costs of crossing boundaries. These costs may be direct, for example import duties and extra insurance cover, or indirect, such as time lost through waiting at customs posts (it can take days for commercial vehicles to get across some eastern European borders, for instance).

Given all these pressures, the cost dimension cannot be ignored. The challenge is to find the balance between cost and added value. In some situations there may be little choice. Who wants to be the manufacturer who cannot supply a small replacement part for a capital plant breakdown that is holding up a car assembly line? In other situations, costs will have to be carefully monitored against the achievement of agreed customer service objectives. There is often a trade-off between cost and customer service, offering many possibilities for the marketing manager (Christopher, 1990).

Logistics management

There are limitations to the distribution concept described above, as it fails to reflect the inward flow of materials and parts that also have an impact on the costs and the quality of customer service provided. While it is not argued that marketing should control these inbound logistics, marketers need to be involved in their design and planning to ensure an integrative approach. A definition of *logistics*, amended from Bowersox (1978) is:

> 'The process of strategically managing the movement and storage of materials, parts and finished inventory from suppliers, through the firm and on to customers.'

Logistics, therefore, is an all-embracing concept that focuses on the physical movement and transformation of goods all the way from the source of supply to the point of consumption. Horley (1993) argues that a shift from a PDM to a logistics perspective could lead to significant benefits, including improved customer service, stock minimisation at all levels in the distribution chain, no costly stockouts, and finally, a lower total cost for all members. Companies are increasingly using logistics to lower costs, yet raise the standards of service to customers. Computers can be customised at the last minute, to match new orders or the market they are supplying, while in book distribution external logistic centres enable rapid selection, packing, transport, invoicing and collection using one provider. In the car industry and for some fmcg products the results of effective supply chain management are becoming even more important in lowering costs. Some companies are now experimenting with international stock-free delivery chains, the ultimate form of JIT. This means that products from Belgium, for example, are delivered straight on to a production line in Germany with no supporting buffer stock. Similarly, fmcg suppliers may be required to deliver to a distribution warehouse on a cross-docking basis just as a load is being consolidated to send to a particular supermarket. With such pressures to eliminate stockholding costs, suppliers need fault-free supply chains to remain competitive (Batchelor, 1994).

The difference between logistics management and PDM can be seen in Fig 14.2 which shows the all-embracing role of logistics compared with the narrower remit of PDM. Byrne and Markham (1993) highlighted the vital linkage between logistics management and customer service. That linkage is further emphasized through the following scenario. A retailer blames the wholesaler or manufacturer for a delayed part (a physical distribution problem), when it is actually the supplier of the castings to the manufacturer who is the ultimate cause (a logistics problem). Customers may care little; all they know is that they have a service problem, but the marketing manager in the manufacturing organisation needs to look backwards as well as forwards in finding a solution to that problem.

This example shows the integrative nature of logistics and the difficulty of managing it as it cuts across different functions within a business as well as across different businesses, linking supply sources with demand. It is primarily a framework for guiding forecasting, planning and strategies rather than just another self-contained

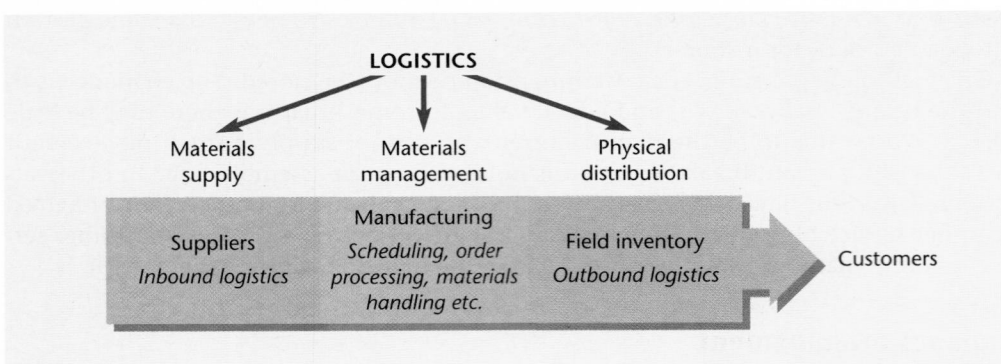

FIGURE 14.2

Physical distribution management and logistics

business function. It is therefore important that regular and reliable information is allowed to flow between all the connected parts and that no one part, whether internal or external to the organisation, is allowed to impact unduly and negatively on the others. The supplier who fails on the delivery of castings may subsequently, albeit indirectly, affect the relationship between the manufacturer who uses those castings and its customers, and so on down the line to the end consumer.

The logistics system will, of course, vary from organisation to organisation. In a bank or financial services operation, most of the inward-bound materials are money and supplies. Logistics, in terms of movement and storage activities, may not be a significant part of the product cost. This contrasts with producers such as Apple, Volvo or BMW who purchase both raw materials and components from many different sources, and then move finished goods to widely geographically spread markets and customers. Logistical costs will still vary widely, however, depending on the kind of manufacturer or market concerned. The key variables that will influence the scale and complexity of the logistics process are shown in Fig 14.3.

Within a channel of distribution, logistical costs will vary from member to member, reflecting the roles undertaken. Whether at this macro level (i.e., the combined logistics of the whole channel of distribution), or at a micro level (i.e., the logistical concerns of one channel member), it is important to focus on the total cost rather than to pursue blinkered strategies that lower costs in one area, only to raise them in another. A decision to close local depots, for example, might increase transportation costs and even inventory costs if the level of goods in transit increases. The effectiveness of this approach, particularly when other organisations are involved, will depend

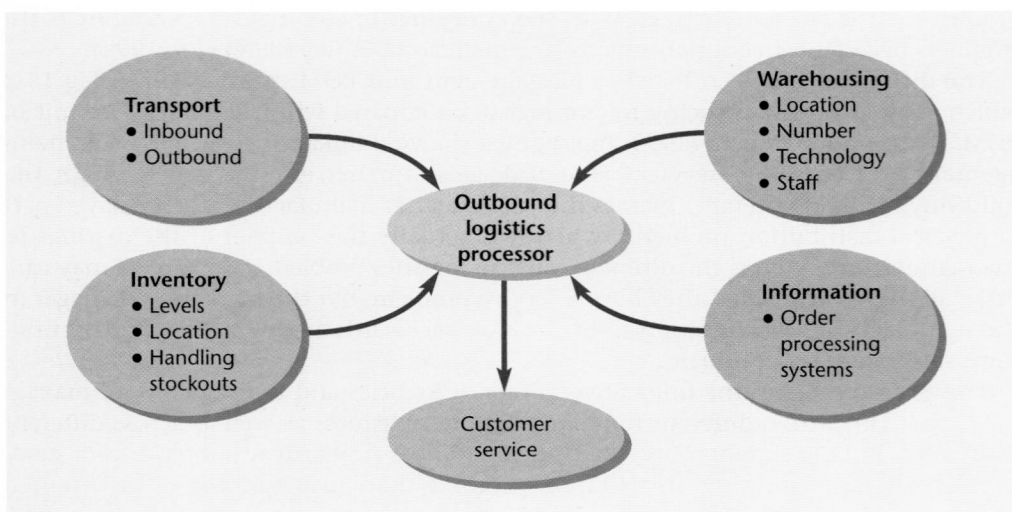

FIGURE 14.3

Influences on the logistics process

Apple Hollyhill

The Apple Hollyhill manufacturing facility in Cork, Ireland, supplies Apple Macintosh computers across Europe. Manufacturing is strongly market driven, and is supported by a European replenishment system called ARP (Apple Replenishment Programme). This system, based in the Netherlands, nightly examines the contents of finished goods warehouses and distribution sites across Europe. This forms the basis for flexible or revised production plans which are communicated to Ireland and to the vendors who supply components to Hollyhill. The system can also call off stock for delivery. The computer system used to plan logistics develops orders for suppliers and plans a production programme to meet demand associated with over 500 different product configurations and 21 different languages.

The Netherlands office also issues the appropriate manifest or pick list, quantity instructions, truck destinations and even how the goods should be arranged in the vehicle or in the warehouse. With increasing moves towards JIT and the overnight replenishment of European distribution, the manufacturing plant has virtually no manufacturing work in progress. However, Apple plan to go even further. They now wish to introduce direct distribution in Europe, thus eliminating finished goods warehouses. This will mean squeezing the supply chain further by taking 10 days out of the cycle, resulting in a saving of 20 per cent in manufacturing costs. The overall objective is to carry intelligent information on demand and replenishment, but not to carry stock.

Source: Allen and Rothery (1994).

on the nature of the contractual relationships, ranging from informal through to highly prescribed and controlled, and the willingness to work as a system rather than as discrete elements. Many of the issues discussed in Chapter 4 regarding buyer–seller relationships will influence the nature of the supply chain and the sharing of logistical costs. There will be considered further in the next section.

Total logistics cost concept

Implicit within a logistics perspective is the notion that decision making concerning the movement and storage of materials should be done as a whole rather than in discrete parts (Sussams, 1991). There are a number of cost areas that should be considered as part of the logistics and distribution system. These cost areas are often interdependent, because as costs decrease in one area, the costs in another may increase. For example as the number of stockholding points increases, the cost of holding inventory will also rise, but the cost of transportation may fall as not only are fewer goods moved, but they are moved shorter distances to the end user.

That example may apply at either the macro or the micro level. A channel of distribution consisting of a number of co-operative and integrated members may take an overview of warehousing or distribution depots relevant to the whole channel, and make logistical decisions which may increase the costs of one member, but will decrease the costs and increase the overall efficiency of the entire channel. The member bearing the increased direct costs may be rewarded in other ways, by increased business or increased profit margins to offset the increased operating costs, for example. At the micro level, an organisation may simply look at its own internal cost effectiveness. The trade-off principle can be seen in the hypothetical example shown in Fig 14.4. The ideal number of distribution outlets is three, when transportation costs are considered alongside inventory costs. Although neither cost in itself is at a minimum, the total logistics cost is minimised for the system as a whole.

FIGURE 14.4

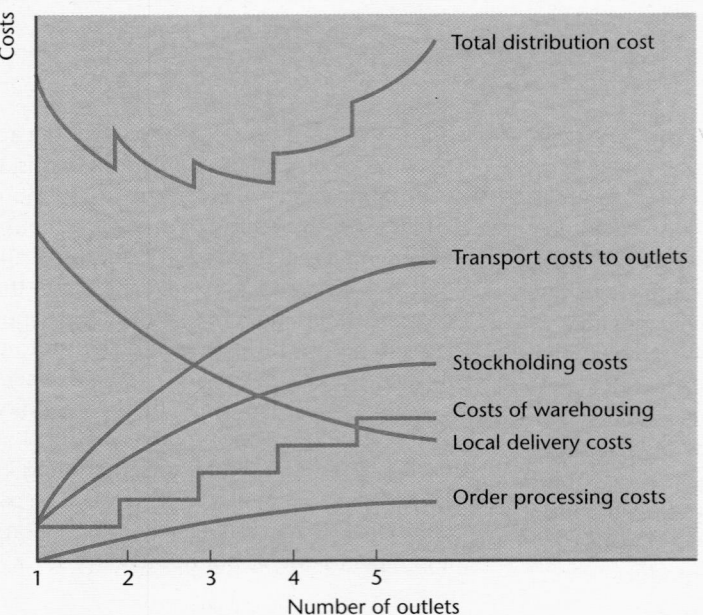

Costs

Total distribution cost

Transport costs to outlets

Stockholding costs

Costs of warehousing

Local delivery costs

Order processing costs

1   2   3   4   5

Number of outlets

Source: Adapted from Christoper (1990).

*Set in the heart of
the countryside, this
Benetton distribution
centre uses robotics
to provide an
efficient service to its
retail outlets.*

Example

Woolworth in the UK needed a
system that could manage the flow
of 4000 to 5000 containers per
annum coming mainly from the Far
East to supply 800 UK stores. By
working closely with P&O they were
able to benefit from an integrated
freight management system that
enabled careful inventory planning
in the UK to minimise replenishment time (Salak, 1993).

A full understanding of the impact of
logistics costs often demands a considerable quantity of accounting data and
the use of decision-support systems to
consider the full range of variables and
the effect of 'what if?' scenarios. The
use of IT has opened up considerable
potential for logistics operations.

However, the principle remains the
same: it is the system cost rather than
the individual functional cost that is
critical. A number of the main cost
areas are briefly considered below.

Source: Benetton UK Ltd.

Benetton

Benetton presents an excellent example of how a global logistics concept can be put into operation in a situation where over 6000 stores in more than 80 countries need a regular supply of garments responsive to changing tastes and fashions. At the heart of the logistics operation is a rapid and applied use of IT to integrate the whole supply chain. Although garment design is in-house, manufacturing tends to be subcontracted to over 450 organisations working to rigorous standards and Benetton-specified production schedules. By using IT they are able to delay the final decision on dyeing until clear information is available on preferred colours, thus ensuring a closer match between supply and customer demand. The Robotic Distribution Centre receives garments that are already packed in one of two standard boxes which are barcoded and preaddressed to customers. Through a fully automated process the boxes are moved to the storage and dispatch area which can store up to 250 000 boxes and can process 12 000 boxes per day.

Shipment is then made direct to the retailers without any use of distributors, wholesalers or regional warehouses. Benetton also went into a joint venture in freight forwarding, as a direct result of the international orientation of its business, to manage and smooth the paperwork flow as carriers cross national boundaries. Various cost trade-offs have been made in this system, not least the decision to have one highly efficient warehouse rather than a number of less automated centres, with a knock-on effect on stockholding. Similarly, order processing costs per garment have been reduced through automation, although transport costs may be somewhat higher. Another main trade-off derives from the decision not to use intermediaries but to supply direct. Effectively, that channel decision influences the rest of the logistics agenda.

Source: Dapiran (1992).

Order processing and administration

Order processing and administration are the areas associated with writing, receiving, acknowledging and processing an order, through to invoicing and confirmation statements, as well as credit checking.

Inventory

Inventory is often a major feature of an organisation's assets. Inventory can be in transit or in storage, represented by work-in-progress. Typical costs include financing (the cost of money tied up in stock, storing work-in-progress, insurance etc.), write-offs (depreciation, wastage etc.) and other losses.

Transport

Transport can be either *trunk*, representing bulk movement over a distance between manufacturer and customer or between manufacturer and distribution point, or *local*, representing relatively small shipments to the final user. An example is the postal system. Bulk mailing is undertaken by lorry, rail or air, while delivery to the doorstep is by small van or even on foot.

Outlet

Outlet costs are the capital and operating costs incurred in maintaining facilities to store and handle products.

Warehousing. Warehouse costs relate to the purchase and rental of space and the associated infrastructure for picking and packing stock efficiently. The increasing use of computer systems to guide picking has allowed greater use of random storage systems, as companies seek to increase space utilisation. Goods can be stored wherever there is room, and the computer system can quickly identify where they are, thus reducing the need for the more disciplined and orderly storage that a manual system would dictate.

Materials handling. Costs concerned with the materials handling system are concerned with the physical processing of orders into economic shipment sizes in line with customer service expectations and functionally sound protection for movement. This includes palletisation and loading.

CUSTOMER SERVICE CONCEPT

The output of logistics and physical distribution is the level of service that the customer receives. This can be defined in many ways, according to the specifics of the product-market situation. The challenge is to match the level of **customer service** provided with the need to constrain costs within planned levels. Too high a level of service could lead to excessively high costs that cannot be covered through pricing. Too low a level of service may enable a close control of costs but little positive response from potential customers. The key is to find the balance through careful research, planning and experimentation.

Customer service can be defined as the interaction of all the factors that affect the process of making products and services available to the buyer. These factors, although situation specific, cover such areas as inventory levels, delivery frequency, consistency and reliability of delivery, ease of order administration and the time taken from order placement through to satisfactory installation or consumption. From a study of customer service practices, LaLonde and Zinzer (1976) concluded that customer service variables could be categorised into three areas: pre-transactional, transactional and post-transactional.

Pre-transactional variables

Pre-transactional service activities relate to the corporate policies and procedures that establish the frameworks and administrative systems to achieve the desired levels of customer service. Implicit in this is the setting of customer service standards that can act as a benchmark for measuring achievement. Typical standards cover such areas as reliability, consistency, time, stockouts and accuracy. In practical terms, they might be translated into goals such as:

- 99 per cent of orders fulfilled satisfactorily
- all refunds made within one week of goods receipt
- all orders processed to dispatch within 24 hours
- all orders delivered within 48 hours
- all lunches served within 10 minutes of order.

These standards derive from the competitive position planned and the expectations of the target customers. Different market segments will respond to customer service provision in different ways. Part of the standard-setting process, therefore, must be the assessment of the costs of provision and whether the additional costs can be recovered from that market segment. The standards set for customer service thus need to be linked with the strategic marketing plan to provide a cost-effective market impact. This will require effective integration of all the activities that are undertaken from order entry through to delivery, to avoid suboptimisation and weak links. It is critical that these standards are clearly communicated to staff to ensure compliance.

Example

Fresh fruit and vegetable producers selling through supermarkets find that customer service standards are tightly controlled by the larger retail groups. The supply chain, which also includes importers, prepackers and haulage companies, can be difficult to manage when produce is scheduled many months ahead and when price and quality standards are agreed in advance. In such circumstances, unforeseen changes in the weather can easily lead to supply difficulties. Some supermarkets, such as Sainsbury and Tesco, are seeking closer supplier partnerships to manage the logistics chain better, and this includes having some intermediaries in the chain monitoring quality. Ordering systems are improving throughout the chain with faster checkout data, but the real pressure for change is for fresher produce and longer shelf life to avoid wastage. These standards are virtually all driven by the supermarkets (Shapley, 1995).

Transactional variables

Transactional service activities are the main dimensions of the implementation phase that actually creates customer service. The concern with physical distribution and administration provides performance measures against the predetermined standards. The main elements, shown in Fig 14.5, are discussed below.

Order cycle time

Time is an important measure in physical distribution. The order cycle time relates to the total time between placing an order and satisfactory receipt of the product. The lower the cycle time, the faster stock can be replenished and the lower the inventory

FIGURE 14.5

Customer service and transactional variables

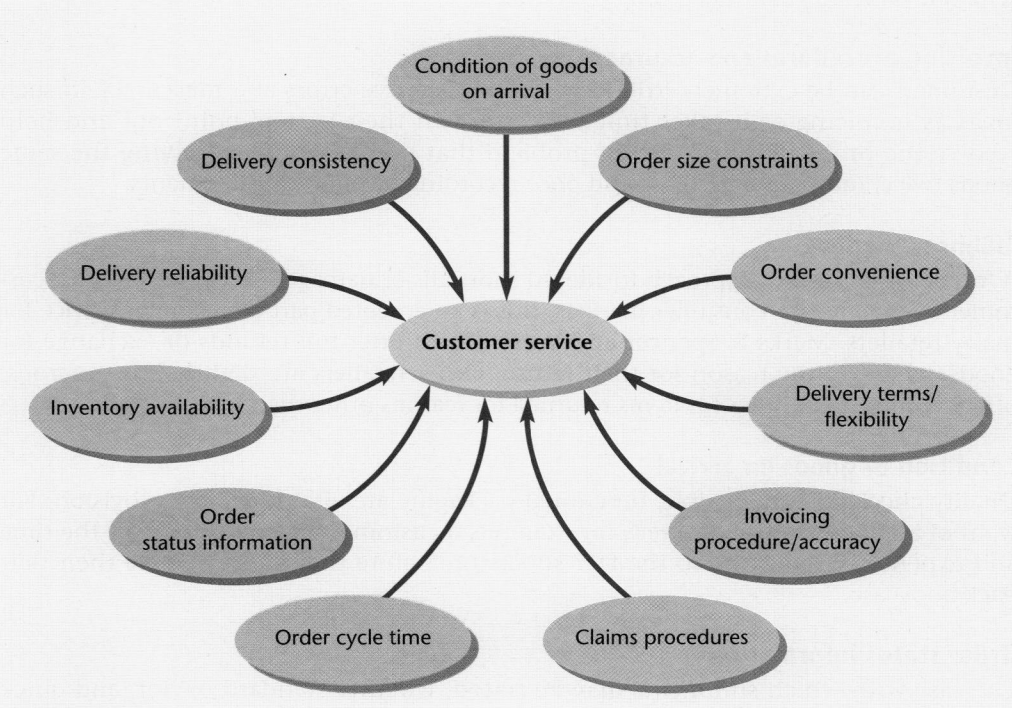

levels that need to be held by the customer. Included in order cycle time is the whole process of administration, delivery and installation, where appropriate.

Consistency and reliability of delivery
Delivery must be on time, orders must be filled accurately and goods received in prime condition. In some situations, it is better to have a slightly longer delivery period that is guaranteed, rather than one that may be quicker but could be vulnerable to delays.

Inventory availability
The availability of inventory refers to the range and depth of stock normally held which provides the essential input to delivery. The balance is between stocking in depth on the faster moving, volume products and retaining a sufficient level of stock of, or at least fast access to, slower moving items. Finding parts for obsolete products is always a challenge if their supply is erratic.

Order size constraints
Some companies implement a minimum order policy. This can penalise light users, but reflects the high administrative and delivery costs on small order sizes.

Ordering convenience
Different customers want different convenience standards. These could relate to opening hours, the use of non-cash alternatives or ease of booking.

Delivery times and flexibility
The issues of delivery times and flexibility highlight whether the delivery is on the customer's or the supplier's terms. Customers operating just in time (JIT) systems clearly need to be able to specify their delivery requirements. On smaller, less crucial orders, however, it may be necessary for the customer to accept the standard delivery schedule with no guaranteed time of arrival.

Invoicing procedures and accuracy
Customers can be extremely irritated by administrative errors and inaccuracy in such areas as invoicing as it takes time and effort on their part to point out and help resolve the problem. The kinds of problem that may occur are receiving the same goods twice, inaccurate invoices and poor recording of financial statements.

Claims procedure
A 'no questions asked' approach to alleged shortfalls or damaged stock is critical for customer confidence. In consumer markets, this is an accepted part of customer service for many retailers. Marks & Spencer and W. H. Smith offer full refunds or exchange for goods, whatever the reason for their return. Other retailers are slightly less generous, offering only credit notes for items returned for reasons other than product faults.

Condition of goods on arrival
Quality checking and sensible, functional packaging are vital to service provision. For want of a missing dowel or screw, for example, a customer may need to incur the time and expense of returning to the DIY superstore before they can assemble their flat-pack bookcase.

Order status information
The ease with which shipments may be traced, whether standard or not, and quick identification of where they are delayed or lost, are important means by which to reassure the customer of the management effectiveness of the whole process. This was highlighted in the Woolworth example mentioned earlier on p. 538.

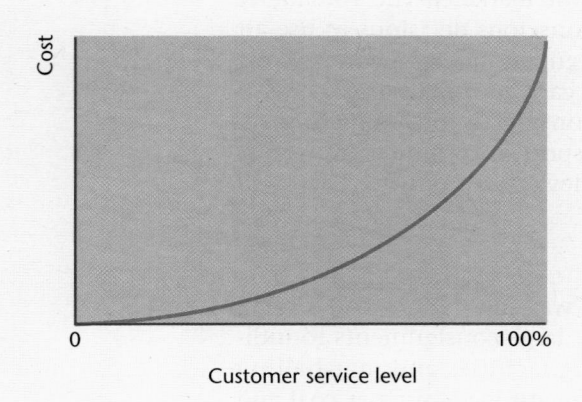

FIGURE 14.6

The cost of customer service

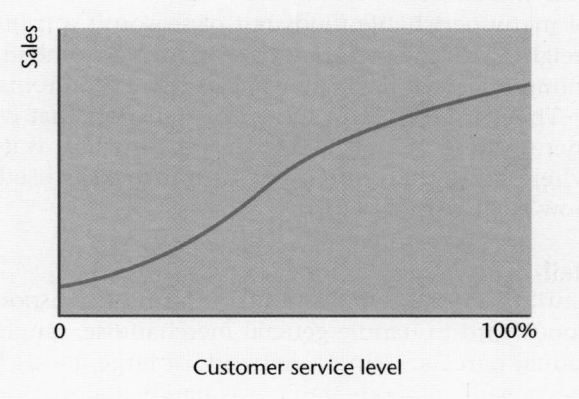

FIGURE 14.7

Customer sensitivity to service

In 1992, consultants A. T. Kearney undertook a study of 1000 shippers and carriers across Europe to establish developments in customer satisfaction with the logistics process. It provides an interesting insight into quality improvements on various service dimensions. A consistent raising of standards is shown, but it can also be seen that there is still room for improvement in most areas (Byrne *et seq.*, 1994). Often, the pursuit of the higher levels can bring a disproportionate cost increase.

Post-transactional variables

Post-transactional service activities relate to the support given to the product while it is in use. Typical areas include product guarantees, installation support, replacement parts and servicing and the efficient handling of complaints. The sale does not end with delivery. If the buyer cannot use the product properly or if there are delays when something goes wrong, it can be a major source of frustration and dissatisfaction. This is especially important when the purchase represents an essential input into the buyer's own product.

The above elements constitute the cost areas that arise from providing a level of service. Costs, or the margin required, set the parameters within which service levels can be planned. As service levels move towards 100 per cent standards, the costs of provision increase disproportionately, as shown in Fig 14.6. At very high service levels, the stockholding levels and transport urgency increase dramatically, without necessarily increasing the customer's willingness to respond by paying higher prices. Figure 14.7 shows that customer sensitivity to high levels of service does not necessarily translate into sales, although it may well enhance loyalty levels. Customers themselves may be prepared to trade service off against cost considerations within agreed parameters.

LOGISTICS FUNCTIONS

The major cost items identified at Fig. 14.3 on p. 536 will now be considered in more detail, to demonstrate the key decisions that relate to customer service provision and maintaining a total cost perspective.

Transportation

Transportation is central to any logistics system, moving goods in time and place, thus providing the means to service urgent replacement or for maintaining inventory levels within a channel system. The selection of alternative modes of transport has different cost and service outcomes that can be used creatively by the marketer. The availability of many perishable foods out of season is a tribute to conscious decisions to use air freight, with the premium price involved. Some market segments are happy to pay premium prices for the benefits of all year round tomatoes or early new potatoes.

There are five main modes of transport that can be considered for product movement. These are rail, road, air, pipeline and water transport. **Intermodal transport**, where more than one mode of transport is used provides a sixth option. Each will now be discussed in turn.

Rail

Until the 1960s, rail was a major form of transport. Most wayside stations had a small goods yard to handle general merchandise, ranging from large consignments to individual parcels. Using a network of large goods handling facilities and marshalling yards, general goods traffic was handled alongside bulk freight loads such as coal and steel. In 1938 the total output of coal in the UK was 228 million tonnes, of which 68 million tonnes were transported by other transport modes and 160 million tonnes travelled by rail. At that time, the leading industries provided the major part of the railways' freight revenues. Things have now changed dramatically in Europe, in most European countries railways are now primarily used for the movement of heavy, bulky items over relatively long distances. Typical products include coal, oil, minerals, chemicals, timber etc. Containerisation is used for the bulk movement of goods from port to user or distribution point to distribution point. SNCF in France structures its rail freight business around seven commodity businesses: intermodal, coal and steel, agriculture, forestry and paper products, petrol and chemicals, foodstuffs and distribution.

The main benefit of rail transportation is the ability to move full train loads, thus reducing the costs of marshalling and materials handling. The longer the distance, the more rail comes into its own as a competitive mode, as it often is in transcontinental traffic in North America and Australia.

Example

Some organisations maintain their own rail networks linked with the national system. Foster Yeoman ship aggregates in bulk from their quarry in Somerset to distribution points and users in the UK using five of their own locomotives. One contract was to supply 1.3 million tonnes of aggregate for use in the construction of the second river Severn crossing near Bristol, and involved 725 trainloads over six months. Others deliberately locate plant or depots adjacent to the rail system for ease of loading and unloading. Rheinbraun AG operate a 300 km rail system west of Cologne to move brown coal and spoil from four open cast sites to nearby power-stations and other industries in the area fuelled by brown coal.

The growth of rail freight across Europe is closely linked with increasing pressure on governments to restrict the use of heavy lorries, especially where rail alternatives are available. In the UK there is less pressure for change, but the decline of many traditional industries has taken its toll on bulk traffic generated. In 1948 in the UK the rail freight tonne miles travelled was 21.6 million, but by 1988 it had dropped to 11.1 million.

Example

The continued drop in sales put considerable pressure on British Rail to downsize its freight operation before privatisation. An example of the problems BR faced was Shell's decision to change from using rail to using the road, for the bulk movement of oil products from its refinery at Grangemouth near Edinburgh to the West Highlands. They regarded it as a government problem to decide whether heavy loads could be moved by road rather than rail, despite the environmental issues involved. Given that there was no legal restriction on this kind of road traffic, Shell made their decision on purely commercial grounds.

However, the Channel Tunnel may provide a much-needed boost to BR's freight fortunes. Of the 35 freight trains planned to leave the UK each day, 22 are intended to be intermodal trains, nine will be linked to the automotive industry, and four are for conventional freight.

Road

The key advantage of road based systems is their flexibility through national road networks.

The advantages of direct delivery to the final customer, whether for catalogue goods to consumers or for large capital plant, are clear for local deliveries over relatively short distances. Many operators in the haulage business are small organisations that work closely within their local business environment. This local operation enables regular collection and often fast delivery not possible by other modes. This has a consequential benefit on inventory costs and service levels. However, the demand for integrated logistics services including warehousing and inventory management is creating new opportunities for value added services that may benefit larger, better financed suppliers (Markham and Aurick, 1993).

Example

It is long-distance trunk haulage by road that is causing debate across Europe. In an effort to reduce traffic levels at congested points, to improve the environment and to avoid continued investment in more motorways that generate yet more traffic, such as experienced with London's M25, pressures are building to restrict the use of greater numbers of larger capacity lorries. In 1994, Germany imposed an annual charge of DM 1500–2500 for all lorries of 12 tonnes and above using the German motorways. Whether this will act as a major deterrent remains to be seen.

Even more controversial is the ongoing 'debate' between the Swiss government and the EU. Given the difficult terrain and costly upkeep of the main

A familiar sight on Britain's motorways, Eddie Stobart's trucks provide an important link in the distribution process.

Source: Eddie Stobart Ltd.

north – south autobahns, pressure has been building to prevent all lorries of 40 tonne glw (gross laden weight) from crossing the Alps by road. More recently the Swiss also voted to ban all transit road freight within ten years. Furthermore, the state is not permitted to introduce any road construction projects that can expand transit freight capacity. The main aim is to encourage more intermodal traffic (as discussed below), using the railway system. To further this aim, a new 56 km Gottard base tunnel and a new 123 km railway line are set to open by 2006, to be followed by a new link under the Lotschberg a few years later. The future growth of European long-haul trucking is, therefore, open to some speculation. Through the use of intermodal arrangements or even direct rail, the main development areas may be in short- rather than long-haul traffic.

The growth of organisations such as European Freight Information Services helps road haulage. These organisations act effectively as 'dating agencies' for the 425 000 road haulage companies in Europe who are seeking a return load, rather than travelling home from a long haul empty. This will encourage greater efficiency, as 25 per cent of all trucks are on the road empty (Lloyd, 1995).

Air

Although the common public perception of airports is that they are for moving large numbers of passengers, preferably to the sunshine, there is also significant freight movement from major and many minor airports. The decision of cross-channel ferry operators to ban the movement of live cattle to the Continent from the UK, was partly responsible for the decision by some exporters to use air transport. Air freight is one of the most costly of the transport modes but this cost must be weighed against the service benefits and lower inventory levels that compensate, to some extent. Items that are very valuable, relatively light and not bulky, such as flowers, jewellery, and electronic parts are ideal for air transport. Air freight also has the benefit of speed, which may be crucial in the case of perishable goods being transported over long dist-ances. The quantity of goods carried is only restricted by the constraints imposed by handling and the capacity of aircraft, but the new generation of cargo planes can carry up to 100 000 kilos.

Where unit costs are high for industrial parts that are fairly slow moving, but could be required by a customer in a hurry, it may be possible to offer a 12-hour door-to-door service in the EU now that trade barriers have been removed. This means that some stock can be held centrally in Europe, within a short distance of a major airport and provision made for rapid handling and dispatch.

Example

Rasterops Corporation, a US hardware and software supplier for desk top publishing, found that renting a space near Schipol airport in Amsterdam enables the freight forwarder to provide general office services, packaging and handling, leading to higher service levels as the goods are further distributed from Schipol to the rest of Europe (Toll, 1993). This airport markets itself as the 'gateway to Europe'. Not only is it a major international and European hub, but it has built a large infrastructure of such facilities as bonded warehouses to encourage its use as a major international distribution centre, as used by Rasterops.

Pipeline

A pipeline is a specialist form of transport usually for crude oil, associated products and natural gas. Other types of pipeline carry bulk items such as coal, and grain in a suspended state. Although there is a major investment involved in the building of a pipeline, once established, it is inexpensive to operate, rarely causes operational problems and usually preserves and delivers the product in first class condition. In Europe, the oil and gas from the North Sea is shifted by pipeline to Norway and the UK, rather than by oil tankers. The pipeline linking the former Soviet Union with Germany was part of a much wider trade deal to enable greater penetration of German products into Russia.

Water

Water transport for transcontinental trade offers, in many cases, the only economically viable option. For destinations as different as the Canary Islands, which depends on a wide range of vessels to import most of its needs, and a steel terminal on Teesside that directly receives bulk shipments of ore from Australia, *sea transportation* rules. The main decisions to be made concern the carrier, the economics of carriage with different vessel types, the most appropriate point of entry and suitable unloading facilities. The longterm changeover to deep draught vessels has seen city ports such as Bristol and Rotterdam give way to harbours such as Avonmouth and Europort that can receive larger, deeper vessels that need more room for manoeuvre and better handling facilities.

Inland water transportation still plays some role in Europe. It is still a low-cost means of moving low-value products in bulk. Typical products include oil, coal, sand and gravel. Despite the relatively slow journey times and the usual need for further handling at the nearest port of destination, a network of rivers, canals and inland seas do provide a green means of transportation, keeping heavy vehicles off the roads and comparing favourably with rail in terms of the cost per tonne moved. In the Netherlands, the Rhine, the Meuse and the Schelde, along with an extensive network (4800 km.) of canals, provide an important link to industrial centres such as the Ruhr area of Germany.

Example

Neckermann, one of Germany's largest mail order companies, decided to place greater emphasis on inland waterways for distribution in order to lower costs and to be more environmentally friendly. They make particular use of the Rhine and Main rivers from Rotterdam to the three Neckermann warehouses in Frankfurt. They estimated that costs dropped from DM 2.6 million for road intensive transport to DM 1.2 million for rail/water (*Business Europe*, 1994).

Over a half of the Rhine's transport volume is moved by Dutch carriers, making effective use of Rotterdam, the world's busiest port, which enables direct offloading on to barges. The Rhine provides access for barges as far as Strasbourg in France and Basle in Switzerland and a number of riverside industries use it extensively. The river port of Strasbourg has extensive facilities and associated direct user industries in the fields of grain, timber, oil and coal distribution. A similar pattern of use can be seen on a number of the other great rivers of Europe. The embargo on certain exports to Serbia highlighted the role of the Danube in providing a direct link to the Black Sea. A number of industries have also grown up in Bulgaria and Romania based upon inland water transport.

There are obvious limitations to the further use of inland water transportation. No new canals are being built in Europe and larger vessels cannot navigate the more difficult systems. The demand for higher levels of customer service means that the main areas of use will probably continue to be the type of products currently carried.

Intermodal

Intermodal transportation refers to the situation where either combined or co-ordinated transport modes are offered, either as a commercial service or tailormade for an organisation. The aim is to get the benefits of each mode of transport without the obvious disadvantages, for example the bulk movement economies of rail with the flexibility of road. The basic principle is for lorry container loads to move to a rail-head, be loaded by highly mechanised equipment on to rail, and then at the rail destination be unloaded again to lorries for the trip to the final destination. This form of transport is likely to grow significantly in the next few years with the opening of the Channel Tunnel and the increasing integration of eastern Europe. The most popular variant of intermodal transportation is road–rail, although some ship–rail or ship–road transportation has been a major mode for export trading.

Intermodal traffic growth is a major part of EU trade. A network of road–rail connections laces Europe. For example in Italy, the international block train services for container or swapbody (containers that can be transferred from road to rail) traffic has recently been increased with a nightly shuttle between Milan and Lyon, three times a week from Chemnitz to Naples and Rome, twice weekly from Bremerhaven to Milan and a nightly service from Trieste to Budapest.

Example

The Channel Tunnel is likely to stimulate the growth of intermodal transport to and from the UK. A number of services have started or are about to start using the freight forwarding services of ACI and CTL from the UK, and Continental operators such as Unilog for the Belgium to UK service. Planned routes from Wembley, which acts as the main UK sorting point, are to Strasbourg and Basle, Lyon, Avignon and Perpignan, Milan, Brussels and Cologne. Up to 22 services are planned daily in the near future as traffic grows. The service to Brussels features swapbody carriers, the lightweight containers used for internal European transport, and with an eight-hour transit expected, a highly competitive service can be offered.

However, another form of intermodal transport, ROLA, the drive on–drive off railway wagons for accompanied trucks and truck and trailer rigs, is being cut back in parts of Europe as a result of the decline in demand. In Germany, services have been cut because the high costs of maintaining specialist rolling stock and the additional cost to hauliers have made it less competitive. However, in Austria and Switzerland, government restraints on lorries transiting these countries has led to an expansion. For example there are 12 daily workings through the Brenner pass each weekday.

Selection of transport mode

This consideration of alternative transportation modes highlights the need to select the most appropriate one very carefully in the light of the corporate context and distribution channel or end user needs. Each mode offers advantages and disadvantages, the significance of which will ultimately depend upon the particular organisational situation. Usually, the selection of one mode involves a trade-off between sometimes conflicting criteria. The decision normally involves a balance between the cost of service and the performance expected within the channel, or by the end customer. As shown at pp. 540 *et seq.*, performance in customer service can be measured by a number of dimensions such as time, reliability, security, frequency, capability and accessibility, all of which can be influenced by the choice of transport mode.

The main criteria affecting *transport choice* are now summarised:

Cost criteria

Costs are the most visible of the criteria. Tariffs are often published on a per route or per kilometre basis. For example, the basic cost of using an intermodal link with

Milan will be readily available, although some negotiation may be possible for heavier use. However costs cannot be considered in isolation; they must be weighed against benefits. One of these is bound to be whether the cost of a faster delivery will enable a higher price to be charged to the receiver. Alternatively, the higher cost of swifter delivery may be offset against lower inventory levels or otherwise absorbed by the supplier in the interests of forming a better relationship with the customer.

Transport costs vary from product to product and between different industries. An overall average is around 6–8 per cent of total costs, although the range goes up to nearly 15 per cent (chemicals and foodstuffs). This indicates the wide variances and the potential gains to be made from finding more cost-effective transport alternatives, both within and between modes. Traditionally, the railways have not been interested in loads of less than 50–100 tonnes, equivalent to approximately three lorry loads. Thus road transport would be favoured for smaller loads.

Performance criteria

Performance criteria relate to the value added to the customer on dimensions that they find important for the type of purchase. These criteria tend to be purchase, rather than customer, specific. The standards expected from buying coal may be different from those demanded for a critical production line component. The coal buyer might be satisfied with frequent regular delivery in bulk as cheaply as possible, favouring rail or sea freight, whereas the component buyer might demand fast response at short notice, thus favouring doorstep delivery by road or air freight.

Time

The transit time of goods refers to the total time that elapses between a carrier being notified that there are goods to be picked up and transported, and final receipt of these goods by the customer. This total perspective is important because although one mode of transport may offer fast point-to-point transit time, any inefficiency at either end may reduce the overall benefit. When the Channel Tunnel first opened, some tabloid newspapers celebrated by testing whether it was faster for an individual business traveller to get from a specified point in London to a specified point in Paris more quickly by air than by road. By the time the journey to the airport, check-in procedures, baggage collection and the journey from the airport had been taken into account, there was actually little difference. Similarly, among the reasons the railways lost much of their general merchandise trade were delays in loading and unloading, and the time of the trip to the final destination.

Reliability

Transit time *per se* may be less important than the certainty that the goods will arrive where, when and how they were expected. Even if the transit time is less by one mode of transport than by an alternative, if the alternative proves to be a more reliable and consistent service, it can be planned into the logistics system. Lost sales arising from late or damaged goods are poor compensation for a day's quicker delivery. Higher levels of reliability enable inventory levels to be lowered, as the holder can always be assured of rapid replenishment once minimum levels have been reached.

Linked with reliability is the ability of the carrier to find out quickly the status of goods in transit. The railways are computerised to trace the location of individual wagons and loads, and hauliers often implement similar systems associated with their ordering and collection systems.

Security

Most carriers are responsible for the security and condition of goods in transit. If they are lost or damaged, provided reasonable security and packaging have been maintained, the carrier will be liable to compensate the customer. Particular difficulties exist when international borders are crossed, especially into countries where materials handling and security are less rigorous than in the EU. However, whatever the cause of the loss, the final customer may be less than sympathetic with a manufacturer who uses insecure systems and carriers. Although responsibility for insurance cover for goods in transit will have been agreed between the buyer and seller as part of the original contract, the administration and delays involved in making a claim are not welcome to either party.

Frequency

The scheduling of transportation may have a major impact on the mode decision, especially in more critical supply situations. Many of the large supermarkets deliver on a daily basis to their stores, using their own lorries. This enables order picking and dispatch to follow store turnover closely on individual lines. The less frequent the collection and delivery service, the greater the buffer stock needed to met unforeseen events, and the greater the potential for total transit time to increase.

Capability

Most transportation modes have strengths and weaknesses in offering material handling and carrying facilities to meet client needs. Until the growth of road haulage in the 1960s, a fleet of specialist wagons were retained by the railway operators to move such diverse goods as fish under controlled temperatures, cattle and livestock, and even tar from the gas works. The same principles apply today, although on much reduced traffic levels and product ranges. Many of the bulk loads use specialist oil, coal or other wagon types for ease of transport and automatic materials handling. In Italy, Casaralta of the Firema group has developed a lorry piggyback wagon that twists to assist in loading tractor units and trailer rigs complete. It is claimed that within three minutes the platform can be manoeuvred into position, the unit loaded onto a train and realigned.

Accessibility

Finally, accessibility to railheads, airports or a water system is bound to influence the modal choice. It is interesting to compare access to railheads in the UK which has

Poland still has many local rail collection and delivery points to encourage the movement of goods by rail.

been restricted to a small number of collection points with that in Switzerland, where government and canton policy enables many small stations to have efficient goods handling facilities, often designed for the local trade area. Without direct access, rail transportation only becomes economic if the distance to be travelled by rail is far enough to justify the costs of road handling and delivery at either end.

There are wide variations across Europe in the use of road haulage as compared with other modes of transport, ranging from around 90 per cent of goods in the UK, to 55–60 per cent in France and Germany, and much lower percentages in central Europe.

Example

ICI Paints found that by switching to rail for distribution to continental Europe, the high fixed cost of transloading could be recovered on longer journeys of over 400 kilometres. Similarly, Spillers estimated that it would take 40 to 50 lorries to cover one train load to Scotland from Cambridgeshire. However, Birds Eye prefer road transport so that they can properly monitor products requiring temperature-controlled conditions, for which any breakdown could be costly. SKF also prefer road transport because of the additional speed on high-value products and the possible costs of delay. Generally, in continental Europe, especially France, Germany and Switzerland, rail access and infrastructure and even a rail transport 'culture' provide more opportunity than often found in the UK (*Business Europe*, 1993b).

Order processing

Order processing refers to activities that are parallel to the physical distribution flow, but still related to it. The process starts with the placement of an order. This may be by electronic on-line systems, written, telephone or fax orders made directly by the customer, or orders collected and passed on by the sales force. After placement, an order has to be entered into the company system to trigger subsequent action. This information processing and administration activity is critical to the picking and delivery flow of goods.

Where there are scheduled activities going on, a particular order may extend the planned production schedule horizon by a few months, but not create an immediate problem for the picking and dispatch operation. In other situations, the order may be the final outcome of considerable design and concept development discussion that may have involved prototype production and testing. In fast-moving consumer or organisational product situations, the order entry triggers delivery rather than production processes.

If there is a demand for immediate dispatch, the next phase is a credit and inventory check. Part of this checking process is designed to eliminate block delivery to problem accounts, and to ensure that appropriate prices and terms are being specified. Upon acceptance of the order, the documentation stage which drives the delivery and payment process can proceed. This may include order confirmation, giving picking instructions, downdating inventory levels to ensure the same product is not sold twice, and raising the invoice according to the terms agreed, whether cash on delivery, credit card or account.

Once the documentation stage has been completed, the picking, packing and transport scheduling can proceed, either to a general journey plan or tailormade to the customer's order. In some cases, special carrier services may be used to meet urgent demands or to raise the general levels of service provided. Freight forwarders might also be used. They are facilitating agents who fulfil a very specialist niche, particularly in international trade. If a company sells goods abroad (especially to customers

EDI – a central part of the logistics system

Logistics and physical distribution systems are increasingly making use of electronic data interchange (EDI) to replace paper and improve the flow of communication in supply chains. For Colgate, for example, customer service and effective logistics management are critical ingredients in its marketing strategy. Its European headquarters is based in Brussels, but each European country has a Colgate presence. This means that distribution networks have to be designed to deal with cross-border supply and product movement. There are, however, problems with toothpaste because although it is widely demanded, different countries want different flavours and want packaging in their own language. An important consideration in designing the logistics system, therefore, is finding the balance between the need for standardisation to ease production and distribution and the need to respond to local variances.

The kind of European system Colgate envisages means that an order can be received in any country and the goods can be shipped from any one of Colgate's factories and distribution points around Europe. From the customer's perspective, however, the service is local. This means developing common systems for purchasing, inventory management, invoicing and order processing systems. These systems are multi-currency and multi-language. Orders from customers can be received through EDI and invoices can use the same method to improve the speed of information transfer. This has become even more critical as Colgate is creating JIT relationships with suppliers who, therefore, need sound and timely information about Colgate's order requirements. This information is based in turn on orders from Colgate's customers and sales forecasts.

Unimerchants is an importer of pasta, tomato puree, olives and other foods from Italy which supplies multiple retail chains such as Budgens and Kwik Save. The company spent £200 000 on an EDI system to enable it to control its own warehouse system and, as part of its marketing strategy, to provide raised levels of customer service. The system enables Unimerchants to respond more quickly to customer orders, in terms of both order processing and goods shipping. The system has enabled it to control its supply chain more tightly.

Similarly, Harris Logistics uses EDI to control its relationship with the Safeway retail chain. Harris is responsible for delivering goods to 50 Safeway superstores and to the retailer's regional distribution centres. EDI enables a close interface between Harris' and Safeway's systems and enables shorter lead times through faster, more timely distribution.

Sources: Murphy (1996); Pontin (1993/94).

outside the EU), then there is considerable planning and paperwork to be done to make sure that the goods arrive in the right place at the right time. The freight forwarder can make shipping arrangements, make sure that the goods arrive at the docks or the airport in good time, raise the necessary documentation (bills of lading, for example) and check that all is in order, so that the goods will not be held up by red tape *en route*. Meanwhile, other arrangements may need to be made to receive payment and if necessary, to instigate account follow-up. It could be argued that the order cycle is complete only after the customer has paid.

These various stages are outlined in Fig 14.8. In some cases, the whole process may be almost instantaneous. An order placed at Argos, the retail catalogue shopping business, is processed simultaneously with payment as soon as stock availability has been verified. Instructions are issued on-line to the stock room behind the scenes, and the goods are brought forward for immediate collection by the customer. The whole order processing cycle may take less than five minutes. Large retail chains, their regional distribution depots and their suppliers are increasingly linked, to make the order processing cycle a much faster and more efficient operation. All of this has been made possible by the use of computer-based systems which can handle order processing, transport planning, production planning, inventory levels and account management as part of an integrated system. Such integration is becoming increasingly essential where high-volume transactions are involved.

FIGURE 14.8

Stages in order processing

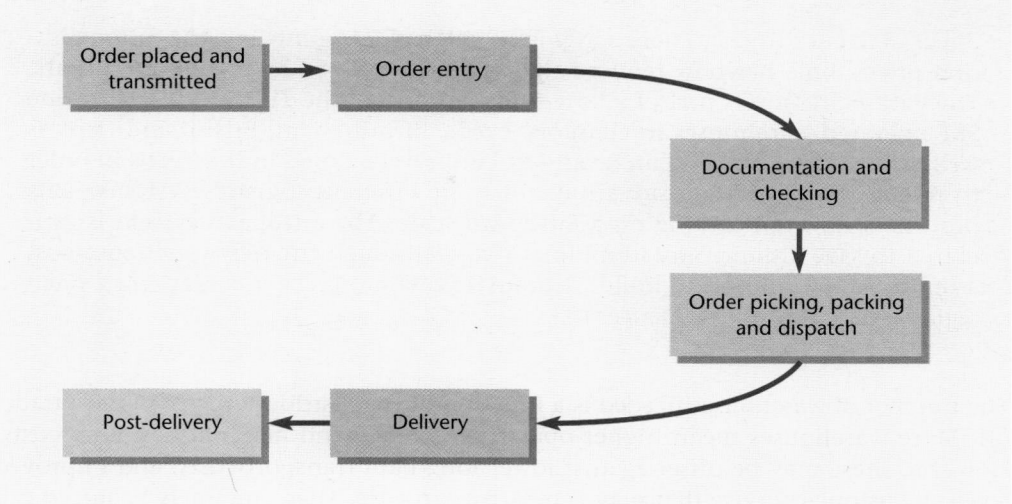

Warehousing

Warehousing is an important link in the physical distribution chain. It enables goods to be stored and subsequently moved according to customer demand. The type and role of the warehouse will vary according to the demands of the product. In Slovakia, Tokai wine is stored by a number of vineyards deep underground in barrels held at a constant temperature. This assists the maturing processes of the wine. Raw timber is often kept at large open sites graded according to the type of wood pending subsequent processing. Other products are completely contained in secure, environmentally controlled surroundings to preserve them in first-class condition. However, the main role of the warehouse remains the same: to help provide the level of customer service agreed in the marketing plan by enabling a rapid supply or resupply of products from locations considered appropriate for responding to that demand.

The main decision facing manufacturers and intermediaries is whether a warehouse is needed at all, and if so, what kind of warehouse it should be. The growth of JIT systems has reduced the need for the level of investment in warehousing that was necessary when safety stocks had to be held. In an ideal situation, JIT removes the need for warehousing, but the reality is that even retailers cannot function reliably or efficiently without any warehousing function at all. Warehouses play an important role in smoothing out the imbalances between supply and demand. Take, for example, apples. In the absence of adequate controlled-temperature storage, the market would be awash with local apples in the autumn, yet they would be in scarce supply in the spring unless expensive imported alternatives were introduced. Of course, the storage of goods can be taken to extremes as, for example, where EU intervention has created wine lakes, butter mountains etc. in an effort to regulate the market. However, again, the practice relies on warehouses that can meet preservation needs.

Warehouses may be primarily used to store goods, but they also enable further handling, such as sorting into appropriate storage areas, picking and order assembly, further packing, palletisation or containerisation and, not least, receiving and loading transportation. Increasingly, these tasks are being automated.

Example

SKF's decision to build a single European distribution centre in Belgium to save costs and reduce delivery times is indicative of some of the changes taking place in warehousing policy across Europe. The new distribution centre will handle direct deliveries to customers. Originally SKF had 24 points but the rationalisation programme has now reduced these to five world-wide distribution points. This rationalisation is part of a long-term strategy. In the 1970s in the UK alone SKF operated warehouses in Glasgow, Leeds, Birmingham, Bristol and Kent as well as the main plant in Luton. All but Luton were closed in the 1980s in order to reduce costs and take advantage of more efficient logistics systems. This process is now continuing on a European scale. The European system is estimated to save around Skr250 million a year although the new warehouse cost around Skr200 million to build. It holds 15 000 products, a far cry from small regional depots (*Business Europe*, 1993a).

The number of warehouses needed is a function of the distribution cost–service trade-off. More warehouses mean higher operating, storage and material handling costs. However, these may be offset against lower long-haul transport costs, and improved levels of customer service that may generate more sales. These are finely balanced calculations, especially as customer responsiveness cannot be measured before the event, only estimated. If the decision is taken to operate warehouses, it will be necessary to consider the location of customers and acceptable order cycle times. The location decision will also reflect the accessibility of motorways or other transport modes, such as airports, for both inbound and outbound distribution. For example the SKF warehouse is on the European motorway network just 15 kilometres from the Netherlands border and just 35 kilometres from Germany.

There are three main warehouse types: public warehouses, private warehouses, and distribution centres.

Public warehouses

Rather than own warehouses, an organisation may rent space and possibly inventory support services to handle goods on its behalf. These services may include receiving, picking, reshipping and co-ordinating between the organisation and the next stage in the channel or the end customer. The main advantage of this method is that the cost relates to usage rather than the fixed and variable operating costs of an owned facility. This could be especially important where volumes are relatively small, but the service demands are high, or where a market is being developed and it is necessary to offer a local inventory base. Also, with seasonal products, usage can be varied through the year, and this may be cheaper than incurring a relatively fixed overhead. Using an independent warehouse operator, therefore, allows the organisation to tap into a network of warehouses that can be used flexibly to meet changing needs. In addition, the warehouse operator will have expertise in maintaining storage conditions and in arranging insurance and perhaps even transportation.

The nature of these warehouses varies. Some specialise in certain product types, such as food products or electrical products. This means that they are able to offer appropriate storage and control facilities, along with handling and redistribution services. Others may accept general merchandise from a wide variety of customers. Even more specialised, bonded warehouses hold imported goods or products on which duty is due. The goods are not released to their owners until all duties and taxes have been paid, thus enabling the owners to delay payment to the relevant authorities until cust-omer orders are received. This type of warehouse is especially common near airports and harbours. It is important to remember that in all public warehouses, title to the goods remains with the user of the service.

Private warehouses

Private warehouses are owned and operated by an organisation within the channel of distribution, whether a manufacturer, a wholesaler or a retailer. The owner is responsible for all the costs associated with the warehouse, fixed and variable. Despite these costs, the warehouse may be designed with the channel's specific requirements in mind and include full computer integration with other members of the channel. The buildings themselves may be bought or rented, and can represent a long-term commitment to the market being served. That very commitment is also a potential problem, because if an organisation owns a facility, then it can become locked into that location, despite the possibility of better ones, perhaps near a new road or industrial development. Furthermore, organisations being serviced by such a facility may view its closure as a sign of lack of commitment to customer service. The major high street retailers and out of town superstores tend to use this kind of facility.

Distribution centres

Distribution centres may be either public or private, but because of the specialised investment sometimes needed, they tend to be public. The whole emphasis is on speed and efficiency rather than storage. While stock may be held for short periods, the aim is to achieve rapid unloading, sorting and redistribution down the channel. Location is critical, to ensure rapid materials handling. Distribution centres are often single-storey buildings with an open external space enabling lorry manoeuvrability. These centres are likely to grow in popularity as the need for service and fast stock movement increases. By breaking bulk from large shipments down to smaller quantities on a consolidated basis, distribution costs can be minimised, yet a full range of product lines can be offered.

Example

Hewlett-Packard operates two major distribution centres in Europe, Grenoble for PCs and Boeblingen near Stuttgart for peripheral products and supplies. These receive orders from customers throughout Europe and ship out by road within 24 hours. These warehouses have replaced inventory at country level.

Materials handling

Materials handling is essentially an internal operation concerned with moving products into, around and out of the warehouse or manufacturing operation. Materials handling is an integral part of a warehouse operation. The complexity of handling thousands of lines, with increasingly high labour costs, means that mechanisation is playing an ever more major role. This typically includes automatic picking equipment, mobile platforms, cranes, conveyors and forklift trucks. Some automated warehouses can handle large volumes of goods using robotic equipment and a computerised control centre. In some *retail* warehouses, such as IKEA, some of the picking and handling responsibility for all but the heaviest items has been transferred to the consumer. Given the labour costs inherent in materials handling, the capital infrastructure and the costs of lost or damaged stock, materials handling needs careful planning.

Materials handling efficiency is linked with the functional aspects of packaging and pack size, considered earlier at pp. 278 *et seq*. The use of forklifts and automated conveyor systems requires careful thought to what kind of palletisation and packing is suitable for open or sealed movement. Similarly, containerisation for road, road–rail

and sea can avoid the necessity of handling individual items before and during transit. The whole thrust of materials handling is to handle the product as few times as possible in as large a quantity as possible and with as much automation as possible.

Inventory management

Inventory management is central to the problem of how to balance customer service against physical distribution costs. Too much stock, although it will permit a high level of product availability, which may please customers, will result in high carrying and obsolescence costs. Too low a level of stock may result in frustrated customers, brand switching and eventually lost market share. Inventory management can also generate internal conflict between the marketing department which wishes to maximise choice and availability, the production department, where longer or continuous runs assist lower unit costs but do not necessarily produce the range required in a timely manner, and the finance department which is seeking to keep costs down through lower inventory levels.

Inventory costs

There are a number of costs associated with holding inventory. Some are readily apparent, as they can be seen in the warehouse. Others are spread through the organisation whether in distribution, marketing or manufacturing. The main costs are:

- *carrying costs*: the costs of financing stock, which are related to cash flow and borrowing, and thus to interest rates

- *stock servicing costs*, including insurance and duties payable
- *storage costs*, which relate to the use of space and handling
- *obsolescence and wastage costs*, due to loss, damage and perishability.

There are other less obvious costs that are associated with being out of stock when orders are received. These relate to the processing of unfulfilled orders, and the need to back-order and monitor until the order is eventually fulfilled. Quite apart from these are the opportunity costs associated with the loss of a customer who decides to source from elsewhere.

Stock movement

Inventory is an asset on an organisation's balance sheet, and can often account for up to 50 per cent of its total working capital value. Careful management is necessary to ensure that stock moves quickly in order to avoid mark-downs (i.e., selling off unwanted goods cheaply) and obsolescence. Part of that management is the need to be clear about the purpose of carrying inventory in the first place. There are various reasons, including:

1 maintaining security stock where supply and demand cannot be accurately predicted;
2 offering better customer service;
3 enabling longer production runs;
4 enabling greater use of purchasing and transport economies of scale; and
5 covering any unforeseen contingencies that would impact on the smooth flow of materials into production or warehouses.

Stock level

Establishing the level of stock to hold has been the subject of much consideration. As already discussed, holding either too much or too little stock can be dangerous and/or inefficient. Allowing stock levels to fall too low may jeopardise customer satisfaction, and waiting to reorder until a dangerously low level has been reached is risky, given that it takes time to replenish stock. Figure 14.9 shows the **reorder point** model of stock control, which triggers reordering at a stock level somewhat higher than the danger level, so that by the time the new stock is received, the danger level has only just been reached with the old stock.

FIGURE 14.9

Stock control: reorder point method

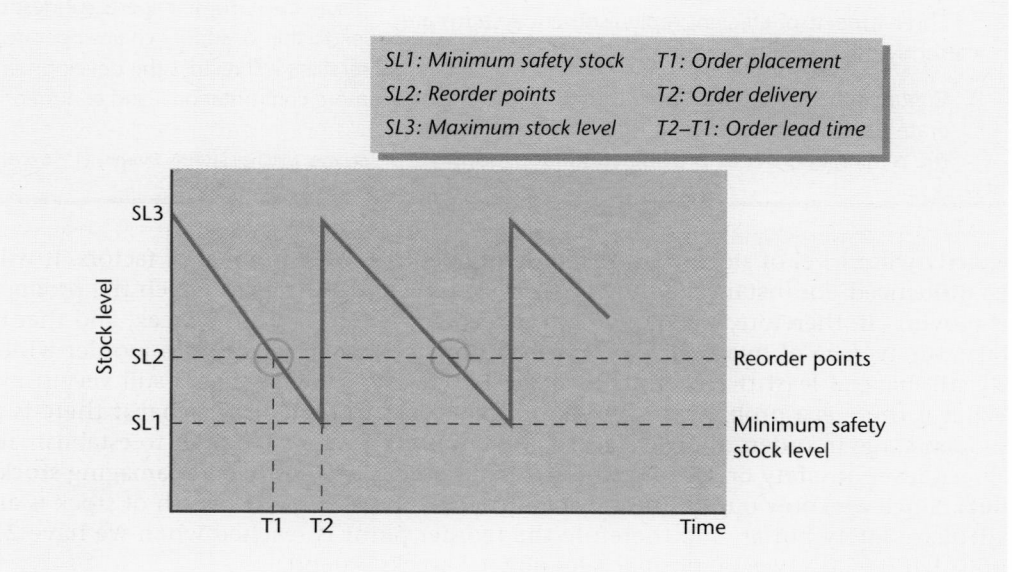

SL1: Minimum safety stock	T1: Order placement
SL2: Reorder points	T2: Order delivery
SL3: Maximum stock level	T2–T1: Order lead time

Efficient consumer response

Retailers and manufacturers across Europe are still undecided whether efficient consumer response (ECR) is another fad from the USA or whether it will fundamentally affect the nature of European buyer–seller relationships in the same way that JIT affected organisational markets a few years ago. ECR is about ensuring that the supply chain works in a co-ordinated manner to ensure that the retailer is well served with product without imposing unnecessary strain and inefficiency on the manufacturer. It is concerned with logistics, but also extends to include promotions, assortment and product development. According to Coopers and Lybrand, ECR principles could generate savings of $33 billion for European supply chains, the equivalent of 5.7 per cent off consumer prices, 4.8 per cent off operating costs and 0.9 per cent off inventory costs. For that reason, a number of leading European retailers and their suppliers, such as ASKO Deutsche Kaufhaus, Tesco, Danone, Nestlé and Mars are actively examining the potential of adopting ECR.

At the heart of ECR is the need for retailers and manufacturers to work more co-operatively than they have done in the past. Adopting a better managed supply chain for branded products could be in the interests of both manufacturers and retailers, not only the discounters, but also the trend towards home shopping. Often, however, the first step is to co-operate to ensure more efficient replenishment of inventory and greater use of electronic data interchange (EDI). At Tesco, for example, all ordering is by EDI and suppliers are expected to be networked.

Three aspects of efficient replenishment systems are currently being piloted in Europe:

1 *Continuous replenishment* means that suppliers generate their orders using inventory data supplied by the retailer in order to provide continuous supply rather than batch delivery. Service levels have improved as a result of the system and inventory and warehouse space costs have lowered;

2 *Cross-docking* is used with fresh produce in particular. At distribution centres, stocks are co-ordinated through the IT system to ensure that the arrival of inbound trucks from suppliers and the departure of retailers' trucks are so close that goods can move from one to the other without going into stock. This means that stock can move easily within the distribution centre. Although trials have shown a loss of transport efficiency, operating costs overall can fall and the shelf life of fresh goods can be increased by up to three days.

Wavin Trepak, a logistics operator from the Netherlands dealing in fresh produce, developed a standardised crate that is fully stackable and can be handled by robots. This system is important for its dealings with Albert Heijn, one of the leading Dutch retailers, as the crates can be rolled straight from the lorry on to the sales floor. This system is also easier for cross-docking;

3 *Roll-cage sequencing* enables products to be stored in the distribution centre by category. This enables easier handling in the distribution centre and results in better packed pallets that are easier for the retail store to deal with. In trials, 200 extra labour hours were incurred in the distribution centre, but this was offset by a saving of 700 hours in stores.

Despite these gains from taking a supply chain perspective, some experts suggest that the traditional leadership of supply chains operated by many UK retailers will restrict the development of ECR in favour of more confrontational and control-orientated methods.

Sources: Mitchell (1996); Murphy (1996); Whitworth (1996).

Exactly what level of stock triggers reordering depends on a number of factors. It will be influenced, for instance, by the order cycle time and the rate at which the product is moving. If, therefore, we know that on average we sell six units a week, and that it takes an average of two weeks to replenish our stock, then we need to reorder while we still have at least twelve units in stock. Leaving it as late as that is still very risky. What if there is a problem and it takes three weeks to replenish? What if there is a sudden surge in orders and we start selling ten units a week? We need to establish an agreed level of **safety or security stock** to avoid potentially costly and damaging **stock-outs**. Since we know our business, we may decide that 1.5 weeks' worth of stock is an adequate safety buffer, and therefore the reorder point is reached when we have 21 units left (i.e., two weeks' normal sales plus 1.5 weeks' safety).

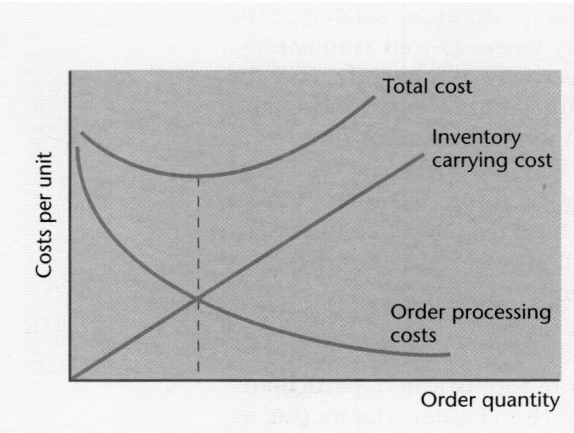

FIGURE 14.10

The economic order quantity model

Reorder models

There is also the problem of how much stock to order at one time. There are conflicting forces here, pulling the organisation in different directions. On the one hand, customer service levels can be kept high, and order processing costs can be kept low (because the organisation does not reorder so frequently) by holding large stocks and maintaining high safety margins. On the other hand, smaller stocks, while potentially lowering service levels, through the risk of stockouts and raising order processing costs with more frequent reordering, do minimise stockholding costs. The economic order quantity model, shown in Fig 14.10, tries to trade off these two alternative, finding a happy medium between them.

The economic order quantity model shows the ideal theoretical relationship between order processing costs and inventory carrying costs to reveal the order quantity size that minimises total costs. However, this model takes an internal, purely economic perspective, in that no reference is made to the impact on customer service levels of compromising on safety stocks. Depending on the desired service levels, the actual order quantities may not necessarily reflect the lowest total cost.

The most appropriate reorder model will depend on the nature or predictability of demand. If stock moves in large, discrete blocks rather than on an almost continuous flow basis, the reorder point model (*see* Fig 14.9) risks generating either too large or too small a safety stock.

Another model uses a mixed approach based on Pareto analysis, which states that 80 per cent of our sales are accounted for by 20 per cent of our products, as shown in Fig 14.11. Those 20 per cent of items (group A) making up 80 per cent of sales are carefully monitored to ensure high levels of customer service through maintenance of high safety stocks. Slower moving items (group B) are stocked in much smaller quantities, with a much lower safety margin, although contingencies may exist for rapid delivery using special transport services. Even more sophisticated models have emerged that focus on materials requirements planning. These include careful systems integration of demand forecasts, distribution requirements, production schedules and associated resource planning. The creation of a close relationship between materials requirements planning and production scheduling, taking into account agreed replenishment times, means that there can be an efficient link between scheduling raw materials or parts requirements and production needs and outputs, minimising stockholding along the way.

FIGURE 14.11

Pareto analysis and stock management

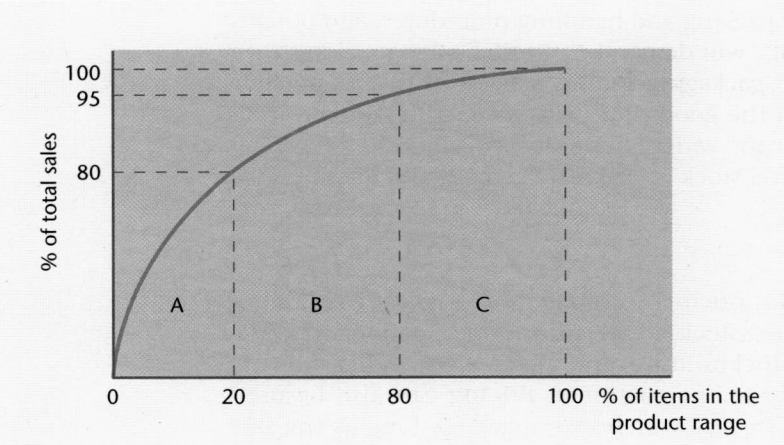

Other techniques have also emerged adopting similar principles (McDaniel *et al.*, 1992). The JIT concept aims, as the name suggests, virtually to eliminate safety stock, with parts arriving just as they are needed in production, as was seen in the example of Apple (*see* p. 537). The order requirements can be so tight as to specify the unloading point and time of day. If the JIT system is to work effectively, suppliers must be able to respond appropriately. This means ensuring complete reliability in quality and delivery terms, as well as making a full commitment to customer service. The supplier effectively assumes the risk for supply security and the carrying of safety stock. A small injection moulder in Ireland, for example, supplying into a JIT system, decided to carry some permanent reserves as a buffer against transport or production difficulties. This was considered preferable to the risks of letting the customer down and potentially losing future business. It must be emphasized that the adoption of JIT systems assumes high degrees of co-operation and trust between supplier and buyer, and the development of longer-term partnerships characterised by closeness and regular communication.

Inventory levels management

The management of inventory levels is becoming ever more sophisticated, particularly in fast moving environments, as has been seen throughout this chapter. The increasing use of IT, whether in a retail store or at an order processing point, helps to tighten inventory control or even in some cases to eliminate inventory altogether. However, poor inventory management still happens, leading to visible problems such as:

1 mark downs and sale rails;
2 late customer delivery;
3 stockouts and extended order cycle times;
4 accepting orders for stock that the system indicates should be on the shelf but is not;
5 stock as an increasingly high percentage of total assets; and
6 falling stock turnover levels.

All of these problems are signs that the inventory management system has not functioned to its original expectation.

MARKETING STRATEGY AND PHYSICAL DISTRIBUTION

This chapter has largely looked at the importance of physical distribution planning as a means of improving customer service. It is equally important, however, to plan PDM in line with rest of the marketing mix.

Product

Clearly PDM decisions will be affected by the nature of the product and the range of products dealt with. Perishable goods, for example, such as fruit and vegetables will bring the need for controlled storage and rapid distribution to the fore; fragile goods, such as glassware, will dictate particular packing and handling procedures, and potentially dangerous goods, such as chemicals, will demand controlled storage, along with specialist transport. Product design and packaging should make it as easy as possible to store, handle, identify and transport the goods, but without sacrificing flair, individuality or customer needs. The greater the variety of products dealt with, the greater the inventory problems, in terms of space, stock levels, management and distribution.

Pricing

As discussed fully in Chapters 10 and 11, pricing decisions should reflect the level of service provided. Slow-moving but valued stock might, for instance, command a premium price to cover the costs of stockholding and reward the seller for the convenience of immediate availability to the customer. Pricing can also be used creatively to shift slow-moving stock, freeing warehouse space. As long as the sale price covers the variable costs of manufacture or value added, it may well be worth sacrificing profit to dispose of goods that are chalking up long-term stockholding costs and taking up space that would otherwise be occupied by faster turnaround items.

Promotion

Promotion is a way of articulating the promises that the organisation wants to make to the customer. Those promises, however, must always be fulfilled. This means that the physical product must always be available when the sales representative or the advertising say it will be. It also means that the back-up infrastructure must always be in place to respond to the customer. If an organisation runs a television advertisement inviting people to place a credit card order by phone, then the phone lines must be available and open, and the order processing system set up to deal with each caller quickly but thoroughly. There is more on this in Chapter 19, on direct marketing.

When promotion and logistics do not coincide, the results can be both embarrassing and expensive.

> ### Example
>
> Mercury 1-2-1, the mobile phone operator, offered free international phone calls on Christmas Day 1994 as a promotion to recruit new customers. Although they had increased the number of lines available for that day, and therefore had thought through the logistics connected with delivering the promotion, they had completely underestimated the number of calls people would want to make and the duration of those calls. As a result, in addition to coping with a moderate amount of poor publicity, Mercury 1-2-1 are having to pay compensation to many thousands of disappointed customers who did not manage to make even one call.

Physical distribution management and logistics are, therefore, yet more integrated elements of the overall marketing task. As with any other marketing responsibility, they are part of a dynamic environment and need to be audited, monitored and changed to help to keep the organisation's competitive edge as sharp as possible.

CHAPTER SUMMARY

This chapter looked at the processes of physical distribution and logistics that carry goods from manufacturers to consumers. Physical distribution is about the handling, storage and movement of outbound goods, including order processing and transportation. The channels of distribution may include facilitators such as transportation and warehousing specialists. Logistics includes the handling of inbound materials and components, as well as managing outbound inventory, effectively linking supply sources with demand. Logistics can thus provide a framework for guiding planning, forecasting and strategic thinking.

The design of the logistics system will vary depending on the type and size of the organisation, and thus its costs will also vary widely. The main factors affecting the total logistics cost include order processing and administration, stock held or moving through the system, transport and outlet costs relating to warehousing and materials handling.

The overall aim of logistics and PDM is to provide customer service, but this has to be balanced against the cost. The higher the level of service offered, the higher the costs incurred. Thus the organisation or the members of the distribution channel must be careful to match the level of service with actual customer needs, avoiding unnecessary costs.

Transportation is obviously central to any logistics system. There are five main modes of transport: road, rail, air, water and pipeline. Each has its own costs, advantages and disadvantages. In reality, *intermodal transport* is likely to be used, for instance taking a container by lorry to a railhead, then by train to a port, then on to a ship bound for an export market. Intermodal transport builds on the strengths and practicality of each mode of transport, building an overall system that is as efficient yet as cost effective as it can be. This might require trade-offs, for example speed against cost. The main criteria that affect transport choice, and might provide the basis for trade-offs, are cost, performance criteria, time, reliability, security, frequency, capability and accessibility.

Order processing is also an important part of the logistics system. Orders may be placed through sales representatives or come directly from the customer to the sales office. In some cases, orders might trigger production processes, but in others, they might simply trigger delivery from stock. The use of computerised systems can make the whole order placing and processing system much faster, more accurate and more reliable, especially where buyer and seller are linked on computer networks.

Warehousing allows goods to be stored at strategically sited locations until they need to be moved to fulfil customer demand. This helps to ensure a rapid response when the need arises. Warehouses can be designed to keep the product in optimum condition through, for example, temperature and humidity control. They can also act as a sorting point, so that goods can be delivered in bulk and then broken down into smaller lots, repacked or containerised to suit the next stage in their journey to the end consumer. Warehouses might be sited to take advantage of road networks or the location of customers. Materials and goods handling is an integral part of any warehousing operation. In large complex operations it might be a highly mechanised process, which has implications for the way in which products are packed for ease of bulk handling.

Inventory management is a critical activity, which has to strike a balance between holding enough stock to meet customer needs, but not holding so much that it becomes a cost and storage burden. Stock might be held in order to provide a better and more responsive level of customer service, to give buffer stocks where demand is unpredictable, to cover unforeseen contingencies or to take advantage of economies of scale through bulk purchasing or transport. A number of models exist to help with stock control by calculating optimum stock levels and reorder quantities. *Pareto analysis*, by concentrating on the fastest moving or most important items, allows managers to prioritise which products need the highest safety stocks maintained. JIT takes stock control to its limits by eliminating safety stocks almost completely, and relying on suppliers to deliver at specific times. Many retailers use automatic computerised stock control systems to trigger stock updating whereby products are scanned through the checkout and are reordered once stock levels reach a certain low point.

PDM influences and is influenced by the other elements of the marketing mix. The perishability or fragility of the *product*, for example, will affect the speed with which it needs to be distributed and the ways in which it can be handled. PDM influences the functional aspects of packaging in terms of its robustness and ease of handling. The greater the variety of goods, the greater the logistics problems involved. *Pricing* might reflect either the savings made by the efficiency of PDM or the costs involved in providing high levels of customer service and convenience. *Promotion* might make promises about delivery or freshness of the product, for example, that PDM then has to be able to live up to.

Key words and phrases

Customer service	*Logistics*	*Safety stock*
Facilitators	*Order cycle time*	*Stockout*
Intermodal transport	*Physical distribution*	
Inventory management	*Reorder point*	

QUESTIONS FOR REVIEW

14.1 List the range of functions undertaken in *physical distribution management*.

14.2 What are *facilitators*, and what specific functions do they provide within PDM?

14.3 How does *logistics* differ from PDM?

14.4 What are the main *cost areas* of logistics?

14.5 What are the three groups into which *customer service* can be categorised, and what kinds of services does each group cover?

14.6 Outline the stages in *order processing* and discuss their contribution to customer service.

14.7 How and why does *holding inventory* incur costs?

14.8 How do *JIT systems* affect inventory control and management?

14.9 To what kinds of problems can *poor inventory management* lead?

14.10 Summarise the ways in which PDM interacts with the elements of the *marketing mix*.

QUESTIONS FOR DISCUSSION

14.1 Draw up a table which lists each of the five main *modes of transport*, summarises their advantages and disadvantages, compares their relative costs per kilometre, and gives an example of an appropriate use of each mode.

14.2 What are the main criteria affecting *transport choice* and how might they impact on transporting:

(a) coal to a power-station;
(b) fruit to a supermarket;
(c) components to a car factory; and
(d) cash for wages from a bank to a factory?

14.3 *Road transport* has come under increasing criticism on environmental grounds. To what extent do you think this should influence organisations' transport policy?

14.4 To what extent and why do you think *warehousing* can contribute to effective and efficient PDM?

14.5 Critically evaluate the limitations of the stock control models presented at pp. 556–560.

Putting some fizz into supply chain management

The scale of the physical distribution problem facing some organisations can be quite astounding. For example Britvic's UK national distribution centre, handling such brands as Tango, 7Up and Pepsi, handles 1.5 billion cans per year, with over 700 lorries arriving and departing per day. Cadbury's national distribution centre near Birmingham stores 93 000 pallets of chocolate in a 36 000 m² centre. That is enough space for 50 million Easter eggs and 250 different lines of chocolate! Working on this scale, successful operations can only be ensured through careful planning and use of sophisticated technology and systems. The concern is not only to maintain smooth day-to-day running, but also to reduce lead times, enhance customer service levels, and minimise stockholding levels. Warehousing and distribution has become a very sophisticated business for some operators.

The Britvic centre has a 50 000-pallet capacity, six bays for receiving goods inward, and 19 despatch bays. Goods are sent to retailers and wholesalers throughout the UK. The centre makes considerable use of IT to manage a custom-built automatic materials handling system. The system stores orders from the Britvic order processing system, maintains stock control, assembles a range of orders according to shipping instructions, as well as managing stock picking and despatch. Such a system has considerable advantages for customers. The supermarket chain Safeway, for example, no longer has to source individual Britvic brands by the truckload from the factory. Instead, Safeway can order specific quantities of different products which will then be delivered on a consolidated basis to Safeway's own regional distribution centres. Safeway's centres are, in turn, responding to orders from individual stores.

Cadbury's decision to centralise its distribution operations at Minworth near Birmingham replaced 12 centres around the UK. Cadbury's had found that maintaining so many centres was costly because of duplicated stockholding, duplicated overheads and additional transportation complexity. The Minworth location, near the M1, M5, M6 and M40 motorways, meant that major customers could still be supplied efficiently and within their service requirements without the need to maintain so many mini locations. The investment cost was £24 million, but provided a facility that is more than repaying the initial investment. The warehouse is one of the largest chilled warehouses in Europe and it is claimed to represent 5 per cent of the UK's total cold storage capacity. Particular attention was given in the warehouse design to aisle width, storage flexibility and crane design to allow high-volume order picking and pallet handling systems. Even when goods arrive at the warehouse, automatic vehicles, using underfloor guidance systems, enable the automatic movement of goods under complete computer control.

The above examples show that electronic data transfer is at the centre of distribution operations in facilitating fast exchange of information. This means that there must be a continuous flow of information to enable faster and more appropriate decisions to be made when assembling loads, thus further reducing stock levels held in the retail outlet.

Source: Murphy (1996).

Questions

1 Why are sophisticated IT systems important for distribution centres such as those operated by Britvic and Cadbury's?

2 What services are these distribution centres providing to the retail trade?

3 In what ways might these distribution centres reduce costs for:
(a) the manufacturers; and
(b) the retailers?

4 What are the relative advantages and disadvantages of having one large distribution centre rather than a series of regional centres when dealing with fmcg products such as chocolate and soft drinks?

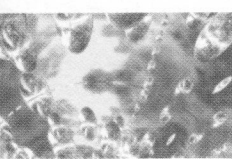

Fording the Channel

The opening of the Channel Tunnel gave a number of companies the opportunity to reconsider their European transportation arrangements. The Ford Motor Company moves car parts on a daily basis from its plant near Valencia in Spain to Dagenham in the UK. Originally, goods were transported by rail from Valencia to Zeebrugge and then by sea to the Ford wharf at Dagenham. Although the parts were containerised, Ford still incurred extra costs in transferring from rail to sea, and of course the process meant time delays.

The Channel Tunnel provides a new direct rail route from Valencia to Dagenham without the need to swap the mode of transport during the journey. Rather than suffer the problems of operating its own service as some other companies do, however, Ford decided to appoint a freight forwarder to take over full responsibility for managing the flow. The five-year contract was awarded to Transfesa, a Spanish freight forwarder with considerable rail traffic experience. Ford could not match their experience in operating 20 regular block trains and in dealing with 15 different railway administrations across Europe. Such experience is essential in view of the different requirements of national railway authorities across Europe. In this case, the forwarder was dealing with the Spanish national railway (RENFE), the French national railway (SNCF) and Railfreight Distribution in the UK.

The problems that the forwarder had to deal with were not just the administrative paperwork involved in transferring goods from one rail company to another. There are some very practical problems when trying to organise pan-European distribution within a rail infrastructure that is definitely not pan-European. In the first place, Spanish railways operate on a 1668 mm. broad gauge track rather than the standard European gauge of 1438 mm. This means that either axles have to be changed at the Spanish–French border before goods can proceed, or the goods or containers have to be transferred to wagons with standard gauge axles. Both options were evaluated and Transfesa decided to build wagons for the Ford contract with changeable axles, to enable speedier transfer.

Second, railway operating requirements meant that the train length could not exceed 450 metres. This meant that the 30-wagon train currently used by the forwarder would have been too long. Rather than incur increased haulage costs, therefore, the wagons that were built especially for the contract were shorter. Thus it was possible to retain a 30-wagon train with the same haulage costs as for the forwarder's existing train.

Finally, handling problems at either end meant that the containers would have to be purpose built so that they could be stacked to fit into the limited storage space at the Valencia site. Traditional bodies for road and rail use could not be stacked. At Dagenham, Transfesa also had to invest £500 000 on new lifting gear for the swapbody containers (containers that could be transferred from road to rail).

The decision to use rail throughout did, therefore, involve additional costs that Transfesa decided to absorb as part of the five-year contract. The saving for Ford is that the 2000 kilometre journey is often covered in 37–39 hours, well short of the time taken by the original rail–sea method. This has a direct benefit in lowering the costs of the logistics system created by having different manufacturing sites around Europe.

Source: *Modern Railways* (1994).

Questions

1 Why is a smooth and fast logistics operation essential for Ford in this case?

2 What difference do you think the opening of the Channel Tunnel made to the European logistics operations of organisations like Ford?

3 Why did Ford choose to award a contract for the Valencia–Dagenham logistics function to an outside company rather than handle it themselves? Are there any risks in doing this?

4 Transfesa have clearly invested a great deal of capital in this five-year contract. What are the potential risks and rewards for them?

REFERENCES TO CHAPTER 14

Allen, P. and Rotherby, B. (1994), 'An End to Work in Progress', *European Purchasing and Materials Management*, 3, pp. 209–15.

Batchelor, C. (1994), 'Relentless Drive to Reduce Costs', *Financial Times*, 21 September, p. I.

Bowersox, D. (1978), *Logistics Management*, MacMillan.

Business Europe (1993a) 'Logistics for Europe', *Business Europe*, 12–18 April, p. 7.

Business Europe (1993b), 'Euro-Logistics: Choosing Between Road and Rail', *Business Europe*, 2-8 August, pp. 6–7.

Business Europe (1994), 'Why Neckermann Chose the Rhine Option', *Business Europe*, 34(3), p. 7.

Byrne, P. M. *et al.* (1994), 'New Priorities for Logistics Services in Europe', *Transport and Distribution*, February, pp. 43–8.

Byrne, P. M. and Markham, N. J. (1993), 'Only 10% of Companies Satisfy Customers', *Transport and Distribution*, December, pp. 41–5.

Christopher, M. (1990), *The Strategy of Distribution Management*, Heinemann.

Cooper, J. (1994), 'Jeux Sans Frontieres', *Purchasing and Supply Management*, March, p. 4.

Dapiran, P. (1992), 'Benetton – Global Logistics in Action',

International Journal of Physical Distribution and Logistics Management, 22(6), pp. 7–11.

Horley, R. C. (1993), 'Integrated Transport', *Logistics Information Management*, 6(1), pp. 42–5.

LaLonde, B. J. and Zinzer, P. (1976), *Customer Service: Meaning and Measurement*, National Council of Physical Distribution Management.

Lloyd, C. (1995), 'Freight Hauliers Load Up On Line', *Sunday Times*, 8 January.

McDaniel, S. *et al.* (1992), 'The Effect of JIT on Distributors', *Industrial Marketing Management*, 21, pp. 145–9.

Markham, W. J. and Aurick, J. C. (1993), 'Shape Up and Ship Out', *Journal of European Business*, 4(5), pp. 54–7.

Mentzer, J. T. *et al.* (1989), 'Physical Distribution Service: A Fundamental Marketing Concept?', *Journal of the Academy of Marketing Science*, 17 (Winter).

Mitchell, A. (1996), 'Two Sides of the Argument', *Marketing Week*, 16 February, pp. 26–7.

Modern Railways, (1994). 'Ford's Spain–UK Chunnel Train', *Modern Railways*, December, pp. 730–1.

Moffat, L. A. R .(1992), 'Consumer Electronic Products: Trends in European Distribution', *International Journal of Physical Distribution and Logistics Management*, 22(7), pp. 13–24.

Murphy, Y. (1996), 'Focus on Warehousing and Distribution', *The Grocer*, 3 February, pp. 53–73.

Pontin, M. (1993/94), 'Single Market Strategy', *European Purchasing and Materials Management*, 2, pp. 115–17.

Robson, P. (1993), 'Tibbett & Britten: Going Places', *Purchasing and Supply Management*, September, pp. 16–17.

Salak, J. (1993), 'When Your Carrier Delivers the Goods', *International Business*, 6(9), pp. 30–2.

Shapley, D. (1995), 'Fresher and Faster Links', *The Grocer*, 28 October, pp. 37–8.

Sussams, J. E. (1991), 'The Impact of Logistics on Retailing and Physical Distribution', *International Journal of Retail and Distribution Management*, pp. 19(7), 4–9.

Thomas, J. (1994), 'Mountain High, River Wide', *Distribution*, May, pp. 62–6.

Toll, E. (1993), 'Get Smart', *International Business*, 6(9), pp. 29–30.

Whitworth, M. (1996), 'Be Sceptical, But Don't Be Left Behind', *The Grocer*, 3 February, pp. 26–7.

Part VI

■ ■ ■

PROMOTION

Communication and the Promotional Mix **15**

Advertising **16**

Sales Promotion **17**

Personal Selling and Sales Management **18**

Direct Marketing **19**

Public Relations, Sponsorship and Exhibitions **20**

What is marketing if it isn't communication? The philosophy of marketing (discussed in Chapter 1) as the interface between an organisation and the outside world, particularly its customers, implies that all marketing activities are destined to communicate something to someone, somewhere. This communication may be direct and tangible, an advertisement for example, but it may also be indirect and intangible: think about the ways in which price communicates with a potential buyer, for instance.

There is certainly synergy between direct and indirect communication. Advertising messages centred on product quality can be reinforced by tacit communication though price and packaging, or a sales representative's credibility can be enhanced by what is implicitly communicated by the product's performance. In practice, the direct and indirect elements of communication are inseparable, but in the following six chapters, the emphasis is on the overt means by which organisations communicate.

Chapter 15 introduces the concept of communication and its application in marketing and also looks at some of the factors influencing and organisation's choice of promotional mix elements. Each of these elements is then explored in more detail in Chapters 16 to 18 look at advertising, sales promotion and personal selling, defining the tools and techniques used within each area, their appropriate use and the problems of implementation. Chapter 19 examines direct marketing; an increasingly important means of injecting a personal touch back into mass markets. Finally, Chapter 20 explores public relations, sponsorship and exhibitions – all of which are now recognised as valuable marketing communication techniques.

■   ■   ■

15 Communication and the Promotional Mix

LEARNING OBJECTIVES

This chapter will help you to:

1 understand the importance of planned communication in a marketing context;

2 appreciate the variety and scope of marketing communication objectives;

3 explain the use of promotional tools in the communication process;

4 identify the factors and constraints influencing the mix of communications tools an organisation uses; and

5 define the major methods by which communications budgets are set.

INTRODUCTION

The promotional mix is the direct way in which an organisation attempts to communicate with various target audiences. It consists of five main elements, as shown in Fig 15.1. Advertising represents non-personal, mass communication; personal selling is at the other extreme, covering face-to-face personally tailored messages. Sales promotion involves tactical, short-term incentives that encourage a target audience to behave in a certain way. Public relations is about creating and maintaining good quality relationships with many interested groups (for example the media, shareholders and trades unions), not just with customers. Finally, direct marketing involves creating one-to-one relationships with individual customers, often in mass markets, and might involve mailings, telephone selling or electronic media. Some might classify direct marketing activities as forms of advertising, sales promotion or even personal selling, but this text treats direct marketing as a separate element of the promotional mix while acknowledging that it 'borrows' from the other elements.

Ideally, the marketer would like to invest extensively in every element of the mix. In a world of finite resources, however, choices have to be made about which activities are going to work together most cost effectively with the maximum synergy to achieve the communications objectives of the organisation within a defined budget.

FIGURE 15.1

The elements of
the promotional
mix

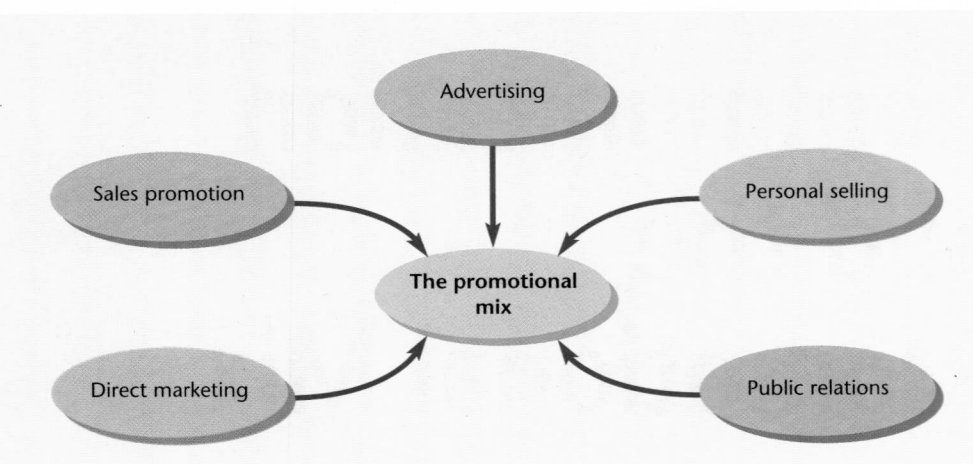

Budgets obviously vary widely between different organisations, and depending on the
type of product involved and the communications task in hand.

> ### Example
>
> Coca-Cola Schweppes Beverages in trying to improve the UK profile of its
> Dr Pepper brand in early 1996 was reported to be spending £100 million mainly
> on television advertising and sales promotion, distributing product samples
> (Marshall, 1995). Contrast that with the expenditure of the Banana Group, a fed-
> eration of the four main UK banana importers, which has spent only £3 million
> over 10 years, mainly on public relations activities such as sponsoring the UK's
> leading cycle racing team (*The Grocer*, 1995).

This chapter, along with the five that follow it, will aim to explain why such choices
are made.

Each element of the promotional mix has its own chapter which discusses in some
detail the element's strengths and weaknesses and its appropriate use. This chapter,
therefore, provides a more general strategic overview by focusing on the marketing
communications planning process. This helps to emphasize some of the influences
that shape an appropriate blend within the promotional mix, allowing the marketer
to allocate communication resources most effectively.

Communication, even mass market advertising, begins and ends with people,
which means that it has plenty of scope for going wrong. The first part of this chapter,
therefore, takes a look at communications theory from first principles, building up a
simple model of communication. This is then applied in a marketing context to highlight the danger areas where marketing communication efforts can fail. These
concepts may appear to be very abstract or theoretical, but they nevertheless form an
important foundation for applied decision making and may make the difference
between success and failure.

On the basis of these concepts, the main focus of the chapter is on developing a
planning framework within which the managerial decisions on communication activity can be made. Each of the elements of the simple communication model is
incorporated into this framework, whether implicitly or explicitly, with a view to
minimising the danger of misunderstanding and failure. Each stage in the planning
flow is discussed in turn, with particular emphasis being given to relevant issues and
the kind of promotional mix blend which might subsequently be appropriate. It is

becoming increasingly important for organisations to design and implement effective marketing communications strategies as they expand their interests beyond their known domestic markets.

COMMUNICATIONS THEORY

Schramm (1955) offers a seminal definition of **communication** which serves as a sound basis for developing a model of communication:

> '**The process of establishing a commonness or oneness of thought between a sender and a receiver.**'

Communication model

Superficially, communication is a very simple process which we all do all the time and take for granted. It would seem from the definition above that all you need is someone to send a message and someone to receive it, as shown in Fig 15.2.

FIGURE 15.2

The basic elements of communication

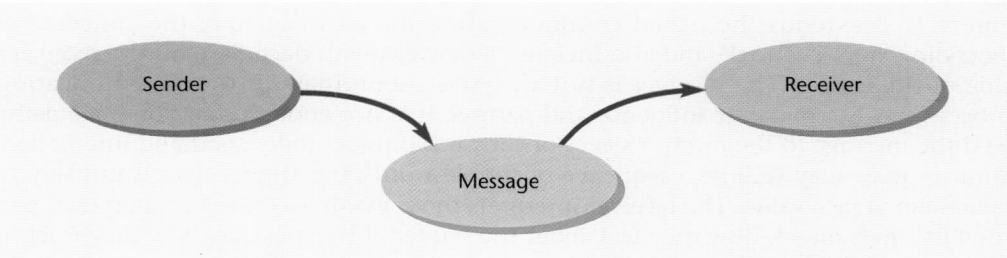

However, even the three apparently simple elements of Fig 15.2 raise a number of questions which Fig 15.2 does not deal with.

Encoding the message

Put yourself in the position of having to tell a professor that an assignment will not be handed in on time. The intent of the message is clear enough, but *what* precisely are you going to say and *how* exactly are you going to say it? Here are some alternatives. (This situation is, of course, purely hypothetical. The authors do not hold themselves responsible for the consequences of your using any of these approaches in reality!)

- 'I can't hand in my assignment on time. I'll deliver it on Friday.' (assertive/assumptive)
- 'I'm sorry, but I haven't quite finished my assignment yet. Please can I hand it in on Friday?' (apologetic/appealing)
- 'I've done it, honestly, but the dog ate it, so I need to print it out again – would Friday be all right?' (possibly honest ...)

There are many, many more alternatives. The point is that, as the sender, you would assess each of these alternative approaches in order to predict their likely effect on the receiver of the message. Naturally, you would choose the one most likely to achieve the desired outcome. This relies on your perceptions of the receiver's attitudes, character and state of mind. The third excuse might be appropriate for a professor with a soft-hearted, sympathetic (or gullible) streak, whereas the second excuse would appeal to an honest, straightforward, no-nonsense type. The first excuse guarantees you a 'fail' from any self-respecting academic. In other words, you make a choice as to how you **encode** the message, first so that it will be understood by the receiver and second, to increase the chances of achieving the objectives of the communication.

Communication channel

A further complication arises when you consider the means by which the message is relayed to the receiver, that is, the choice of **channel of communication**. Will you deliver the message yourself, verbally, or will you leave a note and run away? The choice of channel might affect the success of the communication. The verbal method allows you to assess the response to your initial message, giving you the flexibility to try again with a different approach, if at first you don't succeed. It also gives you the opportunity to employ non-verbal communication to reinforce the message. The tone of voice used (assumptive, quietly polite or pleading), the look in the eyes (hostile, guilty or pleading) all communicate in their own right, and need to be consistent with the verbal message. The written message, on the other hand, is moderated by its legibility (typewritten or handwritten), and perhaps the physical characteristics of the paper. It does not offer the quick flexibility of message and response that the verbal method has.

Decoding

Figure 15.3 extends the initial communication model to include the concepts of 'encoding' and 'channel', and also includes a new element, **decoding**, on the receiver's side of the model. The receiver is not a passive subordinate in the communication process, but is a dynamic influence and partner. It is not enough that you have delivered the message to the receiver's eyes or ears; it has to be understood and interpreted. Your message may well be a sequence of simple words, but the receiver is unlikely to take them at face value. The receiver interprets those words according to their own personality, their mood, how they feel about the sender of the message, how they react to the way in which the message has been sent or worded, and their own needs and wants. So if, for example, you try to use the second excuse, 'I'm sorry, but I haven't quite finished my assignment yet. Please can I hand it in on Friday?', it might be decoded as:

- 'I am a lazy student and I never hand work in on time – here I go again.'
- 'I am normally a conscientious student, but I genuinely have a problem and I am trying my best to solve it as soon as possible with the least inconvenience to you.'
- 'I'm being honest with you, so do me a favour.'

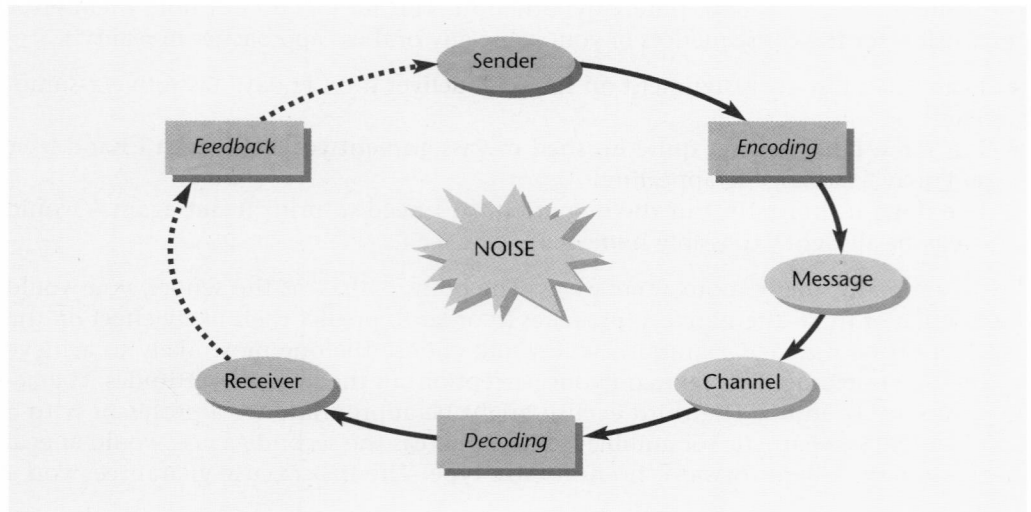

FIGURE 15.3

A simple communication model

The decoding depends entirely on the receiver's perceptions, and whether the receiver is willing to accept a verbal request or would prefer formal written contact. All this in turn can have a profound effect on the *response* offered. The first decoding option might lead to a flat and unequivocal refusal to comply with the request; the second to a more sympathetic 'Yes, certainly, Friday will do, and do you want to tell me what the problem is?', while the third might elicit a more cynical 'Just this once, but you'd better be on time with the next one'.

Feedback

Whatever the response, it provides **feedback** to the sender on whether the message has been received, understood, interpreted as desired and acted upon appropriately. Satisfactory feedback may close this communication episode, whereas unsatisfactory or ambiguous feedback may cause the sender to want to communicate further, going round the model again.

Noise

The final element of the model is **noise**. This consists of all extraneous activity and influences which might interfere and distort information at any point in the communications process. There could literally be physical noise – crackles on a telephone line, other people talking, traffic, background noise etc – which could blot out or distort a part of the intended message. There are, however, other less obvious sources of 'noise' which nevertheless have the same sort of interfering effect, such as the paper running out or crumpling up in a fax machine (thereby distorting or obscuring the message), or perhaps other events distracting the sender's or receiver's attention ('I'll read this message later. I have a train to catch').

Shared meaning

To return to the definition of communication offered at the beginning of this section, the model developed here demonstrates that the process of achieving 'commonness or oneness of thought', or shared meaning between sender and receiver, is not quite as easy and straightforward as it might appear. 'Shared meaning' is more than the successful transmission of words from one party to another, but requires sound mutual understanding of each other, and the active participation of both sender and receiver.

So what has all this to do with marketing? 'Shared meaning' has everything to do with marketing, since an organisation must understand what its market wants, and a market must understand what an organisation is offering and how that will fulfil their needs and wants. There must be two-way communication between buyer and seller if that is to be accomplished. Even a brief attempt to apply the simple communication model in a marketing context highlights some important lessons for the marketer. We look at each of the main components in turn:

Sender

The sender of a marketing message may be the organisation, perhaps in conjunction with an advertising agency, which wants to communicate a message to a defined audience.

Receiver

The receiver of a marketing message may be the individuals within that audience. A pharmaceutical company, for example, might target doctors or pharmacists, whereas a holiday company such as Saga would target the over-50 age group.

Message

The message is what the sender wants the audience to know or understand as a result of receiving the communication. This might be: 'Buy one of our holidays because we understand your needs', or 'This is our new product', or 'Don't drink and drive'.

Encoding

Encoding is where the sender's understanding of the receiver pays dividends. Does the target market only need information? Does it want to be entertained? Persuaded? Threatened? What kind of imagery appeals to this target segment? Artistic? Abstruse? Amusing? What choice of music or voice-over will best enhance the effect of the message in the mind of the target? There are many difficult questions relating to what to say and how to say it which can only be answered through clear knowledge of the target market.

The potential Saga holidaymaker might respond to relaxing scenes, such as almost deserted sunny beaches or gentle activities like rambling, rather than the frenzied disco scene more reminiscent of a Club 18–30 holiday. The core message in each case is actually the same, 'Buy one of our holidays because we understand your needs', but the encoding is appealing to different perceptions of what makes a good holiday.

Channel

The channel is the means by which the encoded message is passed on to the receiver. There are many different choices, for example television, print, or personal contact. Again, what is most appropriate can only be established through knowledge of the target market.

Decoding

The decoding phase is a difficult one for the marketer, who can only trust that the right message, encoding and channel decisions have been made in order to increase the chances of the message being interpreted as desired. This becomes particularly problematic where there are mass markets and subtle, sophisticated messages. The more marketers aggregate and generalise behaviour, the less predictable becomes the response of the individual, and the more complex the message, the less likely it is that it will be interpreted by each individual exactly as desired.

As mentioned at pp. 100 *et seq.*, individuals tend to interpret incoming messages very differently, depending on their personalities, experience, interest and knowledge, among other things. Selective perception, for example, means that people will hear what they want to hear, or what is of specific interest at that time, and disregard the rest of the communication. With television advertising in particular, people are exposed to so much of it, so often, that they have learned to screen it out or ignore it. This means that there is greater pressure on the sender to develop messages which are encoded in such a way that they can break through those defences and be interpreted appropriately.

In the highly competitive fizzy drinks market, Tango's high profile creative communication has proved to be very successful.

Source: Britvic Soft Drinks Ltd/Howell Henry Chaldecott Lury.

Feedback

Feedback is how the recipient of the message responds to it. This might mean overt action, such as purchasing a product or requesting more information, but it might also be less overt, involving the generation of awareness and the development of attitudes. A great disadvantage of any kind of mass communication, such as television advertising, is that feedback can be slow and painful to collect. This contrasts with face-to-face communication where feedback can be assessed immediately. Even if the intent of the message was to sell the product, sales figures only tell part of the story and more detailed investigation is required to try to establish the role of advertising in those sales and the effectiveness of the message. Meaningful feedback is itself the result of a planned communication effort on behalf of the organisation to collect it.

Since marketing communication is an expensive activity, it is important to monitor the outcomes of what is done and, if necessary, modify or change some aspect(s) of the communication process. Even before mass communication takes place, organisations often test their advertising messages with a limited audience to see whether they achieve what was intended.

Example

In transferring the US margarine brand 'I Can't Believe It's Not Butter!' into the UK market, Van den Bergh intended to use the US television advertising as a follow-up to a UK press campaign. Pre-testing the advertisements, however, showed that the brand character communicated by the US advertisements conflicted with that established by the press campaign, and therefore a different message, encoded differently, had to be developed.

Noise

Noise covers any factors which interfere with any aspect of the communication process between sender and receiver. An obvious interference with the receipt of an advertising message, for example, is if the intended receiver is not watching the television when the advertisement is broadcast! Many people regard the commercial breaks as opportunities to make a cup of coffee, or to 'channel hop'. Such behaviour poses a big problem for advertisers. There are no easy answers to this, other than scheduling the advertisement at the beginning or end of a commercial break and starting it with some incredible attention grabbing device. Other 'noise' includes the clutter of other advertising messages, particularly for competing products, which the receiver is trying to process. The impact of a message may be reduced if it is surrounded by equally stimulating and exciting messages, and there is even the risk of messages becoming confused with each other in the receiver's mind. Noise thus either causes the message to be distorted in the receiver's mind or to fail to reach the receiver's attention at all (Mallen, 1977).

The lessons from this application of the model are fundamental to successful and cost-effective marketing communication: know your target market inside out, define exactly what response you would like from the target market and invest in the mechanisms to monitor and evaluate the actual response you get. This all indicates the need for thorough and logical planning of the organisation's communications activities. The following sections take up this theme, and offer a framework within which marketing communications decisions can be developed and justified.

COMMUNICATIONS PLANNING MODEL

Figure 15.4, adapted from Rothschild's (1987) communications decision sequence framework, includes all the major elements of marketing communications decision making and links closely with the theory of communications discussed above. Given the complexity of communication and the immense possibilities for getting some element of it wrong, a thorough and systematic planning process is crucial for minimising the risks. No organisation can afford either the financial or reputational damage caused by poorly planned or implemented communications campaigns.

Each element and its implications for the balancing of the promotional mix will now be defined and analysed in turn. The first element is the situation analysis, which

FIGURE 15.4

The communications planning flow

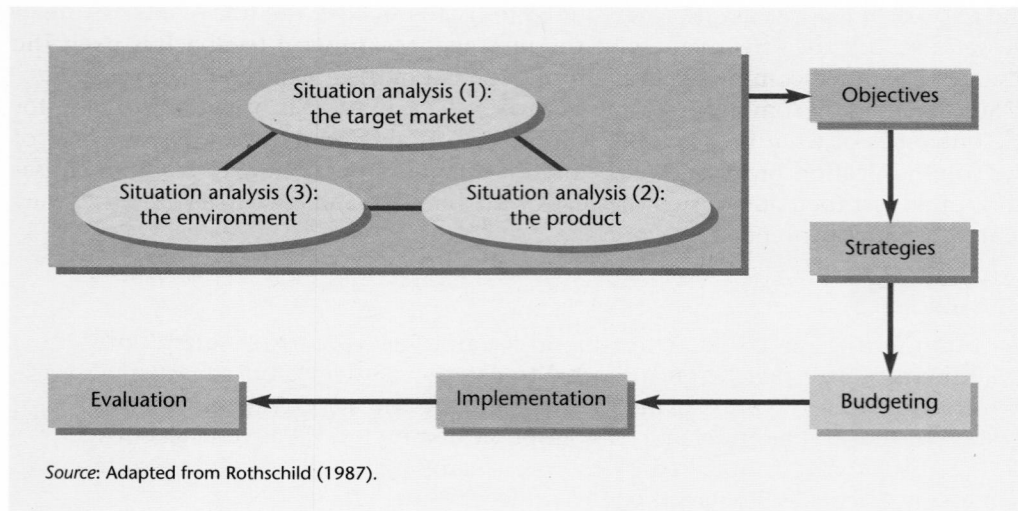

Source: Adapted from Rothschild (1987).

has been split into three subsections: the target market, the product and the environment. Bear in mind, however, that in reality it is difficult to 'pigeon hole' things quite so neatly as this might imply, and there will, therefore, be a lot of cross-referencing.

Situation analysis (1): The target market

Organisational or consumer market

The *target market* decision most likely to have an impact on the balancing of the overall promotional mix is whether the market is a consumer market or an organisational market. Recalling the comparison made in Chapter 4 between consumer and organisational markets, Table 15.1 summarises the impact of the main distinguishing features on the choice of promotional mix. The picture that emerges from this is that

TABLE 15.1

Organisational *vs* consumer market marketing communications: Characteristics and implications

Organisational	Consumer
Fewer, often identifiable customers • *Personal and personalised communication feasible*	Usually mass, aggregated markets • *Mass communication, e.g. television advertising, most efficient and cost effective*
Complex products, often tailored to individual customer specification • *Need for lengthy buyer–seller dialogue via personal selling*	Standardised products with little scope for negotiation and customisation • *Impersonal channels of communication convey standard message*
High-value, high-risk, infrequent purchases • *Need for much information through literature and personal representation, with emphasis on product performance and financial criteria*	Low-value, low-risk, frequent purchases • *Less technical emphasis; status and other intangible benefits often stressed; incentives needed to build or break buying habits*
Rational decision-making process over time, with a buying centre taking responsibility • *Need to understand who plays what role and try to influence whole buying centre*	Short time scale, often impluse purchasing by an individual or family buying unit • *Need to understand who plays what role and to try to influence family*

FIGURE 15.5

Organisational *vs* consumer promotional mix

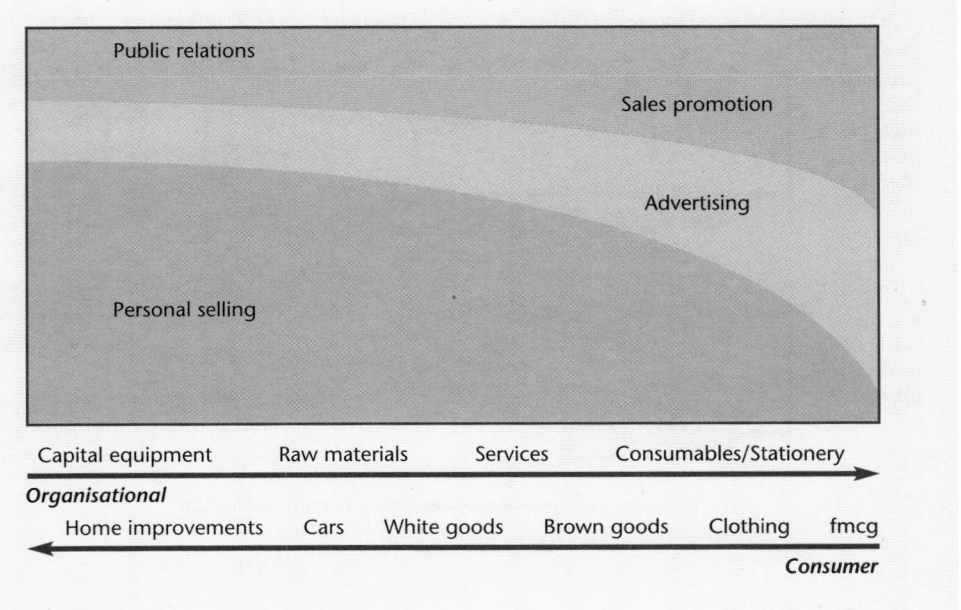

organisational markets are very much more dependent on the personal selling element, with advertising and sales promotion playing a strong supporting role.

The converse is generally true in consumer markets. A large number of customers each making relatively low-value, frequent purchases can be most efficiently contacted using mass media. Advertising, therefore, comes to the fore, with sales promotion a close second, while personal selling is almost redundant. Figure 15.5 shows this polarisation of organisational and consumer promotional mixes. This does, of course, represent sweeping generalisations about the nature of these markets, which need to be qualified. The product itself, for instance, will influence the shape of the mix, as will the nature of competitive and other environmental pressures. These will be addressed later (pp. 582 *et seq.* and 586 *et seq.*).

Push or pull strategy

Remember, however, that even consumer goods marketers are likely to have to consider organisational markets in dealing with channels of distribution. Figure 15.6 offers two strategies, push and pull, which emphasise different lines of communication (Olver and Farris, 1989). With a **push strategy**, the manufacturer chooses to concentrate communications activity on the member of the distribution channel immediately below. This means that the wholesaler, in this example, has a warehouse full of product and thus an incentive to use communication to make a special effort to sell it quickly on to the retailer, who in turn promotes it to the end consumer. The product is thereby pushed down the distribution channel with communication flowing from member to member in parallel with the product. There is little or no communication between manufacturer and consumer in this case.

In contrast, the **pull strategy** requires the manufacturer to create demand for the product through direct communication with the consumer. The retailers will perceive this demand and, in the interests of serving their customers' needs, will demand the product from their wholesaler who will demand it from the manufacturer. This bottom-up approach pulls the product down the distribution channel, with communication flowing in the opposite direction from the product!

The reality is, of course, that manufacturers take a middle course, with some pull and some push to create more impetus for the product.

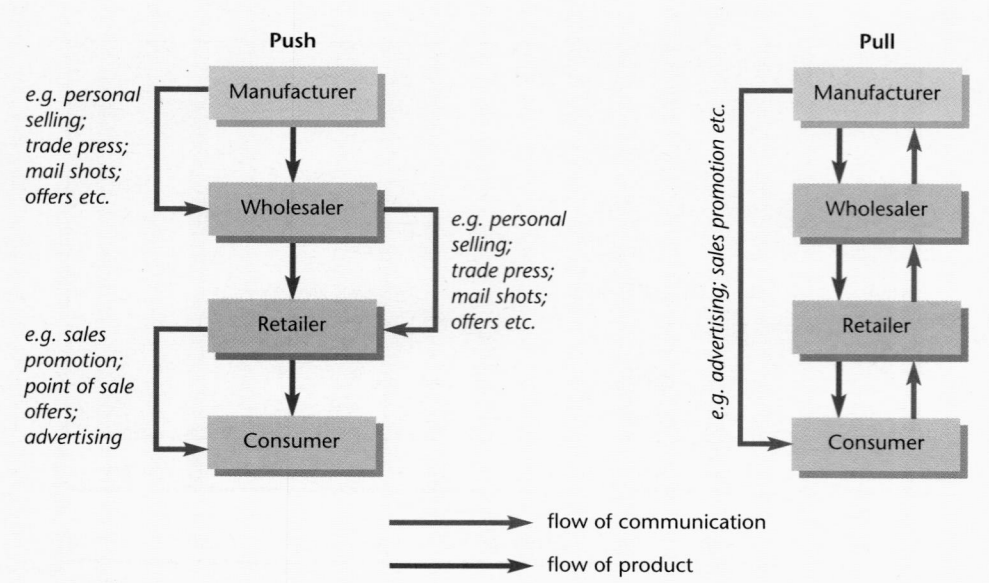

FIGURE 15.6

Push–pull strategy

Push

Pull

e.g. personal selling; trade press; mail shots; offers etc.

Manufacturer

Wholesaler

e.g. personal selling; trade press; mail shots; offers etc.

Retailer

e.g. sales promotion; point of sale offers; advertising

Consumer

Manufacturer

Wholesaler

Retailer

Consumer

e.g. advertising; sales promotion etc.

flow of communication

flow of product

MARKETING IN ACTION

A model market

Airfix's decision to spend £500 000 on consumer and trade promotion might not seem particularly significant compared with the multimillion pound spends of some consumer goods companies. For Airfix, however, it was important because it ended a 20-year absence from spending on any form of advertising, and even then, their previous spending was limited to trade communication only. The company, established in 1919, is one of the oldest and best-known brands for model-making kits and accessories. The range includes kits for planes, ships, military hardware, and not least, trains. Most youngsters have had some contact with an Airfix kit during their lives, whether as a one off present or as part of an ongoing hobby. Brand awareness had thus reached high levels by the 1990s, but market share was declining because of the impact of new competitors and the lack of any trade marketing support. This support was little more than a catalogue and occasional stickers for window displays etc. Airfix relied on the trade to display its products prominently and to create an impact at the point of purchase. The trend in the market towards larger toy shops, however, meant that the main retailers wanted products that could just be stacked high and would sell quickly and in large numbers with the minimum of retailer effort. Add to that the competitive threats, both from alternative

hobbies and from other model kit companies, and it is easy to see why Airfix had to rethink its approach and start to focus on selling the product to the consumer.

In 1994 Allen McGuire and partners bought Airfix along with Humbrol, manufacturer of paint for models. Previously, consumers had had to buy kits and paints separately, but after the acquisition it became possible to sell both in one kit. The kits were repackaged to provide a more modern appearance. To support that, Airfix also sought to give the products a more mass market appeal by selling through mail order and through retailers such as Toys 'Я' Us. Although the toy market has become more sophisticated in recent years, especially with the growth of electronic toys, the appeal of Airfix is that with care, anyone can build a fine model. The target is the 8–14 year old age group. It was somewhat surprising, therefore, that the first advertisement featured two sexy models, only one of which was built from a kit. The message was 'Super Models of the Year', with one model holding the other! It remains to be seen whether the campaign message can achieve the repositioning objectives, and appeal sufficiently to the target market to create sales.

Source: Richards (1995).

Traditionally, toothpaste for sensitive teeth had been marketed on a push strategy by using direct mail and personal selling aimed at dentists and allied professionals. Stafford Miller's Sensodyne brand had been the market leader in this segment for 20 years, with much success in the sense that most dentists recommend Sensodyne and are resistant to competitors' efforts to change this. However, research showed that half the population never visited the dentist, and therefore the push strategy was not affecting the other half. A decision was made, therefore, to communicate for the first time with the general public through television advertising. The first test advertising appeared in 1982, leading to an increase in sales of 40 per cent in the test region, and advertising spend has been increasing steadily since then. In 1992, Beecham as a competitor tried to break Sensodyne's dominance using a similar push–pull approach, with 30 per cent of their effort going into direct push activity with dentists and 70 per cent into consumer-orientated pull advertising (Sambrook, 1992).

Buyer readiness of the target market

In terms of message formulation, a further tempering influence on communication with consumers will be the **buyer readiness** stage of the target market. It is most unlikely that a target market is going to undergo an instant conversion from total ignorance of a product's existence to queueing up at the checkout to buy it. Particularly in consumer markets, it is more likely that people will pass through a number of stages *en route* from initial awareness to desire for the product. A number of models have been proposed, for example Strong's (1925) AIDA model, which put various labels on these stages, as shown in Fig 15.7, but broadly speaking, they all amount to the same sequence:

Cognitive. The cognitive stage involves sowing the seeds of a thought, i.e., catching the target market's attention and generating straightforward awareness of the product: 'Yes, I know this product exists.'

This NEC poster focuses tightly on a specific target group.

In preparation for the 1993 UK launch of their new Mondeo model, for example, Ford Motors used television and press advertising simply to get the brand name known.

Source: Travis Sennett Sully Ross.

Affective. The affective stage involves creating or changing an attitude, i.e., giving the consumer sufficient information (whether factual or image based) to pass judgement on the product and to develop positive feelings towards it: 'I understand what this product can do for me, and I like the idea of it.'

> ### Example
>
> Some attitudes are extremely hard to change; Iran may not appeal to many people as a tourist destination, but nevertheless the tourist board is using advertising to try to overcome preconceptions about the place.

Behaviour. The behaviour stage involves precipitating action, i.e., where the strength of the positive attitudes generated in the affective stage lead the consumer to desire the product and to do something about acquiring it: 'I want this product and I'm going to go and buy it.' Many press advertisements which incorporate a mail order facility are operating at this level.

The speed with which a target market passes through these stages depends on the kind of product, the target market involved and the marketing strategies adopted by the organisation. Nevertheless, each stage becomes increasingly more difficult to implement, since more is being asked of the consumer. Generating awareness, the first stage, is relatively easy as it involves little risk or commitment from the consumer, and may even operate unconsciously. The second stage needs some effort from consumers if it is to be successful because they are being asked to assimilate information, process it and form an opinion. The third and final stage requires the most involvement – actually getting up and doing something which is likely to involve paying out money!

The **Strong (1925) theory** proposed these stages as forming a logical flow of events driven by marketing communication. Advertising, for example, creates the initial awareness, stimulates the interest and then the desire for the product, and only then does trial take place. In other words, the attitude and opinion are formed before the consumer ever gets near the product. There is, however, another school of thought that maintains that it does not always happen like that. The **weak theory** (Jones, 1991) accepts that marketing communication can generate the awareness, but then the consumer might well try the product without having formed any particular atti-

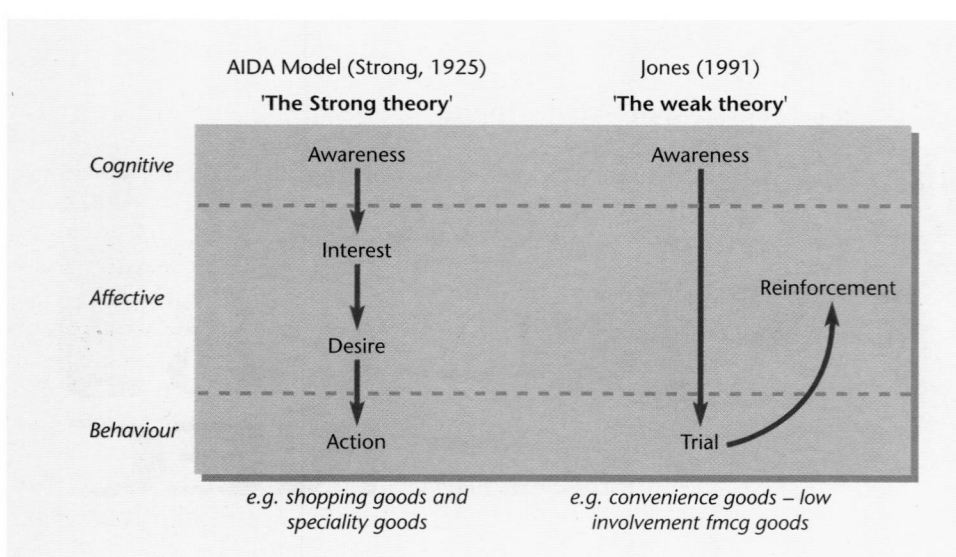

FIGURE 15.7

Response hierarchy models

tude or opinion of it. Only then, after the purchase and product trial, does the marketing communication begin to contribute to attitude and opinion working alongside consumer experience of the product. This would make sense for low- involvement products, the frequently purchased boring goods that it is difficult to get emotional about, such as washing powder.

A consumer might see a television advertisement for a new brand of washing powder and then forget about it until the next trip to the supermarket. The consumer sees that new brand on the shelf and thinks, 'Oh yes, I saw an ad for that – I'll give it a try' and buys a packet. Having tried the product, the consumer might decide that it is quite good and then start to pay more attention to the advertising content as a way of legitimising and reinforcing that opinion.

Whatever the route through the response hierarchy, the unique characteristics of each stage imply that differing promotional mixes may be called for to maximise the creative benefits and cost effectiveness of the different promotional tools. Figure 15.8 suggests that advertising is most appropriate at the earliest stage, given its capacity to reach large numbers of people relatively cheaply and quickly with a simple message. Sales promotions too can bring a product name to the fore and can also help in the affective stage; using a sample which has been delivered to the door certainly generates awareness and aids judgement and recognition of a product. Adding a coupon to the sample's packaging is also an incentive to move into the behaviour stage, buying a full-sized package.

When Tetley introduced instant tea into the UK market, samples delivered to homes included not only the product itself for trial, but also considerable information about the product to overcome initial hostility to the concept, illustration of the brand logo and packaging for recognition and a coupon to encourage consumers to look for the product and purchase a full-sized pack.

Notice, that in Fig 15.8 the role of advertising diminishes as the behaviour stage moves closer and personal selling comes to the fore. Advertising can only reiterate and reinforce what consumers already know about the product, and if this wasn't enough to stimulate action the last time they saw/heard it, it may not do so this time either. At this point, potential buyers may just need a last bit of persuasion to tip them over the edge into buying, and that last kick may be best delivered by a sales representative who can reiterate the product benefits, tailoring communication to suit the particular customer's needs and doubts in a two-way dialogue. With many fmcg products sold in supermarkets, however, this is not a feasible option, and the manufacturer relies on the packaging and, to some extent, the sales promotions to do the selling at the point of sale without human intervention. The washing powder brand Radion therefore has bright orange packaging which stands out on the supermarket shelf, commanding attention. This issue will be readdressed at p. 582.

In reality, individuals within the target market may pass through the stages at different times or may take longer to pass from one stage to the next. This means that it may be necessary to develop an integrated promotional mix which recognises that the

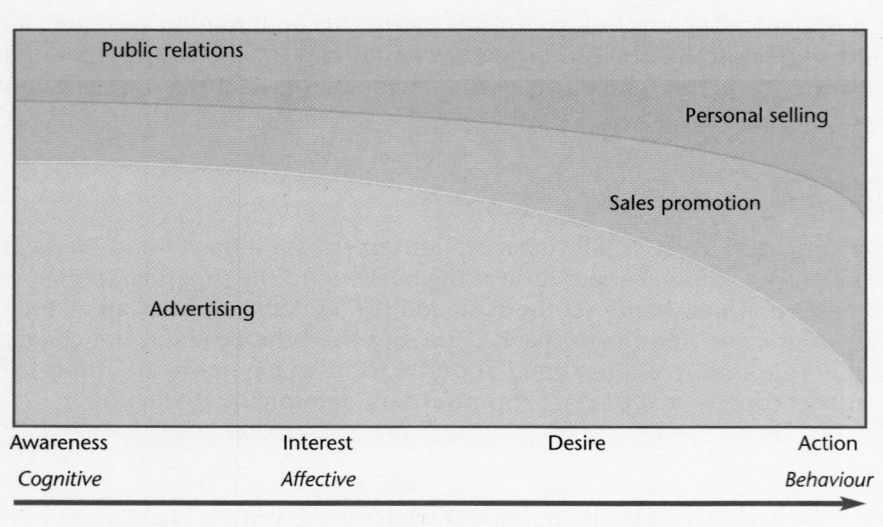

FIGURE 15.8

Buyer readiness stages

various elements are appealing to sub-segments at different readiness stages with imagery and content tailored accordingly. The implementation of the various elements may be almost simultaneous, with some fine tuning of the campaign over the longer term.

Knowledge of the target market is an important foundation stone for all of the communications decision that you are going to make. The more you know about the people you want to talk to, the more likely you are to create successful communication. This does not only mean having a clear demographic profile of the target market, but also means having as much detail as possible about their attitudes, beliefs and aspirations, and about their shopping, viewing and reading habits. It is also important to understand their relationship with your product and their perceptions of it. This will be explained in relation to communication objectives at pp. 587.

This could be a good time for you to look back at Chapter 5 and revise some of the methods of segmenting markets, whether consumer or organisational, since the criteria by which the target market is defined (including product-orientated criteria) may well have a strong influence not only on the broad issue of balancing the promotional mix, but also on the finer detail of media choice and creative content.

Situation analysis (2): The product

Inextricably linked with consideration of the target market is consideration of the *product* involved. This section will look again at the area of organisational and consumer products in the light of the influence of other product characteristics, and then explore the specific influence of the product life cycle on the promotional mix.

Organisational and consumer products

It is simplistic in the extreme to define a product either as an organisational purchase, for which personal selling must be the best way to sell it or as a consumer product, which must be advertised. Other product characteristics or the buying habits associated with the product may make such a distinction meaningless.

At one end of the consumer product spectrum, a frequently purchased, low-involvement, low unit price bar of chocolate would not, of course, warrant such an

An illustration of this 'grey area' is the sale of double glazing to domestic house-holders. Strictly speaking, this is a consumer market, in that the product is being purchased by individuals or families for private consumption. There are, however, a number of features which suggest that this particular product has more in common with typical organisational purchases than with other consumer goods. It is an expensive, infrequent purchase with a high level of technical personalisation required to match the product exactly with the customer's needs. It involves a fairly rational decision-making process which takes place over time, and there is a high demand for product information and negotiation before commitment to purchase is made. To the buyer, it is a high-risk purchase which may well involve several members of the family (effectively acting as a buying centre) and will almost certainly involve a great deal of persuasion, reassurance and dialogue from a sales representative.

All these product and customer-orientated characteristics completely override the superficial definition of a consumer product and point to a different kind of promotional mix. Advertising plays a role in generating awareness of a double glazing company's existence and in laying the foundations for corporate and product image building. It also prepares the way for the sales representative, since a potential customer who has seen an advertisement for a sales representative's company will have an impression of what kind of company this is, and will feel less uneasy about the sales representative's credibility and trustworthiness. The personal selling element is, however, the most important and effective element of this mix because of the need for information, product tailoring and negotiation in the affective and behaviour stages. It is also cost effective in relation to the likely value of a single order.

investment in personal selling to millions of end consumers, even if such an exercise was logistically possible. The marketing would be more likely to conform to the standard mix, emphasizing mass communication through advertising.

Another example chosen to illustrate the grey area between consumer and organisational markets is that of day-to-day consumable office supplies, such as pencils, pens and paperclips, for small businesses. This has more in common with the chocolate bar than the double glazing, although technically it is an organisational product, in that it is used to support the production of goods for resale. Compared with most organisational purchases, it is a routine rebuy, a low-priced, low-risk, low-involvement purchase, probably delegated to an individual who goes out to the nearest stationer's or office supplies retailer at lunchtime with the contents of the petty cash tin. Personal selling of such a range of products to that buyer who belongs to a large and ill-defined target market (there are thousands of small businesses, in every kind of activity and market, and geographically widespread) and who makes such small value purchases is simply not cost effective. At best, personal selling should be targeted at the stationer's or the office supplies retailer.

These two examples above serve as a warning that some organisational products behave more like consumer products and vice versa.

The product life-cycle stage

One further product characteristic which may affect the approach to communication is the *product life-cycle stage* reached (*see* pp. 294 *et seq.*). Since the overall marketing objectives tend to change as the product moves through each stage, it is likely that the specific communications objectives will also change. Different tasks need to be fulfilled and thus the balance of the promotional mix will alter.

Introduction. With the launch of a new consumer product, it is likely that there will be high initial expenditure on the promotional mix. Advertising will ensure that the product name and benefits become known and spread quickly among the target market, while sales promotions, perhaps based on coupons and sampling, help to generate trial of the product. Sales promotions will also be used in conjunction with intense personal selling effort to gain retailer acceptance of the product.

Example

The German company, Storck, which manufactures the confectionery brand Werther's Original spent £3.5 million on consumer-orientated advertising to launch the product in the UK in 1992. It appears, however, that this was insufficient to impress the retailers and pull the product down through the distribution chain, since few were initially willing to stock it (Bidlake, 1992). In an already crowded market, perhaps more thought should have been given to a better balance of push and pull strategies to ensure a stronger foundation for the product's launch.

MARKETING IN ACTION

Hooper's Hooch

Heavy advertising is not necessarily compulsory for the pull strategy of a consumer product launch. When Hooper's Hooch was launched in the UK in 1995 as the first alcoholic lemonade, the communications strategy centred around public relations and point of sale promotions in pubs. This was possible and successful for a number of reasons. Some of it was due to the sheer novelty value of the product and the extra media coverage of the debate about whether alcoholic lemonade is an 'ethical' concept or not. The campaign was also well tailored towards its target market of drinkers aged over 18 who like to 'discover' new products rather than being bombarded with pressure to try them. It also had the effect of generating a cult feel around the product as well as a great deal of word-of-mouth recommendation.

As the product entered the growth stage, more competitors entered the market, such as Two Dogs and Lemonheads. This, combined with the fact that the novelty of the product launch began to wear off in late 1995, meant that the communications emphasis for Hooper's Hooch shifted towards poster advertising. An initial £1 million spend aimed to retain the trendy cult image while creating more mass market appeal at the same time.

Meanwhile, pressure groups such as Alcohol Concern began to receive a great deal of publicity for the view that these products were actually encouraging under-age drinking. The prominence of words such as 'lemonade' and 'cola' on their packaging could, it was suggested, mislead people into thinking they were less alcoholic than they really were (they are actually as strong as some beers), and the use of cartoon characters on the packaging could also attract children to the product. The brewers then had to mount their own PR campaigns to reassure the public that they were not specifically targeting the under-18s. Nevertheless, the Advertising Standards Authority asked Bass to remove its lemon cartoon character from any future poster advertisements.

Source: Benady (1996); Marsh (1995).

Growth. Communications activity is likely to be a little less intense as the product begins to find its own impetus and both retailers and consumers make repeat purchases. There might also be less emphasis on awareness generation and information giving, and more on long-term image and loyalty building. As competitors launch similar products, it is important to ensure that differential advantage is maintained, and that customers know exactly why they should continue to buy the original product rather than switching over to a competitor. This could mean a shift towards advertising as a prime means of image creation that works over a longer period.

Maturity. The maturity stage is likely to be a defensive or holding operation since competitors with younger products may be threatening to take custom away from the product. Most people know about the product, most people (apart from a few laggards) who are likely to try it already have done, so. Thus the role of communication is reminding (about the brand image and values) and reassurance (about having chosen the right product), probably through mass advertising. In organisational markets, this stage is likely to be about further developing and consolidating relationships with customers in preparation for newer products in your portfolio.

Decline. Marketing communication is not going to rescue a product that is clearly on its way out; it can only stave off the inevitable for a while. The majority of consumers and, for that matter, distributors, will have already moved on to other products, leaving only a few laggards. A certain level of reminder advertising and sales promotion might keep them in the market for this product for a while, but eventually even they will drift off. There is little point in diverting resources which could be better used on the next new product.

Example

Both Nike and Reebok have changed their creative strategies for their advertising as their products and reputations have become established and known in the maturing sportswear market. Neither now needs to emphasize the performance or specifications of the products, but rather the status value and psychological benefits of owning those brands. There is still, however, aggressive competition between them, maintaining high advertising spends. Similarly, Martini, as a mature product in the alcoholic drinks sector, concentrates its communications strategies on depicting the chic lifestyle, sophistication, self-confidence, success and status of its drinkers.

The above analysis assumes that a product takes an unexceptional course through the classical stages of the life-cycle. Many consumer goods, however, are revamped at some time during the maturity stage to extend their life cycle. In such a case, there is every reason to rethink the communications package and treat the process more like a new product launch. There is much to communicate both to the trade and to the consumer about the 'new improved' brand, the increased value for money, the enhanced performance, more stylish looks or whatever aspects are being emphasized. In a sense, this stage is even more difficult than the new product launch as the marketer has to tread a fine line between overturning old preconceptions about the product, convincing the market that there is something new to consider and confusing and alienating existing users who might think that the familiar, comforting brand values have been thrown out.

The lifecycle concept, as discussed at pp. 300 *et seq.* does have its problems, and in the context of marketing communication, unthinking, rigid application of it as a primary basis for communications planning is dangerous. If a product is assumed to be mature/declining, then the application of a communications package appropriate to

Skoda cars faced the problem of communicating its 'new improved' product to the market. Early feedback on their 1995 UK campaign to reposition their cars seemed to indicate that little impact had been made on the non-Skoda driver and that their loyal customer base were alienated by it. The loyal customers felt that the Skoda was becoming a different (and more expensive car) and it no longer appealed.

that stage may well hasten its demise. There are other, more relevant factors, both internal and external, which should have a far greater bearing on the planning process. Some of the external factors will now be discussed.

Situation analysis (3): The environment

Again, some revision of an earlier chapter might stand you in good stead here. Chapter 2 analysed the marketing environment in some detail. This section will, therefore, only look at ways in which environmental elements specifically impact on communications.

Social and *cultural* aspects of the environment will mostly impact on the message element of communication. What is said about the product and the scenario within which it is depicted in advertisements will reflect what is socially acceptable and culturally familiar to the target market. There must be something that they can recognise, identify with and/or wish to aspire to, if they are going to remember the message, and particularly if they are expected to act on it. This reinforces what was said at p. 576 about the necessity knowing the target market well.

The Polish washing-up liquid, Pollena 2000 tried to capitalise on a strong nationalistic streak in its target market as a defence against foreign brands threatening the market dominance it had throughout the Communist era. The advertising message positioned the product as an old and faithful indigenous friend which should not be cast aside just because of political and economic changes.

Organisations are particularly keen to spot changes and shifts in social mores and then to capitalise on them, often creating a bandwagon effect. The 'green' issue is a good example of this. Many companies perceived that there was pressure on them to produce environmentally friendlier products, but rather than lose time in developing really new alternatives (and risk lagging behind their competitors), a few simply created new advertising messages and emphasized green-orientated product claims on their packaging to create the desired image. However, questionable approaches such as labelling washing-up liquid 'phosphate free' when that kind of product doesn't ever contain phosphate anyway, and emphasizing that packaging can be recycled when the recycling facilities do not exist have been widely publicised, leading to confusion and suspicion in the consumer's mind about all green claims. Peattie (1992) offers a concise, but thorough review of green marketing communication and how it should be done.

A more general criticism of advertisers' influence in the social and cultural area is in their alleged use and reinforcement of stereotypes. The advertisers argue that they simply reflect society as it is, and that it is not their business to change it – they *respond* to the customer's changing attitudes and life-style. Should there, however, be concern that if people see stereotypes being constantly presented through advertising as the norm, and even as states to be aspired to, then maybe the impetus to question their validity and to break them will be less urgent? This is a complex 'chicken and egg' debate which you may want to pursue for yourself outside these pages. There are no easy answers to this one.

To be fair to the advertisers, the whole area of stereotypes does perhaps present one of the great insoluble dilemmas of mass communication. In moving away from one stereotype, it is too easy to replace it with another. Because the advertiser is trying to appeal to a relatively large number of individuals (even in a niche market), it is impossible to create an image that reflects every member of the target market in detail. What emerges, therefore, is a superficial sketch of the essential characteristics of that group and its aspirations, i.e., a stereotype! Thus the stereotypical housewife who lives in the kitchen and is fulfilled through the quality of her cooking has been usurped at the opposite extreme by the equally unrealistic power-dressing, independent dragon of the board room with the slightest whiff of Chanel and femininity. The advertisers cannot, it seems, win.

No communications plan can be shaped without some reference to what the *competition* are doing or are likely to do, given the necessity of emphasizing the differential advantage and positioning of the product in relation to theirs. This could affect every stage of the planning from the definition of objectives, through the creative strategy, to the setting of budgets. These themes will be taken up under the appropriate headings later in this chapter, and will also feature in the chapters on the individual tools of the promotional mix.

Another important factor to take into account is the *legal/regulatory* environment, as discussed in Chapter 2. Some products are restricted in where they can be advertised. In the UK for instance, cigarette advertising is not permitted on television. Other products are restricted in when they can be advertised. Restrictions may also exist about what can be said or shown in relation to the product. In the UK, alcohol advertisements cannot show anyone apparently under the age of 21, nor are they allowed to imply that you will not be socially acceptable unless you use this product. Toy advertising similarly cannot imply a social disadvantage of not owning a product, and must also indicate the price of the toy. More generally, advertising aimed at children cannot encourage them to pester their parents to purchase (not that they normally need encouragement). Some regulations are enshrined in law, while others are imposed and applied through monitoring watchdog bodies such as the Advertising Standards Authority. Professional bodies, such as the UK's Institute of Sales Promotion or The Direct Marketing Association, often develop codes of practice to which their members undertake to adhere. As yet, no unified codes have been developed that apply across Europe.

Objectives

Now that the background is in place and there exists a detailed profile of the customer, the product and the environment, it is possible to define detailed objectives for the communications campaign.

Table 15.2, based on the work of DeLozier (1975), summarises and categorises possible communications objectives. The first group relate to awareness, information and attitude generation, while the second group are about affecting behaviour. The final group are corporate objectives, a timely reminder that marketing communications planning is not only about achieving the goals of brand managers or marketing managers, but also about the contribution of marketing activity to the wider strategic good of the organisation.

What Table 15.2 does not do is to distinguish between short-, medium- and long-term objectives. Obviously, the short-term activities are the most pressing and are going to demand more detailed planning, but there does still need to be an appreciation of what happens next. The nature and character of medium- and longer-term

TABLE 15.2

Possible communications objectives

Area	Objective
Cognitive	Clarify customer needs Increase brand awareness Increase product knowledge
Affective	Improve brand image Improve company image Increase brand preference
Behaviour	Stimulate search behaviour Increase trial purchases Increase repurchase rate Increase word of mouth recommendation
Corporate	Improved financial position Increase flexibility of corporate image Increase co-operation from the trade Enhance reputation with key publics Build up management ego

Source: Based on DeLozier (1975).

objectives will inevitably be shaped by short-term activity (and its degree of success), but it is also true that short-term activity can only be fully justified when it is put into the context of the wider picture.

> **Example**
>
> The Corfu Tourism Promotion Board has a longer-term aim of moving Corfu upmarket as a holiday destination. In marketing communication terms, this is likely to be a gradual process with the communications strategy developing over time as investment in facilities and infrastructure begins to take effect.

Finally, Table 15.2 also stresses the importance of precision, practicality and measurability in setting objectives. Vague, open objectives such as 'to increase awareness of the product' are insufficient. Who do you want to become aware of the product: the retail trade; the general public, or a specific target segment? How much awareness are you aiming to generate within the defined group and within what time-scale? A more useful objective might therefore be 'to generate 75 per cent awareness of the product within three months among A, B and C1 home-owners aged between 25 and 40 with incomes in excess of £25 000 per annum who are interested in opera and the environment'.

Until such precise definitions of objectives have been made, the rest of the planning process cannot really go ahead – how can decisions be made if you don't really know what it is you are aiming for? Precise objectives also provide the foundation for monitoring, feedback and assessment of the success of the communications mix. There is at least something against which to measure actual performance.

Strategies

Having defined objectives, it is now necessary to devise strategies for achieving them. The analysis done so far may already have established the broad balance of the promotional mix but there is still the task of developing the fine detail of what the

Olive oil

Olive oil is a product typically associated with the Mediterranean countries, and is widely used in cooking to give a distinctive flavour and smell. Most of the two million producers in the EU are to be found in Greece, Spain and Italy, and olive oil is regulated as part of the common agricultural policy. Sales of olive oil have been growing rapidly in the non-producing countries. In the UK, for example, retail sales of olive oil are around £57 million and with profit margins of between 35 per cent and 40 per cent, the big multiple retailers have taken a keen interest in its promotion. The product occupies a premium position, because of an increased interest in Mediterranean food and because of its healthy image. UK market growth during 1996 was thus estimated to be over 10 per cent.

In the UK, retailers were finding demand for olive oil relatively inelastic, despite a stream of price rises. Shelf space had grown to an average two metre frontage dedicated to the product range. Consumers in the UK, however, appear to fall into two groups: those who know about the different oils, their origins and their applications, and the vast majority of the population who do not. Italian products tend to be slightly favoured in the UK, but there is no particular market leader and the majority of buyers do not perceive any major brand differences. Compared with France and Spain, the UK market has been cushioned from the more competitive conditions found in supermarkets where price competition and sales promotion are far more prevalent. Whereas olive oil sells in the UK for about £8 per litre, in France's Carrefour supermarkets £4 per litre is more normal. In Spain, with a per capita consumption of

10 litres a year, a retail price of around £5 is usual. In countries such as Spain, own-label products are increasingly undercutting branded prices and consumers are more knowledgeable about olive oils.

It was against this background that in 1995 the EU decided to run a generic pan-European campaign to promote the use of olive oil. This was part of an effort to make producers more active in terms of marketing and more responsive to customer preferences. Whereas they had previously run campaigns country by country, the decision to find a common appeal across Europe seemed a logical development within the context of the SEM. A £19 million spend was suggested, with specified amounts to be spent in each country. The purpose was to encourage greater use of olive oil and to increase consumer awareness of its cooking possibilities. The whole project soon ran into criticism, however, because the agencies bidding for the contract were not sure quite what was required. In the briefing, the EU sponsors of the campaign talked about developing a publicity campaign, but did not distinguish between advertising, public relations and other areas of the promotional mix that could be included. They also said that they did not want the campaign to appear as if it was a marketing strategy, but as 'generic and philosophical'. Agencies were left speculating on the meaning of that phrase and wondering why the campaign's sponsors had such an aversion to overt marketing principles in what seemed to be a fairly straightforward marketing communications task.

Sources: Crosskey (1996a, 1996b); Dwek (1995).

actual message is to be, how best to frame it and what medium or media can be used to communicate it most efficiently and effectively.

Designing the message content, structure, and format poses questions for managing any element of the promotional mix. Message content is about what the sender wants to say, while message structure is about how to say it in terms of propositions and arguments. The message format depends on the choice of media used for transmitting or transferring the message. This will determine whether sight, sound, colour or other stimuli can be used effectively. These are important themes which will be further addressed in the context of each element of the promotional mix in the following five chapters. A money-off sales promotion, for example, is certainly appropriate for stimulating short-term sales of a product, but will it cheapen the product's quality image in the eyes of the target market? Is the target market likely to respond to a cash saving, or would they be more appreciative of a charity tie-in where a donation is made to a specific charity for every unit sold? The latter suggestion has the added benefit of enhancing corporate as well as brand image, and is also less easy for the competition to copy.

Crocodile: will consumers snap it up?

The Freedown Food Company started its life as a supplier of venison but soon diversified into more exotic meats such as emu, crocodile and kangaroo. Persuading current customers in the restaurant trade to try the more exotic products on a one-off basis was not too difficult and, in the event, there were many repeat orders. However, the company saw this as only the beginning. The longer-term aim was to get these meats accepted by both consumers and the retail trade. This was not an easy communications task. The products are very unusual and the bigger retailers would be reluctant to stock them unless they could be sure of demand. Consumers, however, need the products to be available if they are to try them and develop a taste for them.

In this kind of situation, a mixed push–pull strategy is likely to be the most appropriate. Part of the strategy implemented by Freedown was to give butchers and cookery writers, as credible message sources in the eyes of the general public, information packs, including recipes. Consumers are more likely to listen to these 'expert' sources, and to accept what they say as unbiased, than to accept the content of an advertisement. Experts can reassure the consumer about the product benefits and tell them how to use the product without seeming to be patronising or to be trying a 'hard sell'. By creating awareness and interest among the general public, the butchers are contributing to the *push* strategy, and the cookery writers to the *pull* strategy. Additionally, cookery writers who are seen to be featuring these products could carry influence with the retailers. The restaurateurs also play an important role as expert and trustworthy sources. Consumers who can be persuaded to try the meat, deliciously prepared, as a daring item on a menu might then want to try cooking it for themselves at home.

Freedown could not rely solely on these activities, which are a kind of PR that help to establish the products as more mainstream and might help to persuade the retailers that consumer demand could exist. Direct face-to-face negotiation with the multiple retailers was, nevertheless, still critical for gaining acceptance and listing of the products. By September 1996, Tesco had agreed to stock kangaroo, and other supermarket multiples were waiting to see how the combination of awareness generating activities and product availability translated into sales.

Sources: Barnard (1996).

Example

Scott distributed money-off coupons for its Andrex brand of toilet tissue which gave the consumer 15p off the price of a pack and promised 5p to The Guide Dogs for the Blind Association for every coupon redeemed. This was a particularly appropriate partnership, as Andrex uses labrador puppies in its advertising campaigns.

With advertising in particular, the organisation might use a character or a celebrity to communicate a message on their behalf to give it **source credibility**. The audience will see the spokesperson as the source of the message and thus might pay more attention to it or interpret it as having more credibility (Hirschman, 1987).

Example

The use of celebrities can be a high-risk strategy. There is, for instance the risk of a celebrity falling out of public favour or tarnishing their own image. When Michael Jackson was the target of child abuse allegations, Pepsi dropped him from their advertising campaigns. Similarly, Estée Lauder must have been rather worried when Liz Hurley, the £1 million 'face' of their cosmetic brands, was the target of much unkind publicity as a result of her boyfriend, Hugh Grant, being arrested with a prostitute.

Nevertheless, a crisis can be turned to the advertiser's advantage. The footballer Eric Cantona hit the world headlines for all the wrong reasons when he attacked a member of the crowd who had allegedly been shouting racist abuse. Nike stood by Cantona, and instead of dropping him from their advertising campaigns, they revised their approach to show a repentant Eric condemning racism and violence in football (Teather, 1995). Even if celebrities behave themselves, there is still the risk that the personality will overpower the brand or that a 'promiscuous' celebrity (i.e., one who advertises several different products) will leave the audience confused. Harry Enfield, with his various comedy characters, for example, has been involved in advertising Mercury, Dime Bar, Worthington's beer, and KP Hula Hoops. There is, therefore, no distinct brand associated with him.

Whether the spokesperson, or presenter of the message, is a well-known celebrity or an invented character, it is important to link their characteristics with the communication objectives, as seen in Table 15.3.

The marketing manager might also have to decide whether or not to use personal or impersonal media. Table 15.4 compares the marketing advantages and disadvantages of a range of media, from informal word of mouth contact such as friends recommending products to each other through to a formal professional face-to-face pitch from a sales representative.

Whichever element of the communications mix is being used, the important consideration is to match the message and media with both the target audience and the defined objectives. These issues are covered in further detail for each element of the mix in the following chapters.

TABLE 15.3

The VisCAP model of presenter characteristics and communication objectives

Presenter characteristics	Communication objectives
Visibility • How well known the presenter is	Brand awareness

Credibility
(i) Expertise
  • Knowledge about the product category
(ii) Objectivity
  • Reputation for honesty and sincerity
	Information and attitude building
	• Both low and high involvement products
	Information and attitude building
	• High involvement products

Attraction
(i) Likeability
  • Attractive appearance and personality
(ii) Similarity
  • To target audience members
	Changing attitudes towards the brand
	• Low involvement products
	Changing attitudes towards the brand
	• High involvement products

Power • Authoritative occupation or personality	Create intention to purchase

Source: Based on Rossiter and Percy (1987).

TABLE 15.4
Comparison of personal and impersonal media for communications

	Word of mouth	Sales representative	Personalised mail shot	Mass media advertising
Accuracy and consistency of delivery	Questionable	Good	Excellent	Excellent
Likely completeness of message	Questionable	Good	Excellent	Excellent
Controllability of content	None	Good	Excellent	Excellent
Ability to convey complexity	Questionable	Excellent	Good	Relatively poor
Flexibility and tailoring of message	Good	Excellent	Good	None
Ability to target	None	Excellent	Good	Relatively poor
Reach	Patchy	Relatively poor	Excellent	Excellent
Feedback collection	None	Excellent – immediate	Possible – depends on response mechanism	Difficult – costly and time consuming

Personal ←――――――――――――――――――――――――――――――――――→ Impersonal

Budgeting

Controlled communication is rarely free. The marketer has to develop campaigns within (often) tight budgets, or fight for a larger share of available resources. It is important, therefore, to develop a budgeting method that produces a realistic figure for the marketer to work with in order to achieve objectives. There are six main methods of budget setting, some of which are better suited to predictable, static markets, rather than dynamic, fast changing situations.

Judgemental budget setting

The first group of methods of determining budgets are called **judgemental budget setting** because they all involve some degree of guesswork.

Arbitrary budgets. Arbitrary budgets are based on what has always been spent in the past, or for a new product, on what is usually spent on that kind of thing.

Affordable method. The affordable budget, closely linked to the arbitrary budget, is one which, as its name implies, imposes a limit based either on what is left over after other more important expenses have been met or on what the company accountant feels to be the maximum allowable. Hooley and Lynch (1985) suggest that this method is used in product-led rather than in marketing-led organisations because it is not actually linked with what is to be achieved in the market-place.

Percentage of past sales method. The percentage of past sales method is at least better in that it acknowledges some link between communications and sales, even though the link is illogical. The chief assumptions here are that sales precede communication, and that future activities should be entirely dependent on past performance. Taken to

Launching something as new and as different as Le Shuttle required 'investment' levels of advertising in order to gain rapid awareness.

Source: Le Shuttle.

its extreme, it is easy to imagine a situation in which a product has a bad year, therefore its communication budget is cut, causing it to perform even more poorly, continuing in a downward spiral until it dies completely. The judgmental element here is deciding what percentage to apply. There are industry norms for various markets, for example in the cosmetics industry, 20 per cent or more is a typical advertising/sales ratio, whereas for industrial equipment it could be lower than 1 per cent. However, this is only part of the picture. The industrial equipment manufacturer might well invest much more in its sales force. Such percentages might simply be the cumulative habits of many organisations and thus might be questionable in their wisdom when considered in the context of the organisation's own position and ambitions within the market.

Percentage of future sales method. None of the budgeting methods so far considered takes any account of the future needs of the product itself. However, the percentage of future sales method is an improvement in that communications and sales are in the right order, but again there is the question of what percentage to apply. There is also an underlying assumption about there being a direct relationship between next year's expenditure and next year's sales.

Data-based budget setting

None of the methods examined so far has taken account of communications objectives – a reminder/reinforcement operation is much cheaper than a major attitude change exercise – or indeed of the quality or cost effectiveness of the communication activities undertaken. There is a grave risk that the money allocated will be insufficient to achieve any real progress, in which case it will have been wasted. This then paves the way for the second group of techniques, called **data-based budget setting** methods, which eliminate the worst of the judgmental aspects of budgeting.

Competitive parity. The competitive parity method involves discovering what the competition are spending and then matching or exceeding it. It has some logic in that if you are shouting as loudly as someone else, then you have a better chance of being heard than if you are whispering. In marketing, however, it is not necessarily the volume of noise so much as the quality of noise that determines whether the message gets across and is acted upon.

Marketing magazine's weekly Adwatch feature used to look at the ratio of advertising spend to awareness generated for each of the leading brands in a particular market. In the coffee sector (*Marketing*, 1993), Nescafé's Gold Blend had almost £6 million spent on it, generating 77 per cent awareness at a cost of about £75 000 per awareness point. The standard Nescafé brand, however, spent nearly £9 million on generating only 69 per cent awareness at a cost of almost £130 000 per awareness point. Although this kind of analysis is simplistic and should not be taken too seriously, there is undoubtedly a stronger creative approach in the Gold Blend advertising which has captured the public imagination and made the advertising spend far better value for money.

If it is to have any credibility at all, then the competitive parity method must take into account the competitors' own communications objectives, how they compare with yours and how efficiently and effectively they are spending their money. For all you know, the competitors have set their budgets by looking at how much *you* spent last year, which takes you all back into a stalemate similar to that of the arbitrary budget method.

Objective and task budgeting. The final method of budgeting, and arguably the best, is objective and task budgeting. This is naturally the most difficult to implement successfully. It does, however, solve many of the dilemmas posed so far and makes most commercial sense. It requires the organisation to work backwards. First, define the communications objectives then work out exactly what has to be done to achieve them. This can be costed to provide a budget that is directly linked with the product's needs and is neither more nor less than that required. A new product, for example, will need substantial investment in marketing communication in order to gain acceptance within distribution channels, and then to generate awareness and trial among consumers. A mature product, in contrast, might need only 'maintenance' support which will clearly cost much less. The only danger with objective and task budgeting, however, is of ambition overtaking common sense, leading to a budget that simply will not be accepted.

The art of making this technique work lies in refining the objectives and the ensuing budget in the light of what the organisation can bear. It may mean taking a little longer than you would like to establish the product, or finding cheaper, more creative ways of achieving objectives, but at least the problems to be faced will be known in advance and can be strategically managed.

Hart (1993) indicate that 68 per cent of larger industrial advertisers claimed to use the objective and task method for their budget, as opposed to the 4 per cent who used percentage of sales turnover and the 14 per cent who chose an arbitrary sum. Overall, across the whole promotional mix, organisations are likely to use some kind of composite method that includes elements of judgmental and data-based techniques (Fill, 1995).

Positioning the budgeting element so late in the planning flow does imply that the objective and task method is the preferred one. To reiterate, there is no point in throwing more money at the communication problem than is strictly necessary or justifiable in terms of future aims, and equally, spending too little to make an impact is equally wasteful.

Implementation and evaluation

The aim of planning is *not* to create an impressive, aesthetically pleasing document that promptly gets locked in a filing cabinet for a year. It is too easy for the planning process to become an isolated activity, undertaken as an end in itself with too little thought about the realities of the world and the practical problems of making things happen as you want them to. Throughout the planning stages, there must be due consideration given to 'what if ...' scenarios and due respect given to what is practicable and manageable. That is not to say that an organisation should be timid in what it aims to achieve, but rather that risks should be well calculated.

Planning also helps to establish priorities, allocate responsibilities and ensure a fully integrated, consistent approach, maximising the benefits gained from all elements of the communications mix. In reality, budgets are never big enough to do everything, and something has to be sacrificed. Inevitably, different activities will be championed by different managers and these tensions have to be resolved within the planning framework. For example, many organisations are reappraising the cost effectiveness of personal selling in the light of developments in the field of direct marketing.

Example

It is also true that plans should not be cast in stone; there is a need for flexibility to take account of changing circumstances. The unexpected can interfere even with the best laid plans. Van den Bergh must have thought that they had a routine new product launch on their hands with the margarine brand, 'I Can't Believe It's Not Butter!', planning a heavy emphasis on TV advertising and short-term sales promotion to give the product a kick-start in the market. At the last minute, however, they were informed by the Independent Television Commission that their advertising could not appear on TV because the Butter Council complained that it broke EC rules. The crisis was turned to the brand's advantage by switching much of the planned TV advertising budget to national press advertising, and the creative theme was adapted to 'This commercial has been banned from British television: as usual it all comes down to a question of taste'. The situation also generated a large amount of PR and editorial discussion as to whether the 'ban' was appropriate or not. All of this led to curiosity among consumers, whether through sympathy or a desire to find out just how buttery the brand really was. Initial sales exceeded all expectations and retailers found themselves running out of stock. Although this is clearly an unusual situation, it does underline the vulnerability of planning and the need for creative flexibility in implementation (Gofton, 1992).

An equally important activity is that of collecting feedback. You have been communicating with a purpose and you need to know at least whether that purpose is being fulfiled. Monitoring during the campaign helps to assess early on whether or not the objectives are being met as expected. If it is really necessary, corrective action can thus be taken before too much time and money is wasted or, even worse, before too much damage is done to the product's image.

It is not enough, however, to say that the promotional mix was designed to generate sales and we have sold this much product, and therefore it was a success. The analysis needs to be deeper than this – after all, a great deal of time and money has been invested in this communication programme. What aspects of the promotional mix worked best and most cost effectively? Was there sufficient synergy between them? Do we have the right balance within each element of the mix, for example choice of advertising media? Are consumers' attitudes and beliefs about our product the ones we expected and wanted them to develop? Have we generated the required long-term loyalty to the product?

It is only through persistent and painstaking research effort that these sorts of question are going to be answered. Such answers not only help to analyse how perceptive past planning efforts were, but also provide the basis for future planning activity. They begin to shape the nature and objectives of the continued communication task ahead and, through helping managers to learn from successes and mistakes, lead to a more efficient use of skills and resources. The following chapters will discuss some of the techniques and problems of collecting feedback on specific elements of the promotional mix, and Chapter 6 is also relevant in a more general sense.

COMMUNICATIONS PLANNING MODEL: REVIEW

Rothschild's (1987) model of the communications planning process (see Fig 15.4) is an invaluable framework as it includes all the major issues to be considered in balancing the promotional mix. In reality, however, the process cannot be as clear-cut or neatly divided as the model suggests. Planning has to be an iterative and dynamic process, producing plans that are sufficiently flexible and open to allow adaptation in the light of emerging experience, opportunities and threats.

It is also easy, when presented with a flow chart type of model like this one to make assumptions about cause and effect. There is a great deal of logic and sense in the sequencing of decisions indicated by this model: definition of target market defines objectives; objectives determine strategies; strategies determine budgets, and so on, but in reality, there have to be feedback loops between the later and earlier elements of this model. Budgets, for instance, are likely to become a limiting factor which may cause revision of strategies and/or objectives and/or target market detail. Objective and task is the preferred approach to budget setting, but it still has to be operated within the framework of the resources that the organisation can reasonably and justifiably be expected to marshal, as discussed earlier.

The concluding messages are, therefore, that the planning process:

1 is very important for achieving commercial objectives effectively and efficiently;
2 should not be viewed as a series of discrete steps in a rigid sequence;
3 should not be an end in itself, but should be regarded as only a beginning;
4 should produce plans that are open to review and revision as appropriate;
5 should be undertaken in the light of what is reasonably achievable and practicable for the organisation;
6 should be assessed with the benefit of hindsight and feedback so that next year it will work even better.

Chapter 22 looks at marketing planning more generally, and will further discuss the techniques and problems of implementing plans within the organisational culture.

CHAPTER SUMMARY

Communications theory indicates that there a number of dynamic elements involved in a piece of communication, each of which has the potential to make the process break down. In a marketing context, these risks have to be understood and minimised, given the importance of effective communication to the success of products and given the level of investment often required for marketing communication activity.

As a means of systematically identifying and managing the risks and opportunities inherent in communication, a framework for planning is presented and discussed. The main stages are:

1 *Analyse the situation* in terms of the target market (its characteristics, its buying habits, its state of mind), the product (the type of product, its life cycle stage) and the external environment (social, regulatory and competitive influences in particular). The outcomes of this analysis may indicate that particular elements of the promotional mix are especially appropriate or cost effective.
2 *Define objectives* for the communication. Again, particular objectives lend themselves to particular techniques, thus shaping the promotional mix. Objectives must, however, be precise, practical and measurable.
3 *Define strategies* for how the objectives are going to be achieved, through what activities, media and messages. These strategies have to be closely matched with situation and objectives.
4 *Set budgets*. Budgets often constrain the activities that can be undertaken feasibly. There are many ways of setting budgets, but the recommended 'objective and task' method closely relates expected expenditure with communication objectives for the budgeting period and thus, if implemented intelligently, will lead to more efficient allocation of resources.
5 *Implementation and evaluation*. This stage involves putting the plan into action, monitoring its progress against what is expected, and assessing performance through information gained from detailed market research. Flexibility in implementation is nevertheless important as problems and opportunities emerge over time.

This framework should not, however, be treated as a rigid series of steps to be gone through once a year. It is an iterative and dynamic continuous process which should aid rather than constrain decision making.

Key words and phrases	
Buyer readiness	*Judgemental budget setting*
Channel of communication	*Noise*
Communication	*Pull strategy*
Data-based budget setting	*Push strategy*
Decoding	*Source credibility*
Encoding	*Strong theory of communication*
Feedback	*Weak theory of communication*

QUESTIONS FOR REVIEW

15.1 What are the five main elements of the *promotional mix*?

15.2 Define *encoding* and *decoding*, and discuss their role within the communication model.

15.3 How might an understanding of the *theoretical model of communication* help a marketing manager?

15.4 What are the stages in the *marketing communications planning flow*?

15.5 How does a *push* strategy differ from a *pull* strategy, and in what circumstances might each be appropriate?

15.6 What are the three broad stages of *buyer readiness*, and how might the balance of the promotional mix vary between them?

15.7 How and to what extent might the *product life-cycle* concept influence the balance of the promotional mix?

15.8 What are the main categories of *marketing communication objectives*?

15.9 What are the six main methods of *budget setting*?

15.10 Why is the *post-implementation evaluation* of marketing communication plans important? What areas should the evaluation cover?

QUESTIONS FOR DISCUSSION

15.1 Within a marketing communications model, give three specific examples of *noise*, outlining how it might disrupt the communications process.

15.2 How and why might the balance of the promotional mix differ between:

(a) the sale of a car to a private individual; and

(b) the sale of a fleet of cars to an organisation for its sales representatives?

15.3 For each of the STEP factors of the marketing environment, give three examples of influences on the promotional mix.

15.4 What are the main advantages and disadvantages of *objective* and *task* budget setting compared with the other methods?

15.5 To what extent do you think that the advantages of using a systematic planning process for marketing communications outweigh the disadvantages?

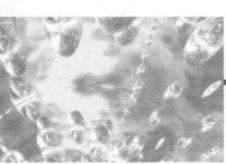
Riverdance

The 39th annual Eurovision Song Contest held at the Point Theatre, Ireland, in 1994 saw the birth of a music and dance sequence that has taken the world by storm. Although it was just seven minutes long and was intended only to fill the time until the judges made their minds up about the songs in the contest itself, the *Riverdance* sequence stole the show and had far more impact than any other act featured that night.

The initial briefing to Bill Whelan, the composer of *Riverdance*, was to produce a musical piece that would not only demonstrate Irish culture to an international television audience of 300 million, but also offer high entertainment value. Given Dublin's location by river and sea, an aquatic theme was thought appropriate. The Riverdance sequence involved a troupe of 20 dancers with the lead duo of Jean Butler and Michael Flatley, soon to become household names. Media comments after the show were largely very positive. Corr (1994), for example, said:

'Combined with Bill Whelan's music, the machine gun feet of Michael Flatley and Jean Butler conjured up visions of a mystic and proud nationality, and reawakened a Celtic revival, providing a fast, sexy link between our dissolving heritage and the genius of a pop moment. So, Riverdance has taken its place in Irish folk history, with a rush of national pride – up there with U2 who conquered the globe in the eighties.'

The combination of ballet, tap, Flamenco and traditional Irish dancing was a big hit. The platform offered by Eurovision, both literally and from a promotional perspective, led to wide public acclaim. A single and a video were produced, and immediately on its release, *Riverdance* became the best selling single in Ireland for 18 weeks. After a Royal Command Performance premiere in London at the beginning of 1995, it rose to seventeenth position in the UK singles chart. It was also broadcast on Top of the Pops on BBC television on 12 January 1995. At that time all proceeds from the video sales were donated to the Irish Rwanda Relief Fund.

By this time, however, not all commentators were prepared to give unreserved acclaim to *Riverdance* as a piece that should make a long-term impact on the Irish arts and culture scene. By the cultural purists, it was regarded as 'Broadway with a dash of Irish dancing', a highly professional, clever dance routine designed to have commercial appeal to a wide audience.

Although there could be no market research or pre-testing because it was a gala performance at a television mega event, the large, captive audience, along with the 'halo effect' of being associated with the Eurovision Song Contest, created high consumer interest. People wanted to learn more about the artists and to acquire *Riverdance* on sound or video. *Riverdance* then developed into a theatrical production in its own right. *Riverdance: The Show* has run across Europe, and also on Broadway. The show first gave 20 performances in Dublin, to which sponsors and critics were invited, and from that came the subsequent tours that sometimes involved parallel productions. Flatley saw no bounds to success at that time:

'I believe that there is room in the market place for an artists' show like Riverdance. I'm absolutely certain with the number of people involved, the hard work and the expertise that we have, that we can bring Riverdance to the top. We're certainly considering an awful lot of things, even Riverdance: The Movie ... We want to take what we've done to another level and showcase a new flavour of what this particular form of Irish art has.'

The problem for *Riverdance* all along has been how best to capitalise on the initial impact created and how far to develop or diversify the 'core product'. This would make a great deal of difference to its positioning as either a piece of high culture or a piece of popular entertainment. This in turn has implications for the marketing communication strategy adopted.

Source: Adapted from a case prepared by Professor Barra O'Cinneide, University of Limerick, including Corr (1994).

Questions

1 Is the *Riverdance* phenomenon more of a 'push' or a 'pull' strategy?

2 Outline the promotional mix likely to have been used to sell the video of the show.

3 What are the particular problems of marketing communication for a stage show and what kind of promotional mix is this likely to indicate?

4 There has been much debate as to whether *Riverdance* is 'a showbiz fad' or a serious piece of culture. What difference would it make to the communications planning flow if it was thought to be culture rather than showbiz?

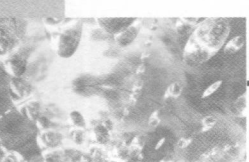

Le Shuttle

Le Shuttle was launched in December 1994 as the vehicle-carrying service between Folkestone and Calais through the Channel Tunnel. The planned market share was expected to grow to 50 per cent within a few years of launching the service. This was to be gained primarily from the ferries, although it was also envisaged that new traffic would be generated because of the improved cross-channel service. By June 1996, Le Shuttle's share had reached around 40 per cent despite fierce competition from the ferries. In order for Eurotunnel to achieve profitability, however, it is critical that Le Shuttle's market share continues to grow towards the original target.

Although all elements of the marketing mix have been used to promote Le Shuttle, including price discounts of up to 50 per cent, a loyalty scheme, duty-free promotions and improved services, marketing communications play a particularly important part in the overall strategy. In 1995, around £11 million was spent on television advertising and a further £3 million on press advertising, inserts and direct mail. The 1995 theme was the 'Fantastic Journey', using swordfish on motorbikes and crabs in cars travelling alongside a real family. The campaign was run in the national press, on television and on posters. Most of Le Shuttle's advertising tends to be pan-European, although around 50 per cent is spent in the UK whence 70 per cent of demand originates. Considerable effort also had to be put into fostering good press relations. This was designed not only to ensure that the media relayed positive messages about Le Shuttle's service benefits, but also to try to dampen or deflect interest in negative stories. Eurotunnel's major financial difficulties, delays, leaks and any other problems always seemed to attract media attention. However despite intense marketing communications activity in 1995, demand did not achieve the planned levels and too many customers were still confused about the difference between Eurostar and Le Shuttle.

The battle between the ferries and Le Shuttle intensified in 1996. Rather than simply allowing Eurotunnel to move in and take market share, the ferry companies decided to make a fight of it. Sweden's Stena Line, with around 20 per cent of the market, planned to introduce a new generation of ferries with a marketing emphasis on speed and the travel experience. The *Stena Emporeur* is the largest ferry to operate on

the channel service and additionally, the catamarans are faster than conventional ferries. The leading ferry operator P&O, with 35 per cent of the passenger market, has placed particular emphasis on the 'on-board experience', as have the other ferry companies. P&O has increased retail space by up to 70 per cent to accommodate a wider range of shops and duty-free facilities. About one-third of its revenue on the services comes from retail sales, including on-board shopping, entertainment and eating. According to Pat Hollis, the P&O ferry director,

> 'Since the early 1990s, there have been major changes in passenger trends; we were once perceived to be carriers of people, now the concept is that the crossing is an experience in its own right.'

At the same time, fares were heavily discounted and despite the success of the on-board sales, profits were being squeezed because of the impact of the competition from Le Shuttle. The ferry experience, which was heavily promoted, contrasts sharply with Le Shuttle. With Le Shuttle, travellers have to use the terminal buildings *before* their car is loaded on to the train, and the actual travel experience is strictly functional, but fast, beyond the terminal. There is of course a dilemma in that the more Le Shuttle promotes its own terminal retail operations, the longer the passenger spends at the terminal and the longer, therefore, the overall journey takes.

In order to combat the ferries' emphasis on 'the cruise experience', Le Shuttle's 1996 £10 million advertising campaign went high tech. The campaign sought to draw a parallel between travelling by Le Shuttle and travelling on a space shuttle. The television advertisement showed the experience from the perspective of a small boy on a 'space' mission, pretending to be an astronaut undergoing a countdown at NASA, in this case on one of 100 'missions' a day! The main rationale for the campaign was to emphasize the speed and excitement of the journey as well as highlighting Le Shuttle's comparatively advanced technology when compared with the familiar ferry. The campaign mainly featured on television but was also echoed in the national press and other media. It was intended to develop a range of merchandising and entertainment packs, based on the advertisement, to be sold through Le Shuttle terminals. The purpose of the various sales promotion activities was to bring the advertising experience to life.

While most experts consider that Le Shuttle will eventually win the battle, especially after the abolition of duty-free shopping in 1999, the battle over the next few years still promises to be highly interesting. In 1995, P&O matched Le Shuttle's advertising spend and Stena spent £4.4 million. There is still much spare capacity on the channel crossing. Ultimately, a ferry is a mobile asset that can soon be moved away on to other routes. Le Shuttle, however, does not have that flexibility! Nevertheless, the ferries will fight to retain their share on this route and marketing communications will be central to all players' marketing strategies. The ferries will not give in lightly.

Sources: Crawford (1996); Lane Fox (1995); Marsh (1996); Patey (1996).

Questions

1 Why is marketing communication so important for Le Shuttle?

2 How have the various elements of the promotional mix been used in Le Shuttle's marketing communications strategy?

3 What do you think is Le Shuttle's main target segment and how has that influenced its communications?

4 How has the launch of Le Shuttle changed the ferry companies' approach to communication, and why?

5 What are the potential risks of focusing on advertising in particular as a major competitive weapon in a head-to-head battle between two large operators such as Le Shuttle and P&O?

REFERENCES TO CHAPTER 15

Barnard, S. (1996), 'Watching Brief', *The Grocer*, 14 September, p. 15.

Benady, D. (1996), 'Soft Targets', *Marketing Week*, 19 January, pp. 28–9.

Bidlake, S. (1992), 'Storck Sours UK Sweets', *Marketing*, 16 April, p. 2.

Corr, A. (1994), 'Riverdance – The Musical', *RTE Guide*, 30 December, pp. 8–9.

Crawford, A. (1996), 'Le Shuttle Reviews Pan-Euro Account', *Campaign*, 16 February, p. 1.

Crosskey, P. (1996a), 'Olive Oil Trade Braced for Summer Squeeze', *The Grocer*, 23 March, p. 64.

Crosskey, P. (1996b), 'Value Speaks Louder than Words', *The Grocer*, 20 April, pp. 42–3.

DeLozier, M. W. (1975), *The Marketing Communications Process*, McGraw-Hill.

Dwek, R. (1995), 'Oiling the Cogs', *Marketing*, 22 June, p. VI.

Fill, C. (1995), *Marketing Communications: Frameworks, Theories and Applications*, Prentice Hall.

Gofton, K. (1992), 'Battering Butter', *Marketing*, 26 November, p. 20.

The Grocer (1995), 'Changing the Habits of a Lifetime', *The Grocer*, 16 December, p. 45.

Hart, N. A. (1993), *Industrial Marketing Communications*, Kogan Page.

Hirschman, E. C. (1987), 'People as Products: Analysis of a Complex Marketing Exchange', *Journal of Marketing*, 51(1), pp. 98–108.

Hooley, G. and Lynch, J. E. (1985), 'How UK Advertisers Set Budgets', *International Journal of Advertising*, 3, pp. 223–31.

Jones, J. P. (1991), 'Over Promise and Under Delivery', *Marketing and Research Today*, 19 (Nov.), pp. 195–203.

Lane Fox, H. (1995), 'Whatever Happened to the Channel Tunnel?', *Marketing*, 14 September, pp. 24–5.

Mallen, B. (1977), *Principles of Marketing Channel Management*, Lexington Books.

Marketing (1993) 'Adwatch Sector Survey: Coffee', *Marketing*, 25 February, p. 10.

Marsh, H. (1996), 'Le Shuttle's Space Booster', *Marketing*, 6 June, p. 12.

Marsh, H. (1995), '"Soft Booze" Focuses Spend Below-the-Line', *Marketing*, 23 November, p. 10.

Marshall, S. (1995), 'Tasting, Tasting ...', *Marketing*, 30 November, p. 11.

Olver, J. M. and Farris, P. W. (1989), 'Push and Pull: A One-Two Punch for Packaged Products', *Sloan Management Review*, 31(Fall), pp. 53–61.

Patey, T. (1996), 'Battle of the Channel That Breaks Every Rule', *The European*, 20–26 June, p. 21.

Peattie, K. (1992), *Green Marketing*, Pitman Publishing.

Richards, A. (1995), 'Airfix Ad Debut Spreads Appeal', *Marketing*, 8 June, p. 5.

Rossiter, J. R. and Percy, L. (1987), *Advertising and Promotion Management*, McGraw-Hill.

Rothschild, M. L. (1987), *Marketing Communications: From Fundamentals to Strategies*, Heath.

Sambrook, C. (1992), 'Getting Tough in a Sensitive Market', *Marketing*, 2 April, pp. 22–3.

Schramm, W. (1955), *Process Effects of Mass Communication*, University of Illinois Press.

Strong, E. K. (1925), *The Psychology of Selling*, McGraw-Hill.

Teather, D. (1995), 'Stars Bring Unknown Risk to Endorsement', *Marketing*, 6 July, p. 6.

16 Advertising

LEARNING OBJECTIVES

This chapter will help you to:

1 define advertising and its role within the promotional mix;

2 appreciate the complexities of formulating advertising messages and how they are presented for both print and broadcast media;

3 differentiate between types of advertising media and understand their relative strengths and weaknesses;

4 appreciate the role played by advertising agencies and the importance of cultivating good agency–client relationships; and

5 understand the stages in the management process of managing advertising activities.

INTRODUCTION

The average European is bombarded daily with an ever increasing number of advertising messages, whether on television, radio, print or posters. Branded goods, machine tools, restaurants, AIDS prevention and thousands of other goods, services and messages are all promoted through advertising. The battle is to attract and hold attention so that the advertising has the opportunity to generate the desired effects. Rarely can this be achieved by one advertisement.

Example

Sellers often develop a campaign which links together a number of advertisements in different media, to work alongside other means of promoting their businesses. A supermarket chain, for example, might use national television advertising to establish the general image of the store in terms of its price competitiveness or its customer service policy. This might be reinforced with poster advertising within the catchment area of a particular store, which might also give details about how to find the nearest store. Press advertising might then be used to communicate short-term specific offers. National press advertising would focus on generally available offers (for example 'A half price bottle of wine with every chicken purchased in any of our stores this weekend') while the local press would feature store specific offers and perhaps money-off coupons. The promises contained within any of these advertisements, however, whether about service, specific products or offers, can then be reinforced by point of sale material.

Regardless of the type of organisation, and whatever the mix of media used, any promises made must be consistent between different advertisements and must be delivered when the customer demands them. This implies a high level of integration between advertising decisions and their implementation and the rest of the marketing mix elements.

This chapter examines the role of advertising in the promotional mix and the important aspects of message design and media selection in the development of successful campaigns. The stages in developing an advertising campaign are then presented, along with the main management decisions at each stage. Sometimes, these decisions are made in conjunction with the support of an external advertising agency, while in other organisations the campaign process is controlled almost exclusively in-house. The decision to use an agency and the importance of the client–agency relationship are thus also considered within the chapter.

THE ROLE OF ADVERTISING IN THE PROMOTIONAL MIX

Advertising can be defined as any paid form of non-personal promotion transmitted through a mass medium. The sponsor should be clearly identified and the advertisement may relate to an organisation, a product or a service. The key difference, therefore, between advertising and other forms of promotion is that it is impersonal and communicates with large numbers of people through paid media channels. Although the term 'mass media' is often used, it has to be interpreted carefully. The proliferation of satellite and cable television channels, along with the increasing number of more tightly targeted special interest magazines mean that, on the one hand, advertising audiences are generally smaller, but, on the other, the audiences are 'better quality'. This means that they are far more likely to be interested in the subject matter of the advertising carried by their chosen medium. A publication such as *Classic CD*, for example, carries advertising from a wide range of recording companies, both large and small, who see this medium as a cost-effective way of reaching a much larger concentrated group from their target market than any other medium, even television, could generate.

Advertising normally conforms to one of two basic types: product orientated or institutional (Berkowitz *et al.*, 1992), as shown in Fig 16.1. A product-orientated advertisement focuses, as the term suggests, on the product or service being offered, whether for profit or not. Its prime task is to support the product in achieving its marketing goals.

Product-orientated advertising can itself take one of three alternative forms, **pioneering, competitive,** or **reminder and reinforcement** advertising.

FIGURE 16.1

Types of advertising

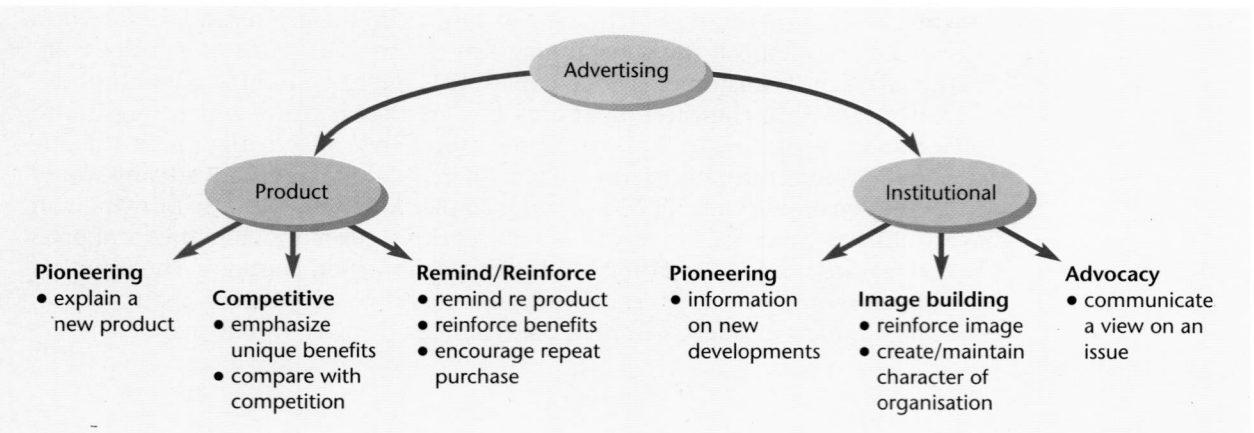

Pioneering advertising

Pioneering advertising is used in the early stages of the life-cycle when it is necessary to explain just what the product will do and the benefits it can offer. The more innovative, technically complex and expensive the product is, the more essential this explanation becomes. Depending on the product's newness, the prime emphasis might well be on stimulating basic generic demand rather than attempting to beat competition.

> **Example**
>
> When Wash and Go was first launched the advertising had to achieve two main objectives. First, it had to explain the concept of combining shampoo and conditioner in one bottle, and second, it had to convince the consumer of the time-saving benefits of such a product. Hence the television advertisements centred on young, active, busy people wanting to get away from the leisure centre as quickly as possible once they had finished their sporting activity. 'Take two bottles into the shower? Not me! I just wash and go.' Once this message was successfully established, it was much easier for competitors and supermarket own brands to enter the market with their own 'two in one' products. Wash and Go very kindly pioneered and effectively opened up a new segment of the hair care market.

As can be seen from the above example, the prime emphasis in the advertising is to provide enough information to allow potential buyers to see how this product might relate to them, and thus to stimulate enough interest to encourage further investigation and possibly trial. Further aspects of this use of promotion were considered in Chapter 8.

Competitive advertising

Competitive advertising is concerned with emphasizing the special features of the product or brand as a means of outselling the competition. Usually the seller seeks to communicate the unique benefits, real or imaginary, that distinguish the product and give it its competitive edge. Given that most markets are mature and often crowded, this type of advertising is very common and very important.

> **Example**
>
> In the coffee market each brand is subtly trying to hint that it uses the best quality beans, or that it has the richest or the smoothest taste, or that it represents the best value for money, or that it is the one favoured by the most discerning and sophisticated coffee drinkers. Nescafé, for example, reinforces its advertising with the messages on the jar label: 'best beans, best blend, best taste', 'richer aroma', and 'coffee at its best'. At the premium end of the market, the emphasis is more on sophistication, as portrayed in Nescafé Gold Blend's romantic soap opera series of advertisements. The launch of the French brand Carte Noire, 'un café nommé désir', in the UK took this kind of positioning even further, with a £6 million campaign in the style of perfume or fashion advertising (Barnard, 1996).

At least with coffee the consumer can try the different brands and then decide which one really delivers what they want.

With financial services, it is not particularly easy to switch brands. Also, because the products are so intangible and so similar, the consumer has problems in differentiating between different banks. Their advertising, therefore, is geared towards building a more human and caring face as well as an image of forward thinking, positive activity (hence slogans such as 'The bank that likes to say YES', 'The action bank', 'The listening bank'). The problem is, however, that consumers feel that the promises and imagery of the advertisements are not delivered in reality, and thus actually become even more cynical about the banks (Benady, 1994).

This underlines one of the critical features of good and effective advertising: it must have truth at its core. Advertising simply cannot be used to create a false image because as soon as consumers try the product or service for themselves, they will compare the reality against the advertising promises and pass judgement.

Comparative advertising

A form of competitive advertising that has grown in significance in recent years is **comparative advertising**. This means making a direct comparison between one product and another, showing the advertiser's product in a much more favourable light, of course (Muehling *et al.*, 1990). Alternatively, the comparison may be more subtle, referring to 'other leading brands' and leaving it up to the target audience to decide which rival product is intended. Initially, it was thought unwise to use a direct comparison approach as it gave a free mention to competitors and was likely to bring about a 'knocking copy' reaction. However, advertisers have now realised that in a competitive world even if they do make a comparison with the market leader which already has high awareness levels, the effect need not be negative.

Through careful selection of the benefits and judgement criteria to be emphasized, a comparative advertisement might encourage a perception of relative superiority,

MARKETING IN ACTION

Foden Trucks

Vehicle advertising can be legitimately and overtly comparative, as long as it compares vehicles on measures that either have been established through standard testing procedures, such as fuel consumption, or can be easily verified, such as spare parts costs. Foden Trucks, for example, advertised their 2000 series in early 1995 on the basis of 'Less Weight, More Profit'. To reinforce that message, the advertisement compared the prices of a 'basket of spares' for various manufacturers' trucks. The Foden basket was cheapest at £537 whereas, at the other end of the scale, the Seddon Atkinson basket cost £826. Both Iveco and Leyland Daf were over £700. Clearly, the spares included were carefully selected to give the best comparison from Foden's point of view, and the cost of spares is only one of many criteria that a truck buyer is going to consider.

In this advertisement, however, the comparison serves to attract attention and to give the reader a gentle reminder that the purchase price is not everything. The advertisement is, in fact, quite subtle in hinting at value for money backed up with hard figures without actually mentioning a purchase price at all! Just to confuse the reader, however, in the same issue of *Truck*, Iveco claim that their vehicle is the most fuel efficient and the most productive, with Foden coming fourth out of five.

Source: Truck (1995).

despite the selectivity used. The advertiser must be careful with this approach to avoid abusing the competition or presenting false comparisons. Thus any comparative product appeal must be made with care from a legal perspective. Any claims must be clearly sustainable.

A competitor might well see all this as a challenge and run their own comparative advertising to redress the balance. In extreme cases, ill-considered comparative advertising might lead to claims of unfair practice and to legal action.

Example

First Direct, the telephone banking service, tried a tentative form of comparative advertising with a campaign centred around the theme of 'Tell me one good thing about your bank'. Although the comparison was indirect and did not name specific competitors, it nevertheless upset a few other banks. National Westminster Bank, for example, was rather annoyed at the implication that people were generally dissatisfied with their banks, and responded with national press advertising listing 'thousands of good things' about its own service (*Marketing*, 1996a).

Reminder and reinforcement advertising

Reminder and reinforcement advertising tends to operate after purchase. It reminds customers that the product still exists and that it has certain positive properties and benefits. This increases the chances of repurchase and sometimes might even persuade consumers to buy larger quantities. The main emphasis is not on creating new knowledge or behaviour but on reinforcing previous purchasing behaviour, and reassuring consumers that they made the right choice in the first place.

Such advertising alongside product usage does help the consumer's learning experience. Frequent exposure to advertising that emphasizes just how long a bottle of Fairy Liquid lasts makes the washer-up look at the bottle in their own kitchen and think, 'Yes, it has actually been there a while...' Complete victory to the advertiser. consumers that they made the right choice in the first place.

This kind of advertising clearly relates to those established products in the mature stage of the product life-cycle where the emphasis is on maintaining market share at a time of major competition. It is also important if the weak theory of advertising, outlined at p. 580, is accepted. That would mean that post-purchase reminder, image building and reinforcement advertising actually create the attitudes and preferences that lead to further purchases. Consumers might be vaguely aware of a brand name because they have seen advertisements although they do not consciously remember them. This might be enough to make them pick up that product in the supermarket, almost as an impulse purchase, and try it. Then, they begin to take more notice of the advertisements and begin to learn about the product benefits, relating them to their own usage, as in the Fairy Liquid example mentioned above.

Institutional advertising

In contrast, **institutional advertising** is not product specific. It aims to build a sound reputation and image for the whole organisation to achieve a wide range of objectives with different target audiences. These could include the community, financial stakeholders, government and customers to name but a few. A number of these issues are picked up in Chapter 20 as they form an important part of a public relations campaign.

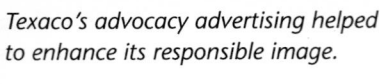
Texaco's advocacy advertising helped to enhance its responsible image.

Source: DMB&B

Institutional advertising may be undertaken for many reasons, as shown in Fig 16.1, for example pioneering, in the sense of presenting new developments within the organisation, image building, or advocacy in the sense of presenting the organisation's point of view on an issue. Some institutional advertising might be linked with presenting the organisation as a caring, responsible and progressive company. These advertisements are designed to inform or reinforce positive images with target audiences. Others may adopt an *advocacy* perspective indicating the organisation's view on a particular issue for political, social responsibility or self-interest reasons. There will be more on this in Chapter 20, on PR.

Example

Texaco, the petrol company, wanted to raise its profile to compete with Shell, Esso and BP. It decided to do this through promoting the issue of child road safety with the theme, 'Children Should Be Seen and Not Hurt'. The television advertisement featured an empty school, representing the 600 children killed or badly injured on Britain's roads every year, and linked into a poster and point of sale campaign offering free reflective stickers that could be attached to children's bicycles or clothing. The campaign was reinforced through the availability of car window stickers, catalogues of child road safety products and information leaflets at the point of sale. According to Texaco's advertising agency, DMB&B, the campaign as a whole was appreciated by a wide range of publics, including politicians and schools, and resulted not only in the distribution of 15 million stickers, but also in an increase of 280 per cent in Texaco's rating as 'a company that puts something back into the community' (DMB&B, 1995a).

Advertising within the marketing mix

The above categorisation of product and institutional advertising broadly describes the direct uses of advertising. Within the marketing mix, advertising also plays a less direct but equally important role in supporting other areas of marketing activity. In organisational markets, advertising often directly supports the selling efforts of the sales team by generating leads, providing information on new developments to a wider audience more quickly and creating a generally more receptive climate prior to the sales visit.

Similarly, with sales promotion, a short-term incentive offer may be actively advertised to encourage increased traffic. For example airlines offering 'two for one' deals or a free ticket competition frequently support their promotions with media advertising. Furniture stores too make frequent use of television and press advertising to inform the public of short-term promotional price cuts or low/no interest financing deals to stimulate interest in furnishing and to draw people into stores that they might not otherwise have thought of visiting at that particular time.

More strategically, advertising may be used to reposition a product for defensive or aggressive reasons in order to improve its competitive position. This may be achieved by demonstrating new uses for the product or to open up new segments, either geographically or benefit based.

Example

Budweiser, despite being the best selling beer in the USA, had made little impact on the UK market by 1990. Research showed that UK consumers associated the brand with the more negative aspects of 1980s US culture. An advertising campaign was therefore developed to associate the brand with more evocative and romantic US imagery, such as the blues, the wide open spaces and freedom and independence. By 1993, the positioning of the product had changed so that its American roots had become a valued, differentiating feature rather than a hindrance and it was the most popular premium lager among 18 to 24 year olds (DMB&B, 1995b).

In other situations, advertising may support other marketing mix activities to spread demand or to reduce sales fluctuations. The problems of seasonality are well known in the services field, whether in relation to holidays, restaurants or cinemas. Combined with pricing, advertising may seek to spread or even out demand patterns, saving the service provider from having to accept periods of marked under-utilisation of capacity. The various cross-channel ferry companies, for example, advertise low-priced deals and 'booze cruises' to France during the winter to boost passenger numbers.

Overall, advertising's role within an organisation depends on a range of contexts, environments and competitive challenges, and may even change within the same organisation over time. The detailed role of advertising will be specified in the marketing plan, which will clearly specify objectives, resources, activities and results expected. These issues will be revisited at pp. 636 *et seq.*, where the stages in developing an advertising campaign are considered.

FORMULATING THE ADVERTISING MESSAGE

The essence of communication, as outlined in the previous chapter, is to decide what to say, to whom, by what means and with what results. This section centres on the very demanding decision area of designing an appropriate message, with the emphasis on the message content, its tone and how it can then be presented for either print or broadcast communication.

Message

Before producing an advertisement you need to know who the target audience is and you need to give careful consideration to what you want to say to them. This requires

TABLE 16.1
Advertising slogans

Company	Slogan
British Telecommunications	'It's Good to Talk'
Coca-Cola	'Coke Is It'
Ford Cars	'Everything We Do Is Driven By You'
Guinness	'Pure Genius'
Peugeot	'The Drive of Your Life'
Tango	'You Know When You've Been Tango'ed'
Toyota Cars	'The Car in Front is a Toyota'

a sound understanding of the targets, their interests, needs, motivations, lifestyles etc. In addition, there needs to be an honest appraisal of the product or service to determine the differential characteristics or benefits that are worth highlighting to achieve the desired results. Table 16.1 shows a range of succinct advertising slogans that convey some complex and sophisticated messages.

Message formulation
Clearly, marketing and promotional objectives are at the heart of message formulation. If the prime objective is to generate awareness, then the message must offer clear information to alert the audience to what is on offer. If the objective is to stimulate enquiries, then the focus would need to be on moving the customer through to action, making sure that the response mechanism is clear and easy to use (more of this in Chapter 19). There also needs to be consistency between the product positioning (*see* pp. 308 *et seq.*) desired and the content and style of the advertisement.

The main aim in message design and execution is to prepare an informative and persuasive message in terms of words, symbols and illustrations that will not only attract attention but retain interest through its presentation so that the target audience responds as desired. Grabbing and holding attention may mean making someone watch an entire 30-second television advertisement, read a long, wordy print advertisement, or simply dwell long enough on a non-verbal graphic image to start thinking about what it means. Whatever the medium or the style of communication, it is therefore essential that the message is understandable and relevant to the audience.

Themes
Sometimes the message may be sent out through both broadcast and print media using the same theme. In other cases, a number of different messages may be communicated in different ways over the length of the campaign.

Example

Daewoo, the Korean car company, uses both broadcast and print media to communicate its approach to customer focus and how it differs from other car companies. The overall messages are the same and support each other, but the print advertisements can go into more detail and cover a number of points whereas the television advertisements have to be shorter and more focused if viewers are to remember them.

The formation of the SEM created new opportunities for the adoption of pan-European messages. Some organisations such as Coca-Cola, Martini and Benetton have, for many years, standardised their basic advertising messages throughout

Europe. Their view is that their products appeal to market segments, based on factors other than geography, which exist across the whole of Europe. These segments are based on age, life style, beliefs and attitudes. Such transnational life style segments tend to be the exception rather than the rule, however. It is very difficult in practice to develop pan-European messages that can appeal to the variety of different national cultures and attitudes that still exist across Europe.

MARKETING IN ACTION

Pan-European advertising – east and west

The growth of pan-European media and increasing sophistication in identifying pan-European segments is having an important impact on the development of advertising campaigns. PepsiCo decided that it needed to give Pizza Hut a boost across Europe, since it was faced with declining sales and a growing public perception of the brand as just another American fast food chain. Rather than go for country by country advertising, PepsiCo decided to pool resources for the first pan-European Pizza Hut advertising. The campaign eatured Cindy Crawford and Linda Evangelista, at a cost of £350 000 each. Both were filmed enjoying the new Stuffed Crust Pizza that was to be promoted as part of the campaign. Selecting these supermodels was deliberate, in order to convey a young personality for Pizza Hut consistent with its 20 to 30-year old target audience across Europe. The campaign rolled out across Europe in April 1995 with the same advertisement used everywhere. The two models were talking together in a Pizza Hut restaurant while eating a stuffed crust pizza. The total cost was £13 million, including making and screening the campaign, far more than any one country could afford to spend, given the cost of production. Pizza Hut, by adopting a single campaign and a single message, was thus able in a dual-purpose campaign to improve its image and position, at least in the short term, in a range of prime European markets.

Another American company, Xerox, had an even more challenging task in developing a pan-European campaign to cover the newly opened markets across eastern Europe. The need for the campaign arose from the increased competitive pressure caused by new brands entering the market, especially from Japan. It was decided that a pan-eastern-European campaign would be developed to emphasize the brand strengths of Xerox with end users, as well as to consolidate its position with dealers. Market research indicated that customers had to be convinced about why they

should pay more for a printer or photocopier, as normally they would simply buy on price. This meant that the campaign had to provide a justification for higher prices, focusing on such factors as product quality, after-sales service and dealer support networks.

The real challenge, however, was how best to communicate across all the eastern European countries, as there are many different cultures and languages. These factors, as well as the availability of different media, were all special considerations in designing the campaign. Strong visual messages were selected that transferred across boundaries with little verbal explanation. One advertisement showed a list of Xerox dealers by name and address, while also showing a pair of binoculars in case the viewer wanted to find a competitor! Standardising the images in the advertisements so that they would be consistent with local conditions in each country was no easy task. In Moscow, for instance, a dealer was in a 14th-floor flat, while in Warsaw there were proper premises, but they were not averse to repairing a machine in the middle of the shop.

The campaign was fully integrated to cover advertisements, direct mail, sales promotion aids and point of sale materials. Xerox found, however, that in one case, a dealer was actually selling the freebie carrier bags. Despite these difficulties, the campaign appeared to have been a success and sales levels re-established themselves. No image or attitudinal change research was undertaken to assess the deeper impact of the activity.

By 1996, Xerox was running the same campaign in eastern Europe as in the EU, with only slight adaptation to suit local circumstances. This partly reflects the maturing of some of the eastern European markets, and partly reflects the fact that the earlier campaigns had established sufficient brand awareness to pave the way for more sophisticated messages.

Sources: Lee (1996); Parker (1996) .

Message execution

The execution of the message can also be a problem. A survey of over 200 European brand managers showed that over 50 per cent believed that it was difficult to standardise advertising programmes (Kapferer and Eurocom, 1992). Research has also shown that British advertising shows a sophisticated humour and is high on emotional content. German advertising, in contrast, has much less humour and is more straightforward and informative (Munzinger, 1988). Language barriers too can prevent the effective translation of sophisticated messages from one culture to another. Nevertheless, this can be avoided by largely visual advertising, such as Renault's 'Papa–Nicole' series, which completely avoids complicated dialogue. One other solution is to develop fairly bland, inoffensive advertising that can easily be understood and adapted. The same images will be used in different countries with any verbal elements translated into the local language.

> ### Example
>
> Television advertising for Ricola cough sweets from Switzerland, for instance, shows simple, stereotypical images of Switzerland (the Matterhorn, men in ethnic costume blowing long horns, mountain pasture etc.) then cuts to an English voice-over describing the product's 13 herbal ingredients. The Ricola advertisement deliberately plays on its Swiss heritage and can be used across Europe because other Europeans can relate in similar ways to the Swiss stereotype shown.

Other organisations go to the opposite extreme and use universal images, familiar in any Western culture, that cannot be associated with any particular country. This brings us back to advertisers such as Benetton and Martini, as well as US companies such as Coca-cola, IBM and 3M.

The attraction of having a single pan-European approach is the cost savings in development and production of advertising, but this has to be balanced against the potential loss of creativity. It also makes the potentially dangerous assumption that advertising objectives are the same across different countries. Many of these issues are equally applicable to wider international marketing and will thus be discussed further in Chapter 25.

Creative appeals

After the marketing issues of message content have been considered, the creative task can proceed. It is here that agencies can play a particularly major role in the conceptualisation and design of messages that appeal effectively. Two broad dimensions of **creative appeal** guide advertisement production. One dimension is rational or emotive appeals, and the other is whether the advertisement is product or customer focused.

Rational appeals centre on some kind of logical argument persuading the consumer to think or act in a certain way. However, often it is not just a case of *what* is said, but also *how* it is said. The bald logic in itself may not be enough to grab and hold the consumers' attention sufficiently to make the message stick. How it is said can introduce an *emotional appeal* into the advertisement to reinforce the underlying logic of the message. The concern here is not just with facts but also with the customer's feeling and emotions towards what is on offer. It is often the emotional element that gives the advertisement an extra appeal.

Fear is not, of course, the only kind of emotional appeal. Positive emotions can be equally effective in creating memorable and persuasive messages, which do not necessarily need any solid rational basis in order to be effective. Humour and sex are particularly powerful tools of the advertiser, particularly in appealing to people's needs for escapism and fantasy. A few examples of positive emotional appeals are shown in Table 16.2. Emotional appeals are especially useful when it is difficult to create a meaningful difference and superiority with more rational appeals.

It may be argued that television is better at creating emotional appeals, as it is more lifelike, with sight, sound and motion to aid the presentation, whereas print is better for more rational, factually based appeals.

Product-orientated appeals

Product-orientated appeals centre on product features or attributes and seek to emphasize their importance to the target audience. The appeals may be based on

TABLE 16.2
Positive emotional appeals

Product	Slogan
Allure (a perfume brand from Chanel)	'Difficult to define. Impossible to Resist'
Carte Noire (coffee)	'Un Café Nommé Désir'
Comfort (fabric conditioner)	'When I wear Denims, I Can Feel the Silk'
Henara (hair colourants)	'Freeing the Forces of Nature'
Hermés (perfumes)	'The Secret World Where Every Woman Is the Spirit of Light'
Lux (soaps and shower gels)	'I'm Not Rita Hayworth–I Am Me'
National Lottery	'It Could Be You'
Nike	'Just Do It'
Twinings Tea	'To Increase the Relaxing Properties of Our Camomile Tea, Add 40 Gallons of Hot Water' (alongside a photo of a woman drinking tea in a hot steamy bath).

product specification (air bags or side impact protection bars in cars, for example), price (actual price level, payment terms or extras), service (availability) or any part of the offering that creates a potential competitive edge in the eyes of the target market. Taken to its extreme, this might lead to comparative advertising, as discussed at p. 606.

With a product-orientated appeal, there are several options for specific message design strategy. These include:

How to solve a problem. As already discussed, solving a problem can be tied in with an emotional appeal, perhaps with fear of the consequences of not tackling a problem such as body odour or bad breath, for example. The product-orientated element of the advertisement shows how the product provides the solution. In a less emotional way, business-to-business advertising can also focus very effectively on problem solution.

Example

Yves Cougnaud advertises in French business magazines, showing how its modular buildings can provide a fast and cost-effective solution for growing companies with space problems.

Product comparison. Product comparision forcefully emphasizes the product's superiority when compared either directly with a competing brand or generally with other products in the same class. Such an approach was shown in the Foden trucks example mentioned earlier on p. 606.

Slice of life. Slice of life advertisements demonstrates how the product fits into a lifestyle which either approximates that of the target market or is one with which they can identify or to which they can aspire.

Example

The family shown in the Oxo advertisements is meant to be fairly realistic, with squabbling children, an overworked and harassed mother, and mum and dad having the occasional row. Bisto and McDonald's have been even more daring in portraying life as it actually is by showing single and divorced parents in their advertising. Meanwhile, Gillette's 'the best a man can get' advertisements put together images of emotional events in men's lives, although the overall effect was rather like a Hollywood piece of fantasy. The Renault 'Papa–Nicole' advertising also depends on fantasy, a slice of rich, idle life in a chateau in a warm climate.

News, facts and testimonials. News, facts and testimonials offer hard information about the product or proof through 'satisfied customers' that the product is all it is claimed to be. Such approaches tend towards the rational, and may be endorsed by a celebrity or by supporting explanation and examples. Magazine advertisements trying to sell goods that the target market might perceive to be the more expensive, or goods that sound too good to be true, or goods that a customer would normally want to see or try before purchase, often use testimonials from satisfied customers. These might help to alleviate some of the doubt or risk and encourage the reader to respond to the advertisement.

> **Example**
>
> An advertisement for the Oreck lightweight vacuum cleaner begins by setting up its credibility by giving the number sold since 1963, then moves into the features and benefits, and finishes with quotes from satisfied customers that reinforce the key benefits, trying to achieve a 'word of mouth' effect. The idea is that if it is good enough for 'Mrs J. Thorpe (Sheffield)', then it is good enough for me (*Sunday Express Magazine*, 1996).

Advertorials. In magazines and trade publications, news and fact-based approaches can also take the form of **advertorials**. These are designed to fit in with the style, tone and presentation of the publication so that the reader tends to think of them as extensions to the magazine rather than as advertisements.

> **Example**
>
> Farmers Seeds Federal published an eight-page 'newsletter' within *Farmers Weekly*, an agricultural trade magazine. Although its graphic design and colour scheme distinguished it from the rest of the magazine, the length and pitch of the articles within the newsletter were similar. Some of them were factual and purely informative, while others told stories about the success of individual farmers using these products (*Farmers Weekly*, 1995).

The overall objective is that the reader's attention should be able to flow naturally from the magazine's normal editorial content into and through the advertorial and out the other side, maintaining interest and retention. This is particularly effective where the advertorial is short.

> **Example**
>
> Böhler, an Austrian special steel company, placed a one-page advertorial in *European Purchasing and Materials Management* which looked and read just like any of the editorial content of that issue. The reader would have to be very alert to notice the words 'sponsored statement' at the top of the page.

Customer-orientated appeals

Customer orientated appeals are focused on what the consumer personally gains through using this product. Such appeals encourage the consumer by association to think about the benefits that may be realisable through the rational or emotional content of the advertisement. Typically, they include:

Saving or making money. Bold 2, for example, could sell itself simply on the product-orientated appeal that it incorporates both a washing powder and fabric conditioner in its formulation. In fact, its advertising takes the argument further into a customer-orientated appeal, demonstrating how this two-in-one product is cheaper than buying the two components separately, thus putting money back in the purchaser's pocket.

This is also a strong appeal in cost-conscious organisational markets. Lucas Engineering and Systems Ltd offer consultancy to other businesses in the field of purchasing management. Their advertising emphasizes cost saving as the main benefit to be gained from using Lucas, suggesting that a '1 per cent cut in purchase costs can boost profits by as much as 15 per cent'.

Fear avoidance. The use of fear avoidance appeals is a powerful one in message generation and has been extensively used in public, non-profit-making promotions, for example AIDS prevention, anti drinking and driving, anti-smoking, and other health awareness programmes. Getting the right level of fear is a challenge: too high and it will be regarded as too threatening and thus be screened out, too low and it will not be considered compelling enough to act upon.

Example

Every year around Christmas, the UK government sponsors an advertising campaign to prevent drinking and driving. Over the years, the messages, based around fear of the consequences of drinking and driving, succeeded in raising public awareness generally but were not making the desired impact on the core target audience of 20–35-year-old males. The problem was that the audience felt that for such horrible things to happen, the driver had to be absolutely blind drunk, and since they themselves were never in that state, the message did not apply to them. From 1992 onwards, therefore, the tone of the fear campaign was altered. The overall theme of 'Drinking and driving wrecks lives' was retained, but the guilty drivers in the advertisements were made much more ordinary and much closer to sober!

The 1994 campaign, for example, pointed out that 'even great blokes can kill', featuring a driver who had only 'had a quick one' and then been responsible for killing the parents of two young children (DMB&B, 1995c). In 1995, the campaign changed direction slightly by showing the damage that 'a quick one' can do to the driver himself. The television advertisement showed a young man, clearly paralysed and brain damaged, being spoon-fed liquidised food by his worn-out mother. With each spoonful, she is encouraging him with, 'Come on, Dave, just one more'. In the background as a ghostly echo, pub noises can be heard, specifically a group of lads having a good time and encouraging each other with, 'Come on, Dave, just one more'. The message that even a small amount of alcohol can be dangerous began to get across and the audience began to believe that this could happen to them. The message made all the more impact by focusing on what could happen to *me* (i.e., a largely selfish concern) rather than on what I could do to an unknown third party (i.e., appealing to a sense of responsibility or duty).

Security enhancement. A wide range of insurance products aimed at the over-50s are advertised not only on the rational basis that they are a sensible financial investment, but also on the emotional basis that they provide peace of mind. This is a customer-orientated appeal in that it works on self-interest and a craving for security. Stairlifts are also sold on the basis of security enhancement, with the implication that they make going up and down stairs easier for the elderly. The advertisements also suggest that with a stairlift, the elderly will be able to retain their independence and remain in their own homes longer, a great concern to many older people.

Self esteem and image. Sometimes, when it is difficult to differentiate between competing products on a functional basis, consumers may choose the one which they think will best improve their self-esteem or enhance their image among social or peer groups. Advertisers recognise this and can produce advertisements in which the product and its function play a very secondary role to the portrayal of these psychological and social benefits. Perfumes, cosmetics and toiletries clearly exploit this, but even an expensive technical products such as a car can focus on self-esteem and image.

The Ford Fiesta featured in print advertisements headlined, 'Escape Hatch' with body copy such as, 'Conformist? Not you. Blinkered? Hardly. Prejudgemental? Never.' The final tag line was, 'New Fiesta. Not for the small-minded.

Usage benefits–time, effort, accuracy etc. An approach stressing usage benefits is very similar to a rational, product-orientated appeal, but shows how the consumer benefits from saving time, or gains the satisfaction of producing consistently good results through using this product. Such savings or satisfactions are often translated into emotional benefits such as spending more time with the family or winning other people's admiration. They even work in organisational advertising.

Siemens advertises its industrial lighting systems not only on their energy cost savings, but also on the basis that they help to create a less stressed work-force that will be more productive.

Execution of consumer-orientated appeals

The execution of consumer-orientated appeals, particularly those with a high emotional content, provides more scope for creative imagination. Approaches may include:

Humour. The series of advertisements centred around the slogan, 'I bet he drinks Carling Black Label' showed people (and once a squirrel) performing comically impossible feats to the admiration of a couple of onlookers. Underlying the genuinely funny entertaining structure of the advertisements, though, was the implication that the Carling Black Label drinker is confident, resourceful, witty and admired, which may well appeal to the aspirations of its young male target market.

Sex. Although it is rare these days to see the overtly offensive sexual portrayal of women in advertising, more subtle sexuality is still rife. As long as people are interested in sex, and as long as they feel insecure about their ability to be successful in relationships, then advertisers will find a role for sex in selling products.

An advertiser may hint that using a particular brand of deodorant, skin cleanser, aftershave or toothpaste will increase your attractiveness. Alternatively, the effect might be more subtly erotic, such as in the Cadbury's Flake advertisements which imply a fantasy-based, self-indulgent pleasure that could be interpreted as bordering on the sexual (it is important to note, however, that this interpretation is strictly in the mind of the beholder and is not explicitly presented on the screen).

As a final point, it is interesting to see that after many years of being criticised for exploiting women, advertisers are redressing the balance and becoming increasingly willing to exploit men.

> **Example**
>
> The 'himbo' is almost as common an image as the 'bimbo' used to be. An example of this is the Diet Coke television advertisement, showing female office staff crowding round a window to drool over a rather handsome construction worker having his '11:30 Diet Coke break'.

Animation. Cartoons have an almost universal appeal. As well as using well-known celebrities such as Bugs Bunny or Tom and Jerry to endorse products, advertisers can create exclusive animated characters who can inhabit invented worlds and do impossible things.

> **Example**
>
> The adventures of Kellogg's Tony the Tiger, who advertises Frosties, have entertained for over 30 years. Tony also offers the brand a strong, readily identifiable character which can be used both for advertising and as a platform for sales promotion activities. Cartoon characters also have the advantage that while they do not age, they are nevertheless adaptable as the tastes and demands of the target audience mature. Tony's appearance and character are not the same now are they originally were.

Music, visual atmosphere. Any emotional effect can be enhanced or reinforced by careful choice of music and/or visual setting. Maxell cassette tapes, for example, used a parody of the song, 'The Israelites', entitled 'Me Ears Are Alight' to demonstrate the clarity of their product. The humour and the point of the message, however, depended on the audience's ability to identify the original song. Classical pieces have also been successfully used to create moods in advertisements. British Airways has adopted the Flower Duet from *Lakmé* as its theme, while in British minds, Dvorak's New World Symphony will forever conjure up images of Hovis bread. Music and strong visual imagery can, of course, serve a useful purpose in international markets by conveying emotion and mood without language problems (Appelbaum and Halliburton, 1993).

Once the decisions on message design and execution styles have been made, the framework exists for more detailed consideration of message presentation. We now turn therefore, to presentation for print media, and then to broadcast media.

Print presentation

The final design of the words, illustrations, symbols and layout completes the message design and execution stage. Whatever the design selected, readers must be attracted to the message and their interest retained for sufficient time to enable them to reach a conclusion. Print is passive, and so it must, by its creativity, create an active and involved reader, whether using a directory, newspaper, magazine or sales literature.

Copywriting

Copywriting is the creative task of putting together the verbal elements of the message. This includes the headlines, any subheadings, body copy and captions. The headline is the main means of attracting attention to the page. Often the first thing read, it will determine whether the reader will be bothered to continue. At its least subtle, the headline aims to communicate a benefit to the reader as an incentive to read on. Where the basic message is very straightforward and rational, the headline might follow suit. 'PC Price Madness' and '50% Off Sale!' are both headlines signalling the type of advertisement that shows lots of different products along with slashed prices, and messages such as 'buy now while stocks last' or 'hurry, sale ends Saturday'.

However, headlines are often a little less direct in their execution, particularly where the appeal is more subtle or emotionally based. If we take a selection of print advertisements for cars, for example, 'There's no such thing as an average person' (Peugeot 405); 'Radical departure' (SsangYong Musso); 'The only bumps you'll feel are goosebumps' (Honda Civic Coupe), we see that they either set the mood for the advertisement or seek to raise curiosity, and the incentive to read on emerges from the desire to find out what on earth this is all about. Headlines are not, however, presented in isolation. They can link with an illustration or body copy to stimulate further involvement.

Example

The Mitsubishi Shogun's headline 'The kids hate it. They've never had a day off school' means little unless it is read alongside the illustration of the car coping easily with a snowbound country lane. Between them, they manage to give a 'slice of life' feel to the advertisement as well as emphasizing a key benefit of the vehicle.

Following on from headlines, tag lines or sub headings either offer further explanation, or act as a bridge to the main body copy. The body copy is the main part of the text in the advertisement. It should flow from the headlines and build upon the propositions that need to be made. The length will vary and in some cases will be minimal. Assuming that the advertisement has not been deliberately designed to work with just a headline and a strong illustration, the body copy has to retain the interest of the reader through to the conclusion. A large percentage of readers will not get past the headline, but for the small percentage that do, the copy has a persuasive and informative job to do.

Example

In the Shogun advertisement, mentioned earlier, the body copy reads as follows:

'I never quite saw the appeal of an off-roader. That was until I discovered just what the Shogun was like on the road. It's safe and comfortable with masses of room. But best of all, it's fun. For me and the kids. It's got a 3 litre V6 engine which means there is plenty of power whenever you need it. (I chose the automatic version. It's easier in traffic.) It's guaranteed for any amount of miles for

3 years, it has a 6 year anti corrosion perforation warranty and the 3 year pan-European breakdown and recovery service that starts at my front door. It's really reliable. And I feel so safe sitting there high up above the traffic. Rupert says it is the only off-roader to have a Super Select transmission system that is able to change between 2 and 4 wheel drive at speeds up to 62 mph. And it's great fun in the mud and snow. But that's Rupert. He's a bit of a kid too. To find out more, including your nearest Shogun Centre, clip the coupon or call free 0800 123 363.'

Guidelines for good copy

There are a number of guidelines in generating good copy which are reflected in the Shogun advertisement.

Sell the benefits. Copy should sell the benefits to the reader, whether product orientated or emotional.

Example

The Shogun body copy not only describes the technical features of the vehicle but also converts them into benefits to the owner, even using the magic words, 'which means that ...' at one point. 'Safe', 'fun', 'reliable', 'comfortable' are more likely to make an impact on the casual reader than '3 litre V6 engine' and other highly technical descriptions.

Mitsubishi Shogan – understanding the customer.

THE KIDS HATE IT. THEY'VE NEVER HAD A DAY OFF SCHOOL.

Source: Butler Lutos Sutton Wilkinson.

Communicate to the individual. The copy should communicate to an individual not to a mass audience. The message should suggest to the reader that the copy has been especially prepared for them. This means using examples and language relevant to the target audience. Remember that they are not obliged to stay with the advertisement all the way to the end. They will stop reading it as soon as they get bored or decide that it's not really talking to them.

> **Example**
>
> The Shogun advertisement has been written in the first person, almost in the style of neighbours chatting over a cup of coffee. That immediately makes it more personal and welcoming to the target audience of middle class upmarket housewives. It is also likely that the target audience is conservative, and does not necessarily enjoy driving for its own sake, and may clock up lower than average miles per year. She may view the car simply as a functional means of moving the children around, but because she is rather uneasy about driving in poor weather conditions or in heavy city traffic, she wants a car that will take as much stress as possible out of driving.
>
> The reader of the Shogun advertisement may not necessarily see herself as a Sylvia married to a Rupert (who is probably a merchant banker or a barrister), living in a converted Cotswold farmhouse complete with an Aga, two children (Tristan and Isolde) and a black labrador, but she can enjoy the scenario. She might even go as far as thinking 'If this car is good enough for someone like that, then it's good enough for me'.

Be credible. Copy must be credible, but without using clichés such as 'great prices' and 'best in town'. Credibility is important as it encourages the reader to accept the essence of the sales arguments presented, whether or not they are in the market at that time.

> **Example**
>
> In the Shogun advertisement, the claims made for the vehicle are not unreasonable. The technical specifications and warranties are purely factual, and the benefits to the driver are entirely believable within the context of the character who is supposed to be telling her story.

Keep the message simple, clear and concise. It may not be necessary to cover all the issues in one advertisement. Selectivity and a clearly focused attempt to explain may be sufficient to get the basic message across. This does not mean that the advertising has to be boring. People expect advertising to tell them what they need to know in a digestible, but nevertheless entertaining form. Dull copywriting, however worthy the content, will not retain interest. Imagine how much more boring the Shogun advertisement would have been if it had just been an impersonal list of product features.

The copy must flow from point to point and end in a clear call for action, whether to reflect, enquire or buy. The copy should always end with some request for action. Note that the Shogun advertisement ends with a freephone number and the option of sending off for more information by mail. The specific copy generated will depend also on the overall style. It may be straight copy, but often involves some combination with pictures, artwork and illustrations, and thus the synergy between all the separate elements needs to be carefully thought through, as in the Shogun advertisement.

Finally, the sponsor of the advertisement is usually clearly identified, through the use of words, logos, trade marks or organisation details. Thus the Mitsubishi Motors logo appears at the top left of the Shogun advertisement, with the Shogun logo at the top right.

If the advertisement is designed to generate a direct response from the reader, then the prominence of phone numbers or the design of a reply coupon should be carefully considered. Chapter 19 on direct marketing takes up some of these issues further.

Layout

The **layout** refers not just to the words but also all the artwork, including photography, drawings and logos. The layout shows how the copy and illustration(s) hang together from a rough concept stage through to the final agreed advertisement. This format enables a number of creative ideas to be explored before a final, irrevocable decision is made. The illustrations can sometimes be even more powerful than the headline, particularly as colour reproduction techniques have improved. Often illustrations communicate more symbolism to the reader than words.

Outdoor hoarding and magazine advertisements for Silk Cut cigarettes have no verbal content whatsoever, other than the statutory health warnings. Even the brand name does not appear; the viewer or reader is expected to recognise what has become a characteristic graphic style for that product.

Illustrations can be photographs, tables and charts, line drawings and graphs, or indeed any type of non-copy content, including free attachments, such as the scented cards included in perfume advertisements.

Finally, the overall design of the advertisement must be attractive and must encourage the reader to follow through. To achieve this requires, apart from an understanding of what makes the reader tick, a sound understanding of print production processes and the aesthetics of the layout proposed. The aesthetics include the balance between the advertisement elements, the focal point of attention, the eye movement for the reader, the relative proportions of the elements and the unity of style and moods generated.

Broadcast presentation

Broadcast presentation includes television and radio commercials. In contrast to print production, broadcast presentation has no layout, but a script to guide the dialogue, narration, sound effects and music. This ultimately includes the production details to cover camera work etc. where appropriate. The script enables discussion between the creative and marketing staff before the expensive commitment to shooting or recording. Once agreed, the script is developed into a *story board*, which has three components: the main scenes and actions, the written description of what occurs and the audio effects. Although at this stage it is still a static format, not using sight, sound or motion, it is a pragmatic response to the problem of incurring production costs at an exploratory stage.

After the initial agreement, the storyboard goes through further stages of refinement prior to final shooting. A number of formats are possible with television commercials. Some advertisements adopt a documentary kind of style, with either an

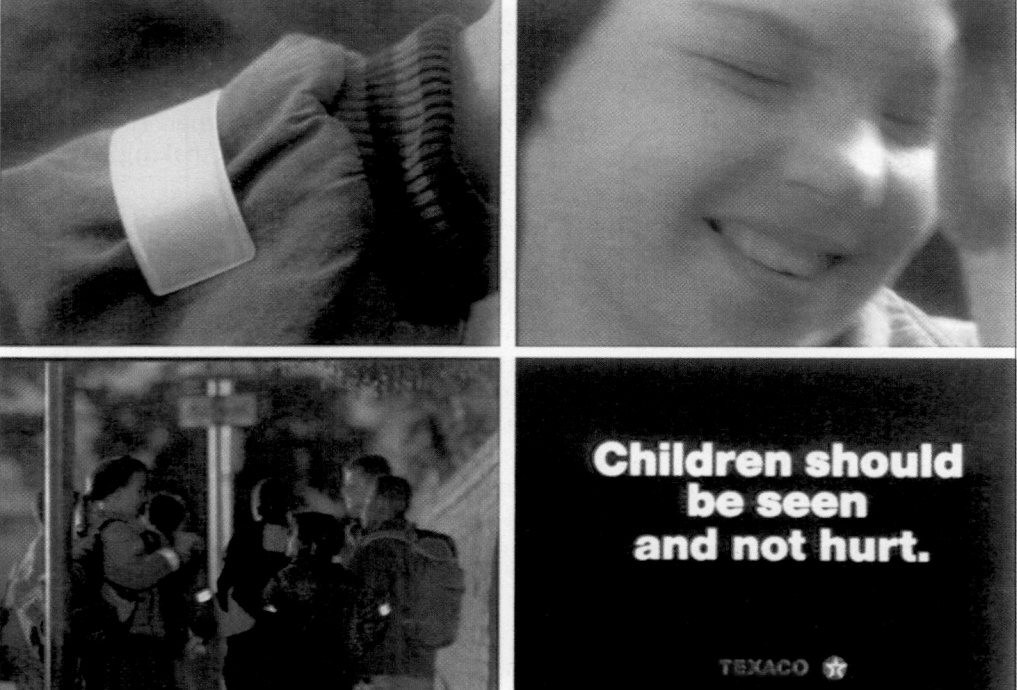

These frames from a Texaco advertisement will have started life as sketches on a storyboard.

Source: DMB&B.

announcer or an expert telling the audience authoritatively about the product on offer. Similarly, demonstrating the product in use gives rational credibility to its claims, especially when its performance is compared with that of rival products. Moving towards a more emotionally based format, some advertisements use a testimonial approach, in which a 'satisfied customer' or a celebrity swears that the product is wonderful. The kind of advertisement that begin with staements like, 'I used to have dandruff until I discovered Head and Shoulders' or end with things like, 'So, Mrs Bloggs, you definitely won't swap your one box of new improved Daz for two boxes of your old powder?' falls into this category.

Animation, as discussed at p. 618 above, clearly lends itself to television advertising, and can be used to inform, to entertain, or to create product image, just as well as using live people can. Much television advertising, though, uses a slice of life type of approach to demonstrate the product in context, with strong inputs of emotion and humour to increase the audience's involvement and entertainment impact.

Example

The PG Tips tea chimpanzee series of advertisements has become a much-loved British institution, as the chimps re-enact humorous problems from everyday life which can be resolved with a cup of tea.

Advertising for most branded products is trying to pre-sell the goods, so the advertisement has to be sufficiently impressive for its impact still to be felt some time later when consumers actually get to the supermarket.

Guidelines for broadcast presentation

There are a number of guidelines to assist in the commercial writing process. Clearly, whatever is shown must attract and hold viewers. It is important that the story is told in an entertaining yet relevant manner. This means using interesting ways of showing people interacting with the product.

The success of the Nescafé Gold Blend advertisements hinged around the use of the soap opera format. The viewer was drawn into the romantic story line, in which the coffee played a central role in bringing the lovers together. The brand then became associated with romance and sophistication, thus making a clear positioning statement.

In addition, the first few seconds of the commercial need to gain attention, in the same way as the headline in print must. This may be by a direct challenge or an unusual or evocative scene or music. There is, however, sometimes a conflict between aesthetic values and selling in advertising. An advertisement might use stunning special effects, broadcast images that remain in the mind, or create a minor masterpiece of cinematic art, but if the viewer cannot understand the commercial message or if they cannot match the correct product or service with the advertisement, then it has failed.

Advertisers do face problems if they want to avoid clichés or what might be seen as stereotypical advertisements for the sort of product involved. Car advertisements, for example, are typically about speed, performance, status or safety.

When Peugeot launched its new 406 model, it wanted to get out of that rut. Peugeot felt that consumers, saturated with technical data, saw most competing cars within a particular class as very similar in terms of performance and specification etc. To stand out from the crowd, therefore, the Peugeot 406 advertisement used powerful and emotional imagery in which the car itself played an almost incidental role. The television advertisement was shot in black and white, although some shots featured a little girl in a red coat (a reference to the film *Schindler's List*) and focused on the passing thoughts of the Peugeot driver. The impact came from images such as the girl in the path of a skidding lorry, a man giving a kiss (or possibly the kiss of life – it is deliberately ambiguous) to another man, and a protester in front of a tank. The purpose was to focus on drivers as individuals, making them feel special. This is consistent with Peugeot's slogans, 'The Drive of Your Life' and 'There Is No Such Thing as an Average Person'.

Some might call all this 'powerful art', but it remains to be seen whether it has the desired effect for Peugeot. To maximise the impact, the initial advertisement was three minutes long and shown simultaneously on every commercial terrestrial and satellite station serving the UK (Snowdon, 1996).

Overall, with television the objective is to create 30 or 60-second dramas, vignettes or jokes that are as heavily loaded with emotional connotations as with product benefits. The big advantage of television is that it does enable feelings to be attached to the product. The more lively the imagery and believable the advertisement, the greater the effect may be. In a similar way, radio has the benefit of creating lively images in the mind.

ADVERTISING MEDIA

Advertising media are called upon to perform the task of delivering the message to the consumer. The advertiser needs, therefore, to select the medium or media most appropriate to the task in hand, given their relative effectiveness and the budget available. Table 16.3 shows the percentage of total advertising spend by medium in

TABLE 16.3
Advertising expenditure across Europe: Percentage spend by medium, 1992

	TV	Print	Radio	Cinema	Outdoor	Total
Austria	27.3	52.1	13.4	0.5	6.6	100.0
Belgium	28.7	51.6	5.5	1.2	13.0	100.0
Denmark	13.4	82.1	1.4	1.2	1.9	100.0
Finland	18.2	74.3	4.6	0.1	2.9	100.0
France	29.5	51.2	6.6	0.6	12.0	100.0
Germany *	16.1	76.3	3.6	0.9	3.1	100.0
Greece	59.0	31.9	5.9	0.3	3.0	100.0
Ireland	28.6	52.4	12.3	0.4	6.2	100.0
Italy	49.5	40.9	3.5	0.2	5.9	100.0
Luxembourg						
Netherlands	15.6	72.2	2.4	0.4	9.4	100.0
Portugal	39.8	31.5	7.6	11.8	9.3	100.0
Spain	28.8	55.2	10.5	0.7	4.6	100.0
Sweden	8.7	86.0	–	0.7	4.6	100.0
United Kingdom	31.7	62.2	2.0	0.6	3.6	100.0

*Former West Germany.
Source: Euromonitor, 1995, p. 340. Reprinted with kind permission

different European countries in 1992. It is interesting to note that print takes a higher percentage than television in many countries. This is a stark reminder that most organisations either cannot afford expensive television advertising or find it inappropriate. Print media, such as local and national newspapers, special interest magazines and trade publications, have thus become the primary focus for most organisations' advertising efforts.

This section will look further at each advertising medium's relative merits, strengths and weaknesses, but first defines some of the terms commonly used in connection with advertising media.

Some definitions

Before we proceed to examine the advertising media, several basic terms need to be defined.

Reach

Reach is the percentage of the target market that is exposed to the message at least once during the relevant period. If the advertisement is estimated to reach 65 per cent of the target market, then that would be classified as 65. Note that reach is not concerned with the entire population, but only with a clearly defined target audience. Reach can be measured by newspaper or magazine circulation figures, television viewing statistics or analysis of flows past advertising boarding sites, and is normally measured over a four-week period.

Ratings

Ratings, otherwise known as TVRs, measure the percentage of all households owning a television that are viewing at a particular time. Ratings are a prime determinant of the fees charged for the various advertising slots on television.

Frequency

Frequency is the average number of times that a member of the target audience will have been exposed to a media vehicle during the specified time period (Fill, 1995).

Opportunity to see

Opportunity to see (OTS) describes how many times a member of the target audience will have an opportunity to see the advertisement. Thus, for example, a magazine might be said to offer 75 per cent coverage with an average OTS of three. This means that within a given time period, the magazine will reach 75 per cent of the target market, each of whom will have three opportunities to see the advertisement. According to White (1988), it is generally accepted that an OTS of 2.5 to three is average for a television advertising campaign, whereas a press campaign needs five or more. An OTS figure closer to 10 is probably a waste of money, as the extra OTSs are not likely to improve reach by very much and might even risk alienating the audience with overkill!

Ideally, advertisers set targets to be achieved on both **reach** and **frequency**. Sometimes, however, because of financial constraints, they have to compromise. They can either spend on achieving breadth of coverage, that is, have a high reach figure, or go for depth, that is, have a high level of frequency, but they cannot afford both. Whether reach or frequency is better depends entirely on what the advertisement's objectives are. Where awareness generation is the prime objective, then the focus may be on reach, getting a basic message to as many of the target market as possible at least once. If, however, the objective is to communicate complex information or to affect attitudes, then frequency may be more appropriate. An advertiser trying to encourage brand switching, for example, in an fmcg market may find that it takes several exposures to the advertisement before the idea of trying a different brand takes root in the consumer's mind.

Of course, when measuring reach, the wider the range of media used, the greater the chances of overlap. If, for instance a campaign uses both television and magazine advertising, some members of the target market will see neither, some will see only the television advertisement, some will see only the print advertisement, but some will see both. Although the overall reach is actually likely to be greater than if just one medium was used, the degree of overlap must enter into the calculation, since as a campaign develops the tendency is towards duplicated reach.

Television

Television's impact can be high as it not only intrudes into the consumer's home but also offers a combination of sound, colour, motion and entertainment that has a strong chance of grabbing attention and getting a message across. Provided that the television is actually switched on, the message in vision or at least sound is being delivered. That does not, however, necessarily mean that anyone is there watching or listening. One of the perennial problems in television advertising is the 'empty armchair' syndrome – the tendency of people to go to the bathroom, make a cup of coffee or do a thousand and one other things while the advertisements are on. Even if they stay in the same room, they might be chatting or otherwise making their own entertainment, distracting them from the advertising.

Nevertheless, television advertising does present a tremendous communication opportunity, as the figures for television ownership across Europe, shown in Table 2.6, indicate. Television enables a seller to communicate to a broad range of potentially large audiences. This means that television has a relatively low cost per thousand (the cost of reaching a thousand viewers) and that it has a high reach, but to largely undifferentiated audiences. Some differentiation is possible, depending on the audience profile of the programmes broadcast, and thus an advertiser can select spots to reach specific audiences, for example during sports broadcasts, but the advertising is still far from being narrowly targeted.

The problem, therefore, with television is that its wide coverage means high wastage. The cost per thousand may be low, and the number of thousands reached may be very high, but the relevance and quality of those contacts must be questioned. Television advertising time can be very expensive, especially if the advertisement is networked nationally. Actual costs will vary according to such factors as the time of day, the predicted audience profile and size, the geographic area to be covered, the length of time and number of slots purchased and the timing of negotiation. All of this means that very large bills are soon incurred.

Example

In 1993, in France alone, Procter & Gamble spent almost 687 million francs on television advertising; Nestlé France spent 662 million francs, and Henkel France, 410 million (Brillet, 1994).

Quite apart from the cost involved, television is a low-involvement medium. This means that although the senders control the message content and broadcasting, they cannot check the receiver's level of attention and understanding because the receiver is a passive participant in what is essentially one-way communication. There is no guarantee that the receiver is following the message, learning from it and remembering it positively. Retention rates tend to be low, and therefore repetition is needed, which in turn means high costs.

Furthermore, the amount of time allowed for advertising is usually strictly controlled, which tends to force up the rates for prime time advertising and to increase the competition for the best slots. The prime slots in the UK and Germany, for example, are often booked over six months ahead, and yet in Spain, advance booking does not extend beyond a few weeks. The number of commercial stations available is also low, as shown in Table 16.4, further emphasizing the limited amount of airtime. This also means that individual television stations can be attractive to advertisers, and can develop large market shares. When a single television station, such as TV1 in France, has a 42 per cent share of television audiences, it is perhaps not surprising that it attracts over 50 per cent of total television advertising revenue (Brillet, 1994).

The growth of internationally broadcast cable and satellite television channels is changing the shape of television advertising by creating pan-European segment interest groups. MTV, for example, has opened up communication with a huge youth market linked by a common music culture.

Nevertheless there are still problems with cable and satellite. The levels of penetration differ across Europe. For example it is high in the Netherlands, Belgium and Switzerland, but still low in France, Italy and Spain. Also, demand is still weak for true pan-European programmes, and there is not always the flexibility to concentrate on specific geographic markets through these channels. Thus you advertise to the whole of Europe or none of it. Last, but not least, there is the language problem. Whether the channel broadcasts

TABLE 16.4
Number of commercial television stations across Europe, 1992

	National commercial television	Public service television
Austria		1
Belgium	3	1
Denmark		1
Finland		1
France	2	3
Germany *	5	2
Greece	2	1
Ireland		1
Italy	4	1
Luxembourg		1
Netherlands	1	1
Portugal	2	1
Spain	3	1
Sweden	2	1
United Kingdom	1	3

*Former West Germany.
Source: *Euromonitor*, 1995, p. 344. Reprinted with kind permission.

in English, German or French, it is automatically going to exclude a large number of people throughout Europe who do not understand the language.

Radio

Radio has always provided an important means of broadcast communication for smaller companies operating within a restricted geographic area. It is now, however, beginning to emerge as a valuable national medium in the UK because of the growth in the number of local commercial radio stations operating and the creation of national commercial stations such as Classic FM and Atlantic 252. Table 16.5 shows the number of national and local commercial radio stations across Europe.

While still not as important as television and print, in general terms, radio can play a valuable supportive role in extending reach and increasing frequency. Despite being restricted to sound only, radio still offers wide creative and imaginative advertising possibilities, and like television, can deliver fairly specific target audiences. Narrow segments can be attractive for specialist products or services.

> ### Example
>
> Classic FM, with its programming of classical music, has created a new radio listening segment of older, affluent potential customers who otherwise would be difficult and expensive to contact as a group. Advertisers of financial products, home furnishings and other 'exclusive' products have found a very cost-effective medium.

Compared with television, radio normally offers a low cost per time slot. However, as a low-involvement medium, it is often not closely attended to, being used just as background rather than for detailed listening. More attention might be paid, however, to the car radio during the morning and evening journey to and from work. Nevertheless, learning often only takes place slowly, again requiring a high level of

TABLE 16.5
Number of commercial radio stations across Europe, 1992

	National commercial radio	Public service radio	Local commercial radio
Austria	3	1	11
Belgium	2	3	680
Denmark			200
Finland			57
France	3		1249
Germany *			137
Greece			500
Ireland	1	1	23
Italy		1	1000
Luxembourg		1	
Netherlands		1	200
Portugal	2		300
Spain	3	1	800
Sweden			
United Kingdom	2		107

*Former West Germany.
Source: Euromonitor, 1995, p. 344. Reprinted with kind permission.

repetition, carrying with it the danger of counter-productive audience irritation at hearing the same advertisements again and again. Radio is, therefore, a high-frequency medium. Television for the same budget will provide more reach, but far less frequency. The choice between them depends on objectives, and brings us back to the earlier 'reach vs frequency' discussion. Large advertisers can, however, use the two media in conjunction with each other, with radio as a means of reminding listeners of the television advertisements and reinforcing that message.

Example

In France, both Renault and Citroen feature in the top ten of television advertising, with spends of nearly 280 and 217 million francs respectively. They also feature in the top ten list of radio advertisers, spending 169 million francs each in 1993 (Brillet, 1994).

One of the main problems with radio is still that there are many commercial stations. Furthermore, the advertising slots tend to be grouped together, creating clutter, and it is difficult to build reach and make an impact. Nevertheless, the costs of production can be low, comprising scriptwriting and delivery. This, combined with the potential of a local orientation, means that radio is still accessible and attractive to the small business advertiser.

Cinema

Cinema is not a major medium, but can be used to reach selected audiences, especially younger and male. In the UK, for example, nearly 80 per cent of cinema goers are in the 15–34 age group. The improvement in the quality of cinema facilities through the development and marketing of multiplexes has led to something of a resurgence in cinema audiences over the last 10 years or so. Advertising revenue for cinemas has also risen accordingly. In 1995, for example, cinema advertising revenue in the UK was £63 million compared with only £53 million in 1994 (Lane Fox, 1996).

A cinema audience is a captive audience, sitting there with the intention of being entertained. Thus the advertiser has an increased chance of gaining the audience's attention. The quality and impact of cinema advertising can be much greater than that of television, because of the size of the screen and the quality of the sound system. Cinema is often used as a secondary medium rather than as a main medium in an advertising campaign. It can also screen advertisements, rated consistently with the film's classification, that would not necessarily be allowed on television.

Magazines

The major advantage of a printed medium is that information can be presented and then examined selectively at the leisure of the reader. A copy of a magazine tends to be passed around among a number of people and kept for quite a long time. Add to that the fact that magazines can be very closely targeted on a tightly defined audience, and the attraction of print media starts to become clear. Advertisers also have an enormous range of types and titles to choose from. Table 16.6 shows the numbers of consumer publications in various European countries in 1990.

There are several different types of magazine carrying advertising.

TABLE 16.6

Number of audited consumer publications across Europe, 1990

	Audited publications
Austria	200
Belgium	130
Denmark	48
Finland	60
France	827
Germany *	2500
Greece	300
Ireland	60
Italy	250
Luxembourg	
Netherlands	96
Portugal	200
Spain	900
Sweden	150
United Kingdom	1600

*Former West Germany.
Source: *Euromonitor*, 1995, p. 343. Reprinted with kind permission.

General and news-based magazines

With publications such as *Time*, *The Economist*, and *Reader's Digest*, an advertiser needs to ensure that the readership profile matches closely with the target segment, given the general orientation of these magazines. Further selectivity may be possible through regional or country editions.

Special interest magazines

There exists an enormous number of special interest magazines, each tailored to specific segment. As well as broad segmentation, by sex (*Bild der Frauen* for women in Germany; *Playboy* for men anywhere), age (*Just 17* for teenagers; *The Oldie* for the over-50s in the UK) and geography (*The Dalesman* for Yorkshire and its expatriates), there are many narrower criteria applied. These usually relate to lifestyle, hobbies and leisure pursuits, and enable a specialist advertiser to achieve a very high reach within those segments.

Trade and technical journals

Trade and technical journals are targeted at specific occupations, professions or industries. *Industrial Equipment News*, *The Farmer*, *Accountancy Age*, and *Chemistry in Britain* each provide a very cost-effective means of communication with groups of people who have very little in common other than their jobs.

Whatever the type of publication, the key is its ability to reach the specific target audience. New technology has created this diversity of magazines to suit a very wide range of targets.

Magazines have other benefits. Some may have a long life, especially special interest magazines which may be collected for many years, although the advertising may lose relevance. Normally, though, an edition usually lasts as long as the timing between issues. The regular publication and the stable readership can allow advertisers to build up a campaign with a series of sequential advertisements over time to reinforce the message. An advertiser may also choose to take the same slot, for example the back page which is a prime spot, to build familiarity. The advertiser may even buy several pages in the same issue, to gain a short burst of intense frequency to reinforce a message, or to present a more complex, detailed informational campaign that a single or double-page spread could not achieve.

> ### Example
>
> There has been an interesting growth in international rather than purely national magazines. *Vogue*, for instance, is a recognised name across the world, yet produces different editions to suit the different tastes of various geographic regions. Airlines also have to cater for international readerships with their in-flight magazines. BA issues *Business Life* to frequent flyers, *High Life* on certain routes and *Sinbad* for Middle Eastern routes. These magazines carry advertising not only for the airline, but also for hotels, car rentals, computers and business services etc. Long-haul flight magazines also include direct response advertising (*see* Chapter 19), capitalising on the bored captive audience. Although these in-flight magazines conform to high standards in production, their circulation and readership can obviously vary considerably.

Magazines also have one potentially powerful advantage over broadcast media, which is that the mood of the reader is likely to be more receptive. People often save a magazine until they have time to look at it properly, and because they are inherently interested in the magazine's editorial content, they do pay attention and absorb what they read. This has a knock-on effect on the advertising content too. People also tend to keep magazines for reference purposes. Thus the advertising may not prompt immediate action, but if readers suddenly come back into the market, then they know where to look for suppliers.

Improvements in print and paper technology have enabled high-quality advertising to be produced, which is especially important if the product is to be shown at its best. Advertisements for food, clothing, holidays, cosmetics, for instance, are all looking to provoke a strong positive emotional desire ('Oooh, that looks nice') through the stimulus provided by the graphic image. Some magazine advertising is almost an art form.

The specific cost of a magazine advertising slot will vary according to a number of factors. These include its circulation and readership profile, the page chosen and the position on the page, the size of the advertisement, the number of agreed insertions, the use of colour and bleed (whether the colour runs to the edge of the page or not), and any other special requirements.

The growth of truly international magazines is partly restricted by language. English-language publications are clearly fine for US and UK markets, and to some extent for business segments in Europe, but the proportion speaking English in Europe is widely variable. Figures quoted by de Mooij (1994) suggest that 72 per cent of people in the Netherlands understand English, 44 per cent in Germany and just 12 per cent in Spain. Balkanair, the Bulgarian national airline, compromises by printing all its in-flight magazine articles in both Bulgarian and English on facing pages (presumably either halving the content or doubling the cost in the process).

Newspapers

The main role of newspapers for advertisers is to communicate quickly and flexibly to a large audience. National daily papers, national Sunday papers and local daily or weekly papers between them offer a wide range of advertising opportunities and audiences. Table 16.7 shows the number of daily and Sunday national newspapers available in each European country in 1993.

Classified advertisements are usually small, very factual and often grouped under such headings as furniture, home and garden, lonely hearts etc. This is the kind of advertising used by individuals selling their personal property, or by very small businesses (for example a one-woman home hairdressing service). Such advertisements are a major feature of local and regional newspapers. *Display advertising* has wider variations in size, shape and location within the newspaper, and uses a range of graphics, copy and photography. Displayed advertisements may be grouped under special features and pages: for instance, if a local newspaper runs a weddings feature it brings together advertisers providing the various goods and services that the bride-to-be would be interested in. Such groupings offer the individual advertisers a degree of synergy. Local newspapers are an important advertising medium, not only for small businesses, but for national chains of retailers supporting local stores and car manufacturers supporting local dealerships. In the UK in 1993, local press advertising represented 20 per cent of all advertising expenditure and was the second largest medium after television (Syedain, 1995).

During the daily scan for news, readers may notice advertisements and with repetition they may eventually remember them. When a reader is actively seeking information then the newspaper, especially the classified section of a local paper, may be a prime source of products or services.

The main problem with newspaper advertising is related to its cost efficiency – if the advertiser wants to be more selective in targeting. Wastage rates can be high, as

TABLE 16.7

Number of national daily and Sunday newspapers across Europe, 1993

	Dailies	Sundays
Austria	5	
Belgium	15	
Denmark	7	5
Finland	17	
France	7	2
Germany *	63	3
Greece	11	8
Ireland	8	5
Italy	14	14
Luxembourg		
Netherlands	6	
Portugal	6	3
Spain	6	
Sweden	4	
United Kingdom	12	12

*Former West Germany.
Source: Euromonitor, 1995, p. 341. Reprinted with kind permission.

newspapers can appeal to very broad segments of the population, and the newspapers' readership research often does not deliver sufficient detail about who reads what and why (Dignam, 1995). Furthermore, compared with magazines, newspapers have a much shorter life span and can have problems with the quality of reproduction possible. Although colour and photographic reproduction quality in newspapers is rapidly improving, it is still inferior to that offered by magazines, and can be inconsistent. The same advertisement, for instance, published in different newspapers or on different days can take on varying colour values and intensities, and be more or less grainy or focused.

Advertising hoardings and outdoor media

The last group of advertising media includes posters and hoardings, as well as transport-orientated advertising media (advertising in and on buses, taxis and trains and in stations). Table 16.8 shows the number of outdoor advertising sites in various European countries in 1992.

Whatever the type of outdoor medium used, the purpose is generally the same: to provide quickly digestible messages to passers-by or to provide something for a bored passenger to look at. As with any medium, the advertising may be a one-off, or it may be part of a multimedia campaign. An advertisement at an airport for a nearby hotel would be a one-off, but long-term campaign with a very focused purpose, whereas a hoarding advertising a car would probably be only one element tied into a campaign with a theme extending across television, print and direct marketing as well.

Advertising posters range from small home-made advertisements to go on a noticeboard, to those for giant hoardings. This section concentrates on the latter group. Hoarding sites are normally sold by the month. Being in a static location, they may easily be seen 20–40 times in a month by people on their way to and from work or school etc. In the UK, over one-third of poster sites are taken by cigarette, car or drink advertisers. The reach may be small, but the frequency can be quite intense. They can, however, be affected by some unpredictable elements, out of the control of the advertiser. Bad weather means that people will spend less time out of doors, and are certainly not going to be positively receptive to outdoor advertising. Hoardings and posters are also vulnerable to the attentions of those who think they can improve on the existing message with a bit of graffiti or fly posting.

Nevertheless, hoardings offer an exciting medium with great deal of creative scope, capitalising on their size and location. Backlighting, for example, can give a clearer, sharper image, while the potential of video hoardings to create moving, changing messages opens up many possibilities. The latter is especially valuable for attracting passers-by to a restaurant or leisure facility, for example. It pays, however, to be careful in the location of such ultra-creative billboards, since to be the cause of multiple pile-ups by distracting drivers' attention is not desirable PR!

Size is one of the greatest assets of the advertising hoarding, creating impact. Over 80 per cent of hoarding space in the UK is taken by 4-, 6- or 48-sheet sites (a 48-sheet hoarding is 10 feet by 24 feet). Also, sites can be selected, if available, according to the match between traffic flows and target audience. However, in appealing to a mobile audience, the message needs to be simple and thus usually links with other elements of a wider campaign, either for generating initial awareness or on a reminder and reinforcement basis.

Finally, there are the *transport orientated media*. These include advertisements in rail or bus stations, which capture and occupy the attention of waiting passengers who have nothing better to do for a while than read the advertisements. Similarly, advertising inside

TABLE 16.8
Number of outdoor advertising sites across Europe, 1992

	Sites
Austria	118800
Belgium	100000
Denmark	15165
Finland	110000
France	400000
Germany *	375798
Greece	9080
Ireland	5484
Italy	289000
Luxembourg	
Netherlands	75000
Portugal	22100
Spain	28000
Sweden	12250
United Kingdom	119455

*Former West Germany.
Source: Euromonitor, 1995, p. 346. Reprinted with kind permission.

Source: Simons Palmer Denton Clemmow & Johnson.

The combination of a well-known personality and a dramatic visual makes this Nike poster difficult to ignore.

trains, taxis and buses has a captive audience for as long as the journey takes. In Switzerland, McDonald's have taken this to the extent of franchising railway catering carriages. Advertising on the outside of vehicles, perhaps even going so as far as to repaint an entire bus with an advertisement, extends the reach of the advertisement to anyone who happens to be around the vehicle's route.

USING ADVERTISING AGENCIES

It is not surprising, given the complexity and expense involved, that many organisations employ an agency to handle the development and implementation of advertising programmes. It is important, however, to select the right kind of agency, not only in terms of their practical ability to do what needs to be done and to solve the problems that need to be solved, but also in terms of their creativity, their culture and their ability to empathise with the product and its target market. In this section, therefore, we will examine briefly the different types of advertising agency, then we discuss criteria for selecting an agency, and finally, there will be a few thoughts on client–agency relationships.

Full service agencies

Full service agencies provide a full range of services, including research, creative work, artwork, media buying etc. Larger agencies might also have subsidiaries or sister companies in the sales promotion, PR or direct marketing fields. If a client's account is not large, the agency may bill separately for creative work. With large accounts, some discount can be achieved through the 15 per cent agency commission earned for media buying. Using a full service agency does not mean that the client abdicates all responsibility, but that the advertising is developed jointly. The advantages are that specialist skills can be drawn on as needed; new, different perspectives on the communication problem may be gained; and the client can change agencies if not satisfied. Using a full service agency is also easier to manage and control, and there is less risk of sensitive information leaking out, because everything is self-contained (Smith, 1993). As with any buyer – supplier liaison, however, the quality of the relationship, trust and understanding are all very important.

Limited service agencies

Limited service agencies tend to specialise in one or a small number of parts of the total process. Within advertising, agencies may specialise in creative work, media buying or advertising research, for example. Such agencies may bid on a speculative basis, receiving a fee only for the proposals selected. The advantage of the limited service agency is that it enables the client to select the best talent to suit their various needs. It does, however, mean more work in co-ordinating the effort involved, and there is a risk of information leaks as more different organisations become involved (Smith, 1993).

A few very large organisations might prefer to develop their own expertise in-house, with dedicated staff to manage the campaign. The in-house department may provide the full range of services or supplement their skills from external sources such as limited service agencies with particular specialisms. At the opposite extreme, there are special difficulties for smaller businesses, as they do not have the expertise or the amount of money to spend to attract significant agency interest. In such a business the owner or the individual responsible for all marketing may handle media and campaign development.

Working in-house gives the advertiser more control and there is no risk of over-dependency on an outside agency. It may even save money, although an in-house department may not have the same media purchasing power as an agency. The organisation will, however, have to be sensitive to potential gaps in its expertise, as well as the risk of becoming too blinkered in its approach to its own advertising. Using outside agencies does at least bring fresh and objective minds to the problem.

Selecting an agency

Clearly, selecting an agency is very important since an agency's work can potentially make or break a product. Different writers suggest different checklists against which to measure the appropriateness of any given agency. The following list has been compiled from the work of Smith (1993), White (1988), and Wilmshurst (1985) and is also shown in Fig 16.2.

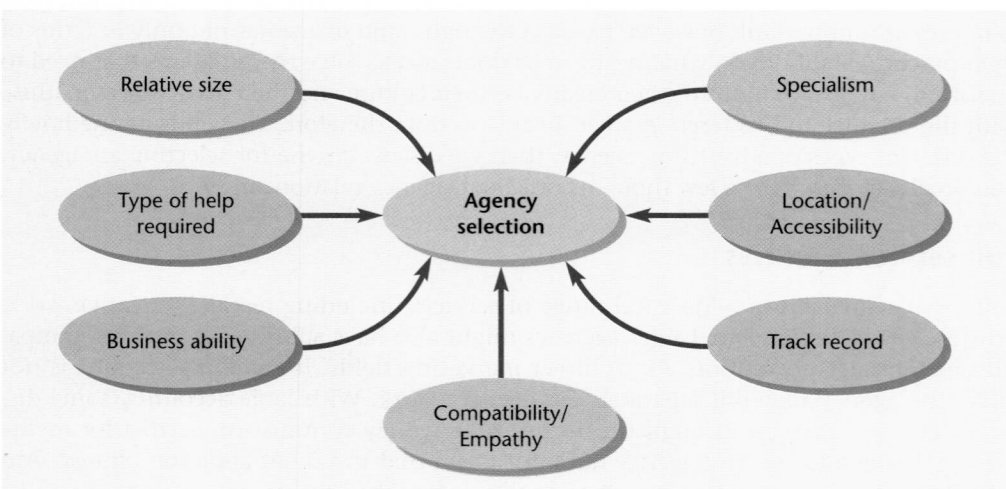

FIGURE 16.2

Criteria for selecting an advertising agency

Relative size of agency and client

As already mentioned, it might be useful to try to match the relative sizes of the client and the agency, certainly in terms of the proposed advertising spend. This is to ensure the right level of mutual respect, attention and importance. The client might also want to think ahead strategically, and choose an agency that will either grow with the client or be able to meet increased future needs. This might mean coping with a bigger account or coping with international advertising.

Location and accessibility

A smaller business with a limited geographic market might prefer to work with a small agency which has deep local knowledge and understanding. A larger business, wishing to keep a close eye on what the agency is doing and thus wanting frequent face-to-face meetings with the account team, might also find it more convenient to use an agency located nearby.

Type of help required

Clearly, a client wants an agency that can supply the kinds of services and expertise required. The client might want a full service agency, or just specialised help in media buying, for example. Any prospective agency thus needs to be measured against its ability to deliver an appropriate package.

Specialism

Some agencies have a reputation for specialising in particular products or services, for example higher education advertising or financial services advertising. Some clients might find this attractive on the basis that they can be sure the agency has detailed knowledge of the relevant marketing and competitive environments. Others, however, might find it off-putting. They might feel that the agency works for the client's competitors or that they are 'stale' from doing too much work in one field. Nevertheless, a degree of relevant experience in some related area might be a good indicator of an agency's ability to handle this new account.

Track record

Regardless of whether the agency specialises in particular types of advertising or not, a new client is going to be interested in its track record. How has the agency grown? Who is on its client list? How creative is its work? How effective is its work? Does it seem able to retain its clients, generate repeat business from them and build strong relationships?

Compatibility, empathy, and personal chemistry

Compatibility and empathy are about corporate culture and outlook and about individual personalities. Clearly a client wants an agency that is sympathetic to what the client is trying to achieve and can find the right way of talking to the target audience. A great deal of this depends on client–agency communication and the ability of the agency personnel who will be working on the account to get on well with the individuals from the client company with whom they will be liaising. It is quite legitimate, therefore, for the client to ask just who will be working on the account.

Business ability

Advertising is extremely expensive and so a client wants to be reassured that their agency can work within budget, cost effectively, efficiently and within deadlines. This might, therefore, mean looking at their research and planning capabilities. Furthermore, a client should make sure that they understand the basis upon which they will be charged by the agency and precisely what is and is not included.

TABLE 16.9

Advertising agency–client relationships

10 factors likely to cause relationship breakdown	Respondents citing factor (%)	10 factors likely to promote a positive relationship	Respondents citing factor (%)
Unreliable delivery	48	Mutual trust	51
Lack of personal chemistry	44	Creative excellence	47
Poor creative performance	40	Understanding the brand	46
Lack of proactive thinking	34	Proactive thinking	38
Poor communication	26	Long-term partnership	23
Lack of strategic input	24	Working within budget	20
Going over budget	23	Continuous improvement	20
Poor business results	19	Planning effectiveness	19
Inability to learn from experience	19	Senior management contact	16
Over-priced production	14	Respect for deadlines	15

Source: The Marketing Forum 1995. Reprinted with kind permission.

The client–agency relationship

Whatever the type of agency used, a good relationship is essential. With sound briefing, mutual understanding, and an agreed system of remuneration, the agency becomes an extension of the organisation's own marketing team. Co-operation may depend upon mutual importance. For instance, a large client working with a large agency is fine, but a small client dealing with a large agency may become lost. There may be other constraints affecting agency choice. If an agency deals with a competitor, for example, then the conflict of interest needs to be avoided.

Research undertaken at the Marketing Forum 1995 by Richmond Events Ltd and published in *Marketing* (1996b) among both agencies and clients looked at the factors most likely to cause a breakdown in client–agency relationships, and the factors most likely to promote a positive relationship. The top ten factors cited in each category are shown in Table 16.9.

It is clear that ability to deliver the goods, in terms of timing, creative content and within budget, is crucial to success. Communication and developing deeper mutual understanding and trust are also important if the agency is going to diagnose, understand and solve the client's advertising problem. If these points are taken out of the advertising agency context, they can be seen to be the fundamental criteria for any good buyer–supplier relationship.

DEVELOPING AN ADVERTISING CAMPAIGN

It almost impossible that one free-standing advertisement in the press or on television would be sufficient to achieve the results expected, in terms of the impact on the target audience. Normally, advertisers think about a campaign which involves a predetermined theme but is communicated through a series of messages placed in selected media chosen for their expected cumulative impact on the specified target audience. The elements of the campaign are expected to integrate synergistically so that each advertisement placed both supports and is supported by the others. Campaigns can run for varying lengths of time, for a few weeks, for a season, or for many years with little change in formulation. The annual drink – drive campaigns discussed earlier at p. 616, for example, change their approach and message slightly every year, although the broad thrust is always consistent. They also tend to focus mainly on the few weeks around Christmas and New Year.

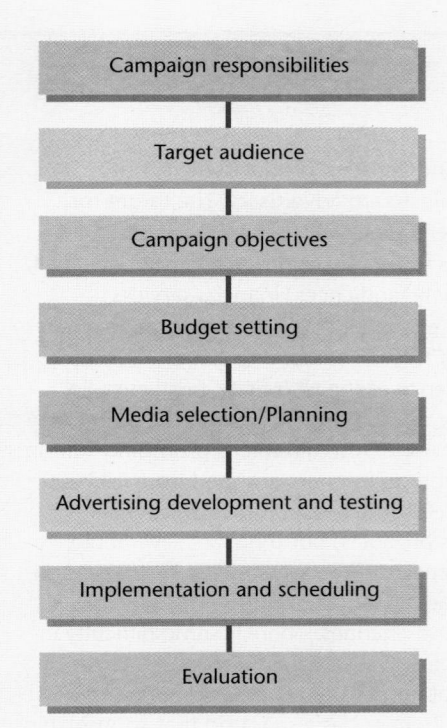

There are a number of stages in the development of an advertising campaign. Although the emphasis will vary from situation to situation, each stage at least acknowledges a need for careful management assessment and decision making. The stages are shown in Fig 16.3 and are discussed in turn below.

Deciding on campaign responsibilities

This is an important question of organisational structure and 'ownership' of the campaign. If management is devolved on a product basis, then overall responsibility may rest with the brand or product manager. This certainly helps to ensure that the campaign integrates with sales promotion, selling, production planning etc, since the brand manager is very well versed in all aspects of the product's life. If, however, management is devolved on a functional basis, then the responsibility for an advertising campaign will lie with the advertising and promotion manager. This means that the campaign benefits from depth of advertising expertise, but lacks the involvement with the product that a brand manager would supply. Whatever the arrangement, it is essential to define who is ultimately responsible for what tasks and what elements of the budget.

FIGURE 16.3

Stages in developing an advertising campaign

Example

In the motor industry, companies such as Renault, Ford and Vauxhall/Opel have enormous advertising budgets covering many different car models. All three of these companies have decided, therefore, to create brand teams each of which has direct responsibility for one or two models. Vauxhall, for example, created five teams (Corsa and Tigra; Astra; Cavalier and Calibra; Omega and off-roaders; and finally, light commercial vehicles. Each team consists of a marketing manager and two brand managers and is responsible for its own advertising and marketing and ultimately for meeting its profit targets (Snowdon, 1995). The advantage of this kind of delegation is that the team has a tight focus and thus the interests of the individual car models will be looked after. It is thus also likely that the advertising campaigns will be tightly focused. The disadvantages, however, are that there might be some loss of overall corporate consistency in the different campaigns, and that the advertising agency has to work with five different teams rather than with one.

Selecting the target audience

As discussed at pp. 576 *et seq.*, knowing who you are talking to is the foundation of good communication. Based on segmentation strategy, the target audience represents the group at whom the communication is aimed within the market. In some cases, the segment and the target audience may be one and the same. Sometimes, however, the target audience may be a subdivision of the segment. If, for instance, an organisation served a particular hobby segment, different approaches to advertising would be taken depending on whether they wanted to talk to serious, casual, high spenders, low spenders, general interest or specific interest subgroups. This underlines the need to understand the market and the range of target audiences within it.

Christian Cable TV

The launch date for the first mainstream Christian television channel in the UK was expected to be 14 October 1996. Critical to its success is the ability to attract viewers and advertisers. The new channel planned to occupy the moral high ground on many issues and to present high quality programmes with a Christian theme or at least with appropriate content for a Christian audience. Sex, violence, drink and antisocial behaviour are out, unless they are associated with an informed debate. In the USA, Christian cable channels achieve very high viewing figures. Ark 2, the new UK channel, was hoping to emulate that success, not by 'bible bashing' and preaching, but by being 'entertaining, challenging and engaging', according to the chief executive.

The target audience for the new channel was not restricted to church goers. That would have locked them into less than 10 per cent of the British population who attend church. The bigger target was the 70 per cent who believe in God, the mainstream audience, who could be persuaded to view the channel if the scheduling and programming was carefully managed. Building a regular audience is important for any commercial broadcaster, as that is primarily what interests advertisers. The new channel did not just want Christian product sellers, but appropriate mainstream advertisers. The target for advertising revenue in the first year was just £1.5 million, but has to be viewed in the context of a small, albeit high quality, audience. Financial services companies, for example, could be interested in an audience with Christian values and low credit risks.

If the experience of the UK's first Christian radio station, Premier, is used as an example, the going may not be easy for Ark 2. After Premier's promising start in 1995, the number of listeners dropped from 193 000 per quarter to 109 000. Most of the advertisers are selling religious products, but there are several big, mainstream names such as Sainsbury's, *The Times* and *The Economist* advertising alongside Christian organisations and charities. There is some difficulty in meeting all advertisers' scheduling requests, as the audience do not appreciate advertising during religious services. Premier has also found that sponsorship has become a far bigger contributor to overall revenue than expected. Ark 2, therefore, hoped that a careful mix of sponsorship and advertising from commercial and charity organisations would enable them to achieve their objectives in the first year.

Sources: Griffiths (1996); Simpson (1996).

A profile of the target audience increases the chances of successful promotion and communication. Any details, such as location, media viewing (or listening or reading) habits, geodemographics, attitudes and values can be used to shape the propositions contained within the campaign or to direct the creative approach and media choice.

> ### *Example*
>
> An advertising agency thinking about advertising a brand of watches in different European countries found from research that in general, Italians treat watches like fashion accessories, and might own several to co-ordinate with different outfits. In contrast, Germans assess watches according to the sophistication of their technology and the number of different functions built in, whereas the British just want a functional and reliable way of telling the time. Clearly, these differences in target market attitudes towards watches will lead to fundamentally different advertising approaches for the brand in those countries.

In organisational markets, the focus is likely to be on understanding the decision-making processes and buying centre membership (*see* Chapter 4), to help create an industry-based segmentation and communication approach.

Whatever the type of product, if the assessment of the target audience is incomplete or woolly, there may be problems in directing campaign efforts later.

Gates Energy Products aimed its advertisements for its Hydritech batteries specifically at designers of cellular telephones.

Campaign objectives

Communication objectives were considered at pp. 587 *et seq.*, and provide a clear view of what the advertising should accomplish. These objectives need to be specific, measurable and time related. They must also indicate the level of change sought, defining a specific outcome from the advertising task. If there are no measurable objectives, how can achievements be recognised, and success or failure judged?

Most advertising is focused on some stage of a response hierarchy model, such as those presented in Fig 15.7. These models highlight the stages in the process of consumer decision making from initial exposure and awareness through to post-purchase review. Issues such as liking, awareness or knowledge, preference and conviction are important parts of that process, and advertising can aim to influence any one of them. These can thus be translated into advertising objectives with measurable targets for awareness generation, product trial and/or repurchase, attitude creation or shifts, or positioning or preferences in comparison with the competition.

These objectives should be driven by the agreed marketing strategy and plan. Note the difference between marketing and advertising objectives. Sales and market share targets are legitimate marketing objectives as they represent the outcomes of a range of marketing mix decisions. Advertising, however, is just one element contributing to that process, and is designed to achieve specific tasks, but not necessarily exclusively sales.

Campaign budgets

Developing a communication budget was considered at pp. 592 *et seq.* Look back to these pages to refresh your memory on the methods of budget setting. Remember that there is no one right or wrong sum to allocate to a campaign, and often a combination of the methods proposed earlier acts as a guide.

Often the setting of budgets is an iterative process, developing and being modified as the campaign takes shape. There is a direct link between budgets and objectives such that a modification in one area is almost certainly likely to have an impact in the other. Even if the underlying philosophy of the budget is the 'objective and task' approach, practicality still means that most budgets are constrained in some way by the cash available. This forces managers to plan carefully and to consider a range of options in order to be as cost effective as possible in the achievement of the specified objectives.

The first job is to link marketing objectives with the tasks expected of advertising and promotion. Targets may be set, for example, in relation to awareness levels, trial and repeat purchases. Not all these targets would be achieved by advertising alone. Sales promotion, and of course product formulation, may play a big part in repeat purchase behaviour.

Increasingly, computerised models are being introduced to relate objectives and budgets more closely. However, there is still room for managerial judgement and common sense, operating from experience and knowledge of what makes customers and competitors tick. It has been argued that establishing the budget for advertising and marketing is as much a political process as a management task (Piercy, 1987).

Media selection and planning

The various media options were considered individually at pp. 624 *et seq.* The large range of alternative media needs to be reduced down to manageable options and then scheduling (discussed at p. 642) planned to achieve the desired results. The resultant media plan must be detailed and specific. Actual media vehicles must be specified, as well as when, where, how much and how often. This means planning bookings by date, time and space. The plan is the means by which exposure and awareness levels can be achieved. The important aim is to ensure a reasonable fit between the media vehicles considered and the target audience so that sufficient reach and frequency is achieved to allow the real objectives of the advertising a fighting chance of success. This is becoming more difficult as audience profiles and markets change (Mueller-Heumann, 1992).

There are two main approaches to reaching the target audience. The first is a 'shot-gun' approach which aims to reach a large number of people across all segments, whether targets or not, accepting that there will be considerable waste. Much television advertising falls into this category. The second approach aims to achieve a close match between the target audience and the advertising media, such as would be the case with a hobby or specific interest group. This approach assumes that the advertiser has a good understanding of the segments and that the media exist for reaching them.

The profile of activity is specified in the media plan which summarises the choices made regarding medium, vehicle and scheduling. The plan has an important role to play in integrating the campaign effort into the rest of the marketing plan and in communicating requirements clearly to any support agencies.

A number of considerations guide the selection of media, as shown in Fig 16.4. These are discussed briefly below.

Campaign objectives

The media selected must be such as will ensure consistency with the overall objectives for the campaign in terms of awareness, reach etc.

Target audience

The target audience is critical to guiding the detailed media selection. As close a fit as possible is required between medium and audience.

Competitive factors

A consideration of the competition includes examining what they have been doing, where they have been doing it, and with what outcomes. A decision may have to be made whether to use the same media as the competition or to innovate.

FIGURE 16.4

Factors influencing media selection

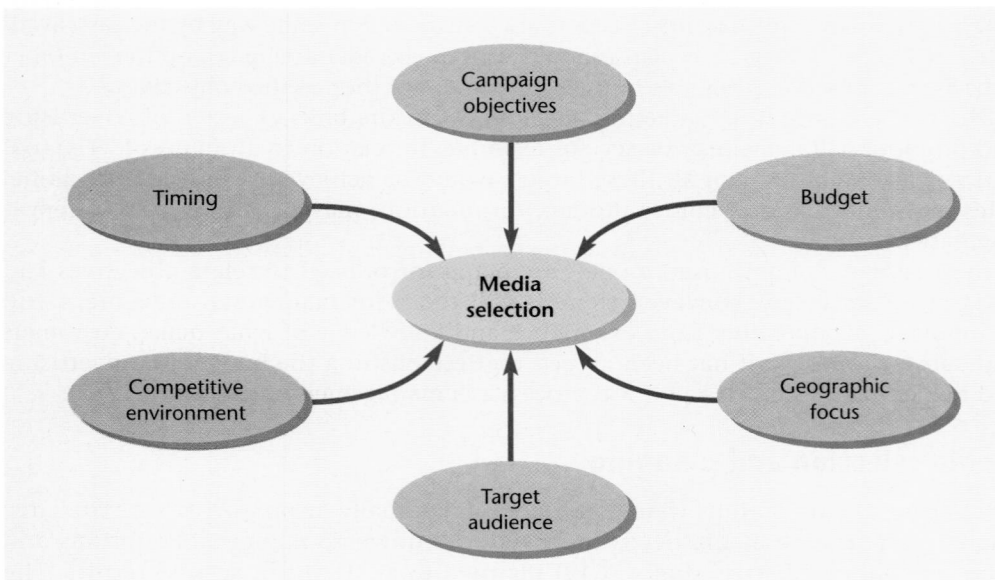

Geographical focus

The target audience may be international, national or regional, and sometimes a selection of media or vehicles may have to be used to reach dispersed groups within the target audience.

Budget constraints

As discussed at p. 639, practicality and affordability usually enter into the planning at some stage. A proposal of 20 prime time slots on television might well give the chief accountant apoplexy and have to be replaced with a more modest print campaign which makes its impact through stunning creativity.

Timing

The plan needs to take into account any lead in or build-up time, particularly if the product's sales have a strong element of seasonality. Perfumes and aftershaves, for example, look to Christmas as a strong selling period. Advertisers of these products use glossy magazine advertising all year round, but in the weeks up to Christmas, add intensive and expensive television campaigns (it's a good job we don't have smellyvision yet) to coincide with consumers' decision making for gifts. Similarly, timing is important in launching new a product, to make sure that the right level of awareness, understanding and desire have been generated by the time the product is actually available.

As with any plan, it should provide the reader with a clear justification of the rationale behind the decisions, and should act as a guide as to how it integrates with other marketing activities.

Advertising development and testing

At this stage, the advertisements themselves are designed and made, ready for broadcasting or printing. The creative issues involved have already been covered elsewhere within this chapter. As the advertisement evolves, **pre-testing** is often used to check that the content, message and impact are as expected. This is particularly important with television advertising which is relatively expensive to produce and broadcast, and also would represent an extremely public embarrassment if it failed.

Tests are, therefore, built in at various stages of the advertisement's development. Initial concepts and storyboards can be discussed with a sample of members of the target audience to see if they can understand the message and relate to the scenario or images in the proposed advertisement. Slightly further on in the process, a rough video of the advertisement (not the full production – just enough to give a flavour of the finished piece) can also be tested. This allows final adjustments to be made before the finished advertisement is produced. Even then, further testing can reassure the agency and the client that the advertisement is absolutely ready for release. Print advertisements can similarly be tested at various stages of their development, using rough sketches, mock-ups and then the finished advertisement.

White (1988) suggests a number of questions that pre-testing advertisements might answer, and these are summarised in Fig 16.5.

Pre-testing is a valuable exercise, but its outcomes should be approached with some caution. The testing conditions are rather artificial, by necessity, and audiences (assuming even that the testers can assemble a truly representative audience) who react in certain ways to seeing an advertisement in a theatre or church hall might respond very differently if they saw that same advertisement in their own homes under 'normal' viewing conditions.

FIGURE 16.5

Information gained from pre-testing advertisements

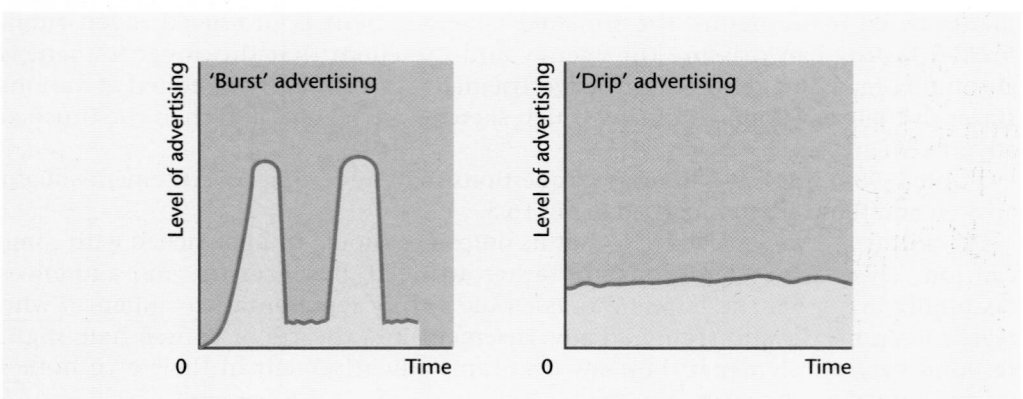

Implementation and scheduling

In the implementation phase, a number of professional experts may be needed to develop and deliver the advertising campaign. These will include graphic designers, photographers, commercial artists, copywriters, research specialists and, not least, media and production companies. The role of the advertising manager is to co-ordinate and select these professionals within a budget to achieve the planned objectives.

A key part of the implementation phase is the scheduling of the campaign. This describes the frequency and intensity of effort and guides all production decisions. There are many different scheduling patterns (Sissors and Bumba, 1989). Sometimes, advertising takes place in *bursts*, as shown in Fig 16.6. This means short-term, intense advertising activity, such as that often found with new product launches. Most organisations do not have the resources (or the inclination) to keep up such intense advertising activity indefinitely, and thus the bursts are few and far between. The alternative is to spread the advertising budget out more evenly, by advertising in *drips*, also shown in Fig 16.6. The advertising activity is less intense, but more persistent. Reminder advertising for a frequently purchased mature product might take place in drips rather than bursts.

A number of factors will help to determine the overall schedule, as shown in figure 16.7. These are discussed in turn, briefly, below.

Marketing factors

Marketing factors might influence the speed of the impact required. An organisation launching a new product or responding to a competitor's comparative advertising might want to make a quick impact, for example.

FIGURE 16.6

Advertising expenditure strategies: 'bursts' and 'drips'

FIGURE 16.7

Factors
influencing
advertising
schedules

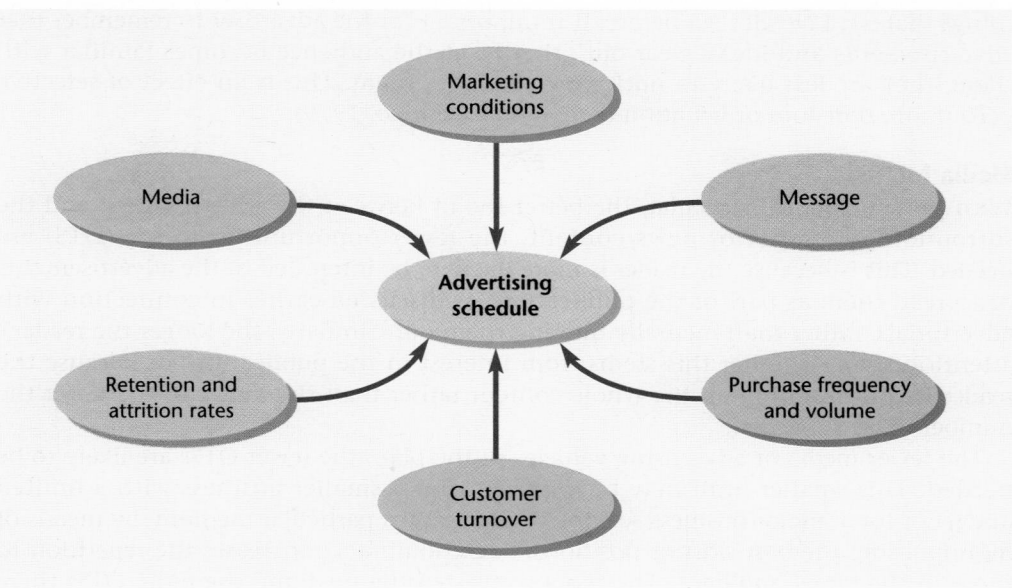

The turnover of customers in the market

If turnover of customers is high, then there is a need to advertise more frequently to keep the message available for new entrants into the market.

Purchase frequency and volatility

If demand is highly seasonal or perishable, then the scheduling might provide for a short period of high-frequency advertising. The peak time for advertising perfumes and toys, for example, is in the run-up to Christmas. Similarly, various chocolate products peak at Easter or Mother's day, for example. Alternatively, there may be a link with brand loyalty. Higher loyalty may need less frequency, provided the product is not under competitive attack. This is, however, a dangerous assumption.

Retention and attrition rates

If the danger of forgetting is high, then the advertiser is likely to need a more active campaign implemented at regular intervals. Different groups learn and forget at different rates. Therefore these retention and attrition rates of the target audience are yet another assessment that needs to be made.

Message factors

A campaign for a new product may need more repetition than one for an established product, because of the newness of the message. More generally, simple messages, or those that stand out from the crowd demand less repetition. Similarly, smaller advertisements or those placed in less noticeable spots within a print medium may need more frequency to make sure they are seen.

In broadcast media, however, there is some debate over the relative effectiveness of 10, 30 and 60-second slots. It seems that longer is not always better. Ten seconds may be sufficient to generate awareness, through a short sharp impact. Two 30-second slots may be more powerful than one of 60 seconds. However, such a general debate is rather meaningless, since so much depends on the context of the advertising. If there are many other messages (and particularly if they are direct competitor's messages) in the pool, then a much greater impact will have to be made just to create awareness. Finally, impact is not just an issue of how many seconds you buy, it is about what you do with them. A 10-second blast of something stunningly novel and memorable is going to achieve far more than 60 seconds of an advertisement that is a rehash of things that we have all seen before. It is important for the advertiser to remember that advertisements and ideas 'wear out', that is, as the audience becomes familiar with them, they are less likely to notice or remember them. This is an effect of selective perception, boredom or irritation (Petty and Cacioppo, 1979).

Media factors

With print media in particular, the better the fit between the advertisement and the surrounding editorial or news content, the fewer opportunities to see (OTS) are needed. This is because the reader is more likely to be interested in the advertisements or to read them as part of the publication, as discussed earlier in connection with advertorials, rather than mentally filtering them out. Similarly, the longer the reader's attention span, whether this stems from interest in the publication, or because the reader is concentrating on the whole content rather than skimming it, the fewer the number of OTSs needed.

The fewer media or advertising vehicles in the plan, the fewer OTSs are likely to be needed. This smaller limit may be important for a smaller business with a limited budget or for a major business seeking to dominate a particular medium by means of monopolising the best slots or positions. Such dominance increases the repetition to those in the target audience. The more congested the medium, the more OTSs there need to be, to cut through the background 'noise'.

Forgetting is part of our daily lives, and so any campaign must seek to minimise forgetting. Time is an important factor, and without reminder advertising or other promotional support, the tendency is to forget. There are exceptions, however. For a consumer durable product, for example, the high involvement necessary may assist in decreasing the rate of forgetting because the purchaser has put a great deal of time and conscious effort into making the decision, as discussed in Chapter 3.

None of this makes one media plan better than another. It depends upon objectives and the particular market circumstances prevailing. If the product is new or seasonal a more intensive effort may be appropriate. The scheduling plan may, of course, evolve over time. During the introduction stage of the product life cycle an intensive burst of advertising will launch the product, and this may then be followed by a more spread out campaign as the growth stage finishes. Creating awareness in the first place is expensive, but critical to a product's success.

Campaign evaluation

The evaluation is perhaps the most critical part of whole campaign process. This stage exists not only to assess the effectiveness of the campaign mounted, but also to provide valuable learning for the future.

There are two stages in evaluation. *Interim evaluation* enables a campaign to be revised and adjusted before completion to improve its effectiveness. It enables a closer match to be achieved between advertising objectives and the emerging campaign results.

Alternatively or additionally, *exit evaluation* is undertaken at the end of the campaign. A number of **post-tests** are possible, and some of them are defined below.

Aided (prompted) recall

In aided (prompted) recall pictures of advertisements are shown to a sample audience Questions are asked about whether they have noticed these advertisements on television, the radio or in print. The research may go further to investigate level of comprehension.

Unaided (spontaneous) recall

In sponteneous, or unaided recall, questions are asked about what advertisements the respondent has noticed recently. No clues are given, so this exercise is much harder for the respondent to do. Sometimes, however, the exercise may be focused on a specific product area, but it is still up to the respondent to remember what advertising they have seen or heard.

Attitude tests
Questions are formulated to measure the respondent's attitude to a product. An attitude test may take place both before and after the advertising campaign so that the level of attitude change effected by the advertising can be measured.

Enquiry Tests
The success of the advertising is measured by the number of requests for product information, premiums or sales visits generated. The enquiry test is a simple measure, and is especially useful for, small businesses with small budgets, who need to make sure that their advertising works harder. Early in a new campaign, a direct response mechanism (see Chapter 19) may be deliberately built in to see what interest is being generated. This gives feedback before the campaign is expanded.

Sales tests
Sales tests are a form of controlled experiment in which an advertising campaign may be run in one area, but not in another. Although it is difficult to keep all other things equal, the running of such a test does give some indication of the impact of the advertising on retail sales etc.

The method of evaluation selected will depend on the original objectives. If these are related to awareness or attitude change, then recognition, recall tests or attitude change tests are appropriate. If the purpose is to influence sales or market share, then the number of enquiries received or sales tests may be used, although neither of these may be a fair assessment, because advertising is only one of many factors contributing to sales. It must be remembered that just because a product's advertisement is recognised or its details are recalled, purchase does not necessarily follow. The consumer might not be able to find anywhere convenient that sells the product, or they might find the price a little too high, or they might be well disposed towards the product, but have even stronger feelings about the competition. These constraints emphasise the need for a fully integrated marketing mix with all its elements working in harmony with each other.

CHAPTER SUMMARY

Advertising is a non-personal form of communication with an identified sponsor, using any form of mass media. It can relate to products, communicating their features, benefits and competitive advantage, or it can relate to organisations, contributing to a strong corporate image or communicating a corporate view on an issue. Advertising can thus help to create awareness, build image and attitudes and then reinforce those attitudes through reminders. It is an invaluable support for other elements of the promotional mix, for example by creating awareness and positive attitudes towards an organisation in preparation for a sales team, or by communicating sales promotions. Advertising also has strategic uses within the wider marketing mix. It can contribute to product positioning, thus supporting a premium price, or it could help to even out seasonal fluctuations in demand.

The advertising message is extremely important. It has to be informative, persuasive and attention grabbing. It has to be appropriate for the target audience and thus speak to them in terms they can relate to. There are several types of creative appeal that advertisers can use: rational, emotional and product centred. Once the message and its appeal have been decided, the advertisement has to be prepared for print or broadcasting. In either case, the advertisement has to be relevant to the target audience, making a sufficient impact to get the desired message across and to get the audience to act on it.

The advertiser has a wide choice of media. Television has a wide reach across the whole population, but it can be difficult to target a specific market segment precisely. Radio can deliver fairly specific target audiences, and is an attractive medium for smaller companies operating in a defined geographic area covered by a local radio station. Cinema is a relatively minor medium delivering captive, well-profiled audiences. It can make a big impact on the audience because of the quality of the sound and the size of the screen.

Print media broadly consist of magazines and newspapers. Magazines tend to have well-defined readerships who are receptive to the content of advertisements relevant to the magazine's theme. Magazines tend to have a long life span, with each copy being passed around several readers, each of whom is likely to make time to read the publication 'properly'. Newspapers, on the other hand, have a very short life span and are often skimmed rather than read properly. A reader is unlikely to read through the same copy more than once. Outdoor media includes advertising hoardings, posters and transport-related media. They can provide easily digested messages which attract the attention of bored passengers or passers-by. They can generate high frequency as people tend to pass the same sites regularly, but can be spoiled by the weather and the ambience of their location.

Since advertising is so expensive and often requires a lot of creativity if it is to attract attention and communicate a complex message, advertising agencies are often used to provide expertise. Choosing an agency is an important task, and an organisation needs to think carefully about the relevant criteria for choice. Once the client has signed up an agency, it is then important to continue to communicate and to build a strong mutual understanding, with both sides contributing according to expectations.

Managing advertising within an organisation involves a number of stages. First, campaign responsibilities need to be decided so that the process and the budget are kept under proper control. Once the target market and their broad communication needs have been defined, specific campaign objectives can be developed. Next, the budget can be set in the light of the desired objectives. Media choices, based on the habits of the target audience, the requirements of the planned message and the desired reach and frequency, can then be made. Meanwhile, the advertisements themselves are developed. Testing can be built in at various stages of this development to ensure that the right message is getting across in the right kind of way with the right kind of effect. Once the advertising has been fully developed, it can be implemented. Both during and after the campaign, managers will assess the advertising's effectiveness, using aided or unaided recall, enquiry tests or sales tests, depending on the original objectives.

Key words and phrases

Advertising	*Frequency*	*Pre-testing*
Advertising media	*Full service agencies*	*Reach*
Advertorial	*Institutional advertising*	*Reminder and reinforcement advertising*
Comparative advertising	*Layout*	
Competitive advertising	*Limited service agencies*	*Slice of life*
Copywriting	*Pioneer advertising*	*Story board*
Creative appeal	*Post-testing*	

QUESTIONS FOR REVIEW

16.1 In what ways can advertising support the other elements of the promotional mix?

16.2 What is *comparative advertising* and what are the risks of using it?

16.3 What are the different ways in which *product-orientated appeal*s can be used?

16.4 Define *reach* and *frequency*. Why might there be a conflict between them in practice?

16.5 What can *radio* offer as an advertising medium to a small business?

16.6 What advantages might *cinema advertising* have over *television*?

16.7 In what ways can *magazines* be a better advertising medium than *newspapers*?

16.8 What are the relative advantages and disadvantages of:

(a) full service advertising agencies;

(b) limited service agencies; and

(c) handing advertising in-house?

16.9 Describe the *stages* in developing an advertising campaign.

16.10 What can an advertiser gain from *pre-testing* advertisements?

QUESTIONS FOR DISCUSSION

16.1 Find examples of advertising that uses:

(a) a rational appeal; and

(b) a fear appeal.

Why do you think the advertisers have chosen these approaches?

16.2 What are the guidelines for good copy for a print advertisement? Find a print advertisement and discuss the extent to which it conforms with those guidelines.

16.3 Find a current advertising campaign that uses both television and print media. Why do you think both media are being used? To what extent is each medium contributing something different to the overall message?

16.4 Find out the cost of:

(a) a 30-second advertising slot on your regional commercial television channel at 8 p.m. on a weekday evening;

(b) a 30-second slot at the same time on your local commercial radio station;

(c) a full-page advertisement in your local newspaper; and

(d) a full-page advertisement in a national daily newspaper.

16.5 Develop a checklist of criteria against which a prospective client could assess advertising agencies. Which criterion would you say is the most important, and why?

Nike

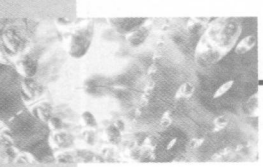

Nike, when it was a recent entrant to the UK sports shoe market, decided on a hard-hitting and intensive campaign in order to create brand awareness in an area dominated by Adidas and Reebok. To generate awareness, it was necessary to make an impact on the young people who were targeted to become the brand-loyal customers of the future. This group, however, can be less sensitive to advertising and other means of promotion than many other market segments. A further problem was the creation of a powerful enough message to stand out from the rest. Competitors had already been in the market much longer than Nike and had tied up deals with a number of the leading sports people and teams to establish high levels of brand awareness and desirability. These competitors did not feel the need to spend heavily on media advertising, preferring to focus on sponsorship and product endorsement.

The approach adopted by Nike was to spend heavily on media advertising and posters. In 1995, Nike's spend was £1.25 million, with 69 per cent on television, 10 per cent on press and 21 per cent on poster advertising. The focus of these campaigns was not on overtly promoting Nike's product benefits as great shoes for great sports people, but on the emotions and attitudes associated with sport. 'Kick it', for example, was an advertisement showing the passion, pride and joy associated with soccer, while 'Just do it' followed a similar theme, communicating the highs of sportsmanship. Taking a powerful moral stance, Nike also used Les Ferdinand and Eric Cantona in an advertisement calling for the elimination of intolerance and racism in soccer.

Nike's association with the 'bad boy' of English football, Eric Cantona, nearly backfired in 1995 when he was sent off for attacking a fan during a match at Crystal Palace. Despite an extended ban imposed by the FA and criminal prosecution resulting in a community service order, Nike continued with Cantona's £250 000 a year sponsorship and actually managed to turn it to their advantage. After condemning his outburst of kung fu kicking, they developed a 'Punished' campaign, run after Cantona's return from suspension. One poster showed a back view of Eric in full Manchester United strip leaving jail with the slogan, 'He's been punished for his mistakes. Now it's someone else's turn.' Nike's campaign could even have been instrumental in helping Cantona's rehabilitation in a very public manner. 'Punished' was

also converted into 10 000 teeshirts, all of which sold within a week.

Nike developed a number of other campaigns consistent with their overall theme and market positioning. The campaigns mainly follow the same formula of rarely showing footwear and never 'hard selling' the shoes themselves. The '66' campaign featured a picture of Cantona in front of an England flag with the line, '66 was a great year for English football. Eric was born', drawing on England's 1966 soccer world cup win. In the build up to Euro '96, around £1.25 million was spent on a poster campaign featuring such imagery and slogans as 'Italy's goalkeeper: Easiest job in Europe' and Cantona, again with a powerful, aggressive expression saying, 'I've worked hard to improve English football. Now it must be destroyed', with the French colours in the background.

Nike's Euro '96 campaign was not without problems, however. Cantona was, surprisingly, not picked for the French squad, which somewhat diluted the effect of the poster. On a similar theme, Nike had developed a poster featuring Holland's Patrick Kluivert and the slogan 'Quit Now, Venables'. These posters had to be removed after England beat Holland 4–1. Another poster featuring Newcastle United team mates David Ginola and Les Ferdinand ('Friendship Ends 6/96') also ran into problems when Ginola was not selected for France, and Ferdinand did not play in any of England's early matches in the tournament. After scrapping all these posters, Nike must have thought that it was on safer ground with a poster featuring a referee ('History. Make It or Be It'). Unfortunately, the referee pictured was injured in an early game and could not referee the final. Nike's advertising agency's chairman was philosophical about it all. Interviewed in June 1996 during the Euro '96 tournament, he said:

> 'In the advertising world you either lead or you follow. If you lead, as Nike do, then inevitably you take chances. The original posters were chosen three months ago and the new one [the referee] three weeks ago' (Craig, 1996).

Some of Nike's rivals and their advertising agencies were reported as being rather cynical about Nike's misfortunes. They felt that Nike knew that it would win either way. If the posters had worked as intended, then it would have been very powerful advertising and Nike would have benefited from it. The posters did not work, but Nike had benefited anyway from all the publicity their failure generated.

In addition to the poster campaign, a much more controversial television campaign was launched in April 1996, to be screened across Europe before and during the Euro '96 tournament. In the advertisement, a team of 11 famous soccer players (with the mix changing slightly in different countries to reflect local heroes), including Cantona, are up against a team of frightening mythical beasts in an amphitheatre. The clash between the two teams is violent, with plenty of smoke, flames and the 'forces of darkness'. Good eventually triumphs, as Cantona scores the winning goal by kicking a fireball past the monsters' evil goalkeeper. The advertisement was judged to be so frightening that Denmark banned one version of it altogether, and the UK regulatory authorities insisted on one scene being cut out and even then would not allow the advertisement to be screened during children's programmes.

All these promotional campaigns appear to have been outstanding successes. By 1996, Nike claimed that its brand awareness was ahead of Reebok and Adidas, and that Nike's footwear sales increased by 50 per cent between 1994 and 1996. Nike had thus become firmly established as a leading sports footwear brand, despite its late entry into the UK market.

Sources: Bainbridge (1996); Craig (1996); Gray (1996); Hall (1996); *Marketing* (1995); *Marketing Week* (1996); Pinder (1996).

Questions

1 Why do you think the youth market is a particularly difficult one for advertisers to communicate with?

2 What are the potential advantages and disadvantages of using a celebrity such as Eric Cantona in advertising?

3 Why do you think Nike chose not to focus more on product-orientated advertising, for example showing the shoes and explaining their technical superiority over the competition?

4 Analyse the 'forces of darkness' advertisement in terms of its target audience, its objectives, the message itself and the creative appeal used. Can the use of this kind of frightening or controversial imagery be justified?

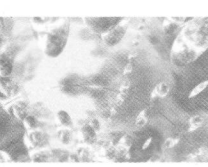

CASE STUDY 16.2

Anti-drugs advertising

Fighting drug taking through the use of promotional campaigns is of concern to most EU governments, although different governments have different views on how best to combat drugs. All governments, however, recognise the dangers of drugs to health and the need not only to educate existing users of the possible side effects, but also to prevent people from becoming users in the first place. At times it must seem like a losing battle when it has to be fought against the powerful counter-forces of peer pressure and the apparent legitimisation of drugs in some aspects of popular culture. The cult film *Trainspotting*, for example, has a much-quoted line describing the highs possible from drug taking as 'Take the best orgasm you've ever had, multiply it by a thousand and you'll still be nowhere near'.

In the UK, although the awareness of the dangers of hard drugs has increased, helped by such campaigns as 'Heroin screws you up', this has been offset by the increase in so-called recreational drugs such as ecstasy, LSD, cannabis and speed. Despite no marketing and advertising, but thanks to very effective distribution, recreational drug taking is even starting to take revenue away from alcoholic drinks on nights out. Several brewers have reported a decline in alcohol sales to young people.

The Health Education Authority (HEA) representing the UK government's Department of Health has been given the task of combating recreational drug taking alongside hard drugs. More sophisticated drugs consumers might well not be addicts and might well feel in control, but they are still at risk from possible side effects that might not be known to them. There is also the risk that recreational drug taking may lead users towards experimenting with harder drugs. The HEA uses many of the promotional techniques used by commercial organisations to ensure that their message gets through to the target audience. That audience is well understood, thanks to various research projects that examine behaviour and attitudes towards drug taking among young people.

At the heart of any campaign is the need to let consumers know what different drugs can do to their users. This cannot, however, be achieved by occupying the moral high ground, by quoting legal arguments or even by suggesting extreme danger. All of these approaches can be counter-productive, and could even enhance the habit by raising the bravado factor by suggesting 'forbidden fruit'. The approach adopted has to encourage young people to make up their own minds not to take drugs. It has to be presented as a health issue rather than as a political one. The campaign selected by the HEA in 1996 focused on the need to give information to help people make their decision with the theme, 'Know the Score'. In one advertisement, graphic images are shown to demonstrate how drugs can lead to spots, insomnia and poor hair condition.

Care must also be taken over the choice of advertising media used. Young people do not want to be embarrassed by having to see such advertisements in the presence of their parents, and so advertising in youth magazines and on the radio allows a more personal, direct appeal in privacy.

The 1996 campaign cost £5 million, and the first part of that was directed at ecstasy takers, with further drug-specific campaigns to follow directed against LSD and amphetamines. Twelve advertisements were scheduled for the youth press and six 50-second advertisements were scheduled for radio. Mothers will also be targeted to encourage them to talk through the problem if they suspect that their children are

taking drugs. Apparently, fathers are less able to play a sympathetic, listening, consultative role. Television was not selected, as the HEA did not want to glamourise drug taking by showing drug taking situations at parties and discos and reinforcing the reference group behaviour. Despite these efforts, the scale of the spend could yet prove to be inadequate for making serious progress in changing behaviour within the target group.

Sources: *Campaign* (1996); Green (1995); Jones (1996).

Questions

1 What messages are the anti-drugs campaigns trying to get across, and what are the problems of turning those messages into advertisements?

2 Do you think the message approaches described in the case are appropriate?

3 What media are best for communicating these messages to the target audience, and why?

4 Why is it more difficult to make a success of a public health advertising campaign than an ordinary consumer product campaign?

REFERENCES TO CHAPTER 16

Applebaum, U. and Halliburton, C. (1993), 'How to Develop International Advertising Campaigns that Work: The Example of the European Food and Beverage Sector', *International Journal of Advertising*, 12(3), 223–241.

Bainbridge, J. (1996), 'Ads are at Risk When the V Chips are Down', *Marketing*, 4 April.

Barnard, S. (1996), 'Will She Prove Vulnerable to Gallic Charm?', *The Grocer*, 20 January, p. 32.

Benady, A. (1994), 'Bank Agencies Back CA on Ads', *Marketing*, 8 December, p. 8.

Berkowitz, E. N. *et al.* (1992), *Marketing*, Irwin.

Böhler (UK) Ltd (1994), 'Advantages All Along the Line', *European Purchasing and Materials Management*, No. 3 1994, pp. 82–83.

Brillet, T. F. (1994), 'La Télé Encaisse La Crise', *Marketing Vente*, Juillet/Août 1994, p. 30.

Campaign (1996), 'Duckworth Finn Drugs Ads Raise Health Issues', *Campaign*, 23 March, p. 10.

Craig, O. (1996), 'Nike Scores a £1m Own Goal', *Sunday Times*, 23 June, p. 24.

De Mooij, M. (1994), *Advertising Worldwide: Concepts, Theories and Practice Of International, Multinational and Global Advertising*, (2nd ed.), Prentice Hall.

Dignam, C. (1995), 'Papers Set Sights on Snatching Ad Income', *Marketing*, 22 June, p. 7.

DMB&B (1995a), *A DMB&B Case Study: Texaco*, DMB&B.

DMB&B (1995b), *A DMB&B Case Study: Budweiser*, DMB&B.

DMB&B (1995c), *A DMB&B Case Study: Drink – Drive*, DMB&B.

Farmers Weekly (1995), 'Seed Matters', advertorial published in *Farmers Weekly*, 3 November, between pp. 58 and 59.

Fill, C. (1995), *Marketing Communications: Frameworks, Theories and Applications*, Prentice Hall.

Gray, R. (1996), 'Putting the Show on the Road', *Marketing*, 20 June, pp. 27–9.

Green, H. (1995),'Can the HEA Curb Drug Culture by Means of Ads?', *Campaign*, 4 August, p. 13.

Griffiths, A. (1996), 'Can Christian Cable Launch Keep Afloat?', *Marketing*, 6 June, p. 9.

Hall, E. (1996), 'Violent Nike Spot Sees Cantona Combat "Evil"', *Campaign*, 29 March, p. 7.

Jones, H. (1996), 'Thrills and Pills', *Marketing Week*, 23 February, pp. 38–9.

Kapferer, J. N. and Eurocom (1992), 'How Global Are Global Brands?', *ESOMAR Seminar on the Challenge of Branding Today and in the Future*, Brussels: 28–30 October.

Lane Fox, H. (1996), 'UCI Plans First Branding Blitz', *Marketing*, 18 January, p. 4.

Lee, J. (1996), 'Pizza Hut Fattens Up on Euro Ad Strategy', *Marketing*, 6 June, p. 7.

Marketing (1995), 'Campaign of the Week: Nike', *Marketing*, 6 April, p. 7.

Marketing (1996a), 'Banks Scrap in Public', *Marketing*, 4 January, p. 3.

Marketing (1996b), 'Divided They Stand', *Marketing*, 11 January, pp. 22–3.

Marketing Week (1996), 'Advalue: Nike Football Campaigns', *Marketing Week*, 26 April, pp. 36–7.

Muehling, D. D. *et al.* (1990), 'The Impact of Comparative Advertising on Levels of Message Involvement', *Journal of Advertising*, 19(4), pp. 41–50.

Mueller-Heumann, G. (1992), 'Markets and Technology Shifts in the 1990s: Market Fragmentation and Mass Customisation', *Journal of Marketing Management*, 8(4), pp. 303–14.

Munzinger, U. (1988), 'Ad*Vantage/AC-T International Advertising Research Case Studies', *ESOMAR Seminar on International Marketing Research*, 16–18 November.

Parker, D. (1996), 'The X Files', *Marketing*, 8 March, pp. 73–4.

Petty, R. E. and Cacioppo, J. T. (1979), 'Effects of Message Repetition and Position on Cognitive Responses, Recall and Persuasion', *Journal of Personality and Social Psychology*, 37(Jan), pp. 97–109.

Piercy, N. (1987), 'The Marketing Budgeting Process: Marketing Management Implications', *Journal of Marketing*, 51(4), pp. 45–59.

Pinder, C. (1995), 'Nike Keeps the Faith in 'Bad Boy' Cantona', *Marketing*, 2 February, p. 5.

Simpson, M. (1996), 'Ark 2 Ready to Sail into UK Christian Waters', *Marketing Week*, 7 June, pp. 14–15.

Sissors, J. Z. and Bumba, L. (1989), *Advertising Media Planning*, (3rd edn.), NTC Business Books.

Smith, P. R. (1993), *Marketing Communications*, Kogan Page.

Snowdon, R. (1995), 'Specialist Units to Oversee Car Model Budgets', *Marketing*, 18 May, p. 1.

Snowdon, R. (1996), 'Peugeot Shock Ads in Top Spot', *Marketing*, 1 February, p. 5.

Sunday Express Magazine (1996) Advertisement for Oreck Vacuum Cleaner, *Sunday Express Magazine*, 4 February, p. 60.

Syedain, H. (1995), 'Local Challenge', *Marketing*, 26 January, p. 31.

Truck (1995), Advertisement for Foden Trucks; advertisement for Iveco Trucks, *Truck, January*, pp. 22 and 16–17 respectively.

White, R. (1988), *Advertising: What It Is and How To Do It*, McGraw-Hill.

Wilmshurst, J. (1985), *The Fundamentals of Advertising*, Heinemann Professional Publishing.

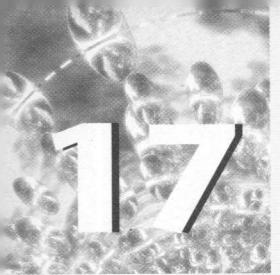

17 Sales Promotion

LEARNING OBJECTIVES

This chapter will help you to:

1 define sales promotion and appreciate its role in the communications mix through the objectives it can achieve;

2 understand the range of available methods of sales promotion in consumer markets and their objectives;

3 understand the range and objectives of sales promotion methods used by manufacturers to stimulate retailers;

4 appreciate the role of sales promotion in other organisational markets and how sales promotion overlaps with other elements of the communications mix; and

5 gain an overview of the issues involved in the sales promotion planning process and their implications for the application and practice of sales promotion methods.

INTRODUCTION

Traditionally the poor cousin of advertising, sales promotion actually covers a fascinating range of short-term tactical tools that can play a vital complementary role in long-term promotional strategy. Its aim is to add extra value to the product or service, over and above the normal product offering, thus creating an extra inducement to buy or try it. Although individual sales promotions are usually regarded as short-term tactical measures, sales promotion generally, as an element of the promotional mix, is increasingly being recognised as a valid strategic tool, working alongside and supporting other promotional elements.

Example

Heinz, for instance, to commemorate the 100th birthday of its baked beans, issued a set of four branded mugs sold for £7.99 as a self-liquidating promotion. Heinz felt that because mugs are used every day by all the family, they are a good way of getting a brand message across without being too intrusive (Oliver, 1995b).

Shell combined tactical and strategic objectives in its smart card promotion. In strategic terms, issuing drivers with cards upon which points can be collected electronically, depending on the value of purchases, encourages long-term customer loyalty and allows Shell to build a database to target its most valuable customers. In tactical terms, short-term extra incentives, perhaps targeting particular groups of customers, can be built into the scheme periodically. This kind of loyalty scheme certainly is a long-term commitment and investment in sales promotion. Shell are reported to have spent £20 million on the necessary hardware and software (Burnside, 1995).

This chapter will define more clearly what sales promotion is, and what strategic role it can play within the promotional mix. It considers in detail the various methods associated with consumer, organisational and trade promotions, discussing what each can contribute towards given marketing objectives. If new products are planned, for example, a number of sales promotions may be designed to encourage product trial. If competitive activity is increasing, then sales promotion efforts may be directed at retaining customer loyalty and generating repeat purchases. The chapter will not, however, only look at the implementation issues, but also consider the management concerns that lie behind sales promotion. To be effective, sales promotion programmes must be carefully planned and managed. There are many examples of what can go wrong under poor planning and management, the most spectacular recent example of which was the Hoover free flights sales promotion in the UK, (*see* p. 674). The key management issues will be considered from a campaign development perspective.

THE ROLE AND DEFINITION OF SALES PROMOTION

According to the Institute of Sales Promotion, **sales promotion** is:

> '... **a range of tactical marketing techniques designed within a strategic marketing framework to add value to a product or service in order to achieve specific sales and marketing objectives.**'

The word 'tactical' implies a short sharp burst of activity that is expected to be effective as soon as it is implemented. The fact that this activity is *designed within a strategic marketing framework* means, however, that it is not a panic measure, not just something to wheel out when you do not know what else to do. On the contrary, sales promotion should be planned into an overall communications mix, to make the most of its ability to complement other areas such as advertising and its unique capacity to achieve certain objectives, mostly tactical, but sometimes strategic (Davies, 1992).

The key element of this definition, however, is that the sales promotion should *add value to a product or service*. This is something over and above the normal product offering that might make the buyer stop and think about whether to change their usual buying behaviour, or revise their buying criteria. As the rest of this chapter will show, this takes the form of something tangible that is of value to the buyer, whether it is extra product free, money, a gift or the opportunity to win a prize, that under normal circumstances they would not get.

Perhaps the main problem with the definition is that the area of sales promotion has almost developed beyond it. The idea of the short-term tactical shock to the market is very well established and understood, and will be seen to be at the heart of many of the specific techniques outlined in this chapter. With the development of relationship marketing, that is, the necessity for building long-term buyer–seller relationships, marketers have been looking for ways of developing the scope of traditional sales promotion to encourage long-term customer loyalty and repeat purchasing behaviour. Loyalty schemes, such as frequent flyer programmes or the Shell smart card, for instance, are sales promotions in the sense that they offer added value over and above the normal product offering, but they are certainly not short-term tactical measures – quite the opposite. Wilmshurst (1993) clearly states that creatively designed sales promotions can be just as effective as advertising in affecting consumers' attitudes to brands. This means, perhaps, that the definition of sales promotion needs to be revised to account for those strategic, franchise-building promotional techniques thus:

FIGURE 17.1

Communication links through sales promotion

> **'... a range of marketing techniques designed within a strategic marketing framework to add extra value to a product or service over and above the 'normal' offering in order to achieve specific sales and marketing objectives. This extra value may be of a short-term tactical nature or it may be part of a longer-term franchise-building programme.'**

The rest of this section will focus on the objectives that sales promotion can achieve. Sales promotion objectives are best discussed in the context of the relationship within which they are happening, as shown in Fig 17.1. The techniques linked with these objectives will be discussed in much more detail in later sections of the chapter.

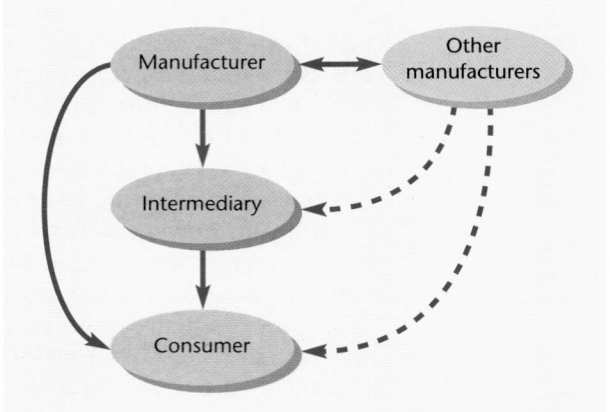

Manufacturer–intermediary (trade promotion)

FIGURE 17.2

Manufacturer–intermediary sales promotion objectives

The intermediary provides a vital service for the manufacturer in displaying goods to their best advantage and making them easily available to the consumer. Any individual intermediary, however, performs this function for a number of manufacturers, and so a manufacturer might wish to use sales promotion techniques to encourage the intermediary to take a particular interest in particular products for various purposes. However, depending on the balance of power between manufacturer and intermediary, the manufacturer might have little choice in the matter. Intermediaries might expect or insist upon sales promotions before they will co-operate with what the manufacturer wants.

As shown in Fig 17.2, and discussed below, trade promotions revolve around gaining more product penetration, more display and more intermediary promotional effort. As Fill (1995) points out, however, this might cause conflict between the manufacturer and the intermediary since the intermediary's prime objective is to increase store traffic. The level of incentive might thus have to be extremely attractive!

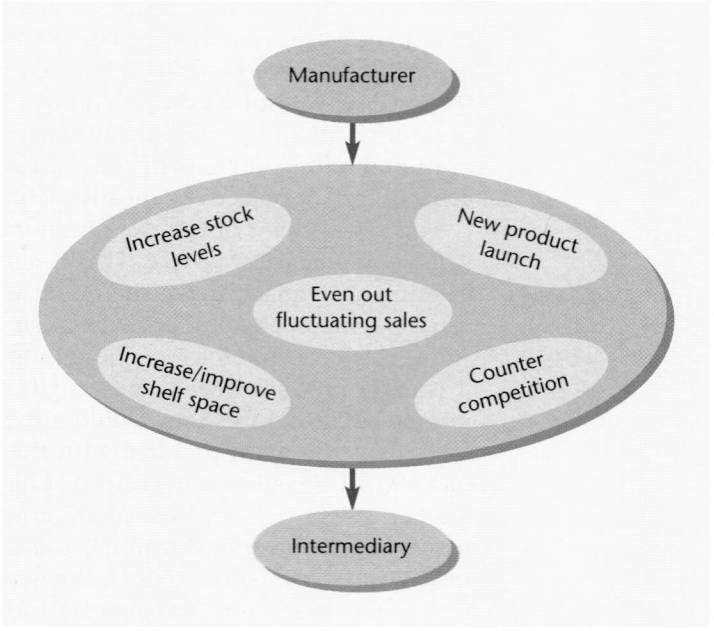

Trade promotions

The winners in the various categories in the Trade Promotion section of the 1996 Institute of Sales Promotion (ISP) Awards show that creativity is not confined to consumer-orientated promotions. Sellotape, for example, set up a National Lottery syndicate for wholesalers and cash and carry operators. Intermediaries bought into the syndicate by collecting tokens from promotional packs. The more tokens, the greater the share in the syndicate. In the event, the syndicate won enough money on the lottery to ensure that all participants got a cash prize.

Cellnet wanted to motivate mobile phone dealers to push more business in its direction rather than to Orange or Vodaphone. Since Cellnet already had a sponsorship deal with Damon Hill, the racing driver, it decided to centre the promotion on motor sport. All the dealers were sent packs signed by Hill. The packs contained sheets to record sales, and individual sales staff were rewarded with gift vouchers for every new sale made. They also had the chance to win a car. The best performing outlets won group trips to motor sport events and the owner of the best performing outlet won a trip to the Portuguese Grand Prix.

Unipath makes pregnancy testing kits sold over the counter at pharmacies. The company wanted to target pharmacy sales assistants so that they would learn more about the company's products and be able to give customers more accurate and appropriate advice. A magazine called *Talking Point* was produced which had articles about women's health issues, competitions and product information. It was sent to pharmacy assistants on a specially compiled database. The information in the quarterly magazine helped the reader to enter competitions, including one for the 'sales assistant of the year'.

Source: Marketing (1996).

Increase stock levels
The more stock of a particular product that an intermediary holds, the more committed they will be to put effort into selling it quickly. Furthermore, intermediaries have limited stockholding space, so the more space that your product takes up, the less room there is for the competition. Money-based or extra-product based incentives might encourage intermediaries to increase their orders, although the effect might be short lived and in the longer term might even reduce orders as intermediaries work through the extra stock they acquired during the promotion.

Gain more and better shelf space
There is intense competition between manufacturers to secure shelf space within retail outlets. Demand for shelf space far outstrips supply. Intermediaries are, therefore, willing to accept incentives to help them to allocate this scarce resource to particular products or manufacturers. Again, this may link with money- or product-based trade promotions, but could also be part of a joint promotion agreement or a point of sale promotion, for instance. The quality of the shelf space acquired is also important. If a product is to capture the consumer's attention, then it needs to be prominent. This means that it must be displayed either at the customer's eye level or at the end of the aisles in a supermarket where the customer is turning the corner and all the trolley traffic jams occur. There is keen competition for these highly desirable display sites, also called *golden zones*, and again, intermediary-orientated sales promotion may help a manufacturer to make its case more strongly.

New product launch
The launch period is a delicate time in any new product's life, and if the distribution aspects of the marketing strategy are weak, then it could be fatal. A new product needs to be accepted by the appropriate intermediaries so that it is available for all those consumers eager to try it. To the trade, however, a new product is a potential risk.

What if it doesn't sell? Trade promotions (particularly with a push strategy – *see* pp. 577 *et seq.*) can reduce some of that risk. Money-based promotions reduce the potential financial losses of a product failure, while '**sale or return**' promotions remove the fear of being left with unsaleable stock. Sales-force support, meanwhile, can reassure the intermediary that staff are ready, willing and able to sell the product and fully understand its features and benefits. This is particularly appropriate with more complex, infrequently purchased items, such as electrical goods.

Even out fluctuating sales

Some products, such as lawnmowers, ice-cream, and holidays suffer from seasonality. While the design of the product offering or the pricing policies adopted can help to overcome these problems, sales promotion can also play a part. If manufactures are able to encourage intermediaries to take on more stock or to push the product harder during the 'quieter' periods, sales can be spread a little more evenly throughout the year. This process can also be enhanced by a related consumer-orientated promotion, so that the manufacturer is gaining extra synergy through simultaneous push and pull activity.

Counter the competition

It has already been indicated that a manufacturer is competing with every other manufacturer for an intermediary's attention. Sales promotions, therefore, make very useful tactical weapons to spoil or dilute the effects of a competitor's actions. If, for instance, you are aware that the competition is about to launch a new product, you might use a trade sales promotion to load up a key intermediary with your related products, so that at best they will be reluctant to take on the competition's goods, or at worst, they will drive a much harder bargain with the competitor.

Retailer–consumer (retailer promotions)

In the same way that manufacturers compete among themselves for the intermediary's attention, retailers compete for the consumer's patronage. Store-specific sales promotions, whether jointly prepared with a manufacturer or originating solely from the retailer, can help to differentiate one store from another, and to entice the public in. Retailers also try to use sales promotions in a longer-term strategic way to create store loyalty, for example through card schemes that allow the shopper to collect points over time that can be redeemed for gifts or money-off vouchers. There are many reasons why retailers use sales promotion and these are summarised in Fig 17.3.

FIGURE 17.3

Retailer–consumer sales promotion objectives

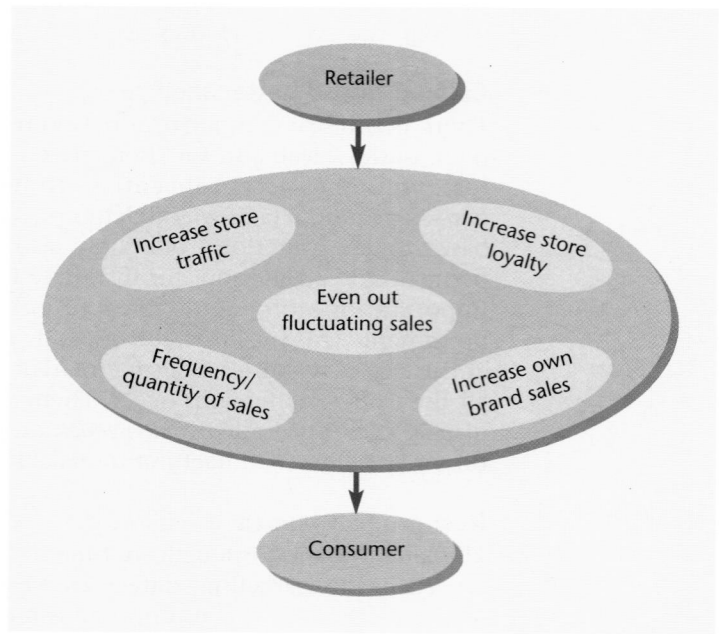

Increase store traffic

A prime objective for a retailer is to get the public in through the shop door. Any kind of retailer-specific sales promotion has a chance of doing that. Money-off coupons delivered from door to door or printed in the local newspaper, for example, might bring in people who do not usually shop in a particular store. Such promotions

These collectable models of old Co-op vans provide an effective repeat purchase incentive.

Source: Christopher Thorburn Associates.

might also encourage retail substitution, giving shoppers an incentive to patronise one retailer rather than another. An electrical retailer might advertise a one-day sale with a few carefully chosen items offered on promotion at rock bottom prices. This bait brings potential customers to the store, and even if the real bargains have gone early, they will still look at other goods.

Increase frequency and amount of purchases

Even if a customer already shops at one retailer's outlets, the retailer would prefer them to shop there more often and to spend more.

Example

Both Sainsbury's and Safeway have in the past used sales promotions to encourage customers to visit more regularly and spend more. The general idea is that the customer has a collecting card which is stamped every time they spend more than a certain amount. Once the card is full, the customer is then entitled to a reward, such as money off their shopping or discounts on holidays. A tight time limit is put on the completion of the card, meaning that the customer has to visit much more often (to acquire the right number of stamps) and to spend much more (to qualify to get a stamp on any one visit). The hope is that this creates shopping habits that stay with the customer beyond the end of the promotion. This has been superceded by the electronic loyalty card.

Increase store loyalty

Supermarkets in particular use sales promotion as a means of generating store loyalty. The kinds of activities outlined in relation to increasing the frequency and amount of purchases help towards this, as does a rolling programme of couponing and money-off offers. The problem with this type of promotion, however, is that it risks creating a 'deal-prone' promiscuous customer who will switch to whichever retailer is currently offering the best package of short-term promotions. To counteract this, some retailers have introduced loyalty schemes using smart cards.

In the UK, Tesco was the first with its Clubcard, and Safeway soon followed with its ABC card. Shoppers thus have an incentive to shop regularly at a particular retailer in order to accumulate points. Using the customer database, coupons and money-off vouchers can be regularly issued and delivered to the customer's own home, thus creating a stronger, more personal retailer–customer link. (*see also* Case Study 17.2)

Increase own brand sales

As discussed at pp. 272 *et seq.* and p. 521, retailers are increasingly investing in their own brand ranges. These are, therefore, legitimate subjects for a whole range of consumer-orientated promotions. These promotions do not have to be overtly price or product based.

Sainsbury's promoted their own-brand goods with a subtle mix of advertising and sales promotion. A series of recipes were broadcast in the UK, featuring well-known celebrities such as Kiri Te Kanawa. Each recipe prominently relied on Sainsbury's own brands, and was backed up with a free recipe card available in-store. In addition, at least one of the ingredients which featured in whatever recipe was currently being advertised would usually be on a price-reduced special offer.

Even out busy periods

In the same way that manufacturers face seasonal demand for some products, retailers have to cope with fluctuations between the very busy periods of the week or year, and the very quiet times. Offering sales promotions that apply only on certain days or within certain trading hours might divert some customers away from the busier periods.

Debenham's department stores occasionally have 'Blue Cross Sales' where goods marked with a blue cross sticker qualify for a discount on the marked price. These sales tend to run for only one or two days, usually Wednesdays and Thursdays, to get people shopping on the quieter days.

Manufacturer–consumer (manufacturer promotion)

While it is obviously important for manufacturers to have the distribution channels working in their favour, there is still much work to be done with the consumer to help ensure continued product success. After all, if consumer demand for a product is buoyant, that in itself acts as an incentive to the retail trade to stock it, effectively acting as a pull strategy. There are many reasons why manufacturers should use sales promotions to woo the consumer, and some of these are outlined below and summarised in Fig 17.4.

Encourage trial

The rationale in encouraging trial is similar to that discussed earlier in relation to the intermediary and new product launches. New products face the problem of being unknown, and therefore, consumers may need incentives to encourage trial of the product. Samples help consumers to judge a product for themselves, while coupons,

FIGURE 17.4

Manufacturer–consumer sales promotion objectives

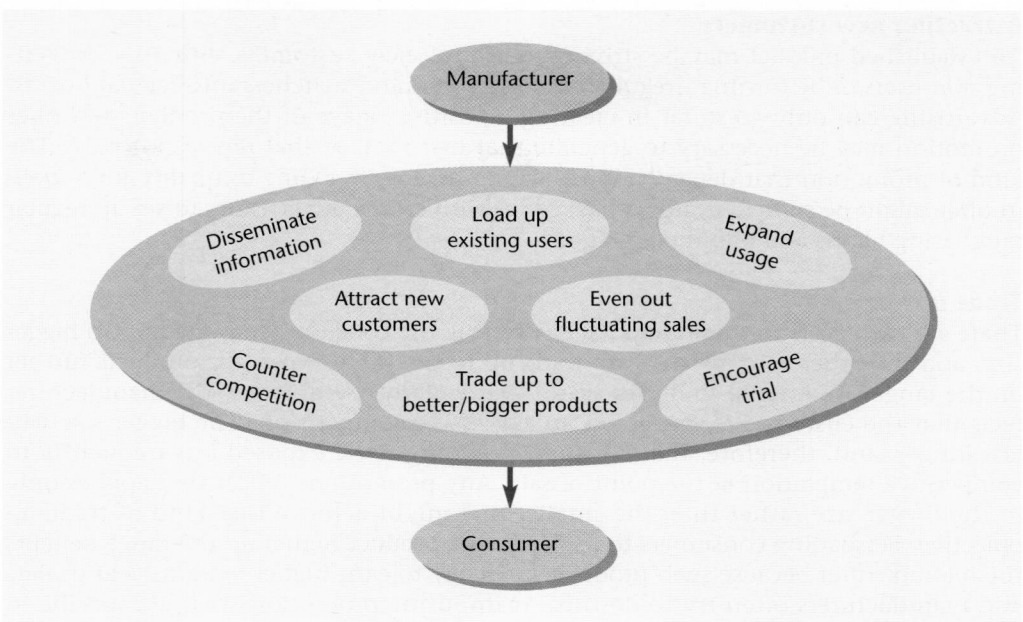

money off, and gifts reduce the financial penalty of a 'wrong' purchase. A survey, reported by Summers (1994) claims that 85 per cent of consumers say they have bought new products because of receiving free samples to try, 75 per cent because of money off offers, and 62 per cent because of money-off coupons or vouchers. Sales promotions thus play an important role in the early stages of a product's life.

Expand usage

Expanding usage involves using sales promotion to encourage people to find different ways of using more of the product so that, of course, they purchase more.

Example

Be-Ro flour produces a low-priced cookery book, available by mail, of reasonably simple, but tasty day-to-day recipes, using its products. This encourages a wider range of more frequent home baking, and therefore, more consumption of Be-Ro products. Wash & Go shampoo tried to expand usage of its product within households by distributing one-use samples on a door-to-door basis in opaque wrapping with the words 'For Men Only'. Perceived largely as a female-orientated product, this sales promotion was clearly trying to reinforce a wider user base.

Disseminate information

Sales promotions can be used effectively as a means of getting information across to consumers. Even a small sample pack distributed door to door, for example, not only lets the consumer experience the product, but also gives the manufacturer a chance to tell that consumer quite a lot about the product's features and benefits, where to buy it, and related products in the range. While advertising can do the same sort of information dissemination, it is easily ignored. If the consumer is tempted to try the sample, then they may take more notice of the information with it, and only then pay attention to the advertising.

Attracting new customers

An established product may be striving to acquire new customers, either by converting non-users or by turning irregular customers or brand switchers into regular buyers. Advertising can only go so far in creating a positive image of the product, and sales promotion may be necessary to generate that first trial, or that repeat purchase. The kind of promotion that depends on collecting tokens over time to qualify for a mail-in offer might be sufficient, if it is backed up with strong advertising, to set up regular purchasing habits and brand preference.

Trade up

There are two facets to **trading up**. One is getting the consumer to trade up to a bigger size, and the other is to get them to trade up to the more expensive products further up the range. Trading up to bigger sizes is particularly useful where the manufacturer feels that the customer is vulnerable to aggressive competition. The bigger size will last longer, and, therefore, that consumer is going to be exposed less frequently to competitive temptation at the point of sale. Any promotional effort that applies only to the bigger size rather than the smaller one might achieve that kind of trade-up objective. Persuading consumers to trade up to a product higher up the range benefits the manufacturer because such products are likely to earn higher margins. Car dealers and manufacturers often try to do this. Again, using promotions that are specific to one model or product in the range, or using increasingly valuable and attractive promotions as the range goes up can help to focus the customer's mind on higher things. Price-based promotions are probably not a good idea in this case, because of the risk of cheapening the product's image.

Load up

Loading up is partly a defensive mechanism to protect your customers from the efforts of the competition. A customer who is collecting tokens or labels towards a mail-in offer with a tight deadline, or who finds a cut-price offer particularly seductive, might end up with far greater quantities of the product than can be used immediately. Effectively, that customer is now out of the market until those stocks are used up. This is a two-edged sword: the advantage is that they are less likely to listen to the competition; the disadvantage is that you will not be selling them any more for a while either, as you have effectively brought your sales to that customer forward. Of course, if that customer was originally a brand switcher, or a non-user, then you have gained considerably from loading them up.

Even out fluctuating sales

Evening out fluctuating sales links with the comments made above in relation to manufacturer–intermediary sales promotions. If seasonality is a problem, then sales promotion aimed at the consumer could help to even out the peaks and troughs a little.

Countering the competition

Again, the concept of countering or spoiling competitors' activities was introduced in the discussion of manufacturer–intermediary sales promotions. Diverting the consumer's attention through your own promotion can dampen the effects of the competitors' efforts, particularly if what they are doing is not particularly creative in its own right. Also, as discussed in at p. 350, a well chosen, regionally based sales promotion can seriously distort, or introduce an element of doubt into the results of a competitor's test marketing.

Manufacturer–manufacturer (business promotion)

The relationship between manufacturers in the area of business promotion is less clear- cut than any of the other relationships studied so far. When we look at the negotiation of large contracts between organisations, we see that many of the activities that in other circumstances have been classed as sales promotions, such as discounts, added extras and time-limited offers, tend to be included in personal selling as part of the negotiation process leading to the final deal. Manufacturer–manufacturer sales promotions are also tightly linked to trade exhibition attendance, which will be considered in detail in Chapter 20.

Even the freebies, such as calendars, corporate neckwear, and golfing holidays do not class as sales promotions, as they do not link directly with specific products for sale. They are part of the wider area of relationship building between organisational buyers and sellers. A 1994 survey found that 80 per cent of companies are likely to send calendars, 54 per cent send pens and 53 per cent send diaries to customers at Christmas (Oliver, 1994).

Sales promotion objectives: Overview

The previous subsections have looked at sales promotion objectives within specific commercial relationships. They covered a wide variety of objectives, all of which fall into three broad categories as shown in Fig 17.5: communication, incentive and invitation. These are discussed in turn below.

Communication

Sales promotion has a capacity to communicate with the buyer in ways that advertising would find hard to emulate. Advertising can tell people that a product is 'new, improved', or that it offers certain features and benefits, but this is conceptual information, which people may not fully understand or accept. Sales promotion can, for instance, put product samples into people's hands so that they can judge for themselves whether the claims are true. Learning by one's own experience is so much more powerful and convincing than taking the advertiser's word for it.

As Chapter 15 made clear, grabbing attention is an important starting point for any communication. Thus an on-pack sales promotion, for instance, particularly one that prominently features the word 'FREE', draws the product to the shopper's attention and perhaps makes them receptive to the product's underlying message.

Incentive

The incentive is usually the central pillar of a sales promotion campaign. The potential buyer has to be given encouragement to behave in certain ways, through an agreed bargain between seller and buyer: if you do this, then I will *reward* you with that.

FIGURE 17.5

Sales promotion objectives: overview

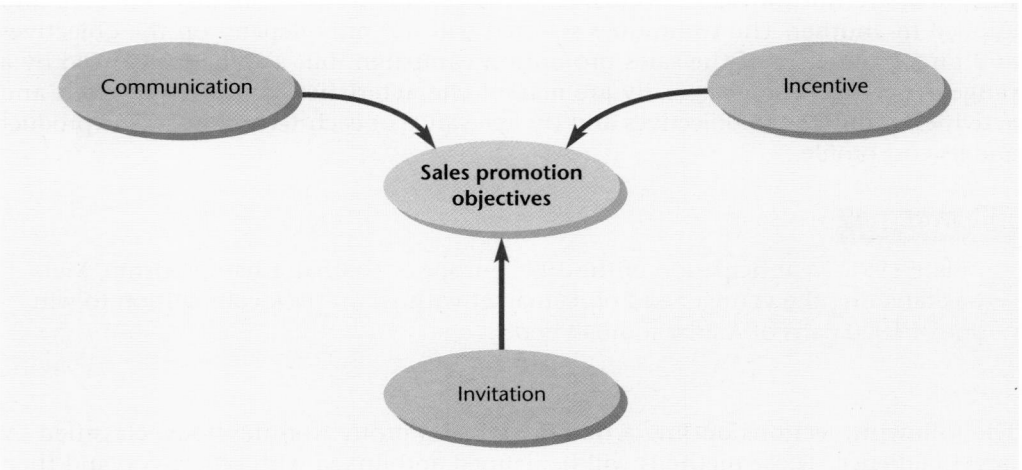

With consumers, the aim may be to encourage brand switching or to fortify wavering existing customers by providing additional rewards and increased value to those who try or repeat buy. If extra benefits are provided, the price-conscious or premium-conscious customer may be attracted. Similarly, the objective may be to reward those customers who are normally loyal to the brand or producer, but perhaps are the target of competitive action. Occasional rewards for the more frequent purchaser, or those who purchase in larger quantities, can help to maintain their loyalty and goodwill.

The intermediary too needs incentives as encouragement to stock the product in quantity and to sell it enthusiastically to the end buyer. Like consumers, intermediaries may be price or premium conscious, and incentives help them to swing towards particular brands or manufacturers.

Invitation

The promoted product is saying, 'Buy ME, and buy me NOW.' The promotion is, therefore, an invitation to consider this product, to think about your buying decision, and to do it quickly. The ephemeral nature of most sales promotions reinforces the urgency of taking up the invitation immediately. It prevents the buyer from putting off trial of the product, because the 'extra something' will not be around for long. For the consumer, in particular, the point of sale represents the crucial decision-making time. A product that is jumping up and down, shouting, 'Hey, look at me!' through its sales promotion is offering the clearest possible invitation to do business.

Communication, incentive and invitation are all linked together. Elements of all three are present in the objectives of most sales promotions, but their mix and emphasis may change, depending on target audiences and circumstances. Peattie and Peattie (1995) highlighted how sales promotion not only is strong in the fmcg area but also can be applied to services marketing, especially through the use of competitions and loyalty schemes.

Within the three main categories of sales promotion discussed earlier in this section (consumer, retail trade and organisation-orientated sales promotions), there are a number of possible techniques for achieving defined objectives. The techniques in each area are not mutually exclusive; ideas can be drawn from any one area and applied in another. The techniques selected will not only depend on the objectives and target audience of the sales promotion campaign, but also be influenced by a range of factors. These typically are market characteristics, competitive levels and activities, promotional objectives and the relevance of each technique to the product and its cost profile.

Example

In late 1995, in anticipation of the 1996 European Football Championship, Mars was targeting the younger end of its market with an on-pack competition to win one of 1000 pairs of Adidas football boots.

The following sections outline a number of sales promotion methods, classified by target audience. These methods will be defined and linked with objectives, and then specific examples of applications will be discussed. The list of methods described is not necessarily exhaustive. Sales promotion is an inherently creative area, subject to development as new ideas are introduced. Nevertheless, the following sections do cover the core methods, both established and emerging.

CONSUMER SALES PROMOTION METHODS (1): MONEY BASED

Money-based sales promotions are a very popular group of techniques used by manufacturers or intermediaries. Sometimes they work on a 'cash back' basis (*see* p. 666), but more often they are immediate price reductions, implemented in various ways, designed as a short-term measure either to gain competitive advantage or to defend against competitive actions. Such price reductions must be seen to be temporary or else the consumer will not view them as incentives. Furthermore, if money-based methods are used too often, consumers will begin to think of the promotional price as being the real price. They will then think of the product as being cheaper than it really is, and adjust their perceptions of positioning and quality accordingly (Gupta and Cooper, 1992).

Another drawback of this group of sales promotions is that because money-based sales promotions are so common among consumer goods, it is very difficult to raise much enthusiasm about them in the market. The main problem is the lack of creativity that usually accompanies these methods. It is also far too easy for a competitor to copy or match a money-based promotion, and thus any competitive advantage may be short lived.

It is also important to remember that money-based promotion can be an expensive way of putting money back in the pockets of people who would have bought the product anyway. If an organisation offers 10p off a product, then that costs the organisation 10p per unit sold in addition to the overhead costs of implementing the offer. In other words, in most cases money-based sales promotions cost the organisation their full cash value, unlike many of the merchandise offers, yet the long-term effect (especially if the technique is over used) may be to cheapen the value of the product in the consumer's eyes (Jones, 1990). Effectively, this is a form of indirect price competition, and as discussed in Chapter 11, any price reduction needs to be balanced by volume increases in sales, and also needs to be balanced against the product's reputation. Generally speaking, with money-based sales promotions, the short-term increase in sales needs to offset the extra marketing, distribution and handling costs associated with the promotion, as well as the lost revenue from those who would have purchased anyway (i.e., if you use a 20p coupon against a £1 product that you would have purchased anyway, then for the manufacturer, that is 20p lost revenue rather than 80p extra revenue).

In their favour, however, money-based promotions are relatively easy to implement, they can be developed and mobilised quickly, and they are readily understood by the consumer. They appeal to many consumers' basic instincts about saving money, and the value of 10p off a price, or £1 cash back, is easy for the consumer to assess. If the objective of the exercise is to attract price-sensitive brand switchers, or to make a quick and easy response to a competitor's recent or imminent actions, then this group of methods has a part to play. The range of money-based methods is summarised in Fig 17.6.

Reduced price offers (1): Shelf

Retailers frequently implement reduced price offers at the point of sale of the product. Although nothing appears on the product itself, the consumer is drawn to the surrounding notices or leaflets advertising the offer.

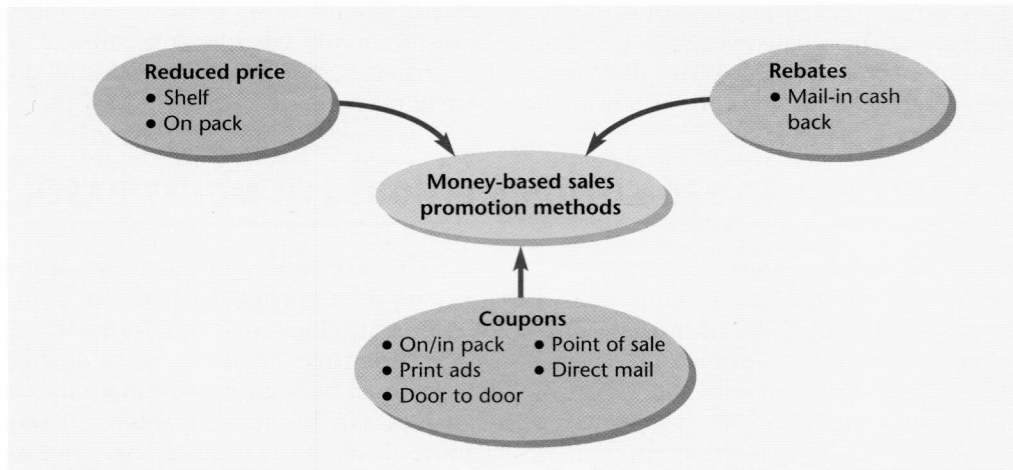

FIGURE 17.6

Money-based sales promotion methods

> ### Example
>
> Leaflets were distributed around the shopping area of Schiphol Airport advertising the fact that for one week only, certain retailers would be offering discounts and gifts to customers paying for other purchases with a Mastercard.

Such offers do have a sense of urgency about them, because consumers cannot be sure that the same offer will be available next time they visit that outlet, so they must take advantage of it immediately. They are very simple and quick to implement, costing only what it takes to notify the customers about the offer and the amount given back to the consumer through the reduced price. Local press advertising might be used to communicate a whole range of such offers, available this week only, to help increase store traffic.

> ### Example
>
> Supermarkets have found themselves drawn into making short-term reduced price offers in response to the discounters. In 1995, Tesco reduced the price of its Value Line washing-up liquid to 7p per litre to match Lidl and Netto. Although such price reductions do tend to be short lived, there is a real danger that they will encourage some of Tesco's customers to trade down. A 500ml bottle of standard own label liquid retailed at 69p, while the top of the range brands, such as Fairy and Persil, were 79p (*The Grocer*, 1995). In early 1996, the price war turned to cans of baked beans which began to sell in some supermarkets for as little as 3p each, not even enough to pay for the packaging.

Reduced price offers (2): On pack

The second type of reduced price offer features on the product pack itself. The offer is likely to originate from the manufacturer, but sometimes takes the form of a joint promotion between the manufacturer and one particular retailer. Greater expenditure and a longer lead time is required here, as the packaging has to be printed specially for the offer. Again, it is a simple kind of sales promotion, with a sense of urgency, as is a shelf-based offer. Sometimes, reduced price is presented to the customer as a **trial price** when a product is being launched, as discussed at p. 415.

Coupons

Coupons are a more complex form of money-based sales promotion. They are printed vouchers which the consumer takes to a retail outlet and uses to claim a set amount of money off a product. Their use is widespread and flexible, and Table 17.1 shows the top 10 sectors within which coupons were used in the UK in 1994 (Gofton, 1995). A manufacturer can issue coupons applicable to one specific product or a range of products, redeemable at any retail outlet stocking the product. Retailers issue coupons redeemable only in their stores either against specific products or against any basket of shopping totalling more than a stated sum. Joint coupons, specifying both retail outlet and manufacturer's product, are also used.

Coupons are distributed using a variety of means. They are printed within advertisements, on leaflets delivered from door to door, on inserts within magazines and newspapers, through direct mail, at the point of sale and on packs. Table 17.2 gives 1994 UK figures for the percentage of coupons distributed through each medium, and for each medium's share of coupons redeemed (Gofton, 1995). It is interesting to see that although in- or on-pack coupons account for less than 10 per cent of coupons distributed, they constitute nearly 40 per cent of redemptions. This presumably is because the coupons will be reaching many people who already like and use the product and will therefore be motivated to buy it again, using the coupon. Effectively, this is a reward for current users. In contrast, coupons distributed through mass media perform less well. Newspapers and magazines between them account for nearly 45 per cent of coupons, but only 11 per cent of redemptions. There is much wastage with these media because many readers will not be even remotely interested in the coupon's product and those who are interested have to remember to keep the magazine, cut the coupon out, take it to the shops and use it.

The technology is also now available to allow retailers to issue coupons at the checkout, as an integral part of the bill issued to the customer. Checkouts that use laser scanning equipment can analyse the purchasing profile of the current customer, and issue coupons against the next purchase of something that has already been bought, or against a related product, or even against the retailer's own-brand equivalent of a purchased manufacturer's brand.

Manufacturers issue coupons with a number of reasons in mind. They act as a kind of *pull* strategy, creating an upturn in consumer demand for the product, thus encouraging retailers to stock and prominently display the brand. By telling them what is available and by reducing the financial risks of purchase, coupons can help the consumer get round to trying a product, to making a subsequent purchase, or to trade up, either to larger sizes or to products further up the range. The main problem for manufacturers is misredemption. Some supermarkets, overtly or covertly, will accept any coupon at the checkout, regardless of whether the consumer has actually bought the coupon's product or not. Preventing this from happening is extremely difficult.

Retailer-specific coupons aim to bring consumers into those outlets, and to keep them coming back. Like manufacturer coupons, retailer coupons can also have product-based aims. These may include encouraging consumers to try own brand products, to repurchase or to trade up. As a part of the supermarkets' loyalty schemes, retailer-specific

TABLE 17.1

Top 10 sectors using coupons in the UK in 1994

Rank	Sector
1	Alcoholic drinks
2	Soft drinks
3	Household products
4	Sauces, pickles and spreads
5	Toiletries
6	Frozen foods
7	Beverages
8	Meat, fish and poultry
9	Biscuits
10	Breakfast cereals

Source: NCH Promotional Services.

TABLE 17.2

Shares of coupon distribution and redemption by medium in the UK in 1994 (per cent)

	Distribution	Redemption
Magazines	25.0	6.0
Newspapers	19.8	4.9
Door to door	14.2	13.1
In/on pack	9.4	39.1
In-store	23.8	18.3
Direct mail	4.1	13.4
Other	3.7	5.2

Source: NCH Promotional Services.

coupons are distributed through direct mail to scheme members. It seems, however, that although the coupons are personalised by having the shopper's name printed on them, a standard set of coupons is issued to all scheme members. This led to Tesco receiving many complaints in the early stages of its Clubcard scheme from vegetarians who had received chicken vouchers!

For whoever issues the coupon, redemption rates are crucial, and can vary from 1 per cent with coupons in advertisements to around 20 per cent with coupons appearing on or in packs (Gofton, 1995). Not surprisingly, it has been found that the higher the coupon value, the greater the interest and redemption. Geographical variations in redemption may also be found. Within the UK, for example, rates tend to be higher in the north than in the south (Wilmshurst, 1993). Overall, the UK is following the lead of the USA where couponing has become one of the main forms of sales promotion because of its flexibility and its direct application to the brand. In 1995, 4.4 billion coupons were distributed in the UK, of which 36 per cent were issued by retailers (Gofton, 1996).

Coupons are subtly different from the other money-based promotions already discussed. With shelf and on-pack price cuts, the offer is open to all purchasers, and there is a very direct link between the price cut and the product which may cheapen the brand. A coupon does not look like a price cut, mainly because the price quoted at the shelf or on the product remains intact. The coupon is also a little more selective, in that only those who collect a coupon and remember to redeem it qualify for the discount.

However, to counter that, coupons are very common, and consumers are overexposed to them. Unless a coupon carries a significant discount on the product, or applies to something intrinsically new and exciting, it is difficult as a consumer to be enthusiastic about them. Increasingly, coupons are being used by people who would have purchased anyway, so the rate of favourable brand switching or recruitment of new users might not be as high as the manufacturers hope. If coupons are being applied to mature products and being redeemed mainly by existing buyers, then all the manufacturer is doing is reducing profits (*see* p. 419).

Rebates

A **cash rebate** or 'cash back' scheme involves a little more work and loyalty from the consumer. Tokens or labels have to be collected from packaging, involving a number of purchasing episodes, and then mailed in to qualify for either hard cash or a substantial coupon (retailer or product specific). This is similar to gift-based schemes, but this involves cash rather than gifts or merchandise. In this case, the 'prize' is widely accepted and valued, and handling costs are considerably reduced.

Example

Turtle Wax ran a Cash in a Flash promotion in 1995–6 in which purchasers of their Colour Magic car polish could claim £2 back with proof of purchase. To add further excitement, the promotion promised that the cash would be sent out within 48 hours of receiving the claim, although the agent handling the redemptions said that 80 per cent of claims were turned around within four hours (Cobb, 1995e).

However if the amounts of money are small, the customer may not develop much interest and may not bother to redeem the offer. It has even been argued (Fill, 1995) that rebates can sometimes be viewed negatively by the customer, who might see them as inconvenient and too much trouble to claim. To some consumers, rebates might even suggest low-quality products that need special help to sell them. For an established product which is well known in terms of image and quality, however, a rebate scheme might achieve a number of things. It is not seen as a direct price cut to all purchasers, and therefore is less likely to taint the image than other methods so far discussed. The customer is working for the rebate through repeat purchases and the effort of collecting and mailing the tokens, and thus the rebate will be valued when it comes. Depending on the time limit put on the sales promotion and the number of tokens required to qualify for the rebate, it may be possible to increase the number and frequency of purchases, even if it is only existing buyers who take advantage of the offer. Because it is a mail-in offer, the manufacturer gets the added benefit of customer names and addresses, offering future potential of direct marketing (more of this in Chapter 19).

> ### Example
>
> When Persil did a rebate offer, they not only asked for labels, but also for till receipts showing the product purchases. If consumers responded to this on a large scale, there is potentially a lot of rich information to be had out of this. Most supermarkets now issue itemised till receipts, so the manufacturer can see what other products consumers buy with their Persil, where they purchased (always the same outlet or a variety?), how frequently they purchased, when they purchased (even down to the time of day), the total number of items purchased and the amount spent on each shopping trip. This may not constitute scientifically rigorous market research, but it certainly gives a quick and dirty feel for shopping habits, and might indicate directions for future promotional activities with a more specific focus.

Rebates do not only apply to manufacturer products. Look back to p. 657, where retailer cash rebate schemes aimed at increasing the value and frequency of purchasing was discussed.

CONSUMER SALES PROMOTION METHODS (2): PRODUCT BASED

One of the risks of money-based promotions that was constantly reiterated in the previous section was the ease with which consumers could relate the promotion to price cutting, and thus the image of the product could, in their eyes, be cheapened. One way of overcoming that problem is to opt for a promotion centred on the product itself. The first method discussed in this section, extra product, demonstrates how this works. The second method, sampling, shows how a product-centred technique can achieve a much greater range of difficult objectives than any money-based activity. Figure 17.7 summarises **product-based sales promotion** methods.

Extra product

There are two main alternatives for the 'extra product' technique.

Extra Free
The 'extra free' technique involves offers such as Sainsbury's '20% EXTRA FREE' own-brand cans of chopped tomatoes. Just in case the consumer has trouble conceptualising what 20 per cent looks like, the primarily blue label had a contrasting red band around the top giving a rough indication of the bit of the can that was free. If that was not sufficient, the red band also carried the words '480 gram for the price of 397 gram' in smaller writing. Similarly, Ovaltine's blue-coloured boxes of Options hot

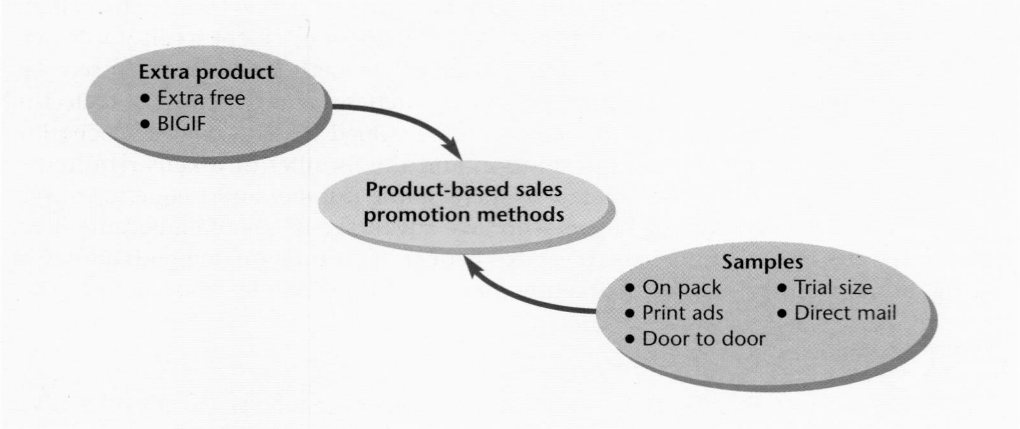

FIGURE 17.7

**Product-based
sales promotion
methods**

chocolate powders carried a bright yellow flash on the front proclaiming, '30 %
EXTRA FREE, 13 sachets for the price of 10'.

Obviously, such offers require changes in the packaging graphics to communicate
the offer, and may even involve major changes in the physical size of the package to
accommodate the extra product. If Sainsbury's tomatoes are normally sold in 400-
gram cans, then producing a 480-gram can will require planned production changes.

A money-based promotion might put 20p back in the consumer's hand; a product-
based promotion might give them 20p's worth of extra product free. To the manufacturer, either option rewards the buyer with 20p, but the buyer's perceptions of the two
are very different. 20p in the hand is 'giving something back', whereas extra product
free is clearly 'giving something in addition' and in the consumer's mind, might be
valued at a good deal more than 20p. These product-based promotions, therefore,
break the link between promotion and price. This method may be especially attractive
as a response to a competitor's price attack, as it can shape the value image of a product without a direct price war

BIGIF or BOGOFF

In contrast to offering extra free product within a single package, the **BIGIF** (Buy 1 Get
1 Free) or the BOGOFF (Buy One Get One For Free) offers centre on bigger rewards,
and are aimed primarily at loading up the customer. Effectively, the offer is saying
'100% EXTRA FREE'. As discussed at p. 660, manufacturers may have a particular
interest in making sure that the consumer has a kitchen full of their brands, as a
means of making them less sensitive to the competition and getting them used to
having that product around.

Retailers are increasingly using a variation on this method, based around bulk purchasing, making the offer, 'Buy two and get a third one free' (B2G3F? – it doesn't
quite have the same ring as BOGOFF, does it?). Sometimes the hurdle is even higher.

> **Example**
>
> Supermarkets occasionally offer 800g cans of Pedigree Chum dog food on a 'buy 6
> and get the 7th can free' basis. Consumers do not tend to see this as a backdoor
> price cutting exercise, because they accept without question that bulk buying is
> cheaper and there is no reflection on the product's image or quality.

These offers may need shorter lead times than the 20 per cent extra free type, because
they do not involve major changes to the packaging. Two ordinary packs can be

Sampling kids

Sampling is a very powerful sales promotion technique. Allowing people to try the product for themselves and thus to judge it for themselves is a convincing way of communicating product benefits. Marketers who are targeting children, however, have to be very careful with sampling. Handing out samples of products in-store is a common form of sample distribution. But while there is no problem in stopping adults in store and giving them 'freebies', children are much more vulnerable. Marketers would not want to be accused of encouraging children to take sweets from strangers, nor would they want to give kids anything that their parents might object to or that might trigger a medical condition. Whereas an adult might have the sense to ask whether a sample contains a certain substance that could trigger an allergy, for example, a child might just accept the sample in blind faith. FDS Field Marketing, an agency

that handles promotional sampling, thus instructs its personnel not to hand out anything to children under 16 without a parent's or teacher's consent.

Fox Confectionery, a part of the Nestlé group, manufactures a number of brands of children's sweets. The company's market research has discovered that most children try new products as a result of hearing about them on the playground grapevine. Thus it is crucial for Fox to get samples of products into children's hands so that they can tell others about how good the product is. In 1996, Fox ran sampling exercises at the theme parks Alton Towers and Chessington World of Adventure. All the samples, however, were only handed out at the exits to the parks, and only if a parent or responsible adult gave permission.

Source: Croft (1996b).

banded together away from the main production line if necessary. In the case of the retailers' B2G3F offers, no banding is needed at all. The offer is made through notices at the shelf, and the computerised checkout is programmed to make the discount automatically when the required number of items have been scanned through.

Samples

Using a 'host' brand to distribute samples of another of the organisation's brands can benefit both products.

Where the main objective is to persuade people to try a product, sampling is often used. People can experience the product for themselves at little or no financial risk and decide on their own evidence whether to adopt the product and buy the full-sized pack or not. **Samples** are thus popular and effective. Seventy per cent of households claim to use the free samples that come through the letterbox. The added bonus, particularly with those samples distributed away from the point of sale, is that the sample's packaging can teach the consumer about the product's benefits, and through graphics that relate directly to the full-sized pack, aid brand recognition in the store.

Source: Christopher Thorburn Associates.

The costs of sampling can be very high. The packaging has to be specially designed and produced, and then there are the costs of distribution. The aim is the future generation of sales, and if it takes a sample to convert a 'possibly would buy' into a 'definitely will buy', then it is a justifiable expense.

In the area of traditional sampling, a one-use or one-portion sample is usually sufficient, and there are a number of ways in which it can be distributed. These are discussed below.

In 1995, Pepsi Max used sampling as part of a wider marketing campaign aimed at the 16 to 24 age group, and succeeded in getting 470 000 consumers to try the product, followed up by a high level of repeat purchasing. The samples were not, however, distributed by any of the conventional means discussed below, but through a travelling roadshow over a two-month period. The sales promotion agency which developed the scheme claimed:

> 'It was "in your face" sampling to reflect the style of the advertising ... it was intrusive and impactful, and, as it was highly targeted, did not suffer from any of the negative connotations of traditional sampling' (Oliver, 1995a, p. XVIII).

A roadshow was also used by Coca-Cola in launching Fruitopia. A combination of the roadshow and door-to-door sample drops meant that 750 000 consumers tried the product (Bond, 1995).

On-pack

If a manufacturer is launching a new product in a range, then samples could be given away with existing products. The objective is to inform existing customers of the new product and to allow them to try it. The problem is that this type of promotion is limited to those who buy the existing product. If new customers are required, then usually other mechanisms must be used.

William Grant managed to overcome the problem of on-pack sample distribution in launching its new whisky brand Black Barrel. In a pan-European 'Taste the Difference' promotion, anyone who ordered a Scotch or Irish whisky or bourbon was also given a free glass of Black Barrel. Effectively, the new brand was being given away with its competitors' products!

Trial sizes

To recoup some of the costs of producing the samples, they can be sold in retail outlets at a minimal price. Sold as products in their own right, they may attract a wider audience than simply those who already purchase the same manufacturer's existing brands. The small cost is insignificant to the consumer, who still sees it as a relatively risk-free way of trying something different. As with on-pack distributions, it is a good mechanism for introducing new products, or new colours or flavours within an existing product line.

Nescafé produced **trial sizes** of its coffee brands in 22g jars, to encourage trial. Just before Christmas 1995, these small jars were even being sold in sets, with one of each type of coffee, as gift packs.

Print media

Because print media allow the targeting of fairly narrowly profiled audiences, this can be an efficient way of distributing samples to potential buyers. Cosmetics and toiletries, for example, are often sampled through women's magazines. Some samples associated with print media have become very significant in their own right. Computer magazines give away demonstration disks featuring various types of software.

Example

The April 1994 copy of *Computer Buyer* gave away a playable demonstration disk of Pinball Fantasies, substantial enough to provide plenty of satisfying entertainment, but limited enough to encourage purchase of the full game. Even if the software does not appeal, the purchaser still has a free disk that can be reformatted.

Similarly, *Classic CD*, a monthly magazine specialising in classical music, gives away a full length (around 70 minutes) CD with every issue, every month, featuring tracks from recent releases. Free CDs regularly feature material from EMI, Phillips, RCA, Deutsche Grammophon, Sony and Hyperion, among others. For the record companies, this is an unbeatable way of whetting the appetite of potential buyers, and for consumers, the CD makes excellent listening, and acts as an audible shop window, reassuring them that they will like particular recordings. This is sampling at a very sophisticated level.

Direct mail

Samples that are small, light and non-perishable can be distributed by direct mail, either to people already on a mailing list, or to those who respond to an offer made in an advertisement.

Example

Maxwell House distributed a leaflet within Sunday newspaper colour supplements with two one-cup sachets of coffee. Having sampled the coffee, the consumer could then mail in for a free voucher for a jar of Maxwell House in return for admitting which brand they currently used. Mailing samples to existing customers means that the samples get into the hands of people who are likely to appreciate them and be converted to the new product. Using direct response advertising allows the organisation to know who has received the samples, and to start building a relationship with them.

Door-to-door

Door-to-door distribution is a popular, but expensive way of distributing samples. Delivering the sample to the house means that you are not dependent on particular existing purchasing patterns (in terms of either store or brand preference), you are not depending on the consumer to notice the sample-in store, nor are you asking them to pay towards the sample. Effectively, you are putting the sample directly into their hands in an environment where it is likely to be remembered and used. Some targeting is possible, using geodemographic segmentation to prioritise distribution areas (*see* pp. 175 *et seq.*), but generally, this is mass sample distribution.

Samples might be distributed through the letterbox, or more expensively through a personal call. Personal calls make sure that samples only go to those households that will use them and can also be used for more extensive market research data collection.

Example

When Persil Power was launched in the UK market in 1994, more than two-thirds of UK households received a sample pack as part of the wider marketing communications strategy.

They also ensure that the sample is put into the hands of a responsible adult rather than being eaten on the doormat by the dog or abducted by the children!

CONSUMER SALES PROMOTION METHODS (3):

GIFT, PRIZE OR MERCHANDISE BASED

A wide range of activities depend on the offer of prizes, low-cost goods or free gifts to stimulate the consumer's buying behaviour. Holidays, brand-related cookery books, mugs or clothing featuring product logos, and small plastic novelty toys are among the vast range of incentives used to complement the main product sale.

Example

The Danish nappy manufacturer, Libero, gives a baby book to new mothers in hospital. Inside the book is an invitation to join Libero's Baby Club so that further marketing communication can be sent, including other promotional incentives, direct to a relevant target audience (Pearce, 1996).

There are many ways in which these incentives can be offered, each with a different impact and its own objectives, as summarised in Figure 17.8.

Self-liquidating offers

Self-liquidating offers invite the consumer to pay a small amount of money, and usually to submit specified proofs of purchase, in return for goods which are not necessarily directly related to the main product purchase. The money paid usually is just enough to cover the cost price of the goods and a contribution to postage and

FIGURE 17.8

Gift, prize or merchandise-based sales promotion methods

handling, and thus these promotions become self-financing if the expected number of customers takes them up.

Often, such a promotion is used to reinforce the brand name and identity of the products featuring the scheme.

Example

An apron with the Bisto logo on it is a daily reminder of the brand. Similarly, Batchelor's Cup a Soup offered an exclusive mug, featuring the brand logo, for £3.99 and two tokens. As a sales promotion, this serves the usual purposes of attracting attention and encouraging sustained purchase of the product. Beyond that, however, the obvious relationship between the soup and the mug underlines the essential brand values of convenience and self-indulgence communicated initially through the product's TV advertising line, 'You only get a hug from a Batchelor's mug'. Consumers value mugs, as they are useful things to have around, and they also value clothing. Carlsberg Tetley ran a self-liquidating promotion for surfing shorts. Similar shorts retail in the shops for about £12, but the promotion offered them for £4.99 plus five ringpulls. Tee-shirts and sweat-shirts are also popular and mean that the customer can act as a walking advertisement for a product. Le Shuttle Tee-shirts are popular with lorry drivers, while photographs of Princess Diana wearing a Virgin Atlantic sweatshirt are estimated to have generated brand exposure equivalent to several million pounds worth of advertising. Where the price charged for the goods becomes higher than that needed to cover the basic costs of the offer, then the offer ceases to be purely a sales promotion, and the goods become a product in their own right (Cummins, 1989).

The problem with most self-liquidating promotions is that response levels tend to be low, as consumers have to be prepared to spend money and make an effort to benefit from the offer. Furthermore, the premium itself has to be very interesting and different to get a good response. Plain mugs can easily be purchased cheaply from discount stores, but brand-specific ones that can only be sourced through the promotion, like the Batchelor's offer, have something more attractive about them. They are 'exclusive', and they are only available for a limited time, hence the incentive value.

Free mail-in

In the case of a free mail-in, the consumer can claim a gift, free of charge, in return for proofs of purchase and perhaps the actual cost of postage (but not handling charges or the cost of the gift itself).

Example

Kitchen Devils, the kitchen knives brand, offered a free chopping board in return for the barcode from one of their products, a till receipt showing its purchase, and 52p in stamps to contribute to postage. As kitchen knives are by no means frequently purchased, inexpensive fmcg goods, asking for only the one proof of purchase in return for a substantial premium is reasonable. In contrast, fmcg brands such as breakfast cereals are more demanding. Weetabix offered a die cast metal performance model car in exchange for 12 tokens and a 20p contribution to postage. The tokens were deliberately adjusted to the different pack sizes: two on the 24-biscuit pack, and six on the 72-biscuit pack. This offer demanded multiple purchases, and given that there were six different cars to collect within the offer's time limit, there was a clear intention to establish intensive Weetabix loyalty and usage within households.

Free mail-ins have increased in popularity in recent years. The free goods attract the consumer and encourage a higher response rate, and the responses potentially provide the organisation with direct marketing opportunities. The main aim, however, in sales promotion terms is to encourage the consumer to make enough additional purchases to collect the necessary proofs of purchase within a carefully assessed time period. If the Weetabix offer mentioned above ran for only one month, few consumers would collect enough even for one car, never mind all six! The frustration of not quite managing to collect enough to meet an offer deadline, or of feeling coerced into buying unreasonably large quantities of goods in a short space of time, might turn consumers against a brand.

Example

Synergy between the product, the premium and the target market might also be important. Chopping boards are likely to be appealing to someone who is interested in purchasing a kitchen knife. The Weetabix cars were aimed at the product's end users and influencers (the children) rather than the purchasers themselves (the parents). A more adult-orientated cereal brand, Shredded Wheat, offered a free admission voucher to any National Trust property in exchange for 10 tokens. This promotion ran at the same time as the Weeabix car offer, but had a very different appeal.

Of course, the promotion is only free to the consumer. The promoter has to consider carefully the merchandise costs, postage, packing, processing and even VAT. All of this has to be put into the context of the likely response rate so that the total cost of the promotion can be forecast and an appropriate quantity of merchandise can be ordered and available when the promotion begins.

Example

The Hoover free flights deal (two tickets to the US free if you purchase a Hoover product) is a good example of what can happen when the forecasting goes wrong, and there is insufficient 'merchandise' for claimants. This promotion resulted in many dissatisfied customers, litigation, and a great deal of extra expense to Hoover, not to mention damaging PR.

Free inside or on pack

Offering free gifts contained inside or banded on to the outside of the pack can make a big impact at the point of sale because the reward is instant, and the purchaser does not have to make any special effort to claim it. One-off gifts are designed to bring the consumer's attention to a product and to encourage them to try it. The offer might shake them out of a routine response purchase and make them think about trying a different brand.

In-pack promotions

In-pack promotions are often used in child-orientated breakfast cereals and, to stimulate repeat purchase, the gifts often form part of a related series.

The costs of in-pack gifts can be high, especially when offered with food products. There may be limitations on size, materials, toxicity, protection and smell in order to conform to hygiene standards. These costs, as well as the direct promotion costs, must be considered.

On-pack promotions

Gifts attached to the outside of the pack are less constrained, and again, provide an immediate reward for purchase. They may even be more attractive than in-pack gifts, as the purchaser can actually see and evaluate the gift in advance.

Free with product

'Free with product' is similar to an on-pack offer, except that the gift is not attached to the product but has to be claimed at the checkout. The forerunner of current practice was the plastic daffodil free with soap powder in the 1950s. There are often logistical and practical difficulties for high-volume supermarkets in using this method, so its use has declined somewhat. Laser scanning checkouts, however, do allow supermarkets to run their own versions of this kind of offer. The consumer, for example, might be invited at the point of sale to buy a jar of coffee and claim a free packet of biscuits. The computerised checkout can tell whether the conditions of the promotion have been met and automatically deducts the price of the biscuits from the final total.

Customer loyalty schemes

Given the increasingly high cost of creating new customers, organisations have turned their attention to ways of retaining the loyalty of current customers. Major international airlines have their frequent flyer schemes, many different retail and service organisations give away air miles with purchases, and petrol stations and supermarkets issue smart cards through which customers can accumulate points as

TABLE 17.3

The 11 Ps of loyalty marketing

1	Pricing	Be customer specific – reward the best
2	Purchases	Make product-specific offers
3	Point flexibility	Occasionally offer double points, for example
4	Partners	Develop alliances with other retailers
5	Prizes	Weekly prize draw for cardholders, for example
6	Pro-bono	Allow customers to convert points into charity donations
7	Personalisation	Direct mail, specifically targeted at customer
8	Privileges	Invite cardholders to special events, for example
9	Participation	Invite best customers to take part in new variations of scheme
10	Pronto	Generate offers at the point of sale
11	Proactive	Use information to predict/pre-empt customer behaviour

Source: Woolf, as quoted by Mitchell (1995).

mentioned earlier. All of these schemes are designed to encourage repeat buying, especially where switching is easy and generic brand loyalty is low. Brian Woolf, an American database marketing expert, proposes eleven rules for getting the best out of a loyalty scheme. These are outlined in Table 17.3.

Price promotions can be dangerous in that they encourage consumers to become price sensitive, and are easily copied by competitors. Tokens, points, and stamps that can be traded in for other goods are all ways of adding value to a product, while avoiding costly price competition. They are thus known as **alternative currencies**.

Trading stamps

Trading stamps are a long-established example of alternative currency. The number of stamps awarded at the point of sale is directly proportional to the value of purchases made. The stamps can be redeemed at the customer's convenience for gifts. Supermarkets and petrol stations widely participated in these schemes until the 1970s. The problem with stamps was that they tended to drive prices upwards at a time when straight price discounting was a more attractive alternative for the consumer.

Points and tokens

In place of trading stamps, new variants have emerged.

Example

Mobil operate a Premier Points collecting scheme in which accumulated points can be redeemed for goods at Argos stores. Motorists are issued with smart cards which can be credited with an amount by electronic transfer according to their spend at participating petrol stations. Every 10p spent on fuel attracts a credit point under a system that is far easier and more convenient to use than sticking stamps in books. Of course some shoppers will still buy on lowest price, but others are happy to accumulate points towards a free gift. Supermarket loyalty schemes work on a similar basis.

One of the problems with loyalty schemes, however, is the sheer number of them. When every airline has a frequent flyer scheme and when every supermarket has a loyalty club, then the competitive edge is lost. As reported by Cobb (1995b), for example, airlines are generating a very small level of extra sales through their loyalty schemes, and some petrol companies are spending up to £10 million a year on schemes that

Tesco gained considerable marketing advantage when it introduced its Clubcard loyalty scheme.

Source: Tesco Stores plc.

only attract 10 per cent of their customers. Furthermore, there is evidence that the loyalty generated by such schemes is questionable. Mitchell (1995) reports a MORI poll that found that 25 per cent of loyalty card holders would switch to a rival scheme if the benefits were better. Mitchell also questions whether the benefits gained outweigh the cost of such schemes, when hardware, software, administration and implementation costs are taken into account.

Nevertheless, loyalty schemes are fast becoming an established part of the marketing scene. The next logical progression is to think about pan-European schemes. There are both cultural and legislative difficulties with this, however. Those in the industry feel that pan-European schemes can at present be built around a broad strategy, but need to incorporate sufficient tailored flexibility to allow for different countries' cultures and legislation covering promotional activities. Sony, for example, has a scheme operating in 23 countries, but only in terms of educational, display and brochure material (Cobb, 1995a).

Contests and sweepstakes

Gifts given free to all purchasers of a product necessarily are limited to relatively cheap and cheerful items. As Hoover found out, giving away expensive freebies to all purchasers is uneconomic. **Contests and sweepstakes**, therefore, allow organisations to offer very attractive and valuable incentives, such as cars, holidays and large amounts of cash, to very small numbers of purchasers who happen to be lucky enough to win. Such promotions might be seen as rather boring by consumers, unless there is something really special about them.

Example

Trebor gave six competition winners the chance to 'Jet into Space' by taking them to Russia and allowing them to take the controls of a Sikorski fighter jet. Allied Domecq achieved an increase of 28 per cent in store traffic at Schiphol airport's duty free shop with an interactive video play and win promotion with T-shirts and shopping vouchers as prizes. They claim that this promotion increased sales of some brands by 200 per cent and 800 per cent (Burnside, 1995).

Contests

Contests have to involve a demonstration of knowledge, or of analytical or creative skills to produce a winner. Setting a number of multiple choice questions, or requiring the competitor to uncover three matching symbols on a scratch card, or asking them to create a slogan, are all legitimate contest activities.

Example

A Volvo dealership wanted to attract car buyers by offering them the opportunity to win £5000 if they bought a Volvo from that dealership during March 1994. On completing the contract for the purchase of the car, each buyer then had to answer three simple questions and complete a slogan to qualify them for the competition.

Sweepstakes

Sweepstakes do not involve skill, but offer every entrant an equal chance of winning through the luck of the draw. Additionally, they must ensure that entry is open to anyone, regardless of whether they have purchased a product or not. Thus *Reader's Digest* prize draws have to be equally open to those not taking up the organisation's kind offer of a subscription. Similarly, if the Volvo dealership mentioned above had not introduced the competition element (through the questions and slogan), their £5000 draw would have had to be open to anybody, making it a much less attractive and exclusive incentive to purchase.

Such activities are popular with both consumers and organisations. The consumer gets the chance to win something really worthwhile, and the organisation can hope to generate many extra sales for a fixed outlay. With price or gift-based promotions, the more you sell, the more successful the promotion, the more it costs you because you have to pay out on every sale. With competitions and sweepstakes, the more successful the activity, the more entries it attracts, yet the prizes remain fixed. The only losers with a popular contest or sweepstake are the consumers, whose chances of winning become slimmer! However, at some stage consumers may become bored with such activities, especially if they do not think they have any reasonable chance of winning. At that point, a more immediate, but less valuable incentive might be more appropriate.

All contests and sweepstakes are strictly controlled in the UK under the Lotteries and Amusements Act 1976, and a code of sales promotion practice guides the presentation and administration of such schemes. It is essential for an organisation to seek professional legal and expert advice to avoid any allegation of illegal or questionable practice that could backfire on the promoter. Despite the problems and the need for caution, contests and sweepstakes can, however, provide a lift to flagging product interest and generate additional awareness. Table 17.4 summarises some of the issues on which decisions need to be made before such promotions can be implemented.

TABLE 17.4
Contests and sweepstakes: Issues for decision

- Communicating the promotion – on/in pack? leaflet? print media? etc.
- Prize structure and description
- Prize limits
- Entry conditions
- Proof of purchase requirements
- Eligibility and geographic restrictions
- Supplementary rule availability
- Entry method – mail? phone?
- Closing date
- Selection criteria for winner
- Tie breaker
- Notification of results

CONSUMER SALES PROMOTION METHODS (4): STORE BASED

This section looks more generally at what can be done within a retail outlet to stimulate consumer interest in products, leading perhaps to trial or purchase.

Point of sale displays

Sales promotion at the point of sale (**POS**) is critical in situations where the customer enters the store undecided or is prepared to switch brands fairly readily. Many different POS materials and methods can be used. These include posters, displays, dispensers, dump bins and other containers to display product. New technology has further changed POS promotion with flashing signs, videos, message screens and other such attention-seeking display material. Interactive POS systems can help customers to select the most appropriate offering for their needs, or can direct them to other promotional offers.

Thomas Cook, the travel agent, for example, uses a system that helps customers to select holidays, while Daewoo uses interactive screens to help consumers 'design' the car they want.

The main objectives of POS promotion are to inform the customer and to persuade them to try or retry the product. In some areas it has been suggested that up to 55 per cent of purchasing decisions are made in-store. This means that the manufacturer has to ensure the product 'talks from the shelf' to attract attention. Cadbury's claim that illuminated or moving POS promotional displays can achieve a 40 per cent increase in sales (Cobb, 1995c).

However, as seen in Chapter 13, retailers are increasingly dominating the shelves in their own stores. It is they who decide on the co-ordinated image for the store and strictly control the use of manufacturer-inspired POS material. They want impact, but do not want their stores to look like a loose collection of POS jumble, nor do they want too many flimsy tacky-looking cardboard displays.

Example

Adidas supply retailers with units that can display up to 25 sports shoes and that are flexible enough to adjust for different ranges and interchangeable graphics. Similarly, but on a smaller physical scale, Revlon have produced a display unit for cosmetics that stands on a counter. It has 80 variations to allow it to be used across Europe, the Far East and the Americas in all types of stores (Cobb, 1995d).

Demonstrations

In-store demonstrations are a very powerful means of gaining interest and trial. Food product cooking demonstrations and tasters are used by retailer and manufacturer alike, especially if the product is a little unusual and would benefit from exposure (i.e., cheese, meats, drinks etc.). Other demonstrations include cosmetic preparation and application, electrical appliances, especially if they are new and unusual, and cars. These demonstrations may take place within the retail environment, but the growth of shopping centre display areas provides a more flexible means for direct selling via a demonstration.

Organisations sometimes use **field marketing agencies** to handle in-store demonstrations and other promotional activities. The agency may well hand out samples and demonstrate products, but they also make sure that products are properly displayed and check where they are positioned on the shelf, particularly in relation to the competition.

METHODS OF PROMOTION TO THE RETAIL TRADE

Manufacturers of consumer goods are dependent on the retail trade to sell their product for them. Just as consumers sometimes need that extra little bit of incentive to try
a product or to become committed to it, retailers too need encouragement to push a
particular product into the distribution system and to facilitate its movement to the
customer. Of course, many of the consumer-orientated activities considered in previous sections help that process through pull strategies.

Some trade promotions are tightly linked with consumer promotions to create a synergy between push and pull strategies.

The main push promotions are variations on price promotions and direct assistance
with selling to the final customer. These will now be looked at in turn.

Allowances and discounts

Allowances and discounts aim to maintain or increase the volume of stock moving
through the channel of distribution. The first priority is to get the stock into the
retailer, and then to influence ordering patterns by the offer of a price advantage. All
of the offers discussed here encourage retailers to increase the amount of stock held
over a period, and thus might also encourage them to sell the product more aggressively. This may be especially important where there is severe competition between
manufacturers' brands.

Individual case bonuses

The most popular form of trade price promotion is the one whereby a retailer or distributor is offered a price reduction on each unit or case purchased (for a limited period only). The advantage of this method is that it is very flexible to introduce and drop, especially with the widespread use of direct ordering systems by phone, fax or computer.

Volume allowances

An allowance or discount could depend on the retailer fulfiling a condition relating to volume purchased. The allowance may take several forms. It could, for instance, be a fixed amount per case provided that an agreed number of cases are purchased. Thus a retailer buying a minimum of 20 cases of a product, for instance, might qualify for a 2 per cent discount on the order total that is not offered to the retailer who only buys 19 cases. Alternatively, the allowance might only apply to those cases purchased over and above the minimum order threshold. Thus the retailer gets no discount on the first 20, but does get a 2 per cent discount on the 21st and subsequent cases. Allowances might also operate on smaller quantities quoted in units.

> **Example**
>
> In the run-up to Christmas 1995, Courage Beer was offering retailers 28 cans for the price of 24 on its John Smith's Bitter and Foster's brands, and 24 cans for the price of 22 on other lager brands and John Smith's Draught.

Discount overriders

Discount overriders are longer-term, retrospective discounts, awarded on a quarterly or annual basis, depending on the achievement of agreed volumes or sales targets. These may be applicable to an industrial distributor selling components as a retail outlet. Although the additional discount may be low, perhaps 0.5 per cent, on a turnover of £500 000 it would still be an attractive £2500.

Count and recount

Count and recount is also a retrospective method in that it offers a rebate for each case (or whatever the stock unit is) sold during a specified period. Thus on the first day of the period, all existing stock is counted and any inward shipments received during the period are added to that total. At the end of the period, all remaining unsold cases are deducted. The difference represents the amount of stock actually shifted, forming the basis on which a rebate is paid. Figure 17.9 shows an example of the calculations involved. This method is not easy to administer and is, of course, potentially time consuming to operate.

Free merchandise

The equivalent of the consumers' BIGIF (*see* p. 668), but on a larger scale, this method involves the offer of free merchandise in return for an agreed level of purchases, for instance buy 10 cases and get another two free. Indirectly, this is a price-based promotion in the retailer's eyes, as it effectively reduces the average cost of all the cases purchased of that brand. The free merchandise need not necessarily be the product itself.

> **Example**
>
> Scottish Courage Brands offered free Foster's carrier bags, themselves featuring a T-shirt offer to retailers. To qualify, the retailer had to buy 20 cases of certain Courage beer and lager brands to get 100 carrier bags, 15 cases to get 75 bags, and 10 cases to get 50 bags.

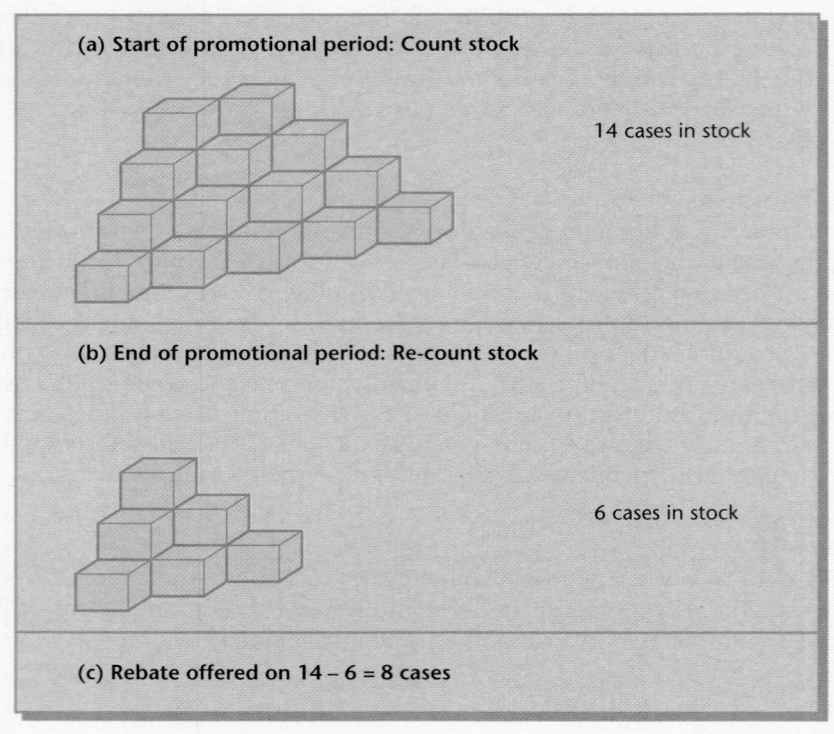

FIGURE 17.9

Count and recount rebate

(a) Start of promotional period: Count stock

14 cases in stock

(b) End of promotional period: Re-count stock

6 cases in stock

(c) Rebate offered on 14 – 6 = 8 cases

Price-based promotions aimed at the trade are less risky than those aimed at consumers, as the organisational buyer will view them as legitimate competitive tactics rather than using them judgementally to make emotive evaluations of the product. Price promotions appeal to the trade because they make a direct and measurable impact on the retailer's cost structure, and the retailer has the flexibility to choose whether to keep those cost savings or to pass them on to the end consumer. However, in common with price-promotions offered to the consumer, trade-orientated price promotions do have the disadvantage of being quickly and easily copied by the competition, leading to the risk of mutually destructive price wars.

Selling and marketing assistance

A number of manufacturer-supported sales and marketing activities assist the reseller by means of promotion at both local and national level.

Co-operative advertising

In co-operative advertising a manufacturer agrees to fund a percentage of a retailer's local advertising, as long as the manufacturer's products are featured in at least part of the advertisement. Normally, the support is limited to media buying rather than creative costs, and is usually set in proportion to the value of product purchased by the retailer from the manufacturer. However, in some cases, standard broadcasting messages or advertising designs, which can be adapted by agreement, are made available to the reseller.

Co-operative advertising support can be very costly, and thus the manufacturer needs to think very carefully before offering it, as it can potentially put far greater pressure on the manufacturer's own promotional budget than some of the methods previously discussed. A further problem arises from the sometimes unco-ordinated

Wetsuit technology provided a heavily branded incentive designed to improve enjoyment of the product itself.

Source: Christopher Thornburn Associates.

advertising programme that may develop. In some regions there may be overlap but in others the retailer may have little interest in media advertising, resulting in incomplete coverage.

Although in theory manufacturer support may result in better advertising, attempts by resellers to crowd a print advertisement with products, often with price promotions, tend to undermine the position and value of some goods – fmcg brands in particular. Rather than leaving the control of the advertisement in the hands of an individual reseller, therefore, some manufacturers prefer to develop dealer listings. These are advertisements, controlled by the manufacturer, which feature the product and then list those resellers from whom it can be purchased. These are particularly common with cars, higher value household appliances, and top of the range designer clothing, for example.

Merchandising allowances

Using money to provide merchandising allowances rather than for funding advertising may have a more direct benefit to the manufacturer. Payment is made to the retailer for special promotional efforts in terms of displays and in-store promotions such as sampling or demonstrations. This is especially attractive if the product moves quickly and can sustain additional promotional costs.

Sales-force support: Consumer markets

A manufacturer may wish to offer training or support for a retailer's sales representatives who deal directly with the public. Such assistance is most likely to be found in connection with higher priced products of some complexity, for which the purchaser needs considerable assistance at the point of sale. Cars, hi-fi equipment and bigger kitchen appliances are obvious examples of products with substantial technical qualities that need to be explained. With perfumes and fine fragrances, on the other hand, personal service at the point of sale is seen as an important reinforcement of the luxury of the purchase. Manufacturers of such products need retail sales assistants to be well versed in the features and benefits of the products, to be aware of how to match those features and benefits with each customer's needs, and not least, to be enthusiastic about selling the products.

Free training

Free training helps to forge a closer relationship between manufacturer and both retailers and their staff, as well as fulfilling the objective of giving the sales assistants the necessary knowledge base. Even so, such training may not be enough to instil enthusiasm for selling the product and so, to gain an extra selling edge, further incentives aimed at the retailer's sales team might be necessary.

Sales contests

Various prizes, such as cash, goods or holidays, may be used in sales contests to raise the profile of a product and create a short-term incentive. Unfortunately, the prizes often need to be significant and clearly within the reach of all sales assistants if they are to make any real difference to the selling effort. This is especially true when other competitors may adopt similar methods.

Premium money

Other more direct incentives than those already mentioned are also possible. Additional bonuses, i.e., premium money, may be made available to sales assistants who achieve targets. These are useful where personal selling effort may make all the difference to whether or not a sale is made. However, the manufacturer needs to be sure that the cost is outweighed by the additional sales revenues generated.

SALES PROMOTION TO ORGANISATIONAL MARKETS

As the introduction to this chapter made clear, sales promotion in its strictest sense is inappropriate to many organisational markets. The role of discounts and incentives in organisational selling is dealt with in other parts of this book, most notably Chapters 4, 11, and 18. Discounts and incentives are applicable in situations where the buyer and seller are in direct contact and there is room for negotiation of supply conditions. Of course, where organisational marketing starts to resemble consumer marketing, for example in the case of a small business buying a range of standard supplies from a wholesaler, much of what has already been said about manufacturer–consumer or retailer–consumer sales promotions applies with a little adaptation.

The issue of sales-force support for retailers selling on to consumers was discussed at p. 683. This same issue will now be looked at from the point of view of an organisational market, as an example of how the same basic techniques and philosophies behind sales promotion can be subtly adapted to a different kind of market.

In industrial distribution situations, it is even more important than in consumer markets for the distributor's sales representatives to have full product knowledge and commitment. As the distributor is likely to carry many product lines, the sales representative is unlikely to be knowledgeable about all products and applications, and thus training through manuals and briefings funded by the manufacturer are likely to assist in selling to the end customer. That takes care of the knowledge base, but even that might not be enough, and the provision of sales aids and a formal sales training programme might need to be introduced for the distributor's salesforce. As well as providing detailed training, the manufacturer's own sales force may undertake joint visits with the distributor's representatives to raise the profile of the product in selected areas. Not only does this directly support the selling effort and provide valuable feedback on customer problems, it also enables informal advice to be given on the best methods of presenting the product and service.

JCB

JCB decided that it needed to give a boost to its sales of earthmoving and construction machines so it invited a group of 200 or more UK distributors and their top customers to the Torrequebrada Hotel in Malaga. The event was not only a sales conference, but also a forum in which to demonstrate over 30 different machines which were either being introduced for the first time or part of a relaunch. Similar events were held for distributors from France, Italy, Germany and Spain. In total, some 1500 delegates were involved in a series of back-to-back conferences, the cost of which was claimed to be into six figures.

JCB operates in highly competitive international markets, against the likes of Caterpillar from North America and Komatsu from Asia. Caterpillar's sales are almost ten times greater than JCB's. The JCB strategy is to compete in three main product segments: the compact segment, the mid-range segment and the heavy duty segment – in which JCB is a partner in a joint venture with Sumitomo. JCB has even developed its organisation's marketing structure to follow this split in order to reflect the differences between customer types. Whereas small businesses predominate as customers in the compact segment, sales of the big machines often involve extensive discussions and negotiation with professional buyers.

The sales promotion event was seen as an important part of relationship building with dealers and customers, as well as an opportunity to demonstrate products. Although national events could have been organised, or promotions centred around individual distributorships, an event like this generates a much greater impact, as well as giving JCB a captive audience undistracted by the pressures of day-to-day business. Taking northern Europeans to Spain during a temperate March could also have been an attractive feature of the event!

Source: Gofton (1994).

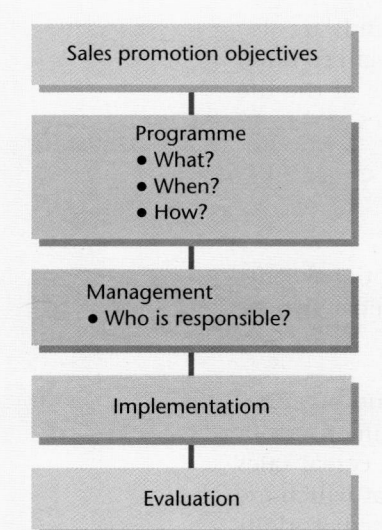

FIGURE 17.10

The sales promotion management process

MANAGING SALES PROMOTION

When we look at the range of objectives (*see* pp. 653–663) achievable through sales promotion, we see that the flexibility and directness of many of the methods described are particularly valuable to the marketing manager as part of a co-ordinated promotional programme. Whereas advertising can produce longer-term results, sales promotion can complement that by providing an immediate POS impact that is very important in attracting and keeping loyalty, especially in retail situations.

This statement should not, however, be taken as in any way undermining the strategic role that sales promotion can also play in the promotional mix. In building and maintaining a brand identity, sales promotion (particularly when the techniques used are not price based) can play a role in adding value to the brand, supporting and enhancing its character. Although the specific objectives and themes of sales promotion may alter during the life of the brand, that invaluable support role will not, and thus even if sales promotions only have a short-term impact, they should, in aggregate, contribute towards the long-term objectives of the product.

All of this implies that sales promotions have to be carefully thought through, and properly designed to fit in with wider market efforts, both corporate and brand specific. Sales promotion thus has to be planned and managed, and the various stages in this process are outlined in Fig 17.10 and discussed below.

Objectives

As the earlier sections of this chapter have shown, many different sales promotion techniques exist to address a wide range of objectives. The definition of appropriate sales promotion objectives should emerge from a much wider strategic marketing communication plan. Any sales promotion programme undertaken has to fit harmoniously with other activities within the promotional mix, as well as making a positive contribution to achieving the overall objectives of the product's marketing mix.

The actual sales promotion techniques employed will themselves depend on the objectives defined and the context within which the sales promotion will take place.

The choice between price and non-price sales promotions may be crucial as the product's life-cycle runs its course. In the early stages, when trial by consumers and retail trade acceptance is vital, the focus may be on samples, coupons and introductory price cuts. Clearly communicating such price cuts as 'trial' or 'introductory' helps to avoid the danger of cheapening the brand's quality.

Example

Sainsbury's, in introducing its own brand Classic Cola, needed to generate trial of the product so that customers could judge the taste for themselves. This was partly done through a massive effort with displays in the stores: posters, banners, and end of aisle displays all over the store, not just in the normal soft drinks area. The shopper could not fail to notice the launch. The main incentive, though, was price based. The 2-litre bottle sold at a trial price of 59p, compared with Coca-Cola's £1.10.

As the brand develops, so the focus of sales promotion objectives may shift to reminders of the product and retaining loyalty, especially if competing brands are also coming on to the scene. This may be an appropriate point at which to begin to build additional brand value with gifts and competitions. In the mature stage of the life cycle, price competition may become more intense and so special bonuses and price promotions may predominate.

Programme

In the development of a sales promotion campaign, as with any other promotional activity, there must be a clear link between the activity, its objectives and the target audience.

Target market

The earlier parts of this chapter distinguished between consumer, trade and organisational sales promotions, but even within those broad categories, the specific needs of different *market segments* need to be considered. A number of breakfast cereal sales promotions, for instance, were mentioned earlier in this chapter, some of which are targeted at children (as users and influencers) and some of which are targeted at adults (as purchasers and users). Similarly, consumers vary in their degree of sensitivity to price and coupon offers. Market segmentation, therefore, can help to determine what kind of sales promotion might be most appropriate, and can also be a major guide to the likelihood of a sales promotion's achieving its objectives.

Campaigns and costs

After the definition of the target audience and sales promotion objectives, a shortlist of alternative *campaigns* can be developed according to the budget available. Unlike a media budget, the sales promotion budget can have far-reaching impact across the organisation, which if not carefully assessed can lead to a resource-intensive campaign. This problem is compounded in that the final cost of the campaign may not be known until it is over. Coupon redemption rates, gift take up and cash backs, for instance, are difficult to estimate in advance.

There are two main types of *cost* category in sales promotion.

Communication cost. Communication cost relates to all the costs incurred in bringing the sales promotion to the target groups. These typically include artwork, print costs (including special packaging), media support and distribution.

Fulfilment cost. Fulfilment cost relates to the cost of handling the campaign and financing the programme offers, whether rebates, prizes, merchandise or discounts. As we saw earlier, even free gifts incur postage and packaging costs. Forecasting redemption rates, and therefore fulfilment cost, is notoriously difficult and depends on both internal and external factors, such as trade support, competitive activity and the effectiveness of the rest of the promotional mix. It is often useful to develop a scenario of likely outcomes for budget outline purposes.

Implementation

As with any communication programme, the duration, intensity, coverage and timing of the campaign needs to be finalised according to the tasks in hand. Although an individual offer may be short-term to gain impact and retain interest, it may itself be a part of a planned series of developing promotional activity, and thus has to be slotted into its appropriate place. Many child-orientated breakfast cereals, for example, permanently feature sales promotions, beginning a new one as soon as the old one ends. These promotions are varied, appealing to different age groups, and utilising different techniques. If the current sales promotion is a free in-pack gift, the next is more likely to be a longer-term mail-in offer. These cereal brands have got to the point where the sales promotion is an expected part of the product offering; it is a shock not to find an offer on the back of a cereal pack!

Guidelines

A number of principles need to be followed to ensure good practice, as outlined by the UK Institute of Sales Promotion and shown in Table 17.5.

TABLE 17.5
Guidelines for good sales promotion practice

Legality	Check any statutory controls/restrictions, e.g. on contests/sweepstakes
Code of practice	What you do should reflect the spirit as well as the letter of the law
Consumer's interests	Deal fairly with the consumer and do not exploit them
Consumer satisfaction	Do not disappoint consumers by raising unrealistic expectations
Fairness	Treat all individuals and participating groups equally
Truthfulness	Do not mislead or deliberately confuse the consumer
Limitations	Exclusions and limitations should be clearly communicated
Suitability	Ensure that the promotion is inaccessible to inappropriate groups where necessary, e.g. children
Administration	Handle consumer queries and responses quickly and efficiently
Responsibility	Prime responsibility lies with the promoter!

Source: Institute of Sales Promotion.

Pan-European guidelines on ethical practice and harmonisation of laws and regulations have not yet been achieved. This means that different countries allow different types of promotion or restrict activities in different ways. Table 17.6 summarises the position as at 1992.

Management

The responsibility for sales promotion will depend partly on the company's policies on the use of external agencies, and partly on the use and demands of sales promotion campaigns.

Using an outside agency brings greater flexibility and fresh ideas into sales promotion campaigns. For the smaller organisation, there may be little choice but to use outside help as an extension of the in-house marketing expertise. However, the agency will need to be clearly briefed and at times managed to ensure that an appropriate type and standard of service is achieved. This is especially true if ongoing assistance is needed to decide on campaign modifications and review. These will often be costed on a time basis.

In-house provision will depend on the structure of the organisation's marketing department. Responsibility may rest with the product manager, marketing services manager, marketing manager or promotions manager. The important points are that there should be direct accountability for sales promotion decisions, and that they are properly integrated and managed within the context of the marketing plan. Clearly, creating in-house sales promotion facilities enables the acquisition and development of skills that can reinforce subsequent campaigns.

Evaluation

Given the range of sales promotion methods available and the increasing spend on such techniques, it is important to assess thoroughly the effectiveness of the programmes developed. This assessment should cover whether the objectives have been met and whether the results were achieved cost effectively. A number of sources can be used:

1 *Sales-force feedback*. Being in the front line, the sales force can quickly get a feel for how a programme is being received by the trade.
2 *Sales data*. Although sales data are a crude measure, early indications of increased shipments may show that a sales promotion is beginning to take off.
3 *Retail audits*. Audits such as Neilson will track changes in distribution, stock levels and market share during and immediately after the campaign.
4 *Consumer audits*. These will indicate changes in customer behaviour, especially that concerned with trial and repeat purchase during the promotion period.
5 *Redemptions*. These are a direct measures of the campaign, such as the number of coupons returned, free gifts claimed, numbers entering the contest etc. These should not be viewed in isolation, but within the context of the campaign and its overall objectives.

However, as with any promotional evaluation, the results cannot be looked at in isolation. Other elements of the mix and the relative level of competitor activity will all play a part in shaping overall results. Only by commissioning pre and post-campaign research can the underlying influences be identified, and the impact on users and non-users of the product assessed.

Joint promotions

Sometimes, the risks and costs of sales promotion can be shared with other organisations by entering into **joint promotions**. If the two products or services have synergy,

TABLE 17.6
European sales promotion regulations: What can and cannot be done

Technique	UK	Ireland	Spain	Germany	France	Denmark	Belgium	Netherlands	Portugal	Italy	Greece	Luxembourg	Austria	Finland	Norway	Sweden	Switzerland
On-pack price cuts	Yes	Yes	Yes	Yes	Yes	Yes	Yes	Yes	Yes	Yes	Yes	Yes	Yes	Yes	Yes	Yes	Yes
Banded offers	Yes	Yes	Yes	Poss	Yes	Poss	Poss	Yes	Yes	Yes	Yes	No	Poss	Poss	Poss	Poss	No
In-pack premiums	Yes	Yes	Yes	Poss	Poss	Poss	Poss	Poss	Yes	Yes	Yes	No	Poss	Yes	Poss	Poss	No
Multiple purchase offers	Yes	Yes	Yes	Poss	Yes	Poss	Poss	Yes	Yes	Yes	Yes	No	Poss	Poss	Poss	Poss	No
Extra product	Yes	Yes	Yes	Poss	Yes	Yes	Poss	Poss	Yes	Yes	Yes	Yes	Poss	Yes	Yes	Poss	Poss
Free product	Yes	Yes	Yes	Yes	Yes	Yes	Yes	Yes	Yes	Yes	Yes	Yes	Yes	Yes	Yes	Yes	Yes
Reusable/alternative-use pack	Yes	Yes	Yes	No	Yes	Poss	Poss	Yes	Yes	Yes	Yes	Yes	Poss	Yes	Yes	Yes	Yes
Free mail-ins	Yes	Yes	Yes	Poss	Yes	Poss	No	Poss	Yes	Yes	Yes	Poss	No	Poss	Poss	No	No
With-purchase premiums	Yes	Yes	Yes	Poss	Poss	Poss	Poss	Poss	Yes	Yes	Yes	No	Poss	Poss	Poss	Poss	No
Cross-product offers	Yes	Yes	Yes	No	Poss	Poss	Poss	Poss	Yes	Yes	Yes	No	No	Poss	Poss	Poss	No
Collector devices	Yes	Yes	Yes	No	Yes	Poss	Yes	Poss	Yes	Yes	Yes	No	Poss	Yes	No	No	Yes
Competitions	Yes	Yes	Yes	Poss	Yes	Yes	No	No	Yes	Yes	Yes	Poss	Yes	Yes	Yes	Yes	No
Self-liquidating premiums	Yes	Yes	Yes	No	Yes	No	No	No	Yes	Poss	Yes	No	No	Poss	No	Yes	No
Free Draws	Yes	Yes	Yes	No	Poss	No	No	No	Yes	Poss	Yes	No	No	Yes	No	No	No
Share outs	Yes	Yes	Yes	Poss	Poss	No	Yes	Yes	Yes	Poss	Yes	No	Poss	Poss	Poss	No	No
Sweepstake/lottery	Poss	Poss	Poss	No	Yes	No	Yes	Yes	Poss	Poss	Poss	No	Poss	Yes	No	No	No
Money-off vouchers	Yes	Yes	Yes	No	Yes	Poss	Yes	Yes	Yes	Poss	Yes	Poss	Poss	Poss	No	Poss	No
Money off next purchase	Yes	Yes	Yes	No	Yes	No	Yes	Yes	Yes	Poss	Yes	No	No	Poss	No	No	No
Cash backs	Yes	Yes	Yes	Poss	Yes	Yes	Yes	Yes	Yes	No	Yes	Yes	Yes	Yes	Poss	Yes	No
In-store demos	Yes	Yes	Yes	Yes	Yes	Yes	Yes	Yes	Yes	Yes	Yes	Yes	Yes	Yes	Yes	Yes	Yes

Source: IMP Europe.

if they appeal to a similar target audience, or if the two organisations operate on a similar philosophy, then a joint promotion can make a big impact, benefiting both organisations and their customers.

Example

For Christmas 1994 Guinness teamed up with the travel agent Going Places to offer discount vouchers for holidays with Guinness multipacks. Guinness wanted a travel promotion to emphasize escapism, and Going Places wanted to communicate with potential customers through the supermarket (Bond, 1994). Travel promotions are popular, and thus Thomas Cook, the travel company, has set up a specific division, Thomas Cook Promotions, to offer joint promotions, as well as providing a fulfilment service for organisations wanting to offer travel-related incentives as a solo promotion or as sales-force incentives, for example.

If a joint promotion is to be successful in all respects, then not only must the right partners be working together, but they must also be clear about what each is bringing to the promotion and how the costs are to be allocated. Joint promotions are not an excuse to try to get someone else to pick up the bill. In many cases, each partner might even pay as much as they would have done for a solo campaign in order to achieve the benefits of reaching a larger audience with a better proposition. Cummins (1989) suggests six factors which help to create successful joint promotions, and these are summarised in Table 17.7.

TABLE 17.7
Factors influencing successful joint promotions

Factor	How to implement
Involve everyone	Include senior management from both parties
Make realistic promises	Only promise what you can deliver
Avoid unplanned changes	Make sure you know at the start what you are committed to
Build in good liaison	Maintain communication and develop problem-solving processes
Bargain realistically	Maximise **mutual** benefit at **reasonable** and **fairly shared** cost
Be proactive	Do not sit back and expect the other party to do everything!

Source: Adapted from Cummins (1989).

CHAPTER SUMMARY

Sales promotion is part of a planned marketing communications strategy that is mainly used in a short-term tactical sense, but can also contribute something to longer-term strategic and image-building objectives. Sales promotions offer something over and above the normal product offering that can act as an incentive to stimulate the target audience into behaving in a certain way. Manufacturers use promotions to stimulate intermediaries and their sales staff, both manufacturers and retailers use them to stimulate individual consumers and manufacturers might use them to stimulate other manufacturers.

The methods of sales promotion are many and varied. In consumer markets they can be classed as either money based (for example, money off), product based (for example, buy one get one free), or gift, prize or merchandise based (for example, a free toy inside a box of cereal). Customer loyalty schemes in particular have become increasingly popular in the retail trade and in service industries. The problem with them is, however, that as they become more common, they lose their competitive edge and consumers become as disloyal as they were ever inclined to be. Given the high costs of setting up and running such schemes, their cost effectiveness might be questionable. Manufacturers stimulate retailers and other intermediaries by offering money back, discounts, free goods, and 'sale or return' schemes, among other methods. They also offer sales-force incentives to encourage a more committed selling effort from the intermediary's staff.

Any sales promotion programme has to be planned, implemented and managed. The first stage is to be clear on its objectives, and how those fit into the wider marketing strategy. Then, within the design of the actual programme, the manager must be clear about who the target audience is, what the most appropriate methods of sales promotion are for reaching that audience given the stated objectives, and how much all that will cost. The manager also has to determine the operational issues, such as the timing, duration, intensity and coverage of the promotion, as well as defining any qualifying criteria. All this should be done within current laws and guidelines. The organisation has to decide whether to handle the promotion in-house or to use an agency. Either way, there should be clear definition of who is responsible for what. Once the sales promotion has run its course, its performance should be assessed and analysed in order to learn from its successes and mistakes. A final issue of sales promotion management is whether to enter into joint promotions with other organisations. Where there is natural synergy between the partners, and a clear division of costs and responsibilities, joint promotions can be very successful. Both organisations can reach a wider audience with a far better proposition than they could have afforded working alone.

Key words and phrases

Alternative currencies	Field marketing agencies	Sale or return
BIGIF	Joint promotion	Sales promotion
Cash rebate	Loading up	Samples
Contests and sweepstakes	Money-based sales promotions	Self-liquidating offers
Co-operative advertising	POS	Trading up
Count and recount	Product-based sales promotions	Trial price
Coupons		Trial sizes

QUESTIONS FOR REVIEW

17.1 What is *sales promotion* and in what ways does it differ from advertising?

17.2 What are the main objectives of *manufacturer sales promotions* aimed at consumers?

17.3 Why do manufacturers offer sales promotions to *retailers*?

17.4 How do the objectives of *retailer–consumer* sales promotions differ from those of *manufacturer –consumer* sales promotions?

17.5 What are the main forms of *money-based sales promotions* aimed at consumers and what are their advantages and disadvantages?

17.6 What specific objectives can BIGIF and similar types of sales promotion achieve?

17.7 How do *self-liquidating offers* differ from *free mail-in offers*, and in what circumstances might each be appropriate?

17.8 What is *count and recount*? Why might a retailer prefer it to a *buying allowance*?

17.9 Outline the key stages in the *sales promotion management process*.

17.10 Once the broad form of a sales promotion has been determined, what specific details need to be sorted out before it can be *implemented*?

QUESTIONS FOR DISCUSSION

17.1 Research a recent new product launch by a manufacturer in a consumer market. What role did sales promotions play in that launch?

17.2 Choose an fmcg product area (breakfast cereals or hot chocolate drinks, for example) and analyse the sales promotions currently offered on the range of available brands in terms of the methods used, duration, size of reward etc.

17.3 To what extent are the sales promotion methods used in consumer markets equally applicable in organisational markets?

17.4 What kinds of sales promotion are:

(a) '20% extra free';

(b) 'send in £9.99 plus five proofs of purchase to get a branded sweatshirt'; and

(c) 'when you open the product packaging, look to see if there is a cheque for £5 000 inside'?

Why might manufacturers use them?

17.5 Find three examples of joint sales promotions and discuss the benefits for the organisations concerned and their customers.

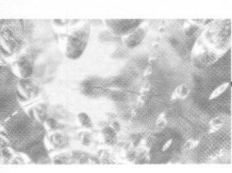

Student banking

A prime target market for UK bankers is the student segment. As young people go to college or university, they usually gain greater financial independence and have to learn the art of careful cash management. They thus need bank accounts. There is much competition for this segment, despite the fact that it is not particularly profitable for the banks. The real attraction of the student segment for banks is their longer-term above-average earning potential. Customer loyalty to banks can often be high, so once a consumer has decided which bank to use, it can be difficult to encourage them to switch allegiances. At the early stage of the bank–customer relationship, therefore, the banks put up with incurring the costs of providing the full range of facilities that students need, without earning much in return through overdraft charges, as student overdrafts are generally charged at lower preferential rates. The banks also feel that they have a social responsibility not to allow young people to get into so much debt that they cannot cope financially.

In the UK, with a steady reduction in student grants and an increased focus on student loans and parental support, it is often difficult for the less well off student to survive. In contrast to the USA, where there is a tradition of working through college and if necessary taking a year or two longer over the degree, in the UK the tradition is for a fast-track degree and only very casual work, often in the evenings, or especially during the vacations. In the UK, the current maximum grant for a student living away from home is £1710 whereas it actually costs around £4200 a year to keep a student if accommodation, subsistence, books, clothes etc. are taken into account. The average graduate in 1995, according to a Barclays Bank survey, left college with a £2930 debt, a 31 per cent increase on the 1994 figure.

Barclays has emerged as a market leader in the student segment, despite a history of problems in the 1960s and 1970s when students were urged to boycott Barclays in protest against the company's South African interests. In some instances, Barclays was prevented from coming on to campuses during freshers' weeks and other forums for meeting new students. Since then, Barclays has successfully used a series of promotional campaigns to attract students. Locating branches or cash dispensers on campuses, offering subsidised banking and making presentations to student groups are all part of the marketing armoury. A timely talk on 'managing your budget' during induction week, for example, can act as a soft sell, even though the bank's products or services are not overtly promoted.

Barclays has been especially strong in using sales promotion to attract new accounts. This approach was considered important as students often could not differentiate between the core offerings of the major banks. In the late 1980s and early 1990s, incentives such as gift vouchers, filofaxes, clothes and CDs all played a part in building a strong market position. As the 1990s progressed, however, the focus switched to service and the various financial products that students might need during their course of study. Barclays, along with the other main banks, offers an interest-free overdraft of up to £1000. Interest on credit varies between 1 per cent at Lloyds Bank and 3.25 per cent at the Bank of Scotland. Cash incentives are also given for opening an account ranging from £40 cash at Barclays to £30 at Lloyds. Student insurance, free credit cards and travel money deals also form part of the packages that banks make available to students, although again the banks have to balance social responsibility against competitiveness. They place particular emphasis on developing relationships with the student so that they can work together to avoid financial problems and, of course, build loyalty.

Most promotions are heavily displayed at the point of sale, especially in branches close to campuses. The literature provides application details or serves as a guide to further discussion. There is, however, still further scope for imaginative incentive campaigns. Barclays offered a 'Rent Free' promotion as an incentive for students to visit their local branch and to open an account. The scratch-card-based promotion enabled a student to win £2500, a year's rent. The promotion, supported by media advertising, was successful in generating branch traffic. There were seven winners nation-wide. With a share of just below 30 per cent in the student segment, it is essential for Barclays to maintain its innovative promotional edge.

Sources: Bruce (1996); Croft (1996a).

Questions

1 What kinds of sales promotions do the banks use in the student segment and what are they trying to achieve?

2 Why do you think the banks have tended to move away from gift-based promotions to money-based offers?

3 What are the problems of using sales promotions in such a highly competitive, concentrated market?

4 How might the use of sales promotion methods differ for a financial services product compared with an fmcg product?

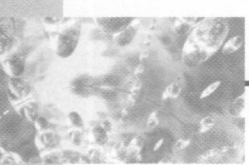

Supermarket loyalty cards

The major UK supermarket multiples have long competed with each other using sales promotion techniques, such as price offers, BIGIFs and free recipe cards available in-store. One or two also used promotions designed to encourage longer-term loyalty and regular shopping habits. These tended to take the form of issuing cards which were stamped at the checkout every time the customer spent more than a certain amount. When the card was full, the customer qualified for a discount. These 'mini-loyalty schemes' were only used infrequently and did not allow the retailer to track individual shoppers or to analyse their buying patterns and preferences.

Permanent loyalty schemes which allow the retailer to capture and analyse customer data on an ongoing basis began to emerge in the UK supermarket sector in 1995. The technology to handle the massive amounts of data about customers and the minutiae of their daily shopping habits existed, and Tesco, the first of the major multiples to develop such a scheme, decided that the time was right to do it.

To participate, customers have to register, filling in a short form giving details about themselves and their domestic situation. They then receive a Clubcard which is swiped through the checkout every time they shop so that points are accumulated electronically, depending on the amount spent. Every quarter, the customer receives a statement showing how many points have been collected, and turning them into money-off vouchers. Effectively, the Clubcard scheme translates into a 1 per cent discount on the customer's shopping. If the customer spends £500 over the three-month period, then a £5 money-off voucher is sent out at the end of it. The quarterly mailing can also be used for sending out product information and sending product-specific money-off coupons.

Tesco was taking something of a risk in doing this, as nobody could be completely sure that supermarket shoppers would respond to it, or that it would actually make any difference to their behaviour. As things turned out, however, being first into the supermarket loyalty scheme market gave Tesco a head start over the others. By June 1996, it had eight million cardholders and had extended the scheme not only to its own petrol forecourts, but also to B&Q DIY stores and Lunn Poly travel agencies. A year after the launch, Tesco was also starting to use the database it had built up to make tailormade offers to individual customers. Tesco was also using the offer of extra Clubcard points as short-

term promotional incentives on specific products at the point of sale.

Analysing and using the massive amounts of data on record takes time, and 18 months after Clubcard was introduced, Tesco was still learning about what might be possible and feasible. In the early days of Clubcard, for example, all cardholders received the same offers and information. By Christmas 1995, Tesco had managed to segment its database by age and family status. This allowed better tailored offers to be made. Similarly, Tesco can segment all its vegetarian customers or all its diabetic customers and make suitable offers to them.

Initially, other supermarkets, Sainsbury's in particular, were sceptical of what Tesco was doing and were not convinced that it would succeed. So while Safeway soon followed Tesco's lead and introduced its ABC card, Sainsbury's was more tentative. It did trial its own Savercard in 50 outlets, but never extended this to a full national scheme. The big question is whether these cards attract new customers or make any difference to loyalty among existing customers. Research, undertaken by Taylor Nelson AGB, showed that Sainsbury's Savercard did not appear to have increased loyalty among cardholders, suggesting that it was just rewarding existing customers without necessarily changing their behaviour in any way. Taylor Nelson AGB also suggested that Tesco had successfully used the Clubcard launch and associated promotions to get its card into the hands of non-customers, as well as increasing the spend and loyalty of existing ones. Thus the Clubcard scheme helped Tesco to increase its turnover by 25 per cent, and achieve a 15 per cent growth in profits, despite giving away an estimated £40 million in Clubcard benefits to customers in 1995.

In June 1996, Tesco launched the next phase of its Clubcard: Clubcard Plus. This is a kind of credit card, in that holders pay a fixed sum every month into their Clubcard Plus account and then can use the card to do their shopping and even to withdraw cash at the checkout. A credit facility, up to the same sum as the usual monthly payment, is also available on the card. Whenever the customer's Clubcard Plus account is in credit, however, interest is paid on the balance.

Two weeks after Tesco launched Clubcard Plus, Sainsbury's finally launched a full national loyalty card of its own, called Reward. It cost £15 million to launch, including £5 million on press and television advertising. To offset these costs, Sainsbury's hoped that Reward would lead to an increase of 3 per cent in sales and that it would take customers away from Tesco. The target for its first six months was 6.3 million cardholders. Although Reward gives only 1 per cent discount (as Clubcard does), it is different in that it also allows customers to turn their points into air miles. Sainsbury's also had plans to move into financial services (similar to Clubcard Plus).

Sources: Curtis (1996); *The Grocer* (1996); Reed (1996); Wilson (1996).

Questions

1 What factors have led the supermarkets towards these kinds of loyalty scheme and what do they hope to achieve from them?

2 What are the practical problems of setting up, managing, and maintaining a promotion like this?

3 Tesco has already segmented its cardholders by age and family status. What other variables could it use and how might these be used in other promotional activities?

4 To what extent and how do you think that the retailers and consumers might benefit or suffer from the long-term continuation of these schemes, once the novelty has worn off?

REFERENCES TO CHAPTER 17

Bond, C. (1995), 'Unforgettable and Lots of Fun', *Marketing*, 26 October, pp. III–IV.

Bond, C. (1994), 'Dangerous Liaisons', *Marketing*, 1 December, pp. 28–9.

Bruce, J. (1996) 'Don't Take Student Life for Granted', *Daily Express*, 12 June, p. 41.

Burnside, A. (1995), 'A Never Ending Search for the New', *Marketing*, 25 May, pp. 31–5.

Cobb, R. (1995a),' Barrier Blues', *Marketing*, 6 April, p. VIII.

Cobb,.R. (1995b), 'Testing the Ties', *Marketing*, 6 April, p. XVIII.

Cobb, R. (1995c), 'Technology on Display', *Marketing*, 22 June, pp. 27–30.

Cobb, R. (1995d), 'POPAI Gets Right to the Point', *Marketing*, 28 September, pp. 37–40.

Cobb, R. (1995e), 'Dancing to a Faster Tune', *Marketing*, 26 October, p. VI.

Croft, M. (1995). 'Field of Endeavour', *Marketing Week*, 12 May, pp. 46–9.

Croft, M. (1996a), 'Student Banking Grows Up', *Marketing Week*, 10 May, pp. 87–8.

Croft, M. (1996b), 'Young, Free and Sample', *Marketing Week*, 31 May, pp. 43–5.

Cummins, J. (1989), *Sales Promotion: How to Create and Implement Campaigns That Really Work*, Kogan Page.

Curtis, J. (1996), 'Loyal Following', *Marketing*, 6 June, pp. 23–5.

Davies, M. (1992), 'Sales Promotion as a Competitive Strategy', *Management Decision*, 30(7), pp. 5–10.

Fill, C. (1995), *Marketing Communications: Frameworks, Theories and Applications*, Prentice Hall.

Gofton, K .(1994), 'JCB Digs for Marketing Gold', *Marketing*, 14 April, pp. 28–9.

Gofton, K. (1995), 'Vouching for an Old Friend', *Marketing*, 9 March, p. XI.

Gofton, K. (1996), 'Coupons Flourish as Distribution Shifts', *Marketing*, 7 March, p. 12.

The Grocer (1995), 'Washing-up Liquid War Hits New Low: 7p A Litre', *The Grocer*, 2 December, p. 9.

The Grocer (1996), 'How Many More Cards Will be Put on the Table?', *The Grocer*, 22 June, p. 4.

Gupta, S. and Cooper, L. G. (1992), 'The Discounting of Discount and Promotion Brands', *Journal of Consumer Research*, 19 (Dec.), pp. 401–11.

Jones, P. J. (1990), 'The Double Jeopardy of Sales Promotions', *Harvard Business Review*, September/October, pp. 141–52.

Marketing (1996), 'Trade Promotions', *Marketing – Sales Promotion Awards Supplement*, 9 May, pp. XIV–XV.

Mitchell, A. (1995), 'Preaching the Loyalty Message', *Marketing Week*, 1 December, pp. 26–7.

Oliver, B. (1994), 'Growth of the Gift Guru', *Marketing*, 27 October, pp. 32–6.

Oliver, B. (1995a), 'Maximising Your Market Impact', *Marketing*, 9 March, pp. XVII–XVIII.

Oliver, B. (1995b), 'Handle with Flair', *Marketing*, 17 August, pp. 30–2.

Pearce, M. (1996), 'Loyalty in a Foreign Climate', *Marketing*, 4 April, pp. III–V.

Peattie, K. and Peattie, S. (1995), 'Sales Promotion – A Missed Opportunity For Services Marketers?', *International Journal of Service Industry Management*, 6(1), pp. 22–39.

Reed, D. (1996), 'Benefits System', *Marketing Week*, 12 January, pp. 41–5.

Summers, D. (1994), 'Sample the Soap, Buy the Brand', *Financial Times*, 2 June, p. 17.

Wilmshurst, J. (1993), *Below The Line Promotion*, Butterworth-Heinemann.

Wilson, R. (1996), 'Join the Club', *Marketing Week*, 12 January, pp. 47–52.

18

Personal Selling and Sales Management

LEARNING OBJECTIVES

This chapter will help you to:

1 appreciate the role that personal selling plays in the overall marketing effort of the organisation;

2 define the tasks undertaken by sales representatives;

3 differentiate between types of sales representative;

4 analyse the stages involved in the personal selling process and understand how each one contributes towards creating sales and developing long-term customer relationships;

5 appreciate the issues, responsibilities and problems involved in sales management.

INTRODUCTION

Many organisations employ sales forces to help in the promotional process. Whether that sales force takes a primary role in creating customers and then servicing their needs, or whether it simply receives orders at the point of sale will vary according to the type of product, the type of customer and the type of organisation. As Chapter 15 suggested, personal selling will probably play a much bigger role in the promotional mix of a high-priced infrequently purchased industrial good, for example, than in that of a routinely purchased consumer product.

Nevertheless, personal selling is important in some consumer markets. Car manufacturers spend many millions on advertising, but the purchase decision is made and the final deal negotiated at the showroom. The sales assistants thus play a very important role, particularly in guiding, persuading and converting the wavering customer without being too pushy. To do this, the sales assistant not only needs to know the product well, but also needs to be trained to judge the state of mind and the motivations of the potential customer so that a sale is made rather than lost. In the car industry, failure at this stage lets the whole glossy marketing process down. The sales representative selling assembly robots to a car manufacturer faces a slightly different situation. The task is still to try to encourage the buyer to make a decision to buy and then a decision to buy from you. In this case, however, the selling process will involve extensive discussion with operational and financial staff, and might include co-ordination between the seller's own staff and the buyer's decision-making unit, in such areas as technical specification, trials and installation. This is a high-level, demanding job, but still needs sound product and sales training and an understanding of customer psychology. Many of these issues were discussed in Chapter 4. In some situations, product differences might be very small and the fit between the buyer's needs and the seller's offering very close for several competing packages. The sales representative may then make the difference through the way in which the process is handled and the degree of trust and respect generated.

Regardless of whether the sales force is selling capital machinery into manufacturing businesses, fmcg products into the retail trade or financial services to individual consumers, the principles behind personal selling remain largely the same. This chapter will address those principles and show how they apply in different types of selling situation.

As a foundation for discussing the deeper issues concerning personal selling, it is important first of all to establish a definition of what personal selling is, and to look at the different roles it can play and the objectives it can achieve. This can then be put into the context of the wider promotional mix to show how personal selling differentiates itself from the other elements and how it complements them. From this, the chapter moves on to look at some of the skills and techniques involved in selling, using a framework that traces the selling process through from identifying likely prospects to making the sales and following it up. Having looked at selling from such a practical point of view, it is important to round off the picture by considering some of the managerial issues surrounding personal selling. These include the problems of selecting sales representatives, their training, deployment, compensation and evaluation.

THE DEFINITION AND ROLE OF PERSONAL SELLING

According to Fill (1995, p. 6), **personal selling** can be defined as:

> An interpersonal communication tool which involves face to face activities undertaken by individuals, often representing an organisation, in order to inform, persuade or remind an individual or group to take appropriate action, as required by the sponsor's representative.

As a basic definition, this does capture the essence of personal selling. *Interpersonal communication* implies a live, two-way, interactive dialogue between buyer and seller (which none of the other promotional mix elements can achieve); *with an individual or group* implies a small, select audience (again, more targeted than with the other elements); *to inform, persuade or remind ... to take appropriate action* implies a planned activity with a specific purpose.

Note that the definition does not imply that personal selling is only about making sales. It may well ultimately be about making a sale, but that is not its only function. It can contribute considerably to the organisation both before and, indeed, after a sale has been made. As a means of making sales, personal selling is about finding, informing, persuading and at times servicing customers through the personal, two-way communication that is its strength. It means helping customers to articulate their needs, tailoring persuasive selling messages to answer those needs, and then handling customers' responses or concerns in order to arrive at a mutually valued exchange. As a background to that, personal selling is also a crucial element in ensuring customers' post-purchase satisfaction, and in building profitable long term buyer–seller relationships built on trust and understanding (Miller and Heinman, 1991).

One final thought on the definition: personal selling need not be a face-to-face activity. Think of it more as a voice-to-ear activity! Recent years have seen big growth in telephone selling techniques and teleconferencing as cost-effective alternatives (Smith, 1993). Remember too that although personal selling depends primarily on the spoken word, audio-visual aids and demonstrations are often used to enhance that, providing a much more stimulating experience for the potential buyer.

Having thus defined the broad essence of personal selling, it is now appropriate to discuss where and how it fits in to the overall promotional mix.

Chapter 15 has already offered some insights into where personal selling fits best into the promotional mix. We discussed how personal selling is more appropriate in organisational than consumer markets at p. 576, while p. 583 looked at its advantages in promoting and selling high-cost, complex products. The discussion at p. 581 also notes that personal selling operates most effectively when customers are on the verge of making a final decision and committing themselves, but still need that last little bit of tailored persuasion.

All of that discussion in Chapter 15 is relevant here for putting personal selling into context, but there is more to be said. By looking at the major characteristics of personal selling, it is possible to compare it in more detail with the other elements of the promotional mix, highlighting its complementary strengths and weaknesses. The characteristics to be examined are impact, precision, cultivation and cost.

Impact

If you do not like the look of a TV advertisement, you can turn it off, or ignore it. If a glance at a print advertisement fails to capture your further attention, you can turn the page. If an envelope on the doormat looks like a mail shot, you can put it in the bin unopened. If a sales representative appears on your doorstep or in your office, it is a little more difficult to switch off. A person has to be dealt with in some way, and since most of us subscribe to the common rules of politeness, we will at least listen to what the person wants before shepherding them out of the door. The sales representative, therefore, has a much greater chance of engaging your initial attention than an advertisement can.

It is also true, of course, that an advertisement has no means of knowing or caring that you have ignored it. Sales representatives, on the other hand, have the ability to respond to the situations they find themselves in, and can take steps to prevent themselves from being shut off completely. This could be, for instance, by pressing for another appointment at a more convenient time, or by at least leaving sales literature for the potential customer to read and think about at their leisure. Overall, you are far more likely to remember a person you have met or spoken to (and to respond to what they said) than you are to remember an advertisement. In that respect, personal selling is very powerful indeed, particularly if it capitalises on the elements of precision and cultivation (*see* below) as well.

Precision

Precision represents one of the great advantages of personal selling over any of the other promotional mix elements, and explains why is it so effective at the customer's point of decision making. There are two facets of precision that should be acknowledged: targeting precision and message precision.

Targeting precision

Targeting precision arises from the fact that personal selling is not a mass medium. Advertising can be targeted within broad parameters, but even so, there will still be many wasted contacts (people who are not even in the target market; people who are not currently interested in the product; people who have recently purchased already; people who cannot currently afford to purchase etc). Advertising hits those contacts anyway with its full message, and each of those wasted contacts costs money. Personal selling can weed out the inappropriate contacts early on, and concentrate its efforts on those who offer a real prospect of making a sale.

Take a simple organisational situation, for instance. A brochure sent to a potential industrial buyer through the post may be addressed to an inappropriate person in the organisation and be put in the bin, the purchasing director's secretary may open the mail and decide not to pass it on, or it may be addressed to someone who is no longer employed within that organisation. In contrast, personal contact with the organisation can establish the identity of the best person to talk to and whether the organisation is even remotely interested in doing business. Both of those issues can be followed through with persistence until satisfactory answers are received. Thus the personal selling effort can then begin properly with a fighting chance of achieving something.

Message precision

Message precision arises from the interactive two-way dialogue that personal selling encourages. An advertisement cannot tell what impact it is having on you. It cannot discern whether you are paying attention to it, whether you understand it or whether you think it is relevant to you. Furthermore, once the advertisement has been presented to you, that is it. It is a fixed, inflexible message, and if you did not understand it, or if you felt that it did not tell you what you wanted to know, then you have no opportunity to do anything about it other than wait for another advertisement to come along that might clarify these things. Because personal selling involves live interaction, however, these problems should not occur. The sales representative can tell, for example, that your attention is wandering, and therefore can change track, exploring other avenues until something seems to capture you again. The representative can also make sure that you understand what you are being told and go over it again from a different angle if you are having difficulty with the first approach. Similarly, the representative can see if something has particularly caught your imagination and tailor the message to emphasize that feature or benefit. Thus, by listening and watching, the sales representative should be able to create a unique approach that exactly matches the mood and the needs of each prospective customer. This too is a very potent capability.

Cultivation

As chapter 4 implied, the creation of long-term mutually beneficial buyer–seller relationships is now recognised as extremely important to the health and profitability of organisations in many industries. The sales force has a crucial role to play in both creating and maintaining such relationships. Sales representatives are often the public face of an organisation, and their ability to carry the organisation's message professionally and confidently can affect judgement of that organisation and what it stands for. Sales representatives can also do something that advertising cannot: they can develop personal relationships with people in client organisations. Turnbull (1990) highlighted the information exchange capability and the technical and commercial roles played by sales representatives. These help to reduce the social and cultural distance between buyer and seller. Such relationships can smooth the way to easier interorganisational negotiation, and they can also make information gathering much easier. A sales representative can potentially find out a great deal more about an organisation's purchasing philosophy by having a friendly chat over a drink with his friend, the purchasing manager from XYZ & Co., than any formal inquiry or survey. Accepting the contention (see pp. 155 *et seq.*) that organisational decision making can be affected by less rational human motivations means that the interpersonal bonds between organisations must be fully encouraged and exploited (Cunningham and Homse, 1986).

Cost

All the advantages and benefits discussed above come at a very high cost, as personal selling is extremely labour intensive. In addition, costs of travel (and time spent travelling), accommodation and other expenses have to be accounted for. It can thus cost anything from £50 000 upwards to keep a sales representative on the road for a year. The actual time spent actually selling to the customer, however, has been estimated at just 6 per cent of total time, with 50 per cent spent travelling, 20 per cent on administration and 24 per cent making the call (McDonald, 1984). Although there are likely to be wide variances between organisations, these figures suggest that organisations have to be sure about what their sales force is for, and what it is actually doing that could not be achieved equally well by other means. Only then can the high investment in personal selling be justified as a cost-effective use of resources.

Many organisations spend more on this element of the promotional mix than on any other, particularly in organisational markets. Estimates vary, but it is suggested that the number of sales representatives employed in various capacities is very large indeed. In the USA, for example, it has been estimated that around 10 per cent of the work-force is employed in positions that involve some kind of personal selling (Zikmund and d'Amico, 1993).

TASKS OF THE SALES REPRESENTATIVE

There is a tendency to think of the sales representative in a one-off selling situation. What the discussion in the previous sections has shown is that in reality, the representative is likely to be handling a relationship with any specific customer over a long period of time. The representative will be looking to build up close personal ties because much depends on repeat sales. In some cases, the representative might even be involved in helping to negotiate and handle joint product development. All of this suggests a range of tasks beyond the straight selling situation.

Clearly, the nature of the selling task and the range of activities that the sales representative becomes involved with will vary according to many factors. The more complex, technical or expensive the product, the more time the representative will have to spend in clarifying what is required, working with the customer to select the right product offering for the situation and ensuring satisfactory post-purchase performance. With routine, low-priced, frequent purchases, the sales representative's role becomes much more administrative, just filling in the order forms. In a dynamic, fast-changing market, the representative may be briefed to take on an information-gathering role, finding out through personal contacts who is saying what to whom, and what moves are likely to be planned.

Figure 18.1 summarises the range of typical tasks of the sales representative, each of which is defined below.

Prospecting

Prospecting is finding new potential customers who have the willingness and ability to purchase. For Rentokil Tropical Plants, for example, the role of the sales representative is to contact a range of potential clients including offices, hotels, shopping centres and restaurants to design and recommend individual displays of tropical plants on a supply and maintenance basis. Prospecting is an important task, particularly for organisations entering a new market segment or for those offering a new product line with no established customer base. For example many central European manufacturers have had to build a whole new customer base since the loss of the Russian market. They are trying to open EU markets by deploying specialist sales staff or agents.

Informing

Informing is giving prospective customers adequate, detailed and relevant information about products and services on offer. In organisational markets, once contact

FIGURE 18.1

Typical tasks of
the sales
representative

has been made with prospects, the sales representative needs to stimulate sufficient information exchange to ensure a technical and commercial match that is better than the competition.

Persuading

Persuading is helping the prospective customer to analyse the information provided, in the light of their needs, in order to come to the conclusion that the product being offered is the best solution to their problem. Sometimes, presenting the main product benefits is sufficient to convince the buyer of the wisdom of selecting that supplier. On other occasions, especially with purchases that are technically or commercially more complex, the persuasion might have to be very subtle and varied, according to the concerns of the different members of the buying team.

Installing and demonstrating

Particularly with technical, organisational purchases, the buyer may need consider-able support and help to get the equipment installed and to train their staff in its use. The sales representative may join a wider team of support personnel to ensure that all this takes place according to whatever was agreed and to the customer's satisfaction. The representative's continued presence acts as a link between pre- and post-purchase events, and implies that the representative has not stopped caring about the customer just because the sale has been made.

This role is also relevant for organisations supplying the retail and wholesale sectors. Area merchandisers for DeLonghi household appliances, for example, are required to support the selling effort with in-store merchandising, training retail staff and making product presentations in store.

Co-ordinating within their own organisation

The role of the sales representative is not just about forward communication with the buyer. It is also concerned with 'representing' the customer's interests within the selling organisation. Whether concerned with financial, technical or logistical issues, the sales representative must co-ordinate and sometimes organise internal activities on a

With complex civil engineering projects such as the second Severn Crossing, building and maintaining relationships with key specifiers and influencers is a major selling task.

project basis to ensure that the customer's needs are met. At Duracell, the UK market leader in batteries, a national account manager is responsible for all aspects of the relationship with the large grocery chains. This includes external roles of display, distribution and promotional planning as well as internal co-ordination of logistics and product category management. Similarly in SKF, an account manager for high-volume users would be expected to co-ordinate technical problem solving, supply schedules, logistics and contractual matters.

Maintaining relationships

Once an initial sale has been made, it might be the start of an ongoing relationship. In many cases, a single sale is just one of a stream of transactions and thus cannot be considered in isolation from the total relationship. An important role for the sales representative is to manage the relationship rather than just the specifics of a particular sale. This means that in many organisations, more substantial and critical relationships have a 'relationship manager' to handle the various facets of the buyer–seller evolution (Turnbull and Cunningham, 1981). In some cases, the sales representative might have only one relationship to manage, but in others, the representative might have to manage a network based in a particular sector. Northern Foods PLC, when seeking a national account manager for Northern Dairies, wanted someone to handle all aspects of just two major accounts. This is a role that involves considerable team working, both internally and externally.

Information and feedback gathering

The gathering of information and the provision of feedback emphasizes the need for representatives to keep their eyes and ears open, and to indulge in two-way communication with the customers they deal with. 'Grapevine' gossip about what is happening in the industry might, for example, give valuable early warning about big planned purchases in the future, or about potential customers who are dissatisfied with their current supplier. Both of these situations would offer opportunities to the organisation that heard about them early enough to make strategic plans about how to capitalise on them. In terms of relationships with existing customers, sales representatives are more likely than anyone to hear about the things that the customer is unhappy about. The representative is in an ideal position, therefore, to make sure something is done to reassure the customer or to put the defect right before the customer's dissatisfaction gets out of hand. It is well worthwhile for the representative to report back even minor problems to give central management as detailed a picture as possible about reaction to products and offerings.

This feedback role is even more important when developing business in export markets, where the base of accumulated knowledge might not be very strong. Personal contacts can help to add to that knowledge over time (Johanson and Vahlne, 1977).

Monitoring competitor action

The representative works out in the field, meeting customers and, in all probability, competitors. As well as picking up snippets about what competitors are planning and who they are doing business with, the representative can provide valuable information about how their organisation's products compare with those of the competition in the eyes of the purchasers. During the course of sales presentations, prospective customers can be subtly probed to find out what they think are the relative strengths and weaknesses of competing products, what they consider to be the important features and benefits in that kind of product, and how the available offerings score relative to each other (Lambert *et al.*, 1990).

Thus while selling remains the central activity for a sales representative, the roles of prospecting for new customers, maintaining communication links with customers, servicing customers' needs before and after sale, and information gathering, are no less important in enhancing the selling process and maximising the investment in such a labour-intensive promotional element.

FORMS OF PERSONAL SELLING

It has already been suggested that different market situations and different product and customer types will vary the demands made on a sales force. These variations relate to the amount of selling effort that needs to be done and the degree of selling skill needed to identify and satisfy customer needs. It is important to identify the level of selling required because the more an organisation demands of its sales force in terms of expertise or skill in handling important long-term customer relationships, the more it has to pay them. There is simply no point in employing a high-quality group of professional sales people who can undertake all the roles defined in the previous section if all you want them to do is sit by the phone and fill in order forms. That is an inefficient waste of resources.

Accepting, then, that not all sales representatives will be required to fulfil all those roles, it is possible to define three broad categories of sales representative: the **order taker**, the **order maker** and **sales support** (Moncrief, 1988).

Order takers

As the title implies, order takers tend to have a somewhat administrative role. They either have a regular set pattern of customer contact, or wait for customers to contact them or to come to them. Generally, they are only concerned with routine or low involvement purchasing. This category can be further divided into two subgroups.

External order takers

External order takers are mainly concerned with processing orders where initial contracts have been agreed. The buyer–supplier relationship already exists, and most of the concern is with reordering and stocking up. In such cases, the important details of the transaction are already known (pricing, discounts, product offering) and so the representative's role is simply to note details of quantity required and make sure the order is duly processed. In selling to major retailers it is usual for the initial contact to be handled by other, more senior sales people.

The external order taker is typical in selling to retailers, and may have perhaps one or two added functions. A junior sales representative with a confectionery manufacturer, for example, might be given responsibility for visiting garage forecourt shops not only to replenish stock, but also to check displays to make sure the organisation's products are being given adequate space relative to the competition. The job involves a minimal amount of new selling. The external order taker may also be involved in arranging in-store displays, or in helping the customer to implement special promotions.

Where a steady routine of order taking has been established, the customer may become dependent on the predictability of the representative's visit to keep their own shelves stocked and thus their own business running smoothly. The importance of the external order taker, therefore, as representing the familiar, friendly, and reliable face of the supplier should not be underestimated.

> ### Example
>
> Wrangler employ Retail Service Representatives to visit major multiples and key accounts to undertake in-store merchandising, handle sales orders and information needs, organise product awareness training for store staff and co-ordinate all aspects of point of sale activities.

Inside order takers

Inside order takers remain within the confines of the employing organisation and wait for customers to come to them. Again they can commonly be found in retailing and distribution. A retailer might telephone to a manufacturer requesting an urgent delivery of stock. The inside order taker will receive and process that request. A sales assistant working within a retail store waiting for a customer to come through the door is also an inside order taker.

The role of inside order takers may vary. Some will need to be able to answer simple questions, take orders, check delivery and complete transactions. At the other extreme, all that is needed is a telephone sales clerk to handle all incoming calls and to take orders with the minimum of customer contact. An inside order taker of the latter type is likely to be employed either with well-understood products in a straight rebuy situation, or where the buying situation is not at all complex. For example, mail order catalogue companies now use inside order takers to handle telephone sales. The consumer phones up, gives their personal details and the product order to the telephonist who inputs the data into a computer and can thus immediately tell the customer whether the goods are still available and confirm the order.

Although order taking may seem to be a low level activity, it is nevertheless an important sales function. It is true that order takers do rely on other sales staff or the general marketing effort for contacts, but they represent an efficient means of processing and servicing large numbers of customers properly.

The essence of order taking is not to get involved in detailed explanation, negotiation or new selling. Where the sales representative's role does extend to include those things, or includes product demonstration, such as trying to sell a car to a consumer, then the sales representative moves into the next category, order makers.

Order makers

The order maker is what most people understand by the term 'sales representative'. The order maker has to find prospective customers, identify customer-specific problems and needs, sell the appropriate product, then assist with installation and training. In other words, the order maker has to take on most of the roles outlined at Fig. 18.1 above.

The order maker therefore needs a good understanding of each prospective customer's situation and how the product or service being sold can match with that. Order making demands a high level of creativity, the ability to explain and persuade, and the ability and willingness to build relationships with customers. These requirements clearly have implications for the kinds of skills needed and training needed to develop a truly professional approach to the job.

There are two broad facets of order making. One is the generation of new business, requiring an ability to identify and make initial contact. The second is a focus on enhancing the long-term relationship with an existing customer, not just by keeping them topped up with supplies of the current product they already purchase, but by extending the range of products they buy. If they buy more of the same, that is order taking; if they buy products that they have never bought before, that is order making. This means a very close relationship with customers and an in-depth appreciation of their situation and problems.

> ### Example
>
> Digital have senior account managers to handle major customers. An important part of their role is to analyse the industry and business objectives of those customers and then translate them into applications and solutions through integrated systems. A requirement for those occupying such roles is experience of the user industries, whether manufacturing or service.

Attracting new customers can be very demanding. Potential buyers are approached by sales representatives from many organisations, so why should they listen to you or treat you any more kindly than any of the others? Furthermore, when economic times are hard, there is much buyer inertia, meaning that they will put off buying for as long as possible, and then only buy what they really need. The representative has to find a way of cutting through this inertia. Even if the buyer does listen and is willing in principle to purchase, the time taken between the initial contact and the first significant order places great strains on the sales representative, especially in a market where there may be many alternative products.

Maintaining existing customers can also be very demanding. The representative must not only protect those customers from the competition, but also ensure that the ongoing purchase pattern is maintained and even improved with new applications and technology. The representative has also to be alert to opportunities arising from existing customers – don't forget that customers can be a great source of new ideas.

Although order making can be very effective in creating the new customers that keep an organisation moving forward and growing, it is nevertheless a costly part of promotion. The organisation needs to reserve the order making effort for worthwhile prospects and high-profile customers, and not waste it on routine follow-up work.

Is the sales rep an endangered species?

A sales representative is an expensive asset for an organisation to maintain. Representatives need cars, computers, mobile phones, samples, presentation equipment and administrative support. They also run up bills for hotel accommodation and entertaining clients. When economic times are hard, therefore, many organisations cut their sales forces or rationalise them to save on costs. Other factors have also led to a reduction in the number of sales representatives. In consumer goods markets, for instance, there has been a reduction in the number of small independent retailers and a corresponding increase in the share of business taken by the big multiples. The bigger retailers tend to have computerised stock control systems with on-line ordering, so that there is no need for a representative to visit individual branches so often (if at all). HP Foods, for example, had between 70 and 100 sales representatives in the 1970s. In the 1990s, the number has been slimmed down to 12 business development executives who each manage a portfolio of national and regional accounts. The largest proportion of HP's orders, however, come in via computers or the telephone.

There is, of course, still a role for the representative in consumer goods markets in visiting smaller retailers both to take orders and to help with promotional events or point of sale displays. Many organisations, however, find it cheaper and more efficient to use contract sales staff from field marketing agencies for such tasks. The benefit of contract staff is that the organisation only has to pay for them when they want them, and can have as large or small a 'sales force' as a particular task or project requires. Contract sales staff tend to work in small territories and thus have established close relationships with the retailers and other customers that they regularly visit.

Some organisations might worry, however, that because contract sales staff are not employed by them full time, there might be questions about their loyalty and motivation. Agencies are well aware of this and try to overcome it by setting up quality control systems to monitor the performance of their staff in the field, and ensuring that staff are fully and properly briefed at the start of an assignment. To try to engender 'loyalty' to the task in hand, the agency will also ensure that a member of staff is only working for one client in a particular product market at a time. Because of the amount of time contract staff spend in the field and because of the wide range of customers and product types they deal with, these agencies can amass a wealth of data about what is going on in the market that a company's own sales force would not have either the time or the resources to collect. Agencies can thus feed information back to clients, providing an additional benefit to their service.

Although contract selling is used widely in fmcg and pharmaceutical markets, it is less well established in financial services, an area that has long depended on face-to-face selling. This is partly because of the minefield of legislation and regulation surrounding the sale of financial service products, and partly because the products themselves are so complex. The financial services companies thus feel that they prefer to maintain tighter control over who sells their products and how.

So, the sales representative might not be about to become extinct. What is certain is that organisations are rethinking how they manage and organise their sales forces and their selling processes. Thus the role and the tasks of representatives will change, and how they are employed might change, but they will always be needed in some capacity.

Source: Rines (1995).

Sales support

Sales support is a broad term encompassing a variety of staff whose role is to augment the efforts of the mainstream sales force. Sales support staff could, for example, take on the burden of locating and initially screening potential new customers, passing that information on to the sales force so that the real selling process can begin. They may also provide sales training, provide technical support or take care of after-sales service.

There are two interesting categories of support staff worth mentioning.

Missionary sales representatives

Missionary sales representatives focus on a particular market segment or product to give enquiries and sales an initial lift. They do not generally work with the selling organisation's customers, but with the customer's own customers. Pharmaceutical companies, for instance, use missionaries to persuade general practitioners to prescribe new drugs for their patients. The actual sales of the drugs, however, are made by the conventional sales force to pharmacists or wholesalers. The missionary is effectively implementing a *pull strategy* (as defined in p. 577), by communicating with groups a couple of stages further down the distribution chain than their own organisation or its direct customers. Figure 18.2 summarises how the missionary approach works.

Sales engineers

Sales engineers, on the other hand, are directly concerned with the organisation's customers and the end users of its products. Their concern is with the technical or application problems of the product. They could be called in at any stage of sales process. Particularly with a complex organisational product, in the early stages of the selling process they may have to advise on systems design. Later in the process, they might help with installation, training or even maintenance.

Often, these support staff can pick up early warning of problems and emerging opportunities, so they need to have good links with the main sales force, and the organisation needs to have mechanisms in place to make sure that the knowledge they pick up in the field is shared and used.

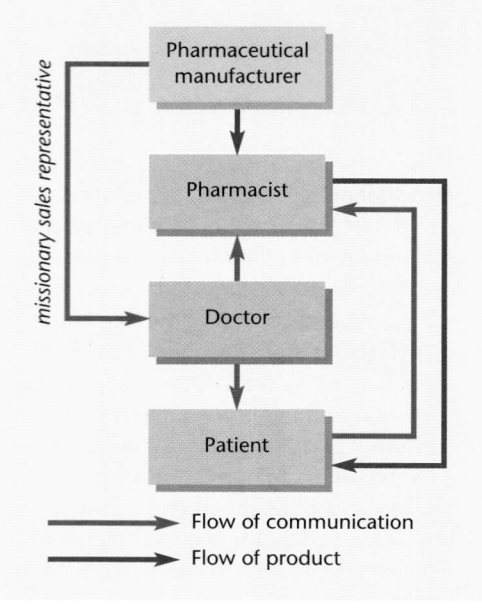

FIGURE 18.2

The role of the missionary

THE PERSONAL SELLING PROCESS

Many textbooks, videos and gurus claim to offer the secret to successful sales presentations. In reality, there is no one approach that is right for all situations, nor is there any one approach that is right for all types of sales representative. This is hardly surprising, because the essential strength of personal selling is the human contact, and the infinite flexibility of the sales representative to create a unique and tailored approach for each prospective customer. At the heart of the sales process is the sales representative's ability to build a relationship with the buyer that is sufficiently strong to achieve a deal that benefits both parties. As shown in Chapter 4, organisations need to buy if they are to achieve their objectives. In many situations the major decision relates to *supplier choice* rather than whether or not to buy. The sales representative's role is to highlight the attractions of the specification, support, service and commercial package on offer. Differences between products, markets, organisational philosophies and even individuals will all have a bearing on the style and effectiveness of the selling activity.

Although it has just been suggested that personal selling does not lend itself to a prescribed formula, it is possible to define a number of broad stages through which most selling episodes will pass (Russell *et al.*, 1977). Depending on the product, the market, the organisations and individuals involved, the length of time spent in any one of the stages will vary, as will the way in which each stage is implemented (Pedersen *et seq.*, 1986). Nevertheless, the generalised analysis offered here provides a useful basis for beginning to understand what contributes to successful personal selling.

Figure 18.3 shows the flow of stages through a personal selling process. It does not begin with meeting the customer; that itself is the outcome of an earlier pre-contact

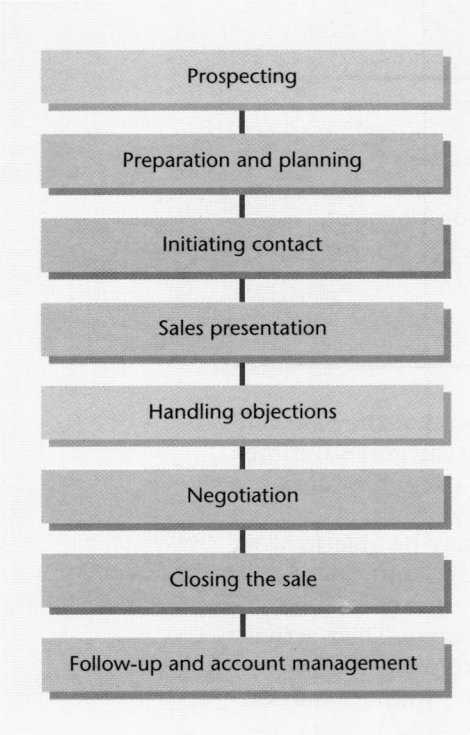

FIGURE 18.3

**The personal
selling process**

stage in which the prospective customer has to be identified. The actual selling stages themselves end with closing the sale, but the model also proposes the extra, necessary stage of following up to ensure a satisfied customer in the post-purchase period. Clearly, at any stage of such a complex human activity things can, and often do, go wrong. Although **conversion rates** between enquiry and real orders vary considerably, it is always useful, if the process ends in failure to make a sale, to look at each stage of the process to establish just where things went wrong. The various stages in the personal selling process are discussed in full below.

Prospecting

Before sales representatives can get down to the real job of selling something, they have to have someone to sell to. This means that there has to be some sort of mechanism for identifying and locating prospects, matching up the prospects' likely needs with what the selling organisation has to offer. In some organisations, perhaps those selling an industrial product with a specific application to a relatively small number of easily defined organisational customers, this will be a highly structured activity, involving sales representatives and support staff, and will lead to the representative going out on a call knowing that the prospect is potentially fruitful. In contrast, double glazing companies often employ canvassers to walk the streets knocking on doors to see if householders are likely prospects. This is not a particularly efficient use of the representatives' time, as most people will say that they are not interested, but in promoting an infrequently purchased, high-priced product, yet in a mass market, it is difficult to see what else in the way of prospecting they can do. Consumers seeing advertising for double glazing might get as far as thinking, 'I must get round to doing something about that bathroom window', but because of the expense and the mess involved, it is too easy to put it off and not respond. More direct stimulation, such as that provided by personal selling, is needed to turn that lethargy into 'I will do something'.

The latter example also shows that prospecting is especially difficult with one-time purchases where there is a constant need to replenish contacts. Once a household has bought double glazing, it is not going to repeat the purchase for many years, and so the organisation is constantly starting from scratch, putting considerable resources and efforts into prospecting. In a market where there is the potential for large repeat sales, prospecting may be a smaller part of selling role, confined to replacing declining or lost customers.

In an organisational rather than a consumer market, the sales representative needs a prospect bank, a pool of potential customers to be drawn on as appropriate. This bank is often a combination of company-inspired and self-researched names and details of prospects. Table 18.1 identifies the wide range of sources of prospects.

Company-inspired prospects are taken from a wide range of sources which can be categorised into three types. First, there are potential customers who have made enquiries or responded to advertising, but not been followed up already. Second, there are those who have already been approached in an exploratory way, for example through telemarketing, and look promising enough to deserve further encouragement. Third, and most problematic, are the lists of names. These lists might be purchased from a list broker or be compiled from a trade directory or a list of organisations attending a particular trade exhibition. While these lists will conform to broad

TABLE 18.1

Sources of prospects

Company inspired	Sales representative inspired
• Sales records	• Scanning directories
• Invoices	• Referrals – direct or via sales support staff
• Advertising responses	• Observation of new developments
• Exhibitions and trade show lists	• Watching the media
• General enquiries	• Cold calling
• Lists from telemarketing campaigns	
• Purchased lists	

criteria relating to the types of organisations or people on them, so that they are generally relevant to the seller, they are still 'colder' than the first two categories outlined above. This is because there is no means of telling whether those on the list are even in the market for your sort of product, never mind whether they are ready, willing and able to do business with you. Telemarketing support staff may be able to work through such a list and convert some of the names on it into the second category to save the sales representative from much pointless **cold calling**.

Sales representatives may have to develop their own prospect banks. Their activity falls into two broad classes. First, there may be referrals, either from word of mouth from contacts outside the organisation, or from the telemarketing support staff discussed above. These are 'warm' contacts. Second, they can also compile lists from directories, or from scanning the media for relevant company news that might open up an opportunity. As with the telemarketers above, this might lead to a session of preliminary cold calling (by phone or in person) to establish whether this person or organisation really is a viable prospect.

In summary, there are three stages in prospecting:

1 Generating lists of **leads**, i.e., those individuals or organisations who could be prospective customers.
2 An initial assessment of whether each lead can be developed into a **prospect** i.e., somebody who is likely to want and can afford to buy the product. This screening is often done prior to a visit.
3 This third stage often only comes after initial contact has confirmed that there is a need (whether the prospect realises that there is a need or not) and that the prospect has the ability, if so motivated, to purchase. This is a **qualified prospect**.

The outcome of this stage of the selling process is a qualified prospect list from which more targeted selling effort can proceed.

Preparation and planning

Identifying a qualified prospect is only the beginning of the process. Before the real selling begins, it is very important to obtain further information on the prospect in order to prepare the best and most relevant sales approach and to plan tactics.

In selling to an organisational customer, this may mean scanning a number of company reports, assessing the norms for that industry in relation to likely buying criteria and needs. Analysing the prospect's company report might promise indications of the strategic direction in which it is moving, as well as revealing its financial situation. It is also necessary to think about the kind of purchasing structures that the representative is going to have to work through, identifying the most likely influencers and decision makers. In industrial situations, for example, a key question may be whether to target the engineering staff early on to get their technical support for the product, encouraging them to re-specify their needs in your favour, or whether to try to motivate the formal buyers to consider alternative sources (i.e., you). Look back at p. 152 to remind yourself about the structure and importance of the buying centre in organisational purchasing behaviour. In addition to finding out who to concentrate on, it is also useful to find out as much as possible about the application of the product and the features and benefits required. This allows the representative to construct a **sales presentation** that will be relevant to the buyer and thus will have more chance of engaging their attention and being persuasive.

Sales representatives in organisational markets are fortunate that sufficient information exists about their buyers to allow them to prepare so well in advance. In consumer markets, it is more likely that representatives have to think on their feet, analysing customers while they are face to face with them. If a couple walk into a car showroom, the sales representative has to work out how serious they are about buying, what alternatives they are considering, what their decision-making criteria are, how price sensitive they are, who the main user will be, and who has the ultimate decision making responsibility. As if that wasn't enough, there is also the problem of working out the best product offering and deal to match those needs and that profile. If, in the course of a 10- or 20-minute encounter, the sales representative makes any misjudgement about that couple and their needs, then in all likelihood the sale is lost.

Where it is possible, therefore, doing the homework is essential, and it often needs to be very thorough, especially in situations involving large, complex projects with stiff competition. Also, if the competition are already well entrenched in doing business with a prospect, it is even more important to find out as much as possible in advance, since getting that customer to switch supplier will probably be an uphill task unless you can find the right approach with the right people.

Initiating contact

Making the first contact with the prospect is a delicate operation. There are two ways of approaching this stage. First, the initial telephone call which qualifies the prospect may be used to solicit an appointment. Failure to achieve that means that the selling process cannot begin. The phone call should not, however, be allowed to draw the sales representative into detailed discussion, as it is unlikely that serious and fruitful dialogue can take place without the use of sales aids and direct contact. Before the telephone call, an introductory letter may be sent to introduce the sales representative and the organisation so that the phone call does not come as a total surprise, but there still remains the important objective of making an appointment.

The second approach is to use cold calling. This means turning up on the doorstep in the hope that someone will see you, as the double glazing sales representative does. This can be very wasteful in terms of time and travel. There is no guarantee that the representative will get access to the key people, who probably would not in any case be able to spare time without a prior appointment. Even if the representative does get access, it is unlikely that a properly tailored sales presentation will have been prepared if there has not been preliminary contact with the prospect. Cold callers are often seen as time wasters, and do not do themselves or their organisations any favours in the eyes of the prospects.

Once an approach has been made and an appointment made, the next stage is the initial call. This helps the representative to discover whether the initial assessment of the customer's likely need is borne out in practice. In these early meetings, it is important to build up rapport, mutual respect and trust between buyer and seller before the more serious business discussion gets underway. The time spent in establishing this relationship is well spent. It helps to build a solid foundation for the later stages of discussion.

The challenge at this point is to demonstrate to the prospect that it is worthwhile to talk about their needs, and to entertain the idea of revising their product purchasing specifications or their current practices. The danger here is of allowing the meeting to develop into a detailed product discussion before the prospect's real needs have been fully explored. In some cases, establishing these needs may mean undertaking a more detailed survey of current usage or application before a more formal sales presentation takes place. Remember that customers do not buy products, they buy solutions to problems. The product should be presented to the prospect within the context of how that product is a solution to an agreed problem, not as the sole and abstract object of the discussion.

Again, it must be stressed that it is not easy to generalise. Different products, applications, competitive states, organisational and even individual characteristics are all likely to have an impact on the length and depth of the exploration of customer needs.

The sales presentation

At last, the representative has enough insight and information to allow the preparation of the sales presentation itself which lies at the heart of the selling process. The ease of its preparation and its effectiveness in practice owe a great deal to the thoroughness and quality of the work done in the earlier stages. The objective of the sales presentation is to show how the product offering and the customer's needs match. The presentation must not be product orientated, but be concerned with what the product can do for that particular customer. In other words, do not sell the features, sell the benefits.

Three approaches are possible, although there is a tendency to rely mainly on the third one.

Stimulus–response
The stimulus–response approach works on the simple assumption that given the right stimulus, the customer will respond in the right way. It is most appropriate in consumer markets where people are buying low-risk, low-involvement products. In McDonald's, for example, the sales staff will always suggest a drink or french fries if you only ask for a burger. The stimulus is the suggestion of a drink, and that is meant to prompt you into making an instant decision and saying yes to something that otherwise you might not have asked for. Similarly, although buying a pair of shoes can be more of a limited decision-making process (in that they cost a bit more than a burger, and are purchased less frequently), the stimulus–response technique is also used to prompt the purchase of the less expensive extras such as laces and polish.

Formula selling
Formula selling involves training representatives in a standard approach so that they can follow a rigid set of rules as the 'ideal method' to cover the relevant (and irrelevant!) points and achieve results. Formula selling is becoming increasingly less common. One reason for its decline is that customers are wise to it. Another is that it is relatively ineffective and inefficient as it does not feed off an essential strength of personal selling, namely tailoring the message to the customer.

This approach, therefore, usually means that the representative imparts a standard bundle of information to a set pattern, regardless of circumstance and needs. Its last bastions are in door-to-door selling and telemarketing. Its biggest problem is that it does not allow spontaneity and feedback from the customer, nor does it encourage interaction between buyer and seller. The customer feels that the representative has a set speech to get through, come what may, and begins to resent that they are not being consulted, yet are expected to provide a passive audience to listen to material of doubtful relevance.

Need satisfaction

The most widely used approach, and probably the most effective is need satisfaction, even though it is more difficult to implement. It involves listening to the customer, asking questions to identify needs, assessing their reactions and tailoring the presentation to suit the circumstance. It is a problem-solving approach.

In organisational markets, the need-satisfaction technique should be well under way by the selling stage if the preparation has been done properly. The customer's reaction to the sales presentation should concern matters of fine detail, to be explored and resolved. It should not to throw up surprises about needs and wants for the representative to have to deal with. In contrast, in a consumer market, selling cars for example, the representative is on more of a knife edge, and the listening and questioning at this stage is incredibly important to establish the customer profile and needs. Clearly, such an approach would not be appropriate in a McDonald's retailing situation where a large number of customers choosing from a very limited range of low-risk product options need to be handled quickly.

In some organisational selling situations, it could even be suggested that the sales representative is acting in a consultative role, using a wider knowledge of the customer's industry to propose informed solutions to the customer's problems. Some advertising agencies, such as Barker's, specialise in advertising for the higher education sector. By building up sound experience of the advertising needs of universities and colleges, especially when recruiting students, they are able to demonstrate a wide and detailed appreciation of the market. Of course the limiting factor is that some universities would prefer not to use the same agency as their primary competitors (*see* p. 635).

Whatever the broad approach taken, there may be some practicalities to be handled as part of the presentation. The representative may have to demonstrate the product, for example. The product or sample used must look right, and will need to be explained, not in technical terms, necessarily, but in terms of how it offers particular benefits and solutions. A demonstration is a powerful element of a sales presentation, because it gets the prospect involved and encourages conversation and questions. It provides a focus that can dispel any lingering awkwardness between buyer and seller. Also, in getting their hands on the product itself, or a sample, the prospect is brought very close to the reality of the product and can begin to see for themselves what it can do for them. Even in a consumer market, this is important. The car dealer takes prospective buyers out for a test drive so that they can experience the 'feel' of the car, and better imagine themselves owning it. The buyers feel that they are judging the car for themselves, and not just

Often, a sales representative will make use of presentation aids to dramatise a sales pitch.

Source: Christopher Thorburn Associates.

taking the sales representative's word for it. The test drive tells most prospective car buyers much more about the character of the vehicle than half an hour of peering under the bonnet listening to detailed technical specifications from the dealer.

Even where it may be difficult to demonstrate the product, other involvement devices may be used. In organisational markets particularly, it may be possible to visit existing customers who have purchased similar products or systems. This gives the opportunity to see the product in application, and to talk to someone who is reasonably unbiased not only about the product, but also about their experience of the seller's after-sales service and ability to honour their promises.

If none of that is possible, then at least the presentation should incorporate plenty of audio-visual aids to keep the attention of the prospect and to prevent any danger of monotony creeping in. Involving members of the sales support team may also help to provide a more detailed and interesting picture for the prospect, and help to answer any of the wider questions or needs that might arise.

Handling objections

It is indeed a rare and skilful sales representative who can complete an entire sales presentation without the prospect coming out with words to the effect of 'that's all very well, but ...'. At any stage in the selling process that involves the customer, objections can, and probably will be made. These may arise for various reasons: lack of understanding; lack of interest; misinformation; a need for reassurance; or from genuine concern. The sales representative must be prepared to overcome objections where possible, as otherwise the sale is likely to be lost completely. If the customer is concerned enough to raise an objection, then the representative must have the courtesy to answer it in some way. Homespun wisdom among seasoned sales representatives argues that the real selling does not begin until the customer raises an objection.

Table 18.2 summarises typical objections that occur time after time, regardless of the specific selling situation. Some objections are so predictable that it should be possible to anticipate them and answer them even before the customer gets around to raising them! It is important to develop counter-arguments. For example, many customers in many different types of market will raise an objection to the effect that the whole thing is too expensive for them. Whether this is a real concern or a last ditch attempt to provoke the representative into price concessions is irrelevant. The representative must have an answer to it, perhaps using it as an opening to discuss credit or leasing terms, or to reiterate the savings made by switching to this product or investing in it.

TABLE 18.2
Typical objections

- Your company
- Your product
- Your service
- Your pricing
- You
- You are not competitive enough
- Delivery delay
- I can't afford it
- I don't need it

Organisations that do not subscribe to the formula approach to selling often do train their sales staff to handle specific objections that commonly arise in their field in a set way. The following are a selection of objection handling techniques commonly used in personal selling. Each is appropriate for a different kind of objection.

Ask the objection back

If the prospect comes out with something vague, then it is appropriate for the representative to ask for further elaboration, either to define the objection better, or to find out whether the objection is real or a stalling excuse. Exploring the objection also allows the representative and the customer to define whether the objection is fundamental or peripheral.

If a buyer says 'I think your product is not as good as product x', the sales representative should explore what is meant by the use of the word 'good'. This could cover a whole range of different areas in the competitive offering. The representative's response may therefore be designed to explore in more detail the underlying problem by asking 'In what way is it not as good?'

Agree and counter

Agreeing with the objection and countering it is often called the 'yes, but' technique. Where the objection is founded in fact, all the representative can legitimately do is agree with the substance of it, then find a compensating factor to outweigh it. Thus if the prospect argues that the product being sold is more expensive than the competition's, the representative can reply with, 'Yes, I agree that value for money is important. Although our product is more expensive initially, you will find that the day-to-day running costs and the annual maintenance add up to a lot less ...'. Such a technique avoids creating excessive tension and argument, because the customer feels that their objection has been acknowledged and satisfactorily answered.

Boomerang

A variation on the previous technique involves turning the objection into a reason for buying. Thus if the prospect says something like, 'This model's getting a bit old; I think I'd be better going for the new generation', then the sales representative might reply with, 'This model's technology has been around for a number of years, and that's the very reason why you should buy it. It's tried and trusted – our customers have five million of these components in service and the failure rate is less than 0.5 per cent. The new generation model is twice the price and yet to be proved in practice'.

Feel, felt, found

The previous techniques have all answered rational objections, based on some aspect of the product or the deal. If the prospect retreats from rationality, and appears to be making fairly inarticulate, emotional objections, perhaps demonstrating a lack of confidence in their decision-making ability, then this is the appropriate technique to use. Thus the prospect says, 'Well, I accept what you say, but I just don't feel certain about this.' To this the representative replies, 'I understand how you feel. Many other people have felt like that, but they've found that buying this product was actually the best decision'. In other words, the representative is offering the empathy, sympathy and reassurance that will bolster the prospect's confidence in the purchasing decision.

Denial

Denial is a dangerous technique to use unless you are very sure of your ground and your prospect. All the previous techniques have been careful not to contradict the prospect, but have all demonstrated diplomacy and sympathy with the prospect's point of view. Denial, on the other hand, involves telling the prospect that they are wrong. To reduce the risk of antagonising the prospect, any denial must be accompanied with proof of why the objection is wrong or misinformed. Even with proof, the prospect might still be offended that the representative has dared to contradict them, or might feel that somehow they have been made to look foolish, and the therefore decide to take their business elsewhere.

An indirect denial might take some of the edge off the situation. If, for example, the prospect says, 'I've heard that you failed to fulfil your delivery promises to Bloggs & Co.,' the representative, rather than using the direct denial of, 'No, that's not true', which is defensive and potentially antagonistic, might initially ask the objection back with a reply such as, 'Where have you heard that, then?' The dialogue that follows this might allow the representative to discredit the source of the rumour or to set the facts straight without overtly telling the prospect that they are wrong. If the situation is handled well, the prospect may conclude that they were wrong, and the representative is saved from awkwardness.

All in all, handling objections requires a very careful response from the representative. He must not see objections as a call for him to say just anything to clinch the sale, since doing so will only lead to legal or relationship problems later. The representative must assess the situation, the type of objection and the mood of the customer and then choose the most appropriate style of response, without overstepping any ethical boundaries in terms of content. It is critical that the winning of the argument used to overcome the objection does not lead to a lost sale. Objections may interrupt the flow of the sales process either temporarily or permanently, and unless they are overcome, the final stages of the selling process cannot be achieved.

Negotiation

Some aspects of negotiation have already been covered at pp. 435 *et seq.*, since the trade-off between price and the package offered does tend to be the main subject of most negotiation. To put negotiation in its proper context within the selling process, this subsection broadens the view of negotiation, emphasizing the effect of the relative balance of power between the two parties on their negotiating positions.

Once the main body of the sales presentation is drawing to a close, with all the prospect's questions and objections answered for the time being, the selling process may move into a negotiation phase. Negotiation is a 'give and take' activity in which both parties try to shape a deal that satisfies both of them. Negotiation assumes a basic willingness to trade, but does not necessarily lead to a final deal. The danger for the sales representative, of course, is that a deadlocked or delayed negotiation phase may allow a competitor to enter the fray.

There are two types of negotiation:

1 *The co-operative or win–win negotiation.* This assumes that by trading concessions, a better deal can result for both parties. Concessions need not centre on price alone. They can take in issues like delivery schedules, delivery or insurance costs, product specifications, trade-ins or credit terms. For example, the buyer may agree to pay the delivery charges, in return for the seller's agreement to offer an extended warranty. The technique is to trade something that is relatively cheap for you, but is valuable to the other party. Thus an extended warranty costs little to the seller in reality, but means peace of mind and potential repair cost savings to the buyer.

   This type of negotiation is especially prevalent when longer-term relationships are being built up. The seller might consider it worth giving away major concessions on a first deal in order to ensure future business from that buyer. There is little point, as a seller, in driving a hard bargain for short-term gain if the long-term relationship flounders as a result.

2 *The competitive negotiation.* The hard bargain focused on short-term gain is appropriate and typical in one-off situations. Rather than seeking a better deal for both parties, the emphasis is on gaining as much advantage as possible over the other party. It still may mean some trading of concessions, especially those that cost you little but are of value to the other party.

Despite the fact that deals are becoming more complex, sales staff are still expected to be able to negotiate. If they are going to be given the power to negotiate on behalf of the organisation, then they need clear guidelines on how far they are permitted to go in terms of concessions, and what the implications of those concessions would be. An extra month's credit, for example, could be quite expensive, particularly for an organisation with short-term cash flow problems, unless it is traded for another prized concession. This effectively means that the sales representative needs financial as well as behavioural training in order to handle complex and sometimes lengthy negotiation.

There are some matters that the representative can consider that might help to establish a successful negotiating position.

The obvious judgement to make concerns the *relative power balance* between buyer and seller. If the buyer has many alternative options, and does not appear to be particularly eager to have that representative's product specifically, then that representative might have to be prepared to give away a considerable amount of ground in order to make a sale. The activities of the competition might also affect what goes on between this buyer and this seller. If the competition have been very aggressive and have already made attractive offers to the buyer, then this seller might feel obliged to make a better offer, depending on how badly the sale is wanted. The only means of saving this situation is if the seller is astute enough not to get locked into purely price-based comparisons with the competition. The representative should, if possible, define the 'better offer' in terms of features, benefits and peripherals other than price, in order to create an offering that is less easy for the competition to copy or undercut, and to blur the distinction between competing products somewhat.

It is, of course, possible that the balance of power lies in the hands of the selling organisation, if it has a unique product, service or expertise to offer that would be difficult to source elsewhere. If that is the case, the seller can afford to be a little less accommodating in terms of concessions.

Another important consideration is the sales representative's assessment of the *limits* within which each party is negotiating. Both parties will enter the negotiation with some idea of their minimum and maximum boundaries in terms of what they want to get and what they are prepared to give way on. The buyer, for example, has minimum performance criteria to which the product must conform, and a maximum price that the organisation is prepared to pay for it. At the same time, the buyer will also have an upper price limit in mind, along with an idea of the extras desired, whether these relate to the product specifications or to peripheral service offerings, the provision of which would justify moving up closer to that limit. The selling organisation too will have defined minimum requirements, in terms of the rock bottom price they are prepared to go down to, and the maximum they are prepared to give away in concessions. It is a delicate judgement, but if the seller can work out when the buyer is close to their absolute limit, it can make all the difference between a sale and a lost sale. Attempting to push the buyer beyond their threshold means that there is a real risk that they will withdraw from the process.

Body language can be an important indicator of a prospect's state of mind. Is the seller (on the left) pushing this prospect too far?

Source: Pitman Publishing.

As a final point, it must be said that negotiation need not be a separate and discrete stage of the selling process. Negotiation may emerge implicitly during the process of handling objections, or may be an integral part of the next stage to be discussed, closing the sale.

Closing the sale

The closing stage of the personal selling process is concerned with reaching the point where the customer agrees to purchase. In most cases, it is the sales representative's responsibility to **close the sale**, to ask for the order. If the sales presentation has been well prepared, if the customer's questions and objections have been satisfactorily handled and if the negotiation issues have been largely resolved, then closure should flow quite naturally with no problems.

Where the representative is less sure of the prospect's state of mind, or where the prospect still seems to have doubts, the timing of the closure and the way in which it is done could affect whether a sale is made. Try to close the sale too soon, and the buyer might be frightened off, leave it too long, and the buyer might become irritated by the prolonged process and all the good work done earlier in the sales presentation will start to dissipate.

Watching the buyer's behaviour and listening to what they are saying might indicate that closure is near. The buyer's questions, for example, may become very trivial or the objections might dry up. The buyer might go quiet and start examining the product intently, waiting for the representative to make a move. The buyer's comments or questions might begin to relate to the post-purchase period, with a strong assumption that the deal has already been done.

A representative who thinks that the time to close is near, but is uncertain, might have to test the buyer's readiness to commit to a purchase. Also, if the prospect seems to be teetering on the edge of making a decision, then the representative might have to use a mechanism to give the buyer a gentle nudge in the direction of closure.

There are many ways of closing the sale (Jacoby and Craig, 1984), and a number are considered below.

Alternative close

The representative may offer the buyer a number of alternatives, each of which implies an agreement to purchase. The buyer's response gives an insight into how ready they are to commit themselves. Thus if the representative says, 'Would you like delivery to each of your stores or to the central distribution point?', there are two ways in which the buyer might respond. One way would be to choose one of the alternatives offered, in which case the sale must be very close, since the buyer is willing to get down to such fine detail. The other response would be something like, 'Wait a minute, before we get down to that, what about …', showing that the buyer has not yet heard enough and may still have objections to be answered.

Assumptive close

In the assumptive close the sales representative assumes that the customer will buy and carries on into the details of the transaction. The representative will say, 'I'll arrange for delivery within two weeks then', to which the buyer can agree without argument, agree, but argue for one-week delivery time, or disagree and pull the dialogue back into the negotiation or objection handling stages.

Time pressure close

A buyer who is clearly on the edge of a decision may be triggered into action by being offered a limited response time. Thus a suggestion that this is the last item in stock and that if the buyer does not agree to purchase it now, the seller might not be able to source another, could be a powerful incentive to act. Threats of imminent price rises, stockouts, or of the type 'sale ends Saturday' can all increase the sense of urgency, but do run the risk of being challenged by the buyer. The representative needs to be sure that the time pressure can be justified.

The ease of bringing the sale to a close, and the type of closing problems that might arise, will depend on the commercial complexity of the transaction. Sometimes, negotiating a trial order or agreeing to 'sale or return' on goods may reduce the risks of purchase sufficiently to bring the sale to some kind of close. In some situations, the initial commitment to purchase may itself trigger a range of complex negotiations to finalise the deal.

Follow-up and account management

The sales representative's responsibility does not end once a sale has been agreed. As implied earlier at pp. 702–03, the sales representative, as the customer's key contact point with the selling organisation, needs to ensure that the product is delivered on time and in good condition, that any installation or training promises are fulfilled and that the customer is absolutely satisfied with the purchase and is getting the best out of it.

At a more general level, the relationship with the customer still needs to be cultivated and managed. In an organisational market, contacts made with the range of staff involved in the buyer's decision-making unit need to be nurtured. Where the sale has resulted in an ongoing supply situation, this may mean ensuring continued satisfaction with quality and service levels. Even with infrequently purchased items,

---

MARKETING IN ACTION

The sales force and IT

One of the roles of the sales force mentioned in this chapter is that of information gathering. In many sales forces, however, although representatives might well be recording information, it is not being disseminated within the organisation. Part of the problem is that information is not being recorded formally and systematically. Even if the sales force does use IT, the systems often are geared too much towards order taking and are not sufficiently flexible to allow the recording of qualitative observations and snippets of conversation.

Group 4, the security company, however, upgraded its IT system to get more useful background information from its sales force. The company recognises the need to know what a prospect is thinking, and to find out exactly why a particular sale is won or lost. Is it price, quality, service, or what? Once the company can get to the bottom of the reasons, it can start to strengthen its sales and marketing efforts. Stanley Tools is similarly equipping its sales representatives with the IT means to record useful information about prospects. It gives Stanley the potential to measure, for example, the effects of a sales promotion on an outlet by outlet basis. Not only does this allow Stanley to create better promotions in

the future, but it also gives them a database of customers with whom, perhaps, more effort needs to be made to gain better results from promotions.

IT in the field can help the sales force in more mundane ways, of course. As well as ensuring the accurate and systematic collection of information, it can help to reduce the time the representative spends on administration and in planning calls. It can certainly help to improve the representative's efficiency in front of the customer, in the sense that product information can be called up on a laptop computer immediately. Using spreadsheets, for example, the representative can also provide instant, informed quotes for the customer, or explore 'what if?' scenarios with them, all of which could provide an important competitive edge and clinch the conversion into a definite sale.

Overall, then, IT can help to improve the quality and flow of information within the organisation. It can also help the representative to utilise time better and thus spend far more time in face-to-face contact with customers. As the cost of maintaining and operating the sales force increases, this is a very valuable benefit.

Sources: Coopers and Lybrand (1994); Norris (1995).

ongoing positive contact helps to ensure that when new business develops, that supplier will be well placed. In the case of the consumer buying a car, the sales representative will make sure in the early stages that the customer is happy with the car, and work to resolve any problems quickly and efficiently. In the longer term, direct responsibility usually passes from the representative to a customer care manager who will ensure that the buyer is regularly sent product information and things like invitations to new product launches in the showrooms.

In the organisational market, an important role for the sales representative is to manage the customer's account internally within the selling organisation, ensuring that appropriate support is available as needed. Thus the representative is continuing to liaise between the customer and the accounts department, engineering, R&D, service and anyone else with whom the customer needs to deal.

Turnbull (1990) highlighted six important ways in which personal contact can help to maintain effective relationships with customers. These are shown in Fig 18.4 and discussed briefly in turn below. At various times in the selling process the buyer and seller may perform different activities in support of each of the following aspects of personal contact.

Facilitating information exchange

Facilitating information exchange goes beyond hard data concerning the product, and relates to relatively confidential information that can lead to a deeper assessment. Such sensitive information will only be exchanged, however, where there is experience, trust and respect built up through a history of personal contact.

Facilitating assessment

Personal contact, coupled with the free exchange of information, enables the buyer to assess the product and commercial offering in order to make a decision on selecting a supplier.

Facilitating negotiation and adaptation

Facilitating negotiation and adaptation will vary from relatively simple commercial negotiation through to complex technical and commercial discussion to find a fit between the buyer's and seller's respective needs. These discussions could include ways of adapting a product, manufacturing processes and delivery systems.

Crisis insurance

Some personal contacts might only be activated at a time of difficulty and thus could be said to amount to crisis insurance. A supplier to a large buyer, for example, might

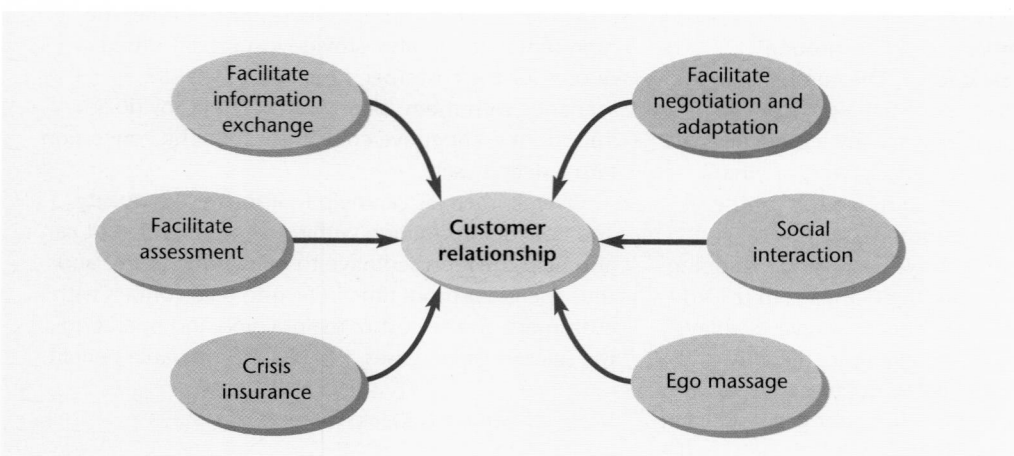

FIGURE 18.4

The role of personal contact in maintaining good customer relationships

only plan to meet with the buyer's managing director once a year, out of courtesy. However, if difficulties do arise in the meantime, that contact may be activated as a form of security or insurance, with a direct appeal to intervene.

Non-commercial social interaction

Although most buyer–seller interpersonal interaction takes place within an organisational context, there might also be some private social interaction that will affect the commercial relationship. This might include membership of other social groups, such as a church or sports clubs.

Massaging the ego

An extension of the social and crisis insurance contacts is 'massaging the ego', whereby higher level contact is sought or offered from time to time to enhance one party's feelings of self-importance. Some buyers might, therefore, appreciate a visit once a year from the seller's sales director as a demonstration of the value of their account.

SALES MANAGEMENT

The previous section concentrated on the mechanics of selling something to a prospective buyer. That is important, certainly, because if the selling process does not work well, then there will be no sales and no revenue. Somebody has to show the customer the benefits of dealing with that particular seller. No matter how good the product or the other promotional elements are they have to be sold.

Equally important, however, is the management of the sales force. Whether in a multinational organisation or a small company, the selling effort needs to be planned and managed. In a very small business, the owner, perhaps with some assistance, may undertake most of the selling and manage it by default. In a larger organisation, a sales manager will be assigned the tasks of achieving sales results through formal management of a sales force. Whatever the size or the character of a business, sales management provides an essential link between the organisation's strategic marketing plans and the achievement of sales objectives by the representatives in the field. Sales management ensures that the selling effort fits with the overall tasks specified in the marketing plan and strategy.

Again, it is difficult to generalise about the specific tasks of sales management, as they will obviously vary between different organisations and different markets. A number of areas which are commonly found are, however, examined in this section. These include establishing a sales plan and strategy; specifying and recruiting sales representatives; training and developing staff; motivation and compensation policies, and finally, controlling and evaluating the selling effort.

Example

British Midland Airways, the UK's second-largest airline, organises its sales force around a general sales manager. The sales manager is responsible for the control, direction and motivation of a team of national account managers who deal with corporate clients and a team of regional managers who are responsible for developing the retail travel sector across Europe.

Sales planning and strategy

The sales plan outlines the objectives for the selling effort and the details of how the plan should be implemented. This plan itself arises from, and must fit closely with, the marketing objectives set for products and market share etc. In designing and implementing the sales plan, there are three interrelated decisions to be made.

Specifying the sales objectives

There are two types of sales objective to be specified. The first is the general sales targets to be achieved by the sales force as a whole. The second is the definition of sales targets specific to individuals or groups within the sales force.

Setting sales objectives provides an essential yardstick against which to measure progress and to motivate and influence the selling effort. Normally, quantitative measures are used to specify exactly what is required. At the level of the total sales force, the targets will be in terms of sales value and/or volume. Setting objectives in sales and profit terms is often necessary either to avoid the dangers of chasing low profit sales or to lessen the temptation to reduce margins to generate more sales volume but less gross profit (*see also* Chapters 10 and 11).

Using market share as a basis for sales targets, rather than sales value or volume, carries its own risks. The reasons are similar to those outlined at p. 639 in the discussion of advertising objectives. Although the sales force's efforts are very important for achieving sales, the effectiveness of that selling effort is also affected by other factors. These include such matters as price levels, company image, product specification and the support of other promotional techniques. While measures of product sales compared with the nearest competitor and year-on-year market share changes are useful indicators of selling performance, they must not be seen in isolation.

For the individual sales representative, many of the same measures still apply. Often, at this level, the sales objectives are called **sales quotas**, and again they are defined in sales value or volume terms. However, it is often useful to clarify these objectives further, perhaps by breaking them down into a number of targets relating to specific product ranges. Where a wide variety of products is offered, there may be weaker ones that need to be highlighted in the setting of objectives, either to boost their sales by setting ambitious targets, or to direct the sales force's attention away from them by setting low targets.

Targets for individual sales representatives need not only relate to selling quantities of products. Performance targets might be agreed in terms of the number of sales calls, the number of new accounts recruited, the call frequency, call conversion rates (i.e., turning prospects into buyers), or selling expenses.

Detailing the sales organisation

Decisions have to be made about organising the sales force. Flexibility in this area depends on whether the organisation already has a sales force or whether one has to be created.

A newly appointed sales manager would normally inherit an existing sales force. One priority for the new manager would be to review the current structure and establish whether it could be modified. Obviously, in a new organisation there are more options available, as the manager does not have to think about the costs of dismantling any existing structure.

For new organisation, a more fundamental question may be raised about whether a direct sales force is required at all. An organisation may decide to sell through an independent agent (*see* p. 456) to increase coverage, for example. To do this the organisation must be sure that the agent has the necessary expertise and selling effort. There is little point in losing one's own sales force or opting out of ever setting one up, if the only gain is poorer performance, whatever the savings in salaries and expenses.

Assuming that the selling effort is to be managed internally, the sales manager has four broad choices for organising the sales force: geography, product, customer type, customer importance. Each of these will now be discussed in turn.

Geographical structure. In a European context, a geographical structure normally means dividing Europe up into its individual nations, then subdividing each nation by region, then, if necessary, further dividing each region into sales territories. Thus France, for example, would be a national sales area, Alsace would be a regional division within it, and Strasbourg would be a final subdivision with its own sales representative. Sales representatives are assigned to each geographic territory according to a formula described later (*see* Fig.18.5), and represent all or a specified number of company products within that territory. The focus on one area has the advantage of minimising travel costs and avoids the danger of call duplication that exists in the other methods discussed later. In addition, having representatives familiar with the local economy encourages a more knowledgeable approach for identifying and exploiting new opportunities. This could be an advantage in situations where the product or service is sold to a wide range of different customers who are geographically scattered, for example financial services. However, if the organisation operates in a specialised, geographically concentrated industry, or if detailed technical product knowledge is needed then the geographical option has more limited appeal.

Product-based structure. As an alternative to the geographic approach, a product-based structure means that individual sales representatives specialise in selling only a limited number of products from the organisation's total range. This kind of structure allows the organisation to develop experts in particular product technologies who can act as consultants or problem solvers as well as sales representatives. A product-based structure may also be appropriate where the organisation offers a wide range of very diverse products in its portfolio.

This approach enables the organisation to recruit more selectively and to develop expertise within its sales force that could give a competitive edge. The disadvantages mirror the advantages of the geographic option. Travel costs increase, as a single representative may have to service customers across Europe. This also has implications for travelling time (and the more time spent travelling, the less time spent selling). Furthermore, the representative may have to acquire a much wider range of knowledge about local conditions and culture relating to the various customers visited. Finally, duplication of calls may increase, because if one customer wants to purchase a wide range of the seller's products, two or three different representatives with different product responsibilities may have to call.

Customer-based structure. A customer based structure, in contrast, is designed to reflect the needs of different types of customers, rather than being product centred. This might mean dividing customers by industry, so that one representative deals with the automotive trade, while another deals with aerospace. This has an attractive logic, as organisations within a particular industry may well have similar needs, similar applications and similar problems. The representative can develop detailed industry knowledge and form long-term personal relationships with customers. Another way of classifying customers is by the nature of their business, that is, whether they are manufacturers or resellers. Each category would require a very different selling approach, because there are fundamental differences in their buying motives.

Whatever the classification system used, the customer-based approach does ensure a better match between the support and expertise needed by the customer and the skills of the sales representative. However, although call duplication may be low, the potential for geographically spread customers means higher travelling and customer servicing costs.

Customer importance. Finally, a variant of the customer-based approach is a structure based on the size or importance of the customer. The Pareto effect (discussed at p. 559) will identify the important strategic role played by a small number of important customers. If 20 per cent of our customers account for 80 per cent of our business, then that 20 per cent deserve the best care and attention we can offer them. If the major accounts are selected for special attention, the better sales representatives can focus on improving buyer–seller relationships, selling in depth, and co-ordinating the efforts of all the selling organisation's personnel to achieve a high service level for those customers. Those representatives become advanced forms of customer specialists, and where there are very large accounts, may represent only one account.

> ### Example
>
> BASF employ a national account manager to deal with audio, video and camcorder tapes with the regional multiples. They also have sales executives who deal with independent trade customers and retailers through a network of sales territories.

Even in a small business, the owner may choose to retain and maintain a personal relationship with the more important customers, delegating the other accounts to the sales representative(s).

There is clearly no one universally applicable and appropriate organisational structure. Sometimes, a mixed structure may be best, combining geographic and major customer specialisation. Johnson & Johnson, for example, employ regionally based territory sales managers for its UK consumer products, but with specific responsibility for certain types of customer, such as independent pharmacies and wholesale cash and carries. This allows the organisation to benefit from the advantages of both types of allocation, while reducing the effect of their disadvantages. The chosen structure will be the right one as long as it reflects the objectives and marketing strategy of the firm. Increasingly, the internationalisation of organisations is causing a reconsideration of the way in which sales are structured across national and EU borders (Hill and Still, 1990). The important point is not to see the sales structure as fixed, but regularly to assess its relevance and its ability to achieve its objectives. If the structure appears to be failing in any way, then questions must be asked and answered, and management may have to be prepared to modify their approach.

Establishing sales coverage and deployment

A further decision has to be made on the ideal size of the sales force. A number of factors need to be considered, such as the calling frequency required for each customer, the number of calls possible each day, and the relative division of the representative's time between administration, selling and repeat calls (Cravens and LaForge, 1983). All these matters will have an impact on the ability of the sales force to achieve the expected sales results from the number of accounts served. For a smaller business, the issue may be further constrained by just how many representatives can be afforded!

Figure 18.5 shows a formula commonly used to assess the size of a sales force. Within the formula, there are several underlying deployment and coverage issues. For example, call frequency will vary according to the size of the decision-making unit within the buying organisation and the frequency of purchase. It may be possible to vary the call frequency depending on the customer's potential and careful use of non-personal communication, such as mail shots etc.

Closely linked with the issue of sales force size is the problem of dividing the whole sales area into individual territories. The size, shape and sales potential may well vary between territories, and these need to be considered when setting sales targets and coverage policies.

The size and deployment of the sales force is not a fixed thing, but must be varied according to emerging opportunities and analysis of resource efficiency. The growth of telemarketing along with the increasingly high cost per personal sales call have made some organisations think much more carefully about where, when and how to employ the sales team.

FIGURE 18.5

Calculating the size of a sales force

The inputs

C = Number of customers
F = Average call frequency per customer per year
L = Average number of calls per representative per day
N = Average number of selling days per representative per year

The calculations

Stage 1 $T = C \times F$ = Total number of calls per year
Stage 2 $D = T/L$ = Total number of selling days required per year
Stage 3 $S = D/N$ = Number of sales representatives required

Example

If: C = 300 (number of customers)
     F =   4 (average call frequency per customer per year)
     L =   3 (average number of calls per representative per day)
     N = 133 (average number of selling days per representative per year)

Then: $T = 300 \times 4 = 1200$ = Calls per year
       $D = 1200/3 = 400$ = Selling days required and
       $S = 400/133 = 3.01$

Thus 3 sales representatives are needed

MARKETING IN ACTION

'The Man From the Pru'

'The Man from the Pru' is an advertising slogan that the Prudential, a UK financial services company, has long been trying to put behind it. This has not been an easy task. The man from the Pru is a warm, cosy image, evoking the days when the insurance man (or woman) used to call on customers at their homes every week to collect premiums and update their payment books. Just because the company is trying to shed this image does not mean that it is any less dependent on personal selling, however. Although many financial service companies, including the Pru, have moved towards telephone-based sales and account management, there is still a role for sales forces.

The Pru still uses 100 independent financial advisers to sell its pensions, savings, PEPs and other investment products. For selling its insurance products, in 1990, the company had a sales force of 10 000 but the number was down to 6500 by 1995. One of the Pru's major problems is that 60 per cent of its policyholders earn less than £10 000 a year, and are unlikely to buy products other than through a door-to-door sales force. This segment is less profitable than higher earning segments, yet is also more expensive to service. The Pru thus has problems competing against rivals who have smaller sales forces, and calculates that its policies cost the customer 25 per cent more, just to pay for the sales force. Another problem that the Pru faces is that little information seems to filter upwards from its massive sales force. It has six million policyholders, but no meaningful central database. It has names and addresses, but no means of segmenting its customers according to purchasing habits or needs.

By 1996, the Pru was trying to restructure its operations to get a better co-ordinated and planned balance between the traditional sales force aspect of the business and the expansion of telephone selling through Pru Direct. Brierley (1996) is of the opinion that so far:

The company [has been] unwilling to make difficult decisions about its sales force and unwilling, or unable, to invest in direct technology.

That could be about to change.

Sources: Brierley (1995; 1996).

Recruitment and selection

As with any recruitment exercise, it is important to begin by developing a profile of who the organisation is looking for. A detailed analysis of the selling tasks should lead to a list of the ideal skills and characteristics of the representative to be recruited. As mentioned at p. 704–06, there are significant differences between order takers and order makers, so the recruiter must at least know where the recruit is to fit in and what tasks they will be undertaking.

Many researchers have attempted to identify the ideal mix of traits that go to make up the super sales representative (Mayer and Greenberg, 1964; Lockman and Hallaq, 1982). The lists of traits rarely agree, contain a huge range of characteristics, and furthermore centre on matters that are difficult to discern and measure in an individual. The challenge for the sales manager is to relate those lists to the specific needs of the recruiting organisation. This means understanding the market, understanding what customers want from representatives, defining selling requirements, and analysing why certain existing representatives appear to be more successful than others. Table 18.3 lists the attributes of sales representatives typically appreciated by buyers.

A common dilemma is whether previous experience is an essential requirement. Some organisations prefer to take on recruits new to selling, then train them in their own methods rather than recruit experienced representatives who come with bad habits and other organisations' weaknesses. Others, especially smaller organisations, may deliberately seek experienced staff, wishing to benefit from training programmes that they themselves could not afford to provide. The eventual choice will depend on the organisation's decision on what they require in terms of such factors as age, background, experience, qualifications etc. A supplier of greeting cards, personalised stationery and postcards etc. considered the most important factors to be experience in sales, a background in retail greeting cards and direct experience of selling into similar outlets. A large car dealer when seeking a new car sales representative demanded two years new car sales experience as a minimum although a parallel trainee position highlighted the need for someone who was articulate, with an outgoing personality.

Formal sales training is an important means of developing selling skills.

Source: Pitman Publishing.

TABLE 18.3
Sales representative attributes typically appreciated by buyers

- Thoroughness and follow-up
- Knowledge of seller's products
- Representing the buyer's interests within the selling organisation
- Market knowledge
- Understanding the buyer's problems
- Knowledge of the buyer's product and markets
- Diplomacy and tact
- Good preparation before sales calls
- Regular sales calls
- Technical education

The actual selection process needs to be designed to draw out evidence of the ability of each candidate to perform the specified tasks, so that an informed choice can be made. The cost of a poor selection can be very high, not just in terms of recruitment costs and salary, but also, and perhaps more seriously, in terms of lost sales opportunities or damage to the organisation's reputation. In view of the importance of making the right choice, in addition to normal interview and reference procedures, a number of firms employ psychological tests to assess personality and some will not confirm the appointment until the successful completion of the initial training period.

Training

The recruitment process generally only provides the raw material. Although the new recruit might already have appropriate skills and a good attitudinal profile, training will help to sharpen both areas so that better performance within the sales philosophy of the employing organisation can be developed. Sales force training applies not just to new recruits, however. Both new and existing staff, even well established staff, may need skills refinement and upgrading.

Training may be formal or informal. Some organisations invest in and develop their own high-quality training facilities and run a regular series of introductory and refresher courses in-house. This has the advantage of ensuring that the training is relevant to the organisation and its business, as well as signifying an ongoing commitment to staff development.

Other organisations adopt a more *ad hoc* approach, using outside specialists as required. This means that the organisation only pays for what it uses, but the approach carries two serious risks. The first problem is that the training may be too generalised and thus insufficiently tailored to the organisation's needs. The second problem is that it is too easy for the organisation to put off training or, even worse, to delete it altogether in times of financial stringency.

Finally, a third group use informal or semi-formal 'sitting with Nelly' on-the-job coaching. This involves the trainee observing other representatives in the field, and then being observed themselves by experienced sales representatives and/or the sales manager. There is nothing quite like seeing the job being done, but with this approach the organisation needs to take great care to deal with a number of points. One concern is to ensure that such training is comprehensive, covering all aspects of the job. Another concern is to ensure that bad habits or questionable techniques are not passed on. The main problem with this kind of on-the-job training is that the training is not usually done by professional trainers. Therefore the quality can be variable, and there is no opportunity for fresh ideas to be introduced to the salesforce.

There are a number of dimensions that can be covered by training programmes, depending on the training needs identified by the organisation. Programmes may need to cover the organisation's products (and those of the competition), company information (relating to their own organisation, its competitors and their key customers), applications, market information, and not least, developing greater competency in selling and negotiation skills and techniques. It is the job of the sales manager to determine the relative emphasis in the training, its location, who participates, the length of a programme and the overall fit between the training budget, training outcomes and sales objectives.

L'Oreal found success with behavioural event interviewing, a process that enables a detailed analysis to be made to match the traits of successful sales people with those of potential applicants. By focusing on key competencies they were better able to select and develop skills with new staff (McClelland, 1994).

The commitment to sales training varies widely.

Example

A small Irish distributor of fire equipment employing around 10 sales people preferred to train its sales representatives on the job with the sales manager doing the training. Formal sales training occurred only occasionally and rarely involved tailormade programmes for the industry. This contrasts with Xerox and IBM where extensive in-company training programmes are organised at induction and at regular intervals for refresher purposes.

Motivation and compensation

Any sales effort needs well-motivated sales people. Apart from the fact that enthusiastic and motivated representatives will sell better, effective sales people are often in high demand by other employers.

Example

Transarc Corporation, a USA-based software organisation operating world-wide was prepared to offer a base salary of up to £45 000 and of up to £90 000 on achieving target earnings to attract highly successful software technology sales people as part of its European expansion plans in 1995.

An organisation will not only want to motivate new recruits to join its sales force, but also have an interest in making sure that they are sufficiently well rewarded for their achievements that they will not easily be poached by the competition (Cron *et al.*, 1988). There are many ways that the sales team can be motivated to achieve outstanding results and rewarded, but they are not all financially based. A supplier of business services offered a £15 000 basic salary, rising to £21 000 on achieving target earnings, a Peugeot 306, mobile phone, pension and life assurance as part of its package.

Even a sense of belonging to a team can be important. Selling can be a lonely activity. Imagine spending your working life out on the road, with mostly only telephone contact with the sales manager, enhanced by the occasional meeting. It is not easy to maintain enthusiasm for the job, or to feel that your work is valued under such conditions. Bringing representatives back to HQ regularly for team meetings, seminars and briefings may help to foster the team spirit. It provides an opportunity for the team to share views and experiences, and allows clear two-way communication regarding achievements and expectations. Training programmes can also play a part in reassuring employees that they are valued, and in bringing teams back together again.

By involving the representatives in managerial activities such as developing their own territory sales plan, the organisation gains in two ways. First, it can plan with the benefit of the representative's knowledge and experience of the territory, and second, it gives the employee a greater sense of control over their own working as well as a feeling that there is open and co-operative management. Providing representatives with mechanisms for regularly feeding back updated intelligence into the organisation, through a direct data link, makes them feel that they are offering more than just selling expertise and can thus assist in developing positive motivation.

Sometimes, sales managers can create an element of healthy rivalry among sales representatives through sales contests. If the rewards are seen as valuable and achievable, contests can renew a representative's interest in doing a good job. Household goods, holidays or cash bonuses, for example, are tangible and attractive motivators. These contests do not necessarily have to be focused on sales figures. They can be targeted at one or more of a range of important activities, such as creating new accounts, quota achievement by area or product, and increased penetration of existing accounts. These incentives can easily be self-financing if they are taken seriously by the sales force.

Example

Legal and General, in response to the growing criticism of hard selling in the financial services sector, decided to scrap commission for the managers of self-employed sales agents, emphasizing instead compliance with regulations and response time in handling enquiries (*Sunday Times*, 1994).

The activities outlined so far have consisted of positive reinforcements, but unfortunately, some organisations choose to use penalties, and the fear of their implementation to motivate. Demotion and dismissal are extreme responses to poor performance, occurring where an organisation is happy to adopt a hire and fire philosophy rather than investing in staff through careful selection and comprehensive, ongoing training. Some organisations in the financial services sector have a reputation for employing sales people in order to benefit from their network of personal contacts and then, when these are exhausted, they are more than happy to terminate sales people's employment if their performance starts to drop.

Pay still remains a vital ingredient in attracting and retaining a committed sales force. The purpose of an effective sales force compensation scheme is to provide the sales manager with the flexibility to focus the efforts of the sales force on the achievement of the sales goals.

Three main methods of compensation exist: straight salary, straight **commission**, and a combination of salary and commission. Each method implies a number of advantages and disadvantages, which are listed in Table 18.4. The straight salary compensation plan is where a fixed amount is paid on a salary basis. This is most appropriate when the organisation wants to encourage representatives to spend time developing quality relationships with customers, or where the product sold is technically demanding. The straight commission compensation plan means that earnings are directly related to the sales and profit generated. This encourages a 'sell it quick and move on' attitude, appropriate to low-involvement, uncomplicated products. Finally, the most popular method is the combination plan, involving part salary and part commission. The selection of the most appropriate method will partly be determined by the nature of the selling tasks, and the degree of staff turnover that can be tolerated given the training and recruiting costs.

TABLE 18.4

Comparison of compensation plans

	Commission only	*Salary only*	*Part salary/part commission*
Motivation for rep. to generate sales	High	Low	Medium
Motivation for rep. to build customer relationship	Low	High	Medium
Motivation for rep. to participate in training	Low	High	Medium
Cost effectiveness for organisation	High	Potentially low	Medium
Predictability of cost to organisation	Low	High	Medium
Predictability of income for the rep.	Low	High	Medium
Ease of administration for organisation	Low	High	Low
Organisation's control over rep.	Low	High	Medium
Organisation's flexibility to push sales of particular products	High	Low	High
Overall, best where …	• Aggressive selling is needed • There are few non-selling tasks	• Training new reps • Difficult sales territories exist • Developing new territories • There are many non-selling tasks	• Organisation wants both incentive and control • Sales territories all have similar profiles

The overall challenge for the sales manager in this area is to find an appropriate balance between income and incentives, taking into account the pressures of the selling task. This requires a knowledge of the market and the sales staff. Although not all effective sales representatives make the transition to become effective sales managers, it is normal for the sales manager to have had direct experience in selling.

Performance Evaluation

Given that many sales representatives work away from an office base, the monitoring and control of individual selling activity is a vital function in the sales management role. No valid evaluation can be made without information about performance and the selling effort. Call reports, as part of a systematic means of gathering account information (*see* Chapter 6), form the basis for the weekly monitoring of an individual sales representative. They are also valuable, from a strategic point of view, in assessing the general impact of marketing polices at account level. Call reports usually specify who was contacted on the visit, the topics of discussion, particular problems arising, competitive activity and general progress towards the account objectives. Sometimes, these reports are linked to a call plan so that the sales manager can compare planned coverage with actual coverage, and can even assist in advance.

The sales representative's performance can be measured in both quantitative and qualitative terms. Quantitative assessments can be related to either input or output measures, usually with reference to targets and benchmarks (Good and Stone, 1991). Input measures assess activities such as the number of calls and account coverage. Output measures focus on the end rather than the means, and include measurement of sales volume, sales development, number of new accounts and specific product sales.

To create a rounded picture of the sales representative's performance, qualitative measures that tend to be informal and subjective are also used. These could include attitude, product knowledge, appearance and communication skills. Using them in conjunction with quantitative measures, the sales manager may be able to find explanations for any particularly good or bad performance underlying the quantitative evidence of the formal results achieved (McAdams, 1987).

TABLE 18.5
Calculating sales performance

Quantitative measure	Means of measuring
Productivity	
Calls per day	Number of calls/number of days worked
Calls per account	Number of calls/number of accounts
Orders per call	Number of orders/total number of calls
Account development and servicing	
Account penetration	Accounts sold to/total number of accounts available
Sales per account	Total sales value/total number of accounts
Average order size	Total sales value/total number of orders
Expenses	
Sales expenses	Expenses/sales made
Cost per call	Total costs/total number of calls made

Either way the assessment can form the basis of a deeper analysis to encourage a proactive rather than reactive approach to sales management. Table 18.5 outlines a number of simple formulae that can be used to assess performance with a view to designing corrective plans or staff development programmes. The analysis might indicate that action needs to be taken on call policy, training or motivation or even that problems may lie not with the sales force, but with the product or its marketing strategies.

Developments in IT are making the task of communicating with and receiving information from the field sales force more effective. This means that trends can be identified sooner, and corrective action planned and implemented more quickly and with more authority.

CHAPTER SUMMARY

Personal selling concerns interpersonal contact between buyer and seller with the aim of encouraging the buyer to behave or think in a certain kind of way. Although it can be an expensive and labour-intensive marketing communication activity, it has a number of advantages over other forms of communication. It makes an *impact*, because it involves face-to-face contact and is less likely to be ignored; it can deliver a *precise and tailored* message to a target customer who has already been checked out to ensure that they fit the right profile; it helps the *cultivation* of long-term buyer–seller relationships.

The roles undertaken by sales representatives are many and varied. They *prospect* for new customers; they provide customers with relevant and detailed *information*; they *persuade* customers to buy; they help to *demonstrate and install* products; they *represent the customer's interests* within the selling organisation; they help to *maintain good buyer –seller relationships* over time; they *collect information and feedback* from the field, and they *monitor* what the competition are doing in the field and how customers feel about the competition. Clearly, these roles will vary depending on the size of organisation, the type of market and the nature of the sales representative. Some will be order takers, some order makers and some will act in a support role.

The personal selling process can be a long and complicated marketing activity to implement. The process starts with the identification of prospective customers, and then the representative has to do as much background work on the prospect as possible in order to prepare an initial approach and a relevant sales presentation. Initial contact breaks the ice between buyer and seller, allowing an appointment to be made for the real selling to begin. The sales presentation will give the representative the opportunity to present the product in the best possible light, using a variety of samples and audio-visual aids, while allowing the customer to ask questions and to raise any objections they may have. Negotiating the fine details of the deal may lead naturally to closing the sale, and then all that remains is for the representative to ensure the customer's post-purchase satisfaction and work towards building a long-term relationship leading to repeat business and further purchases.

Sales management is an important area of marketing, and involves a number of issues. *Sales planning and strategy* means making decisions about sales objectives, both for the organisation as a whole and for individual sales representatives or teams. *Recruitment* and training are also both important aspects of sales management, and *training* too concerns the sales manager. Apart from benefiting from training programmes, sales representatives have to be properly *motivated and compensated* for their efforts. This means not only designing an appropriate and attractive package of pay and other benefits, but also making sure that representatives are fully involved in the life of the organisation generally and more specifically, in any decisions involving themselves. A natural part of all this is *performance evaluation*. Sales managers need to ensure that representatives are achieving their targets, and if not, why not.

Key words and phrases

Closing the sale	*Order maker*	*Qualified prospects*
Cold calling	*Order taker*	*Sales presentation*
Commission	*Personal selling*	*Sales quotas*
Conversion rates	*Prospecting*	*Sales support*
Leads	*Prospects*	

QUESTIONS FOR REVIEW

18.1 What is *personal selling* and how does it differ from other elements of the promotional mix?

18.2 What are the major *advantages* of personal selling and what can they contribute to the marketing effort?

18.3 What are the typical tasks of a *sales representative*?

18.4 How might the implementation and importance of each of those tasks vary between *organisational* and *consumer* markets?

18.5 Why might a sales representative's role include co-ordination within the selling organisation?

18.6 What is the difference between an *order taker* and an *order maker*?

18.7 What are the stages in the personal selling process?

18.8 Why is preparation and planning so important a part of the personal selling process?

18.9 How might the sales representative tell whether or not a prospect is ready to *close a sale*?

18.10 What are the main issues that the sales manager must consider as far as sales *planning* and *strategy* are concerned?

QUESTIONS FOR DISCUSSION

18.1 Give examples of three different kinds of sales support staff and analyse their contribution to the personal selling effort.

18.2 In what ways do you think a sales representative could make the sales presentation more relevant and interesting for the prospective customer?

18.3 What techniques might a sales representative use to counter the following objections:

(a) 'Your competitor's product is a lot cheaper ...'
(b) 'I don't think my wife would like it if I bought this ...'

(c) 'I've heard that your service engineers are very inefficient.'

18.4 Summarise the relative advantages of allocating sales responsibilities on the basis of:

(a) geographic regions,
(b) product-based criteria; and
(c) customer-based criteria.

18.5 Find 20 job advertisements for sales representatives and summarise the range of characteristics and skills sought. Which are the most commonly required and to what extent do you think that they are essential for a successful sales representative?

Buying a car

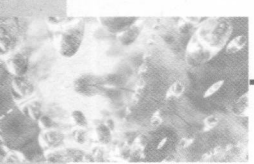

Although the events related in this case are true, the names, prices and product details of the various companies concerned have been changed.

In the early 1990s, life in the retail car market was fairly grim in the UK. Because of adverse economic conditions, consumers had neither the cash nor the motivation to buy new cars. Interest rates were quite high, and therefore it was too expensive to borrow money to pay for a car, unless a dealer was prepared to offer cheap or interest-free finance deals. Besides this, the economic outlook was not very good, and few people were confident that they would still be in work in a year's time. They felt, therefore, that it made sense to save, and to make the old car last a year or two longer until things began to pick up again.

One of the peculiarities of the UK car market is that the registration letter denoting the year of registration always changes on 1 August. This means that the market is somewhat seasonal, with a large percentage of new car sales taking place in August, and this is followed by a relatively quiet autumn. The motorist who is not desperate to be the first in the neighbourhood sporting the new registration letter can, therefore, often find a good bargain in the autumn. Dealerships can be generous in their price discounts or trade-in allowances as they try to keep car sales moving during the quieter periods. This effect can be even greater during years when the market generally has been depressed and the car manufacturers have used 1 August as a major promotional tool to stimulate sales. In those circumstances, most people who were interested in buying are likely to have taken advantage of the summer promotions and there will thus be even fewer buyers around in the autumn.

In one such year, Jane wants to buy a car in October. She has a fairly laid back attitude to this: if she can't have a black, series 7 BMW (which she certainly cannot afford), then she does not particularly care what she has as long as it is not absolutely at the bottom of the market. She envisages spending around £9000–£10 000. Her buying criteria are based on price/value for money, the dealership's geographic convenience (for servicing) and her assessment of the 'customer care' orientation of the dealership. She is also anxious to have the car quickly, therefore, availability is also a key criterion. She has no vehicle to part exchange, so it will be a cash sale financed from savings and a bank loan. She has already spoken to the bank manager who has agreed to make the loan. Although the interest rate is marginally higher than with some of the schemes offered by the car dealerships, she thinks that she will negotiate a better price for the car as a cash buyer.

Having looked at a number of consumer car magazines, such as *What Car?*, and with due respect for her financial situation, she has narrowed the choice of makes down to Company A and Company B. Company A's 1.2 litre GLS hatchback model, a fairly recent model, looks very promising in terms of style and performance on paper, but Company B's 1.2 litre GLX five-door model seems like good value (and with the imminent introduction of a new replacement model, there may be bargains to be had). She now feels that it is time to visit the dealers. Jane enlists the help of her friend, Peter, for moral support, and they set off in Peter's three-year-old car, a 2.0 litre executive model from Company A.

Wednesday, 9 October

Evans' Cars, the Company A dealership, occupies a prime town-centre site, offering both sales and servicing facilities. Fred, the sales representative, is polite, courteous and well-informed. The 1.2 litre GLS hatchback soon drops out as a contender, since Fred is adamant that there is a 5–10 week waiting list for delivery, which Jane feels to be unacceptable. Preliminary negotiation on price encourages Jane to think that maybe she can afford to go up the range and consider the less flashy, but bigger-engined 1.4 litre saloon which could be available within seven days. Fred doesn't put any sales pressure on at this stage, but offers to arrange a test drive (but not now). He makes sure that Jane and Peter have his card and plenty of brochures. As they leave, Fred suddenly remembers to ask for their names, but doesn't take a telephone number.

After leaving the Company A dealer, Jane seems pretty sure that she wants the 1.4 saloon, but is worried by the price tag. The offer on the 1.4 litre saloon is £10 490, down from an original price of £11 240.

The next stop is the Company B dealer, Smiffy's Motors, located on an industrial estate on the edge of town. It is closer to Jane's home than Evans' Cars, and also offers servicing facilities from the same site. Darren is a young sales representative, without much experience. The news on the 1.2 litre GLX five-door model is not cheerful. The only one they have in stock is a very bottom of the range, overpriced 'limited edition' fun version, designed to titillate the summer market. It looks pretty sad in the dim October drizzle. Once Darren picks up the negative attitude from Peter and Jane, he begins to knock the vehicle, using words like 'tinny' and 'plasticky'. However, all is not lost. As before, there does seem to be scope to negotiate one's way up the range to a 1.6 litre GL. There is a red one in the showroom, and Jane seems quite taken with it. Darren cannot arrange a test drive there and then, so Jane and Peter promise to phone him in the morning to discuss the matter further. They leave, armed with brochures and Darren's card, but Darren hasn't a clue who they are.

Assessing the situation, Peter and Jane decide that the Company B model seems the more promising line to pursue in terms of value for money, despite a daunting showroom price tag of £12 450, since Darren gives the (unspoken) impression that there is considerable leeway on price.

Thursday, 10 October

Peter phones Darren, and talks about price, dropping a hint that Evans' Cars are offering something special on Company A's 1.4 litre saloon. Darren trots off to the Sales Manager, who eventually authorises Darren to make an offer at £10 400, cash (i.e., no part exchange involved). Peter is secretly delighted, but isn't going to accept on the spot. Instead, he plays it cool, and says he'll talk it over with Jane and with Evans' Cars, then be in touch.

Friday, 11 October

Peter phones Darren and arranges a test drive for Monday afternoon. Meanwhile, he and Jane have agreed that she should buy the Company B 1.6 litre GL, assuming that the test drive goes well, and they want to get the whole deal finalised on Monday, insisting on delivery by Friday.

Monday, 14 October

Jane and Peter turn up as arranged. No Darren – he is away on a course for the day. No test drive has been arranged. Jane and Peter have to be persistent and create a noisy scene in the showroom to persuade the Sales Manager to wheel the showroom model out on to the road and put trade plates on it for a test drive. The harassed Fleet Sales Representative is pressganged into accompanying them, but he will not get involved in Darren's sale. The car handles well on the road, and they make it clear that they want to close the sale today, but nobody is interested. The Sales Manager scuttles off to get the bodyshop manager to look at some paintwork damage that Peter has pointed out on the car, and Jane and Peter are left standing alone in the middle of the showroom. They are on the verge of walking out and going back to Evans' Cars.

Questions

1 You are Darren, and you arrive on Tuesday morning to hear from the Fleet Sales Representative what happened on Monday. What are you going to do?

2 As the Sales Manager, how would you have handled the situation on Monday?

3 Assess Darren's approach to selling. What did he do right and what did he do wrong?

4 Why do you think that Peter took over the negotiation on Thursday (even though it was Jane who was buying the car) and why did he not accept the £10 400 offer immediately?

5 What should Jane and Peter do next? What can they learn from their experience and how can they turn it to their advantage?

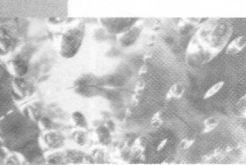

CASE STUDY 18.2

Irish Fire Products

Irish Fire Products (IFP), based in the west of Ireland, is a distributor for a range of fire extinguishers, fire blankets, sprinkler systems and other fire prevention accessories such as alarms, signage and doors. Most of the products sold are of relatively low value compared with an integrated fire prevention system designed to a customer's specific requirements for protecting commercial premises. Despite the low technology used, IFP, a small business, has prospered for over 20 years, competing with other distributors across Ireland as well as with the direct sales forces of companies such as Nu-Swift and Chubb. The market is mature, with most growth coming from the demands of new legislation. More recently, some customers have been increasingly looking for more sophisticated systems that IFP does not provide.

The company employs around 25 staff. Half are based in the headquarters and warehouse in administrative and logistics functions, and the rest are sales staff and support engineers. A wide range of stock is carried, including many different brands of extinguisher designed to combat different types of chemical and material fires. Goods are normally despatched within a few days of the receipt of an order, and often the sales representative will undertake delivery and installation. Overall, customer service and prices are considered comparable with what competitors are doing, although IFP is concerned about some new entrants to the market who do not give good advice to customers and often sell on price. IFP's owner, Mike Dalton, considers these 'cowboys' to be a threat because they have low overheads which he cannot match. The costs of entering the market are low, and sometimes former salesmen start their own businesses with minimal stock and sales support. In replacement situations, he has found that an increasing number of customers are prepared to buy on price rather than on the pre- and post-sales service offered. Although sales are just about holding up, margins are increasingly being pressurised.

Most organisations need some form of fire prevention and fire control systems. Legislation and safety regulations determine the exact specification demanded. The selling process itself differs, depending on whether it is repeat or new business. Regular customers tend to repeat buy with minimal shopping around, unless the value of the item is high. In some cases the sales representative makes additional sales by comparing current equipment against changing fire regulations and changes in material risks. Recommendations are then made to the customer. Customers can vary from a small restaurant or shop to industrial premises, universities and large organisations. Many purchasing decisions cannot be deferred for long because of the insurance and legal implications of being caught out by fire inspectors.

Even where IFP had not supplied a particular prospect before, if a gap in provision was identified, there was a good chance of converting the sale. This also works in reverse from time to time, when other sellers gain sales on the basis of price, once the need has been established. If the sale cannot be closed quickly, there is always the risk of a customer going elsewhere. In new business situations, especially with building extensions and new premises, the demands on the sales representative are sometimes greater because of having to sell through architects and technical experts, as well as having to quote against competition and negotiate the final deal. These customers are often as much concerned with specification match, overall fire system effectiveness, and after-sales service as they are with taking the lowest price.

Mike Dalton decided early on that the key to his business was an aggressive and motivated sales force. There is a range of brochures, often supplied by the manufacturer, and directories are used, but otherwise, little advertising and few other promotional methods are employed. By 1995, IFP had 10 sales representatives, a national sales manager, a field sales manager based in Dublin, and two sales support engineers who could be used for diagnosis or installation. The national and field sales managers are also expected to handle the major accounts, along with Mike Dalton, leaving the rest of the 10 000 or so potential accounts to the sales team. All the sales team are men, as Mike Dalton has found from his experience that women lack the technical credibility to deal with buyers. He also prefers sales representatives to have had previous sales experience, although there are some exceptions in the team.

For the first three months after appointment, each sales representative is paid a low salary plus commission, but after that it is commission only, although an average sales representative can gross over IR£1700 per month plus personal use of company van or car. Mike Dalton feels that the system employed is right because it keeps the sales team on their toes. With up to 1000 potential accounts per territory and many more unknown prospects, the financial motivation to encourage more cold calling is thought to be essential. Most of the sales team are happy with the arrangement and, even if a bad patch is hit after the trial period, the owner will often provide short-term advances on commission. It is never a long-term problem, as poor performance is normally dealt with by the termination of the representative's contract. The sales managers are paid by part commission and part salary and they are responsible for mentoring the sales team and dealing with any problems.

Although most of the sales team had some previous sales experience, most needed product training in fire prevention and control equipment before starting to sell. This training is normally done by the owner or the sales manager on the premises for two weeks before the representative takes over a territory. No formal sales training system is in place, although from time to time one or two day courses are run by staff from the local university. These courses cover general sales topics and tend to be seen as part of the annual sales meeting rather than part of a comprehensive skills development programme. Overall, most of the sales team tend to adjust to the uncertainty of commission-only sales and some have been in their jobs for several years. The sales managers have both worked their way through the ranks as super salesmen and so are well versed in giving advice to less experienced colleagues in the job. The managers are particularly concerned with keeping call

rates up, at least 10 per day is a minimum expectation, as well as encouraging high standards of product presentation. Over a two-year period, the turnover of sales staff has been around 25 per cent, a figure that the owner is comfortable with.

It is against this background that Mike Dalton contemplated the most appropriate actions for maintaining market position and countering the growing comprehensive threat.

Questions

1 What kind of remuneration package is used with the sales representatives? What are the problems with it?

2 IFP wants to encourage sales representatives to do more cold calling. Is the company going the right way about achieving this? What else can be done?

3 Is the training programme adequate? What should go into a formal sales training programme?

4 How can Mike Dalton fight the pressure from the more sophisticated integrated systems at one end of the market and the cowboys at the other? What are the implications for the sales force?

REFERENCES TO CHAPTER 18

Brierley, S. (1995), 'Man From Pru Fights for Public Assurance', *Marketing Week*, 15 September, p. 25.

Brierley, S. (1996), *'Pru's Failing Vision', Marketing Week*, 26 January, pp. 32–3.

Coopers & Lybrand (1994), 'Computers in Marketing', *Marketing*, 17 March, pp. 27–30.

Cravens, D. W. and LaForge, R. W. (1983), 'Salesforce Deployment Analysis', *Industrial Marketing Management*, July, pp. 179–92.

Cron, W. L. *et al.* (1988), 'The Influence of Career Stages on Components of Salesperson Motivation', *Journal of Marketing*, 52 (July), pp. 179–92.

Cunningham, M. T. and Homse, E. (1986), 'Controlling the Marketing – Purchasing Interface: Resource Development and Organisational Implications', *Industrial Marketing and Purchasing*, 1(2), pp. 3–27.

Fill, C. (1995), *Marketing Communications: Frameworks, Theories and Applications*, Prentice Hall.

Good, D. J. and Stone, R. W. (1991), 'How Sales Quotas are Developed', *Industrial Marketing Management*, 20(1), pp. 51–6.

Hill, J. S. and Still, R. R. (1990), 'Organising the Overseas Salesforce: How Multinationals Do It', *Journal of Personal Selling and Sales Management*, 10 (Spring), pp. 57–66.

Jacoby, J. and Craig, S. C. (1984), *Personal Selling*, Heath.

Johanson, J. and Vahlne, J. E. (1977), 'The Internationalisation Process of the Firm: A Model of Knowledge Development and Increasing Foreign Market Commitments', *Journal of International Business Studies*, 8(1), pp. 23–32.

Lambert, D. M. *et al.* (1990), 'Industrial Salespeople as a Source of Market Information', *Industrial Marketing Management*, 19, pp. 141–5.

Lockman, B. D. and Hallaq, (1982), 'Who Are Your Successful Salespeople?', *Journal of the Academy of Marketing Science*, 10 (Fall).

McAdams, J. (1987), 'Rewarding Sales and Marketing Performance', *Management Review*, April, pp. 33–8.

McClelland, D. (1994), 'Hiring Top Performers', *Selling*, May, pp. 34–5.

McDonald, M. H. B. (1984), *Marketing Plans*, Butterworth-Heinemann.

Mayer, M. and Greenberg, H. M. (1964), 'What Makes a Good Salesman', *Harvard Business Review*, 42 (July/Aug), pp. 119–25.

Miller, R. B. and Heinman, S. E. (1991), *Successful Large Account Management*, Holt.

Moncrief, W. C. (1988), 'Five Types of Industrial Sales Jobs', *Industrial Marketing Management*, 17, pp. 161–7.

Norris, S. (1995), 'Gathering Strength', *Marketing Week*, 16 June, pp. 53–6.

Pedersen, C. A. *et al.* (1986), *Selling: Principles and Methods*, Irwin.

Rines, S. (1995), 'Forcing Change', *Marketing Week*, 1 March.

Russell, F. A. *et al.* (1977), *Textbook of Salesmanship*, (10th edn) McGraw-Hill.

Smith, P. R. (1993), *Marketing Communications*, Kogan Page.

Sunday Times (1994), 'Is the Hard Sell on the Way Out?', *Sunday Times*, 19 October.

Turnbull, P. W. (1990), 'Roles of Personal Contacts in Industrial Export Marketing' in D. Ford (ed.), *Understanding Business Markets: Interaction, Relationships and Networks*, Academic Press.

Turnbull, P. W. and Cunningham, M. T. (1981), *International Marketing and Purchasing: A Survey Among Marketing and Purchasing Executives in Five European Countries*, MacMillan.

Zikmund, W. G. and d'Amico, M. (1993), *Marketing*, (4th edn) West.

19 Direct Marketing

LEARNING OBJECTIVES

This chapter will help you to:

1 understand what direct marketing is and why it has risen in importance in recent years;

2 review the various methods used in direct marketing, appreciating their relative strengths and problems in implementation;

3 analyse direct marketing's contribution to achieving marketing communication objectives, and how direct marketing can integrate with other elements of the promotional mix;

4 appreciate the broad issues involved in managing a direct marketing campaign; and

5 appreciate the importance of creating and maintaining a database of customers and understand the importance of using the database as a direct marketing tool.

INTRODUCTION

Over the past decade, direct marketing has grown to become a major element of the communications mix, emerging from relatively specialised beginnings in traditional mail order and what is derisively labelled 'junk mail'. It can now play an important supporting role, adding an extra dimension to the other elements of the promotional mix. Look at the increasing number of television and print advertisements, for example, which offer some kind of direct response mechanism (phone or mail) to encourage direct dialogue between supplier and customer, over and above the 'normal' objectives of the advertisement. Direct marketing can also be used as a central strategy in its own right as a means of attracting and retaining customers.

Example

An insurance company, Direct Line, created differential advantage in the highly competitive field of motor insurance through a marketing strategy centred on direct marketing. They cut out the insurance broker, thus selling to individuals who contact them on a freephone number, forging direct and sustainable links between buyer and supplier. Their advertising is designed to promote the name and the phone number and to encourage people to contact them. In this case, the advertising is the tool of direct response, rather than the direct response mechanism being an afterthought tagged on to a normal advertisement.

As the Direct Line example implies, direct marketing is more than just 'junk mail'. It encompasses a wide range of commonly used techniques, not only direct mail, but also telemarketing, direct response mechanisms and mail order. The later part of this chapter will look at each of those areas, as well as the use of new interactive communication and computing technology. The main aspects of managing direct marketing campaigns will be explored, starting with the need for careful targeting and working through the construction and maintenance of customer databases. Finally, a number of legislative issues will be discussed, as European governments and the EU seek to regulate the excesses of direct marketing.

First, however, the chapter will begin by defining exactly what direct marketing is, and then examining its role in the marketing plan.

THE DEFINITION OF DIRECT MARKETING

The US Direct Marketing Association has defined **direct marketing** as:

> **An interactive system of marketing which uses one or more advertising media to effect a measurable response at any location.**

This is quite a broad definition which does, however, capture some basic characteristics of direct marketing. **Interactive** implies two-way communication between buyer and seller, while *effect a measurable response* implies quantifiable objectives for the exercise. *At any location* implies the flexibility and pervasiveness of direct marketing, in that it is not inextricably linked with any one medium of communication, but can utilise anything (mail, phone, broadcast or print media) to reach anyone anywhere. What this definition does not do, however, is to emphasise the potential of direct marketing as a primary means of building and sustaining long-term buyer–seller relationships.

It is, therefore, proposed to extend this definition to form the basis of the content of the rest of the chapter:

> **An interactive system of marketing which uses one or more advertising media to effect a measurable response at any location, forming a basis for creating and further developing an ongoing direct relationship between an organisation and its customers.**

The key added value of this definition is the phrase *ongoing direct relationship*, which implies continuity and seems to contradict the impersonal approach traditionally offered by mass media advertising. Is it really possible to use mass media in a mass market to create a relationship with a single customer? Is it really possible to capitalise on the advantages of personal selling that arise from one-to-one dialogue to build and sustain that relationship without the need for face-to-face contact?

If the answer to those two questions is to be 'yes', then the problem becomes one of information gathering and management. To create and sustain *quality* relationships with hundreds, thousands or even millions of individual customers, an organisation needs to know as much as possible about each one, and needs to be able to access, manipulate and analyse that information. The database, therefore, is crucial to the process of building the relationship. We will look in some detail at the issues of creating, maintaining and exploiting the database at pp. 769 *et seq.*

Direct marketing is being used increasingly across a wide range of both consumer and organisational markets. In particular, in consumer markets, it has always been a central feature of the marketing strategies of book clubs which have seen phenomenal growth over the past few years and are now expanding into CDs, videos and computer software. Even in the relatively conservative financial services industry, there has been a marked increase in the direct selling (see the Direct Line example earlier) and direct marketing of a wide range of banking facilities and insurance. The next

section of this chapter looks more closely at the characteristics and conditions that have led to both the enthusiastic adoption of direct marketing by organisations, and its acceptance by their customers.

THE RISE OF DIRECT MARKETING

There are a number of reasons for the rapid growth of direct marketing, connected with the changing nature of the customer, the marketing environment, and in particular, technological development.

Changing demographics and life-styles

In practical terms, many more women are now working, and therefore have less time for shopping, preferring to use what little spare time they have for other leisure activities. Direct marketing, therefore, offers the convenience of shopping by phone or mail with a minimum of effort, particularly if it is possible to use a credit card for easy payment.

An additional feature of direct marketing that makes it increasingly accepted by consumers is its ability to bring specialist goods within reach. Someone with a particular interest in railways, for example, might find that their local bookshop has a very limited range of titles, and that it takes time (and money) to travel to a place with an appropriate bookshop. Joining a railway, industrial history or general history book club solves many of those problems by bringing the specialist range into the customer's own home.

Increased customer confidence

The big benefit of using direct marketing to build an ongoing relationship with an individual customer is that as time goes on, the customer's trust and confidence in the organisation build up. The hardest job is to get the initial purchase, but once customers have had one successful and satisfactory experience, they will be much more receptive and willing to try again. A shrewd direct marketer can capitalise on this by analysing a customer's purchasing habits in order to tailor future offerings to fit that customer's profile, and by gently nudging the customer upmarket into more expensive purchases.

A further aspect to consider is the customer's self-confidence. Some customers prefer to have a discreet direct relationship with organisations, and to make their purchases by mail order. Adult incontinence products, for example, are widely available through pharmacists, yet many customers purchase by mail to avoid what they see as the embarrassment of having to ask for the products or being seen to purchase them.

Increasing competition

Direct marketing offers organisations the opportunity to create loyal customers. If customers have entered into dialogue with an organisation, and have had their needs and wants met through a series of tailored offerings, then it is going to be quite difficult for the competition to poach those customers. Furthermore, using techniques such as direct mail, an organisation can communicate at length and in depth with its customers personally and relatively privately. In contrast, a television or print advertisement is limited in its scope, has to appeal to a much broader segment, and is seen by the competition (who can then work to counter its effects immediately) as soon as it is screened or published.

Media fragmentation

The increasing number of advertising media available, particularly for organisations looking towards pan-European markets, presents both problems and opportunities. It is a problem because the reduced reach per medium makes advertising less attractive for general mass communication. It is an opportunity for direct marketing because audiences are fragmenting into better profiled groups. The growth of specialist magazines and reading patterns, along with more specialist satellite TV channels, such as MTV, make it easier to locate a defined segment. It also makes it more cost effective to build in direct-response mechanisms, because a higher proportion of the audience reached will be interested, and thus a relatively high response rate might be expected.

Increasing media and sales costs

Communication is becoming very expensive. Personal selling is too slow and involves a high cost per call, and is inappropriate for most consumer markets. With traditional advertising, it can be difficult to make the kind of impact that actually leads to action, and thus the outcomes and cost effectiveness of an advertising campaign can be difficult to define (Barton, 1994). Direct response advertising, followed up by direct mail activity, prompts the customer into action, providing measurable results which allow the cost effectiveness of targeting predetermined receptive audiences to be properly judged.

New distribution channels

Many of the types of direct marketing that have been mentioned not only affect approaches to communication, but also have an impact on the use of distribution channels. Until recently, one of the big drawbacks of mail order was the length of time that a customer had to wait for the delivery of goods. Improvements in the management of logistics (*see* Chapter 14) and increasing competition among carriers means that delivery times have been cut from the old-style 'allow 28 days' to 48 (or even 24) hours, with increased reliability and reduced costs. Combining all that with the convenience factor, cutting out the time and hassle of crowded shopping centres, and the potential of increased merchandise selection, we can begin to see why direct distribution is increasingly becoming acceptable.

Increasing computer power and lower data processing costs

It is now realistic for even the smallest company to develop and manage some kind of customer database relatively cheaply. The costs (and size) of the hardware have reduced dramatically, while the power and quality of both hardware and software have increased. Thus it is now possible to hold a vast amount of detail on each individual customer, and it is relatively quick and simple to update and analyse the data held to create better marketing strategies for both existing and future customers.

Impact of new communication technology

There is little point in making any effort to elicit a direct response unless the capability exists to handle the volume of responses generated. With telephone response, for example, it is now possible using automated systems to handle many hundreds of calls simultaneously, reducing the risk of losing potential respondents through the frustration of failing to get through quickly. It is also necessary to keep the costs of response as low as possible for both the organisation and its customers. Freephone numbers and freepost addresses represent the most attractive option for the customer. Both British Telecommunications and the Post Office are aware of the opportunities that direct marketing offers them as 'middlemen' (or facilitators), and will work with organisations to agree a package that represents the most efficient and cost effective use of their services.

> ### Example
>
> Costs can also be reduced by centralising telephone-based services. Hilton Hotels, for example, established a call centre in Brussels to handle telephone reservations from eight different European countries. The service uses an international freephone service provided by Belgacom, the Belgian telecommunications company, and calls are automatically routed to an appropriate operator depending on their country of origin (Mirbach, 1994).

A final, but extremely important development in communication technology, which has yet to achieve its full potential in most of Europe, is the use of interactive computers in home shopping. This exciting development is discussed further at p. 763 below.

Many of the issues mentioned in this section are interrelated. Consumer attitudes to direct marketing have, for example, mellowed as technology has allowed organisations to target personalised mailshots more appropriately, so that what is received through the letter box is less likely to be dismissed outright as 'junk'. The pioneering work of organisations such as the *Next Directory* in developing upmarket, high quality merchandise, and successfully developing the logistics to fulfil a promise of 48-hour delivery has also revolutionised UK attitudes to mail order. This has in itself provided the impetus for greater commitment and investment in direct marketing by a wide range of organisations.

The discussion so far has talked generally about the concept of direct marketing, with passing reference to specific areas such as direct mail and direct response, among others. The next section, therefore, looks more closely at each of these areas, and their individual characteristics. Figure 19.1 gives an overview of the range of direct marketing areas.

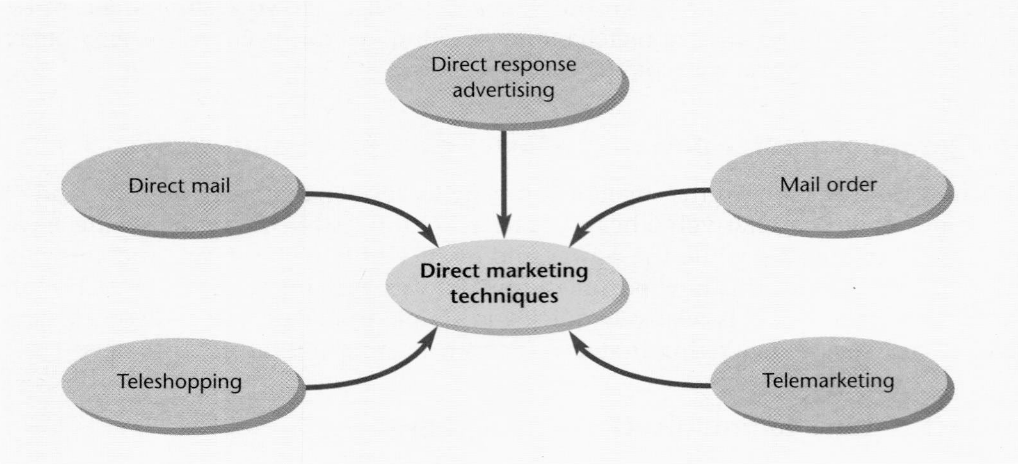

FIGURE 19.1

The range of
direct marketing
techniques

TECHNIQUES OF DIRECT MARKETING

The scope of direct marketing is very wide. It utilises what might be called the more traditional means of marketing communication, such as print and broadcast advertising media, but it has also developed its own media, through mail, telecommunications and modem. Each of the main techniques in direct marketing will now be considered in turn.

Direct mail

Direct mail is material distributed through the postal service to the recipient's home or business address to promote a product or service. What is mailed can vary from a simple letter introducing a company or product through to a comprehensive catalogue or sample. Many mailshots incorporate involvement devices to increase the chances of their being opened and read, through stimulating curiosity.

Example

Cross Products wanted to get computer games developers to visit their stand at an exhibition in the USA. So they mailed a can opener, representing the organisation's games programming tool, to 220 games developers world-wide. The message was that if the can opener was taken to Cross's stand at the exhibition, the games developer could claim a discount on the programming system. Ninety can openers came back to the exhibition, and the cost per response to Cross was £39 (*Marketing*, 1995a).

The ultimate involvement device, however, surely must be the one used by the direct marketing agency M-S-B+K. The agency wanted to get interviews with marketing directors in order to sell its services. Marketing directors, however, receive a great many mailshots and thus it is a challenge for an agency to cut through the clutter and get its approach noticed. This agency rose to the challenge by sending a live carrier pigeon to 15 marketing directors. They were told either to release the pigeon and confirm that a meeting with the agency would be arranged, or to eat it! Fortunately for the pigeons, all 15 came back safely and 12 meetings actually were arranged (*Marketing*, 1995a).

Most direct mail is unsolicited. Organisations compile or buy lists of names and addresses, and then send out the mailshot. The **mailing list** used may be cold, that is, where there has been no previous contact between the organisation and the addressee, or may reflect various selection criteria based on data held about previous or existing customers.

Direct mail is widely used in both consumer and organisational markets. The financial services sector, for example, sends out mailshots to encourage people to apply for credit cards, mortgages, loans and insurance quotes. The pharmaceutical and medical supplies companies send out mailshots to doctors, pharmacists and dentists, partly to make them aware of what is available, and partly to pave the way for a later call from the sales representative. Consultants, contractors and suppliers similarly target organisational buyers and decision makers. Sometimes, different members of the distribution channel can work together.

Direct mail has the problem that it has suffered from bad PR. All of us as consumers can probably think of a couple of examples of direct mail we have received that have been completely inappropriate, and misconceptions about direct mail's effectiveness are often based on such personal experiences of receiving 'junk'. Historically, this has arisen partly from the lack of flexibility and detail within databases, and partly from poor marketing thinking. In the earlier days of direct mail, marketers were obsessed with the power of databases to generate vast numbers of contacts and to process personalised mailshots at high speed. This created a false bonus in going for volume rather than concentrating on more carefully targeted use, since it was as easy to send 100 000 mail shots as 10 000. If the organisation was looking for a predetermined response rate, then there was an advantage in mailing larger numbers of mailshots, even though the majority were wasted. This then led to resentment among those receiving vast quantities of inappropriate material, and the labelling of direct mail as ineffective junk. Increasingly, though, marketers are using the information at their disposal more intelligently, and mailing smaller groups of well-defined prospective customers, using better designed creative material. They are also keeping their databases more current, and so a household should not receive direct mail addressed to people who moved away or died over a year ago. In theory then, an individual should be receiving less direct mail, but what they do receive should be of prime relevance and interest. This should then prompt a 'quality' response (Wilmshurst, 1993).

There is evidence to suggest that direct mail is more effective than its reputation gives it credit for. It is estimated that 83 per cent of direct mail is opened (91 per cent in organisational markets), and that 68 per cent of it is read and 31 per cent passed on (Royal Mail, 1994). This is heartening, but it may not be enough. Think about the hierarchy of effects models shown in Fig. 15.7, and how direct mail fits into those. Using the AIDA model as an example, opening the envelope begins the *awareness* stage; reading the content generates *interest* and *desire*, and finally, the mailshot clearly defines what subsequent *action* is expected. The main objective is to move the recipient quickly through all the stages from awareness to action. The key is not simply the opening of the envelope, but whether the content can pull the reader right through to the completion of action. As a consolation prize, if the recipient reads the content but chooses not to respond, there may still be an awareness or interest effect which may 'soften up' the customer for subsequent mailings, or, in organisational market, a sales visit.

Advantages of using direct mail

There are a number of advantages of using direct mail.

Targeting. Using the post code system, targeted campaigns can be developed based on geodemographic criteria. Combine that with the depth of knowledge held about existing customers, and even more detailed targeting can be achieved. Similarly, with organisational lists, targeted efforts at specific, named individuals within organisations is possible. Even purchased lists can be used for clearly targeted campaigns. The London Herb and Spice Company wanted to create awareness of its fruit teas and so used a mailshot aimed at 90 000 users of competitive products.

When operating on a European basis, however, it must be remembered that regulations on list broking vary from country to country. Laws are more lenient in the Netherlands and France than in the UK and Germany. In the UK list broking is allowed, subject to notifying the subject ('Please let us know if you do not wish to receive offers from other carefully selected companies'), while in Germany heavy regulation reduces the number of lists available.

Personalisation. With new technology in ink jet imaging, laser printing and electronic processing, large numbers of personalised mailings can be undertaken regularly. Although the novelty of receiving mailshots that begin 'Dear Mrs Shufflebottom, You will be the envy of Railway Terrace, Heckmondwyke, if you take advantage of our wonderful offer ...' has worn off, there is still an undeniable intimacy about personalisation that other advertising media cannot achieve.

> ### Example
>
> American Express wanted to persuade high-spending holders of its ordinary green Amex card who had been members for five years or more to upgrade to gold card status. A personalised mailshot on high quality paper persuaded them that they were very special and privileged to be invited to join the 'inner sanctum' of gold card holders. The target response rate was 5 per cent but the actual response was nearly 10 per cent (*Marketing*, 1995a).

Response rates. Depending on the quality of the database and the selection criteria underpinning the mailing list, the response rate for direct mailing can be high. This has already been seen in the examples mentioned earlier, such as the pigeon stunt, the children's hospital appeal, and the Amex customer upgrade exercise. All of this is a product of the personal, confidential, selective and flexible nature of direct mail.

Flexibility. The creative scope of what can be included in a mailshot is very flexible, allowing varied and interesting campaigns, which can even be phased if required. This flexibility extends to frequency, size, colour, length, copy, layout and quality, as well as the inclusion of videos, CDs, gifts, samples or pigeons.

Attention seeking. Even if only for a brief moment, the mailing holds the attention of the reader far more exclusively than advertising. An involvement device that requires the recipient to do something (a competition scratch card; something that needs careful unfolding; a video to play; a pigeon to clean up after) reduces the chances of the mailing being discarded unread. The RSPCA tried a mailshot without a video to 7000 top donors and achieved a 5.4 per cent response with an average contribution of £63. A mailshot including a video was sent to another 1000 on the same list, and that produced a 23 per cent response with an average donation of £77. With new lightweight video cassettes that last for only ten plays, the cost per video can be reduced to 60p per shot, making this a potentially very cost-effective approach, opening up many more creative opportunities for message formulation (*Marketing*, 1993).

Developing a direct mail campaign

It must, however, be stressed that a mailshot is only as good as the data underpinning it. If, for example the mailing list contains many small firms which frequently change their address, or an area of high turnover in residential property, then its quality and its ability to deliver a satisfactory response rate are questionable.

The mailing list is the first of a number of specific areas in developing a direct mail campaign that need to be examined.

Mailing list management. A list is a collection of names and addresses of individuals or companies grouped together on predetermined criteria. Getting the list right (i.e., fit for its purpose) is a major challenge. Direct mail must have accurate targeting, drawing on the same concepts as market segmentation, discussed in Chapter 5.

Lists are either internal or purchased. Internal lists can be compiled from a variety of sources, including past and present customers, enquirers, prospects or compilations from published sources, for example through a systematic scan of trade directories, telephone books etc. Thus Great Ormond Street hospital was able to identify and extract a subset of lapsed donors from its own database. Lists can also be purchased from other organisations who maintain customer databases and wish to trade information.

Example

The *London Review of Books*, in seeking to generate new subscriptions, used subscription lists from other publications as well as lists of 'mail responsive' individuals. These lists covered overseas markets as well as the UK (*Marketing*, 1995a).

Lists purchased from external sources need to be carefully checked to make sure that they are relevant and up to date. Next time you fill in a reply coupon, look to see if it has small print at the bottom to the effect that: 'We may wish to pass your details on to other carefully selected companies'. Unless you tick the box stating that you would rather deny them this privilege, your details are liable to be sold on to another company. Organisations also exist which specialise in consumer research and list compilation.

Example

In March 1994, ICD Marketing Services could offer you lists based on virtually anything you could think of. The lists range from occupation (for example

329 998 clerical workers), through specific brand purchasing habits   (16 682 users of Colgate Blue Minty Gel toothpaste), to newspaper reading habits (123 421 purchasers of *The Times*), health (8860 sufferers from stomach ulcers) and leisure interests (1 336 728 pub goers, or if you prefer, 324 people who have travelled more than five times from the UK to Continental Europe by car).

In the UK, the Post Office offers a Postcode Address File that contains almost every postal address (business and domestic) and postcode in the UK. This file can be used with a mainframe to enable easy selection of geographically based mailing lists. It does not, however, offer a wealth and depth of detail about the lifestyle of those who live at each address. Similar systems have been developed across Europe.

Creative implementation. Designing the content of a mailshot is the realm of a well-briefed copywriter. It is certainly not simply an extension of letter writing. The prime objective of most mailshots is to generate a response, which really means that the recipient's attention and interest have to be engaged quickly, if a rapport is to be established. Even if the recipient starts to read, there is still the danger of distraction and rejection. Personalisation, involvement devices, benefit orientation and flow are therefore critical to holding the reader.

Example

Accolade, a computer games company, sent a mailshot to young games purchasers to help launch three new games. It was designed to look and read as though it was an unofficial printout generated by hackers who had got into Accolade's computer, and then hastily stuffed into an envelope. It generated a 60 per cent response rate and sales targets were exceeded by 300 per cent. The agency that designed it, Impact FCA!, claimed that

'The strategy of offering an endorsement from illegal hackers was credible and powerful to a cynical youth market. The copy and art direction were raw and unorthodox' (*Marketing*, 1995a, p. 46).

The envelope or packaging can also be part of the creative appeal. Placing a message on the outside of the envelope might increase the chances of its being opened, as well as building some sense of anticipation. Teaser messages, coloured envelopes, windows to show a glimpse of an incentive, whether it is a gift or a prize draw, all assist in this process. Thus the Great Ormond Street Hospital mailshot had the words 'Link up with them this Christmas' on the outside of the envelope with the 'Link up' presented as a logo written in paper chains.

It should be noted, however, that some organisations take an opposite view. Some consumers will dump an envelope, unopened, straight into the bin, if it is obviously a piece of direct mail. The strategy, therefore, is to make the envelope as innocuous and unobtrusive as possible, so that the recipient has to open it to make sure that it isn't something important. Once the envelope is opened, there is a greater chance that the content will be read. The Amex mailshot was sent in a plain white envelope with just the Amex logo on it. The existing card holders at whom the mailshot was targeted would have assumed that it was something to do with their account.

The response mechanism is also important, especially for business-to-business direct mail where the main objective is often to generate leads rather than sales *per se*. Response cards not only assist the ease of reply, but also the initial qualification of leads. They can be used to gain additional information on the buyer prior to contact,

TABLE 19.1

Number of items of direct mail received per head of population, 1991

	Number of items		Number of items
Austria	–	Italy	–
Belgium	80	Luxembourg	–
Denmark	49	The Netherlands	60
Finland	46	Portugal	5
France	55	Spain	23
Germany *	56	Sweden	75
Greece	–	United Kingdom	38
Ireland	14		

* Former West Germany
Source: Euromonitor (1995), p. 347.

to assess whether the contact is worth following-up, and what kind of follow up is most appropriate. Reply-paid cards should not be an add-on, but a well thought out means of improving the quality of leads generated.

Table 19.1 shows the amount of direct mail received per head of population across Europe. It is interesting to note that the more developed markets have a higher number of mailings than the countries of southern Europe where the infrastructure for communication is less well advanced. Interestingly, in eastern Europe direct mail is in its infancy, but can still attract high levels of readership, as long as a practical, offer-specific orientation is taken.

Direct response advertising

Direct response advertising appears in the standard broadcast and print media. It differs from 'normal' advertising because it is designed to generate a direct response, whether an order, an enquiry for further information or a personal visit. The response mechanism may be a coupon to cut out in a print advertisement, or a phone number in any type of advertisement. This area has grown in popularity in recent years as advertisers seek to get their increasingly expensive advertising to work harder for them. Research has shown that around 20 per cent of all television advertisements in the UK carry direct response mechanisms (Fry, 1995), although in the USA it is nearer to 50 per cent.

By using advertising media, direct response advertising's initial targeting, unlike that of some of the other forms of direct marketing, relies much more on an assessment of the medium's reader or viewer profile than on a pre-prepared mailing list. Responses to such advertising, however, can then be used as a database for other forms of direct marketing in the future.

Types of direct response advertising

An analysis of a typical Sunday newspaper colour supplement shows a range of approaches to direct response advertising. Table 19.2 summarises the breakdown of the advertising in one particular magazine, showing the split between normal and direct response advertising. The direct response group is further categorised in terms of the range of response mechanisms, and whether the organisation or the customer pays for the response. Throughout the rest of this discussion, the costs are considered from the consumer's perspective, that is, 'freepost' means free to the respondent, and, 'pay post' means that the respondent has to pay normal postage rates. However, before considering further the question of who should pay, we provide a few examples from some of the categories defined in Table 19.2.

TABLE 19.2

Breakdown of direct response mechanisms in print advertisements (number of advertisements featuring each combination of response mechanisms)

Mail		Telephone			
		Freephone	*Pay phone*	*No phone*	**TOTAL**
Coupon	*Freepost*	4	5	3	12
	Pay post	3	5	0	8
No coupon	*Freepost*	0	0	0	0
	Pay post	1	6	0	7
No post		1	1	2	4
TOTAL		9	17	5	31

Freepost (coupon) and freephone

Citroën, advertising their ZX Estate car offered either a freephone number to call or a coupon to mail in for more information. The coupon attempts to qualify the lead by asking current make of car, its registration, the intended replacement date and whether it is company or privately owned. Collating such information across all respondents might also indicate trends or clusters that can be researched further. The responses might show, for instance, that a significant number of respondents are looking to trade up from their current model, or that they do not currently drive an estate car. This information might influence the way in which Citroën chooses to approach those potential customers, as well as perhaps providing evidence of the effectiveness of the advertising in reaching the planned target segments.

Pay post (coupon) and pay phone

The French Tourist Office, in conjunction with P&O Ferries tried to generate interest in western France, with a small cut out coupon tucked away at the bottom of the advertisement, requesting the respondent's name and address only (that is, there was no qualification of leads). Alternatively, the respondent could have called a full cost telephone number (not a freephone).

Pay post (no coupon) and pay phone

The French Tourist office example above a more serious attempt at direct response generation than an advertisement for Portugal as a business conference destination, which had no specific response mechanism, although an address was given along with fax and telephone numbers in very small print at the bottom.

Freepost and pay phone

Bonusprint, a photo developing company, glued a freepost envelope to their full page advertisement to make it as easy as possible for readers to order photographic prints at special reduced prices, and claim their free photo album. The loosely attached envelope attracts attention to the advertisement, because it changes the weight and the feel of the page, thus making it difficult to ignore, while the free album offer further encourages response. The envelope has all the necessary information about prices etc. on it so that if it becomes detached from the advertisement, it could still be used. Given the nature of the response sought in this case, getting people to put their films in the envelope and post them, the lack of a freephone response mechanism is entirely understandable.

Freepost (coupon) and freephone

Unlike the first example (Citroën), in which the sought response was a request for further information, this one is about selling off the page. Franklin Mint are a company specialising in selling moderately expensive 'collectables' through direct response advertising. In conjunction with Fabergé, they offered a 'collector egg in crystal clear glass, enamel and accents of gold' for £125, payable in 10 equal installments. The sale was made entirely through a full page colour advertisement featuring a photograph and brief description, but a 30-day money back guarantee provided reassurance for the more risk-averse customer. Paying in installments also reduces the perceived risk, and since the initial payment was only £12.50, it downplayed the actual price, making response more likely.

Pay post (coupon) and freephone

Harrods are also using direct response advertising to generate sales, offering a range of cosmetics by mail order. Furthermore, with the purchase of two or more products, a black holdall containing travel sizes of a further range of useful cosmetic items were sent free. The gift was being used to create a sense of urgency, since the offer was only open for two weeks. The advertisement prominently featured the free gift rather than the purchased cosmetics which were presented only in list form. Again, response is made easier by offering the facility to respond by mail or on a freephone line for direct ordering, both with credit card payment.

Approaches to direct response advertising

As all these examples show, some organisations approach direct response much more seriously than others. The ones who expect the consumer to pay for a phone call or postage, or who expect the consumer to compose a letter rather than filling in a coupon, are immediately putting up barriers to response. Why should consumers make any undue effort, or even pay directly, to give an organisation the privilege of trying to sell them something? In the light of that view, organisations either need to have incredibly compelling direct response advertising that makes any effort or cost worth while, or, more realistically, they need to minimise the effort and cost to the potential customer. Schofield (1994) confirms that certainly in organisational markets, response should be as easy as possible. The easier the response, the greater the number of enquiries and the greater the conversion rate and revenue per enquiry.

Direct response advertising on television

The use of direct response advertising on television is beginning to grow. Some products are marketed on satellite channels across Europe using toll free telephone support. CDs and tapes, for example, are actively promoted on the music channel. Holiday companies use a toll free line to receive requests for brochures, while the insurance industry is starting to appreciate the value of direct response television advertising to generate requests for quotes. If the advertisement is being used to sell off the screen (as opposed to simply generating enquiries), and hard cash is wanted, the risk limit is around £10–£15, and the product must be easily demonstrated and explained.

> **Example**
>
> The Korean car manufacturer, Daewoo, uses direct response television advertising as a means of generating enquiries. The agency handling the responses has 100 operator lines, but can activate another 100 if necessary. The operators take details and send out information packs, but more complex enquiries can be routed through to Daewoo. Between April and October 1995, Daewoo claims that 250 000 responses were received (Fry, 1995).

Different media and more creative approaches encourage direct response.

Book Club Associates used door drops and a television campaign to supplement its normal magazine insert approach.

The soft drink brand, Apple Tango, ran a direct response television advertising campaign, presented in Tango's characteristically eccentric style, asking people to phone in if they had been seduced by Apple Tango. Around 500 000 calls were received.

> ### Example
>
> Even the phone number used can help generate responses, especially with radio advertising where the listener might have to remember a number after only hearing it rather than seeing it.
>
> Forte hotels, for example use the number 40 40 40, of course, while the insurance company Guardian Direct, reminding people of the owl in their logo, use 28 28 20 (too-whit, too-whit, too-woo).
>
> Similarly, BUPA's Dental Cover service has the number 230 230 (tooth hurty, tooth hurty).
>
> Since Forte introduced the 404040 line as part of a programme to centralise its telephone reservation system, it claims to have improved its conversion of enquiries into sales from 25 per cent to 40 per cent (Summers, 1995b). Some numbers are memorable in their own right, without strong links with the company or brand. Disney has 000000, for example, and the insurance company Scottish Widows has 678910.

Direct response has only been possible because of allied developments in the widespread use of credit cards which makes remote ordering easier, the use of freephone numbers, and improvements in response handling techniques and technology. However, the principles of advertising described in Chapter 16 still have to be applied while the specific elements of direct response messages and media are considered. There is a feeling, however, that the UK market is not properly exploiting direct response, especially through television. Fry (1995) reports the opinion of the head of a direct marketing consultancy who cited the following seven reasons why television-based direct response is less effective than it should be:

- poor forecasting of response
- lack of co-ordination
- ill-considered calls to action
- over-optimistic promises to respondents

The headline gets the attention: the telephone number gets the response.

Today, a snail in the slow lane. Tomorrow, a road warrior on the information super-highway.

D∉LL   0344 720000.

Source: Travis, Sennett, Sully, Ross.

- failure to carry the creative message through from the advertisement to the handling of the respondent
- inappropriate evaluation of effect
- inadequate follow-up.

Telemarketing

While direct response advertising and direct mail both imply the use of an impersonal initial approach through some kind of written or visual material, **telemarketing** makes a direct personal, verbal approach to the potential customer. However, although this brings benefits from direct and interactive communication, it is seen by some as extremely intrusive. If the telephone rings, people feel obliged to answer it there and then, and tend to feel annoyed and disappointed if it turns out to be a sales pitch rather than a friend wanting a good gossip. It can be very difficult to curtail a telemarketing call without resorting to rudeness, and many people feel awkward about doing that. At least a piece of direct mail can be dismissed and put in the bin quickly and without leaving a feeling that someone has been offended in some way.

Telemarketing, therefore, can be defined as any planned and controlled activity that creates and exploits a direct relationship between customer and seller, using the telephone.

Example

American Express wanted to increase the number of supplementary cards (extra cards on an account for use by husbands, wives or other trusted individuals) issued on existing Amex accounts. A telemarketing campaign was implemented in seven European countries, managed centrally from the UK, but tailored to meet the needs of the different geographic markets. The campaign on average achieved 17 per cent take-up of supplementary cards, with the highest take-up generated by France (23 per cent) and the UK (21 per cent) (*Marketing*, 1995b).

The American Express campaign is an example of **outbound telemarketing**, where the organisation contacts the potential customer. **Inbound telemarketing**, where the potential customer is encouraged to contact the organisation, is also popular. This is used not only in direct response advertising, but also for customer care lines, competitions and other sales promotions.

Example

Nestlé used a freephone number to encourage people to request samples of its Blend 37 coffee in the UK. Callers were asked about their coffee purchasing habits, and thus Nestlé at least gained a little bit of market research in return for its samples.

Scope for telemarketing

Telephone rental or ownership is high across Europe, as shown in Table 19.3, and thus if an appropriate role can be defined for telemarketing within the planned promotional mix, it represents a powerful communication tool. As with personal selling (*see* p. 699), there is direct contact and so dialogue problems can be addressed. Similarly,

TABLE 19.3
Telephone ownership across Europe, 1990/1

	% of households		% of households
Austria	85.0	Italy	89.0
Belgium	79.0	Luxembourg	75.0
Denmark	87.0	The Netherlands	96.0
Finland	79.0	Portugal	52.0
France	94.0	Spain	66.0
Germany *	89.0	Sweden	97.0
Greece	75.0	United Kingdom	88.0
Ireland	53.0		

* Former West Germany
Source: Euromonitor (1995), pp. 392–5.

the customer's state of readiness to commit themselves to a course of action can be assessed and improved through personal persuasion, and efforts made to move towards a positive outcome. Telemarketing can also be used to support customer service initiatives.

> **Example**
>
> Abbey National Direct has a system that recognises the telephone number from which an inbound call originated and can route the call to the staff member who dealt with that customer last time they called (McKenzie, 1995). This clearly allows the customer to develop a more personal relationship with the organisation as well as providing consistency. As the one-to-one relationship develops, it also becomes easier for the staff member to try to sell other financial services products to that customer.

Nevertheless, outbound telemarketing in particular is still not widely accepted by consumers and is often seen as intrusive. Where customers have an existing relationship with an organisation, however, and where the purpose of the call is not hard selling, they are less suspicious. A survey in 1994 showed that 47 per cent of people said that they would be happy to receive customer service calls at home, with only 16 per cent completely hostile to the idea (McKenzie, 1995).

Marketing tasks. It would be misleading, however, to imply that telemarketing is only about high pressure selling. As a form of personal selling, it certainly lends itself to that kind of application, but there is a whole range of marketing tasks that can be performed using telemarketing methods. As Table 19.4 shows, telemarketing has a clear role at an operational level, not only making sales, but also improving distribution, customer service, technical support, information gathering and credit control. A particular challenge is to integrate it creatively into the rest of the promotional mix.

Customer care. Another growth area for telemarketing is customer care lines. Ideally, these are set up to allow customers

TABLE 19.4
Applications of telemarketing

- Generate leads
- Screen leads before follow-up
- Arrange appointments for representatives
- Direct sales
- Encourage cross/up selling
- Dealer support
- Account servicing
- Market research
- Test marketing

Example

Inbound telemarketing was used successfully by Tango, the soft drink brand, as a key part of its marketing communication strategy. Television advertisements and promotional packs offered consumers the chance to acquire their own Tango rubber doll which, incidentally, could be filled up with water and squirted. What was particularly interesting about this promotion was that it was a self-liquidating offer (*see* p. 672) in which the cost of the doll was included in the telephone call charge. The call was not just used functionally, to take customer orders for the doll, it also provided seven minutes of Tango-orientated entertainment for the caller, thus reinforcing the brand image (*Marketing*, 1995a).

to make direct contact with an organisation to ask questions or pass comment on products and their use. Care line numbers are included in advertisements and on packaging. Rines (1994), however, reports a survey that indicated that in the UK only 8 per cent of branded products carry a care line number, whereas in Germany the figure is 15 per cent, in France 30 per cent and in the USA 83 per cent. It is argued, however, that the quality of care line service in the UK is better. Many USA care lines simply consist of a recorded message, whereas UK care lines are staffed by real people!

The organisation can benefit from its care line in a number of ways, but particularly from the potential to build a database of callers and their profiles.

Example

In 1992, Boots the pharmacy chain, provided a care line service predicting pollen counts for hayfever suffers. Over 12 weeks, nearly 107 000 freephone calls were received and Boots were able to build a database for the future direct marketing of appropriate remedies and other related hayfever products. Furthermore, the care line benefited the corporate image, as the company was perceived to be providing a valuable free service (Rines, 1994).

Limitations on telemarketing

In addition, and again in common with personal selling, there are limitations on the practical application of telemarketing, and a number of operational and regulatory issues have to be considered:

Operational issues. For inbound calls in particular, the organisation has to ensure that the system is designed to cope with the expected volume of calls and can handle them speedily and efficiently. Potential customers who cannot get through at all, or who are kept waiting, are likely to give up trying. The problem is made worse by the fact that 80 per cent of responses to a direct response television advertisement, for example, will be made within 10 minutes of the advertisement being screened. After 12 minutes, the response rate is likely to be negligible (Slingsby, 1994). Most telemarketing is handled by specialist bureaux that have the technology to cope with 2000 calls simultaneously, and if that is insufficient, they can network with each other to provide up to 12 000 lines (Cramp, 1995).

Another issue, partly operational and partly strategic, concerns the kind of line to use. Providers such as British Telecommunications offer a number of options to the marketer, some of which are free or cheap to the caller, others of which carry a premium rate charge. The options offered by BT are summarised in Table 19.5, which also gives an indication of the type of marketing activities they might support.

Clearly, freephone numbers are most attractive to the customer, but do incur costs for the organisation providing the service.

TABLE 19.5
British Telecommunication's telemarketing services

Product	Caller pays	Cost to provider	Revenue earned	What's it for?	Who uses it?
Freefone 0800	Nil	12p per minute (daytime), 9p per minute (cheap)	–	Lead generation, order taking, customer care direct response TV	Freemans, Racing Green, American Express, Rank Xerox, Boots, Amstrad, BUPA, PPP, Apple, Forte
International Freefone 0800	Nil. In some countries the local rate charges apply	Price per minute charged (varies by country)	–	To give presence in overseas markets at minimum cost	Thomas Cook, Shell, American Express, Marriott Hotels
Lo-call 0345	Local rate	9p per minute (daytime) 6p per minute (cheap)	–	Inbound ordering line, customers support	Children in Need, Next, Porsche Cars (GB), Royal Mail
Nationalcall 0990	National long-distance rate	Nil	–	Direct response TV information line, brochure line	Walt Disney, Center Parcs, Eurotunnel
Value Call Services					
0891	45/50p per min	–	26.28p per minute	Information line, subsidising promotional costs	Ford, RAC
0894	25p or 50p per call (flat rate)	–	Base rate of 12.22p or 26.63p per call	Brochure requests, coupon replies Ideally using ACH to limit call duration	Benetton, Radio Atlantic 252
0897	£1 or £1.50 per min	–	Base rate of 64.62p or 97.2p per minute	High-value information, e.g. consultancy, legal services, accountancy and technical professions	Music by Fax, FT Cityline

*All services also incur a quarterly rental fee and connection charge. Call charges are subject to volume discounts.
Source: British Telecommunications plc. For more information Freefone 0800 660099.

Example

Music Sales uses an 0897 number which allows them to recoup the cost of the sheet music as part of the telephone charge, and similarly, the Tango doll promotion recouped its costs through use of an 0891 number. The BBC, in contrast, wanted to distribute packs related to a television series on adult literacy. It was decided that it was best to ask viewers to phone in to request a pack, as people with literacy problems would probably be reluctant to write in. It was also felt that the freephone number was best, because the target audience was largely from the lower income brackets and would not wish to pay for a call (*Marketing*, 1995b).

Outbound telemarketing has its own set of problems. As already mentioned, cold calling for sales purposes is not popular with the public, and has increasingly become the subject of regulation and restriction. In Germany, most cold calling is banned whereas

Automated call handling

Technology can make a significant contribution to improving the efficiency of inbound telemarketing. Automated call distribution systems, for example, route incoming calls to the first available line or operator, thus minimising any waiting time. Adding a further dimension to the service, automated call handling (ACH) triggers prerecorded messages, or puts the caller into an interactive dialogue with a computer. At its most basic, ACH can tell the caller that there is a queue and that their call will be dealt with as soon as an operator is available. Alternatively, it can record customer details so that an operator can call the customer back at a less busy period. In interactive mode, the caller can use a push button touchtone phone to 'talk' to a menu-driven computer ('Press 3 on your phone if you want ticket sales, 5 for arrival and departure information, or 9 for any other enquiry') which eventually either delivers the information or service that the customer wants or routes them through to an appropriate live operator.

ACH handles not only enquiries, but also sales as well. MGM cinemas, for example, use ACH for ticket sales as does British Airways. For a company called Music Sales, ACH even delivers the product! Music Sales sells sheet music and has developed a 'music by fax' service for some of its products. Customers who have a copy of the company's catalogue note the code numbers of the sheet music they want. They then phone through to an ACH system and use the telephone keypad to enter the codes. The required sheet music is retrieved from the computer's memory and sent straight down the line to the customer's fax machine. The cost of the music is determined by the length of time the transaction and transmission take and is added directly to the customer's telephone bill.

The problem with such ACH services, however, is their impersonal nature. A Henley Centre survey (as reported by Cramp, 1995), *Teleculture 2000,* showed that although 70 per cent of people are confident in using the telephone, only 30 per cent are confident about leaving messages on answerphones. Not surprisingly, people thus prefer to deal with a live operator, although speed and convenience are also extremely important. Over time, and with the benefit of experience, perhaps consumers will eventually begin to appreciate the benefits of ACH. Organisations will, however, need to ensure that they do not lose direct contact with customers or become too faceless. ACH systems are currently only useful for fairly straightforward transactions. Because they are menu-driven, it takes time to work through all the options with the caller, who might become impatient or confused. Also, the longer the call, the more expensive it becomes.

Sources: Cramp (1995); *Marketing* (1995b); Rines (1995).

in the UK it is permitted, although organisations are not allowed to use automatic dialling systems that play prerecorded sales messages. Outbound customer service calls are useful, however. These might, be used as an after-sales follow-up to check that customers are satisfied with their purchases. They might also be integrated into a longer-term relationship marketing strategy.

Example

Next Directory, for example, tried an experiment with 'welcome calls', made to new customers just after receipt of their first order. After six months, it was found that 92 per cent of those customers who had been 'welcomed' were still active, against only 86 per cent of those who had not received a welcome call. Furthermore, the welcomed customers were spending about 30 per cent more (*Marketing*, 1995b).

Whatever the purpose of outbound telemarketing, it is important to ensure that the operators making the calls are well trained, knowledgeable and courteous. Well-targeted and carefully prepared lists of numbers to call can help to reduce the irritation factor to those called, although pre-screening can be difficult. It can be especially annoying or upsetting to get calls for people who have died or who have moved away. Technology can help to deal with the volume and efficiency of outgoing calls. A central computer dials a number and routes the call to an operator when a reply is detected. If the number called is engaged, or if an answering machine is reached, the computer terminates the call and puts that number to the back of the queue to try again later (McKenzie, 1995).

Regulatory issues. Pan-European telemarketing is not easy, partly because of language and cultural differences, and partly because of the variation in what is and what is not allowed in different countries. By the end of 1995, the EU had been working for nearly four years on developing the Distance Selling Directive, an attempt to harmonise regulations to make cross-border direct marketing easier. The original proposals would have meant a complete ban on cold calling by telephone and on unsolicited e-mail. Lobbying by the direct marketing industry, however, managed to get these bans dropped from the proposals. Instead, e-mail can still be used in unsolicited approaches, but prior consent is needed for telephone cold calling. In practice, this actually means that the caller has to identify themselves and the purpose of the call at the beginning, then presumably the recipient has the opportunity to give consent to the continuation of the call (Teather, 1995b; Marsh, 1996).

Another mechanism to protect the consumer from unwanted communication is the use of **telephone preference services**. In the UK, for example, consumers can register with a central agency if they do not wish to receive cold calls. The problem is, however, that currently not all organisations are members of the voluntary scheme, and thus consumers will continue to get calls from non-subscribing businesses. The scheme also excludes calls to business numbers, market research calls and customer service calls. Similar schemes exist in parts of Europe, for instance in the Netherlands, and the EU is looking to impose preference schemes on all member states eventually (Summers, 1995a).

Mail order

Mail order, as the name suggests, involves the purchase of products featured in advertising or selected from a catalogue. The goods are not examined before ordering, and thus the advertisement or the catalogue has to do a good sales job. Mail order companies promote themselves through any media, and receive orders through the mail, by telephone or via an agent. Direct selling through one-off, product specific advertisements (such as the Franklin Mint operation) has largely been covered at pp. 749 *et seq.* under direct response advertising. This section will therefore concentrate on the mail order catalogue sector.

In the 1960s, the mail order catalogue in the UK was a very heavy and comprehensive document, selling absolutely everything a household could possibly need from clothes, through to toys and power tools, on extended credit. Catalogues were mainly aimed at the poorer sections of society who could not afford to buy things for cash when they wanted them. Mail order catalogues ran on an agency system in which the agent sold to friends and earned commission on sales. The agent was responsible for collecting the owed money weekly. The main strengths of the traditional catalogue were as shown in Fig 19.2.

Weaknesses of traditional catalogues
Traditional catalogues did, however, have their weaknesses, and these are discussed below.

Lack of speed. Catalogues asked customers to allow 28 days for delivery, and it often did take as long as that for orders to be processed and deliveries made. That lead time was in addition to the time taken for an order to pass through the postal system and be delivered to the organisation. It also took a long time before customers would be informed that an item was out of stock, and then they would have to go through the whole ordering process again.

FIGURE 19.2

The traditional strengths of mail order

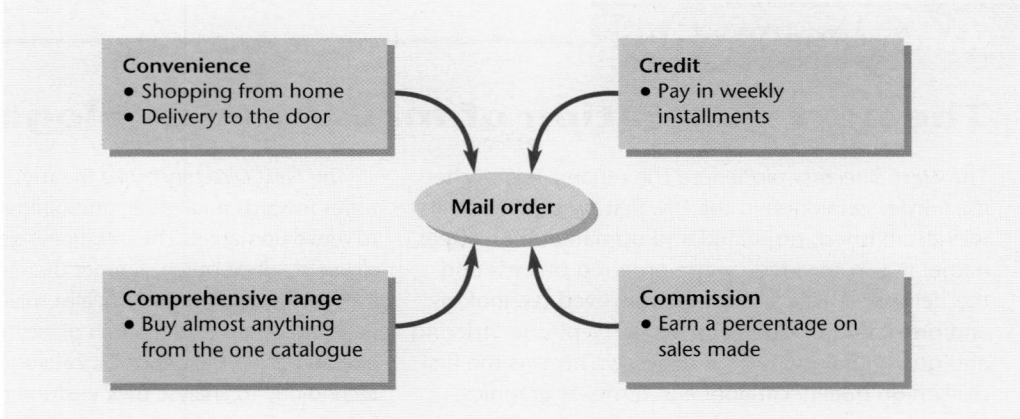

Downmarket image. The range and quality of merchandise, the emphasis on credit, and the presentation of the catalogues meant that mail order was seen very much as a preserve of the C2, D and E socioeconomic groupings.

Lack of targeting. Although the general image was downmarket, there was historically little effort to target catalogue offers closely to customer needs. Catalogues were generalists, so each customer was offered everything. This meant that a great deal of what was offered, including mid-season promotions, was irrelevant to many customers.

The agency system. Many customers just did not want the bother of running an agency. The paperwork and the debt collection involved made it unattractive, even when commission was being earned. Customers wanted to be able to purchase for themselves and their immediate families, with as little administrative responsibility as possible.

Modern mail order catalogues

Figure 19.3 shows how modern catalogues, particularly the new generation pioneered by the likes of the *Next Directory*, have largely dealt with the weaknesses of their predecessors.

FIGURE 19.3

How modern catalogues overcame mail order's weaknesses

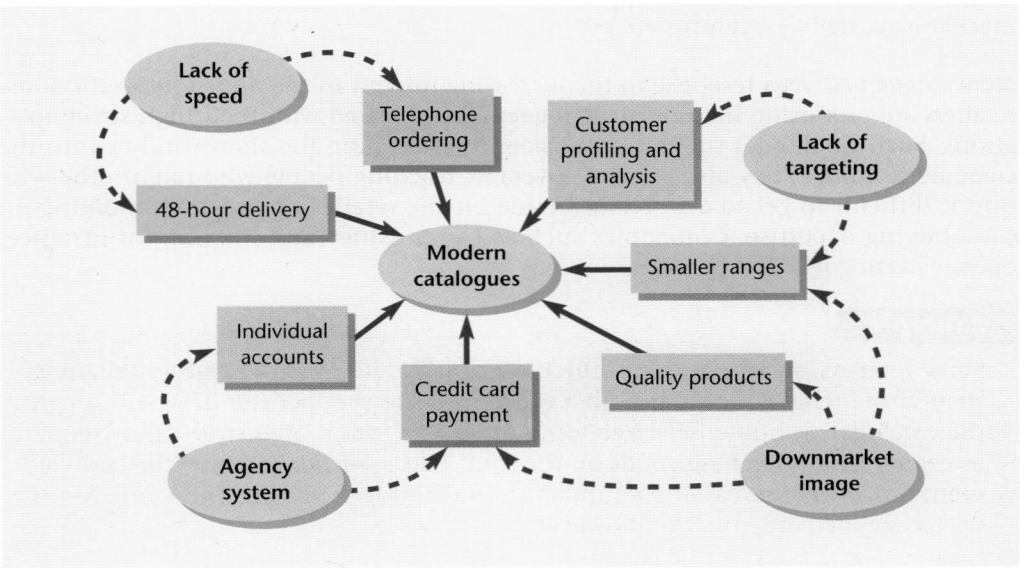

The next generation of mail order catalogues

The *Next Directory* pioneered the renaissance of the mail order catalogue in the UK, first by trading on its well-established, respected and upmarket high street name. It also speeded up the ordering process and the delivery logistics, through improved technology and distribution systems, to allow telephone ordering and guaranteeing 48-hour delivery. This was the first really high quality catalogue in terms of graphics, photography and the inclusion of fabric swatches. Most importantly, Next Directory targeted the young, trendy end of the market with high disposable income. Forty per cent of its customers were in the A and B socioeconomic groups.

The *Next Directory* broke the mould in terms of attitudes towards mail order, and opened the way for others to move upmarket. The traditional generalist catalogues still exist, albeit much slimmer than in the past, but there is now a wide range of specialist mail order publications, covering goods from garden plants to toys, books and clothing. Even the generalist catalogues now have the technology to analyse their customers' profiles and buying habits and can, therefore, make tailored, relevant individual offers. Payment systems are much more flexible, allowing cash payment, credit if customers want it, or the use of credit cards if they prefer, while the agency system has been pushed into the background.

There are now two main types of catalogue.

Non-store catalogues. Non-store catalogues are catalogues which do not have links with high street retail outlets. The catalogue is the sole 'shop window'. Traditionally, catalogues carrying the full range of household and fashion goods have been seen as downmarket, and they have found it difficult to move upmarket in the consumer's eyes.

Following Next's example, a number of new smaller catalogues of specialist clothing, such as Lands' End and Racing Green, aimed at a more upmarket audience, have emerged. Other catalogues in DIY, business to business goods, computers and many other sectors also now exist, and there is greater acceptance among more affluent segments of buying from smaller, more targeted catalogues rather than the larger, more traditional blockbusters.

This kind of catalogue is really a form of distribution channel, in that the operator performs the tasks of merchandise assembly, marketing and customer service. The important thing is to find the selection of merchandise appropriate to the market niche served, and to design an appealing kind of service package (in terms of ordering mechanisms, delivery, returns etc.).

Store catalogues. As a response to the increasing interest in the non-store sector, some retailers are producing their own catalogues clearly linked with their high street operations. Such catalogues support retail sales by extending the shop window into the customer's home. They also expand coverage, reaching people who might otherwise find it difficult to get to a store, and trade on the retailer's reputation, building on their buying expertise. Companies such as Laura Ashley and Habitat, for instance, operate catalogues.

Example

Some retailers, such as Argos in the UK and IKEA, have gone as far as designing their entire retail concept around a catalogue. The shopper can browse through the catalogue at home, select goods and then go into a high street 'showroom' to examine and purchase goods on the spot. This seems to combine the best elements of both the catalogue and the retail outlet. Neither IKEA nor Argos operates a mail order service, however.

TABLE 19.6

Typical advantages of mail order over retail outlets

Advantages of shops over mail order	Advantages of mail order over shops
Can see/touch goods	Delay payment
Can try on/test goods	Choose at leisure
No delay in acquiring purchases	Choose at convenience
Easy to return goods	Easy to return goods
Easy to compare prices	Saves time
Cheaper	No pestering
Shopping is enjoyable	Shopping is not enjoyable
Advice/service available	Home delivery of purchases

Advantages and disadvantages of mail order

Regardless of the type of operation, the basis of the mail order business is the catalogue. As a major selling tool, a great deal of thought and effort is required to get it right and tailor it to the target market. The main advantages of mail order to the consumer are convenience and efficiency and, for some, easy credit. This is especially valuable in areas remote from larger city centres where regular shopping trips are difficult. For the organisation, by avoiding expensive high street locations and the associated display and personal selling costs, the opportunity is provided for a wider variety of lower cost offerings. However, unless catalogues are updated regularly, and unless shoppers are happy not to experience the 'fun' of trial and shopping around for speciality items, the catalogue range may still not suit the more discerning shopper. Table 19.6 shows the perceived advantages and disadvantages of mail order over retailing from the consumer's perspective.

Mail order across Europe

Table 19.7 shows the level of mail order sales in various EU countries and the share of the retail market that mail order takes. While Italy seems to have the weakest mail order sector, Germany certainly seems to have the strongest. Much of this is due to Otto Versand, the biggest mail order conglomerate in the world. Its catalogue is something of an institution in Germany, and has maintained its edge by pioneering high-quality service levels and developing targeted speciality catalogues. Otto Versand generates almost half of its sales outside Germany, however. As already mentioned, it owns Grattan in the UK, as well as 3 Suisse in France, Postalmarket and Euronova in Italy, and Spiegel, Eddie Bauer and West Hampton in the USA. It also has interests in Hungary and Japan, and is developing other eastern European and Far Eastern markets (Miller *et al.*, 1994).

Although there are over 2000 mail order operators across Europe, most of them specialise in narrow ranges of high-quality products. In terms of sales, however, the sector is dominated by the wide-ranging generalists. Table 19.8 shows the top five mail order com-

TABLE 19.7

Mail order sales and retail market shares in selected EU countries

	Sales ($ billion) 1993	Share of Total retail sales 1992 (%)	Share of Total non-food sales 1992 (%)
Austria	1.0	2.5	3.5
France	4.2	1.3	2.1
Germany	22.4	5.7	8.3
Italy	1.1	0.3	1.4
The Netherlands	1.3	2.0	3.0
UK	6.3	2.0	3.2

Source: Euromonitor (1995).

panies and their 1991 turnover. Like Otto Versand, most of them have expanded internationally largely through acquisition and joint ventures rather than simply by distributing their catalogues across borders. La Redoute is the exception, in having set up operations from scratch in Portugal, Belgium, Spain and Norway although goods are supplied from a central depot in France. Cross-border operations and ordering for mail order companies are not easy because of legal, banking and taxation differences, as well as language, taste, pricing and currency problems.

TABLE 19.8
Europe's Top 5 mail order companies, 1991

Rank	Company	Country	Turnover (bill. ECU)
1	Otto Versand	Germany	10.3
2	Quelle Schikedanz	Germany	7.7
3	GUS	UK	3.2
4	La Redoute	France	2.7
5	Littlewoods	UK	1.2

Source: Based on Shipman (1993).

Nevertheless, some mail order companies do try to develop a pan-European identity. Lands' End capitalised on its American origins to present a consistent image in a number of different European markets with catalogues targeting the well-educated, affluent, over-35-years-old audience. Different catalogues are produced for each country to overcome some of the problems outlined above, such as language and pricing, but the print advertisements that invite potential customers to send off for a catalogue are basically the same, with small variations for cultural differences. Lands' End operates in the UK, Germany, France, the Netherlands, Japan and Australia (Siler and Mussey, 1994).

Penny Plain targets an upmarket niche with high quality, hand-made designer fashion through mail order.

Source: Penny Plain.

TABLE 19.9
Cable and satellite penetration across Europe, 1992

Per cent of households owning TV		
	Cable	Satellite
Austria	24.5	11.1
Belgium	86.9	0.7
Denmark	54.5	3.9
Finland	38.5	1.2
France	5.2	0.6
Germany *	37.0	9.8
Greece		0.3
Ireland	39.1	2.5
Italy		0.1
Luxembourg	64.3	
The Netherlands	87.7	3.9
Portugal		1.0
Spain	5.3	0.9
Sweden	49.6	5.8
United Kingdom	3.0	10.4

* Former West Germany
Source: Euromonitor (1995), p. 349.

Teleshopping

Developments in communications technology in telephone, cable and satellite television, radio, and the Internet have enabled a further revolution in home-based shopping or **teleshopping**. The Internet worldwide has seven million computers connected to it, representing around 40 million users (*Marketing Week*, 1995). On the Internet, it is possible to access product information, select goods and then complete the transaction by credit card, all using a home computer. In the UK, for example, Barclays Bank operates an Internet site called Barclay Square which is effectively an electronic shopping mall. Retailers such as Argos, Toys 'Я' Us, Victoria Wine, Interflora and Eurostar all sell goods and services there. As the number of households and businesses with the ability to access the Internet rises, it will become a more attractive proposition for retailers and other types of organisation with goods to sell.

On a more domestic scale, French teleshopping has benefited for several years from the Minitel system, sponsored by France Telecom, using a terminal linked with the telephone. Around six million French households are linked to Minitel, which accounts for around 14 per cent of all French home shopping (Coad, 1993). This system is especially used by La Redoute, the largest French mail order and teleshopping company, and generates over one-third of the firm's turnover.

Cable and satellite television networks are also gaining ground in Europe. Direct marketing through these media can vary from fairly standard one-off advertisements screened during a normal commercial break, to slots featured in dedicated home shopping programmes or channels, usually involving product demonstration, often to a live audience. The main problem with developments in this area is not the capability of the technology, but the willingness of consumers to participate. Much depends, of course, on the number of homes connected to either satellite or cable systems, and there are variances across Europe, as shown in Table 19.9.

THE ROLE OF DIRECT MARKETING IN THE PROMOTIONAL MIX

The previous sections have defined the nature of direct marketing, and some of the tools and techniques involved. This section draws all that together to look at how direct marketing fits in with the other elements of the promotional mix. Although, as previous sections have shown, direct marketing can overlap with advertising, the key distinction between direct marketing and the other elements of the promotional mix is the personalised direct approach that relies on another communication channel, such as telephone, mail or computer link. At the centre of the activity is a direct response from the customer. For example, a successful mail campaign depends on accurate personalised targeting and a response mechanism that can prompt further contact. It requires action by the customer to generate a measurable response to the promotional effort.

Objectives of direct marketing

There are a number of tasks that direct marketing can perform, depending on whether it is used for direct selling or supporting product promotion. The tasks may be related

Castle Cement sweeps telemarketing awards

Each year, British Telecommunications sponsors the Telemarketing Awards in conjunction with *Marketing* magazine. In 1996, Castle Cement won the award for the most outstanding sales promotion using tele marketing, and also won the manufacturers' telemarketing category.

There is nothing especially glamorous about the cement business. Castle supplies cement in either tankers or bags from its six factories around the UK. Its market share was estimated to be about 25 per cent of the UK market, with a turnover of around £140 million. In 1994, the company launched a new type of cement called Multichem but found that product awareness after one year was very low, especially compared with its major competitor, Mastercrete. It therefore decided

to use telemarketing to reverse the fortunes of the product. The campaign ran from June until December 1995 and involved contacting 13 000 builders nation-wide in an effort to influence end user demand. During the campaign, Castle introduced Multichem product benefits as well as a sales promotion offering price discounts and a holiday competition. The promotion was also used to find out more information about customer purchasing habits.

As a result of the campaign, Castle found that corporate and product awareness was raised, sales started to grow, and the company had developed a useful database of end users for further promotional activity.

Source: *Marketing* (1996).

to ongoing transactions and relationships with customers. At its most basic, therefore, direct marketing can fulfil the following objectives.

Direct ordering

Direct marketing aims to enable direct ordering, whether by telephone, mail or, increasingly, by direct computer linkage. The use of credit cards, passwords and specific account numbers all make this possible. All kinds of direct marketing techniques can be used to achieve this, but the example of Music Sales, mentioned earlier is particularly interesting as it both takes the order and delivers the product immediately.

Under the EU's proposed Distance Selling Directive, however, customers will have the right to change their minds within seven working days and withdraw from the contract. It will be the supplier's responsibility to make sure that customers have details of how to annul the transaction and to make any refund within 30 days.

Information giving

Direct marketing aims to open a channel of communication to enable potential customers to ask for further information. Information may be given verbally by a sales person, or through printed literature. Again, many techniques can achieve this objective, including customer care lines.

Example

PPP, a private medical insurer, launched a 24-hour medical advice line staffed by trained nurses, pharmacists and other specialists to help reassure and inform its customers (Teather, 1995a).

Visit generation

Direct marketing aims to invite a potential customer to call in and visit a store, show or event with or without prior notification. Nissan, for example, used direct mailshots targeted at fleet buyers to encourage them to visit the Nissan stand at the UK Motor Show.

Trial generation

Direct marketing aims to enable a potential customer to request a demonstration or product trial in the home, office or factory.

Achieving the objectives of direct marketing

These objectives can be achieved through a variety of means. They can be regarded as stages in the selling process from making the initial contact to creating a loyal customer. In some cases, the selling company may directly seek business, perhaps by using the telephone to contact lost or former customers, or by introducing a direct on-line ordering system for regular volume customers, such as dealers and distributors. In other cases, the response may come from the customer as a result of other promotional efforts, such as advertising or sales promotion campaigns.

How and when to use direct marketing

Initiation

An important decision in direct marketing is how best to use it at various stages of the relationship with the customer. The earliest stage, *initiation*, can be very difficult, as it involves creating the initial contact and making the first sale. A combination of appealing advertising and sales promotion techniques may be used, for example, to overcome the potential customer's initial apprehension and risk aversion. Thus in its introductory offer, a book club may reduce the customer's perceived risk through drastic price reductions on the first order (any four books for 99p each), and further specifying a period within which the books may be returned and membership cancelled without obligation. Alternatively, a sale on credit or even a free trial may ease the initial fears of the customer, despite the high administration costs. Any of these methods makes it easier for the customer to part with their cash on the first order, thus opening the opportunity for a longer-term relationship.

Relationship building

Most direct marketing is in fact aimed at the *relationship stage* customer. This is when the seller has started to build a buying profile, supported by more widely available non-purchase specific data. This enables a steady flow of offers to be made, whether by telephone, mailshots or catalogue updates. Customers are also likely to be more responsive at this stage, as they have established confidence in product quality and service performance.

> **Example**
>
> Avery Office Products run a loyalty scheme, Avery Club, and a customer care line. The club works like many other loyalty schemes in which customers earn points for purchases made. The points are redeemable at Argos catalogue stores. The freephone customer care line receives about 1000 calls a week and enables the company not only to sort out customers' problems, but also to gain valuable information and new product and service ideas (Gofton, 1995).

Combination selling

Finally, combination selling results from using contacts gained from one medium, such as a trade exhibition, for regular contact by direct marketing means. This could be the mailing of special offers, price lists, catalogues or telephone calls to gain a face-to-face meeting etc. The direct marketing activity is therefore used in combination with other methods. As mentioned earlier, Boots used the contacts generated by its pollen count care line to provide a mailing list for material on hayfever remedies and other related products. Similarly, Avery used information from its care line to target a subgroup of customers with colour inkjet printers.

MANAGING A DIRECT MARKETING CAMPAIGN

If direct marketing is going to create, build and maintain relationships with new and existing customers, then it needs to be carefully targeted and managed. A failure in any one of the main areas may result in inappropriate messages directed at the wrong targets. The main stages in the development of a direct marketing campaign are outlined in Fig 19.4 and considered in turn below.

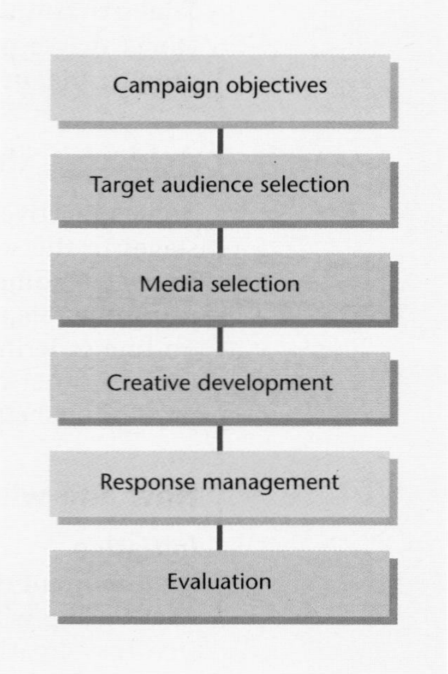

Campaign objectives

As with all marketing activities, the definition of objectives provides an important foundation, guiding subsequent management decisions. Direct marketing objectives must be linked with wider marketing and promotional objectives, and their definition must relate to target audiences and measurable results. Desired outcomes may be expressed in terms of market awareness, number of responses sought or conversion of enquiries into sales.

Campaign objectives

Target audience selection

Media selection

Creative development

Response management

Evaluation

FIGURE 19.4

Managing a direct marketing campaign

Prospects and target selection

Prospects can be in a number of states:

1 *possible prospects*: a broad pool of potential customers about whom little is known;
2 *probable prospects*: a list selected through qualification on some predetermined criterion;
3 *unconverted enquiries*: those who have had previous contact with the organisation, showing an interest in its products, but who have not yet committed themselves;
4 *former or lost customers*: those who have purchased in the past, but not recently;
5 *existing customers*: those with an established pattern of custom who are still actively purchasing.

Generally, the nearer the top of that list a prospect falls, the higher the cost per sale. Existing customers will need much less persuasion and incentive to buy than a completely unknown, 'cold' prospect. Note too that information held on present customers can always assist in the targeting of new customers. By identifying the key characteristics of the most valued existing customers, such as demographic, geodemographic and psychographic details (look back to Chapter 5 to brush up on the definitions of these terms), media preferences, products purchased and response profiles, qualification criteria can be defined for screening out the best new prospects, along with an offer that is most likely to appeal to them.

As p. 747 indicated, commercial market research data agencies can provide lists of qualified prospects. The European Direct Marketing Association, for example, provides an international list search service and can also provide details of European list brokers. The sheer volume of information held is surprising and also gives some cause for concern in terms of privacy. CCN database, for example, holds information on 43 million consumers that can be analysed by lifestyle, age, gender, creditworthiness, postcode, purchasing habits or any combination of these. All of this information assists in profiling and helps not only to understand behaviour, but also to predict it.

Information systems are slowly, but inexorably, moving from geodemographic level data down to the individual household level.

Accessing even geodemographic data is, however, less easy in some European countries. Census data (the foundation of most commercial databases) and standards vary in format and timing, and postcode systems may not be so flexible. For example Germany does not have such a closely pinpointed postcode system as the UK. In Germany, whole cities are often treated as homogeneous for postcode purposes, therefore undermining one of the main methods for direct targeting. Variations in systems mean that we are still some way from having a pan-European database, but international lists are becoming available through conference attendance, car rental, freight companies, hotels and publishers. In practical terms, there are some difficulties in designing pan-European software for database management. Issues of salutation differences, gender, titles, use of first names, and different address structures need to be covered. Locally produced software may not easily adapt.

Media selection

After the initial selection of the target customer group, the most appropriate media need to be selected to generate the planned response. The full range of media discussed in Chapters 15 and 16 are available, but their use will be influenced by the size and profile of audience reached, availability, the predicted cost per sale, and their general cost effectiveness for implementing a multimedia or single medium campaign. In terms of cost, for example, Fill (1995) estimates that to reach a decision maker in an organisation, telephone selling would cost about £10, direct mail about £1.50 and a personal sales call about £175. Although these figures are very generalised, they do underline the importance of cost effectiveness and the need to justify media choices in terms of objectives and expected benefits.

The choice of medium will also depend on what stage in the buying process the prospective customers have reached. Three main stages can be identified.

1 *Response initiation*: The initial contact, generating an expression of interest, can be achieved through almost any medium, for example broadcast and print advertising, magazine inserts, mailshots, or door-to-door leaflet drops. We have already looked at the various response mechanisms (freephone, freepost etc.), and discussed their role in generating the desired outcome (*see* pp. 747 *et seq.*).
2 *Information and action*: Responding to the customer's request for more information and, where necessary, fulfilling the order and delivery process involves more direct contact from seller to buyer. Appropriate media include direct mail, telephone, point of sale information, and the sales force (particularly in organisational markets).
3 *After sales*: Once customers have been created, it is important to keep in touch with them and promote new offers from time to time. Again, the seller needs to be proactive through media such as direct mail, telemarketing, and the sales force.

Experience with direct marketing suggests the importance of an integrated multimedia campaign (Eisenhart, 1990). This means ensuring that the best combination of techniques is used to move the potential customer through to a sale.

Creative development

Depending on the nature of the direct marketing campaign, a brief may be developed for either internal specialists or external consultants. This brief is similar to that used in advertising and sales promotion, and relates the target customers' needs with marketing objectives and product benefits on offer. There are a number of areas that need to be addressed, as shown in Fig 19.5. These are discussed in somewhat more detail below.

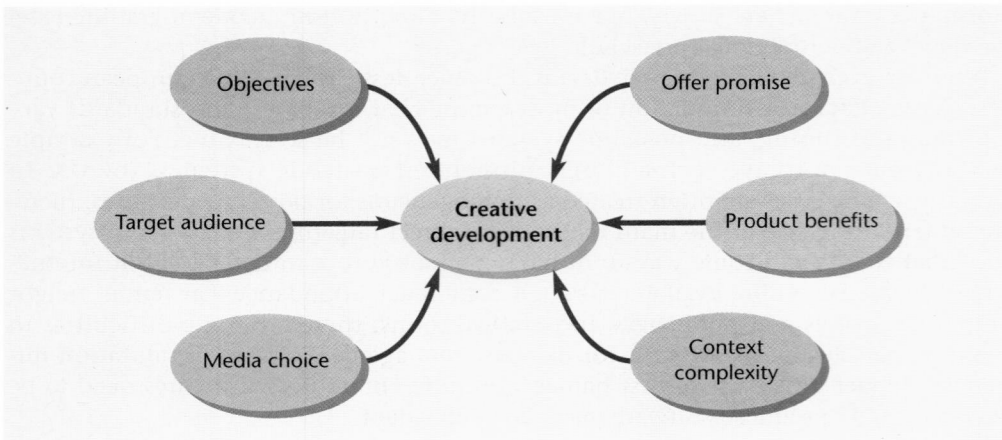

FIGURE 19.5

Issues influencing
creative
development

1 *Objectives*: these indicate what the campaign is expected to achieve and defines the required response targets;
2 *Product benefits*: these describe the key features and relate them to the potential benefits that can be promoted;
3 *Target audience*: this profiles the audience to provide a sound 'feel' for the typical customer;
4 *Offer promise*: this encompasses the key benefits to offer and how they can be supported;
5 *Tone of communication*: the tone will be influenced by the media selected. The formality and communication style need to be specified;
6 *Layout, graphics, scripts*: the physical look of the offer is important for attracting and retaining attention, especially if the campaign is likely to be given only a short period to make an impact. The offer must end by encouraging action relating to the campaign objectives. At a very practical level, it must also be remembered that advertisements used in a campaign may require more space in different countries because of language differences. Compared with English, languages such as Italian and Spanish require 20–25 per cent more space, and German and Scandinavian need 25–30 per cent more. This is quite apart from the normal concerns about translating words and phrases literally from one language to another;
7 *Positioning*: this concerns relating the offer to the many other competitor efforts in the customer's mind;
8 *Restrictions*: any legal and corporate restrictions need to be identified and complied with;
9 *Action*: as the key to direct marketing is action, the mechanism and ease of responding need to be carefully considered.

Response management

One of the major advantages of direct marketing is that the response is direct and usually happens within a limited time span.

Example

Digital sent out a mailshot to 60 000 potential customers in France, Germany, Italy, Spain and the UK, to promote its software tools. They estimate that sales worth £2.3 million were generated as a result within a short period.

A number of ratios can be developed to analyse responses to help increase effectiveness. These ratios include:

- cost per enquiry
- cost per order
- response rate
- conversion rate from enquiry to order
- average order value
- renewal or repeat order rate.

With direct marketing campaigns a unique code can be given to distinguish specific advertisements or promotions. This enables patterns and trends to be identified and these can be used to predict further responses based on customer profiles.

DATABASE CREATION AND MANAGEMENT

Any organisation with a serious intention of utilising direct marketing needs to think very carefully about how best to store, analyse and use the data captured about its customers. This means developing a **database** with as detailed a profile as possible about each customer in terms of geodemographics, lifestyle, purchase frequency and spend patterns. In organisational markets, information might also be held about decision makers and buying centres. Whatever the kind of market, the deeper the understanding of the customer the easier it is to create effective messages and products. However, if database usage goes wrong, it can cause some unfortunate errors, for example offering maternity wear or prams to old age pensioners. When the database works well, it can help to offer products that will appeal to the target audience and generate a response, enabling relationships to build and prosper.

This section looks at some of the issues connected with database creation and management, as summarised in Fig 19.6. Note that the end of the first cycle, customer recruitment and retention, is the start of a stronger second cycle, based upon better, recorded information and subsequent targeting.

FIGURE 19.6

Database creation and management

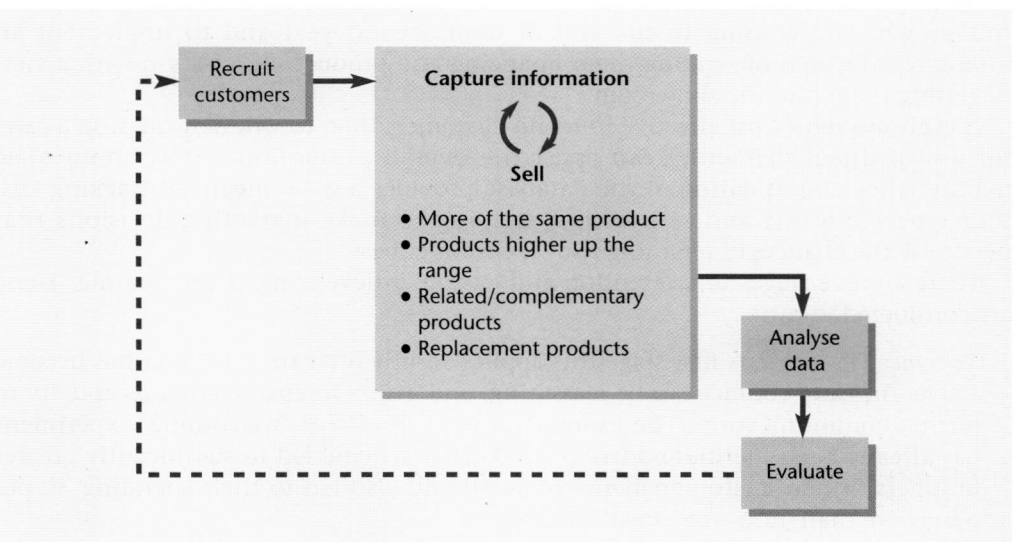

Customer information

Although internally developed databases are nearly always more appropriate than those available externally, they do take time to develop and maintain. External lists can be purchased, with over 4000 being available in the UK and some 20 000 in Europe. The selection of the most appropriate list depends upon purpose and selection criteria. Geodemographic profiles, such as ACORN and Mosaic, highlight the areas offering the highest probability for identifying the best targets, based on a combination of neighbourhood and demographic detail such as family, education, occupation etc.

The assembly and management of an up-to-date database provides the necessary foundation for future campaigns (Burns, 1995). Typical information contained in a database describes customer profiles. Through analysis and model building, its predictive potential can be exploited. The first part of Table 19.10 summarises the kind of information that helps to create a rich profile of existing customers, and the second part tracks the developing buyer– seller relationship.

TABLE 19.10
Customer information for database building

- Contact name
- Company name (if applicable)
- Type of company (if applicable)
- Address
- Geodemographic profile
- Psychographic profile

- Previous contacts
- Previous responses
- Purchases actually made
- Frequency of purchases
- Value of purchases
- Types of purchase
- Media responsiveness
- Promotional responsiveness

Keeping customers and reselling to them

As with any marketing effort, the continuation of exchanges will depend upon how well needs have been satisfied, service provided and value offered. However, the real challenge for direct marketing is to continue to communicate actively with the customer and win further orders after the initial contact has been made. This can be achieved by keeping in regular contact and developing a range of initiatives to encourage further orders. These could be further sales of the same product, sales of new offers, or cross-selling into related product areas to maximise the returns from established contacts.

Classifying the customer list to reflect loyalty, purchase activity, susceptibility to future offers and age of listing can help to determine the best way of approaching future communication and offers. For example individual car owners tend to change cars every two or three years, and therefore it might be appropriate to identify customers who are coming to the end of their second year and to implement an intensive campaign of sending them financing and product information with a view to getting them into the showroom.

It is always more cost effective to retain customers than to win new ones, so a careful use of direct marketing can assist the overall promotional programme. The maintenance and updating of the database provides a good means of tracking customer needs, wants and satisfaction, helping to make marketing decisions that maximise the chances of retaining a loyal customer base.

There are five stages in a retention and customer development programme. These are considered in turn.

1 *Welcome*: The obvious first stage this applies shortly after the customer has become active. An early contact can be reassuring, and assists in engendering receptivity to further communication. The example of *Next Directory's* 'welcoming' experiment has already been mentioned (*see* p. 757). That scheme led to significantly greater numbers of new customers being retained and also led to their spending 30 per cent more than 'non-welcomed' customers.

2 *Selling up*: Apart from normal repeat business, such as occurs with customers of a book club, organisations should encourage the customer to adopt a better or higher

valued model. This approach would be appropriate for a wide range of products and services including cars, cameras and credit cards. American Express, for example, was mentioned earlier as using direct mail to encourage green Amex cardholders to trade up to gold card status (*see* p. 746). The timing of contact will depend upon the expected replacement period for the product.

3 *Selling across*: The selling across stage is where an organisation tries to sell a wider range of products than those in the area originally selected. A customer who purchases car insurance from a particular company might subsequently receive mailings about house insurance or private health cover, for example.

4 *Renewal*: With products that involve annual or regular renewal, such as motor insurance, the timing of appropriate and personalised communication around the renewal date can reinforce repeat purchases.

5 *Lapsed customers*: Customers may be temporarily dormant or permanently lost. A continuation of communication may be appropriate for a period of time so as not to lose contact, especially if reorder frequencies are high.

The Internet provides a mechanism for direct one-to-one browsing and selling.

Take a trip around our virtual store!

Order PC software using our NEW 1-800 Number!
It's the quick and easy way of getting the software you want...delivered right to your doorstep!

Check out all our hot new toys throughout the store...just in time for the new year.

Find out about our new Toys"R"Us VISA® card and how to get yours!

Learn how to choose the right toys with The Toy Guide For Differently-Abled Kids

... and lots more!

 Click TOYS AT THE TOP to find all our best-sellers in 9 subcategories. You'll find color photos in addition to full product descriptions so you can learn all about the toys everyone's talking about!

 Our PLAY IT SMART section is full of toys and software that not only help kids learn...they're fun to play with, too! We've broken these toys into specific categories to help make your choices easier!

NEW: Order our PC software through our 1-800 Number. A wide variety of titles to choose from!

Source: Toys 'Я' Us.

Review and recycle

As implied above, once a database is up and running it should be monitored, reviewed and evaluated periodically to make sure that it is working well and achieving its full potential. This is not just about 'cleaning' the database (i.e., making sure that it is up to date and that any individuals who have disappeared without trace are deleted from it), but also about data analysis. As part of the strategic planning process, the organisation can look for opportunities to cross-sell to existing customers or to get them to trade up, for instance. Managers can also review whether the nature and frequency of contact is sufficient to achieve full customer potential. Perhaps more importantly, they can assess whether they have recruited the kind of customer expected and whether targets have been met.

All of this analysis can be used to plan the continuation of database building. Although the organisation will be trying primarily to hold on to the customers it already has, there will inevitably be some wastage as customers lose interest, or as their tastes and aspirations change, or as they move house without telling anybody. That wastage, as well as the organisation's own growth aspirations, mean that new customers will have to be sought. Learning from the first implementation of the cycle, managers can assess whether the 'right' kind of media were used to attract the 'right' kind of desired customer. They can refine their profiling and targeting in order to improve response rates and perhaps attract even more lucrative customers. They can review which promotional offers or which kinds of approach were most successful and repeat those with new customers, or try similar activities again.

Ideally, as the organisation builds its relationship with customers over time, and as it repeats the cycle of recruitment and retention with increasing numbers of customers, it should learn and become better at serving its customers' needs. This can only happen, however, within a framework of tight planning, management, analysis and control.

CHAPTER SUMMARY

Direct marketing has made considerable progress in recent years in overcoming its poor image as being just 'junk mail'. It now includes a wide range of tools and techniques, all designed to create one-to-one relationships between organisations and their customers, and to allow organisations to tailor increasingly more relevant offers to individual customers. Direct marketing has become more important in recent years for several reasons, including changing consumer lifestyles, competitive pressure, technological advances and the general move towards relationship marketing.

There are several approaches to direct marketing that an organisation might consider. Direct mail can be very effective in stimulating responses from very tightly defined target audiences made up either of existing customers or of new ones. Direct response advertising uses broadcast and print media with the aim of stimulating some kind of response from the target audience. Such advertising can thus be used to create a new database of interested customers who can then be targeted by other direct marketing methods in the future. Telemarketing specifically covers the use of the telephone as a means of creating a direct link between organisation and customer. Outbound telemarketing is generated by the organisation, whereas inbound telemarketing is where the organisation encourages individuals to contact them. The telephone provides a quick, easy and cost-effective response mechanism, and can be used both to increase the impact and creativity of advertising and sales promotion, and to provide a human character for the organisation.

Mail order catalogues now target their customers with 'specialogues', providing narrow selections of better quality goods that suit the customer's profile. More streamlined ordering and administration systems, coupled with a reduction in delivery lead times, have revitalised the mail order sector and made it much more attractive and convenient for busy, higher income households. Some catalogues are solely mail order operations, while others are developed by retailers as a means of extending their established high street business. The most recent development is the catalogue showroom, such as Argos. Within the mail order sector, some organisations expand their operations internationally, usually through the acquisition or partial acquisition of a foreign company.

Part of mail order's new appeal is its use of the telephone to speed up transactions. The caller can find out if a particular item is in stock and, if required, make payment immediately by credit card. This principle has been further developed to open up the teleshopping industry. Satellite channels sell the same goods across Europe in this way, and there are whole channels on cable and satellite devoted to home shopping. The latest manifestation of teleshopping, however, is the Internet. Information and goods can be traded from computer to computer.

Direct marketing thus takes a variety of forms and can achieve a wide range of objectives. As well as direct ordering of goods, it can support the sales effort with information campaigns and after-sales customer care initiatives. It can also pave the way towards sales by inviting potential customers to try out products or to make appointments to see sales representatives.

To achieve all this, however, the direct marketing campaign should be well planned, designed and executed. The campaign objectives should be clearly laid out and measurable. The target audience should also be clearly defined. This in turn leads to the selection of the most appropriate media and message. Media choice is also influenced by the campaign's objectives. Once the advertisement or other material has been developed, the organisation has to ensure that all the likely responses can be handled quickly and efficiently. The planning process should also allow for the response to the campaign to be measured and evaluated so that lessons can be learned for the future. Organisations reap the best benefits from direct marketing when they use responses to build databases so that any one campaign or offer becomes just one of a series of relationship-building dialogues. It is important, however, to create and maintain a database that can cope with a detailed profile of each customer and their purchasing habits and history.

Key words and phrases

Database	*Inbound telemarketing*	*Telemarketing*
Direct mail	*Mailing list*	*Telephone preference services*
Direct marketing	*Mail order*	
Direct response advertising	*Outbound telemarketing*	*Teleshopping*

QUESTIONS FOR REVIEW

19.1 What is *direct marketing*?

19.2 What general issues have led to the rise in popularity of direct marketing?

19.3 Summarise what you consider to be the key success factors for a *direct mail campaign*.

19.4 What is *direct response advertising* and what are the relative advantages and disadvantages of using:

(a) television;
(b) radio; and
(c) print media

for it?

19.5 In what ways can *telemarketing* support and enhance the other elements of the promotional mix?

19.6 How do 'modern' *mail order* operations differ from the 'traditional' approach?

19.7 Why might high street retailers want to run mail order operations in parallel with, and under the same trading name as their stores?

19.8 What is *teleshopping* and through what media can it be offered to customers?

19.9 Explain the role that direct marketing can play in both creating and retaining customers.

19.10 Define the main stages in managing a direct marketing campaign.

QUESTIONS FOR DISCUSSION

19.1 Collect three pieces of direct mail and for each one assess:

(a) what you think it is trying to achieve;
(b) how that message has been communicated;
(c) what involvement devices have been used to encourage the recipient to read the mailshot; and
(d) how easy it is for the recipient to respond in the required way.

19.2 Using Table 19.2 as a framework, carry out your own analysis of the advertising in a magazine. Discuss examples of good and bad direct response advertising from that magazine. What overall conclusions can you draw?

19.3 To what extent, and why, do you think that outbound telemarketing should be controlled by legislation or codes of practice?

19.4 For each of the techniques of direct marketing outlined in Fig. 19.1, assess their relevance to:

(a) consumer markets; and
(b) organisational markets.

19.5 Imagine that you are a customer of a mail order CD club. Specify what information about yourself the club's database should ideally hold. Which bits of that information would be of greatest use to the organisation in designing an appropriate offer for you?

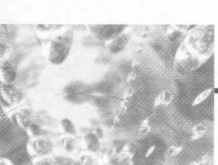

Hyatt International Hotels

The Hyatt International Group operates 68 hotels in 35 countries, in addition to Hyatt Hotels Corporation's 103 locations in the United States. Hyatt is a good example of an organisation that has come to appreciate the power of direct marketing in enabling it to keep in touch with its customers and to target particular groups with special promotions.

It is perhaps surprising how long it has taken the hotel sector to build and utilise databases of their customers. Unlike many retail operations, hotels can gain a considerable amount of information about a customer from both registration and checking-out systems. The customer's name and address are obviously available, but the hotel can also use information such as the type of credit card used, the range of services purchased, the length of stay, whether a business account is used, food preferences, and even the choice of morning paper. All of this can be stored and analysed for marketing purposes. In other industries, such wealth of detail about customers is of such value that marketers are prepared to buy the information for targeting purposes. Hotels, however, have been slow to exploit the information potentially available to them. This could be due partly to the sheer quantity of information gathered about each customer and partly to failure to link operating systems with marketing systems. The Hyatt International Group, however, is changing all that.

Rather than focus on all its customers, Hyatt, at each of its hotels, segmented the most profitable from the least profitable customers. The most profitable group, consisting of about 10 per cent of guests, spend over £10 000 per year, while a further 72 per cent manage to spend around £800. Previously, Hyatt had been marketing to both groups as if they were the same, but clearly the two segments would have very different responses and potential. The most profitable customers were targeted both to retain loyalty and to build stronger relationships with them. The loss of a profitable, loyal customer would be far more significant than the loss of an occasional user. One such targeted campaign was the 'Hyatt Great Deals' package which aimed to fill the hotels during the traditionally quiet times of year (January and February). The campaign was also successful in encouraging Hyatt customers to use a wider range of locations. Of the responses to the winter deal in Hong Kong, for example, 72 per cent represented new business, and the remaining 28 per cent would probably have stayed there anyway. Through database analysis, Hyatt estimated that overall, this promotion generated £10 million additional revenue.

Much still needs to be done to build a fully integrated system. At present, each hotel's database is separate, so the real benefits of a co-ordinated international direct mailing campaign have not yet been realised.

Source: Curtis (1996).

Questions

1 What kind of data could a hotel capture about its guests and how might this be of use to the hotel's marketers?

2 In what ways might the direct marketing approach to a £10 000 a year customer differ from the approach to an £800 a year customer?

3 What advice would you give to Hyatt's marketing department about what problems to look out for in setting up a centralised, co-ordinated database?

4 What are the potential problems facing Hyatt when eventually it is able to think about a co-ordinated international direct mail campaign?

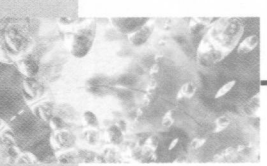

Into the Internet

The potential audience for Internet shopping is wide in terms of its age and socioeconomic profiles. A survey reported by Wilson (1996) suggested that over 20 per cent of all UK shoppers, for example, envisage using electronic shopping over the next few years. Interest in electronic shopping does tend to be greater among younger age groups. Nearly 35 per cent of 15–24 year olds are interested as opposed to approximately 15 per cent of 55–64 year olds. In socioeconomic terms, over 30 per cent of ABs are interested, compared with only 16 per cent of DEs. By the year 2000, it is estimated that electronic shopping could be accounting for about 5 per cent of UK shopping expenditure, about £7.25 billion. In 1995, the German Internet shopping market was the largest in Europe, but by 2000 the UK and France are expected to catch up, as CD-ROM penetration increases, and become major markets. Compared with total mail order expenditure, however, Internet shopping will still be small, but as Newbold (1996) points out, it will be delivering a different kind of audience and will still be developing as a new distribution channel in its own right.

The interest might well be there, therefore, but that still has to be turned into action. In the mid-1990s, the Internet still has a few problems, such as speed. It is often still quicker to order by phone than interactively, even assuming that the customer can find their way to the relevant Internet site immediately. It is also felt that the price of the hardware necessary for accessing the Internet will have to fall further to encourage a much wider audience.

Potential customers (both in consumer and organisational markets) and suppliers are also worried about the Internet's security. Customers are reluctant to transmit credit card or other financial details and thus many companies are holding back from actually selling goods over the Internet. Software companies are working on cryptography, and the view in 1996 was that, by 1998, the Internet would be much more secure. This is essential, because the benefits of electronic commercial transactions go beyond just convenience and time saving. It is estimated that on average it costs £65 to produce a paper invoice and process the payment, whereas the same transaction dealt with electronically only costs £6.50 (Cane, 1996). Some industry experts, however, feel that the insecurity concern is just a perception rather than a reality. They say that it is far more risky to give a credit card number out over the telephone or to leave a carbon copy of

card details in a store. Additionally, a hacker would need about £10 000 worth of equipment to 'hijack' credit card details from the Internet. Nevertheless, the perception of insecurity is there.

Another problem is the lack of interaction between the customer and the goods. Part of the pleasure of 'real' shopping is the ability to handle goods and to choose the freshest, the ripest, the biggest or whatever. Shopping via the Internet also takes away the stimulation of the retail environment. The smell of baking bread in the supermarket or the smell of fresh fruit and vegetables stimulates impulse purchases. Even with non-edible products such as cars, the Internet can only offer an unsatisfying, remote experience. It can present technical data about a vehicle, its performance and the options available, and it can show pretty pictures of the car. What it cannot do is replace the showroom experience, where the buyer can sit in the driver's seat and fantasise, smell the leather upholstery and then take the car for a test drive.

Nevertheless, the major car manufacturers are enthusiastic about the Internet as a means of targeting key segments and of building direct relationships with potential customers. It is estimated that up to two million Internet users in the UK and up to 25 million worldwide have professional or business backgrounds, with high disposable incomes. BMW sees its Internet site as an integrated part of its total marketing package rather than as a replacement for it. A presence on the Internet not only implies that BMW is at the forefront of technology, but also gives them the opportunity to offer what the company called 'tactical entertainment' such as downloadable branded screen savers. Furthermore, the site encourages visitors to register, thus giving BMW demographic data and a potential sales lead, and in return customers get up-to-date information and details of their nearest dealership.

Kay (1996) claims that electronic shopping can help the consumer to obtain more information about the range of choices available within a particular market, but otherwise does little more (and perhaps even less) than conventional retailing. It should, therefore, be ideal for making complicated, relatively high risk, bulky purchases such as washing machines which tend to involve a fairly extensive information search and have to be delivered to the buyer's home. Yet people still prefer to visit a showroom to see and touch the available models (although they are unlikely to see them actually working) before making a decision.

As at mid-1996, the major UK supermarket chains were only tentatively using the Internet as a means of selling goods. Sainsbury's and Tescos, for example, were only selling wine and flowers through this medium. In its first year of operation, Sainsbury's Wine Direct service was only accounting for a disappointing 0.5 per cent of the company's total wine sales. Safeway was in the process of considering an on-line ordering service, but ASDA claimed to have no plans for it. The launch of a new food and drink Internet site called Channel 11, planned for July 1996, could change that. It was hoped that this site would attract the major multiples, and of course, if one of them found it successful, the others would soon follow.

Whatever the type of organisation or product, and whatever the objectives of setting up an Internet site, there are a few general guidelines to follow:

1 the branding on the site must be consistent with what is presented through more conventional media;

2 the site must be an integrated part of a total marketing communication effort;

3 the information must be kept up to date;

4 pages that take too long to download because of detailed graphics run the risk of losing visitors' attention, and similarly, complicated menu systems within the site will also frustrate them;

5 there should be a direct response mechanism, and any responses must be dealt with promptly.

Sources: Cane (1996); Fletcher (1996); *The Grocer* (1996); Kay (1996); McGookin (1996); Newbold (1996); Rosen (1996); Wilson (1996).

Questions

1 What are the main barriers to Internet shopping and how can they be overcome?

2 What kinds of products do you think can best be sold direct over the Internet, and why?

3 How can the Internet help to improve relationships between companies and their customers and potential customers?

4 Will the Internet ever take over from other forms of direct marketing and from conventional retailing?

REFERENCES TO CHAPTER 19

Barton, H. (1994), 'Mailshot in the Arm', *Marketing Week*, 9 September, pp. 49–51.

Burns, J. (1995), 'Developing and Implementing a Customer Contact Strategy', *Managing Service Quality*, 5(4), pp. 44–8.

Cane, A. (1996), 'Net's Rivals Feel the Squeeze', *Financial Times*, 26 February, p. 15.

Coad, T. (1993), 'Variations on a Theme', *Marketing*, 21 October, p. 36.

Cramp, B. (1995), 'Automatic for the People', *Marketing*, 16 November, pp. 33–5.

Curtis, J. (1996), 'Checking in for the Data Revolution', *Marketing*, 9 May, p. 27.

Eisenhart, T. (1990), 'Going the Integrated Route', *Business Marketing*, December, pp. 24–32.

Euromonitor (1995), *European Marketing Data and Statistics 1995*.

Fill, C. (1995), *Marketing Communications: Frameworks, Theories and Applications*, Prentice Hall.

Fletcher, W. (1996), 'Home Shopping Takes a Tumble from its Trolley', *Financial Times*, 2 January, p. 11.

Fry, A. (1995), 'Channels of Communication', *Marketing*, 5 October, p. III.

Gofton, K. (1995), 'Addressing Customer Needs', *Marketing*, 26th October 1995, pp. 38-9.

The Grocer (1996), 'Surfing For Groceries on the Internet', *The Grocer*, 8 June, p. 12.

Kay, J. (1996), 'The Coming Age of a Shop for All Markets', *Financial Times*, 1 March, p. 12.

McGookin, S. (1996), 'BMW Drives on to the Internet', *Financial Times*, 18 January, p. 18.

McKenzie, S. (1995), 'Engaging Tactics', *Marketing Week*, 10 March, pp. 19–24.

Marketing (1993), 'The DMA – Royal Mail Direct Marketing Awards 1993', a supplement to *Marketing*.

Marketing (1995a). 'The DMA – Royal Mail Direct Marketing Awards 1995', a supplement to *Marketing*.

Marketing, (1995b), 'Telemarketing Awards 1995', a supplement to *Marketing*, 22 June.

Marketing (1996), 'Telemarketing Awards 1996', a supplement to *Marketing*, 20 June.

Marketing Week (1995), 'Internet Watch', *Marketing Week*, 8 December, p. 16.

Marsh, H. (1996), 'Is the Number Up for Direct Advertising?', *Marketing*, 4 January, p. 7.

Miller, K. *et al.* (1994), 'Otto the Great Rules Germany', *Business Week*, 31 January, pp. 70J–70K.

Mirbach, S. (1994), 'Brussels is Site of Choice for Hilton Call Center', *Telemarketing Magazine*, 13(2), pp. 40–2.

Newbold, L. (1996), 'New Markets Needed for Internet Shopping', *Marketing Week*, 7 June, pp. 26–7.

Raphel, M. (1992), 'Where's the Retail Direct Mail Revolution?', *Direct Marketing*, December, pp. 42–5.

Rines, S. (1994), 'Dial and Error', *Marketing Week*, 18 November, pp. 11–14.

Rines, S. (1995), 'Smooth Operators', *Marketing Week*, 30 June, pp. 45–57.

Rosen, N. (1996), 'Interaction with the Right Style', *Marketing*, 16 May, pp. 39–42.

Royal Mail (1994), *Direct Action*, CW Editorial Ltd.

Schofield, A. (1994),'Alternative Reply Vehicles in Direct Response Advertising', *Journal of Advertising Research*, 34(5), pp. 28–34.

Shipman, A. (1993), 'Catalogue of Woes', *International Management*, March, pp. 50–1.

Siler, C. and Mussey, D. (1994), 'Lands' End Dons Plan for European Growth', *Advertising Age*, 19 September.

Slinsby, H. (1994), 'Line Management', *Marketing Week*, 13 May, pp. 47–50.

Summers, D. (1995a), 'Wrong Number', *Financial Times*, 2 February.

Summers, D. (1995b), 'Calling on Memory', *Financial Times*, 9 March.

Teather, D. (1995a), 'Facelift for a Serious Operation', *Marketing*, 12 October, p. 13.

Teather, D. (1995b), 'Dialling the European Code', *Marketing*, 16 November, p. 37.

Wilmshurst, J. (1993), *Below The Line Promotion*, Butterworth-Heinemann.

Wilson, R. (1996), 'Security Alarm', *Marketing Week*, 26 January, pp. 49–53.

20 Public Relations, Sponsorship and Exhibitions

LEARNING OBJECTIVES

This chapter will help you to:

1 define PR and the areas of marketing activities it covers;

2 understand its role in supporting the organisation's activities and in reaching various groups, or publics, with differing interests and information needs;

3 outline the techniques of PR, their appropriateness for different kinds of public, and how they might be evaluated;

4 appreciate the importance of corporate identity, why organisations might wish to change identity, and the processes involved in change;

5 understand the role of sponsorship in the marketing communications mix and the benefits and problems of different types of sponsorship;

6 appreciate the contribution that exhibitions can make to achieving marketing objectives and how to exploit them to the full.

INTRODUCTION

Looking back to Chapter 2 and the discussion there on the marketing environment, it is clear that organisations need to be concerned about much more than just their trading relationships with their target markets. Customers are important, but a business as a whole cannot function effectively without the support and co-operation of its financial backers, its employees and trades unions, its suppliers, the legal and regulatory bodies to which it is answerable, interested pressure groups, the media, and many more groups or 'publics' which have the ability to affect the way in which the organisation does business. There is no direct trading relationship between the organisation and many of the publics listed above, which means that the objectives of whatever communication takes place are centred more on explaining what the organisation stands for, and creating a strong, positive corporate image than on a hard sell.

Public relations (PR) is the area of marketing communications that specifically deals with the quality and nature of the relationship between an organisation and its publics. Its prime concern is to generate a sound, effective and understandable flow of communication between the organisation and these groups so that shared understanding is possible.

> **Example**
>
> Rhône-Poulenc used PR to communicate its responsible and caring attitude within the farming industry. It used its annual report, press releases and publicity to contribute to the ethical farming debate, providing well researched facts and figures to key audiences (Burnside, 1995a).

As the range of publics implies, PR has a broad brief and a difficult objective to achieve. While publicity or press relations can make a major contribution, PR utilises a much wider range of activities, which this chapter will cover. First, however, it is important to discuss in more detail exactly what PR is, why it is so important, and what is involved in its management. Then the chapter will go on to look in more detail at some specialist areas of PR, including corporate identity, sponsorship and trade exhibitions. Through this, the chapter will show how PR interacts with other areas of the promotional mix to create a synergy, and how it can sometimes draw on techniques such as advertising in achieving its objectives.

THE DEFINITION OF PUBLIC RELATIONS

First, we discuss some formal definitions of PR and the activities covered by PR, and then we proceed to a more focused overview of the various publics which might be of interest to an organisation.

Public relations defined

Stanley (1982, p. 40) defined **public relations** as:

> **A management function that determines the attitudes and opinions of the organisation's publics, identifies its policies with the interests of its publics, and formulates and executes a programme of action to earn the understanding and goodwill of its publics.**

The Institute of Public Relations (IPR) is rather more succinct in its definition:

> **The deliberate, planned and sustained effort to institute and maintain mutual understanding between an organisation and its publics.**

The latter is, nevertheless, a more useful definition which gets close to the core concern of PR, which is *mutual understanding*. The implication is that the organisation needs to understand how it is perceived in the wider world, and then work hard to make sure, through PR, that those perceptions match its desired image. Two-way communication is essential to this process. Another interesting element of this definition is the specific use of the word *publics*. Advertising, in its commonest usage, is usually about talking to customers or potential customers. Public relations defines a much broader range of target audiences, some of whom have no direct trading relationship with the organisation, and thus PR encompasses a wide variety of communication needs and objectives not necessarily geared towards an eventual sale. Advertising can certainly be used as a tool of PR, but as this chapter will show, it is not the best communication method for many publics or objectives. Finally, the definition emphasizes that PR is *deliberate, planned and sustained*. This is important for two reasons. First, it implies that PR is just as much of a strategically thought out, long-term commitment as any other marketing activity, and second, it counters any preconceptions about PR simply being the *ad hoc* seizing of any free publicity opportunity that happens to come along.

The essence of PR, as stated in the introduction, is to look after the nature and quality of the relationships between the organisation and its various publics. This means that PR covers the management of a range of activities that create and maintain the character and status of the organisation in the eyes of those who matter. It includes, therefore, activities such as:

- the creation and maintenance of corporate identity and image
- the enhancement of the organisation's standing as a corporate citizen, through activities such as arts and sports sponsorship, charitable involvement and community initiatives
- the communication of the organisation's philosophy and purpose, through activities such as open days, visitor centres and corporate advertising
- media relations, both for the dissemination of good news stories and for crisis management, including damage limitation
- attendance at trade exhibitions, which helps to forge stronger relationships with key suppliers and customers as well as enhancing the organisation's presence and reputation within the market.

All of these activities will be discussed in this chapter, but before we do that, it is important the look in more detail at just *who* the various publics are.

Publics defined

A **public** is any group, with some common characteristic, with which an organisation needs to communicate. Each public poses a different communication problem, as each has different information needs and a different kind of relationship with the organisation, and may start with different perceptions of what the organisation stands for (Marston, 1979).

Example

A university has to develop relationships with a wide range of publics. Obviously, there are the students and potential students and the schools and colleges that provide them, both nationally and internationally. The university also has to consider, however, its staff and the wider academic community. Then there are the sources of funding, such as local authorities, the government, the EU and research bodies. Industry might also be a potential source of research funds, as well as commissioning training courses and providing jobs for graduates. It is also important for a university to foster good press relations. Local media help to establish the university as a part of its immediate community, national media help to publicise its wider status, while specialist publications such as the *Times Higher Education Supplement* reach those with a specific interest and perhaps even the decision makers within the sector.

A number of different publics, which relate generally to any kind of organisation, are shown in Fig 20.1 and discussed below. It is, however, important to remember that any individual may be a member of more than one public. This means that although the slant and emphasis of messages may differ from public to public, the essential content

What publics do You think Fiat Ferroviaria, manufacturer of the Pendolino, has to communicate with?

Source: Fiat Ferroviaria.

and philosophy should be consistent. Appropriate techniques within PR for communicating with a range of different publics will be looked at later (*see* pp. 787 *et seq.*).

Commercial

The commercial group includes anyone who has some kind of trading relationship with the organisation, or those who trade in competition with them. It obviously includes, therefore, customers, suppliers and competitors. The main role of PR in relation to this group is to act in synergy with other sales-orientated marketing communication, such as advertising and personal selling. Public relations can be used to convey product information, through editorial coverage in trade magazines, for example, to reinforce attitudes and opinions, or to offer reassurance about product choice, as well as providing a wider umbrella of positive corporate image.

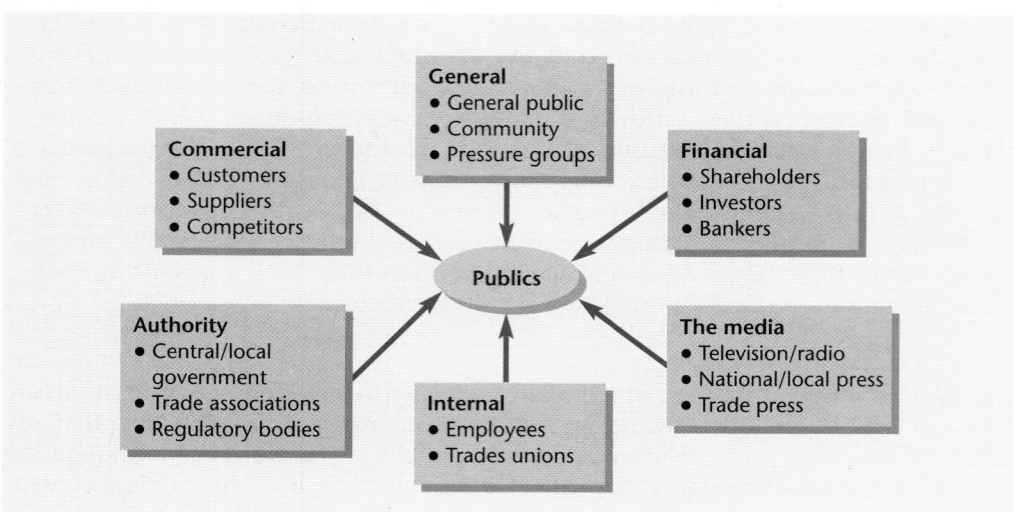

FIGURE 20.1

Publics

Internal

The internal group consists of those who work within the organisation, and support organisations represented within the workplace. It covers, therefore, management, administrative staff, production operatives, and trades unions. Internal PR is important for keeping employees informed about what the organisation is doing, for boosting morale, engendering a sense of belonging, and helping to reinforce the desired corporate culture.

Financial

Members of the financial group have some kind of financial interest in the organisation. The group therefore consists of shareholders, potential investors, bankers and the wider financial community. Public relations contributes towards instilling confidence in the organisation, which means that current investors are less likely to pull out, potential investors are more likely to invest and bankers will be more flexible. It goes without saying, however, that PR cannot be used to disguise a basically unsound business, but it might help to buy a little tolerance or flexibility from creditors or backers. Public relations also comes into its own during take-over battles, such as Granada's take-over of Forte and Trafalgar House's failed take-over bid for Northern Electric, where both sides were trying to influence the outcome and persuade shareholders to make a decision about whether or not to sell out.

Authority

'Authority' is a loose label that covers those who have the power, whether statutory or voluntarily given, to influence the way in which an organisation conducts itself. Central and local government, trade associations and regulatory bodies are all included. Maintaining good relationships with these groups might give the organisation a louder voice in consultation on drafting proposed rules or legislation, or at least give sufficient advance warning of what is in the pipeline to allow them to prepare fully for its implementation or to lobby against it.

The media

The media are an important group because most members of the other publics listed here will take notice of what the media are saying. The media, which include TV, radio, national and local press, and trade and professional press, are both a public in their own right and a tool of PR. Good media relationships are essential, whether the organisation wants to feed 'good news' stories to other publics or to minimise the risk of very hostile media reaction in a crisis.

Customers or potential customers are influenced by the non-advertising messages they see or hear in the media, whether on the news, in consumer programmes or as features, and may well change their attitudes and purchasing habits as a result. Over a period of several weeks in late 1995, for example, the media kept the 'mad cow disease may be transmitted to humans' story in the headlines, fuelling public fear. This then led to a significant decrease in consumer demand for beef. *The Grocer* (1995a) reported that in the 12 weeks up to 9 December 1995, beef sales were 15 per cent lower than in the equivalent period the previous year.

Mad cow disease should be seen as a part of the marketing environment that affects all beef producers and retailers equally. Sometimes, however, negative events are linked with particular organisations. Product tampering scares (such as glass in baby food), product faults (such as washing powder damaging clothes), or what are perceived to be unethical practices are seen as newsworthy items which could seriously damage an organisation's standing if the coverage is allowed to run on unchecked. The organisation needs to have a mechanism for putting its own side of the story and limiting the damage. Similarly, on the positive side, an organisation with good news to tell, such as job creation, winning a large contract or the launch of an innovative new product, will crave media attention to spread the story far more widely than an advertising budget could, and to give the story more credibility.

General

The final group covers the general public at large. This group includes the local community, special interest groups and in particular, opinion formers and leaders. It is now accepted that organisations need to be seen as good corporate citizens and have to play a part in the communities in which they are based. Public relations can help this process by, for example, making sure that a company's sponsorship of a local young athlete, environmental project or community group is adequately and positively publicised. It is also clear that organisational activities are under increased public scrutiny from pressure groups who are prepared to publicise and lobby against what they see as unacceptable practices. The nuclear power industry, for instance, is constantly having to use PR to defend itself against a barrage of vocal anti-nuclear pressure groups, while the chemical industry has to deal with environmental groups. Opinion leaders and pressure groups alike have the power to influence public opinion which, in turn, can seriously affect sales or lead to pressure on 'authority' to regulate, legislate or restrict operations.

Not all publics will be regarded by an organisation as having equal importance. Some will be seen as critical, and be given priority in targeting PR activities, while others will just be left ticking over for the time being. As the organisation's situation changes, the priority given to each of the publics will have to be reassessed (Wilmshurst, 1993).

> ### Example
>
> When the UK's water supply industry was about to be privatised, the PR priorities were to persuade potential shareholders that the new water companies would be dynamic, efficient, profitable businesses worth investing in. During the 1995 drought, however, the companies found themselves having to use PR in a very defensive way. The government and the financial media accused them of having put short-term profits and shareholders before investment in infrastructure; customers accused them of delivering a substandard service at extortionate prices, and shareholders became somewhat nervous.

Even in the quietest and most stable of industries, the membership of each public will change over time, and their needs and priorities will evolve too. This process of change emphasizes the need to monitor attitudes and opinions constantly, and thus to identify current and future pressure points early enough to be able to defuse or control them.

THE ROLE OF PUBLIC RELATIONS

As with any marketing activity, managers must be sure that PR integrates with the rest of the organisation's promotional efforts, and that it is clearly related to wider company objectives. Cutlip *et al.* (1985) distinguished between **marketing PR** and **corporate PR**. Although the two are not mutually exclusive, there may be differences in their scope and objectives.

Marketing PR

Marketing PR may be used for long-term strategic image building, developing credibility and raising the organisation's profile, to enhance other marketing activities. When used in this way, it becomes a planned element of the wider promotional mix, working in synergy with the others (Gray, 1994). A new product launch, or the introduction of a big new innovative advertising campaign, for instance, might benefit from planned PR aimed at specific audiences through specific media to generate interest and awareness.

Example

Playtex spent £300 000 on advertising for its Wonderbra. The advertisements, featuring headlines such as 'Hello Boys', and 'Or Are You Just Pleased to See Me?' were sexy, funny and somewhat more upfront than traditional lingerie advertisements. Because of this, and because of a deliberate strategy of attracting media attention, Playtex was able to generate publicity equivalent to an estimated £18 million advertising spend.

Corporate PR

It is possible to use corporate PR as part of a long-term relationship building strategy with various publics or as a short-term tactical response to an unforeseen crisis. By definition, short-term circumstances are somewhat unpredictable, and therefore any organisation needs to have contingency plans ready so that a well-rehearsed crisis management team can swing into action as soon as disaster strikes. This means, for example, that everyone should know who will be responsible for collating information and feeding it to the media, and that senior management will be properly briefed and trained to face media interrogation. Such measures result in the organisation being seen to handle the crisis capably and efficiently, and also reduce the chances of different spokespersons innocently contradicting each other or of the media being kept short of information because everyone thinks that someone else is dealing with that aspect. Although the duration of the crisis may be short, and thus the actual implementation of PR activities is technically a short-term tactic to tide the organisation over the emergency, the contingency planning behind it involves long-term management thinking.

Example

One of the problems is foreseeing what kind of crisis might occur. Wellcome, the pharmaceutical company, did have crisis management plans ready in case of any incidence of product tampering or adverse side effects from their drugs. They were not prepared, however, in 1993 for the publication of a research study that cast doubt on the efficacy of AZT, Wellcome's anti-AIDS drug. This had a devastating effect on the company, causing its share price to collapse. This was because, as Bond (1995a) reports, when AZT was launched as the first real contender in the AIDS treatment market, the medical profession, AIDS groups and the media had all built up their hopes and the hype around the drug. Wellcome had never made unrealistic claims for the product, but it had allowed the hype to spiral, presumably because it provided positive PR. Thus when the critical study was published, it burst a particularly large bubble. Wellcome tried to argue with the media, claiming that the study was statistically questionable, but:

> 'Journalists wanted a concise soundbite but they got a lengthy academic polemic. And Wellcome's defensive tactics only reinforced its perceived role as the villain pitched against the heroic independent medical research teams' (Bond, 1995a, p.36).

In hindsight, Wellcome recognise that they would have been better advised to keep the message to the media simple and to concentrate on persuading opinion leaders within the AIDS community.

Mad cows and Englishmen

In March 1996, the British beef industry was taken by surprise at the speed and intensity of reaction to the UK government's acknowledgement of a possible link between BSE (mad cow disease) and the human equivalent, CJD. BSE had been around for nearly a decade, but had had little impact before this announcement. Within days, the national press were coming up with headlines such as, 'Could it be worse than AIDS?' and 'Don't eat beef says consumer watchdog' and front-page deathbed scenes of the victims of CJD. Eating beef was seen as a high risk pursuit, even though changes in meat processing in the early 1990s had actually eliminated most of the risks. The crisis developed quickly. McDonald's withdrew British beef from their fast food restaurants, beef was withdrawn from many school menus, and a Europe-wide ban was imposed on British exports in order to restrict the problem to the UK. Consumer confidence in beef appeared to be shattered.

The scare soon affected beef prices. Within hours of the admission of a possible link, livestock prices dropped sharply at auction markets. Ironically, young bull prices dropped the most even though the meat most at risk was thought to be from old female cattle. The multiple retailers started to adjust their beef stocks, and some began to increase purchases of poultry and bacon, in anticipation of changing consumer needs.

The messages coming from the government and the Meat and Livestock Commission (MLC) did little to allay consumer fears. The Health Secretary, Stephen Dorrell, claimed that there was no actual proof of a connection between BSE and CJD, but nevertheless, the government was willing to slaughter millions of cattle if advised to do so by scientists. During an   interview on radio, he also refused to answer a question about whether he would feed his own children with beefburgers! The MLC, representing the industry, could not understand what all the fuss was about. To them, the danger had passed as BSE was originally caused by cattle eating contaminated feed that had been banned several years previously. Strict controls had been introduced to ensure that infected meat did not enter the food chain. The MLC quoted the latest research proving their point, and then expected beef sales to return to normal as soon as the press lost interest. Unfortunately for the MLC, it would appear that few people were listening to them.

By early April the news of mad cow disease had spread around the world. In Denmark, beef sales dropped significantly, until labelling showing the country of origin was introduced. Concern was also expressed for those Danes who had lived in the UK in the 1980s. The Greeks impounded 40 tonnes of British beef, the Canadians withdrew it from the supermarkets, and although the French initially ignored the problem as being confined to the UK, with no impact on them, they still stepped up plans to clearly mark the country of origin on meat. In Austria, sales of beef dropped by 15 per cent to 20 per cent, even though it was a BSE-free country. The Germans insisted that all beef had a certificate of origin. However, despite these measures, consumer confidence was affected in many countries and beef sales suffered, regardless of the meat's origins. One month after the scare broke, beef consumption had dropped by 40 per cent in France, 55 per cent in Germany but just 10 per cent in Holland and Denmark. Ironically, in the UK, sales started to recover.

In the UK, the major retailers decided to continue to support British beef and even though sales were shifting towards imported meat, a series of price promotions helped to maintain volume. At Sainsbury's, for example, prices were halved and some stores sold out. Consumer confidence started to recover and an element of defiance against European pressure started to take hold. In all cases, however, retailers had to give clear assurances at the point of sale and on product labelling that the meat was of prime quality and that it was safe.

Although confidence had been hit, the MLC could have been right in its assumption that the problem would be short lived. However, the disruption caused to the market, consumers and government during that time was considerable. It is interesting to recall the facts that actually fuelled the scare. Comparative figures are given in Table 20.1.

Table 20.1
Statistics on BSE and CJD, 1994

Country	Cases of BSE Reported	Cases of CJD (alleged)
United Kingdom	157 000	54
Germany	4	58
France	12	47
Italy	2	30

The trade magazine *The Grocer* concluded that the relationship between CJD and BSE could actually be negative, thus making it safer to eat British beef!

Sources: P. Barrett (1996); *The Grocer* (1996a–1996g).

As the above examples show, given PR's wide range of uses and applications, it might be very easy to drift into activities without a clear sense of purpose. It is, therefore, very important to define clear objectives as a rationale for action and as a yardstick against which outcomes and achievements can be measured (Stone, 1991).

TECHNIQUES IN PUBLIC RELATIONS

The PR manager has a range of techniques and activities to draw on, limited only by imagination. The first area to look at is that of **publicity** and **press relations**, a major concern within the PR remit. Other external communications and internal PR will then be discussed. While considering techniques, it is important to relate them to the target publics and the PR objectives for which each is appropriate. The range of techniques is summarised in Fig 20.2.

Publicity and press relations

Public relations and 'publicity' are often mistakenly used as interchangeable terms. Publicity is, however, simply one of the tools available for achieving the overall PR objective of creating and maintaining good relationships with various publics. Publicity is thus a subset of PR, focused on generating media coverage at no cost to the organisation. In other words, publicity happens when the media voluntarily decide to talk about the organisation and its commercial activities.

All areas of the mass media can be used for publicity purposes. Within the broadcast media, apart from news and current affairs programmes, a great deal of publicity is disseminated through chat shows (authors plugging their latest books, for instance), consumer shows (featuring dangerous products or publicising companies' questionable personal selling practices, for instance), and special interest programmes (motoring, books, clothing etc.). Print media also offer wide scope for publicity. National and local newspapers cover general interest stories, but there are many special interest, trade and professional publications that give extensive coverage to stories of specific interest to particular publics. It must also be remembered that sections of the media feed each other. National newspapers and television stations may pick up stories from local media or the specialist media and present them to a much greater mass audience.

Generating good publicity

Publicity may be unsought, as when the media get the smell of scandal or malpractice and decide to publicise matters which perhaps the organisation would rather not

FIGURE 20.2

Techniques in public relations

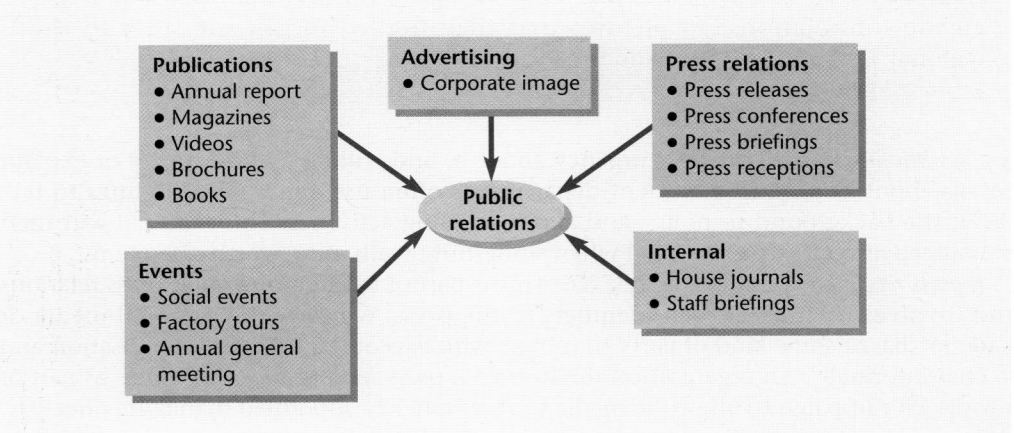

have publicised. To reduce the risk of bad publicity, however, most organisations cultivate good press relations, and try to feed the media's voracious appetite with 'good news' stories that will benefit the organisation. This can be done through a number of mechanisms.

Press releases. Traditionally, press releases consist of a one-page, brief outline of the essential facts behind a story, with a contact name and number being provided for those who wish to obtain more information. It is also common practice to back up a press release with photographic and video material to encourage the media to take up a story.

Many organisations have created snippets of video material which are made available to television news agencies, for example. These snippets feature fairly bland shots, such as the production line, or exteriors of the factory or head office, appropriate for backing a wide range of stories about the organisation. Thus a news story about Vauxhall Opel's latest wage agreement will be backed by footage, provided by the company, of diligent workers on the assembly line. The availability of such material means that the organisation's story is more attractive to the news agency and that they may give it more air time because they have the pictures to fill out the news item without having to go to a lot of trouble. The news agency can either use the material as it is or edit their own interviews or other coverage into this footage.

Unfortunately, the majority of press releases end up in the news editor's bin. This is partly because organisations produce far too many of them, often covering pretty mundane events, and partly because they are often produced with little imagination. The news editor needs an 'angle' that captures the imagination and might provide the focus for an interesting story.

Press conferences. One of the problems with press releases is that they are used so frequently and it is difficult to make yours stand out from all the others that land on an editor's desk every day. This might make organisations look for more personal contact with the media to make a bigger impression.

A *news conference* could be used where there is a major story to announce or where a crisis has erupted and there is a need to update the media from the organisation's point of view. Journalists gather to receive information and to ask questions so that they can then go away and write up the material quickly.

Example

When Samsung announced that it was to build a new factory in Cleveland, a news conference was held in the presence of executives from Samsung and representatives of the various regional bodies, such as the Northern Development Company who had helped to put the deal together. The media were able to get all the information and pictures that they needed to run the story in the regional and national print and broadcast media.

A *press briefing* has slightly less urgency about it, and will be used to clarify or explain details about a story. Government departments often use daily press briefings to talk about the background to policy and about ongoing activities. This material will then be sourced as contextual material when something really newsworthy happens.

A *press reception* is even more relaxed. This is part of maintaining good press relations and involves inviting chosen members of the press, whether the national media or trade media, to some kind of party to mingle with executives from the organisation and to chat informally. An organisation might hold a press reception, for instance, as part of a wider PR campaign to allow the media to meet a newly appointed managing director.

Involving the media. Press releases and the other methods of feeding information to the press do work well, but sometimes more can be gained by going a little further and getting the media more involved in what is happening.

When P. J. Holloway became the sole UK distributor for fans made by the German firm Rosenberg Ventilation, if they had simply issued a press release, they might have gained limited coverage in the trade press. Instead, they invited key journalists to visit Rosenberg's manufacturing facility in Germany. As a result of this extra investment in press relations, they found that their coverage was considerable and much more complimentary comments than they could have expected otherwise were made about the product benefits.

Advantages of publicity over advertising

The media are obviously very powerful, not only as a public in their own right, but also as a third party channel of communication with other publics. It may be argued that advertising can do just as good a communication job, in spreading good news to mass audiences, but publicity has a few advantages.

Credibility. Advertising is paid for, and therefore publics have a certain cynicism about the bias within the message. Publicity, on the other hand, is seen as free, coming from a neutral third party, and therefore has more credibility. An advertisement can tell you that a particular make of car has especially good roadholding capacity, and you may or may not choose to believe it, but if a newspaper's motoring correspondent or the BBC's *Top Gear* programme conclude that the car demonstrates good roadholding, then that constitutes neutral expert opinion and thus carries more weight.

Reach. To make sure that the widest possible audience is reached with advertising would involve a multimedia strategy that would be extremely expensive to implement. A good PR story that captures the imagination of the media so that it gets wide coverage across both print and broadcast media can achieve an incredible level of reach (*see* p. 625) at a fraction of the cost, and might even make an impact on sections of the audience who wouldn't normally see or absorb advertising.

Excitement. Publicity, by definition, is about news. Whatever is being publicised is of current and topical concern and therefore generates its own excitement. Once a story starts rolling, it can gather its own momentum as the media start vying with each other to generate the most coverage or to find a new angle on the story. Extensive media coverage of the concern over the so-called alcopops (alcoholic lemonades and colas) is one such example.

Disadvantage of publicity over advertising

These advantages do, however, need to be balanced against the big disadvantage, which is: *uncontrollability*. Whereas advertising gives the advertiser complete control over what is said, when it is said, how it is said and where it is said, the control of publicity is in the hands of the media. The organisation can feed material to the media, but cannot guarantee that the media will adopt the story or influence how they will present it (Fill, 1995). The outcome of this might be, at worst, no coverage at all, or patchy coverage that might not reach the desired target publics. Another potential risk is that of distortion of the story.

When British Telecommunications unveiled its new corporate image to the press, they probably wanted the emphasis to be on what it meant for the future of the organisation and how it represented a fundamental change in customer service attitude. What they actually got from certain sections of the media was ridicule of the new logo and 'shock horror' speculation on the likely cost of the exercise.

It is not true to say that there is no such thing as bad publicity. The risks of negative coverage can, however, be minimised by the maintenance of ongoing, good press relations, and by setting up a crisis management plan so that if disaster strikes, the damage from bad publicity can be limited and even turned to advantage.

Other external communication

Other forms of external communication are also used for PR.

Advertising

Advertising can be used as a tool of PR, although it is something of a grey area. The kind of advertising to which we are referring here is not the selling or promoting of a specific product or range of products, but the type that concentrates on the organisation's name and characteristics. As previously suggested, although this sort of advertising lacks the impartiality of publicity, it makes up for it in terms of controllability. As a means of helping to establish and reinforce corporate image, it is certainly effective, and as a mass medium, will reach members of most publics.

Philips, for example, felt that it needed to refresh its corporate image because its brand was seen as 'too technical'. Mass media advertising, therefore, was used to reach opinion leaders in consumer markets to generate a more user-friendly image.

Events

An organisation can host or participate in various events for PR purposes. As well as press conferences, mentioned above, the organisation may host other social events. If they have just opened a new factory, for instance, they may hold a party on the premises for key shareholders, employees, customers and suppliers. Such one-off events will also, of course, create media interest.

An important public is the one with a financial interest in the organisation. The organisation's annual general meeting is an important forum for both shareholders and the financial media. Efficient administration and confident presentation can help to increase credibility (although none of that can disguise a poor financial position)

Some organisations open their doors to the general public quite regularly, allowing factory tours, and some have even gone as far as building dedicated visitor centres on site, for example Cadbury's Chocolate World, the Sellafield nuclear plant visitors centre, and Tetley's Brewery Wharf. Such facilities help to involve the public in the work of the organisation, so that they may understand it better, and thus to forge a stronger, more human relationship between organisation and public. Lego have taken this concept a step further by diversifying into Legoland theme parks which are 'products' in their own right, not just PR generators.

Publications

An organisation can commission a wide range of print and video material to support its PR efforts. Videos can be used, as already mentioned, to support press coverage, or can be sent to potential customers or clients to give them a flavour of how the organisation operates. Most universities, for example, will have a recruitment video to send out to schools and colleges to give a more three-dimensional feel for the place than the prospectus alone can manage. At the other end of the university education process, university careers offices stock corporate videos and brochures of organisations looking to recruit graduates.

Annual reports. An important publication is the organisation's annual report, distributed primarily to shareholders and the financial media, but often sent out to anyone who expresses an interest in the organisation. Like the annual general meeting, it is an opportunity to present the organisation in the best possible positive light and to make public statements about the organisation's achievements and its future directions.

Company histories. As a one-off exercise, organisations may even decide to publish their 'autobiographies'.

Example

To celebrate its one hundredth birthday in 1987, Johnson and Johnson published a beautifully produced full colour history of the company. This was distributed with the compliments of the company to all its senior employees world-wide and to key influencers and decision makers among its customers.

MARKETING IN ACTION

Corporate magazines

Corporate magazines, such as *Healthwise*, distributed to Norwich Union Healthcare's policy holders, and *O Magazine*, distributed to subscribers to the Orange telephone network, are a growth area of PR. Nikon's *Pro*, for example, is aimed at professional photographers and is a pan-European publication in three languages, designed to act as an umbrella to bring together diverse professional markets. These magazines are an aspect of relationship marketing and are designed to keep the organisation's name in the customer's mind as well as providing product information in a 'soft sell', easily digestible way. Some magazines are distributed free as a means of encouraging loyalty to existing customers on databases, but some do charge. *Sainsbury's – The Magazine*, for example, is available for purchase within Sainsbury's supermarkets. Others, such as Sony's *The Official PlayStation Magazine*, try to broaden their appeal by selling through newsagents.

The production of corporate magazines, contract publishing, has become increasingly popular with all kinds of organisations, and was estimated to be worth around £100 million in the UK in 1995. Nevertheless, it should be approached with caution and with clear objectives, since it involves considerable investment. *The Boots Magazine*, retailing at 95p in Boots stores, closed after only three issues. Its disappointing performance may have been partly due to poor marketing in-store and partly because its content did not really appeal to the target market or capture its imagination. Nevertheless, store-specific magazines for which the customer pays can be successful. In February 1995, it was estimated that *Sainsbury's – The Magazine* had a circulation of around 260 000, while that of *Tesco's Recipe Collection*, at that time with a cover price of 30p, was nearer 450 000. Unlike the Boots magazine, Tesco's publication was well displayed in the store and was supported by media advertising.

Sources: Bond (1995b); Fletcher (1995a); Massey (1995).

The University of Luton, to celebrate its achievement of university status, published in 1994, *A Hatful of Talent*, a history of the institution, available for purchase through bookshops. Clearly, such a publication primarily has local interest, and would be used to raise the profile of the organisation in its immediate region. The launch of the book and the distribution of complimentary copies to local dignitaries provided additional PR opportunities.

Lobbying

Lobbying is a very specialised area, designed to develop and influence relationships with 'authority', particularly national and EU governmental bodies. Lobbying is a way of getting an organisation's views known to the decision makers, and trying to influence the development and implementation of policy.

The tobacco industry has used lobbying of MPs and MEPs to try to stall any move towards a total ban on cigarette advertising. Similarly, in the UK, brewers are lobbying to try to get the government to reduce the taxation levied on alcoholic beverages. This is to help them even out the price differential between the UK and continental Europe, which currently encourages 'bootleggers' to buy UK brands much more cheaply abroad and then bring them back for resale.

Internal communication

Although employees and other internal publics are exposed to much of the PR that is directed to the external world, they do need their own dedicated communication so that they know what is going on in more detail, and they know it before it hits the wider media (Bailey, 1991). This emphasis on keeping people informed rather than in the dark reflects quite a major change in employers' attitudes towards their employees. It is important for motivation, as well as being a means of preparing people for change and strengthening corporate culture. Two main areas of communication are considered below.

House journals and newsletters

Presented in the style of newspapers or magazines, these are a vital form of communication. Not only can they cover the important trivia of workplace gossip (Maureen from purchasing is getting married on Saturday; marketing beat accounts at five-a-side soccer last weekend; Albert from maintenance will be retiring next month after 50 years' service) which keeps the place vibrant and alive, but they can also be used for crucial managerial communication. Few people would want to read a long working paper written by the managing director on quality management or production targets, but most would at least glance at a well-illustrated, short, clearly written summary of the important points presented in journalistic style. The **house journal** can help to draw disparate parts of an organisation together, renewing a sense of belonging, as well as providing information. This can be particularly important in large organisations, such as retailers, whose staff work in geographically dispersed branches. Mothercare, for example, has launched *First*, a quarterly, eight-page, full colour magazine for all its staff.

Briefings

Briefings provide a good mechanism for face-to-face contact between management and staff, and of increasing staff involvement and empowerment. Frequent, regular departmental or section meetings can be used to thrash out operational problems and to pass communication downwards through the organisation. Less frequently, once a year perhaps, more senior management can address staff, presenting results and strategic plans, and directly answering questions. Internal staff briefings are also likely to feature in a crisis management plan. If staff are hearing disaster and scare stories in the media, then they need to be reassured and given full and accurate information about what is being done. After all, their jobs may be at stake.

EVALUATION

Any PR programme should have begun with specific objectives relating to specific publics, and in order to learn from the experience, needs to end with an evaluation of success or failure (Palin, 1982). Haywood (1984) suggests seven commonly used measures of results, some of them qualitative, others less so. They are summarised in Fig 20.3, and discussed below.

Not all of these measures will be appropriate for all PR campaigns. The choice of method depends on the defined objective of the PR programme and the target publics involved. In all PR campaigns, however, it is important to define objectives at the start and to define the means by which outcomes will be measured. It is also important to ensure that those measures adequately identify the contribution of PR against the compelling background of other marketing techniques.

Budget

FIGURE 20.3

Evaluating public relations

Budget is a straightforward assessment of whether the planned activity has been completed within the given budget and time-scale. This seems fine as a measure of management planning and control, but it does not say much about the quality of the activity or whether it actually made any appreciable difference to anything. Thus it provides no measure of the activity's cost effectiveness.

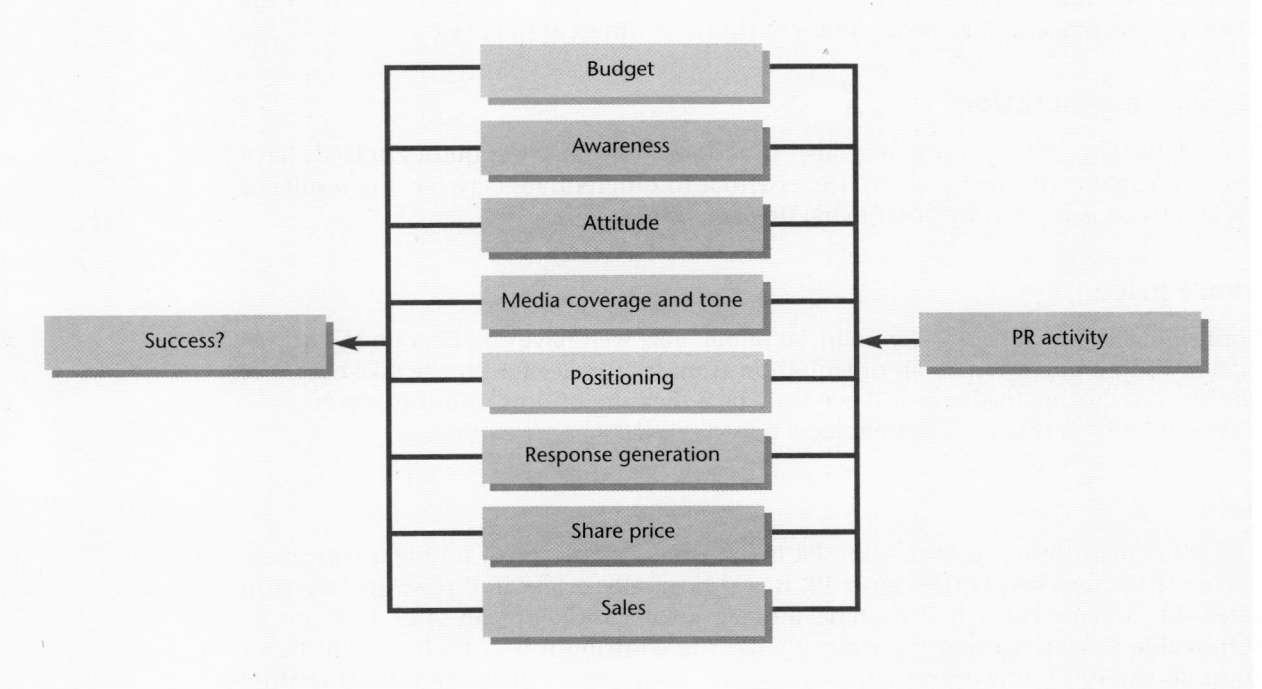

Awareness

Using standard market research techniques (*see* Chapter 6), an organisation can try to establish whether there has been any increase in awareness of the organisation among the target publics. Care must be taken, however, to try to differentiate between the effects of PR and those of other marketing activities, and also to establish where the synergies between them lie.

Attitude

Building on the identification of changes in awareness, research can establish not only the levels of awareness and knowledge, but also how target publics now feel about the organisation, and to what extent the PR has affected this. Ideally, this post-PR research should be compared with the pre-PR position to give a clearer picture of how far and how deeply the PR has penetrated attitudes.

Media coverage and tone

There are two facets to media evaluation in relation to a PR programme. The first is simply finding out how much media coverage the PR generated. This can be measured in air time or column inches, for instance. It is, however, dangerous to be unduly impressed by the sheer *quantity* of coverage; getting the message into the right medium for the target public is much more important.

The second, and harder part, is assessing the *tone* of the coverage, whether it emphasized the right aspects of the story, whether it was generally favourable, and whether the coverage was suitably prominent. There are many subjective elements within such an assessment, and it might best be combined with the attitude research, to look at coverage from the point of view of its effects rather than its quantity.

Positioning

Evaluating position means assessing how the PR activity has affected the positioning of the organisation in relation to its competitors. Again, this may be linked with the attitude research, and may mean different things to different publics.

Response generation

It is relatively easy to quantify response, in terms of how many enquiries or leads have been generated, although, again, it is essential to differentiate between the results of PR and those generated by other marketing activities.

Share price

Some PR activities aimed at the financial public may well have an effect on the organisation's share price. Where an organisation is under threat of a hostile take-over bid, the level of dealing in shares will certainly be a measure of how well the organisation has used PR to persuade its shareholders not to sell out.

Sales

The ultimate measure in evaluating PR is the effect on sales. The problem with measuring this, however, is that most PR is not normally orientated towards affecting sales. As so many other matters have a much greater influence on sales, it might be impossible to state with any certainty what the contribution of PR has been. In an unusual situation, however, such as a product tampering scare, when the story hits the media there will inevitably be a sharp drop in sales, and any slowing or reversal of that decline is likely to be an outcome of the quality of the PR response to the crisis. In such a case, direct attribution is possible with some confidence.

CORPORATE IDENTITY

Source: The Prudential Assurance Company Ltd.

The Pru's new corporate identity was accompanied by some fundamental changes in company culture.

Corporate identity refers to the way in which an organisation chooses to present itself to the world. It reflects the character and philosophy of the organisation, emphasizing those characteristics that it would most like to be associated with (Abratt and Shee, 1988). Although an organisation's logo is the most visible face of its identity, this only the tip of the iceberg, since the logo should emerge from a deeply ingrained culture. Changing a logo without changing the culture correspondingly is a cosmetic waste of time, and publics will soon recognise that under the fresh veneer lie the same old attitudes.

The creation of new companies as a result of privatisation is a clear opportunity for revising both culture and identity. The 'new' company wants to signal to its external publics that it is a competitive entrepreneurial business and to its internal publics that a fresh start with new attitudes is being made. The privatisation of the British Airports Authority, for example, completely changed its operating structure and its mission. A new identity as BAA linked all its diverse areas of business, presenting a coherent fresh face to its investors, customers, suppliers, employees and other publics.

Reasons for changing identity

The 1980s saw a boom in the corporate identity business, as organisations both large and small became aware of the importance of presenting a sharp image to their various publics. They realised that they needed to manage and plan their identities rather than letting an image evolve by accident (Bernstein, 1984). There are many reasons why organisations eventually decide to develop or change their corporate image, as shown in Fig 20.4 and discussed below.

FIGURE 20.4

Reasons for changing corporate identity

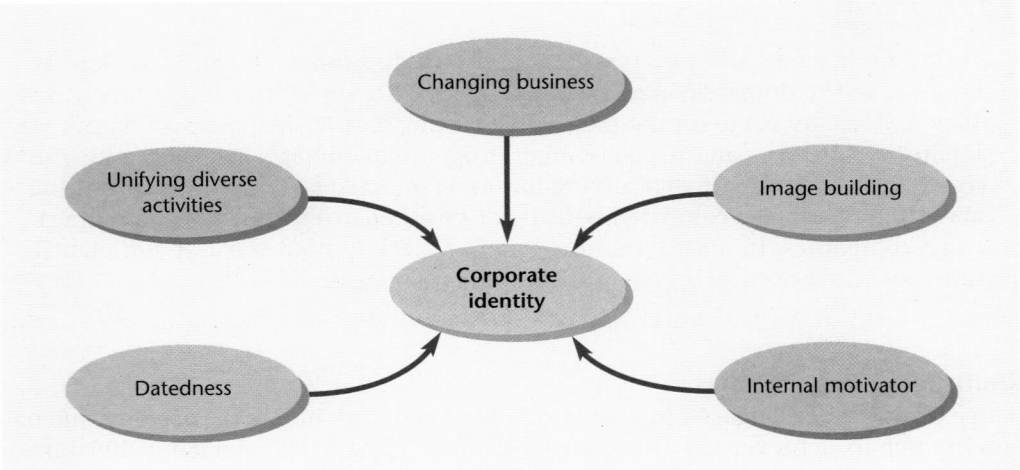

Datedness

An existing identity may come to look old fashioned and it may be considered to be having an adverse effect on publics who see it as a sign of an organisation that is being left behind.

Example

The solution to a dated identity, as ICI found in 1987, may simply be a subtle redesign of the existing identity to freshen it and modernise it, without losing its essential recognisability.

Changing or developing business

Some organisations find that their existing identities are no longer appropriate because of the way their business has evolved. As mentioned earlier, privatisation creates a strong motivation for rethinking corporate identity.

Example

British Telecommunications, for example, found that their old logo (a T in a circle) was not sufficiently dynamic for its post-privatisation business and that people still associated it with the old, allegedly inefficient BT. A new identity was commissioned to reflect the fundamental changes that had taken place in the management and customer service culture of the organisation.

Other privatised companies in industries such as water and electricity also took the opportunity for radical corporate redesign to emphasize their new-found status and to disassociate themselves from any lingering poor reputation of the state-owned industries. Mergers or acquisitions might also trigger an identity change. A merger between Smit, a Dutch offshore contractor and Brown and Root, an American underwater engineering company, created an entirely different kind of organisation from either of its parents. This was reflected in its new identity and logo as Rockwater.

Differentiation

Linked with the previous point is the fact that, as markets become more competitive, organisations strive to differentiate themselves from the competition. While this is obviously done at product and promotional levels, it is also done through corporate identity.

Example

Differentiation is another reason for British Telecommunications' identity change. In the domestic market, BT lost its monopoly status and competitors such as Mercury came on the scene. This meant that BT had to work harder to retain its customers and needed a high profile public image. The company also found itself increasingly diversifying into foreign markets, and thus had to think about how its image compared with those of other world-wide telecommunications companies. In an international arena, the T symbol was not sufficiently different and proved to be very difficult to register legally.

Unifying diverse activities

Large organisations engaged in a wide variety of activities have a particularly fine balancing act to achieve. On the one hand, they want each operating division or subsidiary company to have a certain degree of autonomy and to be seen as a specialist in its own field, yet on the other hand, they still want the divisions or subsidiaries to be seen to have the backing of the wider organisation and to benefit from its standing and reputation. An umbrella style of corporate identity can allow the divisions or subsidiaries to retain their own names and character, but visibly draws them all together under a unified house style that marks them as being related to each other.

> ### Example
>
> Unification was one of the reasons behind the identity change of the Prudential Corporation, one of the UK's largest financial institutions, in the mid-1980s. At the time, it had seven operating divisions, trading under different names, and many people who were customers of two or more of these divisions were often not aware that they were related in any way! This has been solved by the implementation of a uniform identity across all divisions, clearly marking them as part of the Pru (Traverso and White, 1990).

Image building

Clearly, a prime motivation for working on corporate image is to communicate a desired image. Careful thought about the elements of the image and the impression they convey can lead to an effective change in attitudes. This can be reinforced by using effective PR and advertising to explain the meaning of the new identity when it is launched.

Internal motivator

Finally, a corporate identity exercise, if managed properly, can be a useful means of effecting internal changes in attitudes. The process of thinking about identity, as discussed below, makes the organisation as a whole look at where it is and where it is going, and what it means to work for that organisation. Launching a new identity can represent a fresh start, or a renewed sense of purpose and direction.

FIGURE 20.5

Stages in the corporate identity change process

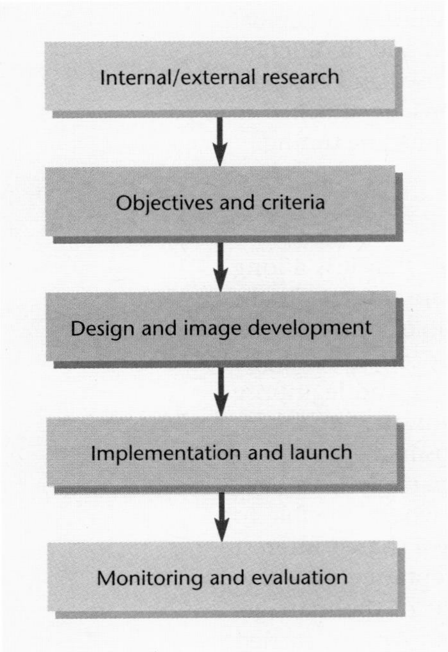

The change process

There are many good reasons for going ahead with a change in corporate identity, but the exercise is only as good as its implementation. It is a sufficiently specialised area to warrant the involvement of professional corporate identity consultants who will oversee the whole process. This subsection deals with the change process.

Figure 20.5 outlines the broad stages involved in the change process, each of which is discussed below.

Research

Before the identity change process can begin, it is essential to carry out research both internally and externally, with a variety of important publics, to establish exactly how the organisation is currently viewed, and what kind of organisation those publics would ideally like to see. Until this is done, the extent and direction of change required will be uncertain.

Setting objectives and criteria for the new identity

A formal statement sets out what the identity is to achieve and what characteristics it is to reflect. This will be based on the research undertaken, and will balance the needs of the various external publics consulted with the organisation's internal mission statement and future direction.

Design and development of the new image

It is in the design and development stage that the words and concepts are translated into a visual image. The design team may come up with a number of alternative design solutions, which may have to be tested with focus groups to see whether they evoke the right responses and which one is liked most. In practical terms too the identity has to be sufficiently flexible to be used in a variety of contexts, such as on stationery, vehicles, uniforms and products, for example. It also has to work in a range of media, in both colour and monochrome, and the logo itself has to work in a variety of sizes. This stage may take some time and involve a lot of reiteration, but it is worth it to get the design elements right. An organisation expects to have to live with a new identity for a long time. BAA for example, mentioned earlier, had to apply its new image to the exterior of airport buildings, interior signs, stationery, corporate and sales literature, souvenir merchandise, vehicles, luggage trolleys, uniforms and much more.

Implementation and launch

Much work is involved at the implementation and launch stage – in making sure that the new identity is properly installed and utilised throughout the organisation and that it is recognised and understood by internal and external publics. Staff briefing sessions are needed in order to explain the new identity and how it is to be applied and used, and then there are the practical problems of, to name but a few, replacing all the organisation's stationery stocks, repainting the fleet of delivery vans and informing all the interested publics about the new identity. The sheer scale of this task may mean that it is impossible to unveil the new identity overnight and thus a gradual roll-out during a transition period may have to be adopted.

Even if there has been a gradual roll-out, there is still likely to be an official launch date when the new identity is properly recognised and takes over from the old one. This is a good excuse for extensive advertising and a whole range of PR activities to inform publics and to reassure them that the good things they valued about the organisation have not been lost.

Monitoring and evaluation

Finally, it is important to monitor the implementation and evaluate the effects of the new identity as it settles down. This means ensuring that everyone in the organisation is applying the identity correctly and consistently, and that they are adhering to the guidelines laid down for its use (part of the design process will be the production of a manual showing exactly how the identity should be applied on different items and in different contexts). It also means carrying out research to assess how well recognised and accepted the identity has become among various publics, and what connotations are attached to it. The outcomes of this may mean going back to the design team for some fine tuning.

Problems with the change process

Even the brief description of the change process presented here shows that it is a long and potentially difficult task to redesign a corporate identity. There are several pitfalls that can make that task even more difficult, if not downright impossible, and these are summarised in Fig 20.6. It is essential, for example, for the whole process to have the full commitment of top management. If they are not prepared to drive and legitimise the exercise then there is no reason to expect anyone else in the organisation to take it seriously, or for it to take on anything other than the character of a cosmetic exercise.

It is not enough, however, just to have the commitment of top management. Staff at all levels of the organisation need to know what is going on and where possible to participate in the process, even if only at the research stage. Creating a shared interest and ownership of the new identity is essential for its eventual acceptance. If a new identity is not accepted, then it has to be the fault of some element of the management process. Perhaps the preparatory research was badly carried out (or not carried

FIGURE 20.6

Reasons for the failure of an identity change

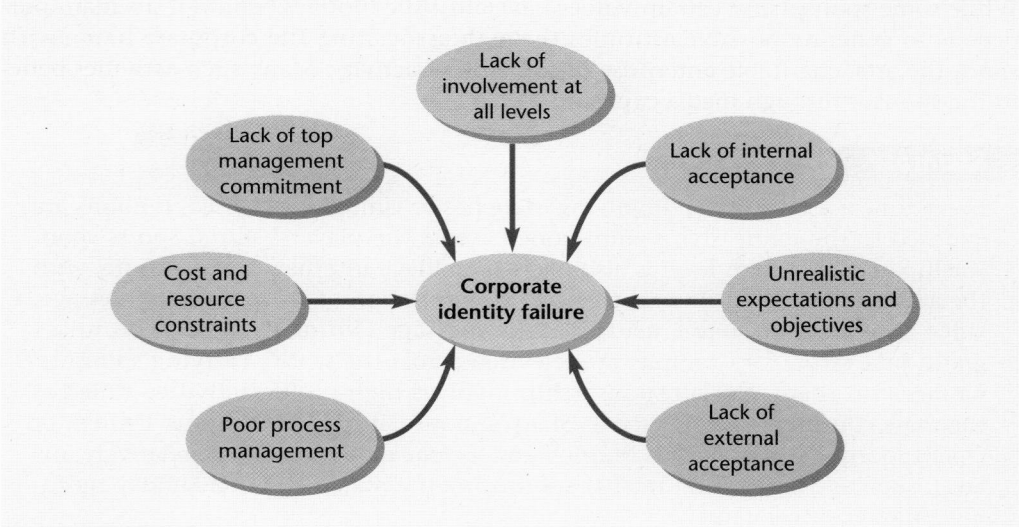

out at all) or misinterpreted. The design stage may have been skimped so that an identity was hurriedly chosen and implemented without enough thought or staff involvement. Another danger area is the implementation and launch. Perhaps staff were not given adequate briefing about the new identity or perhaps PR and other communication aimed at external publics was inadequate.

To be successful, corporate identity change needs to have, as well as top management commitment to the philosophy of change, if the right person managing it on a day-to-day basis. This is an important project and should not be given to a junior trainee as something to do between making cups of tea for the office manager. The person in charge needs to have sufficient authority and managerial skills to make it all happen and to win over the doubters. Entrusting the project to a suitably experienced manager reduces the risk of the exercise falling apart because of inadequate research, poor planning, poor control or a lack of attention to detail.

Given the ideals of commitment, thoroughness and participation already suggested, it is clear that this kind of exercise cannot be done cheaply. It is an expensive investment in the organisation's future and well-being. If management start putting unrealistic cost constraints on the work, then it is likely that corners will be cut and the outcomes will be poor and disappointing. There is a danger that management will view an identity change as a cheap way of avoiding facing up to more fundamental organisational problems. It cannot be emphasised enough, however, that corporate identity should not be used as a cosmetic means of papering over cracks. Changing identity does not compensate for bad management, inadequate or inappropriate products or a poor attitude to customer service. If an organisation has problems of this type, then it needs to do something rather more radical than simply changing the name and/or the logo. If the organisation is unrealistic about what corporate identity can do for it, then the exercise will be a failure.

SPONSORSHIP

Sponsorship is defined by Wilmshurst (1993, p. 367) as:

> . . . the provision of financial or material support by a company for some independent activity . . . not usually directly linked to the company's normal business, but support from which the sponsoring company would hope to benefit.

While some sponsorship certainly does have altruistic motives behind it, its main purpose is to generate positive attitudes through associating the corporate name with sport, the arts, charitable enterprise or some other activity. Many such activities benefit the sponsor through media exposure.

> ### Example
>
> Every time a soccer match involving Manchester United is televised, millions are exposed to the name Sharp emblazoned across the players' shirts. Sports sponsorship at such a high level is also likely to achieve international exposure, with the added benefit that there is no need for translation of an advertising message, since the corporate name usually *is* the message (Norman, 1991). Formula 1 grand prix races, for example, are televised across the world, carrying sponsors' names with them. Not all sponsorship involves high-profile activities aimed at the mass consumer sector, such as Sharp's sponsorship of Manchester United, or Opel's sponsorship of Bayern Munich and AC Milan. Some may be relatively low level, such as a small local retailer sponsoring the match ball at a Sunday morning amateur soccer game.

Sponsorship grew in popularity during the 1980s, partly because of its attractiveness as a supporting element in the promotional mix, and partly because of the growing cost of media advertising compared with the potentially greater coverage of various sports and arts activities (Meenaghan, 1991). Its growth was also helped by the tobacco companies using it as a means of achieving exposure in spite of the ban on television advertising.

There is a clear distinction between sponsorship and patronage (Wilmshurst, 1993). Patronage is the giving of gifts in whatever form, with no intention to influence the commercial success of the company. Examples might include supporting a local hospital, or allowing company sports facilities to be used by outside groups. Sponsorship does seek a return, however indirect it may be, on the investment, although it is mainly about image building rather than selling the product as such. Despite this business orientation, sponsorship may involve only indirect influence on the target audience. The name of the sponsor may only be incidental to the proceedings, for instance the Lloyds Bank-sponsored BAFTA awards, and there may be no mention at all of products or services. This creates a challenge for the marketing manager, as the effects of sponsorship tend to be long-term and, although sponsorship may reinforce a company name, it need not support any understanding of the product ranges on offer. The effect on sales, therefore, is often unclear unless the sponsorship is supported by a promotional campaign or a series of events is planned during a concentrated period.

Types of sponsorship

Four main areas of sponsorship have attracted most interest: sport, broadcast sponsorship, the arts and cause-related marketing.

Sport

With the widespread appeal of sport across all ages, areas and lifestyles, it is perhaps not surprising that sports sponsorship has grown in popularity. This is especially true when it is linked to the televising of the events. The mass audiences possible through television, for even some minority sports, enable the widespread showing of the sponsor's name.

A major sponsor of the arts, Midland Bank reaches large numbers of ABs with targeted sponsorship.

Source: Midland Bank plc.

Example

Perrier France sponsors the French Open tennis championships, which are viewed world-wide, and similarly, Vittel's sponsorship of the Monte Carlo Athletics Grand Prix meeting gained international media coverage (Walker, 1994).

Many sports attract heavy television coverage and so although the typical sponsoring costs may be high, in comparison with the cost of direct television advertising, such sponsorship can actually be very cost effective.

Example

Heineken sponsored the Rugby World Cup on a world-wide basis. It was estimated that in the UK, the television coverage of the event would deliver an audience of 83 per cent of all men within a month, each of whom would be exposed to the Heineken name at least 22 times (Miles, 1995). This audience would consist not only of individual consumers, but also of those involved in wholesaling, retailing and the licensed trade.

Sponsorship of sport has the added benefit that although people may ignore commercial breaks, they do pay attention when a 'real' programme is on, and therefore may be more likely to absorb the sponsor's name.

Walker (1994) estimates that in 1993, UK companies spent over £250 million on sports sponsorship within a sector that world-wide is growing at 10 per cent per year. One of the problems, however, is that as events become bigger and more international in their coverage, sponsorship becomes more expensive. There is thus a danger that as events such as the Olympic games take on more official sponsors in order to cover their costs, the impact for any one of those sponsors becomes less. The 1995 Rugby World Cup had seven main sponsors in addition to Heineken, including Visa, Toyota and Coca-Cola. Nevertheless, it was estimated that the Rugby World Cup would have had a world-wide television audience of three billion, which perhaps makes sharing the sponsorship worthwhile.

Example

Highland Distillers use rugby sponsorship to promote their brand of whisky, The Famous Grouse. As well as being one of the World Cup's sponsors, The Famous Grouse is also the sponsor of the Scottish team. The organisation chose rugby in the late 1980s partly because at that time rugby was underexploited in terms of sponsorship, and partly because they felt that the profile of the rugby enthusiast was similar to that of a whisky drinker. Both audiences are largely male, aged between 25 and 40 and in the A and B socioeconomic groups, hence some synergy exists (Buxton, 1995).

If the sponsorship of tournaments does not appeal, then there is always the option of sponsoring individual athletes or players, or of sponsoring teams or leagues.

Example

In the UK, soccer is a prime target for corporate sponsors, who can come in at a level that suits their budgets. At the top end of the game, Carling lager spent £15 million to sponsor the Premier League, thus guaranteeing themselves all kinds of media coverage, not least whenever the football results were announced. Sponsoring an individual team comes a little cheaper. Buchanan (1995) estimates that to sponsor one of the top six Premier League clubs, such as Manchester United, can cost up to £1 million, whereas a top third division side might cost around £60 000. Clearly, a team like Manchester United generates vast PR potential for its sponsors. It attracts huge crowds to its matches, features regularly in UK televised matches as well as in the sports media, and achieves European exposure too. Nevertheless, even one of the smaller clubs, if carefully chosen, can create exposure.

On a more limited basis, companies can sponsor match programmes, balls, or even the corner flags. Smaller or non-league clubs are appealing for local businesses who want to reinforce their role in the community, and even large organisations can value this.

Example

Hutchison Communications sponsor Darlington which is not one of the higher profile clubs in the league, simply because it is their local club and they want to contribute to the local community. The name of Ericcsson Mobile Phones, painted across the roof of the stand at Brentford Town football club, is seen by many of the 47.6 million air passengers flying in and out of Heathrow every year!

All of this works well as long as the sport and the individual clubs continue to maintain a 'clean' image. A riot in the stands or a punch-up on the pitch generate the kind of publicity and media coverage of the type, 'What kind of depths has the game sunk to' that sponsors will not want to be associated with. The fracas between Eric Cantona and a member of the crowd in January 1995, for example, hit the headlines across the world for all the wrong reasons. This, however, is one of the risks of any kind of celebrity endorsement.

The main advantage of sports sponsorship remains the ability to reach large audiences, and sometimes to communicate with audiences that normal advertising scheduling would find difficult.

Example

The A and B socioeconomic groups can often be reached through sponsorship of tennis and golf tournaments (Wilmshurst, 1993). Golf, however, is a very expensive sport to sponsor but does have a very upmarket and global appeal. The whisky brand, Johnnie Walker, spends £11 million on golf around the world, while Benson and Hedges International spent £650 000 on prize money alone in 1994 (Wighton, 1995). Volvo's next four years sponsoring the European tour will cost them about £20 million.

Despite the rising costs, organisations can still gain a lot of value for money, quite apart from the media coverage.

Example

Toyota sponsors the Toyota World Match Play Championship at Wentworth. The competition is used as a focus for a much wider range of marketing activities, such as incentives, promotions and corporate hospitality aimed at key distributors and fleet buyers from around the world. To spread the impact of the event throughout the year, Toyota dealers sponsor tournaments at their local clubs, with the winners getting the opportunity to play in a pro-am competition at Wentworth just before the main championship begins (Wighton, 1995).

Broadcast sponsorship

Broadcast sponsorship, sponsoring programmes or series on television or the radio, is a relatively new area in the UK. In 1993, it was thought to be worth around £70 million with television specifically accounting for £40 million (Carter, 1994). In 1995, television sponsorship was about £50 million, and was estimated to be growing at about 15 per cent a year (M. Barrett, 1996). This is still, however, a minor proportion of the channels' commercial income, representing just under 2 per cent of their total advertising revenue. This figure varies from channel to channel. MTV, a satellite channel with a pan-European youth audience, generates 10 per cent of its advertising revenue from sponsorship, whereas for the terrestrial Channel 4, the figure is only 1 per cent (M. Barrett, 1996).

In other parts of Europe, the level of sponsorship is much higher than in the UK. Some in the industry claim that the restrictions imposed by the Independent Television Commission (ITC) are too tight. The ITC rules say, for example, that an organisation cannot sponsor programmes directly relating to their products (but a 'good match' is acceptable.

Thus, Lego's sponsorship of *Tots TV* was acceptable, but PPP (a private medical insurance company) were asked to terminate their sponsorship of *Peak Practice*, a medical drama, because of a potential conflict of interest.

Furthermore, a sponsor's products cannot feature in the show, nor can sponsors have any editorial control over the programme's content. Satellite has a little more flexibility and is allowed to incorporate the sponsor's name into the programme title and to have up to two minutes of sponsor's credits. However, the ITC rules are taken from an EU Directive and are thus the same as those imposed in other parts of Europe, although they may be enforced more rigorously in the UK. In 1994, for example, the ITC fined Granada TV £500 000 for repeatedly breaching product placement rules in its breakfast programme (Fry, 1995). The ITC is in the process of reviewing the rules, and may be prepared to relax them somewhat to make sponsorship a little more appealing to industry (Barrett, 1995).

Even within the current regulatory framework, broadcast sponsorship still has much to offer. As with advertising, of course, it is reaching potentially large audiences and creating product awareness. Further than that, however, it also has the potential to help to enhance the product's image and message by association. *London's Burning*, a drama series about fire fighters, for example, is sponsored by Commercial Union, an insurance company. Another advantage of broadcast sponsorship is that viewers are under the impression that the sponsorship actually goes towards funding the programme, a belief that creates an enormous amount of goodwill towards the company on the part of viewers (Carter, 1994). To get the best out of broadcast sponsorship, however, it should be integrated into a wider package of marketing and promotional activities. This might mean using characters or themes from the programme in promotional materials. This was one of the reasons behind Cadbury's bid in early 1996 to become the first sponsor of *Coronation Street*, a popular soap with a regular audience of 18 million. Part of the proposed £10 million deal would be the right to use characters from the programme in other marketing activities (*Marketing*, 1996).

One of the fears broadcasters have, particularly when thinking of large deals such as Cadbury's and *Coronation Street*, is that advertising revenues will fall. If Cadbury's spend £10 million on sponsorship, will they then spend £10 million less on standard advertising? Perhaps one of the potential advantages for broadcasters is that sponsorship allows them to build better relationships with advertisers, and thus they might be able to negotiate sponsorship packages that guarantee a certain level of advertising spend too.

The arts

Arts sponsorship is a growing area, second only to sport in terms of its value in the UK. In 1994, arts sponsorship was worth around £50 million, and it is predicted to rise to £60 million by 1999 (Denny, 1995b). The art forms covered range widely from music, including rock, classical and opera, to festivals, theatre, film and literature. Table 20.2 shows the kinds of activities covered by arts sponsorships and their value.

Sponsorship in kind is an interesting growth area. As Thorncroft (1995c) reports, for example, London Underground donated free advertising space for a festival; Ibstock Building Projects supplied clay for sculpture, and British Steel have given structural steel for building galleries. Similarly, Derwent Valley Holdings have donated office space to The Orchestra of the Age of Enlightenment, along with £30 000 of other sponsorship money.

> ### Example
>
> According to Mintel, Marks & Spencer is by far the most active sponsor of the UK arts, with 194 events and organisations sponsored during 1994/95. Both Pepsi and Coca-Cola are active in supporting rock music, while classical orchestras benefit from funding from companies like British Telecom, which has a

£1.8 million arts sponsorship programme, and BMW (Denny, 1995b). Such polarisation is hardly surprising, considering the likely target audiences for those organisations. Funding might, of course, relate to specific activities or projects rather than being a general contribution to costs. The City of Birmingham Symphony Orchestra's 1991 recording of Haydn's Creation, for example, was sponsored by Croft Original sherry. The costs of making such a large-scale recording can be very high, and the recording company, in this case EMI, would be very happy to share those costs in return for featuring the sponsor in the sleeve notes and on the cover. Another possibility is to commission a new work. The Woolwich Building Society, for example, paid £5000 to John Dankworth to compose the Woolwich Concerto for clarinet.

Arts sponsorship is not just about music or 'safe options', however. Häagen Dazs has sponsored an *avant garde* contemporary art exhibition at the Tate Gallery; Beck's Bier similarly sponsors *avant garde* artists; Toshiba has a £500 000 sponsorship of the Institute for Contemporary Arts; Absolut Vodka sponsors art graduates, and Barclays Bank sponsors a competition for new playwrights (Hewison, 1995).

TABLE 20.2

Sponsorship by art form in the UK, March 1993–March 1994

	Cash sponsorship £m	Sponsorship in kind £m	Total sponsorship £m
Music	9.65	0.86	10.51
Museums	5.78	1.17	6.95
Opera	6.22	0.05	6.27
Festivals	5.19	0.94	6.13
Theatre	5.03	0.57	5.60
Awards/competitions	3.44	–	3.44
Dance	2.37	0.11	2.48
Film	2.64	0.36	3.00
Visual arts	2.19	0.24	2.43
Arts centres	1.48	0.18	1.66
Services	0.10	0.02	0.12
Heritage	0.64	0.08	0.72
Literature	0.38	0.06	0.44
Photography	0.30	0.16	0.46
Crafts	0.01	*	*
Other	3.34	1.37	4.77
Total	48.76	6.16	54.92

* Under £5000
Source: ABSA/Mintel, reproduced with kind permission.

What all of these companies have in common is that they are trying to reach the young intelligentsia, potentially a lucrative market for them, as well as trying to enhance their own images as sophisticated, forward-looking organisations. A wider, if perhaps somewhat less discerning, youth audience can be reached through rock music. Youth audiences are notoriously difficult to reach and to communicate with

Music sponsorship

If a company wants to create an impression on the youth market, it could well decide to enter into music sponsorship. In 1996, some 750 000 people were estimated to have attended around 12 major music festivals, such as Mastercard's Masters of Music festival which featured Eric Clapton, Bob Dylan, Alanis Morissette and The Who performing in Hyde Park. As they reach an audience that is sceptical of mainstream above the line promotion, music and sport have both emerged as powerful ways of marketing communication.

The important consideration for marketers in deciding whether to sponsor these events is understanding the link between the product and the music. To gain maximum value, it is necessary to ensure that the event features in all aspects of the communications mix, including packaging, advertising and sales promotion. This means exploiting the association before, during and after the music event.

Sponsoring festivals can be particularly useful in boosting unprompted awareness among the target group. The benefit of association between the brand and the event is often enough to justify involvement, but where that can be extended it can add further value to the sponsorship. Sometimes, this can be achieved by a spin-off recording that is released soon after the event.

The purpose of Virgin's V96 festival at Chelmsford was to promote Virgin's newly acquired stake in Eurostar. A special train brought fans from continental Europe, using special tickets that could only be purchased at a Virgin Megastore. The event was also used to launch Virgin's new record label, V2 Records.

Although music sponsorship has not yet reached the high levels of sports sponsorship, it is likely to feature more strongly in the future as more companies identify its potential for communicating with a notoriously difficult audience.

Source: Curtis (1996).

---

because of their cynicism about advertising. Even sponsorship can backfire, since, as Thorncroft (1995a) reports, the under-25s react against over-branding by sponsors. Carlsberg, the lager brand owned by Allied Domecq, seems to have overcome this hurdle, and has successfully sponsored both the Reading Festival and the Monsters of Rock concert. In 1995, Carlsberg spent around £300 000 on rock music sponsorship (Thorncroft, 1995a).

Example

Lloyds Bank is an active patron of the arts with a particular wish to reach the youth audience. At various times, Lloyds has been involved with the BAFTA film and television awards, the Lloyds Bank Film Challenge, the Clothes Show Live exhibition, the British Fashion Awards, and the Young Musician of the Year (Tait, 1995). It is also the title sponsor, with an investment of £1 million, in Knebworth '96, a major one-day rock festival. Lloyds aborted its sponsorship of Knebworth '95 because it felt that the bands involved were not sufficiently high profile. Despite this setback, Lloyds still hopes to benefit from the 1996 event, reaching an audience of 18 to 45 year olds, not only through television and radio broadcasts, videos and recordings, but also through the distribution of free tickets to young account holders, corporate hospitality at the event and tickets as incentives to young bank staff members.

Even at this level, however, sponsorship is not easy, nor is it guaranteed success.

Mazda Cars met with problems in large-scale sponsorship of a festival set up as a commercial entity. They invested £250 000 in the Stately Homes Music Festival, which not only proved unpopular with its dealerships, thus presumably failing to achieve corporate hospitality objectives, but also ran into financial difficulty, meaning losses for its sponsor (Thorncroft, 1995b).

With arts sponsorship there are a number of opportunities to present the sponsoring organisation, including on stage, in programmes, through associated merchandise including videos and CDs, around venues, and even on tickets. There are also advantages in hosting key customers and suppliers at high profile events, by offering the best seats and perhaps hosting a reception during the interval or after the show.

The popularity of the arts has grown in recent years. While the attractiveness of highbrow cultural activities to A, B and C socioeconomic groups is evident, their ever widening appeal has created new opportunities to reach different target groups in a quality way. Despite this, however, the arts cannot be complacent about their importance to corporate sponsors. During difficult trading times, organisations such as IBM and British Gas have been known to cut their arts budgets substantially. Thorncroft (1995d) also points to a change in corporate thinking, with a shift in emphasis towards supporting charities and 'good causes' with more immediate public appeal rather than the arts, which might be perceived as élitist. He refers also to the difficulty of assessing the marketing benefits of arts sponsorship, and the fact that it is easier and cheaper to purchase tailormade corporate hospitality packages than to sponsor one's own event. Nevertheless, he does see some positive signs. Sponsorship from large, London-based organisations may be falling, but there is growth in the sponsorship of regional and local arts groups from smaller, provincial based organisations.

Cause-related marketing

Linkages between organisations and charities benefit both parties. If, for example, a company runs a sales promotion along the lines of 'We'll donate 10p to this charity for every token you send in', the charity gains from the cash raised and from an increased public profile. The consumer feels that their purchase has greater significance than simple self-gratification and feels good about having 'given', while the company benefits from the increased sales generated by the promotion and from the extra goodwill created from associating its brands with a good cause. It is a kind of indirect sponsorship.

J&B Rare Scotch Whisky associated itself with raising money to help endangered species such as the black rhino by making a donation for each promotional bottle sold. The impact of such activities is greater if there is a clear synergy between the brand and the charity, or at least if the charity has a particular appeal to the same target audience as the brand. Pet foods and animal charities are natural partners, for example, and Tesco's 'Computers for Schools' promotion appeals to the supermarket's family shoppers, directly benefiting their own communities.

Not all **cause-related marketing** is linked with sales promotions, however. Many large organisations set up charitable foundations or donate cash directly to community or charitable causes. Others might pay for advertising space for charities, whether on television, radio, press or posters. This is important at a time when consumers are becoming more conscious of the ethical and 'corporate citizenship' records of the companies they patronise.

> ### Example
>
> As Richards (1995) reports, Procter & Gamble have themselves benefited from their investment in community orientated projects, such as crime prevention and drugs awareness. They have strengthened their corporate image and their relationships with other businesses and their local authority as well as with national government. This in turn means that they have a greater say in what happens in their own community. Their charitable works have also generated a considerable amount of positive PR, and P&G even feel that it has made recruitment of employees easier.
>
> British Airways, as a global operator, teamed up with UNICEF, a global charity. A scheme encouraging long haul passengers to donate unwanted foreign coins raised over £1 million in one year. The airline also 'donates' unfilled seats on flights to UNICEF personnel and allows the charity to use any spare cargo space (Fletcher, 1995b).

Organisations clearly do not just take an altruistic view of their charity involvement. As with any other marketing activity, it should be planned with clear objectives and expected outcomes. Midland Bank, for example, has a clear charities policy to screen and select which causes should receive donations or other support. In terms of focusing its efforts on clearly defined areas, Midland assessed broad sectors in terms of their media and public appeal, their marketing potential and their topicality. The outcome of this was that Midland selected youth, the elderly and disability as priority areas. Then individual charities were assessed to select one within each of those three sectors that would receive substantial support for a specific project over a three-year period (Lane Fox, 1996). The idea behind all this is one of partnership, with mutual responsibility and accountability, rather than a one-off donation of the type, 'Here's the cash, do what you want with it'.

The role of sponsorship

Despite the connotations of charity, community support, entertainment and fun, sponsorship is still a serious commercial tool for the marketing manager. As with any other promotional activity, it is important to specify clearly the objectives of pursuing a sponsorship campaign and to plan the activities carefully to ensure that they are relevant and that they are achieved. Evaluation, however, can be a problem with sponsorship, as it is often used in support of other promotional activities, and thus isolating the sponsorship effect may be difficult.

Sponsorship offers the potential to support the broader PR strategy, both directly and indirectly. Directly, it can provide a venue for meeting key customers or suppliers in an informal setting, or more generally improve awareness and attitudes towards the sponsoring company. Indirectly, it can support employee, government and community relations through emphasizing the sponsor's enlightened sense of social responsibility and good corporate citizenship. Furthermore, it can support wider marketing objectives through increasing product awareness and even enhancing product and corporate image.

A number of factors need to be considered before a sponsorship decision is made, as summarised in Fig 20.7.

The first consideration is *relevance*, which is perhaps the most important factor. There needs to be a match between the chosen sponsorship and the target audience that the organisation is seeking to influence.

Example

Tango's sponsorship of *The Word* on Channel 4 was an ideal partnership since both were trying to create a rather outrageous image to appeal to the youth market. McDonald's and Burger King's commitment to children's charities and projects to help teenagers match their desired images as family-orientated companies with a responsible attitude. Occasionally, however, relevance can be a burden. The ruling body controlling women's tennis turned down a three-year $10 million offer of sponsorship from Tampax for fear of losing other sponsors of individual tournaments within the tour (Thompson-Noel, 1995). This appears to be an incredible decision, coming from a sport that was quite happy to accept cigarette sponsorship (from Philip Morris' Virginia Slims brand) for many years.

The *length of impact* made may also be a consideration. One-off events, unless they are very high profile such as Lloyds Bank's sponsorship of Knebworth '96, mentioned earlier, tend not to have the capacity to build the continuity and establish the name familiarity that sponsoring a series of events would bring. Nevertheless, as Toyota have shown with their handling of the Toyota World Match Play Championship at Wentworth, mentioned earlier, other promotional activities and events can be linked into the main one to increase and spread the impact.

Uniqueness might be desirable, but as already mentioned, it is not always possible to be a sole sponsor, especially for large international events or where the costs are very high. There is an expectation, for example, that the sponsorship of grand prix racing and its teams will be shared by a range of companies, both within and outside the motor industry. It is difficult, therefore, for any one sponsor to establish a higher profile than the rest unless a particular driver keeps winning. With the Rugby World Cup, however, Heineken managed to raise its profile by not only being one of the competition's sponsors, but also sponsoring the UK television coverage of the tournament for £2 million. This was reinforced by on-pack promotions and point of sale posters emphasizing the link.

FIGURE 20.7

Factors influencing sponsorship choice

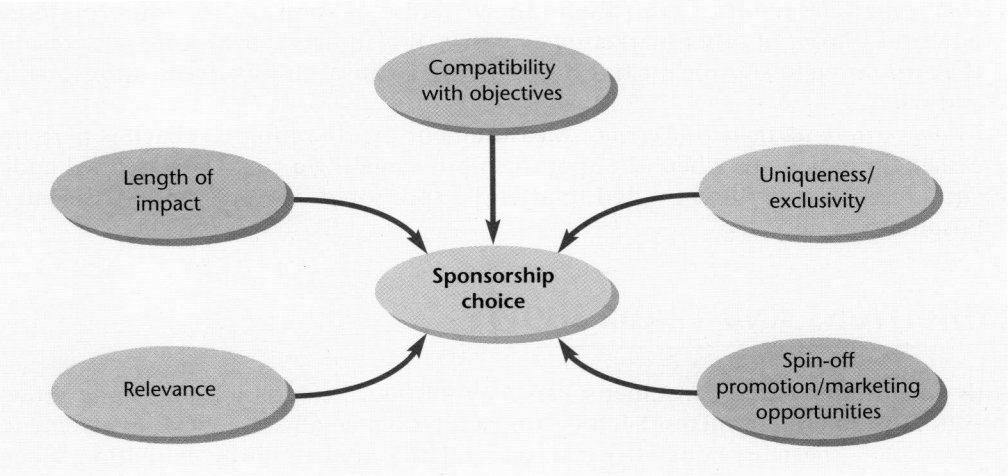

Compare all that with the unique benefits derived by Coca-Cola from its sole sponsorship of the English soccer league cup competition. The competition extends over most of the season, and when each round of results is announced, it is always under the title of The Coca-Cola Cup, with no sponsorship confusion.

It is also important to consider the potential for *spin-off promotion* and other marketing activities from the sponsorship. Sporting and cultural events provide a focus for corporate hospitality, as well as an opportunity for sales promotion themes. A company sponsoring the Olympics, for example, might run an on-pack competition to win a trip to the games. Events might provide internal marketing opportunities as well. Lloyds Bank, for example, realised that the opportunity to attend Knebworth would be a good incentive for rewarding their highest performing staff, many of whom are under 30 and would relate to this kind of event. Charity sponsorship can provide employees with a focus for fundraising efforts, thus helping to encourage a sense of community (and fun) within the workplace.

Finally, it is always important to ensure that the activity is *compatible* with the sponsor's overall promotional objectives. It is easy to get involved with sponsorship because the MD loves soccer or fancies a guaranteed box at the opera for the season. This will cloud judgement over the real fit with the commercial objectives, and call the cost effectiveness of the sponsorship into question. In this sense, sponsorship decisions should be as calculated and unemotional as any other advertising decision. Midland Bank's seemingly clinical approach to selecting charities to support actually ensures that its money is as well spent as possible and that all parties will gain the maximum benefit from it. It is extremely unlikely that the bank or its chosen charities will feel disappointed with either the outcome of the sponsorship or the other party's attitude or commitment.

EVALUATING SPONSORSHIP

Whatever type or method of sponsorship is used, however, it is important to establish the most appropriate means of evaluating results. A number of methods are possible.

1 *Media exposure measurement*. Establishing how much air time on television or radio, or how many column inches in the print media were given to the event is one measure. The problem is, however, that this measurement takes place after the event, and at best can help to decide whether to continue with future involvement.
2 *Assessing communication results*. Pre-and post-tests on awareness, image etc. can be undertaken to assess whether the sponsorship was noticed and what improvement it made to awareness levels, attitudes and opinions about the sponsor.
3 *Measuring sales results*. Given the indirect nature of sponsorship amid the more powerful impact of other marketing activities, it is unlikely measuring sales results that would yield significant findings proving a causal link between sponsorship and sales.
4 *Feedback from participating groups*. Measurement by obtaining feedback is perhaps easiest to implement where the sponsorship is targeting a small well-defined audience, for example those invited to attend a sponsored concert and its associated hospitality.

EXHIBITIONS AND TRADE SHOWS

Both organisational and consumer sellers may introduce **exhibitions and trade shows** into their promotional mixes. Such events range from small-scale local involvement, for example a specialist bookseller taking a stall at a model railway exhibition, to an annual national trade show serving a specific industry, such as the DIY and Home Improvement Show, or Pakex for the packaging industry. In either case, the exhibition may become an important element of the year's marketing activities, as this section will show. Even those who specialise in organising and supporting exhibitions have their own exhibitions!

> ### Example
>
> Show 95 brought together all kinds of specialists from stand contractors to designers, lighting specialists and even carpet suppliers. The target audience was organisations which were going to be attending trade exhibitions themselves and needed to purchase goods and services to support their attendance. To boost the appeal of the show, a series of seminars was also offered, giving advice on all aspects of exhibition attendance and management, for example budgeting, design, dealing with visitors to the stand, tracking sales leads, evaluating success, and exhibiting overseas (Bryant, 1994).

Benefits of attending and participating in exhibitions

Benefits for the small business

Exhibitions and shows can be of particular importance to the smaller business which may not have the resources to fund an expensive marketing communications programme. The exhibition can be used as a cost-effective means of building more 'presence' and reputation with the trade, and to generate potential sales leads. Small businesses in the UK, however, seem less inclined to use exhibitions than those from other European countries. According to Hall (1995), in 1994 UK small businesses spent about 10 per cent of their marketing budgets on exhibiting whereas the French spent 20 per cent and the Italians 30 per cent.

Benefits of international exhibitions

International exhibitions can be particularly valuable because they bring together participants from all over the world who might otherwise never meet, and can thus lead to export deals.

Exhibitions are a major showcase for motor manufacturers and generate enormous spin-off publicity.

Source: Daewoo Motors.

Alimentaria 96, with its theme of Mediterranean diet, took place in Barcelona and involved 3500 exhibitors from 50 countries. To help visitors focus on whatever interested them, the exhibition was divided into nine separate sections including, for example, frozen foods, meats, beverages and wine. A database in the exhibition's business centre allowed visitors to access information about participants, their businesses and their brands.

For those who want a smaller, more focused exhibition, then ISM, held in Cologne in 1996, brought together over 1200 suppliers of cakes, biscuits and confectionery (*The Grocer*, 1995b).

Cologne also hosted Domotechnica in 1995, an exhibition of white goods, featuring 1250 manufacturers from 50 countries. Two major exhibitors there were Whirlpool and Electrolux. Whirlpool was there to make a brand leadership statement, while Electrolux was there to launch 100 new products (Gofton, 1995a).

Trade exhibitions and shows

Although some exhibitions, such as the Motor Show, the Ideal Home Exhibition, and Clothes Show Live, are open to the general public for part or all of their duration, the serious business of exhibiting takes place in organisational markets. The National Menswear Exhibition may be less well known to the consumer than Clothes Show Live, but it is of far greater importance to manufacturers and retailers in making sure that the right goods reach the right shops at the right time.

For the manufacturer, attending exhibitions provides a formal opportunity to display the product range and to discuss applications and needs with prospective customers in a neutral environment. Depending on the type of show and the care that an organisation puts into planning its presence there, an exhibition provides a powerful and cost-effective way of getting the message across and making new contacts that may subsequently turn into sales.

Comparison of the benefits of exhibitions and personal selling

Despite the increasing cost of attending shows, a number of benefits can be gained from attendance, which will be compared with what can be achieved through personal selling, the main alternative in organisational marketing.

Product launch and demonstration

An exhibition, as well as providing an organisation with an opportunity to launch or test market new products, enables it to set up working demonstrations of products. This gives potential customers the chance to have hands-on experience of the product

Black & Decker used the DIY and Home Improvement Show in 1995 to launch a new range of consumer power tools to independent retailers. Black & Decker staff demonstrated the tools, but visitors to the exhibition were also given the chance to try them out (Burnside, 1995b).

and can act as a focal point for discussing applications with individuals or small groups. With a product that is bulky or difficult to set up, a sales representative cannot always provide such demonstrations when visiting potential customers.

Learning experience

The event allows the exhibitor to be present alongside major competitors, learning of new developments and trends and even making comparisons. Taking time to visit other exhibitors' stands can provide a wealth of information that sales representatives would not necessarily pick up in their day-to-day operations.

Lead generation

A valuable aspect of an exhibition is that it concentrates many potential new customers in one place over a short period of time. A small company with a small sales force simply does not have the time or resources to generate and follow up large numbers of geographically dispersed leads from scratch. At an exhibition, potential buyers come to you because they are interested, and an initial face-to-face meeting can take place. Even if that meeting does not directly generate a sale, the ice has been broken, the lead has been qualified, and the relationship can be further developed by the sales force after the exhibition. The advantage of an exhibition as a lead generator becomes even more obvious with international events. For a UK company, the cost of attending an exhibition in Frankfurt might be higher than that of one held in London, but the time and effort saved, not to mention the uncertainty involved in trying to locate and follow up foreign leads, should more than compensate. Attendance at a foreign exhibition can be an excellent way for an inexperienced organisation to find its first export customers.

Relationship building

Even with existing customers, goodwill and relationship building can be furthered if customers are invited to the exhibition stand. Hospitality is an equally important element of the exhibition, and many organisations host parties or receptions for key customers, suppliers or the trade press to foster good relationships. There are also informal, personal networks to develop, renew and refresh. As discussed in Chapter 4, personal relationships between people who work for different organisations within an industry can help to spread information around as well as improving the commercial relationship between their firms.

Visitors' sense of purpose and absorption in the atmosphere

An exhibition takes place in a neutral location over a clearly defined period of time. It is important enough to draw in decision makers and people within an industry who might otherwise be difficult to see. People are there because they want to be, and are there for the purposes of gathering information and making contacts. The atmosphere can be vibrant, busy and fun, heightening the sense of excitement and stimulation. All of this adds to the visitor's sense of enjoyment and fulfilment. The sales representative, on the other hand, could be calling on someone, in their own workplace, who is extremely busy and reluctant to be seen. The representative might have problems attracting and retaining attention and interest, because the phone never stops ringing, or the manager has made it clear that time is precious and there is a problem on the production line that really must be sorted out immediately.

Market presence

A reasonable objective, particularly for a small company or a new entrant into an industry, is to build awareness, both of the organisation and of the products offered. The larger multi-product company commonly finds that, although the company and its main products are known, there may be several 'blind spots' in the range and thus the exhibition can be used to display them. By comparison, there is a limit to what the sales representative can achieve in this respect. The representative can certainly try to display the full product range to a customer or potential customer, but in terms of raising the organisation's profile within the industry, it would take a long-term determined effort by the entire sales force to achieve as much as a single three-day exhibition could.

PR spin-offs

As the high point in an industry's year, the major national or international exhibition will receive a great deal of publicity within the trade press at least. An organisation with a particularly creative stand or with something exciting to unveil at the show should be able to generate substantial coverage. Some shows generate much more widespread publicity. The Motor Show in the UK, for example, usually has a whole BBC programme devoted to it on a Sunday afternoon when the exhibition is on. This gives valuable air-time to a wide variety of exhibitors, presenting their stands and products to a mass audience.

The hospitality aspects discussed earlier are also a part of the PR effort, whether they centre around customers and suppliers, or cultivating trade press relations.

Corporate boost

Although working at an exhibition can be exhausting, it is different from the day-to-day jobs that most people do. Even for sales representatives, it provides an opportunity to work with colleagues rather than alone, and to meet customers without the slog of travelling. Participating in an exciting event, benefiting from the hospitality, and getting together with old acquaintances, all help to boost morale, especially if the exhibition has been a commercial success too.

Importance of exhibitions to organisations

Given these potential benefits it is perhaps surprising that exhibitions do not take a more prominent role in organisations' marketing plans. The overall figures for UK business generally are no more impressive than those for small businesses (quoted earlier). Exhibitions only take up about 8 per cent of the marketing budget of UK organisations, whereas the figures for other countries are: France, 17 per cent, Germany, 21 per cent, Japan, 25 per cent and the USA, 26 per cent (John, 1996). Nevertheless, the exhibition sector in the UK is quite healthy, as shown in Table 20.3 which demonstrates how the number of exhibitions and visitors in the UK evolved between 1991 and 1994.

In terms of performance, the two major UK venues, the NEC in Birmingham and Earls Court in London, compare very favourably with the other 12 members of the European Major Exhibition Centres Association (Gofton, 1995b). Table 20.4 shows how they rank against each other on various criteria.

According to John (1996), over 100 000 companies exhibit at UK events, of which 18 per cent are from overseas. Furthermore, 10 per cent of UK exhibition visitors are foreign, further underlining the role of exhibitions in helping to generate export leads.

TABLE 20.3

Number of UK exhibitions and visitors, 1991–1995

	1991	1992	1993	1994	1995
Exhibitions	660	672	671	691	733
Visitors (millions)	9.39	9.15	9.51	10.28	9.71

Source: Exhibition Industry Federation, reprinted with kind permission.

TABLE 20.4
International exhibition venues

Note: Venues are in rank order on each criterion. 1 = highest, 14 = lowest.

	No. of exhibitions	Gross exhibition area	No. of exhibitors	No. of visitors	Turnover 1994
NEC Birmingham	1	5	2	2	4
Earls Court	2	12	7	4	3
Paris	3	3	4	1	6
Milan	4	1	3	6	2
Utrecht	5	11	9	10	5
Brussels	6	10	11	3	10
Madrid	7	13	6	5	9
Barcelona	8	9	8	8	11
Frankfurt	9	2	1	9	1
Leipzig	10	7	12	14	12
Paris-Nord	11	4	5	11	8
Basle	12	6	13	12	7
Bologna	13	8	10	7	13
Lyon	14	14	14	3	14

Source: European Major Exhibition Centre Association, reprinted with kind permission.

Table 20.5 looks more closely at the results of a survey undertaken by the Exhibition Industry Federation (EIF), showing outcomes and attitudes to exhibitions by sector.

Reasons for attending exhibitions

The EIF also looked at the reasons why organisations attend exhibitions. These are shown in Table 20.6 alongside the remarkably similar results of a US survey reported by Hart (1993). There has to be more of a reason to attend the show than 'our competitors do' or 'we always go'. Nevertheless, the cost of exhibiting needs to be considered in comparison with alternative ways, if indeed there are any, of achieving the same objectives.

TABLE 20.5
Exhibition statistics by sector

	Engineering	Computing	Food
Cost per contact (£)	41	35	62
Cost per sale (£)	215	161	182
Average annual budget (£'000)	25.0	44.8	20.3
Spend per exhibition (£'000)	7.4	n/a	3.0
How worthwhile (%)			
Exceptionally	2	3	7
Very	33	35	48
Fairly	40	38	31
Marginally	19	17	14
Not	2	4	0
Under review	3	3	2

Source: Exhibition Industry Federation, reprinted with kind permission.

TABLE 20.6
Why organisations use exhibitions

UK survey	Per cent	US survey	Per cent
Sales leads	83	Gain qualified leads	71
Presence in the market	70	Maintain Image	63
Launch new products	35	Intensify awareness	60
Direct selling	25	Presence in the market	56
		Launch new products	31
		Direct selling	25

Source: UK survey: Exhibition Industry Federation; US survey: Hart (1993).

There are many factors to consider before deciding to attend an exhibition. Some of the more important criteria are (Wilmshurst, 1993):

- type of visitors and previous attendance patterns
- participation by main competitors
- advice from agents, trade and local representatives
- exhibition organiser's and independent assessment of previous events
- the promotion and organisation of the event
- the expected costs to be incurred and the objectives to be realised from the event.

Importance of planning for exhibitors

These reasons for attendance are put into sharp perspective by an examination of the reasons for poor exhibition performance (Dudley, 1990), as shown in Table 20.7. These areas of potential disappointment clearly demonstrate that central to any exhibition decision is the willingness to plan fully, well in advance of the event, including making sure that all participating personnel are fully briefed to handle the event for its duration. Inadequate preparation, even down to poor stand lighting and decor or a shortage of support material, is going to detract from the performance and pull at the event. If added to that there is a parismonious approach that tries to cut costs through poor quality space, displays and too few staff, it is easy to see how disappointment might arise.

TABLE 20.7
Reasons for poor exhibition performance

- Inadequate statement of objectives
- Poor quality visitors
- Bad location of the stand
- Ineffective stand quality/design
- Poor personnel performance
- Lack of follow-up of leads/enquiries
- Ignoring the competition: they get the visitors
- Poor recognition of company by buyers
- Poor corporate identity leading to low recall
- Poor organisation/control of exhibition logistics
- Inadequate staffing arrangements
- Inadequate budget/cost controls

Source: Dudley (1990).

Preparation might also mean co-ordinating the exhibition with the selling effort, making sure that sales representatives invite customers to visit the stand for example, or with advertising, by featuring participating in the exhibition in advertisements. In all cases, accurate records need to be kept of the visitors to the stand so that the sales force can follow up leads within a short period of time to take full advantage of the contacts. An exhibition should not be seen as an opportunity for the sales force to get away and have a good time, although enjoyment is not precluded! A sobering thought for those inclined to treat exhibition attendance as a holiday is provided by the following statements:

> '**A 100m² stand costing around £30 000 in visible costs is an investment of £10 000 a day or £1000 for every hour the show is open and that is before you have included the thousands of pounds of hidden costs**'
> (Richard John of consultancy ECS, quoted by Bishop, 1995).

Finally, more flexible mobile exhibitions, whether taking the form of specially fitted caravan, or a shopping centre display or a display set up in a hotel room, provide many of the advantages of meeting potential customers without the costs associated with high profile, national exhibitions.

CHAPTER SUMMARY

Public relations is about the quality and nature of an organisation's relationships with various interested publics. These might well include customers and suppliers, but also include shareholders, trades unions, the media, government and other regulatory bodies and pressure groups, among many others. Public relations performs an important supporting role, providing a platform of goodwill and credibility from which other marketing activities can develop and be enhanced. Public relations becomes particularly important in limiting the damage and repairing credibility when a crisis strikes an organisation.

Publicity and press relations are important areas of PR. The media can be valuable in communicating messages to all kinds of publics and even in influencing opinion. Publicity, 'free' media coverage, has the added bonus of being seen as objective and therefore more credible. Organisations are therefore anxious to foster good press relations so that they might be treated less critically should they suffer a 'bad news' crisis. Press releases and press conferences are commonly used ways of getting information to the media, as well as means of fostering personal relationships with key journalists. There are, however, more controllable methods of PR. Advertising can be used to build corporate image and attitudes, and special events and publications can also target key publics. Given the variety of PR methods available, however, it can be very difficult to evaluate PR's success.

Corporate identity is an important consideration for any organisation. Its identity communicates its values and its character, and thus should be strong, clear and distinctive. A desire to change an identity may arise for a number of reasons, but it is not just a cosmetic issue of designing a pretty new logo. It needs extensive research to find out why the old identity was not working and to establish the criteria for the new one. The development of the new image ideally needs to be done in consultation with employees at all levels and, where appropriate, in all divisions of the organisation to make sure that it will be suitable and acceptable from all perspectives. The implementation and launch also need meticulous planning to ensure that all the practical and perhaps even emotional problems of the change are avoided. Finally, the new image should be monitored and evaluated once it has been launched to ensure that it is recognised, properly understood and accepted. Where the change process is not properly planned and managed, problems can occur. Identity change thus needs top management commitment and support and cannot be hurried.

Sponsorship is used by many organisations as a means of generating PR and enhancing both their image and their other marketing communications activities. Sponsorship might mean involvement with sport, the arts, broadcast media or charities or other good causes. Both parties should gain. The sponsor benefits from the PR spin-offs from the activities and the public profile of the organisations and/or events it supports, while those receiving the sponsorship benefit from cash or benefits in kind. Sponsorship might be corporate or brand specific, and the sponsor's involvement might be plainly obvious or quite discreet. Evaluating sponsorship is not easy, but there are a few guidelines for avoiding disappointment. These include the match between the parties concerned, the expected outcomes, potential spin-offs and compatibility with the sponsor's wider marketing objectives.

Exhibitions and trade shows vary from small local events to major national or international shows. They bring together a wide range of key personnel in one place at one time, and can thus generate great many potential sales leads cost effectively. Sometimes it can be important to be seen at certain high profile exhibitions, among the major competitors, in order to make a statement about one's presence in the market. From the exhibitors' point of view, the main reasons for being there are to generate qualified sales leads and to reinforce the organisation's presence and image in the market. For exhibition attendance to be successful, however, the organisation should ensure that it is a planned element of the overall marketing mix and that it has clear objectives and purposes. It is important to invest adequate funds to make a suitable impact on the show's visitors and to prepare staff carefully so that they make the most of the opportunities offered at the exhibition. After the exhibition, it is crucial that any leads generated are followed up quickly before the visitors have the chance to forget the good impressions made by the organisation.

Key words and phrases

Cause-related marketing	Marketing PR	Public relations
Corporate identity	Press relations	Sponsorship
Corporate PR	Public	Trade shows and exhibitions
House journal	Publicity	

QUESTIONS FOR REVIEW

20.1 What is *PR* and in what ways does it differ from other elements of the promotional mix?

20.2 Differentiate between *marketing PR* and *corporate PR*. To what extent do you think this is a useful distinction?

20.3 List the advantages and disadvantages of *publicity*.

20.4 In what ways can organisations feed material to the media, and in what kind of circumstances might each be appropriate?

20.5 Outline the potential benefits of developing a *corporate magazine*, such as those discussed at p. 791.

20.6 Why might an organisation want to change its *corporate identity*?

20.7 Briefly describe the stages an organisation should go through in changing corporate identity, explaining why each one is important.

20.8 Why might the lack of top management commitment to a corporate identity change mean the failure of the whole exercise?

20.9 What can *sponsorship* offer that media advertising cannot?

20.10 What factors might contribute to successful *exhibition attendance*?

QUESTIONS FOR DISCUSSION

20.1 At p. 781 a range of different publics are mentioned with which a university might have to create and maintain relationships. Draw up a similar list for your own university or college and:

(a) briefly outline what aspects of the institution's activities might be of particular interest to each of those publics; and
(b) suggest appropriate PR methods for each of them.

20.2 Find a corporate story that has made the news recently. It might be a 'crisis', a take-over battle, job losses or creation, new products or big contracts, for instance. Collect reports and press cuttings from a range of media on this story and compare the content. To what extent do you think that:

(a) the media have used material provided by the organisation itself?; and

(b) the story has developed beyond the control of the organisation?
(c) Imagine yourself to be the organisation's PR manager. Write a brief report to the managing director outlining what you feel to be the benefits and disadvantages of the coverage your organisation has received, and what you think should be done next regarding this story.

20.3 Assess the Midland Bank's approach to choosing the charities that benefit from its cause-related marketing outlined at p. 808.

20.4 What are the dangers of sponsorship from the recipient's perspective?

20.5 Draw up a table outlining alternative methods for evaluating PR, sponsorship and exhibitions, and the potential pitfalls of those methods.

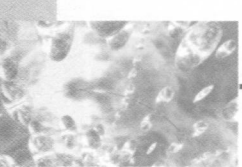

Shell, Greenpeace and Brent Spar

After a four-year decision-making process, Shell (UK) finally decided how they would handle the disposal of a redundant oil rig, Brent Spar. The detailed technical and legal assessment led them to one favoured option, to tow it into the North Atlantic and sink it, a course of action which would be legal under the terms of the Oslo–Paris Convention agreed by European governments.

Disposing of a 65 000 tonne, 150m unwanted steel and concrete structure is not easy. The only alternative to deep sea disposal was to break the rig up onshore and to recycle such material as was suitable for recycling. This option, however, costs more and could also have negative environmental side effects. Unfortunately, what Shell had not taken into account was international public opinion and how it could be shaped by pressure groups such as Greenpeace. Shell's handling of the situation provides powerful insights into the role of public relations in trying to manage an issue in which the public might not understand the detailed technical arguments but nevertheless develops strong emotional views.

Had it not been for the intervention of Greenpeace, the dumping might have gone unnoticed. In January 1995, Giys Thieme, Greenpeace's North Sea campaign logistics co-ordinator noticed Shell's intention to dispose of Brent Spar, but initially was unable to gain much interest in taking action because of the tough financial situation facing the organisation. Despite Greenpeace's annual income of £89 million, any battle with Shell pitches them against an organisation with global sales of £84 billion. It took until April 1995 before sufficient support was gained to allow Greenpeace to plan an occupation of the rig in protest against Shell's plan. The intention was to turn Brent Spar into Greenpeace's North Sea operations headquarters. A sum of £600 000 was allocated for the project, and it was expected that this budget might have to be doubled eventually.

When selecting an issue to fight on, Greenpeace looks for simplicity, both in the project itself and in the message it sends out to the public. The main priority was to maximise publicity, in order to attract the public support and sympathy that can create the necessary pressure for change.

The battle really began on 30 April when Brent Spar was boarded by Greenpeace activists, just ahead of Shell's disposal workers. The headquarters communication centre was soon established. It included satellite telephones for downloading photographs and video footage to the media centre in Frankfurt, and there was a support team

for photography and film work. Linked with this direct action, lobbying then began to persuade a wide audience that onshore disposal was the option Shell should have taken. The Internet, press and posters were all used, as were attempts to maximise media coverage. In the UK, the initial response was not very great. Public sympathy was difficult to mobilise and the press did not appear to be taking much notice of the issue. It was not until the campaign was extended to include Germany, Denmark and the Netherlands that matters started to advance. The level of environmental sensitivity appeared to be higher in these countries then in the UK, and media coverage soon followed and public support grew rapidly. It was not long before politicians, such as Chancellor Kohl of Germany and Sweden's Environment Minister Anna Lindh (who commented that 'The sea must not be used as a rubbish dump'), were publicly questioning the dumping option. The eviction of those who were occupying the rig and the use of water cannon against another attempted occupation using helicopters helped to create a view, rightly or wrongly, of 'big business versus the environment'.

The UK Prime Minister, however, still strongly supported Shell's position. Shell was thus firm that the dumping would proceed with the government's full support, despite growing public pressure in the UK. With an armada of ships, the Brent Spar was eventually towed towards the drop zone with two protesters still on board.

The main focus of the protest then took a decisive twist when motorists began to boycott Shell petrol. In Germany, petrol revenue dropped by between 20 per cent and 30 per cent when the boycotting started in June. Greenpeace had asked for a boycott for just one day, but the public mood extended that voluntarily. The powerful German Green party, consumer groups and even the church had joined the Greenpeace cause. The Brent Spar dumping was portrayed as a battle that had to be won to avoid the seas being used as a dumping ground as other North Sea oil rigs were decommissioned.

Shell was surprised about the protest and the public reaction. In the UK, the company had spent three years lobbying the British government, presenting the case for the dumping option. Shell had won the lobbying battle but then found itself in a PR war. While Shell had the technical and logistical ability to proceed with the dumping, with the full support of the UK government, it was less certain that it could afford to pay the PR price. The president of Shell openly admitted that the company had underestimated the strength of consumer response and that the brand image had been badly damaged as a result of the affair. The company was caught between implementing what it still firmly believed to be the best environmental and technical option and the consequences in prime European markets of doing so. There were allegations that Greenpeace had deliberately misled the public with faulty scientific analysis of the pollution spin-off from dumping, but Shell could not regain the PR high ground in the short-term.

By the end of June the tugs were turning around to bring the rig back for onshore disposal in Norway. The power of public opinion and the consumer boycott had hurt Shell. They had concluded that enough was enough. In early September it emerged that Greenpeace had in fact got its analysis wrong and had miscalculated the amount of oil remaining on the rig. Greenpeace had written to Shell to apologise, but still maintained that its campaign had still been justified in principle. The pressure group denied that the apology had damaged its image in any way.

Sources: Cowe (1995); Denny (1995a); Hobsbawm (1995); Kearney and McKie (1995); Mayer (1995); Pilkington *et seq.* (1995); Vidal (1995a; 1995b).

Questions

1 Which 'publics' was Shell having to deal with during the course of this issue?

2 What different PR techniques have been used by the various parties in this case and how effective were they?

3 What advantages and disadvantages does a pressure group like Greenpeace have in dealing with a large global company such as Shell?

4 What lessons can both Greenpeace and Shell learn from this situation?

CASE STUDY 20.2

Antique exhibitions

The growth of specialist exhibitions has changed the way in which people buy antiques. The rising costs of maintaining premises faced by antique dealers meant that a significant number were moving out of shop-based retailing. Selling from a shop also gave dealers problems in making sure that they were communicating with the right customers at the right time, and the onus was on customers to be highly active in specifying their wants to the dealers and in undertaking regular browsing and shop visits. Exhibitions not only reduce the dealer's operating costs, but also attract many more potential customers than a single store could because of the range of goods and dealers on show. Customers might also feel more relaxed browsing among the crowds at an exhibition than in a quiet shop where they might be the only customer and might therefore be the object of too much attention from the staff.

The scene has changed with the growth of fine art and antiques fairs such as those held in the UK and in Amsterdam and Maastricht. Olympia in London runs three fairs per year, which it is claimed can generate as much as £21 million worth of orders each. In some cases, half the annual turnover of an exhibiting dealer could be made at such fairs, so it is crucial that they present the best image possible. Most stands are of a high quality, showing a wide range of merchandise in room-like settings. Although dealers do sometimes sell to each other at the shows, the majority of visitors are consumers looking for that special piece or just for a bargain. The Olympia shows attract international audiences, as the events are big enough to encourage customers to make a special visit, despite the cost of travel. The key to the success of many fairs is the degree of organisation that takes place in attracting customers to come on the day. Exhibitors do not necessarily just want sheer numbers of visitors, but prefer a targeted effort to attract those customers who are most likely to buy. For the Olympia fairs, the organisers send out direct mailshots to potential customers selected from lifestyle databases as likely antiques purchasers.

Despite the undoubted success of these fairs, however, there are some problems emerging which could yet have an impact on further development. A disadvantage of any busy fair is that less time can be spent with each customer, unlike in a shop setting. Although the product itself is central to any antiques purchase, there is often a need to provide customers with reassurance about its value, and some price negotiation might be necessary. At a busy show it is often difficult to concentrate on such personal selling when there are three or four other customers on the stand. One dealer estimated that he used to have 50 visitors a week in his shop, but attracted 18 000 at an exhibition! A lost customer could easily buy from any of the other 3000 to 4000 exhibitors at a typical fair.

Another problem concerns the mushrooming growth in such exhibitions, which, combined with craft fairs, provide a plethora of opportunities for both dealers and potential customers. Not only might customers start to suffer 'exhibition fatigue', but dealers' costs might also start to rise again as the number of shows at which they exhibit goes up. Furthermore, at some of the more popular fairs, exhibition fees for dealers can be quite high. All of this might lead to some rationalisation in the market, with a reduction in the number of events. The casualties are likely to be some of the smaller shows.

They are less well equipped to target and attract specific segments of visitors and so there can be no guarantee that sufficient trade will be generated to justify the costs of exhibiting and the direct costs of transport, display and staffing.

Source: Bryant (1995).

Questions

1 What factors have led to the growth of exhibitions as a means of selling antiques?

2 What are the potential advantages and disadvantages to (a) the dealer and (b) the customer of buying and selling in this way?

3 What can the exhibition organiser do to try to ensure the success of an event?

4 What other consumer goods could be sold in this way?

REFERENCES TO CHAPTER 20

Abratt, R. and Shee, P. S. B. (1988), 'A New Approach to the Corporate Image Management Process', *Journal of Marketing Management*, 5(1), pp. 63–76.

Bailey, J. N. (1991), 'Employee Publications' in P. Lesly (ed.), *The Handbook of Public Relations and Communication*, (4th edn.), McGraw-Hill.

Barrett, M. (1995), 'Please Adjust Your Sponsorship', *Marketing*, 30 November, pp. 21–25.

Barrett, M. (1996), 'Vision of the Future', *Marketing*, 6 January, pp. 29–30.

Barrett, P. (1996), 'Beef Industry Takes Stock', *Marketing*, 28 March.

Bernstein, D. (1984), *Company Image and Reality: A Critique of Corporate Communications*, HRW.

Bishop, L. (1995), 'Happy Returns', *Marketing*, 7 December, pp. 29–31.

Bond, C. (1995a), 'Emergency Services', *Marketing*, 12 October, pp. 35–8.

Bond, C. (1995b), 'Contract Title Fight', *Marketing*, 26 October, pp. 31–7.

Bryant, S. (1994), 'Making a Stand', *Marketing*, 8 December, p. 34.

Bryant, S. (1995), 'Fine Art and Fair Trade', *Marketing*, 30 March, pp. XIV–XV

Buchanan, K. (1995), 'Match of the Day', *Marketing*, 17 August, pp. 20–2.

Burnside, A. (1995a), 'Keeping Your Eyes on the Prize', *Marketing*, 22 June, pp. XVII–XVIII.

Burnside, A. (1995b), 'Knowing the Right Time and Place', *Marketing*, 19 October, pp. VI–IX.

Buxton, J. (1995), 'Conversion for The Famous Grouse', *Financial Times*, 2 February, p. 20.

Carter, M. (1994), 'Frame, Set and Match', *Marketing Week*, 4 November, pp. 45–8.

Cowe, R. (1995), 'Shell Chief Laments PR Failure in Move to Dump Brent Spar', *Guardian*, 15 September, p. 21.

Curtis, J. (1996) 'Pumping up the Volume', *Marketing*, 13 June, pp. 30–1.

Cutlip, S. *et al.* (1985), *Effective Public Relations*: Prentice Hall.

Denny, N. (1995a), 'Oil and Troubled Waters', *Marketing*, 29 June, p. 13.

Denny, N. (1995b), 'Businesses Queue Up to Sponsor the Arts', *Marketing*, 7 September, p. 13.

Dudley, J. (1990), *Successful Exhibiting*, Kogan Page.

Fill, C. (1995), *Marketing Communications: Frameworks, Theories and Applications*, Prentice Hall.

Fletcher, K. (1995a), 'Magazines Drive the Brand Home', *Marketing*, 6 April, pp. XI–XVI.

Fletcher, K. (1995b), 'Good Cause and Effect', *Marketing*, 20 July, p. 31.

Fry, A. (1995), 'Spreading Across the Small Screen', *Marketing*, 18 May, pp. VIII–X.

Gofton, K. (1995a), 'Hot Stuff in the Kitchen Wars', *Marketing*, 30 March, pp. III–IV.

Gofton, K. (1995b), 'Showing Off Abroad', *Marketing*, 13 July, pp. 23–4.

Gray, R. (1994), 'Ads Pack More Punch with PR', *Campaign*, 6 May, pp. 33–7.

The Grocer (1995a), 'Beef Sales Dropping', *The Grocer*, 23 December, p. 9.

The Grocer (1995b), 'Feature: Exhibition Update', *The Grocer*, 23 December, p. 14.

The Grocer (1996a), 'Death Knell for Beef Industry', *The Grocer*, 23 March, p. 5.

The Grocer (1996b), 'Markets Tell a Different Story to Retail Outlook', *The Grocer*, 23 March, p. 61.

The Grocer (1996c), 'Retailers Shift and Reorder', *The Grocer*, 6 April, p. 9.

The Grocer (1996d), 'The Media Stampede Flattens the Facts', *The Grocer*, 6 April, p. 12.

The Grocer (1996e), 'CJD: UK 54 v Europe 144,' *The Grocer*, 13 April, p. 5.

The Grocer (1996f), 'Market Turmoil Fuels Volatile Price Swings', *The Grocer*, 13 April, p. 5.

The Grocer (1996g), 'Calls for Brussels Cash to Restore Confidence', *The Grocer*, 27 April, p. 73.

Hall, C. (1995), 'Get a Fair Share Abroad', *Daily Express*, 26 June, p. 39.

Hart, N. A. (1993), *Industrial Marketing Communications*, Kogan Page.

Haywood, R. (1984), *All About PR*, McGraw-Hill.

Hewison, R. (1995), 'Out to Change the Message on a Bottle', *Sunday Times*, 28 May, p. 10.

Hobsbawm, J. (1995), 'Rough Sea of Publicity', *Guardian*, 26 June, p. 10.

John, R. (1996), 'How To Steal the Show', *Marketing*, 4 January, pp. 19–23.

Kearney, J. and McKie, R. (1995), 'Motorists Shun Shell Over Sinking of Rig', *Observer*, 18 June, p. 1.

Lane Fox, H. (1996), 'Good Cause, Better Effect', *Marketing*, 11 January.

Marketing (1996), 'Cadbury Backs Coronation Street', *Marketing*, 11 January, p. 1.

Marston, J. E. (1979), *Modern Public Relations*, McGraw-Hill.

Massey, A. (1995), 'Contracts With Killer Looks', *Marketing*, 2 February, pp. IX–X.

Mayer, S. (1995), 'Brent Spar – Forcing Home Environmental Responsibilities', *Energy Economist*, pp. 11–14.

Meenaghan, T. (1991), 'The Role of Sponsorship in the Marketing Communications Mix', *International Journal of Advertising*, 10, pp. 35–47.

Miles, L. (1995), 'It's Marketing Jim, But Not as We Know It', *Marketing*, 18 May, pp. III–VI.

Norman, D. (1991), 'The Sponsorship Contribution', in M. Nally (ed.), *International Public Relations in Practice*, Kogan Page.

Palin, R. (1982), 'Operational PR', in W. Howard (ed.), *The Practice of Public Relations*, Butterworth-Heinemann.

Pilkington, E. *et al.* (1995),'Battle of Giants, Big and Small, Fought with High Technology and Skillful PR', *Guardian*, 22 June, p. 4.

Richards, A. (1995), 'Does Charity Pay?', *Marketing*, 21 September, pp. 24–5.

Stanley, R. E. (1982), *Promotion: Advertising, Publicity, Personal Selling, Sales Promotion*, Prentice Hall.

Stone, N. (1991), *How to Manage Public Relations*, McGraw-Hill.

Tait, S. (1995), 'The Bank that Likes to Say 'Yo!'', *The Times*, 17 March, p. 32.

Thompson-Noel, M. (1995), 'Tampax Knocked Off the Tennis Court', *Financial Times*, 27 February, p. 11.

Thorncroft, A. (1995a), 'Ten Years of Motivation', *Financial Times*, 3 February, p. 13.

Thorncroft, A. (1995b), 'Now for Something Completely Different, Please', *Financial Times*, 7 April, p. 17.

Thorncroft, A. (1995c), 'Contemporary Backers Feel Safe at the Tate', *Financial Times*, 5 May, p. 15.

Thorncroft, A. (1995d), 'Companies Tackle New Pragmatism', *Financial Times*, 7 July, p. 21.

Traverso, M. and White, J. (1990), 'The Launch of the Prudential's Corporate Identity' in D. Moss (ed.), *Public Relations in Practice: A Casebook*, Routledge.

Vidal, J. (1995a), 'Hell for Shell as Fury Spills on to the Forecourts', *Guardian*, 17 June, p. 27.

Vidal, J. (1995b), 'Greenpeace Admits Mistakes Over Brent Spar', *Guardian*, 6 September, p. 2.

Walker, J. A. (1994), 'Treasure Chests', *Marketing Week*, 4 November, pp. 37–42.

Wighton, D. (1995), 'FT Guide to Golf: The Price of Playing', *Financial Times*, 20 July, p. XXVII.

Wilmshurst, J. (1993), *Below-the-Line Promotion*, Butterworth-Heinemann.

Part VII

MARKETING MANAGEMENT

Strategic Marketing **21**

Marketing Planning, Management and Control **22**

In offering you a detailed and comprehensive introduction to the important elements of marketing, this book has had to take a 'pigeon hole' approach, treating each element as a separate entity. Throughout the text, however, it has been made clear that all these elements are   interdependent and must be integrated into a consistent and coherent overall strategy.

This section, therefore, serves two purposes. First, in Chapter 21, issues of strategic marketing and competitive strategy are addressed. Increasingly, marketing managers are expected to play an additional role in supporting the corporate planning process by focusing on the important areas of product market strategy and marketing resource allocation as well as the more traditional mix management perspectives. Chapter 21, therefore, also outlines the interface between corporate and marketing planning frameworks, and how each influences and is influenced by the other. Second, Chapter 22 examines the marketing planning process, and the role it plays in providing a structured framework within which marketing actions can be undertaken. The importance of planning, based on sound assessment of the organisation's present position, both internal and external, as stressed in Chapter 15 on marketing communication, cannot be understated.

■　　■　　■

21 Strategic Marketing

LEARNING OBJECTIVES

This chapter will help you to:

1 define marketing strategy and the internal and external influences affecting it;

2 understand the various types of portfolio model used to develop a strategic view of the organisation and the competitive context within which it operates;

3 outline different strategies for achieving growth and their appropriate use;

4 differentiate between types of competitors, appreciate the perspectives from which they can be analysed, and start to define appropriate strategies for dealing with them; and

5 understand the concept of competitive positioning and the range of strategies and tactical actions broadly appropriate for achieving and maintaining a position.

INTRODUCTION

So far, this book has looked at the practical aspects of marketing, from identifying consumer needs and wants through to designing and delivering a product package that aims to meet those needs and wants, and maintains customer loyalty despite the efforts of the competition. The tools that make up the marketing mix are, of course, critical for implementing the marketing concept. Each one adds value to the overall offering, contributing towards a competitive edge that will attract the target market. What exactly constitutes the best mix to adopt varies from situation to situation and must be the subject of research, experimentation and management judgement. In Chapter 8 (p. 316), we saw how Mercedes with the launch of the 190, was able to move into a lower price segment though a careful programme of product development and pricing, while the key to the success of adult soft drinks in Chapter 5 (p. 175) was their ability to target their marketing effort carefully to appeal to the 'cola fatigue' segment. So far, the focus on the marketing mix elements has largely been operational and orientated to the short-term. Managers must, however, think of their operational marketing mixes in the context of wider, more strategic questions, such as:

- Which markets should we be in?
- What does our organisation have that will give it a competitive edge? (This need not necessarily come directly from marketing.)

- Do we have the resources, skills and assets within the organisation to enable planned objectives to be achieved?
- Where do we want to be in five or even 25 years' time?
- What will our competitors be doing in three or five years' time?
- Can we assume that our current *modus operandi* will be good enough for the future?

These concerns are strategic, not operational, in that they affect the whole organisation and provide a framework for subsequent operational decisions. The focus is on the future, aligning the whole organisation to new opportunities and challenges within the changing marketing environment, as discussed in Chapter 2. The list of questions suggested above seem deceptively simple, but finding answers to them is, in fact, a highly skilled and demanding task. The future welfare of the whole organisation depends on finding the 'right' answers. As Chapter 2 showed, trends within the marketing environment can be difficult to spot, and even if the organisation does see them, their implications can still be unclear and contradictory. This is particularly true where the competition are concerned. Even the best laid plans can be severely disrupted by competitive action, especially when the competition refuse to act predictably or to play by 'the rules' as you define them. Thus there is a constant need for information gathering, updating and analysis as a fundamental part of the strategic planning in the first place, and then as a part of monitoring and controlling the implementation of those plans.

Gaining an understanding of the external environment is not enough in itself. The organisation also has to take a long hard look at its internal resources, assets and skills to assess whether the organisation is sufficiently well equipped to meet the challenges of the external environment. Strategic marketing planning thus might have long-term implications for the direction and shape of the whole organisation rather than just impacting on the operational management of the marketing mix elements themselves. The strategic marketer is, therefore, a catalyst for change through highlighting the need to create a better fit between the market's needs and the capabilities and resources of the organisation. The stakes are high, for the organisation that gets it wrong can face very serious consequences, particularly if long-term investments in plant, machinery or product development have been made on the basis of a particular interpretation of the marketing environment.

MARKETING IN ACTION

Grolsch

Grolsch, the Dutch brewer, is an example of how strategic marketing decisions can lead to long-term investment and corporate change. In the 1990s, Grolsch felt that to compete effectively within its market, it needed to build a strong European-wide specialism in premium brands. This led to a corporate commitment and decision to pursue a policy of expansion through acquisition. Thus Grolsch purchased Wickuler, a German brewery as big as its own, and Ruddles brewery in the UK. The Ruddles purchase provided the capacity to enable Grolsch to achieve its objective of becoming one of the top five premium lager brands in the UK, despite fierce competition from brands such as Budweiser, Beck's, Holsten Pils and Stella Artois.

In the UK, the Grolsch brand had grown during the 1980s from being a £1 million, marginal niche brand to a brand worth over £80 million. The Ruddles acquisition provided an opportunity to achieve an even stronger competitive position on the back of the growth of the strong lager (5 per cent proof or more) segment. Furthermore, there were plans to expand the Ruddles brand to strengthen the Dutch brewer's position in the wider UK beer market even more. These are marketing strategies that clearly involve long-term commitment and a relatively long lead time of three to five years before their prime objectives can be achieved.

Source: Meller (1992).

This chapter first introduces strategic marketing issues by defining some of the commonly used terms and showing how they fit together. Some, however, will not be considered in depth until the next chapter. A number of techniques have been developed for analysing strategic marketing problems, especially those concerned with the interface between the products offered and the dynamics and structure of the related markets. Product portfolio and market attractiveness models are therefore considered at pp. 836 *et seq.* There then follows a review of a variety of strategic options that are closely related to marketing issues. These include growth directions, developing and maintaining a competitive position and deciding on how to compete, ranging from direct attacks to almost independent decision making regardless of competition. Competitive strategies and their impact on marketing are then explored. This area has grown in importance in recent years, reflecting the increased level of competition in many markets, often on an international scale. Chapter 22 will then build further upon this chapter by examining the implementation of strategic and operational marketing through the planning process.

DEFINITIONS AND PERSPECTIVES

Marketing strategy cannot be formulated in isolation. It has to reflect the objectives of the organisation and be compatible with the strategies pursued elsewhere in the organisation. This means that marketers must refer back to corporate goals and objectives before formulating their own strategy, to ensure consistency, coherence and relevance.

It would be inappropriate to imply, however, that marketing strategy is always subservient to corporate strategy. Many aspects of marketing actually influence corporate strategy. In a marketing-orientated organisation, the needs of customers and the maintenance of competitive edge are important ingredients in formulating corporate strategic direction and priorities. Furthermore, the product is at the heart of the business and thus marketers' product decisions, for instance deletion, modification or range

Linn's niche marketing strategy targets the high performance, top end of the hifi market.

Source: Linn Products Limited.

extension are likely to have a major impact on the organisation as a whole. In this context, the strategic aspects of marketing are likely to have a major (but not exclusive) impact on the formulation of corporate strategy, as seen in the Grolsch case earlier.

> **Example**
>
> The interaction between marketing strategy and corporate strategy is clearly seen in the case of Linn Products, a manufacturer of hi-fi systems based in Scotland. They targeted the high performance, top end of the market across Europe and designed their whole marketing strategy around that position, although they realised that the market segment would be relatively small. They knew that they did not want to be the cheapest, but the best, a tough claim in a market that has competitors such as Mission. In corporate terms, to live up to this promise and to implement this marketing strategy, the organisation had to be sure that it could handle relatively small production volumes made to very high quality specifications, deliver the high level of customer and technical service required and still make a profit (Southam, 1993: Anne Young, Linn Products Limited).

The two-way process between marketing and corporate strategy is shown in Fig 21.1.

To help to clarify the two-way interaction, the rest of this section is divided into two. First, we provide an overview of some of the different, and often overlapping internal strategic perspectives, both corporate and marketing specific, that marketers have to consider in their strategic thinking. We then examine some of the broader factors that affect the formulation of marketing strategy in practice.

Strategic marketing frameworks

This subsection outlines some of the strategic perspectives of the organisation, starting with the broad picture required by corporate strategy, then gradually focusing down towards the very specific detail of marketing programmes.

Corporate strategy

Corporate strategy concerns the allocation of resources within the organisation to achieve the business direction and scope specified within corporate objectives.

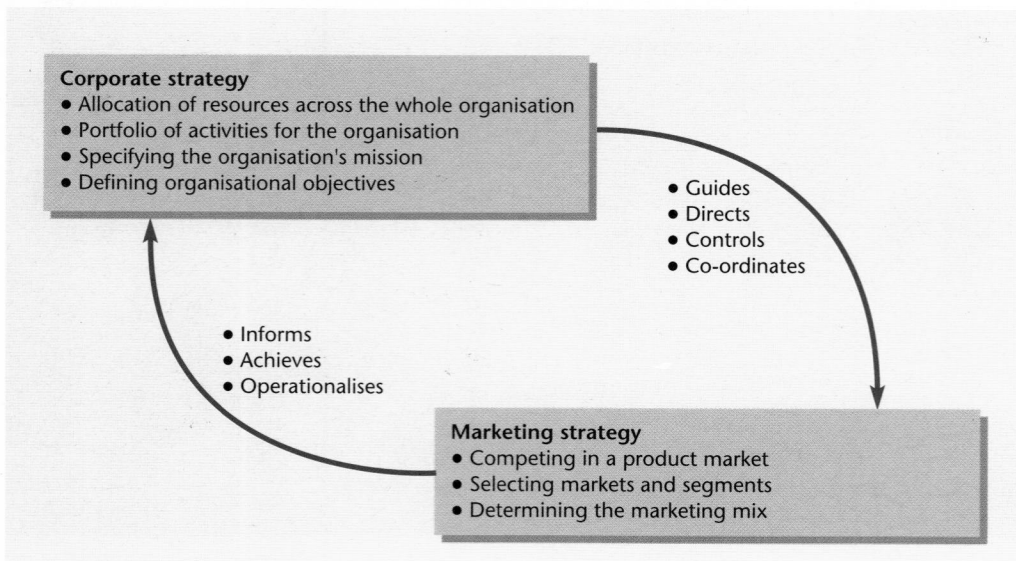

FIGURE 21.1

The two-way influence between marketing and corporate strategy

Although the marketing department is primarily responsible for responding to perceived marketing opportunities and favourable competitive environments, it cannot act without the involvement of all other areas of the organisation too. Corporate strategy, therefore, helps to control and co-ordinate the different areas of the organisation, finance, marketing, production, R&D etc., to ensure that they are all working towards the same objectives, and that those objectives are consistent with the desired direction of the business as a whole.

Although the techniques for corporate planning may vary between different sizes and types of organisation, the objective is always the same: to match targeted opportunities with resources, focused activity and strategies. Typical issues of concern to corporate planners might thus be market expansion, product development priorities, acquisition, divestment, diversification and maintaining a competitive edge. In a smaller firm, the planning process could be fairly straightforward but for a larger firm with distinct business areas, this planning might mean making tough decisions about resource allocation and strategic priorities, which might create a degree of internal conflict.

Example

Corporate planning often does work closely with strategic marketing. BMW wanted to strengthen its overall corporate position by moving into larger volume, less specialised markets, while retaining a niche position for the highly successful existing BMW range. There would have been a risk, if this had been done under the BMW name, of compromising the positioning of the more 'executive' cars within the marque. The corporate decision to acquire Rover cars in the UK meant that BMW maintained an uncompromised presence in its traditional £15 000+ market, and also gained a foothold with Rover's existing cars in the £5 000 to £15 000 bracket. The acquisition also strengthened the corporate position by spreading both the risks and opportunities arising from involvement in new market segments (Dwek, 1994).

Interestingly, this began to change in 1996. It was reported that Rover was having problems competing against European and Asian models in the lower price brackets, and therefore BMW was taking Rover upmarket into the premium price sector. Experts seemed to be sceptical about whether the full range of Rover products could be repositioned convincingly with a more luxury image. Barrett (1996) reported one industry analyst as saying:

> 'It takes years to establish a premium brand. Rover is a dog, no pun intended, as a luxury brand. Rover as a name just does not have cachet as far as I'm concerned. Short of sticking a BMW badge on them I don't see how it is going to happen' (Barrett, 1996 p. 13)

To help to make the corporate planning process more manageable, larger organisations often divide their activities into **strategic business units** (SBUs). An SBU is a part of the organisation that has become sufficiently significant to allow it to develop its own strategies and plans, although still within the context of the overall corporate picture. SBUs can be based on products, markets or operating divisions that are profit centres in their own right. Each SBU might face very different marketing environments, achievement targets, strategies and competitors. Given that SBUs might have different growth and financial profiles, it is important at corporate level to assess both the current performance and future potential of each SBU and then decide overall priorities and resource allocation.

Competitive strategy

Competitive strategy determines how an organisation chooses to compete within a market, with particular regard to the relative positioning of competitors. Unless an organisation can create and maintain a competitive advantage, it is unlikely to achieve a strong market position. In any market, there tend to be those who dominate or lead, followed by a number of progressively smaller players, some of whom might be close enough to mount a serious challenge. Others, however, are content to follow or niche themselves (i.e., dominate a small, specialist corner of the market). As we show later (*see* p. 859), there are many ways of competing, and the choice of competitive strategy guides subsequent detailed corporate and marketing strategy decisions.

Example

There are various forces that influence the competitive positioning of an organisation, including established competitors, new competitors, market conditions and the trade. The vineyard region of Bordeaux is internationally renowned for fine wines. After a period of growth in the 1980s, more recent years have seen considerably increased competition, not just from traditional French sources such as Beaujolais and Côtes de Rhône, but also from new competitors entering the market. Market conditions also changed, both in export markets and in the domestic French market. Although sales volume in Belgium and Switzerland changed little in the early 1990s, in the UK sales dropped considerably, not only because of new alternative wines from South Africa and Australia, but also because of a flood of relatively cheap wines from eastern Europe and South America. The higher priced position that Bordeaux occupies is vulnerable to any shift in spending during a recession.

In the domestic French market, the massive buying power of the supermarkets put further pressure on the Bordeaux producers by keeping prices down. This means that increasing marketing expenditure might not have been a feasible option, because the producers would not be generating sufficient profit margin to pay for it and could not charge premium prices. Some good wines, because of the supermarkets' power, are selling in France for as little as 9 francs, and only one brand, Malezan, which sells four million bottles a year, has managed to maintain a price of 20 francs (Faith, 1993). This all restricts the producers' ability and flexibility to compete as they would wish.

Marketing strategy

The marketing strategy defines target markets, what direction needs to be taken and what needs to be done in broad terms to create a defensible competitive position compatible with overall corporate strategy within those markets. It is, therefore, concerned with many of the aspects considered in buyer behaviour (Chapter 3 and 4), as well as the decision to target particular market segments (Chapter 5). Marketing mix programmes can then be designed to best match organisational capabilities with target market opportunities. Many of the cases and examples highlighted in Chapters 7–20 showed how various marketing mix strategies were used to achieve marketing objectives. Chosen strategies will vary, depending on the context (compare, for example, two case studies, the German Diesel Railcar (Case study 7.2) and Riverdance (Case study 15.1)) but they all share the same marketing-orientated philosophy.

Marketing plan

It is in the marketing plan that the operational detail, turning strategies into implementable actions, is developed. The **marketing plan** is a detailed, written statement specifying target markets, marketing programmes, responsibilities, time-scales and resources to be used, within defined budgets. Most marketing plans are annual, but their number and focus will vary with the type of organisation. The plan might be geographically based, product based, business unit based, or orientated towards specific segments. An overall corporate marketing plan in a large organisation might, therefore, bring together and integrate a number of plans specific to individual SBUs. Planning at SBU level and then consolidating all the plans ensures that the corporate picture has enough detail, and allows overall implementation and control to be managed.

Marketing programmes

Marketing programmes are actions, often of a tactical nature, involving the use of the marketing mix variables to gain an advantage within the target market. These programmes are normally detailed in the annual marketing plan, and are the means of implementing the chosen marketing strategy. Linn hi-fi systems, mentioned earlier in this chapter, found that an advertising campaign of £250 000 using quality journals, a direct mail programme, an annual brochure and a bi-annual magazine, were appropriate actions for stimulating trial and maintaining customer relationships. Programmes provide clear guidelines, schedules and budgets for the range of actions proposed for achieving the overall objectives. These are determined within the framework of the overall marketing plan to ensure that activities are properly integrated and that appropriate resources are allocated to them.

Influences on marketing strategy

Figure 21.2 outlines the various influences on an organisation's marketing strategy, each of which is then be discussed in turn.

Organisational objectives and resources

Marketing strategists need to be guided by what the organisation as a whole is striving for – what its objectives are and what resources it has to implement them. Some organisations might have very ambitious growth plans, while others might be content with fairly steady growth or even no growth at all, that is, consolidation. Clearly, each of these alternatives implies different approaches to marketing.

> ### Example
>
> Aston Martin, the prestigious British car maker, has a long history of hand-made sports cars, linked with such names as James Bond and Prince Charles. For many years, fewer than five cars per week were produced and total production between 1914 and 1992 totalled fewer than 12 000 cars. In 1987, Ford purchased a 75 per cent stake in the company and slowly began to influence the company's

FIGURE 21.2

Influences on marketing strategy

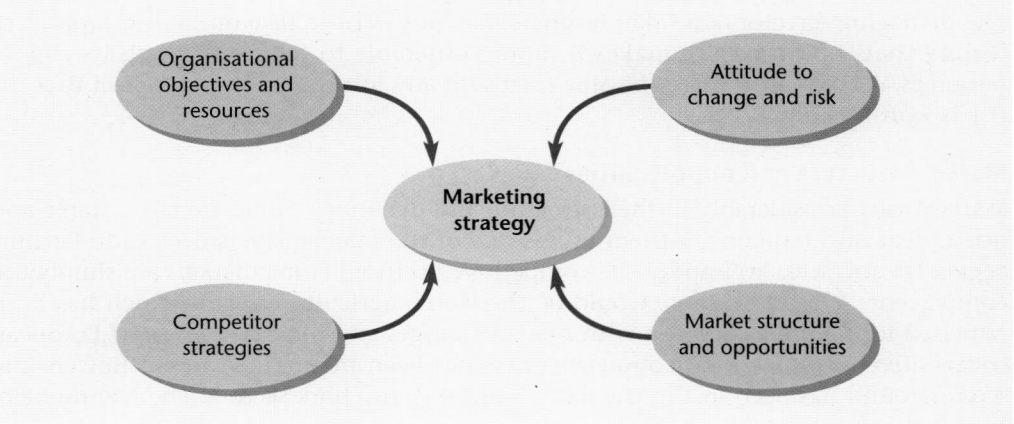

traditional approach. The objective was to expand production to around 700 cars per year and to produce a downmarket version to sell at around £75 000 (as opposed to £132 000 for the standard car). This dramatic increase in planned production led to a reappraisal of the marketing effort, including such activities as dealer support, special pick-up and assistance services across Europe, free advanced driving tuition, as well as enhanced promotional activity (Dwek, 1992).

Resources are not only financial. They also include skills and expertise, in other words any area of the organisation that can help to add value and give a competitive edge. The exploitation, through marketing, of things that the organisation does well, such as manufacturing, technical innovation, product development or customer service, might help to create non-financial assets such as reputation and image, which are difficult for competitors to copy.

Example

Holderbank SA, based in Switzerland, is Europe's largest cement supplier. For any cement company to survive, economies of scale in production, ongoing supplies of quality raw materials and low transport costs are critical. For this reason, it is common to find companies operating from several locations near to raw materials and customers rather than using centralised production. Holderbank has therefore acquired many national and regional companies, but a key distinguishing strength, the company claims, arises from its concentration on high quality levels and production efficiency in the cement business. This contrasts with competitors such as Ready Mix Concrete and LaFarge Coppee who consider themselves to be in the construction business and sell a wider range of products to the same customer base. In a market that has not experienced dramatic innovation and which changes primarily with the economic cycle, such a focus on key skills and strengths might be highly appropriate (Lynch, 1994).

As the cases of Aston Martin and Holderbank show, marketing strategies do need to be compatible with corporate objectives and to capitalise on available resources.

Attitude to change and risk

The corporate view on change and risk often depends on the approach of top management. Risk tolerance varies widely from individual to individual, and from management team to management team. Managers will also, of course, be guided by the nature of the organisation and their interpretation of its business environment. The managing director of a small business may not want to take on high-risk projects, feeling that the firm's size makes it more vulnerable to failure through its lack of resources. A larger firm might be able to absorb any losses, and therefore feel that the risk is worth taking.

Market structure and opportunities

Markets vary considerably in their structure and dynamics. Some are fairly stable and not a great deal happens in them unless one of the major players decides to become aggressive and seeks to improve its competitive position. Some markets are simply too complacent. A good example would be the Dutch agriculture sector which has been criticised for failing to keep up with market changes and increased levels of European competitiveness. Although competitiveness has been maintained in cut flowers and seeds, ground has been lost in the dairy, vegetable and pork sectors. The real problem

Tele Danmark makes international calls

Tele Danmark, and the five state-owned regional telephone companies which were merged to create it in 1990–1 have experienced rationalisation, privatisation and deregulation in recent years, but by the mid-1990s, it was internationalisation that formed a central part of its strategy. The telecommunications industry throughout Europe was experiencing considerable change, with increased liberalisation in most markets. This meant that previously protected, often state-owned organisations, were suddenly faced with the potential for intense competition. This reflected the EC's fears that telecoms prices across Europe were too high; that there was too little innovation, and that sometimes telecoms markets were plain uncompetitive. The EC was keen to expose telecoms operators to competition, and thus privatisation had either taken place already or was expected to be achieved by 1998, not only in Denmark but also in Germany, the UK, Greece, Belgium, the Netherlands, Italy and Portugal.

Tele Danmark, the Danish telecommunications company, was a relatively small player in European terms, but had adopted an aggressive policy of international expansion since its privatisation. This strategy was designed to offset the problems of being attacked in its own market and to spread its customer base as a long-term defence. In the mobile market, for instance, it was locked into a price war with Sonofon, part of GN Store Nord. Sonofon appeared to have won that war, in that its subscriber base had increased to 270 000, but in achieving that, it made a DKr 1.27 million loss.

By 1996, Tele Danmark had acquired a 16.5 per cent stake in the Belgian national telecom group, Belgacom, as part of a consortium. Not only did this add a new revenue stream, it also created some synergy in routing traffic and in equipment purchasing. Tele Danmark had also expressed an interest in Telecom Eireann and Mobilkom, Austria. The strategy was Scandinavia first, Europe second, and other international development third, in descending order of priority. The company had a stake in mobile phone companies in Hungary, Lithuania, Ukraine and Poland as part of an attempt to gain an early position in potentially fast developing markets. Among the most important of Tele Danmark's efforts in Scandinavia was its membership of a consortium offering telecommunication services to the business sector in Sweden. In Germany, it has a company that resells telecommunication capacity, because prices are higher in Germany, while other interests further afield include Hong Kong and there was the possibility of expanding into China.

Achievements were still modest, with international revenue just DKr 224 million from a total turnover of DKr 18.8 billion in 1995. However, the strategy appeared to be working. As margins and share would be increasingly threatened in the domestic market following full liberalisation after 1 July 1996, the deliberate policy of pursuing international opportunities would minimise the long-term effects of increased competition in the domestic market.

Sources: Barnes (1996a; 1996b); Cane (1995); Reuters (1996).

has arisen from changes in the marketing environment, as consumers have sought a wider variety of products and higher product specifications, and European supermarket buyers have sought greater efficiency. In the cheese sector, for example, only one new cheese has been successfully launched from the Netherlands (Leerdammer) since 1980, while Denmark and France have both been highly successful in launching ranges of feta and mozzarella cheeses (van de Krol, 1994a).

The impact of the increasing internationalisation of organisations is that previously dormant markets can be suddenly transformed into dynamic competitive arenas by the entry of a new, foreign competitor. This can be seen in the UK construction industry. Companies suffered badly in the 1990s, partly because of the depressed state of the construction market generally, but also because of increasing difficulties in competing with European, Japanese and American rivals entering the UK market. For many years, contracting was often a national and sometimes even a regional business with a large number of smaller firms. With the arrival of international competitors, most of whom, such as Bouygues (France) and Skanska (Sweden), are much larger, smaller firms are finding it harder to win contracts and to do battle in European markets (Lynn, 1996).

Often, such turbulence only happens over a limited period until a new *status quo* is reached through a new market structure that redefines relative market shares. In the case of construction, that could mean considerable rationalisation within the UK industry. Sometimes, the turbulence is created by innovation and new product technology that again has the potential to redefine how players actually compete. In some growth markets, turbulence can be high until the market stabilises and competitors become more entrenched, leaving fewer opportunities for new entrants.

Example

Stafford Millar identified and exploited a distinct market niche in toothpaste with its brand Sensodyne. For many years, it was unrivalled and captured around 80 per cent of the sensitive tooth market. In the 1990s, however, the market burst into life with the entry of brands such as Macleans Sensitive, Mentadent S, and supermarket own-label brands. They all took their share of the growing market. The impact on the market leader, however, was less pronounced than one would expect, as increased promotion encouraged greater trial and switching from standard toothpaste brands (Sambrook, 1992).

Competitor strategies

The competitive structure in different product markets will vary to create conditions of strong or weak competition. In markets such as the sensitive toothpaste segment, the dominant competitor has a major influence over the level and nature of competition. Challenges can still arise, but nevertheless, within constraints set by governmental competition policy and public pressure, a dominant competitor is effectively able to decide when and how to compete. The dominant competitor is likely to be confident that it has sufficient strength through its market position, volume sales, and thus perhaps through its cost base to fight any serious challenger successfully.

Example

Intel, the computer chip manufacturer, dominates its markets through size and speed. It dominates world manufacturing capacity and has geared up its R&D to shorten the development time for new generations of chips. Through its dominant strength, Intel has developed a strong capacity in motherboards and chip sets for PCs, regardless of the individual brand name of the final computer sold. This has created a situation that competitors find increasingly difficult to overcome.

Achieving such dominance provides a strong basis for competitive advantage as it makes building, sustaining, and defending a market position relatively easier. The strategies that lead to this will be explored in the next section.

STRATEGIC MARKETING ANALYSIS

Strategic marketing planning makes use of a number of analytical models that help to develop a strategic view of the business, and thus can be used as decision-making aids. The various models outlined below can be applied either to SBUs or to individual products, and thus the use of the word 'product' throughout the discussion should be

Williams Holdings decides to refocus its product portfolio

The Williams Holdings group is an example of a conglomerate business that covers a range of disparate product areas that are largely unrelated and appear to offer little scope for marketing or manufacturing synergy. In recent years, however, it has been reassessing its portfolio and concentrating on a smaller number of areas where it can gain marketing, R&D, and distribution savings through some sharing and integration.

Williams is a major international force in fire protection, which world-wide is worth £6 billion per year and is growing at between 5 per cent and 15 per cent per year because of the impact of increasingly stringent fire regulations. The purchase of the French company Sici and Siddles strengthed its international position and enabled Williams to claim 12 per cent of the world market for fire equipment. It also enabled Williams to combat competition from such large or specialist operators as Tyco International (USA), Chubb (UK) and Nohmi Bosal (Japan). Williams is actively developing its portfolio to offer one of the most complete ranges available. The systems cover detection, fire-fighting equipment, fire engines, and fire extinguishers for the home. The fire protection market is seen as a major area for development, and accounts for around one-third of turnover.

Building products in Europe and North America represent approximately a further 50 per cent of turnover, and include such product areas as Rawlplugs, Polyfilla and paint, among others. Because of the importance of the sales from this division, there is a concern that Williams is locked in to the building and construction industry which can be very volatile and cyclical. Efforts are being made, therefore, to develop new areas. Security products such as locks is one priority area. Williams already owns Yale, and has been acquiring ailing businesses with a view to managing a turnaround. In 1996, for example, it purchased Folger Adam in the USA, which was into prison security and high security windows, both very specialist product niches. The purchase of Mondena locksmiths in Italy projected Williams to number two in the market.

Outside these three core areas, it is rumoured that other businesses in the conglomerate could be available for sale to the right buyer, as they are considered peripheral to the core business. Some are loss making and others, although generating cash, do not fit the group's long-term portfolio strategy. These areas include home improvement companies (fitted kitchens, fences and conservatories) as well as electronics companies (specialising in microswitches, motors and timers for use in cars, consumer electronic products and office equipment). Although a number of these companies are performing well, the lack of fit within the conglomerate group means that they had to be sold. The conglomerate is in the process of refocusing.

Sources: Buckley (1996); Tieman (1996a, 1996b, 1996c).

taken to mean either. The fundamental concept of many of these models is that although products may be managed as individual entities on an operational basis, strategically they should be viewed as a **product portfolio**, that is, a set of products, each of which makes a unique contribution to the corporate picture. The strategist needs to look at that corporate picture and decide whether, for example, there are enough strong products to support the weak ones, whether the weak ones have development potential or whether there are appropriate new products in development to take over from declining ones.

Example

In 1992, Nestlé decided to define its business in terms of strategic brands rather than technologies such as frozen or canned foods. Four key strategic brands worldwide, plus two product areas that cover brands that differ between countries, were defined as SBUs. Nescafé (coffee), Nestlé (confectionery), Friskies (petfood) and Buitoni (pasta) are the worldwide brands that act as business units, with soups and sauces (Crosse & Blackwell; Maggi) and milks and creams (Carnation; Nestlé) also receiving special attention. Each SBU's strategic direction is determined centrally, even though local differences are allowed. Each SBU offers different opportunities and problems on a global scale, but the taking of a portfolio approach has meant that more focus and control can be brought to bear in the development of a large, complex business (Bidlake, 1992b).

Managing SBUs or a product portfolio means that management have to consider products *relative* to each other and ensure that each is fulfiling its allotted strategic role and that the overall balance is right. Management might decide, for example, that the strategic role of a mature product is to generate revenues to provide the stability and investment needed for a risky new product. The new product's role on the other hand, might be to become sufficiently well established within the next three years to take over from the mature product as it declines.

Product portfolio analysis: the Boston Box

Sometimes referred to as the **Boston Box**, or the BCG matrix, the Boston Consulting Group (BCG) market growth–relative market share model, shown in Fig 21.3, assesses products on two dimensions. The first dimension looks at the general level of growth in the product's market, while the second measures the product's market share relative to the largest competitor in the industry. This type of analysis provides a useful insight into the likely opportunities and problems associated with a particular product.

Market growth reflects opportunities and buoyancy in different markets. It also indicates the likely competitive atmosphere, because in high-growth markets there is plenty of room for expansion and all players can make gains, while in low-growth markets, competition will be more intense since growth can only be achieved by taking share away from the competition. The model assumes a range of between 0 per cent (or decline) and 25 per cent growth (or more, if relevant to a particular industry). Some fine tuning is possible to reflect market circumstances.

Market share position is measured on a logarithmic scale against the product's largest competitor. Thus a relative share figure of 0.2 means that the product only achieves 20 per cent of the market leader's sales volume, a potentially weak competitive position. Similarly, a share figure of 2 would mean that the product has twice the market share of its nearest rival. A share figure of 1 means roughly equal shares, and therefore joint leadership.

FIGURE 21.3

BCG matrix

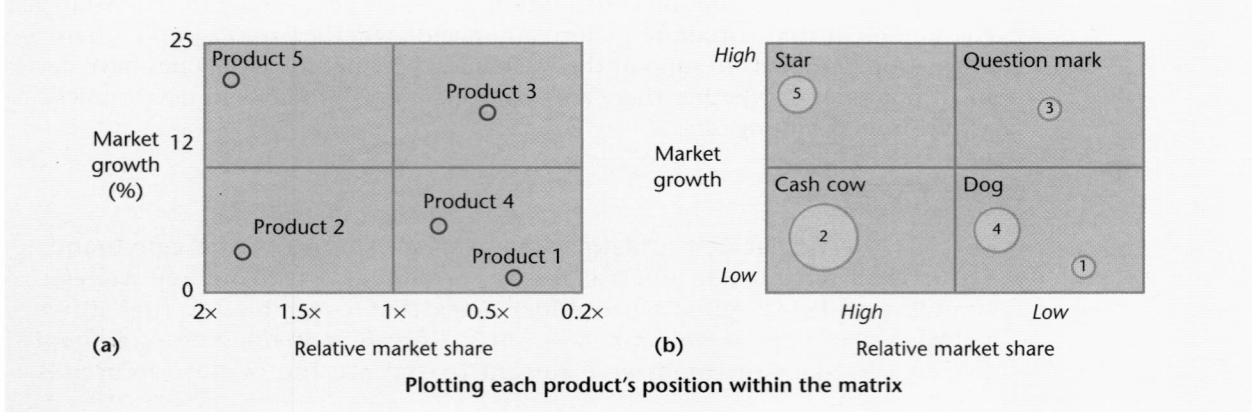

Plotting each product's position within the matrix

Figure 21.3(a) gives an example of the resultant matrix after all the products of an organisation have been thus analysed. The next stage is to plot the products within a simpler four cell matrix that reflects the differing competitive positions, as shown in Fig 21.3(b). Each cell offers different types of business opportunities and imposes different resource demands. The general labelling of the cells as 'high' and 'low' gives an instant and sufficient feel for each product's situation, and the circle that represents each SBU's contribution to the organisation's total sales volume provides a further indication of the relative importance of different products. In Fig. 21.3(b), for example, Product 2 can be seen to be the biggest contributor to overall sales volume, whereas Product 1 contributes very little.

This model provides a guide to the most appropriate corporate investment and divestment options. The 'ideal' model is one where the portfolio is reasonably balanced between existing strength and emerging opportunity. The great advantage of the model is that it forces managers to reflect on current and projected performance, and to ask important questions about the continued viability of products, their strategic role and the potential for performance improvement.

We now look in turn at each cell of the matrix.

Dog (low share, low growth)

A dog holds a weak market share in a low growth market, and is likely to be making a loss, or a low profit at best. It is unlikely that its share can be increased at a reasonable cost, because of the low market growth. A dog can be a drain on management time and resources.

> **Example**
>
> Quaker Foods decided to drop its Wholegrain Feast cereal just two years after its launch. Some £7 million was spent on television and press advertising in 1994, partly to establish the brand. However, such heavy advertising could not be maintained and the product failed to achieve the required market impact (*Marketing Week*, 1996a).

The question, therefore, is whether or not to shoot the dog, that is, withdraw the product. Much depends on the strategic role that the dog is fulfilling, and its future prospects. It may, for example, be blocking a competitor (a guard dog?), or it may be complementing the company's own activities, for example, creating customers at the bottom of the range who will then trade up to one of the organisation's better products (a guide dog, or a sheep dog?). Otherwise, a dog may be worth retaining if management feel that there will be an upturn in the market soon. It may also be possible to retain the product with less marketing support (which might improve the profits, but is unlikely to help its market share), or to reposition it into a narrower segment where it is more highly valued.

> **Example**
>
> In Quaker's case, it was felt that Wholegrain Feast had too narrow an appeal, and was perceived as being too healthy and not sufficiently tasty. On that basis, therefore, it was decided that the product would be dropped and replaced with Crisp Grain Feast, which would be formulated and positioned to overcome the problems.

Question mark (low share, high growth)

The high market growth of a question mark is good news, but the low share is worrying. Why is relative market share so low? What is the organisation doing wrong, or what is the competition doing right? It may simply be that the question mark (also sometimes called a problem child or a wild cat) is a relatively new product that is still in the process of establishing its position in the market. If it is not a new product, then it might just need far more investment in plant, equipment and marketing to keep up with the market growth rate. There is also a risk, however, that a question mark with problems might absorb a great deal of cash just to retain its position.

> ### Example
>
> The market for vegetarian foods is growing as more consumers take up the vegetarian option. Mintel predicted a UK market growth of over 13 per cent in 1995. Such growth, fuelled by changing consumer tastes and attitudes to healthy eating as well as fears about BSE and salmonella, is stimulating a number of new products, especially from those seeking niches. The industry is fragmented, with just a few mainstream manufacturers such as Birds Eye Wall's, Marlow Foods (Quorn), and Ross Young, along with a large number of smaller manufacturers seeking to specialise in specific niches, such Abel Eastern's veggie naan breads or the New Covent Garden Soup Company. The success of these brands is partly a result of differentiation and partly a result of opening up a niche that is sufficiently large, sustainable and defendable (McClintock, 1996).

Some of the alternatives for question marks, such as dropping or repositioning, are the same as for the dogs, but there are some more creative options. If the product is felt to have potential, then management might commit significant investment towards building market share, as mentioned above. Alternatively, if the organisation is cash rich, it might seek to take over competitors to strengthen its market position, effectively buying market share.

Star (high share, high growth)

A star product is a market leader in a growth market. It needs a great deal of cash to retain its position, to support further growth and to maintain its lead. It does, however, also generate cash, because of its strength, and so it is likely to be self-sufficient. Stars could be the cash cows of the future.

In the vegetarian food market, some products have already achieved a strong position and are well placed to build further as the market expands. The Vegetable Cuisine range from Birds Eye is a major contributor to the company's estimated 50 per cent share of the added value vegetarian market, while Ross Young claims 27 per cent of the frozen meat-free market.

Cash cow (high share, low growth)

As market growth starts to tail off, stars can become cash cows. These products no longer need the same level of support as before since there are no new customers to be had, and there is less competitive pressure. Cash cows enjoy a dominant position generated from economies of scale, given their relative market share.

> ### Example
>
> Philips have two international cash cows in their portfolio: lighting and televisions. Both have provided the cash necessary to fund the introduction of such innovations as CDs, laservision and digital compact cassettes. However, Philips' cash cows are increasingly under pressure from Japanese competition in relatively stable markets.

The management focus here is on retention and maintenance, rather than on seeking growth. Management might be looking to keep price leadership, and any investment will be geared towards lowering costs rather than increasing volumes. Any excess cash can be diverted to new areas needing support, perhaps helping to develop dogs and question marks into stars.

Two further categories were proposed by Barksdale and Harris (1982):

War horses (high market share, negative growth)

War horses are market leaders, but their cash generating position is under threat because of negative market growth. Management options depend on whether the decline is terminal or temporary. If it is terminal, then the strategy should be to harvest for as long as possible, offering minimal marketing support, as most volume comes from repeat sales based on loyalty. Any investment, whether in promotion or plant, should look for a swift payback. If the decline is temporary, it is probably worth riding the storm, maintaining support to enable cash generation to continue.

Dodos (low share, negative growth)

As the name implies, the dodo product is almost certain to become extinct, as low share of a declining market means that sales volumes are dwindling away. Management needs to undertake regular reviews of returns generated, adopting a contribution-based approach to such a product. As soon as the product's contribution becomes negative, it is a candidate for early termination.

MARKETING IN ACTION

Aérospatiale and Dassault take off

The merger between the state-owned Aérospatiale and the private company Dassault, the two leading aircraft manufacturers in France, caused considerable controversy. It involved politicians at the highest levels, as well as the companies' chief executives, in the search for an agreement on a new combined civil and military company, French Aerospace. Dassault made fighters such as Mirage and Rafale, while Aérospatiale was renowned for its role in the successful European Airbus. The rationale presented by the government was that to compete successfully with larger US firms, a merger would provide a Fr. 60 billion company with greater combined strength. This combined strength would also give the two companies a better chance of survival, an issue of great concern to the government as any employment loss in this sector would be capable of generating grave public concern. As an added bonus, the state also would only need to supply orders to one company rather than to two. The merger could also be the forerunner of a new pan-European company that would also involve the British and Germans to meet US competition on more equal terms.

Most of Aérospatiale's turnover came from the Airbus programme, and the regional turbo props, the ATR 42 and 72, that were produced in a venture with Alenia from Italy. Aérospatiale also had a share in Eurocopter Holdings (helicopter production), which was a leading player worldwide, with its products having military applications such as the Tiger anti-tank and ground support helicopter for the French and German armed forces. Other activities included missiles, weapons systems, and ballistic missiles. It was also the lead company in the Ariane space programme.

There was, therefore, little product overlap between the two companies. Aérospatiale generated 72 per cent of its business from the civil sector, with a tradition of working with foreign companies in all areas except ballistic missiles. Dassault operated primarily in the military sector, which is often bound in secrecy, only rarely encouraging co-operation with other companies outside France. From a commercial perspective, Dassault's priority was to ensure that the air force and navy budgets allowed 300 Rafales to be ordered over the next few years.

The main area for synergy resulting from the merger was research and development. The two companies have 4500 R&D staff between them, which could be rationalised in a merger. There were few other obvious benefits from the merger that would directly lead to savings or synergy, as the two companies tended to operate in very different markets.

Sources: Buchan (1996); Tillier (1996); Verchere (1996).

English China Clays
sets sail towards the
next century with a
streamlined portfolio
of SBUs.

Source: English China
Clay International.

Example

English China Clays have undergone a revolution in their portfolio in recent
years. They had developed not just in the production of kaolin, calcium carbon-
ate and ball clay, their traditional businesses, but also into construction materials,
aggregates and housebuilding, as well as specialised drilling fluids for the oil and
gas industries. They found, however, that to remain competitive, a number of the
businesses required investment well beyond the capability of the company. The
portfolio had become unbalanced. In 1993 they divested the building materials
division, worth about £350 million and the group's second largest operation. The
funds released were used to strengthen the industrial minerals and speciality
chemicals core business through higher value added, improving the service orientation and seeking higher-margin business. This clearly demonstrates the need to
analyse the SBUs in portfolio terms as a means of supporting the strategic development of the business as a whole (Lorenz, 1995).

Once the BCG matrix has been developed for an organisation, it can be used to assess
the strength of the company and its product portfolio. Ideally, a strong mix of cash
cows and stars is desirable, although there may be embryonic stars among the dogs
and question marks. The situation and the portfolio become unbalanced where there
are too many dogs and question marks and not enough cash cows to fund new developments to allow them to break out of those cells. There is also a risk dimension to all
this. The organisation as a whole is vulnerable if there are too many products with an
uncertain future (question marks).

Four main assumptions underpin the BCG model:

1 gains in market share are made by investing in a competitive package, especially
  through marketing investment;

2 market share gains have the potential to generate cash surpluses as a result of economies of scale and the learning curve;

3 cash surpluses are more likely to be generated when products are in the maturity stage of the life-cycle;

4 the best opportunities to build a strong position occur during a market's growth period.

Abell and Hammond (1979), however, identified a number of weaknesses in the BCG model and its assumptions, for instance that cash flow and cash richness are influenced by far more than market share and industry growth, and that return on investment (ROI) is a more widely used yardstick of investment attractiveness than cash flow. Although it is conceptually neat, the BCG matrix does not adequately assess alternative investment opportunities when there is competition for funds, as for example, when it is necessary to decide whether it is better to support a star or a question mark.

Market attractiveness model: the GE matrix

Developed first by General Electric (GE), the market attractiveness–business position portfolio assessment model was designed to overcome some of the problems of models such as the BCG matrix.

FIGURE 21.4

GE matrix

The **GE matrix** adds more variables to aid investment decision appraisal. It uses two principal dimensions, as seen in Fig 21.4: *industry attractiveness* (the vertical axis) and *business strengths* (the horizontal axis). Within the matrix, the circle size represents the size of the market and the shaded part the share of the market held by the SBU.

The first dimension, industry attractiveness, is a composite index determined by market size, rate of growth, degree of competition, pace of technological change, new legislation and profit margins achieved, among others. The second dimension, business position, is another composite index, comprising a range of factors that help to build stronger relative market share, such as relative product quality and performance, brand image, distribution strength, price competition, loyalty, production efficiency etc. Both dimensions need to work positively together, since there is little point in having a strong position in an unattractive market, or a weak position in strong market.

Within the matrix, there are three zones, each implying a different marketing and management strategy:

1 *zone 1 (high attractiveness, strong position)*. The strategy here should be investment for further growth;

2 *zone 2 (medium attractiveness)*. Because there is a weakness on one dimension, the strategy here should be one of selective investment, without over-committing; and

3 *zone 3 (least attractive)*. Either make short-term gains or proceed to pull out.

The main areas of concern with this model are linked to methodology and the lack of clear guidelines for implementing strategies.

Shell's directional policy matrix

Shown in Fig 21.5, the **Shell directional policy matrix** has two dimensions, competitive capabilities and prospects for sector profitability. The nine cells of the matrix offer different opportunities and challenges, so that placing each product in an appropriate cell provides a guide to its strategic development.

FIGURE 21.5

Shell matrix

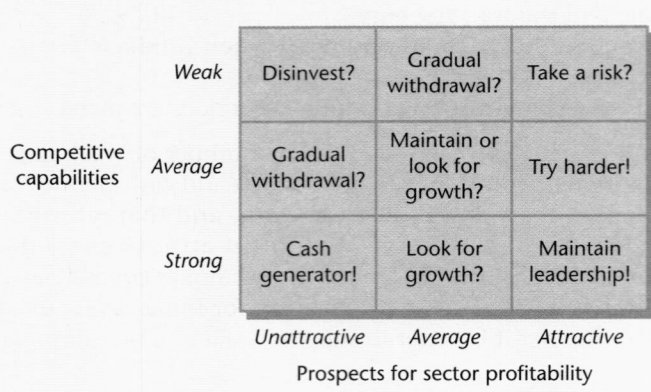

Review of models

Portfolio models have been criticised, but they have, nevertheless, been useful in forcing managers, especially in large complex organisations, to think more strategically. They can certainly be used as diagnostic tools to give an overview of the current position and to stimulate debate on what could happen if direction is not changed. These models do not, however, give solutions about what strategies should be adopted, and they need to be supported by clear action plans. The main problem with them is the rather simplistic use of variables that contributes to the axes and the decision rules sought from the models. The preoccupation with market share is of particular concern, since it might be just as valid to consolidate and perform better as to pursue high-growth, high-share business. The models also fail to consider the synergies between businesses, where one may support another.

In some situations, it might be more appropriate to focus on a small number of areas, and perform really well in these than to over-extend in the pursuit of market share or market growth. In many markets, a set of businesses survive with little reference to market share as niche operators. They might, therefore, develop attractive returns without necessarily seeking market share for its own sake or incurring the costs and risks associated with the pursuit of relative sales volume. This is also true in situations where technological change and obsolescence can quickly erode any significant advantage gained.

> **Example**
>
> Lilliput has built a highly profitable company based on a range of cute cottage models to adorn the living-room. The key to its success is in creating brand and market awareness rather than in preparing moulds and painting the output. The organisation now employs 600 people and is resisting the temptation to diversify other than by acquiring related product lines. The company has little concern for market share, but in retaining its position as a niche operator, it is a classic example of successful positioning (Darwent, 1994).

Some methodological weaknesses emerge when the models are implemented in practice:

1 how to weight the variables for a composite index such as that which the GE model uses. Different managers could have different opinions about how to weight variables, leading to very different looking matrices for the same organisation;
2 the guidelines used to distinguish zones or cells are open to some debate. Different rules may apply in different situations;

3 the measures used on each matrix also need careful examination. Often, the preoccupation with market share, SBUs and production suggest a bias away from the smaller business and the service business. In a small business, share may be of minimal importance compared with dependable niches. The service business has very different operational concerns from a manufacturing organisation, given the focus on service performers and facilities rather than production lines.

Although these models are commonly described in text books, they are not so widely used in practice. They are conceptually easy to design, but very difficult to implement effectively. They require considerable management skill and judgement, because of their focus on the identification of variables, weighting decisions and future changes, rather than just on present, tangible, measurable factors. Thus although they can be useful planning tools, they still have some way to go to achieve widespread use. Where they are used at all, there is often a tendency to use them as diagnostic tools rather than as predictive tools. Their real advantage is their focus on corporate objectives, and the contribution that marketing decision making makes to that process. Above all, however, it must be remembered that they are tools to assist decision making, not a series of rules that lead to inevitable conclusions and decisions.

GROWTH STRATEGIES FOR MARKETING

The previous section looked at the corporate perspective on strategic planning, presenting a number of models that can guide marketing strategy development. This section examines a number of different strategies that organisations might adopt if their priority is *growth*. It is important to remember, however, that growth is not always a priority. In many small firms, for example, survival or sustaining the *status quo* might be the main objective. In other situations, standing still might be the right strategy if the market is starting to tighten up. The preoccupation with growth, therefore, should not be assumed to be relevant to all organisations all the time.

Managing growth is not without problems, because of the demands it imposes on management time and resources, and not least because of the additional risks created. For those who are facing growth opportunities, and who have the capabilities to exploit them, a number of options are available. The product–market matrix proposed by Ansoff (1957) provides a useful framework for considering the relationship between strategic direction and marketing strategy. The four-cell matrix shown in Fig 21.6 considers various combinations of product–market options. Each cell in the **Ansoff matrix** presents distinct opportunities, threats, resource requirements, returns and risks, and will be discussed in the next two subsections.

FIGURE 21.6

Ansoff's growth matrix

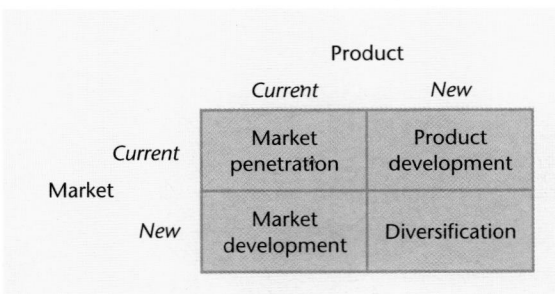

Source: Ansoff (1957).

Intensive Growth

Three cells of the Ansoff matrix offer opportunity for sustained growth, although each one has different potential according to the market situation.

Market penetration

The aim of **market penetration** is to increase sales volume in current markets, usually by more aggressive marketing. This means using the full range of the marketing mix to achieve greater leverage.

The priority for Wrangler in the UK in 1993 was to improve its position in the £1.2 billion jeans market. The market was dominated by Levi's with over 20 per cent share, followed by Lee and Wrangler. Any significant penetration would have to be achieved at the expense of the other leaders. Wrangler aimed to achieve this by developing a £2 million campaign positioning their jeans away from fashion wear and more towards casual wear, aiming at a wider target audience than the traditional youth market (Benady, 1993). By 1996, however, Levi's was reported to be holding 26 per cent of the market, with Lee and Wrangler about equal on 7 per cent each. Wrangler's 1996 campaign was the first move in a shift in focus back towards a core market of consumers in their early twenties (Simpson, 1996).

Market development

Market development means selling more of the existing product to new markets, which could be based on new geographic segments or could be created by opening up other new segments (based, for example on age, product usage, lifestyle or any other segmentation variable). Danish firms control nearly half of the world's market for wind turbine machines. Companies such as Vestas Wind Systems and Nordtank Energy Systems depend heavily on achieving growth by developing new markets. A key part of their success will be the speed with which wind power is adopted. Experts such as the International Energy Authority predict that the market will have tripled by the year 2000 to around 12 000 megawatts, while others suggest that there could be a growth to 200 000 megawatts by the year 2010. Developing the market around the world with proven technology is clearly a priority for manufacturers (Heller, 1995).

Product development

Product development, as covered in Chapter 19, means selling completely new or improved products into existing markets. The luxury chocolate market has been growing as consumers become increasingly willing to pay premium prices for quality. Not all of the UK and Irish market has been captured by Belgian luxury chocolate producers, however. Lir Chocolates from Ireland, specialists in hand made chocolates, developed a new brand, Cliona, exclusively for the Irish multiple chain Quinnsworth (Murphy, 1996).

Diversified and integrative growth

Growth through **diversification** takes place outside the value chain, for example developing new products and new markets, whereas growth through integration takes place within the chain, for example making components yourself rather than buying them in.

Specialist Computer Holdings (SCH) achieved very rapid growth in its computer sales and service group by moving into mail order computer sales and through the Byte chain of computer stores. This integrative growth was partly organic and partly through acquisition. By developing in unfamiliar, but related technology areas (diversification growth) it increased its turnover from £95 million to £229 million in three years, with further growth expected (Smith, 1996).

Both diversification and integration might involve radical new departures into unknown technical, managerial or marketing areas.

Growth through diversification

Diversification, the final cell in the Ansoff Matrix, happens when an organisation decides to move beyond its current boundaries to exploit new opportunities. It means entering unfamiliar territory in both product and market terms. One of the major attractions of this option is that it spreads risk, moving the organisation away from being too reliant on one product or one market. It also allows expertise and resources to be allocated synergistically, for example theme parks diversifying into hotel accommodation, or airlines diversifying into tour packages. Calori and Harvatopoulos (1988), in a study of diversification in France, found both offensive and defensive reasons for diversification, with outcomes such as a stronger financial position or greater synergy with existing operations. The danger is, of course, that the organisation spreads its effort too widely into areas of low expertise, and tries to position itself against more specialist providers.

There are two main types of growth through diversification:

Concentric diversification. Concentric diversification happens where there is a link, either technological or commercial, between the old and the new sets of activities. The benefit is, therefore, gained from a synergy with current activities. An organisation could, for example, add new, unrelated product lines to its portfolio, but still use the same sales and distribution network. In reverse, SCH, as mentioned in the example on p. 846, added new distribution methods to existing product technology.

Conglomerate diversification. The conglomerate diversification route is taken when an organisation undertakes new activities in markets that are also new. This involves risks in both the product development area and gaining acceptance in the market place.

Example

American Express decided to become a multi-product business, building on its image and experience with certain lifestyle segments gained through its credit cards. Not only was direct banking piloted in Germany, but consideration was also given to mobile phone services, travel products and private health care. The common thread for the diversification was the use of the Amex name.

Growth through integration

Meanwhile, integrative growth means staying within the same value chain, but entering new roles or processes either to ensure greater control of the overall process or to gain expansion. There are a number of options.

Backward integration. The focus in backward integration is on guaranteeing the quantity and quality of supply within acceptable cost guidelines. This could mean looking closely at raw materials, semi-processed materials, components or services supplied. A large manufacturer of vehicle refrigeration units in Ireland, for example, acquired the capacity to produce one of the components. This meant that these components were now made in-house, thus effectively terminating supply arrangements with some local small suppliers. Marks and Spencer, in contrast, does not seek formal ownership of its suppliers, but firmly controls their operations through tight specifications, prices, quantities and exclusivity agreements.

Backward integration might not be undertaken by choice. Suppliers may not be able to meet the buyer's specifications, or the buyers might want access to the supplier's technology to allow them to redesign and control the specification, for example.

Forward integration. Forward integration occurs where the organisation sets up or acquires dealers, distributors, wholesalers or retailers in order to control the distribution process in terms of physical supply, inventory, selling effort etc. This could also include controlling the major customers for your product.

Example

Cockerill Sambre, the major Belgian steel producer, set up companies further down the distribution channel to process their products for specific applications. Phoenix Works produces coating and galvanizing sheet steel, Polypal produces industrial storage systems and Polytuile produces roof coverings of steel sheeting (Lambin, 1993).

Horizontal integration. The objective of horizontal integration is to absorb competitors, to strengthen either market coverage or market position. This route might result in cost savings if, for example, product distribution overlap can be eliminated and a common distribution network used. Within the greeting card industry, for example, larger producers tend to acquire the more successful smaller operators who find it difficult to break out of confined niches as they lack the distribution and merchandising strengths to deal with the larger retailers. In other horizontal acquisitions, the partners may be complementary rather than direct competition.

Example

Samas, a Dutch office furnishings company, acquired a majority stake in Schaerf, a German office manufacturer. This will provide a 10 per cent share of the European market. Schaeff makes wooden office desks primarily for the German market but also for eastern Europe, whilst Samas focuses mainly on the Netherlands, France and Britain. The combined strength gives each of them access to markets where previously they were not strong (van de Krol, 1994b).

Each of the alternative growth strategies is summarised in Table 21.1.

Other 'no growth' options

Not all strategies have to be growth orientated. *Harvesting* is a deliberate strategy of not seeking growth, but looking for the best returns from the product, even if the action taken may actually speed up any decline or reinforce the no growth situation. The objective is, however, to make short-term profit while it is possible. Typically, products subjected to harvesting are likely to be cash cows in the mature stage of their life-cycles (*see* pp. 294 *et seq.*), in a market that is stable or declining, as considered at pp. 836 *et seq.* Harvesting strategies could involve minimal promotional expenditure, premium pricing strategies where possible, reducing product variability and controlling costs rigidly. Implementing such strategies helps to ensure that maximum returns are made over a short period, despite the potential loss of longer-term future sales. Effectively, the company is relying on the short-term loyalty of customers to cushion the effect of declining sales.

In more extreme cases, where prospects really are poor or bleak, *entrenchment or withdrawal* might be the only options. A timetable for withdrawal or closure would be developed and every effort made to maximises returns on the remaining output, in the full

TABLE 21.1
Alternative growth strategies

Intensive growth

- Market penetration
- Market development
- Product development

Diversified growth

- Concentric diversification
- Conglomerate diversification

Integrative growth

- Backward integration
- Forward integration
- Horizontal integration

Brylcreem was for a number of years regarded as a cash cow by SmithKline Beecham. Other than for brief relaunch periods, little was spent on promoting the hair control brand. However, when Sara Lee purchased the brand in 1993, a decision was made to reposition the brand towards a younger age group through 'sensual imagery' featuring a couple in intimate encounters, with an advertising strapline of 'Control yourself'. Sara Lee considered that a revitalised brand that was supported rather than milked could produce growth, and did not accept that further growth was not an economic option (Nicholas, 1994).

knowledge that harm will be done to sales volume in the short term. Some care should, however, be exercised when considering withdrawal, as highlighted in our discussion of dogs (*see* p. 839). Although the profit potential may be poor and the costs of turn-around prohibitive, the loss of a product in a range may affect other parts of the range adversely. Thus entrenchment, protecting the product's position as best you can without wasting too many resources on it, might be the most appropriate course of action.

Sometimes brands might be allowed to die slowly rather than be subjected to a firm decision to terminate.

The Scottish Courage brewery decided to concentrate its activities on its main national brands with the result that the minor 'second tier' brands were allowed to decline until final withdrawal. The marketing budget on such brands as Gillespie's Stout and Home Bitter were planned to be transferred to more popular brands such as Fosters and John Smith's. The withdrawal of a marketing budget could be regarded as making further decline and marginalisation of a brand inevitable (Benady, 1996).

MARKETING AND COMPETITIVE STRATEGY

No organisation operates in isolation. The organisation is not free to develop a business and marketing strategy without reference to the competitive environment. In recent years, the analysis and development of competitive strategy has become a major area of concern in many markets, reflecting the changing economic environment, and especially the internationalisation of trade. Competitors are an important factor that will influence the eventual success or failure of a business in any market. Ignore competition, and the likelihood of being taken by surprise or of being caught out by a strong new product or a major attack on a loyal customer base is very great and can create severe problems. That is why it is important to consider systematically a number of aspects of competitive behaviour.

Competitor analysis

Competitor analysis is a systematic attempt to identify and understand the key elements of a competitor's strategy, in terms of objectives, strategies, resource allocation and implementation through the marketing mix. A sound understanding of these areas enables stronger defences to be built and sustainable competitive advantage to be created and, not least, provides a foundation for outmanoeuvring the competition to gain share or market position.

At the macro level, Porter (1979) in his Five Forces Model defined the competitive forces that operate in an industry. They are:

- the bargaining power of suppliers
- the bargaining power of customers
- the threat of new entrants
- the threat of substitute products and services
- the rivalry among current competitors.

Porter's five forces form a useful starting point for undertaking a competitive analysis, in particular because they encourage a very wide definition of competition. Competition is not just about established, direct competitors at end-product level, but also about indirect and future competitors and about competition for suppliers. Before the development of the Channel Tunnel, the cross-channel ferry companies felt little need to compete aggressively with each other. Once the concept of the tunnel became a reality, however, they were shaken into action because of the perceived competitive threat.

The Porter model gives a sound foundation, but there are still several areas that should be analysed, if there is to be a full appreciation of competitors.

Competitor identification

As the Porter model implies, the identification of competitors is often broader than it first appears. The exercise should look at potential competitors, focus on the extent to which market needs are being satisfied and look at the needs that are emerging, as well as evaluating the activities and capabilities of the obvious competition. Latent or new competitors can take a market by surprise.

There are several types of competitors:

- *Similar specific* – same product, technology, and target market, for example Sega *vs* Nintendo
- *similar general* – same product area, but serving different segments, for example Häagen Dazs *vs* Wall's ice-cream
- *different specific* – same need satisfied by very different means, for example Eurostar *vs* British Airways between London and Paris
- *different general* – competing for discretionary spend, for example a holiday *vs* a new car.

An organisation needs to decide with whom it is really competing, and from which category of competition the major threats are emerging. A market leader might base its marketing strategy on the overall stimulation of demand (i.e., tackle the *different general* competitors, on the basis that it will pick up the largest share of any new business created), while a minor player might be more concerned with taking share from *similar specific* competition.

Any organisation should take a wide view of who it is competing with. Small local shops discovered the hard way that they were competing with the supermarket multiples. The process can, however, work the other way round: it is possible for what appears to be a small niche operator to shake up a market. Häagen Dazs, for example, entered the UK by opening up a whole new 'adult indulgence' segment in the ice-cream market which grew so fast that it caused existing players to rethink their marketing strategies.

Competitive clusters

Once competitors are identified, it might be possible to group them into clusters, depending on their focus and strategy. Figure 21.7 shows, how advertising agencies can be clustered.

The vertical axis in Fig 21.7 covers a geographic spectrum. At one end are the purely local, typically small operators, perhaps based in a town or city. Then come regional agencies, for example based in Lyon or Leeds, that may have some national accounts. These are followed by national agencies that operate throughout the country, and are often based in the capital. European agencies handle European accounts, working through a network of offices in other capitals, while at the far end of the spectrum are the international agencies, operating from major world capitals. The horizontal axis covers the range of services, beginning with the specialists (handling,

FIGURE 21.7

Strategic groupings: Advertising agencies

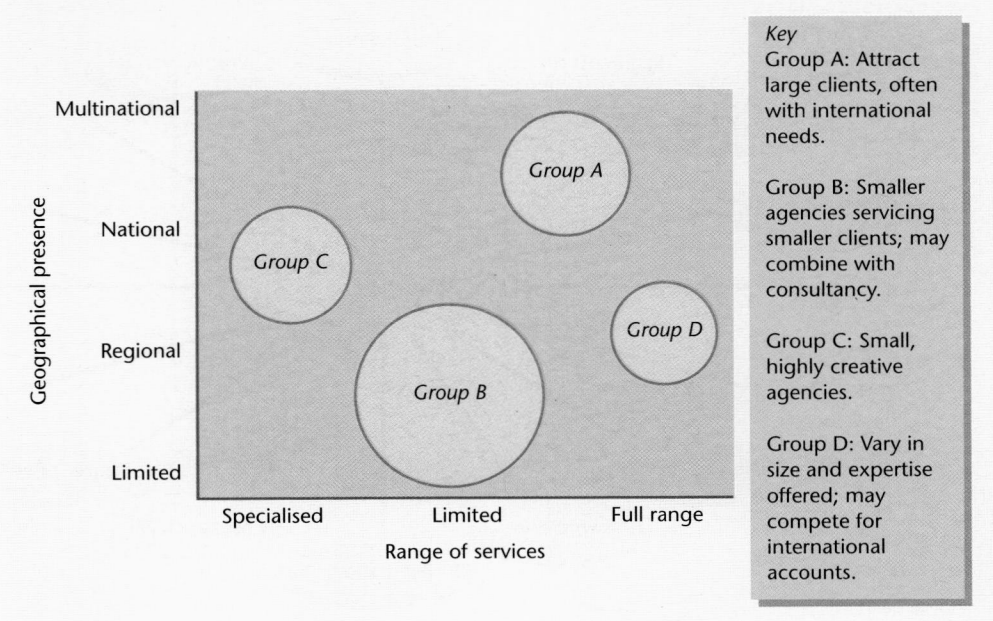

for example only one task, such as media buying or one type of advertising, such as direct response). Limited service agencies handle mostly advertising work, but not research or wider aspects of marketing, while full range agencies offer most services directly or by affiliation. Finally, diversified agencies offer all marketing services on a 'one stop shop' basis.

Once the clusters have been identified, the strong and weak competitors in each group can then be considered, and strategic opportunities defined. It is clearly easier to enter the market as a local, specialised or limited service agency than as a major international player, but subsequent evolution may be possible. It is important to remember, however, that there might still be competition between different clusters. A local agency could bid for a national contract, for example, but might find it difficult to convince a potential customer that they have the expertise, resources and track record.

There are a number of different characteristics that can be used for identifying strategic clusters, as shown in Fig 21.8. This can provide a useful framework for identifying opportunities, but remember that in order to implement the technique, the organisation needs detailed competitor information, not just on financial performance but also on segments served and marketing strategies etc.

Competitive strengths and weaknesses

Examining a competitor's strengths and weaknesses provides a valuable insight into their strategic thinking and actions. A full range of areas should be examined, for example manufacturing, technical and financial strengths, relationships with suppliers and customers and markets and segments served, as well as the usual gamut of marketing activity. It is particularly worth undertaking a detailed review of the product range, identifying where volume, profits and cash come from, where the competitor is the market leader, where it is weak and where it seems to be heading.

Of course, the required information may not all be readily available. Shared customers or suppliers can be a useful source of information, but the organisation might also have to make use of secondary data, especially sales reports, exhibitions and press cuttings etc. The analysis of this information should be considered in the context of *critical success factors*. These are the factors or attributes that are essential if an organisation

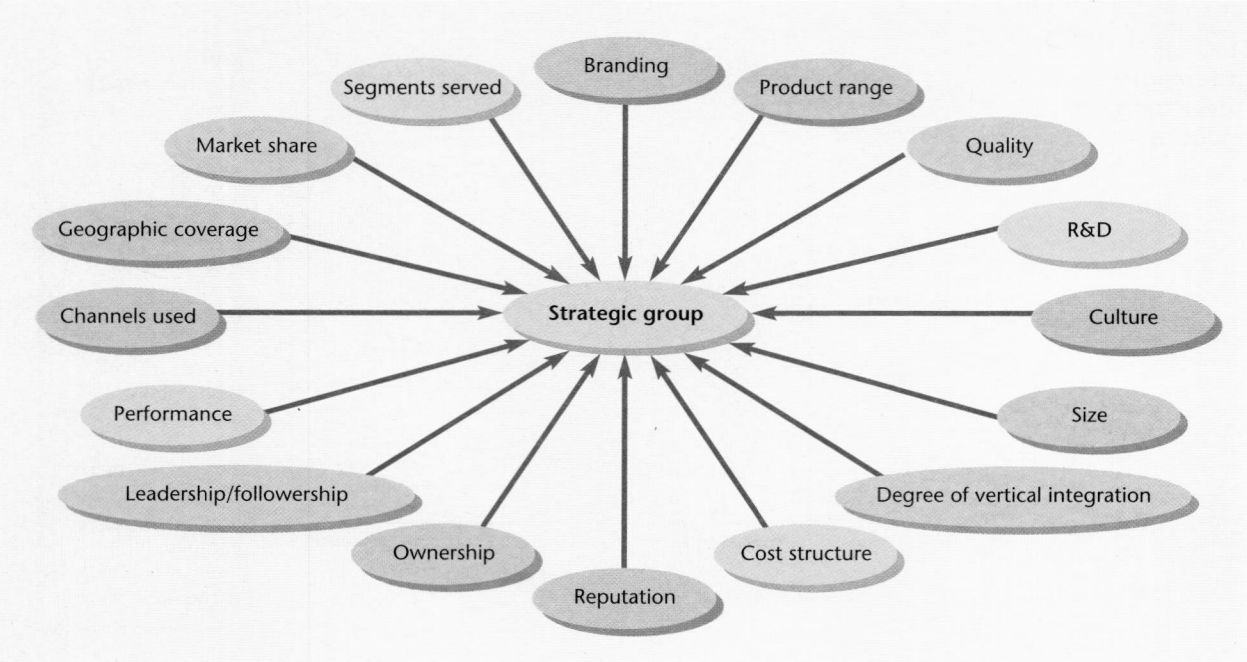

Source: Adapted from Wilson *et al.* (1992).

FIGURE 21.8

Characteristics that define strategic groups

Example

ICI might consider improving its competitive position in the bulk chemicals market by benchmarking itself against its best international competitors in each of its businesses. By examining its own performance in such areas as purchasing, supply, chain management and manufacturing, it could identify areas that require efficiency improvements (Smith, 1995). Similarly, in the 1980s, Rank Xerox benchmarked its performance against Japanese brands such as Canon. Xerox found that its lead times in product development were twice as long, defects per 100 machines were seven times higher, it used nine times more production supplies and in some areas unit manufacturing cost was close to the selling price. This formed the basis of a major change within the organisation, transforming efficiency (Johnson, 1992).

---

is to have any chance of success in a particular industry. Often, they evolve around technology, image, finance, service, quality, distribution, management or the skills of the work-force. Each competitor can be rated on each factor to assess their strong and vulnerable points. This information can be used later to plan and launch an attack.

Competitors' objectives and strategies

It is important to understand what drives competitors, what makes them act as they do. Most firms have multiple objectives beyond the simple notion of profit. Objectives could relate to cash generation, market share, technological leadership, quality recognition or a host of other things. Sometimes developing an understanding of a competitor's product portfolio provides a valuable insight into likely competitive objectives. Once you understand their objectives, you have strong clues about how their strategy is likely to unfold in terms of their positioning, marketing mix and vulnerable points for attack, or your best means of defence. Furthermore, if you can assess the relative importance of their objectives, you can go further in assessing their likely future plans and their reaction to market or competitive events. Competitive retaliation, for example, is likely to be more intense if the competitor has a strong vested interest in the market, such as profit contribution, growth, opportunities etc.

Example

Polar, the former Polish state-owned manufacturer of refrigerators and washing machines, found itself open to competition from a wide range of sophisticated western imports after the 1990 liberalisation of trade. Output initially slumped to 50 per cent of 1989 levels, but a strategy of product improvement, new manufacturing methods and not least an improved distribution strategy helped to restore the company's fortunes. It recognised that it could create a potential competitive advantage over the new suppliers if it could build a distribution network offering high standards of product distribution and service quickly. This has proved to be a strong defence against foreign competitors who find it difficult to operate within a relatively backward distribution network, especially given the need to build channels from scratch (Robinson and Dobrowolski, 1995).

Competitive reaction

It is very important to be able to assess competitors' responses to general changes in the marketing environment and to moves in major battles within the market. These responses could range from matching a price cut or an increase in promotional spend, through to ignoring events or shifting the ground completely. An organisation can learn from experience how competitors are likely to behave. Some will always react swiftly and decisively to what is seen as a threat, others may be more selective depending upon the perceived magnitude of the threat.

Example

The Swiss based pharmaceutical group Ares-Serono and Organon International, a subsidiary of the Dutch group Akzo, found themselves in direct conflict with each other. Both wanted to be the first company to the market with a revolutionary new drug to overcome infertility. The drug was designed to stimulate egg production in women and sperm production in men. With a potential market worldwide of $500 million and 20 per cent year on year growth expected, the battle to be first to market with a proven product from large-scale clinical trials was intense (Hecht, 1993).

TABLE 21.2
Useful information about competitors

- Sales
- Customers
- Products
- Advertising and promotion
- Distribution and sales force
- Pricing
- Finance
- Management
- Anything else ...

Source: Wilson *et al.* (1992).

It is not always easy to predict competitive reaction, as it is likely to be influenced by a range of factors, including cost structures, relative market positions and the stage reached in the industry or product life cycle.

Competitive information system

The above discussion of competitor analysis demonstrates the need for a well-organised and comprehensive competitor information system. This would be part of the MIS discussed in Chapter 6. Often, data need to be deliberately sourced on an ongoing basis, collated, analysed, disseminated and discussed. Then, management at all levels can learn what is happening. They may dispute the findings or the data may provide a basis for seeking further insights. It is impossible to provide a complete checklist of areas that need to be considered, but Wilson *et al.* (1992) provide useful guidelines, as shown in Table 21.2.

Clearly, information is the key to outmanoeuvring and limiting the threats of competition, and should be gathered and analysed on both an individual competitor and competitive cluster basis.

Alternative competitive strategies

It has been argued that organisations should select a generic strategy that provides the direction for subsequent operational decisions, including marketing (Porter, 1980). Three **generic strategies** are proposed, as shown in Fig 21.9. Each one imposes different pressures on the organisation to ensure that resources and capabilities are consistent with the requirements of the strategic alternative selected. The expectation is, however, that the vigorous pursuit of the chosen strategy will create a *sustainable competitive advantage*. The three alternatives are cost leadership, differentiation and focus. Each one is now considered in turn.

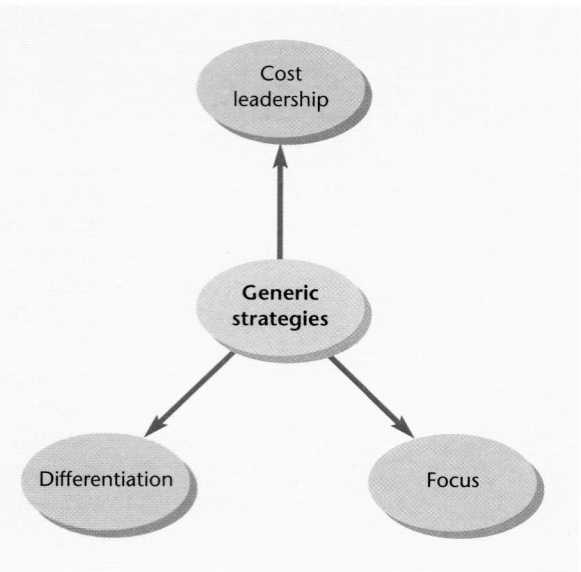

FIGURE 21.9

Generic strategies

Cost leadership

Through the strategy of cost leadership, the organisation seeks a cost advantage over its competitors. This might involve efficiency drives, tight cost controls or a preoccupation with low-cost production. It almost certainly means a ruthless attack on waste, in the drive to gain cost advantage. It might mean investment in production to achieve productivity gains, or it might mean investment in marketing to ensure that adequate sales volumes are achieved.

A focus on the good health of the nation could be the right strategic medicine for BUPA, the private healthcare company.

Source: Ogilvy & Mather.

The Bonas Machine Company based in the north east of England specialises in the textile machinery business and has around 50 per cent of the world market for electronic Jacquard weaving machines. These machines enable looms to weave patterns and designs into the cloth. From the late 1980s, the company has had the strategic objective of being the world's lowest cost producer for Jacquard type machines. This meant a series of major changes in manufacturing and supplier management to get costs down and enable the objective to be achieved (New and Wheatley, 1995).

In the above example, the low-cost position was designed not so much to cut prices as a market leader, but to offset aggressive international competition. The problem with cost leadership is, however, that it tends to put undue emphasis on price. A cost leader can entertain a price war and, with a more efficient cost base, can contemplate winning. Cost leadership can also give a defensive cushion. A competitive supply market might, for example, encourage a powerful buyer to demand yet lower prices. The cost leader can deliver on those prices, and perhaps still retain a small advantage. Such a focus on costs and price can also have the advantage of making it less attractive for new entrants to come into the market.

In short, the firm with cost leadership will feel the pinch last. There are two main sources of cost leadership, productivity and linkage effectiveness.

Productivity. There are a number of ways within a manufacturing environment to reduce and maintain low or lower average unit costs compared with the competition. *Economies of scale* suggest that as production volume increases, unit costs decrease. Plant and equipment might be more efficient or be able to cope with additional volume without a proportional increase in overheads and support services. A 20 per cent increase in production volume does not mean a 20 per cent increase in staffing, R&D or supplies management costs. The increased production gives more volume over which to spread fixed costs, thus lowering the average unit cost.

Such economies of scale may be linked with higher overall annual volumes, or an ability to better utilise capacity to the full over the course of the year if the overall capacity is fixed. Many service providers, including airlines and hotels, face problems in how to fill off-peak capacity. Often it is the ability to solve this problem that will determine overall success.

The *experience curve* is another means of building a low cost base. This concept suggests that as cumulative volume increases, so does experience in manufacture, which might mean less wastage or higher productivity, and thus have a beneficial influence on cost. In other words, the more you do something, the more proficient you become at it. That benefit will only be achieved, however, if management responds to the opportunity for cost reduction created.

This means that through learning to produce, specialise, and innovate in process design, improving the performance of production equipment, and redesigning or standardising production, the operation becomes more efficient and the opportunities for cost reduction increase. The Boston Consulting Group estimated that as cumulative output doubles, average cost is reduced by 15–20 per cent. This favours those firms aggressively seeking market share gains, as they can enhance further their competitive position.

Of course, there are limits to how far cost efficiencies can be gained through economies of scale and learning. Economies of scale arise from the size of operation and volume produced compared with competitors. There may come a point where the economies of scale turn to diseconomies, as a result of unmanageable size and complexity. Learning curve effects arise from cumulative effects over time, regardless of operational scale. The benefits of learning might lead to further scale effects as the market position of the cost leader increases. In many ways, the efficient organisation will be chasing ever smaller gains in average unit costs. The biggest gains are often to be had during the launch and early stages of a new product, not during the maturity phase.

Linkage effectiveness. Not all gains come from production itself, whether the operation is a factory or a hotel. Some can derive from linkages with other areas of the organisation, the supply network and customer and channel interfaces. Large production volumes need successful marketing and logistics to ensure their efficient throughput to customers. In particular, pricing and distribution strategies and promotional approaches need to generate a sufficient flow of trade. Mass production requires mass distribution to keep goods flowing.

Working closely with suppliers to ensure timely and competitive component and materials supply can be a source of cost saving. The need to reduce inventories both before and after the production line emphasizes the role of 'just in time' systems, supplier partnerships, efficient physical distribution and the right dealer network or channel. All of there are essential if the cost advantages created in production are actually to reach the market place. Some organisations go further and integrate supply lines either horizontally (thus sharing costs in some areas, for instance physical distribution), or vertically, by controlling suppliers and the distribution network. Not all control and gains from integration have to be based on legal ownership. Managed supply chains based on supplier dependency, such as those created by large retail multiples, can achieve many of the same results without the problems of ownership.

Problems of cost leadership. There are, however, several problems with a cost leadership position:

1 The focus is on cost as a competitive weapon rather than on the range of other factors that customers might find important. Some customers will be prepared to pay more for added value or a stronger brand image.
2 The focus is purely on product cost, not the total cost of purchase to the customer, including after-sales costs, change costs and usage costs.
3 As we saw in Chapters 10 and 11, price is the easiest of the marketing mix variables to replicate in the short term, and price wars are rarely beneficial to all suppliers in the long run.
4 The cost leader may become more resistant to change, becoming locked into obsolete or less relevant production technology. New technology can erode both the scale effect and the benefits of learning. The benefits of the technological efficiency gained might thus become the cause of inertia and eventual demise.

Differentiation

The second generic strategy is differentiation. In order to succeed, an organisation must offer something to the buyer that the buyer values, and which is different from the rest. This differentiation is usually defined in terms of better performance, better design or a better fit with the customer's needs. The tradition within Germany's long-established piano manufacturers is to seek high quality and excellent design in the face of stiff competition from the Far East. Manufacturers such as Bechstein in Berlin, Steinway in Hamburg and Bluthner in Leipzig have all resisted the temptation to go downmarket, and although the market is relatively small the industry has survived (Dempsey, 1994). The value added must be sufficient to command a price premium, but that in no way means that the organisation can forget about costs. The offering still needs to be competitive, and the organisation must justify the price–value relationship.

The aim is to create an edge over rivals, and to have a differentiation package that is sustainable over time. In marketing, this can be 'real' (e.g., a product design feature) or 'imaginary' (a strong brand image or advertising campaign). People really do have to believe that there is a difference. Remember, though, that this approach might not achieve market leadership, even if the product is regarded as superior. Buyers might still be prepared to accept second best at a lower price.

The main advantage of a differentiation strategy is that it takes the focus away from price, and therefore might lead to the possibility of charging a price premium. It might also generate buyer loyalty, reducing their tendencies towards substitution or switching. The organisation does, however, have to think through the marketing activity that supports this strategy very carefully, and must plough back any price premium into sustaining its position. In the case of Aston Martin, mentioned earlier (p. 833) and Ferrari, with prices around £100 000 it is essential that the design, image, performance and service package justify the asking price.

The sources of differentiation can emerge from any area of the market offering:

● *product*: branding; innovation; quality; specification; design; image; patents
● *price*: price positions; price value combinations
● *place*: intensive distribution, exclusive distribution; back-up, service support
● *promotion*: creativity; spend
● *service*: strong trusting relationships with customers; adaptation; transaction-specific investments.

The difficulties with this approach stem from environmental changes. More experienced consumers may see through 'imaginary' differences, and even question the value offered for the price premium. As the market matures, imitators might reduce margins (think, for example, about IBM's loss of market share in personal computers), and it becomes more difficult to retain the level of marketing investment required. New types of competitors might also disturb the *status quo*, for example telephone banking, or chains of opticians offering 'your glasses in one hour or less'.

Focus

An organisation adopting a focus strategy is deliberately selective, focusing on a narrow group of customers, rather than on the whole market. There are many ways of selecting appropriate segments, but the organisation building a long-term strategy needs to ensure that they are durable. The philosophy here is to do a little thing thoroughly and well by meeting the needs of a clearly defined group far better than any one else. Focus in itself might not be enough, however, and the organisation might have to combine it with cost leadership or differentiation to build advantage.

> ### Example
>
> Wolfking is a small Danish manufacturer specialising in machinery for the food processing industry. Eighty-five per cent of its turnover comes from exports and it has become a market leader in the meat industry. Wolfking's machinery is used by butchers, supermarkets and processors of all kinds of meats and meat products. The focus on the meat industry has been the basis of its success, although the specialised product range developed also has supported its reputation for quality (Barnes, 1994).

If a focus strategy is to succeed, the organisation must understand segments thoroughly, how their needs are changing and what range to offer. If you are not serving a segment more effectively than your competitors, then you are in a poor position. To some extent, the scope for focus strategies has been opened up by the advent of the SEM. It is easier now for organisations to adopt a European market segmentation approach. Similar segments may exist in different countries, and thus although the segment may be small in each country, aggregated across Europe, it becomes an attractive option. Imagine, for example, the pan-European segments for premium brands of designer clothes, sports cars, fragrances and jewellery. An organisation operating in one of these segments might adjust its offering slightly to reflect local differences, but the key is the focus on a pan-European segment. It could be possible to define subsegments, perhaps based on natural clusters, for example Nordic, German or Iberian markets, but the danger here is that the segmentation becomes purely geographic rather than behavioural.

The risk with this segmentation approach is that the segments identified might not be sustainable long term, or might be undermined locally by competition. Although there is pressure on larger organisations to take a fairly standardised approach across Europe, with minor implementation variances, there is still room for the smaller business to compete. Many small organisations, perhaps with a local or regional orientation, survive alongside larger suppliers because of their local presence, local service and responsiveness and differentiation to reflect specific local characteristics, for example food taste, or the need for personalised attention.

Choice of generic strategy

The actual choice of generic strategy depends upon three criteria:

- the fit between the demands of the strategy and the organisation's capabilities and resources
- the main competitors' abilities on similar criteria
- the key criteria for success in the market and their match with the organisation's capabilities.

Once these criteria have been assessed, the organisation can select the best strategy to build a strong position. In some cases, an organisation might not have a free hand, since the nature of the marketing environment and the competitive stances already taken by other firms might force a particular strategic direction.

Assuming, however, that an organisation does have a free choice, it should take into account its potential sources of advantage and how they might best be used to exploit each alternative strategy. These sources of advantage might be:

1 *skills*. The question of skills concerns the hiring, training and development of key staff, who could be in R&D, selling, quality assurance or any area that could help to implement a particular strategy;
2 *resources*: The issue of resources refers both to the level and deployment of resources, for example promotional spend, R&D investment, financial reserves, production facilities and market coverage, and to brand strength;
3 *relationships*: The quality and long-term stability of supplier–customer relationships provides an asset that is durable in the face of many of the short-term pressures that are created by new entrants and competitors. Such relationships might tend to favour a focus strategy, for example.

Whichever strategy an organisation chooses, there must be ruthless commitment to it. Half-hearted implementation will mean that the strategy is ineffective and the organisation will be vulnerable to attack. Trying to implement parts of all three strategies in some kind of hybrid is equally dangerous. The organisation might then have to deal with the worst of all worlds: having no cost advantage, poor differentiation and an inappropriate or fuzzy focus. Nevertheless, there is some interrelationship between the three strategies. Although differentiation is the opposite of a cost leadership strategy, because differentiation incurs costs, a dominant position achieved through differentiation may itself help to achieve volume economies in manufacturing and distribution.

Furthermore, even if the commitment to the chosen strategy is strong in theory, it can still be difficult to stick to it in practice. If cost leadership is the chosen strategy, then beware of the customer requesting special modifications. Although flexible manufacturing methods are enabling more scope for variation during the assembly process, such customising needs to be within defined cost parameters. Despite the fact that Cummins produce a specified range of diesel engines, for example, they are also able, through flexible manufacturing, to accommodate some variability for customer specification, including colour, features and even packaging. However, Cummins would not be in the business, within a mass production system, of building prototypes and limited batch produced lines. Similarly, if differentiation is the chosen, strategy there are risks in the pursuit of the low price option. If the focus strategy is to be implemented on a pan-European basis, then decisions have to be taken on how much adaptation can be allowed for local needs in different countries.

COMPETITIVE POSITIONS AND POSTURES

A final stage in the determination of a competitive strategy is to decide how to compete, given the market realities, and how to either defend or disturb that position. This means that the organisation has to consider its own behaviour in the context of how competitors are behaving, and select the most appropriate strategy that will enable overall objectives to be achieved. Two aspects need to be considered, competitive position and competitive posture. **Competitive position** refers to the impact of the organisation's market position on marketing strategies, whereas **competitive postures** are the strategies implemented by organisations in different positions who want to disturb the *status quo*.

Competitive positions

An organisation's competitive position usually falls into one of four categories, according to its relative market share. The four categories, and the kinds of marketing strategies that go with them, are shown in Fig 21.10 and are now considered in turn.

FIGURE 21.10

Competitive position and strategy

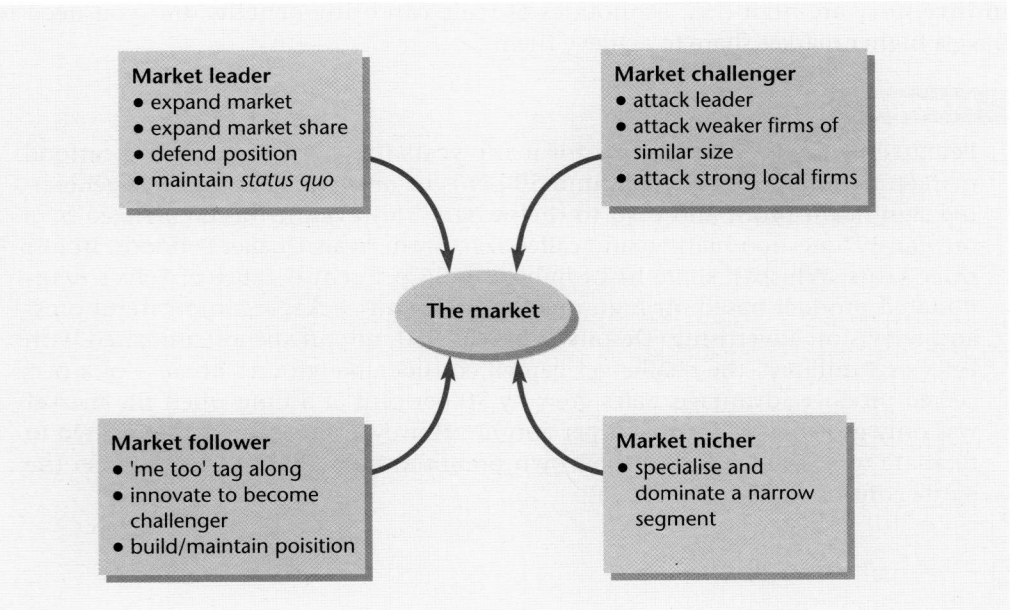

Market leader
- expand market
- expand market share
- defend position
- maintain *status quo*

Market challenger
- attack leader
- attack weaker firms of similar size
- attack strong local firms

The market

Market follower
- 'me too' tag along
- innovate to become challenger
- build/maintain poisition

Market nicher
- specialise and dominate a narrow segment

Market leader

In many industries, one organisation is recognised as being ahead of rest in terms of market share. Its share might only be 20–25 per cent, but that could still give it a dominant position. The market leader tends to determine the pace and ways of competing in the market. It sets the price standard, promotional intensity, the rate of product change and the quality and quantity of the distribution effort. Effectively, the market leader provides a benchmark for others to follow or emulate.

Market leadership can be at company, product group or brand level. Hellmans claims over 50 per cent of the UK mayonnaise market, just ahead of a series of own-brand products. Chivers Hartley are market leaders in jams and marmalades, and Otto Versand are Germany's market leader in mail order. In each case there are a number of rivals, so the power associated with being a leader might not necessarily be very great, especially if markets are defined from a European rather than a domestic perspective.

Market leadership lends itself to a number of strategic alternatives, none of which is mutually exclusive:

- *expand total market* by creating new uses, new users, or more intense use
- *expand market share* via the marketing mix. This assumes that share and profit are related
- *defend position* against challengers, through continuous innovation, or through expanding the range to get more shelf space. This strategy has been seen in many high-profile marketing battles between leaders and challengers, such as Coke *vs* Pepsi, Avis *vs* Hertz, Unilever *vs* Proctor & Gamble.
- *seek stability* and retention of customer base, as have organisations such as Kodak, Benetton, Nestlé, and L'Oréal.

Market challengers

Market challengers are organisations with a smaller market share, but who are close enough to pose a serious threat to the leader. However, an aggressive strategy can be costly, if the challenger is thinking of attacking where there is uncertainty over winning. Before making a concerted effort to steal share, therefore, the challenger needs to ask itself whether market share really matters so much, or whether there would be greater benefit from working on getting a good ROI from existing share. Dolan (1981) found that rivalry is greater where there is stagnant demand (i.e., growth can only come through stealing share from competitors), and where fixed costs or investment in inventory are high (i.e., economies of scale can bring benefits, but you need to have a higher market share to achieve them).

Example

Pedigree Petfoods' Whiskas was for many years the clear leader in the catfood market. In 1989, it retained around 50 per cent of the market and was generating significant profit and cash to the owners. However, it was challenged by a previously 'question mark' brand called Felix from rivals Quaker Petfoods. In just three years, Whiskas' share had tumbled to 35 per cent because of Felix's reformulated product based on high quality, premium packaging and careful press and television advertising. Despite Whiskas' £10 million spend (compared with Felix's £3 million), the challenger gained considerable ground because of a perceived product advantage. Sales grew by 30 per cent at a time when the market was only growing by 2 per cent per annum. However, the leader was prepared to retaliate with the launch of their own premium brand Select Cuts, and so the battle continued (Bidlake, 1992a).

Assuming that the decision is made to attack, there are two key questions: where to attack, and what the likely reaction will be. There are several options:

- attack the market leader
- attack weaker firms of a similar size
- attack firms who are strong but very local.

It is never easy to attack leaders, who tend to retaliate through cutting prices, or by investing in heavy promotion etc. It is, therefore, a high risk, but high return route. The challenger needs a clear competitive advantage to exploit to be able to neutralise the leader. In the case of Felix, it was by product improvement. The challenger might also have to be prepared to absorb short-term losses as a result of defending against the leader's retaliation. Again, Felix had to increase its advertising spend considerably to attack the leader. The moral of this story is not to enter the fight unless you are really convinced you can win and are prepared to invest in the battle.

Market followers

Given the resources needed, the threat of retaliation, and the uncertainty of winning, many organisations favour a far less aggressive stance, acting as market followers. There are two types of follower. First, there are those who lack the resources to mount a serious challenge and prefer to remain innovative and forward thinking, without disturbing the overall competitive structure in the market by encouraging open warfare. Often, any lead from the market leader is willingly followed. This might mean adopting a 'me too' strategy, thus avoiding direct confrontation and competition.

Example

Holiday Autos car rental company in the UK offered to provide cheaper rentals in overseas destinations than the main renters such as Hertz and Avis. Although prebooking was essential, their progress became sufficiently threatening for Hertz to run a discounting campaign, offering similar prices.

The second type of follower is the organisation that is simply not capable of challenging, and is content just to survive, offering little competitive advantage. Often, smaller car rental firms operate in this category by being prepared to offer a lower price, but not offering the same standard of rental vehicle or even peace of mind should things go wrong. A recession can easily eliminate the weaker members of this category.

Hammermesch *et al.* (1978) and Saunders (1987) found that some market followers seek deliberately to build and maintain that position through a range of strategies, which include careful and narrow segmentation, highly selective R&D and a focus on quality, differentiation and profitability rather than on cost and share gains.

Market nichers

Some organisations, often small, specialise in areas of the market that are too small, too costly or too vulnerable for the larger organisation to contemplate. Niching is not exclusively a small organisation strategy, as some larger firms may have divisions that specialise. The key to niching is the close matching between the needs of the market and the capabilities and strengths of the company. The specialisation offered can relate to product type, customer group, geographical area or any aspect of product/service differentiation.

Lobb shoes cost over £1000 per pair. There is no opportunity for mass production to achieve such a premium position, serving customers wanting something very different. The UK market represents only 25 per cent of Lobb's sales, with the rest going mainly to the USA, Arabs and Japanese. Lobb, however, also experiences the difficulties of operating right at the top of the market. Scope for growth is limited, because of the exclusivity of the product and the necessity for hand crafting. Because of the low volumes, profits are very modest. Moving downmarket or making the production more efficient would undermine the whole reputation of the business. However, Lobb survives on a small and loyal customer base, in some cases from generation to generation. The key to their success is quality, reputation, history and tradition (Rigby, 1995).

Problems occur with this strategy if others challenge by entering a well established niche, or the niche disappears as a result of innovation and change. One of the problems faced by Sock Shop, the niche hosiery retailer, for example, was that larger retailers such as Marks & Spencer encroached on their niche by providing equally wide and deep hosiery assortments at competitive prices, thus eroding the differential advantage of the niche operator.

Competitive postures

The previous section considered the underlying rationale for defending, attacking or ignoring what is going on in the market from the point of view of an organisation's relative market position. This section examines *how to attack* or *how to defend* a position. A number of analogies from texts on warfare have been used (*see* e.g., Kotler and Singh, 1981) to describe the various options and the difficulties associated with them. Four broad postures are considered here, although the final two owe their roots to diplomacy rather than warfare.

Aggressive strategies

Aggressive strategies are implemented when one or more players in a market decide to challenge the *status quo*. Again, the question of who to attack, when to attack and where to attack all need to be answered carefully in the context of the resources needed, the competitive reaction and the returns to be gained at what cost. Even in warfare, head-on assaults can be costly and do not always succeed. Five broad aggressive strategies can be contemplated, as shown in Fig 21.11.

Frontal attacks. A challenger contemplating a head-on attack in marketing terms needs to be very well resourced relative to the market leader. A full-scale attack means matching and winning on all the competitive variables such as price, mass distribution, product features and the rest. A more limited frontal attack may pick off some customer groups who could be more vulnerable to a new offering, for example, those who are more service conscious.

The wet shaving market has seen a number of upheavals over the past 20 years. Bic launched a full frontal attack on Gillette and Wilkinson by innovating with a disposable razor offering convenience, regular repurchases and low prices. Bic built volume rapidly with mass advertising and distribution across a wide range of retail outlets. It took three years for Gillette and Wilkinson to retaliate with their own disposables. However, by launching a full frontal attack, Bic gained around one-third of the market (but less than 20 per cent in value).

FIGURE 21.11

Attack strategies

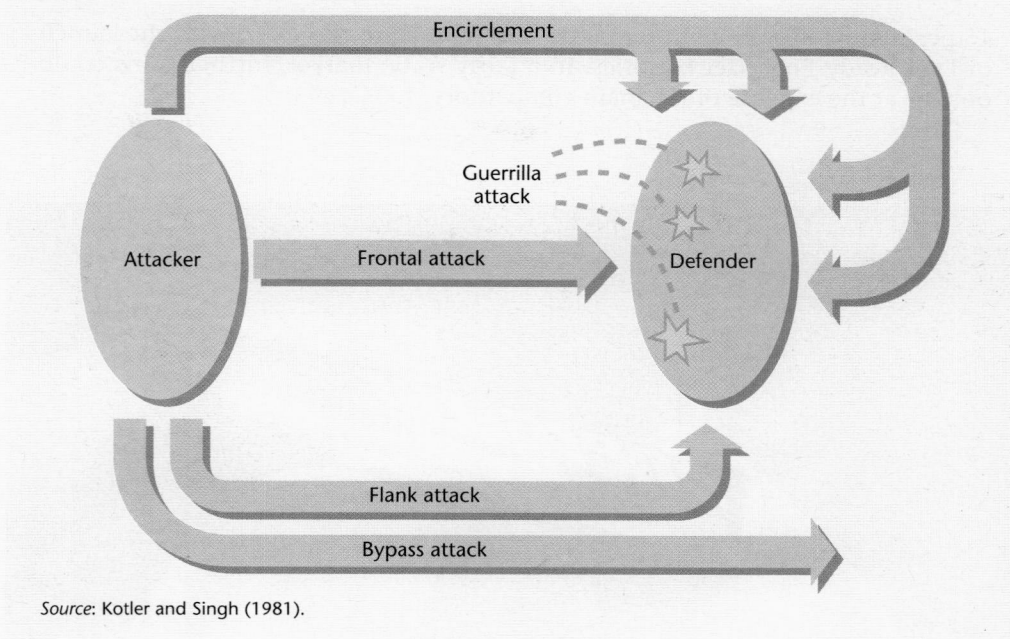

Source: Kotler and Singh (1981).

Flank attack. Many successful attacks occur because the enemy has been outflanked and its strategy has been disrupted. By attacking particular segments, product weakness areas or poor distribution facilities, progress can be made despite the overall strength of the competition. Such tactics are called technological flanking and segmental flanking.

> ### Example
>
> Continuing with the example of the wet shaving market, by the 1990s, Gillette and Wilkinson considered that the time was right for launching a further retaliation by introducing premium wet shave systems. A segment had developed that was ready for further quality improvements, such as wetness combined with closeness and safety. It was estimated that 71 per cent of men preferred a wet shave. Exploiting this trend, they introduced Sensor and Protector respectively which were designed to put pressure on Bic, should significant numbers of consumers switch away from the economy option. Another important part of the strategy was to secure prominent display and space with retailers, through both television advertising and trade press adverts (Bevan, 1992).

Flank attacks can lead to encirclement if the poorly defended segment is used by the challenger to build an image and reputation in the market in preparation for a further attack in an area of direct concern to the leader.

> ### Example
>
> Ever Ready had a dominant position in the battery market in the 1970s. At the end of the decade, Duracell launched alkaline batteries which lasted much longer than zinc batteries despite having a premium price. Although Ever Ready countered in 1982 with Gold Seal, it still protected its zinc brands for less demanding applications. Despite the counter-attacks, by the end of the 1980s, Duracell had over 50 per cent of the alkaline market and Gold Seal had less than

15 per cent. However, a further battle was declared in the 1990s with the launch of Ever Ready Energizer batteries. In a fairly static market, further gains could only be at the expense of the main competitors (Toor, 1993).

The Ever Ready Energizer is a powerful product in a competitive market.

Source: Energizer Ever Ready.

Encirclement attack. Encirclement means launching an attack on many fronts with rapidity and force so as to spread panic and overwhelm the opposition. It is difficult to defend a position with enough concentrated force and effect when faced with an all-out attack on all sides. Although short-term losses may be experienced by the challenger, the outcome might eventually be significant advances in market share. This could be achieved by the pure breadth of range, such as that offered by Seiko watches, aggressive pricing at consumer and retail levels, heavy pull promotion, and a relentless drive to attack segments either on a sequential or a parallel basis.

Bypass attack. A bypass attack is one where there is no effort made to engage the enemy in direct conflict, but the tactic is to move on and perhaps surround and slowly reduce the power base of the leader. In a commercial setting, the focus could be on unrelated products in the same market segment as the leader, new geographical markets, and always seeking a competitive edge through technological advances.

Example

Digital technology developed by Casio enabled them to bypass Seiko in watches. Similarly, it is only because Ever Ready responded that it avoided a complete encirclement on technological grounds by Duracell.

Guerilla attack. Guerrilla action is a well known strategy for a small group operating against a much more powerful force that it dare not meet head-on. In business, the purpose of such a strategy is to make short-term marginal gains that can still be important for the smaller organisation, although not very significant to the larger operator. It could mean bursts of activity, perhaps in price promotions, dealer loadings or geographically concentrated campaigns, or even in recruiting some of the market leader's key staff. It is about hitting poorly defended targets hard, and then quickly retreating.

Defensive strategies

Defensive strategies might be adopted by a market leader under attack, or by a market follower or nicher put under pressure by competitive activity. Even a challenger needs to reflect on likely competitive retaliation before committing itself to aggressive acts. Figure 21.12 shows a range of possible defences.

Fixed position defence. One option is to sit tight and defend the current position. This can be risky, in that such defences might then be bypassed rather than attacked directly. In commercial terms, the organisation that seeks to hold position without adopting fresh ideas can run into trouble. Land Rover, for instance, failed to do product-market development, sticking with its largely agricultural segment, while Japanese manufacturers attacked on price and the leisure vehicle image.

Mobile defence. Rather than defending existing products, the focus in mobile defence turns to broadening the market appeal and even diversifying away from that market, as the cigarette companies have done. This means, however, that an organisation must be prepared to redefine its priorities and the type of business it is in, and keep an open mind. It does not mean a retreat, but it does reduce vulnerability, and opens up new segments, for example developing bicycles into item for the health and leisure segments.

Flanking defence. In military situations, the rear or flank is often seen as a weak area. If it is attacked, this can turn the course of a battle.

FIGURE 21.12

Defence strategies

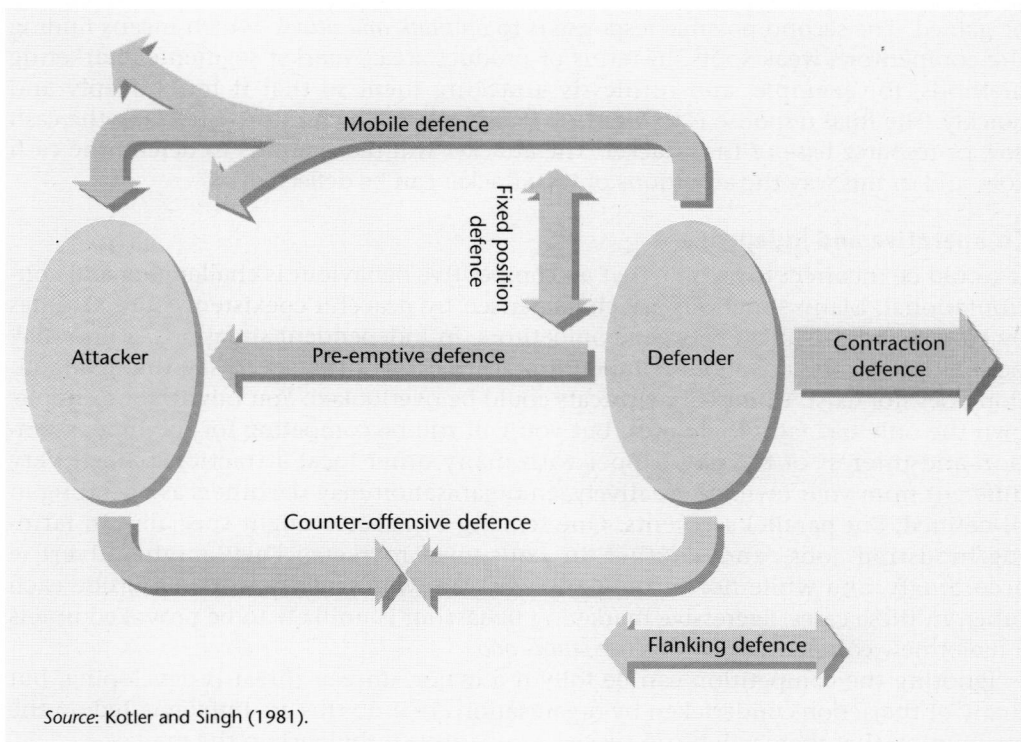

Source: Kotler and Singh (1981).

In the potato crisps market, Smith's Crisps dominated in the early 1960s with a product distributed through pubs, appealing to adults. Golden Wonder attacked the flank by entering the market with a product targeted as a children's snack, and sold through supermarkets and sweet shops.

The lesson, therefore, is to ensure that there are no weak spots emerging that would allow a competitor to find an attractive segment.

Contraction defence. In contraction defence rather than risk the threat of being overwhelmed in one major defensive position, an organisation undertakes a selective withdrawal, to delay or even offset the attacking force. In commercial terms, that could mean withdrawing from marginal segments and areas where the presence is small and cannot be defended. This might mean that in areas where strengths do exist a better, more concentrated fight can take place. When under threat, the core business must be defended at all costs.

Pre-emptive defence. The phrase 'the best form of defence is to attack' is now a recognised business strategy. If an organisation feels that it might soon be under attack, rather than wait for that to happen, it takes deliberate aggressive actions. This might mean a particular marketing mix emphasis, for example advertising, dealer loaders, or new products. Alternatively signals can be sent that any attack would be vigorously defended.

Counter-offensive defence. Once hostilities have begun, a number of counter-offensive measures can be taken in defence. Many of these actions are aggressive, but retaliatory. Three responses are possible. First, *head to head confrontation* means matching action with action. This, incidentally, is how price wars start. It does not just centre on price moves, however: it might also mean investing as much in advertising as the competition or launching a similar new product. It shows that no competitive advantage can be gained. The second possible response is to *outflank and attack*, which means finding the competitor's weak spots, in terms of product areas, market segments, marketing methods, for example, and ruthlessly attacking them so that it hurts deeply and quickly. The final response is to *hit where it hurts most*, which means attacking the cash cow or resource base of the attacker. The attacker will make efforts to defend the cash cow, and in this way the attentions of the attacker can be deflected.

Co-operative and independent

It would be incorrect to assume that all competitive behaviour is challenging and confrontational. Many situations are characterised by peaceful coexistence and at times by co-operative alliances between competitors. In independent situations, a firm may neither know nor care about competition. That does not mean to say that competition does not exist. Competitive threats could be overlooked. You might, for example, own the only bee farm in an area, but you will still be competing for the time, attention and interest of the day tripper with many other local attractions, albeit very different from your own. Alternatively, an organisation may see others as operating in ill-defined, but parallel segments. One fencing contractor might specialise in farming/industrial jobs, and another in consumer markets. They might advertise accordingly, and while not turning any work away, peacefully work alongside each other. In these cases, aggressive marketing behaviour is unlikely to be provoked unless a major new competitor disturbs the *status quo*.

Ignoring the competition can be folly if a major, unseen threat is developing, but many of the actions undertaken by organisations that do this are implemented on the assumption that there will be no special competitive turbulence in the market.

Strategic alliances were briefly covered in Chapter 13 (p. 521 *et seq.*) in the context of retailing. Strategic alliances occur when organisations seek to work together on projects, pooling expertise and resources. This could include R&D (*see* the Yorkshire Water and Siemens example at p. 357), joint ventures or licensing arrangements, sometimes on a world-wide scale. Many large construction projects demand that different firms work together to provide a turnkey package. The alliance can be general, on many fronts or specific to a certain project.

Not all joint ventures work out as expected, however. After ten years of participating in a joint venture in the construction and earthmoving sector, Volvo decided to buy out its partner Clark Equipment to form the Volvo Construction Equipment Corporation from the formerly jointly owned VME Group. The purchase added to the financial strength of Volvo as the operating margins from VME exceeded those earned from both Volvo trucks and the automotive division. Another advantage of the purchase was the ability to co-operate more closely in engine development. It was also felt that the Volvo name would be a marketing advantage in a highly competitive market dominated by Caterpillar with a worldwide share of 34 per cent compared with VME's 5 per cent (Baxter and Carnegy, 1995).

Example

Campari and Bols-Wessanen agreed to form a strategic alliance in which the Dutch-owned company Bols purchased a stake of around 33 per cent in Campari. One of the main advantages was the synergy created in developing international activities in terms of distribution and marketing. Outside Italy, the companies have duplicate production facilities in some countries. In Switzerland, for example, Cyner aperitif was under Dutch control while Campari was under the control of the Italians. There would clearly be opportunities for both parties in an alliance if a common approach could be developed (Hill, 1994).

Joint ventures and alliances are also widely used as a means to enter the former communist bloc countries of eastern Europe. In Pravdinsk in Russia, the Volga Pulp and Paper mill has prospered from German investment of $160 million in new machinery. The mill, based on plentiful supplies of timber and low-cost labour, can now compete with other international competitors. Meanwhile the Pravdinsk Radio Factory, once the town's main employer, has not found an international partner. With the guaranteed supplies to the military all but gone and an infrastructure that does not enable effective international competition based on technology and quality, the work-force has been halved and is on short-time working. Attempts to diversify into emergency vehicles appear to be based more on hope than on detailed market analysis (Channel 4 News, 20 February 1996).

Finally, *collusion* is where firms come to an 'understanding' about how to compete in the market. Legislation prevents this from extending to deliberate price fixing, as witnessed in the UK's cement industry, where a number of firms were prosecuted and executives jailed.

CHAPTER SUMMARY

This chapter has been concerned with marketing strategies, the longer term consideration of where the organisation wants to be and how it can get there using its products and its marketing mixes. The implication of this is that marketing strategy is intertwined with the wider issue of corporate strategy. Marketing strategies will not only be influenced by corporate goals, but also by competitive strategy. The organisation has to decide how it wants to position itself relative to the competition, whether it wants to be perceived as a leader, a follower or a niche operator, and how it wants to deal with competition. Marketing strategy thus creates, maintains and reinforces corporate positioning and how it is perceived, by using the elements of the marketing mix to capitalise on strengths, overcome weaknesses, defend against threats and exploit opportunities within the business environment. Outcomes of this analysis are the marketing plan that specifies the overall direction of the organisation and marketing programmes that spell out the operational tasks to be undertaken in order to implement the plan.

Central to this is as deep an understanding of competitors as possible, since only then can competitive advantage be deliberately created and maintained, and defences put in place to protect it. Models such as Porter's five forces can help to analyse competitive structures systematically and provide a starting point for building strategies. In designing marketing strategies, it is also important to understand how competitors are likely to react and the implications of that reaction on the successful implementation of the strategies. The depth of information thus required underlines the need for a comprehensive and well-maintained information system.

In terms of the strategies themselves, there are broadly three generic options. The first is cost leadership, seeking to gain a cost advantage over the competition. An alternative is to seek differentiation, offering something different, better or more valued by the customer than that offered by the competition. The third generic strategy, a focus strategy, means concentrating on one specific segment of the market and serving it thoroughly. The actual choice of generic strategy depends on the organisation's capabilities and resources, the nature of the competition faced and the key factors for success in that market. In practice, it might be difficult to stick rigidly to one of these strategies alone and there might have to be some flexibility.

Strategic marketing planning often revolves around analysis of the organisation's product portfolio. The Boston Box provides a diagnostic tool which can act as a basic foundation for strategic decisions. The Boston Box does, however, have its critics because of its emphasis on the desirability of market growth and high market share. Other portfolio models, such as the GE matrix and the Shell directional policy matrix have therefore been developed to try to overcome some of the Boston Box's weaknesses by redefining the axes in more detail, increasing the number of cells, and thus trying to be more specific about associated courses of action.

Where growth opportunities are identified, there are a number of alternative strategies available as defined, for example, by the Ansoff matrix. Not all strategies revolve around the concept of growth. Harvesting, associated with cash cows, means reaping the benefits of a product without actively seeking growth for it. Entrenchment, protecting a current position, might be appropriate for a dog deemed essential to the overall portfolio, while withdrawal might be considered for a completely useless dog.

An organisation also needs to consider competitive position and competitive posture. Competitive position defines an organisation as a market leader, a market challenger, a market follower or a market nicher. Competitive posture is about how to attack or defend a position. This covers aggressive strategies for attacking competitors in different ways, and defensive strategies to be used when the competition attacks.

Competition need not always involve confrontation, however. It is possible to work co-operatively with competitors or other organisations. Strategic alliances or joint ventures, have become increasingly appreciated as ways of exploiting synergies between organisations and opening up new opportunities that neither party would have the resources to pursue alone.

QUESTIONS FOR REVIEW

21.1 Define the main factors influencing organisations' *marketing strategy*.

21.2 What is a *product portfolio* and what is the point of *portfolio analysis*?

21.3 Define the four cells of the *Boston Box*.

21.4 How does the GE matrix define *industry attractiveness* and *business position*?

21.5 What are the problems of implementing portfolio models in practice?

21.6 Which three cells of the Ansoff matrix offer *growth opportunities*?

21.7 Differentiate between three different types of *integrative growth*.

21.8 What issues might an organisation take into account when undertaking *competitive analysis*?

21.9 What are the three *generic strategies* and how might each be implemented?

21.10 Define the four different types of *competitive position*.

QUESTIONS FOR DISCUSSION

21.1 To what extent do the cells of the Boston Box reflect the stages of the product life-cycle (PLC)? What does the Boston Box offer as an analytical tool that the PLC does not?

21.2 For each cell of the Ansoff matrix, find and discuss an example of an organisation which seems to have implemented that particular growth strategy.

21.3 Choose an organisation and apply Porter's

five forces to its industry or market. What are the implications of your findings for your chosen organisation's strategic development?

21.4 To what extent do you think that market leadership is the best competitive position to aspire to?

21.5 Discuss the relative merits and appropriate use of each of the competitive postures described in this chapter.

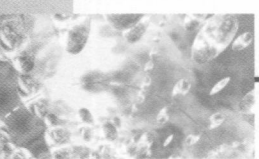

Chuft Toys and Gifts

Chuft Toys and Gifts, launched in 1992, is a small business manufacturing a range of specialist wooden toys. After graduating, both partners in the business became quickly disillusioned with working in large companies and met each other by chance while backpacking in Australia. Although their degrees were in production engineering and product design technology, their first business venture was developing a backpacker's travel guide based on their first-hand experiences. This guide still survives today. However Chuft, the young entrepreneurs' second venture, was the real basis for developing a full-time business. Sales grew from £150 000 in the first year to £500 000 by year four.

The initial product was a wooden steam train whistle which they designed. The prototype and first production run were produced in a draughty garage at the home one of the partners. They both enjoyed the fun of designing and establishing the most appropriate way of manufacturing the early batches. They approached the heritage line, the North Yorkshire Moors Railway, which agreed to place a pilot order in its station shops to see how well the whistles sold. To everyone's surprise 30 whistles were sold in one weekend. Chuft thus made the transition from being a possible enterprise to being a trading concern. The partners managed to raise capital for production machinery and found premises in an Enterprise Centre. Although resources were tight, they had just sufficient to build a basic business infrastructure.

Four years on, the company now sees itself as primarily being in the gift market. The steam train whistle, with a few variants, is still the company's core line, although other products have also been developed, including low-priced wooden novelties and puzzles and 'equilibria', balancing wooden clowns. Another range is 'Toys With Noise', a tractor, a traction engine, a steam engine, a fire engine and a police car, each of which makes a suitably characteristic noise when pushed or blown. Chuft also markets a whistling train, comprising a wooden locomotive, caboose and carriage as a boxed set. The locomotive whistles when you blow into the cab.

A common characteristic of all the toys and gifts is the high quality of the materials and finish, and the attention paid to packaging, which follows a strong, unified and coherent design and image. Considerable thought has gone into the colours, materials, information provided and not least the shape of the packaging, so that it stands out in display areas and communicates the product's quality. Wooden toys and gifts tend to be bought on impulse rather than as planned purchases. Although cheaper alternatives are available, the quality positioning commands an above average price and this is supported by a selective distribution strategy.

Finding the best price and trade margin took some time, a few mistakes, and considerable trial and error. Initially, the toys were exhibited at national and regional toy and trade fairs. The partners decided to expand further, however, by carefully selecting outlets that valued premium quality rather than cheap products. These included preserved railways, Harrods, Jenners (Edinburgh), the National Trust and other heritage sites. One of the partners was responsible for selling while the other managed production. They did not meet very much sales resistance, as they allowed retailers to try small pilot orders to assess whether larger volume sales could be realised.

While they expanded steadily in the home market, the first export enquiries were received. This was a source of surprise to the partners. Attendance at exhibitions generated the enquiries that soon led to further trial orders. There was no plan to move into exports or to modify their activities to suit export markets. Orders from these buyers were taken on a reactive basis, with the view 'Why refuse an order?' This exposed the partners to some of the problems of exporting, including documentation and procedures. From these initial export orders, a number of buyers suggested that they themselves should become agents for Chuft in their own markets. Chuft did not feel that it had the resources to become directly involved in developing new markets, so any arrangement with foreign intermediaries was considered appropriate.

Although no major changes in the marketing mix took place for export customers, a number of new decisions had to be made. First, changes were made to the product packaging to emphasize 'Heritage' and 'Britishness' as the selling point, thus taking into account comments from the foreign buyers. New languages such as French, Japanese and German were introduced to the packaging. Price setting was never very sophisticated, but the partners decided to apply a standard discount, with little variation for the volume of order. Agents were selected mainly on the strength of trust and a feeling that they were reliable, rather than on any kind of objective criteria. Regardless of trust, however, Chuft always insisted on cash in advance for export orders.

Exports have grown to 30 per cent of output, although profit margins are tighter than in the domestic market. This volume is considered useful for spreading the load of the factory and in reducing the effects of concentrating on just one market. The main markets are Japan, America and Germany, although other European markets also provide some sales. The partners do not want to sell to developing countries and are determined not to be swamped by US demand.

The future challenge for the business is in keeping the product range fresh. Life cycles are tending to become shorter as the range increasingly moves into novelty products. Despite the success, there are still many other problems to overcome. Deciding on whether to manufacture or subcontract, obtaining suitable premises as production expands, achieving production efficiency and assembling the resources to hit a market harder than has been possible in the past, have all become priorities. Although the business now employs 20 people, sales are still handled by the partners. There appear to be many opportunities for further expansion, but the need to develop a sound strategy to enable further growth to be properly managed is starting to occupy the partners' minds. They think that they have reached a crossroads. Should they continue to expand, should they consolidate, or should they seek radically new options?

Source: Adapted from a case prepared by Gerry Kirkwood.

Questions

1 What do you think are the problems facing two young graduates wanting to start a new business?

2 To what would you attribute Chuft's initial success?

3 Assess Chuft's approach to market development.

4 Where does Chuft go from here? What do you think might be the main dangers facing this firm?

CASE STUDY 21.2

Boots' strategic headaches

Boots is a long-established household name in the UK and is increasingly developing a presence in European and international markets. From its roots as a retail pharmacy business, it has become not only a major pharmacy and personal health care retail chain, but also a contract manufacturer, and has diversified its retailing interests to include such areas as DIY, car spares and accessories, and a chain of superstores specialising in products for babies and young children. Pre-tax profits in 1996 were reported to be around £500 million, in spite of the sale of its profit-making pharmaceutical business to BASF. Despite its size and strength, however, Boots faced three major strategic marketing problems in 1996, all of which stem from managing the organisation's strategic portfolio of businesses and adjusting them to new opportunities and threats. Each one is now considered in turn.

Combating new and reinvigorated competition in the domestic UK market

Boots the Chemist, the core retail chain within the group, is without question the cash cow. It generates between 75 per cent and 80 per cent of the pre-tax profits from the group and provides the resources for new development in other areas. A key part of its dominant strength in the pharmacy sector is Boots' success in developing and marketing own-label products produced by Boots Contract Manufacturing. The chain of 1200 stores has a market leader position, but increasingly this is under threat from:

(a) supermarket own-label products;

(b) the aggressive development of the Superdrug chain with its 720 stores; and

(c) the possible merger of Lloyds and Unichem which would create a retailer with many more outlets than Boots.

The supermarket chain ASDA caused a storm in 1995 when it began unilateral price cutting on health, beauty and over the counter (OTC) medicines as an opening shot in seeking the removal of Resale Price Maintenance (RPM) on these products. With RPM the pharmaceutical manufacturers have the right to set the prices for their products and retailers are legally obliged to charge those prices. By 1996, ASDA had still not managed to force an end to RPM on OTC medicines. Nevertheless, although Boots feels confident that its market position is so strong that it can respond to any serious competitive threats on price and product promotion, it is also strengthening its market position by operating a two-track distribution policy. While it has always retained a major high street and shopping centre presence, it is also opening small community pharmacies at the rate of around one per week. Overall, therefore, the strategy in this sector is to defend its position while building in new areas.

Finding and opening new international markets

Boots Healthcare International (BHI) was launched a few years ago to develop the company's capacity to supply the OTC pharmaceutical trade on an international scale. It could, therefore, be regarded as a business unit alongside other areas such as Boots the Chemist and Boots Contract Manufacturing. In that capacity it has required considerable investment, as the international market, especially in Europe, is a tough one. In contrast to in the UK, multiple pharmacies are not legal in southern Europe and are discouraged in northern Europe. This means considerable investment for BHI in developing sales and distribution networks through doctors and independent pharmacists. At another level, within BHI there are four key product categories, Strepsils throat pastilles, Nurofen pain killer, Optrex eye treatment and E45 skin cream. Each of these brands has different profit and share potential in a competitive European market dominated by such organisations as SmithKline Beecham and Glaxo Wellcome, and therefore BHI has to look carefully at balancing and managing this portfolio.

Nurofen and Strepsils are available in 130 countries, and £74 million was spent in 1995–6 on developing and marketing these products. As part of the process of international brand building, BHI developed line extensions in Europe, such as Nurofen Plus and Nuroflex. It takes time to gain the necessary approvals to sell an OTC product in a market, and it also takes time and money to build distribution to OTC outlets, as well as to communicate with pharmacists and doctors. These products are, therefore, still only generating small profits, but BHI has high hopes for the future as the health care market is seen as a major opportunity that fits well with the business.

Moving out of loss-making businesses

Boots, as part of its diversification strategy, also moved into new retail areas such as Do It All (DIY), Halfords (car spares and accessories), and Fads and Homestyle (interior decoration). When Boots took over Halfords, it also inherited the Payless DIY chain as part of the package. In 1990, Boots agreed to merge Payless with W. H. Smith's Do It All chain as a joint venture. The idea was that the joint strength would enable them to compete more effectively against the larger players such as B&Q, Sainsbury's Homebase, Texas and Wickes. Unfortunately the problem was timing. After the prop-

erty boom of the 1980s, the early 1990s saw a slump in demand as the UK economy failed to respond to various incentives to encourage growth. The smaller DIY stores suffered the effects of the recession more than the larger operators did, thus putting pressure on the likes of Do It All. Do It All had thus become a major problem to its joint owners Boots and W. H. Smith.

Things became so desperate for Do It All in 1996 that W. H. Smith was alleged to be paying Boots £50 million just to get out of the venture and rid itself of the problems. This move reflected the problems of high dependency on leased property, which could cost the partners as much as £300 million each if the whole store network were to be closed down. The losses in the chain were around £10 million per year and the choices for the continuation of the enterprise appeared to be stark. Either find a buyer for the whole Do It All business (and even sell it with Fads and Homestyle as a package in order to cut the losses), or invest heavily to turn the business around in the context of an improving property market. This would mean, however, improving its competitiveness against the strong players in the market. Stores in poorer locations were already being closed so that more effort could be given to refurbishing and marketing the better outlets.

In the other areas of its portfolio, properties are increasingly generating a profit. By becoming involved in the development of shopping centres and retail parks, Boots can not only take a prime site, but also receive income as the property developer. The £40 million shopping centre in Harrow, London, is a good example of the benefits in pursuing such a strategy.

So, overall Boots is actively involved in managing its business and product portfolios with varying degrees of success. It is, however, the resources generated by its core business that are enabling the organisation to develop BHI, as well as coping with the drains of the Do It All chain.

Sources: Brierley (1996); *Marketing Week* (1996b); Oram (1996); Pitcher (1996).

Questions

1 Which growth strategies has Boots employed? To what extent do you think they are appropriate? What problems do you think Boots might have faced in implementing them?

2 Using the cells of the Boston Box, indicate roughly how you would categorise each of Boots' SBUs?

3 For each of those SBUs, what do you think is the most appropriate strategy for the future? What might cause problems in implementing those strategies?

REFERENCES TO CHAPTER 21

Abell, D. E. and Hammond, J. S. (1979), *Strategic Market Planning*, Prentice Hall.

Ansoff, H. I. (1957), 'Strategies for Diversification', *Harvard Business Review*, 25(5), pp. 113–25.

Barksdale, H. C. and Harris, C. E. (1982), 'Portfolio Analysis and the PLC', *Long Range Planning*, 15(6), pp. 74–83

Barnes, H. (1994), 'Market Leader in Meat Machinery', *Financial Times*, 7 June, p.13.

Barnes, H. (1996a), 'Financial Operations Bolster Tele Danmark', *Financial Times*, 19 March, p. 24.

Barnes, H. (1996b), 'International Lines Keep Tele Danmark Busy', *Financial Times*, 13 June, p. 31.

Barrett, P. (1996), 'Rover Tries New Tricks', *Marketing*, 9 May, p. 13.

Baxter, A. and Carnegy, H. (1995), 'Gaining Ground in the Earthmover Industry', *Financial Times*, 13 March, p.19.

Benady, A. (1993), 'Wrangler Rides on the All-American Dream', *Marketing*, 9 September, pp. 20–1.

Benady, D. (1996), 'Scottish Courage Clears Out Brands', *Marketing Week*, 9 February, p. 7.

Bevan, S. (1992), 'Closer to a Wet Shave Success', *Marketing*, 27 August, pp. 22–3

Bidlake, S. (1992a) 'Felix: Number One By a Whiska?' *Marketing*, 3 December, pp. 22–4.

Bidlake, S. (1992b), 'Nestlé Adopts the Personal Touch', *Marketing*, 19 November, pp. 24–6.

Brierley, S. (1996), 'Boots Seeks to Build Healthy Global Share', *Marketing Week*, 9 February, p. 23.

Buchan, D. (1996), 'Political Dogfight Nears its End', *Financial Times*, 2 July, p. 15.

Buckley, S. (1996), 'Williams Makes Security Buys', *Financial Times*, 26 March, p. 24.

Calori, R. and Harvatopoulos, Y. (1988), 'Diversification: Les règales de conduite', *Harvard – L'Expansion*, 48 (Spring), pp. 48–59.

Cane, A. (1995), 'A Permanent Revolution', *Eurobusiness*, September, pp. 51–5.

Darwent, C. (1994), 'Lilliput Learns About Growth', *Management Today*, April, pp. 63–4.

Dempsey, J. (1994), Quality is the key to a More Upbeat Tempo', *Financial Times*, 7 September, p. 23.

Dolan, R. J. (1981), 'Models of Competition: A Review of Theory and Empirical Evidence' in B. M. Enis and K. Roering (eds.), *Review of Marketing*, American Marketing Association.

Dwek, R. (1992), 'The Supercar Stoops to Conquer', *Marketing*, 5 March, pp. 24–5.

Dwek, R. (1994), 'BMW Turns the Niche into Mass Market', *Marketing*, 10 February, pp. 25–7.

Faith, N. (1993), 'Rivers of Fine Wine', *EuroBusiness*, June, pp. 38–41.

Hammermesch, R. G. *et al.* (1978), 'Strategies for Low Market Share Business', *Harvard Business Review*, 56 (May–June), pp. 95–102.

Hecht, F. (1993), 'The Baby Business', *EuroBusiness*, May, pp. 36–7.

Heller, R. (1995), 'Denmark Tilts at Windmills', *EuroBusiness*, November/December, pp. 36–8.

Hill, A. (1994), 'Campari Stirred as the Dynasty Adds a Dash of Dutch,' *Financial Times*, 11 October, p. 2a.

Johnson, G. and Scholes, K. (1993), *Exploring Corporate Strategy*, (3rd edn.) Prentice-Hall.

Johnson, M. (1992), 'Rank Xerox Seeks a Sharper Image', *Marketing*, 20 August, pp. 16–17.

Kotler, P. and Singh, R. (1981), 'Marketing Warfare in the 1980s', *Journal of Business Strategy*, 2 (Winter), pp. 30–41.

Lambin, J. J. (1993), *Strategic Marketing*, McGraw-Hill.

Lorenz, A. (1995), 'English China Clays' New Chemistry', *Management Today*, October, pp. 48–52.

Lynch, R. (1994), *European Business Strategies: The European and Global Strategies of Europe's Top Companies*, Kogan Page.

Lynn, M. (1996), 'Building's Decline and Fall', *Management Today*, February, pp. 28–32.

McClintock, L. (1996), 'To Bean Or Not To Bean ...', *The Grocer*, 27 January, pp. 47–8.

Marketing Week (1996a), 'Quaker Ditches Wholegrain Feast Despite £7 Million Launch Blitz', *Marketing Week*, 9 February, p. 8.

Marketing Week, (1996b), 'Boots' Long March', *Marketing Week*, 7 June, pp. 36–9.

Meller, P. (1992), 'Tapping Grolsch's Premium', *Marketing*, 23 July, pp. 18–19.

Murphy, Y. (1996), 'Small Objects of Desire', *The Grocer*, 20 January, pp. 41–2.

New, C. and Wheatley, M. (1995), 'Excellence in the Round', *Management Today*, November, pp. 96–126.

Nicholas, R. (1994), 'Brylcreem Rolls Out Bad Boy Ads', *Marketing*, 30 June, p. 5.

Oram, R. (1996), 'Boots Halves Cash Pile in £300 Million Share Buy-back', *Financial Times*, 28 June, p. 23.

Pitcher, G. (1996), 'Boots Will Have its Work Cut Out Trying to Rebuild Ailing Do It All', *Marketing Week*, 14 June, p. 25.

Porter, M. E. (1979), 'How Competitive Forces Shape Strategy', *Harvard Business Review*, 57(2), pp. 137–45.

Porter, M. E. (1980), *Competitive Strategy*, Free Press.

Reuters (1996), 'Mobile Woes Hit GN Store Nord', *Financial Times*, 21 March, p. 14.

Rigby, R. (1995), 'Simply the Best,' *Management Today*, December pp. 70–2.

Robinson, A. and Dobrowolski, R. (1995), 'Appliance Maker Sees Off Rivals', *Financial Times*, 28 March.

Sambrook, C. (1992), 'Getting Tough in a Sensitive Market', *Marketing*, 2 April, pp. 22–3.

Saunders, J. (1987), 'Marketing and Competitive Success', in M. J. Baker (ed.), *The Marketing Book*, Macmillan.

Simpson, M. (1996), 'Superior Jeans', *Marketing Week*, 16 February, p. 36.

Smith, D. (1995), 'The Long Slow Grind to Profits', *Management Today*, October, pp. 61–4.

Smith, D. (1996), 'The Secrets of Hypergrowth', *Management Today*, February, pp. 60–4.

Southam, H. (1993), 'Turning the Tables at Linn', *Marketing*, 20 May, pp. 20–1.

Tieman, R. (1996a), 'Williams Set to Sell Electronics Side to Managers for about £80 mill', *Financial Times*, 17 June, p. 22.

Tieman, R. (1996b), 'The Hot Future in Fire Protection', *Financial Times*, 18 June, p. 20.

Tieman, R. (1996c), 'Williams in £71mill MBO Disposal', *Financial Times*, 18 June, p. 20.

Tillier, A. (1996), 'The Uneasy Marriage of Dassault', *The European*, 29 Feb–6 March, p. 19.

Toor, M. (1993), 'Energizer: The Birth of a Brand', *Marketing*, 4 March, pp. 20–1.

Van de Krol, R. (1994a), 'Dutch Agriculture Urged to Act on Competitiveness and Quality', *Financial Times*, 18 October, p. 32.

Van de Krol, R. (1994b), 'Samas Makes German Purchase', *Financial Times*, 28 December, p. 16.

Verchere, I. (1996), 'Why Merger Will be Difficult', *The European*, 29 February–26 March, p. 19.

Wilson, R. M. S. *et al.* (1992), *Strategic Marketing Management*, Butterworth-Heinemann.

22 Marketing Planning, Management and Control

LEARNING OBJECTIVES

This chapter will help you to:

1 understand the different types of plan found within organisations and the importance of formal planning processes;

2 define the stages in the marketing planning process and their contribution to sound, integrated plans;

3 appreciate the various methods of estimating or forecasting both market and sales potential;

4 outline alternative ways of structuring a marketing department and their advantages and disadvantages;

5 understand the need for evaluation and control of marketing plans and their implementation, and the ways in which this can be achieved.

INTRODUCTION

Much of this text so far has been concerned with the development of competitive advantage through the careful design and implementation of an appropriate and integrated marketing mix. After selecting the most appropriate target markets, the organisation can create an offering that is of value to the chosen market segment(s) through a tailored package of pre-sale, consumption and post-sale benefits. This is a dynamic process because the marketing environment changes, competitive actions change, and not least, customer needs and preferences are also liable to change. This process of matching between the organisation and all aspects of the environment cannot be left to chance since it requires careful planning and management. Marketing, at both strategic and operational levels, plays an important part in that process.

The previous chapter looked at marketing planning's contribution to the process of matching organisational capability to the environment strategically. The products offered, the markets targeted and the basis of competitive advantage all have a major impact on company success and the operational plans of the various functions within the organisation. Marketing planning, alongside other areas such as financial and production planning, are part of the functional planning that takes place at divisional, business unit or individual company level. Its aim is to ensure that marketing activities are appropriate to the achievement of corporate objectives, can be implemented within resource limits and are capable of creating and sustaining a competitive position.

Example

The Cott Corporation was developing a new product, a drink designed to counter the effects of alcohol, in early 1996 (Marshall, 1996). In order to bring this product to the market, careful marketing planning and co-ordination would be necessary. From a corporate point of view, the new product would be consistent with the company's desire to be innovative, but would also be costly to develop and launch. Thus corporate agreement on resource allocation to the project is likely to have been necessary, as well as the incorporation of the new product into the longer-term corporate plans. To launch the product, the marketers will have to estimate market and sales potential, and then develop strategies for getting it into appropriate distribution channels. They will also have to decide who their target market is, and how to convince them of the product benefits. Contingency plans will have to be developed, so that Cott will know what to do if, perhaps, there was to be a backlash against the product from anti-alcohol campaigners or if competitors were to enter the market.

The first part of this chapter examines some of the issues associated with designing a planning system for marketing and how it fits into the organisational planning process. Then, the various stages of the marketing planning process are discussed in detail. Although the implementation of the planning process may vary from situation to situation, the outline given here at least demonstrates the interrelated nature of many planning decisions. Attention then turns to the important role of forecasting, which is sometimes neglected, but is nevertheless a fundamental part of the planning process. Poor forecasting increases the likelihood of formulating inappropriate plans, whether at a strategic or operational level.

The chapter then moves on to examine other managerial issues associated with managing marketing. Making sure that the organisational structure of the marketing function is appropriate, for example, is essential to the achievement of the tasks specified in the plans. Within any kind of structure, the degree of specialisation, motivation, responsiveness and expertise of staff will be a major factor in determining how well and how successfully those tasks are performed and completed. Finally, issues of marketing control and analysis are considered. Without adequate and timely control systems, even the best laid plans may be blown off course without managers realising the seriousness of the situation until it is too late to do anything about it.

STRATEGIC MARKETING PLANS AND PLANNING

Planning can be defined as a systematic process of forecasting the future business environment, and then deciding on the most appropriate goals, objectives and positions for best exploiting that environment. Organisational and functional strategies and plans provide the means by which the organisation can set out to achieve all that. All organisations need to plan, otherwise both strategic and operational activities would at best be unco-ordinated, badly focused and poorly executed. At worst, the organisation would muddle through from crisis to crisis with little sense of purpose, until eventually competition would gain such an advantage and demand reach such a low level that continuation would just not be viable.

Planning is therefore an activity, a process in business that provides a systematic structure and framework for considering the future, appraising options and opportunities, and then selecting and implementing the necessary activities for achieving the stated objectives efficiently and effectively. The marketing plan provides a clear and unambiguous statement concerning what strategies and actions will be implemented, by whom, when and with what outcomes.

It is important to distinguish between *plans*, the outcomes of the planning process, and *planning*, the process from which plans are derived. While the process of planning is fairly standard and can be transferred across functions and organisations, there are often wide variations in the actual use of plans to guide strategy and operations. This is partly because there are several different types of plan that can emerge from a planning process. The next subsection looks in detail at some of them.

Types of plan

Plans can be developed to cover many different aspects of an organisation. In some cases, they may be designed and developed as part of an integrated corporate system of long-term planning, encompassing the whole organisation, while in others, they may be used to address specific short-term issues of concern. Plans may be differentiated in terms of a number of features. These are as follows:

Organisational level

Managers are involved with planning at all levels of an organisation. The concerns of managers, however, change at higher levels of the organisation, and the complexities affecting planning also change. The more senior the manager, the more long-term and strategic becomes the focus. At the highest level, the concern is for the whole organisation and how to allocate resources across its various functions or units. At lower levels, the focus is on implementation within a shorter-term horizon, and on operating within clearly specified parameters. The marketing director may thus have a particular concern with developing new innovative products and opening new segments, while the sales representative may have to focus on sales territory planning to achieve predetermined sales and call objectives.

Time scale

Plans may be short-, medium-, or long-term in focus. '*Short term*' normally means the shortest period of time appropriate to the operations of the organisation. Normally, this is one year, or in some industries, such as fashion, one season. Such plans are usually about implementation, the achievement of specified objectives and allocating clearly defined responsibilities. *Medium-term plans* are more likely to cover a one- to three-year period. The focus is not so much on day-to-day operations and detailed tactical achievement, as on renewal. This involves the redesign and redefinition of activities to create, maintain and exploit competitive advantage. This could include the opening up of a new market, a new product innovation, or a strategic alliance to improve market position, for example. *Long-term* plans can be anything from three to 20 years, with the time-scale often dictated by capital investment periods. If it takes 10 years to commission, build and earn a payback on a major capital project, such as a new manufacturing plant or new machinery, then the planning horizon will have to be extended to take into account the various influences that could affect the feasibility of the project. Long-term plans are nearly always strategic in focus and concerned with resource allocation and return.

The definition of short- and long-term is variable. When Carte Noire was launched in the UK, the marketing plan for its first year aimed to gain between 2 per cent and 3 per cent of the total instant, ground and roast coffee sectors. That share was forecast to be worth £15 million for the first year, but the longer-term plans were aiming for £35 million by 1998 (Barnard, 1996). In contrast, the aircraft industry would consider 1998 to be a very short-term horizon, since they are looking to meet demand for aircraft well into the next century.

Regularity

Most longer-term plans have annual reviews to monitor progress. Shorter-term plans are often part of a hierarchy linking strategy with operations. Some plans, however, are not produced regularly as part of an annual cycle, but are campaign, project or situation specific. A *campaign plan*, for example, might have a limited duration to achieve defined objectives. As seen in Chapter 16, advertising is normally linked to a theme built into an integrated campaign covering perhaps media advertising, sales promotion, selling, distribution and pricing. *Project plans* are specific to particular activities, perhaps a new product launch, a change in distribution channels, or a new packaging innovation. These activities are of fixed duration and are not necessarily repeated.

Contingency plans are efforts to cater for the 'what if?' questions that emerge in more turbulent environments. Planned responses to any possible scenarios that might occur are prepared. A major new competitor entering the market, a supply shortage or a radical product innovation from a competitor could all affect the best laid plans. By thinking through the implications and alternatives before the crisis arises, a number of options can be identified to support management if the scenario really materialises.

By 1998 Carte Noire plans to have a £35 million share of the UK coffee market.

Focus

Plans will vary in their focus across the organisation. *Corporate plans* refer to the longer-term plans of the organisation, specifying the type of business scope desired and the strategies for achieving it across all areas of the business. The focus is on the technology, products, markets and resources that define the framework within which the individual parts of the organisation can develop more detailed strategies and plans. *Functional or operational plans* are, therefore, developed within the context of the organisational corporate plan but focus on the implementation of day-to-day or annual activities within the various parts of the organisation.

Organisational focus

Plans will vary according to the nature of the organisation itself. A number of alternative ways of organising marketing are considered later (*see* pp. 901 *et seq*.) If the organisational focus is on products, then plans will also take that focus, while if markets or functional areas are emphasised, plans will reflect that structure. For example, a functional organisational marketing

Source: Kraft Jacobs Suchard.

plan will have distinct elements of pricing, advertising, distribution etc. If SBUs are formed, then there is immediately a requirement for a two-tier planning structure: (a) considering the portfolio of SBUs at a corporate level, and (b) for each SBU, looking at the more detailed organisational design. Similarly divisional, regional, branch or company plans may all be used in different circumstances.

Planning: Benefits and problems

There are several benefits to be gained from taking a more organised approach to planning marketing activity. In summary, the benefits can be classified as relating to the development, co-ordination, or control of marketing activity, as shown in Fig 22.1.

Despite the obvious benefits, we cannot assume that all organisations practice planning, and even those that do might not achieve all the results they expect. Planning in itself does not guarantee success. Much depends on the quality of the planning, its acceptance as a fundamental driving force within the organisation, and the perceived relevance of the resulting plans. There are thus many ways in which the process can go wrong.

One major pitfall is a tendency to become technique orientated, losing sight of what planning is actually for. The production of big, complex, multicoloured BCG or GE matrices becomes an end in itself, and too little time and attention is devoted to working out what they mean and their implications for strategic decision making and planning. There is also a risk that because techniques produce clear, pretty pictures, with things neatly pigeonholed, managers take them too literally, and look for formulaic solutions. 'This product is a dog, therefore *we must* do THIS or THIS.' Such attitudes stifle creativity and ignore the true complexity of the world. Techniques such as the BCG matrix were never meant to be used in this way; they act as guides, they stimulate debate, but they do not offer pat solutions.

Finally, managers can become very fond of certain techniques. This is dangerous because any one technique only gives a partial insight, and occasionally looking at things from a new perspective can add new dimensions. That is not to suggest, of course, that the organisation should go to the opposite extreme of concentrating too

FIGURE 22.1

Benefits of planning

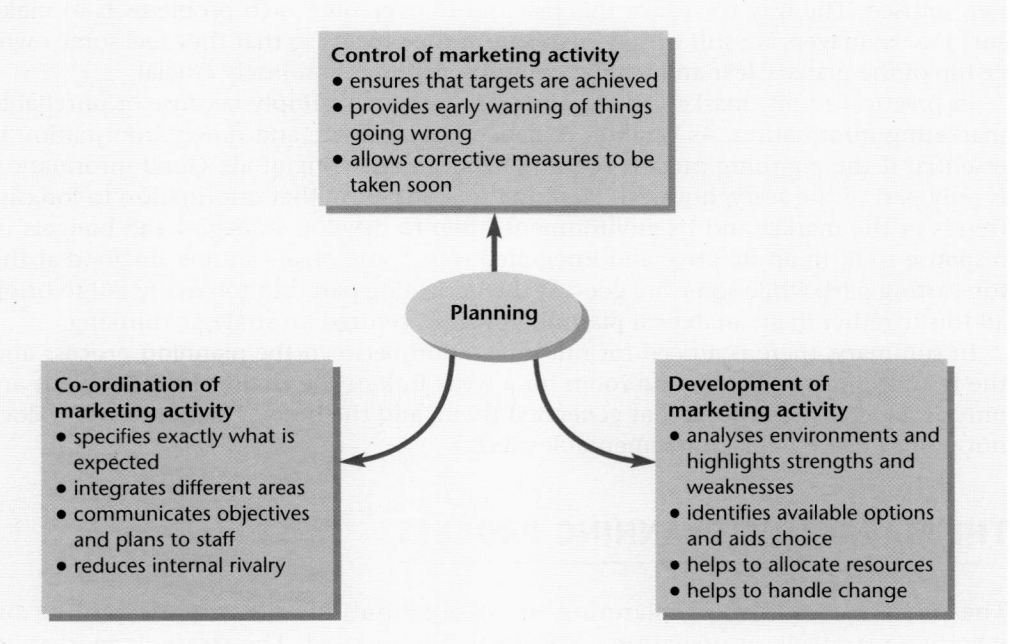

Behind the Hollywood glitter

The US film industry is an example of an attempt to bring budgeting and planning processes together. This has happened because of the huge costs involved in making films, and thus the need to minimise the risks of failure. The Hollywood studios research their audiences and use concept testing (as discussed in Chapter 9) which might well lead to revising the plot and script of the film. Even after the film is shot, it is test marketed and in one or two cases, this has led to a re-shooting of the film's ending. As well as making sure that the film itself is market orientated, the studios make detailed marketing plans for its launch. The marketing effort might begin up to a year before the film is released, and usually peaks in the two weeks surrounding the film's cinema launch. Furthermore, the marketing planning will also take into account the need to earn revenue from the branded merchandise, character licensing and the video release.

Nevertheless, it is a rather sobering thought that huge budgets and systematic commercial planning do not guarantee a film's success. *Waterworld* cost $200 million and *Judge Dredd* cost $70 million, yet neither achieved its targets. In contrast, *Four Weddings and a Funeral* cost only $3.5 million (considered a very low budget in the industry), had very little marketing input, yet managed to gross $250 million at the box office world-wide. This is a timely reminder that the best laid plans are subject to the unpredictability of the market's response. In general, the more the product relies on an emotional or psychological response from the target market, the greater the unpredictability.

Source: Goodridge (1995).

much on the planning process itself. Too many techniques may just confuse the real issues, creating a fog around the whole process. A complementary portfolio of carefully chosen techniques needs to be defined, and regularly reviewed for appropriateness.

Another potential problem arises perhaps from embracing planning rather too eagerly. The urge to set up dedicated planning departments can divorce the professional planner from the managers who have to live with the resulting plans and implement them. Differentiating so clearly between the planner and the manager is far more likely to lead to plans that are not valued and end up locked in a filing cabinet, unused. The way to reduce this risk and to overcome such problems is to make sure that managers are still wholly involved in the process so that they feel some ownership of the plans. Clear and regular communication is absolutely crucial.

In practical terms, marketing planning can fall down simply because of unreliable marketing information. As Chapter 6 made clear, accurate and timely information is essential if the planning process is going to mean anything at all. Good information is only part of the story, however. Planning is about using that information to forecast trends in the market and its environment, then to develop strategies and budgets in response to it, in an iterative and integrated way. Some organisations are good at the forecasting part, while some are good at the budgeting part, but too many fail to bring all this together in an analytical planning process, centred on strategic thinking.

In summary, there is a need for full integration between the **planning process** and the resulting plans. There is no room for a weak link in the chain, since the plans are only as good as the process that generated them, and the process is pointless if it does not result in acceptable, implementable plans.

THE MARKETING PLANNING PROCESS

The process of marketing planning in an organisation will vary, depending on whether a strategic or operational perspective is adopted. The **strategic marketing**

plan differs from an **operational marketing plan** on two key dimensions, according to Abell (1982). First, the strategic marketing plan deals with the total strategy in a market linking customers, competitors and organisational capability. Operational marketing plans, on the other hand, normally deal with the marketing mix strategy that will be used to gain leverage in a market. The strategic marketing plan, therefore, guides all planning and activities at a functional level not just in marketing, but across the whole organisation. Second, strategic marketing plans tend to be prepared at an SBU or company level, while the operational marketing plan is more often concerned with products and market segments.

Example

Pilkington Glass developed long-term corporate strategies aiming to make it the number one or number two supplier in selected geographic markets. Essential to achieving this was a detailed review and restructuring of its marketing positioning and activities (Lorenz, 1996a). The longer-term strategic marketing plans would, therefore, have defined the desired position and outlined the strategies for getting there (e.g., improving margins, increasing control over distribution channels and increasing the added value of the products), whereas the operational marketing plans would have told managers precisely how to put that into practice.

The previous chapter dealt with many of the issues associated with the strategic marketing plan and its contribution to the overall strategic management process in an organisation. In the corporate planning process, marketing acts as a critical link between customers, competitors and the strategic direction and objectives of the organisation. Thus appraising opportunities, market attractiveness, competitive positioning and portfolio management are important tools in the corporate planning process. The marketing plan, however, although well subsumed in the strategic planning process, still operates as a means of integrating activities, scheduling resources, specifying responsibilities and providing benchmarks for measuring progress.

The purpose of marketing planning has been defined as:

> **to find a systematic way of identifying a range of options, to choose one or more of them, then to schedule and cost out what has to be done to achieve the objectives.** (McDonald, 1989, p. 13)

If this definition is to work in practice, an organisational structure is needed to ensure that the process is properly managed. Without such a structure, there is a danger that key stages may be omitted, or given insufficient attention. Although the structure will vary according to the complexity and variability of the organisation, and the emphasis may vary according to the turbulence in the environment and the resultant challenges facing the organisation, a number of broad phases in the planning process are likely to operate in any case. The main stages in the planning process are shown in Fig 22.2 and each stage is considered in turn. The early stages of this planning process form part of strategic marketing planning.

Corporate objectives and values

Corporate objectives are at the heart of the planning process, since they describe the direction, priorities and relative position of the organisation in its market(s). These objectives help to create guidelines for marketing plans, since the output of the corporate planning process acts as an input into the marketing planning process.

Objectives are normally presented in terms of different kinds of targets.

FIGURE 22.2

**Stages in the
planning process**

Quantitative financial targets

Quantitative financial targets are items such as market share (by value), sales, profit and ROI, over a set time period. These could be broken down into specific targets for each of the various organisational units. Therefore within a university, the student number targets (the equivalent of sales targets) could be allocated across different faculties, and these will in turn determine the financial allocations.

Philosophical targets

Philosophical targets are likely to be contained within a mission statement. A mission statement represents a vision of where the organisation is today and where it wants to be in the future. It expresses the core values of the organisation and is intended to guide functional and business unit areas in their strategic development. It should encompass segments served, the needs to be fulfilled in the market, and the technological or service character of the organisation (Abell, 1982). It should encapsulate the distinctive and principal values of the organisation, but from a market rather than a product orientation.

Day (1990) identified four characteristics of a well thought through mission statement:

- *Future orientated*: linking the future with its impact upon the business
- *Reflecting the values and orientation of the leader*: providing support and clear guidelines to staff
- *Stating strategic purpose*: indicating the direction and strategy to be followed, the targets and competitors to beat
- *Enabling*: providing clear guidelines to managers lower down the organisation in their preparation of SBU or functional plans.

To Wensley (1987), mission statements should be 'short on numbers and long on rhetoric but remaining succinct'. The mission statement provides the essential guidelines for managers in making their day-to-day decisions and when preparing operational plans. Nevertheless, the corporate mission statement needs to be supported by quantitative and qualitative targets that reflect this mission.

Example

Mission statements vary in length, complexity and philosophy. KFC, for example, wants 'to provide families with affordable, delicious chicken-dominated meals', whereas McDonald's '... will provide great tasting food backed up by excellent operations and friendly service in a relaxed, safe, and consistent restaurant environment'. Pepsi's takes a little more deciphering: 'we will be an outstanding company by exceeding customer expectations through empowering people guided by shared values'. Lada cars, however, must win a prize for clarity and straightforwardness, with its mission 'to provide the lowest price and best value for money in Britain' (Thomas, 1995).

Qualitative targets

Qualitative targets include items such as service levels, innovation and scope. These rarely have just one objective, but are often found in a mixture with defined priorities. Drucker (1955) highlighted eight areas, as shown in Fig 22.3.

Whatever the type of objective, they all must be realistic, achievable within a specific time-scale, and cited in order of priority. This will lead to a hierarchy of interlinking objectives. In any case, objectives should reflect the competitive and market positions considered in Chapter 21. In practice, however, defining objectives is often a case of managing trade-offs, such as those suggested by Weinberg (1969) in Table 22.1.

The outcome of this stage should be a clear statement of what is expected of the functional units within the organisation and their plans.

TABLE 22.1
Trade-offs in setting objectives

- Short-term profit *vs* long-term growth
- Profit-margin *vs* market positioning
- Direct sales effort *vs* market development
- Penetrating existing markets *vs* developing new ones
- Profit *vs* non-profit goals
- Growth *vs* stability
- Change *vs* stability
- Low-risk *vs* high-risk environments

Source: Weinberg (1969).

The marketing audit

Audit is a term more commonly used in financial management to describe the process of taking stock of an organisation's financial strengths, weaknesses and health, through checking and analysing changes in its assets and transactions over a given period. The philosophy of the **marketing audit** is very similar, in that it systematically takes stock of an organisation's marketing health, as the formal definition implies:

FIGURE 22.3

Qualitative targets

> [The audit] is the means by which a company can understand how it relates to the environment in which it operates. It is the means by which a company can identify its own strengths and weaknesses as they relate to external opportunities and threats. It is thus a way of helping management to select a position in that environment based on known factors. (McDonald, 1989, p. 21).

The marketing audit is really the launching pad for the marketing plan, as it encourages management to reflect systematically on the environment and the organisation's ability to respond, given its actual and planned capabilities. The marketing audit, just like its financial counterpart, first and foremost is about developing a shared, agreed and objective understanding of the organisation. It thus concerns such questions as:

1 What is happening in the environment? Does it pose threats or opportunities?
2 What are our relative strengths and weaknesses for handling and exploiting the environment?
3 How effective are we in implementing marketing activity?

In order to answer such questions, managers have to look at both environmental variables (i.e., an external audit) and operational variables (i.e., an internal audit).

The **external audit** systematically looks at the kinds of issues covered extensively in Chapter 2 as the STEP factors. Sociocultural changes, such as in the demographic make-up of a market, or in public concerns or attitudes, may well influence the future strategic direction of an organisation. The early identification of technological change might also change strategic direction, as the organisation plans ways of exploiting it to make cheaper, better or different products ahead of the competition. Economic and competitive factors are both, of course, very important. Low disposable incomes among target customers may force the organisation towards more rigorous cost control or into changing its product mix, while high interest rates on organisational borrowing might delay diversification or other expansion plans. Competition also has to be analysed very carefully on all aspects of its marketing activities, including its response to STEP factors and its choice of target markets. Finally, the external audit should note what is happening in terms of the legal and regulatory frameworks, whether national or European, that bind the organisation.

MARKETING IN ACTION

The car park environment

National Car Parks (NCP) is the UK's biggest car park operator, with nearly 600 sites. If it was to undertake an external audit, it might raise the following issues, among others:

1 *Competition*: a number of rivals from mainland Europe and the US have entered the UK market.
2 *Negotiating for sites*: increased competition means that acquiring new sites or even renewing the leases on existing ones is more difficult. On the other hand, competitors who are struggling provide an opportunity for NCP to pick up sites and contracts.
3 *Management contracts*: many site owners (local authorities, airports, hotels, shopping centres etc.) now prefer to award management contracts to car park operators, rather than giving them complete autonomy over the car park operation. NCP's traditional approach has been one of autonomy, and its competitors have been faster to accept management contracts.
4 *Security*: both the general public and the police are pressurising car park operators to install increasingly sophisticated security systems.
5 *Shopping habits*: the rise of out of town shopping with ample free parking not only pulls shoppers away from town centres, NCP's traditional territory, but also highlights the high cost of town centre parking. 'Park and ride' schemes operated from edge of town sites into the centres might provide an opportunity for NCP in co-operation with local authorities.

Source: Foster (1996).

The **internal audit** focuses on many of the decision areas discussed in Chapters 3–20 and their effectiveness in achieving their specified objectives. It is not just, however, a *post mortem* on the 4Ps. Auditors will also be interested in how smoothly and synergistically the 4Ps fit together, and whether the marketing actions, organisation and allocated resources are appropriate to the environmental opportunities and constraints.

Table 22.2 summarises the issues that a marketing audit should consider.

TABLE 22.2
Marketing audit issues

- Macro environment: STEP factors (*see* Chapter 2)
- Task environment: *competition, channels, customers* (*see* Chapter 3–5)
- Markets (*see* Chapter 21)
- Strategic issues: *segmentation, positioning, competitive advantage* (*see* Chapter 5 and 21)
- Marketing mix (*see* Chapter 7–20)
- Marketing organisational structure and organisation (*see* Chapter 22)

The audit should be undertaken as part of the planning cycle, usually on an annual basis, rather than as a desperate response to a problem. The audit is a systematic attempt to assess the performance of the marketing effort, looking from the present backwards, although when it is done thoroughly, it can be a time-consuming activity. To help the audit process, it is critical to have a sound marketing information system covering the marketing environment, customers, competitors etc., as well as detail on all areas of the organisational marketing effort, as outlined in Chapter 21.

The main risk in undertaking the marketing audit is a lack of objectivity. This may arise from being too close to the situation to see it clearly, or from a fear that if the audit is too objective, a manager's past decision-making might be criticised. The use of external consultants could overcome these problems, but nevertheless, going through the process itself internally can be a valuable experience for managers.

Example

Bridon PLC, a manufacturer of wire and rope, undertook an extensive internal audit as part of its move towards becoming a marketing led company. Some of the problems that it highlighted were (Fraser, 1995):

1 *Inconsistency*: different subsidiaries, divisions and distribution centres were presenting themselves to customers in different ways, so that there was no consistency between product specifications, sales literature etc. A corporate identity project was therefore commissioned to create an umbrella image that would inject the necessary consistency world-wide.

2 *Internal competition*: in some markets, different divisions of Bridon were competing with each other for the same customers.

3 *Product quality and new product development*: it was felt that product quality and consistency could be improved, and that it was taking too long to get new products through to the market. Additionally, R&D was felt to be too remote from customers. Measures were taken to bring marketing, R&D and customers closer together, with the result that a new product project took only eight months from start to finish rather than five years!

4 *Customer service*: the organisation felt that it was taking too long to get products to customers and that customer queries were not being efficiently dealt with. To overcome these problems, a new ordering and scheduling system was developed, as well as a simplified administration system that brought all the information about an individual customer together.

Marketing analysis

The marketing audit is a major exercise which ranges widely over all the internal and external factors influencing an organisation's marketing activity. It generates, therefore, a huge amount of material that has to be analysed and summarised to sift out the critical issues that will drive the marketing plan forward.

SWOT analysis

The commonest mechanism for structuring audit information to provide a critical analysis is the **SWOT analysis** (strengths, weaknesses, opportunities, threats).

Strengths and weaknesses. Strengths and weaknesses tend to focus on the present and past, and on internally controlled factors, such as the 4Ps and the overall marketing package (including customer service) offered to the target market. The external environment is not totally ignored, however, and many strengths and weaknesses can only be defined as such in a competitive context. Thus, for example, our low prices may be seen as a strength if we are pricing well below our nearest competitor in a price sensitive market. Low prices may, however, be a weakness if we have been forced into them by a price war and cannot really sustain them, or if the market is less price sensitive and our price is associated with inferior quality when compared with higher priced competitors in the minds of the target market.

Opportunities and threats. Opportunities and threats tend to focus on the present and the future, tending to take a more outward-looking, strategic view of likely developments and options. Thus the organisation that is the price leader in a price-sensitive market might see the opportunity to get its costs down even further as a means of maintaining its position and pressurising any challengers. The challenger's SWOT analysis would define that same scenario as a threat, but might see an opportunity in opening up a new, non-price-sensitive segment. Many opportunities and threats emerge from the marketing environment, when shifts in demographic and cultural factors are taken into account, when developments in emerging markets, such as eastern Europe, are analysed, when, in fact, the implications of anything included in Chapter 2's STEP factors are considered.

Understanding the SWOT analysis

The SWOT analysis, therefore, helps to sort information systematically and to classify it, but still needs further creative analysis to make sense of it. The magnitude of opportunities and threats, and the feasibility of the potential courses of action implied by them, can only really be understood in terms of the organisation's strengths and weaknesses. If strengths and weaknesses represent 'where we are now' and opportunities and threats represent 'where we want (or don't want) to be' or 'where we could be', then the gap, representing 'what we have to do to get there' has to be filled by managerial imagination, as justified and formalised in the body of the marketing plan.

Marketing objectives

As the previous subsection implied, the desire to exploit strengths and opportunities, and to overcome weaknesses and threats, gives a foundation for the definition of marketing objectives. Objectives are essential for clearly defining what must be achieved through the marketing strategies implemented, and also provide a benchmark against which to measure the extent of their success. **Marketing objectives** do, however, have to be wide ranging as well as precise, as they have to link closely with corporate objectives on a higher level but also descend to the fine detail of products, segments etc. They must, therefore, be *consistent*, with each other and with corporate goals,

West Coast Fish Products is a small fish processing company in Ireland, which smokes salmon, trout and mackerel, using a special blend of woods, herbs and spices to achieve a distinctive flavour. Although its main market is in Ireland, it is looking towards European markets, especially Germany and Switzerland. Even though it is a small company, it uses a formal approach to marketing planning, identifying priorities for marketing strategy development. Its SWOT analysis revealed the following issues:

1 *Strengths*

    (a) reputation for quality in raw materials and processes;
    (b) value-added products using herbs;
    (c) knowledge of the market and contacts in Germany, France and Switzerland;
    (d) good location for accessing raw materials.

2 *Weaknesses*

    (a) no formal organisation for marketing;
    (b) emphasis on quality and production rather than on systematic market development;
    (c) buyers tend to initiate contact – company not sufficiently proactive;
    (d) limited resources for intensive market development;
    (e) most competitors have larger market share;
    (f) remote European location means higher transport costs and reduces shelf life of products by up to seven days;
    (g) retail and catering trade dominated by a few large customers.

3 *Opportunities*

    (a) increasing European consumption of smoked salmon;
    (b) fish seen as a healthy product, low in fat and cholesterol;
    (c) contract catering sector relatively underdeveloped;
    (d) the rural, green image of Ireland reflects positively on Irish food products;
    (e) government aid programmes for small businesses in exporting, marketing etc.;
    (f) new potential in US and Japanese markets.

4 *Threats*:

    (a) seasonal demand, peaking at Christmas;
    (b) domestic Irish market relatively small;
    (c) smoked salmon regarded in Ireland as luxury speciality food;
    (d) pressure on prices in domestic market from retail and catering buyers;
    (e) low levels of supplier loyalty;
    (f) highly competitive European market (80 competitors in Ireland alone) with strong competition from Norway and Denmark in particular;
    (g) market pressure to raise quality standards, especially with smoked salmon;
    (h) business vulnerable to impact of disease and pollution in fish stocks;
    (i) tougher European legislation affecting processing, additives, handling, marketing etc.;
    (j) variety of tastes and demands (colour, saltiness, dryness etc.) across different European markets.

From this profile, marketing objectives could then begin to be formulated.

attainable, in that they can be achieved in practice and their progress can be measured, and *compatible* with both the internal and external environments in which they are to be implemented. These criteria are generally applicable, despite the fact that marketing objectives can vary over time and between organisations.

Guiltinan and Paul (1988) identified four fundamental areas within which marketing objectives may be defined:

1 achieving market share growth or maintenance;
2 the maintenance or improvement of profitability;
3 establishing an opening marketing position;
4 maximising cash flow, harvesting.

Whatever the basis of the objectives, they cannot be left at such a descriptive level. It is not enough to say that our objective is to increase our market share. That leaves too many questions unanswered, such as:

● Volume (i.e., focus on quantity) or value (i.e., focus on revenue) share?
● How much more share?
● For which products?
● In which segment(s)?
● At which competitor's expense?

It is essential to quantify and make explicit precisely what is intended. Even when those questions have been answered, the objective is still quite general, and a number of detailed subobjectives, which will perhaps relate to constraints or parameters within which the main objective is to be achieved, should be also defined. The main objective of increasing market share, for example, may have subobjectives relating to pricing. Thus the marketing manager might have to find a way of increasing market share without compromising the organisation's premium price position.

Example

For West Coast Fish Products, introduced earlier, the primary broad marketing objective might be to improve its profitability in the domestic Irish market through more effective and efficient marketing. It might also strive to improve its marketing position in selected European markets. With limited resources, however, this can only be done if there is a disciplined approach to developing one or two markets in depth rather than seeking orders from a wide geographic area. Detailed marketing objectives would then have to be defined that outline quantified targets relating specific products to specific markets.

Marketing strategies

A marketing strategy is the means by which an organisation sets out to achieve its marketing objectives. The main areas of focus are the definition of the target market and the marketing mix employed. They are not only described in qualitative terms, but are also specified in terms of the resources required and the structure and allocation of responsibility for implementation.

In terms of the target market, the planner needs to ensure that the right group has been selected, matching with the conclusions drawn from the SWOT analysis. The organisation should, of course, be able to make an attractive offering to that segment, and have the expertise to create and sustain differential advantage, whether it is looking for defendable niches or to compete head-on in a crowded mass market segment. Chapter 5 looked more closely at segmentation bases and target market selection. The choice of target segment will be influenced by the competitive structure of the

TI rethinks its portfolio

Tube Investments (TI) is a remarkable example of a company that completely overhauled its portfolio over a period of 10 years and still emerged making a profit. In 1986, sales exceeded £1 billion and the company, despite its name, was not a main player in its original tube business, or indeed in any organisational markets. Most of its sales were from consumer products such as Creda and New World cookers, Russell Hobbs kettles, Gloworm heaters and Raleigh bicycles. Although sales levels had held up, profits were being heavily squeezed by strong competition from imports.

In 1986, a new chairman, Sir Christopher Lewinton, started a complete reversal of the company's fortunes. Most of the consumer products divisions were sold and replaced with a new portfolio, primarily from acquisitions. Sales in 1995 exceeded £1.5 billion and pre-tax profits rose from £43.5 million in 1986 to £200 million in 1995. At the root of these changes were key decisions on corporate capability and mission. TI had its basic roots in engineering, not consumer goods. This meant that it did not really understand consumer markets and buyer behaviour, thus making it vulnerable to those who did. The new mission statement was:

'to be an international engineering group concentrating on specialised engineering businesses, operating in selected niches on a global basis.'

Each of the key businesses had to have sustainable technological and market share leadership. The search for technological leadership was compatible with the drive to move from basic production into areas with a high knowledge and service content.

To implement the mission, several major changes were required. Businesses were bought and sold. Creda, for example, was sold to GEC in 1987, and most of the consumer products followed. Two purchases, John Crane Hougaille from the USA, the world leader in mechanical seals, and the Bundy Corporation, a specialist in small diameter tubing for the motor and refrigeration industries, formed the basis of the new portfolio. These two companies, with further associated acquisitions in 1995 accounted for 80 per cent of TI's sales. Dowty Aerospace, purchased in 1992, however, has not been without its problems, primarily because of a slump in aviation market demand soon after the acquisition. The company was especially interested in the landing gear business, where it was the world leader, along with the polymer engineering division, which appeared to have excellent long-term prospects.

Further changes can be expected in the portfolio. Mechanical seals, automotive tubing and air-landing gear are all in mature, long-term low-growth markets. With plans to reach a steady 5 per cent to 10 per cent growth over the late 1990s, TI might well have to make further acquisitions. The opportunity for further share gain from service and value-added products would not be sufficient to achieve those objectives. There are plans for greater differentiation at Crane and Bundy by taking on higher value products, but these are likely to assist only in retaining market position.

Sources: Financial Times (1996); Lorenz (1996b).

---

market, and thus by the organisation's choice of competitor against whom it wants to compete, and how. This in turn links with generic competitive strategies and the concept of competitive positioning, as outlined in Chapter 21 (pp. 854 *et seq.*).

In reality, an organisation will be presented with a range of strategic options, relating to its defined objectives. Some will be related to increasing volume (as in Ansoff's product and market matrix presented in Fig 21.6), while others relate to improving profitability and holding on to what the organisation already has (reducing costs, increasing prices, changing the product mix, streamlining operations etc.).

Within each area examples of actions might be to:

1 *Improve product packaging*: Trebor Bassett revised the packaging of its Liquorice Allsorts brand in spring 1996. Supported by promotional activity, the 'facelift' was expected to increase the brand's sales by between 20 and 30 per cent.
2 *Alter prices*: when *The Times* cut its cover price to 20p in 1993, its daily circulation was just under 400 000. Although the price gradually increased, by January 1996,

The Times was still 10p cheaper than any of its rivals and had a circulation of just under 700000.

3 *Improve productivity*: as seen at p. 833 when Ford took over Aston Martin, one of the first objectives was to increase productivity as a means of improving both the cost profile of the organisation and sales volumes.

4 *Standardise*: the Boss Group uses a common chassis for a range of different lift trucks. By standardising the component, the organisation can achieve cost efficiency in both logistics and manufacturing, yet can still offer a wide range of trucks to meet different customer needs.

5 *Change sales or customer mix*: Sellotape still derives over half its sales from its original product launched in the 1930s, but it has gradually developed a more segmented approach, to change both the product and customer mix. There are products for DIY, children, gift wrapping, and general home stationery, as well as a brand aimed at the small office.

Example

For West Coast Fish Products, the strategy might be to occupy a narrow niche with high quality, clearly differentiated, unique products. Within the domestic Irish market, this would mean increasing the promotional effort targeted at top class restaurants and hotels, and opening up a new segment of high-class catering services. This is not just a question of promotional activity, of course, but also needs to be carried through to product appearance, packaging, delivery and order processing etc. Prices, however, are under pressure from competitive forces, so it might be difficult to accompany any push upmarket with a corresponding price increase. In the international market, the priority is to fine tune the marketing mix strategy to meet the needs of selected European wholesale and retail markets.

Marketing programmes

Whereas the previous stage was about designing marketing strategies, this one is about their detailed implementation. The marketing programme will precisely specify actions, responsibilities and time-scales. It is the detailed statement that managers have to follow if strategies are to be put into operation, as it outlines required actions by market segment, product, and functional area. Within the marketing programme, each mix element is considered individually, covering all the decision areas outlined in Chapters 7 to 20. This is in contrast to the marketing strategy itself, which stresses the interdependency between elements of the mix for achieving the best synergy between them. Now, the individual strands that make up that strategy can be picked out, and for each functional area, such as pricing, managers can go through planning processes, audits, objectives, strategies, programmes and controls.

On the basis of the overall marketing strategy, managers can emphasize those areas of comparative strength where a competitive edge can be gained, strengthen those areas where the organisation is comparable with its competition, and work to develop further or overcome those where the organisation is more vulnerable. The key challenge at the end of it all, however, is to ensure that the marketing mix is affordable, implementable and appropriate for the target segment. With that in mind, and given the dynamic nature of most markets, managers will also have to review the mix on a regular basis to make sure that it is still fresh and still serving the purposes intended.

Marketing budgets

The marketing plan must specify and schedule all financial and other resource requirements, otherwise managers might not be able to accomplish the tasks set. This

West Coast Fish Products drew up a series of planned actions for the main segments served. In the domestic Irish market, for example, the programme aimed at the trade segment might entail:

- sales visits to the top 25 hotels and restaurants
- sales visits to 30 large catering companies
- attendance at relevant trade shows and fairs
- improving design, labelling and durability of packaging
- improving logistics to reduce order processing and delivery times
- launching a new line of fresh eels
- encouraging bigger average order size to improve sales volume and efficiency.

In each case, responsibility will have to be allocated, resources specified, schedules drawn up and activities described in much more detail. For this company, it might well mean that the directors have to spend time meeting customers and developing new business rather than concentrating on the manufacturing processes.

is partly about costs, such as those of the sales force which include their associated expenditures, advertising campaigns, dealer support, market research etc., and partly about forecasting expected revenues from products and markets. In determining budgets, managers need to balance precision against flexibility. A budget should be precise and detailed enough to justify the resources requested and to permit detailed control and evaluation of the cost effectiveness of various marketing activities, yet it also needs the flexibility to cope with changing circumstances.

We discussed budget setting, and some of the issues surrounding it, in Chapter 15 in a marketing communications context (*see* pp. 592 *et seq.*). Many of the points made there are more widely applicable, particularly the relative strengths and weaknesses of objective and task budgeting compared with methods based on historical performance (for example basing this year's budget on last year's with an arbitrary 5 per cent added on).

Marketing controls and evaluation

Control and evaluation are both essential if managers are to ensure that the plans are being implemented properly and that the outcomes are those expected. As part of the planning process, therefore, managers will have to specify what will be measured, when, how and by whom. Although the defined marketing objectives provide the ultimate goals against which performance and success can be measured, waiting until the end of the planning period to assess whether they have been achieved is risky. Instead, managers should evaluate progress regularly throughout the period against a series of benchmarks reflecting expected performance to date. If, for example, the overall objective is a 20 per cent increase in volume sales over 12 months, managers might expect after three months to see at least a 5 per cent improvement on the equivalent figure for the previous year, as strategies begin to take effect and gather momentum. At that three-month staging post, managers can then decide whether their strategies appear to be well on target for achieving objectives as planned or whether the deviation from expected performance is so great that alternative actions are called for.

Control and evaluation can take either a short- or a longer-term perspective. In the short-term, control can be monitored on a daily basis through reviewing orders received, sales, stockturn, or cash flow, for example. Longer-term strategic control focuses on monitoring wider issues, such as the emergence of trends and ambiguities in the marketing environment. This has strong links with the marketing audit, assessing the extent to which the organisation has matched its capabilities with the environment and indeed the extent to which it has correctly 'read' the environment.

This whole area of control and evaluation will be considered in greater detail at pp. 905 *et seq*.

MARKET POTENTIAL AND SALES FORECASTING

The extent to which plans can be successfully implemented depends not only on managers' abilities in setting and implementing strategies, but more fundamentally on their ability to predict the market accurately. This means two things: first, assessing the market potential, that is working out how big the total cake is, and second, forecasting sales, that is calculating how big a slice of that cake our organisation can get for itself. The following subsections will look at both of these areas, especially the factors influencing their calculation and the methods used.

Market and sales potential

The concept of **market potential** is very simple, but in practice it is very difficult to estimate. Market potential is the maximum level of demand available within the total market over a given period, assuming a certain level of competitive marketing activity and certain conditions and trends in the marketing environment. This definition immediately raises problems in calculating a figure for market potential, as it involves many assumptions about competitors and the environment, needs a precise definition of 'the market' and requires methods of quantifying the variables concerned.

Market potential

We now look more closely at some of the difficulties in estimating market potential.

Maximum level of demand. The calculation of maxium level of demand should be product or service specific, and means calculating the demand if all possible buyers were to purchase to their fullest realistic extent in terms of volume and frequency. It is an idealised concept that is difficult to measure, for many reasons. For example, any individual's decision about whether to purchase, how much and how often is, in practice, influenced by many factors. One factor is marketing activity, such as campaigns encouraging product substitution or increased consumption. If market potential is partially dependent on marketing effort, then a range of alternative 'maximum levels of demand' become immediately possible.

Total market. The potential total market is really a question of boundaries. In the same way that calculation of profit can vary according to the way in which an accountant interprets the rules, total market size can vary according to the definitions used to mark market boundaries.

> ### Example
>
> In the early 1990s, the traditional toy industry was reviewing its definition of the market following the success of Sega and Nintendo. An article in *Marketing* (Toor, 1992) made the valid point that children are leaving the traditional toy market earlier and earlier, and that their needs, wants and consumption choices are broadening. This means that toys are competing directly with clothing, trainers, videos, electronic games etc. for children's disposable income. As an industry expert said, the toy manufacturers '[have] got to consider themselves in the youth gift market, not just the toy market' (Toor, 1992 p.19).

The Australian Tourist Commission used pan-European advertising to improve its sales potential.

Source: DMB&B.

Level of competitive activity and trends in the marketing environment. As we showed in Chapter 2, the marketing environment is a very dynamic and complex phenomenon that has a fundamental impact on the organisation. A change in any aspect of the marketing environment can, therefore, have a corresponding effect on market potential. A government decision to reduce the tax levied on unleaded petrol, for instance, making it cheaper than Four Star, dramatically increased motorists' demand for the unleaded product. This in turn meant that oil companies had to revise their predictions of total demand for both unleaded and Four Star. Competitors can also implement strategies that change the nature of the market as a whole, either by opening up new segments, increasing demand through marketing communication efforts, or by launching new products that effectively create a new market.

Over time, market potential will change, depending on the forces at work. All of these forces are beyond the organisation's control, yet the organisation has to try to predict them. It is also important when looking at the environment to be clear about the time period being considered, the stage of growth reached by the market, and the rate of change, especially in technology that is likely to impact upon the environment. Clearly, the further ahead the organisation is looking, the greater the uncertainty in predictions. The mobile phone industry, for example, is relatively young and still growing. It is very difficult to predict how the rate of growth will progress over time and at what point saturation will be reached. Much of this depends on how the competitive structure of the market evolves and what further technological innovations are introduced. Predictions of market potential, therefore, vary from eight million to 12 million subscribers in the UK by the end of the 1990s (Reguly, 1995).

Sales potential

Even after the potential has been estimated for the market as a whole, an organisation will then need to determine its own **sales potential**, that is, the share of the market that it could reasonably expect to capture. Obviously, sales potential is partly a result of the organisation's marketing effort and its success in attracting and holding customers. Although the level of total market potential will create a ceiling for an organisation's individual sales potential, in reality sales potential should be based on a clear understanding of the relative success of individual organisations' marketing efforts. The decision to launch a new range or to increase promotional expenditure could help to raise the level of sales potential. As already mentioned, in some situations the actions of an individual organisation can increase the potential for all competitors by expanding the market potential as a whole. Thus if a major player in the market or a number of competitors increase their promotional spends, that might stimulate the market for all competitors, not just those undertaking the marketing effort.

Having a clear idea of market and sales potential provides a useful input to the marketing planning process. It is especially important for planning selling efforts and allocating resources. The allocation of sales force effort, and the establishment of distribution points and service support centres, for example, can reflect sales potential rather than actual sales, thus allowing scope for expansion. Similarly, sales potential can also be used to plan sales territories, quotas, sales force compensation and targets for prospecting.

Estimating market and sales potential

The methods used for estimating sales and market potential will vary, depending on just how new or innovative the product or service is, and how mature the market is. The two main groups of methods discussed here are *breakdown*, that is, working from the aggregate level of the whole market down to the segment of interest, and *build up*, that is, starting with individual customers then aggregating up to industry or market totals.

Breakdown methods

Breakdown methods fall into two main groups: those based on total market measurement and those based on statistical series analysis.

Total market measurement. The total market measurement method begins with any total industry or market data that may be available from secondary research, and then breaks that information down to market segment level and thence to the organisation's own sales potential. This method relies heavily on the availability of a long series of data on industry sales volume and consumption by segments within that market, but rarely are such complete and detailed data available. Potential is thus often estimated from what data are available and then adjusted to take account of the current marketing environment. Once market and segment potentials have been established, sales potential can be derived by estimating competitors' relative market shares and then calculating how those might change as a result of expected actions, for example a new product launch.

Statistical series analysis. Statistical series analysis is a means of calculating potential for market segments. It is based on developing a statistical relationship, correlating sales and key factors influencing them. The success of this method depends on identifying the right factor or combination of factors (i.e., statistical series) to use in the analysis. Cox (1979), for example, quotes the case of a company trying to establish potential for production machinery. The analysis was based on a single factor, the number of production employees within each industry using that kind of equipment. Several other statistical series, such as expenditure on new equipment and value of products shipped, had been tested but discarded. In some industries, the appropriate factor to use is fairly obvious. The potential for building material sales in a region, for example, is closely related, as one might expect, to the number of building contracts and the size of their floor area. The calculation might further be influenced by weightings which reflect managerial judgements on the relative importance of segments and the likely effect of other environmental factors on the future development of those segments. Thus knowledge that the authorities in a certain region are about to invest in an extensive campaign to attract new industry into its neighbourhood might make the building materials company weight that region more highly than a similar region with lower future growth prospects.

Build up methods

There are three main methods for aggregating data to produce reliable market and sales potential figures: census, survey, and secondary data.

Census. The census method is based on a detailed consideration of every buyer and potential buyer in a market. This may be difficult, if not impossible, in mass consumer markets, but is more feasible in industrial situations, where demand might be concentrated and orders infrequent but of high value. With large capital plant, such as turbine generators or aircraft engines, for instance, a census could provide a good indication of market and sales potential as the customer base is very small. The market potential is effectively the sum of all the potentials estimated for individual purchasers.

Survey. The survey method is more widely used in consumer markets where a representative sample (look back at Chapter 6) of consumers are asked about their purchase intentions. This information can then be used as a basis for calculating total market or sales potential. The main problem, however, is that respondents might lie about their

MARKETING IN ACTION

Bouygues backs its forecasts

Mobile phones is one of the fastest growing product sectors in Europe. The total number of subscribers was around 16 million in 1995, with the possibility of a further rise to 30 million by the end of the decade. Penetration rates are quickly expected to grow to around 40 per cent of the market in Europe. Deutsche Morgan Grenfell predicts a rosy future for the mobile market even in France, which experienced a slower than average start, allegedly because of high connection fees and tariffs. Growth in the number of subscribers in France is forecast to grow from 1.37 million in 1995 to 8.64 million by the year 2000. This would mean a penetration of 11.8 per cent of the market compared with the current level of around 2.4 per cent.

These projections for the French market seemed so attractive to Bouygues, a group with interests in construction and television, that in 1996 it decided to enter the mobile market. This was despite the presence of two well-established operators, France Telecom (65 per cent share) and Generale des Eaux (35 per cent), who had invested in market development without any significant returns. All three were hoping for the same explosive growth in the French mobile market that was already under way in other European markets.

The penetration in Germany was already 4.6 per cent, in Italy 6.8 per cent, and in the UK 9.4 per cent. This reflected a far greater use in non-business situations in those countries, a phenomenon that had not yet reached France.

Bouygues believed that it could benefit from market development by targeting individual consumers and setting prices accordingly, rather than competing for the business customer. An advertising campaign costing Fr 65 million aimed to open the segment, and tariffs included three hours of free calls within a 100 km radius. In planning for the share that Bouygues expected to gain, it had also to take into account the technical feasibility of linking potential subscribers to the network. Initially, coverage was restricted to the Paris region, but expansion to cover 50 per cent of the population by 1997 and 90 per cent by 2000 was expected. This would be an important factor in determining the sales growth, and could represent a competitive advantage. Either way, the entry into the market is based upon a careful assessment of trends and the factors that influence both market growth forecasts and predicted share.

Sources: Owen (1996); Zoller (1995).

intentions, or fail to follow them through in the future. Consumers might well be genuine in saying that yes, they do intend to replace their car within the next 12 months, but an unexpected redundancy, repairs to the roof of the house, or the allure of an exotic holiday might cause them to revise their intentions. Even more problematic is establishing intent to purchase a particular brand. A consumer might genuinely intend to replace their car with a Ford, but if at the time of the actual purchase Renault or Volvo are running a particularly attractive promotion, then ... who knows?

Secondary data. Finally, secondary data can be used to establish sales and market potential. Internal sales records can be used to predict individual customers' purchasing on the basis past behaviour. In this approach, the sales potentials are produced first and the market potential is then derived from those figures.

Market and sales forecasting

Marketing often plays a central role in preparing and disseminating **forecasts**. This is perhaps one of its most important functions, as the sales and market forecasts provided are the basis of all subsequent planning and decision making within most areas of the organisation. Whether the organisation is a car manufacturer forecasting the demand for each model, a tour operator forecasting demand for specific destinations, or a university forecasting numbers of full-time, part-time and overseas students by programme area, the forecast is the starting point for all subsequent decisions. Get it wrong and the whole organisation can be caught out by major capacity or cash flow problems. In fashion markets, for example, it can be very difficult to forecast what styles are going to sell in what quantities, hence the popularity of 'end of season' sales as retailers try to sell off surplus stock. Holiday companies also find forecasting difficult, and again find themselves selling off surplus holidays at a discount right up to departure dates.

Forecasting and planning are, however, different functions. Forecasting attempts to indicate what will happen in a given environmental situation if a specific set of decisions and actions is implemented with no subsequent changes. Planning assumes that the environmental situation, especially that relating to the competitive arena, can be influenced, or at least better dealt with, by changing management decisions and actions. The focus of planning is, therefore, on alternatives and outcomes. Of course,

Rock Circus faces the difficult task of forecasting demand for a day visitor attraction (see also Case Study 3.1*).*

Source: Madame Tussaud's Rock Circus.

there needs to be interaction between planning and forecasting, so that forecasts can be revised to take account of the new conditions likely to be created by the implementation of proposed plans.

There is no such thing as a rigid or absolute forecast. Different forecasters using different forecasting methods are almost certain to come up with different results. Forecasts should, however, share some common characteristics, as suggested by Wheelwright and Makridakis (1977). They should:

- be based upon historical information from which a projection can be made
- look forward over a specific, clearly defined time period
- make clearly specified assumptions, since uncertainty characterises the future.

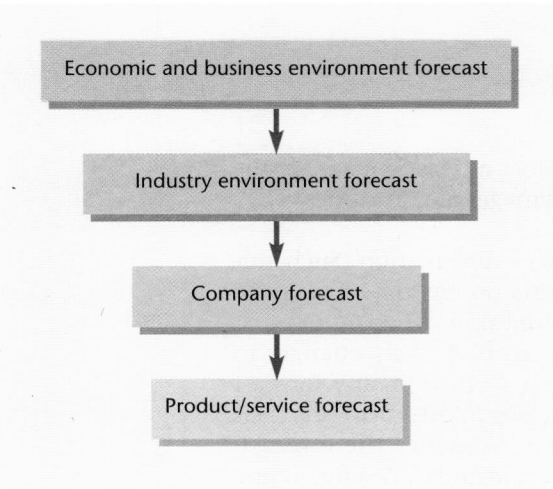

Forecasts often evolve from the general to the specific through a process of information assessment, sharing and iteration between senior staff, professional planners and line managers. This evolution allows managers to arrive eventually at a forecast based on an agreed set of assumptions regarding the industry and market environment, and compatible with planned effort at a corporate level. The process of reconciliation between the 'specialists' and line managers in sales and marketing is important for generating commitment and a sense of responsibility for the forecasts agreed.

If forecasts are to be operationally relevant, they should progress through four levels of detail, so that formulating assumptions, identifying key trends, and operational planning and decision making can all be included. These four stages, proposed by Wolfe (1966), are shown in Fig 22.4.

FIGURE 22.4

Four-stage approach to forecasting

Each stage clearly builds on the previous one, and thus the impact of changes can be traced throughout the process. A range of methods can be used for forecasting, depending on the stage being undertaken. Each method differs in its cost profile, complexity in preparation, rigour, and ability to generate the range of projections needed to plan the next stage. The following subsection looks at a number of forecasting methods.

Forecasting methods

Forecasting methods fall into two main groups. *Qualitative techniques* are often used in the earlier stages of forecasting to describe the likely changes and to help define more precisely the assumptions used. *Quantitative techniques* tend to be used in the later stages, when production schedules and financial planning require hard numbers upon which to make plans. All these techniques are shown in Fig 22.5.

Qualitative methods

Qualitative methods do not rely on hard, statistical data, but centre on 'soft' data based on expertise, knowledge and judgement. There are several methods of qualitative forecasting.

Management judgement. Management judgement is perhaps the riskiest source, as it relies on the people at the top or on experts within the organisation to predict what will happen. While the people involved may have a wealth of expertise and knowledge between them, there is a risk that they are too close to the organisation, its way of doing things and its markets to be truly objective. Their assumptions and prejudices may lead to an incomplete or inaccurate picture. Although management

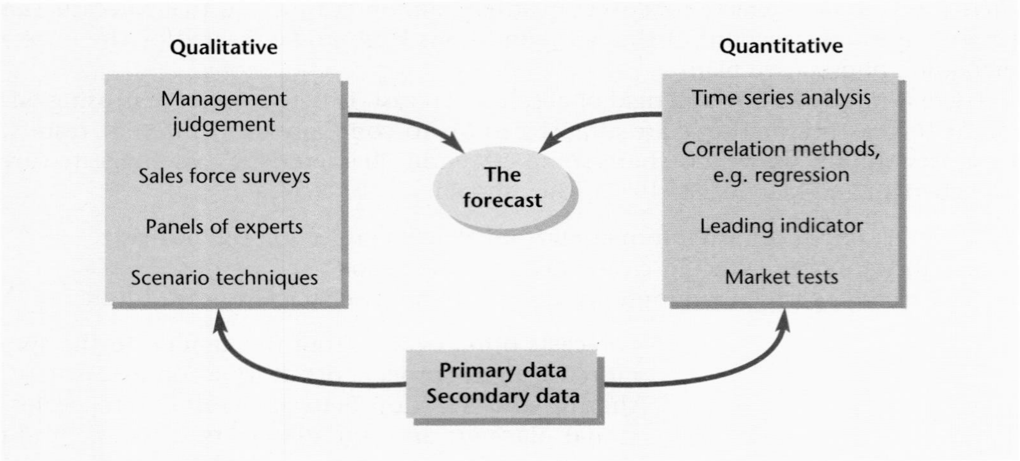

FIGURE 22.5

Forecasting
methods

Qualitative | Quantitative

Qualitative
- Management judgement
- Sales force surveys
- Panels of experts
- Scenario techniques

The forecast

Quantitative
- Time series analysis
- Correlation methods, e.g. regression
- Leading indicator
- Market tests

Primary data / Secondary data

judgement does not lead to rigorous forecasts, however, it does at least encourage the systematic analysis and justification of available data and management attitudes.

Sales force surveys. Sales force surveys can provide a wealth of information. Such surveys involve asking sales representatives to provide forecasts on customers, dealers, accounts etc. The sales force is a valuable source of expert opinion, since representatives are very close to customers on a daily basis, and will learn of likely changes in purchasing intentions early. As with a primary research survey, however, any forecast derived from this method should be treated with caution. In addition to any bias introduced by the customer, the representatives might also influence the forecast, either through naivety or through consideration of their own agendas. A naive representative, for example, underestimating barriers and constraints, might assume that when our new product is launched, sales to certain customers will boom. More insecure representatives might prefer to underestimate future demand and overestimate the barriers so that their own performance will look better. The cynical representative, on the other hand, might underestimate future demand because sales targets and bonus arrangements depend on it. Thus the more pessimistic the forecast, the lower the sales target and the sooner the bonuses start to accrue.

Representatives might thus be over-optimistic or pessimistic, or protective of their own position and interests, but rarely realistic. Management do, of course, recognise these biases, and try to make allowances for representatives' involvement, motivation and realism. Nevertheless, the sales force survey is still an attractive technique as it slots into the existing structure of the organisation, and can easily provide forecasts for individual customer groups, sales territories, areas, operating divisions or products.

Panels of experts. Panels of experts consisting of specially chosen eminent industrialists, economists, management consultants or academics, for example, may be asked for their opinions. These individuals are chosen for their sound knowledge and opinions of a market or its environment, and the membership of the panel will be balanced to represent a range of areas of expertise. The panel will be presented with forecasts and views of the future, and then asked to comment. The quality of the results will depend upon the quality and commitment of the experts used, but even the best experts get it wrong sometimes.

Scenario techniques. Scenario techniques aim to provide a complete picture of trends and events to create a more integrated and complete view of alternative situations. Although a panel of experts can be used for such a purpose, the main method used tends to be the Delphi technique. The *Delphi method* pools expert opinion, on the assumption that group opinion is better than that of an individual. It is especially useful for very long-range forecasting and technological forecasting. The experts used are not brought together, and they do not know who else is involved. Each one is questioned on issues and trends, then the collective responses are distributed to all members of the team with a further, more detailed questionnaire. This process is repeated until a rounded profile is obtained, the median of the group response. The main problem is potential bias, as members are influenced by feedback from the collective responses. For short-term, organisation-specific forecasts, the same approach can be used involving the sales team and managers.

Quantitative methods

The majority of quantitative techniques are concerned with the analysis of historical data to establish trends and make projections for the future based on a time series. More sophisticated models have also been developed, however, that aim to reflect the complex interactions between variables that help explain cause and effect, thus enabling the organisation to be better prepared for an uncertain future.

Time series analysis. Time series analysis is a means of using historical data to predict the future. Analysis of historic data can reveal patterns in the organisation's sales figures. These patterns include the following.

1 *Trends*: extrapolation of data on a straight or curved line basis can give a broad view of the general direction in which sales are moving.
2 *Cycles*: these reflect periodic changes in patterns over a period of time. It is important to analyse the reasons for cycles. Some may be caused by external factors, such as fluctuations in the economy leading to upturns and downturns in business, while other short-term fluctuations could reflect the outcomes of successful marketing activities. Cycles may last years or months, and tend to recur. The UK's construction industry is used to 'boom and bust' cycles linked with the state of the UK economy. When the economy is depressed, nobody wants to build new offices, factories, supermarkets or other retail space. Furthermore, a long-term depression in the housing market means that there is little building work in that sector either. Normally, when the economy recovers, the construction industry follows close behind. In early 1996, however, the UK industry was worried because although the economy was showing signs of picking up, construction remained depressed. This was partly because UK companies are felt to be less efficient and less competitive than foreign companies who are succeeding in winning many large contracts.
3 *Seasonality*: this covers shorter-term fluctuations around an overall trend, and may even be observed on a daily or weekly basis, if the organisation wants to get down to that level. Obviously, some markets are naturally highly seasonal, such as summer holidays, toys as Christmas gifts and gardening products, and any forecasting is going to produce pronounced seasonal effects.
4 *Random factors*: these are very difficult to predict, but nevertheless, any forecast is going to have to make allowances for the effects of strikes, riots, civil commotion and acts of God, as the insurance industry would put it.

At the end of this detailed analysis of trends and patterns, managers are better able to estimate the sales forecast for the coming period, perhaps giving pessimistic, optimistic and expected figures. Time series analysis builds on long-term trends and short-term fluctuations, and can be smoothed exponentially, placing more emphasis on recent data. The problem with time series analysis, as with any technique based on historical data, is that it assumes that things will carry on steadily into the future without any major deviation. This might be a reasonable assumption if the market concerned is stable and predictable, but a highly dangerous assumption in unstable, fluctuating markets.

Correlation method. If time series analysis is felt to be inappropriate, the forecaster might prefer to use a correlation method (or statistical demand analysis). Techniques such as multiple regression are, like time series analysis, based on historical data but instead of assuming that sales are simply a function of time, they try to identify other factors that influence sales. Thus, for example, sales of domestic conservatories might be expressed as a function of a number of other variables:

$$Q = f(x_1, x_2, x_3),$$

where Q is the quantity of conservatories demanded,
  x_1 is disposable income,
  x_2 is the cost of borrowing and
  x_3 is the number of households with gardens, but without conservatories.

By analysing statistically a series of historic data relating to Q and x_1 to x_3, an equation can be developed which gives the best explanation of the quantitative relationship between sales and the other variables involved. Thus analysis might reveal that

$$\text{Sales} = c + 3(x_1) + 50(x_2) - 0.05(x_3).$$

It would then be possible to forecast future sales by inserting estimated future values of x_1 to x_3 into this equation, or to forecast sales in a different region, for example, by inserting known values of x_1 to x_3 from that region.

This type of method can be difficult to implement, since it needs an extensive historic data bank to work with if the best possible equation is to be devised. Managers still need to exercise a certain degree of caution when using such equations. The forecast is never going to be 100 per cent accurate, and there is still the underlying assumption that the relationship between all the variables is going to continue into the future in the same way as it has in the past. The main problem with using an equation like this for forecasting, however, is the estimation of future values of x_1 to x_3. Any unforeseen swings in their behaviour might render the whole forecast meaningless.

Leading indicators. Leading indicators are useful for shorter-term forecasting. These indicators give advance warning of trends and changes in the marketing environment so that the organisation can adjust or plan accordingly. The definition of the key indicators will vary from industry to industry. A carpet manufacturer, for example, might look at the rate of new business start-ups or the amount of new office space being developed (on the basis that new businesses might want to carpet their new offices). In consumer markets, the leading indicators might be house sales, the rate of new house building, or even trends in average disposable income or unemployment levels. These all affect consumers' willingness and ability to buy new carpets, and will have an on impact the type, quality and price of carpets the manufacturer produces.

Market tests. Market tests, as discussed at pp. 349 *et seq.* give an insight into real behaviour rather than focusing on intentions. They are very useful as a part of new product development and launch programmes, and can help to forecast likely future performance. Managers need to be sure, however, that the structure of the test and the area in which it takes place are as truly representative of the target market and the planned marketing mix as possible.

Overall, the more cross checking of forecasts that takes place using different techniques, the more tailor-made the techniques to suit the industry, the organisation's product and its target market's purchasing characteristics, the better and more reliable the forecast will be.

Primary research. Primary research looks outside the organisation by surveying customers. In an organisational market, key customers could be asked their opinions of trends and how their own consumption patterns are likely to change. In consumer markets, a sample of consumers within a segment could similarly be surveyed, although this is more likely to be part of a bigger quantitative survey. In either case, it is essential that the research is sufficiently deep to allow the assumptions underlying the respondent's opinion to be thoroughly understood. Respondents are not always willing, however, to give information or may simply not know much about the issues raised. There is also a risk that organisational customers may feel that they are being asked to reveal commercially sensitive information which might be used against them in future negotiations. This may lead to non-response or to lies! Respondents may even be over-optimistic about their own intentions so that when customer intentions to purchase are aggregated, the resulting forecast is far too high.

Secondary data. Some secondary data can also be used to help create a general picture. Organisations can make use of published research data (*see* pp. 210 *et seq.*), such as those published by Euromonitor, to validate their own understanding of the way the market is moving, to raise new issues, and to act as a basis for further detailed investigation. Similarly, publications by various banks and government bodies provide the kind of background information on economic and industrial trends, demographics, and social trends that can lead to a deeper understanding of the marketing environment.

ORGANISING MARKETING ACTIVITIES

Effective marketing management does not happen by itself. It has to have the right kind of infrastructure and place within the organisation in order to develop and work efficiently and effectively. First, therefore, we discuss the role and place of the marketing department within the organisation as a whole. That is followed by an overview of different ways of structuring a marketing department, and then finally, we consider issues surrounding the implementation of marketing plans.

Organisational location of marketing

Central to the marketing philosophy is a focus on customer needs. As discussed in the early chapters of this book, marketers act as an interface between customers and other functions within the organisation. By understanding markets, customers' needs and wants and the ways in which they are changing and why, the marketer is providing essential information for planning corporate direction and the activities of other functions within the organisation. The production department, for example, needs to know what products will be demanded, with what variations, to what specifications, in what quantities and when, so that they can plan to produce them. Most, if not all, of these decisions will be marketing driven.

So that marketing can fulfil its role effectively, therefore, and be taken seriously, marketing managers should be equal in status to senior managers from other functional areas. They also need to work closely with other managers, not just for information exchange, but also on joint projects, for example new product planning and development, inventory management, physical distribution or logistics management.

It is important, however, to distinguish between a functional marketing department and marketing orientation as a management philosophy. A small organisation might not have a marketing department as such, but it can still practise a marketing orientation very effectively through the closeness of its relationships with its customers and its responsiveness to their needs. In contrast, any organisation can have a marketing department, yet not be truly marketing orientated. If that marketing department is isolated from other functional areas, if it just there to 'do advertising', then its potential is wasted. Marketing orientation permeates the whole organisation and *requires* marketing's involvement in all areas of the organisation.

Whether or not there is a marketing department, and how it is structured, depends on a number of factors. These might include the size of the organisation, the size and complexity of the markets served, the product and process technology and the rate of change in the marketing environment. There are several ways of incorporating and structuring marketing within the organisation, and these are discussed below.

Organisational alternatives

In thinking about how marketing might be organised, it is important to be clear about the tasks involved in marketing. Marketers have to research and analyse markets and customers. They have to forecast sales and then plan, develop, implement and manage elements of the marketing mix. They also have a wider corporate role in supporting the organisation's strategic development, interfacing with other functions. The marketer's focus is not just on today, but on the future as well. These tasks open up a number of choices for organising staff, delegating authority and responsibility and specifying line management relationships. The purpose is to clarify who makes what decisions and who is responsible for their implementation, and to ensure that all this is done at an appropriately senior level with proper monitoring and control.

There are four main choices for structuring marketing management within a department, focusing on function, products, regions or segments. The marketing department might also choose to develop a matrix structure, allowing an equal focus on both function and products, for example. These are all shown in Fig 22.6. The organisation might, of course, choose not to have a formal marketing department at all. Each of these choices is discussed below.

Functional organisation

A functional department is structured along the lines of specific marketing activities. This means there are very specialised roles and responsibilities, and that individual managers have to build expertise. Such a department might have, for example, a market research manager, an advertising and promotions manager and a new product development manager, each of whom will report to the organisation's marketing director.

FIGURE 22.6

Forms of marketing organisation

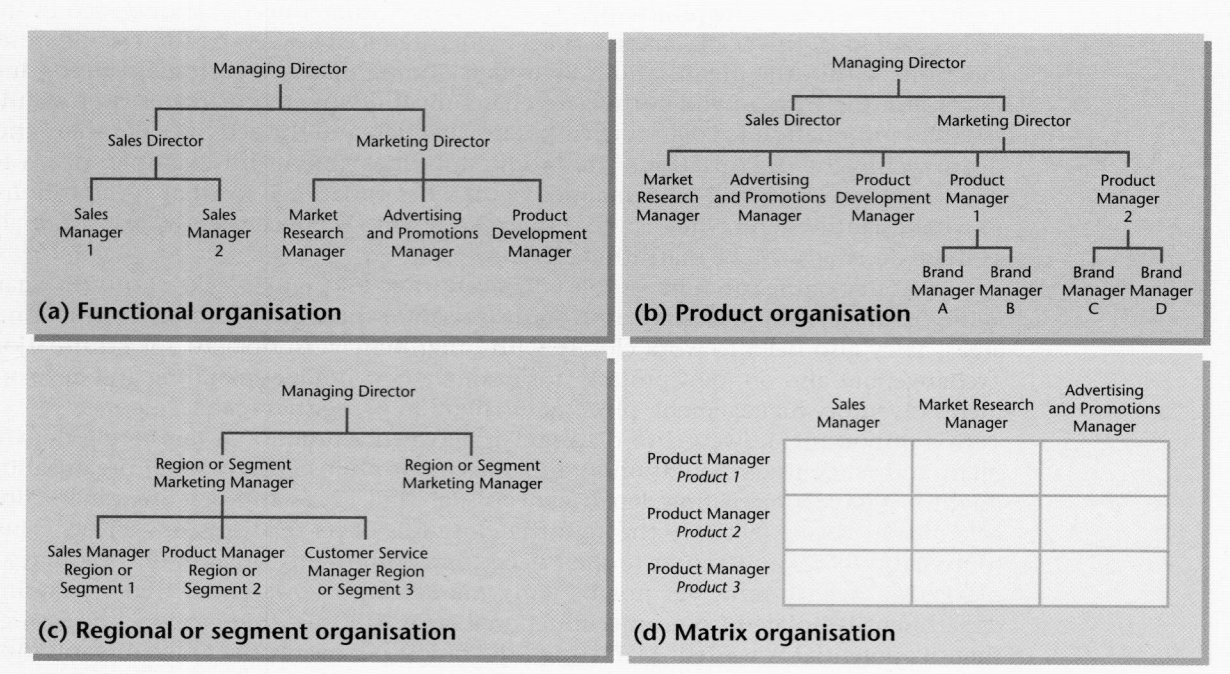

(a) Functional organisation

(b) Product organisation

(c) Regional or segment organisation

(d) Matrix organisation

This system works well in organisations where the various business functions are centralised, but problems can arise where they are decentralised. Then, functional marketing tasks have to be co-ordinated across diverse areas, with greater or lesser degrees of co-operation and acceptance.

Product organisation

Giving managers responsibility for specific products, brands or categories of product might suit a larger company with major brands or with diverse and very different product interests. The manager, reporting to a product group manager or a marketing director, builds expertise around the product, and is responsible for all aspects of its development, its strategic and marketing mix planning and its day-to-day welfare. Other specialist staff, such as market researchers, might be involved as necessary to help the product manager.

The product, brand or category management approach is very popular in fmcg markets. It gives clear lines of management responsibility, but there is still a need for a central function to co-ordinate the overall portfolio. As mentioned at pp. 320–1, there are potential problems with internal rivalry as managers seek to champion their own brands. A little healthy rivalry is not necessarily a bad thing, but it must not be allowed to get out of hand or to cloud management judgement.

The typical tasks of a product or brand manager include:

- the development of competitive strategies and plans consistent with corporate objectives
- the production of annual marketing plans, forecasts and budgets
- the design and development of support strategies for the sales and distribution team
- the gathering or commissioning of primary and secondary data on the product, market, competitors etc.
- management of the product in terms of innovation, modification and deletion.

The main problem with product organisation is working with other functions, such as production, finance etc. to get the resources, attention and effort that the product needs. There is also the risk that too many management layers will be introduced, hence the move towards category management (i.e, responsibility for a group of brands) rather than individual brand management.

Regional organisation

An organisation with its activities spread over a wide geographic area, or one operating in markets with distinct regional differences, might find regionally based marketing responsibility attractive. The regional marketing manager, along with a support team, will make all marketing decisions relevant to planning and operations in that territory. There will then be some mechanism for co-ordinating regional efforts at a national or international level to ensure consistency and strategic fit. As larger organisations become more international, this approach is becoming more common. The main benefit is that local managers develop the knowledge and expertise to know what is best for their region. They can then develop the most appropriate, fully integrated marketing mix package, as well as contributing intelligently to the organisation's overall strategic planning for that region.

Regionally based marketing departments are particularly attractive to organisations with a great emphasis on selling in the field, where close co-ordination and control are necessary. It is also appropriate for service industries, such as hospitality, where local conditions may differ and where, again, close control and co-ordination of service delivery is required.

Segmental organisation

An organisation that serves diverse groups of customers with very different needs might choose to develop marketing teams dedicated to each of those groups. This is because

Restructuring marketing departments

In 1994, many marketing consultants and large commercial organisations were questioning the effectiveness of marketing departments. It was said that many product managers had no real concept of commercial realities, that marketing departments had become unimaginative and lacked ideas, that marketing departments were not doing enough to drive their companies forward.

Mitchell (1994) suggests a number of reasons for this, including the emergence of more demanding customers (both trade and consumer), and the changing advertising media landscape. All of this means that marketing is no longer as straightforward as it once may have been, and perhaps some marketers are failing to appreciate this and adapt to this change. Mitchell also raises the interesting issue of the effects of globalisation and pan-European strategies on marketing organisational structures. National marketing departments may no longer have the same autonomy as before.

The structure of the marketing function has, of course, also changed as different approaches to corporate design have been introduced to deal with such problems. Management layers have been removed, and 'empowerment' and 'multi-functional team working' have led to less hierarchical structures and less rigidly defined functionally orientated job descriptions. These changes have the potential to bring some of the creativity back into marketing thinking, and to delegate some of the responsibility for marketing decision making to those who are actually implementing such decisions. Many organisations, such as Unilever, Unipart, Vauxhall UK and Philips have moved towards various kinds of team-based matrix structures. (*See*, for example, p. 637.)

Others have streamlined the upper echelons of the marketing organisation in order to make it easier to plan and get things done. Procter and Gamble (P&G), for example, announced in March 1995 that it was restructuring its organisation. Its problem was that it wanted to launch as many global brands as possible, and be first into the market with them, but the current structure was felt to be hindering that process. The main change, therefore, was the creation of four executive vice-presidents (one for each operating region – North America; Europe; the Middle East and Africa; Asia and Latin America) each one reporting to P&G's number 2 executive and each one responsible for all product categories within their respective regions. Then, within each region, regional vice-presidents were appointed with specific responsibility for a particular product category (for example laundry and cleaning products).

At a strategic level, this kind of structure shortens the length of lines of communication and concentrates knowledge and expertise into the hands of fewer people. The number 2 executive is obtaining a total global picture, while the executive vice-presidents have a total picture for all product categories in their own regions. This would not have happened under the old structure, in which knowledge was more fragmented because it was spread across many more executives. This new structure seems to combine the best of both geographic and product-based structures. Working together under the executive vice-president for the region, the regional vice-presidents for the different products can share ideas and expertise, find synergies, and co-ordinate their efforts within the context of wider corporate objectives.

Sources: Mitchell (1994); Richards (1995).

the marketing decision making and the marketing mixes have to be tailored to the individual needs of segments in which the competitive threats may be very different.

A brewery, for example, will market to the licensed trade (for instance pubs and clubs) and the retail trade (for instance supermarkets and off licences) very differently; a manufacturer of wound dressings will market differently to the hospital sector and to the pharmacist; a car dealer will market differently to the family motorist and to a fleet buyer. The volume purchased by individual customers within the same segment might create differences that are reflected in the marketing effort. An fmcg manufacturer will create a different kind of marketing mix and customer relationship with the top six multiple supermarket chains than with the many thousands of small independent grocers.

The marketing manager for a particular segment or customer group will have a range of specialist support staff and will report to a senior marketing manager or director with overall responsibility for all segments.

Matrix organisation

A matrix approach allows the marketing department to get the best of more than one of the previous methods of organisation. It can be particularly useful in large diverse organisations or where specialists and project teams have to work on major cross-functional activities, for example PR, new product development or marketing research programmes.

Our Indian recipes are a secret. Everyone knows the rewards.

Pukka people pick a pot of Patak's.

Source: Travis Sennett Sully Ross.

No department

Of course, another option is not to have a department at all. Small organisations might not be able to afford specialist marketing staff and thus perhaps the owner finds himself or herself performing a multi-functional role as sales representative, promotional decision maker and strategist rolled into one. If a small organisation does decide to invest in marketing staff, the recruit might be put into an office-based administrative support role or into a sales role.

Sales-driven organisations

Some organisations are still driven by sales. They might have a few very large customers, and be selling a complex technology. In such a case, the role of marketing is relegated to a support role that is largely concerned with PR and low-key promotional activity. Other organisations, particularly those currently or previously in the public sector, are still in the process of developing marketing departments. Universities, for example, are reappraising the role of marketing. Although they might have marketing departments, many of the key variables are beyond the control of their marketing managers. For example, academics, with or without the benefit of market research, develop and validate new courses; in another area, domestic full-time student fees and student numbers are agreed with the government. Often, universities see the marketing department's role as purely functional, handling student recruitment fairs, prospectuses, schools liaison, and advertising. In short, there is no guarantee that having a department means there will be a marketing orientation in the organisation.

CONTROLLING MARKETING ACTIVITIES

Control is a vital aspect of implementing marketing plans, whether strategic or operational. It helps to ensure that activities happen as planned, with proper management. It also provides important feedback that enables managers to determine whether or not their decisions, actions and strategies are working appropriately in practice.

Strategic control takes a wide, long-term view, considering whether the overall marketing strategy is actually driving the organisation in the desired direction. This is normally assessed through the marketing audit process outlined at pp. 883 *et seq.* and is often conducted on an annual basis, either as a special *ad hoc* process or as part of the marketing planning cycle. *Operational control* takes a shorter-term view, checking whether detailed, functional marketing programmes are actually working in practice. These checks can take place on a daily basis if necessary, and certainly happen frequently enough to determine whether problem areas are developing. Operational control needs to pick up problems early, before too much damage is done, so that corrective action can be taken more easily. Designing an effective control system to suit the needs and characteristics of the organisation is a critical part of managing marketing effort.

The marketing control process

The marketing control phase, shown in Fig 22.7, is not an afterthought to be bolted on to the end of the planning process, but should be designed as an important part of that process. In setting marketing objectives, it is important to define them in terms of detailed time-specific goals against which performance can be measured. This makes the task of control more manageable, since those areas where serious deviation is occurring can then be easily diagnosed. Management effort can thus be focused on areas of greatest need rather than being spread too thinly.

FIGURE 22.7

Marketing control

When setting performance targets for marketing activities, however, it is important to ensure that they are realistic, that they can be measured and that the measurement criteria used are meaningful and relevant. This is especially important where managers' performance is partly judged by their achievement of the agreed targets. Typical measures might be sales volume or value, the number of new customers created, the number of enquiries generated, stock turnover, satisfaction surveys or relative market share. The MIS system considered in Chapter 6 should provide the essential flow of information that enables performance to be measured as well as highlighting emerging problem areas. This flow of data must, therefore, be timely and sufficiently detailed to allow deeper analysis.

As soon as the control mechanism shows that a gap is opening between proposed targets and actual achievement, managers can start to look for reasons why this is happening. Sometimes, the reasons might be obvious, for example a stockout in a particular region or the loss of a major customer. In other situations, however, further research might have to be commissioned to support deeper analysis of the underlying causes. If, for example, a brand's market share continues to decline despite increased marketing effort, managers might start asking serious questions about customer responsiveness and the brand's competitive positioning.

Unless managers can be sure about why performance is off-target, they cannot reliably define the right corrective actions. In some cases they might decide that no corrective action needs to be taken, in others they might devise a programme of major or minor changes to bring the marketing strategy back on track. Where a regional stockout occurs, the solution may be obvious, but if brand share is declining unexpectedly, a fairly radical revision of the brand's marketing strategy might be called for. Failure to achieve targets does not, however, mean automatic condemnation of the marketing plan and its manager. It could be that targets were hopelessly optimistic, in the light of the emerging market conditions. Alternatively, other departments within the organisation, for example production or logistics, may have failed to achieve their targets.

Managers should, however, be wary of overreaction. A certain amount of deviation is to be expected since no forward plan can be absolutely right. Part of the planning process is to agree what the threshold is between tolerable and intolerable deviation. Real customers buying real products in a real competitive market do not necessarily behave to order, and therefore some flexibility and patience should be exercised. There is also sometimes a lag effect between implementing marketing action and seeing the results of that action. Declaring a crisis and taking corrective action too soon might well be counterproductive. If, however, a major event happens that represents discontinuous change, corrective action might have to be taken long before its effects start to show in the computer printouts.

Methods of evaluating operational performance

There are several ways of evaluating marketing performance, two of which, sales analysis and costs and profitability analysis, are discussed here.

Sales analysis

Sales analysis is at the heart of any performance control system, as it most directly relates to the product and is likely to be widely understood across the organisation. Through the ordering and invoicing system, sales data can be accumulated within the MIS. These data include future order files, current sales, and sales history by product and perhaps even by individual customer, giving detailed information on location, price, quantity etc. Sales analysis can thus provide a ready measure of performance to date, and through analysis of the variances between expected and actual performance, it can form a basis for planning remedial actions.

Sales analysis can be broken down into various subdivisions for more refined analysis, as shown in Fig 22.8.

Sales analysis can also be linked with market share analysis, reflecting general trends within the industry. It is possible for an organisation to have increasing sales, but to be losing market share (because competitors' sales are growing faster). Equally, it is possible to see a decline in sales at the same time as market share is rising (because competitors' sales are declining faster). In some situations, for example during harvesting and strategic withdrawal, an organisation might be happy to see both sales and share declining, as long as short-term profits are maintained or improved. Linking sales analysis with market share analysis is useful for putting the organisation's performance in its proper competitive context. It could give indications

FIGURE 22.8

Bases for sales analysis

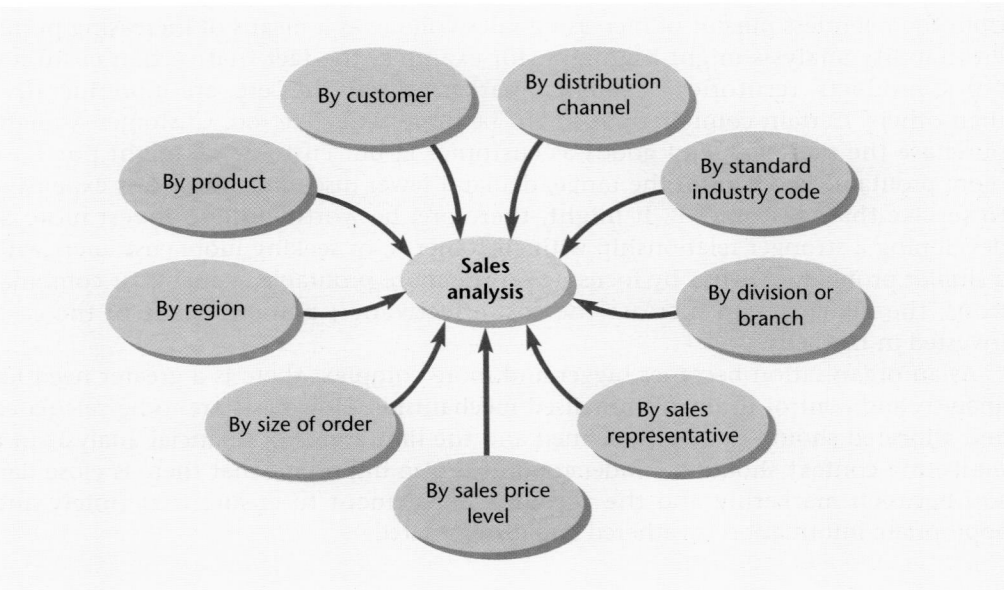

of how well a marketing mix has been formulated, as well as raising debate about the controllable and uncontrollable factors at work in the market.

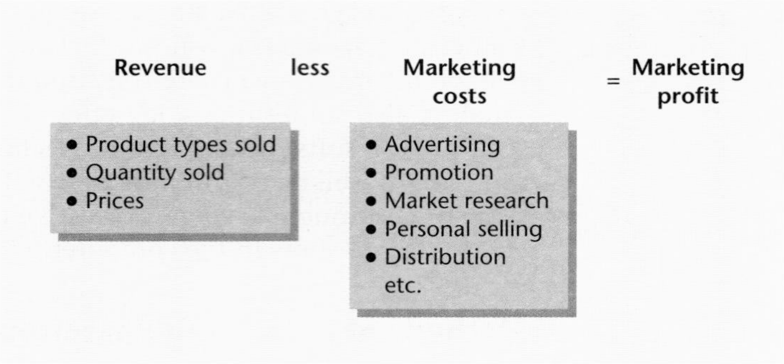

Marketing costs and profitability analysis

Fig 22.9 shows the three controllable elements of marketing that contribute towards profit and that those that create costs (Wilson *et al.*, 1992). Thus marketing profitability is created by what is sold, in what quantity and at what price, but reduced by the costs associated with achieving those results.

| Revenue | less | Marketing costs | = Marketing profit |

- Product types sold
- Quantity sold
- Prices

- Advertising
- Promotion
- Market research
- Personal selling
- Distribution etc.

FIGURE 22.9

Marketing costs and profit

Although the categories of costs seem to be reasonably straightforward, it can be difficult in practice to identify and control some aspects of marketing costs. Wilson *et al.* (1992) suggest a number of characteristics of marketing costs that make them difficult to estimate, allocate or evaluate, a few of which are discussed below:

1 *Long term or lagged effects:* an advertising campaign running now might only start to generate sales next year and the effects of that advertising might last much longer than the campaign itself. How should this be reflected in terms of profitability analysis?

2 *Joint costs:* some costs, for example corporate advertising or trade exhibition attendance, will be spread across different products, sales territories or segments etc. Then there are the indirect central costs, such as general administration, some of which will be apportioned to the marketing department. What is the fairest way of allocating all these shared costs?

3 *Isolating effects*: marketing results are achieved as a consequence of an integrated marketing mix and thus it can be difficult to isolate the influence of one activity and evaluate its financial efficiency. This is particularly true where there is close synergy between elements, for instance between advertising and sales promotion.

Despite such difficulties, it is important for strategic planning purposes to try to assess profitability by customer group, product, sales territory etc., rather than just measuring sales. Conducting such assessments encourages managers to move away from the relentless pursuit of increasing sales volume as a means of increasing profit. Profitability analysis might highlight, for example, the fact that certain customer types, products, territories, segments, marketing activities etc. are more lucrative than others. Certain combinations might be more attractive too. Customer A might purchase the same value of goods as customer B, but customer A might purchase more profitable goods from the range, demand fewer discounts, or be less expensive to service than customer B. It might, therefore, be worthwhile to invest more in developing a stronger relationship with customer A, or seeking more customers with a similar profile to A. Thus by focusing on the more profitable elements or combinations, the manager can increase the cost effectiveness and efficiency of the cash invested in marketing.

As an organisation becomes bigger and more complex, there is a greater need for analysis and control through formalised mechanisms. How costs are to be calculated and allocated should be clearly defined and the limitations of financial analysis in a marketing context should be understood. It is also important that there is close liaison between marketing and the accounts department to ensure that timely and appropriate information is gathered and disseminated.

CHAPTER SUMMARY

Marketing planning is about developing the objectives, strategies and marketing mixes that best exploit the opportunities available to the organisation. Planning should itself be a planned and managed process. This process helps organisations to analyse themselves and their marketing environments more systematically and honestly. It also helps organisations to co-ordinate and control their marketing activities more effectively. There are, however, risks in allowing planning to become an end in itself, as its managers might then become too technique orientated or too formulaic in their approach. It might also encourage the rise of the 'professional planner'. Planning should, therefore, be a flexible, dynamic activity that is fed with accurate, reliable and timely information, and is not divorced from the managers who have the day-to-day responsibility for implementing the plans.

Marketing plans can be strategic or operational. The plans help to integrate activities, schedule resources, specify responsibilities and provide benchmarks for measuring progress. There are eight main stages in the planning process: corporate objectives, the marketing audit, marketing analysis, setting marketing objectives, marketing strategies, marketing programmes, controls and evaluation and budgeting.

In order to construct realistic plans, managers need to estimate what total market demand could be, and what their own organisation's sales potential within that market might be. The whole area of forecasting is an important one for marketers. The more accurate the view of the future, the more appropriate the plans are likely to be. Forecasts can be general or specific, qualitative or quantitative. There are a number of forecasting techniques. The qualitative group includes management judgement, sales force surveys, expert opinion and scenario techniques. Quantitative techniques include time series analysis, multiple regression, leading indicators and market tests.

In order to fulfil its function properly, the marketing department should have a central role within the organisation, with senior management of equal status to those in other functional areas. It is also important, however, that the marketing philosophy pervades the whole enterprise, regardless of the size or formality of the marketing department. There are several approaches to structuring the marketing department itself. These are the functional, product based, regional, segmental or matrix approaches.

As marketing plans are being implemented, they have to be monitored and controlled. Strategic control concerns the longer-term direction of marketing strategy, whereas operational control assesses the day-to-day success of marketing activities. Using information gathered in the monitoring process, the actual achievements of marketing strategies can be compared with planned or expected outcomes. Managers can then analyse gaps and decide whether they are significant enough to warrant corrective action. Although this can be a quantitative analysis, it should still be looked at in the context of more qualitative issues concerning customer needs and synergies between customers, markets or products.

Key words and phrases

Control and evaluation	*Market potential*	*Planning process*
Corporate objectives	*Marketing audit*	*Sales potential*
External audit	*Marketing objectives*	*Strategic marketing plan*
Forecasts	*Operational marketing plan*	*SWOT analysis*
Internal audit		

QUESTIONS FOR REVIEW

22.1 Why do organisations need *marketing planning*?

22.2 Define the stages in the *marketing planning process*.

22.3 What is a *SWOT analysis*?

22.4 To what general criteria should 'good' marketing objectives conform?

22.5 What is the difference between *marketing strategies* and *marketing programmes?*

22.6 Define *market potential*.

22.7 What is the difference between *breakdown* and *build up* methods of assessing market potential?

22.8 What are the:

(a) *qualitative;* and
(b) *quantitative* techniques

of forecasting?

22.9 What are the four main choices for structuring the marketing department?

22.10 How can *operational performance* be evaluated?

QUESTIONS FOR DISCUSSION

22.1 What is the mission statement of the university or college at which you are studying? From your general knowledge of the organisation and your experience as a customer, discuss the extent to which you feel it is fulfilling its mission.

22.2 Using whatever information you can find, develop a SWOT analysis for the organisation of your choice. What are the implications of your analysis for the organisation's short- and long-term priorities?

22.3 Discuss the importance of market and sales forecasting in the marketing planning process and outline the relative advantages and disadvantages of three different forecasting methods.

22.4 What kind of marketing organisational structure would be appropriate for each of the following situations and why?

(a) a small single product engineering company;
(b) a large fmcg manufacturer selling a wide range of products into several different European markets;
(c) a pharmaceutical company manufacturing both prescription and 'over the counter' medicines.

22.5 Discuss the role played by control and evaluation in both the planning and implementation of marketing strategies and programmes.

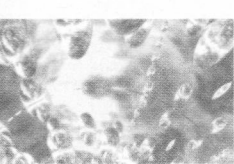

DHL – a global brand

DHL started life as a company in 1969, handling express document deliveries between San Fransisco and Honolulu. From these humble beginnings, DHL has grown to the extent that it is now a truly global organisation operating in 200 countries. With 35 000 employees world-wide, and its own fleet of over 10 000 distribution vehicles, including 170 aircraft, DHL has almost a 50 per cent share of the $10 billion international air express industry.

DHL has developed its own organisational structure to serve the global market, which it has called 'corporate symbiosis'. This approach encompasses the empowerment of DHL personnel at a local level, at the same time recognising the interdependence of the parts of DHL as a corporate whole. This symbiotic approach has a direct impact on DHL's marketing activities. It means that on a global level, corporate management is determined to project the core values of the brand, while the local management has a free hand to promote these values in the most culturally appropriate way. As Chris King, regional brand manager for Europe and Africa says,

> We're essentially a decentralised organisation. In Nigeria, 496 of the 500 employees are Nigerian.

A key to global dominance for DHL's of strategic alliances, most prominent of which are with Japan Airlines (JAL), Lufthansa, and Nisshio Iwai, one of Japan's foremost trading houses. Toyota's just-in-time manufacturing in the UK, for example, is made possible by a combination of JAL's long-haul services and DHL's express delivery service. DHL's global position is further strengthened by its virtual ownership of the word *worldwide*, a position no doubt envied by its rivals Federal Express and United Parcel Service. According to Glyn Jones, commerical director DHL UK:

> DHL is practically synonymous with the air express industry ... it has almost become a generic in its own right – "I've DHL-ed it!".

When a new product is created, DHL has a policy that it feeds off the master brand DHL. So in the name of the new brand, 'DHL' is always followed by something that succinctly describes exactly what the service is, hence *DHL WorldMail,* and *DHL European Union Express.* There are several core values with which DHL promotes its brand. Key to its strategy is the promotion of the service as fast and reliable, providing value for money, as well as its excellent customer relations. Consistent with this quality of service, DHL is priced near the top of the market. As part of its strategy to maintain brand loyalty,

DHL has initiated a process of customer automation through the installation of PC-based systems to help its major customers worldwide with export documentation.

The need to create a global DHL brand personality is of paramount importance. According to Glyn Jones:

> A major focus for DHL is not merely image management, but also reputation management.

A recent UK survey revealed a 70 per cent spontaneous recall rate for the DHL name among businesses. It was also revealed that spontaneous recall among all adults in the UK had increased from 12 per cent to 26 per cent between 1990 and 1995. The 1994 pan-European campaign, 'We Keep Your Promises', using media such as television, radio and press, was a successful attempt to convert awareness to usage. As a result, European sales rose by an average of 20 per cent.

Glyn Jones sees continual investment in service improvements as the key factor in contributing to long-term brand growth. DHL spends approximately 10 per cent of its marketing budget on research, and the emphasis is placed on identifying who its customers are and what motivates them. Information technology is also an area for investment with an integrated programme of activities designed to harness IT to the task of making DHL easier to do business with. DHL has, for example, also been looking at ways in which the Internet can be turned to its advantage. EDI (electronic data interchange) and electronic mail could pose a massive threat to DHL, especially as a significant portion of its business is in worldwide document delivery and DHL aims to turn this potential threat into a significant opportunity.

Adapted from a case prepared by Anthony Allen and Alan Smith, University of Teesside.

Sources: Allen (1995); DHL Corporate Literature; *Media and Marketing Europe* (1994); Ries and Trout (1993).

Questions

1 Why is marketing planning so important for an organisation such as DHL?

2 Identify the key factors in the global marketing environment that are likely to have an impact on DHL's marketing planning.

3 Is the global approach to branding the best strategy to take DHL into the next millennium?

4 How could DHL evolve to meet threats such as electronic mail?

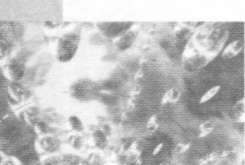

Filofax

Although the Filofax became the symbol of the 1980s that no respectable yuppie could do without, its history as a product goes back to 1921 when it was first invented and then launched as a business venture. The system underpinning Filofax is simplicity itself, consisting of a looseleaf ring binder and a series of printed sheets for insertions, such as diary sheets, meeting reports, finances and expenses, preprinted information sheets, and address book sheets. It represents an almost complete personal organiser. Back in 1921, of course, such refinements and potential had not yet been realised. At that time it was a niche product, especially popular with priests and clergy responsible for the forward planning of events ranging from baptisms to funerals. Its use soon expanded into the military, where it became an essential purchase at the British Army Staff college. It also began retail distribution through specialist religious book shops and church suppliers. Its main purpose in those days was to provide a flexible system for recording names, addresses and dates of future events.

Things could well have continued that way, if David and Lesley Collischon had not decided in 1976 that the concept could have a far wider range of options and markets than those covered at that time. After setting up a rival firm, they decided to take up an opportunity to buy Filofax. The timing was perfect; the status-conscious, symbol orientated 1980s were right for the imagery that Filofax could generate. The addition of new information sheets, the upgrading of the cover (often leather) to suggest prestige and status all helped to make a statement about the owner. The more comprehensive the Filofax information, the more skilled the owner in being able to use it and not least, its overall thickness, were just as important as status symbols as mobile phones were to become a few years later. Sales mushroomed from £100 000 in 1980 to £12 million by 1987. Filofax was in fashion in many European markets.

The decline of Filofax's fortunes by the end of the 1980s was even more rapid than its rise. Profits slumped to a £1 million loss in 1989, and share prices fell from 200p to 13p. Filofax was in trouble. The cause went far deeper than the recession that hit its prime target market, the young yuppies, in the late 1980s when financial markets entered a period of turbulence and city shakeouts started. Problems such as difficulties in managing rapid growth were also quoted, along with over-staffing, poor sourcing and the increasing reluctance by consumers to pay the Filofax premium price. It was the growth of new competition, however, that hit Filofax particularly hard. The premium product position left an attractive gap at the bottom end of the market, so competitive products with plastic covers, limited standardised ranges, and copycat ranges all had a lower cost structures and much lower prices. Filofax's margins and sales volume both became depressed.

In addition to undertaking rationalisation and regaining a firm control of the business, Filofax responded to the new threats by re-emphasizing its brand identity and launching new products under that brand name. It was, of course, helped by having the 'generic' name for the sector. New versions specialised in lifestyle rather than business Filofaxes, targeting groups such as students and housewives. The Filofax name was also introduced on to the front cover again in order to build the brand seriously in all its markets. The company felt that it needed to communicate the benefits of paying more for a quality brand rather than opting for the cheaper alternatives. Another part of the strategy was to acquire and build business outside the personal organiser sector. The company acquired an office stationery brand and greeting cards business, both of which were compatible with Filofax's distribution strengths.

By 1996, sales had recovered. The company now sells 30 million Filofaxes a year into over 40 countries, with its major export markets including Japan, France, Germany and Sweden. Recent expansion has taken it into the Baltic States and South Africa and it is also seeking to buy more distribution companies in continental Europe. In 1995, it paid £6 million for its major UK rival Topps, in order to build its strength to a UK market share of 85 per cent. Sales are now over £40 million with pre-tax profits restored to around £6 million. It has managed to cling on to its position as a quality, high margin product that communicates a similar message in many markets. The next major challenge may not be far away, however, as electronic organisers fall in price and become more widely available.

Sources: Jones (1996); Martinson (1996).

Questions

1 What kinds of factors is Filofax likely to cover in its external audit?

2 From the information in the case, outline a rough SWOT analysis for Filofax. What do you think represents:

   (a) its biggest opportunity; and

   (b) its biggest threat,

and why?

3 What marketing strategies might Filofax include in its planning to help it capitalise on its opportunities and overcome its threats?

4 How might a company like Filofax control and evaluate its marketing activities?

REFERENCES TO CHAPTER 22

Abell, D. F. (1982), 'Metamorphosis in Market Planning,' in K. K. Cox and V. J. McGinnis (eds.), *Strategic Market Decisions*, Prentice Hall.

Allen, A. (1995), *An Analysis of Global Branding Strategies,* unpublished undergraduate dissertation, University of Teesside.

Barnard, S. (1996), 'Will She Prove Vulnerable to Gallic Charm?', *The Grocer*, 20 January, p. 32.

Cox, W. E. (1979), *Industrial Market Research*, Wiley.

Day, G. S. (1990), *Market Driven Strategy*, Free Press.

Dolan, R. J. (1981), 'Models of Competition: A Review of Theory and Empirical Evidence' in B. M. Ennis and K. J. Roering (eds.), *Review of Marketing*, AMA.

Drucker, P. F. (1955), *The Practice of Management*, Heinemann.

Financial Times (1996), 'The Lex Column: TI Group', *Financial Times*, 13 March, p. 24.

Foster, M. (1996), 'NCP Fights for its Space', *Management Today*, February, pp. 54–8.

Fraser, I. (1995), 'Imperfect Science', *Marketing Business*, September, pp. 36–9.

Goodridge, M. (1995), 'A Dead Cert?', *Marketing Business*, November, pp. 12–15.

Guiltinan, J. P. and Paul, G. W. (1988), *Marketing Management: Strategies and Programs*, McGraw-Hill.

Jones, H. (1996), 'Fax of Life', *Marketing Week*, 10 May, pp. 53–4.

Lambin, J. J. (1993), *Strategic Marketing*, McGraw-Hill.

Lorenz, A. (1996a), 'Pilkington Picks Up the Pieces', *Management Today*, March, pp. 37–41.

Lorenz, A. (1996b), 'Why TI Group Went West', *Management Today*, April, pp. 35–8.

Lynn, M. (1996), 'Building's Decline and Fall', *Management Today*, February, pp. 28–32.

McDonald, M. H. B. (1989), *Marketing Plans*, Butterworth-Heinemann.

Marshall, S. (1996), 'Cott's Solution to Demon Drink', *Marketing*, 29 February, p. 13.

Martinson, J. (1996), 'Topps Purchase Helps Filofax to 33% Advance', *Financial Times*, 18 June, p. 19.

Media and Marketing Europe (1994), *Media and Marketing Europe*, October, EMAT Business and Computer Applications Ltd.

Mitchell, A. (1994), 'Dark Night of Marketing or a New Dawn?', *Marketing*, 17 February, pp. 22–3.

Owen, D. (1996), 'Lines to Profit Still Open as Bouygues Enters the French Mobile Market', *Financial Times*, 19 June, p. 31.

Reguly, E. (1995), 'Status Symbol Connects to Real World', *The Times*, 4 January, p. 25.

Richards, A. (1995), 'P&G Divides to Rule', *Marketing*, 23 March, p. 15.

Ries, A. and Trout, J. (1993), *The 22 Immutable Laws of Marketing*, Harper Business.

Thomas, L. (1995), 'Millions Spent on Firing Firms with Missionary Zeal', *Sunday Times*, 26 March.

Toor, M. (1992), 'Is the Game Over for Toys?', *Marketing*, 9 April, pp. 18–19.

Weinberg, R. (1969), 'Developing Marketing Strategies for Short Term Profits and Long Term Growth', paper presented at Advanced Management Research Inc. Seminar, New York.

Wensley, J. R. C. (1987), 'Marketing Strategy' M. J. Baker (ed.), in *The Marketing Book*, Heinemann.

Wheelwright, S. C. and Makridakis, S. (1977), *Forecasting Methods for Management*, (2nd edn.) Wiley.

Wilson, R. M. S. *et al.* (1992), *Strategic Marketing Management*, Butterworth-Heinemann.

Wolfe, H. D. (1966), *Business Forecasting Methods*, Holt, Rinehart and Winston.

Zoller, E. (1995), 'Mobiles Market Opens Up', *Eurobusiness*, September, pp. 67–8.

Part VIII

MARKETING APPLICATIONS

Services Marketing **23**

Marketing and the Smaller Business **24**

International Marketing **25**

Current Perspectives in Marketing **26**

This final part of the book has been included because it is recognised that a broad introduction to a subject such as marketing has to generalise. In some respects this is a strength – it is hoped that the variety of industries, products and experience illustrating this text has been both entertaining and informative for you. This breadth and variety do, however, make it more difficult to envisage how all the elements of the marketing mix mesh together in specific practical applications. Part VII began the integration process, but this part takes it further, in looking at specific situations and types of organisation.

As many of the examples cited in the text so far have related to physical products, Chapter 23 centres on services marketing, such as banking, travel and tourism, and personal services. Marketing tends to be thought of as belonging in large, profit-making businesses. To redress this, Chapter 23 also looks at the non-profit sector where organisations such as charities, the police, medical and other public services are increasingly adopting a marketing orientation and marketing strategies. Chapter 24 takes the small business perspective, providing a sympathetic analysis of the real difficulties of adopting and applying some marketing techniques sometimes on extremely limited resources. Chapter 25 looks at the problems, pitfalls and rewards of international marketing, both within Europe and further afield.

The final chapter of the book looks at a number of the current issues in marketing from a senior management perspective. While much of marketing theory is now well established, it has to be applied in changing and dynamic environments which means that different applications or issues of implementation may become particularly topical at any one time. Chapter 26 considers a number of such issues of interest largely through interviews with senior managers, showing how the field is evolving. This further helps to integrate the preceding material and sheds more light on the problems of making the theory work in practice.

■   ■   ■

23 Services Marketing

LEARNING OBJECTIVES

This chapter will help you to:

1 define the characteristics that differentiate services from other products and outline their impact on marketing;

2 develop an extended marketing mix of 7Ps that takes the characteristics of services into account and allows comprehensive marketing strategies to be developed for services;

3 understand the importance of interactive and internal marketing for service products and their impact on issues of quality and productivity;

4 understand the special characteristics of non-profit organisations within the service sector, and the implications for their marketing activities.

INTRODUCTION

The focus of this chapter is on the marketing of services, whether sold for profit or not. Service products cover a wide range of applications. In the profit-making sector, services marketing includes travel and tourism, banking and insurance, and personal and professional services ranging from accountancy, legal services and business consultancy through to hairdressing and garden planning and design. In the non-profit-making sector, services marketing applications include education, medicine and charities through to various aspects of government activity that need to be 'sold' to the public.

Marketing these kinds of services is somewhat different from marketing physical products. The major marketing principles discussed in this book, segmenting the market, the need for research, sensible design of the marketing mix and the need for creativity, strategic thinking and innovation are, of course, universally applicable, regardless of the type of product involved. Where the difference arises is in the detailed design and implementation of the marketing mix. There are several special factors that provide additional challenges for the services marketer.

This chapter will, therefore, examine in detail the special aspects of services that differentiate them from physical products. It will then look at the issues involved in designing the services marketing mix and the marketing management challenges arising from its implementation. Finally, the whole area of marketing services in the non-profit sector will be considered.

PERSPECTIVES ON SERVICE MARKETS

Services are not a homogeneous group of products. There is wide variety within the services category, in terms of both the degree of service involved and the type of service product offered. Nevertheless, there are some general characteristics, common to many service products, that differentiate them as a genre from physical goods. This section, therefore, explores the criteria by which service products can be classified, and then goes on to look at the special characteristics of services and their implications for marketing.

Classifying services

There are few pure services. In reality, many product 'packages' involve a greater or lesser level of service. Products can be placed along a spectrum, with virtually pure personal service involving few, if any, props at one end, and pure product that involves little or no service at the other. Most products do have some combination of physical good and service, as shown in Fig 23.1. The purchase of a chocolate bar, for example, involves little or no service other than the involvement of a checkout or till operator. The purchase of a gas appliance will involve professional fitting, and thus is a combination of physical and service product. A new office computer system could similarly involve installation and initial training. A visit to a theme park or theatre could involve some limited support products, such as guides and gifts, while the main product purchased is the experience itself. Finally, a visit to a psychiatrist or a hairdresser may involve a couch, a chair and some minor allied props such as an interview checklist or a hair-dryer. The real product purchased here, however, is the personal service manufactured by the service deliverer, the psychiatrist or the hairdresser.

Tangibility is not the only way of classifying service products. Lovelock (1996) suggests several other ways of grouping services along dimensions that might have implications for the marketing mix employed in designing and delivering the service. These include how the service is delivered, the extent to which supply is constrained or demand fluctuates, the degree of involvement of people and facilities in the service, the level of customisation, the relationship between the service organisation and its customers, the duration of the benefits of the service and the duration of the service delivery.

Special characteristics of service markets

Five main characteristics, as shown in Fig 23.2, have been identified as being unique to service markets (*see*, e.g., Sasser *et al.*, 1978; Cowell, 1984).

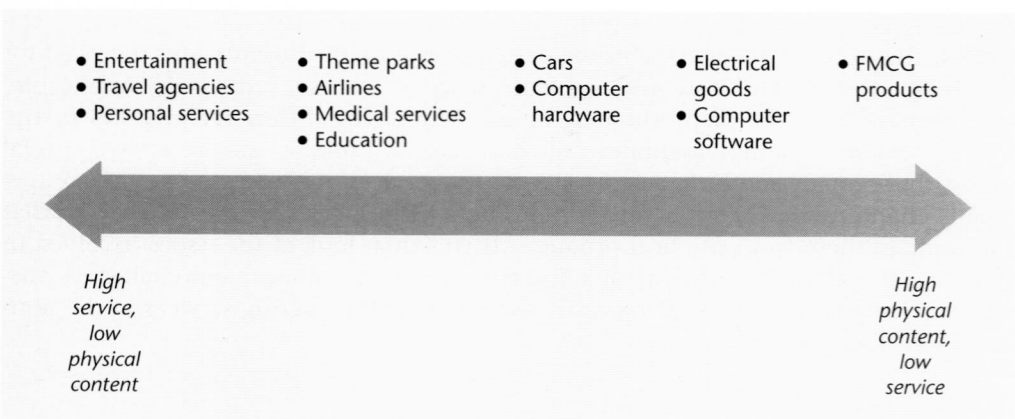

FIGURE 23.1

The product spectrum

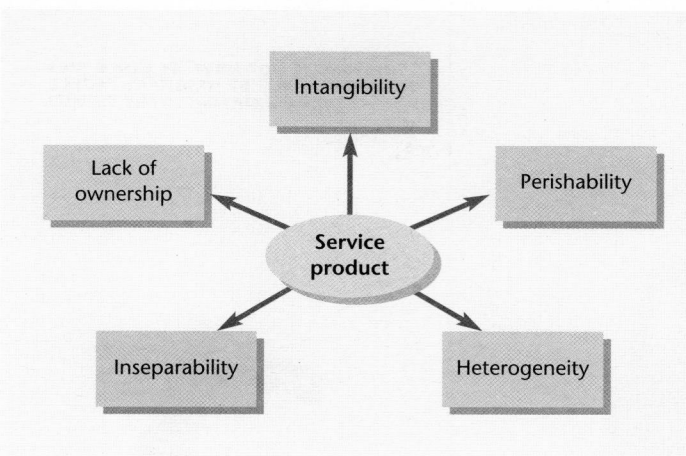

FIGURE 23.2

Characteristics of service markets

Lack of ownership

Perhaps the most obvious aspect of a service product is that no goods change hands, as such, and therefore there is no transfer of ownership of anything. A legal transaction does still take place; an insurance company agrees to provide certain benefits as long as the premiums are paid and the terms and conditions of the policy are met. A car rental company allows the customer full use of a vehicle for an agreed length of time, subject to some restraints on named drivers and type of usage, but the ownership of the vehicle remains with the rental company. A train seat can be reserved for a journey, but it is not owned. A subscription to the National Trust provides rights of access free of charge but no actual share in the ownership of its properties. The access, use or experience of the service is, therefore, often time specific, usage specific and subject to contractual terms and conditions.

The lack of ownership raises the issue of the transient nature of the purchase. Most service products involve some kind of 'experience' for the customer. This might be surrounded by props, for example a stage, lighting and sound systems, a lecture theatre, an insurance policy, a vehicle or a room, but these only serve to enhance or degrade the experience of the service. The faulty fuel gauge which means that the car hirer runs out of petrol in the most remote location, the hotel room next to the building site, the ineffective microphone at a concert all spoil the memory of the service consumed. Most service products are about the expectation of 'temporary use' and the memories arising therefrom, for example, the stories of the annual holiday in Marbella or trekking through the Himalayas.

The growth of timeshare provides an interesting case where the service package includes partial ownership of something. The customer does purchase a share in a holiday property, but is also purchasing the timeshare operator's services in administering and maintaining the property. The operator might also provide an exchange service, whereby the customer can join a network of owners to swap timeshares. With services that do not involve ownership, frequent flyer programmes, membership clubs and loyalty schemes can encourage customers to feel a sense of ownership and belonging to the service product.

Intangibility

A visit to a retail store reveals an inviting display of products to purchase. These products can be examined, touched, tried on, sampled, smelt or listened to. All this can help the customer to examine what is on offer and to make choices between competing brands. The consumer regularly uses the whole range of senses to assist decision making (*see* Chapter 3). Touch, sight, sound, smell and taste are powerful influences on consumer purchasing, enabling them to assess what is being offered, to weigh up value, and to develop the confidence to act. This is especially important before the purchase is made, but even after the sale the product can be assessed in terms of its use, its durability and whether it lives up to general expectations. If there is a fault with a physical product, it can be returned or exchanged.

With service products, it is far more difficult to use the senses in the same way as a means of making a purchase decision because the actual service experience can only take place after that decision has been made. The heart of a service is the experience created for the customer, whether individually as with a personal service such as dentistry or

HISTORY IS NOT MADE BY KINGS AND
PRESIDENTS, BUT BY ORDINARY PEOPLE
DOING EXTRAORDINARY THINGS.

History is happening all around us.

Ask any news reporter who has spent years in the field which, of all the things they have witnessed in their long careers, left the most lasting impression.

We predict that they will not start telling you about the coronation of a king, or a speech by a president. Instead they will recall a face, or remember a person. Maybe the first person who climbed the Berlin Wall, the student who stopped a column of tanks in Tiananmen Square, or the distraught face of a fire man at the Oklahoma bombing.

All of these are images captured and broadcast to the world by CNN International. In most cases, they feature people whose names will never find a place in the history books.

The history books are wrong. The real history of the world is happening all around us in the lives of millions of ordinary people.

In capturing these images, CNN International is reporting and recording history as it happens.

Tune your TV set to CNN International and see ordinary people turning news into history before your eyes.

CNN INTERNATIONAL.

A Turner Company FOR INFORMATION ABOUT CNN INTERNATIONAL PLEASE CALL ATLANTA +1 404 827 1700 OR NEW YORK +1 212 852 6500

Source: Travis Sennett Sully Ross.

This powerful and memorable image helps to add a tangible quality to CNN's cable and satellite news service.

hairdressing, or as a group experience, such as a lecture, a show or a flight. In many cases, once the purchase decision has been made, all the customer will receive is a ticket, a confirmation of booking or some promise of future benefit. The service experience itself is intangible, and is only delivered after the customer is committed to the purchase.

Despite the problem of **intangibility**, the potential customer can make some kind of prior assessment of the service product. Using available tangible cues, the customer can assess whether a particular service provider is likely to deliver what is wanted. The actual cues used and the priority given to them will vary according to the customer's particular needs at the time. In choosing a hotel, for example, a customer might look at:

1 *Location*: if the customer is on holiday, then perhaps a hotel near to the beach or other tourist attraction would be preferred, or one in a very peaceful scenic setting. A business traveller, in contrast, might look for one that is convenient for the airport or close to the client being visited.
2 *Appearance*: a customer's expectations about a hotel are likely to be affected by its appearance. Does it look shabby or well kept? Is it too big or too small? Does it look welcoming? What is the decor like, both internally and externally? Do the rooms seem spacious enough and well appointed? Those who are familiar with the Parador hotel chain in Spain will realise what an impact can be made by building a hotel around the conversion of historic buildings such as castles and stately homes.
3 *Additional services*: the customer might be concerned about the peripheral aspects of the service on offer. The tourist who will be spending two weeks in a hotel might be interested in the variety of bars and restaurants provided; hairdressing, laundry or creche facilities; shopping and postal services; or the nightlife. The business traveller might be more concerned about car parking, shuttle buses to the airport, or fax and telephone provision.

4 *Customer handling*: if the potential customer contacts the hotel for further information or to make a reservation, the quality of the handling they receive might affect the purchase decision. Courtesy and friendliness will make a good impression, as will a prompt and accurate response to the query. This kind of efficiency implies a commitment to staff training and good operating systems to assist easy access to relevant information and the speedy processing of bookings.

MARKETING IN ACTION

Multiplex cinemas

A visit to the cinema has been revolutionised over recent years, and further changes are still expected as efforts continue to be made to upgrade the customer experience. It is not very long ago that going to the cinema meant a choice of one main feature and a 'B' film and that was all. Stern-faced usherettes guided you with their torches towards a seat (usually the one you did not want), then they doubled up as ice-cream sellers during the interval (until they ran out of stock). Parking was usually non-existent, as cinemas were located in town centres, and queueing was the norm for more popular shows as no advance booking was possible. The seating was not particularly comfortable, and the whole episode was not very customer friendly. It is perhaps not surprising that cinema audiences declined over many years as people switched to new leisure pursuits.

All that has now changed in many cinemas, as marketing strategies have become far more orientated towards the needs of the consumer. This is very evident from a visit to a multiplex cinema, a format which has been a major influence in the rise in cinema attendances in the UK. Box office revenues increased by 80 per cent between 1989 and 1995, despite the increase in alternative leisure pursuits. Around 100 million tickets are sold each year and this number is expected to grow to 155 million by 1999. At the heart of this growth has been the popularity of a product concept centring on the multiplex. A multiplex is a large building containing a number of small, individual cinemas around a central circulation area. A multiplex can thus show 12 or more different films at any one time and can seat up to 3500 customers in total. The size of the individual cinemas varies, so that, for example, blockbusting new releases can be put into bigger ones or even be shown in two cinemas at once, reflecting the expected popularity of the film. The seating in all the cinemas is invariably of a high standard.

Pre-booking is possible, at least to guarantee entry although not necessarily to have a specific seat allocation, and there is plenty of opportunity to purchase a wide range of snacks in the central circulation area while you wait to be admitted to the cinema itself. Parking is rarely a problem, as most multiplexes are on large out of town sites. Whereas town centre sites tend to attract primarily a local audience, multiplexes tend to pull audiences from greater distances. Careful marketing, through advertising and brochures, for example, ensures that people know what range of films is on offer at any one time. Once customers are in the cinema, trailers for forthcoming features also help to encourage 'repeat purchases', keeping more regular cinema goers aware of new releases.

Most of the large operators, Odeon, UCI, Showcase Cinemas, and more recently Virgin, already operate multiplexes in the UK. Two new entrants were expected in 1996: Warner Cinemas was expected to build a multiplex in Stevenage, and the US chain AMC was planning to build 2000 screens across Europe. In 1996, there were around 75 multiplexes in the UK, all of which had been opened within the previous 10 years. Many are located in new leisure parks alongside discos, bingo halls, ten pin bowling alleys, and food outlets. Seventeen leisure parks were already open in the UK in 1996 with a further 17 planned. Each one costs between £15 million and £25 million to develop. Virgin is also considering developing a 17-screen multiplex cinema.

Efforts to upgrade the customer experience are not over yet. Bars and catering are expected to be upgraded further, even though on many sites a number of fast food franchises have been licensed. Improved booking systems are likely to be introduced to speed up pre-booking (with seat allocations) and payment, in some cases using the Internet. Although the supply of quality cinema viewing is increasing, the service enhancement is still essential as part of the package to encourage cinema goers to visit more often by making it easier and more pleasant for them.

Sources: Daneshkhu (1996); Murphy (1996); Rawsthorn (1996).

In a wider sense, marketing and brand building are also important, of course. These help to raise awareness of a hotel chain's existence and positioning, and differentiate it from the competition. These communicate the key benefits on offer and thus help the customer to decide whether this is the kind of hotel they are looking for, developing their expectations. Advertising, glossy brochures and other marketing communications techniques can help to create and reinforce the potential customer's perception of location, appearance, additional services and customer handling, as well as the brand imagery. Strong marketing and branding also help to link a chain of hotels that might be spread world-wide, giving the customer some reassurance of consistency and familiarity. A business traveller in a strange city can seek out a known hotel name, such as Novotel, Holiday Inn, Sheraton, Campanile, or Formula 1, and be fairly certain about what they are purchasing.

The more intangible the product, the greater the pressure on marketers to create what tangibility they can. This makes it easier for the consumer to do some pre-purchase evaluation and gives them the confidence to buy. The secret of franchising's success is to make a service offering tangible so that the customers know what to expect before purchase, regardless of the geographic location of the outlet.

Example

Pizza Hut's menu, decor, servers, order processing, equipment, cooking procedures etc. are all standardised (or allow minor variations and adaptations for local conditions), creating a consistent and familiar experience for the customer all over the world. Customers thus have a strong tangible impression of the character of Pizza Hut, what to expect of it, and what it delivers.

One of the greatest problems of intangibility is that it is difficult to assess quality both during and after the service has been experienced. Customers will use a combination of criteria, both objective and subjective, to judge their level of satisfaction, although it is often based on impressions, memories and expectations. Different customers attach significance to different things. The frequent business traveller might be extremely annoyed by check-in delays or the noise from the Friday night jazz cabaret, while the holidaymaker might grumble about the beach being 20 minutes' walk away rather then the 5 minutes promised in the brochure. Memories fade over time, but some bad ones, such as a major service breakdown or a confrontation with service staff, will remain. In a restaurant, assessing the quality of the food or the cleanliness of the cutlery might well be straightforward and consistent between different customers, but atmosphere, music and interaction with the serving staff are much more individual and subjective.

Perishability

Services are manufactured at the same time as they are consumed. A lecturer paces the lecture theatre creating a service experience that is immediately either consumed or slept through by the students. Manchester United, Ajax, or AC Milan manufacture sporting entertainment that either thrills, bores or frustrates their fans as they watch the match live. Similarly, audiences at Covent Garden or La Scala absorb live opera as it unfolds before them. With both sport and entertainment, it is likely that the customer's enjoyment of the 'product' is heightened by the unpredictability of live performance and the audience's own emotional involvement in what is going on. This highlights another peculiarity of service products: customers are often directly involved in the production process and the synergy between them and the service provider affects the quality of the experience. A friend might tell you, 'Yes, it was a brilliant concert. The band were on top form and the atmosphere was great!' To create such a complete experience, the band and their equipment do have to perform to the expected standard, the lighting and sound crews have to get it right on the night, and the venue has to have adequate facilities and efficient customer handling processes. The atmosphere, however, is created by the interaction between performer and audience and can inspire the performer to deliver a better experience. The customer therefore has to be prepared to give as well as take, and make their own contribution to the quality of the service product.

Perishability thus means that a service cannot be manufactured and stored either before or after the experience. Manufacture and consumption are simultaneous. A hotel is, of course, a permanent structure with full-time staff, and exists regardless of whether it has customers or not on a particular night. The hotel's service product, however, is only being delivered when there is a customer present to purchase and receive it. The product is perishable in the sense that if a room is not taken on a particular night, then it is a completely lost opportunity. Room 503 for the night of Friday, 19 April 1996 is a unique, time-dependent service product. The same is true of most service products, such as airline seats, theatre tickets, management consultancy or dental appointments. If a dentist cannot fill the appointment book for a particular day, then that revenue-earning opportunity is lost for ever. In situations where demand is reasonably steady, it is relatively easy to plan capacity and adapt the organisation to meet the expected demand pattern.

Even where demand does fluctuate, as long as it is fairly predictable, managers can plan to raise or reduce service capacity accordingly. A larger plane or an additional performance might be provided to cater for short-term demand increases. It can be more difficult, however, if there are very marked fluctuations in demand that might result in facilities lying idle for a long time or in severe overcapacity. The profitability of companies servicing peak hour transport demands can be severely affected because vehicles and rolling stock are unused for the rest of the day. Airlines too face seasonal fluctuations in demand.

Example

Balkanair mothballs a number of its holiday jets over the winter, as the Black Sea resorts in Bulgaria virtually close down and there is little demand from foreign tourists. Sports and entertainment can be hit by unpredictable demand fluctuations. A football team that hits a run of bad luck can see its crowd fall to 5000 but still have to maintain a 50 000 seater stadium. More drastically, a West End show that gets universally bad reviews might have to end its run early because it cannot fill the theatre on a regular enough basis.

Sometimes, of course, changes in demand or events within the marketing environment mean a flood of extra customers. This can put severe strain on the service delivery system and on capacity, if the service provider cannot respond in sufficient time. AIDS help lines in the UK were suddenly put under severe short-term strain in 1996 when the results of a certain brand of HIV test were found to be unreliable. Charities and mainstream medical services found themselves having to set up extra telephone lines, get hold of extra counsellors, gather up-to-date information, and deal with publicity in order to cope efficiently with a surge in queries. In happier circumstances, success might lead to increased demand. A non-league football team experiencing a good cup run might 'borrow' a bigger and better equipped ground for a fixture against a high profile opponent, or a show that gets good reviews and good word of mouth recommendations might extend its run or insert extra performances.

The concept of perishability means that a range of marketing strategies is needed to try to even out demand and bring capacity handling into line with it. These strategies might include pricing or product development to increase demand during quieter periods or to divert it from busier ones, or better scheduling and forecasting through the booking and reservation system. Similarly, the capacity and service delivery system can be adapted to meet peaks or troughs in demand through such strategies as part-time workers, increased mechanisation or co-operation with other service providers. These will be considered in more detail later (*see* pp. 936–40).

Inseparability

Many physical products are produced well in advance of purchase and consumption, and production staff rarely come into direct contact with the customer. Often, production and consumption are distanced in both space and time, connected only by the physical distribution system considered in Chapter 14. Sales forecasts based on reasonable expectations of changes in demand provide important guidelines for production schedules. If demand rises unexpectedly, opportunities might well exist to increase production or to reduce stockholding to meet customer needs.

As has already been said, with service products, however, the involvement of the customer in the service experience means that there can be no prior production, no storage and that consumption takes place simultaneously with production. The service delivery, therefore, cannot be separated from the service providers and thus the fourth characteristic of service products is **inseparability**. The terminology used to order a service product might vary: booking, making an appointment, reserving a seat or prepaying an entrance fee. All of these terms, however, imply that the customer is being granted legitimate access to consume a service experience at an agreed time and place in the future, with the co-operation and participation of the provider.

Inseparability means that the customer often comes into direct contact with the service provider(s), either individually, as with a doctor, or as part of a team of providers, as with air travel. The team includes reservations clerks, check-in staff, aircrew and perhaps transfer staff. In an airline, the staff team has a dual purpose. Clearly, they have to deliver their aspect of the service efficiently, but they also have to interact with the customer in the delivery of the service. An unco-operative check-in clerk might not provide the customer's desired seat, but in contrast, a friendly empathic air hostess can alleviate the fear of a first time flyer. The service provider can thus affect the quality of the service delivered and the manner in which it is delivered.

While the delivery of a personal service can be controlled, since there are fewer opportunities for outside interference, the situation becomes more complex when other customers are experiencing service at same time. The 'mass service experience' means that other customers can potentially affect the perceived quality of that experience, positively or negatively. As mentioned earlier, the enjoyment of the atmosphere at a sporting event or a concert, for example, depends on the emotional charge generated by a large number of like-minded individuals. In other situations, however, the presence of many other customers can affect aspects of the service experience negatively. If the facility or the staff do not have the capacity or the ability to handle larger numbers than forecast, queues, overcrowding and dissatisfaction can soon result. Although reservation or prebooking can reduce the risk, service providers can still be caught out. Airlines routinely overbook flights deliberately, on the basis that not all booked passengers will actually turn up. Sometimes, however, they miscalculate and end up with more passengers than the flight can actually accommodate and have to offer free air miles, cash or other benefits to encourage some passengers to switch to a later flight. At theme parks, much more time can be spent waiting to get on to a ride than on the ride itself during times of peak demand. Although attempts are made to manage that situation by providing information about waiting times, planning the queueing procedure to give the impression of constant forward movement, and providing entertainment while people wait, customers would still prefer shorter queues and less competition for the park's facilities.

What the other customers are like also affects the quality of the experience. This reflects the segmentation policy of the service provider. If a relatively undifferentiated approach is offered, there are all sorts of potential conflicts (or benefits) from mixing customers who are perhaps looking for different benefits. A hotel, for example, might have problems if families with young children are mixed with guests on an over-50s holiday. Where possible, therefore, the marketer should carefully target segments to match the service product being offered. By attracting like-minded individuals, not only will the service experience be enhanced for all customers, but there will also be less opportunity for those seeking a peaceful retreat at a hotel being disturbed by a Club 18–30 all-night rave!

Finally, the behaviour of other customers can be positive, leading to new friends, comradeship and enjoyable social interaction, or it can be negative if it is rowdy, disruptive or even threatening. Marketers prefer, of course, to try to develop the positive aspects. Social evenings for new package holiday arrivals, name badges on coach tours, and warm-up acts to build atmosphere at live shows all help to break the ice. To prevent disruptive behaviour, the service package might have to include security measures and clearly defined and enforced 'house rules' such as those found at soccer matches. Of course, there can be real problems for marketers in keeping some segments apart, for example in soccer grounds.

The implications of inseparability for marketing strategy will be considered at pp. 932–4.

Heterogeneity

With simultaneous production and consumption and the involvement of service staff and other customers, it can be difficult to standardise the service experience as planned. **Heterogeneity** means that each service experience is likely to be different, depending upon the interaction between the customer and other customers, service staff, and other factors such as time, location and the operating procedures. The problems of standardising the desired service experience are greater when there is finite capacity and the service provided is especially labour intensive. The maxim 'when the heat is on the service is gone' reflects the risk of service breakdown when demand puts the system under pressure, especially if it is unexpected. This might mean no seats available on the train, delays in serving meals on a short-haul flight, or a queue in the bank on a Friday afternoon.

Sometimes, the differences are more subtle but they can still affect the perception of service performance. On one day, a lecturer might deliver an entertaining and informative lecture but on the next day, perhaps suffering from the effects of a late night, the performance might be well below average. Following an inconsistent soccer team can be a roller coaster; a great match and a convincing win one week, but an eminently forgettable performance the next. A multi-location service provider might regularly provide excellent service in one branch, but very poor service in another. There can also, of course, be inconsistencies between different service providers. Within a single branch of a bank, some clerks can be bright, friendly and helpful, while others will be surly and offer service grudgingly. Some travellers assess the check-in staff at an airport to decide which one looks more likely to turn a blind eye to excess luggage or to allocate the best seats!

Some of the heterogeneity in the service cannot be planned for or avoided, but quality assurance procedures can minimise the worst excesses of service breakdown. This can be done by designing in 'failsafes', creating mechanisms to spot problems quickly and to resolve them early before they cause a major service breakdown. Universities, for example, have numerous quality assurance procedures to cover academic programmes, staffing and support procedures that involve self-assessment, student evaluation and external subject and quality assessment.

Not all service breakdowns are caused by the service provider, but, whatever their cause, they can still fundamentally affect the quality of the service experience.

TABLE 23.1

Generic differences between services and physical goods

1 The nature of the product
2 Customers' involvement in the production process
3 People as part of the product
4 Greater problems in maintaining quality
5 Harder for customers to evaluate
6 Absence of inventories
7 Relative importance of time factors
8 Structure and nature of distribution channels

Source: Lovelock (1996).

Technical problems with a plane are the responsibility of an airline, but not the fog, air traffic delays or problems with the baggage handlers. A state agency might have responsibility for promoting regional tourism, but is dependent on the hotels, guest houses, tourist attractions, taxi drivers and other service providers to deliver the required service to a proper standard for the region's tourism to develop.

Management, therefore, has to develop ways of reducing the impact of heterogeneity. To help in that process, they need to focus on operating systems, procedures, and staff training in order to ensure consistency. New lecturers, for example, might be required to undertake a special induction programme to help them learn teaching skills, preparing materials and handling some of the difficulties associated with disruptive students. Managers have to indicate clearly what they expect of staff in terms of the desired level of service. This must cover not only compliance with procedures in accordance with training, but also staff attitudes and the manner in which they deal with customers. Many franchising chains have successfully managed growth, yet maintained service consistency and control through the careful design of the operating manual, extensive staff training, and regular monitoring and feedback.

Lovelock (1996), however, feels that these characteristics are somewhat over-generalised and are not necessarily applicable to all service products. An alternative list of eight generic differences between physical products and services, summarised in Table 23.1, is therefore suggested as a more practical approach. This list does, nevertheless, include many of the concepts discussed above, albeit under different labels.

The characteristics of service products, regardless of how they are defined, create problems for marketers. They have to build and maintain competitive advantage through service design, delivery, differentiation and efficiency, while providing consistent service regularly. The next section, therefore, looks in more detail at the impact of the particular characteristics of service products on the design and implementation of the marketing programme.

SERVICES MARKETING MANAGEMENT

So far, this chapter has looked at the characteristics of service products in a very general way. This section looks further at the implications of those characteristics for marketers in terms of formulating strategy, developing and measuring quality in the service product and issues of training and productivity.

Services marketing strategy

The traditional marketing mix, consisting of the 4Ps, forms the basis of the structure of this book. For service products, however, additional elements of the marketing mix are necessary to reflect the special characteristics of services marketing. Shown in Fig 23.3, these are:

- *people*: whether service providers or customers who participate in the production and delivery of the service experience
- *physical evidence*: the tangible cues that support the main service product. These will include facilities, the infrastructure and the products used to deliver the service
- *processes*: the operating processes that take the customer through from ordering to the manufacture and delivery of the service.

Any of these extra marketing mix elements can enhance or detract from the customer's overall experience when consuming the service. However, despite the special considerations, the purpose of designing an effective marketing mix remains the same whether for services or physical products. The marketer is still trying to create a differentiated, attractive proposition for customers, ensuring that whatever is offered meets their needs and expectations. All seven of the services marketing mix elements will now be considered in turn.

Product

From a supplier's perspective, many services can be treated like any other physical product in a number of ways. The supplier develops a range of products, each of which represents profit-earning opportunities. A hotel company might treat each of its hotels as a separate product with its own unique product management requirements arising from its location, the state of the building and its facilities, local competition, and its strengths and weaknesses compared with others in the area.

FIGURE 23.3

The services marketing mix

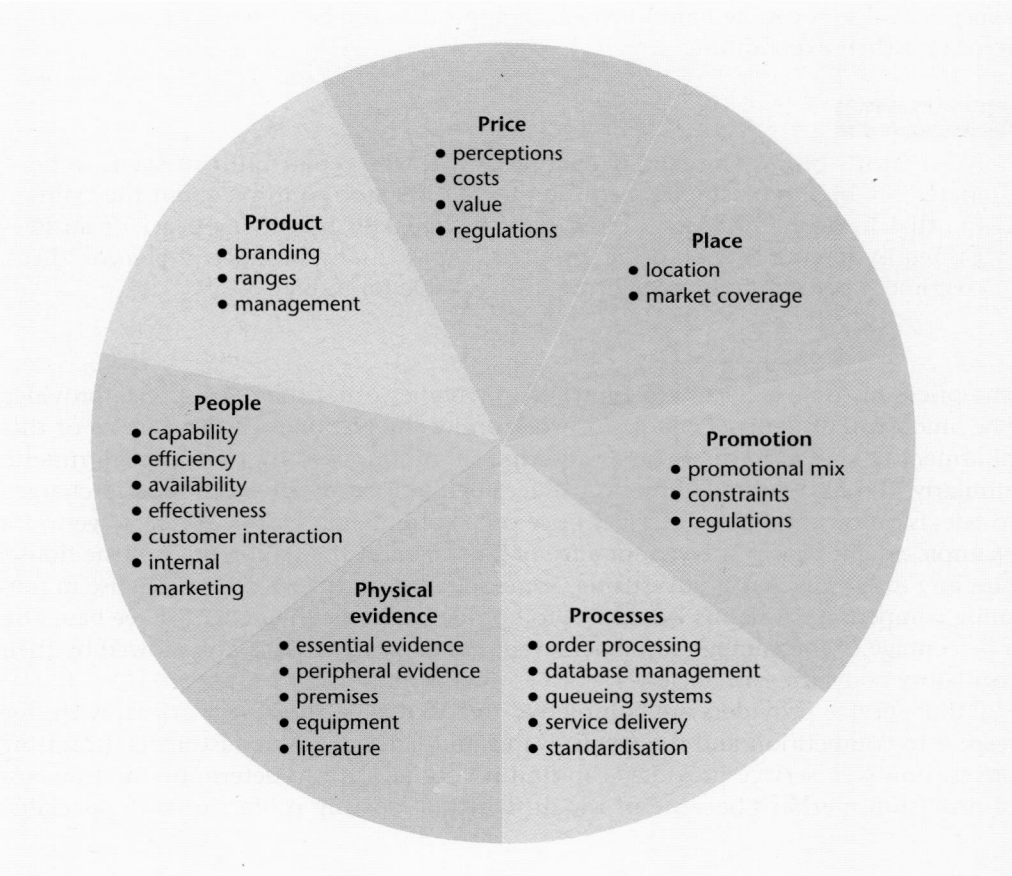

These products might, of course, be grouped into product lines and SBUs based on similarities and differences between them, just as physical products can be.

Similarly, an insurance company might have many different policies on offer, including pension plans, endowments, life insurance, house buildings and contents insurance, and motor or holiday insurance. Each one again might be considered as a product or as part of a range.

Many of the product concepts and the decisions concerning them which were discussed in Chapters 7 to 9 apply equally to services and physical products. Positioning, branding, developing a mix, designing new services and managing the product life cycle are all relevant.

Example

British Airways seeks to brand itself as a friendly, reliable and professional airline; Formula 1 positions itself as a no frills, low cost motel chain; Sky television offers a range of satellite channels to cover sport, news, movies and other entertainment. Services can be repositioned too. Spain, for example, is trying to reposition itself and change its appeal because of too many new competitors in the sea, sun, sand and cheap alcohol segment of the market. Spain now wants to be regarded as a destination that still offers good value, but a wider range of tourist attractions and cultural activities.

Price

Because services are intangible, their pricing can be very difficult to set and to justify. The customer is not receiving anything that can be touched or otherwise physically experienced, so it can be hard for them to appreciate the benefits they have gained in return for their expenditure.

Example

A solicitor's bill or the labour charges added to a repair bill can seem to be incredibly high to customer, because they do not stop to think about the training that has gone into developing professional skills nor of the peace of mind gained by having the job done 'properly'. As with any product, therefore, the customer's perception is central to assessing value for money.

The prices of some services are controlled by bodies other than the service provider. The amount that dentists charge for work under the National Health Service or that pharmacists charge to dispense a prescription are imposed by central government. Similarly, the BBC is funded by licence fees determined by government and charged to television owners. Other services price on a commission basis. An estate agent, for example, might charge the vendor a fee of 2 per cent of the selling price of the house, plus any expenses such as advertising. Some solicitors in the UK who specialise in pursuing compensation claims would like to be able to charge their clients a fee based on a percentage of the compensation achieved, but currently that is not allowed by their regulatory body, the Law Society.

Other service providers are completely free to decide their own prices, with due respect to competition and the needs, wants and perceptions of customers. In setting prices, however, service providers can find it very difficult to determine the true cost of provision, perhaps because of the difficulty of costing professional or specialist skills, or because the time and effort required to deliver a service varies widely between different customers, yet a standard price is needed. Perishability might also affect the pricing of professional services. A training provider, for example, who has little work on at the moment might agree to charge less than the normal daily rate, just to generate some income rather than none.

In service situations, price can play an important role in managing demand. By varying the price, depending on the time at which the service is delivered, service providers can try to discourage customers from purchasing at the busiest periods. Customers can also use price as a weapon. Passengers purchasing airline tickets shortly before the flight or visitors looking for a hotel room for the night might be able to negotiate a much lower price than that advertised. This is a result of the perishability of services: the airline would rather have a seat occupied and get something for it than let the flight take off with an empty one, and similarly, the hotel would rather have a room occupied than not. In 1996, tour operators decided to delete certain holidays from their brochures to avoid the situation faced in previous years where they had to discount heavily to maintain reasonable capacity levels.

Place

According to Cowell (1984), services are often supplied direct from the provider to the customer because production and consumption are simultaneous. Direct supply allows the provider to control what is going on; to differentiate through personal service; and to get direct feedback and interaction with the customer. Direct supply can take place from business premises, such as a hairdresser's salon, a solicitor's office, or a university campus. Some services can also be supplied by telephone, such as insurance and banking services. Others are supplied by the service provider visiting the customer's home or premises, such as cleaning, repair of large appliances, equipment installation and servicing, or home hairdressing services.

Whatever the mode of direct supply, it can cause problems for the service provider. It limits the number of customers that can be dealt with and the geographic coverage of the service. For sole traders or small businesses who particularly value the rapport and personal relationships built up with regular clients, this might be perfectly acceptable. Businesses that want to expand might find that direct supply involving the original proprietor of the business is no longer feasible. Professional service businesses, such as accountants or solicitors, might employ additional qualified staff to expand the customer base or to expand geographic coverage.

Other service businesses such as fast food outlets, domestic cleaners, or debt collection agencies might opt to expand by franchising, an area which will be further discussed in Chapter 24. Some services will decide to move towards indirect supply through intermediaries paid on a commission basis. Thus, the local pharmacist might act as an agent for a company that develops photographic film; a village shop might collect dry cleaning; insurance brokers distribute policies; travel agencies distribute holidays and business travel, and tourist information offices deal with hotel and guest house bookings. In some of these cases, the main benefit of using an intermediary is convenience for the customer and spreading the coverage of the service. In others, such as the travel agency and the insurance broker, the service provider gains the added benefit of having their product sold by a specialist alongside the competition.

Place is not just important for delivering the service. It also covers access to reservation and information systems. Travel agents, for example, have direct computer links with tour operators and other central reservation systems that are not available to the consumer. The tour operator benefits from being able to distribute information cost effectively and having its holidays sold by trained agents. The growth of Teletext, interactive shopping and the Internet might revolutionise this aspect of the services marketing mix still further.

Promotion

Marketing communication objectives, implementation and management for services are largely the same as for any other product. There are a few specific issues to point out, however. As with pricing, some professional services are ethically constrained in what marketing communication they are allowed to do. Solicitors in the UK, for example, are allowed to use print advertising, but only if it is restrained and factual. An advertisement can tell the reader what areas of the law the practice specialises in, but it cannot make emotive promises about winning vast amounts of compensation for you, for example.

Service products face a particularly difficult communications task because of the intangibility of the product. They cannot show you pretty pack shots, they cannot whet your appetite with promises of strawberry and chocolate flavoured variants, they cannot show you how much of this amazing product you are getting for your money. They can, however, show the physical evidence, they can show people like you apparently enjoying the service, they can emphasize the benefits of purchasing this service. Testimonials from satisfied customers can be an extremely effective tool, because they reassure the potential customer that the service works and that the outcomes will be positive. Linked with this, word of mouth communication is incredibly important, especially for the smaller business working in a limited geographic area. Overall, if the service provider can use communication to build a reputation for quality, reliability and trustworthiness, then it is well on the way to overcoming potential customers' doubts and overcoming intangibility.

Finally, it must be remembered that many service providers are small businesses, who could not afford to invest in glossy advertising campaigns, even if they could see the point of it. Many can generate enough work to keep them going through word of mouth recommendation and advertisements in the *Yellow Pages*. Much depends on the level of competition and demand in the local market for the kind of service being offered. If the town's high street supports four different restaurants, then perhaps a more concerted effort might be justified, including for example, advertising in local newspapers, door-to-door leaflet drops and price promotions. Local service outlets that are franchises are likely to benefit from large scale national corporate promotion, designed to create a consistent image for all branches. Nevertheless, franchisees might also have some discretion and flexibility to do their own communication tailored specifically to local conditions.

It is important to remember, however, that customers are likely to use marketing communication messages to build their expectations of what the service is likely to deliver. This is true of any product, but as will be discussed at pp. 932–4, because of intangibility, the judgement of service quality is much more subjective. It is based on a comparison of prior expectations with actual perceived outcomes. The wilder or more unrealistic the communication claims, therefore, the greater the chances of a mismatch that will lead to a dissatisfied customer in the end. The service provider does, of course, need to create a sufficiently alluring image to entice the customer, but not to the point where the customer undergoing the service experience begins to wonder if this is actually the same establishment as that advertised.

People

Services depend on people and interaction between people, including the service provider's staff, the customer and other customers. As the customer is often a participant in the creation and delivery of the service product, there are implications for service product quality, productivity and staff training. The ability of staff to cope with customers, to deliver the service reliably to the required standard and to present an image consistent with what the organisation would want, is a vital concern to the service provider. This is known as *internal marketing*, and will be discussed later at pp. 934 *et seq*. The role of the customer in the service is known as *interactive marketing*, and will be discussed at pp. 932 *et seq*.

Physical evidence

Physical evidence comprises the tangible elements that support the service delivery, and give clues about the positioning of the service product or give the customer something solid to take away with them to symbolise the intangible benefits they have received. Shostack (1977) differentiates between *essential evidence* and *peripheral evidence*. Essential evidence is central to the service and is an important contributor to the customer's purchase decision. Examples of this might be the type and newness of aircraft operated by an airline or of the car fleet belonging to a car hire firm; the layout and facilities offered by a supermarket (*see* pp. 515 *et seq.* for more on this), or a university's lecture theatres and their equipment as well as IT and library provision. Peripheral evidence is less central to the service delivery and is likely to consist of items that the customer can have to keep or use.

> ### Example
>
> Banks provide wallets to keep bank statements in; retailers provide carrier bags; hairdressers or dentists give appointment cards; insurance companies provide leaflets that explain in plain language (with pictures) the main benefits of their insurance policies, and hotels often provide a variety of toiletries (bearing their logo, of course) for the guest to take away. Such items can enhance the service or ease its delivery, adding value to it in small ways that the customer appreciates. As a minor example, Lloyds Bank issues left-handed cheque books to customers who request them. This is peripheral evidence designed to show that the service provider cares about the needs of minority groups of customers, and perhaps as a small point of differentiation from the other major banks.

Processes

Because the creation and consumption of a service are usually simultaneous, the production of the service is an important part of its marketing as the customer either witnesses it or is directly involved in it. The service provider needs smooth, efficient customer friendly procedures. Some processes work behind the scenes, for example administrative and data processing systems, processing paperwork and information relating to the service delivery and keeping track of customers. Systems that allow the service provider to send a postcard to remind customers that the next dental check up or car service is due certainly help to generate repeat business, but also help in a small way to strengthen the relationship with the customer. Other processes are also 'invisible' to the customer, but form an essential part of the service package. The organisation of the kitchens in a fast food outlet, for example, ensures a steady supply

MARKETING IN ACTION

Novotel design

Any physical evidence, whether essential or peripheral, can help to create an image of quality and communicate the provider's market positioning. The hotel chain Novotel, for example, understands the importance of physical evidence in its market. It felt that the image of its hotels and their rooms was rather tired, bland and boxy and was contributing to a loss of market share. A designer was brought in to refresh the whole look, from the look of the car parks and gardens, through to the rooms and the staff uniforms, over a five-year project. The brief also included music, lighting and smells, as well as fine detail such as the design of ashtrays. A new £32 million corporate image is also part of the strategy to make customers think again about what Novotel offers.

Source: Jolley (1995).

of freshly cooked burgers available for counter staff to draw on as customers order. Well designed processes are also needed as the service is delivered to ensure that the customer gets through with minimum fuss and delay and that all elements of the service are properly delivered. This might involve, for example, the design of forms and the information requested, payment procedures, queueing systems or even task allocation. At a hairdressing salon, for instance, a junior might wash your hair while the stylist finishes off the previous customer, and the receptionist will handle the payment at the end.

Banks, for example, have thought seriously about ways of making their services more accessible to their customers. Telephone banking, for example, with processes designed to protect customer security and to provide 24-hour coverage,

Source: Direct Line.

allows customers easy access to their accounts from their own homes whenever they want it. In addition to this, the banks are also experimenting with on-line banking so that customers can access their accounts through PCs. National Westminster Bank's Bankline, for example, means that small businesses can manage their own transactions without the need for contact with any bank staff (Barrett, 1996).

Direct Line gives customers easy and convenient access to a wide range of financial services from the comfort of their own homes.

Interactive marketing: Service quality

Central to the delivery of any service product is the *service encounter* between the provider and the customer. This is also known as **interactive marketing**. This aspect of services is an important determinant of quality because it brings together all the elements of the services marketing mix and is the point at which the product itself is created and delivered. Quality issues are just as important for service products as they are for a physical product, but service quality is much more difficult to define and to control. These difficulties arise from the essential intangibility of the service, the fact that it is produced 'live' and the involvement of the customer in the production process. Because there is no physical product to look at and measure, service quality assessment is largely dependent on the customers' perceptions of what they have received and the extent to which that has fulfiled or exceeded their expectations. Authors such as Devlin and Dong (1994) and Zeithaml *et al*. (1990), for example, stress the importance of customer perceptions and use them as the basis for frameworks for measuring service quality.

Measuring service quality

Some aspects of the service product can, of course, be measured more objectively than others. Where tangible elements are involved, such as physical evidence and processes, quality can be defined and assessed more easily. In a fast food restaurant, for example, the cleanliness of the premises, the length of the queues, the consistency of the size of portions and their cooking, and the implementation and effectiveness of stock control systems, can all be 'seen' and measured. Whether the customer actually *enjoyed* the burger, whether they *felt* that they had had to wait too long, or whether they *felt* that the premises were too busy, crowded or noisy are much more personal matters and thus far more difficult for managers to assess.

A particular group of researchers, Berry, Parasuraman and Zeithaml, have developed criteria for assessing service quality and a survey mechanism called SERVQUAL for collecting data relating to customer perceptions (*see*, e.g. Parasuraman *et al*. 1985;

Zeithaml *et al.*, 1988; Zeithaml *et al.*, 1990). They cite 10 main criteria which between them cover the whole service experience from the customer's point of view:

1 *Access*: how easy is it for the customer to gain access to the service? Is there an outlet for the service close to the customer? Is there 24-hour access by telephone to a helpline?

2 *Reliability*: are all the elements of the service performed and are they delivered to the expected standard? Does the repair engineer clean up after himself after mending the washing machine and does the machine then work properly? Does the supermarket that promises to open another checkout when the queues get too long actually do so?

3 *Credibility*: is the service provider trustworthy and believable? Is the service provider a member of a reputable trade association? Does it give guarantees with its work? Does it seem to treat the customer fairly?

4 *Security*: is the customer protected from risk or doubt? Is the customer safe while visiting and using a theme park? Does an insurance policy cover all eventualities? Will the bank respect the customer's confidentiality? Can the cellular telephone network provider prevent hackers from hijacking a customer's mobile phone number?

5 *Understanding the customer*: does the service provider make an effort to understand and adapt to the customer's needs and wants? Will a repair engineer give a definite time of arrival? Will a financial adviser take the time to understand the customer's financial situation and needs and then plan a complete package? Do front line service staff develop good relationships with regular customers?

Those first five criteria influence the quality of the *outcome* of the service experience. The next five influence the quality of the *inputs* to the process to provide a solid foundation for the outputs.

6 *Responsiveness*: is the service provider quick to respond to the customer and willing to help? Can a repair engineer visit within 24 hours? Will a bank manager explain in detail what the small print in a loan agreement means? Are customer problems dealt with quickly and efficiently?

7 *Courtesy*: are service staff polite, friendly and considerate? Do they smile and greet customers? Are they pleasant? Do they show good manners? Do service staff who have to visit a customer's home treat it with proper respect and minimise the sense of intrusion?

8 *Competence*: are service staff suitably trained and able to deliver the service properly? Does a financial adviser have extensive knowledge of available financial products and their appropriateness for the customer? Does a librarian know how to access and use information databases? Do theme park staff know where the nearest toilets are, what to do in a medical emergency or what to do about a lost child?

9 *Communication*: do service staff listen to customers and take time to explain things to them understandably? Do staff seem sympathetic to customer problems and try to suggest appropriate solutions? Do medical, legal, financial or other professional staff explain things in plain language?

10 *Tangibles*: are the tangible and visible aspects of the service suitably impressive or otherwise appropriate to the situation? Does the appearance of staff inspire confidence in the customer? Are hotel rooms clean, tidy and well appointed? Do lecture theatres have good acoustics and lighting, a full range of audiovisual equipment and good visibility from every seat? Does the repair engineer have all the appropriate equipment available to do the job quickly and properly? Are contracts and invoices easy to read and understand?

It is easy to appreciate just how difficult it is to create and maintain quality in all 10 of these areas, integrating them into a coherent service package. Parasuraman *et al.*

(1985) suggest that there are four barriers to service quality, all of which are the fault of the service provider, and all of which will affect the customer's perception of the service experience. These barriers thus mean that there is a mismatch between what customers expected and what they perceived to be actually delivered.

1 *Misconceptions*: management misunderstands what the customer wants and thus delivers an inappropriate or incomplete service product.
2 *Inadequate resources*: if a service provider is trying to cut costs, for example, the customer might suffer. There could be long queues because there are too few staff available, premises might be ill equipped or shabby, or administrative support systems might start to break down. Students are often all too familiar with the effect of large classes and increasing staff–student ratios in many universities.
3 *Inadequate delivery*: lack of training or poor recruitment might lead to staff with poor knowledge or with no real interest in the customer. This might mean that elements of the service package are not delivered at all or delivered in a very cursory and inadequate way.
4 *Exaggerated promises*: a service provider desperate to gain customers in a highly competitive environment might be tempted to be somewhat economical with the truth. In some cases, when choosing a hotel in a foreign holiday resort from a brochure, for example, customers can only really test the validity of the promises made after they have committed themselves to the purchase. The true picture emerges as the service is being consumed. Thus a hotel brochure might boast that it is within five minutes walk of the beach and that all rooms have a sea view. Unless customers have been to the resort before, or can get word of mouth verification from friends, relatives or travel agents who have stayed there, the fact that they would have to be Olympic sprinters to get to the beach in five minutes and that they would need to stand on a chair with binoculars to see the sea might emerge too late. In this case, expectations are being raised that simply cannot be fulfiled. The customer's perception of service quality is therefore bound to suffer.

In summary, Fig 23.4 shows the service experience and the factors that affect consumers' expectations of what they will receive. The criteria that influence their perception of what they actually did receive are also shown, as well as the reasons why there might be a mismatch between expectations and perceptions.

Internal marketing: Training and productivity

Because of the interaction between customers and staff in the creation and delivery of a service, it is particularly important to focus on developing staff to deliver high levels of functional and service quality. This does not mean a take-over of personnel and operational management functions by marketing, but marketers must work closely with these line managers to ensure that the right staff are recruited, inducted and trained and that they then perform to the service standards set. The pay and rewards system employed can also help to boost staff morale and encourage them to take a positive approach to service delivery. Defining the ideal profile and right remuneration package for staff is not easy.

Example

Harris (1995) compares London Underground's practices with those of British Rail. He points out that London Underground pays more than British Rail to staff in equivalent jobs because it wants to recruit better qualified staff. Harris quotes one post for which British Rail was asking for candidates to be qualified to A level standard whereas London Underground wanted only candidates educated to Master's degree level for a similar job. He is also critical of remuneration policies which mean that many railway staff can only earn a reasonable level of take home pay if they accept significant amounts of overtime, suggesting that

'... low wages and long hours do not improve morale, and a workforce with low morale is not likely to give a good service'. (Harris, 1995, p. 626).

Staff training

Many service failures actually do stem from staffing problems. To minimise the risk of failure, therefore, it is important to identify all functions that involve customer contact and to train and remunerate staff for these functions accordingly. As Table 23.2 shows, some staff have direct or indirect involvement in the creation of the service product, and some staff are visible, whereas others are invisible to customers.

Staff who have direct involvement are those who come into contact with a customer as a key part of service delivery. In an airline, these might be air hostesses and stewards, check-in staff, and those at the enquiries desk. Indirect involvement covers all staff who enable the service to be delivered, but do not normally come into contact with the customer. They affect the quality of the service delivery through their impact on the efficiency and effectiveness of the operating system and the standards and performance possible from the facilities and infrastructure. Examples might include aircraft catering staff, cleaning and maintenance staff, ground staff at sports venues, banks' computer systems staff and railway signalmen.

Visible staff (both those with direct involvement and those with indirect involvement with the customer) are in the front line of service delivery. Not only are they concerned with the practical aspects of service delivery to the required standards, but

FIGURE 23.4

Service quality: Expectations, perceptions and gaps

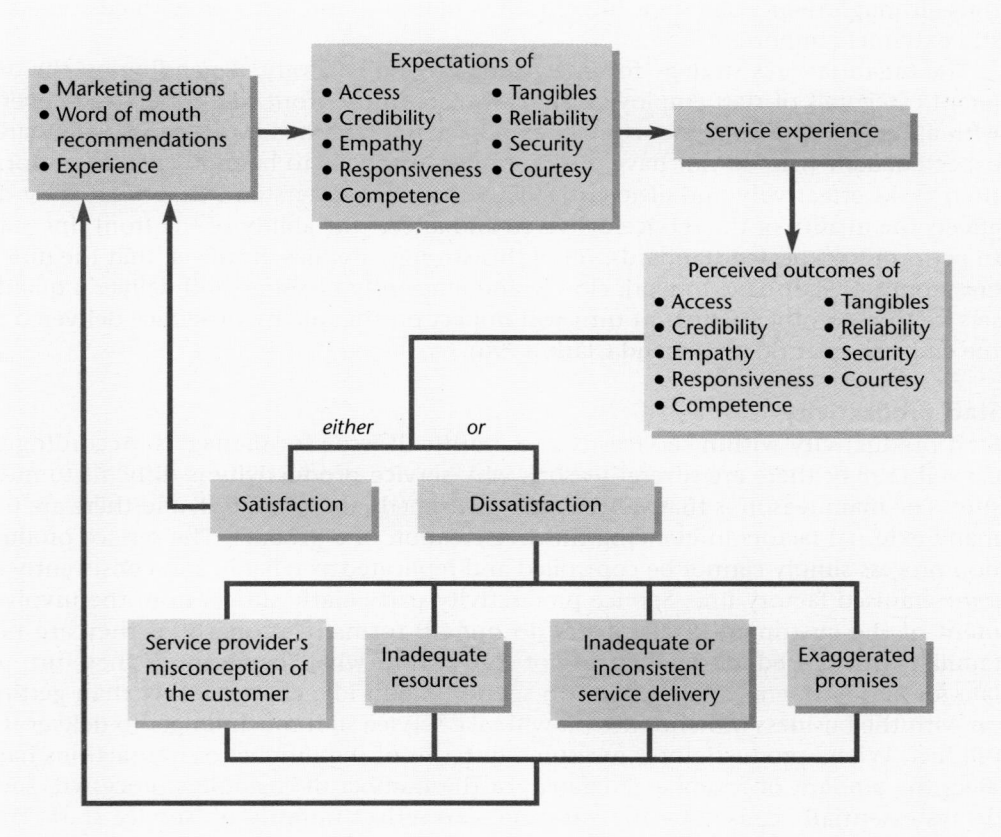

TABLE 23.2

Staff in the service function

	Visible to the customer	Invisible to the customer

Direct involvement	• Airline cabin crew
	• Cashiers
	• Sales assistants
	• Medical staff
	• Receptionists
		• Telephone based services
		  – order takers
		  – customer helplines
		  – telephone banking

Indirect involvement	• Hotel chamber maids • Supermarket shelf fillers	• Office cleaners • Airline caterers • Administrative staff

their appearance, interpersonal behaviour and mannerisms will also make an impression on the customer. Airlines, for example, will pay particular attention to a cabin attendant's personal grooming and dress standardisation to ensure a consistent visual impact. Dress is often used to help the customer identify visible staff, both those directly involved in the service, such as aircraft cabin crew, and those who are indirectly involved, such as stewards at soccer matches or security staff, for example.

Indirect visible staff also include people such as the cleaners at McDonald's, chamber maids in hotels, or staff supporting the cashiers in banks. Invisible staff might or might not have direct contact with customers. Staff who take telephone bookings or those who deal with customer queries on the telephone are heard, but not seen. In some cases, these staff might be the only major point of contact for the customer, and thus although their visibility is limited, their ability to interact well with customers is still extremely important.

The organisation's strategy for **internal marketing** will vary, depending on the different categories of staff employed. Staff who are in the front line of service delivery, with a high level of customer contact, will have to be trained to deliver the standards expected. Staff who do not have direct contact still have to be motivated to perform their tasks effectively and efficiently. They have to understand that what they do affects the quality of the service delivered and affects the ability of the front line staff to perform to expected standards. All of this strongly implies, however, that the different groups of staff have to work closely and efficiently together, and deliver a quality service to each other, which in turn will impact on the quality of service delivered to the end customer (Mathews and Clark, 1996).

Staff productivity

Staff productivity within services is also a difficult issue for managers. According to Cowell (1984), there are several reasons why **service productivity** is difficult to measure. The main reason is that services are 'performed' not 'produced' and there are too many external factors influencing this live creation of a product. The service production process simply cannot be controlled and replicated as reliably and consistently as a mechanised factory line. Service productivity particularly suffers from the involvement of the customer. If customers do not fill forms in properly, if they are not familiar with procedures or they do not really know what they want, if they turn up late for appointments, if they want to spend time in idle chatter rather than getting on with the business in hand, then it will take service staff much longer to deliver the product. Where productivity is measured in terms of the number of transactions handled, the amount of revenue generated, or the number of customers processed, such delays essentially caused by the customer can reflect unfairly on service staff. This raises the whole question, however, of what constitutes appropriate and fair measures of service productivity. A customer who is given a great deal of individual help or who feels that service staff have taken time for a friendly chat with them might well feel that they have received a much better quality service and appreciate not being treated with cold bureaucratic efficiency. It might be worth tolerating a slightly longer queue if you feel that you will be treated with care, respect and humanity when you get to the front of it. Definitions and measures of productivity therefore need to be flexible and sympathetic, striking a fine balance between the customer's needs and the business's need to work efficiently.

None of this absolves managers from looking at ways in which service productivity can be improved. There are several possibilities for delivering services more efficiently without necessarily detracting too much from their quality.

Staff. Through improved recruitment and training, staff can be given better skills and knowledge for dealing with customers. A clerk in a travel agency, for example, can develop a better knowledge of which tour operators offer which resorts so that the key brochures can be immediately pulled out in response to a customer query. Library staff can be fully trained in the use and potential of databases and on-line search mechanisms so that customers can have their problems solved immediately without having to wait for a 'specialist' to return from a lunch break. Improving the staff profile might also allow more delegation or empowerment of front line service staff. A customer does not want to be told, 'I can't do that without checking with my supervisor' and then have to wait while this happens. Staff should be given the responsibility and flexibility to deal with the real needs of customers as they arise.

Systems and technology. The design of the service process and the introduction of more advanced technology can both help to improve service productivity.

Example

Aircraft cannot take off until all passengers are properly seated and all cabin baggage is properly stowed away. Traditionally, airlines have managed this by allowing passengers sitting at the rear of the plane to board first so that they can move quickly down to their seats without pushing past the front passengers. This meant, however, that passengers with seats next to the aisles were constantly having to move in and out of their seats to let window passengers in, causing disruption and delay.

Lufthansa, therefore, decided that this was still inefficient and introduced a new boarding system whereby passengers sitting at window seats are invited to board first. They could get their luggage stowed and settle into their seats without being disturbed, leaving space clear for those seated next to the aisle to sort themselves out without distractions. It is hoped that this new system will speed up the boarding process and reduce the risks of the flight missing its take-off slot.

Technology combined with well-designed systems can be very powerful. Libraries, for example, have used technology to improve their productivity. Laser scanning barcodes in books make it far quicker to issue or receive returned items than with the old manual ticketing systems. This has also allowed them to improve the quality of their service. The librarian can immediately tell you, for instance, which books you have on loan, whether or not another reader has reserved a book you have, and which other reader has borrowed the book you want. Some technology means that the service provider need not provide human interaction at all. In the financial sector, 'hole in the wall' cash machines, for instance, give customers 24-hour, 7-days-a-week access to their bank accounts, usually without long queues, and because of the way these machines are networked they provide hundreds of convenient access points. As discussed at p. 757, British Airways, for example, uses automated call handling (ACH) for customers' telephone enquiries. Standard queries, such as arrival and departure times for specific flights and some ticket sales, can be dealt with by a menu-driven computer system without the need for a 'live' human operator, if the customer is calling from a touchtone telephone.

Within service premises, post offices, banks and supermarkets all use express tills or checkouts, for instance, to process customers with small or straightforward transactions faster. Supermarkets also use laser scanning of barcodes not only to help in stock control but also to move goods through the checkout more quickly. The problem with this, however, is that the customer still intrudes. Customers pack their shopping bags at their own pace, and then have to fumble in purses or wallets for enough cash or for a credit card to pay for it all.

Reduce service levels. Reducing service levels to increase productivity can be dangerous if it leads to a perception of reduced quality in the customer's mind, especially if customers have become used to high levels of service. Reducing the number of staff available to deliver the service might lead to longer queues or undue pressure on the customer to move through the system more quickly.

Example

If a busy doctor's surgery introduces a system that schedules appointments at five minute intervals, one of two things might happen. A doctor who wants to maintain the schedule might hurry patients through consultations without listening to them properly or allowing them time to relax enough to be able to say what is really worrying them. Patients might then feel that they have not got what they came for and that the doctor does not actually care about them. Alternatively, the doctor may put the patient first, and regardless of the five-minute rule take as long as is needed to sort out the individual patient. The patient emerges satisfied, but those still in the waiting room whose appointments are up to half an hour late might not feel quite so happy.

Reducing service levels also opens up opportunities for competitors to create a new differential advantage. As discussed in Chapter 13, discount supermarkets such as Aldi, Netto and Lidl keep their prices low partly through minimising service. Thus there are few checkout operators, no enquiries desk, and nobody to help customers pack their bags. The more mainstream supermarkets have been able to use this as a way of emphasizing the quality of their service, and have deliberately invested in higher levels of service to further differentiate themselves. Thus Tesco, for example, promised its customers that if there were more than two people in a checkout queue, another checkout would be opened if possible. Tesco also announced that it was taking on extra staff in most of its branches, simply to help customers. These staff might help to unload your trolley on to the conveyor belt or pack your bags, or if you get to the checkout and realise that you have forgotten the milk, they will go and get it for you.

Customer interaction. Productivity might be improved by changing the way the customer interacts with the service provider and its staff. It might also mean developing or changing the role of the customer in the service delivery itself. The role of technology in assisting self-service through cash machines has already been mentioned. The whole philosophy of the supermarket is based on the idea of increasing the customer's involvement in the shopping process through self-service.

Customers might also have to get used to dealing with a range of different staff members, depending on their needs or the pressures on the service provider. Medical practices now commonly operate on a group basis, for example, and a patient might be asked to see any one of three or four doctors. If the patient only wants a repeat prescription then the receptionist might be able to handle it, or if a routine procedure is necessary, such as a blood test or a cervical smear, then the practice nurse might do it. The role of students in the delivery of educational services has also evolved, partly as a means of improving academic staff productivity. Student-centred learning for example, means that students are encouraged to take more responsibility for their own education, with academic staff providing the broad structure, ongoing guidance and assessment rather than handing out the whole learning experience to a passive audience on a plate. This has led to a greater degree of partnership between staff and students, and in many ways has actually improved the quality of the service delivered.

If any measures are taken that relate to the nature of customer involvement and interaction, the service provider might have a problem convincing customers that these are for their benefit and that they should co-operate. Careful use of marketing communications is needed, through both personal and non-personal media, to inform customers of the benefits, to persuade them of the value of what is being done and to reassure them that their co-operation will not make too many heavy demands on them.

Reduce mismatch between supply and demand. Sometimes demand exceeds supply. Productivity might well then be high, but it could be higher still if the excess demand could be accommodated. Some customers will not want to wait and might decide either to take their business to an alternative service provider or not to purchase at all. At other times, supply will exceed demand and productivity will be low because resources are lying idle. If the service provider can even out some of these fluctuations, then perhaps overall productivity can be improved.

Hotels such as this Parador in Spain lower their prices in the off-season in order to maximse occupancy.

The service provider might be able to control aspects of supply and demand through fairly simple measures. Pricing, for example, might help to divert demand away from busy periods or to create extra demand at quiet times. Off-peak or off-season tariffs, prices or fares or time-specific promotions ('10 per cent off the price of a haircut on Wednesday afternoons between now and Christmas', for example) might help to achieve this. An appointment booking system too might help to ensure a steady trickle of customers at intervals that suit the service provider. The danger is, though, that if the customer cannot get the appointment slot that they want, they might not bother at all. Finding alternative uses for staff and facilities during quiet times can also create more demand and increase productivity. Universities, for instance, have long had the problem of facilities lying idle at weekends and during vacations. They have solved this by turning halls of residence into conference accommodation or cheap and cheerful holiday lets in the vacations, or hiring out their more attractive and historic buildings for weddings and other functions at weekends, with catering provided.

If the service provider cannot or does not wish to divert demand away from busy times, then the ability to supply the service to the maximum number of customers will have to be examined. If the peaks in demand are fairly predictable, then many service providers will bring in part-time staff to increase available supply. There might be limits to their ability to do so, however, which are imposed by constraints of physical space and facilities. A supermarket has only so many checkouts, a bank has only so many tills, a barber's shop has only so many chairs, a restaurant has only so many tables. Nevertheless, part-time staff can still be useful behind the scenes, easing the burden on front line staff and speeding up the throughput of customers.

In other situations, physical constraints are less important.

Example

A business school operating a modular scheme might find that there are substantial numbers of students wanting to take marketing options. This might not put too much pressure on the weekly lecture programme, since as long as a large enough lecture theatre is available, a lecturer can talk to 200 students as easily as to 50. The problems arise with the number of seminar groups to be serviced and part-time staff might be brought in to take some of the burden off full-time staff. Physical facilities are not likely to pose too many problems in this case, especially if staff and students are prepared to tolerate less popular timetable slots such as 4 p.m. on a Friday!

Internal marketing is an extremely important element of service creation and delivery. As Heskett *et al.* (1994) suggest, there is a direct link between employee satisfaction and productivity, customer satisfaction and loyalty, and profit. If service creation and consumption are inseparable, then it is logical to assume that staff attitudes, efficiency and competence are also inseparable from the customer's judgement of quality, and thus satisfaction.

NON-PROFIT MARKETING

The marketing concerns of **non-profit organisations**, including those in the public sector, became increasingly important over the 1980s and 1990s for a number of reasons. In the UK, the government pursued a deliberate policy of exposing public sector services to commercial market forces and of increasing their autonomy and accountability.

Charities too have found that the environment within which they operate has changed. There are many more charities competing for attention and donations, and the attitudes of both individual and corporate donors has changed. The case of the corporate donor was discussed earlier at pp. 807–8. Thus all sorts of organisations that have not traditionally seen themselves as 'being in business' have had to become more business-like, fighting for and justifying resources and funding.

This section, therefore, discusses the characteristics that differentiate non-profit from profit-making organisations. Then, the implications for marketing will be explored.

Classifying non-profit organisations

TABLE 23.3
Non-profit organisations

Public sector	Private sector
Public hospital	Private hospital
University	Private school
Public library	Charity
State railway	

As suggested above, non-profit organisations can exist in either the public or private sectors, although the distinction between them is rather blurred in some cases. A hospital that treats both National Health patients and private patients, for example, is involved in both sectors. Table 23.3 gives examples of organisations in both sectors.

Characteristics of non-profit organisations

Clearly, all non-profit organisations operate in different types of market and face different challenges, but they do have a number of characteristics in common that differentiate them from ordinary commercial businesses (Lovelock and Weinberg, 1984; Kotler, 1982). These are as follows.

Multiple publics. Most profit-making organisations focus their attention on their target market. Although they do depend on shareholders to provide capital, most day-to-day cash flow is generated from sales revenue. Effectively, therefore, the recipient of the product or service and the source of income is one and the same. Non-profit organisations, however, have to divide their attention much more equally between two important groups, as shown in Fig 23.5. First, there are the customers or clients who receive the product or service. They do not necessarily pay the full cost of it. A charity, for example might offer advice or help free to those in need, whereas a museum might charge a nominal entry fee that is heavily subsidised from other sources. Thus clients or customers concern the non-profit organisation largely from a *resource allocation* point of view. The second important group is the funders, those who provide the income to allow the organisation to do its work.

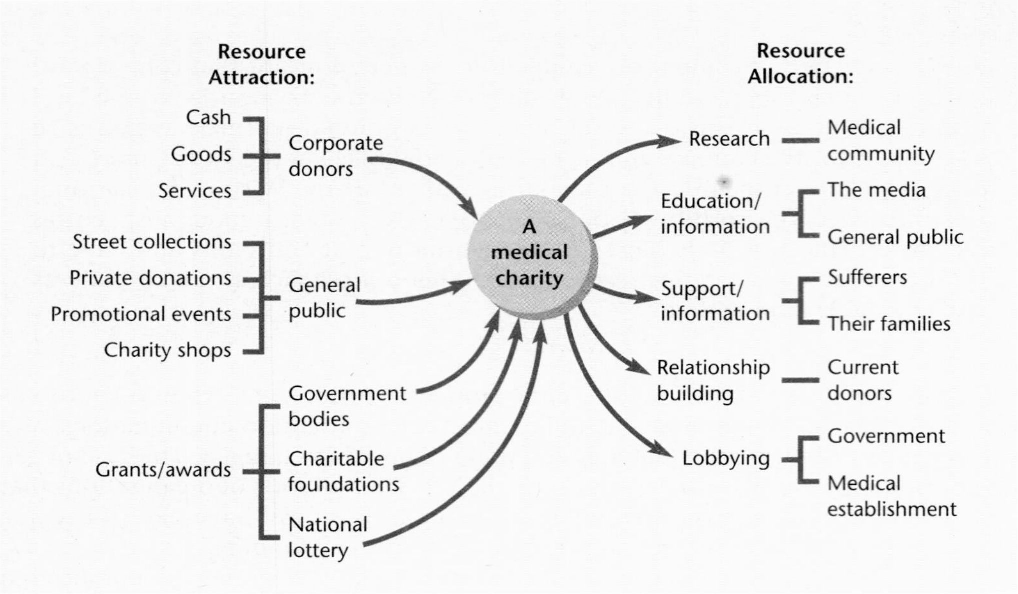

FIGURE 23.5

Non-profit
organisations:
Multiple publics

Multiple objectives. One definition of marketing offered earlier in this book is to create and hold a customer at a profit. As we have seen, there are many different ways of achieving this and many possible subobjectives on the way, but in the end for most organisations it is all about profit. As a result success criteria can be fairly easily defined and measured. In the non-profit sector, however, there might be multiple objectives, some of which could be difficult to define and quantify. They might concern fundraising, publicity generation, contacting customers or clients (or getting them to visit you), dispensing advice, increasing geographic coverage or giving grants to needy clients.

Example

An art gallery will want to get visitors through its doors, but might equally be concerned with lobbying for more cash from the UK government's Arts Council to cover its day-to-day running and maintenance costs. Then, it might want to raise funds from various sources to help to buy a particular painting that is about to come up for auction and it might also want to find a commercial sponsor for a one-off exhibition of pre-Raphaelite paintings. In parallel with all that, it might also want to run a series of education programmes for schools and colleges.

Service rather than physical goods orientation. Most non-profit organisations are delivering a service product of some sort rather than manufacturing and selling a physical product. Many of the services marketing concepts already covered in this chapter therefore apply to them. In some non-profit bodies, the emphasis is on generating awareness about a cause, perhaps to generate funds, and giving information to allow people to help themselves solve a problem. Particularly where charities are concerned in generating funds, donors as a target audience are not directly benefiting from their participation in the production of this service, other than from the warm glow of satisfying their social conscience. This contrasts with the more commercial sector, where the customer who pays gets a specific service performed for their benefit (a haircut, a washing machine repaired, a bank account managed for them etc.).

Fundraising and image creation

A hospice in the north of England cares for children who are dying of cancer. In order to buy even better equipment and to support its counselling work it needs to raise funds in addition to those provided through the National Health Service. The hospice's name and purpose is well known in the locality, and so regular 'flag days', collecting donations on the streets, are well supported. Every weekend, instant prize scratch cards are also sold in local high streets to maintain a more regular flow of funds. Special events are staged to raise money for specialist pieces of equipment, and these are well advertised in local media, such as newspapers, radio and on public transport. Again, these events tend to be very generously supported by the public.

The hospice has also adopted a cuddly hedgehog character as its logo, and this appears on all publications and publicity material. Soft toys of the character have also been manufactured, which can be bought either from the hospice itself or at the various events. The character also appears on Christmas cards and tea towels. The tea towels are sold through local schools for £2.95 each. The pupils of a school draw pencil sketches of themselves and their teachers and these are printed on the towels along with the hospice's logo.

With thanks to Helen Bussell, University of Teesside.

Public scrutiny and accountability. Where public money is concerned or where organisations rely on donations, there is greater public interest in the activities and efficiency of the organisation. To maintain the flow of donations, a charity has to be seen to be transparently honest, trustworthy and to be producing 'results'. The public wants to know how much money is going into administrative costs and how much into furthering the real work of the charity.

Marketing implications

In general terms, the same principles of marketing apply equally to non-profit organisation as to any purely commercial concern. There are, however, a few specific points to note. A non-profit organisation might have quite a wide-ranging **product portfolio**, if the needs of both funders and customers or clients are taken into account. Their products might, for instance, vary from information, reassurance and advice to medical research and other practical help such as cash grants or equipment. Donors might be 'purchasing' association with a high profile good cause or the knowledge that they have done a good deed by giving. Because the products vary so much, from the extremely intangible to the extremely tangible, and because there are so many different publics to serve, a strong corporate image and good marketing communication are particularly important to pull the whole organisation together.

If dispensing information and advice, or increasing the profile of a cause are central objectives of the non-profit organisation, then **marketing communication** is an essential tool. This might mean using conventional advertising media, although that can be expensive for organisations such as smaller charities unless advertising agencies and media owners can be persuaded to offer their services cheap or free as a donation in kind. *Publicity* can also be an invaluable tool for the non-profit organisation, not only because of its cost effectiveness, but also because of its ability to reach a wide range of audiences. Publicity might encourage fundraising, help to educate people or generate clients or customers. Association with high-profile commercial sponsors can similarly help to spread the message, through publicity, sponsored fundraising events or joint or sponsored promotions.

In sectors where a non-profit organisation offers a more clearly defined product to a specific target segment within a competitive market, then a more standard approach to marketing communication might be used. A university, for example, is offering degree courses to potential students. As discussed elsewhere in this book, it might use advertising media to tell potential students why this is the best place to study; printed material such as the prospectus, brochures and leaflets to give more detail about the institution, its location and the courses on offer; visits to schools and education fairs to meet potential recruits face to face, and publicity to increase awareness and to improve its corporate image.

Pricing is applied somewhat differently in the non-profit sector than in the commercial world. As mentioned earlier, those providing income might be totally different from those receiving the product. It is accepted in most areas of the non-profit sector that the recipient might not have to bear the full cost of the service or product provided. In other words, the recipient's need comes first rather than the ability to pay. In the profit-making sector it is more likely to be the other way around: if you can pay for it, you can have it. Non-profit pricing, therefore, might be very flexible and varied. Some customers will not be asked to pay at all, others will be asked to make whatever donation they can afford for the service they have received, others will be charged a full market price. A UK university, for example, receives government funding for UK and EU

MISSING

We can help

Over 70% of the vulnerable missing cases reported to us are found. We care, we listen in confidence and give all the help we can to families of missing persons. But we respect that everyone has the right to go missing.

MESSAGE HOME 0500 700 740
For those who have gone missing this confidential helpline enables you to let those left behind know that you are safe and well.

Can you help?

We are successful because, as an independent charity we open doors that the authorities can't. But we rely entirely on public donations to continue our work. A donation of any size is most welcome.

0500 700 700
FREE CALL
NATIONAL MISSING PERSONS HELPLINE

Roebuck House, 284-286 Upper Richmond Road West, London SW14 7JE.
Registered charity No 1020419.

Like many charities, NMPH has to attract resources from a wide range of donors and then allocate them to its various activities and services.

students to cover tuition costs, but other foreign students are charged full cost fees. Companies who purchase training courses from the university will also be charged the going commercial rate on a profit-making basis, with any surplus being ploughed back into the university.

Issues of distribution, process and physical evidence, where applicable, are similar for non-profit organisations to those of other types of organisation. The organisation has to ensure that the product or service is available when and where the customer or client can conveniently access it. This might or might not involve physical premises. Clearly, non-profit institutions such as universities, hospitals, museums and the like do operate from premises. They face the same issues as any other service provider of making sure that those premises are sufficiently well equipped to allow a service to be delivered and to deal with likely demand. They also have to realise that the premises are part of the marketing effort and contribute to the customer's or client's perception of quality. Prospective students visiting a university on an open day might not be able to judge the quality of the courses very well, but they can certainly tell whether the campus would be a good place for them to live and work, whether the teaching rooms are pleasant and well equipped, and how well resourced the library and IT facilities seem to be.

Some non-profit organisations that focus mainly on giving information and advice by mail or by telephone do not, of course, need to invest in smart premises. Their priority is to ensure that customers or clients are aware of how to access the service and that enquiries are dealt with quickly, sympathetically and effectively.

Example

A charity providing support to AIDS victims and their families might advertise its telephone helpline or mail address through leaflets available from health centres, libraries and Citizens' Advice Bureaux, as well as through more mainstream advertising media.

MARKETING IN ACTION

The National Missing Persons Helpline

The National Missing Persons Helpline (NMPH) was registered as a charity in the UK in 1992. It was set up because at any one time there are up to 250 000 people 'missing' in the UK, yet there was no central body to offer advice and support to missing persons' families, to co-ordinate information on missing people, or for missing people to contact for help. Although many people do 'go missing' on purpose and do not wish to be found, others disappear because they are distressed, ill or confused and need help and reassurance to solve their problems. A few are the victims of abduction.

The NMPH, therefore, offers a number of services, including:

- a national 24-hour telephone helpline for families of missing people
- a confidential 'Free Call Message Home' 24-hour telephone helpline so that missing people who do not want to be 'found' can at least leave a message to reassure their families that they are all right
- a national computerised database of missing people
- searching for missing people, using contacts among the homeless population, and advertising and publicity
- an image-enhancing 'age progression' computer that can create a photograph of what someone who has been missing for several years, might look like now.

The charity's 'customers' are not just missing people and their families. The police find the NMPH and its database invaluable in assisting with identifying corpses and helping with missing persons cases generally.

In marketing terms, the NMPH has a few problems, many of which are common to many non-profit organisations. Its main one is generating a steady and reliable flow of income. The NMPH does not charge for its services, even to the police. It hopes, of course, that those who have benefited from the service will make a donation, but this is unlikely to cover the full cost. It thus relies heavily on cash donations, corporate donations of goods and services, fundraising and promotional events. It is particularly dependent on some of the 'donations in kind' it receives, in order to carry on its work effectively. In 1993–4, for example, Carlton Television and Meridian Broadcasting between them donated the equivalent of £3 million in television air time, and *The Big Issue* magazine donated £78 000 of advertising space.

Maintaining this sort of high profile through marketing communication is vital not only for the continuing work of the NMPH, but also to help build the charity's image to maintain a flow of donations. The NMPH has a particular image problem in that it is not involved in any matter that the general public find easy to relate to or to sympathise with (compared with animals', children's, or medical charities, for instance). This, therefore, is why it might make better use of its famous patrons such as the Duchess of Gloucester, Richard Branson, Sir Cliff Richard, Gaby Roslin and Gordon Roddick (co-founder of The Body Shop) to strengthen its public profile.

Sources: NMPH literature; briefing given by Elaine Quigley at Buckinghamshire College, February 1996.

CHAPTER SUMMARY

Many goods include some element of service as part of their product package, but those for which service is a major element of what the customer is buying are known specifically as *service products*. Although the variety of service products is very wide, everything from air travel to accountancy, fast food to pharmacies and doctors to degrees, all of them share some common characteristics that differentiate them from other types of product. With service products, for instance, there is often no transfer of ownership of anything, because a service is intangible. Services are also perishable, because they are generally performed at a particular time and are consumed as they are produced. This means that they cannot be stored in advance of demand, nor can they be kept in stock until a customer comes along. The customer is often directly involved in the production of the service product and thus the manufacture and delivery of the product cannot be separated. It also means there is extensive interaction between the customer and the service provider's staff. Finally, because of the 'live' nature of the service experience and the central role of human interaction, it is very difficult to standardise the service experience.

These peculiar characteristics of services have implications for marketing strategies and management. The normal model of a marketing mix consisting of the 4Ps is useful, as far as it goes, and many of the principles associated with the 4Ps and physical products are also appropriate to services. Overall, however, the 4Ps are insufficient, and an additional 3Ps, people, processes and physical evidence have been added to deal with the extra dimensions peculiar to services. *People* takes account of the human interactions involved in the service product; *physical evidence* looks at the tangible elements that contribute either directly or indirectly to the creation, delivery, quality or positioning of the service; and *processes* defines the systems that allow the service to be created and delivered efficiently, reliably and cost effectively.

Service quality is an important but difficult issue for managers, because it is hard to define and measure. Judgement of quality arises largely from customers' comparisons of what they expected from various facets of the service with what they think they actually received. Management can ensure that the service product is designed with the customer's real needs and wants in mind; they can make sure that it is adequately resourced; they can make sure that it is delivered properly; and they can try not to raise unrealistic expectations in the mind of the customer. In the end, quality is a subjective issue. Different customers will pick up on different aspects as being of prime importance, and the same customer might even react differently to the same service on different occasions.

Staff are an important element of service and its delivery. The service provider has to ensure that staff are fully qualified and trained to deal with customers and their needs, and to deliver the service reliably and consistently. The emphasis that is put on this will vary depending on whether staff have direct or indirect involvement with customers, and whether they are visible to customers or not. Like quality, productivity is a difficult management issue because of the live nature of services and the involvement of the customer in the process. Managers have to think and plan carefully in terms of staff recruitment and training, systems and technology, the service levels offered and the way in which customers interact with the service, to try to maintain control and efficiency in the service delivery system. Trying to manage supply and demand can also help to streamline productivity.

Non-profit organisations, which might be in the public or private sector, form a specialist area of services marketing. They differ because they are likely to serve multiple publics; they have multiple objectives that can often be difficult to quantify; they offer services, but the funder of the service is likely to be different from the recipient of it, and finally, they are subject to closer scrutiny and tighter accountability than many other organisations. It is also possible that where non-profit organisations are in receipt of government funding or where their existence or operation is subject to regulation, there will be limits placed on their freedom to use the marketing mix as they wish. Pricing or promotion, for example, might be prescribed or set within narrow constraints.

Key words and phrases

Heterogeneity	*Internal marketing*	*Services*
Inseparability	*Non-profit organisations*	*Visible staff*
Intangibility	*Perishability*	
Interactive marketing	*Service productivity*	

QUESTIONS FOR REVIEW

23.1 What are the main characteristics that distinguish *services* from physical products?

23.2 How can *tangibility* be introduced into service products?

23.3 Define *inseparability* and its implications for the service product.

23.4 What are the 7Ps of the services marketing mix?

23.5 What are the 10 criteria that affect customers' perceptions of service quality?

23.6 Define the barriers to service quality.

23.7 What is *internal marketing* and why is it important in service products?

23.8 In what ways can service *productivity* be improved?

23.9 In what ways do non-profit organisations differ from other types of business?

23.10 Why might a non-profit organisation's approach to pricing differ from that of other types of business?

QUESTIONS FOR DISCUSSION

23.1 Discuss the impact of perishability on the management and marketing of a service business.

23.2 Choose a service business and analyse its marketing offering in terms of the 7Ps.

23.3 Design a short questionnaire for assessing the quality of service offered by a local dental practice.

23.4 In what ways might the following service organisations define and improve their productivity:

(a) a theme park;
(b) a university;
(c) a fast food outlet?

23.5 What do you think might be the main sources of revenue for the following types of non-profit organisation and what revenue generation problems do you think each faces?

(a) a small local charity;
(b) a National Health Service hospital;
(c) a public museum?

The Education Catering Service

The Local Government Act of 1988 introduced market forces to the operation of the UK's local government services. Compulsory competitive tendering was to be applied to a number of local authority services which had previously enjoyed virtual monopoly status. This meant that local authority departments and agencies would be required to bid for contracts, against outside competition, to carry out services traditionally performed by local authorities.

Cleveland County Council's Education Catering Service (ECS) used to be the sole provider of meals for state-run schools in the county. When compulsory competitive tendering was introduced, ECS naturally wanted to win the school meals contract in order to maintain its position. It recognised the importance of providing a midday meal for pupils and believed that it was the organisation best suited to offer this service.

As market principles were to be introduced into the provision of school meals, ECS decided to meet the challenge by adopting marketing techniques. However, its commitment that 'each pupil has the opportunity to obtain a midday meal that is balanced, nutritionally sound and adequate for his/her needs' would underpin any strategy adopted. ECS was, therefore, clear on the core product it was offering. A less clear aspect was identifying the customer. Was it the pupil consuming the meal or the parent paying for it? The school also played an important role, as it collected dinner money and provided dining facilities (usually school halls or classrooms used for teaching during the rest of the school day).

As ECS was so dependent on the goodwill of the schools, the co-operation of head teachers was sought early on in the campaign. The County Education Officer sent a memo to all head teachers highlighting the importance of school meals, informing them of the planned marketing strategy, and inviting closer liaison with the school cook. The assistance of school cooks in educational programmes directed at publicising healthy eating was also offered. School cooks and those concerned with the management of ECS attended a short training course on marketing. They were also informed of the likely impact of the 1988 Local Government Act and the new marketing strategy.

Existing recipes and menus were closely evaluated. Schools were offered a choice of menus and service systems. Head teachers could opt for a centrally planned, single choice meal (which allowed for local variations) delivered to the pupil's dining table, or a cafeteria system with either a limited or a more extensive choice of menus. In secondary schools, a cash cafeteria system with all elements individually priced could be provided to allow pupils greater choice. There would be a standard charge for each meal, but with free meals for those pupils who qualified. Prices for providing the catering service were, however, to reflect the full cost of implementing the service and maintaining the required standard.

To promote ECS and the concept of healthy eating, a cartoon chef called Eric (Eating Right In Cleveland) was introduced. He would appear in all publications and publicity material. A series of bright posters, in which Eric featured prominently were made available to schools.

ECS was successful in winning the contract to supply Cleveland Education Authority schools with meals. Although take-up rates for meals are fairly high compared with those in other parts of the UK, increasing numbers of children are opting not to eat a school dinner.

Case prepared by Helen Bussell, University of Teesside.

Questions

1 One difficulty facing ECS was deciding who the customer was. Identify all the different groups who would have an interest in the product offered.

2 For each of the groups you defined in question 1, outline how their needs and priorities in terms of a school meals service might differ.

3 Outline the 'competition' facing a school meals provider such as ECS. Can marketing help ECS to overcome the competitive threat?

4 Evaluate ECS's marketing strategy. Has ECS adopted the 'right' approach?

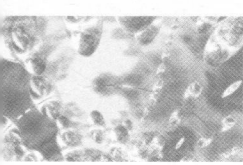
Day visitor attractions

Having a good day out is a preoccupation of many Europeans who have the cash and the leisure time to 'get away from it all'. The range of attractions that caters for this demand has grown considerably over the last 10 years and the prospects for further growth are considerable. Day visitor attractions can range from a cultural and historical experience at Westminster Abbey or Nôtre Dame through to the manufactured service experience of places like Legoland where 'the imagination knows no bounds' and a safe 'land within a land' has been created. Disneyland too, with its rides, shows and escapism, has achieved international fame.

Three examples of successful day visitor attractions are presented within this case study to highlight the typical marketing problems of maintaining interest and visitor levels once the initial launch has taken place and customers have sampled the delights on offer. Although the product they are selling is 'fun and escapism', these are commercial organisations that have to make the same sort of strategic decisions as any industrial or consumer goods operator.

Aillwe Cave, Ireland

Aillwe Cave is situated in the remote Burren region of Ireland, famous for its limestone scenery, cultural heritage and spring flowers. Although it cannot match the grandeur of many other European caverns, the heritage of the cave systems in the Dordogne of France, or the commercialisation of the Cheddar caves in the UK, it has became a major day visitor attraction along the west coast of Ireland.

Although the cave has been open for around 16 years, the problem is keeping up a regular flow of customers. This is necessary to sustain the capacity needed and to generate sufficient revenue to plough back into further development, both in the cave and elsewhere on the site. Particular attention has been given to maximising the amount that consumers spend on their visits. This is achieved by careful routing of pedestrian flows through the gift shop and nearby restaurant, as well as developing a cheese making facility as a form of agritourism. Visitors can see the cheeses being made and make purchases. The finished cheese products are also branded for sale in speciality stores.

It is attention to detail in terms of the visitor experience that has helped to make Aillwe a successful enterprise. While some bear remains and other prehistoric remnants have been found on the site, the human and geological interest, although comparing well with other Irish cave systems, cannot hope to match the intrinsic interest of better developed systems. Aillwe makes up for this, however, through employing and training well qualified staff who can almost be called 'actors' as they build up atmosphere during the guided tours. Their driving principle is to offer an impeccable product experience, delivered right first time. They are even flexible enough to handle tours in another language, as long as they have advance notice. Considerable attention is also given to the physical infrastructure to ensure that buildings and materials blend in with the local environment. A litter free policy is vigorously enforced throughout the site.

From a marketing perspective, the challenge is to attract visitors in the first place. Research has shown that half of the visitors are Irish, and they often make repeat visits with the extended family. The rest of the business, however, comes from European and American tourists. Aillwe advertises in a range of tourist guides and employs a full-time promotions assistant to develop literature, handle PR, implement mailings and organise group tours. Signposting is also very important to attract passing trade, with advertising hoarding and signs starting 25 km from the site.

The main strategic priority is to decide how to expand the business. Should it be by developing the cave site further or by developing new day visitor attractions such as a wildlife park, an aquarium or a butterfly farm? Either way, the approach to promoting and delivering the service experience would remain the same.

Tivoli Gardens, Denmark

The Tivoli Gardens in Copenhagen, founded in 1843, could be regarded as one of the first generation of theme parks. Situated in the centre of Copenhagen, it offered the classic arts, including a famous orchestra that employed 150 musicians in the summer months, and offered light entertainment, fairground rides, a variety of restaurants and a wide display of shrubs and flowers. For many years, it offered all the ingredients for an entertaining day out. Unfortunately, over the past 30 years, the number of visitors to the park has been falling, from five million in the 1950s to 3.5 million in the 1995 season. As the Tivoli Gardens is a publicly owned and quoted company, the painful drop in turnover and profit has been all too obvious. Although it was one of the world's most visited parks, its problems were mounting.

The reasons for the decline suggested by Tivoli range from changing consumer location patterns, with the shift to the suburbs, lack of parking space (it is in a city centre location), the growth of new leisure pursuits and not least the problems of a season only four months per year. Options for reversing the decline include opening at Christmas as well as between May and September, spending more on promotion and even licensing the concept elsewhere. A Tivoli park was expected to open in Japan in 1997. The idea of adding new rides and entertainment was rejected, as Tivoli is happy to play on an image which has been described as 'quaintly old fashioned'.

Lightwater Valley, UK

Lightwater Valley describes itself as the 'Ultimate Country Theme Park'. Situated close to Ripon in North Yorkshire, it is well placed to attract day visitors from the large conurbations in the UK's north east region and West Yorkshire. The catchment area within a two-hour drive is something like eight million people and a significant proportion of visitors actually come from that catchment area. The park is open from April to October and is best known for its three 'white knuckle rides': the Rat, Soopa Loopa and the Ultimate. Like most theme parks, all rides are free after the entrance fee has been paid. Again, like many other theme parks, revenue is generated not only from entrance fees, but also from retailing and restaurants.

Lightwater Valley is no different from other theme parks in targeting the family market segment. While the greatest appeal may be to children and teenagers, the 16–25 year old age group are especially attracted to the 'white knuckle rides'. In 1994, the Ultimate roller coaster featured in the *Guinness Book of Records* as the longest one in the world, being over 2 km long and covering 44 acres of land. This ride alone acts as a major pull to the park. Meanwhile, the Rat ride goes through a mock sewer system underground, an illusion reinforced by dripping water and almost complete darkness. The family adventure side of the park offers small roller coasters, water splash rides, a crazy golf course, a miniature railway and a boating lake. In addition there are areas for young fun, catering outlets and retail shops for toys, jewellery, pictures and china, as well as restaurants.

Although the physical infrastructure is an important part of the service experience, the experience is also strongly influenced by the staff. Lightwater has to be very mindful of this area, as most staff are seasonal. Staff have to be competent enough to handle the safety aspects, as well as dealing with customers. There is a particular focus on inducting and training new staff at the start of each season. The organisation has gained an 'Investors in People' award, reflecting the care given to developing staff.

Sources: Carnegy (1995); company literature.

Questions

1 Outline the issues facing a theme park under each of the elements of the services marketing mix.

2 One of Aillwe Cave's target markets is groups of foreign tourists. How might Aillwe's marketing approaches to this segment differ from those aimed at the domestic Irish family segment?

3 What are the benefits to the Tivoli Gardens of remaining 'quaintly old fashioned'?

4 If Lightwater Valley wanted to attract more visitors, what sorts of marketing actions could it take?

REFERENCES TO CHAPTER 23

Barrett, P. (1996), 'Money Markets', *Marketing*, 25 April, pp. 18–19.

Booms, B. H. and Bitner, M. J. (1981),' Marketing Strategies and Organisation Structures for Service Firms', in J. Donnelly and W. R. George (eds.), *Marketing of Services*, American Marketing Association. .

Carnegy, H. (1995), 'Tough Times for a Historic Park', *Financial Times*, 6 November.

Cowell, D. (1984), *The Marketing of Services*, Butterworth-Heinemann.

Daneshkhu, S. (1996), 'Leisure Parks Fund Launched', *Financial Times*, 10 February, p. 9.

Devlin, S. J. and Dong, H. K. (1994), 'Service Quality From the Customers' Perspective', *Marketing Research*, 6(1), pp. 5–13.

Harris, N. G. (1995), 'Do Passengers Complain Too Much?', *Modern Railways*, October, pp. 626–7.

Heskett, J. L. *et al.* (1994), 'Putting the Service–Profit Chain to Work', *Harvard Business Review*, March/April, pp. 164–74.

Jolley, R. (1995), 'Designer Brings Style to a New-Look Novotel', *Travel Trade Gazette*, 24 May, p. 9.

Kotler, P. (1982), *Marketing for Non-Profit Organisations*, (2nd edn), Prentice Hall.

Lovelock, C. H. (1996), *Services Marketing*, (3rd edn), Prentice Hall.

Lovelock, C. H. and Weinberg, C. B. (1984), *Marketing for Public and Non-Profit Managers*, John Wiley and Sons.

Mathews, B. P. and Clark, M. C. (1996), 'Comparability of Quality Determinants in Internal and External Service Encounters', in *Proceedings: Workshop on Quality Management in Services VI*, Universidad Carlos III de Madrid: 15–16 April.

Murphy, C. (1996), 'Front Seat for Cinema Brands', *Marketing*, 28 March, p. 15.

Parasuraman, A. *et al.* (1985), 'A Conceptual Model of Service Quality and Its Implications For Future Research', *Journal of Marketing*, 49(Fall), pp. 41–50.

Rawsthorn, A. (1996), 'UCI Set to Open Six More Cinema Complexes', *Financial Times*, 30 January, p. 18.

Sasser, W. E. *et al.* (1978), *Management of Service Operations: Text, Cases and Readings*, Allyn & Bacon.

Shostack, L. G. (1977), 'Breaking Free From Product Marketing', *Journal of Marketing*, 41(April), pp. 73–80.

Zeithaml, V. *et al.* (1988). 'SERVQUAL: A Multiple Item Scale for Measuring Consumer Perceptions of Service Quality', *Journal of Retailing*, 64(1), pp. 13–37.

Zeithaml, V. *et al.* (1990), *Delivering Quality Service: Balancing Customer Perceptions and Expectations*, The Free Press.

24 Marketing and the Smaller Business

LEARNING OBJECTIVES

This chapter will help you to:

1 understand the special characteristics of a small business;

2 describe how marketing assists small business development from start up to maturity;

3 appreciate the impact of franchising as both a means of business expansion and a means of distribution;

4 identify the main stages in setting up a franchise operation.

INTRODUCTION

Although marketing principles apply equally across all organisations regardless of their size, the application of marketing often varies greatly. A large business with a well-defined management structure and a strong resource base applies marketing principles very differently from a small firm with limited resources and managerial skills trying to establish itself or grow in the market-place. Compare the situation facing a large fmcg organisation launching a new product with that of a new business starting up in the same market.

The large organisation is likely to have assessed the market carefully in terms of customer needs and competitive positions. Product development will probably have taken place over a period of time, including concept testing, prototype development and test marketing. By the launch date, sufficient research and analysis should have been undertaken to enable the organisation to be fairly sure that it has developed the best image and price position for the product. Distribution is likely to be achieved through supermarket chains, if there is clear evidence of the manufacturer's proposed promotional commitment and track record of successful product launches. Physical distribution is likely to be relatively straightforward, using existing systems. In short, the expertise, contacts and sheer resource power generate both the management commitment and strategic marketing integration that help to reduce the risks of failure. Of course, many products do still fail in spite of this, especially in saturated markets.

In contrast, a new small business faces an entirely different prospect. A significant lack of resources and a lack of expertise often means that many of the testing and trial stages in product development are limited or, in some cases, even overlooked altogether. This is made worse by inadequate market research. Secondary research calls for skill in searching and analysis, but even then might be too dated or too general to be really useful. Primary research requires careful design and a level of investment that many small businesses either cannot afford or cannot see as being necessary. When the product is launched, the consequences of poor research and testing become evident. Inappropriate positioning might lead to difficulty in becoming established, inconsistent or badly located price points, or even more critical, failure to gain distribution. Chapter 12 considered the dominant role of supermarkets in the distribution channel for fmcg products and the demands they make on their suppliers. New brands from unknown companies and brands that are not supported with comprehensive promotional and merchandising campaigns might never even get past the starting block. It is not surprising that a high percentage of new start businesses fail within two years. Despite the odds, however, some do succeed – especially where a more innovative strategy is adopted.

This chapter examines the marketing approaches and issues facing the small business sector that is so dominant across Europe. After a brief consideration of the definitions and nature of small business, the focus will shift to marketing decision making in the various stages of a small firm's development from launch to maturity. Although there is some dispute over the actual stages of development and the criteria that should be used to describe them, small business marketing strategy will nevertheless be shown to evolve as the organisation changes and grows. Finally this chapter provides a detailed consideration of franchising. For many, the franchise route is attractive for new business formation, but the decision to enter such a relationship has major implications for the marketing strategies of both the franchisor and the franchisee. Of course, some very large international organisations such as McDonald's or Pizza Hut can hardly be called small businesses. Under their umbrella, however, independent entrepreneurs running single outlets as small businesses can thrive.

THE NATURE OF SMALL BUSINESSES

According to Burns (1989a), **small businesses** are easier to describe than to define. Perhaps that is not surprising, given that the small business sector includes a large number of organisations at different stages in their development, displaying different strengths and weaknesses and operating in different markets. From a UK perspective, the Bolton Committee (Bolton, 1971) suggested a number of characteristics that describe rather than define small business:

- having a relatively small share of the market
- being owned in a personalised way, rather than through a formal management and governance structure
- being independent from outside control, thus enabling fully autonomous decision making.

Small share of the market

Marketing implications arise from all three criteria. A small share of the market means that a small business cannot influence either supply or prices in the same way as a market leader could. As previous chapters have suggested, however, much depends on how the market is defined. An organisation with a small share of a generally defined national or international market might nevertheless hold a dominant position in a specifically defined segment.

Systemcare is a niche operator that employs 45 staff. As a market leader in the provision of software solutions for the wholesale and distribution industries, the company has steadily grown in terms of sales turnover and space requirements from modest beginnings in 1988. After a management buyout in 1993, renewed emphasis was placed on product development and finding additional niche markets as a means of maintaining growth.

Personal ownership

Many small businesses are characterised by the fact that the owner of the business is closely involved with many facets of the operation. That kind of involvement is obviously intense in a sole trader or family business. However, even where 30 or 40 staff are involved, it is not uncommon to find the owner at the heart of all the strategic decisions and in many operational issues. That might mean repairing machinery in the morning and negotiating with a major customer in the afternoon. If the owner is not careful, however, this can lead to too much time being spent on operational fire fighting, and not enough priority being given to strategic marketing and external activities (Pettitt and Kirkwood, 1986). As a result of this involvement, it could be argued that if you want to assess the marketing strategy of a small firm, then look at the interests and focus given to it by the owner. To some owners marketing is central, and winning customers and serving their needs well is paramount. To others, marketing is a necessary evil to be undergone after the much more pleasurable act of producing something. The reality for many owners is that they are market analysts, strategists, sales representatives and service deliverers all rolled into one, but many still enjoy their time on the shop floor most of all. Only as the business grows and a more formal organisational structure starts to form can the owner manager start to delegate and use specialists where appropriate.

Independence

Finally, the independence of the small business means that there is no external interference. A wholly owned subsidiary, for example, might have its decisions influenced by a remote management board. The subsidiary might make its own promotional decisions, for instance, but have product range and pricing decisions imposed by the parent organisation. Many manufacturing subsidiaries of multinational corporations actually have little control over product development and specification. The small business thus has much more autonomy in its decision making, but of course cannot benefit from the resources and expertise of a parent company.

In franchised relationships, however, the autonomy of the small business becomes more questionable. A franchise is sometimes described as a contractual relationship between two independent entities, in which the franchisor blueprints the package that the franchisee offers to the end customer. The reality is that the contractual relationship often rigidly defines most of the strategic and operational marketing issues. The franchisee thus has little strategic autonomy, and sometimes even limited operational marketing autonomy.

Other differentiating factors

There are other approaches to describing the difference between large and small firms. Wynarczyk *et al.* (1993), for example, suggest that the level of uncertainty, the approach to innovation and organisational evolution are important factors that help to distinguish between large and small businesses. Each of these factors again has implications for marketing strategy.

Uncertainty

The degree of *external uncertainty* facing the small firm is thought to be greater than that facing the larger organisation. This might arise from having to accept market prices rather than influencing them; having a limited customer and product base; and the diversity of objectives set by small business owners. Without a diversified base of activity, any organisation can be vulnerable to sudden and unexpected changes in the business environment. Unlike the larger organisation, the smaller firm may not have the resources to shift its focus easily onto other areas of activity to overcome the difficulty.

There are also issues associated with *internal uncertainty*. In a smaller firm, the motivation and aspirations of the owner are key influences on the organisation's strategy and performance. In a larger business, owners seeking to control the organisation have to persuade and work through a number of senior and middle managers, sometimes creating internal conflict. There is no such problem in the small organisation, unless succession or partnerships are involved. In the small firm, ownership, control and management are often in very few hands, sometimes closely associated with the founding family.

Innovation

It has traditionally been thought that small firms are at the cutting edge of innovation (Schumpeter, 1934). A greater degree of flexibility, a higher tolerance of risk and a willingness to enter non-standard niches are all held to support small firms' innovative approaches. By providing specialisation in product or service terms the smaller firm can exist alongside the larger operator. The smaller firm might be highly successful in bringing non-standard technology to a market, but unless the venture is carefully planned and resourced, the small business might lack the resources to exploit the opportunity effectively. Many small firms appear to practise continuous and incremental innovation rather than going for radical change (Carson *et al.*, 1995). Given the scale of R&D investment now needed in many markets, smaller firms are finding it increasingly difficult to achieve any real breakthroughs. This is especially true where rapid penetration of worldwide markets is needed to beat the competition early. There is clearly a major difference between product or service invention and the commercialisation of that invention.

MARKETING IN ACTION

A reason to celebrate

Celebrations is a small business that is all about fun. The combination of disco music, dance floors, dining, DJs and a few streamers thrown in for good measure are the key ingredients of this new business's innovation. The owners began in business in 1991, operating a catering and sandwich bar on the south coast of England. This was soon followed by a prototype business called Jokers which offered a fun night out on specially organised party nights or for special occasions. The idea was not new, as fun theme dining was already popular in the USA. What the entrepreneurs did, however, was to transfer the idea to the UK successfully and then to package the concept commercially as the Celebrations franchise after a three year pilot period. The package did have to be fine tuned in terms of the entertainment and food options offered, and the marketing and business format. The claim made to potential franchisees is that 'the customers get their kicks and the franchisee gets the profits – and they all end up celebrating'. It remains to be seen how successful the offering will be for franchisees. Jokers/Celebrations have, however, already shown an innovative approach.

Source: Franchise International (1996b).

The truly innovative small firm is the exception rather than the rule, however. Most small firms are technologically very unsophisticated and make little, if any, contribution to technological change. They can often be characterised as 'me too' organisations, drawing on ideas developed and tested elsewhere.

Firm evolution

Finally, a small firm can be distinguished from a large one by its tendency to evolve more quickly and change, often with step-like growth as particular projects achieve success. This could be caused by taking on a new product range, deciding to enter a new market niche, or winning a significant new order. Each might require fundamental change within the business if it is to exploit the opportunity. This kind of evolution clearly has implications for management structure and decision making.

Example

C. D. Welding in the north east of England was launched in 1988 to offer specialist welding services on site. The idea was developed from the owner's previous career experience as a welding inspector. Since 1988, the business has gained larger and larger contracts, usually on a regional basis. This included working on the large Tees Barrage project. To cope with these changes, capacity had to be improved, new premises found and more sophisticated quality systems introduced. The process of diversification then began, building on experience and reputation. The precision engineering sector, using CNC machines, represented a further new challenge for the business.

Resource scarcity

Other factors differentiating small businesses centre around aspects such as resource scarcity, whether in management expertise, finance or the sales base. While all such factors have a certain intuitive appeal, they are virtually impossible to apply accurately to define the small business population. For those looking for a quantitative and easily applied test, the *number of employees* has emerged as the main criterion for distinguishing small firms. It benefits from being easily transferable across different EU member states and indeed beyond.

A consensus is emerging across the EU for defining different types of enterprises. This is important for comparative purposes and when seeking to develop policies for assisting smaller firms in such areas as technology transfer and marketing. The classification based on the number of employees (Storey, 1994) is:

- micro-enterprises: 0–9 employees
- small enterprises: 10–99 employees
- medium enterprises: 100–499 employees
- large enterprises: over 500 employees

These definitions are not sector specific and the top limit of 99 employees means that the definition of small business encompasses both very small new starters and more established enterprises. There are wide differences across Europe, and using this definition, the vast bulk of employment and output in Greece, Spain, Finland, Ireland and Portugal would be classified as small. Nevertheless, for comparative purposes, the EU definition is probably the best available at a general level. In specific sectors, however, it might be appropriate to develop one's own definition, such as that proposed by Curran *et al.* (1991), who looked at small firms in the service sector. Increasingly, researchers are having to define small firms in a manner appropriate to their research topic (Storey, 1994). Debating size differences is only relevant if it is linked with issues of performance and management.

Small firms, however they are defined, are a dominant force across Europe. Italy, Greece, Portugal and Spain have a higher percentage of their work-forces employed in small business, with a correspondingly larger number of enterprises per 1000 inhabitants than the rest of the EU. In contrast, the UK, former West Germany and the Netherlands tend towards larger organisations in terms of share of employment. Overall, small firms comprise 95 per cent of all enterprises in the EU. All of this, of course, is very general and conceals wide variations across different sectors.

Despite this level of economic and political significance, many of the special marketing problems faced by the small firm as it starts and grows are often ignored, unlike those of the larger organisation. This chapter, therefore, now turns to marketing decision making during the evolution of an enterprise.

THE STAGES IN SMALL BUSINESS DEVELOPMENT

Marketing decisions play a critical part in launching and developing a business. Although most businesses fail because they cannot meet their financial commitments, a more detailed analysis often shows that it is a failure to make sufficient impact in the market, whether in volume or price terms, that is the root cause of the difficulty.

The business launch and development process can be generalised as a model, as shown in Fig 24.1. This model reflects the same basic concept as the product life-cycle (**plc**) model considered at p. 294. As with the **plc**, different businesses might exhibit very different *profiles*. Some might not even get as far as the start-up stage, if the initial business assessment appears to be too problematic. As a result of a combination of marketing, financial or operational problems, others might never get beyond the survival stage. Eventually, the owners might decide that the returns are not sufficient to justify all the risks and hours expended. The lucky and well-managed businesses, however, might continue to grow into ever larger organisations, becoming significant players in their industries. Many well-known organisations such as Marks & Spencer, Ford and Olivetti are proud of their roots in the street market or the small workshop. The secret is to spot those organisations that are still capable of significant further growth.

The *rate of development* of a small business might also vary depending on the nature of the industry, its stage of maturity and the degree of innovativeness of the new product or service idea. In the high-technology and innovative service sectors, growth can be very rapid indeed because of the faster rates of product adoption and acceptance. However, given that most businesses in Europe are small rather than large, the achievement of growth and significant size is the exception rather than the rule. The majority of micro-enterprises start small and stay small throughout their existence. They either do not want to grow or lack the marketing and management impact to manage the transition (Gallagher and Miller, 1991).

Marketing in each of the five stages in the development will now be considered in turn.

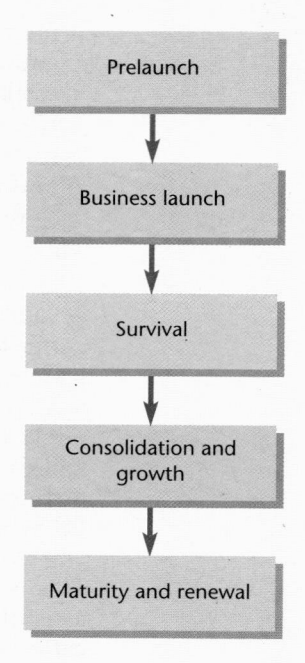

FIGURE 24.1

Business launch and development stages

Marketing in the prelaunch stage

The prelaunch stage covers the period up to the start of trading. There might be a few months or several years between an individual first having the idea for a business venture and the launch of the business itself. People start their own businesses for many different reasons. The common perception is that they are driven by a desire to succeed, and to experience independence and wealth through self-enterprise. They spot a market opportunity and then use their talent to build the necessary resources and organisational expertise to exploit it effectively (McClelland, 1961). While there are some entrepreneurs who conform to that model, studies suggest a much wider range of motivations (Vesper, 1980; Birley, 1989). For many entrepreneurs, it is not 'pull' factors but 'push' created by unemployment, frustration from being in a dead-end job or other unexpected shocks to career or life development patterns. The impact of bereavement, emigration, divorce or college failure can trigger the desire to start a business, for instance. This latter group is less likely to be opportunity or wealth driven and more intent on making a living and surviving. Consequently, they might be far less market orientated. Many even lack any idea about which might be the best product or market area to enter. To this group, the idea of the entrepreneur as an innovator is rather a remote concept.

Why people start in business

Understanding why people start in business can help to explain the subsequent approach to marketing and strategic development. Cooper (1981) provided a useful reference framework for influences on the entrepreneur's start-up decision. Broadly, three groups were proposed: **antecedent influences**, the **incubator organisation**, and environmental factors. These are detailed in Fig 24.2.

FIGURE 24.2

Influences on the start-up decision

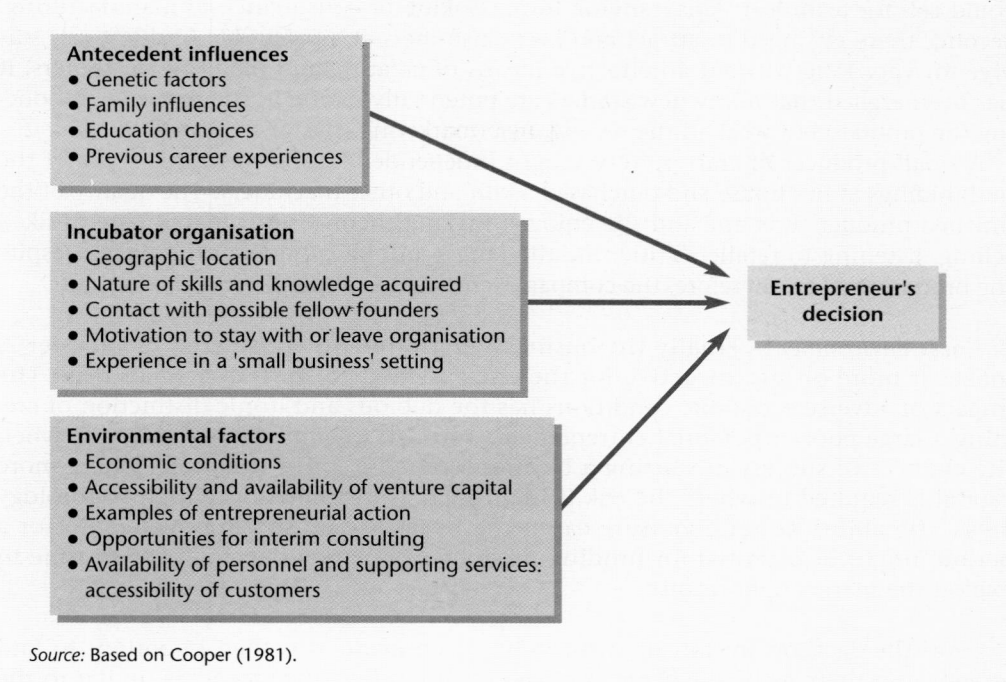

Source: Based on Cooper (1981).

Antecedent influences. Antecedent influences arise from the entrepreneur's previous personal and career development, including such factors as personality traits and education. These help to encourage the individual to consider self-employment as an option and to prepare them for it. An exposure to a family-run business, for example, is often a major influence on the desire to enter that or another business. It might also help the individual to appreciate the marketing skills and approaches necessary for success. Career factors can also be important. If the prospective entrepreneur has studied marketing, there will be a more solid foundation for marketing decision making. The entrepreneur will have a better understanding of the marketing environment, competition and the dynamics of interacting with customers and the trade. Without those insights, the prospective entrepreneur has a great deal of learning to do in a short period of time!

The incubator organisation. Following on from the previous point, the incubator organisation is the organisation for which the prospective entrepreneur worked before making the decision to become the independent. This organisation provides a very detailed exposure to a particular sector. In an ideal sense, the greater the exposure to the range of business functions and the incubator's internal and external environment, the better prepared the entrepreneur. This could cover anything and everything, including invoicing systems, quality control, packaging, the strategic focus on potential customers, new trends or alternative service or product formulations. A number of new entrepreneurs come from the industry in which they were previously employed. It is, however, very difficult to generalise about this. Cross (1981), for example, found that individuals previously employed in small firms were up to 12 times more likely to start their own enterprises than those working in organisations employing over 500. In contrast, Keeble *et al.* (1992) found in the business service market that an individual previously working in a large firm was more likely to start their own business in the same sector.

Skills necessary for starting a business. Two sets of skills could be considered essential for a successful start-up. First, there is the ability to produce the product or service to the specification demanded by the market. Without that, everything else is irrelevant. This could call for technical skills, ranging from cooking or consultancy to manufacturing. Second, there is a need to attract and keep customers at a profit. No business can survive for very long without an effective means of creating and retaining customers. It has been argued that many new starters are potentially strong in the first area (producing the product) but weak in the second area (marketing it) (Carson *et al.*, 1995).

A small producer of craft pottery sought independence. She converted some of the outbuildings at her house and purchased a kiln and other machinery. The quality of the finished products was fine and she enjoyed making them. Unfortunately, she disliked selling, listening to retailers criticising the range, and haggling over the price. Despite the product quality, therefore, the company remained as a small, part-time business.

Business environment. Finally the business environment, considered in Chapter 2, makes it more or less attractive for the entrepreneur to start up a small firm. The impact of adverse economic conditions has the dubious and ironic distinction of creating a large pool of potential entrepreneurs through unemployment at a time when the chances of success in starting a business are reduced. In situations where more capital is required or where the risk is high, such as in some of the high-technology areas, the ability to raise venture capital, if necessary by sharing ownership for a period, might be essential for funding product and market development in time to exploit the market opportunity.

Once the decision to start in business has been made, it is then important to find an idea and then assess the chances of success carefully. This process is similar to the new product development factors discussed in Chapter 9. This concerns far more than marketing issues, and includes, for instance, staffing, finance, operations, premises etc. Sometimes, these matters are formally described in a business plan, but unfortunately many new businesses fail to give them serious consideration, and many assumptions and poorly researched decisions are used as a substitute. It is, however, often the marketing decisions that will determine the success of the business launch. The battle in any start-up situation is to generate sufficient revenue from customers before the initial reserves are exhausted.

The nature of the initial business plan will be determined, in part, by the innovativeness of the product or service idea. If the idea is genuinely innovative in the planned market (even if it has been transferred from other geographical markets), the main focus should be on developing or transferring the concept and on developing the most appropriate marketing mix for local conditions. This might mean a detailed examination of current demand for whatever alternatives are currently available in that market, and their usage (*see* pp. 180 *et seq.*). The broad parameters of the marketing mix might then become evident from this comparative research, but what is actually at issue is whether that marketing mix is sufficiently targeted and resourced in the most effective manner. It must be compatible with the skills and resources of the prospective entrepreneur.

In many situations, the 'new' idea is far from innovative and could be described as yet another 'me too'. Whether video rental stores, kissogram agencies or engineering fabricators, the market may well be saturated already at the time of entry. Here, the key decision is not so much whether the concept will work, but whether a gap exists in the market for another entrant. In a growing market there might be a gap, but the threat of over-capacity and excessive competition might have a fundamental effect on potential financial returns. It is surprising how frequently marginal pricing will be used by the smaller business in order to survive a little longer in a static and declining market. This reflects the difficulty of differentiating through product specification and in some sectors, the reluctance of the consumer to pay more for higher service levels.

There are a number of sources of new product or service ideas, as detailed in Fig 24.3. Some ideas arise from hobbies, as the potential entrepreneur finds out from experience what is and is not currently available, and where the gaps are in the market.

FIGURE 24.3

Sources of new
business ideas

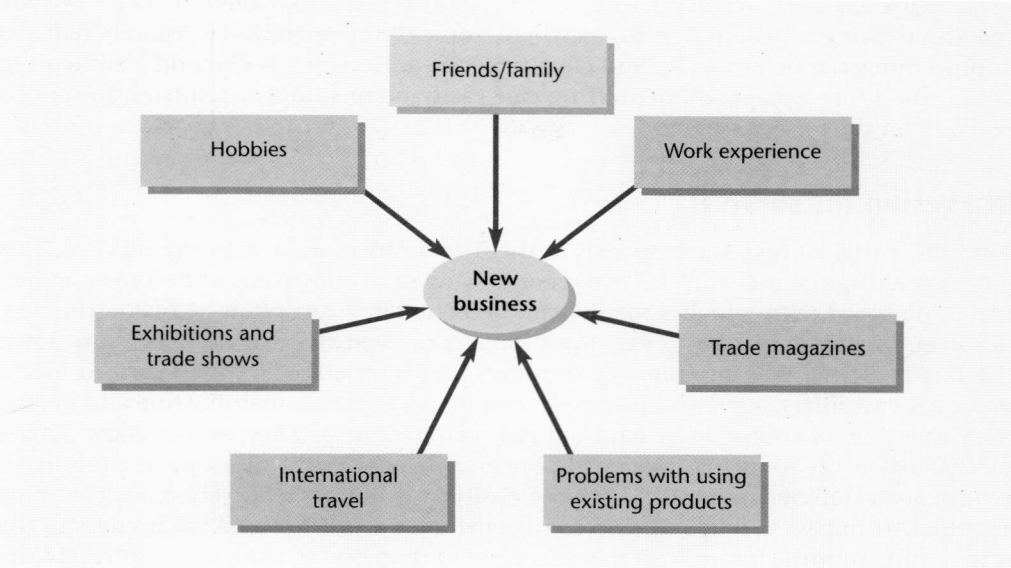

Other ideas arise from previous work experience, as detailed earlier, especially where a high level of customer contact has exposed the budding entrepreneur to new opportunities. This might be combined with a deliberate search for new product opportunities within the boundaries of the entrepreneur's experience. Another group of entrepreneurs are simply able to take experiences from one environment and conceptually transfer them to another. Thus although the idea is 'new', it has been proven elsewhere. This might be an especially important source of new service product ideas as demonstrated in the Celebrations case discussed at p. 955.

Whatever the source of the new business idea, however, there has to be a trigger that stimulates the prospective entrepreneur into acting on the idea and deciding to start a business. This could be any of the push or pull factors mentioned earlier.

Particularly in situations where there is potentially a great deal of competition, there has to be a clear understanding of why the launch will be successful. Market assessment and research should provide some insights into competitor vulnerability and weaknesses, and the sensitivity of potential customers to alternative marketing mix offerings. The entrepreneur should understand whether the focus should be on niching, service differentiation, pricing, branding or heavy promotional spending.

For the inexperienced marketer, none of these decision areas is easy. Consider, for example, the problems of researching the market if the resources available for start-up are severely limited. In such a case, the prospective entrepreneur might have to accept the high level of risk inherent in using low-cost research. Rather than employing a market research agency for systematic, organised and methodologically sound research, it might be necessary to compromise. Heavy reliance on secondary data, meetings with those operating in the same sector in a different geographical market and concept tests with potential buyers (on a limited scale), might provide useful insights, but all these techniques have their limitations.

An important part of this process is the testing of the product or service idea. With a tangible product, it might be possible to undertake trials to iron out any problems before the full launch. In some cases, these might take the form of bench tests to minimise the risks of outright failure on specification and performance grounds. This might be followed or replaced by trials involving a sample of customers. The main risk, however, is of another organisation stealing the idea, if it is truly innovative. Many new starters do not have the resources to defend against such acts from larger, better resourced competitors. Testing the product on real customers at the launch can prove to be even more costly and risky for the entrepreneur.

Service ideas are much more difficult to test, as was discussed in Chapter 9. Where the idea is being transferred from elsewhere, some of the operational risks are reduced as procedures can be drawn up and clearly specified. However, if demand is difficult to assess, the level of capacity or staffing can easily be misjudged, resulting in serious pressure on the service system.

Marketing for survival

After the initial launch, the emphasis in the new business is on ensuring survival. This means creating the niche in the market and using marketing tools to become competitive. The speed with which a market can be penetrated can often be over-estimated, however. Customer loyalty to existing suppliers or even risk aversion can slow down the rate at which new products or suppliers will be tried. The time taken to locate potential customers, agree specifications, negotiate contracts, manufacture and deliver the goods and, of course, to be paid can put considerable pressure on cash flow. This is particularly acute for a manufacturing business, where lead times can be prolonged. Service and retail businesses can generate positive cash flows relatively quickly, as long as sufficient impact is made, thus creating customer awareness and willingness to try. It took nine months for an Irish manufacturer of diamond cutting heads to receive its first significant revenue from a customer. In contrast, a small bakery or take-away business could generate customer revenue on day one.

Several marketing factors will influence the ability to achieve a successful launch.

Perceived, valued product differences

It is relatively easy for the entrepreneur to think that what is being offered is clearly differentiated from the competition and will be of value to the customer. The first few months of business will prove whether that belief is justified or not. Often the difference either is not perceived by the customer, or does not matter to them. Thus the product offering is not valued and fails. A farmer decided to try to diversify, and introduced a boot warmer element. Just the thing for a cold winter's morning, he decided. Unfortunately, customers thought otherwise and the product failed.

Size of market niche

Even when some customers do find the product of interest, the size of the niche may be too small to generate a sufficient volume of initial or repeat business. A small business owner decided that there was an opportunity for a premium-priced pet hotel in her town, offering first-class facilities for dogs. Although she did attract some customers, the volume of business was never sufficient to make it viable. Customers were not prepared to pay double the price charged by perfectly acceptable alternative service providers.

Sometimes, the opposite might be true, and the market potential can prove to be too large. Full exploitation of the opportunity is beyond the resources of the individual operator. Better capitalised and more experienced operators might quickly move in and start to dominate the market.

Market entry strategy

Marketing is often unco-ordinated at this stage, so the market entry strategy rarely turns out as planned. Areas of particular focus should include ensuring that product quality is maintained on a consistent basis and that there is a match between the product positioning and its price. Too low a price might mean that the business is not generating enough revenue to support marketing effort, and too high a price might not attract enough customers. A well thought out entry plan in which all aspects of the mix are co-ordinated increases the chances of success. Rarely do the owners of small firms have a sufficient grasp of all the marketing tools, however, to create an impact. A small manufacturer of handcrafted wooden furniture decided to use local advertising to attract customers, but was soon disappointed to realise that despite the unusual designs, insufficient numbers of customers were visiting the workshop. He soon worked out that he needed to open a retail shop to display his merchandise and to attend regional craft fairs.

Ability to attract key customers

In manufacturing situations, the business launch is often based on promises of orders from one or two key customers. In some cases, these customers might include the entrepreneur's former employer or the former employer's customers. Attracting firm orders from these key customers could be crucial to the successful launch of the business. If the entrepreneur is completely unknown, it could take some time for potential customers to overcome the risks of dealing with an unproven supplier. The key requirements for winning orders are likely to be a combination of the product offered and the way it is presented to the potential customer. Often, this latter point is overlooked (Pettitt and Kirkwood, 1986).

Competitive reaction

It is surprising how often a small business start-up plan fails to take into account the likely reaction of competitors to a new entrant. Although clear market leaders might not be particularly bothered, other recent entrants and smaller operators might well increase their own marketing effort to combat the new threat. Their actions could put pressure on margins from price competition and the need for increased promotional effort from the new business. These two forces might not be compatible for the vulnerable and stretched new business, and might result in stunted growth.

Distribution coverage

The best-laid launch plans can be thrown off course if the entrepreneur cannot gain distribution coverage. As outlined in Chapters 12 and 13, retailers occupy a dominant position in many channels and they are highly selective over which new products to stock. If the range is new, unproven and not supported with advertising and sales promotion, the new business might have little chance of achieving sales volume objectives. Distributors and wholesalers might also be selective about stocking a new product and even if they do choose to stock it, they might not actively promote it. Direct distribution options are often not viable, for the cost efficiency reasons discussed in Chapter 12. One small manufacturer did, however, find success by approaching Harrods with a range of unusual co-ordinated bedding and curtains for nurseries. A trial order was placed that subsequently turned into regular business.

Awareness and interest generation

Generating awareness and interest is often a major challenge for the new business. Given the crowded nature of many advertising media, as discussed in Chapter 16, a new business with a limited budget could find it very difficult to make any impact in the market. In organisational markets, the priority is likely to be to develop a campaign of personal sales visits, with sales letters and publicity material supporting direct sales. In a micro-enterprise, it is often the entrepreneur who undertakes this task, and so his or her personal skills and expertise in making appointments, generating interest and closing sales could be critical. In consumer markets, the priority is often to create a basic level of awareness. Local media are often used, with the business graduating from the classified small advertisements to the display columns as resources grow.

Flexibility and responsiveness

During the start-up period, the entrepreneur has to learn very quickly from experience and to try new ways of doing things. The business plan should have provided a general match between customer needs and the small business offering, but the start-up period enables the fine tuning to take place. Sometimes the changes can be very radical indeed as new opportunities are perceived. A shop selling reproduction antique furniture found that by opening a high quality coffee shop at the back of the premises in the high street they were able to increase cash flow and stimulate sales of the furniture. Entrepreneurs that cannot learn face failure.

Marketing factors are, of course, not the only consideration during this stage of development. All the business functions have to be well managed, and mistakes can easily be made. Cash flow has to be planned and managed, production scheduled, stock control mechanisms implemented and supplies linked with output. Difficulty in any area could lead to barriers and blockages to survival. Businesses that cannot overcome the barriers might survive a year or two and then perhaps give up the struggle, if cash reserves do not build because of either poor inflows or poor expenditure management. Others move into the consolidation and growth stage.

Marketing for consolidation and growth

The next stage occurs after the small business starter has survived the first year or so and has reached a position of having built a customer base and adjusted to the unexpected aspects of the launch. The character of the business might have already changed by this stage as a result of new market opportunities, redefinition of target segments or changes in the product or service concept that have emerged from practical experience. The first priority after survival is to consolidate any progress made. This might mean encouraging repeat purchases and expanding the customer base sufficiently to provide some security. Unfortunately, it is very easy for a smaller business at this stage to drift into a significant trading relationship with a major customer as a result of which dependency starts to develop. The attractions of regular cash flow from a major customer are very tempting, but if the customer base is not diversified, the small business is extremely vulnerable to sudden changes in policy and buying patterns.

Chuft Toys and Gifts expanded and diversified its product range as the business grew.

Consolidation is important for any business that wants to continue, and assumes some kind of ongoing balance between cash inflows and outflows. Many small business owners are happy to stay at that level because they do not want to have to tackle the problems of growth, or they feel that they do not have the capability to manage growth. Consider the differences in management skills and style needed for running one retail store compared with operating 10 stores, for instance. The price for not moving far beyond survival might, however, be fairly low personal returns and a degree of vulnerability to external forces. Curran *et al.* (1993) found, for example, that entrepreneurs in the service sector recognised that their own pay was often very poor compared with what they could be earning as employees of large businesses.

Only a small percentage of small businesses plan and achieve rapid growth. Storey (1994) argues that there are three key influences on the growth rate of a small firm:

1 *The entrepreneur's background and access to resources*: there are many factors in the background of entrepreneurs that can influence the success of the business. Factors such as previously acquired skills,

education and experience might all play a part, but the central factor is often the motivation of the entrepreneur. Those who were 'pushed' into self-employment through redundancy tend to be less growth orientated than those starting a small business for the attractions of independence and wealth (Kinsella *et al.*, 1993). Education, previous managerial experience and group (rather than solo) start-ups have all been pin-pointed as creating faster growth. Research continues in this area, however, and studies often contradict each other because of the heterogeneity of the small firm population.

2 *The organisation and its characteristics*: evidence suggests that the smallest firms are less likely to grow (Hakim, 1989) than larger businesses with between 25 and 49 employees. Accessible rural locations, offering proximity to customers and suppliers, tend to favour growth, in contrast to more remote areas.

3 *The quality of the strategic decisions taken*: strategic marketing decisions made once the business has been launched and has survived the difficult early period are of particular importance. Of course, many other strategic areas also affect growth prospects, such as the equity structure, staff availability and training, and technological sophistication.

The marketing areas that can be significant to the growth of a business are:

Product development and adaptation

Once the product concept has been proven and has become established in the market, it might be necessary for the entrepreneur to start to develop the original idea or to think about broadening the product range. Companies that are excessively focused on one product can be as vulnerable as those who are dependent on one major customer.

The ability of the entrepreneur to adapt or to develop new product areas will partly depend on how aware they are of the need for change and the available opportunities. Those who tend to focus inwards too much could be less alert to new product opportunities.

Example

A dentist decided to diversify his operation by going into the design and manufacture of gum shields for sports players. Being only too familiar with the impact of sports injuries on teeth, he felt that he could design a better method of protection than was currently on offer.

A critical factor in the growth of a smaller business was the ability to adapt products to meet changing customer needs, regulations and competitive offerings. Sometimes these changes are step-like in terms of impact, because of the relative scale of investment required. In the gum shield situation, for example, it was all or nothing, because of the investment required for manufacturing and gaining market trial.

Market development

The need to reconsider the market niche pursued will depend on whether it is large enough to sustain the growth. Many small food producers in Ireland soon have to look towards mainland European markets in order to achieve reasonably attractive sales volumes (*see*, for example, the case of West Coast Fisheries in Chapter 22). The domestic Irish market niche, given the state of competitive activity, might be less attractive than larger, perhaps less price sensitive segments elsewhere.

Even in larger and better developed markets, the niche, however attractive, might soon be exhausted, and so other options have to be considered. For a retailer, this might mean opening another store in another area, whereas a manufacturer might seek new segments and applications. In some situations, this might involve a deliberate policy of reducing the degree of concentration on just a few customers. Westhead and Birley (1993) found that the most rapidly growing firms often had the lowest level of customer concentration. The specialist niche that was so important for the business launch could soon become a straitjacket for the growing enterprise.

Strength of competitive positioning

As the business starts to grow, the risk of more serious competitive reaction might start to emerge. This process can sometimes be hastened by the buyer who decides to source from the new supplier or decides to give that supplier a percentage of business on a dual or treble sourcing arrangement. The entrepreneur who is active rather than passive in the market-place will learn more quickly about possible retaliation and plan new strategies accordingly. The passive seller might become blind to the possible threats and become more vulnerable as a result.

The strength of the market position will be an important determinant of the ability to anticipate and withstand competitive reaction (Wingham and Kelmar, 1992). If there are real product or service advantages, a close match between customer specifications and the product offering, or a clear added value position, it can be harder for competitors to retaliate. Small firms, however, often only have a local advantage that will be tested as they move into a larger market area. The first orders outside the home region can be considered as 'exports' because the operating environment can be more hostile.

One of the major risks for the smaller firm is becoming embroiled in price competition. Rarely do they have the back-up resources or sales volumes to win. The net effect of a local price war is likely to be depressed margins that can stunt further growth because of their knock-on effect on funds available for investment in marketing or production. Sometimes, the printing industry for example sees heavy price competition at a local level in order to maintain or improve local share.

Professionalisation of marketing

At this stage of development, it might be necessary for the entrepreneur to manage the transition from being an owner-operator, undertaking many of the tasks in the business, to being an owner-manager. The owner-manager can no longer do everything and has to delegate in order to meet the increases in demand. At this stage, marketing will have to be taken seriously, perhaps for the first time. The exact roles to be undertaken will, of course, vary depending on the industry, the level of resources, commitment to continued growth and not least, whether trading is with consumer or organisational markets.

Example

A small producer of custom-made business software packages reached the stage of professionalising marketing after just 12 months of operation. The owner had previously handled most of the sales to a small customer base of around eight accounts, but the organisation soon outgrew the potential demand from these accounts. In order to expand the customer base, the owner made the first significant investment in marketing by recruiting of a marketing assistant to handle research, customer identification and promotional material such as mail shots. Soon afterwards, a sales representative was recruited to expand the number of customers. Unfortunately, the expansion did not work and the company could not develop outside its region. It closed less than a year later as a result of cash flow difficulties. In a small business, increasing the number of staff can cause financial strain more easily.

In addition to deciding to employ marketing support or sales staff, an entrepreneur will have to decide when to take the first steps towards developing a marketing plan. He or she could have been driven to do so by the pressure to prove to a lender that the level of sales build could be maintained. Often, the sophistication and reliability of market information and forecasts may be suspect, but time and experience are likely to improve these aspects.

Sustaining growth

In order to sustain growth, an entrepreneur will have to learn how to use the marketing mix to good effect. If the organisation operates in a consumer market, very careful scheduling of media is required. Mass media are usually well beyond the limited resources available to a small organisation. Instead, targeted media such as specialist magazines can provide more effective communication, and direct marketing might also offer attractive and cost-effective options. In organisational markets with clearly defined customers, the entrepreneur will be a need to ensure that regular contact is maintained and that suitable promotional material and exhibitions are used to support the selling effort.

Where an organisation uses intermediaries, it will be crucial at this stage to gain their support. This might mean gaining distribution or encouraging intermediaries to promote the product more heavily. Only by developing trade promotion policies can growth be maintained.

All the above forces interact to encourage or restrict the development of the small firm. To cope with these forces, the entrepreneur must change and respond to emerging opportunities. The whole process will be highly demanding in terms of time and expertise. Those who are better able to adapt and manage the market threats and opportunities will be better able to move into the final stage.

Marketing for maturity and renewal

The maturity stage marks the end of the transition from start-up to established enterprise. The size and profile of the micro-enterprise may have evolved to become a small business or even a medium enterprise with a management structure. At this stage, many of the marketing principles described in this book can become practical possibilities. As the organisation grows, specialist staff in sales and marketing might be recruited, although the entrepreneur might still keep a close watch on key customers.

The critical decision at this stage is whether to move forward with growth or whether to consolidate and primarily seek to retain market share.

> ### *Example*
>
> A packaging company specialising in shoe boxes decided not to seek further growth but to maintain sales to its established customer base. This was possible for a number of years because there was no significant market change. But there are risks in this approach. The company dealt with customers primarily by telephone and only visited them once every 18 months or two years. The company had little information about new opportunities or specification changes even within its core market, let alone the threat of new competition.

No growth does not, therefore, also mean no change (Gibb and Scott, 1985). Even to stand still, because of turbulence and market forces, the entrepreneur might have to respond to new competitive threats, changes in customer needs and market dynamics. This could mean new products, product development and finding new customers to compensate for any losses. If there is no change and stagnation sets in, a decline may soon follow.

Velden Engineering manufactures a wide range of component parts and assemblies for aircraft, medical and switchgear markets. Founded in the 1970s, the business grew steadily by ensuring that quality and new technology were offered, and more recently by its willingness to supply tested assemblies that could go straight into JIT (Just in time) systems. By welcoming supplier partnerships and changing and improving the operation to meet new demands, Velden has been able to achieve a turnover of £2 million, with 60 employees.

MARKETING IN ACTION

Small businesses move into international markets

Small businesses occupying narrow niches or those with products that are easily transferable across national boundaries have to decide, at some point during their development, whether to pursue export opportunities. AirRide, a UK company formed in the 1990s to sell 'intelligent chairs,' had to learn to handle international markets very early in its life. Morellato, on the other hand, a maker of watch straps from the Veneto region of Italy, expanded into other EU markets slowly, based on a successful formula worked out in its home market. We now contrast the experience of these two small companies.

AirRide's 'intelligent chair' enables the occupant to be turned, rolled or twisted, usually in front of a wide screen television. The net effect is that there is a greater feeling of realism, perhaps simulating a space ride or other forms of dramatic movement. Entertainment parks and cine-motion theatres are obvious customers, and that meant that a global perspective was needed very early in the business's development if it was to break into the £200 million worldwide simulator market. One of the major orders was to supply the chairs for an entertainment system in a Hong Kong hotel. This order was worth £350 000. There could also be applications in virtual reality systems in the next generation of home or packaged entertainment.

The product uses air – rather than hydraulic-based systems, and this results in savings in capital outlay and in maintenance. Each chair costs £6000, although with volume sales the cost could come down to £2000 per chair. The inventor wanted nothing to do with commercialisation, and so sold the product design and concept to AirRide, based in West Sussex. The inventor preferred to accept royalties on sales rather than having to bother with marketing and production problems. Commercialisation has proceeded apace, with sales expected to be £3.7 million in 1996, £10 million forecast for 1997 and £20 million plus by 1999. Most of these sales will be from exports, with licensing rather than direct sales as the preferred route

in large difficult markets such as Japan.

The fast track export approach is in contrast with Morellato's international development. It has now become a world leader in a very specialised product niche: leather straps and metal bracelets for watches. The company was founded in the 1930s, but was taken over by the Carraro family in 1954. Subsequent development has been carefully controlled and slow, and has never involved alliances and mergers. It was only in the years between the mid-1980s and the mid-1990s that sales began to grow significantly, from L17 billion to L90 billion, largely due to export sales.

The strategy employed by Morellato has been to focus on design and production, ensuring differentiated products that are cost effectively produced. As cross-border movement became easier, the company built a small manufacturing plant in Hungary, an eight-hour drive from Morellato's plant in Italy. The Hungarian plant enables access to low-cost production. The marketing strategy has also been carefully formulated to exploit the company's strengths. It has avoided contracts with watch manufacturers in order to steer clear of over-dependency on particular customers and lower-priced contracts. Instead, it has focused on supplying retail outlets for watch strap replacement. To implement this strategy, however, the company had to incur additional selling costs in building a distribution and customer service network. The strategy worked in Italy, where Morellato gained a 40 per cent share, and was then replicated in other EU markets. In the 1990s, it set up its own distribution company in Spain and Germany. By branding the products, based on design and range, it has successfully managed the transition into a medium-sized enterprise.

In both examples, marketing has been central to business development. The main differences are first, commitment to the speed of change, and second, the necessity to move into exports early.

Sources: Graham (1995); Marsh (1996).

Other entrepreneurs will also continue to seek growth through other means. Exporting might become a major priority, and this will be considered in Chapter 25. Bijmolt and Zwart (1994), in a study of Dutch SMEs, found four groups of exporting SMEs. The first group, largely unsuccessful exporters, exported only a small fraction of their sales, and were not interested in pursuing further opportunities. The second group were prepared to react to export opportunities, but did not go out of their way to find them. The third group took a positive and proactive stance towards exporting, and were experiencing success as a result. The final group also sought to be proactive but were less successful in their achievements.

The growth stages presented in this section are by no means universal. High-growth companies can move very quickly through the stages, often by large incremental steps as new projects are introduced. Others might stabilise very early and change very little, in line with the owner's wishes. This could mean that marketing is always treated on an *ad hoc* basis, is poorly informed and is not integrated into the organisation. The attitudes, expertise and objectives of the owner or ownership team will be paramount.

Many small businesses have to run very hard just to survive. Many do not make it. Storey (1994), makes the generalisations that younger rather than older businesses are more likely to fail; very small micro-enterprises are more vulnerable than larger ones; and most interestingly, those that grow soon after starting have a better chance of survival. It is interesting to consider some of the managerial deficiencies that can cause failure. The small business might fail if:

- it cannot identify the target market or target customers
- it cannot delineate its trading area
- it cannot delegate
- it considers advertising an expense not an investment
- it has poor knowledge of pricing and strategy
- it has an immature understanding of distribution channels
- it does not plan.

(adapted from Burns, 1989b).

Marketing is indeed at the heart of small business development.

FRANCHISING

As mentioned in Chapter 12, a **franchise** is a kind of vertical marketing system with a contractual relationship between the **franchisor** and the **franchisee**. Generally, it means that the owner of a product, trade mark, process or service licenses another person or organisation to use, buy, sell or operate it in exchange for some form of payment. This might be in the form of a royalty, a licence fee or a commitment to purchase products at supplier dominated prices. Franchising is therefore both a distribution method through which market coverage can be extended and a business system through which enterprises can launch or grow. Table 24.1 highlights a number of the better known international franchises.

> **Example**
>
> Marco Leer from the Netherlands specialises in leather upholstery refinishing. After several years of R&D, the owner found an innovative way of mixing and applying paint to leather upholstery. This significantly reduced labour costs and created an opportunity to standardise prices. Soon after the launch in the Netherlands, the owner decided that franchising was the best method of

expansion. He first appointed franchisees in other parts of the Netherlands, then in Europe, where there soon were 14 franchises across Belgium, Germany and Switzerland. The emphasis then turned to world-wide expansion. The key ingredients of the package for franchisees are detailed business and technical training, field support and advice over finding a suitable business location. It is the product concept, however, that lies at the heart of a franchise system that has led to business success (Franchise International (1996b).

TABLE 24.1
International franchisors

Franchise name	Product/ Service	Number of countries served
Applewoods	Bodycare/ Home fragrance	20
Dunkin' Donuts	Snacks/ Beverages	24
Fourth R	Children's computer education	16
Q–Zar	Laser tag game sites	45
Subway	Sandwiches	30+
Worldwide Refinishing	Bath resurfacing	22
Yogen früz	Frozen Yoghurt	33

Although franchising is primarily a method of marketing goods and services, it can also offer a small business a route for achieving more rapid growth, as seen in the Marco Leer case. From a slightly different perspective, it can also provide a prospective entrepreneur with a *quasi*-independent entry into a market with a tried and tested concept. Such an entrepreneur might be new to franchising or even new to business, but can nevertheless bring a bundle of skills and competencies acquired in a previous career.

Franchising concepts

The essence of franchising is the relationship between the two parties, the franchisor – the manufacturer, concept owner or supplier, and the franchisee – the recipient or purchaser of the franchisor's offering. There are five types of franchise relationship (Barrow, 1989).

Distributorships

This category of relationships was considered in Chapter 12. A distributor sells products and/or provides service on behalf of the originating organisation while remaining independent of it. The products involved could be computer hardware, cars, electrical components, or after-sales service. Often, the contractual agreement provides the distributor with territorial rights and the originating organisation's support in marketing, management, staff training and general business advice. The originating organisation is also likely to specify the range and level of stock, as well as imposing or influencing the marketing methods used. Although taking up a distributorship is not reserved exclusively for a smaller business and the capital requirements for entry might vary considerably, this route is popular for new enterprise as the initial financing requirement is likely to be relatively small in such areas as computing, with most resources going into stock and premises.

La Compagnie des Petits

The first shop belonging to La Compagnie des Petits opened in March 1992. Founded by three partners who all had experience in the textile industry, the purpose of the store was to offer children's clothing that was of good quality, well designed and fashionable, but not too expensive. By 1994, the chain had expanded to include 20 stores, five of which had been franchised out when the owners decided to share their experience. The results from the franchises were sufficiently promising, with provisional turnover of around Fr 2.5 million, for the company to advertise for further franchises.

In its advertisement, the company offers potential franchisees premises, fixtures and fittings, as well as professional advice and support. It also claims to offer attractive gross margins on goods sold. Because it manufactures its goods in countries with low labour costs, and supplies its franchisees at cost price, gross margins of around 45 per cent are possible. The company's research suggests that the average spend in one of its stores is Fr 350, on goods priced between Fr 30 and Fr 350 Fr.

As one might expect, the company, as a franchisor, says that it is looking for motivated people who want to take the welfare of an enterprise into their own hands. The franchisor claims too that because of their stake in the business, the franchised stores in the chain perform much better than the wholly owned branches. The company thus wants to establish a real partnership with its franchisees, developing an extensive network without losing sight of the interests of the individual franchisee.

Franchisees, however, have to be able to raise sufficient finance to set themselves up in business. The franchisor will find and equip the premises, and in 1994, was asking for Fr 4000 per square metre for the rights to the franchise, a one off 'entry fee' of Fr 50 000, and investment in opening stock of around Fr 290 000. Then, once the franchise was up and running, a quarterly royalty of 3.5 per cent of turnover was also payable.

Source: Franchise Magazine (1994).

Licence to manufacture

A licence allows the licensee to produce a product, as specified by the licensor, and then to sell it in a specified territory. This arrangement might include access to otherwise secret formulae, operating processes or brand names. Often, the specification is rigidly controlled, quality standards are imposed and, where appropriate, servicing levels detailed. Before licences are granted, however, it is important to establish protection for patents and trade marks. That is relatively easy compared with protecting areas such as know-how and systems. Like a distributorship, licensing is not the exclusive territory of small enterprises. A number of larger organisations in central Europe are actively seeking licensing and joint venture agreements with EU partners as a means of strengthening know-how and product portfolios. Licensing can be attractive to both parties, especially in international markets. It is a relatively cheap means of expansion and, for the smaller business, it can be a valuable way of enhancing a product range by bringing in new and innovative technology. International licensing will be considered in more detail in Chapter 25.

Celebrity endorsement

Celebrity endorsement is linked to branding (*see* Chapter 7) and promotion (*see* p. 590). The manufacturer seeks the endorsement of a well-known celebrity, perhaps in the sports or entertainment area, in return for a royalty payment on sales. Effectively, the celebrity is franchising their name. Often, the product is named after the celebrity such as Arnold Palmer golf clubs and Pavarotti perfume. Rarely, however, can small businesses afford the endorsement fees required for well-known sports or entertainment personalities.

Trade marks

Trade marks were considered at p. 267. Trade marks are distinctive names, symbols, marks, slogans, colours or packaging shapes or designs that readily identify a company's product, component or service. The mark can be used for a fee as part of a clear licensing agreement as to its use.

Business format franchise

The franchising of a business format has emerged as the most potent and dynamic growth area in western Europe in the last 20 years. It provides opportunities for small, independent entrepreneurs, without a novel idea, to enter business and is an attractive route for existing business with a proven concept to expand.

The **business format franchise** implies access not only to a product concept, but also to a comprehensive package that enables the product or service to be delivered in a standardised way, regardless of location. The package or format might include a wide range of different requirements and supports.

Example

Highway Windscreens offer a three-in-one franchise. Windscreen replacement, emergency glazing and security film are all part of the format. For an investment of £38 000, the format includes specified territory, training, fully fitted out vehicles, marketing support, business support services, BS5750 registration and ongoing product development. Although the services have to be delivered to specified quality standards, the format includes the key ingredients to increase the franchisee's chances of successful launch and business development.

The business format therefore includes such issues as intellectual property rights relating to trade marks, trade names, shop signs, designs, copyrights, know-how or patents. All of these can be used to market more effectively, thus facilitating the resale of goods or the provision of services to end users.

Types of business format franchise. There are four main types of business format franchise:

1 *Executive*: this involves white-collar orientated businesses, such as consultancy, estate agencies and personnel recruitment, where the franchisee usually visits the client to perform the service.
2 *Retail*: the franchisee operates from premises either in prime locations or from carefully selected sites. Examples of this type of franchise are fast food, picture framing and wine stores. Many of the issues considered in Chapter 13 apply to this group. Investment can be high, but so too can the returns.
3 *Distribution*: these franchisees often operate from vans delivering to retailers or direct to the public. Products include greeting cards, tools and pet accessories. The sales territory is normally firmly specified.
4 *Job*: these tend to be service franchises where the franchisee performs a service on the customer's premises. They often operate from a home base with a van. Cleaning, repairs and security services are all good examples.

The business format contract. A number of elements are incorporated into the business format franchise, providing the basis for the content of the contractual agreement and the mutual responsibilities created (Mendelsohn, 1992):

1 The contract should specify the nature and terms of the relationship. This should cover its duration, the geographical extent of any exclusive sales territory and the franchisee's and the franchisor's mutual expectations and responsibilities.

2 The franchisor must have developed a successful, proven business format system with an identified brand name before offering it to franchisees. This is normally a requirement of the various national bodies that register and regulate bona fide franchises. It protects potential franchisees from the small minority of unethical franchisors who would take money from franchisees and leave them with an unproven concept that will quickly fail.

3 The franchisor should train the franchisee in the system before opening and fully assist in the planning and implementation of the opening.

4 The franchisor should maintain a business relationship with the franchisee through ongoing support in marketing and management. Such a relationship is important in the early stages of the franchise when the franchisee is still learning the business.

5 The franchisee is permitted, under the control of the franchisor, to use the brand name and to operate the business system in a defined geographic area. The franchisee is allowed to benefit from the goodwill created.

6 The franchisee should make a capital investment to launch the business.

7 The franchisee should legally own the business. This means that the consequences of business failure will fall primarily on the franchisee rather than on the franchisor.

8 The franchisee must pay the franchisor for the rights acquired and the ongoing services provided. This is normally by a combination of licence fee, royalty or mark-up on supplies purchased.

Business format franchising can help the aspiring entrepreneur to start a new business in a new area. By providing the innovative idea and a potentially successful formula, franchisors are active in encouraging this route into self-employment. Typical advantages for the franchisee are the independence of ownership, control over one's own working environment and the freedom to guide one's own destiny. In the view of Felstead (1991), however, the degree of independence is highly variable depending upon the design of the system, varying from high to low discretion franchising, as shown in Table 24.2.

TABLE 24.2
Variations in franchise independence

	High discretion/ 'Soft' franchising	Low discretion/ 'Hard' franchising
Controls on and nature of the productive process	High service content/low product content	Low service content/ high product content
	High level of expertise at the point of consumption	Low level of expertise at the point of consumption
	Exclusive territory served by mobile operation	Single fixed store location
	High levels of local advertising/low levels of national advertising	Low levels of local advertising/high levels of national advertising
Revenue payments	Low royalities	High royalties
Ownership of the means of production	Absence of trade secret/special equipment/special products	Trade secret/special equipment/special products
	Weak 'ties' on physical means of production	Strong 'ties' on physical means of production

Source: Felstead (1991).

The scope and growth of franchising

Although franchising is often regarded as a relatively recent phenomenon, its origins can actually be traced back to the tied house system in British brewing in the eighteenth century. Although such arrangements did not demonstrate the characteristics of a business format system, their roots lay in exclusive purchasing arrangements. The modern genesis of franchising, especially of the business format type, can be traced back to the USA with the Howard Johnson restaurant chain in the 1930s, which was followed by many other well-known franchises. Some of the early franchises centred on product and trade names in such areas as petrol retailing and soft drinks bottling. Most of the major growth in the USA, however, has been through business format franchising. The magazine, *Franchise International* (1996a) has estimated that in the USA 40 per cent of all retail sales and 10 per cent of GNP is accounted for by franchised systems. There are around 750 000 franchisees and over 3000 franchisors. They give rise to a combined turnover of $950 billion. Over 450 franchisors currently offer international systems, with double that figure developing plans over the next few years. However, these figures conceal the marked concentration in the franchise industry. It has been estimated that 56 companies account for 48 per cent of all franchise system sales, each with over 1000 franchised units.

Europe has also experienced the franchise revolution. Many of the trends that fuelled growth in the USA have also been seen in Europe. Growing disposable incomes, urbanisation and home-centred families have all played their part in creating more service-orientated operations. Franchising is particularly well suited to services and people-intensive activities, especially where geographical proximity is needed. In Europe, it has been estimated that there are 120 000 franchisees belonging to around 3000 franchise systems with a total annual turnover of $80 billion (*Franchise International*, 1996a; 1996b).

The impact of franchising in Europe has been greatest in France, the Netherlands and the UK. The leader is France, with over Fr 185 billion revenue from nearly 30 000 outlets and over 450 networks. Germany has 25 000 franchisees in 500 franchised systems with a turnover of DM 20 million. Franchising is also now spreading into central and eastern Europe, especially in the fast food sector operated by the well-known international franchisors. In Hungary, KFC has four stores, McDonald's is well established and Dunkin' Donuts have 14 outlets. The latter company is also planning nearly 40 stores in Poland and 10 in the Czech Republic and Slovakia.

In the UK, a recent estimate for business format franchising indicated around 370 franchisors, 18 000 outlets and a turnover of £4.5 billion per annum. (National Westminister Bank and BFA, 1993).

Example

Not only are the long-standing names such as McDonald's and Wimpy (fast food), Dyno-Rod (drain cleaning and hygiene) and Servicemaster (carpet and upholstery cleaning) all well represented, but there are many new names, such as Hoggies (spit roast specialists), The Local Artist, and VDU Techclean services. Some of the UK-owned franchises have become internationally renowned. The Body Shop, established by Anita Roddick in 1976, operates in 41 countries with over 1 000 franchised outlets.

The survey by National Westminster Bank and the British Franchise Association (NatWest/BFA, 1989) identified the five largest areas of franchising activity, as measured by the number of franchised systems:

- business and professional services: 42 per cent
- print: 15 per cent
- food and drink: 14 per cent
- home improvement and cleaning: 14 per cent
- transport and leisure: 8 per cent.

The actual percentage figures should be treated with some caution, as exits and new entrants can lead to fluctuations and further variations can be caused by changes in the criteria used. Within each area, some franchises are almost job franchises, with only limited investment potential, whereas others are fast food or hotel franchises requiring large investment.

The franchisor's perspective

Benefits

Both small and large companies can expand through franchising. The two main benefits are financial and managerial. From a financial point of view, rapid growth in market coverage and penetration can be achieved using the resources provided by the franchisees. To open a new directly owned outlet would involve an investment both in capital assets (shop fittings, equipment, property etc.) and in working capital for stock and other operating costs. There would also be the risk of failing to achieve sales targets and financial projections. Many of these risks are effectively borne and financed by the franchisees through their start-up capital investment, licence fees and any other royalty payments.

The franchisee also represents a committed management resource. The franchisee becomes the legal owner of the business and will therefore suffer from failure or benefit from success. By applying entrepreneurial skills within the framework of the franchise agreement, the franchisee will have to manage the local operation, promote sales and control resources. It would be very hard for the franchisor to motivate salaried staff to make the same effort, because they would not be running the same personal risks as a franchisee (Barrow, 1989).

There are other benefits from franchising. Of particular importance is the ability to develop economies of scale in purchasing, marketing and corporate image and branding without having a large organisation. Indeed, a small enterprise seeking to expand quickly can gain these benefits on the basis of the franchisees' capital. The important benefit of a business format franchise system, however, is that it can divorce service design and planning from service delivery and operations. The skill for a successful franchisor might therefore lie in opportunity assessment, system design and franchisee recruitment rather than in the technical area of production.

Example

The Subway restaurant chain provides an excellent example of the pace of network development possible through a franchised system. The chain was started in 1965 in the USA by a 17-year-old high school graduate wanting to pay his way through college. Since starting to use franchising in the 1980s, the chain has opened over 1000 outlets a year. Sales are in excess of $3 billion and there are now over 11 500 locations worldwide. Over 300 outlets are outside the USA in places such as Poland, Japan, South Africa and Peru (*Franchise International*, 1996b).

Disadvantages

There are, nevertheless, also problems associated with franchising a business. Some of them relate to handling difficult, ineffective or remote franchisees, especially as they become highly experienced in trading in the system area. This could lead to some questioning of the franchise relationship, if poor or ineffective support is being provided by the franchisor (Pettitt, 1988). Furthermore, if the franchisor is felt to be abusing its power, franchisees might start to group together to negotiate on more equal terms with the franchisor. Reputable and better established franchisors often welcome the formation of formal franchisee groups, as a means of generating feedback and working together to develop a more effective franchise system.

The franchisee's perspective

In some respects, for the franchisee, the decision to start a franchised business is similar to the decision to start a fully independent one. The main difference is the need to select the most appropriate business sector from the franchise opportunities available. Some of the benefits from entering a franchise agreement are generic, in that they are related to the growth prospects in that particular product or service sector. Other benefits might only be realised if a 'good' franchisor is selected, one that offers a first class support package and meets their commitments over time.

Ultimately, the decision is based upon the individual's preparedness to accept a lower return for a lower risk. As indicated in the previous section, many new small businesses fail. This often reflects a lack of preparedness, experience or real and reasonably permanent market potential. Through careful site selection, concept packaging and training, the franchisee entrepreneur does not have to go through the same learning experience and trial and error process. While the returns may be lower, given the need for royalties and other means of remunerating the franchisor, because the concept is entirely proven, the risk in the launch phase might be much lower. The failure rate for franchised systems is often between one-eighth and one-tenth of failure rates of independent ventures.

Advantages of franchising

The main advantages in adopting a franchise are:

1 Participation in a system with an established image, name and reputation, often on a regional or national scale. As shown in Chapter 15, it can take a considerable time to get a company or brand name established in the consumer's mind. The franchisee can cut out much of this building process and where a reputation already exists, it can be traded upon.

2 In well organised systems, the franchisee receives a number of services as part of the start-up package. With the Inter caves system in France these include site selection, planning and launch assistance, training for the franchisee and key staff in all aspects of the business, support in raising finance and where necessary, the best combination of opening stock or supplies, marketing information and launch publicity. Often franchisors can provide special finance facilities for new franchisees.

3 National or regional advertising in addition to any undertaken by the franchisee can play an important role in building a stronger system (brand) identity. Advan, a system based on special vehicles that can display up to 21 illuminated, large-scale colour posters at 15-second intervals, has a series of vans on the road offering mobile advertising services. As part of the package the franchisor has a central telesales team as well as a direct sales team selling to major advertisers. In other situations, mainstream regional or national media might be used.

4 Where supplies or equipment have to be purchased, the franchisee will at least receive considerable guidance to avoid shortages or surpluses. At best, preferential terms might be passed on.

A franchise offers a recognisable corporate image and a proven business and operating system to the franchisee.

Source: Perfect Pizza.

5 Ongoing advice and support might be available for management problem solving, whether in marketing, finance, or any other aspect of business development. Amtrack Express Parcels goes further by covering all invoicing, cash flow and debt collection services for its franchisees.

6 New product development can also be important if a stream of product or service improvements would help the franchisee to keep the product portfolio fresh. Trophy offers a mobile pet food delivery service using over 250 franchisees, providing a door-to-door service. Each franchisee carries over 250 product lines which are changed on a regular basis to maintain customer interest.

7 Some territorial protection will be offered if franchisees are given defined licence areas in which to trade. Of course, that is no protection from competitors operating within other franchise systems or independent operators. A Domino's Pizza franchise does not mean protection from Pizza Hut, Pizzaland or indeed non-pizza fast food outlets.

Problems in franchising

Despite the advantages of franchising which might contribute to an increased likelihood of success, there are potential problems that also need to be considered by the prospective entrepreneur before signing the franchise agreement. Perhaps the greatest problem arises from the contract itself.

1 The contract has to ensure systems compliance. This means rigorous control over the product range offered, its quality and specification, its delivery and the way in which it is marketed. Much of the freedom to experiment and adjust to the local environment might well be denied to a franchisee. In more mature franchise

chains, such as Prontaprint, some local flexibility might be allowed, but in most franchise chains, close control is exercised.

2 The option always exists for the independent operator to expand, sell out, or cease trading according to personal objectives. Most franchisors, however, require that any franchise transfer can only be made with their approval, and that they must approve any new franchisee. Similarly, restrictions on market development might limit growth. Although EU competition law prohibits franchisors from delineating where franchisees can draw customers from, it does not affect their ability to restrict the number of new licences or to define broad sales territories.

> ### Example
>
> McDonald's might only operate one or two pioneering outlets in Polish cities, but in a medium-sized city in the USA over 20 or 30 franchises might have been awarded.

3 A fundamental tension can creep into the franchise relationship. The franchisor might seek to increase volume in the system to achieve greater market presence and to raise royalties based on turnover. The franchisee might be more interested in return on investment than in chasing extra turnover for lower margins.

4 Any loss of reputation or poor decision making by the franchisor might have negative effects on the franchisee. Some franchisors have been criticised for failing to fully develop their national promotional campaign in support of franchisees. Some franchise systems have failed.

> ### Example
>
> In 1985, the Young's Franchise Group comprising Young's Formal Hire, Pronuptia Wedding Hire and La Mama fashion maternity wear chain went into receivership without warning.

On balance, the advantages and disadvantages of the franchised route are a trade-off between the benefits of being associated with a franchised chain and the costs associated with the loss of complete independence and the ongoing franchisor involvement. Given the worldwide growth of franchising and the fact that many franchisees do renew their agreements when the original contract period expires, it would appear that many entrepreneurs are prepared to sacrifice their independence for lower start-up risk and that they do feel that operating a franchise is worthwhile.

Franchise blueprints and contracts

The key to success in any franchise system is the development and testing of an unusual or attractive market concept, patented equipment and/or a readily identifiable trade mark and image. In the view of Mendelsohn (1992), any business which is capable of being run under remote management is also capable of being franchised. Table 24.3 indicates the wide range of areas that are currently being franchised across Europe. From a marketing perspective, there is really no difference between developing a successful independent business and developing a successful franchise system. The product or service must be valued, differentiated from its competitors by real or imaginary criteria and be sustainable over time. There are, however, some other considerations that are relevant when an entrepreneur is deciding on the appropriateness of the franchising route. The system must be capable of replication according to the franchisor's design. This could include product, service and marketing effectiveness. It

TABLE 24.3

Business areas franchised in Europe

Business area	Specific products/services franchised
Food and drink	sandwiches; pizzas; burgers; petfood; Chinese take-aways; Mexican restaurants; off-licences; sweet shops
Clothing and consumer goods	leisure wear; children's wear; bridal/formal wear; accessories; sports goods and clothing; greeting cards; toiletries
Domestic services	home cleaning; double glazing repair/maintence; upholstery/carpet cleaning; interior decoration; drains clearance
Car services	windscreen replacement; scratch/dent repairs; car cleaning/ valeting; servicing
Personal services	dating agencies; hairdressing; sunbeds; nursing care; party planning
Legal/business services	courier services; stock auditing; utility auditing; office training; computer training; workwear; office cleaning; printing; will writing; property sales.

must also be capable of generating margins that can sustain the continued interest of both franchisor and franchisee.

The decision to build a franchise chain can stem from an existing business seeking to expand or from a new business start-up, where the investment may be large, as is typically found in the fast food business, or quite small as in such areas as domestic services.

> **Example**
>
> A typical job franchise such as Dyno-Rod might require around £18 000 in start-up capital. This compares with a food franchise, such as Fatty Arbuckle's, a themed table service restaurant, where the typical investment is between £100 000 and £200 000 including a £10 000 franchise fee.

In the case of a new start rather than an outgrowth such as the Marco Leer example (*see* p. 969 above), it is normally expected that the franchise package will have been piloted before being offered to potential franchisees. This enables the concept to be fully tried and tested in field conditions.

Launching a new franchising system

There are seven stages in launching a new franchised system, as shown in Fig 24.4.

Developing the franchised business system concept. As indicated above, a franchised business system should offer many of the characteristics of any successful business plus the ability to replicate without the direct intervention of the concept owner. The more complex and technically orientated the business, the greater the difficulty of franchising, because of problems in replicating. The impact of franchising in industrial markets is, therefore, marginal, being reserved mainly for industrial services rather than manufacturing. In contrast, a fast food system can be standardised through the use of similar equipment, kitchen design, premises, raw materials, cooking instructions, food presentation, menu, seating configuration etc.

As with any business launch, it is very important to have a clear idea of the target market and to assess the potential business likely to be generated across a geographical

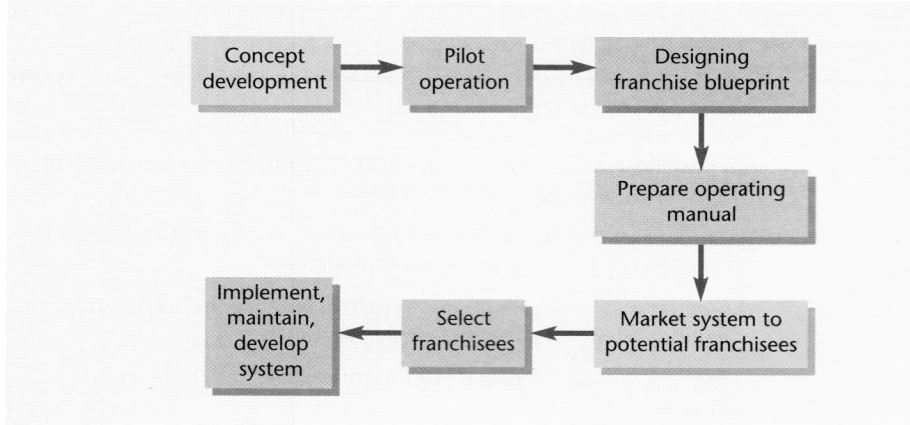

FIGURE 24.4

Stages in launching a new franchised business system

area. In some cases, the availability of suitable premises might be an important consideration. Often a franchisor agrees a town or city and even a site before advertising for franchisees. This might be especially crucial where impulse or passing trade is required.

Undertaking a pilot operation. Before the franchise is offered to a wider audience, it should be piloted in at least one location for at least one year. This enables a full market test to take place, and the package to be fully developed and refined. If the franchisor is new to the trading concept, the experience gained will be invaluable later when advising others on managerial and operational problems. Many national franchise associations insist on a pilot period as a precondition of membership. Without such a pilot the franchisees, if they are prepared to take a chance, are effectively working on a trial and error basis and might not receive the same benefits as they would if they were entering a proven system.

> ### Example
>
> From humble beginnings in Bantry, Ireland in 1986, Pasco Graves had developed his casual fashion retailer business into 45 shops by 1993, five of which were franchised. The stores offer a very distinctive range of bright co-ordinated casual wear for both adults and children. This includes knitwear, T-shirts, casual jackets, jeans, leggings and accessories. By 1989, the business had extended into the UK with sales and profits doubling every year from 1990 to 1992. The initial success of franchising was based on the development of a carefully prepared and tested operational formula. Further franchises are planned, with longer-term significant expansion including 300 international franchises. However the period of piloting and proving the viability of the concept was crucial to its success.

Designing the franchise blueprint. The proven franchise package should be the output of the pilot period. The package represents the **franchise blueprint** for a successful operation, the key factors that are likely to maximise the chances of success. Obviously, these factors will vary from one system to another, depending on innovativeness, positioning and competitiveness.

As mentioned above, an important part of the blueprint will be the site selection, both specifically and in a general trading area. The way in which the area and site decision is made will be similar to that of any other retail location decision, as discussed in at pp. 511–4. Issues of market potential, customers' preparedness to travel, and competition might all play a part in the decision to locate in a particular area. Proximity to other attractions might be important, for example siting a multiplex cinema in an edge of town retail park close to a Burger King and a Pizza Hut. The selection of specific sites might also consider such factors as traffic flow analysis, space requirements, access, parking and, of course, rental or freehold costs. Perfect Pizza, for example, advertises for franchisees both for new territories yet to be developed and to take over existing stores.

Other areas for consideration in the blueprint will be the equipment, layout, service specification, interior design, product range etc. These issues should all be detailed in the development of the operating manual. Similarly, work systems, material requirements, staffing, marketing literature and management systems such as stock control and accounting will have to be tested and included in a refined state in the package. A final part will be the development of a finance package that can help potential franchisees to raise capital. This must allow franchisees to generate a start-up proposal that will survive the close scrutiny of financiers and analysts.

A franchisee might have a better chance of obtaining start-up capital from banks and leasing companies with the franchisor's support than if it was a completely independent business. A Pasco franchise, for example, requires an initial capital investment of £80 000, of which £40 000 must be in liquid assets. The balance can be raised as loan capital with the support of the franchisor.

Some operators decide to adopt a mixed system in which some outlets are franchised and others are company owned. This enables the franchisor to maintain control and contact with the market, and allows for continuing updating of the concept and blueprint.

> ### Example
>
> Bulgari is a jewellery chain based in Italy. It already has over 2500 outlets, but plans to double this number. Of the existing stores, one-third are franchised and the rest are company owned. The decision on which route to follow is often made on the basis of whether local culture mitigates against a corporate Italian approach. Its stores in France and Italy are usually company owned while those in the Middle East are franchised.

Preparing the operating manual. The operating manual is an important document that specifies exactly how the franchisee should conduct the business. It formalises the blueprint that has been developed, and is usually copyrighted to provide extra protection for the concept. Usually, any induction training is built around the **franchise operating manual** which is designed to guide the franchisee in all aspects of the operation.

The manual will vary according to the type of franchise. Operating instructions can be quite specific, down to such details as opening hours, staff schedules, pricing policies, staff duties, service standards, accounting procedures and point of sale promotion. Any standard forms that have to be regularly submitted to the franchisor are provided, along with associated instructions. In situations where the service is more technical and requires careful delivery, a technical supplement might explain in some detail the equipment used and how it must be maintained to ensure high standards.

All franchisees receive the manual and are expected to inform their staff of the relevant parts. In a restaurant franchise, for instance, the level of detail can even include how the food should be arranged on the plate!

Marketing to franchisees. Once the system has been designed and the necessary support made available, the franchisor needs to find and select suitable franchisees. There is little point in recruiting 'unsuitable' candidates, as they are more likely to fail or to demand excessive franchisor time. Poor franchisees might also reflect badly on the reputation of the franchisor. Often, the expansion of the network proceeds slowly in the first year or two in order to fine tune the system and franchisee recruitment.

Franchisors use a variety of methods to reach prospective franchisors. Magazines such as the *Franchise Magazine* are an obvious source, as are franchise exhibitions such as the European Franchise Exhibition, and advertising in general media. Once potential franchisees have made an initial approach, there should be a preliminary screening before a detailed analysis of the suitability of a potential candidate.

Selecting franchisees. The level of detail and formality in the selection phase will often depend on the care taken by the franchisor, the range of alternatives, and the scale of the investment required. In reality, this phase is actually about mutual selection, since the franchisee must also be convinced that the relationship is worth the investment and commitment.

A number of issues might be explored by the franchisor, including the candidate's motivation, commitment, transferable skills, financial resources, career history and ability to adopt a multi-functional entrepreneurial role. Many franchisors develop a franchisee profile to guide their selection. Over time, this can reflect the franchisor's actual experiences of franchisees rather than an idealised profile. Certain skills might emerge ahead of others. Sometimes, these skills are marketing and sales related, reflecting an ability to adopt a planned, proactive approach to market development.

Source: Perfect Pizza.

The franchisor does have a responsibility to avoid selecting unsuitable applicants, despite the temptation of more licence fees. Often, a potential franchisee is investing a significant sum of money, perhaps from savings or redundancy. The loss of this through business failure could be devastating. Ultimately, any franchise system will only sustain itself if all its parts are strong. Rumours of high failure rates amongst franchisees will soon spread and deter potential candidates.

Perfect Pizza offers a tasty opportunity to potential franchisees.

From the franchisee's perspective, the decision to take out a franchise should be treated just like any other investment decision. The franchisee should thoroughly investigate the character and track record of the franchisor, as well as thinking through the feasibility of the franchise itself under different market conditions. The franchisee should be particularly concerned about the level of initial and ongoing support offered by the franchisor in site selection, opening, training and marketing. Often the best source of information is existing franchisees. Any franchisor who is reluctant to provide such contacts might be regarded as dubious. If the system appears to be working well, the real question is whether it will transfer to the area being considered and whether the applicant has the necessary skills and interest to make it work.

The franchise contract specifies, usually very precisely, the obligations of both parties and the basis upon which the agreement may be terminated. It is a legal document, is rarely negotiable and always needs careful scrutiny before signing. Once the agreement is signed it is legally binding for the contract period. The agreement normally specifies (based on Barrow and Golzen, 1990):

Domino's Pizza franchises

Domino's claims to be the biggest home or office pizza delivery company in the world. Some of the figures quoted are astounding. In 1994, it sold 230 million pizzas, including 50 000 tonnes of mozzarella, 77 000 tonnes of tomatoes, and 8000 tonnes of pepperoni. These pizzas are sold through 1100 franchisees with over 5000 stores in 44 countries. In the UK there are over 100 stores trading, with plans to expand further by 20 to 30 per year. Some of these will be located at petrol stations rather than in town.

From a humble beginning in Ypsilanti, Michigan in 1960 sales worldwide have reached $2.5 billion, all based on building a successful franchise system. The motto is deceptively straightforward, 'keep it simple and do it best'. Domino's gives extensive support to its new franchisees to ensure that they have the maximum chance of building their businesses. Initially, the franchisee only has to invest £5000. Domino's will put up the rest of the money. It pays for the site, the lease

and the equipment. Marketing support and advertising is conducted by the franchisor, and centralised buying lowers the costs of ingredients. The main priority is finding good people who will be committed to building their franchise outlet. Staff training and the manual provide guidelines for inexperienced franchisees, but one of the most important factors in selecting applicants is their knowledge of their local environment and a willingness to become involved in that community through schools, churches etc. There is also a preference for franchisees who are prepared to take their turn on deliveries, thus keeping in touch with customers and being able to control the service levels offered a little better. This can be especially important when demand peaks according to the television schedules!

With over 18 per cent of people eating pizzas regularly, Domino's consider that there is still plenty of potential left for expansion.

Source: Fairbairn (1995).

- the nature and name of the activity being franchised
- the franchise territory
- the terms of the franchise
- the franchise fee and royalty
- franchisor responsibilities
- franchisee obligations
- the conditions under which the franchisee may sell or assign the business
- the conditions under which the franchisee may terminate the franchise
- the terms and obligations of the franchisor in similar circumstances.

It is often considered that once the contract has to be quoted, normal working relationships have either become very strained or broken down. Most franchise systems have less confrontational ways of resolving difficulties as they emerge. These include regular meetings and associations of franchisees to represent the collective interest.

Maintaining and developing the franchised system. After the contract has been signed, an initial franchise fee will be payable. This normally reflects a payment for the initial service in establishing a new unit, including site selection and acquisition, training and an element of goodwill in entering an established network. To the franchisor much of this payment represents a direct contribution. Other capital for specified equipment, leases etc. will have to be paid directly or to specified suppliers. In some cases, a turnkey package might be offered in which the whole operation, including equipment, is prepared by the franchisor, leaving the new franchisee to concentrate on staffing, learning new systems and launch marketing. To the franchisor, especially in the early stages, this return for the systems investment can be an important source of income.

Continuing fees are also normally paid in order to cover the provision of ongoing services, especially in advertising, product development and management advice. This is based on a direct fee for management services, a royalty on sales, or a mark-up on goods that have to be purchased from the franchisor. In some cases, a special levy may also be imposed solely for advertising, on the basis that national advertising and promotion benefits all members of the system. Central co-ordination also enables the franchisor to control the form and content of the advertisements for the whole system.

As with any business, the inflow of fees from the franchisees must not only meet the franchisor's profit requirements, but also be able to support the renewal of the franchise system. This can be achieved by new product lines, fresh advertising campaigns, more effective training or any other means of maintaining competitive edge. As it becomes harder to find really innovative service ideas, competition between similar franchise systems and fully independent operators is increasing.

CHAPTER SUMMARY

Small businesses are difficult to define, but do tend to have certain characteristics in common. They have relatively small market shares, their owners tend to be closely involved in all aspects of both strategic and operational management, and they are often fully independent. Small businesses also face a high degree of uncertainty in their environment and can find innovation difficult because of shortage of resources. If they can develop successful projects, however, they can evolve very quickly. In purely quantitative terms, small businesses can be defined as those with fewer than 500 employees.

The four-stage model of small businesses development suggests that marketing plays an important part in the process of starting and developing a business. In the prelaunch stage, the entrepreneur must assess the feasibility and viability of the business idea. During the launch period, it is a fight for survival, ensuring that sufficient sales volume is generated to sustain the business. Many small businesses do not grow, but start small and stay small either because they do not want to grow or because there is no growth in the market. A small percentage of small firms do grow, some very rapidly indeed. This requires a more professional strategic marketing approach to maintain differentiation. The final stage, maturity and renewal, determines whether the business will grow even further to become a medium or large enterprise or stabilise. Stability does not, however, mean that strategic marketing can be neglected. Innovation in products and marketing might still be necessary to maintain the *status quo*. At any one of these four stages, failure can occur. Many of the factors contributing to failure are based in poor marketing.

Franchising represents a way for established businesses with a good idea to grow rapidly and achieve wider geographic coverage, and also a way for individuals to get into business with a relatively low risk. Franchises can involve manufacturing systems, distributorships, retail outlets or service provision. Most franchised systems are governed by a contract which formally lays out both parties' obligations and rights. There is also likely to be a blueprint or manual that can specify a wide range of operating procedures and systems that allow each individual franchise to be operated effectively and to the same standards as others. Failure in franchise situations is lower than for independent small businesses. Although the franchisee must sacrifice a certain amount of independence, the risks are much reduced and the franchisee can benefit from the franchisor's experience and managerial support.

Key words and phrases

Antecedent influences	*Franchise blueprint*	*Franchisor*
Business format franchise	*Franchise operating manual*	*Incubator organisation*
Franchise	*Franchisee*	*Small business*

QUESTIONS FOR REVIEW

24.1 What are the qualitative differences between large and small businesses?

24.2 How is a small business defined in terms of the number of *employees*?

24.3 What are the stages in small *business development*?

24.4 What factors might trigger the decision to *start* a small business.

24.5 Outline the factors that contribute to a successful small business *launch*.

24.6 What factors contribute to *business growth*?

24.7 What are the five types of *franchise relationship*?

24.8 What benefits does franchising offer (a) the franchisor and (b) the franchisee?

24.9 What are the stages involved in developing a new franchised system?

24.10 What factors does a *franchise agreement* or contract usually cover?

QUESTIONS FOR DISCUSSION

24.1 What kind of small business would you like to start? What problems do you think you would face in trying to turn that idea into reality?

24.2 What are the practical problems of designing and implementing a marketing mix in a small business compared with a large business?

24.3 What do you think are the advantages of a business remaining small? What kinds of pressures might push or pull an organisation into growth?

24.4 Develop a checklist of factors that a potential franchisee should consider before deciding to invest.

24.5 Find out about a potential franchise opportunity. How much is the licence fee and what does it include? What benefits would the franchisee derive and what risks would they run if they decided to take up this opportunity?

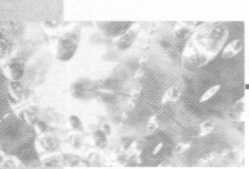

Styles Precision Components Ltd

Styles is a long established precision engineering business in the north-east of England. The founder, George Styles, built up the capability to produce precision engineering components suitable for subsequent use in manufacturing jigs and toolmaking. Most orders were for one-off components or for small batches. After George died in 1987, his son Gordon Styles took control of the business after an extended apprenticeship which had begun in 1983 when he was 18. He was keen to develop his business and started a programme of investment and relationship building with key customers. In the precision engineering field, the quality of the final product is determined partly by the skills of the work-force and the systems of quality assurance in place, and partly by the range and capability of the machines used to manufacture the product. Greater efficiency and better specification capability can often only be achieved by investing in new plant and machinery.

The business developed rapidly from a turnover of £140 000 in 1987, to £540 000 by 1992. The backbone of the success was the strong relationships built up with Nissan and ICI which provided Styles with 80 per cent of its business. Then, within a matter of a few months, disaster struck Styles. Both major customers decided to stop outsourcing their production needs, and so business was lost, even though Styles had not been beaten by competition and had maintained a good relationship with its major customers. In the context of a declining sector and with 3500 other competitors, a number of whom were better placed due to previous investment, Styles' future looked very bleak.

Rather than liquidate the company, Gordon Styles decided to maintain the precision engineering business, and also to diversify into new business opportunity areas associated with rapid prototyping. Manufacturing companies have always required prototypes or models for developing new products. They are needed to verify designs, check functions, form and appearance, as well as for customer testing. Model making is often a skilled task offered by specialists working from two-dimensional drawings. It can be both expensive and time consuming in an era where the premium is often on getting new products to the market quickly and being able to cope with design changes and modifications. Gordon spotted the opportunity for his business by using a technology developed in the USA for rapid prototyping using stereolithography. The machine allows plastic prototypes to be developed quickly from 3D CAD data by using laser beams to 'grow' the

prototypes in a bath of resin. The liquid resin is photoreactive to the laser beam which traces layer upon layer of cross-sections of the model. Each layer is instantly solidified as a result of the photo reaction between laser and resin. From this original resin model, hollow moulds are made and further models can then be cast using stronger materials with a high quality look that resembles the finished products. Typical products generated from the technology include hand-held telephones, artificial knee joints, and lawn mower bodies.

The technical processes were unrelated to the previous business, so the work-force had to be retrained to cope with the new demands. In other ways, however, the new product area was very similar to the past core activity. It was high value, high specification, fast turn-around and compatible with a jobbing culture that dealt as much with design engineers as professional buyers. To Gordon the change was manageable:

> 'Instead of playing Jazz with a trumpet we were playing it with a guitar, but when you know Jazz – you know Jazz.'

The decision to shift to a new product technology required a major rethink on Gordon's part. He needed £580 000 to make the initial investment in a stereolithography machine and vacuum casting equipment. This involved successfully raising money from venture capitalists 3I, gearing up through the banks, and buying with hire purchase. The rebuffs and problems in raising the necessary finance would make case studies in their own right!

By selling to some existing customers and developing new customers, Styles has once again experienced considerable growth. Sales rocketed to £3 million within three years, the number of staff grew to 43, including technicians and research staff to complement the original skilled craftsmen. From a near close down situation, the company has acquired a leading edge technology and has been able to transfer its core values to the new area. Further problems may lie on the horizon, however. Competitors are taking an interest in the technology, and the US manufacturers are contemplating a medium-sized version of the stereolithography machine that will require less entry capital and thus be more readily accessible to other organisations. Despite subsequent investment of £750 000 in more modern equipment, and a reputation as a pioneer in the field, Styles' future is far from certain.

Source: Adapted from a case prepared by Gerry Kirkwood.

Questions

1 What factors led to the problems encountered in 1992? Could these have been avoided or otherwise dealt with?

2 What factors do you think Gordon would have considered when deciding how best to turn the company around?

3 Gordon eventually decided to go for a new product in a new market. What were the risks of doing this and do you think it was the right choice?

4 Where does Gordon go from here? How can he minimise the threat from new entrants?

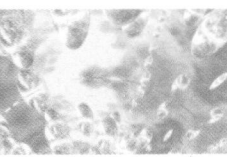

CASE STUDY 24.2

Developing a new franchise proposal: budget-priced hostels

(The name of the company featured in this case has been changed.)

Western Hostels were based in a picturesque part of Ireland, overlooking the Atlantic Ocean. The area was popular with tourists, although the season tended to be short. The business idea for a budget tourist hostel developed from the owners' experience in running a small hotel. They saw two backpackers having breakfast by the side of the road early one morning and after some investigation they realised that there was a gap in the market for accommodation located somewhere between a tent and a bed and breakfast guesthouse on the luxury scale. This gap was not just based on price but also on the customer's preferred accommodation experience. Independent backpackers are not just young people, but come from all age ranges. What they have in common is the desire for a different type of more informal holiday experience.

The entrepreneurs, having done some careful analysis, developed a business plan, and opened a hostel for all age ranges. They were surprised with the scale of the response. It was especially attractive to the French and Germans who were visiting Ireland on walking or cycling holidays. In the main season, the hostel was often fully booked and was turning customers away. Demand was even steady in the shoulder months of March–April and October–November at the beginning and end of the main season. There was little demand in the winter months, so they decided to close for refurbishment and a rest. The owners did not live on the premises, but they did live nearby so that they could keep a watch on the hostel. The cost of the hostel was around IR£100 000 which had been covered by a secured business loan.

The hostel concept was simple. Communal, single sex sleeping, a community kitchen and lounge, all of which allowed plenty of opportunity for guests to mingle and share experiences. The range of facilities was basic, but of high quality, and prices were a little lower than typical bed and breakfast rates. No food was served, although guests could cook their own. Most of the marketing that was undertaken was through travel guides and some specialist hiking magazines. Organised groups such as walking clubs, universities, schools and churches were direct mailed. A few add-on services were offered, for example a rent-a-bike scheme, a *bureau de change*, a limited selection of groceries, stationery etc., along with musical instruments that could also be hired for the evening.

After two seasons the owners contemplated the next stage in development. They became interested in the franchise option after attending a business seminar. Although there were other hostels in Ireland, they were independent and of variable standard. By franchising the product concept to a specified standard and then developing and implementing a brand identity and group marketing, the basis of a successful franchise system seemed possible. The direct experience they had gained would enable them to produce an operating manual, especially covering start-up, maintenance, pricing, promotion and service standards. If a number of franchisees could be found, an advertising royalty could be used to develop a centralised reservation system and to produce a central brochure for key markets. The initial capital would be around IR£50 000 to cover equipping premises with 30 or more beds, and a levy on sales would be also be made. In addition, the property could be acquired by the franchisee on a mortgage basis, so the capital and interest charges could be extended over a longer period.

They thought they knew the main ingredients for a franchise package, but they were still not entirely convinced that it was the best way to expand. Their plan would be for five franchises in Ireland and at least 10 in the UK within five years. Each franchisee could expect to generate around £3000 per week in the high season, based on a price of £12 to £15 per person per night and at least 30 beds. Ancillary sales would add to those revenues. After an advertisement in a franchise magazine, the owners have arranged to meet with three serious franchisee enquiries. They started to prepare for the meeting.

Questions

1 Is franchising the best way forward for this business? What are its alternatives?

2 Is the product concept, as outlined in this case, a good candidate for franchising?

3 If you were one of the potential franchisees at the meeting, what questions would you be asking?

4 What are the next stages the owners will have to go through to create and implement a franchised system?

REFERENCES TO CHAPTER 24

Barrow, C. (1989), 'Franchising', in P. Burns and J. Dewhurst (eds.), *Small Business and Entrepreneurship*, MacMillan.

Barrow, C. and Golzen, G. (1990), *Taking Up a Franchise*, Kogan Page.

Bijmilt, T. H. A. and Zwart, P. S. (1994), 'The Impact of Internal Factors on the Export Success of Dutch Small and Medium Sized Firms', *Journal of Small Business Management*, 32(2), pp. 69–83.

Birley, S. (1989), 'The Start Up', in P. Burns and J. Dewhurst (eds.), *Small Business and Entrepreneurship*, MacMillan.

Bolton, J. E. (1971), *Report of the Committee of Inquiry on Small Firms*, HMSO.

Burns, P. (1989a),'Introduction', in P. Burns and J. Dewhurst (eds.), *Small Business and Entrepreneurship*, MacMillan.

Burns, P. (1989b), 'Strategies for Success and Routes to Failure', in P. Burns and J. Dewhurst (eds.), *Small Business and Entrepreneurship*, MacMillan.

Carson, D. *et al.* (1995), *Marketing and Entrepreneurship in SMEs*, Prentice Hall.

Cooper, A. C. (1981), 'Strategic Management: New Ventures and Small Business', *Long Range Planning*, 14(5), pp. 39–45.

Cross, M. (1981), *New Firm Formation and Regional Development*, Gower.

Curran, J. *et al.* (1991), 'Profiles of the Small Enterprise in the Service Sector', paper presented at the University of Warwick, 18 April 1991.

Curran, J. *et al.* (1993) *Employment and Employment Relations in the Small Service Sector Enterprise – A Report*, ESRC Centre for Research on Small Service Sector Enterprises, Kingston Business School.

Fairbairn, S. (1995), 'Pizza Whizz Steps on the Gas', *Sunday Times*, 15 October, p. 5.

Felstead, A. (1991), "Facing Up to the Fragility of "Minding Your Own Business" as a Franchisee', in J. Curran and R. A. Blackburn (eds.), *Paths of Enterprise: The Future of the Small Business*, Routledge.

Franchise International (1996a), New Year 1996 edition.

Franchise International (1996b), Spring 1996 edition.

Franchise Magazine (1994), 'La Compagnie des Petits Joue La Franchise', advertisement in *Franchise Magazine*, No. 124, October.

Gallagher, C. C. and Miller, P. (1991), 'New Fast Growing Companies Create Jobs', *Long Range Planning*, 24(1), pp. 96–101.

Gibb, A. A. and Scott, M. (1985), 'Strategic Awareness, Personal Commitment and the Process of Planning in the Small Business', *Journal of Management Studies*, 22(6), pp. 596–631.

Graham, R. (1995), 'Big Crocodiles, Small Pools', *Financial Times*, 13 December, p. VI.

Hakim, C. (1989), 'Identifying Fast Growth Firms', *Employment Gazette*, January, pp. 29–41.

Keeble, D. *et al.* (1992), 'Small Firms, Business Services Growth and Regional Development in the United Kingdom: Some Empirical Findings', *Regional Studies*, 25(5), pp. 439–57.

Kinsella, R. P. *et al.* (1993), *Fast Growth Firms and Selectivity*, Irish Management Institute.

McClelland, D. C. (1961), *The Achieving Society*, Van Nostrand.

Marsh, P. (1996), 'In the Hotseat', *Financial Times*, 18 June, p. 10.

Mendelsohn, M. (1992), *Guide to Franchising*, Cassell.

National Westminister Bank and BFA (1989), *Annual Franchising Survey British Franchising Association*.

National Westminister Bank and BFA (1993), *Annual Franchising Survey British Franchising Association*.

Pettitt, S. J. (1988), *Marketing Decision Making within Franchised Systems*, proceedings of the Society of Franchising, San Fransisco, USA.

Pettitt, S. J. and Kirkwood, G. (1986), 'Developing Marketing Within the Owner Managed Firm', paper presented to 31st *Annual World Conference, ICSB*, Denver.

Schumpeter, J. A. (1934), *The Theory of Economic Development*, Harvard University Press.

Storey, D. J. (1994), *Understanding the Small Business Sector*, Routledge.

Vesper, K. (1980), *New Venture Strategies*, Prentice Hall.

Westhead, P. and Birley, S. (1993), *Employment Growth in New Independent Owner Managed Firms in Great Britain*, University of Warwick.

Wingham, D. L. and Kelmar, J. H. (1992), *Factors of Small Business Success Strategies*, School of Management Working Paper 92.01, Curtin University of Technology, Perth, Western Australia.

Wynarczyk, P. *et al.* (1993), *The Managerial Labour Market in Small and Medium Sized Enterprises*, Routledge.

International Marketing

LEARNING OBJECTIVES

This chapter will help you to:

1 understand what international marketing is, and why it is so important to many organisations;

2 appreciate the problems of analysing international marketing environments and selecting markets to enter;

3 define the various available methods of international market entry, outlining their advantages and disadvantages within the context of the broad factors influencing the choice of market entry method;

4 develop an overview of the factors that encourage organisations to adapt their marketing offerings to suit specific international markets, and those that push them towards standardisation; and

5 appreciate the reasons why individual elements of the marketing mix might have to be treated differently in different international markets.

INTRODUCTION

Although international trade has been a feature of civilisation for thousands of years, this century has seen an enormous growth in the scale and complexity of trade across national frontiers. Now, most large organisations and many smaller ones assume that they will have to trade across national boundaries and indeed for many such organisations, international trade is essential for their survival. For some organisations, an international orientation is so deeply ingrained into their strategy and operations that the domestic market in which the corporate headquarters are located is regarded as a relatively minor part of the total trading picture. Others, however, take a much more *ad hoc* approach, simply responding to any export enquiries that might drift in but with no special commitment to developing new markets. In between are those who proactively want to develop an international strand to their businesses. Many smaller firms in Europe have learned and benefited from the potential offered by the SEM and are now actively pursuing marketing opportunities wherever they occur in the world.

Organisations that are looking to expand their customer base internationally, however, face challenges that might be very different from those encountered in domestic markets. Decisions have to be made about the most attractive markets to pursue and develop, the best methods of entering new markets, and how much adaptation of the marketing package is necessary to achieve the desired positioning in the context of local needs and buyer expectations. These decisions are not, of course, too different from those required for domestic markets, and many of the key concepts presented in this book are just as applicable when dealing with Americans, Japanese or Danes. What is different, however, is the practice and implementation of marketing in order to take into account local customs, trading contexts, competition and other special factors that might inhibit or encourage free trade. Some organisations, such as McDonald's and Coca-Cola, choose to ignore any differences and market in the same way internationally, but the majority have to modify their marketing carefully to suit local conditions.

Example

Nestlé is a major global organisation. Its domestic market in Switzerland generates just 2 per cent of its sales and even Europe only generates 40 per cent. Nestlé operates in more than 100 countries and has nearly 500 factories around the world. It does, however, use a wide variety of methods to grow internationally. Acquisitions, for instance, have provided a fast route into some markets. Nestlé has spent over Sfr 20 billion purchasing brands such as Carnation in the USA, Buitoni in Italy, Rowntree's in the UK and Perrier in France, as well as acquiring a host of smaller organisations to strengthen their product portfolio and international market presence. In some markets, joint ventures with the likes of Coca-Cola and General Mills were felt to be more appropriate, while in others it has set up its own directly owned production and marketing facilities. International development can never, however, be considered complete, given the dynamic nature of the environment. Nestlé's next major phase of strategic expansion focuses on the growing markets in the Far East.

Despite being a major international player in the food industry, Nestlé still faces major competition, also on a worldwide scale. Not only must the organisation fight for market share and presence alongside its western competitors such as Unilever, Danone, and Mars but in the Far East it faces competition from such powerful enterprises as President Enterprises Corporation (Taiwan) and the Salim Group (Indonesia). When Nestlé plans its marketing, although it must take national markets into account, the regional and global competitive scenes are important aspects of the strategy formulation. Thus while broad strategies are determined at an international level, they are fine tuned and implemented at a local level to ensure that cats eat Gourmet and humans eat Lion bars in sufficient numbers to achieve the objectives set. This means that a series of carefully integrated marketing positioning and mix decisions are made at a national level under the international corporate strategy umbrella (Hecht, 1996).

At the other end of the spectrum, the first international order was of great significance to Chuft Toys and Gifts, as seen in the case study at the end of Chapter 21. The breakthrough achieved by winning business in the Netherlands was an important stage in that small business's development, helping them to think more creatively about selective positioning in a range of other European markets. The principles of marketing were the same as those applied in the domestic market, but they encountered a series of additional problems in pricing and distribution which had to be overcome before the company could successfully exploit the international opportunity.

This chapter starts with an examination of the rationale for international marketing and the philosophy behind it in different types of organisation. This will help to explain better the motivation and direction that organisations take as they plan their marketing strategies. The next part of the chapter, building on the concepts introduced in Chapter 2, will consider the special environmental forces that affect international markets. Sometimes these forces can become so great that it becomes undesirable, difficult or extremely risky to enter a market. The analysis of environmental forces can help to identify which countries (for example Peru, Ukraine or Vietnam) or regions (for example South America, eastern Europe or South-East Asia) should be given priority in the organisation's international development plans. Having decided on which market(s) to target, the organisation then has to decide on a market entry method. Each method carries its own risks and benefits and is appropriate for different kinds of organisations and situations. We look at this decision area later in this chapter (*see* pp. 1004 *et seq.*). Finally, the more practical issues of designing the international marketing mix are introduced, applying the concepts outlined elsewhere in this book. In this section, the most important issue is balancing the pressure to adapt and modify the marketing mix to suit local needs against the benefits of adopting a standardised approach across a whole range of different international markets to achieve economies of scale and a greater sense of consistency.

THE MEANING OF INTERNATIONAL MARKETING

International marketing is, of course, concerned with marketing across national boundaries. At its simplest, the small business that receives an order to supply its product to a buyer in another country is involved in international marketing. Even in such a simple situation, however, practical problems will have to be solved. Decisions will have to be made, for example, about what currency the price is quoted in and whether it has to cover shipping costs, import duties or other taxes. Special documentation will probably be necessary to enable the product to be shipped and transferred across national boundaries, and then the specific transportation and insurance arrangements will have to be made. The mechanism through which payment for the goods is to be transferred from country to country will have to be agreed between the buyer and the seller and might have to involve their bankers. In some cases, the seller might also have to consider installation and after-sales service arrangements. All these activities differ from normal domestic arrangements in complexity and design.

As soon as the organisation decides to seek markets proactively beyond its own national boundaries, the complexity increases still further. Promotional material and methods will have to be fine tuned to suit the local market environment in terms of language, culture, business practice etc. Successful trading on a longer-term basis might require a physical presence in the market through a sales office or distribution point from which customers can be serviced. Regardless of how committed or long term the presence, however, the principle of simple international marketing still holds: the organisation operates from its home base and supplies customers in a country other than its own. This is *exporting*.

The difficulty with such a simple principle of international marketing, however, is that it can become less applicable as the organisation intensifies its international activity. An organisation might, for example, acquire or set up a manufacturing company to serve the market in a foreign country. That company is part of an international group, but at a local level it does not market across national boundaries but concentrates on its own domestic market. The parent organisation might get involved to a greater or lesser extent in critical issues such as strategic direction, resource allocation or product strategies, but otherwise the manufacturer is largely autonomous. Truly global organisations such as Shell, Rank Xerox and McDonald's, therefore, are likely to have production, distribution and/or marketing organisations to serve different nations or regions. International marketing is, therefore, far more complex and less easy to define than the simple principle suggests. Its complexity

arises not only from operational considerations, but also from the attitude which organisations have towards it. International marketing could be an integral part of the corporate culture or it could be viewed as an add-on extra of less importance than domestic marketing.

Lynch (1994) proposed five broad categories of European organisation that will differ in their attitude and approach towards international marketing:

1 *Local-scale organisations* operate within national or even local boundaries and have little opportunity or desire to trade internationally. This group might include the local garage, a television repair shop or a small metal fabricator, for example. There might be little competitive advantage to be gained in transferring existing skills and experience to new markets. In some cases, 'exporting' could mean trading in another part of the same country rather than going abroad.

2 *National-scale organisations* focus mainly on their own domestic market, but might find a number of changes impacting upon them as a result of the SEM. In the retail sector, for example, such organisations as Leclerc and Karstadt are still primarily national operators in terms of their origins and main markets. Although Karstadt generates around 90 per cent of its sales from its domestic market, it is pursuing opportunities for international expansion based upon its existing expertise.

3 *Regional-scale organisations* might experience some growth with the economic changes in Europe. Rather than operating throughout Europe, their first stage of development may be to operate on a regional scale, for example in Scandinavia or Benelux/Northern Germany. Irish companies, as we shall see (p. 1023, Case 25.1) in the case of Martin Joinery, have a long tradition of exporting to the UK as a first experience of operating beyond national boundaries. UK companies often used to focus on Commonwealth countries as export markets, although there is now more emphasis on Europe.

By operating on a regional scale, a firm gains early experience of operating beyond the domestic market, and is exposed to such issues as cultural differences, administration and logistics within a less hostile setting. Often organisations in this category are in transition as they seek similar niches beyond their domestic markets.

4 *European-scale organisations* It is perhaps in this area that there will be considerable growth over the next 10 years as organisations with a strong national presence expand to take advantage of the single market. Some, such as Siemens AG, (with about 75 per cent of its sales in Europe), BSN (90 per cent of its sales in Europe), Fiat (with about 80 per cent of its sales in Europe) and Marks & Spencer (with about 90 per cent of its sales in Europe) are already at various stages of transition from European to world-scale companies. Others are now seeking to strengthen their European presence from a traditionally strong domestic base, for example Otto Versand (Germany).

5 *World-scale organisations* have a strong European base, but now operate in a range of different world markets on a direct investment, joint venture or exporting basis. Companies such as Shell, Unilever, Pilkington and Glaxo-Wellcome derive a significant proportion of their sales from outside Europe. Often Europe is seen as one geographic market containing segments that transcend national boundaries, and the priority is to compete against powerful international competitors, especially from the Far East and the USA. A successful European base provides a good foundation from which to compete internationally.

The distinction drawn between different types of organisations is important, as it highlights a Europe in transition. It could be argued that within the SEM there is no such thing as exporting, but just one large domestic market. Some organisations might adopt a European niching strategy as a matter of course, and see that as their 'home' market. For others with a national or local bias, moves to expand within Europe would be regarded as significant strategic developments that require major learning and adjustment. To these organisations, the decision to trade elsewhere within Europe differs little from a decision to trade in the USA, which is seen as just as risky and difficult. Although some of the risks and barriers to trade have been eliminated within Europe, others such as language or different distribution and communication channels require a different marketing approach.

Thus international marketing means different things to different organisations. To small organisations and companies which still primarily operate from one main manufacturing base, most marketing involves product movement across national boundaries and the design of a marketing mix for each market. For other organisations, the scale of international operation has become so great that product movement across national boundaries is minimal or part of a carefully planned strategy. To such multinational or transnational organisations, the distinction between international and domestic marketing becomes very artificial from a strategic marketing perspective.

> ### Example
>
> Some organisations manufacture around the world and, like General Motors (GM) and SKF, might concentrate on particular products in different nations as part of their international product strategies. Thus GM's Astra model could be manufactured in Germany and sold into the home market, but it will also be shipped across international boundaries. Similarly, SKF might produce spherical roller bearings in Sweden, selling some in the domestic market and exporting the rest.

The rationale for international marketing

Nations encourage their businesses to export their goods and services as a means of earning the foreign currency to pay for necessary imports, whether oil or oranges. The smaller and less well endowed a nation, the greater the need for foreign trade. But even the more powerful economies in the world still need exports and positively encourage their business communities to generate them. A number of small firms in the USA, for example, have been accused of not giving exporting sufficient priority because of the size and potential of the domestic market.

Apart from the warm glow arising from the sense of having done one's duty as a good corporate citizen in contributing towards the nation's balance of payments, there are other reasons, both positive and negative, why organisations consider international development as an option. For many, there is in fact no choice, unless the objective is to remain a local or national operator. This might be possible where careful positioning or regulation provides a shelter from which the organisation can ignore most of what is happening in the international market-place. In reality, however, few businesses are immune from the impact of international trade. As trade become more liberalised and domestic markets consequently become less well protected, tough and sometimes powerful competitors can enter the market with sufficient resources to take a significant share.

> ### Example
>
> In the 1980s, Chile sought to develop her international sales of wine but made little impact because of quality and marketing problems. In the 1990s, however, Chile increased her efforts in European and North American markets with an offering based on quality, consistency and price competitiveness. In the UK in 1995, 1.3 million cases of Chilean wine were sold, making it the fastest growing wine supplier to the UK. By 1996, Chile had a 2.2 per cent market share in a tough market dominated by the supermarkets, and was beginning to become a serious threat to more traditional exporters to the UK (*The Grocer*, 1996).

Whole industries have been effectively wiped out by the inability of domestic producers to withstand the impact of international competition.

> ### Example
>
> The Japanese have succeeded in achieving dominant world positions in such areas as cameras, consumer electronics, photocopiers and motorcycles, while battles still rage in motor vehicle and financial services markets. Not only did other competitors lose business in their export markets, but they also had problems managing to survive the onslaught on their domestic market.

To ignore or underestimate international competitors and to position poorly against them can, therefore, have serious consequences. Waiting until the competitor has entered and gained a foothold in the market could be too late.

Defending the organisation against the worst effects of foreign competition might involve rather more that just creating a strong positioning strategy for products, however.

> ### Example
>
> In response to the Japanese threat, Ford wanted to restructure and integrate its worldwide operations to enable it to become more competitive. Similarly, SKF undertook major rationalisation and manufacturing concentration to ensure that its cost base was low enough to compete, whereas Bosch relied on technical superiority and close customer relations, even developing plants near its main automotive customers as a means of defence. The threats have not receded but these organisations are better able to survive and to compete on equal terms in the international arena.

There are also positive reasons why organisations might actively pursue international opportunities. Each of these, shown in Fig 25.1, is considered in turn.

Small or saturated domestic markets

If the domestic market is limited in size or has become saturated (in that there are too many suppliers chasing too few customers), the organisation might look towards

FIGURE 25.1

**Reasons for inter-
nationalisation**

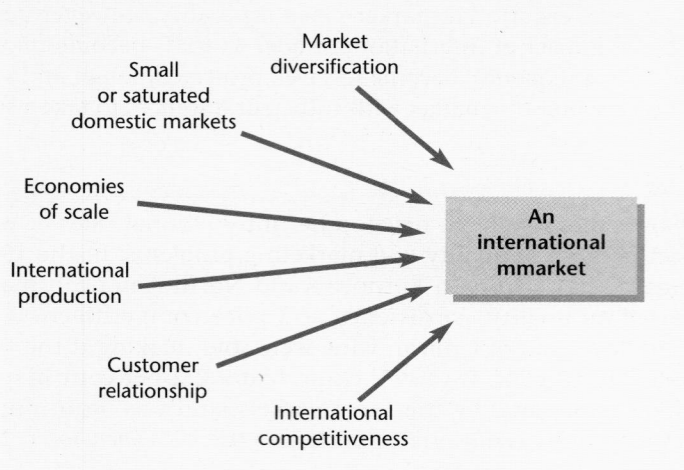

international markets sooner rather than later. An Irish producer of specialist furniture, for example, might soon find that with a domestic population of 3.5 million there are too few potential customers to maintain a viable level of business activity. In this case, the feasibility of exporting and willingness to try it might have been an important part of the business start-up process, as considered in Chapter 24. A similar manufacturer in Germany or Italy might, however, have a much larger domestic market to target before reasonable opportunities are exhausted.

The more an organisation decides to niche, the smaller the segment and the greater the chance of reaching saturation.

MARKETING IN ACTION

Novo Nordisk

Novo Nordisk, although not as widely known among the general public as Carlsberg, is in fact one of Denmark's most successful global companies with a turnover in 1995/96 of DKr 2.15 billion. Like Carlsberg, which generates 80 per cent of its sales outside Denmark, Novo Nordisk only makes 3 per cent to 4 per cent of its sales within Denmark, making it a global operator in the health care market. Its product range includes insulin for diabetes treatments, hormones for hormone replacement, products to combat menopausal and central nervous system disorders, human growth hormones, and industrial enzymes. Product areas are added and divested on an international basis, a strategy that is common in a fast moving industry, where the premium is on getting into a market sector early enough to make significant returns on investment. Thus, a bulk penicillin plant in Italy was divested while new facilities were opened for producing drugs for epilepsy and haemophilia treatment.

The health care market is growing world-wide and the focus strategy adopted by Novo Nordisk has enabled it to lead in some sectors, such as insulin production. It has direct operations in some markets, such as the USA, and in others has chosen to work in alliances. In 1996, it formed a global alliance with Rhône Poulenc Rorer to market hormone replacements in Japan, the joint strength being considered important to build a long-term presence. In the USA, from where Novo Nordisk receives around 15 per cent of its revenue, the operation is primarily a US-managed operation, although it does employ some Danish nationals. The company has an insulin company in New Jersey, an enzyme manufacturing facility in North Carolina, and research groups in Seattle and California.

Sources: Barnes (1996a, 1996b); Guttman (1994).

Montebelluna, in Italy, has become the home of 400 companies specialising in sports footwear, such as roller skates, ice skates, and in-line skates. In these three product areas alone, the town produced three million pairs in 1994. Ski and après-ski boots are also made there. Clearly, the domestic Italian market could not support such a large niche industry, and much of its output is exported, supplying 75 per cent of world demand for ski boots and 65 per cent of demand for après-ski boots (Sullivan, 1996).

Ultimately, the judgement as to whether a market is too small or too saturated lies with the organisation. What might be a comfortable niche for a small business might appear to be not worth the effort of a large organisation. In a mainstream market, if two or three very large organisations hold most of the market share between them, other companies might decide that there is no room for them to develop as they would wish, and thus they might look to foreign markets for opportunities. The significant development of Japanese companies in world markets was partially stimulated by the limited growth potential in the domestic market, where domination had already been achieved.

Ciba, the large Swiss chemical and pharmaceutical company has negligible sales in its home market, but a strong presence throughout Europe, North America and Japan. Pharmaceutical companies, in particular, find it necessary to operate on a global scale to create a big enough market to recoup the astronomical costs of R&D quickly.

Economies of scale

The Ciba example also demonstrates the importance of developing internationally to achieve economies of scale. Serving a large market with high volumes from one plant enables cost competitiveness to be maintained. Thus Ford makes the Fiesta in the UK and makes the Mondeo in Belgium for distribution to the whole of Europe. While the prospect of economies of scale is not necessarily enough in itself to push an organisation into international markets, nor does it guarantee success, it can provide a flexible foundation for developing the international marketing package.

International production

Differential labour costs around the world have been an incentive for some organisations to shift production abroad. Not only do they save on labour and possibly operating costs, but they also save on transport and import costs as well as benefiting from government incentives to encourage inward investment. Furthermore, the organisation might want to develop a regional presence for marketing purposes.

Philips manufactures a number of products in the Far East for export back into Europe, while many car manufacturers locate their plants to take advantage of lower labour costs and government incentives. The town of Montebelluna, mentioned earlier as a centre of sports footwear production, has attracted investment from many large multinationals such as Rossignol and Nike. Some of these multinationals have acquired and developed local companies because of the highly skilled labour and because of the proximity to specialist suppliers who also thrive in the region.

Customer relationships

As customers become more international in orientation, suppliers have to follow suit. Those supplying components to the automotive industry might have to be able to supply standard parts to any one of several manufacturing plants around the world. They might even be expected to expand their own manufacturing operations so that they themselves have plants close to the car manufacturer's locations. In service industries in particular, it might be necessary to locate closer to customers, wherever they might be. The Italian firm Teksid, for example, established manufacturing facilities in Poland initially in order to be close to, and to supply Fiat Polska. Teksid now not only fulfils Fiat's needs, but also manages to export almost 40 per cent of its Polish output (Bobinski and Robinson, 1995). Engineering consulting and testing service providers or advertising agencies, for example, might also feel that they can develop better customer relationships and better service by having branch offices or subsidiaries in a number of foreign markets where potential customers are concentrated.

Market diversification

The broader the range of markets served, the less likely it is that failure in any one market will cause terminal corporate decline. As discussed in Chapter 21, different markets are at different stages of development and competitive intensity, and make different resource demands. If, therefore, the organisation has a well spread portfolio, resources can be shifted for further development, for combating short-term difficulties, or even to allow withdrawal. Central and eastern Europe and the Far East are currently regarded as markets that need investment if a long-term presence is to be built, whereas many western European markets are generally regarded as mature, with any growth arising from aggressive techniques for stealing share from competitors.

Example

Thomson, the French manufacturer of television tubes, invested $33 million in buying a 51 per cent stake in the Polish company Polkolor. By improving quality and developing the labour force, Thomson was able to capture almost 75 per cent of the Polish market and still export 65 per cent of its output. Because of the high production volumes and the relatively low labour costs, this gives Thomson the added bonus of a cost advantage over its international competitors (Bobinski and Robinson, 1995).

International competitiveness

Finally it should not be forgotten that one of the major reasons for international development is the pursuit of market opportunities, with a view to either beating the competition or strengthening one's position against them.

Example

A number of European organisations, such as Heineken, Glaxo-Wellcome and Daimler Benz have proved highly successful in building and defending their position in international markets. In these situations careful marketing planning and environmental appreciation are important prerequisites for the successful entry and penetration of international markets.

Whatever the motivation for entering and developing international markets, a planned approach considerably increases the chances of success. The main stages in that process include identifying opportunities, assessing markets, planning entry, and allocating resources to ensure a match between opportunities, objectives and capabilities.

UNDERSTANDING INTERNATIONAL MARKETS

Once the decision has been made to pursue international development, the organisation has to choose which foreign markets to target. It might already have a shortlist of two or three areas that clearly show potential, but further more detailed analysis is necessary in order to choose between them or to set priorities. Understanding the marketing environments involved can form the basis of detailed market assessment and selection.

International marketing environment

The STEP factors making up the marketing environment have already been covered in detail in Chapter 2. Much of that discussion is as relevant to international markets as it is to the domestic situation. This section, therefore, will simply highlight briefly a few issues under each factor that might influence international marketing decisions and strategies specifically.

Sociocultural factors

As well as the normal consideration of market structure in terms of demographics, the international marketer needs to pay special attention to sociocultural factors, issues of cultural difference. These could affect not only the way in which a product is marketed to consumers, but also the way in which business negotiations are handled. Cultural differences might be seen in terms of language, social structures and mores (including class structure, gender roles and the effect of religion), and prevalent values and attitudes.

Language. Language is a minefield for the international marketer. Many British exporting companies assume (and indeed expect) all foreigners to speak and to negotiate in English. Unfortunately, this arrogance is often misplaced. In much of continental Europe, small and medium-sized companies cannot operate in English, and others resent being expected to do so. It is not unreasonable to expect a marketing orientated organisation to make the effort to deal with customers in the customer's own language.

> **Example**
>
> A small UK firm exporting agricultural supplies and equipment found that after just three months of specialised intensive language training, its staff were able to increase exports to Italy by over 40 per cent. By reducing the language barrier, it gained access to many new customers and relationships with existing customers were improved because they appreciated the effort made to communicate with them.

Language can also be a problem within the marketing mix. As seen at p. 274, brand names do not necessarily transfer easily across borders. Not only might the name itself have an unfortunate meaning or be difficult to pronounce in other languages, but the subtle associative elements of some names might be lost in translation of when used by people ignorant of the original language. Sales brochures and literature, manuals and instruction leaflets have to be carefully translated. Most of us have come across instruction books for Japanese electronic goods which have been translated by someone with a less than perfect grasp of English idiom. At best, this is amusing, but it can irritate and frustrate the customer, and it does not give the best impression of the organisation that has produced it.

Social structures, customs and mores. Social factors can affect what is or is not acceptable in terms of the product itself, its marketing mix, or the business negotiation process. In any consumer market, the marketer needs to understand as much as possible about the individual and the influences of various groups upon them (*see* pp. 100 *et seq.* and 109 *et seq.* to revise these concepts). The role of women in society or the structure and centrality of the family might affect product positioning and what is portrayed in advertising, for example.

Occasionally, however, the zealous drive to adapt marketing approaches to fit with the character of the foreign market can lead to trouble.

Example

Ford wanted to adapt some of its sales literature for the Polish market. One of the photographs showed a group of Ford's UK production workers which included a number of black and Asian people. The company decided that because there are few black or Asian workers in Poland, it would be better if they superimposed white faces on certain individuals. Predictably, this caused deep offence among Ford's UK work-force, leading to confrontation with the unions, the payment of compensation and much damaging publicity.

Business culture also needs to be understood in detail. Negotiating styles and etiquette can differ widely. Figure 25.2, based on Mead (1990), summarises some of the considerations that the international marketer has to take into account.

Values and attitudes. Values and attitudes can affect reaction to a product or to its origins. During the days of apartheid, consumer pressure and trade sanctions imposed by governments meant that South African products were not imported, while consumer boycotts affected those European companies that invested in South Africa. Quite apart from such specific political issues, some cultures are more resistant to foreign goods

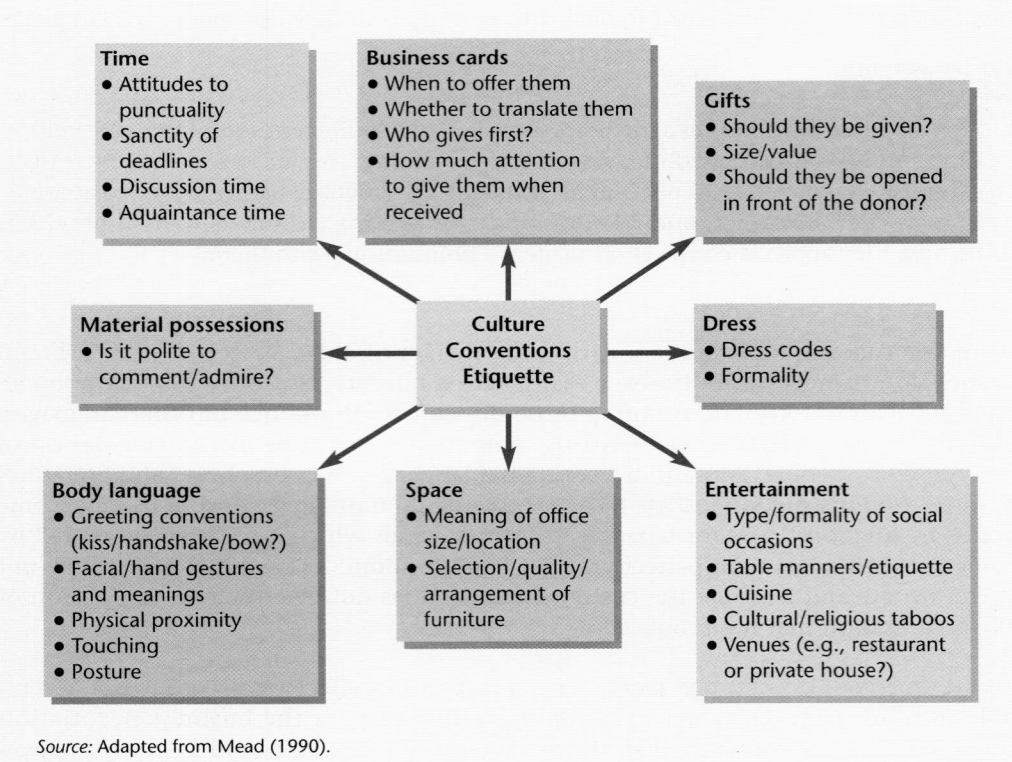

FIGURE 25.2

Behavioural factors influencing business conduct

Source: Adapted from Mead (1990).

than others. As seen at pp. 178 *et seq.* (Paitra, 1993), even within Europe there are different attitudes to the origin of goods. Germans tend to be traditionalists, orientated more towards long established home-produced products, whereas France and Italy are much more open to new foreign ideas.

Nevertheless, some companies do trade successfully using their country of origin as a major international selling point. IKEA, for example, emphasizes its Swedishness because in most countries, Scandinavian design is much admired. Both Burberry and Laura Ashley trade on their Englishness, with an image of quality and quaint heritage. Meanwhile, McDonald's and Coca-Cola carry the American dream around the world. This can backfire, of course, if customers in a foreign market do not hold or believe the 'right' stereotypical images of Englishness or Swedishness. National images can also be damaged by international political events. During the Gulf war, for example, associations with the UK or the USA became a distinct disadvantage for products in some international markets.

Not surprisingly, many organisations prefer to gain international experience initially by choosing countries that are culturally as similar as possible to their own. Thus smaller Irish companies might begin by exporting to the UK while Swedish companies might begin by trading in other Scandinavian markets. This reduces the risks and barriers to market entry and allows the organisation to learn a little about what international marketing means before it launches itself into more far-flung territories.

Technological factors

The stage of technological development that a market has reached can have many implications. A manufacturer of 'ready to microwave' meals might not have much success selling into markets where the penetration of microwave ovens is very low! Similarly, sophisticated computer peripherals or software need markets with an established IT base. Technology available within a market might also affect goods handling, stock control or the preservation of perishable goods. This raises questions as to whether the exporter can work within the existing technological infrastructure or whether investment will have to be made in developing it or finding alternative solutions.

Economic and competitive factors

As might be expected, the international marketer is interested in the size of the foreign market and its market potential. Basic information about per capita disposable income, consumption patterns and unemployment trends can help to paint a background picture of how that market is developing in the longer term. The international marketer will also be interested in inflation, the stability of exchange rates and any exchange control regulations. An exporter wanting payment in hard currencies such as sterling or dollars rather than in the importer's local currency might face problems if the importer's government tightly controls their access to hard currency. The existence and levels of import tariffs, duties and local taxes can also add to the costs and problems of entering foreign markets. We discussed at the impact of VERs on the car market at p. 65. Chapter 2 also discussed the problems of varying VAT rates and excise duties on cross-border trade within the EU.

In terms of competitive analysis, the procedure is the same as for any domestic market, and organisations need to look at the number of competitors, the structure of the market and the sophistication of market positioning and marketing mixes. Of particular interest in foreign markets is the extent to which other exporters have managed to penetrate that market and the problems they have faced in doing so.

Political and legal factors

Some countries are more politically stable than others. In some, a change in government makes little difference to commercial life, but in others the changes can be dramatic. The last thing an organisation needs is to invest in setting up a manufacturing plant in a country with a liberal regime only to have it 'confiscated' by a subsequent hardline government with a hostile attitude to foreign ownership of assets. This is an extreme case, although it must be said that some governments do restrict foreign ownership. This might mean, for example, that the foreign manufacturer has to enter into a joint venture with a local company, with the local company retaining 51 per cent ownership of the joint enterprise.

Political problems do not always arise from specific conditions in the foreign market itself. Individuals and groups in the domestic market might have strong views about trade with certain countries and regimes, as mentioned earlier in relation to South Africa. Action taken by trading blocs and governments working together also have a profound influence. In spring 1996, for example, there was a worldwide ban on the sale of British beef and beef products in response to the 'mad cow disease' crisis which completely devastated a major UK export industry.

Organisations thinking about setting up a manufacturing plant in a foreign country are going to have to look not only at ownership restrictions, but also for example at employment law, health and safety regulations, financial law and patent protection relevant to that market. Any organisation wanting to sell or market a product will also need to know about advertising, sales promotion and direct marketing constraints, pricing regulations, contract law and consumer protection legislation.

Market selection

Once the marketing environment is understood, the organisation needs to look at it in their own context. This means matching the opportunities and threats emerging from the marketing environment with the organisation's own strengths, weaknesses, assets, skills and aspirations. Some of the issues that might be considered are shown in Fig 25.3 and discussed below.

Product fit factors

Is there a gap in the market for our product? Is there demand for our sort of product? Would we have to adapt the product to suit local conditions and if so, how much?

Market factors

Is it a completely undeveloped market, is it still in its growth stage, or has it reached maturity? Is there sufficient potential future demand to warrant our long-term commitment to this market? Are there established distribution channels we can use or would we have to invest in creating them? How long are the distribution channels and how sophisticated is their infrastructure?

Competitive factors

Who are the existing competitors in this market and how well established are they? How intense and how aggressive is the competition? To what extent have existing competitors obtained control over distribution channels? How likely are competitors to react aggressively to our entry into the market and what barriers to entry can they raise?

Entry factors

What market entry methods are feasible for this market, and how much would each cost us? Do we have any established contacts in this market who could help us? What marketing costs are

FIGURE 25.3

Factors influencing international market selection

Eastern Europe strikes back

The popular view is that eastern Europe is an ideal market for EU companies to develop, not only because it is geographically close to their own domestic markets, but also because there is new wealth emerging in these countries. Because of the major industrial overhaul needed in eastern Europe's infrastructure, some western European companies see direct investment or joint ventures as appropriate ways of market entry. This not only allows them to capture the eastern European market, but also gives them a relatively cheap manufacturing base from which to export elsewhere. An example of this was seen earlier in this chapter at p. 998 in the case of Thomson's take-over of the Polish company, Polkolor. Some Eastern European companies are now fighting back, however, and developing EU markets for their own exports.

Chlumcanske Keramicke Zavody (CHKZ), a ceramics works in the Czech Republic has increased its turnover and its exports without the direct involvement of western investors. It has coped with formidable challenges, such as the collapse of its traditional markets, currency volatility, price liberalisation, privatisation, the imposition of VAT, and not least the split of the former Czechoslovakia into two states. The company has had to invest heavily in order to approach western quality and productivity standards. It has also invested in market development in the EU, especially in Germany, and also in other central European states such as Poland. Over one-third of its sales come from exports. One of the other big changes was the restructuring of the product range. The company found that those products that used to be valued in the former Soviet Union were not necessarily acceptable in Germany when up against strong Italian and Spanish competition.

Graboplast from Hungary has gone one step further, and is now seeking to develop through acquisition, especially in the former eastern European states. Around half of its sales now come from exports, especially to the EU. Originally, the company made artificial leather, floor coverings and wallpaper. To succeed since liberalisation, however, has required some major changes in the company's marketing strategy, as well as restructuring. To achieve market penetration, it had to move away from its traditional focus on artificial leather for belts and clothes trimmings, where it did not have a competitive advantage, towards a new focus on areas in internal decorations. While it does have EU market penetration, the priority for the future is to be number one in eastern Europe, where it already generates about 40 per cent of its sales. The company sells through representatives in the Czech Republic, Slovakia, Poland and Russia, and Romania will soon follow. It is also looking to purchase manufacturing operations in these countries, with a view to restructuring purchased companies to establish them for domestic and export penetration.

Sources: Done (1995); Marsh (1995).

going to be incurred in getting established in this market and developing a market share? How similar is the culture in this market to our own, and how well do we understand any differences? Is this going to cause us problems in entering the market?

Resourcing factors

What are we going to have to invest in entering this market? Are we going to have to recruit local staff and/or relocate our own staff? Are we going to have to train staff in languages, export procedures, business culture etc?

Trade restraint factors

What legal and regulatory factors will influence our operation in this market? Do we have to manufacture to different quality or safety standards? Can we use advertising and sales promotion as we would wish? Are there import tariffs or quotas that apply to us? Will we be allowed to repatriate any/all our profits (i.e., take money out of the country)? Are there any constraints on foreign companies operating in this market, for example a ban on foreign ownership of companies?

Throughout the whole process, there is a need for sound market intelligence and information. It is very difficult to undertake detailed research on 180 sovereign states, hence the need for a scan to reduce the shortlist to two or three serious contenders. The screening process will become more detailed as options are eliminated. Early screening will soon reveal the options that are unattractive because of clearly unfavourable environmental forces. Desk research alone can show up markets with low potential, leaving a much smaller number for more detailed investigation. In reality, however, market screening can be random, driven as much by enquiries or knowledge gained through media and personal networks as by systematic research. At some point, however, it is likely that a visit will have to be made to a potential market to see at first hand how it operates and to make preliminary contacts.

MARKET ENTRY METHODS

Once an organisation has decided which are the best markets to enter, it must then decide how to enter. The choice of **market entry method** depends on a number of factors. Paliwoda (1993) cites six main factors, as summarised in Fig 25.4. They are briefly outlined here, but will be further considered as each entry method is discussed later in this section.

1 *Speed*: how quickly does the organisation want to get into the market? Some market entry methods might take many months or even years to plan and implement, whereas others can be put into action almost immediately.
2 *Costs*: how much is it going to cost to enter the market by each method? Do the benefits derived from using one method rather than another justify its higher cost?
3 *Flexibility*: how much flexibility does the organisation want to retain? Some entry methods allow the organisation to leave the market or expand further relatively easily. Others require long-term contractual agreements or long-term financial commitments that could restrict the organisation's future options.
4 *Risk factors*: these are wide ranging, covering all aspects of the marketing environment, but particularly competitive and political risks. Again, some entry methods can help to reduce certain types of risk. Long-term investment in a manufacturing plant in a foreign country, for example, not only helps to overcome import quotas and duties, but also might be viewed more kindly by the government.
5 *Payback period*: there might be pressure from within the organisation to produce a quick return on any investment in a foreign market. If this is the case, acquiring an established manufacturer might be a more appealing option than building a new factory from nothing, if it means that revenues can be generated within one year rather than five years.
6 *Long-term profit objectives*: the organisation has to look ahead to what it wants to achieve in the future and how it can best exploit the opportunities available in the foreign market. The choice of market entry strategy is just the first stage in a longer-term strategic plan for that market.

Of course, much also depends on the nature of the product itself and its market. Some services lend themselves naturally to international franchising, while mass production can make it cost effective to manufacture abroad. As discussed in Chapter 2, Japanese car manufacturers have established manufacturing plants within the EU to overcome import quotas and to delete the costs of shipping finished goods half-way across the world.

FIGURE 25.4

Factors influencing the choice of market entry method

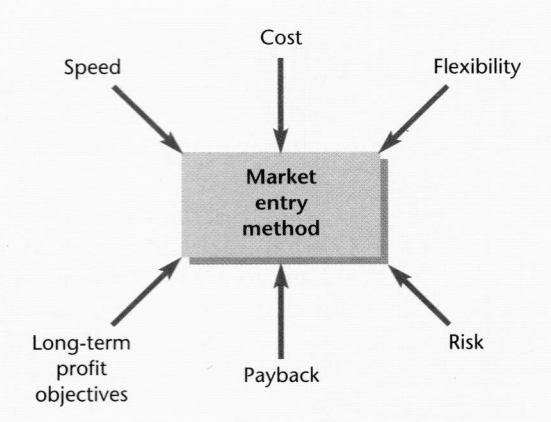

The range of market entry methods from which the organisation can choose is wide and varied, as can be seen in Fig 25.5. When looking at this figure, remember that the definition of *customer* needs to be flexible. In some cases, it might mean an individual consumer or end user, in others it might be a wholesaler or retailer within a longer distribution channel, but in others it might be a manufacturer who is buying in components or raw materials.

The classification of market entry methods is not easy, as there are many relevant criteria, such as the level and type of investment involved and whether it is indirect or direct; whether the goods or services are manufactured or produced at home or abroad; whether the exporter deals directly or indirectly with the buyer, or whether the transaction involves exporting goods and services, knowledge and expertise or investment. For further exploration of these issues *see*, for example, Brooke (1992), Young *et al.* (1989), or Paliwoda (1993). The groupings presented in Fig 25.5 are largely based on Brooke (1992), and will now be discussed in turn.

Trade in Goods and Services

There are two main methods of trading in goods and services: **direct export** and **indirect export**.

Direct export

Direct exporting means that the organisation produces the product at home and then sells to the foreign customer without the use of an intermediary. The seller thus has to take responsibility for finding customers, negotiating with them, processing their orders and arranging shipment and after-sales service.

Clearly, this involves some investment and can represent a big step, especially for the smaller firm. The costs can be high, but at least the seller maintains complete control by selling through its own export department and sales force. The selling effort can be co-ordinated and run from the organisation's home base with sales representatives making trips abroad, or it can be run from a branch sales office located in a foreign country. It depends on the organisation's objectives and the volume of business it expects to handle. Ultimately, the organisation might decide to set up a sales subsidiary, which will be considered at p. 1009.

FIGURE 25.5

Market entry methods

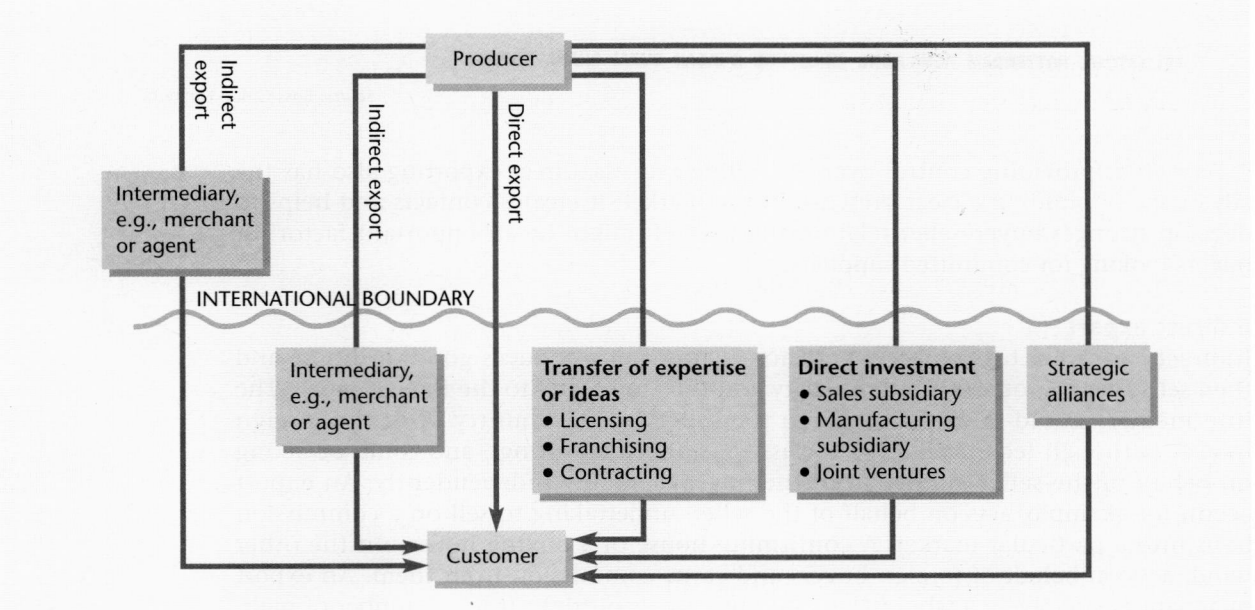

The Boss Group Limited has used a variety of market entry methods in order to develop its global sales.

Source: Boss Group Limited.

As well as providing control over the selling process, direct exporting also has the advantage of building a clear presence in the market. It creates contacts and helps to develop stronger buyer–seller relationships, which might be an important factor for buyers looking for committed suppliers.

Indirect export

Indirect exporting takes place where an organisation produces goods at home and then sells them through an intermediary and thus indirectly to the foreign buyer. The intermediary could be based either in the seller's home country or in the foreign market (although technically this is classed as direct exporting), and could be acting on behalf of the seller, on behalf of the buyer or totally independently. An export agent, for example, acts on behalf of the seller, undertaking to sell on a commission basis into a particular market. A confirming house or a buying house, on the other hand, acts on behalf of foreign buyers and earns commission from them. An export merchant is effectively a wholesaler who buys goods outright from a number of manufacturers and then resells them, perhaps to foreign retailers at a profit. Whether the intermediary is a merchant or an agent, the exporting manufacturer benefits from the intermediary's knowledge of the foreign market concerned, their contacts within the distribution channel, and their experience of how business is done in that country. Similarly, the foreign buyer using a buying agent is also benefiting from the intermediary's knowledge and contacts in the export market.

Because of the reliance on the expertise of an intermediary, indirect exporting is an ideal starting point for a small business entering the international arena. It also carries little risk and little commitment because there is no investment in market development. It can, therefore, be a useful method if the organisation is dealing in small volumes or is somewhat uncertain, either about its own future or whether the product is appropriate for an international market.

Trade in knowledge and expertise

So far, the methods discussed have involved the transfer of goods or services from a domestic producer to a foreign customer. Here, however, we look at the transfer of ideas, concepts and processes, a transfer that is usually carried out so that goods and services can be produced abroad by foreign producers. This gives the originating organisation the benefit of selling a product with a 'made in ...' label that shows that it was produced in the country in which it is being sold rather than one that is overtly a 'foreign' product.

The main methods to be covered here are licensing, franchising and contracting.

Licensing

Licensing can be an attractive option for entering international markets. The licensor grants a licensee the right to manufacture a product, use patents, use particular processes or exploit trade marks in a defined market in return for a royalty payment. Franchising applications of licence agreements are considered separately.

In manufacturing, **licensing** is useful for markets that are very remote or not worth the costs of direct involvement. The domestic manufacturer might be producing up to full capacity in its own plants and might not want to invest in new facilities or to divert capacity for a particular foreign market. Licensing helps to overcome high import tariffs, but also avoids the costs and commitment of direct investment. The licensor does, however, need to be sure that the licensee can handle the necessary production and marketing, otherwise a gap might be left for competition.

Licensing can be a particularly effective way of achieving technology transfer, that is, the movement of technological advance to new nations.

> **Example**
>
> The German bus manufacturer Neoplan, for example, licensed Autobus Zil in Russia to build its buses. To help the technology transfer process, the buses were initially to be built in Neoplan's German plant by Zil staff, with production later transferring to Moscow using imported German components. The ultimate target is to build 1000 buses a year in Moscow (Gibbins, 1994).

Licensing can thus be viewed favourably by foreign governments, as it brings in new technology and helps in the training and skilling of the local work-force. Licensing can also be useful in some specific industrial sectors, such as defence, as a means of winning government contracts.

The financial risk of licensing could be relatively low, as the licensee is the one who will be investing in plant, machinery and marketing. There could, however, be risks to the licensor's reputation if the licensee degrades or abuses the licensor's name or intellectual property. There is also a risk that the licensee, having gained experience, might then decide to go it alone at the end of the contract period and turn into a competitor.

A major strength of licensing is that it combines the skills and knowledge of the licensor with the local contacts and experience of the licensee. Its success, however, is very dependent on whether production quality and marketing effectiveness can be created and sustained. Like any distribution decision, the choice of licensing as an entry strategy is based on a trade-off between the increased coverage and lower risk gained, and the potentially reduced financial returns because of the high level of involvement of the licensee.

Franchising

The previous chapter looked at the impact of franchising across Europe and the development of some large international franchisors such as KFC, Subway, Dunkin' Donuts and Burger King. Some franchisors, such as McDonald's in the UK, have grown through direct involvement between the franchisor and its franchisees. Sometimes, however, indirect methods are adopted that involve a sharing of know-how, resources and marketing effort. McDonald's, for example, preferred to use a joint venture to enter the Russian market because of the alien and relatively unknown nature of the marketing and operating environment. By far the most popular indirect method, however, is the **master franchising** system.

Master franchising. Master franchising means that an individual or organisation in a country is given an exclusive right to develop the franchising system. The master franchisee can then develop a network of sub-franchises on a regional, multiple or individual unit basis. The master franchisee might receive extensive training from the franchisor, not only in operating a unit, but also in franchisee recruitment, staff training and managing a franchised system. It is then the master franchisee's responsibility to use local knowledge and contacts to develop the network in a manner that is satisfactory to the franchisor. The master franchisee earns a percentage of the fees or royalties paid by individual franchisees.

Example

The USA-based franchisor New Horizons, which offers certified applications and network training for business computer users, primarily develops foreign markets through the appointment of master franchisees. Within three years they had developed in 22 countries, the majority, including France, Japan, Malaysia and South Africa involving master franchisees. By adopting this approach, New Horizons has been able to expand more quickly, an important point given the increasing growth of competition between franchised systems and the ease with which many franchised ideas can be adapted. Fast innovation and expansion can be crucial.

Area development agreement. The franchisor might not want to appoint a single master franchisee to cover a whole country. After all, it does put a great deal of power into the master franchisee's hands, and if the master franchisee fails to fulfil their part of the agreement or to maintain high standards among the sub-franchisees, the franchisor stands to lose both reputation and the competitive initiative in that country. The franchisor might, therefore, prefer to enter into *area development agreements* in which several master franchisees are appointed, each with responsibility for a clearly defined regional territory. The agreement might also specify that a certain number of outlets are expected to be opened over a defined period of time in return for the exclusive territory. This approach has all the benefits of the master franchisee system, in terms of reducing the network development costs, the time taken to develop a new market and exploiting the local knowledge of the master franchisees, while reducing the potential losses from a poor master franchisee. Popeye's restaurants operate area development agreements for their expansion into in Europe, Asia and Australia.

Contracting. A manufacturing contract means that the manufacturer contracts with a company in the foreign market to produce or assemble the product on their behalf. This saves the time and costs involved in physically transporting the finished product from abroad. This allows a more flexible approach for entering markets where international logistics costs might otherwise reduce effectiveness and margins. Like licensing, **contracting** also avoids the problems of currency fluctuations and import barriers, but potentially creates a new competitor. Nevertheless, contracting can be particularly useful if the volume of business in the foreign market is too much for direct importation of goods, but not sufficient to warrant direct investment in production facilities. As Gilligan and Hird (1986) make clear, contracting also allows the contractor to retain control over marketing and distribution, unlike licensing.

Management contracts are widely used in service markets, such as hotels. An independent enterprise contracts to operate all the management functions in return for a fee, and occasionally for a share in the profits. The company awarded the contract has responsibility for operational matters such as human resource management, financial control, marketing and service delivery, but does not normally get involved in strategic or policy issues, nor does it have any share in the ownership of the business.

Example

Hilton Hotels have management contracts for a number of hotels around the world, without any equity stake in them. Thus the management team can bring their international knowledge and skills to a local level, helping to develop the market while avoiding the risks associated with capital investment.

The careful use of management contracts can help the 'exporter' to increase market coverage and to develop international segments more quickly.

Investment

This group of entry methods involves a major commitment for the organisation because it involves some level of investment in the foreign market. As mentioned earlier, this might mean simply setting up a sales subsidiary to market and distribute goods imported from the home country, or it might mean acquiring a local company or setting up a new manufacturing facility to produce goods closer to the market, thus avoiding international logistics costs and import barriers. Whatever the type of investment, it certainly helps the organisation to create a presence in the market and to build much closer relationships with customers.

Because investment is such a big decision, there are a number of specific issues to be taken into account. These are summarised in Fig 25.6, which is based on Walsh (1993), and cover the whole range of operational and marketing environmental factors.

Within this section, three particular forms of investment are considered: **sales subsidiaries**, **manufacturing subsidiaries** and **joint ventures**.

Sales subsidiaries

Sales subsidiaries play no part in manufacturing the product, but do take responsibility for marketing, selling and distributing it. They might also get involved in after-sales service. Sales subsidiaries can be especially created or they can be developed from an existing acquired company. Staff, therefore, can either be transferred from the

FIGURE 25.6

**Factors
influencing the
investment
decision**

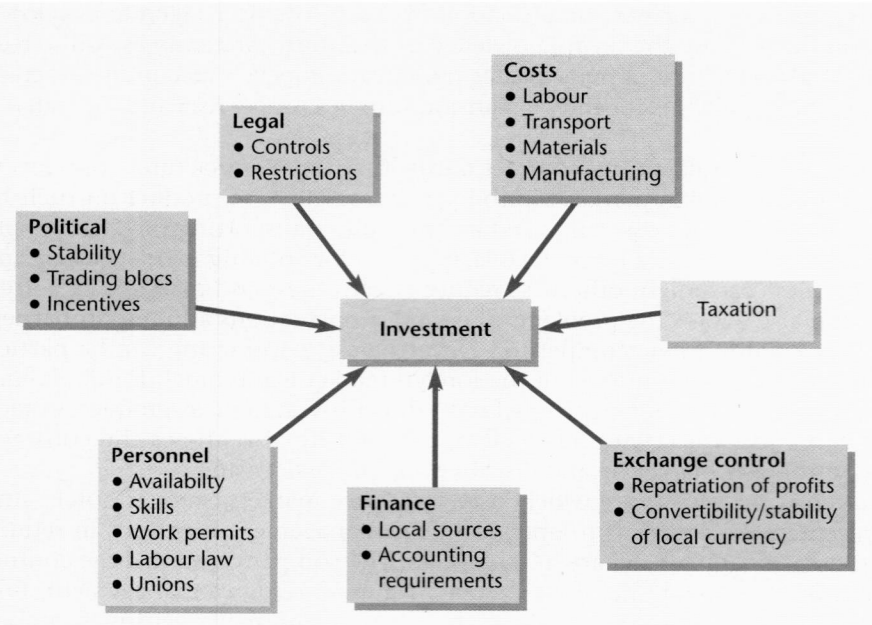

Source: Based on Walsh
(1993).

MARKETING IN ACTION

Barco – projecting the future

Barco is an electronics company based in Belgium that has seen a dramatic turnaround in its fortunes through a carefully designed product and market development strategy. In the early 1980s, Barco faced bankruptcy primarily because of difficulties in its consumer electronics division. Its problem was that it could not achieve sufficient sales volume to be fully competitive. Barco just could not compete with other international companies in such product areas as radios and televisions. Although consumer electronics accounted for 85 per cent of the company's turnover, losses were growing. Barco had also found, however, that it is not easy to change direction in a mass manufacturing operation.

The critical strategic decision, made in 1985, was to switch to high value added niche products, primarily concentrating on professional rather than consumer markets. Since then, sales and profits have grown steadily to BFr 15.1 billion and net profits to BFr 1.8 billion. The 'visualisation and communication' division provides around 53 per cent of turnover from such products as projectors, television studio equipment, satellite receivers and modems. This division was well placed for the media revolution that

swept Europe. The graphic systems division includes prepress systems and software packages for film and transparency image enhancement. Again, the market is highly specialised. This division accounts for 26 per cent of turnover. The automated division, with 16 per cent of turnover, supplies the textile, rubber and plastics markets.

The common thread in all these areas is the ability to create an environment that facilitates product innovation. Around 10 per cent of turnover is ploughed back into R&D, an important point in a market experiencing rapid technological development. As Barco has concentrated on narrower niche markets, it has also been necessary to seek market development, within and beyond Europe. The company needs a larger range of markets to achieve its full potential. Exports have grown significantly in the USA, Asia and Latin America. Barco is already strong throughout Europe, with manufacturing plants in Germany, Switzerland and the UK. As exports continue to fuel growth, further development is expected outside Europe, where the new markets are.

Source: Southey (1996).

parent organisation or recruited locally. With local staff, the organisation acquires local contacts and knowledge, but might have to give product and management training. With transferred staff, the product and management knowledge might well be in place, but local knowledge will have to be developed.

The advantage of selling through sales subsidiaries rather than through the domestic sales force lies in the dedicated local knowledge and expertise that builds up and the closeness to the customer. Also, in the event of failure in that market, any losses can be confined to the subsidiary rather than impacting extensively on the parent company.

Manufacturing subsidiaries

The establishment of manufacturing subsidiaries involves assembling or manufacturing the product in local markets. Again, such an operation can be set up from scratch or developed from an acquisition. It becomes an integral part of the manufacturing base of the host country, and can thus become a significant contributor to the local economy. As discussed in Chapter 2, because of the employment and wealth creation potential involved, many governments are keen to attract this sort of inward investment, offering incentives and grants to manufacturers to set up plants in key regions. Many of these manufacturing subsidiaries themselves export their goods to nearby markets. Japanese cars, for example Nissan and Toyota, manufactured in the UK are exported to other European countries.

Joint ventures

A joint venture is set up when two organisations come together to create a jointly owned third company. The two parents share the ownership, control and profits, as well as the risks. There are many reasons for taking this route. The partners might feel that separately they do not have the necessary resources (whether financial, physical or managerial) to develop or make an impact on a market. This motivation could be especially important if they are up against larger, more powerful competitors. The partners are likely to have complementary assets or skills. One might have cash, the other know-how; one might have technical expertise, the other might be an ailing manufacturing plant at the geographical heart of the market; one might have marketing and distribution skills, the other an unexploited product idea. A joint venture

By the year 2000 the Daewoo Group plans to have 430 sales subsidiaries, 130 manufacturing subsidiaries, 20 R&D centres and 70 branch offices spread across 150 countries.

Source: Daewoo Motors.

might be the only choice if an organisation wants to enter a country whose government is hostile to foreign companies having 100 per cent ownership of any aspect of production (whether physical assets or know-how).

Joint ventures have been an important force in the privatisation and regeneration of the industries of the central eastern European countries. Western companies have been encouraged to invest cash and managerial skills in joint ventures with local companies that provide production facilities that can be updated, labour that can be retrained and access to the market. The partners work together to develop products and markets and share the benefits.

Example

Joint ventures do, however, carry risks, and the whole operation can all go horribly wrong. After four years of planning and negotiation and one year of operation, the Rodacar plant in Varna, Bulgaria closed in May 1996. Rodacar was a joint venture between Rover of the UK and Bulgaria's Daru Car. Despite an investment of $20 million in the plant, the sales of the Maestro model produced fell so far short of expectations that it was a source of embarrassment. Both Rover and the Bulgarian government had different explanations for the failure. Rover blamed the Bulgarian government for lack of support. The government insisted on levying import duties on imported parts, despite an original agreement not to do so. Less directly, the government also signed a free trade agreement with the Czech Republic, thus halving the level of import duties on Skodas. However, Rover's decision to manufacture the Maestro was itself questionable. Not only was it a 1982 model, but it also proved to be too expensive for the mass market and too unsophisticated for those who did have sufficient income to afford a western European car (Troev and Moss, 1996).

This example shows just how exposed to risk the organisation is when entering a market with such a level of commitment. Political, legal and economic issues all add to the normal commercial and marketing problems of operating in relatively unknown environments. Rover's losses might well be limited to their initial $20 million investment in the new company, but that is still a significant amount to lose, not to mention the strategic setback to their plans to compete in a major emerging market.

Nevertheless, joint ventures can be very successful, as long as both partners plan the venture carefully and are clear about their objectives. They also need good communication and mutual understanding of what each party is bringing to the venture, what each one's responsibilities are within it and what each expects to get out of it. Figure 25.7 suggests a number of factors that might contribute towards a more successful joint venture partnership.

Strategic alliances

The term **strategic alliance** is wide ranging, covering any kind of collaborative agreement or activity between two or more organisations. It can include joint ventures, but not all strategic alliances have to be joint ventures. Whereas a joint venture specifically means creating a separate, jointly owned entity, a strategic alliance can be much looser and informal. It could be two companies joining R&D forces to develop a specific product for a specific market, or agreeing to share a distribution channel, or agreeing to sell each other's products. The benefits from a strategic alliance are similar in principle to those derived from a joint venture, in that it brings together complementary assets and skills creating synergy. Strategic alliances do not, however, necessarily carry the same degree of long-term commitment and risk, as there is no

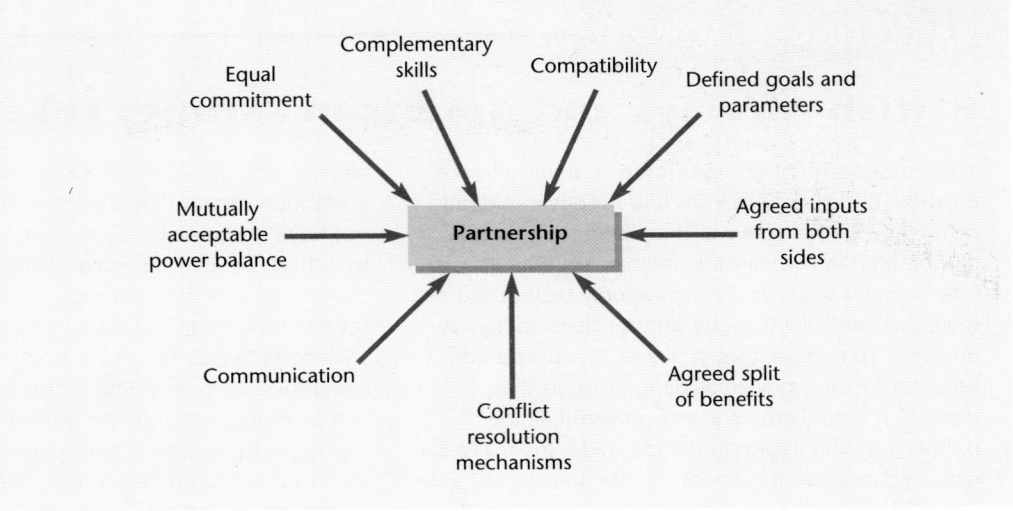

equity stake, just commitment to a specific project or activity. The retail alliances mentioned at pp. 521–3, such as SEDD and Eurogroup, are effectively strategic alliances for the purpose of purchasing more efficiently.

The number of strategic alliances of all kinds has increased rapidly over the last 10 years or so, as competition has become more aggressive, markets have become more global and technology has increased its rate of change. Alliances are particularly prevalent in fast moving, high-technology industries such as defence, communications, pharmaceuticals (all requiring heavy investment in R&D to keep up with the pace of technological change and to deliver necessary innovation) and airlines (under pressure from competition and national protectionism). As Houlder (1995) points out, a strategic alliance can help an organisation to enter new markets, obtain access to expertise and technology and to achieve economies of scale much more quickly. She does, however, sound a note of caution, quoting a survey that suggested that only 17 per cent of US managers thought that alliances were effective while 31 per cent thought they were downright dangerous. The risks arise from ill-matched partnerships, poor definition of the alliance's purpose and the mutual responsibilities involved, or poor implementation of the alliance. Figure 25.7 suggests ways of creating more successful joint ventures, but imagine how much damage can be done when one or more of the factors considered there goes wrong, as they often do in practice. Houlder (1995) sums up the real-world problems neatly:

> There is a dilemma at the heart of alliance-making. Trust, flexibility and commitment are widely seen as the keys to success. But companies dare not blind themselves to the risks involved. Today's ally may be tomorrow's competitor; a joint venture may turn out to be a takeover by the back door. For the growing number of companies engaged in alliances, ambiguity is a fact of life.

INTERNATIONAL MARKETING STRATEGY

Once an organisation has analysed the characteristics of the target foreign market and has decided how to enter it, the next stage is to design the marketing programme. In principle, this is no different from designing a marketing mix in a domestic market. The organisation has to define and select target segments, position the product and decide whether to modify the marketing mix to suit conditions in the foreign market, whether it is close to home in Europe or elsewhere in world. Just because a particular marketing mix is successful in the domestic market, however, it cannot necessarily be

British Airways and American Airlines take off

The announcement of a proposed strategic alliance between British Airways (BA) and American Airlines (AA) was a further move in the changing face of competition in the transatlantic passenger market. International alliances are increasingly being used as a means of controlling routes and for developing new business. To competitors, however, the proposed BA–AA alliance was seen as dangerous, as they thought it would create a very powerful airline partnership that could distort fair trade. Ironically, BA had used a similar argument to criticise the Lufthansa–United Airlines alliance that was designed to seek anti-trust immunity in the USA.

The BA–AA proposal might, at first glance, appear to be straightforward. From April 1997, all BA and AA flights between the UK and the USA would have co-ordinated schedules that would enable smoother transfers for passengers between the two airlines. By placing joint flight codes on their UK–USA flights, they would also share the revenues generated. It would also mean, however, that around 60 per cent of the total transatlantic market, and 70 per cent of flights between London and New York would be covered by the agreement. They would also be able to access parts of each other's database for mailing and promotion purposes. This could seriously affect the competitive position of a number of smaller airlines who are excluded from similar deals. Richard Branson, speaking for Virgin Atlantic, claimed that the BA–AA alliance would be bad for the market, because it could lead to reduced competition and higher fares. Virgin even took out a full-page advertisement in the *Sunday Times* on 7 July, quoting industry experts and newspaper analyses to support their view that the alliance was dangerous for the market.

Transatlantic alliances are not new. Lufthansa and United Airlines already co-operate, as do KLM and North West. Austrian Airlines, Swissair and Sabena are all part of an alliance with Delta. Air France, however, is without a transatlantic partner and therefore does not have the same US access benefits that are enjoyed by others. Alitalia, Sabena and Olympic are also concerned that they will miss out on the profitable transatlantic trade, especially if their domestic customers decide to use London Heathrow as a hub. If passengers on connecting flights in Europe or the USA can be routed through the alliance, clearly there are real opportunities to generate more bookings than if the customer has a free choice. The EC has the right to investigate the alliance under Article 89 of the Treaty of Rome, and by July 1996 had decided to investigate all transatlantic alliances, not just the proposed BA–AA agreement.

The air passenger industry is by its nature international and often meets political problems at an intergovernmental level. There are already a number of discussions going on between Europe and the US governments which set the background for proposed deals such as the BA–AA alliance. European airlines, for example, are not permitted to own more than 25 per cent of a US carrier, although US airlines can own up to 49 per cent of an EU carrier. US airlines can fly between EU cities, but EU airlines cannot fly between US cities. The US government is keen to open up Heathrow to more flights from non-British airlines, even though it is the world's busiest airport. BA, however, considers it important that Heathrow is identified as part of the UK national interest, rather than existing for the convenience of the USA or other countries. It is claimed that the US government is seeking more freedom for an 'open skies' agreement, allowing more internal EU flights to be undertaken by US carriers, as the price for supporting the BA–AA deal.

Sources: Cunningham (1996); de Jonquieres and Skapinker (1996); Rees (1996); Skapinker (1996a, 1996b); Skapinker and Buckley (1996).

successfully transferred elsewhere. A whole range of factors within the marketing environment, for example culture, customs or competition, might point to the wisdom of adapting some or all of the marketing mix elements.

We now look more closely at the pressures affecting the debate on the merits of the standardisation as compared with adaptation, and later we take a more general view of the implementation of the marketing mix in international contexts.

Standardisation or adaptation

The decision on whether to standardise or to adapt is a major one for any organisation operating in more than one environment. There could be conflicting pressures, some of which push the organisation towards adapting the marketing mix to suit local conditions, and some of which push the organisation towards standardisation of the marketing approach, regardless of local market. We look first at pressures leading towards **adaptation**, which are summarised in Fig 25.8.

Pressures towards adaptation

Customer needs. Any organisation has to think carefully about customer needs and wants and the extent to which the marketing mix satisfies them. If those needs and wants are different in an international market, then some adaptation might be necessary. A food product, for example, might have to be flavoured differently, be more or less sweet, be more or less salty, be more or less fizzy, contain less fat, have a different smell or be a different colour to meet the preferences and expectations of the local market. Clothing too might have to be adapted for the local market and use different fabrics, different colours, and be produced in different size ranges. In an earlier chapter (*see* p. 173), for example, it was shown how Gossard, the lingerie company, had to vary its product mixes across Europe to cater for different average sizes, different attitudes towards the purpose of lingerie, and different fabric preferences. Benetton produces garments centrally to the same designs for all its world-wide markets in undyed yarns and fabrics. Batches of garments are then dyed on demand to meet the colour requirements of different markets.

Practical considerations. It is not just customers' aesthetic preferences that prompt adaptation, but practical considerations as well. The paper used for printing postage stamps has to be adapted depending on the climate of the destination country. This is because the gum used in a temperate climate could not withstand the humidity of some Far Eastern countries. The stamps would simply go gooey and be unusable. Similarly, the paper used to wrap soap in hot climates has to be treated with a mould inhibitor.

FIGURE 25.8

Factors influencing the adaptation or standardisation decision

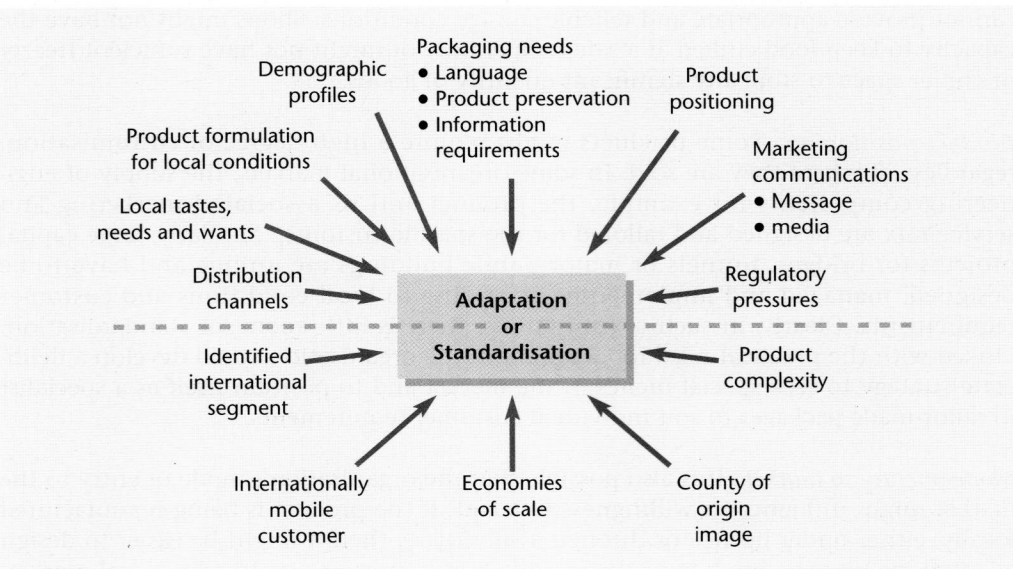

Packaging and communication. It might not, of course, be necessary to go as far as redesigning or reformulating the product itself. The focus of adaptation could be brand imagery, packaging, or marketing communication, for instance. Brand image might have to be adapted to avoid embarrassing connotations in foreign languages or to create a clearer and stronger positioning statement within the local marketing environment. Packaging design can help to reinforce image, but might also have to be adapted in practical terms for the local language or to give instructions relevant to local usage of the product. Nevertheless, some consumer products do manage to standardise their packaging for a number of international markets, regardless of language. Provided that the same brand name is used, it is possible to print lists of ingredients and basic instructions in several languages.

Marketing communication. All of this is likely to follow through into the adaptation of advertising and other marketing communication activities, again to create something to which the local target audience can better relate, and to differentiate the product more clearly. Marketing communication might also have to be adapted to take account of the different buyer readiness stages of different markets. A product that is mature in the domestic market, and only needs reminder advertising and low key promotional activity, might be unknown in a foreign market and need a promotional mix that is much more geared towards awareness, generating trial, and attitude building. Communication might also have to be adapted for the effects of local media availability and consumption habits.

Distribution channels. Another practical consideration is the sophistication and structure of distribution channels. An fmcg producer selling into eastern Europe, for example, will not find the same concentration of retailing in hypermarkets and superstores owned by large chains as in western Europe. This means that the producer has to find ways of achieving geographic coverage through thousands of small independent grocers, which could prove to be difficult and expensive, particularly if the wholesale sector is similarly underdeveloped. Logistics might also have to be adapted, if deliveries are being made direct to small stores rather than to a big retailer's regional depots. Also, if it takes longer to get the product into the shops, perhaps because of poor transport infrastructure to outlying areas, then the producer might have to address issues of product freshness. This problem could be compounded if retailers cannot provide appropriate and reliable storage conditions. Shops might not have the capacity to keep food chilled at a safe temperature or might not have sufficient freezer or chiller space to store any significant quantity of goods.

Product positioning. Some products might require a high degree of customisation, regardless of where they are sold. In some organisational markets, the supply of engineering components for example, the product and its associated marketing and service mix are designed and tailored for the specific customer. Similarly, large capital projects for bridges, tunnels or major public buildings are unique and have to be designed, managed and implemented according to local conditions and customer requirements. Clearly, in such circumstances, there is little room for standardisation. Linked with the practical need for adaptation, the organisation could develop a deliberate strategy to seek special niches in the market and to position itself as a specialist in tailor-made packages to suit individual customer requirements.

Mode of entry to market. It is also possible that the organisation's mode of entry to the market might influence its willingness to adapt. If the product is being manufactured locally, either under licence or through a subsidiary, then it might be easier to design adaptations into the product or the manufacturing process and to allow local marketing managers to adapt the marketing approach to suit local conditions. In an organisation that is more centrally controlled and where more functions, such as R&D

and manufacture, are undertaken by the parent organisation, the more likely it is that there would be a standard marketing approach.

Regulations. Finally, the organisation might be forced towards adaptation by technical or commercial regulations. Toys imported into the EU, for example, have to conform to certain safety standards. Some Far Eastern manufacturers, therefore, have had to adapt their product designs and improve their quality standards or face exclusion from European markets. Regulations might also cover product labelling (relating to weight, country of origin or declaration of ingredients, for example) and product claims (relating to the extent to which it can be recycled, health warnings, nutritional or other alleged benefits). As discussed in Chapter 2, other elements of the marketing mix, such as pricing, sales promotion, advertising and direct marketing are likely to be subject to widely differing regulation in different international markets, and therefore might have to be adapted in order to conform.

Pressures towards standardisation

If an organisation is operating in a market where customer needs and preferences are largely universal, then there might be little enthusiasm for adaptation and **standardisation** might be considered to be preferable. Unfortunately, such markets are not very easy to find. Coca-Cola has virtually created such a market, but even they occasionally adapt the sweetness or fizziness of the product to suit local market preferences.

Identified international segment. What is more likely to happen is that the organisation will define an international lifestyle or usage segment (*see*, for example, the discussion of Euro-segments at pp. 178 *et seq*.) which cuts across geographic borders and allows a standardised marketing mix to be developed.

Example

Finding an international segment is not necessarily easy, but is attempted by brands such as Cadbury's, Wash & Go, American Express, Nescafé, and Carte Noir. Car manufacturers also try to standardise their marketing approaches as much as possible, across Europe at least. Some retailers, particularly the franchised ones, including companies like Benetton, The Body Shop, Toys 'Я' Us, and IKEA also aim for standardisation.

As mentioned earlier, some retailers and product manufacturers use their country of origin as a key element of the product's appeal, and that is clearly going to imply a degree of standardisation.

Economies of scale. Such standardisation does not stem just from the existence of international life-style or usage segments, but also from a practical desire to achieve economies of scale, where possible. If aspects of the marketing mix can be standardised, then costs will be lower. A standardised product with standardised packaging can be produced in larger, more economic quantities and then distributed to a number of different markets. If a product is particularly complex to manufacture or involves sophisticated technology, then the pressure towards standardising it in all markets might be considerable. The costs and implications of trying to adapt could be just too high.

Mobile customers. International service industries aim to standardise their offerings as far as possible, as discussed in Chapter 23. A hotel chain serving business travellers, for example, will want to create a strong international brand image so that experiencing a stay at a Sheraton hotel in Sofia is as similar as possible to a stay at a Sheraton hotel in London. In this case, although the hotels are located in different countries,

FIGURE 25.9

**Five product
adaptation
strategies**

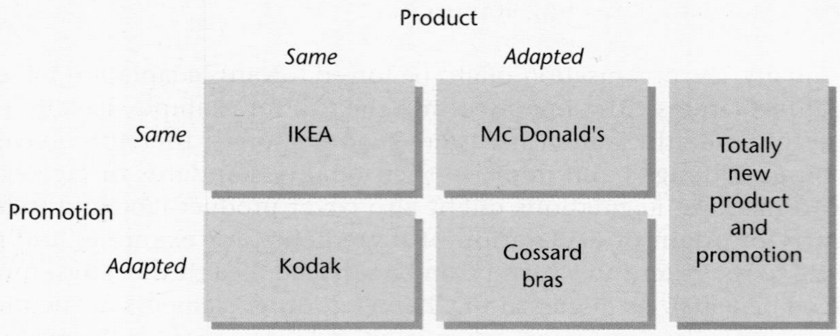

Product

	Same	Adapted	
Same	IKEA	Mc Donald's	Totally new product and promotion
Adapted	Kodak	Gossard bras	

Promotion

Source: Adapted from Keegan (1969).

the market segment served is not geographically tied and thus the product has to be standardised for consistent positioning in the mobile customer's mind. Other products, also targeted at internationally mobile customers, implement a deliberate standardisation strategy. Kodak or Fuji films, for example, have to be immediately recognisable by tourists wherever they are.

Degree of adaptation or standardisation

As this discussion has implied, the degree of adaptation can be total or partial, or there can be no adaptation at all. If the marketing environment warrants it, adaptation could mean a complete overhaul of all elements of the marketing mix. At the other extreme, it could just mean a standardised product with slight alteration to the labelling on the package to make it conform to local regulations. Keegan (1969), looking at adaptation in terms of product and promotion in particular, came up with five alternative strategies, reflecting differing levels of adaptation. These are summarised, with examples, in Fig 25.9. The important point, however, is that any adaptation, however great or small, should be justified by the market or its environment, although its cost effectiveness should also be taken into account. It is equally important that a decision to standardise should be based on an appreciation of different market needs rather than on cultural arrogance.

International marketing mixes

The principles of designing a marketing mix for international markets are the same as those employed in domestic markets. Sound market analysis and understanding should precede any detailed decision making in the selection and scheduling of the marketing tools. As discussed above, the marketing strategy and programme might have to be tailored to exploit strengths and opportunities and minimise weaknesses and threats in the context of the local marketing environment. This includes the need to appreciate the social and cultural influences on consumer decision making, the state of technological capability and the sophistication of distribution channels. Also, as considered at p. 994, the segmentation and positioning strategy will be an important determinant of the shape of the marketing mix.

As a way of summarising many of the points made throughout this chapter, each element of the marketing mix will now be considered briefly.

Product

The specification of the whole product package must be driven by customer needs and wants rather than pure convenience. It might be possible to define a standard product that can be sold across a number of international markets, for example consumer elec-

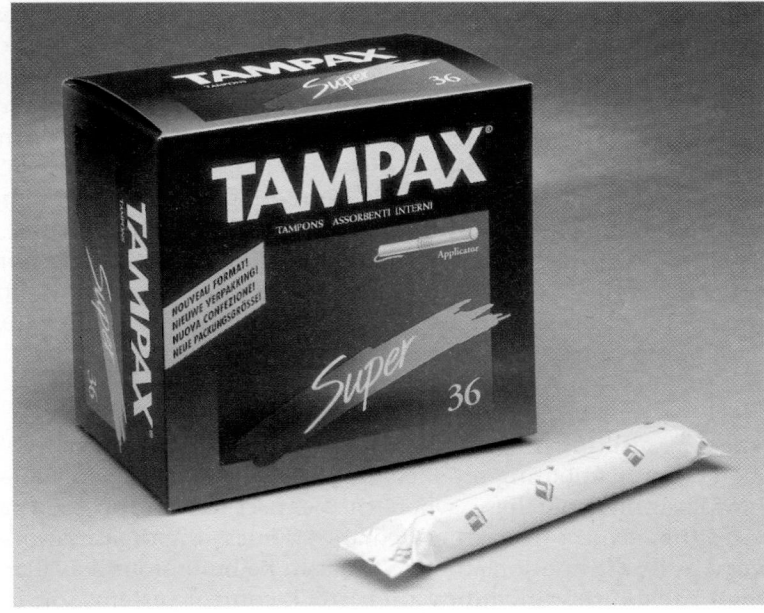

Tampax standardises its product and packaging across international markets using multi-lingual labelling to overcome language barriers.

Source: Tambrands.

tronic goods, kitchen appliances or some toiletries. Otherwise, the product might have to be adapted for local needs in major or minor ways. Packaging and brand imagery are likely to have to be adapted to reflect local culture or to help create a market position that is compatible with the local marketing environment. Packaging might also have to be redesigned to cope with different physical conditions and handling. The climate might be hotter and drier or more humid, or the product might have to be better protected to survive a longer journey time or a longer shelf life, especially if storage conditions within the distribution channel are less than perfect.

Price

In any market, domestic or otherwise, the primary consideration for price is what the market will bear. The organisation has to be aware of the pricing structure within the market, customers' price perceptions and the implications of price for product positioning. A price level that might represent excellent value for money in the home market could seem to be very expensive in a foreign market. Clearly, price perceptions and positioning are partly affected by competitors' approaches to pricing. The organisation thus has strategic decisions to make about whether to match the competitors' prices or to price significantly higher or lower.

The cost structure associated with a product might also change in international markets. If an organisation is exporting goods, it potentially faces higher logistics costs, for example in terms of insurance and transportation, especially if the goods are being sent to quite remote markets. There could also be additional administration and banking costs in arranging shipping and payment. If, for example, a buyer wants to pay for the goods through a letter of credit, then banks have to act as intermediaries, checking documentation and arranging the international transfer of funds. Banks charge for this service, as well as charging for foreign currency exchange. Price might also have to reflect a 'cushion' against fluctuations in exchange rates, to avoid losses.

Selling costs can also be higher, for example if sales representatives are being sent abroad on sales trips or the organisation is attending international trade fairs and exhibitions. In addition to these costs, there is the cost of preparing sales materials, brochures and other sales aids. A great deal of cash might have to be invested in market development before any significant level of orders is generated. This cost will have to be recouped somehow.

Longer-term capital investment in a country can also affect cost structures. Building a manufacturing plant, for example, might lead to a lower unit cost and reduce distribution costs, but nevertheless a return will be expected on the capital. Alternatively, if there is major adaptation and market development activity, there might be pressure to get a faster payback. Where goods are traded between the home organisation and a foreign subsidiary, issues of transfer pricing (as discussed at pp. 439 *et seq.*) arise. If transfer prices are set too low, and cannot be defended in commercial terms, then the organisation might be open to accusations of 'dumping', that is, of exporting goods at unfairly low prices in order to get rid of them outside the home market. Different countries regulate transfer pricing to different extents and in different ways, and thus the organisation should investigate carefully how much flexibility there actually is with transfer prices.

Place

The organisation should develop an appreciation of what is 'normal' in the local market for distributing products similar to its own. This includes an understanding of how customers purchase, where they expect to find the goods and what support services they expect from intermediaries. Unless the organisation is prepared to invest heavily, its distribution strategy needs to be built around available intermediaries and their capabilities, including their stock control systems, on-line ordering capacity, goods handling capacity and storage conditions. Delivery size and frequency will have to be tailored to suit the channel. Logistics thus have to be planned around intermediaries' needs and available modes of transport. They also have to be timed to take into account problems such as crossing borders. Sometimes, for example, it could take lorries two or three days to get across the German–Polish border.

Promotion

Promotional mixes are highly likely to have to be tailored to suit the local environment. Advertising has to conform to local regulations, in terms of both media choice and content. Furthermore, a campaign has to take into account available media and their costs, as well as the target market's media consumption patterns. Sales promotion too, as seen in Chapter 17, is subject to different degrees of regulation. The choice of sales promotion techniques therefore has to respect local regulations and reflect the target market's preferences. In some markets, for example, coupons distributed through print advertisements might stimulate more response than those printed on packs.

Public relations activities, particularly publicity, might call for the services of a local PR agency which knows the media scene and has established contacts. Public relations can be particularly useful if the organisation wants to be seen to be integrating into the local community. Some kind of sponsorship, for example, gives an opportunity to demonstrate a willingness to give something back to the community, and to participate in its life. Finally, personal selling in a foreign market might mean training sales staff in language and culture, including negotiation styles, business etiquette and social interaction. If the organisation does not have an established name in the international market, the sales force could face a great deal of cold calling and rejection. The sales manager, therefore, should take particular care to ensure that the sales force is properly motivated and supported, and that their morale is kept up, especially if they are working a long way from home.

CHAPTER SUMMARY

International marketing is of concern to organisations of all types and sizes, whether they drift into it accidentally through the receipt of unsolicited orders from abroad or whether they treat it as a major planned part of their marketing strategy. International marketing is complex, not only because it potentially involves greater administrative and operational marketing effort, but also because it involves an understanding of marketing environments that might be very different from the domestic market.

There are many reasons why organisations seek international marketing opportunities. The limitations of the domestic market might encourage organisations to look further afield for growth opportunities, or the domestic market could be under threat from foreign competition. International marketing might open up an opportunity to manufacture more cheaply abroad or to develop economies of scale in the home manufacturing operation. Customers who operate internationally might also expect their suppliers to follow and do the same.

Whatever the reason, the choice of foreign market has to be made carefully and a full analysis of the STEP factors should provide a foundation for an informed decision. By comparing a number of possible markets on criteria such as product fit, market factors, competitive factors, market entry issues, resource constraints and trading constraints, an organisation can decide which one presents the best opportunity.

There are many possible market entry methods, and the choice depends on how quickly the organisation wants to get into the market, what it is prepared to invest in terms of time, money and long-term commitment to do so, its willingness to take risks and its financial objectives. Some organisations begin their international careers by direct exporting, selling to a foreign customer or through a foreign-based intermediary, or by indirect exporting, selling through an intermediary based in the domestic market. If an organisation is selling expertise or knowledge rather than goods and services, then available options include licensing, franchising and contracting. Where an organisation wishes to make a long-term commitment to a market or region, then investment might be appropriate, acquiring or setting up manufacturing or sales subsidiaries, or entering into joint ventures or strategic alliances. By having such a strong local presence in the market an organisation might be able to overcome any political hostility to importers and might gain a better understanding of how best to adapt the product and its marketing package to suit local needs.

A major concern for any organisation is whether to standardise or adapt its marketing offering for an international market. If it decides to adapt, it needs to think about which elements of the marketing mix should be adapted and to what extent. Standardisation is attractive, in that it can lead to economies of scale and easier marketing administration, but it can be dangerous unless there are clear indications that it is appropriate within the international marketing environment.

In any market, even if the product can be standardised, it is likely that the price will have to be adapted. Different markets face different cost structures and are subject to different taxes and import duties. Customers might have different price perceptions and expectations. Advertising and other marketing communication activities will face different regulatory environments and might well have to be adapted to conform, quite apart from any cultural differences.

Key words and phrases

Adaptation	*Joint ventures*	*Master franchising*
Contracting	*Licensing*	*Sales subsidiaries*
Direct export	*Manufacturing subsidiaries*	*Standardisation*
Indirect export		*Strategic alliance*
International marketing	*Market entry methods*	

QUESTIONS FOR REVIEW

25.1 Why is marketing in an international context more complex than in the domestic market?

25.2 Define Lynch's five categories of international European organisation.

25.3 Why do organisations internationalise?

25.4 For each STEP element of the marketing environment, outline three factors that might make the international market different from the domestic one.

25.5 What six broad groups of factors should be taken into account when selecting a foreign market?

25.6 What factors influence the choice of *market entry method*?

25.7 Differentiate between *direct* and *indirect exporting*.

25.8 What are the main strengths of *licensing* as a market entry method?

25.9 What are *joint ventures* and what are the risks associated with them?

25.10 Summarise the factors that might create pressure towards *adapting* the marketing mix for a foreign market.

QUESTIONS FOR DISCUSSION

25.1 To what extent do you think that internationalisation is essential for today's organisations?

25.2 Choose an fmcg product from your home market that has not yet become an international product. Decide which foreign market you would like to launch this product in and find out as much relevant information as you can about the marketing environment in that country. What recommendations would you make to the manufacturer of your chosen product about the launch?

25.3 Discuss the problems that small businesses might face in internationalising and the feasibility of the various market entry methods for them.

25.4 Find an example of a successful joint venture in an international market. What benefits have the parties to the venture derived from it?

25.5 Citing examples that you have found, discuss whether standardisation is possible or desirable in international markets.

CASE STUDY 25.1

Martin Joinery

(The name of the company has been changed.)

Martin Joinery was set up in the west of Ireland as a sister company to Michael Martin Ltd, a building contracting firm, in order to provide it with specialised non-standard joinery products. Five years after its launch, the company was still selling virtually 100 per cent of its output to the building firm, which means that it was effectively just a production unit, with no marketing or selling skills. What it produced and how much it produced were dictated by the one large customer. The management became increasingly uneasy about this. The Irish building industry was in decline, and the amount of business coming from Michael Martin Ltd was no longer enough to occupy all the available production capacity. The management, therefore, felt that it had two options. One was to sit tight and wait for the building industry to recover, but that was felt to be too risky. The company could fade away to nothing before that happened. The second option was to develop a strategy that would reduce the dependency on Michael Martin Ltd and would ensure the longer-term viability of the company. Management were willing to make the effort to do this, but needed to work out exactly what the right course of action should be.

One area of concern was the production process. Until that time, the company had tended to employ part-time workers as and when they were needed. The company also had out-of-date production machinery. The management decided, therefore, to buy in new equipment in order to help it move to a situation where it employed fewer workers, but on a full-time basis, in a continuous production process. The management had spotted an automatic window-making machine at a trade exhibition which they felt could make the production process much more efficient and cost effective. It would also increase the range of different window frame types they could produce from two to four, and would make it quicker and cheaper to switch between different sizes and shapes of window frame. This was important because the Irish and UK markets demanded a great deal of variety in window frames, whereas the European market was fairly used to standardisation.

The management did realise that this new machinery alone was not going to solve all their problems. Because of the recession in the Irish building industry, the home market was not likely to absorb all

they could produce, and so new market opportunities would have to be sought. One option was to seek a joint venture with a UK joinery company. The ideal partner would be a company having problems satisfying the UK market because of limited production capacity and strong competition. Martin Joinery felt that they could offer an efficient, fast turnaround, and a cost advantage because of lower corporation tax rates in Ireland. The management got as far as desk research to assess the viability of doing this, when an alternative option emerged.

Through the Irish export agency, Martin Joinery was able to participate in a joint market research exercise along with seven other Irish joinery companies looking for opportunities in the UK market. This research study looked at market definition, market potential, distribution, selling requirements, competition etc. Taking all these aspects into account, the main opportunities seemed to be in doors and windows. Martin Joinery was particularly interested in the windows. Although the UK window market was not necessarily growing, and the wooden frames sector was under pressure from UPVC and aluminium alternatives, and an expected tightening of regulations meant that there could be an opportunity for high specification frames.

The research also showed that an Irish company entering the UK market would need to have at least one UK distribution depot from which products could be despatched quickly. Where products were made in batches to customer requirements, they could be shipped directly from the Irish factory, but products to be delivered and sold through multiple outlets would have to be stored and directly distributed from a UK base. The researchers gave several reasons for this. One was that they could not find a large independent distributor who was prepared to distribute imported products to its range of outlets. Second, distributors were reluctant to hold large stocks and expected the supplier to be able to deliver out of stock items at little notice. Finally, house builders wanted products delivered direct to building sites, again at little notice. Other practical issues arising from the research were the need to work to metric measurements, the need to shrinkwrap the frames and the need to redesign some of the product ranges.

The next stage was to think about a market entry strategy. The agency decided to set up a group marketing project to help some of the Irish joinery companies get established in the UK market. Two of the companies, including Martin Joinery, were selected as having complementary products with a strong chance of success in the UK. The agency proposed to set up a sales and marketing function in the UK to represent the two companies, with a manager appointed on a three year contract. The scheme was set up so that the agency would be paid commission on sales made, with the rate of commission increasing over years two and three of the project. This meant that the agency would bear the risk of the market entry – no sales, no commission – but that it would recoup its investment if the venture succeeded. This support from the agency would give Martin Joinery the opportunity to get itself established and to pay the bulk of its market entry costs after sales had been achieved.

Further research indicated that Martin Joinery's best chance lay with specialised, high performance, non-standard frames made to architects' and builders' specifications.

The principal features of the company's service would be:

- high quality
- small quantities of non-standard or special sizes
- speed of delivery.

The short-term objective was to generate sales among house builders and builders' merchants with standardised products in order to establish a track record for the company, and then to move towards the specification segment later. The long-term objective was thus to capture a share of the specification market (e.g., architects and local authority contracts). Initially, the company also wanted to focus on the south and south-east of England.

Martin Joinery intended to have its products tested in order to gain accreditation under British Standards. The company also felt that with its new machinery, it could a offer customers extra product features as

standard and at no extra cost. The quality was comparable with competitors' products. To build orders quickly, Martin Joinery intended to pitch its prices competitively, compared with the major UK players in the market. Under the agency's group marketing scheme, a UK sales and marketing manager was duly appointed. The manager appointed knew the UK trade well, and took responsibility for setting up a warehousing distribution system and sourcing raw materials more cheaply.

Promotional literature consisted of brochures with specifications and prices for both standard and non-standard ranges. By offering a standard range at competitive prices, the company wanted to gain credibility, but the sales message also emphasized the company's ability to produce high quality, non-standard products, with fast delivery. The main promotional thrust would be through personal selling, and this would be supported by brochures, advertising in trade journals and direct mail to a carefully targeted list.

Source: Based on a case prepared by Martin Thompstone.

Questions

1 What kind of market entry strategy has Martin Joinery used for entering the UK market?

2 What are the potential advantages and disadvantages generally of participating in joint research into a foreign market?

3 Outline the marketing mix used by Martin Joinery to enter the UK market and assess its appropriateness.

4 What would have been the likely risks and rewards of sticking with the original idea of seeking a joint venture in the UK market? Has Martin Joinery made the right choice?

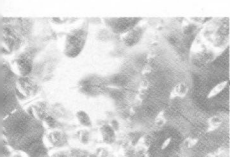

CASE STUDY 25.2

Vinprom-C

Peter Adamov was the chief executive officer of Vinprom-C, a Bulgarian company specialising in wine exports. The company was formed from an alliance of several producers in one region specialising in dry red wines, semi-dry wines, sweet wines and grape brandy. The product was of a high quality, and very competitive in the world wine market. As Bulgaria made the transition to a free market economy in the early 1990s, Adamov faced the problem of preparing the company for privatisation. The market was rather chaotic after the abolition of the state's foreign trade monopoly on wine, and there were a few problems. Many operators lacked marketing and selling expertise, many different agents were trying to sell into the same markets, prices were falling and customers were being lost.

Vinprom-C exported through distributors based in Bulgaria. In dealing with the UK market, for example, in 1993, 52 per cent of Vinprom-C's exports went through the Bulgarian Vintners Company, 45 per cent through Domain Boyar, and the remaining 3 per cent through other distributors. These organisations had exclusive selling rights and did not pass back any extensive marketing information. Vinprom-C's main information sources, therefore, were trade fairs and exhibitions.

The competitive situation was not helped by the fact that there was oversupply in the world wine market, with supply (at 30 billion litres per year) outstripping demand (27 billion litres). New competitors, from Australia, New Zealand, Mexico and other places, were still entering the market. Some producers around the world had nevertheless cut back production, partly because of the oversupply situation, and partly because of the effects of an epidemic of phylloxera disease among the vines. Others cut their costs by moving towards more productive grape varieties. In terms of geographic markets, 70 per cent of the world's wine output was consumed by a relatively small number of countries, France, Italy, Germany, Russia, central and eastern Europe, USA, Argentina and Spain. In most of these places, however, the trend was towards decreasing consumption. The new growth markets for wine were Japan, Finland, Sweden and Germany.

Adamov, from talks with industry experts, felt that achieving price competitiveness was important for success, and that further product diversification was ·needed, targeted at countries with relatively low per capita wine consumption. The two main target groups would therefore be as follows.

Group 1 Large customer countries:

	Annual consumption per capita (litres)
USA	7.7
Japan	0.94
Turkey	0.47
China	0.03
Mexico	0.1

Group 2 Europe:

	Annual consumption per capita (litres)
UK	10.00
Scandinavia	9.00
Russia	6.95
Central and eastern europe	10.00

All these countries were thought to have enormous potential. Their current consumption was relatively low, so there was room for growth, and all had high earning segments. None of them had sufficient local wine production to meet their local market needs. All of these factors made them attractive in both the long and the short term. The European group was particularly attractive because of the culture of wine drinking in these countries, but they did represent fiercely competitive markets, and EU import regulations made it difficult for a non-EU producer such as Bulgaria to penetrate them. As western European markets accounted for 60 per cent of the world's wine consumption between them, they became the prime strategic targets for Bulgarian producers. There were three major problems in penetrating the EU market:

1 *Import duties*: had been imposed to eliminate any price advantage that developing countries might have.
2 *Import ceilings and quotas:* the EU allowed 5 per cent of its wine consumption to be imported. Bulgaria was allowed to export 580 000 hectolitres to the EU, but the brand, quality, origin and authenticity of the grape varieties had to be guaranteed.
3 *Competition from local producers*: within the EU, some local producers qualify for subsidies which give them a competitive price advantage over imported wines.

Nevertheless, Adamov still found the EU attractive, especially the UK market, since Vinprom-C had already had 10 years experience of dealing with the UK, which accounted for 21 per cent of Vinprom-C's exports.

In the mid-1990s, the UK had relatively low wine consumption (11 litres per capita per year, compared with France at 67 litres and Italy at 62 litres), although it was growing. The major competitors for Bulgaria in the cheap wine segment were Hungary, Chile, Argentina, South Africa and Australia. The distribution system for wine in the UK was highly concentrated, with around 12 organisations, dominated by the major supermarket multiples, accounting for 70 per cent of wine sales. They are very demanding in terms of quality, quantity, price and delivery terms, and want changes in assortment as their customers' tastes and demands change.

Another market of which Vinprom-C had experience was eastern Europe (including Russia). Until 1989, eastern Europe had accounted for 93 per cent of Vinprom-C's exports, but after the fall of communism, it all fell apart. By 1994, this market was looking attractive again. Wine consumption was relatively low (5.1 litres), and high-earning segments were starting to emerge. Local production could only meet about 60 per cent of demand, and experts were predicting increasing demand. Adamov was a little worried, however, because this market had been targeted by low-priced low-quality Spanish and Italian producers. Furthermore, these markets are difficult to predict, and at that time, the political situation in some areas was unstable, import regulations were changeable and there was little legal protection for foreign traders.

Source: Adapted from a case prepared by Professor Nicola Yankov, University of Svistov, Bulgaria.

Questions

1 What kind of market entry strategy did Vinprom-C use to get into the UK market?

2 After 10 years' experience in the UK market, is that same strategy still the best for distributing the company's products to the UK? Debate the issue, giving due consideration to alternative courses of action.

3 If Vinprom-C had to make a choice, do you think the company would be better off investing in further development of the UK market or in the eastern European market? Why?

4 One of the potential growth markets of the future was Japan. What do you think would be the problems of planning an entry into that market?

REFERENCES TO CHAPTER 25

Barnes, H. (1996a), 'Novo Nordisk Up 12 per cent Despite Currency Effects', *Financial Times*, 14 March, p. 29.

Barnes, H .(1996b), 'Currency Gains Help 31 per cent Advance at Novo Nordisk', *Financial Times*, 16 May, p. 30.

Bobinski, C. and Robinson, A. (1995), 'Bright Picture on TV', *Financial Times*, 29 September, p. 35.

Brook, M. Z. (1992), *International Management* (2nd edn), Stanley Thornes (Publishers) Ltd.

Cunningham, S. (1996), 'Carriers Storm Warning', *The European*, 13–19 June, p. 1.

Done, K. (1995), 'Well Laid Paths to Profit', *Financial Times*, 22 November, p. 18.

Gibbins, E. (1994), 'Mercedes Move Spurs Market Realignment', *Financial Times*, 16 December, p. III.

Gilligan, C and Hird, M. (1986), *International Marketing: Strategy and Management*, Croom Helm.

The Grocer (1996),'Chileans Make Their Mark on the Wine World', *The Grocer*, 4 May, p. 30.

Guttman, R. J. (1994), 'Danish Business Goes Global', *Europe*, September, pp. 10–11.

Hecht, F. (1996), 'Nestlé Takes on the World', *Eurobusiness*, February, pp. 18–23.

Houlder, V. (1995), 'Today's Friend, Tomorrow's Foe', *Financial Times*, 2 October.

de Jonquieres, G. and Skapinker, M. (1996), 'Brussels Airline Probe Faces Squally Skies', *Financial Times*, 5 July, p. 4.

Keegan, W. (1969), 'Multinational Product Planning: Strategic Alternatives', *Journal of Marketing*, 33 (Jan).

Lynch, R. (1994), *European Business Strategies: The European and Global Strategies of Europe's Top Companies*, Kogan Page.

Marsh, V. (1995), 'A Hungry Phoenix', *Financial Times*, 21 November, p. III.

Mead, R. (1990), *Cross-cultural Management Communication*, John Wiley & Sons.

Paitra, J. (1993), 'The Euro-consumer: Myth or Reality?', in C. Halliburton and R. Hunerberg (eds.), *European Marketing: Readings and Cases*, Addison-Wesley.

Paliwoda, S. (1993), *International Marketing*, (2nd edn), Butterworth-Heinemann.

Rees, J. (1996), 'BA Deal Unlocks Finance Bonanza', *Marketing Week*, 14 June, p. 7.

Skapinker, M. (1996a), 'BA Attacks US-German Anti-trust Move', *Financial Times*, 6 March, p. 4.

Skapiner, M. (1996b), 'EU Still Undecided on Airline Alliance', *Financial Times*, 28 June, p. 6.

Skapinker, M. and Buckley, N. (1996), 'EU May Probe Air Alliances Amid Talks on BA Deal', *Financial Times*, 2 July, p. 1.

Southey, C. (1996), 'Specialisation Sparks Turnround at Barco', *Financial Times*, 28 March, p. 28.

Sullivan, R. (1996), 'A Town that Learnt to Stand on its Own Feet', *The European*, 4–10 April, p. 24.

Troev, T. and Moss, N. (1996), 'Rover Abandons Bulgarian Plant as Chief Executive Resigns', *The European*, 2–8 May, p. 25.

Walsh, L. S. (1993), *International Marketing*, (3rd edn), Pitman publishing.

Young, S. *et al.* (1989), *International Market Entry and Development: Strategies and Management*, Harvester Wheatsheaf.

26 Current Perspectives in Marketing

LEARNING OBJECTIVES

This chapter will help you to:

1 pull together the broad themes of this book;

2 gain an insight into the practical problems that senior managers face in planning and implementing marketing;

3 appreciate the need to integrate the elements of marketing into a coherent strategy within the context of the 'real world' environment;

4 gain an insight into the kinds of marketing jobs taken by recent graduates, and what they feel organisations are looking for in graduate trainees; and

5 start thinking about the future direction of marketing and its emerging issues.

INTRODUCTION

The opening chapters of this book concentrated on defining marketing and on the need for organisations to adopt a marketing orientation. Such an approach puts the customer at the centre of the organisation's attention, and ensures that all employees, not just those working directly in marketing, are aware of their contribution to meeting the customer's needs and wants. It was also established right from the start than an understanding of the marketing environment is crucial if appropriate strategies and marketing actions are to be planned and implemented. The environment affects the structure of markets, the structure of distribution channels, competitive behaviour, customer behaviour and what is feasible and acceptable in terms of the elements of the marketing mix.

Within a marketing-orientated organisation, understanding customers or potential customers is of particular concern. In Part II of the book, therefore, the focus was on buyer behaviour, in both consumer and organisational markets, and on the factors that influence how and why people and organisations buy. This Part also looked at the concept of segmentation, ways of defining sub-groups of customers within a market with common characteristics. By tailoring a marketing offering towards a particular segment, an organisation can better meet that group's needs and wants rather than trying to be all things to all people.

Parts III–VI looked at the individual elements of the marketing mix, product, price, place and promotion, that are used in combination to create an offering that satisfies the customer's needs and wants. The chapters within these Parts were wide ranging, covering basic definitions and concepts, then developing a more managerial, strategic view of how these concepts can be applied in practice. Picking up this strategic thread, Part VII followed with an overview of strategic marketing principles and the importance of planning and managing marketing activities in a controlled way. This helped to bring the elements of the marketing mix together to some extent. Part VIII took this further by looking at some specific specialist applications of marketing. The areas of services marketing, small business marketing and international marketing all draw on the same central body of marketing theory but apply it in very different ways, with different emphases. This underlines again the need to apply marketing with due respect for the environment within which the organisation is working, for the resources which the organisation has at its disposal, and for objectives which the organisation is trying to achieve.

Inevitably, in trying to develop a comprehensive picture of what marketing is this book has, for the most part, had to break marketing down into its component parts, looking at each of them individually. The risk of this approach is that the subject might appear to be a series of loosely linked discrete elements rather than an integrated and interdependent whole. The later chapters, of course, on strategy and specific applications, have presented a more integrated picture, but this needs to be reinforced further. The other problem with a textbook is the need to tailor examples to emphasize the theoretical concepts discussed. The examples and Marketing in Action vignettes, therefore, tend to focus on one narrow aspect of an organisation's marketing practice, perhaps giving that element undue emphasis. The end of chapter case studies are a little fuller, but even they have tended to be topic specific.

The main objective of this chapter is to break free of those constraints, and offer you a series of senior management perspectives in depth that give an insight into the marketing problems and issues facing a variety of organisations in a variety of industries. The striking thing about these perspectives is that they are purely about the practical application and implementation of marketing, and the impact of the marketing environment on strategy. This is not about theoretical concepts, removed from real life. Nevertheless, many of the theories explained in this book are implicit in what the senior managers say. They show the true interaction between elements of the marketing mix, and the very real problems of working within changing, uncontrollable and often hostile environments. All these managers are as much concerned with the future as with the present, and all show a creative flexibility in adapting strategies to suit emerging conditions.

The next five sections thus present the perspectives of five senior managers in very different industries. In order to support and implement their strategic thinking, however, these managers need good staff at all levels of the organisation. As the brief profiles of two recent graduate entrants outlined at p.1047 *et seq* show, even relatively junior managers have important roles to play, not only in making marketing happen on a day-to-day basis, but also in contributing to the strategic direction of marketing. These graduate entrants talk about why they went into marketing, what their jobs entail, and what they think employers are looking for in graduate trainees. This should reassure those of you who are just starting out on your careers that there *is* life after graduation, and that there are rewarding careers to be had in marketing for those who are sufficiently determined and motivated. Finally, the book rounds off with a look towards the future when we present our personal views on the emerging issues that are changing the face of marketing.

The five senior management perspectives now follow. Each one begins with a short introduction to highlight the themes that emerge from it so that you can pick up the threads from the beginning and follow them through as you read. There is a short background profile of each company, and then the managers speak in their own words about their approaches to marketing and their analyses of their own marketing environments. The five organisations are:

- *The Boss Group*: manufactures and markets various kinds of lift trucks, and operates in global organisational markets
- *Wilkinson Sword*: primarily manufactures and markets razors, blades and shaving toiletries in the UK and European consumer markets
- *Vauxhall UK*: manufactures and markets cars and commercial vehicles to both private and fleet customers
- *DMB&B*: one of the world's leading advertising agencies, providing the whole range of marketing communication services to clients in many different industries
- *Continental Microwave Ltd*: manufactures and markets a wide range of high-tech. telecommunications hardware, primarily to broadcasting companies worldwide.

BOSS GROUP LTD

This first management perspective touches on a number of issues that are important in a company supplying global organisational markets. It underlines the importance of 'reading' the marketing environment and developing a strategic position that reduces the organisation's vulnerability. As will be seen in this case, the company initially failed to do this and not only lost out to competitors which were better positioned when recession hit the market, but also left itself open to take-over. Another important point to note is the crucial interaction and interdependence between marketing and production strategies. Without this, there is little chance of designing and producing the kind of products that customers want to buy at prices they are prepared to pay, and that will sell in the volumes necessary to achieve profit and market share objectives. Note too the issues raised about internationalisation and globalisation, especially the problems caused by the company's original imperfect understanding of what a rapidly globalising market would mean to them and what they should do about it.

The company concerned used to be known as Lancer Boss, a name that has been synonymous with the development of the lift truck industry for many years. Lancers Machinery Ltd was established in 1957 by two brothers, Neville and Trevor Bowman Shaw, to manufacture sideloading trucks capable of working in ports, freight terminals, steel stockholding centres, timber yards and other areas needing long load lifting. By developing such a specialist product range, Lancer Boss, as it was then known, grew rapidly to become a leading force in a niche sector in the international materials handling market. As a niche producer, in its early years, its production volume was often fewer than ten units a year. The product range then expanded further, through new designs, so that it also included front loading trucks. This moved Lancer Boss into the volume market as opposed to the specialist producer category.

The steady growth of the company was reflected in 1974 when it entered *The Times'* list of top 1000 companies, and by 1975, 70 per cent of its sales were generated from export markets. In the niche product segment, it had a strong market position, based on sound product design and specifications which resulted in superior product performance. In the front loading sector, however, it was far more difficult to achieve superiority through differentiation. The market was highly competitive, and achieving production efficiency and economies of scale through volume were critical to success. In order to strengthen its market position, Lancer Boss acquired Steinbock GmbH of Moorsburg, Bavaria, Germany's third-largest truck manufacturer. This acquisition strengthened its presence in the European market and added a complementary range of electric frontlifts and warehouse trucks. Further deals were done in 1986 with Komatsu to assemble internal combustion trucks in the UK; with Nissan for the design, development and manufacture of a range of small electric trucks for sale

Dr Robert Bischof believes that a global perspective is crucial to the developement of the Boss Group.

through the Nissan dealer network; and in 1991 with Doosan of Korea to manufacture a series of 2–3 tonne frontlifts under licence.

The early 1990s saw a serious downturn in demand for lift trucks. Lancer Boss reported losses of £3.1 million with no likelihood of recovery for three years. The resultant financial pressures, initially from German and then from British bankers, resulted in the forced sale of Steinbock Boss to Jungheinrich AG, one of the leading lift truck manufacturers in Germany. After a series of complex financial dealings, this was soon followed by the acquisition of Lancer Boss itself after the firm went into receivership. The Jungheinrich purchase meant the end of the last remaining UK truck manufacturer and the new operation began trading as the Boss Group Ltd, marketing the products of Boss (UK), Steinbock (Germany) and MIC (France). This acquisition projected Jungheinrich into the number two position in the world league of lift truck manufacturers and moved it into the sidelift and container handling product sectors. The complementary product range, the Boss reputation and world marketing capability, combined with the engineering, manufacturing and strategic strengths of the German parent, created an opportunity to restore the fortunes of lift truck making in the UK. The new chairman of the Boss Group was Dr Robert Bischof, a former senior manager of Jungheinrich. His remit was to realise the opportunities presented by the acquisition through a careful programme of strategic reformulation and a focus on manufacturing efficiency.

In an interview in 1996, Robert Bischof speculated on what had gone wrong with Lancer Boss, and outlined the basis of his new strategy for the new Boss Group Ltd.

'Lancer Boss had to have a clear view of its competitive strategy if it was to survive successfully through the 1990s in an increasingly tough industry. The company was caught in the middle ground between being a niche producer and being a volume producer. While it was strong in the former area, as soon as it tried to compete in the volume market, it failed to carry through the necessary changes. It was not good enough just to sell more, the company had to review its cost base. Volume means volume. It's no good producing 2000 trucks per year if they are spread across a number of different models. That's not volume. To be highly efficient you have to sell 7000–10 000 trucks per year using a high percentage of common user parts and components. We still have not yet reached that target at Boss, but we are now on 4000 units per year with nearly 70 per cent commonality in parts. Such thinking is essential for survival in the global market place.

'There has been a steady evolution in the market over the past 25 years. When I first joined Jungheinrich in 1967, the company had just begun to take the first steps to expand beyond Germany. Subsidiaries were set up in German-speaking Switzerland and Austria, followed by Holland, Scandinavia, France and southern Europe. What had been successful in Germany, a direct selling and service organisation, was replicated in each of these markets. From the 1970s onwards, sales in the rest of Europe exceeded the home country sales. Jungheinrich had developed from a national company with manufacturing and sales centred in Germany, to a European company with sales and service organisations in 14 European countries.

'Something else happened during that period. Whereas there were about a dozen German manufacturers of lift trucks in the early 1970s, by the early 1990s there were, apart from the niche producers, just two German groups left: the Linde Group and Jungheinrich AG. Something similar happened throughout Europe. France has virtually no indigenous forklift truck industry left after the take-overs of Saxby, Fenwick and MIC. Italy's industry suffered a similar fate, while in the UK, Lansing Bagnall was sold, and we took over Lancer Boss in 1994. It would appear that the rationalisation that has taken place in the industry is not just a series of

random events, but that there are sound reasons for the changes. When markets grow, stronger companies and those who are prepared to take a longer-term view can cope with the costs of setting up and becoming established in a market. They can develop a market share driven policy, forego short-term profit maximisation, survive cyclical market conditions with a wider market spread, and finally they can take over their weakened competitors.

'Lancer Boss did not fully understand the implications of increased globalisation. Whereas it was able to withstand competition in the niche sidelift truck and container handling market, it could not achieve the significant cost efficiencies necessary for developing a volume market share position. In the front loading product sector, it had too many designs, too little cost efficiency and too little standardisation and production investment. It became caught in the middle ground between volume and niche production. The volume markets increasingly became dominated by larger international players, and as markets grow in size and scope, so the number of companies declines. Lancer Boss learnt that lesson the hard way, despite having a fine reputation for quality products and service support.

'Jungheinrich has learnt this lesson. With the acquisition of Boss and Steinbock we are on course for a transition from being a European company to becoming a global company. It has the size to do it, being number two in the world league. But in global markets stretching from Europe to North America, and including the tiger economies of South-East Asia, even large players need strategic alliances and/or further acquisitions to fulfil the conditions of global membership. This means that in marketing terms we can operate not only through the proven formula of direct selling, but also through dealerships, licence agreements and other forms of co-operation.

'To manage the transition to a global company also requires changes in the minds of management and employees, changes that are far more significant than those experienced in the transition from a national to a European organisation. Globalisation does not just mean global marketing, it also means global sourcing and global benchmarking for the best manufacturing locations in the world. In theory at least, anything can be made anywhere in the world; transport costs are typically between 3 per cent and 6 per cent of buying prices, even for shipments that go half-way around the world, because of containerisation. The global perspective thus has to pervade all areas of the business.

'Developing global thinking within a company does not come from textbooks or strategies, it comes from experiencing, seeing, touching and being confronted by the real challenges of foreign attitudes, cultures, ways of working, laws or even the lack of them! In our company we have a deliberate policy of sending as many people from top and middle management as possible out into the world to learn this lesson in reality. For many years it was not possible to persuade a German buyer and a German engineer that others in Europe could also provide quality products and that it might be worth looking outside Germany for innovative solutions. It took us a long time to make the transition from a national level to being a truly European company. We have learnt that the transition to global thinking has to be faster.

'In my opinion not every company will make that transition, because of management, financial and cultural weaknesses, or even just a lack of long-term patience in shareholders. It's a fair bet that our industry will go through another round of weeding out the weaker members and there will be further concentration and rationalisation. Jungheinrich goes into this next round well prepared after the acquisition of Boss. Various changes are already under way to ensure our position. A significant investment programme has already been implemented at the former Lancer Boss plant to create a world class manufacturing centre for lift trucks in the UK. A rationalisation of parts and components has followed, along with the introduction of a common user chassis for a number of models. All this helps to achieve production economies as an aid to competitiveness, but at the same time it allows the flexibility to suit different customer applications.

'Perhaps our greatest challenge is to retain the best qualities of the old Lancer Boss organisation, with its unique combination of British creativity, innovative designs, advanced engineering skills, quality products, marketing flair and customer support, and to combine them with the strengths of Jungheinrich in developing a long-term strategic view that is consistent with the market and the capabilities of the organisation. We still have not achieved all our objectives in managing our transition to a global player, but we are now well down the path to ensuring our success in the coming years.

WILKINSON SWORD

This senior management perspective comes from an organisation with a long and venerable history, and with a deep commitment to innovation. The emphasis here is on the role of market research as a means of preparing new products and their marketing mixes for launch, and as an operational tool for evaluating and monitoring the progress of the corporate brand name and the products that form its sub-brands. There are also interesting insights into the changing nature of market research techniques, as technology opens up new possibilities and makes some traditional techniques almost obsolete.

The company now known as Wilkinson Sword was founded in 1772 as a gunsmith's. Right from the start, it was an innovative company that recognised the need for added value and differential advantage, and was not afraid to evolve to capitalise on emerging opportunities. From guns the company gradually moved into swords, via bayonets. One of the core technologies of sword making is putting an edge on fine steel, hence diversification into cut-throat razors in 1890. Safety razors followed at the turn of the century. In 1918, garden tools were added to the portfolio as consumers began to rebuild domestic lives after the First World War, and in the 1940s, the company went back into armaments. What all of these products had in common was technical and marketing innovation.

The company is now best known for its razors and related products, and it has remained innovative in this area. In 1956, it was the first to put an edge on stainless steel strips, and thus was the first on the market with a double-edged safety razor. Again, it was the first to develop Teflon-coated blades, giving the consumer more shaves per blade, and more comfortable shaves. This particular innovation, in the early 1960s, was very important for the company in terms of competitive position. Before then, its market share was 4 per cent, very small compared with Gillette. By 1970, Wilkinson Sword's share was between 45 per cent and 50 per cent, and by 1975 its share was over 50 per cent of the double-edged blade market which it had pioneered.

In the 1970s, however, the nature of the market changed again, and the competition became tougher. Shaving 'systems', consisting of a permanent holder into which specially designed dedicated blade cartridges can be fitted, were introduced, again pioneered by Wilkinson Sword. Disposable razors also became popular towards the end of the 1970s, and the strong growth of disposables during the 1980s put a great deal of pressure on both double-edged razors and systems. Strong marketing by both Gillette and Wilkinson Sword, positioning systems at the premium-priced, quality end of the market well away from disposables, led to a resurgence of systems in the 1990s. By the mid-1990s, on a world-wide basis, Gillette was the number one player in the market, with Wilkinson Sword and Bic sharing second place. In terms of razors, however, Bic is a one-product company: the good value for money, low-priced disposable razor. Wilkinson Sword feels that Bic is unlikely to expand from that into the premium-priced systems sector.

Bill Scholes, Wilkinson Sword's market research manager, talked about some of the company's problems and approaches to new product development, product management and market research.

'In the 1970s, Wilkinson Sword had 50 per cent of the market for double-edged razors, but it did not have enough cash to reinvest in the market and to develop its position further through other new products. So the company merged with British Match to gain more funds for product development, and this led to a series of take-overs and sell-offs, with Wilkinson Sword passing through the hands of a number of different owners in the last 20 years. Gillette, our biggest competitor, even bought some bits of Wilkinson Sword in Australasia, Japan, the USA and some parts of Europe outside the EU, although the US part was eventually sold back to us. Wilkinson Sword is now owned by Warner Lambert, the US health-care company. Warner Lambert bought us because it already had a razor brand, Schick, which was big in the USA and number one in

Japan with a 70 per cent share, yet had no UK and European presence. Wilkinson Sword was thus an ideal acquisition to fill the gap. Warner Lambert have kept the Schick brand name in markets where it was well established, and the Wilkinson Sword brand in Europe and the UK. There is some dual branding in the Middle East, with Wilkinson Sword and Schick existing side by side, but that is likely to come to an end.

'As far as Wilkinson Sword is concerned, market research is very important as a means of understanding where the market is going, who is doing what, and how our products are progressing. In the 1970s, the early days of systems, it was even more important to see how the brand and the sector were both developing. In those days, retail audits were the main method of research, but they were in their infancy themselves, and their coverage of the market was patchy. There was about 25 per cent of the market "missing". Woolworth's, for instance, sold between 15 per cent and 20 per cent of razors, yet was not included in retail audits.

'So, to fill the gap, we developed the "brand in use" technique, in conjunction with NOP, as a means of continuous progress measurement that covered the whole market. Every two weeks or every month, we'd do a check on what razor brand a sample of consumers was using on that particular day. We'd also do bathroom checks, that is, have a look to see what consumers actually had in the bathroom. We were probably doing this before any of the big market research companies adopted this technique. We had to do it, because many people don't actually know which brand they are using! The proliferation of sub-brands – G2, Contour, Profile etc. – certainly didn't help either. We don't do much of this type of research any more, partly because it is very difficult to conduct, since it's even more difficult to tell what brand of blade is in use, and partly because retail audits have become much better and now cover about 95 per cent of the market. The power of retail audits also means that we don't buy panel data (continuous research) any more. It's too expensive.

'The nature of retail audits is still changing. What used to happen is that companies like Nielsen and IRI compiled data from various sources and then produced retail reports. In a market like ours, however, most of the sales are made through the two big chemist multiples, Boots and Superdrug, and five or six supermarket multiples. Some of these big retailers are starting to offer their own EPOS (electronic point of sale) data for sale directly to people like us rather than to the research companies. This means that we monitor retail data continuously, and get hold of it much more quickly than if it's having to be processed by a third party. We're buying direct from ASDA at the moment, so we can get weekly data on what's happening in their stores in our market, and we can do store-specific tracking if we want. We had a new POS display stand in ASDA, and by tracking those stores that were using it we found that we were selling 100 or more systems a week from the new display compared with four or five from a normal shelf display. We use IRI data still, and we find that the figures we're getting direct from the retailers replicate the IRI data very closely. What we're all waiting for now is to see what Tesco does. If Tesco starts releasing its EPOS data direct, then that is going to cause big problems for the research companies.

'When we launched the FX Performer, which was our first pan-European launch as a Warner Lambert company, we did a great deal of research. We had to research the name particularly carefully, for instance, because we wanted to use the same one across all countries. We had to check out potential names for their meaning in different languages, any negative connotations, and whether they were already in use by other companies. The Schick brand in the USA had launched the same product there under the FX Tracer sub-brand name. We couldn't use Tracer because it was already in use in Europe, but we could use FX, and Warner Lambert was keen that we should do so, as a clear link between the US and European brands. Of course, a brand name on its own is rather meaningless, and at some point you have to bring it together with the product, packaging and positioning concepts and test the whole thing.

'We brought all the elements of FX Performer together in a European-wide simulated test market for this brand, using InfoTech Burke's Bases Test. At the start of a test like this, we gather a panel of 250 or more razor users and we expose them to all the marketing mix elements of the product. If there's no advertisement in existence, then we'll use a concept board to show them the name, the packaging and the main features and benefits of the product. We'll then measure their reactions to various elements, including intention to purchase, on rating scales. Then we give them the product to use for two or three weeks, before recalling them and asking them similar questions again. Effectively, it gives us a pre and post-usage check, and tells us whether the product actually matches up to their expectations.

'In the case of FX Performer, we had wanted to get three points across at the concept stage at the beginning of the test:

- the first totally flexible system blade
- a lubrication strip enriched with aloe vera and vitamin E
- a protective guard wire.

Overall, we were trying to bring these features together to communicate the product's benefits of shaving closeness and comfort. In the post-test we can tell how well these messages have come across through product usage, which ones matter most to the consumer, and which ones need more emphasis in advertising. This sort of testing is really about confirmation and fine tuning. By the start of this test, the various elements should already have been fully tested and refined individually. The product should perform; pack research will have tested its ability to stand out and its impact; the name research will have been done, and it's likely that the advertising agency will already have tested the broad communications concept. So all we're doing here is bringing all that together as a total package for the first time. Given that Bases tests cost anything from £30 000 upwards each, it wouldn't make sense to put completely untried material into them. In practice, it's rare to see a big shift in pre and post-test attitudes and reactions. There'll be some movement, but not much. If pre-test interest is not high, but it's better by the end, then we know that the product is probably OK, but the supporting marketing mix elements are not quite right and we should be able to tell where the problem lies. If post-test results are well down on the pre-test reactions, then we do have a big problem, since we're clearly not delivering on our promises.

'Having done all that, we can then input additional data on expected distribution, advertising spend, likely competitor reactions etc. to come up with sales volume estimates over various time periods. And because it's a simulation, we can do some scenario analysis – What if we increase our advertising spend? What if the competition lower their prices, or increase their advertising spend? We've found that these tests are very accurate, often within 5 per cent of what actually happens when the product is launched. This sort of thing is taking over from traditional test marketing using television regions, which is rarely done now. Whole countries are test markets now! It's actually quite difficult to test market a consumer product in a television region, because of the dominance in the UK of the supermarket multiples. They tend to have centralised distribution and stock control systems, and it's difficult to place a product in some of their stores and not others. They're not too interested anyway in listing a product that is not getting national support from the start. Given that in our market, Boots, Superdrug and five of the supermarket multiples account for about 70 per cent of the blades sold, you can see why we've moved away from test marketing in the field. Getting distribution is difficult enough as it is. None of the manufacturers in our market is dropping any brands, but we're all introducing new ones. This proliferation is putting much pressure on retail space. Thirty years ago there were only two products. Now, a 2m² display can only show 10 per cent of the available ranges. At least in our market we don't have to face the same level of competition for space as some other consumer goods do from retailers' own brands. They've only got about 10 per cent of the market, because it's the kind of product where the consumer wants an established reputation and reassurance.

'On a day-to-day level, we do regular research for monitoring and evaluation purposes. We check out awareness and attitudes towards the Wilkinson Sword brand name regularly, and we track our advertising. We have much lower budgets than Gillette, and so we have to ensure that our advertising is working very hard for us. In the mid-1970s, the Wilkinson Sword image was very strong. We still have a very strong logo, but the overall image needs refreshing and updating to appeal to a younger market. We're particularly targeting the 16- to 34-year-old group and, as well as mainstream advertising, we're using sports ground advertising, which generates high levels of awareness for us.

'We also test out retail displays. Like test marketing, this area is moving into simulation. We used to take groups of consumers into a store and put them in front of a live display. The retailers didn't like it much, but they co-operated. Now we use a virtual reality store, which is much easier and much more flexible.

'We don't actually do a lot of pricing research. In real terms, prices have fallen dramatically, partly because of the pressure from the disposable sector. There's a limit to the price differential *that the customer will tolerate between a system and the equivalent number of disposables. Customers do make mental trade-offs between the price and convenience of disposables and the quality and comfort of systems. Disposables have made a big impact and hold 60 per cent of the market by volume, although it certainly isn't 60 per cent by value. They're virtually giving them away. ASDA have an own-brand of disposable, Gem, which is currently retailing at 23p for five. That compares with around £3.50 for five system blades. We have to be very careful, therefore, to justify the price of systems in terms of product benefits.*

'Our major problem, which is not unique to us, is the available budget. There's never enough cash to do everything you would like to do, so you have to prioritise and spend what you do have carefully. I have to produce an annual market research plan, and I liaise with the marketing department to map out what their market research needs are likely to be for the year and what problems might emerge that would need research. As far as Wilkinson Sword in the UK is concerned, I no longer have to worry about spending on product testing. Warner Lambert do all the R&D in the USA, and all the product testing before we get the product here. We don't have to pay for that initial research out of our budget. We take any new product as given, then put it into our own Bases tests.

'Attitudes to market research vary from organisation to organisation and a great deal depends on senior management. I'm talking very generally, but in some organisations senior management take the attitude that "We know our customer best, and we don't need to spend lots of money to be told what we already know". Attitudes like this are reinforced, unfortunately, by the existence of less creative market research agencies that do indeed spend their time confirming the obvious. That's why I like to stay as far as possible with the same market research agency or research teams. They know our market, they know us and they know what we want. Our organisational attitude is closer to a view that market research is the fuel that drives the organisation and its products forward. We could say that the phenomenal growth in the ladies' razor segment over the last couple of years, for example, has been partly due to the quality and thoroughness of the research we did. We didn't just take a man's product and colour it pink! We researched different product shapes, colours, names and image concepts in order to create something with individual style that appealed to women without patronising them.

'Of course, you have to be careful how you interpret market research, and you have to remember that research is not infallible. When disposables were first launched in the UK we were told that research had shown that they would never get established or take any significant market share! Nevertheless, market research is an essential guide to the future, even if it is an imperfect one.'

VAUXHALL UK

The UK car market is not an easy one for the major manufacturers. Each manufacturer, pursuing economies of scale and market dominance, is trying to take market share away from the others, because there is little new growth in the market. In 1995, for example, the overall UK market grew by only 1.8 per cent, with 1.95 million passenger car sales. Although fleet sales grew by 7.2 per cent, retail sales (to private and small business buyers) actually declined by 2.5 per cent. Vauxhall UK held just over 15 per cent of the total market in 1995 (nearly 300000 cars), with only Ford ahead of it in both the fleet and retail sectors. Vauxhall is owned by General Motors (GM), and is a sister company of Opel. It operates two plants in the UK, at Luton and at Ellesmere Port, manufacturing Astras, Astravans and Vectras (replacing the Cavalier) for the UK, European and world markets. Other Vauxhall models are manufactured at Opel plants in Europe. Overall, Vauxhall employs over 9600 people in the UK.

Within a market that is experiencing low growth and that is concentrated in the hands of relatively few suppliers, it is not surprising that one of the major concerns of marketers working in this industry is customer care and loyalty building. This is likely to become even more important as new entrants from Asia and the Far East increase the amount of competition in a saturated market. In the management perspective that follows, Ian Coomber, Executive Director, Sales and Marketing, Vauxhall UK, talks about the way in which the car market is changing and the problems of creating and maintaining a differential advantage over competitors in the minds of consumers. He then outlines Vauxhall's solution to this through its approach to building relationships with customers. It is also interesting to see how much importance he puts on the role of the retailer in this process, and thus the importance of good manufacturer–retailer relationships.

'There have been two important trends in the car market over recent years: a move away from a focus on a specific product towards building brands, and second, an increasing commitment to customer care.

'The move towards a greater concentration on branding has arisen because it's become increasingly difficult for manufacturers to differentiate their products. This is because regulatory pressures, in terms of safety, fuel efficiency etc. make it almost impossible for a manufacturer to make a fundamentally different product statement. Cars are thus being developed along similar and parallel lines by most manufacturers. What this means, of course, is that differentiation has to come from branding cars and emphasizing their emotional attributes rather than their technical attributes. Vauxhall, for example, has positioned the Astra in the family segment and so we used the baby ad [a convention of babies "demanding" certain features such as safety, pollen filters, and lots of boot space for toys, to make their ideal car] to communicate emotional safety to the family buyer.

'So, the Astra, the Corsa, the Vectra and our other models are being developed as brands in their own right, positioned in different segments, and with different "personalities". What we need to pull these together a little bit and to give the customer the reassurance that these brands have a good pedigree, is to develop the Vauxhall name as an umbrella brand. The emphasis in developing the Vauxhall name, therefore, is on customer care, peace of mind and reassurance. What this does is to build positive feelings towards Vauxhall which is especially useful when we launch a new brand, such as the Vectra, for example. When we launched the Vectra, the initial advertising was designed simply to get the brand name known and make people aware of it. That was all about attention grabbing, and getting across a basic message that here was a new high-tech. car from Vauxhall. Awareness is pretty easy to generate – it just takes a lot of advertising spend. The next stage is a little more difficult. With the Vectra, it had to communicate more about the benefits of the car and what that means to the driver. The objective here was not only to get the potential customer to understand what the car was about, but also to get it high on their mental list of cars they would consider buying. This requires a very clear brand and product statement. The advertising was actually very successful – the Vectra came out first in terms of "consideration" in the mid-range segment.

'We do have to think about our branding in global as well as local terms. The Vectra is a pan-European product and we think about its marketing at two levels: global/European and domestic. What you have to be careful about with pan-European campaigns is ensuring that they are sufficiently well focused. You don't want to work to the lowest common denominator and end up with something that makes little impact on anybody. We agree, therefore, the broad positioning of the product on a pan-European basis, but leave the translation of that positioning into marketing communication activities to each individual country. I see pan-European broadcast advertising media as a mixed blessing. The good news about satellite channels, for instance, is that they deliver highly segmented audiences, but the bad news is that some of these audiences are too specialist and too fragmented. Where will we find the generalist channels that will deliver mass market audiences in the future? Add to that a general increase in consumer cynicism about advertising and their tendency to channel hop or fast forward to miss out the advertisements, and you can see why direct marketing with its tailored, targeted communication has become so much more attractive.

'The second major trend in the motor industry, which further helps to create differentiation, is a move towards greater customer care. This is linked closely with the branding strategies, of course, and is essential. There's no point having wonderful brand images if the customer's actual experience of buying and owning that brand is disappointing. That's why customer care is a core part of the Vauxhall umbrella brand. You can't just advertise it, however; you also

have to deliver it, and that's why we've fundamentally rethought our whole distribution philosophy.

'The change in our UK and European thinking was triggered when we went to the USA to see what (GM) had achieved with the Saturn. This was a new model – it had some innovative features, but what was really different was the way in which it was retailed. What amazed us was how these dealers, who work with all the major manufacturers and are usually quite confrontational, were so enthusiastic about the Saturn. This was because GM had deliberately set out to make customers **enthusiastic** about buying and owning a Saturn, and if that was to be achieved, dealers had to be enthusiastic and so GM had to be prepared to work in much closer partnership with them. GM succeeded in this to the extent that dealers were saying that it was actually fun to sell a Saturn and that GM were a pleasure to deal with.

Source: Vauxhall UK.

In Ian Coomber's view, a strong Vauxhall umbrella brand name provides vital support to brands such as this Corsa.

'So we set up a pan-European task force, not only to look at the Saturn, but also to look at customer care programmes from a wide range of European industries, including banking, for instance, and tried to develop a programme that would suit our markets. In the UK, we launched the "Vauxhall Difference" project. This was about ensuring quality in all aspects of the business, whether visible to the customer or not, and changing the corporate culture towards this concept of enthusiasm that could be passed on to the customer. The thing is that mere customer satisfaction isn't enough any more. If you meet a customer's expectations, so what? That's what they've paid for. You don't go round telling your friends, colleagues and neighbours that a car retailer has managed to service your car properly. But if you can exceed a customer's expectations, by doing something a little extra, that's different and then they might tell others. Much of this happens at the retailer level, of course, in the interaction between the retailer's staff and the customer.

'Our problem, though, is that we do not own our outlets. Our retailers are independent entrepreneurs. We thus had a major task on our hands to persuade them of the validity of the "Vauxhall Difference" and to encourage them to change their ways of selling to customers and delivering after-sales service. One thing we did, for instance, was to set up a democratically elected franchise board, with representatives from our retailers across the country. It meets monthly, and helps to bring our retailers into our business. This board works with us on product specification, distribution, IT and promotional issues, and it's helped to strengthen us. After all, these retailers are front-line experts in what the customer wants and thinks and can give us early indications of any problems, while we are very good at translating that into manufacturing and marketing action. The board is also useful for helping Vauxhall and its retailers to understand each other's problems better and to work together towards solutions. It's all much less confrontational, and although there are, of course, still one or two pressure points, we have the incentive and the means to try to work things out constructively.

'To help our retailers deliver the "Vauxhall Difference", we looked closely at the business processes involved in the retailer's interaction with the customer, before, during and after the sale. What we looked for was "moments of truth", the key points in the relationship when things might go wrong. These include things like: "Customers can't easily find their way to the retailer's premises in the first place", "Customers can't attract the attention of a sales assistant when they want one", "Customers don't want to have to wait three months for delivery of their chosen car", "Customers want their car service completed on time as promised". At any of these points, a customer might experience disappointment and lose whatever enthusiasm they had for Vauxhall. Alternatively, a positive experience could build up their enthusiasm and reinforce brand loyalty.

'We did pan-European research to see which were the most important moments of truth, the ones that really had to deliver a positive experience to the customer. This analysis led us to define 49 standards for our retailers. If these 49 things work well, it will make a positive difference to the customer and exceed their expectations. The retailers then, quite rightly, said that if they were to deliver these 49 things, then we would have to guarantee our practical support. If, for example, we were insisting that a particular type of repair should be completed within 48 hours, then the retailer has to know that we can deliver the relevant parts immediately. Often, the retailer is making promises to the customer on our behalf, and the retailer has to be confident that we can deliver. That, then, led to a further 21 wholesale standards that we have to live up to in order to support our retailers. We've also invested in giving appropriate training to all staff from our retailers. It covers everyone, from senior managers, through the sales staff, to the mechanics and the trainees who wash the cars. We've especially concentrated on retraining sales staff. We want them to put the customer first by diagnosing the customer's requirements and then selling them the most appropriate car for their needs. If there isn't this consultative process, how can we expect enthusiasm from our customers? We don't just stop at the training. We use mystery shoppers, for instance, to check whether it's being put into practice, and if it isn't then we'll work out what the problem is and put it right through refresher training or whatever.*

'We have also started rationalising our retailer network so that it is more efficient and better suited to customer needs. Traditionally in the UK, retailers had single site operations handling both selling and after-sales service. We've found, though, that people are prepared to travel between 10 and 15 miles to buy a car, but only five miles to have it serviced. We mapped the country, taking into account all sorts of demographic and market data, to find out where we needed selling capacity and where we needed servicing capacity. What we're now trying to move towards is a different approach to retailing. In the future, a retailer will have a bigger sales territory, but will be expected to run a core showroom, concentrating on sales and handling all the admin. and purchasing etc., and a series of smaller wholly owned satellite depots, mainly concentrating on servicing. The role of the satellite might vary, depending on local needs. Some will have small showrooms selling new or used cars, for example. We've been running this system in the UK for a couple of years now, and the profitability is pretty good.

'We have to implement this sort of change gradually. Over the years, we've built up a dense national network of retailers and you can't radically alter that overnight without offending anyone. So the streamlining is taking place over time. Whenever a retailer changes hands or closes, it's an opportunity to start again under the new system. It'll take about five years to fully complete the programme, and we'll end up with more outlets overall, but concentrated into the hands of fewer retailers.

'I think there will always be a place for a service-orientated retailer in selling cars. High-tech. interactive direct selling systems are all very well, but they are only electronic catalogues, when all's said and done. Cars are not commodities. They are high involvement products that people get emotional about. Cars always make a statement about their owners, and people want to see, smell, touch and test drive the merchandise before they buy.'

DMB&B

DMB&B is one of the top 10 full service marketing communications groups in the world. It employs 5000 people world-wide, including 2500 in Europe and 600 in the UK. It has 155 offices worldwide in 72 different countries, with 67 offices in Europe. As a communications group, it offers a full range of services, not only in advertising, but also in below the line sales promotion, PR and direct marketing. This senior management perspective, from Mike Dickson, a Board Account Director with DMB&B in London, discusses some of the issues and challenges facing advertisers and their agencies. It emphasizes a changing environment in which agencies, like any other suppliers in organisational markets, are having to adapt to meet their customers' changing needs and to remain competitive. As a consequence of that, and again like other suppliers, agencies are becoming much more involved in their clients' overall strategic thinking and thus are developing deeper relationships with some of them. There are also some interesting insights into the way that companies' attitudes to brands and brand building have shifted over the last few years. Mike also comments on international expansion, both for agencies and their clients, and the changing face of advertising media.

Source: DMB&B

DMB&B offers a full range of integrated marketing communications services anywhere in the world for its clients.

'Integration has been a big buzzword in marketing, not only in terms of creating an integrated marketing mix, but also in terms of developing an integrated communications mix. There is a polarisation taking place within the advertising industry. At one extreme there are the large multinational agencies like DMB&B, with networks around the world and who can undertake a range of marketing communication techniques anywhere in the world for a client. At the other extreme are the smaller more "boutique" type agencies who offer something very special in the way of creativity. The ones in between, who cannot offer either high levels of creativity or global presence, are going to be squeezed out. The big agencies are also well set up to offer integration in marketing communications. DMB&B has brought all its companies, involved in advertising, direct marketing, design, below the line activity, media buying, planning etc., under one roof so that they can group resources and offer a client a total, seamless package that meets all their marketing communication requirements. An agency must be able to develop ideas and then pursue them consistently through all aspects of the communications mix smoothly within an overall strategic framework. Smaller agencies simply cannot offer the breadth of service.

'Another advantage of being a bigger agency with interests across the whole range of marketing communications is that we can see synergies between clients and their needs and can thus arrange joint activities. We set up a joint sales promotion between an airline and a soft drinks company, for example.

'As in many other markets, our clients are demanding more for less. As they have slimmed down over the recession, they have become much more dependent on agencies, not just for advertising but for research, strategic analysis and guidance. Some clients are just demanding all this while remaining very cost conscious, but the more sensible clients are treating their agencies more as partners than as suppliers. This means building closer relationships and bonds between client and agency, and ensuring that the agency has positive involvement in the strategic thinking going on around a product or brand. Marketing and advertising have become so integrated, that agencies really have to see themselves as providing business thinking, not just advertising solutions. We no longer see ourselves as an advertising agency; we are a communications group, and in doing what's best for a client we are quite happy to tell them that they should not be advertising but that they should be doing below the line or PR activities instead, and we can provide those services.

'As far as mainstream brand advertising is concerned, clients' needs and priorities have been changing. Branding has had a bit of a rough ride over the past five years or so. Because of the economic recession, brand owners have tended to concentrate more on short-term tactical thinking for their brands, with more emphasis on price and below the line marketing activity. Mainstream heavy advertising was considered just too expensive when companies were thinking about cost cutting and survival. What this did was to weaken brand strength and open a gap for the retailers to leap into with strong own-brand propositions. Now we're seeing manufacturers return to long-term strategic brand building, and thus the re-emergence of the importance of the brand and brand strength.

'Some companies are approaching brand building in a different way, however. Birds Eye, for example, are consolidating their brands by cutting out sub-brands such as "Menu Master" and uniting all their ranges under one strong Birds Eye umbrella brand. Heinz too, which has traditionally had a very strong corporate umbrella brand, has shifted its emphasis slightly. A couple of years ago it was concentrating on below the line tactical activity and building a loyalty scheme rather than investing heavily in brand advertising. It has pulled back a bit from that extreme and is now putting some effort back into long-term brand building through advertising.

Branding is incredibly important in consumer markets as competition becomes tougher. As we move into the next century, it is clear that in any one product sector there will only be room for two or three brands in the mid-range of the market (i.e., excluding ultra cut-price value brands or top end of the market exclusive products), so any organisation needs to build strong brands to ensure that theirs is one of the two or three winners. A recent survey of 20 large markets showed that in each of them, two or three brands account between them for 60 per cent of that market.'

'In the run-up to 1992 and the SEM, there was a lot of talk about pan-European branding and the need to think "European". The expectation was that it would not just be fiscal, technical and legal barriers that would come down, but also marketing barriers. Pan-European standardisation hasn't quite lived up to expectations, and there has been a bit of a backlash against it. Companies have learnt that you cannot assume that ideas will travel. It might be possible to create a common overall strategy and product position that is applicable across Europe, but almost invariably, marketing communication has to be adapted to suit local conditions. Some of this is to take account of the fact that regulations vary greatly from country to country, and thus marketing communications activities that are perfectly legitimate in one market might not be allowed in another. There are also cultural problems. Styles of advertising vary greatly. In the UK, for example, consumers find advertising that is entertaining and humorous particularly appealing. The Germans tend to go for a more didactic and instructional approach. Italians build passion and sex appeal into the most unlikely product advertising, while the French approach often can best be described as quirky. These are sweeping generalisations, but differences do exist and must be recognised. The reality of the pan-European market is not the dream that we had in the late 1980s. There is much more realism and many pan-European campaigns are driven simply by business concerns, such as economies of scale, rather than a conviction that there is a true pan-European segment out there.

'In handling pan-European campaigns, the best performing agencies are adaptable, according to what their clients want, but normally there would be one central point of leadership that will develop broad ideas that can then be interpreted locally to suit the needs of different countries. Thus the strategic continuity is there, and the risk of producing bland advertising that tries to fit inoffensively into all cultures is avoided. Sometimes, pan-European advertising can be handled on a regional basis rather than a national basis. We developed two campaigns for the Philishave brand: one for northern Europe and one for southern Europe. It is also possible, in rare cases, to define a pan-European segment and centre a campaign on that. This is more likely to happen in youth markets, for example with Levi jeans, or with luxury products like perfumes. At the other extreme, for some products, it is not even easy to define a broad pan-European positioning strategy. In Germany and the Netherlands, for example, Mercedes cars are much more common – they are often used as taxis, for instance – and offer a wider range than in the UK where they are seen exclusively as expensive "executive" products.

'On the wider international front, the market to watch for the future is China. As China opens up, there will be massive opportunities emerging with very rich pickings. It will be similar to what happened when eastern Europe started to open up, but this time, western organisations will have learnt from the mistakes they made in eastern Europe. Some organisations went in with a certain arrogance, assuming that "west was best", and took an extremely patronising approach which was resented by nations that took pride in their own ability to judge and in their own integrity. The best performing agencies in eastern Europe are those who have developed local managers and learned from them rather than imposing western teams.

'The emergence of China reflects the fact that generally, the balance of centres of economic activity is shifting eastwards. Advertising agencies have to be prepared to meet their clients' global needs, and so agencies are setting up in the Far East. Twenty years ago the focus of expansion for agencies was New York, 10 years ago it was Europe, now it is Asian and Pacific Rim countries like Singapore, as we develop in parallel with our clients. South America is a rapidly expanding market too.

'Technology is a fast changing area of marketing communications. The technological convergence of telecommunications means that more material than ever, publishing, entertainment, advertising etc., is going down the same channels and competing for the consumer's attention. Brand names are appearing all over the place, not just in conventional "paid for" advertising or on packaging. There has been an explosion of consumer communications, with a consequent increase in the difficulty of grabbing and retaining consumers' attention. With things like the

Internet, consumers can make an active choice about the messages they receive, and the challenge for advertisers is to use it creatively to get the best out of its interactivity. As yet, they are still learning, but they are getting better at it. It's a big opportunity. It is estimated that within the next three or four years, there will be seven million people in the UK on the Internet and as the cost of the technology comes down, it will become even more accessible. It still has its limitations, though. There's no problem about buying practical, well-defined products such as airline tickets interactively, but it will never replace the glamour of a retail outlet for more psychological purchases where there is a need to interact with the product. It can never replace the human factor, where the customer feels a need for self-expression rather than for convenience.

'Digital cabling has opened up many more channels and opportunities for interactive marketing etc. Advances so far have tended to be technically led, but now organisations are thinking about how these advances can best be applied in a strategic marketing way. Technology is no good unless it is used in the right way. It means speedier communication and more individual targeting as channels fragment into special interest areas, for example travel, sport etc. Of course it is possible to get too clever, and target too narrow a group with the risk of missing out on peripheral members of a segment. You still need broader media that can deliver mass mixed audiences. Sometimes it can be more cost effective to accept wastage and use generalist media, such as GMTV [UK breakfast channel], which reaches a very wide range of different segments simultaneously. As experience develops, there is likely to be some backlash against the fragmentation of broadcast media, and a deliberate move back towards more generalist channels to satisfy advertisers. On a European scale, we have also found that consumers at home feel much more comfortable watching television in their native language, even if they are proficient in English. This too is going to hinder the pan-Europeanisation of broadcast media.'

CONTINENTAL MICROWAVE LTD

This senior management perspective gives a fascinating insight into the problems of a relatively small company operating in a high-tech. global organisational market. A major theme of this book has been the importance of building and maintaining close and lasting supplier–buyer relationships. For this company, that can sometimes be difficult. It has a small customer base, but it is globally spread and there can be many years between orders from any one customer. The role of personal selling is thus emphasized, and there is also an interesting insight into the conflicting motivations and pressures on organisational purchasers. For this company, globalisation has been a major issue and thus market entry methods, the pressures on standardisation and adaptation and the impact of international competition come through strongly.

So, how does a relative minnow in the global communications industry survive against a host of multinationals such as Alcatel, NEC, Siemens, Northern Telecom and Fujitsu? Continental Microwave Ltd (CML), employing around 250 people, has a £19 million turnover, and is a medium sized manufacturer of communications equipment for national broadcasting, PTT and communication establishments world-wide. Its customers include CNN and NBC (USA), BBC and ITN (UK), ORF (Austria), TV2 (Denmark), PTT (Sweden), and the US Navy. It has found a niche in the market to design and manufacture television communication systems, multi-channel telephone systems and digital communication systems along with satellite news gathering equipment. It also grants licences to foreign companies to manufacture products locally. Each order, although containing some standard hardware, is usually tailor-made to suit individual customer specifications and requirements. CML uses terrestrial, satellite and fibre optic media, and typical traffic over its systems is television signals, high quality sound, telecommunications and data transfer. The first complete communications system was introduced in 1982 for transmitting television signals from outside broadcast events, such as sports, accidents and war zones. This product set the world standard and has retained its market position.

CML has between 100 and 150 customers world-wide, although only a small percentage may be active at any one time. The company might only take orders from 10 or 15 customers per year. A typical annual order profile will involve two or three annual projects valued at £2 to £3 million each, 20 valued at around £250 000 each, and a number in the £50 000 to £250 000 bracket. Over 80 per cent of sales are exported to over 70 countries, and most are bound for non-EU destinations. As a contract could be worth several million pounds, it can take a few years to manufacture, and a challenge for the company is how to keep in touch with its customers despite long periods with no orders.

At the heart of the marketing effort are eight 'product managers', who are all trained engineers who have had marketing skills grafted on. Most have been developed through promotion within the company, but some have been recruited because of specialist knowledge acquired in organisations like the BBC and ITN. Because product managers have a considerable degree of autonomy, they are able to make most of the major decisions for their product ranges, as well as selling and pricing the product. They are each given costings, corporate financial targets, minimum prices, recommended prices and subsistence prices so that they can negotiate intelligently with customers. Marketing costs are six per cent of revenue, although around half of that is spent on travel. The selling process normally involves an initial stage in which specifications are established, and from that, a tender can be submitted. In some cases, that can be followed by direct negotiation.

The Managing Director of CML, Ian Aizlewood, outlined the company's marketing strategy and how it is evolving.

'*Markets appear to be becoming ever more competitive. We can handle direct competition from the larger companies, as we can beat them in terms of responsiveness and some superior hardware in our systems. It is the new competitors selling on price that are the problem, as they undercut market prices and make buyers even more price sensitive. We are finding well-qualified technical people with generous redundancy packages banding together as new entrants. They have the obvious initial advantage of low overheads, but the fundamental problem in matching prices arises from their total disregard for ongoing customer relationships.*

'*I am finding that with increased job mobility, buyers may not be in post for more than three or four years and are long gone when serious system capability issues emerge. Some of our systems are designed for a 15- to 20-year life span, and it is a brave buyer who thinks so far* ahead. Job mobility encourages buyers to concentrate on more short-term considerations, such as price, so that they can claim to their bosses how effective they have been. As long as the product purchased meets the specified standards and criteria, the buyer is then able to focus on price. It is surprising how dense buyers can be when it suits them! When faced with a price difference of 50 per cent less, they might not always ask how that can be achieved. They might buy first and only worry about quality standards, after-sales service, non-standard parts, and systems incompatibility in a few years' time. Others will use these prices as a weapon and expect us to move towards it. All of this lowers any price premium we may have and puts the focus on price rather than product differences.

'In addition to the small new entrants, some defence manufacturers in parallel technologies are becoming interested, as their traditional markets decline. The international new entrants cause us a problem in our export markets. Some Italian companies, for instance, arrived from nowhere. A year ago, nobody had heard of them, and now they are popping up everywhere with bids, but so far, fortunately, with little credibility as their prices are 50 per cent to 60 per cent off traditional prices. All these new competitors are causing short-term distortions, and we at CML do not feel that we can respond with similar price cuts. This price pressure has been made worse by stagnant markets, and oversupply in some sectors.

'The problem for us at CML is that our market is world-wide, but in each country there may be only two or three customers. Often, these customers are state owned or controlled, and then it means selling to governments rather than to private organisations. Although this is changing slowly with increased liberalisation and privatisation, most of the time we are involved in high-level selling. We are selling systems solutions to problems, so the emphasis in sales is on being able to respond to and to influence the specifications as well as being able to negotiate and close sales. This puts a great deal of pressure on our sales staff, who in our business are essentially product and pricing managers also. I allow considerable autonomy to these staff. They have complete price discretion, but of course they would have to live with the consequences of bringing back a loss-making deal. Such autonomy is essential, as the minute the sales representative needs to refer back to head office, his credibility is lost, and he becomes no more than a walking catalogue.

'These product managers are all cross-trained so that they can sell anything from our range. We usually promote from within rather than bringing in untried outsiders. Although three product managers have overall responsibility for our three broad product categories, satellite communications, links and broadcast, each supported by an assistant, anyone could handle an enquiry. We do not want rigid boundaries in our team, and they are split on an "advisory area of expertise" basis. This means that no strategic decisions can be taken by the non-expert.

'It is important in a medium-sized company to establish the right culture. We have tried to develop a family culture where all staff feel committed. I am sure that this is a major factor in the low staff turnover that we have had over many years, and often just one or two leave per year. Everyone feels involved. That does not mean that we are unstructured, but we do have a friendly atmosphere that obviates the need for an oppressive hierarchy and excessive layers of management. This does mean good communication in all areas, although it is especially important in the marketing area where we need to share common market intelligence and think through new strategies. I meet with the managers weekly and every month we have a birthday buffet so that anyone with a birthday is invited to a buffet lunch, an excellent way of exchanging new ideas and information.

'Another aspect of our culture that is important for marketing is that all our customers can contact any employee rather than having to go through the marketing department. That again involves potentially everybody in thinking about and appreciating the importance of customers. This philosophy influences how we deal with our marketing staff. We do not offer them any reward over their basic salary, a position that they all actually favour. We are in a serial business where all areas, such as design, production, quality, after-sales service etc., affect the likelihood of a sale. A failing in any area would reduce the chances of a sale.

'An important part of our success has been the ability to work closely with our customers to meet their needs. As problem solvers we are happy to form supplier alliances to ensure that the system delivered meets the expected performance standards. We have been especially successful with the BBC in that regard, where we have some 2000 UHF TV transmitter/transponder stations in the UK. Other UK customers include BT, the Ministry of Defence and the commercial television stations. A lot of our equipment is used during outdoor sports events.

'To keep up with changes in technology, related products in all areas are added to the portfolio every year or so. It normally takes between six and eight months from drawing board to launch. Often, this is driven by particular applications so that competition finds it less easy to counter-attack before we have the product trialed and established. We often have design, manufacturing, test and marketing teams cross-trained in all products so that they can better spot new product opportunities while working with customers. Most new products in our field tend to be incremental in design as this reduces risk and cost.

'We do have to manage the portfolio carefully and sometimes shift our marketing strategy to suit competitive conditions. This is the advantage of having a range of unrelated product areas. If we are facing price or technical competition in one area, we can be aggressive if we want because of better margins from less threatened categories. Alternatively, we can choose not to chase contracts in that area and concentrate on one of the other market areas until the storm passes. Retaining flexibility is essential. Again, all our design and production teams are multi-skilled so that they can transfer easily from one product area to another at very short notice.

'Another important part of our product strategy is the ability to move up and down the value chain. As a product matures, we tend to increase the proportion of in-house manufacture as well as extending options and services such as providing additional frequency bands and ancillary equipment installation. By manufacturing in-house from component level, we have been able to maintain control of our reputation and quality. When we do work with suppliers, we enter into contracts that provide the right environment for a collaborative partnership. The benefits can then be passed on in the guarantees that can be given to customers. The key is keeping our options open in tough, competitive markets. We even supply own-brand products for Philips in the digital link range. They undertake all the marketing functions and order from us in batch quantities, and we gain market access and credibility without significant additional market investment.

'As we are a global supplier, we have to be prepared to sell anywhere. The problem sometimes is finding out what tenders are being sought, as we do not have the resources to invest in this area. Europe has not been a high priority for us as the playing fields are only very slowly becoming level. Germans still buy from German suppliers and the French from French. It is only the British that will buy from the French or the Germans! Part of this is historical and about natural close relationships that had developed long before 1992. The rest is left over from an era when markets were effectively protected by idiosyncratic standards that just somehow favoured indigenous suppliers. The 1996 harmonisation could change all that but it is still very difficult in some European markets. The level playing field in our industry is a myth. Tenders are sometimes written with powerful differentiated requirements favouring preferred suppliers. In Germany, for example, obscure frequency bands must be tolerated and they are very strong on green and pollution-free issues.

'We are moving to meet some of the localised requirements, but that by no means guarantees us business and it is not always viable to respond to these requirements for one-off orders. Although with 1996 harmonisation, type standards in the UK should be good enough for Germany, we have not yet tested it. An added problem in Germany is that there is not one central organisation that influences standards. It is really a series of states, through the Länder, each of which makes its own purchasing decisions. This makes representation difficult.

'There are some parts of Europe where we are more successful, especially where there are no large indigenous suppliers. In Norway, we have picked up £6 million over the past few years and in Belgium we have received an order from the state telecom operator for £2 million. A few years ago that would almost certainly have gone to France, but now the Belgians appear to be more open-minded. Even in France we have made some progress by coming to a preferred supplier arrangement with Thomson to supply them with our satellite products. Any that they sell in the domestic French market will be CML products, so we are making progress in one of the two hardest markets to crack. We had to accept a lower margin on this deal, but we do save on marketing costs.

'Eastern Europe is still chaotic. Although the opportunities in some areas are great, so are the operational and political difficulties. Technical standards are again set to favour politically preferred suppliers, and the purchasing systems have not evolved quickly enough for large-scale capital projects such as ours to be adequately evaluated by professional personnel. At times, orders are determined by who is in power and whether they will be re-elected!

'It is the non-aligned and British Commonwealth countries that represent our prime export focus. In the case of the latter, buyers have often been trained to UK standards and have been working on UK-supplied equipment. That has given us a chance to build a relationship with the key players so that we receive a fair hearing and share a common engineering philosophy when new tenders are being placed. Elsewhere in the non-aligned countries we are often up against very stiff competition. The cost of initial infrastructure building often far outweighs that of subsequent additions and refurbishments and also creates the opportunity for future add-on and new-system sales. There is always keen international interest in these initial contracts when it is known that funds are available.

'We also have to be very careful about regulations, whether imposed by our own government or by theirs! For example, technology transfer arrangements are sometimes part of the deal, as is the need for a local office which is jointly owned with host country directors. Sometimes if we deal with one country we cannot deal with another, especially in the Middle East. We rarely get involved with overseas defence sales as they have a habit of coming back to bite you.

'A major area for development is the Pacific Rim countries, as they are building infrastructure and have the funds. The problem there is that it is a difficult and remote market for us, and the Japanese and Americans are better placed to exploit the opportunities.

'Our market entry and development methods tend to be standard, but we are flexible enough to adapt to local customer requirements. In Belgium, our customers prefer not to deal with agents, because of our geographic closeness. In France, with a similar proximity, they prefer to buy through agents, especially French agents who can add peripheral French engineering. Further afield we expect agents to provide both sales and service support. This may be crucial in Australia and the Far East, due to remoteness. Some of our agents are specialist one-person operations while others, such as those in India, are organisations ten times our size. All, however, have been screened and are normally provided with an exclusive territory.

'Despite national differences, things are changing. International agreements are moving towards technical standardisation; and not before time, when you consider that most communication is international by its very nature. This will leave less room for national government pressure, but it could enable more competitors, differentiated by features rather than performance, to enter the market. In some areas, such as broadcast, with more commercial stations there will be further opportunities for differentiation, as it does not depend, as in satellite, on standard systems. We are probably more fortunate than most when dealing with difficult government actions. We are young, having been formed only in 1973, we are not directly linked to the defence industry and we have the flexibility to adapt to local circumstances. We still convert around 50 per cent of our tenders into sales, but we have to be selective about which projects we are prepared to pursue.

'Another pressure is being able to cope with the need for more rapid product innovation in ever more complex systems. In the same way that Marconi and Alcatel have effectively become project houses managing a series of specialist high-tech. cottage industries, we may have to develop our own supplier networks to cope with the sheer pace of technological change. It is essential that we retain our competitive edge for our niche position, but the more niches there are, the more the product development problems multiply. Within these developments are the increased uses of semiconductor technology. The full impact of this has not yet been realised, but as with Pentium's impact on computer manufacturers, the demands for our creativity will decline. This will again emphasise the systems solution rather than the hardware production side. Digital technology will also have a big impact in improving technical capability and flexibility. We have to keep abreast of all these developments if we are to remain competitive, and this includes new and enhanced supplier partnerships in order to access specialist technologies, and adapting to the changing criteria for winning business. Price can be used as a weapon by our customers, but they are also increasingly demanding on the technical standards and capability of the systems solutions they buy. The future for CML as a niche operator will be very challenging indeed.'

GRADUATE TRAINEES IN MARKETING

The focus of this chapter has been marketing strategy in action. The senior management perspectives have talked about strategic responses to the changing marketing environment, but an important part of designing and implementing those responses successfully is having well qualified, committed, motivated, competent, involved staff at all levels. As the profiles within this section show, developing these qualities starts with recruitment and continues from the first day of a person's employment. The interesting thing about the two graduates featured here is that both of them have been given responsibility very quickly and both are involved in high profile and important aspects of their organisations' marketing decision making. Although both are involved in marketing, they have slightly different perspectives on it. One works in an advertising agency, providing services that help clients to find communications solutions to marketing problems, while the other works for a major manufacturer, and is concerned with all aspects of the marketing mix relating to a particular set of brands. As you will see, there is a contrast between them, yet the fundamental philosophy of what they are doing is very similar.

Another theme common to both of them is that obtaining the job you want in marketing is not just a question of academic achievement. Of course, proving that you can perform under pressure and deliver results is important, but potential employers look beyond that. They need employees who have the drive and potential to succeed; they are looking for self-confidence and maturity; they are looking for articulate problem solvers who can work productively to tight deadlines in teams as well as individually. They also want well-rounded people, who can work hard while maintaining a sense of proportion through an active social life and outside interests. The message from both the graduates featured here is clear: know what you want, then strive to achieve it and do not give up at the first set back. Determination and perseverance are desirable qualities too!

John Hopwood: Brand analyst (Vauxhall UK)

'After leaving school, I spent a year working for Vauxhall. They agreed to sponsor me through university, but they didn't make it easy! They wouldn't guarantee me a job at the end of it unless I got a 2:1 or a First Class degree in a business-related subject. I decided to go to the University of Greenwich to do a BA (Hons) in International Marketing and German. It was a four-year course which included a placement year, which I spent with Opel in Germany, a General Motors company like Vauxhall. I really enjoyed that – it was good business experience and it gave me plenty of opportunity to improve my German! I graduated in 1994, and Vauxhall took me on along with two other graduate management trainees in sales and marketing.

'I started off in marketing communications. I was the Direct Marketing Co-ordinator, and I worked with the Direct Marketing Manager to plan direct marketing activity for all Vauxhall's brands and to manage the entire direct marketing budget for the UK. We'd formulate direct marketing communications strategies and then brief the direct marketing agency. Of course, our strategies had to be consistent with the company's overall marketing communications plans. Some of our work was what we call strategic – building up customer relationships and loyalty, and some of it was tactical – building up individual car brands.

'I then moved on to become an analyst with the team of brand builders working on the Vectra and the Calibra models. We're a small team, and we're responsible for all the marketing decisions for those brands. We decide what market research we want and commission it; we develop the brand's positioning and so we are involved in pricing, product specification, and the image of the brand; and we implement it all! To do all this, it's important that we keep in close touch with our retailers. We talk to them as often as possible and have retailer panels spread across the country so that we can get a feel for customer needs and local differences.

'The graduate programme has been great. I've had a very wide spread of experience very quickly, and I've been given responsibility early. I haven't just worked at head office, though. I spent six weeks working in a Vauxhall dealership in Leeds. I sold new cars, I sold used cars, I worked in the service department and I worked in the bodyshop. I've done everything from front line customer care and selling to washing cars! It might only have been six weeks, but at least it made me appreciate first hand the pressures and problems that our retailers face.

'The language part of my degree has been really useful. We have close links with Opel in Europe and many of our engineers are German. So I'm speaking German nearly every day in liaising with European business teams. It really makes it a lot easier to build relationships with people and to integrate into international teams. The competition for places on graduate entry schemes is very tough and I think having a language as well as a Business degree is really useful.'

'The best bit about working for Vauxhall is the people. There's a real enthusiasm among employees at all levels of the company, and a real belief in our products and what we are trying to do. It's all very team based, so you need to be able to work well together and to interact to get things done. I'm certainly very happy here.'

Kate Hopkins: Account executive (DMB&B)

'I graduated in June 1995 with a First Class BA Honours degree in Business Studies from Nottingham Trent University. Although my degree covered a full range of business subjects, I specialised in marketing and advertising in my final year. I also did two six-month industrial placements during my degree. In the first year, I worked as an account handler in a firm of security printers, and then in my final year, I did six months as the marketing co-ordinator in a tiny electronics firm (three people, including me!). I had to do all the marketing, so I was creating brochures, press releases, advertising – the lot.

'Before I went to university, I had worked for a year in a small advertising agency in Chester, and I knew that I wanted a career in advertising and that I wanted to get into one of the leading agencies. So during my final year, I applied to the top 20 agencies in London. That was tough, because the deadline for graduate applications in advertising is extremely early – round about Christmas, and the application forms are incredibly demanding. Each one took several hours to fill in, and I even had to prepare a video CV. Then the interviews started in January/February. It wasn't easy to go through all that while coping with final year academic work.

'I think that agencies are looking for bright people, in terms of both intellect and personality. You have to be likeable and you have to get on well with people, because this is a people-orientated business. The quality of your thinking matters too. You've got to be a good all rounder who can solve problems creatively by working well with others. Agencies do not seem to be too bothered about your degree classification or even the subject you took, as long as you have the right sort of outlook and personality. My job offer wasn't even conditional on passing my degree! The other three graduate entrants who started at the same time as I did had degrees in economics, history and science.

'The graduate traineeship is a fast track route. It's intensive and it's hard. I started in October 1995, and immediately had six weeks' intensive training, which was broadly a week in each department getting to know who was who, and what the various departments did. Then there was another three weeks or so at a slightly gentler pace, and then I was into my proper role. I had been allocated the accounts I was to be working on right at the start and I had already met my boss and other members of the team. During the first six months, I was given two simulated projects to sharpen my research, analytical and presentation skills. First, I was given a list of companies and I had to assess which one DMB&B should target as a potential client, then I had to outline the strategy that DMB&B should pursue once they had got that account. It was hard work, and I had to present my findings to the Managing Director of the agency and other senior management.

'After six months, I became an account executive which is an all-round role, generally helping to run and manage a client's account on a day-to-day basis. One minute I can be checking that there's a plate of biscuits available for a meeting, and the next I can be included in high level strategic account planning. I'm working on two accounts: Fiat, which is an existing account, and a pitch for a new account. With Fiat, I'm involved in the day-to-day management *of their account, ensuring that everything is happening that should be and that we keep them up to date with what their competitors are doing, and with the results of their advertising. The new business pitch is different. We were briefed in May/June by the client about what they had done with the brand so far and what their future plans were for it. Between then and now (mid-July) we've been undertaking a strategic analysis of the market and working on our creative approach. Part of my role is to turn business information into creative expression by shaping a brief for the creative team to work from. We're presenting to the client soon, so we'll be working all weekend, and putting in 14 hours work a day.*

'The best bit of the job has been having the opportunity to deal directly with clients from day one. I really feel that I "own" the projects that I'm working on and I'm enjoying building relationships with my clients. The biggest shock was the stress and the pressure, particularly on deadlines. There are so many elements to co-ordinate so that they come together in the right order, in the right way and at the right time. At university it was a lot more laid back. OK, if your assignment was late, you could smooth-talk your way around it and it was no big deal. Here, lateness might mean risking £600 000 or more, and it just cannot be tolerated. To meet deadlines means putting in long, hard hours. I also feel that I am under great pressure to prove myself. The agency has invested time and money in me, and I feel that I have to justify that. There are so many people out there who would have liked to have my opportunity.

'At the moment, I am on a two-year contract, and expect to become an account manager after one year. The first year is essentially a learning process, and the agency is not necessarily looking for high powered results, but in the second year, it really is about performance and results. It's the kind of industry in which there are great rewards – if you're good. They say that if you haven't made it by the time you're 30, you might as well get out.

'In retrospect, my advice to anyone who wants a job in advertising is "be determined". Graduate entry is very competitive and you've got to persevere. You need ambition and confidence. You also need to be prepared to invest the time and effort to get your application absolutely right, and submitted on time. I've helped to go through graduate applications in our agency. One single spelling mistake is enough to put an application on the "reject" pile, as is illegible or messy handwriting. This business is all about presentation and attention to detail.'

CONCLUSION

This text has sought to introduce the ideas, principles and technology of marketing as it is practised today by commercial and non-commercial organisations. As an introductory text, its main aim has been to develop a basic knowledge of marketing and to describe just what marketing managers do, why they do it and with what effect. From the range of situations featured throughout the text, it should be clear why marketing has received so much attention in recent years, especially when markets have become increasingly global, dynamic and competitive. Sound marketing is, of course, not enough on its own to guarantee corporate success, but it does have a major contribution to make to the development and operational implementation of an organisation's strategies. There is just no 'right' production strategy, no 'right' financial strategy, and for that matter, no 'right' advertising campaign for a product that customers do not want to buy, because better alternatives are available or because it just does not meet their needs or live up to the promises made for it.

Marketing is thus at the heart of strategic development. The senior management perspectives introduced in this chapter provide a rich, insight in depth into some of the strategic issues facing management, whether they are in a senior general management role or still closely allied to the marketing function. Dr Bischof at the Boss Group, for example, has had to grapple with globalising the company and strengthening its position in world markets against aggressive competition. Ian Aizlewood of Continental Microwave Ltd is concerned with both competitive and technological changes that had the potential to change the company's niche market position. Both are in senior management positions, and both see marketing as central to their future success.

Senior managers who are located within the marketing function are also grappling with changes and priorities to ensure they remain competitive. Mike Dickson at DMB&B emphasised the need for agencies to anticipate and to adapt to developments in the communications industry so that they can provide the kind of ideas and advice that clients expect. This is crucial in a highly competitive market. The motor industry too is fiercely competitive and is likely to remain so. This is not only because of the entry of Asian and Far Eastern manufacturers into European markets, but also because of the potential of eastern European manufacturers to challenge the mature operators who are already having to fight for market share among themselves. If consumers are becoming more resistant to claims about product superiority and are taking much more for granted within a price bracket, it is easy to see why companies like Vauxhall have put more emphasis on their branding and distribution strategies to make them more customer service focused. Finally, Bill Scholes of Wilkinson Sword gave some insights into the changing nature of market research, and underlined its importance in the whole process of developing, launching and managing successful products in competitive consumer markets.

So, what trends, what issues will face marketing managers as we move into the next millennium? There are probably as many answers to this as there are marketing experts. In the midst of change, it is not always easy to distinguish a passing fad or natural evolution from a discontinuous break with the thinking of the past. There have been several critical themes running throughout this book which are likely to become increasingly important as influences on marketing thinking:

Competitiveness

Competitiveness and the creation of competitive advantage have always been core concerns of marketers. The Europeanisation, internationalisation and globalisation of business, however, is intensifying the drive towards competitiveness. As several of the senior management perspectives implied, with markets becoming concentrated in the hands of a few powerful operators, creating a sustainable competitive position and then defending it and developing it is a crucial priority for survival.

Organisations that are caught in weak or ill-defined competitive positions do suffer. Think about the downfall of Lancer Boss, described earlier in this chapter. The Belgian company Barco (Marketing in action in Chapter 25) found out very late that it had stretched itself too far with its product portfolio, and has had to restructure it. Similarly, Williams Holdings (Marketing in action in Chapter 21) had become a slightly unfocused conglomerate and decided to strengthen the areas in which it already had a clear competitive advantage, and to divest those areas in which it did not. Both of these organisations have had to redefine their priorities to build competitive strength on an international scale. The advantages of a clearly thought through differentiation and niching strategy have been demonstrated in this text with examples drawn from numerous product sectors: Lazenby's (sausages – Marketing in action in Chapter 11), Plasser and Theurer (railway track maintenance equipment – Case study 1.2), and Borsalino (hats – Marketing in action in Chapter 12), for instance. Tube Investments (Marketing in action in Chapter 22) in the late 1980s and 1990s completely revamped its portfolio, in a way currently being implemented in a number of central European companies, to find the 'best fit' niches and then to go all-out to build a dominant position in that niche. In many of these examples, the battleground was not the domestic market, but either Europe or a series of priority global markets, especially North America and the Far East.

Technology and quality

Many examples have been presented in this book to demonstrate the impact of technology on what products are made, how they are made and how they are delivered and used. Pressures for productive efficiency, product range improvement and new product development, along with high customer expectations for quality, service and customer care all demand an ongoing review of the use of technology. Customers now expect quality consistency, high standards of service and performance that lives up to the claims made. If a particular organisation can not satisfy these requirements, there are usually many alternative suppliers who can. There appears to be no likelihood of any let-up in these demands and indeed it could be argued that the pace of change will quicken and that expectations will rise still further.

Technology has not just revolutionised organisational markets, but is leading to innovation in consumer and service markets, influencing both products and the quality of customer care initiatives. Madame Tussaud's, for example, used state of the art technology to create Rock Circus (Case study 3.1) and, of course, supermarket loyalty cards (Case study 17.2) and a whole range of direct marketing techniques depend on sophisticated database technology.

Technology is a very powerful force that can change market boundaries, open up opportunities for new entrants and topple a market leader that misses out on a new technology. The impact of CD-ROM, the Internet and other forms of home-based delivery could even make books such as this, in its current form, obsolete in a few years. These challenges mean that companies need to focus on their core capability, using technology to add value in a way that customers want and that competitors can not easily copy.

Entrepreneurial thinking and planning

Many of the changes in the area of thinking and planning demand a deliberately innovative and entrepreneurial approach from decision makers. Adopting an analytical approach to decision making as a form of risk reduction and outcome optimisation is as widely accepted in marketing as in other areas of business. The standard approaches to environmental and business analysis, through environmental scanning and SWOT analysis, have been presented in this book. These techniques are, however, potentially limiting, because they tend to be retrospective and thus lead to projections of the future based only on existing knowledge, systems and perspectives. What is sometimes needed is an entrepreneurial leap that moves the organisation in a fundamentally new direction. Such leaps will, of course, have to be carefully evaluated before any commitment is made, but the inspiration and the vision are important for starting the process rolling.

Such an entrepreneurial leap was seen in the Styles Precision Components case (Case study 24.1). The trigger of lost customers was used to transform the business into a fast growing profitable player in new stereolithography technology. Even on a large company scale, the vision can be a critical factor in deciding new strategic directions. Tube Investments (Marketing in action in Chapter 22), showed how a managerial leader was able to completely change and reprofile the company's portfolio within a relatively short period. In both cases, marketing appraisal and management techniques were employed, but key was the entrepreneurial leap. These are just two cases taken from numerous examples of entrepreneurial thinking cited throughout this text.

Supplier–buyer relationships

Customer relationships are traditionally the focus of marketing, and throughout the book examples of these have been presented. The example of a newly formed relationship was described in Ford's decision to use Transfesa to shift its products from Valencia to Dagenham (Case study 14.2). Continental Microwave Ltd (in this chapter) developed close high-level relationships with the major broadcasting companies to ensure that it could keep up with new developments and changes. German railcar builders had to work closely with DBAG and the *Länder* to design and deliver new prototype railcars for lightly used lines (Case study 7.2). Some relationships fail, however, as we saw in Case study 24.1 when Styles Engineering lost the business from its two major customers within a very short period of time. However, they were able to build new relationships. Even in consumer markets, the text has highlighted the development of schemes such as airline frequent flyer clubs and supermarket loyalty cards as a means of encouraging customer loyalty. The potential for a closer relationship with a large, dispersed customer base has been made possible because of more powerful data collection and analysis systems, as well as direct marketing techniques for maintaining a regular flow of communication.

With the trend towards closer partnerships between buyers and sellers in supply chain management (as described in Chapter 14) and towards developing co-operative partnerships to exploit common opportunities (as described in Chapter 25), the focus on building close interrelationships is likely to intensify. Much of this is the result of increasing competitive pressures, driving organisations to look for strength through synergy and co-operation.

Supplier–supplier alliances and partnerships

As suggested above, a major side effect of the trend towards greater internationalisation and more rapid technological change is that companies' resources are being stretched to maintain or build a strong market position. It has been estimated that over a quarter of all new international ventures in the last decade have been in some form of alliance. This has been demonstrated in the transatlantic air passenger business, where a number of alliances have been formed, culminating in the proposed BA–AA alliance. The underlying rationale was presented in a Marketing in action vignette in Chapter 25, but the main benefit envisaged by the partners was the ability to keep a higher percentage of customers on the alliance's two airlines, thus building more choice and a stronger presence in that market.

A range of co-operative agreements are possible ranging from joint ventures to strategic alliances and contractual agreements on a licensing basis. Some partnerships are market specific, while others represent a more fundamental partnering approach. The Boss Group, for example, manufactures several other lift truck ranges from Italy and Japan, but these do not conflict with their own product range priorities. It is likely that the trend towards forming alliances will continue as companies globalise and seek either a greater presence in markets or greater efficiency in their operation. All these forms of partnership and alliance, however, require different ways of thinking about former competitors or adversaries in some instances and new co-operative forms of behaviour will need to develop. Some alliances do not succeed, such as Rover's joint venture in Bulgaria, (Marketing in action in Chapter 25).

Organisation–society relationships

Organisations cannot work in isolation from the societies in which they operate. Social acceptance and pressure as well as regulatory forces are increasingly becoming major considerations for companies. Some already take an enlightened view of the need for a sense of responsibility for their communities and wider society, while others are becoming exposed in ways that were not considered possible a few years ago. The pressures created go well beyond issues such as pollution and faulty or dangerous products. They involve both personal and business ethics and the values that an organisation transmits through its deeds to the world.

Shell had to face two such dilemmas in 1995, even though it felt vindicated on both the major issues that confronted it. The Brent Spar debate was considered in Case study 20.1, and it became clear after the event that the technical arguments largely supported Shell's initial stance that deep sea dumping of the redundant oil rig was better than dismantling it on land. At the time, however, Shell lost the battle for public opinion. Later in the same year, Shell's involvement in Nigeria became a matter of public and media interest after the judicial execution of Ken Saro-Wiwa, an outspoken critic of the Nigerian military government's environmental record. There was much public debate about whether Shell should continue to operate and invest in Nigeria, since in some people's eyes this was tantamount to condoning the Nigerian government's actions (O'Sullivan, 1996). Shell is certainly not alone among multinationals in having to deal with tensions between commercial and ethical interests.

The underlying issue in the example of Shell, and in other cases past and present such as trade with South Africa in the apartheid era, arms deals with unstable governments, and the supply of powdered baby milk to third world countries, is whether business should be prepared openly to take a moral stance even if it might mean a loss of investment. Can a business be ethically neutral? A survey among 18-to-35-year olds in the UK undertaken in 1995 found that less than 2 per cent would trust a business person to provide moral leadership. If this position is to be corrected, companies are going to have to be far more alert to the ethical dimensions of their actions and anticipate problems before they hit, or better still, prevent their occurrence in the first place. If they can achieve this, not only does it protect the organisation's longstanding reputation as a good corporate citizen (a reputation which it has probably taken many years to develop), but it also avoids extensive and highly public battles with the pressure groups who are waiting for new issues to surface. The task is not easy. For Shell, the duty was to balance the trust and views of Shell's customers, the Nigerian government, the Nigerian people, and company stakeholders, as well as pressure groups.

Environmental responsibility

Linked with the issue of ethics is the question of environmental impact. Companies are becoming increasingly conscious of their impact on the environment through production processes, energy efficiency, materials use, and approaches to recyclability, for instance. While some companies see the green movement as no more than an emerging segment for commercial exploitation just like any other, others have taken a far more considered and positive stance on a wide range of environmental concerns. A number of companies are leading the way in developing a caring approach to the environment.

Mitsubishi established a separate Environmental Affairs Department, first to review the environmental soundness of the organisation's current operations and then to communicate a positive image to society. The organisation recognised that it needed to go far further than required by legislation, which often lags behind public opinion. Komatsu produced a biodegradable hydraulic fluid for its construction machines, rather than risk the danger of conventional fluids getting into groundwater supplies, while Fujitsu has placed considerable emphasis on manufacturing, packaging and recycling (Forbes, 1995). It is not just Far Eastern companies that are environmentally concerned, of course. European organisations, such as Continental Tyres (Marketing in action in Chapter 2), also take this issue very seriously.

A key part of an environmental strategy is the decision to communicate progress made at every opportunity. Shell lost the Brent Spar battle not on facts, but in people's perceptions. The ability to present issues in a scientific, user friendly manner means that environmental issues, as they emerge, can be dealt with through rational debate rather than emotional misinformation. The positive attitudes that can be generated can be important for withstanding criticism in other areas where improvement is still needed and, of course, can lead to more sales if presented in an appropriate manner. Perhaps organisations need to accept that if action can be taken to improve the environment then it should be done regardless, and if the organisation can make marketing capital out of it, then that is an added bonus. The environmental debate will undoubtedly continue. The challenge is to see whether organisations can move beyond superficial gimmicks into a sustained, caring approach to the environment that affects all aspects of business, including marketing.

It is perhaps appropriate that this book should end with some comment on the broader societal and environmental impact of marketing and business decisions. Considerable attention in marketing is focused on retaining and winning market share, and a vast array of proven and new techniques are used in an attempt to achieve desired positions. Some fail, some succeed, and sometimes the same approach can fail now but succeed later. As we have seen, however, marketing managers have to consider more than the immediate customer relationship. Marketing can only operate with the compliance of the society in which it is practised and with willing and involved customers. Even from a competitive perspective, patronage can no longer be assumed, temporarily or on an ongoing basis, in the dynamic environments facing most organisations. Those of you looking to enter the marketing profession will thus have to be prepared to fight hard to win customers, and then treat them with integrity, honesty and respect in order to retain their custom. You will have to be prepared to be flexible and creative in order to deal with the considerable changes triggered by many of the forces described in this text. There is one thing of which you can be sure: marketing managers of the future will indeed live in 'interesting times'.

REFERENCES FOR CHAPTER 26

Forbes, A. (1995), 'Eco-Friendly Image Takes Hard Work', *Asian Business*, December, pp. 48–52.

O'Sullivan, T. (1996), 'Shell Needs More than Slick Solution', *Marketing Week*, 24 November, pp. 22–3.

Glossary

■ ■ ■

(Words which are set in *italics* have their own entries in the glossary, where they are further defined).

4Ps: otherwise known as the *marketing mix*, these are the basic tools of marketing: product, place, price and promotion.

7Ps: an extended *marketing mix* that takes account of the particular characteristics of services markets: product, price, place, promotion, physical evidence, people and processes.

Adaptation: (a) tailoring a product or other aspects of the *marketing mix* to suit the different needs and demands of other markets, usually international; (b) changing production methods or product specifications in an organisational market in order to better meet an individual customer's requirements.

Advertising: a paid form of non-personal communication transmitted through a mass medium.

Advertising media: the means through which advertisements are delivered to the target audience. Media include broadcast media, print media, cinema, hoardings and outdoor media.

Advertorial: a form of print *advertising* that is designed to mimic the editorial content, style and *layout* of the publication in which it appears.

Agents and brokers: *intermediaries* who have legal authority to act on behalf of a seller in negotiating sales, but who do not take title to goods themselves.

Alternative currencies: trading stamps, tokens or loyalty scheme points awarded on the basis of the amount spent by the customer that can be accumulated and then exchanged for gifts or discounts.

Ansoff matrix: a framework for considering the relationship between general strategic direction and *marketing strategies*. The four-cell matrix looks at permutations of new/existing products and new/existing markets.

Atmosphere: (a) the elements that come together to make an impact on retail customers' senses as they enter and browse in a store; (b) creating a feeling appropriate to the character of the store and the desired mood of the customers.

Attitude: the stance that individuals take on a subject that predisposes them to act and react in certain ways.

Augmented product: add-on extras that do not form an integral part of the product but which might be used, particularly by retailers, to increase the product's benefits or attractiveness. Includes guarantees, installation, after-sales service etc.

Awareness: the consciousness that a product or organisation exists.

Behaviour segmentation: grouping consumers in terms of their relationship with the product, for instance their usage rate, the purpose of use, their willingness and readiness to buy etc.

BIGIF: a form of *product-based sales promotion* – buy one get one free.

Boston Box: (also known as the BCG matrix) a tool for analysing a *product portfolio*, plotting relative market share against market growth rate for each product. The resultant matrix classifies products as cash cows, dogs, question marks and stars.

Brand loyalty: occurs when a consumer consistently buys the same brand over a long period.

Branding: the creation of a three-dimensional character for a product, defined in terms of name, packaging, colours, symbols etc., that helps to differentiate it from its competitors, and helps the customer to develop a relationship with the product.

Breadth of range: the variety of different *product lines* either (a) produced by a manufacturer; or (b) stocked by a retailer.

Breakeven analysis: shows the relationship between total costs and total revenue in order to assess the profitability of different levels of sales volume.

Bulk breaking: buying large quantities of goods and then reselling them in smaller lots, reflecting some of the cost savings made through bulk buying in the resale price. A prime function of *intermediaries*.

Business format franchise: allows a *franchisee* access not only to a product concept, but also to a comprehensive package that allows the product or service to be delivered in a standardised way regardless of the location.

Business–to–business marketing: see *organisational marketing*.

Buyer readiness stages: categorise consumers in terms of how close they are to making a purchase or a decision. Stages range from initial awareness, through to interest, desire and, finally, action.

Buyer–seller relationship: the nature and quality of the social and economic interaction between two parties.

Buying centre: a group of individuals, potentially from any level within an organisation or from any functional area, either contributing towards or taking direct responsibility for organisational purchasing decisions. The buying centre might be formally constituted, or be a loose informal grouping.

CAPI: computer aided personal interviewing.

Cash rebate: a form of *sales promotion* usually involving the collection of a specified number of proofs of purchase in order to qualify for a cash sum or for a *coupon*.

Catalogue showrooms: a high street store selling goods through catalogues displayed in the outlet, with the customer collecting goods immediately from a pick-up point on the premises.

CATI: computer aided telephone interviewing.

Cause-related marketing: linkages between commercial organisations and charities that can be used by both parties to enhance their profiles and to help achieve their marketing objectives.

Channel of distribution: the structure linking a group of organisations or individuals through which a product or service is made available to potential buyers.

Channel strategy: decision taken about the allocation of roles within a *channel of distribution*, and the way in which the channel is formally or informally managed and administered.

Closed questions: market research questions which offer the respondent a limited list of alternative answers to choose from.

Closing the sale: the stage of the *personal selling* process in which the customer agrees to purchase.

Cognitive dissonance: a state of psychological discomfort arising when a consumer tries to reconcile two conflicting states of mind, for example, the positive feeling of having chosen to buy a product and the negative feeling of being disappointed with it afterwards.

Cold calling: unsolicited visits or calls made by sales representatives to potential customers.

Collaborative R&D: pooling resources and expertise with one or more other organisations to undertake a research and development project jointly.

Commission: a percentage of the value of goods sold paid as total or partial remuneration to a sales representative or agent.

Comparative advertising: a type of *advertising* that seeks to make direct comparison between a product and one or more of its competitors on features or benefits that are important to the target market.

Competitive advertising: a commonly used type of *advertising* that communicates the unique benefits of a product, differentiating it from the competition.

Competitive edge: having a clear advantage over the competition in terms of one or more elements of the *marketing mix* that is valued by potential customers.

Competitive position: the organisation's strategic position in a market compared with its competitors: leader, challenger, follower or nicher.

Competitive posture: an organisation's means of dealing with competitors' actions in a market, proactively or reactively. Postures can be aggressive, defensive, co-operative or independent.

Competitive strategy: how an organisation chooses to compete within a market, with particular regard to the relative positioning and strategies of competitors.

Concept testing: the presentation of a new product concept, in terms of its function, benefits, design, branding etc., to a sample of potential customers to assess their reactions, *attitudes* and purchasing intentions towards it.

Concessions: also known as stores within stores; trading areas usually within *department stores*, sold, licensed or rented out to manufacturers or other retail names so that they can create their own distinctive trading image.

Consumer decision making: the process that consumers go through in deciding what to purchase, including *problem recognition*, information searching, evaluation of alternatives, making the decision, and *post-purchase evaluation*.

Consumer goods: goods that are sold to individuals for their own or their families' use.

Contracting: a type of *market entry method* whereby a manufacturer contracts with a company in a foreign market to produce or assemble goods on its behalf.

Contests and sweepstakes: a form of *sales promotion* in which customers are invited to compete for a specified number of prizes. Contests must involve a degree of skill or knowledge, whereas sweepstakes are effectively open lotteries.

Continuous innovation: products are upgraded and updated regularly in relatively small ways that make no great changes to the customer's buying behaviour.

Continuous research: research undertaken, usually by commercial market research organisations, on a long-term, ongoing basis, to track changing patterns in markets.

Control and evaluation: mechanisms for ensuring that *marketing plans* are properly implemented, that their progress is regularly measured and assessed and that any deviations are picked up early enough to allow corrective action to be taken.

Convenience goods: relatively inexpensive frequently purchased consumer goods; related to *routine problem-solving* buying behaviour.

Convenience stores: usually small neighbourhood grocery stores that differentiate themselves from the *supermarkets* through longer opening hours and easy accessibility.

Conversion rate: the number of enquiries from potential customers or sales visits made by sales representatives that actually turn into orders or sales.

Co-operative advertising: a form of *sales promotion* targeted at *intermediaries* through which manufacturers agree to fund a percentage of the *intermediary's* local advertising costs as long as the manufacturer's product appears in the *advertising* material.

Copywriting: writing the verbal (written or spoken) elements of an advertisement.

Core product: the prime purpose of a product's existence which might be expressed in terms of functional or psychological benefits.

Corporate chain: multiple retail outlets under common ownership, usually with national coverage.

Corporate identity: the character and image of an organisation, reflecting its culture, that is presented to its various *publics*, including the organisation's name and logo.

Corporate objectives: the overall objectives of the organisation that influence the direction of *marketing strategy*.

Corporate PR: *public relations* activities focused on enhancing or protecting the overall corporate image of an organisation.

Count and recount: a form of *sales promotion* targeted at *intermediaries* through which rebates are given for all stock sold during a specified promotional period.

Coupons: a form of *sales promotion* consisting of printed vouchers, distributed in a variety of ways, that allow a customer to claim a price reduction on a particular product or at a particular retailer's stores.

Creative appeal: the way in which an *advertising* message is formulated in order to provoke the desired response from the target audience. Types of appeal include rational, emotional, product-orientated or consumer-orientated appeal.

Culture: the personality of the society in which an individual lives, manifest in terms of the built environment, literature, the arts, beliefs and value systems.

Data-based budget setting: setting *advertising* or marketing budgets using methods that do not involve guesswork or arbitrary figures. The two main methods are competitive parity and objective and task.

Database marketing: compiling, analysing and using data held about customers in order to create better tailored, better timed offers that will maximise customer value and loyalty.

Decision making unit (DMU): see *buying centre*.

Demographic segmentation: grouping consumers on the basis of one or more *demographic* factors.

Demographics: the measurable aspects of population structure, such as birth rates, age profiles, family structures, education levels, occupation, income and expenditure patterns.

Department stores: large stores, usually located in town centres, which are divided into discrete departments selling a very wide range of diverse goods, from clothing to travel, from cosmetics to washing machines.

Depth of range: the amount of choice or assortment within a *product line*.

Derived demand: where demand for products or components in organisational markets depends on consumer demand further down the chain; for example demand for washing machine motors is derived from consumer demand for washing machines.

Differential advantage: see *competitive edge*.

Diffusion of innovation: a concept suggesting that customers first enter a market at different times, depending on their attitude to innovation and new products, and their willingness to take risks. Customers can thus be classified as innovators, early adopters, early majority, late majority and laggards.

Direct export: selling goods to foreign buyers without the intervention of an *intermediary*.

Direct mail: a *direct marketing* technique involving the delivery of promotional material to named individuals at their homes or organisational premises.

Direct marketing: an interactive system of marketing that uses one or more *advertising media* to effect a measurable response at any location, forming a basis for further developing an ongoing relationship between an organisation and its customers.

Direct response advertising: *advertising* through mainstream *advertising media* that encourages direct action from the audience, for example, requests for more information, requests for a sales visit, or orders for goods.

Direct Supply: a distribution channel in which the producer deals directly with the end customer without the involvement of *intermediaries*.

Discontinuous innovation: represents a completely new product concept unlike anything the customer has yet experienced, and thus involves a major learning experience for the customer with much information searching and evaluation.

Discount clubs: similar to *wholesalers*, but reselling in bulk to consumers who are members of the club rather than small retailers.

Distributors and dealers: *intermediaries* who add value through the provision of special services associated with the selling of a product and the after-sales care of the customer.

Diversification: developing new products for new markets.

DSS: decision support system; an extension of the *MIS* that allows the marketing decision maker to manipulate data to explore scenarios and 'what if ...' questions as an aid to decision making.

Durable products: products that last for many years and are thus likely to be infrequently purchased, such as electrical goods and capital equipment.

Dynamically continuous innovation: the introduction of new products with an element of significant innovation that could require major reassessment of the product within customers' buying behaviour.

Economic and competitive environment: trends and developments in terms of the economic well-being and condition of individuals, nations or trading blocs, including taxation and interest rates etc.; the structure of markets in terms of the number of competitors and their ability to influence the market.

Environmental scanning: the collection and evaluation of data and information from the marketing environment that can influence the organisation's *marketing strategies*.

EPOS: electronic point of sale systems which streamline stock control and ordering systems through barcode scanning and allow the automatic processing of credit card payments for goods.

Eurobrand: also known as a pan-European brand; a brand which is marketed and sold with a standardised offering across a number of different European countries.

Evoked set: the shortlist of potential products that the consumer has to choose from within the purchasing decision making process.

Exchange process: the interaction between buyer and seller in which each party gives the other something of value. Usually, the seller offers goods and services, and the buyer offers money.

Extended problem solving: a *purchasing situation* usually involving a great deal of time and conscious information searching and analysis, as it involves high-priced goods which are purchased very infrequently; the consequences of making a 'wrong' decision are severe and thus the customer is prepared to invest time and effort in the process.

Extending the product line: adding further *product items* into a *product line* to extend coverage of the market, for instance introducing a bottom of the range cut-price version of a product, or developing a premium quality product to extend the top end of the range.

Facilitators: *intermediaries* who undertake *physical distribution* functions such as warehousing, transport, insurance and administration.

Family life-cycle: a model representing the way in which a family's structure changes naturally over time.

Field marketing agencies: agencies which undertake in-store *sales promotions*, *sampling*, and/or the setting up and maintenance of POS material.

Filling the product range: adding further *product items* into a *product line* to fill gaps within the range, for instance introducing additional flavours, pack sizes or packaging formats.

Fmcg products: fast moving consumer goods; relatively low-priced, frequently purchased items, such as groceries and toiletries.

Focus group: a small group of people, considered to be representative of the target segment, invited to discuss openly products or issues at their leisure in a relaxed environment.

Forecasts: estimates of future demand, sales or other trends, calculated using quantitative and/or qualitative techniques.

Franchise: a contractual *vertical marketing system* in which a *franchisor* licenses a *franchisee* to produce and market goods or services to criteria laid down by the *franchisor* in return for fees and/or royalties.

Franchise blueprint: the design of a franchised system in terms of premises, equipment, service specifications, *layout*, suppliers, interior design, product range etc.

Franchise operating manual: a document provided by the *franchisor* based on the *franchise blueprint* specifying exactly how the *franchisee* should conduct the business on a day-to-day basis.

Franchisee: an *intermediary* who holds a contract to supply and market a product or service to operating standards and criteria set by the *franchisor*.

Franchisor: the individual or organisation offering *franchise* opportunities.

Frequency: the average number of times that a member of the target audience will have been exposed to an advertisement during a specified period.

Full service agencies: advertising agencies that provide a full range of services, including research, planning, creative work, advertising production, media buying etc. Such agencies might also offer other marketing communications services such as *direct mail*, *sales promotion*, and *PR*.

GE matrix: a tool for analysing a *product portfolio*, plotting industry attractiveness against business position for each product, resulting in a nine-cell matrix.

Generic strategies: three broad strategic options that set the direction for more detailed strategic planning: cost leadership, differentiation and or focus.

Geodemographics: a combination of *geographic* and *demographic segmentation* that can either give the demographic characteristics of particular regions, neighbourhoods and even streets, or show the geographic spread of any demographic characteristics.

Geographic segmentation: grouping customers in either organisational or consumer markets in terms of their geographic location.

Heterogeneity: a characteristic of *services*, describing how difficult it is to ensure consistency in a service product because of its 'live' production and the interaction between different customers and service providers.

House journal: an internal publication produced by an organisation in order to inform and entertain its employees and to generate better internal communication and relationships.

Hypermarkets: very large self-service *out of town* outlets, 5000 m² or more, stocking not only a wide range of grocery and *fmcg products*, but also other consumer goods such as clothing, electrical goods, home maintenance products etc.

Incubator organisation: an organisation for which an entrepreneur has previously worked, that gives the knowledge and skills necessary for a new *small business*.

Independent retail outlet: a single retail outlet, or a chain of two or three stores, managed by either a sole trader or a family firm.

Indirect export: selling goods to foreign buyers through *intermediaries* such as export agents, export merchants or buying houses.

Industrial marketing: see *Organisational marketing*.

Information overload: having so much information available that the consumer either cannot assimilate it all or feels too overwhelmed to take any of it in.

Inseparability: a characteristic of *services*, describing how service products tend to be produced at the same time as they are consumed.

Institutional advertising: a type of *advertising* that does not focus on a specific product, but on the corporate image of the advertiser.

Intangibility: a characteristic of *services*, describing their non-physical nature.

Interactive marketing: in *services* markets, the encounter and interaction between the service provider and the customer.

Intermediary: an organisation or individual through whom products pass on their way from the manufacturer to the end buyer.

Intermodal transport: using more than one type of transport (road, rail, sea, airfreight etc.) in transferring goods from one location to another.

Internal marketing: the development and training of staff to ensure high levels of quality and consistency in service delivery and support. Internal marketing includes recruitment, training, motivation and productivity.

International marketing: a particular application of *marketing* concerned with developing and managing trade across international boundaries.

Inventory management: controlling stock levels within the *physical distribution* function to balance the need for product availability against the need for minimising stock holding and handling costs.

Joint demand: where demand for one product or component in an organisational market is dependent on the supply or availability of another, for example a computer assembler's demand for casings might depend on the supply or availability of disk drives.

Joint promotion: *sales promotion* activity undertaken by two or more brands or manufacturers jointly, for example collecting tokens from Virgin Cola in order to get two Eurostar tickets for the price of one.

Joint ventures: a jointly owned company set up by two or more other organisations: (a) as a means of *market entry method;* or (b) as a means of pooling complementary resources and exploiting synergy.

Judgemental budget setting: setting advertising or marketing budgets using methods that involve some degree of guesswork or arbitrary figures. Methods include: arbitrary, affordable, percentage of past sales, and percentage of future sales.

Layout: (a) in retailing, the arrangement of fixtures, fittings and goods in the store (b) in *advertising,* the arrangement of the various elements of a print or poster advertisement.

Leads: names, addresses and/or other details of individuals or organisations which could be potential customers.

Learning: the change in behaviour that results from experience and practice.

Licensing: an arrangement under which an organisation (the licensor) grants another organisation (the licensee) the right to manufacture goods, use patents, use processes, or exploit trade marks within a defined market. Often used as an international *market entry method.*

Lifestyle segmentation: grouping consumers on the basis of *psychographic* characteristics.

Limited problem solving: a *purchasing situation* usually involving some degree of conscious information searching and analysis, as it involves moderately high priced goods which are not purchased too frequently, and thus the customer might be prepared to shop around to a limited extent.

Limited service agencies: advertising agencies that specialise in one or just a few parts of the whole *advertising* process; for example they might specialise in creative work, or media buying or advertising research.

Loading up: an objective of *sales promotion,* encouraging customers to advance their buying cycles, i.e. to buy greater quantities of a product in the short-term than normal.

Logistics: the handling and movement of inbound raw materials and other supplies as well as outbound *physical distribution.*

Macro segments: segments in organisational markets defined in terms of broad organisational characteristics such as size, location and usage rates, or in terms of product applications.

Mail order: a form of non-store retailing usually involving a catalogue from which customers select goods, then mail or telephone their orders to the supplier. Goods are delivered to the customer's home.

Mailing list: a list of names and addresses, which can be compiled from organisational records or purchased, used as the basis for *direct marketing* activities.

Manufacturer brands: *branding* applied to goods that are produced and sold by a manufacturer who owns the rights to the brand.

Manufacturing subsidiary: a subsidiary company set up in a foreign market to manufacture or assemble a product.

Mark-up: the sum added to the trade price paid for a product to cover the *intermediary's* costs and profit. Mark-up can be measured as a percentage of the trade price or as a percentage of the resale price.

Market coverage: ensuring that the product is made available through appropriate *intermediaries* so that: (a) the potential customer can access it as easily as possible; and (b) the product is properly displayed, sold and supported within the *channel of distribution.* Market coverage might involve intensive distribution, selective distribution or exclusive distribution.

Market development: selling existing products into new segments or geographic markets.

Market entry methods: ways of getting into international markets, including *direct exporting, indirect exporting, licensing, franchising, sales* or *manufacturing subsidiaries, joint ventures,* or *strategic alliances.*

Market penetration: increasing sales volume in current markets.

Market potential: the total level of sales achievable in a market assuming that every potential customer in that market is buying, that they are using the product on every possible occasion, and that they are using the full amount of product on each occasion.

Market segmentation: breaking a total market down into groups of customers and/or potential customers who have something significant in common in terms of their needs and wants or characteristics.

Marketing: creating and holding customers by producing goods or services that they need and want, communicating product benefits to customers, ensuring that goods and services are accessible, and that they are available at a price that customers are prepared to pay.

Marketing audit: the systematic collection, analysis and evaluation of information relating to the internal and external environments that answers the question 'Where are we now?' for the organisation.

Marketing concept: a philosophy of business, permeating the whole organisation, that holds that the key to organisational success is meeting customers' needs and wants more effectively and more closely than competitors.

Marketing environment: the external world in which the organisation and its potential customers have to exist, and within the context of which *marketing* decisions have to be made.

Marketing mix: the combination of the *4Ps* that creates an integrated and consistent offering to potential customers that satisfies their needs and wants.

Marketing objectives: what the organisation is trying to achieve through its *marketing* activities during a specified period. Closely linked with *corporate objectives*.

Marketing orientation: an approach to business that centres its activities on satisfying the needs and wants of its customers.

Marketing plan: a detailed written statement specifying target markets, *marketing programmes*, responsibilities, time-scales, controls and resources. Plans may be short term or long term, strategic or operational in focus.

Marketing PR: *public relations* activities focused on particular products or aspects of their marketing campaigns.

Marketing programmes: specific marketing actions, specified within the marketing plan, involving the use of the *marketing mix* elements in order to achieve marketing objectives.

Marketing research: the process of collecting and analysing information in order to solve marketing problems.

Marketing strategy: the broad marketing thinking that will enable an organisation to develop its products and *marketing mixes* in the right direction, consistent with overall *corporate objectives*.

Master franchising: a *franchisor* grants an individual or organisation in a particular country or other trading region the exclusive right to develop a *franchise* network by sub-franchising within that territory.

Micro segments: segments in organisational markets defined in terms of detailed organisational characteristics such as management philosophy, decision making structures, *purchasing policies* etc.

MIS: marketing information system; the formalised collection, sorting, analysis, evaluation, storage and distribution of marketing data.

Modified rebuy: goods and services purchased relatively infrequently by organisations which might want to update their information on available products and suppliers before making a repeat purchase decision.

Money-based sales promotions: *sales promotions* that centre around some kind of financial incentive: money-off packs, *cash rebate* offers, or *coupons*.

Motivation: the driving forces that make people act as they do.

Multiple sourcing: the sourcing of a particular *organisational good* or service from more than one supplier simultaneously.

Multivariable segmentation: using a number of different variables to develop a rich profile of a target group of customers.

Negotiation: a give and take process between a buyer and a seller in which precise terms of supply, specification, delivery, price, and after-sales service etc. are agreed.

New product development (NPD): the process of seeking and screening new product ideas, analysing their commercial feasibility, developing and *test marketing* the product and its associated *marketing mix*, launching the product fully, then monitoring and evaluating its initial progress.

New task purchasing: goods and services that are purchased extremely infrequently by organisations, and involve a high level of formalised information collection and analysis before a purchasing decision is made.

Non-durable products: products that can only be used once or a few times before replacement, such as groceries or office stationery.

Non-profit marketing: marketing activities undertaken by organisations which do not have profit generation as a prime corporate objective, such as charities, public sector health care, and educational establishments.

Open-ended questions: market research questions which do not offer a respondent a list of alternative answers. The respondents are encouraged to answer spontaneously and to enter into explanation of their answers.

Order cycle time: the time taken between putting in an order for a product and its satisfactory receipt.

Order maker: sales representatives with responsibility for: (a) finding new customers and making sales to them; and (b) actively increasing the volume or variety of sales to existing customers.

Order taker: sales representatives who either have a set pattern of customer contact or wait for customers to contact them when they want to buy.

Organisational goods: goods that are sold to organisations for: (a) incorporation into producing other products; or (b) supporting the production of other products directly or indirectly; or (c) resale.

Organisational marketing: (also known as industrial marketing or business-to-business marketing) activities directed towards the *marketing* of goods and services by one organisation to another.

Out of town: describes large retail sites located away from the town centres so that they are easily accessible to large numbers of car-borne shoppers.

Outsourcing R&D: commissioning other organisations or research bodies to undertake specific research and development projects, rather than handling them in-house.

Own label brands: *branding* applied to goods that are produced by a manufacturer on behalf of a retailer or wholesaler who owns the rights to the brand.

Penetration pricing: setting prices low in order to gain as much market share as possible as quickly as possible.

Perception: the way in which individuals analyse and interpret incoming information and make sense of it.

Perishability: a characteristic of *services*, describing how service products cannot be stored because they are produced and offered at particular moments in time.

Personal selling: interpersonal communication, often face to face, between a sales representative and an individual or group, usually with the objective of making a sale.

Personality: features, traits, behaviours and experiences that make each person a unique individual.

Physical distribution: the handling and movement of outbound goods from an organisation to its customers.

Pioneer advertising: *advertising* used in the early stages of a *product life-cycle* to explain what a product is, what it can do and what benefits it offers.

Political and regulatory environment: the governmental influences, at local, national and European levels, that inhibit or encourage business; the legal and regulatory frameworks within which organisations have to operate, including national and European law, local by-laws, regulations imposed by statutory bodies and voluntary codes of practice.

POS: point of sale; marketing communication activity, for example *sales promotions,* displays, videos, leaflets, posters etc., which appears in retail outlets at the place where the product is displayed and sold.

Post-purchase evaluation: the stage after a product or *service* has been purchased and used in which the consumer reflects on whether the product met expectations, exceeded them or was disappointing.

Post-testing: evaluation undertaken during or after an *advertising* campaign to assess its impact and effects.

Potential product: what the product could and should be in the future to maintain its *differentiation*.

PR: see *Public relations*.

Premium price: a price which is distinctly higher than average to reflect better product quality, exclusivity or status.

Pre-testing: showing an advertisement to a sample of the target audience during its development to check whether it is conveying the desired message in the desired way with the desired effect.

Press relations: cultivating good relationships between an organisation and the media as an aid to *public relations* activities.

Price: a medium of exchange; what is offered in return for something else; usually measured in terms of money.

Price comparison: using price as a means of comparing two or more products in order to judge: (a) their likely quality in the absence of other information; (b) which offers the best value for money.

Price differential: any difference in the prices charged for the same product to different *market segments* or in different geographic regions.

Price elasticity of demand: the responsiveness of demand to changes in prices. Elastic products are very responsive, so that a price increase leads to a fall in demand, while inelastic products are very unresponsive and thus a rise in price leads to little or no change in demand.

Price negotiation: bargaining between a buyer and a seller to agree a mutually acceptable price.

Price objectives: what the organisation is trying to achieve through its pricing, measured in financial or market share terms, and closely linked with overall *corporate* and *marketing objectives*.

Price perception: a customer's judgement of a price in terms of whether it is thought to be too high, about right or extremely good value for money; this judgement might vary with different circumstances and is often formed in the light of what other alternative products are available.

Price sensitivity: the extent to which price is an important criterion in the customer's decision making process; thus a price sensitive customer is likely to notice a price rise and switch to a cheaper brand or supplier.

Pricing method: the means by which prices are calculated. Methods can be cost orientated, demand orientated, or competition orientated.

Pricing policies and strategies: the overall strategic guidelines for the pricing decision, specifying pricing's role within an integrated *marketing mix*.

Pricing tactics: short-term manipulation of price to achieve specific goals, as for example in *money-based sales promotions*.

Primary research: *marketing research* specially commissioned and undertaken for a specific purpose.

Problem recognition: the realisation, triggered by either internal or external factors, that the consumer or the organisation has a problem that can be solved through purchasing goods or services.

Product-based sales promotions: *sales promotions* that centre around some kind incentive connected with the product: extra product free, *BIGIF*, or *samples*.

Product development: selling new or improved products into existing markets.

Product items: the individual products or brands that make up a *product line*.

Product life-cycle (PLC): a concept suggesting that a product goes through various stages in the course of its life: introduction, growth, maturity and decline. At each stage, a product's *marketing mix* might change, as will its revenue and profit profile.

Product lines: a group of products, closely related by production or *marketing* considerations, that exists within the overall *product mix*.

Product manager: the individual within an organisation responsible for the day-to-day management and welfare of a product or family of products at all stages of their *product life-cycle*, including their initial development.

Product mix: the total sum of all the *product items* and their variants offered by an organisation.

Product orientation: an approach to business that centres its activities on continually improving and refining its products, assuming that customers simply want the best possible quality for their money.

Product portfolio: the set of different products that an organisation produces, ideally balanced so that some products are mature, some are still in their growth stage while others are waiting to be introduced.

Product positioning: developing a product and associated *marketing mix* that: (a) is 'placed' as close as possible in the minds of target customers to their ideal in terms of important features and attributes; and (b) clearly differentiates it from the competition.

Product repositioning: refining the product and/or its associated *marketing mix* in order to change its *positioning* either: (a) to bring it closer to the customer's ideal; or (b) to move it further away from the competition.

Product specification: the criteria to which an organisational purchase must conform in terms of quality, design, compatibility, performance, price etc.

Production orientation: an approach to business that centres its activities on producing goods more efficiently and cost effectively, assuming that price is the only factor important to customers.

Promotional mix: the elements that combine to make an organisation's marketing communications strategy: *advertising, sales promotion, personal selling, direct marketing* and *public relations*.

Prospecting: in *personal selling*, finding new potential customers who have the ability, authority and willingness to purchase.

Psychographics: defining consumers in terms of their *attitudes*, interests and opinions.

Psychological pricing: using price as a means of influencing a consumer's behaviour or perceptions, for example using high prices to reinforce a quality image, or selling at £2.99 instead of £3.00 to make the product appear much cheaper.

Pull strategy: a communications strategy that focuses on the end consumer rather than other members of the *channel of distribution*. Thus a manufacturer might focus on communication to consumers, rather than to wholesalers or retailers, thus helping to pull the product down the channel.

Public relations (PR): a deliberate, planned and sustained effort to institute and maintain mutual understanding between an organisation and its *publics* (Institute of Public Relations definition).

Publicity: a tool of *public relations* focused on generating editorial media coverage for an organisation and/or its products.

Publics: any group, with some common characteristic with which an organisation needs to communicate, including the media, government bodies, financial institutions, pressure groups etc. as well as customers and suppliers.

Purchasing policy: an organisation's preferences, systems and procedures for purchasing including, for example, attitude towards favoured or approved suppliers, *single* or *multiple sourcing*, and rules and guidelines.

Purchasing situation: the context in which a consumer purchasing decision is made, defined by the frequency of purchase, the risks involved, and the level of information searching undertaken: *routine problem solving, limited problem solving*, and *extended problem solving*.

Push strategy: a communications strategy that focuses on the next member of the *channel of distribution* rather than on the end consumer. Thus a manufacturer might focus on communication to wholesalers or retailers rather than to consumers, thus helping to push the product down the channel.

Qualified prospects: potential customers who have been screened to check that they meet relevant criteria as potential purchasers, for example checking their financial status or that they do actually need the product.

Qualitative research: the collection of data that are open to interpretation, for instance on *attitudes* and opinions, and that might not be validated statistically.

Quantitative research: the collection of quantified data, for example sales figures, *demographic* data, purchase frequency etc., that can be subjected to statistical analysis.

Rating scales: a form of multiple choice market research questionnaire question in which respondents are asked to indicate their answer on a scale, for example ranging from 1 to 5 where 5 = 'strongly agree' and 1 = 'strongly disagree' with a given statement.

Reach: the percentage of the target market exposed to an advertisement at least once during a specified period.

Reference groups: groups to which an individual belongs or to which the individual aspires to belong, and which influence the individual's *motivation*, *attitudes* and behaviour.

Relationship life-cycle: the evolution of *buyer–seller* relationships in organisational markets, through stages including awareness, exploration, expansion, commitment and dissolution.

Relationship marketing: a form of *marketing* that puts particular emphasis on building a longer-term, more intimate bond between an organisation and its individual customers.

Reminder and reinforcement advertising: a type of *advertising*, targeted at consumers who have already tried and used the product before, that reminds consumers of a product's continued existence and of its unique benefits.

Reorder point: a stock level which, when reached, triggers an order for further supplies.

Repeat purchase: the purchase and use of a product on more than one occasion by a particular customer.

Retailer: an *intermediary* which buys products either from manufacturers or from *wholesalers* and resells them to consumers.

Rolling launch: the gradual launch of a new product, region by region.

Routine problem solving: a *purchasing situation* usually involving low-risk, low-priced, regularly purchased goods, which does not involve much, if any, information searching or analysis on the part of the buyer.

Routine rebuy: goods and services purchased frequently by organisations from established suppliers, with little, if any, formal decision making involved in the *repeat purchase*.

Safety stock: an agreed level of extra stock held in case of sudden surges in demand or unexpected delays in receiving new supplies.

Sales orientation: an approach to business that centres its activities on selling whatever it can produce, assuming that customers are inherently reluctant to purchase.

Sales potential: the share of a total market that the organisation can reasonably expect to capture.

Sales presentation: the stage of the *personal selling* process in which the sales representative outlines the product's features and benefits.

Sales promotion: usually short-term tactical incentives offering something over and above the normal product offering to encourage customers to act in particular ways.

Sales quotas: the sales targets that a sales representative has to achieve, broken down into individual product areas and specified as sales value or volume.

Sales subsidiaries: a subsidiary company set up in a foreign market to handle marketing, sales, distribution and customer care in that market.

Sampling: (a) a form of *product-based sales promotion* involving the distribution of samples of products in a variety of ways, so that consumers can try them and judge them for themselves; and (b) in market research, the process of setting criteria and then selecting the required number of respondents for a research study.

Sampling process: defining the target population for a market research study; finding a means of access to that population, and selecting the individuals to be surveyed within that population.

Secondary research: data which already exist in some form, having been collected for a different purpose, perhaps even by a different organisation, and which might be useful in solving a current problem.

Self-liquidating offers: a form of merchandise-based *sales promotion* that invites the consumer to send cash, and often proofs of purchase, in return for merchandise. The price charged covers the cost of the merchandise and a contribution to handling and postage.

SEM: single European market; since 1992, completely free trade has been possible between member states of the EU, although the process of harmonising marketing regulations, product standards, tax rates etc. is an ongoing process that has not yet been fully achieved.

Semi-structured interview: a form of market research that involves some *closed questions* for collecting straightforward data and some *open-ended questions* to allow the respondent to explain more complex feelings and *attitudes*, for example.

Services: goods that are largely or mainly non-physical in character, such as personal services, travel and tourism, medical care or management consultancy.

Shell directional policy matrix: a tool for analysing a *product portfolio*, plotting competitive capability against prospects for sector profitability for each product, resulting in a nine-cell matrix.

Shopping goods: consumer goods purchased less frequently than *convenience goods*, and thus requiring some information search and evaluation; related to *limited problem-solving* buying behaviour.

SIC code: standard industrial classification; a means of categorising organisations in terms of the nature of their business.

Single sourcing: the sourcing of a particular organisational good or service from only one supplier.

Skimming: setting *prices* high in order to attract the least price-sensitive customers and to generate profit quickly before competitors enter the market and start to force prices down.

Slice of life: a style of *advertising* that shows how the product fits into a lifestyle that is similar to that of the target audience, or represents a lifestyle that they can identify with or aspire to.

Small business: small businesses are usually defined as those with fewer than 100 employees.

Social class: a form of stratification that structures and divides a society, often on the basis of income and occupation, for marketing purposes.

Social marketing: a marketing focus that is concerned with ensuring that organisations handle marketing responsibly, in a way that contributes towards the well-being of society as a whole.

Sociocultural environment: trends and developments within society as a whole, affecting the *demographic* structure of the population, life-styles, *attitudes*, culture, issues of public and private concern, tastes and demands.

Source credibility: the trustworthiness, likeability, respect or expertise of the perceived source of a marketing message in the minds of the target audience. Source credibility might be transferable to the actual subject of the message, or might at least ensure that the message is listened to.

Speciality goods: expensive, infrequently purchased consumer goods; related to *extended problem-solving* buying behaviour.

Speciality stores: stores which tend to concentrate on one clearly defined product area, focusing on *depth of range*.

Sponsorship: the provision of financial or material support to individuals, teams, events or organisations, outside the sponsor's normal sphere of operations. This might involve sport, the arts, community or charity work.

Standardisation: a deliberate strategy to maintain the same *product* and *marketing mix* across all international markets without adapting it for local conditions.

STEP factors: the four broad categories of influences that create the *marketing environment*: sociocultural, technological, economic and competitive, and political and regulatory.

Stock-out: a situation where an organisation runs out of supplies of a product or component completely.

Store image: the *positioning* of a store in terms of its *branding*, product selection, interior and exterior design, fixtures and fittings, lighting etc.

Storyboard: part of the process of developing a television or cinema advertisement, a storyboard shows sketches of the main scenes in the advertisement, describes what is happening at that point, and what sound effects should be used.

Strategic alliance: a collaborative agreement entered into by two or more organisations with a specific purpose in mind. It might include *joint ventures* or looser arrangements that do not involve any equity stakes.

Strategic business unit (SBU): a group of products, markets or operating divisions with common strategic characteristics, that is a profit centre in its own right. An individual product, market or operating division could also be defined as an SBU if appropriate.

Strong theory of communication: a theory that assumes that marketing communication takes the potential buyer through the *buyer readiness stages* in sequence, thus forming *attitudes* and opinions before a purchase has taken place.

Supermarkets: self-service stores carrying a wide range of grocery and *fmcg products*, with smaller branches located in town centres and larger stores located on *out of town sites*.

Switchers: consumers who are not loyal to any one brand of a particular product and switch between two or more brands within the category.

SWOT analysis: a technique that takes the findings of the *marketing audit* and categorises key points as strengths, weaknesses, opportunities or threats.

Tangible product: the way in which the concept of the *core product* is turned into something 'real' that the customer can interact with, including design, quality, *branding*, and product features.

Targeting: deciding how many *market segments* to aim for and how to do it. There are three broad targeting strategies: concentrated, differentiated and undifferentiated.

Technological environment: trends and developments in the technological field that might: (a) improve production; (b) create new product opportunities; (c) render existing products obsolete; (d) change the ways in which goods and services are marketed; or (e) change the profile of customers' needs and wants.

Telemarketing: using the telephone: (a) to make sales directly; or (b) to develop customer relationships and customer care programmes further. Calls might be: (a) outbound, instigated by the organisation; or (b) inbound, instigated by the customer.

Teleshopping: a form of non-store retailing including shopping by telephone and shopping via computer networks.

Tendering: where potential suppliers bid competitively for a contract, quoting a price to the buyer.

Test marketing: the stage within the *new product development process* in which a product and its associated *marketing mix* are launched within a confined geographic area to get as realistic a picture as possible of how that product is likely to perform when fully commercialised.

Trade shows and exhibitions: centralised events, large or small, local or international, focused on an industry or a product area, that bring together a wide range of relevant suppliers and interested customers under one roof.

Trading up: an objective of *sales promotion*, encouraging customers either to buy bigger sized packs of products, or to buy the more expensive products in a range.

Transfer pricing: prices charged for the exchange of goods and services between different departments or operating divisions within the same organisation.

Trial: the purchase and use of a product for the first time by a particular customer.

Trial price: a very low or minimal temporary price often used for new products to encourage consumers to try them.

Trial sizes: a form of *product-based sales promotion* involving the sale of products in smaller than normal packs, so that consumers can buy and try them with minimal risk.

Unsought goods: goods that consumers did not even know they needed until either (a) an emergency arose that needed an immediate purchasing decision to help resolve it; or (b) an aggressive sales representative pressurised them into a purchase.

Value: a customer's assessment of the worth of what they are getting in terms of a product's functional or psychological benefits.

Value management: the analysis of products and processes to see where the greatest costs are being incurred and where the greatest value is added. This can lead to cost savings and better value for money to the customer.

Variety stores: smaller than *department stores*, variety stores stock a relatively limited number of different product categories, but in greater depth.

Vertical marketing systems: a *channel of distribution* which is viewed as a co-ordinated whole and is effectively managed or led by one channel member. The leadership might be contractual, or derived from the power or dominance of one member, or arise from the ownership of other channel members by one organisation.

Weak theory of communication: a theory that assumes that marketing communication creates awareness of products, but that *attitudes* and opinions are only created after purchase and *trial*.

Wholesaler: an *intermediary* which buys products in bulk, usually from manufacturers, and resells them to trade customers, usually small retailing.

Index
■ ■ ■

Note: This index contains no references to the Glossary, but should be used in conjunction with it. Cross-references are not normally given to entries beginning with closely related words (e.g. marketing/markets); these should be searched in addition.

accessibility
    as criterion of service quality, 933
    as requirement for segmentation, 191
accessory goods (product classification), 261
account management, 719–20
accumulation of products, intermediaries and, 459
ACORN (A Classification Of Residential Neighbourhoods), 175–7, 770
action
    as buyer readiness stage, 183
    direct mail and, 746
Action on Smoking and Health (ASH), 53, 77–8
activities, segmentation and, 177
adaptation, 1015–17, 1018
added extras, 661
administered vertical marketing systems, 473, 479
administration, 539, 551–3
    technology and, 59
adopter categories, 304–5, 333
advantage, relative, perception of, and adoption of products, 306
adversarial approach to suppliers, 158–9
advertising, 114–15, 603–45, 780
    campaign development, 636–45
        stages in, 637
    and children, 118
    comparative, 606–7, 614
    competition and, 640, 742
    co-operative, 682–3
    costs, 278, 624–5, 627, 628, 742
    creative appeal, 612–18
    definitions, 604, 645, 780
    direct response, 739, 742, 749–53
        as proportion of advertising, 749
        telemarketing in, 753
    evaluation of, 644–5
    frequency, 625, 626, 629
    handling in-house, 634
    international aspects, 1000
    and learning, 104
    length of advertisements, 643–4
    media, 624–33, 639–40, 644
    message, 609–12, 643–4
    non-commercial, 616, 649–50, 808, 943–4
    personal selling and, 699, 700
    political and regulatory environment, 73–4, 75–7, 82, 587
    print, 618–22
    public relations and, 780–1
    publicity and, 789–90
    reach, 625, 626, 629
    regulation of, 39
    role in marketing mix, 645
    role in promotional mix, 581, 604–9
    sales promotion and, 660, 661, 664
    scheduling, 642–4
    small businesses and, 963

technology and, 60
    testing, 641, 644–5
    types, 604–8
    wastage rates, 626–7, 631–2
advertising agencies, 633–6, 713
    criteria for selecting, 634–5
    relationships with, 636
Advertising Standards Authority, 75–6, 584, 587
advertorials, 615
advocacy, institutional advertising and, 607–8
affective attitudes, 108
affective stage of buyer readiness, 580–2
affordable method of budget setting, 592
after-sales contact, 95, 463, 543, 757, 767
age, as basis of segmentation, 174, 184
agencies
    advertising, *see* advertising agencies
    field marketing, 679, 707
    idea generation, 343
    mail order, 759
    and sales promotion, 688
agents, 452
    export, 1006
aggressive strategies, 860–1, 862–5, 866
agriculture, 14–15, 834–5
    environmental issues, 38, 40
    ethical issues, 49
    EU and, 64, 74–5
    and perfect competition, 69–70
AIDA response hierarchy model, 183, 184, 304, 579, 580
    direct mail and, 746
air transport, 546
aircraft industry, 147, 327–8
airlines, 67, 74, 924
alcohol, 109, 113, 584
    advertising, 76, 587
    see also brewing
alliances, strategic, 521–3, 866–7, 1012–13, 1054
allowances, 434, 436
    as sales promotion, 680–2
    see also discounts
alternative close (method of closing), 718
alternative currencies, 676
American Marketing Association, definition of marketing, 5, 6–8, 11
Amnesty International, 11
analysis, 235–9
    in idea generation, 343
    marketing costs and profitability, 908
    sales, 907–8
    situation, in communications planning model, 576–87
    statistical series, 894–5
    strategic marketing, 836–45
    SWOT, 886, 1002
animal welfare issues, 49–50
animations, 618
annual reports, 791
Ansoff matrix, 845–8, 889
antecedent influences, 958–9
appeal, types of, 612–18
appearance, and assessment of services, 920
arbitrary budgets, 592
area sampling, 223

arts, pricing, 378
arts sponsorship, 804–7
ASH (Action on Smoking and Health), 53, 77–8
aspirant groups, 115
association, 104
assortment strategy, 454, 459, 514–15
assumptive close (method of closing), 718
atmosphere, 480–1, 492, 515–17
    in advertising, 618
attack strategies, 860–1, 862–5, 866
attention, 102–3, 644
    advertising and, 610
    direct mail and, 746, 747
    sales promotion and, 661, 662
attitudes, 48–54, 99, 103, 107–9, 580
    and behaviour, 108
    changing, 108, 794
    components of, 107–8
    corporate, 834
    international aspects, 1001
    public relations and, 794
    and segmentation in consumer markets, 183
    and target audiences for advertising campaigns, 638
    tests of, in post-testing of advertising, 645
    see also beliefs *and* culture
attribute listing, as method of idea generation, 343
audiences, target, for advertising campaigns, 637–9, 640, 641, 643
audits
    in evaluating sales promotion, 688
    external, 884, 885
    home, 208
    internal, 885
    marketing, 883–5
    retail, 209
augmented product, 254, 255, 256
Austria, 64
availability, 22
average prices, and transfer pricing, 439
awareness
    as aim of advertising, 626, 644
    as buyer readiness stage, 183, 579–82
    direct mail and, 746
    exhibitions and, 813–14
    public relations and, 794
    and routine problem solving purchasing situation, 97
    small businesses and, 963
    as stage of buyer–seller relationship life-cycle, 160

BACC (Broadcast Advertising Clearance Centre), 76
backward integration, 472
banks, 12, 15, 606, 693, 931, 932
barcodes, uses of, 209, 242–3, 520, 937, 938
    see also POS technology
barter, 370
BCG (Boston Consulting Group) matrix (Boston Box), 837–42, 843–5
behaviour, international aspects, 1000, 1001
behaviour segmentation, 180–4
behaviour stage of buyer readiness, 580–2

beliefs, 92, 93, 108
    measuring, 109
    see also attitudes
belongingness and love needs, 105–6
benchmarking, 852
benefits, 104–7, 372
    advertising appeal and, 613–17
    core, 254–5
    and perception of price, 371–3
    personal, 104–7, 372
    and segmentation, 181, 184
bias, 218, 220, 226, 227, 234
bidding, see tendering
BIGIF, 668–9, 681
    see also bulk discounts
biros, 421
birth rates, 41–2, 116
board games, 300–1
body language, 717, 718
    international aspects, 1001
body size, 173
BOGOFF, see BIGIF
bonuses
    for sales assistants, 684
    as sales promotion, 681
bookselling, 391, 401–2
boomerang technique of handling
        objections, 715
Boston Box/Boston Consulting Group
        matrix, 837–42, 843–5
boutique layout, 518, 519
brainstorming, 343
brand loyalty/switching
    sales promotion and, 660
    and segmentation in consumer
        markets, 182–3
brand managers, 320–1, 359
brands/branding, 265–78
    benefits to consumers, 269
    benefits to manufacturers, 269–70
    brand extension, 277
    disadvantages, 271
    discreet, 276
    'essential' brands for retailers, 471,
        479–80, 521
    Eurobranding, 321–3
    fixed endorsed approach, 276
    flexible endorsed approach, 276
    generic, 276
    marks, 268
    monolithic, 276
    names, 267, 274–5, 322, 1000
        court rulings on, 275
    own label, see own label brands
    and price, 377–8
    product life-cycles, 303
    retailers and, 270–1, 471, 479–80, 521
    selling/contracting out, 300
    services and, 928
breadth of range, 497–8, 514
breakdown methods of assessing market
        potential, 894–5
breakeven analysis, 425
brewing, 64, 123, 224
    and variations in duties, 62, 77
briefings, 792–3
briefs, research, 232
British Heart Foundation, 53
broadcast advertisements, 622–4, 626–9
    length, 643–4
Broadcast Advertising Clearance Centre, 76
broadcasting, sponsorship of programmes,
        803–4
brokers, 452
budgets/budget setting, 19, 592–4, 639, 641,
        793, 890–1
build up methods of assessing market
        potential, 894–5
Bulgaria, 12, 13, 465

bulk breaking, 451, 454, 460
bulk discounts, 433
bundle pricing, 422, 430
bursts, advertising in, 642
business(es)
    defining ('what business we are in'), 28–9,
        56, 67, 184–5, 892
        and competitor identification, 850
    size classification, 957
    small, see small businesses
business analysis stage of new product
        development, 346–7
business cards, international conventions
        concerning, 1001
business direction, 827–8
    see also marketing strategy
business environment, see marketing
        environment
business ethics, see ethics
business format franchising, 972–83
business forums, 359
business objectives, 881–3
    and distribution channel strategy, 464–5
    and pricing, 391–4
    see also corporate strategy and objectives
business orientations, 12, 13–17
business promotion (manufacturer–
        manufacturer sales promotion), 660–1
business services, as product
        classification, 262
business to business marketing, see
        organisational marketing
butter, 385, 392
Butter Council, 595
buyer(s)/buying, see customers and
        purchasing
buyer readiness, 183, 579–82
    international aspects, 1016
    see also AIDA model
buyer–seller relationships, 9, 11, 146–7,
        156–61, 262, 1054
    as basis for organisational market
        segmentation, 171
    and choice of competitive strategy, 858
    direct marketing and, 740
    exhibitions and, 813
    JIT systems and, 560
    length of, 158
    life-cycle, 160–1
    negotiation style and, 716
    in organisational markets, 142
    personal selling and, 700, 703, 719–21
    price negotiation and, 436
    see also relationship marketing
buyer-specified products, 262, 318–20, 427
buying allowances, 680–1
buying behaviour, distribution channel
        strategy and, 466
buying centres, 140, 151–3
    personal selling and, 711
buying chains, 496, 507
buying houses, 1006
buying situations, 96–8
    and classification of products, 260
    see also purchasing

cable television, 627–8, 638, 763
call centres, 743
camcorders, 14
cameras, 372–3, 417
campaigns, 878
    advertising, 636–45
        stages in, 637
    sales promotion, 686–7
cannibalising products, 312, 315, 316
Cantona, Eric, 591, 633, 648, 649, 803
capabilities, and distribution channel
        strategy, 464–5
capacity utilisation, 419

CAPI (computer aided personal
        interviewing), 208, 235
capital goods (product classification), 260–1
car dealership/selling, 128, 376, 377,
        449–50, 480, 713–14, 734–5
car prices, international differences, 397, 398
cards, see collecting cards and smart cards
carton technology, 14
cartoons, 618
cash and carry stores, 524
'cash cows', 840
cash discounts, 433–4, 436
cash flow, 409, 410–11
    EFTPOS systems and, 521
    inventory management and, 534
cash rebates, see rebates
catalogue (retail) showrooms, 498, 508
catalogues, 758–60
    see also mail order
catchment, 511, 527
category killers, 506
CATI (computer aided telephone
        interviewing), 208, 234–5
causal research, 206
cause-related marketing, 589, 807–8
    see also non–profit marketing
celebrities, 312, 590–1, 611, 614, 648, 655,
        658
celebrity endorsement, as franchise
        relationship, 971
census method of assessing market
        potential, 895
censuses, 210, 527, 767
Central Europe, see Eastern Europe
Central Statistical Office, 210
chains, buying, 496, 507
challengers, market, 859, 860–1
chambers of commerce, 211
change
    business size and, 956–7
    corporate attitudes to, 834
    and new product development, 337
channel strategy, see under
        distribution channels
channel system competition, 472
Channel Tunnel, 67, 428–9, 549, 565
channels of communication, 572, 574
channels of distribution, see distribution
        channels
charities, 941, 942, 944–5
    charity tie-ins, 589, 807–8
    see also non-profit marketing
Chartered Institute of Marketing,
        definition of marketing, 5, 6, 8, 11
children
    marketing concerning, 98
    and purchasing decision-making, 118–19
    samples directed at, 669
choice
    in pack sizes, 280
    see also product range
CIF (cargo, insurance, freight) pricing, 434
CIM, see Chartered Institute of Marketing
cinema advertising, 629
claims procedures, 542
class, social, 110–11
classes, product, 303
classification data, 225
classified advertisements, 631
climate, 1015, 1019
closed questions, 226–7, 229
closing a sale, 718–19
clothing, reference groups and, 114–15
clubs, business, 359
coercive power, 479, 480
cognitive attitudes, 108
cognitive dissonance, 94
cognitive stage of buyer readiness, 579,
        580–2

cold calling, 709, 710, 711, 756
  in telephone selling, 74
cold mailing lists, 745
collaboration, 56
  see also co-operation
collaborative approach to suppliers, 159
collaborative research and
          development, 357–9, 360
collecting cards, 657
collusion, 867
colour, effects of, 516
combination selling, 765–6
command economies, 12
commercialisation stage of new product
          development, 352–3
commission, 729–30
commitment
  in organisational purchasing, 147, 148
  as stage of buyer–seller relationship
          life-cycle, 160
committees, new product, 360–1
communicability, and adoption of products,
          306
communication, 26, 568, 570–5
  assessing sponsorship results, 810
  concerning services, 930
  and convenience goods, 257–8
  international aspects, 73, 1016
  objectives, 587–8, 639
      see also advertising (campaign
          development)
  personal/impersonal media, 591–2
  presenter characteristics and, 591–2
  as sales promotion objective, 661, 662
  segmentation and, 191
  by service staff, as criterion of service
          quality, 933
      and shopping goods, 259
  and speciality goods, 259
  strategies, 588–91
  theoretical model/theories of, 571–5, 579,
          580–1
  see also advertising, personal selling *and*
          public relations
communication channels, 572, 574
communication costs, in sales promotion
          campaigns, 687
communications planning flow, 576
communications planning model, 575–96
comparative advertising, 606–7, 614
compatibility, perception of, and adoption
          of products, 306
competence, staff, as criterion of
          service quality, 933
competition/competitors, 18
  advertising and, 640, 642, 742
  analysis of response, in new product
          development process, 347
  consumer decision-making process and,
          100
  direct marketing and, 742
  in distribution channels, 470–2
  entry timing, 306–8
  international aspects, 73, 998, 1003
  marketing information systems and, 243
  marketing strategy and, *see* competitive
          strategy
  monopolies and, 67
  monopolistic competition, 69, 389
      and pricing, 388–9
  perfect competition, 69–70
      and pricing, 389, 431
  personal selling and, 717
  price cuts by, 420–1
  price increases by, 422–3
  pricing and, 387–9, 412–13, 414
  product range and, 317
  sales promotion and, 656, 660
  sales representatives and, 704

and selective distribution, 468
  as source of information, 812–13, 851–4
  as source of new product ideas, 340–1
  state ownership and, 69
  and test marketing, 350
competition-based pricing, 431–2
competitions (contests/sweepstakes), 677–8
competitive advertising, 604, 605–7
competitive analysis, 431
competitive clusters, 850–1
competitive edge, 27, 29
competitive environment, *see* economic and
          competitive environment
competitive negotiation, 716
competitive parity method of budget
          setting, 593–4
competitive position, 859–61
competitive postures, 859, 862–7
competitive pricing, 432
      see also tendering
competitive strategy, 831–2, 849–67
  generic strategies, 854–9
  small businesses and, 966
competitive tendering, *see* tendering
competitiveness, 1052–3
competitor analysis, 849–54
competitor identification, 850
complexity, perception of, and adoption of
          products, 306
components, 262
computer aided manufacturing, 58
computer aided personal interviewing
          (CAPI), 208, 235
computer aided telephone
          interviewing (CATI), 208, 234–5
computer systems, 171–2
computers, 14, 307
  direct marketing and, 743
  sales representatives and, 719, 731
      see also databases
conative attitudes, 108
concentrated targeting, 186
concentration of demand, 135–7
concentric diversification, 847
concept testing stage of new product
          development, 345–6
concessions (stores within stores), 500–1
condoms, 248–9
confirming houses, 1006
conflict, 476–8
  underlying, 476
  within distribution channels, 476–8
conglomerate diversification, 847
consultants/consultancies
  on brand names, 275
  idea generation, 343
  and marketing audits, 885
consumer(s), *see* customer(s)
consumer decision making, *see* purchasing
          decision making
consumer demand, and organisational
          markets, 132
consumer goods, 29–30
consumer goods and services,
          user-based product classification
          systems, 257–60
consumer groups, 51–5
consumer markets/marketing
  direct marketing and, 740
  distribution channel structures, 452–4
  organisational markets/marketing
          compared to, 128–9, 576–7
  segmentation in, 172–92
consumer panels, 207–8
consumerism, 51
Consumers' Association, 51, 55, 473
consumption patterns, social class and, 110
contests, 677–8
  sales, 684

contingency plans, 878
continuous innovation, 335–7
continuous research, 207–9
contract selling, 707
contracting, international, 1009
contracting-out research and development,
          357–8, 360
contractual vertical marketing systems, 473,
          479, 496
control, 789
  marketing, 891–2, 905–7
convenience goods, 257–8
  intensity of distribution, 462–3
convenience stores, 507
conversion rates, 709
cooking demonstrations, 679–80
'cooling-off' periods, 260
co-operation, 475
  JIT systems and, 560
  in negotiation, 716
  strategic, 866–7
  within distribution channels, 475
      see also collaboration
co-operative advertising, 682–3
co-operative approach to suppliers, 159
co-operatives, 473
  consumer, 508
      see also buying chains
copycotting, 289–90
copywriting, 619–22
  direct mail, 748
  for direct marketing, 767–8
core benefits, 254–5
core product, 254–5, 256
corporate chains, 495–6
corporate identity, 285, 781, 795–9
  changing, 795–9
      stages of process, 797–8
      top management and, 798, 799
corporate magazines, 791
corporate objectives, 881–3
      see also business objectives
corporate plans, 878
corporate PR, 784, 785
corporate strategy, 830–1
      see also marketing strategy
corporate vertical marketing systems, 472
correlation method of forecasting, 900
cost(s), 317, 423–4
  advertising, 278, 624–5, 627, 628, 742
  advertising basing appeal on, 615–16
  communication, in sales promotion
          campaigns, 687
  customers', 374, 379–80, 422
  of direct marketing, 742
  economies of scale, 855–6, 860, 1017
  of exhibition attendance, 814–15, 817
  of failure, 354
  increases in, and price increases, 422
  intermediaries and, 453, 456, 457, 461
  international aspects, 1019–20
  inventory-related, 556–7
  joint, 908
  marketing, analysis of, 908
  of money-based sales promotion, 663,
          664
  negotiation and, 436–7
  of new product development, 331, 337
  and other choice criteria in purchasing,
          145
  of packaging, 280
  of packaging development, 278
  of personal selling, 700–1, 707, 742
  of physical distribution and logistics-
          related activities, 532, 533–4, 535,
          536–40
  and pricing, 381, 394, 426–8, 440
  of sales promotion, 663, 664, 668, 669,
          675, 676, 682
  of sales promotion campaigns, 686–7

of transportation, 434, 534, 539, 548–9
cost-based pricing methods, 426–8, 440
cost leadership, as competitive strategy, 854–6, 858–9
cost-plus pricing, 427
cost–volume–profit relationship, 423–6
count and recount, 681, 682
counterfeiting, 268
coupons, 658–9, 665–6
  in direct response advertising, 749–51
  redemption rates, 665, 666, 688
  use to compile mailing lists, 747
courtesy, as criterion of service quality, 933
Crawford, Cindy, 611
cream cakes, 108, 109
creative appeal, 612–18
creativity, 343
  in writing for direct mail, 748
  see also idea generation and invention
credibility, as criterion of service quality, 933
credit, 51, 62–3
  intermediaries and, 461
crisis insurance, 720–1
cross-docking, 558
CTN (confectionery, tobacco and news) retailing, 494, 507
culture, 104, 111–14
  international differences, 112–14, 173, 322
    see also language(s)
  organisational, 151
  see also social class
customer(s), 17, 153
  and adaptation/standardisation, 1015, 1017–18
  adopter categories, 304–5, 333
  attracting, sales promotion and, 660
  benefits of branding for, 269
  benefits of direct marketing to, 741, 742–3
  concerns, 48–54
  costs of purchasing, other than price, 374, 379–80, 422
  defining, 168, 169
  dissatisfied, 95
  distribution channel strategy and, 462–4, 466
  effects of other customers, 517, 925
  filming, 219
  handling of, 921
  information needs, 22
  information on, 242–3
    gathering, 9–10, 184
    see also marketing research
  and internationalisation, 998
  market beliefs, 92, 93
  marketing concept and, 12
  needs of, 5, 6
    identifying and monitoring, 21–2, 23, 38, 40
  and new businesses, 962, 963
  and positioning, 309–10
  post-purchase monitoring, see after-sales contact
  and price, 371–3, 428
  relative importance of, 723–4
  right of withdrawal from contract, 764
  sales representatives as source of information from, 702–4
  of services, 938–9
  shopping habits, 258–9
  as source of new product ideas, 341–2
  turnover, advertising and, 643
  understanding of, as criterion of service quality, 933
  views on own label brands, 273
  see also buying and related entries, decision

making, prospects and purchasing and related entries
customer-based organisation of sales force, 723–4
customer bases, 135–6
customer care lines, 754–5, 764, 765–6
customer loyalty schemes, see loyalty schemes
customer-orientated advertising appeal, 615–18
customer retention/development programmes, 70–2
customer service, 540–3
customer service telephone calls, 754, 757
customer-specific coupons, 665
customer-specified products, see buyer-specified products
cynicism, 273

data
  collection, 184
  secondary, 210–14, 896
  types obtainable from questionnaires, 225–6
  see also information and marketing research
data-based budget setting methods, 593–4
data protection laws, 74
databases, 60, 98, 184, 243, 740, 743, 766–7, 769–72
  card schemes and, 9–10
  care lines and, 755
  and decision support systems, 244
  European, 210, 213
  limitations, 745
  sales representatives and, 719
  see also mailing lists
dealers, 451
  retailers and, 451, 453
debt, 51, 62–3
deciders, 153
decision domain conflict, 477
decision making, purchasing, see purchasing decision making
decision-making units, 140, 151–3
  as basis for organisational market segmentation, 171
  personal selling and, 711, 719
decision support systems, 243–4
decline stage of product life-cycle, 298–300, 317–18
  promotional mix and, 585–6
decoding, 572–3, 574
defensibility, as requirement for segmentation, 192
defensive strategies, 862, 865–6
deflecting price cuts, 421
deletion, product, 299–300, 317–18
delisting, 471
delivery, 493
  costs, pricing and, 434
  flexibility, 542
  international aspects, 1020
  and service quality, 934, 935
  times, 542, 742, 758
Delphi technique, 899
demand, 382–6, 408
  concentration/dispersion, 135–7
    and distribution channel strategy, 465–6
  curbing by increasing prices, 422
  curves, 382–6
  derived, 132–3
  elasticity of, 134, 382–6
  joint, 133–4
  marketing and, 8
  in organisational markets, 132–7

patterns of, advertising and, 643
predicting, 8
price and, 376, 422, 428–31
price elasticity of, 134, 382–6
  see also wants
demographic segmentation, 173–5, 178, 181, 184
  see also geodemographics
demographics/demographic environment, 41–6, 116, 527
  direct marketing and, 741
demonstrating, 679–80, 812
  direct marketing and, 764
  in personal selling, 713–14
department stores, 498, 499–501
dependency, 142, 480, 856
depth of range, 497–8, 514
derived demand, 132–3
descriptive research, 205
design
  and positioning, 314–15
  print advertising, 618–22
  product, 282–3, 284–5
  see also layout
desire
  as buyer readiness stage, 183
  direct mail and, 746
desk research, see marketing research, secondary
detergents, 68–9, 89, 90, 92, 364
development, market, as growth strategy, 846
development, research and, see research and development
dichotomous questions, 226–7
Diesel Railcar, German, 290–1, 832
differential advantage, 27, 29
differential pricing, 393, 396–7
differentiated targeting, 186–7
differentiation
  as competitive strategy, 856–7, 858–9
  price, 431
  product, and monopolistic competition, 69
  small businesses and, 960, 962
differentiators, 307
diffusion of innovation, 303–6
direct mail, 744–9
  campaign development, 747–9
  coupons in, 666
  response rates, 746
direct marketing, 739–40, 744–63
  benefits to customers, 741, 742–3
  campaign management, 766–9
  database use, 769–72
  definitions, 740
  objectives, 763–5
    achieving, 765–9
  rise in, reasons for, 741–3
  role in promotional mix, 763–5
  see also relationship marketing
Direct Marketing Association, 76–7, 587
direct response advertising, 739, 742, 749–53
  as proportion of advertising, 749
  response problems, 755
  telemarketing in, 753
direct supply, 452–3, 455
directories, 211–12, 213, 222
discontinuous innovation, 336, 337
discount clubs, 507–8
discount supermarkets, 392, 502–3, 504, 938
discounts, 432–4, 436, 661
  as sales promotion, 680–2
  see also allowances
discreet branding, 276

display (in retail outlets), sales promotion and, 655, 679
display advertising in newspapers, 631
disposable products, 284
dissociative groups, 115
dissolution, as stage of buyer–seller relationship life-cycle, 160–1
distinctiveness, as requirement for segmentation, 191
distribution, 22
  competitive strategy and, 856
  geographic segmentation and, 173
  infrastructure, 463, 464
  intensity, 462–4
  international aspects, 1016, 1019, 1020
  pricing and, 386
  segmentation and, 191
  selective, 463–4
    see also price discipline
  small businesses and, 963
  technology and, 59
distribution centres, 555
distribution channels, 450–6, 461–2
  behavioural aspects, 474–81
  channel strategy, 462–9
    influences on, 464–8
      product characteristics and, 462–4, 466–7
  competition in, 469–72
  conflict in, 476–8
  intermediaries in, 451–2, 456–61
    selection of, 468–9
  mail order, 742
  vertical marketing systems, 472–4
distributors, 451
  retailers and, 451, 453
  see also intermediaries
distributorships, as franchise relationship, 971
diversification
  concentric, 847
  conglomerate, 847
  as growth strategy, 846–7
  internationalisation and, 998
divisibility, perception of, and adoption of products, 306
DMUs, see decision-making units
documentation of orders, 539, 551–3
'dodos', 841
'dogs', 839, 848–9
door-to-door distribution of samples, 671–2
drinks, 34, 47, 172
  see also alcohol and soft drinks
drips, advertising in, 642
DSS (decision support systems), 243–4
dual-income households, 110
dumping, 1020
Dun and Bradstreet directories, 211, 222
durability, 256, 284
duties, 62, 386, 391, 397
dynamically continuous innovation, 336–7

Eastern Europe
  business orientations, 12–13, 14
  and European trading blocs, 64
eating out, 112
Ecolabels, 281
economic and competitive environment, 39, 60–70
  and consumer decision-making process, 100
  international aspects, 1001–2
  marketing information systems and, 243
  and promotional mix, 587
  segmentation and, 190, 192
economic order quantity reorder model, 559
economic status scale, 175
economies of scale, 855–6, 860, 1017
economy, international, 63–5

ECR (efficient consumer response), 558
EDI (electronic data interchange), 552, 558
EEA (European Economic Area), 64
efficient consumer response (ECR), 558
EFTA (European Free Trade Association), 64
EFTPOS (electronic funds transfer at point of sale), 521
  see also POS technology
elasticity of demand, 134, 382–6
electronic data interchange (EDI), 552, 558
electronic funds transfer, see EFTPOS
electronic point of sale technology, see POS technology
emotional appeal, 612–13, 616–17
emotional attitudes, 108
emotional needs, 105–6
employees, 810
  number of, and business classification, 979
  as source of new product ideas, 341, 343
  see also internal publics, sales representatives and under services (staff)
employment patterns, 46
encoding, 571–2, 574
end user segmentation, 181, 184
endorsement, celebrity, as franchise relationship, 971
Enfield, Harry, 591
engineering, relationship to marketing, 20
enquiry tests, in post-testing of advertising, 645
entertainment, international conventions concerning, 1001
entrenchment, 848–9
entrepreneurs/entrepreneurial thinking, 958–61, 964–5, 1053
environment
  marketing, see marketing environment
  physical, international differences, 1015, 1019
  selling, see selling environment
environmental issues, 38, 48–9, 52, 54, 586, 1055–6
  and agriculture, 38, 40
  and clothing, 51, 52, 57
  and consumer decision-making process, 98
  motor industry and, 54, 57
  and packaging, 280–1
  and paper, 342
  and planning permission, 72
  and tourism, 378–9
environmental scanning, 40–1
  and marketing information systems, 243
EPOS (electronic point of sale) technology, see POS technology
ESOMAR (European Society for Opinion and Marketing Research), 239
esteem needs, 106
ethics, 10–11, 49–51, 1054–5, 1056
  concerning organisational purchasing, 138
  in marketing research, 219, 239
  see also environmental issues
etiquette, international differences, 1001, 1020
Eurobrands, 321–3
European Economic Area, 64
European Free Trade Association (EFTA), 64
European organisations, Lynch's categories of, 993–4
European Union (EU)
  and advertising, 595
  advertising expenditure in, 624–5
  and business size classification, 957
  Commercial Communication, Green

Paper on, 73
Common Agricultural Policy, 64, 74–5
demographic information on, 41–6
and design, 283
differences in political and regulatory environment, 70–5, 689
differences in socioeconomic definitions, 110, 174–5
differences in taxation and duties, 62, 77, 391, 396–7, 398
direct mail in, 749
Distance Selling Directive, proposed, 758, 764
and distribution channel strategy, 468
funding from, 63, 65
and labelling, 281–2
lifestyle segmentation covering, 178–80
mail order in, 761–2
marketing research covering, 199, 200, 204, 207, 208
and packaging, 280–1
and pricing, 389, 396–8
and purchasing, 142
sales promotion techniques possible in different countries, 73, 689
social class definitions, 110
sources of information on, 210–11, 212
spending patterns, 44–8
and sponsorship of broadcast programmes, 804
and trade marks, 267–8, 275
transfer pricing policies, 440
value of retail sales in, 493
see also Single European Market
Europeanisation
  of retailing, 521–3
  of segmentation, 178–80, 858, 1017
Europe-wide advertising, 610–12
Europe-wide loyalty schemes, 677
evaluation
  of marketing performance, 891–2, 907–8
  in marketing research, 235–9
  post-purchase, 94–5
  of responses to direct marketing, 768–9
  of sales representatives' performance, 730–1
  of sponsorship, 808, 810
evaluation stage of new product development, 353–4
Evangelista, Linda, 611
evidence
  essential, 931
  peripheral, 931
  physical, 931
evoked set (shortlist), 92, 94–5
evolution, market, see market evolution
exchange process, 6–7, 9, 370
  history of, 11–12
  stimulating, 8
excise duties, see duties
exclusive distribution/exclusivity, 464
  see also price discipline
exhibitions, 351–2, 781, 810–17, 821–2
  business promotion and, 661
  direct marketing and, 764, 765
  franchise, 982
  mobile, 817
  performance at, 816–17
  personal selling and, 812–14
exit evaluation of advertising, 644–5
expansion, as stage of buyer–seller relationship life-cycle, 160
expectations, conflict concerning, 477
experience curve, 855–6
experience curve pricing, 427
experimentation, 221
  see also marketing research
expert power, 479, 480
experts, 899

exploration, as stage of buyer–seller relationship life-cycle, 160
exploratory research, 205
export agents, 1006, 1007
exporting, 992
   direct, 1006
   distribution channels, 454, 456
   exhibitions and, 814–15
   indirect, 1006–7
   international agreements concerning, 63–5
   small businesses and, 968–9
   see also international marketing
extended problem solving purchasing situation, 97
extension, product line, 315–16
external audits, 884, 885
external/internal influences on decision-making process, 100–19
ex-works pricing, 434

facilitators, in physical distribution, 534
facts, as appeal factor in advertising, 614–15
failure, 354–5
   of products, 331, 337, 354–6
families, and purchasing decision-making, 116–19
family life-cycle, 116
Family Market Research Panel, 118
fashion industry, 48, 133, 134, 301–2
   idea generation agencies, 343
fear, 106, 156, 613, 616
feedback
   in communication theory, 573, 574–5
   concerning marketing communication campaigns, 595–6
   in evaluating sales promotion, 688
   intermediaries and, 461
   sales representatives and, 703–4
   on sponsorship, 810
feelings, 108
   measuring, 109
   see also attitudes
Ferdinand, Les, 648
field marketing agencies, 679, 707
field research, see marketing research (primary)
filling the product range, 316–17
filters, 102–3
finance deals, 63
finance departments, 19, 20, 151
financial analysis, in new product development process, 347
financial objectives, 882
   and pricing, 409–11
financial services, 12, 606, 616
financing, intermediaries and, 460–1
fitness, 50
fixed costs, 394, 423
flexibility, small businesses and, 963–4
fmcg
   branding policies, 275–6
   continuous innovation, 336
   introducing, 295
   and loyalty, 96
FOB (free on board) pricing, 434
focus, as competitive strategy, 857–9
followers, market, 859, 861
food
   availability, 491
   health concerns and, 50, 53
   nutritional labelling, 281–2
   price elasticity, 386, 389
   sorting/grading, 459–60
forced relationships technique of idea generation, 343
forecasts/forecasting, 896–901
   methods, 897–901
   planning and, 896

stages, 896–7
forgetting, 643, 644
forms, product, 303
formula selling, 712
forums, business, 359
forward integration, 472
'4Ps', see marketing mix
fragrance, see perfume
France
   care lines, 755
   list broking, 746
   social class in, 110
franchises/franchising, 452, 473, 496, 953, 954, 969–84
   area development agreements, 1008–9
   blueprints, 978, 980–1
   contracts, 972–3, 982–3
   development stages, 979–84
   franchisee's perspective, 976–8, 981, 982, 983
   franchisor's perspective, 975–6, 983–4
   international aspects, 1005, 1008–9
   and legitimate power, 479
   master franchising, 1008
   mixed systems, 981
   operating manuals, 981
   types of relationship, 971–2
free flow layout, 518–19
free gifts, see gifts
free mail-in offers, 660
freefone numbers, 743, 755
freepost addresses, 743, 749
frequency (advertising exposure), 625, 626, 629
Friends of the Earth, 52, 77
fulfilment cost, in sales promotion campaigns, 687
full national launch, 352
full service advertising agencies, 633–4
functional plans, 878
functionality, and perception of price, 371
fur, 49–50

games, 300–1
gatekeepers, 153
GATT (General Agreement on Tariffs and Trade), 65
GE (General Electric) matrix, 842–5
generic competitive strategies, 854–9
geodemographics/geodemographic segmentation, 175–7
   direct mail and, 746
   direct marketing and, 767, 770
   door-to-door distribution and, 671
   and target audiences for advertising campaigns, 638
geographic adjustments to pricing, 434
geographic analysis, for retail locations, 512, 527
geographic concentration of demand, 136–7
geographic organisation, company, 722–3, 724, 903
geographic segmentation, 172–3, 184
   see also geodemographics
German Diesel Railcar, 290–1, 832
Germany
   care lines, 755
   and labelling, 281
   list broking, 746
   mail order in, 761
   political and regulatory environment, 70, 71, 72, 73, 74, 77, 142
   reunification, 63
   rules on packaging, 281
   social class in, 110
   telemarketing in, 756
gifts, 673–5
   in business promotion, 661
   international conventions

concerning, 1001
   packaging as, 675
   in sales promotion, 659
   samples as, 671
Ginola, David, 648
goals, conflict concerning, 476
'going rate', 431–2
golden zones, 655
Good Housekeeping Institute, 55
government bodies, as customers, 131–2
government control, 70–3
government ownership, and competition, 69
government spending, 62, 63, 131–2
grading, 459–60
Great Ormond Street Hospital, 745, 747, 748
green issues, see environmental issues
Greenpeace, 7, 11, 52, 77, 820–1
'grey market' (dubious supply sources), 463
'grey market' (older people), 42
grid layout, 517–18
groups
   focus, and group interviews, 216–17
   social, 109–11, 114–19
growth, 845–8, 860
growth stage of product life-cycle, 296–7
   promotional mix and, 585
guarantees, 286, 542
   see also warranties
guesswork in budget setting, 592–3
gum shields, 217, 965

'harvesting', 299, 848
health concerns, 50, 52–3
   and marketing of pharmaceutical products, 29
Health Education Authority, 649–50
health issues, 616, 649–50
   'neutraceuticals' and, 336
   nutritional labelling, 281–2
   taxation and, 391
health and safety, labelling concerning, 282
heterogeneity, 925–6
hierarchy of needs, Maslow's, 104–7
Hill, Damon, 655
hoardings, 632
hobbies, small businesses and, 960
home audits, 208
home improvements, 15
honey, 387
horizontal competition in distribution channels, 470–1
hospitality, 813, 814
house journals, 792
households
   dual-income, 110
   size, 43–4
   social class and, 110
humour, 104, 617, 618, 623
Hurley, Liz, 590
hypermarkets, 504–5

ICC, International Code of Advertising Practice, 77
idea generation stage of new product development, 339–43
idea screening stage of new product development, 343–5
image, advertising basing appeal on, 616–17
image, store, 515–17
image building, institutional advertising and, 607
imitators and imitative products, 301, 306–7, 335, 338
inbound telemarketing, see direct response advertising and telemarketing
incentives

for employees, 728–30, 810
sales promotion and, 661–2
incomes and spending patterns, 44–8
social class and, 110
incubator organisations, 958–9
independence, 494, 953, 954
as strategy, 866–7
independent retail outlets, 494–5
Independent Television Commission, 71, 76, 595, 803–4
industrial concentration of demand, 135–6
industrial goods, *see* organisational goods
industrial marketing, *see* organisational marketing
industry attractiveness, 842–3
inelasticity, *see* elasticity
influencers, and purchasing, 152
information
advertising and, 605
competitors as source of, 851–4
for customers, 491
on customers, mail-in offers and, 667, 671, 674
direct marketing and, 764, 767
intermediaries and, 461
for lifestyle segmentation, 180
planning and, 880
and purchasing decision making, 89–92, 375
sales promotion and, 659
sales representatives and, 703–4, 719, 731
sources of secondary, 210–14
see also data, environmental scanning, intelligence, marketing information systems *and* POS technology
information control, and survey techniques, 218
information overload, 91
information search, in decision-making process, 89–91
information technology (IT), 719, 731
informing, in personal selling, 701–2
infrastructure, distribution, 463, 464
in-home selling, 509
innovation, 295, 332
advertising and, 605
business size and, 955–6
continuous/dynamically continuous/ discontinuous, 335–6
diffusion of, 303–6
see also new product development
innovators (adopter category), 304, 333
inseparability, 924–5
installation, personal selling and, 702
Institute of Practitioners in Advertising, 76–7
Institute of Public Relations, 76–7
Institute of Sales Promotion, 76–7, 587, 655
institutional advertising, 604, 607–8
institutions, as organisational customers, 132
insurance, crisis, 720–1
intangibility, 918–22
integration
backward, 847
forward, 847
growth through, 847–8
horizontal, 848, 856
vertical, 856
see also vertical marketing systems
intelligence, 243, 343
see also information
intensity of distribution, 462–4
interactive aspect of direct marketing, 740
interactive marketing, 930, 932–4
interactive media, 186, 679
interactive shopping, 8
interest
as buyer readiness stage, 183

direct mail and, 746
interest rates, 62–3
interests, and market segmentation, 177
intermediaries, 18, 128, 130–1, 451–2, 456–61
in exporting, 1006–7
as organisational customers, 130–1
selection of, 468–9
see also facilitators, retailers *and* wholesalers
intermodal transportation, 544, 547–8
internal audits, 885
internal/external influences on decision-making process, 100–19
internal marketing, 930, 934–40
internal publics, 783, 792
internal uncertainty, business size and, 955
international demographic comparison, 174–5
international differences, *see under* culture
international exhibitions, *see* exhibitions
international marketing, 31–2, 990–9, 1002–20
market entry methods, 1003, 1004–13, 1016–17
reasons for pursuing, 994–9
sales promotion techniques allowed, 689
selection of markets, 1002–4
international policies, 63–5
internationalisation, 835–6
of advertising, 610–12
of manufacturing, 1005
of products, 321–3
of retailing, 521–3
see also Europeanisation
Internet, 763, 776–7
intertype competition in distribution channels, 471
interviewing skills, 216, 217, 218, 234
interviews, 215–17, 218–19, 234
selling and, 239
semi-structured, 216
structured, 216
telephone, 217
unstructured, 216
introduction stage of product life-cycle, 295, 584
invention, 332
see also creativity *and* innovation
inventory and inventory management, 58–9, 491, 534, 539, 542, 556–60
sales promotion and, 655
see also JIT systems
investment
international, 1006, 1009–12
purchases as, 372
invitation, as sales promotion objective, 662
invoicing, 542
IT (information technology), 719, 731
ITC, *see* Independent Television Commission

Jackson, Michael, 590
Japan, voluntary export restraint, 65
JIT (just in time) systems, 58–9, 141, 147, 535, 542, 553, 559–60, 856
collaboration and, 159
quality and, 58, 154–5
joint demand, 133–4
joint promotions, 669, 688–90
joint ventures, 1011–12, 1054
judgement, management, as forecasting method, 897–8
judgemental budget setting, 592–3
judgemental sampling, 223
'just in time' systems, *see* JIT

Kluivert, Patrick, 648
knowledge
attitudes and, 108
measuring, 109
Kompass, 211, 222

labelling, 281–2
lager, 123
language(s), 274, 322, 612, 627–8, 631, 768, 999–1000, 1016
launching, 352–3
layout
for direct marketing, 768
of print advertising, 622
of questionnaires, 230
store, 517–20
leaders, market, 859–60
leading indicators, and forecasting, 900–1
leading questions, 228–9
leads, 709–10
exhibitions and, 813, 814
generating, 754
as object of direct mail, 748
qualifying/screening, 750, 754
learning, 103–4
exhibitions and, 812–13
learning curve, 855–6
learning curve pricing, 427
legal environment, *see* political and regulatory environment
legal protection of trade marks, 267–8
legitimate power, 479
licensed characters, 284
licensing, 342
as franchise relationship, 971
international, 1007–8
life-cycle
family, 116
product, *see* product life-cycle
lifestyle, 101, 177–80
social class and, 110
lifestyle segmentation, 177–80, 181, 183, 184
lighting, 516
limited problem solving purchasing situation, 97, 98
limited service advertising agencies, 634
limits, negotiation and, 717
lining, price, 430
linkage effectiveness, 856
list broking, 709, 746, 747–8
list prices, and transfer pricing, 439
loading up, sales promotion and, 660, 668
lobbying, 792
location
and assessment of services, 920
classification of, 513–14
direct marketing and, 740
of organisations, as basis for segmentation, 170
retailers', 490, 511–14
see also place
logistics and logistics management, 532–3, 535–40, 543–60
competitive strategy and, 856
cost areas, 539–40
intermediaries and, 457, 459–60
international aspects, 1016, 1020
mail order and, 742
long channel of distribution, 453–4, 456, 463
love and belongingness needs, 105–6
low involvement purchases, 96–7
loyalty, and segmentation in consumer markets, 182–3
loyalty schemes, 184, 652–3, 654, 656, 657, 675–7, 765
Lynch's categories of European organisation, 993–4

macro segments, 170–1
macroeconomic/microeconomic
    environment, 61–70
magazines, 466
    advertising in, 604, 614, 615, 629–31
    direct response advertising in, 749–52
    samples in, 671
mail, direct, *see* direct mail
mail-in offers, 660, 667, 671, 672–4
mail order, 509–10, 742–3, 758–62
    changes in, 742–3, 758–9
mail services, 434
mail surveys, 217–18
mailing lists, 745, 746, 747–8
    see also databases
maintenance, 284, 437
    as product classification, 262
managed supply chains, 856
management
marketing and, 5, 22–3
    see also organisational environment
    and new product development, 359–61
    organisational aspects, 901–5
    product, *see* product management
    and sales promotion, 688
    sales, *see* sales management
management judgement, as
    forecasting method, 897–8
manuals, purchasing, 138
manufacturer brands, *see* brands/branding
manufacturer–consumer sales promotion,
    658–60
manufacturer–intermediary sales
    promotion, 654–6
manufacturer–manufacturer sales
    promotion, 660–1
manufacturers
    benefits of branding for, 269–70
    benefits of own label brands for, 272–3
    and intermediaries, 457–8, 460–1, 463
manufacturing, internationalisation, 1005
manufacturing subsidiaries, 1011
marginal analysis, 424–5
marginal costs, 423, 424
marginal pricing
    small businesses and, 960
margins, 451, 503–4
    see also mark–up
markdowns, 430–1
market beliefs, 92, 93
market challengers, 859, 860–1
market coverage, 461–4
market development, as growth strategy,
    846
market entry methods for
    international marketing, 1003,
    1004–13, 1016–17
market evolution, 303–8
    see also product life-cycle
market followers, 859, 861
market growth, 838
market information, *see* information *and*
    marketing research
market leaders, 859–60
market managers, 360
market nichers, 859, 861
market penetration
    as growth strategy, 845
    intermediaries and, 468
market potential, 892–6
    methods of assessing, 894–6
market presence, exhibitions and, 813–14
market prices, and transfer pricing, 439
market research, *see* marketing research
Market Research Society, 239
market saturation, 996–7
market segments, *see* segmentation
market share, 838
    pricing and, 411, 419–20

and sales objectives, 722
    small businesses and, 953
market size, and distribution channel
    strategy, 465–6
market structures, 65–70, 834–6
    and pricing, 387–9, 431
market tests, *see* test marketing
marketing, 12, 901
    definitions, 2–11, 22
    and demand, 383–5
    development of, 11–13
    direct, *see* direct marketing
    interactive, 930, 932–4
    internal, 930, 934–40
    organisational aspects, 901–5
    and other aspects of business, 19–22, 896,
        901
    product definition and, 28–9
    scope of, 29–32
    social class and, 111
    social processes in, 9
        see also relationship marketing *and*
            social marketing
    status in business, 901
    targeting, 185–9, 192
        see also segmentation
marketing audits, 883–5
marketing channels, *see* distribution
    channels
marketing communication objectives, 587–8
marketing communications planning,
    575–96
    post-implementation evaluation, 595–6
marketing communications planning flow,
    576
marketing control, 891–2, 905–7
marketing departments, 901–5
marketing environment, 17–20
    elements of, 38–40
        see also STEP factors
    international, 999–1002
    and promotional mix, 586–7
    small business start-ups and, 960–1
marketing information systems, 209, 240–4,
    853
    and control, 906
    information sources, 242–3
marketing mix, 23–7
    advertising and, 608–9, 645
    and defining business, 28–9
    differentiation, and 857
    inseparability, 375
    international aspects, 1013–14, 1017,
        1018–20
    packaging in, 279–81
    physical distribution management and,
        534, 560–1
    segmentation and, 190
    services, 926–32
marketing myopia, 28–9
marketing objectives, *see* objectives
marketing orientation, 12, 13, 15–17, 20–2
    degrees of, 16–17
marketing plan, 832–3
marketing planning
    definitions, 881
    process, 881–92, 905–8
    stages, 882
        see also planning *and* marketing strategy
marketing PR, 784–5
marketing programmes, 833, 890
marketing research, 109, 199–239
    causal, 206
    continuous, 207–9
    defining objectives, 231–2
    descriptive, 205
    door-to-door distribution of samples and,
        671
    ethical issues, 219, 239

exploratory, 205
    field workers in, 234
    international, 204, 207, 208
    interpreting, 235–9
    and positioning, 310–12
    post-testing of advertising, 644–5
    predictive, 206
    and pricing, 431
    primary, 202, 214–30
        and forecasting, 898
    qualitative, 206–7, 236
    quantitative, 207, 235–6
    report preparation and presentation,
        236–8
    research briefs, 232
    secondary, 202, 209–14
        criteria for evaluating, 214
        sources, 209, 210–14;
        use in primary research, 233
    selling and, 239
    sensitive issues, 225, 226, 229
    stages of process, 230–9
    technology and, 59–60
    and test marketing, 349
        see also marketing information
            systems
marketing strategy, 27–9, 827–36, 888–90
    analysis and, 836–45
    analysis of, in new product development
        process, 346
    competitive strategy, 831–2, 849–67
    examples of, 888–90
    growth strategy, 845–9
    international aspects, 1013–20
    pricing and, 391–4
    small businesses and, 962–9
markets, 508
    entry timing, 306–8
    monopolies and, 67
    target, communications planning and,
        576–82
    types, and price, 375–80
        see also business (defining)
mark–up, 426–7
    see also margins
Maslow's hierarchy of needs, 104–7
materialism, 51
materials, 57–9, 261
    handling, 555–6
        costs, 540
matrix structures for company organisation,
    905
maturity stage of product life-cycle, 297–8
    promotional mix and, 585–6
meaning, shared, 573
    see also communication
media, 604, 742
    advertising, 624–33, 639–40, 644
    choice for direct marketing, 767
    relations with, 781, 783–4, 787–9
        see also individual media
media exposure measurement, concerning
    sponsorship, 810
membership groups, 114–15
memory, 103–4
message, advertising, 609–12, 643–4
MFA (multi fibre agreement), 65
micro segments, 170, 171–2
microeconomic/macroeconomic
    environment, 61–70
military spending, 62, 131–2
milk, 395, 477
'milking' strategy, 299
Minitel, 763
MIS, *see* marketing information systems
misconceptions, as barrier to service quality,
    934, 935
mission statements, 882–3
missionary sales representatives, 708

MMC, *see* Monopolies and Mergers Commission
mobile phones, 893, 895
modified rebuys, 141
money-based sales promotion, 659, 663–7, 680–2
monitoring, using EPOS technology, 242–3
monitoring stage of new product development, 353–4
monolithic branding, 276
Monopolies and Mergers Commission, 67, 71, 75, 389–90, 468
monopolistic competition, 69, 389
  and pricing, 388–9
monopoly, 65–7
  and pricing, 387–8
morphological analysis, 343
Mosaic, 770
motivation, 104
  and data collection for marketing research, 234
  gaining data on, 225–6
  Maslow's hierarchy of needs and, 104–7
  and organisational purchasing, 154, 155–7, 356, 372, 700
  and response rates, 218, 226
  of sales representatives, 728–9
motor industry, 40–1, 128
  and dealers, 480
  design, 283
  and environmental issues, 54, 57
  esteem needs and, 106
  international aspects, 65
  withdrawal strategies, 300
multiple choice questions, 227–8
multiple sourcing, 137, 138
multivariable segmentation, 184
music, 196–7
  in advertising, 618
  recorded, formats, 14, 363, 443–4
  in retail settings, 516
  sponsorship of, *see* arts sponsorship
myopia, marketing, 28–9
mystery shopping, 219–20

names, 267, 274–5, 322, 1000
NBA (Net Book Agreement), 391, 401–2
need satisfaction approach to selling, 712–14
needs, 375
  for information, 22
  Maslow's hierarchy of, 104–7
  and new products, 333–4
  psychological, *see* psychological needs
  see also wants
negotiated transfer pricing, 439
negotiation
  business promotion and, 661
  and decision-making process, 93
  intermediaries and, 461
  international aspects, 1000, 1001, 1020
  in personal selling, 716–18
  price, 376, 380, 417, 435–7, 439
  see also objections (handling)
Net Book Agreement, 391, 401–2
Netherlands, the
  list broking, 746
  price control, 70
  social class, 110
'neutraceuticals', 336, 337
new product committees, 360–1
new product development, 331–61
  advertising and, 605, 642
  organisational aspects, 359–61
  price and, 407
  reactive/proactive, 338–9
  small businesses and, 960–2
  stages of process, 339–54
  survival/failure, 331, 337, 354–6

new product launches, sales promotion and, 655–6
new product managers, 360
new products
  exhibitions and, 812
  intermediaries and, 468
  pricing strategies, 415–16
  sales promotion and, 658–9
new task purchasing, 141, 146, 148
  business services and, 262
newness, types of, 332–5
news, as appeal factor in advertising, 614–15
newspapers, 631–2
  samples in, 671
niche markets, 997
  market entry and, 307
  new businesses and, 962, 965–6
  positioning and, 311
nichers, market, 859, 861
noise, in communication theory, 573, 575, 644
non-durable products, 256
non-profit organisations and marketing, 31, 807–8, 940–5
  and definitions of marketing, 6
  examples, 7, 11
  pricing, 378–9, 944
non-random sampling, 223–4
non-store retailing, 499, 509–10
  see also direct marketing *and* personal selling
NPD, *see* new product development
nuclear industry, 108, 109, 790
nutritional labelling, 281–2

objections, handling, in personal selling, 714–16, 718
objective and task budget setting, 594, 639, 891
objectives
  of advertising campaigns, 639
  control and, 906
  corporate, 881–3
  financial, 409–11, 882
  marketing/sales, 409, 411–13, 639, 722, 886–8
    and pricing, 409, 411–13
  short/long-term, 409–11, 413
  see also business objectives
observational research, 219–20
odd–even pricing, 429–30
Office of Fair Trading, 71, 75, 389–90, 391, 473
office stationery, 172
offices, sales, 455
Ofgas, 75
Oflot, 389
OFT, *see* Office of Fair Trading
Oftel, 75
Ofwat, 75
oligopoly, 68–9
  and pricing, 388
olive oil, 589
omnibus services, 208
on-line information services, 210, 211, 213
on-line ordering, 60
on-pack sales promotion, 661
one-price selling, 417
open-ended questions, 216, 226
opera, 196–7
operating supplies, 262
operational control, 905–6
operational marketing plans, 881
operational performance, evaluating, 907–8
operational plans, 878
opinion leaders, *see* innovators (adopter category)
opinions
  data based on, 225

and market segmentation, 177
opportunity to see, 626, 644
order cycle time, 541–2
order makers, 706, 726
order processing, 539, 551–3
order sizes, 542
order status information, 542, 549–50
order takers, 704–6, 726
ordering, on–line, 60
organisation of services, 931–2, 937–40
organisational customers, categories of, 129–32
organisational environment of marketing, 17–22, 896, 901–5
organisational goods, 30
organisational marketing
  definitions, 126–9
  differences from consumer marketing, 128–9
  flows within, 127
  see also relationship marketing
organisational markets
  advertising and, 609
  buying process in, 137–41
    price and, 379–80
    roles in, 148–53
    see also purchasing decision making
  demand in, 132–7
  differences from consumer markets, 132, 134, 135, 137, 139, 140, 576–7
  direct mail to, 748
  direct marketing and, 740
  distribution channel structures, 454–6
  mail surveys, 218
  personal selling in, 710–11
  pricing in, 379–80
  product management for, 318–21
  sales promotion and, 684
  segmentation in, 169–72, 192
  see also relationship marketing
organisational products
  test marketing and, 351–2
  user-based product classification systems, 260–2
organisations, business, *see* business(es) *and* corporate identity
orientations, business, 12, 13–17
original equipment manufacturers, as customers, 130
OTS (opportunity to see), 626, 644
out of town retailing, 504–6
outbound telemarketing, *see* telemarketing
outdoor media, 632–3
outlet costs, 539
outsourcing research and development, 357–8, 360
overbooking, 924
own label brands, 272–3, 274, 521
  and brand loyalty, 182
  conflict concerning, 477
  consumer views of, 273
  and oligopoly, 68–9
  and positioning, 272
  and price, 377–8
  and resale price maintenance, 391
  sales promotion and, 658
ownership
  business, 953, 954
  services and, 918

'Ps', 4/7, *see* marketing mix
pack sizes, 280, 316
  household size and, 43–4
  sales promotion and, 660
  see also trial sizes
packaging, 14, 278–82, 284–5, 542
  environmental issues, 48, 280–1
  and filling the product range, 316
  functions, 279–80

international aspects, 1016, 1018–19
   multilingual, 322
   as promotional gift, 675
   promotional gifts in/on, 674–5
   and repositioning, 314
packing, 491
Palmer, Arnold, 971
pan-European brands, 321–3
pan-European segments, 178–80, 858, 1017
paper, 48, 342
parallel trading, 397, 398
Pareto analysis, 559, 723
partnerships, 1054
   see also joint ventures and strategic
      alliances
parts, 262
party plans, 453, 509
pasta, 376
Pavarotti, Luciano, 971
PDM, see physical distribution management
peer pressure, 98
penetration, market, as growth strategy, 845
penetration pricing, 415, 416
pens, 421
people, as element of services marketing
      mix, 26–7, 930
percentage of future sales method of budget
      setting, 593
percentage of past sales method of budget
      setting, 592–3
perception, 102–3
   conflict concerning, 477
   and positioning, 309–10
   price and, 369–75, 428
perfect competition, 69–70
   and pricing, 389, 431
performance, 283–4
   and positioning, 314–15
perfume, 4, 383, 391, 463
perishability, 922–4
personal benefits, 104–7, 372
personal selling, 698–721
   advantages of, 699–700
   approaches to, 708
   definitions, 698–9
   exhibitions and, 812–14
   extent of, 701
   follow-up, 719–21
   international aspects, 1020
   place in promotional mix, 576–7, 581,
      582–3, 699
   stages in process, 708–21
      preparation and planning, 710–11
   types of, 704–8
   see also sales management and
      telemarketing
personalisation, 746
personality, 101–2, 109
   and organisational decision making, 154,
      155–7, 356, 372, 700
   and organisational market segmentation,
      171
   sales representatives', 726, 727, 728
persuading, in personal selling, 702
petrol, 68, 187–8, 275
   duty on, 391, 893
   environmental issues, 57
   pricing, 68, 373, 374
   supermarkets and, 68, 472
petrol retailers, 188, 507
pharmaceuticals, advertising, 76
phasing out, 299–300, 318
philosophical objectives, 882–3
physical distribution, 532
physical distribution management, 532–5
   logistics and, 535, 536
   and the marketing mix, 534, 560–1
physical evidence (element of services
      marketing mix), 27, 931

physiological needs, 105, 107
pigeons, 744, 747
piloting of questionnaires, 230
pioneering advertising, 604–5, 607
pioneers, 306
pipelines, 546–7
place, 22, 24, 26
   international aspects, 1020
   physical evidence and, 27
   services and, 929
   see also location
place utility, 490
planning, 21–2, 595, 879–80, 1053
   of communication strategy, 575–96
   and customer requirements, 5–6
   definitions, 876–7
   forecasting and, 896
   sales, 721–5
   see also marketing planning
planning permission, 72
plans
   marketing, 832–3
   types of, 877–9, 880–1
PLC, see product life-cycle
Poland, 13
political and regulatory environment, 39,
      70–8
   collusion and, 867
   and consumer decision-making process,
      100
   and distribution channel strategy, 468
   influences on, 77–8
   international aspects, 1002, 1017, 1020
   list broking, 746
   and organisational purchasing, 141–2
   and pricing, 389–91
   and promotional mix, 587
   sales promotion methods and, 677, 678,
      687–8, 689
   and sponsorship of broadcast
      programmes, 804–5
   telemarketing and, 756–7, 758
Porter's five forces, 849–50
portfolio analysis, 837–45
portfolios
   product, see product portfolios
   segmentation variables, 184
   supplier, 160
POS (point of sale) displays, 679
POS (point of sale) technology, 242–3,
      520–1
   and distribution, 242–3, 467, 520
   and sales promotion, 242, 520, 665, 669,
      675
   see also barcodes
positioning, 308–15
   international aspects, 322, 1000, 1016
   pricing and, 411
   public relations and, 794
   retailers and, 515
   services and, 928
postal services, paying/freepost distinction,
      743, 749
posters, 632–3
post-implementation evaluation of
      marketing communications
      planning, 595–6
post-purchase evaluation, 94–5, 217
post-testing of advertising, 644–5
potatoes, 181, 187, 376
potential, market/sales, 892–6
potential product, 254, 255–6
power, 478–80
   balance, 437, 489
   in distribution channels, 461
   and negotiation in personal selling,
      716–17
   sources of, 478–9
PR, see public relations

precipitation, see problem recognition
predictive research, 206
premium price, 373
presenter characteristics, 591–2
press relations, 787, 788–9
pressure groups, 52, 53–5, 72, 77–8, 584
   use of marketing techniques, 7, 11
pressure selling, 260
prestige pricing, 429
pre-testing of advertising, 641
price/pricing, 22, 368–70
   advertising basing appeal on, 615–16
   average, and transfer pricing, 439
   'basic-plus', 417, 422
   bundling/unbundling, 417, 422, 430
   competition and, 387–9
   competitive, 432
      see also tendering
   consumer attitudes to, 100
   consumer/organisational markets
      compared, 380
   contexts, 375–80
   costs and, see under costs
   distribution and, 386
   as element of marketing mix, 24, 25
   geographic adjustments, 434
   influences on
      external, 380–91
      internal, 391–4
   international aspects, 396–8, 1019–20
   marginal, small businesses and, 960
   market tolerance and, 381–6
   misleading, 417
   negotiation, see under negotiation
   non-profit organisations and, 944
   perception and, 369–76, 428
   physical distribution management and,
      560–1
   product life-cycle and, 394
   promotional, 430
   psychological aspects, 372, 373–4, 417,
      429–31
   and purchasing decision making, 154,
      379–80
   quality and, 373–4, 411–12
   relationship to new product
      development, 407
   as scapegoat, 375
   in service markets, 378–9, 412, 928–9
   small businesses and, 960, 966
   stages in setting, 408
   strategies and policies, 407–40
   transfer, 427, 439–40, 1020
   trial, 415–16, 664
price banding, 376
price changes, 418–23, 432–4
   see also price reductions
price comparison, 378
price controls, 70
price cuts, see price reductions
price differentials/differentiation, 393,
      396–7, 431
price discipline, 377, 390, 468
   see also resale price maintenance
price elasticity of demand, 134, 382–6
   see also price sensitivity
price fixing, 867
price followers, 431–2
price increases, 421–3
price lining, 430
price objectives, 408–13
price reductions, 418–21
   coupons and, 666
   as sales promotion method, 663–4
   sales volume needed to compensate for,
      418, 419
price rises, 421–3
price sensitivity, 134, 372–3, 376, 379,
      381–2

and brand loyalty, 182
and business orientations, 14
mark-up and, 426–7
see also price elasticity of demand
price structures, 432
price wars, 412–13, 420, 503
pricing adjustments, 432–4
see also promotional pricing
pricing methods, 426–32
primary research, *see under* marketing
    research
print advertising, 618–22
privatisation, 65–6, 388, 389
and organisational purchasing, 144
prizes, for design, 283, 285
proactive new product development, 338–9
probability sampling, 222–3
problem definition, in marketing research,
    231
problem recognition, in purchasing decision
    making, 88–9, 143–4, 148
problem-solving
advertising appeal and, 613, 614
see also wants
process, as element of services marketing
    mix, 27
processes, services and, 931–2
processing of orders, 539, 551–3
product(s)
as basis for company organisation, 903
as basis for organisation of sales force,
    723
as basis for organisational market
    segmentation, 171
as basis for sales promotion, 667–72
characteristics, and distribution
    channel strategy, 462–4, 466–7
communications planning and, 582–6
consumer/organisational distinction,
    582–3
contracting out, 300
definitions and classifications, 254–62
design, 282–3, 284–5
as element of marketing mix, 24–5
imitative, 301
international aspects, 1002, 1018–19
launching, 352–3
new, 332–7
    see also new product development
physical distribution management and,
    560
services and, 918, 926, 927–8
undifferentiated, 187–8, 275
wants and, *see under* wants
see also brands/branding
product adopter categories, 304–5
product assortment, *see* assortment strategy
product classes, 303
product deletion, 299–300, 317–18
product development, as growth
    strategy, 846
product development stage of new product
    development, 347–8
product differentiation
and monopolistic competition, 69
and pricing, 389
product forms, 303
product items, 264
product life-cycle, 294–308, 309
advertising and, 605, 607
communications planning and, 584–6
and diffusion of innovation, 303–6
length, and new product
    development, 339
and pricing, 394
as self-fulfilling prophecy, 301
services and, 928
small businesses and, 958
and targeting, 189
product lines, 264–5

branding and, 265
depth, 264–5, 315–16
extending, 315–16
length, 264, 315–16
product management, 308–18, 320–3
see also product life-cycle
product managers, 320–1, 359
product mix, 263–5
branding and, 265
and pricing strategies, 417
width, 265
product-orientated advertising, 604–7,
    613–15
product orientation, 13, 14–15
product portfolios, 308, 837–45
new product development and, 338–9
non-profit organisations', 943
portfolio analysis, 837–45
product positioning, *see* positioning
product range, 263–5, 497–8, 514
breadth of, 497–8
depth of, 497–8, 514
filling, 316–17
international aspects, 322
management of, 315–17
sales promotion and, 660
product refreshment, 312, 314
product repositioning, *see*
    repositioning
product specification, 144–5, 148, 154
production
analysis of, in new product development
    process, 346
organisational purchasing and, 150
relationship to marketing, 20, 21
production capacity, pricing and, 419
production era, 12
production orientation, 12, 13, 14
productivity, 855
in services, 936–40
profit/profitability, 6, 373, 374
analysis related to, 908
margins, branding/own brands and, 272
objectives related to, 410
programmes, marketing, *see* marketing
    programmes
project plans, 878
promises, 11, 95
and service quality, 934, 935
promotion, 24, 26
international aspects, 1020
packaging as, 279–80
physical distribution management and,
    561
services and, 930
see also sales promotion
promotional allowances, 434
promotional mix, 569–70
role of advertising in, 604–9
direct marketing in, 763–5
international aspects, 1020
planning model, 575–96
product life-cycle and, 584–6
sponsorship and, 808
strategies, 588–91
telemarketing and, 754
see also individual elements of mix
promotional pricing, 430, 432
see also pricing adjustments
promotions, *see* sales promotion
prospecting, 701, 709–10
prospects, 701–2, 709–10, 766–7
protectionism, 65, 67
'Ps, 4/7', *see* marketing mix
psychographics/psychographic segmentation,
    177–80, 181, 183, 184
psychological influences on
    decision-making process, 100–9
and organisational decision making, 154,
    155–7, 356, 372, 700

psychological needs/benefits, 89, 104–7, 372
psychological pricing, *see under* price/
    pricing
public health, 391
public purchasing, 131–2
public relations, 780–95
advertising and, 780–1
brand-related self-liquidating offers and,
    673
budgets, 793
definitions, 780–4
evaluation of, 793–5
exhibitions and, 814
international aspects, 1020
see also corporate identity,
    exhibitions *and* sponsorship
Public Relations, Institute of, 76–7
public services, 379
pricing, 389
publicity, 787–90
advertising and, 789–90
from exhibitions, 814
international aspects, 1020
non-profit organisations and, 944
see also public relations
publics, 780–4
publishing, 132–3, 391, 401–2
pubs, 326
pull strategies, 577–9, 658, 680
coupons as, 665
missionary sales representatives and, 708
purchasing
attitudes towards, 108
frequency of, advertising and, 643
relationship to marketing, 19
professional, and purchasing
    departments, 139–40, 149–50
see also entries related to buying *and* buyers
purchasing approaches, as basis for
    organisational market
    segmentation, 171
purchasing decision making
consumer, 87–96
and business definition, 100
internal/external influences on, 100–19
price and, 382–6
psychological influences on, 100–9
reference groups and, 114–15, 116–19
retailers' and wholesalers' role in, 491
consumer and organisational markets
    compared, 144, 152
information and, 375
organisational, 142–8, 154–7
choice criteria, 145
personal factors in, 154, 155–7, 356,
    372, 700
price and, 379–80, 385–6
process, 87–96, 142–8, 154–7
purchasing departments and professional
    purchasing, 139–40, 149–50
purchasing manuals, 138
purchasing policy, 138–41
purchasing schedules, 141
purchasing situations
consumer, 96–8
in organisational markets, 141
and buyer–seller relationships, 146
push strategies, 577–9, 680
sales promotion and, 656

qualified prospects, 710
qualitative methods of forecasting, 897–9
qualitative objectives, 882–3
qualitative research, 206–7, 236
quality, 283–6, 1053
as focus in product orientation, 14
and positioning, 309, 313, 314–15
price, perception and, 371, 373–4, 378,
    411–12

and product range management, 315–16
  of services, *see under* services
  tendering and, 438
quality assurance, 58
quality checking, 542
quality control, 58, 154
QUANGOs, 75, 389
quantification of marketing objectives, 888
quantitative methods of forecasting, 899–901
quantitative research, 207, 235–6
quantity discounts, 433
'question marks', 839–40
questionnaires, 217–19, 225–30
  ideal lengths, 229–30
  in interviewing, 216
  layout, 230
  piloting, 230
  question types, 226–9
  question wording, 228–9
queueing, 94–5, 924, 932
quota sampling, 223–4
quotas
  sales, 722
  trade, 64, 65, 74–5
quotations, 146, 372–3
  see also tendering

R&D, *see* research and development
radio, sponsorship of programmes, 803–4
radio advertising, 622, 628–9
Radio Authority, 76
rail transportation of goods, 544–5, 548, 549, 550–1
railways, 35, 64, 67, 145, 290–1, 306, 347
  advertising on, 633
random sampling, 222–3
range, *see* product range
rating scales, 228, 229
ratings, television, 625
rational appeal, 612, 614
raw materials, *see* materials
reach, 625, 626, 629
reactive new product development, 338
rebates, 663, 666–7
  see also loyalty schemes
recall, and evaluation of advertising, 644–5
receptions, 813
  press, 788–9
recommendation, 90–1, 95
recording industry, 318, 363, 443–4
recruitment
  of franchisees, 981–2
  of sales representatives, 726–7, 728
recycling, 280–1, 342
Red Cross, International, 11
redemptions, 665, 666, 688
reference groups, 114–19
referent power, 479, 480
referrals, 710
refilling, 281
refusal to supply, *see* selective distribution
regional organisation of sales force, 722–3
regulatory bodies, 70, 71, 75–7
regulatory environment, *see* political and regulatory environment
reinforcement and reminder advertising, 604, 607, 642
relationship(s)
  buyer–seller, *see* buyer–seller relationships
  within distribution channels, 474–81
relationship marketing, 9, 157–61
  direct marketing and, 765
  free gifts and, 661
  increasing importance, 11
  sales promotion and, 653–4
  telemarketing and, 757
  see also direct marketing
reliability, 284
  as criterion of service quality, 933

reminder and reinforcement advertising, 604, 607, 642
remoteness, and distribution channel strategy, 465–6
reorder models, 559–60
reorder point model of stock control, 557–9
repair, as product classification, 262
repeat purchase, 97
replenishment systems, *see* inventory management
reply-paid cards, 748
reports
  annual, 791
  preparation and presentation of, 236–8
repositioning of products, 312–15
  advertising and, 609
  and distribution channel strategy, 465
reputation, 285–6
resale price maintenance, 391, 871
  see also price discipline
research and development, 55–6, 356–9, 360
  business size and, 955–6
  collaborative, 357–9, 360
  and organisational purchasing, 151, 153
  outsourcing, 357–8, 360
  place in different industries, 337
  place in new product development, 340, 356–9
  relationship to marketing, 20, 21–2
  see also new product development
research, marketing, *see* marketing research
re-sellers, *see* intermediaries
resources, 833–4, 858
  business size and, 957, 964–5
  and distribution channel strategy, 464–5
  and market segmentation, 178
  and service quality, 934, 935
response
  measurability, 740
  mechanisms, 748–51
    see also coupons
  public relations and, 794
response hierarchy model, *see* AIDA
response management, 768–9
response rates to surveys, 217–19, 226
responsibility for goods in transit, 549–50
responsiveness
  as criterion of service quality, 933
  small businesses and, 963–4
retail alliances, 1013
retail audits, 209
retail co-operatives, 473
retail ownership, forms of, 493–6
retailer coupons, 665–6
retailer–consumer sales promotion, 656–8
retailers/retailing, 451
  assortment of goods, 490–1
  and branding, 270–1
  concentration of power, 479–80
  dealers/distributors and, 451, 453
  'essential' for manufacturers, 521
  functions, 490–3
  information and advice role, 491
  location, 490, 511–14
  and mail order, 760–1
  manufacturers' relationships with, 390, 391, 468
  marketing concept and, 12
  need for products, 471
  non-store, *see* non-store retailing
  own-brand products, *see* own label brands
  planning permission issues, 72
  and price, 100, 376–8, 426–7
  sales promotion and, 679–84
  services offered by, 491, 493, 496–7, 503
  and shopping goods, 259
  store image, 515–17
  store layout and display types, 517–20
  strategic alliances, international, 521–3
  types, 499–508, 509–10

retention rates, advertising and, 643, 644
return on investment, 410
revenue, 373
  see also price
reward power, 478–9
risk
  corporate attitudes to, 834
  intermediaries and, 458
  in new product development, 331–2, 356
  in purchasing situations, 141, 146
    consumer, 96–7, 98–9, 306
    with new products, 306, 336–7
    organisational buying, 128, 156, 379
  reducing, 306
Riverdance, 599, 832
road transport, 545–6
robots, 58
ROI (return on investment), 410
ROLA, 548
role conflict, 476
roll-cage sequencing, 558
rolling launch/rolling out, 352–3
routine problem solving purchasing situation, 96–7
routine rebuys, 141, 146, 148
running out (deletion strategy), 318

safety needs, 105, 107
safety standards, 72, 1017
  selective distribution and, 463–4
safety stock, 558
sale or return, 656, 719
sales
  public relations and, 794–5
  sponsorship and, 810
sales analysis, 907–8
sales base, 316
sales-based methods of budget setting, 592–3
sales branches, 455
sales engineers, 708
sales force, *see* sales representatives
sales management, 702–3, 721–31
  international aspects, 1020
sales objectives, 722
  and pricing, 409, 411–13
sales offices, 455
sales orientation, 12, 13, 15
sales planning and strategy, 721–5
sales potential, 892–6
sales presentation, 711, 712–19
sales promotion, 589, 652–90
  advertising and, 609, 660, 661, 664
  cause-related marketing and, 807–8
  definitions, 653–4
  evaluating, 688
  existing customers and, 663, 666
  guidelines for, 687–8
  implementation, 687
  international aspects, 73, 688, 689, 1020
  joint promotions, 463, 688–90
  management process, 685–8
  manufacturer–consumer, 658–60
  manufacturer–intermediary, 654–6
  manufacturer–manufacturer, 660–1
  methods
    aimed at consumers, 663–80
    aimed at organisational markets, 684
    aimed at retailers, 680–4
  objectives, 661–2
  place in communications mix, 653
  place in promotional mix, 581
  political and regulatory environment, 73, 668, 669
  psychological effects, 663, 666, 668, 674
  retailer–consumer, 656–8
  sale or return, 656
  sales representatives and, 719
  services and, 940
  sponsorship and, 810

Sales Promotion, Institute of, 76–7, 587, 655
sales quotas, 722
sales representatives, 707
  co-ordinating role in organisation, 702–3
  and differences between consumer and
    organisational markets, 711
  evaluation of performance, 730–1
  and forecasting, 898–9
  management of, *see* sales
    management
  recruitment and selection, 726–7, 728
  selling process, 708–21
  size of force, 724–5
  as source of information, 719
  support, 60, 683–4
  surveys, use in forecasting, 898–9
  tasks of, 701–4
    recruitment and, 726
  technology supporting, 60
  time use, 701
  training, 727–8
  see also personal selling and sales
    management
sales subsidiaries, 1006, 1009–11
sales support, 707–8, 710
sales tests
  in post-testing of advertising, 645
salt, 189, 334, 389
samples (of products), 94, 658–9, 661,
  669–72
  and children, 119
  in personal selling, 713
sampling (in research), 214, 218–19, 221–4
  sampling unit, 222
  stages of process, 222
sanitary protection (sanpro), 82
satellite television, 627–8, 763
SBUs, *see* strategic business units
scale, economies of, 855–6, 860, 1017
scales
  rating, 228, 229
  semantic differential, 228, 229
scarcity, price and, 373
scenario techniques, 899
scent
  in retail settings, 516
  see also perfume
screening of ideas, stage of new product
  development, 343–5
seasonal discounts, 433
seasonality, 411, 428
  advertising campaigns and, 641, 643
  sales promotion and, 656, 658, 660
  services and, 940
secondary data
  sources, 209, 210–14
  use in assessing market potential, 896
  use in forecasting, 898
secondary research, *see under* marketing
  research
security, 492
  advertising basing appeal on, 616
  as criterion of service quality, 933
  of goods in transit, 549–50
security stock, 558
segmentation, 168–9
  adopter categories and, 333
  advertising campaigns and, 637–9
  as basis for company organisation, 903–5
  benefits of, 189–90
    to customers, 189
  in consumer markets, 172–92
  dangers of, 190
  default, 187
  direct mail and, 747
  and direct marketing, 742, 775
  Eurobranding and, 323
  and focus as competitive strategy, 857–8
  implementing, 184–9

international aspects, 1017
marketing research and, 203
in organisational markets, 169–72, 192
and positioning, 310–12
requirements for success, 191–2
and sampling, 222
social class and, 110
selective attention/perception, 102–3
selective distribution, 390, 391, 463–4, 468
  see also price discipline
self-actualisation needs, 106–7
self-esteem
  advertising basing appeal on, 616–17
  personal selling and, 721
self-interest, advertising basing appeal on,
  616
self-liquidating offers, 652, 672–3
  telemarketing and, 755, 756
self-orientation, and market
  segmentation, 178
seller-specified products, 262
selling
  environment, 492–3
  marketing research and, 239
  need for, 721
  personal, *see* personal selling
  pressure, 260
    see also atmosphere
selling orientation, *see* sales
  orientation
SEM, *see* Single European Market
semantic differential scales, 228, 229
semi-finished goods, 262
semi-structured interviews, 216
sensitivity, 225, 226, 229
  price, *see* price sensitivity
sensory factors in retail settings, 515–17
service backup, 155, 463, 543
service goods, *see* services
service levels, retailers', 496–7
service products, *see* services
services, 30, 257, 918–26
  business, 262
  distribution and, 30
  as element of physical products, 30
  heterogeneity, 925–6
  inseparability, 924–5
  intangibility, 918–22
  marketing, 923–4, 926–40
  perishability, 922–4
  pricing, 378–9, 412
  productivity, 936–40
  products compared to, 918, 926
  purchasing situations, 97
  quality, 313, 932–4
    barriers to, 934, 935
  staff, 933, 934–7
    visible, 935–6
  technology and, 59
  test marketing, 351
services marketing mix, 26–7, 926–32
SERVQUAL, 934–5
'7Ps', *see* services marketing mix
sex, advertising basing appeal on, 617–18
share prices, 794
shared meaning, 573
  see also communication
shelf space, sales promotion and, 655
Shell directional policy matrix, 843–5
shoppers, *see* customers
shopping, mystery, 219–20
shopping products/goods, 258–9
  intensity of distribution, 463
short channel of distribution, 453, 455–6
shortlist/evoked set, 92, 94–5
SIC (standard industrial classification)
  codes, 170–1
Single European Market, 63–4, 73
  and competitive tendering, 131

and duties, 77
whether an export market, 994
and focus as competitive strategy, 857–8
packaging and, 281
pricing and, 396–8
  see also European Union
single sourcing, 137, 138
size
  of organisation, as basis for
    segmentation, 170
  of segments, 191
skills, 858
skimming, 415–16
slice of life advertisements, 614, 623
Slovenia, 15
small businesses, 31, 953–69
  and advertising, 644
  antecedent influences, 958–9
  compared to large organisations, 952–7
  definition, 957
  and distribution channel strategy, 465–6
  and exhibitions, 811
  reasons for failure, 966, 969
  growth, 964–9
  incubator organisations, 958–9
  launching, 958–64
  marketing in, 958–69
  pricing strategies, 432
  stages of development, 958
  starting, 958–61
smart cards, 652–3, 654, 657–8, 675–6
smear campaigns, 364, 374
smells, in retail settings, 516
soap, 270
  see also detergents
social class, 110–11
social groups, 109–11, 114–19
social interaction, international differences,
  1000, 1001, 1020
social marketing, 10–11
sociocultural environment, 38, 39, 41–55
  and consumer decision-making process,
    98, 109–19
  and distribution channel strategy, 468
  international aspects, 999–1001
  and political and regulatory
    environment, 77–8
  and promotional mix, 586–7
socioeconomic definitions, 110–11, 174–5
soft drinks, 34, 175, 184, 185
sorting, 459–60
soup, 181
source credibility, 590–1
sourcing strategy, 135, 137–8
spatial marketing, 512
speciality goods, 259
speciality stores, 498, 505–7
spending patterns, 44–8
sponsorship, 378, 781, 799–810
  and children, 119
  definitions, 799–800
  evaluation of, 808, 810
  international aspects, 1020
  and promotional mix, 808
  relevance, 803–4, 809
  and sales promotion, 810
sport, sponsorship of, 800–3, 804, 809–10
spreadsheets, 244
standardisation, 1015, 1017–18
'stars', 840
statistical series analysis, 894–5
statistical techniques, 235
status, 106, 156
  and market segmentation, 178
STEP factors, 38–40
  and consumer decision-making process,
    98–100, 109–19
  international aspects, 999–1002
  market potential and, 893

as opportunities/threats, 886
and promotional mix, 586–7
see also individual factors; *see also* audits (external)
stimulus–response approach to selling, 712
Stock Exchange, London, 163–4
stock, *see* inventory
stockouts, 558
storage, 491, 492
intermediaries and, 459
store image, *see under* retailing
store loyalty cards, *see* loyalty schemes and smart cards
storyboards, 622–3, 641
strategic alliances, 521–3, 866–7, 1012–13, 1054
strategic business units, 831, 837
strategic control, 905
strategic marketing plans, 880–1
strategy, marketing, *see* marketing strategy
strategy, sales, 721–5
strategy, targeting, 185–9, 192
stratified sampling, 223
strong theory of communication, 579, 580
structured interviews, 216
structures
market, 65–70
and pricing, 387–9, 431
organisational, 901–5
subcontracting, *see* outsourcing
subcultures, 112–14
subsidiaries
manufacturing, 1011
sales, 1006, 1009–11
subsidy, 378
sugging, 239
supermarkets, 502–4, 938
discount, 392, 502–3, 504, 938
sales promotions by, 657–8
supplier dependency, *see* dependency
supplier handling strategies, 158–60
supplier portfolio, 160
supplier selection, 135, 137–8, 146, 148
supplier-specified products, 262
suppliers, 18
supplies, operating, 262
supply chains, 132–3, 134, 856
support, post-purchase, personal selling and, 702
surveys, 215–19, 895–6
survival, 413
pricing and, 392
Sweden, 63, 64, 77
sweepstakes, 677, 678
Switzerland, 64
SWOT analysis, 886, 1002
synectics, 343

tampering, 279
tangibility, as requirement for segmentation, 191
tangible product, 254, 255, 256
branding and, 265
tangibles, and service quality, 933
target audience, for advertising campaigns, 637–9, 640, 641, 643
targeting, 185–9, 192
communications planning and, 576–82
direct mail and, 746, 747
direct marketing and, 766–7
door-to-door distribution and, 671
mail order and, 759
personal selling and, 699–700
sales promotion and, 686
telemarketing and, 757–8
see also segmentation
targets, 639
sales, 722
for sales representatives, 730

see also objectives
task-based budget setting, 594, 639
task forces, 361
Taurus, 163–4
taxation, 62
and price elasticity, 386
and pricing, 391
Te Kanawa, Kiri, 658
team spirit, 728–9
technical sales support, 708
technological environment, 38, 39, 55–60
and consumer decision-making process, 98–9
and distribution channel strategy, 467
international aspects, 1001
technology, 57–9, 1053
choice criteria in purchasing, 145
direct marketing and, 743, 755–6, 757, 763
and intensity of distribution, 463
and product management, 306
retailing and, 520–1
in services, 937–8
telemarketing, 74, 509, 753–8
inbound (defined), 753
limitations on, 755–8
outbound (defined), 753
and other elements of promotional mix, 754
and self-liquidating offers, 755, 756
as support for sales representatives, 710
telephone interviews, 217, 218
telephone preference services, 758
telephone selling, *see* telemarketing
telephone technology, 743, 754, 755–6, 757, 938
teleshopping, 509, 510, 743, 763, 776–7
television
consumer programmes, 54
digital, 5–6
sponsorship of programmes, 803–4
television advertising, 622–4, 626–8
direct response, 751–2, 755
political and regulatory environment, 76
television viewership panels, 208
tendering, 131, 146, 260, 432, 437–9
for research projects, 233
test marketing, 348–52
and forecasting, 901
for services, 351
simulated, 350
test marketing stage of new product development, 349–52
testimonials, as appeal factor in advertising, 614–15
testing
comparative, 51–2
concept, *see* concept testing
franchises and, 980
small businesses and, 961–2
theatre tickets, 373
Thomson, Daley, 312
time constraints, services and, 940
time, international attitudes concerning, 1001
time-limited offers, 661
time-pressure close (method of closing), 718–19
time-related pricing/discounts, 430–1, 433–4
time-related sales promotion, 656, 658, 660, 664
time scales
audits, 885
planning and, 877–8
time series analysis
and forecasting, 899–900
time use, sales representatives', 701
time utility, 490
timeshares, 15, 260

timing of advertising campaigns, 641
title (legal ownership), 458, 492
tobacco, 109
advertising, 76, 77–8
and price elasticity, 386
Tobacco Advisory Council, 78
toiletries, emotional needs and, 106
tokens, 660, 676
for cash rebates, 666, 667
and cause-related marketing, 807
for gifts, 673
total cost, 423
total market measurement, 894
total quality management (TQM), 283
touts, ticket, 373
TQM, 283
trade agreements, international, 63–5
trade-in allowances, 434, 436
trade associations, 70, 76–7
data published by, 211
trade discounts, 433
trade marks, 267–8, 275
franchising, 972
trade names, 267
trade promotion, 654–6
trade shows/exhibitions, *see* exhibitions
trading blocs, 63–5
see also European Union
trading stamps, 676
trading standards officers, 72
trading up
coupons and, 665
sales promotion and, 660
training, 461, 463
as sales promotion, 684
of sales representatives, 727–8
transactional value, 451, 458
transfer pricing, 427, 439–40, 1020
transit time, 549, 550
transport-based advertising media, 632–3
transportation, 460, 491, 543–51
costs, 534, 539, 548–9
modes of, 544–51
travel industry, 469, 473
travellers, services for, 9, 11
trial, and routine problem solving purchasing situation, 97
trial orders, 719
trial prices, 415–16, 664
trial sizes, 280, 670
trust, 157
in distribution channels, 481
JIT systems and, 560

UK
care lines, 755
political and regulatory environment, 70, 71, 72, 73, 74, 75–7
social class in, 110
uncertainty, business size and, 955
undercutting, 421, 471
understanding, public relations and, 780
undifferentiated targeting, 187–8
universities, as organisational customers, 132
unsought goods, 259–60
unstructured interviews, 216
USA, care lines, 755
usage rate, as basis for segmentation, 170–1, 181, 182–3
user base, 659
user-based product classification systems
consumer, 257–60
organisational, 260–2
users
as organisational customers, 129–30
and purchasing, 152
utility
place, 490
time, 490

vacuum cleaners, 282–3
value
    intermediaries adding, 460–1
    price and, 370, 431
    and sales objectives, 722
    sales promotion and, 653, 654
    as selling point, 388
    transactional, 451, 458
    see also price
value added, 128
value management, 379–80
value pricing, 417
Values And Life Style typology, 178
values, corporate, 881–3
variable costs, 394, 423, 425
variation/variety, as consumer demand, 48
variety stores, 501–2
VAT, 62, 391, 396, 398
vending machines, 510
venture teams, 356–7, 360
ventures, joint, *see* joint ventures
VER (voluntary export restraint), 65
vertical competition in distribution
        channels, 471–2
vertical marketing systems, 472–4, 496, 521
    and legitimate power, 479
    types, 472–3

see also integration
video surveillance, 219
videos, 14
    in direct mail, 747
    public relations, 788, 791
VisCAP model of presenter
        characteristics and communication
        objectives, 591
visible staff, 935–6
VMS, *see* vertical marketing systems
volume, and sales objectives, 722
volume allowances, 681
volume sales, 412

waiting, 94–5, 924, 932
wants
    assessing, 5–6
    products and, 14, 15–16, 28, 29
    see also demand
'war horses', 840–1
warehousing, 553–5
    costs, 539–40
warranties, 492
    see also guarantees
Watchdog (television programme), 54
water, 270
water transport, 547

weak theory of communication, 580–1
weighting procedures, in screening ideas for
        new products, 344–5
'welcome' calls, 757, 770
What to Buy for Business, 145
Which? magazine, 51, 55
whisky, 298
wholesale markets, and price, 376–8
wholesaler voluntary chains, 473
wholesalers, 451, 453–4, 459, 523–4
    full service, 523
    functions, 490–2
    information and advice role, 491
    limited service, 524
    mark-up, 426–7
    services offered by, 490–2
win–win negotiation, 716
withdrawal strategies, 299–300, 317–18,
        848–9
women
    advertising and, 106
    survey of attitudes, 99
    working patterns, 468, 741

Yellow Pages, 211
youth markets, 113, 114–15, 805–6

zoned pricing, 434

Index of company names

■ ■ ■

AB Konstruktions-Bakelit, 455
ABB, 437
ABB Henschel, 291
ABB Traction, 438
Abbey National, 144
Abbey National Direct, 754
Abel Eastern, 840
Absolut, 805
Access, 179
Accolade, 748
ACI, 548
Adidas, 115, 274, 648, 649, 662, 679
AEG Schienenfahrzeuge, 291
Aer Lingus, 69
Aeroflot, 108
Aérospatiale, 56, 843
AGB, 208
AGB Dialogue, 178
Ahold, 474, 489, 494, 522
Aillwe Cave, 949
Air France, 69, 74, 403–4, 1014
Air Liberté, 74
Air 2000, 473
Airbus, 467
Airfix, 578
AirRide, 968
Airtours, 473
Airtours International, 473
Akzo, 853
Albert Heijn, 272, 489, 558
Alcoa, 261
Aldi, 115, 392, 395, 494, 502, 522, 938
Alfa Laval, 455
Alitalia, 69, 74, 1014
Allen McGuire, 578
Allied Domecq, 677, 806
Allied Domecq Leisure, 326
Allkauf, 489
AMC, 921
American Airlines, 1014, 1054
American Express, 746, 748, 753, 772, 847, 1017
Amstrad, 528–9
Amstrad Business Direct, 528
Amtrack Express Parcels, 977
Anheuser–Busch, 123
Ann Summers, 453, 509
Ansell International, 248
Apple, 267, 268, 307, 357, 418, 536, 559
Apple Hollyhill, 537
Apple Replenishment Programme, 537
Applewoods, 970
Arc-en-Ciel, 377
Ares-Serono, 853
Argos, 258, 498, 508, 676, 760, 763, 765
Argyll, 489, 494
Ariston, 259
Arjo Wiggins, 275
Ark, 68–9
Ark 2, 638
Arla, 63
Armani, 295
ASDA, 118, 248, 273, 391, 401–2, 480, 484, 504, 527, 777, 871, 1034, 1036
ASKO Deutsche Kaufhaus, 558
Associated Marketing Services, 489
Aston Martin, 833–4, 857, 890
Atlantic 252, 628

Auchan, 485, 494, 502, 505
Audi, 268
Austrian Airlines, 1014
Autobus Zil, 1007
Avery Office Products, 765, 766
Avis, 860, 861

B&Q, 694, 872
Bacardi, 76
Balkanair, 631, 923
Banana Group, 570
Bank of Scotland, 693
Barclays Bank, 693, 763, 805
Barco, 1010, 1052
Barker, 713
BASF, 724
Bass, 224, 333, 472, 584, 591
Batchelor, 181, 673
Baxter's, 181
Bayernwerk, 142
Bechstein, 856
Belgacom, 743, 835
Bell's, 76
Benetton, 496, 522, 538, 539, 610–11, 612, 860, 1014, 1017
Benson and Hedges International, 803
Be-Ro, 659
Bestway, 524
BhS, 501, 521
Bic, 421, 862, 863, 1033
Big Issue, The, 945
Bijttebier, 745
Binns, 500
Birds Eye Wall's, 115, 551, 680, 840, 850, 1041
Black & Decker, 284, 285, 340, 813
Blackwell's Bookshop, 510
Blowspeed, 132
Blue Circle, 188
Bluthner, 856
BMW, 23, 255, 286, 371, 536, 776, 805, 831
Body Shop, The, 48, 49, 51, 186, 270, 974, 1017
Boeing, 56, 204, 467
Böhler, 615
Bols-Wessanen, 867
Bonas Machine Company, 855
Bonusprint, 750
Book Club Associates, 752
Boots The Chemist, 186, 270, 494, 519, 755, 765–6, 791, 871–2, 1034, 1036
Boots Contract Manufacturing, 872
Boots Healthcare International, 872
Borsalino, 466, 1052
Bosch, 264, 265, 283–4, 285, 995
Boss Group, 56, 890, 1030–3, 1054
Boulanger, 502
Bouygues, 895
BP, 68
Braun, 258
Bridon, 885
Britannia, 473
British Aerospace, 56, 62, 140, 327, 328
British Airports Authority, 795, 798
British Airways, 69, 74, 235, 255, 403–4, 618, 630, 808, 850, 928, 938, 1014, 1054
British Broadcasting Corporation, 54, 1044

British Gas, 66, 807
British Midland, 67, 327, 403–4, 662, 721
British Rail, 67, 347, 544–5, 934–5
British Steel, 30, 67, 804
British Telecommunications, 66, 75, 388, 393, 610, 743, 755–6, 764, 790, 796, 804–5, 1046
Britvic, 34, 76, 113, 303, 556, 564, 574, 610, 752, 755, 756, 809
Brooke Bond, 34, 623, 669, 675
Brown and Root, 796
Brush Traction, 438
BSN, 994
Budgens, 552
Bueche Girod, 416
Buitoni, 991
Bulgari, 981
Bulgarian Vintners Company, 1025
Bundy Corporation, 889
BUPA, 752
Burberry, 1000
Burger King, 275, 809, 1008
Burton Group, 501
Butlin's, 298–9
Byte, 846

C&A, 472, 495, 501
C.D. Welding, 956–7
Cabouchon, 509
CACI Information Services, 175, 176
Cadbury, 267, 269, 271, 276, 285, 371, 564, 617, 679, 790, 804, 1017
CAF, 438
Calvin Klein, 295
Camelot, 243, 613
Campanile, 922
Campari, 466, 867
Campbell, 181
Canon, 339, 852
CAPIBUS Europe, 208
Cargo Club, 72
Carlsberg-Tetley, 123, 673, 790, 806, 996
Carlton Television, 945
Carlyle and Forge, 495
Carnation, 837, 991
Carrefour, 485, 494, 502, 504, 505, 589
Carte Noire, 605, 613, 876, 1017
Casa, 56
Casaralta, 550
Casino, 489, 494, 505
Casio, 865
Castle, 393
Castle Cement, 764
Caterpillar, 685, 867
Catteau, 522
CBB Research, 212
CBS, 443
CCN, 176, 766
Celebrations, 955, 956, 961
Cellnet, 372, 655
Chanel, 613
Chivers Hartley, 860
Chlumcanske Keramicke Zavody, 1003
Christian Dior, 266
Chubb, 736, 838
Chuft Toys and Gifts, 870–1, 964, 991
Ciba, 997
Cipem, 485

Citroën, 629, 750, 751
CKD Praha, 145
Clark Equipment, 867
Clark's shoes, 476
Classic FM, 628
Club 18–30, 75, 76, 115, 254
Club Méditerranée, 419
CML, see Continental Microwave
CNN, 920, 1044
Coca-Cola, 34, 114, 175, 266, 267, 289, 294, 610–11, 612, 618, 670, 802, 804, 810, 860, 991, 1000, 1017
Coca-Cola Schweppes Beverages, 570
Cockerill Sambre, 67, 848
Coley Porter Bell, 285
Colgate Palmolive, 96, 99, 119, 270, 271, 322, 323, 552
Comet, 258, 528
Commercial Union, 804
Compagnie des Petits, La, 970
Compt. Modernes, 505
Computerised Marketing Technologies, 177
Continent, 485
Continental Microwave, 146, 1030, 1043–8, 1054
Continental Tyres, 53, 54, 377
Cook, Thomas, 473, 679, 690
Co-operative societies, 494, 657
Coop Schweiz, 523
Cora, 505
Corfu Tourism Promotion Board, 588
Costco, 280, 377, 471, 477, 479, 480
Cott Corporation, 289–90, 876
Cougnaud, Yves, 614
Country Choice, 50
Courage, see Scottish Courage
Courvoisier, 680
Covent Garden Soup, 181, 840
Crane Hougaille, John, 889
Creative Fragrances, 266
Creda, 889
Cross Pens, 256
Cross Products, 744
Crosse & Blackwell, 181, 837
CTL, 548
Cummins, 859
Curry's, 258, 520
Cusson's, 270

Daewoo, 186, 215, 470, 610, 679, 751, 811
Daimler-Benz, 291, 407, 999
Daimler-Benz Aerospace, 327–8
Danone, 558, 991
Daru Car, 1012
DASA, 327–8
Dassault, 843
De Dietrich, 291
Debenham's, 499, 500, 501, 658
Debonair, 74
Decathlon, 502
Del Monte, 14
Delhaize le Lion, 15, 494, 521, 523
Delifrance, 50
Dell, 752
DeLonghi, 702
Delta, 1014
Denim, 74
Derwent Valley Holdings, 804
Deutsche Bundesbahn, 290–1
Deutsche Morgan Grenfell, 895
Deutsche Telekom, 435
Dexion, 458
DHL, 66, 911
Dickins and Jones, 500
Digital, 706, 768
Dillons, 401
Dior, Christian, 266
Direct Line, 739, 740
Disney, 752

Disney World, 286
Dixons, 477, 528
DMB&B, 10, 608, 623, 1030, 1040–3, 1050–1
Do It All, 872
Docks de France, 505, 522, 523
Dohme and Pfizer, 214
Domain Boyar, 1025
Domino's, 983
Donna Karan, 270
Doosan, 1031
Dowty Aerospace, 889
Duarig, 485
Duewag, 291
Dun and Dunstreet, 211, 213
Dunkin' Donuts, 970, 974, 1008
Dunlop, 30
Dunne, 273
DuPont, 133
Duracell, 286, 703, 863–4, 865
DWA, 291
Dyno-Rod, 974, 979
Dyson, 282–3

Eastern Electricity, 155
EasyJet, 74
Economist Intelligence Unit, 213
Economist, The, 638
Ecover, 68–9
Eddie Bauer, 761
Eddie Stobart, 545
Edeka, 489, 494, 496
Edwardian International Hotel, 155
Egger, 429
ELC International, 212
Elektromis of Poznan, 522
Elida Fabergé, 4, 274, 296
Elida Gibbs, 265, 266, 836
Elo Pak, 14
EMI, 443, 805
English China Clays, 842
Ericsson, 55, 357, 802
ESA, 377
Esselunga, 523
Esso, 68, 275
Estée Lauder, 590
Euro Belgium, 74
Euro Panel, 178
Eurocopter Holdings, 843
Eurodisney, 113–14
Eurofreight, 429
Eurogroup, 523, 1013
Euromonitor Publications, 211–12
Euronova, 761
European Passenger Services, 403
European Retail Association, 489
Euroshuttle, 398
Eurostar, 67, 275, 403–4, 429, 600, 763, 850
Eurostart, 275
Evans, 173
Ever Ready, 863–4, 865
Evian, 510

Fabergé, 751
Fads, 872
Farmers Seeds Federal, 615
Fatty Arbuckle's, 979
FDS Field Marketing, 669
Federal Express, 66, 911
Ferrari, 466, 857
Ferrero, 267
Fiat, 145, 158, 303, 439, 994
Fiat Ferroviaria, 145, 782
Fiat Polska, 998
Filofax, 912
Findus, 274
Firema Group, 550
Firestone, 30
First Choice, 473

First Direct, 607
Fisher-Price, 266, 286
Foden Trucks, 606, 614
Fokker, 56, 327–8
Folger Adam, 838
Ford, 144, 186, 267, 269, 270, 276, 283, 397, 417, 464, 565, 610, 617, 637, 833–4, 890, 958, 995, 997, 1000, 1054
Forte, 297, 752, 783
Foster Yeoman, 544
Fourth R, 970
Fox Confectionery, 669
France Telecom, 763, 895
Francis Nicholls, 475
Franklin Mint, 751, 758
Fraser, House of, 499, 500
Freedown Food, 590
French Aerospace, 843
French Tourist Office, 750
Fuji, 1017
Fujitsu, 357

G's Fresh Salads, 14–15
Galeries Lafayette, 499
Gates Energy Products, 639
Gateshead Metro Centre, 508, 513–14
GEC, 889
GEC Alsthom, 437
General Mills, 991
General Motors, 139, 341, 417, 994, 1037, 1038; see also Vauxhall Motors
Generale des Eaux, 895
Gerber, 14
GIB, 522
Gibbs & Dandy, 492
Gillette, 99, 275, 322, 614, 862, 863, 1033, 1056
Glaxo-Wellcome, 785, 872, 994, 999
Global, 522
Globi, 522
GN Store Nord, 835
Going Places, 473, 690
Golden Wonder, 101, 866
Goodyear, 30, 377
Gossard, 173, 174, 1014, 1018
Graboplast, 1003
Graham and Trotmans, 212
Granada, 783
Granada TV, 804
Grattan, 510, 761
Great Frog, 113, 114–15
Great Universal Stores, 494, 762
Greenalls, 326
Grolsch, 828
Group 4, 719
Guardian Direct, 752
Gucci, 106, 466
Guinness, 48, 113, 610, 690
GUS, see Great Universal Stores

H J Hall Sock Group, 187
Häagen Dazs, 24, 25, 523, 805, 850
Habitat, 760
Hagen, 489
Halfords, 360, 470, 872
Handel Communications, 118
Harley-Davidson, 113, 114
Harris Logistics, 552
Harrods, 272, 309, 496, 751, 870, 963
Hasbro, 266, 300
Heinz, 96, 172, 181, 264, 267, 272, 274, 276, 316, 322, 371, 652, 1041
Hellman's, 860
Henkel France, 627
Hennes and Mauritz, 497
Hertz, 860, 861
Hewlett-Packard, 358, 555
High and Mighty, 173
Highland Distillers, 802

Highway Windscreens, 972
Hilton Hotels, 743, 1009
Hitachi, 357
HMV, 443, 490, 493
HMV Direct, 493
Hochtief, 260
Hodder Headline, 401
Hoggies, 974
Holderbank SA, 834
Holiday Autos, 861
Holiday Inns, 922
Holloway, P. J., 789
Homebase, 522, 872
Homestyle, 872
Honda, 65, 619
Hoover, 255, 281, 282, 653, 674, 677
Hotpoint, 255, 259
House of Fraser, 499, 500
Howard Johnson, 974
HP Foods, 707
Humbrol, 578
Hutchison Communications, 802
Hyatt International Hotels, 775

Iberia, 69, 74
IBM, 213–14, 271, 307, 357, 612, 728, 807, 857
Ibstock Building Projects, 804
ICA, 489, 494
ICD Marketing Services, 747–8
Icelandair, 413, 423
ICI, 133, 551, 796, 852
ICL, 357
IKEA, 432, 492, 506, 519, 521, 522, 555, 1000, 1017, 1018
Ilva, 67
Impact FCA!, 748
Independent Grocers' Alliance, 473
Indesit, 255
Ingersoll–Rand, 263, 468
Innovazione, 500
Intel, 358, 836
Inter Caves, 977
Interbrew, 123
Interflora, 763
Intermarché, 494, 504, 505
IRI, 1034
Irish Fire Products, 736–7
Issy Miyake, 295
Italian Railways, 145
ITN, 1044
Iveco, 146, 606

J&B Rare Scotch Whisky, 807
J C Decaux, 202, 203
Jaeger, 314, 500
Japan Airlines, 911
JCB, 685
Jenners, 870
Jeronimo Martins, 489, 504, 522
Jet, 507
Jeyes, 159
Jiffi, 248
John Lewis Partnership, 499
John West Foods, 52
Johnson & Johnson, 151, 322, 724, 791
Jokers, 955
Jungheinrich, 1031–3

Kabo, 83
Kallo Group, 334
Karstadt, 494, 499, 993
Kaufhalle, 501
Kaufhof, 494
Kellogg's, 119, 174, 219, 256, 273, 276, 286, 294, 312, 377, 618, 675
Kettle Foods, 101
Key Note Reports, 212–13
KFC, 140, 882, 974, 1008

Kimberly–Clark, 266
Kinetica, 66
Kingfisher, 494
Kings Hotel (Krakow), 195, 247
Kitchen Devils, 673
Klein, Calvin, 295
Klemm, 468, 469
KLM, 203, 204, 1014
Kodak, 274, 275, 286, 341, 860, 1017, 1018
Komatsu, 685, 1030
Kompan, 283
Kompass, 211, 213
Kovintehna, 15
KP, 101, 591
Kwik-Fit, 217, 360
Kwik Save, 174, 272, 392, 552

La Mama, 978
La Redoute, 762, 763
Lada, 23, 108, 255, 883
LaFarge Coppee, 834
Lamborghini, 253–4, 284
Lancer/Lancer Boss, 1030–3, 1052
Land Rover, 865
Lands' End, 760, 762
Laura Ashley, 12, 495, 516, 522, 760, 1000
Lawson Mardon Group, 159
Lazenby's, 414, 1052
Le Shuttle, 428, 429, 593, 600–1, 673
Leclerc, 494, 505, 993
Lee, 845–6
Leer, Marco, 969–70, 971, 979
Legal and General, 729
Lego, 274, 286, 790, 803
Leroy Merlin, 502
Lever Brothers, 68, 69, 89, 90, 92, 106, 219, 266, 267, 270, 364, 581, 613, 664, 667, 672
Levi, 113, 256, 286, 845–6
Leyland Daf, 606
Libero, 672
Libraire du Commerce International, 213
Lidl, 392, 502, 664, 938
Lightwater Valley, 950
Lilliput, 844
Linde Group, 1031
Linn Products, 829. 830, 833
Lir Chocolates, 846
Littlewoods, 762
Lloyds Bank, 693, 800, 806, 809, 810, 931
Lobb, 862
Local Artist, The, 974
Lofthouse of Fleetwood, 6, 8
London Herb and Spice Company, 746
London International Group, 248
London Review of Books, 747
London Underground, 804, 934
L'Oréal, 728, 860
LOT, 195
Lucas Engineering and Systems, 615–16
Luceplan, 283
Lucerne Hotel and Conference Centre, 444–5
Lufthansa, 74, 911, 937, 1014
Lunn Poly, 473, 694

M-S-B+K, 744
McAlpine, 260
McDonald's, 51, 119, 135, 200, 268, 349, 452, 614, 633, 712, 713, 786, 809, 882–3, 953, 974, 978, 991, 992, 1000, 1008, 1018
McDonell Douglas, 56
Mace, 473, 507
Macleans, 836
McQuillan Engineering Industries, 467
McVitie, 278
Madame Tussaud's, 122, 1053
Maggi, 837

Makro, 524
Malezan, 832
Mama, La, 978
Mammouth, 522
Manlee, 495
Mannesmann, 435
Manor, 499, 500,
Manor House Press, 212
Marco Leer, 969–70, 971, 979
Marie Claire, 99
Market Research Burda, 213
Marks & Spencer, 187, 192, 255–6, 272, 273, 286, 474, 478, 479, 494, 501, 513, 521, 522, 542, 804, 847, 862, 958, 994
Marlow Foods, 840
Mars, 271, 274, 275, 294, 477, 558, 662, 991
Martin Joinery, 993, 1023–4
Martini, 115, 585, 610–11, 612
Master Foods, 183, 477, 478
Mastercard, 664, 806
Matsushita, 357, 363
Matthew Clark Taunton, 123
Maxell, 618
Mazda, 807
MBM Technology, 135
MD Foods, 840
Meadowhall, 513–14
Mercedes-Benz, 271, 286, 316, 827, 1042
Merck, 29
Merck Sharp, 214
Mercury, 66, 591, 796
Mercury 1 to 1, 561
Meridian Broadcasting, 945
Merrydown Wine, 333, 584
Mesa Air, 327
Messerschmitt Belkow-Blohm, 56
Metro, 494
Metronic, 486
Michael Martin, 1023
Michelin, 377
Microsoft, 236, 282, 307, 418
Midland Bank, 801, 808, 810
Miele, 389
Migros, 489, 514
Milk Marque, 395
Minitel, 60
Minolta, 264
Mintel Publications, 212
Missho Iwai, 911
Mitsubishi, 619–22, 1055
Mobil, 676
Mobilkom, 835
Moctezuma, 123
Monaghan Mushrooms, 484
Mondena, 838
Monoprix, 501
Morellato, 968
Moser, 456
Mothercare, 792
Motorola, 357
MRB, 207
MTV, 114, 248, 742
Music Sales, 756, 764
Mustang, 464

National Car Parks, 884
National Westminster Bank, 607, 932
NBC, 1044
NEC, 579
Neckermann, 547
Nedalo, 155
Nekermann, 510
Neoplan, 291, 1007
Nestlé, 17, 18, 20, 34, 115, 264, 265, 266, 271, 273, 321, 322, 381, 382, 558, 594, 605, 624, 627, 669, 670, 753, 837, 860, 991, 1017
Netto, 115, 392, 395, 502, 522, 664, 938

New Covent Garden Soup, 181, 840
New Horizons, 1008
Newman Books, 212
Next, 496, 743, 757, 759, 760, 770
Nielsen, 1034
Nielsen, A C, 207
Nielsen Homescan, 208
Nike, 115, 168, 268, 532, 533, 585, 591,
    613, 633, 648–9, 998
Nikon, 791
Nintendo, 390, 850, 892
Nissan, 65, 72, 764, 1030–1
Nohmi Bosal, 838
Nokia, 357, 439
Nordmann, 500
Nordtank Energy Systems, 846
North West, 1014
Northern Dairies, 703
Northern Electric, 66, 783
Northern Foods, 395, 703
Norwich Union, 296
Norwich Union Healthcare, 791
Novo Nordisk, 996
Novotel, 922, 931
NTC Publications, 212
Nurdin and Peacock, 472, 524
Nu-Swift, 736

Odeon, 921
Office World, 454
Ogilvy and Mather, 99
Olivetti, 56, 958
Olympic, 1014
Olympus Optical Company, 373
Opinion Leader, 213
Orange, 372, 655, 791
Oreck, 615
ORF, 1044
Organon International, 853
Osram, 680
Otto Versand, 510, 761, 762, 860, 994
Our Price, 443
Ovaltine, 667–8

P&O Ferries, 538, 600, 601, 750
Palladium, 485
Pan Am, 413
Pao de Acucar, 504
Pasco Graves, 980, 981
Patak (Spices), 266, 905
Paxman, 347, 348
Payless, 872
Pechiney Rhenalu, 261
Pedigree Petfoods, 266, 271, 668, 860
Penguin Books, 393
Penny Plain, 762
Pepe Jeans, 114
PepsiCo, 7, 34, 114, 140, 175, 266, 271, 289,
    590, 611, 670, 804, 860, 883
Perfect Pizza, 976, 981, 982
Perrier, 510, 801, 991
Peugeot, 267, 610, 619, 624
Philip Morris, 809
Philips, 164–5, 258, 306, 363, 790, 840, 904,
    998
Phoenix Works, 848
Pierre Cardin, 316
Pilkington, 994
Pilkington Glass, 881
Pinault-Printemps, 494
Pirelli, 54
Pirelli Reifenwerk, 377
Pizza Hut, 140, 320, 611, 922, 953
Placette, 500
Plasser & Theurer, 35, 1052
Playtex, 785
Pleroma, 484
Polar, 853
Polkolor, 998, 1003

Pollena 2000, 586
Polygram, 363, 443
Polypal, 848
Polytuile, 848
Popeye's, 1009
Post Office, 66, 438, 743, 748
Postalmarket, 761
PPP, 764, 803
Pravdinsk Radio Factory, 867
Premier, 638
President Enterprises Corporation (Taiwan),
    991
PreussenElektra, 142
Price Waterhouse, 212
Principles, 501, 521
Pringle, 315–16
Printemps, 499
Procter & Gamble, 68, 69, 82, 104, 266, 267,
    270, 273, 275, 322, 364, 457, 605,
    607, 613, 615, 623, 627, 659, 664,
    808, 860, 904, 1017
Promodés, 494, 505
Prontaprint, 978
Pronuptia Wedding Hire, 978
Prudential, 725, 795, 797
PTT (Sweden), 1044

Q-Zar, 970
Quaker Foods, 300, 307, 839
Quaker Petfoods, 860, 861
Quelle, 510
Quelle Schikedanz, 762
QVC, 510

Racing Green, 760
Rackhams, 500
Railfreight Distribution, 565
Railtrack, 35, 437
Raisio, 336
Raleigh, 889
Rank Xerox, 339, 611, 728, 852, 992
Rasterops Corporation, 546
Reader's Digest, 678
Ready-Mix, 834
Reckitt and Colman, 277, 294, 295
Redoute, La, 762, 763
Reebok, 115, 168, 268, 585, 648, 649
Rema, 522
Renault, 283, 300, 356–7, 360, 393, 612,
    614, 629, 637, 994
RENFE, 565
Rentokil Tropical Plants, 701
Research Services (GB), 208
Revlon, 679
Rewe, 494, 496, 523
Rheinbraun, 544
Rheinbrucke, 500
RHM, 50, 267, 618
Rhône-Poulenc, 780
Rhône Poulenc Rorer, 996
Ricola, 612
Rock Circus, 122, 1053
Rockwater, 796
Rolex, 106
Rolls-Royce, 106, 327, 436
Rosenberg Ventilation, 789
Ross Young, 840
Rossignol, 998
Routin, 485
Rover, 286, 397, 831, 1012, 1054
Rowntree, 118, 991
Royal Doulton, 8
Royal Mail, 438
RS Components, 524
RSMB, 208
Russell Hobbs, 889
RWE, 142, 435
Ryanair, 74
Rymans, 454

Saab, 327, 455, 467
Saatchi & Saatchi, 75
Sabena, 69, 1014
Saes Getters, 338
Safeway, 316, 348, 477, 484, 527, 552, 564,
    657, 658, 694, 777
Saga Holidays, 43, 573, 574
Sainsbury, J., 50, 68, 72, 118, 272, 298–0,
    374, 388, 477, 480, 484, 494, 499,
    502, 503, 511, 522, 523, 527–8, 541,
    638, 657, 658, 667–8, 685, 694–5,
    777, 786, 791, 872
St Laurent, Yves, 280, 295
Salim Group (Indonesia), 991
Samas, 848
Samsung, 271, 788
Sandoz, 29
Sara Lee, 849
SAS, 413
Savia, 522
SCH, see Specialist Computer Holdings
Schaeff, 848
Schirolli, 156
Scott Paper, 104, 266, 310, 590
Scottish Courage, 123, 398, 681, 683, 713,
    805, 828, 849
Scottish Enterprise, 359
Scottish Widows, 752
Securicor, 66
Security Backup Systems, 144
SEDD, 523, 1013
Seddon Atkinson, 606
Sega, 390, 850, 892
Seiko, 864, 865
Sellotape, 655, 890
Servicemaster, 974
Sharp, 800
Shell, 68, 374, 507, 544–5, 652–3, 654,
    820–1, 992, 994, 1055
Sheraton, 922, 1017
Showcase Cinemas, 921
Shuttle, Le, 428, 429, 593, 600–1, 673
Sici, 838
Siddles, 838
Siemens, 145, 260, 291, 347, 357, 359, 437,
    617, 867, 994
Singapore Airlines, 436
Skelair International, 468, 469
SKF, 136, 439, 532, 533, 551, 553–4, 703,
    994, 995
Skoda, 109, 314, 586
Sky Television, 928
SLM, 291
Smirnoff, 123
Smit, 796
Smith, W. H., 401, 443, 520, 542, 872
Smith's Crisps, 866
Smith & Nephew, 82, 270
SmithKline Beecham, 29, 263, 274, 280,
    312–13, 336, 579, 849, 872
SNCF, 67, 544, 565
Sock Shop, 192, 497, 514, 862
Soldier Blue, 497
Somerfield, 484
Sonae Group, 504
Sonana, 56
Sonofon, 835
Sony, 20, 271, 275, 301, 305, 306, 335, 338,
    357, 363, 390, 416, 443, 677
Southwest, 74
Spanair, 74
Spar, 474, 496, 507
Spar (Germany), 494
Spear's, 300
Specialist Computer Holdings, 846, 847
Spiegel, 761
Spillers, 551
SsangYong Musso, 619
Stadler, 291

Stafford-Miller, 275, 579, 836
Stanley Tools, 719
Staples, 454
Steinbock, 1030, 1031
Steinway, 856
Stena Line, 600
Storck, 584
Styles, 986, 1053, 1054
Subaru, 397
Subway, 970, 975, 1008
Suchard, 271
SüdBadenBus, 291
Sugro, 454, 467
Sukhoi, 320
Sumitomo, 685
Summers, Ann, 453, 509
Sun Alliance, 745
Superal, 522
Superdrug, 391, 463, 1034, 1036
Superquinn, 489
Swan Hunter, 62, 131–2
Swissair, 1014
Systemcare, 954
Système U, 485, 505

Tambrands, 82, 809, 1019
TAP , 69
Target Market Consultancy, 177
Tate & Lyle, 411
Taylor Nelson AGB, 208, 214, 694
Teijo Pesukoneet, 456
Teksid, 998
Tele Danmark, 835
Telecom Eirann, 835
Telmat, 457
Tengelmann, 494, 504, 522
Tesco, 9–10, 144, 243, 276, 289, 388, 453,
    472, 477, 480, 484, 494, 499, 502,
    503, 511, 522, 527, 541, 558, 590,
    658, 664, 677, 694–5, 777, 791, 938,
    1034
Tetley (brewery), see Carlsberg-Tetley
Tetley (Tea), 231, 581
Tetra Pak, 14
Texaco, 214, 390, 608, 623
Texas, 872
Thermoking, 128
Thomas Cook, 473, 679, 690
Thomson, 473
Thomson , 998, 1003
3M, 301, 306, 612
Tibbett and Britten, 534
Tie Rack, 497, 511, 514
Times Newspapers, 409, 638, 781, 889–90
Tivoli Gardens, 949–50
TNT Express Worldwide, 429
Top Shop, 501

Topps, 912
Toshiba, 805
Total Research, 285
Toyota, 65, 139, 341, 610, 802, 803, 809
Toys 'Я' Us, 506, 510, 520, 578, 763, 771,
    1017
TR Fastenings, 9
Trabant, 253–4, 284
Trafalgar House, 66, 783
Transarc, 728
Transfesa, 565, 1054
Trebor Bassett, 274, 677, 889
3 Suisse, 761
TSB, 90
Tube Investments, 889, 1052–3
Tupperware, 453, 509
Turtle Wax, 666
TV2 (Denmark), 1044
Twinings Tea, 613
Tyco International, 838
Tyreco Trading, 377

UCI, 921
Unigate, 395
Unilever, 18, 20, 34, 860, 904, 991, 994
Unilog, 548
Unimerchants, 552
Unipart, 904
Unipath, 655
United Airlines, 1014
United Distillers, 266, 298, 803
United Parcel Service, 911
Ushers, 741
Usinor Sacilor, 67

Valio, 392
Van den Bergh, 34, 268, 575, 595
Van Dyck Belgian Chocolates, 264
Vauxhall, 102, 358, 376, 377, 438, 637, 788,
    800, 904, 1030, 1037–40, 1049–50
VDU Techclean Services, 974
Veba, 435
Velden Engineering, 155, 968
Vendex, 499, 523
Versand, Otto, 510, 761, 762, 860, 994
Vestas Wind Systems, 846
VG, 496, 507
Victoria Wine, 763
Vilan, 500
Vinprom-C, 1025–6
Virgin, 113, 289, 296, 443, 806, 921
Virgin Atlantic, 673, 1014
Virgin Direct, 16, 28, 296
Virgin Express, 74
Virgin Megastores, 122
Virgin Vodka, 76
Visa, 802

Vitra, 283
VME Group, 867
Vobis, 477
Vodaphone, 372, 655
Vogue, 630
Volga Pulp and Paper Mill, 867
Volvo, 9, 40, 267, 311, 455, 536, 678, 803,
    867
Volvo Construction Equipment
    Corporation, 867
VTN, 460
VW, 109, 314

Waddington's, 300
Walker's Crisps, 140, 266
Wall's, see Birds Eye Wall's
J. Walter Thomson, 219, 220
Warner Cinemas, 921
Warner Lambert, 1034, 1035, 1036
Waterford Crystal, 8
Waterstone's, 401–2
Wavin Trepak, 558
WEA/Warner, 443
Weetabix, 267, 673, 674
Weir Paper Products, 342
Wellcome, see Glaxo-Wellcome
West Coast Fish Products, 887, 888, 890,
    891, 965
West Hampton, 761
Western Hostels, 987–8
Whirlpool Europe, 323
Whitbread, 123, 209, 214, 224, 326, 801,
    802, 809, 828, 999
Wickes, 872
Wilkinson Sword, 862, 863, 1030, 1033–7
William Grant, 670
Williams Holdings, 838, 1052
Wimpey, 437–8
Wimpy, 974
Wolfking, 857
Woolwich Building Society, 805
Woolworth, F. W., 289, 443, 538, 542
Worldwide Refinishing, 970
Wrangler, 705, 845–6

Xerox, 339, 611, 728, 852, 992

Yakovlev, 320
Yakult, 353
Yale, 838
Yogen Fruz, 970
Yorkshire Water, 357, 359, 867
Young's, 978
Yves Cougnaud, 614
Yves St Laurent, 280, 295

Zanussi, 255, 259